# Miscellaneous Writings and Letters of Thomas Cranmer

# The Parker Society.

Instituted A.D. M.DCCC.XL.

For the Publication of the Works of the Fathers
and Early Writers of the Reformed
English Church.

# MISCELLANEOUS WRITINGS

AND

# LETTERS

OF

# THOMAS CRANMER,

ARCHBISHOP OF CANTERBURY,
MARTYR, 1556.

EDITED FOR

**The Parker Society,**

BY THE

REV. JOHN EDMUND COX, M.A., F.S.A.,
OF ALL SOULS' COLLEGE, OXFORD, CURATE AND LECTURER OF STEPNEY.

REGENT COLLEGE PUBLISHING
Vancouver, British Columbia

**Miscellaneous Writings and Letters of Thomas Cranmner**

First published 1846 by the Parker Society, Cambridge University Press
This edition reproduced from the 1846 edition by Regent College Publishing
5800 University Boulevard, Vancouver, B.C. Canada V6T 2E4
www.regentpublishing.com



A cataloguing record for this publication is available from the National Library of Canada

ISBN 1-55361-044-X (Canada)
ISBN 1-57383-215-4 (United States)

# CONTENTS.

# BIOGRAPHICAL NOTICE

OF

# ARCHBISHOP CRANMER.

---

The notice which the editor purposes to give of the Life of Archbishop Cranmer will necessarily be very brief: a full exhibition of the character and conduct of such a man would require a careful and orderly investigation of documents connected with the three reigns of Henry, Edward, and Mary, and a close examination of the leading facts of ecclesiastical history, extending from the days of Wicliffe to his own; while the plan pursued by the Parker Society is only to present a succinct view of such general and prominent features of individual biography as may contribute to the intelligent appreciation of the writings collected in its volumes.

"The Life, State, and Story of Thomas Cranmer," already reprinted in the first volume of this edition of his works, describes his character as it was viewed by his contemporaries. This, together with Strype's Memorials of him, and his Life as written severally by Todd and Gilpin, forms a valuable groundwork for all historians of his times, as well as an important help to assist the general student to a just estimate of his principles, as viewed in connection with the singular and appalling difficulties of his position. These difficulties, candidly considered, will often suggest a satisfactory reply to the obloquy, which either religious or political acrimony has attempted to cast on the name of this illustrious martyr.

Thomas Cranmer was born July 2, 1489, at Aslacton in Nottinghamshire. At an early period of his life he lost his father, but his mother sent him to Cambridge, at the age of fourteen, and entered him at Jesus College, where he succeeded to a fellowship. He devoted the first eight years of his academical career to the acquisition of a knowledge of the questionists of the Church of Rome. In the year 1519 he commenced the study of the scriptures, which he pursued with unremitting assiduity till he reached his thirty-fourth year, i.e. A.D. 1523. In his twenty-third year he had married, by which he forfeited his fellowship; but being appointed reader at Buckingham (now Magdalene) College, he continued to reside and to prosecute his studies at Cambridge. His wife dying about twelve months afterwards, he was reinstated in his former fellowship, which he continued to hold, though much urged by the agents of Cardinal Wolsey to join the new foundation at Oxford, for the endowment of which that prelate suppressed several monastic establishments; but Cranmer preferred to continue divinity lecturer in his own college, which office he held from the time of his proceeding to the degree of D.D.

In 1528 he retired to Waltham Abbey with two pupils, named Cressy, on account of an infectious disorder breaking out at Cambridge. At this time the divorce between Henry VIII. and his queen, Katherine of Arragon, attracted the attention of Cranmer, whose opinion as to the best method of deciding upon the validity of the royal marriage having been represented to Henry, he was summoned to court, when he was required to digest his views in writing: having done this to the satisfaction of the king, he returned to Cambridge, but in a short time afterwards became one of the commissioners appointed from the universities, to determine the cause of the divorce, against the pope's dispensation. Henry VIII. soon after appointed him to the archdeaconry of Taunton, as well as one of his chaplains. In 1529, towards the close of the year, he was sent as an ambassador to the court of Rome, upon the same question, but was compelled to return home about the end of the following year on account of the ill success of his negociations.

In January 153$\frac{0}{1}$, he was sent as Henry's sole ambassador to the court of Charles V., in order to induce the German divines to advocate the cause of his master, when he married a second time, his wife being the niece of Osiander, pastor of Nuremburg. The embassy was unfavourable in its results; but Cranmer was summoned to return to England, to receive the highest appointment in the realm, which could be conferred upon him, namely, the archbishoprick of Canterbury, which had become vacant by the death of William Warham, August 23, 1532. Although he delayed his return to avoid the appointment, and manifested great reluctance to undertake the responsible duties of this high station, he was at length compelled to yield to the determination of the imperious monarch, and was consecrated on the 30th March, 1533, having made a public and repeated protestation before witnesses, "wherein he declared that he intended not, by the oath that he was to take, to bind himself to do anything contrary to the laws of God, the king's prerogative, or to the commonwealth, and statutes of the kingdom[1]." On the 23rd May, in the same year, the new archbishop pronounced judgment in favour of the king's divorce.

The primary concern of the archbishop in the following year, 1534, was to bring about the reformation of the church, and in connection with it, to effect an object which he had long desired, namely, to procure a translation of the bible, and to obtain the royal permission that it should be read by the people. He was also employed in endeavouring to settle the succession to the crown upon the heirs of Anne Boleyn, in which he was vehemently opposed by Sir Thomas More, and Fisher, bishop of Rochester, who in consequence of their refusal to take the oath required in the preamble of the act were beheaded, although Cranmer used every endeavour to prevent that result.

The archbishop about this time commenced the visitation of his province, and met with much opposition from the bishops and clergy, who favoured Romanism, and opposed the progress of the reformation; amongst whom none was more persevering than Stephen Gardiner, bishop of Winchester. He also counselled that the monasteries should be visited, with a view to their dissolution, in order that "new foundations might spring from them, which should be nurseries of learning throughout the realm."

On the 2nd May, 1536, Anne Boleyn was sent to the Tower, and a few days after the archbishop divorced her, by command of Henry VIII., which "he performed by due order and process of law[2]," but evidently with much reluctance.

In the year 1537, Cranmer had the satisfaction of seeing the bible of Tyndale's translation printed in English, and by the assistance of his friend and fellow-labourer in the work of the reformation, Crumwell, lord privy seal, he caused it to be set forth by the king's authority. It had been preceded by that of Coverdale, dedicated first to Anne Boleyn, and afterwards to Jane Seymour. In the following year, 1538, it is supposed that the archbishop, still intent upon advancing the progress of the reformation, addressed a memorial to the king, praying for his countenance and support in the accomplishment of this purpose, as well as his assent to the marriage of the clergy. He succeeded in having the English bible printed with farther revisions; but at this time the influence of the Romish party against his efforts was gaining ground, and so far from his second request being granted, a proclamation was issued against the marriage of the clergy, depriving all who had openly entered into that state of their privileges and offices, and threatening the punishment of fine and imprisonment upon such as in future should do so. Other disappointments also were encountered by the archbishop, amongst which it was not the least, that a conference between the German ambassadors and the English divines, which was held to effect an uniformity of doctrine between the reformed and continental churches, had proved unsuccessful. His urgent applications were set aside by those who were determined, if possible, to restore the power of the Roman catholic church. The result of the mission from Germany proved utterly useless. Every prospect now appeared of a decline of the archbishop's influence at court, through the efforts which were made to obtain a counter ascendancy over the mind of Henry VIII. It was in this year that Cranmer had to take a part in the

[1] Strype's Mem. of Abp. Cranmer, Vol. I. p. 28. Ed. Oxon. 1840. [2] Id. ibid. p. 69.

argument against John Lambert on the bodily presence in the sacrament, the result of which was his condemnation and execution as a heretic; which is one of the grounds of accusation urged against the archbishop by his opponents.

From the year 1538 to 1541 Cranmer had to endure a succession of disappointments, which much tried his spirit. He saw the Act of the Six Articles passed, notwithstanding his opposition to it, and Crumwell, his most intimate friend and associate, beheaded in consequence of the part he had taken in bringing about the marriage of Henry with Anne of Cleves. But although left almost alone, and surrounded by indefatigable adversaries, who were bent upon his ruin, he yet firmly resisted an attempt which was made by them "to extort from him a consent to a set of articles which would have re-established the dominion of error and superstition." In this instance the king still remained his friend, and for a time opposition against him ceased; and he was enabled to secure a royal proclamation enforcing the placing of the bible in the churches throughout the country. In the year 1542, attempts were made by the Roman Catholic party to effect a revision of the English bible; but the archbishop succeeded in defeating the object, by obtaining the consent of the king to have the matter referred to the universities: in twelve months time, however, when the attempt was again renewed, he was unable effectually to resist it; for the king, wearied and perplexed by continued dissension, was induced to sanction the prohibition of Tyndale's English bible, and to limit the privilege of reading the translations of the scriptures, which had previously been granted.

During the succeeding years Cranmer had still to encounter the hatred and opposition of his opponents; but, in 1543, a conspiracy was resorted to which bade fair to destroy his influence, and to render ineffective all that he had hitherto accomplished in the advancement of the Protestant cause. "A succession of meetings were held, a regular scheme was organized, and a voluminous mass of articles were collected by Gardiner and his accomplices, to obtain an advantage over him. The chief accusations brought against him were, that he had discouraged and restrained those preachers who refused to promote the new doctrines of the Reformation, that he had ordered the removal of images, and that he corresponded with the divines of Germany." The accusations, however, were no sooner laid before the king than he suspected the parties who originated them: he immediately shewed them to the archbishop, who solicited that the whole matter might be sifted by a commission, to which the king at once acceded, but insisted upon appointing the primate himself as chief commissioner. The result of the examinations which followed was, that the archbishop's character was cleared, and his adversaries confounded.

In the year 1544 Cranmer succeeded, through his influence with the king, in mitigating the Act of the Six Articles, and effecting a great change in the forms of public devotion, by the introduction of an English Litany, with responses: nevertheless, his further attempts at a reformation were defeated, and he had again, A.D. 1545, to endure another measure of hostility on the part of his adversaries, from which he was only again released by the continuance of the firm friendship of Henry, who in this instance personally defeated their object of sending him to the Tower, by granting him his ring to be produced at any moment of emergency, and by afterwards reproving them for their hostility and malice against him.

On the 28th of January, 1547, Henry VIII. died, at a period of the deepest interest to Cranmer, when he had anticipated the prospect of a speedy abolition of many of the remaining and most notorious abuses of the church of Rome, which hitherto he had been unsuccessful in his efforts to remove. The state of religion at this moment throughout the country was unsettled, and it was evident to himself that he was entering upon a reign which, in its earliest period, could not fail to increase his anxiety and his cares. Edward VI. was but ten years old when he began to reign; and as much of the affairs of state necessarily fell to the charge of the archbishop, he had still to encounter the unceasing opposition of the men who throughout the latter years of the late king's government had never ceased to harass and persecute him. Gardiner still continued his activity, although separated from the government; but Cranmer was enabled to set his machinations at defiance by prosecuting steadily the objects he had in view: and, in order to ascertain the actual condition of the church, he obtained a royal proclamation for a visitation of the whole kingdom, which measure was resolved upon in April, and carried into effect in the following September.

The Reformation was now progressing, and the archbishop's influence became more and more predominant, especially in the deliberations of the clergy. On November 22, he produced an ordinance for the receiving of the sacrament in both kinds, which was unanimously carried; and immediately afterwards obtained an entire repeal of the Act of the Six Articles, and other persecuting statutes, the abrogation of which hitherto he had not been able to procure. This year, 1548, saw the abolition of images, and steps taken for converting the mass into a communion-service in English. Opposition was offered to these proposed changes; but the tide had now set in favour of the progress of the Reformation, and the great work of producing the English Liturgy was finished, and received the final sanction of the legislature on the 15th of January, 1549. The spirit of rebellion was, however, abroad; and while a vast proportion of the inhabitants of the country rejoiced at the changes which were taking place, in Devonshire and Cornwall active opposition was roused by the disaffected, and a formidable revolt broke out, which ended in the signal defeat of the rebels. The part which the archbishop had to take in these events was of a prominent character; and his answer to the demands of the rebels remains as an important and interesting document amongst his many literary labours.

In the month of December, of the same year, an act passed the legislature authorising the marriage of the clergy, which afterwards, A.D. 1552, was confirmed by a declaratory statute that marriages performed under it were valid. From the year 1549 to 1551 the work of reformation still proceeded. "The labour of the most reverend the archbishop of Canterbury," writes Peter Martyr to Bullinger, Jan. 27, 1550, "is not to be expressed. For whatever has hitherto been wrested from them (the bishops) we have acquired solely by the industry, and activity, and importunity of this prelate[1]." He obtained orders for the abolition of popish books of devotion, and effected the completion of the formulary for the ordination of the clergy. He likewise entertained many of the foreign divines at Lambeth, with whom he took counsel in aiding the progress of scriptural divinity. A source of affliction to Cranmer at this season was a spirit of dissension, which spread amongst the reformers themselves, upon the refusal of Hooper, bishop of Gloucester, to wear the episcopal vestments then usually worn. The archbishop was firm in his opposition to these scruples, and resisted the influence which dictated the opposition: a compromise however was in the end effected. In October, 1550, the communion-table was substituted for the Roman catholic altar, to do away the popish idea of a sacrifice, though several of the bishops resisted the change[2].

Proceedings were also taken out against Gardiner, who was deprived of his bishoprick in April, 1551. In this matter the conduct of the archbishop has been animadverted upon, as he undoubtedly took a considerable part in the degradation of his old and inveterate adversary. Gardiner pertinaciously refused to comply with the views of the Reformers. During his imprisonment in the Tower he prepared his treatise on the sacrament, in answer to the archbishop's "Defence of the True Doctrine of the Sacrament," which had attracted great attention, and met with extraordinary success. The primate lost no time in preparing a reply to the bishop of Winchester's confutation, which issued from the press in October, 1551. These works will be found in the first volume of the present collection of the archbishop's writings. Gardiner also replied to this work under the feigned name of Marcus Antonius Constantius, and his rejoinder was published in 1552. It is impossible to say when this contest would have terminated, had Cranmer and Gardiner lived to carry it on. The anxious attention of the former was occupied during his imprisonment about an answer to Marcus Antonius; and three parts of it are said to have been actually written, when the design was cut

[1] Original Letters relative to the English Reformation (Park. Soc.) p. 479—80.

[2] In this year (1550) occurred the burning of Joan Bocher. In the biographical notice prefixed to the writings of Roger Hutchinson published by the Parker Society, there is a statement (pp. iv—v.) relieving the archbishop from the allegation respecting her case so commonly reported to his prejudice.

short by his approaching martyrdom: but not a fragment of his labours is known now to be extant, though unceasing search has been made, if possible, to discover it; and but little doubt now exists that it is irrecoverably lost.

About this time the English Liturgy underwent a revision at the hands of the archbishop, assisted by Ridley, and Cox (afterwards bishop of Ely), in which some of the suggestions of Peter Martyr, Martin Bucer, and others were adopted. The result of these labours was, that the Book of Common Prayer was reduced very nearly into the form in which it stands at the present time, the subsequent changes in Queen Elizabeth's reign having been principally intended to render it less objectionable to the opponents of the reformation. A project of the archbishop for an agreement in religious doctrine between the Anglican and foreign reformed churches about this time was once more attempted, but it again failed; and the design entertained by him, of holding a synod in England, and adopting one Confession for all the reformed churches, was at length finally abandoned.

In the course of 1551, the archbishop received an order of the king in council to compile certain articles of religion: in the May following, 1552, the first draft was completed, and laid before the council. In September it was again revised by the archbishop, and on the 19th of the same month was submitted by him to sir John Cheke, the tutor of Edward VI., and to Mr Secretary Cecil. On the 2nd October the draft was handed over to six of the royal chaplains, viz. Harley, Bill, Horne, Grindal, Perne, and John Knox, the Scottish reformer. On the 20th November it was returned to Cranmer, who again revised it, and returned it to the council, November 24th, with a letter expressing his sentiments thereon, and requesting that all the clergy might be called upon to subscribe to it as the book of articles[3]. The authority here sought was not granted till June 9, 1553, when the king issued his mandate confirming Cranmer's request.

The next project which the archbishop entertained was that of bringing about a reformation of the ecclesiastical laws; but his intention was cut short by the untimely removal of his young master, Edward VI., who died before he could authorise the code which had been prepared for this purpose, and which was printed in the following reign, though never authorised or adopted.

The prospects of the reformation were now wholly darkened. By the accession of Mary to power Cranmer lost not only all hope of completing the work he had so long laboured to perfect, but he soon found that he could expect no mercy at the hands of the successor of Edward VI.; for although he raised his voice against the design for making the Lady Jane Grey queen, yet he did not remain long unmolested after Mary was firmly seated in the throne. Early in the month of August he was summoned before the council, and was commanded to keep his house at Lambeth. On the 27th of the same month he was again brought before the council, and ordered to give in an inventory of his goods; and in the middle of the following September he was committed to the Tower. The archbishop was now prepared for extremities, which he anticipated would quickly follow upon his imprisonment. As the commencement of them, he found himself attainted of high treason by the parliament. This took place in the month of November, and there is reason to believe that he fully expected his execution would speedily have followed. This did not, however, immediately happen, and in the month of March[4], 1554, he was removed to Oxford, with Ridley and Latimer, where disputations were held between these reformers and the Romanist party. On the 20th of April they were condemned, and excommunicated as heretics. Their execution did not, however, even now immediately follow: eighteen months elapsed from the period of their condemnation, before Ridley and Latimer were burned; and there was still a further interval of five months allowed to expire between their martyrdom and that of Cranmer, as he was reserved

---

[3] Vid. Letters CCCV. CCCVII. pp. 439, 40.

[4] Incorrectly stated, Vol. I. p. 391. in the quotation from Foxe, to have been "about the tenth of April:" but Bishop Ridley (Works, Park. Soc. p. 390.) says, "a little before Easter," (which was March 27th.) See also Original Letters relating to the English Reformation, p. 154. where the note, following Foxe, is at variance with the text.

for another trial when the authority of the pope should be restored throughout the realm. On the 12th September, 1555, the archbishop was summoned before his judges, and on the following day the process against him was closed. On the 7th of September, previously to these proceedings, he was cited to appear at Rome within eighty days; and though obedience to this citation was totally impossible, as he was still kept in prison, yet no sooner had the eighty days elapsed, than on the fourth of December, he was sentenced to excommunication at Rome: the pope's final executory letter was dated December 14th, by which it was commanded that he should first be degraded from his archbishoprick, and then be delivered over to the secular powers. It was not till Feb. 14th, 1556, that this degradation was carried into execution; and notwithstanding he appealed to a general council, after having formally withdrawn the recantations he had been induced to make, he was led to the stake, and suffered death for the truth's sake, on the 21st of March, 1556, in the 67th year of his age, and just at the close of the twenty-third from his consecration as primate of all England.

A list of archbishop Cranmer's writings, extracted from bishop Tanner's Biblio theca, has already been given in Vol. I. pp. xxx. xxxi. To this the editor subjoins the following lists:—from Bale's Script. Illust. Mag. Brit. Cat., Todd's Life of Abp. Cranmer, and Jenkyns' Remains of Abp. Cranmer.

*List of Abp. Cranmer's Writings from Bale's "Script. Illust. maj. Brit. Cat. Ed. Basil,* 1559."

INTER occupationes varias in Anglico sermone composuit Cranmerus:

Catechismum Doctrinæ Christianæ. Lib. I. "Excellentissimo principi Edwardo."
Ordinationes Ecclesiæ Reformatæ. Lib. I. "Nusquam excogitatum aliquid erat."
De Ministris Ordinandis. Lib. I. "Clarum est omnibus hominibus."
De Eucharistia cum Luthero. Lib. I.
Defensionem Catholicæ Doctrinæ. Lib. V. "Pro cura Dominici gregis mihi."
Ad Veritatis Professores. Lib. I. "Dominus et Servator noster."
Jura Ecclesiastica tempore Edwardi. Lib. I. "Quoniam regni potestas et legum."
Contra Gardineri Concionem. Lib. I.
Doctrinam Cœnæ Dominicæ. Lib. I. "Servator Noster Christus Jesus."
Contra Transubstantiationis Errorem. Lib. I. "Quatuor audivistis declaratas."
Quomodo Christus adsit in Cœna. Lib. I. "Resoluta jam, ut spero, transub."
De Esu Cœnæ Dominicæ. Lib. I. "Crassus Papistarum error de."
De Christi Oblatione. Lib. I. "Maxima blasphemia et injur."
Homelias Christianas. Lib. I.
Ad Ricardi Smithi Calumnias. Lib. I. "Jam nunc obtinui, candide lec."
Confutationes Veritatum non scriptarum. Lib. I. "Nihil addetis ad verbum, quod."
Locos Communes ex Doctoribus. Lib. XII "Sacræ Scripturæ intellectus et."
De non ducenda Fratria. Lib. II.
Contra Primatum Papæ. Lib. II.
Adversus Papæ Purgatorium. Lib. II.
De Justificatione. Lib. II.
Pias Precationes. Lib. I.
Epistolas ad viros eruditos. Lib. I.

Scripsit ex carcere:

Contra Sacrificium Missæ. Lib. I.
Contra Adorationem Panis. Lib I.
Ad Reginam Mariam. Lib. I.

et alia quædam.

Bibliorum translationes Anglicas pluribus in locis emendavit, præfationesque addidit.

*List of Abp. Cranmer's Writings, from Mr Todd's Life of Cranmer,* Vol. II. p. 519 et sqq.

A LONG Speech in the House of Lords in 1534, discussing the propriety of a General Council, and denouncing the authority of the Pontiff.
A Speech in Convocation in 1536, defending the Opinion of Alexander Aless concerning the Sacraments of Baptism and the Lord's Supper.
Answers to Questions concerning Confirmation, 1537.
Considerations submitted to King Henry in order to a further Reformation, 1537.
Injunctions given at his Visitation of the See of Hereford, 1538.
Preface to the Translation of the Bible, in 1539, first printed in 1540.
Articles intended to be the Doctrine of the Church of England, 1540.
Answers to Seventeen Questions concerning the Sacraments, previously to the publication of the Necessary Doctrine, in 1543.
Three brief Discourses on his Review of the Necessary Doctrine, entitled, Faith, Justification, and Forgiveness of Injuries.
Other Annotations on this Review.
Parts of three other Discourses against the fear of Death, and on Patience in Sickness and Adversity.
Collection of Passages from the Canon Law, to shew the necessity of reforming it, about the year 1544.
Speech to Edward the Sixth at his Coronation, 1546-7.
Speech in Convocation to the Clergy, 1547.
The Homilies on Salvation, Faith, and Good Works, 1547.
Answers to Questions concerning the Mass, 1547.
Additions to the Translation of Justus Jonas's Catechism, 1548.
Against Unwritten Verities, 1548.
Articles to be inquired into at his Visitation, 1548.
Preface to the Book of Common Prayer, entitled, "Concerning the Service of the Church," 1548-9.
Answers to the Fifteen Articles of the Devonshire Rebels, 1549.
Notes for a Homily on the subject of Rebellion, 1549.
Defence of the True and Catholic Doctrine of the Sacrament of the Body and Blood of our Saviour Christ, 1550.
Vindication of the Defence in Answer to Bishop Gardiner and Dr Smith, 1551.
Pious Prayers.
Declaration against the Mass, 1553.
Disputation at Oxford, 1554.
Speech before the Papal Commissioners, 1555.
Appeal to a General Council, 1555-6.
Speech at his Martyrdom, 1555-6.

*List of Abp. Cranmer's Writings as given in "Jenkyns' Remains of Cranmer,"* 4 Vols. Oxon. 1833.

LETTERS.
Collection of Extracts from the Canon Law.
Substance of a Speech on the authority of the Pope, and of General Councils.
Speech in Convocation.
Queries and Answers on Confirmation.
Injunctions for the Diocese of Hereford.
Corrections of The Institution of a Christian Man, by Henry VIII.
Annotations on the King's Book.
Seventeen Questions and Answers on the Sacraments, &c.
Preface to the Bible.

Speech at the Coronation of Edward VI.
Notes and Authorities on Justification.
Homily of Salvation.
——— of Faith.
——— of Good Works.
Queries and Answers on the Mass.
Articles of Visitation for the Diocese of Canterbury.
Articles of Visitation for the Dean and Chapter of Canterbury.
Injunctions to the Dean and Chapter of Canterbury.
Answer to the Devonshire Rebels.
Notes for a Sermon against Rebellion.
Sermon on Rebellion.
Defence of the True and Catholic Doctrine of the Sacrament, &c.
Answer to Rich. Smythe's Preface.
Answer to Gardyner's Explication.
Notes of Gardyner's Errors.
Declaration concerning the Mass.
Disputation at Oxford with Chedsey.
——————— with Harpsfield.
Condemnation, by Weston.
Examination at Oxford before Brokes.
Appeal to a General Council.
Prayer, Exhortation, and Confession of Faith at St Mary's Church.
Confutation of Unwritten Verities.
Appendix.

In bringing this edition of the Writings of Archbishop Cranmer to a close, the editor cannot but express how much he has been indebted to the previous labours of Dr Jenkyns, by whose researches many difficulties have been cleared for him: he would indeed consider it a dereliction of duty, were he not to state that in preparing the reprint of the archbishop's letters for this volume, he has found the chief part of the work amply done before him, which he would here most thankfully acknowledge. Nevertheless he has not thought it right to take any statements upon trust; but in every instance, when it has been practicable, he has collated for himself, having gone over the MSS. in the State Paper Office, the British Museum, and other libraries, and examined them seriatim and verbatim. He is enabled, through the kind assistance of friends, to add several letters of the archbishop to those already published, which have never before been printed in any collection of the archbishop's writings; and in many instances, when it had been left undone by Dr Jenkyns, he has supplied references not previously given.

The editor would be wanting in courtesy, were he not to acknowledge his obligations to various persons who have kindly assisted him; and more especially are his thanks due to the Rev. the masters and fellows of Corpus Christi and Emmanuel colleges, Cambridge; to R. Lemon, Esq., of the State Paper Office; to the Rev. W. H. Cox, vice-principal of St Mary Hall, Oxford; to the Rev. H. Christmas, Sion College; to the Rev. G. Bryan; to the Rev. H. Robbins, Head Master of the Stepney Grammar School; to the Rev. J. Mendham, Sutton Coldfield; to the Rev. S. R. Maitland, librarian of the Archiepiscopal Library, Lambeth; to Mr J. Darling, of the Clerical Library, Little Queen Street, Lincoln's Inn Fields, London; to Mr Black, of the Public Record Office; and, though last not least, to the Rev. J. Ayre, the indefatigable and laborious editor of Becon, Jewel, &c. for the Parker Society, without whose aid the work in several parts would have been far less complete.

*Dec.* 10, 1846.

# ADDENDA ET CORRIGENDA.

Page 17. n. 6. *for* Gardner *read* Gardiner.

36. at the end of n. 1. supply D. Scot. Prol. Sent. quæst. ii. p. 5. Ed. Venet. 1497.

66. l. 7. *after* "another learned man," *supply* [Salcot. Bp. of Bangor.]

155. l. 3. *for* war *read* wax.

210. n. 9. substitute the following:

Antididagma, seu Christianæ et Catholicæ &c. Propugnatio. Ed. Paris. 1545. fo. 34. 2. where is affixed a marginal note: "Cum judicio legenda sunt hæc."— This is a work relative to Archbishop Herman's reformation at Cologne.

298. n. 1. l. 7. *for* 1533 *read* 1523.

457. to n. 6. add: These grounds may be briefly stated as follows:

1. It is clear from the letter that the bearer was high in Cranmer's estimation, and also intimate with P. Martyr. Jewel had been engaged as an assistant to Martyr at Oxford, and had also acted as notary in behalf of Cranmer at his first trial in April, 1554.
2. He was a person of note among the reformers, and one who *left England late*: for the date given by Bullinger either for the letter, or his own note to it, is 1555. Now the exiles had settled at Zurich before Sept. 1554; but Jewel came thither later than the rest.
3. The bearer of the letter was going straight from Oxford to the continent, and to P. Martyr; for Cranmer evidently implies that the friend to whom he entrusted it would deliver it in person to Martyr. And Jewel did actually start from Oxford when he fled abroad, and immediately became Martyr's assistant at Strasburgh, and followed him to Zurich.
4. Jewel had conformed; but evidently repented of this before he left Oxford, though it was not till he reached Frankfort that he made his open confession of penitence. This previous repentance at Oxford accounts for his precipitate flight thence; and also for the caution observed by Cranmer in not mentioning his name; and explains his allusion to the "danger and mischief" occasioned by letters.
5. It is also very intelligible that the fact of Jewel's temporary conformity to the popish articles may have procured him access to Cranmer in his imprisonment; while it seems incredible that any friend of Cranmer and Martyr, *not conforming*, would have been allowed such access.
6. To all this it must be added, that there is no evidence (it is believed) of any other reformer—a friend of Cranmer and Martyr—having been in England and at Oxford so late as the date of this letter.

Post plurimam in Christo servatore nostro salutem. Quando tum demum necessariae sunt literae,
cum aut non satis prudens est nuncius, aut rerum quas significare volumus ignarus, aut non
fidens cui arcana credas: cumque mihi Dei benignitate sese obtulisset hic tabellarius, vir
et prudentia (ut nosti) insignis, et qui rebus in credendis fidissimus sit, et nostrum utriusque
amantissimus, et rerum nostratium scientissimus, ex cujus ore quae hic acta fuerint intelligas omnia:
non necessarium existimavi, ut plura ad te scriberem, praesertim cum scripturae tot pericula
damnaque afferre soleant. Illud tamen unum praeterire tandem non censui (quod expertus didici)
nunquam Deum splendidius illucescere, et clementiae suae, consolationis, aut roboris ac fortitudinis
animi radios, suorum mentibus clarius aut pressius infundere, quam in summis animi corporisque angoribus atque pressuris: ut tum vel maxime sese declaret suorum esse Deum, quum
illos desertissimos praeterisse videtur; tum erigere quum dejicere atque prosternere, tum glorificare quum confundere, tum denique vivificare quum occidere putetur. Ut cum Paulo dicere
liceat, Quando infirmior, tunc fortior sum, et si gloriari oportet, in infirmitatibus meis
gloriabor, in carceribus, in contumeliis, in necessitatibus, in persecutionibus, in angustiis
pro Christo. Faxit obsecro Deus, ut in finem perseverem. Hodie nihil magis animum angit meum, quam quod tractationi M. A. nihil est responsum, ad cujus astutias, praestigias et insanias
redarguendum non defuisset responsio, nisi mihi defuissent et libri et libertas. Proinde tibi
scripsi iterum, nec scire tamen queo quae ad te scripserim, proinde meo nomine salutabis omnes.

Thomas Cranmerus

Haec est manus Archiepiscopi Cantuariensis. Scripsit
haec ex carcere ad D. Pet. Martyrem. M. A.
significant Marc. Antonium, i. e. Wintoniensem 1555

# A CONFUTATION

OF

# UNWRITTEN VERITIES.

[Title-page of the original Edition.]

# ¶ A Confu-
# tatiō of vnwrittē verities, both bi the

holye scriptures and moste auncient
autors, and also probable arguments,
and pithy reasons, with plaine auns-
wers to al (or at the least) to the moste
part and strongest argumentes, which
the aduersaries of gods truth either
haue, or can bryng forth for the profe
and defence of the same vnwritten va
nities, verities as they woulde haue
them called: made by Thomas Cranmer, late Archebishop of Cantorbu-
rie, Martyr of god, and burned
at Oxford for the defēce of the
trewe doctrine of our sauiour Christ, translated
and set forth,
by E. P.

¶ The contentes whereof, thou
shalte finde in the next side
folowinge.

# ¶ A Confutation of
## vnwritten verities, both by the holye
**Scriptures and most auntient authours, and also probable**

Arguments, and pithie reasons, with plaine aunsweres to all (or at the least) to the most part and strongest argumentes, which the Aduersaries of Gods truth, either haue or can bring foorth for the proofe and defence of the same vnwritten Vanities, Verities as they woulde haue them called.

*Made by Thomas Cranmer, late Archebishop of Canterburie, Martir of God, and burned at Oxenforde for the defence of the true doctrine of our Sauiour Christ.*

The Contents whereof, thou shalt finde in the next side following.

(·.·)

*Imprinted at London by Thomas Purfoote*
and are to be solde at his Shop, without Newgate, ouer-against S. Sepulchers Churche.
*Anno.* 1582.

[The "Confutation of Unwritten Verities," is printed from the edition "imprinted at London by Thomas Purfoote, anno 1582," and has been carefully collated with the original edition, published by E. P. in the reign of Queen Mary.]

The Title-page of the original edition of the "Confutation of Unwritten Verities" states that it was "translated and set forth by E. P.;" and upon that of both editions it is said to be "made by Thomas Cranmer, late archbishop of Canterbury." Strype, in his Memorials of Archbp. Cranmer, writes, that "there was another book of the archbishop's against unwritten verities, which I do by conjecture place here, as put forth under this year, or near this time, (A. D. 1547.) The book was in Latin, and consisted only of allegations out of the bible and ancient writers. In queen Mary's days the book was again published by an English exile, naming himself E. P. The title it now bore was, *A Confutation of Unwritten Verities, by divers authorities, diligently and truly gathered out of the Holy Scripture and ancient fathers; by Thomas Cranmer, late archbishop, and burned at Oxford for the defence of the true doctrine of our Saviour. Translated and set forth by E. P.* Before it is a preface of the translator to his countrymen and brethren in England," &c[1].

Dr Jenkyns, in his edition of the archbishop's works[2], pronounces that it certainly was not "made" by Cranmer in its present form: for the preface and some other parts were avowedly written by the translator. "And" (he goes on to say) "it may be doubted, whether it was ever prepared by him for publication at all; no complete copy of it in Latin, either printed or in manuscript, having been yet discovered. The citations, however, of which the work chiefly consists, are for the most part to be found in one of the archbishop's common-place books in the British Museum, arranged under the same heads as in the *Confutation*. And hence perhaps it may be conjectured, that, according to his usual practice, he formed a collection of authorities on the subject for his private use; that this collection fell after his death into the hands of the person designated by the letters E. P., and that it was moulded by him, by addition, omission, and transposition, into the shape in which it now appears." "Under these circumstances," Dr Jenkyns thinks, "it cannot safely be quoted as evidence of Cranmer's tenets, and that perhaps it scarcely ought to be admitted into a collection of his works."

The work, however, has been usually placed amongst the writings of the archbishop; and there is but little doubt, even in the mind of Dr Jenkyns, that the materials, from which "it was composed, were brought together" and prepared by him. The editor has collated the original edition set forth by E. P., with that imprinted at London, A. D. 1582, by Thomas Purfoote, from which copy the piece is printed in this edition, and he has given the different readings in each copy, though adhering as closely as possible in the text to that of A. D. 1582.

Another treatise of unwritten verities, which was published, A. D. 1548, anonymously, is also supposed by Strype to have been written by archbishop Cranmer. Dr Jenkyns[3], however, thinks, as he has not brought forward "any evidence in support of his opinion, and has manifestly fallen into much confusion on this matter," that "his judgment is of no great weight, since Bale, the cotemporary of Cranmer, evidently knew of no other work" of his than that, which was supposed to be written in Latin, A. D. 1547, and afterwards translated and set forth by E. P. Bp. Tanner, in reference to it, says, "that though it was written in Latin, it is evident to him that it was never printed in that language[4]."

---

[[1] Strype, Memorials of Archbishop Cranmer, Vol. I. p. 228. Ed. Oxon. 1840.]

[[2] Vol. IV. p. 144. Ed. Oxon. 1833.]

[[3] Ibid. p. 144.]

[[4] Qui liber Latine scriptus nunquam, ut mihi quidem videtur, in ea lingua impressus fuit. Tanner, Bibliotheca.—"Cranmer."]

Dr Jenkyns[1] thinks, "that it was not unlikely that it was compiled by E. P. out of Cranmer's MS. notes, which are still preserved in the British Museum;" and he also positively asserts that "it is certain, at least, that the preface and the conclusion, together with some parts of the body of the work, must be ascribed entirely to the translator."

The anonymous treatise, which is found in Strype[2], will be printed in an appendix to this edition. For further particulars, relating to these treatises, the reader is referred to Strype, Memorials of Archbishop Cranmer, Vol. I. pp. 228, 570, ed. Oxon. 1840. Ecclesiastical Memorials, Vol. II. part i. pp. 212, 213; Vol. II. part ii. p. 410, ed. Oxon. 1822. Bale, Script. Brit. Catal. p. 691, ed. Basil. 1559. Ames, Typ. Antiq. Vol. I. p. 583, ed. 1785; Vol. III. p. 1563, ed. 1790.

---

[[1] Vol. I. Preface, p. lvi.]

[[2] Strype, Ecclesiastical Memorials, Vol. II. part ii. (Appendix AA. MSS. D. Joh. D. Episc. Elien.) p. 410. Ed. Oxon. 1822.]

# THE CONTENTS.



---

[[3] The words, "of the dead," are not found in the original ed.]

[[4] The Editor is indebted to the edition of Dr Jenkyns, Vol. IV. p. 147, et sqq. for the following valuable information:—"A conjecture has been hazarded in a preceding note, that this *Confutation* was compiled from a collection of authorities still preserved in the British Museum (Royal MSS. 7. B. xi. xii.) A list of the principal heads under which these authorities are arranged, is subjoined. It will assist the reader in forming a judgment on the validity of the conjecture, and will also give him some insight into Cranmer's studies on other subjects. It will be found to be more copious than the Table of Contents which is prefixed to the manuscript in the Museum, and which has been printed by Strype, (Life of Parker, App. No. 23). The additions are distinguished by brackets. The articles marked with an asterisk exist in the original Table, but are not in the same handwriting as the rest.

*Collectiones ex S. Scriptur. et Patribus.*

TABULA REPERTORIA.

1. Sacræ Scripturæ intellectus et utilitas, p. 9.
2. Quod auctorum scripta sine verbo Dei non sunt accipienda pro articulis fidei, p. 15.
3. Scripturæ confirmantes idem, p. 16.
4. Doctores idem probantes, p. 19.
5. Rationes in idem, p. 42.
6. Conciliorum decreta sine Scriptura non sunt accipienda pro articulis fidei, p. 47.
7. Veteres Canones abrogati, p. 48.
8. Ex angelorum oraculis non licet idem facere, p. 53.
9. Nec miraculis idem probare fas est, p. 54.
10. Ne etiam apparitio mortuorum id ipsum satis astruit, p. 59.
11. Sed ne consuetudini hac in re fidendum est, p. 62.
12. Objectiones, quod præter Scripturæ auctoritatem recipiendi sunt novi articuli fidei, p. 65.
13. Traditiones non scriptæ, p. 75.
    *Ex Tertullian. Anglice, p. 93.
14. Rationes in idem, p. 94.
    [Baptismus parvulorum, p. 97.
    Baptizati ab hæreticis non sunt rebaptizandi, p. 98.]
15. Nec miracula, nec Christi professio, nec locus, nec externum aliquod, faciunt hominem sanctum aut Deo gratum, sed observatio mandatorum Dei, p. 99.
16. Novæ doctrinæ, p. 101.
17. In cæremoniis fere omnibus Judæos imitamur, p. 101.
18. Osiander.
19. De sacrificiis Christianorum, p. 103.
20. De sacramentis, p. 115, 121.
21. De charactere, p. 133.
22. De baptismo, p. 147.
23. De eucharistia, p. 211.
    [Pro sacramentariis, p. 259.]
24. De pœnitentia, p. 305, 327.
    *De confessione, p. 351.
25. De satisfactione, p. 384.
26. De matrimonio, p. 397.
27. De ordinibus ecclesiasticis, p. 417, 454, 461.
    [Multa fecerunt Christus et Apostoli quæ hodie apud nos non observantur, p. 474.
    Multi sacerdotalem dignitatem consecuti sunt sine episcoporum consecratione, p. 476.
    Quod ordo sit sacramentum, p. 477.]
28. De unctione, p. 464, 483.
29. De impositione manuum, p. 470.
    [De unctione chrismatis, p. 486.
    De confirmatione sine unctione chrismatis, p. 502.]
30. De confirmatione, p. 506.
31. De extrema unctione, p. 519.

In consequence of a mistake in the paging, there are duplicates of the numbers after 447 in the second volume. These are distinguished in the above list by the letters a and b."]

# THE PREFACE.

WHAT christian heart, dearly beloved countrymen and brethren in our Saviour Christ, 2.
can abstain from deep sobs and sorrowful sighings? What natural and kind-hearted man can forbear weeping; so often as he calleth to remembrance the Lord's vineyard within the realm of England (which he himself had of late so strongly hedged, walled, and fenced round about by the princes of most famous memory, king Henry the eighth, and Edward the sixth, and planted therein the pure vine of his own blessed word by godly preachers, his gardeners,) to be so suddenly broken down, destroyed, wasted, and rooted up by the roots, by the wild boar of the wood and the beasts of the field, that is, by the Romish bishop and his bloody ministers; and now in the same vineyard to see planted, take root, and prosper, brambles, briars, and hemlocks; that is, gross ignorance, naughty doctrine, false worship of God, and such other kinds of most stinking, vile, and filthy weeds? Oh what a sweet and pleasant grape of godly doctrine was then gathered in England, to the great comfort and rejoicing of all them that lovingly tasted thereof! Then was God's word (for that is the sweet and pleasant grape "that maketh glad the heart of man") with great freedom preached, earnestly embraced, and with greedy hearts in all places received.

Isai. v. 2.

Kings and rulers ought to be aiders, and not invaders; helpers, and not hurters; defences, and not offences, to God's people.

Psal. lxxx.[1]

God's word is a sweet and pleasant grape, and comforteth the heart of man to everlasting salvation.

Psal. civ.[1]

Then was God's great glory marvellously advanced. Then the only merits of Christ, then true repentance for our former sins, then trust in God's mercy through the death of our Saviour Christ, with a new christian life, was truly published and preached every where. Then was there the common prayer rightly used, and the sacraments (baptism, I mean, and the holy communion) in such a tongue and language set forth that all people might understand them. Then were they plainly ministered, without any juggling or sorcery, according to Christ's institution and the rule of his holy word: which word at that time had the prize and bare the bell away throughout the whole land.

With that were all pulpits filled, churches garnished, printers' shops furnished, and 3.
every man's house decked. With God's word was every man's mouth occupied, of that were all songs, interludes, and plays made. But, alas! so long, till all was played under the board. But what was the cause of all this? Truly none other thing but our own sins and wickedness. For we were talkers only and not walkers, lip-gospellers, from the mouth outward and no farther. We were even such as the prophet speaketh of, saying, "This people honoureth me with their lips, but are far from me with their hearts." We could speak of God's word and talk gloriously thereof; but in our hearts we were full of pride, malice, envy, covetousness, backbiting, rioting, harlot-hunting, no whit bettered at all than we were before under the pope's kingdom. Nothing was in us amended, but only our tongues; no, nor they neither, if I shall speak rightly and as the truth was in deed. For, besides our communication of scripture, we used detraction of our neighbour, filthy talk, with many proud brags of ourselves. We read not the scriptures, neither heard them, for any amendment of our own wicked lives, but only to make a brag and a shew thereof, to check and to taunt others, yea, and to spy small motes in other men's eyes, but nothing desirous to see the great beams in our own. This, I say, to talk and not to walk, to say and not to do, was not only amongst the unlearned sort, but also amongst the great clerks and chief preachers of God's word. Which thing, as I judge, was the only cause, why God by his just judgment suffered his elect and chosen vineyard to be thus trodden down, rooted up, and miserably afflicted by this bloody boar of Rome, and the fat bulls of Basan, his cruel officers. This is the cause why God hath suffered

But the hearts of the most part were naked, bare, and empty; as the proof now, alas! too well declareth. Sin is the cause why God taketh his word from any people.

Isai. xxix.[1]

Matt vii. 2.[1]

Psal. xxii.[1]

[1 Not in ed. 1582.]

The pope giveth lies for truth, poison for nourishing sustenance, and ministereth death for life.

John vi.

John iv.

this great antichrist to disgrace the merits of Christ's passion, and in place thereof to set up men's merits, and instead of his sufficient satisfaction upon the cross once for all to set up his masses satisfactory for the sins both of the quick and dead. This is the cause that this monstrous beast hath taught the invocation of saints, and the same to be our mediators to God, and satisfiers for our sins. Whereas before, in the forenamed vineyard, was planted Christ Jesus, the true bread that came down from heaven, and that most pure well of the water of life; now, after the rooting of this monstrous and ravenous boar, are upsprung conjured bread, conjured water, to drive away evil spirits and to purge our sins.

Psal. cxv.[1] Jer. x.

Exod. xx. 4.[2]

This bloody boar, besides all mischiefs that he hath done to the vineyard, yet ceaseth
4. he not, with fagot, fire, and all other cruel torments, to constrain and compel men to worship images, the work of men's hands, to kneel to them, to reverence them, to bow to them, and with all manner of obeisance to honour them, clean contrary to God's commandment, who saith: "Thou shalt not make to thyself" (much less then to honour, reverence, and worship them) "any graven image, nor the likeness of any thing that is in heaven above, or in the earth beneath, or in the water under the earth; thou shalt not bow down to them, nor worship them." But yet these shameless wretches be not abashed to say, that images are necessary, because they be laymen's books, teaching them, instructing them, and leading them to the true worship of God. Oh great blasphemy! Oh sacrilege! Oh spiteful robbery! What is blasphemy, what is sacrilege, what is robbery, if this be none? God giveth his word written to be every man's book, and his pure, everlasting, and undefiled commandments as sufficient instructions for all men to the true worship of him. But these earthly wroters (the pope, I mean, and his prelates) as though they were wiser than God, will teach men to worship him with images, although the same be utterly forbidden by God throughout the whole course of his holy scriptures.

God's word is sufficient to instruct all men in the true worship of God, without images. Priests think themselves wiser than God.

These and such other false and feigned doctrines, contrary to the scriptures of God contained in his holy bible, are now blown out, blustered, and yelled forth in every pulpit. Every street soundeth of these; yea, every printer's house is filled with such ungodly baggage; yea, and the same are commanded by public authority (which is much to be lamented) to be set forth, and the sincere doctrine of Christ's holy word clean put to silence, and utterly condemned. Neither may any man reason, or once doubt of their doctrine, under pain of excommunication, nay, rather under pain of burning.

The pope maintaineth his doctrine by fire and fagot, and not by holy[3] scriptures.

A weak refuge, if they were not obstinate and shameless.

And when they be not able (as they are not able at any time indeed) to prove any of these doctrines by the word of God written, then they fly to their unwritten verities, that is, to certain things delivered, as they say, from the apostles by word of mouth, without writing. Which things are to all men uncertain; for no man knoweth certainly, what they are But whatsoever pleaseth them and maketh for their purpose, profit, and lordly ambition, that is an unwritten verity, not to be gainsaid or denied. This is their shot-anchor, bulwark, and extreme refuge, whereunto they fly whensoever they are forced and constrained by God's word. These they make their foundations, whereupon they build and maintain all their superstitions, idolatries and heresies. Which
5. foundations I trust, by God's grace and help, so to shake, both by the open scriptures, by the full consent of all the most ancient writers, and by probable reasons, that the building thereupon shall have a fall.

If unwritten verities were necessary to salvation, then God's word were not sufficient thereunto.

For this is most true, that no unwritten verity is or can be necessary for our salvation: for then should the sacred and holy scriptures, written by the apostles in the Spirit of God, and sealed with their bloods, seem to be insufficient and not able to bring us unto salvation. But what a great blasphemy that should be to God and his most holy Spirit, all men, I trust, that list to read the same scriptures, easily shall perceive. But when these unshamefaced robbers are put to their shifts, urged and forced herein by the open and manifest word written, then have they another starting-hole to

[[1] Misprinted Psalm xx. in ed. 1582.]

[[2] Misprinted in Orig. ed. Exo. xx. 2, and in ed. 1582, Exo. 115.]

[[3] By the holy scriptures, Orig. ed.]

creep out at, crying and yelling, *Templum Domini*, *Templum Domini*, *Templum Domini*, &c. "The church, the church, the church;" affirming in plain words that the church can in no wise err or be deceived. And here they deceive themselves, because they take[4] no distinction or difference of the church. For there are two manner of churches, one true, perfect, and holy in the sight of God, and another false, imperfect, and ungodly. Truth it is, that the true church of God, being grounded and set upon his holy word, (I mean the gospel of grace) cannot err unto damnation. But the other, how shining and glorious soever it appear, if it wander abroad, and be not contained within the compass and limits of the word written, is no true, but a feigned and forged church. That church, as it is without the compass of God's promises made in truth, not only may, but also doth commonly, yea continually err and go astray; for they are not coupled to the head Christ, which is the life, the way, and the truth. Paul, the apostle of God, and elect vessel of salvation, writing to the Galatians, hath these words: "If we," saith he, "or an angel from heaven, preach any other gospel unto you, than that we have preached, hold him accursed:" and yet the papist[5], not fearing the curse of God, dare be bold to teach things which Paul never knew, yea, things clean contrary to his evident and manifest teaching. Such gross ignorance (I would to God it were but ignorance indeed) is entered into their heads, and such arrogant boldness possesseth their hearts, that they are bold to affirm no church to be the true church of God, but that which standeth by ordinary succession of bishops, in such pompous and glorious sort as 6.
now is seen. For if there be, say they, no such outward and visible church, how shall any man know whether he be of the church of Christ, and in the right belief, or no? To this I answer, that if our faith should be stayed upon the outward, glistering, and pompous church, not ruled nor governed by the determinate counsel of God in his word written, we should never be certain thereof, but ever wavering and doubting; which is the gate and ready pathway to desperation, from which God defend his chosen flock!

Jer. vii. 2.

Yea, this is their strong tower and bulwark of defence: and yet weak enough, not being walled about with God's word.

God's true church, because it is grounded upon the word of grace, cannot err in matters of salvation.

The church that wandereth from God's word written may and doth err in matters of faith and salvation.

Galat. i.

The papists fear not God's curse.

"Cursed is he," saith the scripture, "that putteth his trust in man." And why? For "all men," as the kingly prophet David saith, "are liars" in their words, and sinners in their works. By which words it appeareth plain, that there was never man so virtuous, holy, nor so well learned, only the writers of the holy scriptures excepted, but, either of ignorance or of negligence, there escaped some faults in his writings and doings. Yea, the general councils themselves also, that they make so much of, have notably erred, as hereafter shall be declared. Yea, such hath been the truth of those seen churches, that one general council hath condemned another of heresy: moreover, the outward seen church, whereof they brag not a little, hath never since the beginning any space continued in the true doctrine of God. Let us begin at Moses, who was the first lawgiver, and we shall see the state of this outward church, which consisteth in the ordinary succession of bishops, whether it be so as I have said, or no. When Moses was gone up to the mount Sinai to talk with God, and to receive the law at his hands, did not Aaron, the high priest and bishop, with all the people, in the mean space worship the golden calf? Read the book of Judges, and you shall see how the whole outward and visible church fell to idolatry and worshipping of strange gods: as Baal, Astaroth, gods of the Edomites, Moabites, Philistines, and the Syrians. After the reign of king David, how many kings were there, I pray you, in whose time false gods were not openly worshipped? All the kings of Israel served strange gods with the consent of the bishops, priests, and the whole people. And in Juda there passed not three or four kings, after David, in whose days open idolatry was not allowed and practised, by the consent of the kings, bishops, high priests, scribes, and Pharisees. Which of the prophets did not the open and visible church persecute? Where was the visible church in the time of Elias? Were not all that were known, and thought to be of the church, worshippers of Baal; insomuch that Elias thought there had been left alive of God's true church but himself only? And yet, notwithstanding, God had preserved his church, known but only to himself; for he knoweth who are his. Who smote Micheas, the true prophet of God, but the chief priest and bishop Zedechias?

Jer. xvii.

Psal. cxvi.

The general councils have erred, and that in no small trifles.

Exod. xxxii.

2 Tim. ii.

1 Kings xxii.

[4 Make, Orig. ed.]

[5 Papists, Orig. ed.]

And he, with four hundred priests more of his own mind and religion, deceived
7. Achab, and promised him victory over the Assyrians, although God had made them no such promise, but rather had pointed the contrary, as it came to pass. Who commanded Jeremy to be beaten for his true prophesying, but Phashur, the archbishop? Who persuaded with the king that Jeremy, the true prophet of God, was a seditious fellow, and went about to discourage the people in Jerusalem, that they should not resist Nabuchodonozor, king of Babylon, but the priests? Yea, and when the king delivered him out of prison, who but these holy men of the church procured him to be cast again into a deep dungeon, where they would have famished him, if God had not put in the king's heart to take him out and deliver him? These be the fruits and practices of the visible and seen church, which, if it be true that the papists say, cannot err. But whatsoever they say, it forceth not: for we know what the spiritualty, as they call themselves, have been since the beginning, the very expressed image whereof is set forth and declared in the Machabies (as they that read the story shall perceive it well enough) by Alcinus, Simon, Jason, and Menelaus.

Jer. xx

This and such like is the reward of all true preachers and faithful servants of God.

1 Mac. vii.

Now let us come to the new Testament, and see what the visible and known church was under it. Who was the true church, or how was it known to the people, in Christ's time? The high priests, bishops, scribes, Pharisees, and Sadducees, which appeared outwardly and boasted themselves to be the church of God, were indeed, as Christ calleth[1] them, serpents, the generations of vipers, hypocrites, children of hell, painted tombs, persecutors of true religion, and murderers of the prophets, yea, of himself and his apostles; men that shut up the kingdom of heaven, so that neither they would enter therein themselves, nor suffer the poor simple, that were desirous to know the truth, to enter, but excommunicated and thrust them out of the church, as men cast away, as heretics, and forsaken of God, whosoever believed on Christ. Who commanded the apostles that they should preach no more in Christ's name? Who caused Stephen to be stoned, and James to be thrown off the pinnacle?[2] Who gave authority to Paul to bind and bring before them all that professed Christ? Who commanded him to be buffeted? Who accused him before Festus and Agrippa? Who stirred the gentiles against him in all countries where he went to preach, but the church? If you will then needs judge the outward visible church, that sitteth in Moses' chair, (though they do not as the chair requireth,) to be the true church of God, I pray you then tell me, who caused Constantinus, the emperor, to banish Athanasius?[3] Who exiled Chrysostome and many other more godly and well learned bishops, and slew a great number of godly and well learned men, but the
8. priests, by seducing the empress Eudoxia?[4] Who put out the eyes of Constantine, the fourth emperor, and caused him to be slain, because he pulled the images out of the church, being worshipped contrary to God's holy will and commandment, but his own mother, by the counsel of the pope and the bishops, being then taken for the church? Who deposed Henry, the fourth emperor, causing his own son to rebel against him? Who deposed Childericus, the French king, assoiling his subjects from their obedience to him, and made Pipine king in his stead, but the pope and his churchmen?

Matt. iii. xii. xxiii.

Acts iv.

Acts vii.

Euseb. Eccl. Hist. Lib. ii. cap. 22.

Acts ix.

Acts xxv.

Ruffini, Lib. i. cap. 17. Socratis, Lib. vi. cap. 18.

Mark well the fruits of this outward church; and by them ye shall know what they be.

Let us come to our own realm, and speak of things done in our own memory. Who procured king Henry the eighth, in the beginning of his reign, to war against the French king; where, besides the murder committed, adultery was learned, theft and sacrilege practised, lying, swearing, yea, and forswearing, with all other kinds of vices, used, which be the very fruits of war, but the clergy? For the pope, then being in war with the French king, to make his part good and the stronger, procured the bishops of the church of England, being the pope's dear darlings, and chief of the king's council, to entitle the king to his right of the realm and crown of France; and to encourage the young king thereto, the pope accursed the king of France and all his

[1 Called, Orig. ed.]

[2 Eusebius, Eccl. Hist. Lib. II. cap. xxii. p. 61. Ed. Paris. 1659.]

[3 Ruffinus, Eccl. Hist. Lib. I. cap. xvii. xix. pp. 190, 1. Ed. Basil. 1661.]

[4 Socrates, Eccl. Hist. Lib. VI. cap. xvi. p. 724. Ed. Colon. Allobr. 1612.]

aiders and succourers. Then free pardons flew abroad as thick as butterflies in summer: but so free, that the realm thereby and the said warriors[5] was robbed of a great deal of our treasure, and in manner half undone. There was full remission *a pœna et culpa* preached at Paul's Cross, and almost in every sermon through all England; promising, that whosoever died in the pope's quarrel, his soul should be in heaven before his bones were cold. After, when the same king Henry had justly, by the authority of God's word, and the full consent both of the parliament and convocation, abolished the usurped power of the bishop of Rome, then the pope interdicted the whole realm, and sent cardinal Poole from prince to prince, to excite and move them (if he could have brought it to pass) to make open war against the king and the realm; as it appeareth in a sermon preached by Tonstall then[6] bishop of Durham, and set out in print openly: which sermon, and all other tell-truths, opening the abuses and tyranny of the bishop of Rome, are now put to silence. Who were the workers of all these mischiefs? Who, these three years past, hath persecuted, prisoned, and burned so many learned and godly men, only for their true faith's sake, grounded upon God's most holy word, (men worthy to be compared with the old martyrs of
the primitive church, as well for the constancy of their faith, as also for patience and 9.
charity shewed at their deaths,) but the church, as they call themselves? Who, by their cruel tyranny, hath enforced so many notable members of Christ (leaving wife, children, kinsfolk, lands and goods) either to fly into strange realms, or else from town to town, from city to city, only because they would not drink of the venomous cup of the whore of Babylon? Who hath wrought all these wickednesses, but only the mitred prelates and their popish priests?

The pope maketh himself equal to God, yea, rather above him, in this his promise.

This is one of the practices of prelates.

The spiritual man never persecuteth the carnal man, but forgiveth him. Hier. ad Gal. iv.[7]

If we shall allow them for the true church of God, that appear to be the visible and outward church, consisting of the ordinary succession of bishops, then shall we make Christ, which is an innocent lamb without spot, and in whom is found no guile, to be the head of ungodly and disobedient members. Which thing is as impossible as to make God, which is only good, and nothing but goodness itself, to be the author, original, and cause of all evil. For Christ, as he is pure, holy, and perfect, even so must his church and members be, to whom he, as the head, is adjoined and coupled. But if we allow the pope, his cardinals, bishops, priests, monks, canons, friars, and the whole rabble of the clergy, to be this perfect church of God, whose doings are clean contrary, for the most part, to the will and commandment of Christ, left and expressed in his word written; then make we him a sinner, and his word of no effect[9]. For as sweet agreeth with sour, black with white, darkness with light, and evil with good; even so this outward, seen, and visible church, consisting of the ordinary succession of bishops, agreeth with Christ.

Exod. xii. 1 Pet.[8]

Ephes. i. Colos. i.

But here they will ask me, how shall a man know whether he be in the right faith, but by this church? To this Christ shall make answer himself, saying, in the gospel of John, "My sheep hear my voice, and shall not hear a stranger." And where, I pray you, hath Christ left any voice to be heard or followed, but in his word written? "Search the scriptures," saith he, "for they bear witness of me." Where he biddeth you not search unwritten verities, such as the outward, seen, and pompous church shall of their own heads shew you, but the written verities contained in the holy scriptures, "which are profitable to teach, to improve, to amend, and to instruct in righteousness, that the man of God may be perfect and prepared unto all good works."

John x.

John v.

2 Tim. iii.

If thou therefore be desirous to know, whether thou be in the right faith or no, seek it not at man's mouth: for "all men be liars." Seek it not, I say, at a proud, glorious, and wavering sort of bishops and priests; but at God's own mouth, which is his holy word written, which can neither lie, deceive, nor be deceived. Ask, I say, seek, and knock by diligent study and earnest prayer unto God, who hath promised to

Psal. cxvi. God's word only certifieth a man whether his faith be good or no.

10.

---

[5 Warres, Orig. ed.]

[6 Now Bishop, Orig. ed. See Strype, Eccl. Mem. Vol. I. part i. pp. 518, 521. Oxford, 1822. This Sermon was intituled "Against the Pope's supremacy." Bertholet. 1539.]

[7 Nunquam enim spiritualis persequitur carnalem, sed ignoscit. Hieron. in Epist. ad Galat. Lib. II. cap. v. Tom. IX. p. 146. Ed. Francof. 1684.]

[8 1 Pet. ii. Orig. ed.]

[9 None effect, Orig. ed.]

give to all them that ask faithfully of him the certainty of good faith in their conscience, taught and confirmed by the holy scriptures of the old and new Testament.

And here I forbid no man, as though they should not ask and learn of the learned; for that is good and necessary, yea, and allowed by God's truth: but this would I have all men to do, to use discretion and wisdom in this matter, and to know whether they be learned, godly-minded, and able to instruct by the scriptures, or no. And yet, if they be, believe them no further than they can shew their doctrine and exhortation to be agreeable with the true word of God written. For that is the very touchstone which must, yea, and also will, try all doctrine or learning, whatsoever it be, whether it be good or evil, true or false. And let not men of small learning be too curious in asking or moving dark and doubtful questions, which breed contention rather than godly edifying, but let them be content with the plain and open places of the scriptures. Let them rather be earnest to observe the commandments of faith and love, which are plainly set forth in God's book, than to trouble themselves and busy their heads with dark places; for that is a thing that hath done, and also doth displease God very greatly. Yea, I think surely, that these heavy plagues, wherewith God most justly punisheth now this realm of England (which I beseech him, of his infinite mercy, either to take clean away, or else to mitigate them for his elect's sake) cometh not so much from the simple, innocent, and unlearned sort, (which, being beguiled through their simplicity, by the craft and subtlety of the wily papists, do still continue in superstition and idolatry,) but rather for the curious sort, which preach strange and far-fetched doctrines, nothing so much to edifying as to contentious brawling. Yea, I would to God there were not a great number of them, that were and are counted learned, which preach and defend doctrines which themselves know to be untrue and contrary to the evident scriptures. Would God there were not many hundreds of great gospellers sometimes, that had not subscribed with their own hands, and confirmed by their open and public sermons, the contrary of that which they once builded in Christ. And some of such, I know, in persuading privately with their old friends and acquaintance, have confessed no less, but that they have done contrary to the truth, and the good persuasion of their own conscience: and yet the same men counsel their friends, for unity and peace sake, as they term it, but rather, they may say, for fear of loss of goods and life, to obey wicked superstition[1], naughty rites, and damnable laws. But what peace, or what unity is that, that is against God and his Christ? And "what profiteth it a man to win all the world, and lose his own soul?" For "he that loveth his own life more than me," saith Christ, "is not worthy of me." For these men's sakes therefore, that is to say, the stubborn papists, that lead the world in blindness, contrary to their own consciences; and specially for delicate gospellers' sakes, whose wit and virtue is in their tongues, hot disputers, busy talkers, taunters and fault-finders with others, rather than menders of themselves; for these two sorts' sakes chiefly, I say, God heapeth these great plagues, that is, persecution of his word, dearth, danger of war, and people of strange nations, likely to subdue and utterly destroy that our realm, except they repent and amend their lives in time, and become not only forgetful of their former evils, but also diligent workers and true followers of the word, that they have so lightly condemned and refused. Which if they do not, let them be sure that all the plagues which are written in the book of God, and all the blood of his saints, which hath been shed from just Abel unto this present time, shall be poured upon them. But howsoever these men do, let us, dear brethren, whose hearts God of his goodness hath more mercifully touched, repent and amend our former lives, and cease from all dead works, lest we be partakers of the same plagues with them. But thanks be unto our God, that hath so gently ordered us! For this we know, that God suffereth not his people long to follow their own minds, but shortly punisheth them, which is a token of his great loving-kindness toward them. For this grace have we of God more than other people, as it is written, that he suffereth not us long to sin unpunished, like other nations, that when the day of judgment cometh, he may punish them in the fulness of their sins. If we sin, he correcteth us, but he

Try every spirit, but allow none further than they agree with the written scriptures. God's word trieth all things, whether they be good or bad.

Their consciences shall therefore condemn them for so doing, if they repent not in time.

11.

Matt. xvi.

The wit and virtue of delicate gospellers is in their tongues.

Matt. xxiii.

2 Macc. vi.

[[1] Superstitions, Orig. ed.]

never withdraweth his mercy from us; and though he punish us with adversity, yet
doth he never forsake his people: "For whom," as St Paul saith, "the Lord loveth, Heb. xii.
him he chasteneth; yea, and he scourgeth every son whom he receiveth."

But, to leave this digression and come to our purpose again, I will briefly shew
you what the outward face of the church and religion hath been in all ages; even
such as hath pleased the mighty kings, emperors, and rulers of the world. When
Jeroboam set up golden calves at Bethel and Dan, the priests and Levites consented 2 Chron. xiii.[2]
thereto, and all Israel worshipped them, contrary to God's commandment. When 12.
Jesabel had persuaded with her husband about murder, he fulfilled her mind and slew
all the prophets of God that he could come by; only Elias remained that was known
to be the true church, whereas the priests of Baal were four hundred and fifty in
number. Ezechias destroyed the brazen serpent, and restored the true religion and
worship of God; but Manasses, his son, set up idolatry, maintained wicked religion,
and slew them that were good. Josias restored right religion; but Jehoas and Jeho-
achim, his sons, forsook it, and all their priests and subjects with them committed
idolatry. And generally, what religion soever the king would have, that was stablished for his time; so that, as Solomon saith of the judges, so may we say of the
clergy, "Whatsoever saith the prince, that saith the priest."

The will of a woman must be followed, or else all the fat is in the fire.
1 Kings xix.[2]
1 Kings xviii.
2 Kings xviii.
2 Kings xxi.[2]
2 Kings xxiii.
2 Kings xxiv.
As princes would, so all things were done.

But let us once again come to the new Testament. Did not the head rulers of
the church, with the authority of Herod and Pilate, condemn Christ and his doctrine Matt. xxvi. Matt. xxvii.
as erroneous and seditious; and all the people followed, and cried, *crucifige?* Did not
all the emperors before Constantine, being seduced by their bishops and priests, condemn christian religion as heretical, seditious, and traitorous, and for the same mur-
dered many thousands of martyrs? When Constantine was christened, then was the
true religion first set forth and openly preached by public authority: and yet, in the
space between Christ and this godly emperor, God was not without his church, though
it were not known, seen, and so accepted of the world. In this prince's time, and
by his authority, was kept the first and best general Council of Nice[3]; where was set
forth our common creed, containing shortly the chief and most necessary articles of
our belief. This Constantinus' son, Constantius, favouring the error of the Arians, in Theodoreti, Lib. ii. cap. 18.
the council of Arimine, decreed that Christ was not God but man only[4]: and then
to call Christ the Son of God, was by the outward known church, and by a general
council, condemned for an heinous heresy. From that time forth, when painime[5] princes
reigned, idolatry and worshipping of false gods was the public doctrine. When heretics
reigned and bare the rule, heresy was openly preached for God's truth. When the emperors were catholic, then was the true doctrine of the gospel openly preached. And
generally, such as was the faith of the emperors, kings, or other rulers, such did the
priests preach. And if any, by the authority of God's word, preached the contrary, or
withstood their corrupt teachings, straightway he was either deposed from his office,
condemned for an heretic, banished, brent, or put to some other cruel death.

The priests, for the most part, were double-faced, turntippets, and flatterers.

After all these sprung up the pope, that triple-crowned monster, and great anti- 13.
christ, which took upon him authority[6], not only over the clergy, but also climbed
above kings and emperors, deposing them at his pleasure, and settled himself in the
temple of God, that is, in the consciences of men, extolling himself above God, dispensing
with good[7] laws, and giving men leave to break them, and to regard more his decrees
than the everlasting commandments of God. And so it came to pass in time, that
to eat flesh on the Friday, or fasting-day, was counted greater sin than drunkenness,
adultery, or perjury. And why? because his laws were diligentlier and more straitly
looked to, and the offenders thereof sorer punished, than God's laws. Since this antichrist of Rome, I say, was stablished in his full power, whatsoever pleased him, that
was taken for God's law, and that was decreed upon by general council, confirmed

---

[[2] Omitted in ed. 1582.]

[[3] The first Œcumenical, or General Nicene Council, was held at Nice, A.D. 325.]

[[4] Theodoreti, Eccl. Hist. Lib. II. cap. xviii. p. 70. Ed. Colon. Allobr. 1612. The Council of Rimini was held, A.D. 359. Vid. Labbè et Cossart, Tom. II. col. 791. Ed. Lutet. Paris. 1671.]

[[5] Painime: Pagan.]

[[6] An authority, Orig. ed.]

[[7] With God's laws, Orig. ed.]

and ratified by whole heaps of clerks. To speak against that was, and also now is, detestable heresy, and so heinous a crime against the Holy Ghost (if it were true that they say), that it cannot be forgiven either in this world or in the world to come. He that speaketh against any of his decrees must utterly be condemned for an heretic, accursed of God, and damned into hell for ever, without redemption, except he recant, abjure, and deny the truth, and set forth error and false doctrine, and promise with a solemn oath, that he shall never preach, teach, nor defend the truth hereafter.

These be the pope's thunderbolts, wherewith he feareth the people, and maketh them to incline to his ways.

Now let us come to our days. When king Henry the eighth was, as he ought to be by God's law, made supreme head, as well of the clergy as of the laity, he, by the consent of the parliament and convocation, set forth in print a godly book of religion[1], not much varying from that which was enacted in his son's time, Edward the sixth. But when he took displeasure with certain bishops, as they term them, of the new learning, because they would not give their consent in the parliament, that the king should have all abbey lands to his own use, but only such lands as were given by his ancestors, kings of England; and that the residue of those lands should have been bestowed to augment the number of learned men in the universities; to the founding also of grammar schools in every shire of England, where children, most apt to learning, should have been brought up freely, and without great cost to their friends and kinsfolks; to the founding of hospitals, where poor and impotent people should have been sufficiently provided for with physicians and surgeons,
14. which should have ministered physic[2] and surgery freely, not only to them, but also to all other poor folk within this realm; and also in every shire town, and other market towns, where should be thought most meet and fit, to set up divers occupations, most profitable for the commonwealth, where all valiant and sturdy beggars should have been set to work, and if they refused to labour, then to force them thereto by whipping, stocking, and hunger; and the residue of the abbey lands above these should have been reserved in the common treasuries, to aid the king in his wars, or other affairs of his realm, and thereby to have favoured and eased the more his subjects, in taxes, subsidies, fifteenths[3], and loans, and such other like thing[4]:—king Henry, as I said before, upon the displeasure taken, and by the incitation of the old popish bishops, shortly after, by consent of the same, or the most part of them, that were makers of the first book of religion, set forth by open parliament and convocation the Six Articles, as well agreeing with the former parliament and the word of God, as black with white, light with darkness, Christ with Belial, or with antichrist. But after, when he was pacified with these foresaid bishops, considering that they spake against the king's profit, not of malice but of good conscience and zeal to God's glory and the commonwealth, he mitigated the Six Articles, and from that time forth, more and more, restored true religion. And I doubt not but, if he had lived, he would have brought all things to a better state than he left it. But Edward the sixth, his son, succeeding in his said father's place, by the advice of his uncle, the duke of Somerset, the lords of his council, bishops, and the clergy, set forth such a book of religion[5], as without boast or dispraise of other be it spoken, was never a better set forth since the apostles' time.

It was a small matter at that time to be displeased with such men, and so much the more for that they withstood private commodity.

Private commodity and popish subtlety overcame good public policy, and brought in tyranny.

Now, after that God had plagued this realm with the most grievous plague that ever came to it, in taking away from it so godly a king as he was, yea, such an one as hath not been read of, of his age, in any realm, both for wit, learning, soberness, and godliness; in his stead he hath set up queen Mary, who in short time hath pulled down that was not builded in many years, and brought in the bishop of Rome, before justly and by law of parliament abolished, with open perjury of so many, as gave their voices and consent to the same. For they had all made a solemn oath before, never to receive his unjust usurped power into the realm again.

They are all perjured, so many as gave their consent to the bringing in of the bishop of Rome.

---

[1 "The godly and pious institution of a christian man," published 1537, which was superseded by "A necessary doctrine and erudition of any christian man," in 1540; the latter book being in several points less favourable to the doctrines of the reformation than the other.]

[2 Ministered both physic, Orig. ed.]

[3 Fifteens, Orig. ed.]

[4 Things, Orig. ed.]

[5 i. e. the Liturgy.]

Hath she not, being seduced by the perjured prelacies[6], revoked and made of none 15.
effect so many godly laws enacted by parliament, that is, by the consent of the lords both spiritual and temporal, the clergy and common house, yea, and by them that were the chief of king Henry her father's privy council, and setters on of him in the abolishing of the bishop of Rome, even open preachers and writers against the pope's tyranny, with so pithy reasons and strong arguments, as neither they themselves, nor any other after them, shall be able at any time rightly to assoil and answer? Yet these men were chief of counsel, and procurers of the queen, and first workers in the parliament to allure the lords and commons to receive the bishop of Rome again for the supreme head of this realm, contrary to God's law, the laws of this realm, and their own solemn oaths. And not only this, but they have taken away the acts of mortmain and præmunire, and divers other statutes that did bridle the unsatiate[7] covetousness and licentious liberty of the popish priests, and restored the act *ex officio*[8]. Which thing if it should long continue in this state that it is in, the great treasure of this realm should come into the clergy's hands, and a great part thereof should fly to Rome for bishoprics, benefices, appellations, pardons, dispensations, and such other baggage.

The bishops, I warrant you, were none of those: for they cannot err. These are wavering reeds, and perfect weathercocks, that turn with every wind.

By their deeds ye shall know them, what they be.

But (say the papists) when scriptures be hard and doubtful, and seem to be contrary one to another, by mistaking and wrong understanding whereof divers heresies do arise; how shall a man know the truth in such diversity of opinions, both parties grounding themselves upon the scriptures, but only by the church, which (as they say) cannot err? St Augustine shall make answer herein for me, saying on this wise: "Dark places are to be expounded by more plain places; for that is the surest way of declaring the scriptures, to expound one scripture by another[9]." And again he saith, that "in things openly contained in the scriptures are found all things that concern faith, good living, and charity[10]." "And if any thing cannot be tried by the certain and clear places of the scriptures, let man's presumption," saith he, "stay itself, not leaning to either part: for this I am sure of, that if it were requisite to be known upon pain of damnation, there should not lack most plain and clear authorities of the same in the scriptures. But in seeking of the scriptures, let us seek no farther than is left in writing by God our Saviour, lest in desiring too much we lose all[11]." St Chrysostom also saith: "It is not possible that he which with earnest study and fervent desire applieth him to the scriptures of God, should ever be[12] neglected of God; but although we lack a master to teach us, yet the Lord himself, entering our
hearts from above, shall give light into our minds, and pour his bright beams into 16.
our reason and understanding, and open the things that be hid, and teach us those things whereof we be ignorant[13]." "Therefore," saith the same Chrysostom, "if thou wilt enter into the truth of the scriptures, now ask by prayers, now knock by good works, and search the old ancient writers, and ask divers priests, to know which be

In his third book of Christian Doctrine, cap. 28.

In his second book of Christian Doctrine, cap. 9.

In his second book of Merits and Forgiveness of Sins, Tom. vii. cap. ult.

Upon Genesis, cap. xiv. Hom. 35.

In his Unperfect Work, cap. 23.

---

[6 Prelates, Orig. ed. i. e. Bishops Gardner, Bonner, &c. who had previously written and spoken against the Pope's supremacy.]

[7 Unsatiable, Orig. ed.]

[8 Vid. Foxe's Acts and Monuments, Ed. 1583. pp. 418, 19. 523. and 1410; and Strype, Eccl. Memorials, Vol. III. Part I. p. 59; and Life of Abp. Whitgift, Vol. II. pp. 28—32. Ed. Oxon. 1822.]

[9 Ubi autem talis sensus eruitur, cujus incertum certis sanctarum scripturarum testimoniis non possit aperiri, restat ut ratione reddita manifestus appareat, etiamsi ille cujus verba intelligere quærimus, eum forte non sensit. Sed hæc consuetudo periculosa est. Per scripturas enim divinas multo tutius ambulatur. Augustin. De Doctrina Christiana, Lib. III. cap. xxviii. Tom. III. p. 25. Paris. 1635.]

[10 In iis enim quæ aperte in scriptura posita sunt, inveniuntur illa omnia quæ continent fidem moresque vivendi, spem scilicet atque caritatem. Id. Lib. II. cap. ix. Tom. III. p. 12.]

[11 Ubi enim de re obscurissima disputatur, non adjuvantibus divinarum scripturarum certis clarisque documentis, cohibere se debet humana præsumptio, nihil faciens in partem alteram declinando. Etsi enim quodlibet horum, quemadmodum demonstrari et explicari possit, ignorem, illud tamen credo, quod etiam hinc divinorum eloquiorum clarissima auctoritas esset, si homo illud sine dispendio promissæ salutis ignorare non posset. Id. De Peccatorum meritis et remissione. Tom. VII. p. 304.]

[12 Would ever be, Orig. ed.]

[13 Οὐδὲ γάρ ἐστι τὸν μετὰ σπουδῆς καὶ πολλοῦ πόθου τοῖς θείοις ἐντυγχάνοντα περιοφθῆναί ποτε· ἀλλὰ κἂν ἄνθρωπος ἡμῖν μὴ γίνηται διδάσκαλος, αὐτὸς ὁ δεσπότης ἄνωθεν ἐμβατεύων ταῖς καρδίαις ταῖς ἡμετέραις φωτίζει τὴν διάνοιαν, καταυγάζει τὸν λογισμὸν, ἐκκαλύπτει τὰ λανθάνοντα, διδάσκαλος ἡμῖν γίνεται τῶν ἀγνοουμένων. Chrysost. in Genes. Cap. xiii. Hom. xxxv. Tom. IV. pp. 349,50. Ed. Paris. 1718—38.]

the true key-keepers, and which are the false[1]. For all things," saith he, "are plain and manifest in the divine scriptures: whatsoever things are needful are there[2] opened[3]." But if these authors will not satisfy them, then let them use St James' counsel, saying: "He that lacketh wisdom, let him ask it of God, which giveth to all men indifferently, and casteth no man in the teeth, and it shall be given him." For God is not partial, nor regardeth any more a pope than a potter, a cardinal than a carter, a bishop than a butcher, a priest than a pedlar, except his faith and life be agreeable to God's will.

James i.

Whither should a man (desiring to know the truth, and right understanding and worshipping of God) have resorted in Elias his time, when there was no more of the true outward church but he alone? To whom should a man have resorted for counsel of the truth in the time of Jeremy? Of whom should a man have learned the truth in Christ's time, when there was no ordinary succession of bishops in the truth? Should they have learned (think you) the truth of God of the head priests, scribes, and Pharisees? Then you know what a learning they should have had, and how much Christ should have profited them. How should a man have been satisfied of his salvation at Annas, Caiphas, and the rest of the Pharisees' hands? Even so, no doubt, would they have taught and instructed him, that, if he had believed and followed their sayings, Christ and he should never have met. And yet those men bare the image and name of the known church at that time; yea, and the same men condemned him of whom our faith and salvation dependeth, as a seditious fellow, as a traitor to Cæsar, as an heretic, and a blasphemer of God. Christ therefore, to teach us what we should do in matters pertaining to his glory and our own commodity, sendeth his hearers to the scriptures, and not to the church. He said also to the Sadducees, "Ye err because ye know not the scriptures;" and not, because ye believe not the church. He also promiseth his elect, that they shall hear his voice, and not a stranger's voice. If ye be doubtful therefore in any point, resort to the scriptures given from God, and out of them search for the thing whereof thou art ignorant; and, above all things, be not too rash in judgment, neither trust too much in thine own wit.

Matt. xxii. Mark xii.

John x.

17. Ask also counsel of such men whom thou knowest to be well learned and exercised in the same scriptures, and whose conversation thou seest to be agreeable to their words; and yet believe them no farther than they can prove their doctrines and exhortations to answer and agree with God's most holy word. Seek, ask, cry, call, knock, fast and pray, with a constant faith, joining thereto a christian, sober, and a charitable living; and then "he that hath the key of David, who openeth, and no man shutteth," shall (according to his promise) give unto you all that you ask of his Father in his name, and shall send his Holy Spirit into your hearts, who shall lead you into all truth, and put you in remembrance of all those things which Christ hath commanded, needful and necessary for your salvation.

Rev. iii.

John xv.

Whatsoever therefore the church teacheth you out of the canonical books of the bible, believe that; but if they teach any thing beside that, (I mean, which is not agreeable[4] with the same,) believe neither that, nor them. For then they are not the church of Christ, but the synagogue of Sathan and antichrist. For the church of God (as Saint Paul witnesseth) is "builded upon the foundation of the apostles and prophets;" not upon the apostles, but upon the same foundation which they laid, that is, Christ Jesus, and his holy word. And all such unwritten verities as the papists

Ephes. ii.

[[1] Et si velles scripturarum ingredi veritatem, nunc peteres orationibus, nunc quæreres in scripturis, nunc pulsares bonis operibus, nunc interrogares sacerdotes, nunc istos, nunc illos; non investigas qui veri sint clavicularii scripturarum, qui falsi. Id. Opus. Imperf. in Matthæum. Hom. xliv. col. clxxxvii. in cap. xxiii. Tom. VI. This treatise is generally supposed to be spurious. See James' Corruption of Scripture Councils, p. 107. &c. London, 1843. Riveti Critica Sacra. Ed. Genevæ, 1626.]

[[2] Needful there to be opened, Orig. ed.]

[[3] Ergo non sunt scripturæ clausæ....Non ergo abscondita est in scripturis veritas, sed obscura: non ut non inveniant eam qui quærunt eam, sed ut non inveniant eam qui quærere eam nolunt. Id. ibid. col. clxxxvi.]

[[4] Agreeing, Orig. ed.]

have in their mouths, though they seem never so glorious a church to the face of the world, if they be not agreeing (as they are not indeed) to the very word of God, suspect them, yea, rather, I bid you utterly to abhor and reject them. For their outward and seen church may, and doth (as is before proved) commonly err in great and weighty matters. Stand fast therefore to sound and good doctrine, and waver not. And "if any man come unto you, and bring not this doctrine with him, receive him not into your house: bid him not God speed," nor have ought to do with him; but count him as an abject from God and Christ. But cleave ye fast to the sound and certain doctrine of God's infallible word, written in the canonical books of the new and old Testament, which is able sufficiently to instruct you to eternal salvation, through Jesus Christ our Lord. To whom, with the Father and the Holy Ghost, be all honour and praise for ever and ever. Amen.

2 John Epist.

# THE BOOK TO THE READER.

18. *Judge not before*
*Thou know mine intent,*
*But read me throughout,*
*And then say thy fill:*
*As thou in opinion*
*Art minded and bent,*
*Whether it be*
*Either good or ill.*

*I care not for praise,*
*Nor slander untrue,*
*Of man nor of child,*
*Whatever he be:*
*Truth need not to fear,*
*Who doth it pursue*
*With praise or dispraise*
*In any degree.*

*For truth is not bettered*
*By praises at all,*
*Nor harmed by dispraise*
*Of any wight:*
*But goodness or hurt*
*Most surely come shall*
*To him that doth judge*
*Either wrong or right.*

*Read me, then judge me,*
*Therefore I thee pray,*
*Nothing for my cause,*
*But only thine own:*
*For I shall endure,*
*Whosoever say nay,*
*When unwritten truths*
*Shall be overthrown.*

# A CONFUTATION 19.

OF

# UNWRITTEN VERITIES

## BY DIVERS AUTHORITIES DILIGENTLY AND TRULY GATHERED TOGETHER OUT OF THE HOLY SCRIPTURES AND ANCIENT FATHERS.

---

## THE FIRST CHAPTER.

*That the word of God written, contained within the canon of the Bible, is a true, sound, perfect, and whole doctrine, containing in itself fully all things needful for our salvation.*

"YE shall put nothing to the word which I command you, neither take aught therefrom; that ye may keep the commandments of the Lord your God which I command you." Deut. iv.

"You shall not do after any thing[1] that we do here this day, every man what seemeth him good in his own eyes." Deut. xii.

"Whatsoever I command you, that take heed you do only to the Lord; and put nothing thereto, nor take aught therefrom." Ibidem in fine.

"The prophet which shall presume to speak a word in my name, which I have not commanded him to speak, or that speaketh in the name of strange gods, that prophet shall die." Deut. xviii.

"All the words of God are pure and clean: for he is a shield unto all them that put their trust in him. Put thou nothing unto his words, lest he reprove thee, and thou be found a liar." Prov. xxx.

"Hear not the words of the prophets that preach unto you and deceive you: for they speak the meaning of their own hearts, and not out of the mouth of the Lord." Jer. xxiii.

"Whosoever teacheth and keepeth the same, (speaking of his commandments,) shall be called great in the kingdom of heaven." Matt. v. 20.

"Whosoever heareth these my words, and doth the same, shall be likened unto a wise man, that buildeth his house upon a rock; and abundance of rain fell, the floods came, the wind blew, and beat upon the same house, and it fell not, because it was grounded on the sure rock." Matt. vii.

"This people draweth nigh unto me with their mouth, and honoureth me with their lips[2], howbeit their hearts be far from me; but in vain do they serve me, teaching the doctrines and precepts of men." Matt. xv.

"Go ye, and teach all nations, baptizing them in the name of the Father, &c. teaching them to observe all things whatsoever I have commanded you." Matt. xxviii.

"Go ye into all the world, and preach my gospel to all creatures." Mark xvi.

"He that heareth my word, and believeth in him that sent me, hath everlasting life, and shall not come into damnation; but is escaped from death to life." John v.

"Search the scriptures, for in them ye think ye have eternal life, and they are they which testify of me." John v.

"These are written that you might believe that Jesus is Christ the Son of God, and that (in believing) ye might have life through his name." John xx.

"I have spared no labour, but I have shewed you all the counsel of God." Acts xx.

"I have obtained help of God, and continue unto this day, witnessing both to the small and to the great, saying none other things than those which the prophets and Moses did say should come." Acts xxvi.

---

[1 Do anything, Orig. ed.] [2 With lips, Orig. ed.]

Rom. x. "Faith cometh by hearing, hearing cometh by the word of God."

Rom. xiv. "Whatsoever is not of faith, the same is sin."

2 Cor. i. "We be not lords over your faith, but helpers of your joy."

Gal. i. "Though we ourselves, or an angel from heaven, preach any other gospel unto you than that which we have preached, let him be accursed."

2 Tim. iii. "Continue thou in the things which thou hast learned, which also were committed unto thee, knowing of whom thou hast learned them: and forasmuch also as thou hast known the holy scriptures of a child, which are able to make thee learned unto salvation, through the faith which is in Christ Jesu. For all scripture, given by in-
21. spiration of God, is profitable to teach, to improve, to amend, to instruct in righteousness, that the man of God may be perfect, and prepared to all good works."

1 Pet. iv. "If any man speak, let him speak as the words of God."

2 John, Epistle. "If any man come unto you, and bring not this learning, receive him not into your house, neither bid him God speed. For he that biddeth him God speed is partaker of his evil deeds."

Rev. xxii. "If any man shall add unto these things, God shall add unto him the plagues that are written in this book. And if any man shall minish of the words of this prophecy, God shall take away his part out of the book of life, and out of the holy city, and from those things which are written in this book."

---

## THE SECOND CHAPTER.

*That the Writings of the old Fathers, without the written Word of God, are not able to prove any doctrine in religion.*

Doctrine in religion must be grounded upon the scriptures only.

IRENÆUS, Lib. II. cap. 46. "To lean to the scriptures of God (which is the certain and undoubted truth) is to build a man's house upon a sure and strong rock. But to leave that, and lean to any other doctrines (whatsoever they be), is to build a ruinous house upon the shattering gravel, whereof the overthrow is easy[1]."

We may not build our faith upon men's traditions.

Idem, in Epist. 72. "Happy is he that soweth upon the water where the ox and the ass treadeth, that is, upon that people which only followeth the doctrine of both the testaments, and not upon the vain traditions of men."

The apostles taught nothing but that which they learned of Christ.

Tertullian, in the Prescriptions of Heretics, pa. 19. "It is not lawful for us to favour any doctrine at our pleasure, nor yet to choose what any man hath brought in of his own mind. We have the apostles of the Lord for our authors, which did not elect any thing, that they would bring in, of their own heads; but taught faithfully to all nations that doctrine that they had received of Christ. Therefore, although 'an angel from heaven should preach any other thing, let us hold him accursed[2].'"

The first point of belief is, that after the gospel no[3] other thing is to be believed.

And a little after he saith: "We need to use no curiosity after Jesus Christ, nor make further search after the gospel: for when we believe, we desire to believe no more. For first we believe this, that there is nothing else that we ought to believe[4]."

22.

[1 Quia autem parabolæ possunt multas recipere absolutiones; ex ipsis de inquisitione Dei affirmare, relinquentes quod certum et indubitatum et verum est, valde præcipitantium se in periculum, et irrationabilium esse, quis non amantium veritatem confitebitur? Et numquid hoc est non in petra firma, et valida, et in aperto posita ædificare suam domum; sed in incertum effusæ arenæ? Unde et facilis est aversio hujusmodi ædificationis. Iren. Lib. II. cap. xlvi. (xxvii.) p. 155. Ed. Paris. 1710.]

[2 Nobis vero nihil ex nostro arbitrio inducere licet, sed nec eligere quod aliquis de arbitrio suo induxerit: apostolos Domini habemus auctores, qui nec ipsi quicquam ex suo arbitrio, quod inducerent, elegerunt; sed acceptam a Christo disciplinam fideliter nationibus adsignaverunt. Itaque etiamsi angelus de cœlis aliter evangelizaret, anathema diceretur a nobis. Tertull. de Præscript. hæreticor. Cap. vi. p. 204. Ed. Lutet. Paris. 1664.]

[3 None, Orig. ed.]

[4 Nobis curiositate opus non est post Christum Jesum, nec inquisitione post evangelium. Cum credimus, nihil desideramus ultra credere. Hoc enim prius credimus, non esse quod ultra credere debeamus. Id. cap. viii. p. 205.]

Idem, Of the Flesh of Christ, pa. 20. against Apelles, which said that the angels had a bodily substance, which they took of the stars. Tertullian answereth, that "there is no certainty in this matter, because the scripture declareth it not[5]."

There is no certainty in that the scripture defineth not.

The same, to Praxeas. "Let this be a general rule, indifferently determined before and against all heresies: that that is true, whatsoever is first; and that to be forged, whatsoever cometh after[7]." pa. 418.

The law, the prophets, and gospel[6], are the first doctrines, and therefore true.

Origen, in his first homily upon Jeremy. "We must needs call the holy scriptures to witness: for our judgments and expositions without these witnesses are worthy no credit[9]."

Our words, without[8] God's word are not to be believed.

Idem, upon Leviticus, in his fifth homily. "If the holy scripture do not determine any thing, we ought not to admit any other writing for the stablishing of our doctrine: but as for the rest, let us leave it to God[10]."

That which cannot be proved by the scripture, leave to God.

The same, upon the third chapter to the Romans. "After these, as his custom is (meaning St Paul), he doth confirm that he had said by the scriptures, giving also an example to the preachers of the church, that those things which they speak to the people should be armed and maintained by the holy scriptures, and not spoken out of their own judgments. For if he (being such and so great an apostle) thought not the authority of his own words to be sufficient, except he teach those things which he saith to be written in the law and the prophets; how much more ought we little ones to take heed, that when we teach, we utter not our own minds, but the sentences of the Holy Ghost[11]!"

If Paul thought his authority[not sufficient, much more ought we to take heed that we utter not our own minds[12].]

The same, upon Matthew, in his 26th Homily. "No man ought (for the stablishing of doctrine) to use any books that be without the canonical scriptures[13]."

Cyprian, in the exposition of the creed, after that he hath rehearsed the canonical books of the bible, he saith: "These be they which our fathers have included within the canon, out of the which our fathers would the doctrine of our faith to be certain: nevertheless there be other books, which of our elders were not called canonical, but ecclesiastical; as the book of Wisdom, the books of Sirach, Tobie, Judith, Machabees, and other. All which books they would have to be read in the church, but not alleged as of authority to confirm any article of our faith. All other writings they called Apocrypha, which they would in no wise to be read in the church[14]."

All books which be not in the canon of the Bible are called Apocrypha, and are not sufficient to prove any articles of our faith.

---

[5 Igitur probent angelos illos carnem de sideribus concepisse. Si non probant, quia nec scriptum est, nec Christi caro inde erit.... Igitur, cum relatum non sit unde sumpserint carnem, relinquitur intellectui nostro non dubitare, hoc esse proprium angelicæ potestatis, ex nulla materia corpus sibi sumere. Quanto magis, inquis, ex aliqua? Certum est, sed nihil de eo constat, quia scriptura non exhibet. Id. De carne Christi, cap. vi. p. 312.]

[6 And the gospel, Orig. ed.]

[7 Quo peræque adversus universas hæræses jam hinc præjudicatum sit, id esse verum quodcumque primum; id esse adulterum quodcumque posterius. Id. adversus Praxeam. Cap. ii. p. 501.]

[8 With God's words, 1502.]

[9 Μάρτυρας δεῖ λαβεῖν τὰς γραφάς. ἀμάρτυροι γὰρ αἱ ἐπιβολαὶ ἡμῶν καὶ αἱ ἐξηγήσεις ἄπιστοί εἰσιν. Origen. In Jeremiam. Hom. i. Tom. III. p. 129. Ed. Paris, 1733—1759.]

[10 Si quid autem superfuerit, quod non divina scriptura decernat, nullam aliam tertiam scripturam debere ad auctoritatem scientiæ suscipi,......sed igni tradamus quod superest, id est, Deo reservemus. Id. In Levit. Hom. v. Tom. II. p. 212.]

[11 Post hæc vero, ut ei moris est, de scripturis sanctis vult affirmare quod dixerat: simul et doctoribus ecclesiæ præbet exemplum, ut ea quæ loquuntur ad populum, non propriis præsumpta sententiis, sed divinis munita testimoniis proferant. Si enim ipse tantus ac talis apostolus auctoritatem dictorum suorum sufficere posse non credit, nisi doceat in lege et prophetis scripta esse quæ dicit; quanto magis nos minimi hoc observare debemus, ut non nostras cum docemus, sed sancti Spiritus sententias proferamus! Id. In Epist. ad Romanos, Cap. III. Tom. IV. p. 504.]

[12 The words, "If Paul thought his authority," are only found in the margin of the original edition. The remaining clause is in Jenkyns' Cranmer, Vol. IV. p. 175.]

[13 Non ergo debemus ad confirmandum doctrinam nostram nostros proprios intellectus jurare, et quasi testimonia assumere, quos unusquisque nostrum intelligit, et secundum veritatem existimat esse, ni ostenderit eos sanctos esse ex eo quod in scripturis continentur divinis. Id. In Matthæum, Hom. xxv. Tom. III. p. 842.]

[14 Hæc sunt quæ patres intra canonem concluserunt; ex quibus fidei nostræ assertiones constare voluerunt. Sciendum tamen est, quod et alii libri sunt qui non canonici, sed ecclesiastici a majoribus appellati sunt: ut est Sapientia Salomonis, et alia Sapientia quæ dicitur filii Syrach.........Ejusdem ordinis est libellus Tobiæ et Judith, et Machabæorum libri.......quæ omnia legi quidem in ecclesiis voluerunt, non tamen proferri ad auctoritatem ex his fidei confirmandam. Ceteras vero scripturas apocryphas nominarunt, quas in ecclesiis legi noluerunt. Cyprian. Expos. in Symb. Apostol. Capp. xxxvii, viii. col. ccxxiv. Ed. Paris. 1726. This exposition is asserted by the Benedictine editors to be spurious. Ruffinus was probably the author.]

23. Athanasius against the Gentiles. "The holy scriptures, being inspired from God, are sufficient to all instruction of the truth[1]."

Basilius, in his book of Ethics, of his short definitions the 26. "Every word and deed that maketh for the certainty and surety of good men, and the confusion of them that be evil, must be confirmed by the testimony of God's scriptures. And those things, which either in our nature, or in the custom and manner of our life, are manifestly known, must we use to confirm those things which we do and say[2]."

The same, in his short definitions, the first question: "Whether it be lawful or expedient for a man to permit himself to do what he thinketh good, without the testimony of the holy scriptures." His answer: "Seeing that our Saviour saith of the Holy Ghost, 'He shall not speak of himself, but whatsoever he hath heard, that shall he speak:' and of himself he saith, 'The Son can do nothing of himself:' and again, 'I have not spoken of myself, but he which sent me gave me commandment what I should say, and what I should speak; and I know that his commandment is eternal life: therefore those things that I speak, I speak as the Father said unto me:' who is he then that will run into such madness, that he dare once think only anything of himself, seeing that he hath need of the Holy Ghost for his aid, so that both in mind, word, and work, he may be guided in the way of truth, and that he must needs walk in darkness, except he be lightened with the Sun of Righteousness, our Lord Jesus Christ, which shineth upon us with his commandments, as with bright beams? For 'the commandment of the Lord is clear, and giveth light to the eyes.' For of those things that are done, and commonly used among us, some are by God's commandment determined, and plainly set forth in the holy scriptures, and some not expressed. Of those that be expressed by the scriptures, there is utterly no power given to any man (whatsoever he be in the whole world) either to do anything of those that be forbidden, or else to leave undone anything of them that be commanded: seeing that the Lord hath once commanded and said, 'Whatsoever I command you, that take heed ye do, &c.' But of those things that are not expressed, the apostle Paul hath given us a rule, saying: 'I may do all things; but all things are not expedient. I may do all things; but all things edify not[3].'"

No man can dispense with God's law.

Things that be not commanded be indifferent to be used or not used: but yet as charity requireth.

Search no further than the gospel.

Isychius, upon Leviticus, lib. v. cap. 16. "Let us, which would have anything observed of God, search no more but that which the gospel doth give unto us[4]."

24. Chrysostom, upon the 24 cap. of Matthew, Homilia 49. "'When you shall see the abominable desolation stand in the holy place,' (that is) when you shall see ungodly heresy (which is the army of antichrist) stand in the holy places of the church, 'in that time let them which are in Jewry fly unto the hills,' (that is) let them that be in Christendom resort unto the scriptures. For like as the true Jew is a Christian (as

In time of heresy there is no means to try the truth, and the true church of Christ from Antichrist's church, but only by the scriptures.

[1 Αὐτάρκεις μὲν γάρ εἰσιν αἱ ἅγιαι καὶ θεόπνευστοι γραφαὶ πρὸς τὴν τῆς ἀληθείας ἀπαγγελίαν. Athanas. Oratio contra Gentes. Tom. I. p. 1. Ed. Paris. 1598.]

[2 Ὅτι δεῖ πᾶν ῥῆμα ἢ πρᾶγμα πιστεύεσθαι τῇ μαρτυρίᾳ τῆς θεοπνεύστου γραφῆς, εἰς πληροφορίαν μὲν τῶν ἀγαθῶν, ἐντροπὴν δὲ τῶν πονηρῶν..... Ὅτι δεῖ καὶ τοῖς ἐν τῇ φύσει καὶ τῇ συνηθείᾳ τοῦ βίου γνωριζομένοις κεχρῆσθαι εἰς βεβαίωσιν τῶν γινομένων ἢ λεγομένων. Basil. Moralia Ethica. Regula xxvi. cap. i. ii. pp. 434, 435. Ed. Paris. 1637.]

[3 Τοῦ κυρίου ἡμῶν Ἰησοῦ Χριστοῦ λέγοντος περι τοῦ ἁγίου πνεύματος, Οὐ γὰρ λαλήσει ἀφ' ἑαυτοῦ, ἀλλ' ὅσα ἂν ἀκούσῃ, ταῦτα λαλήσει· περὶ δὲ ἑαυτοῦ, Οὐ δύναται ὁ υἱὸς ποιεῖν ἀφ' ἑαυτοῦ οὐδέν· καὶ πάλιν, Ὅτι ἐγὼ ἐξ ἐμαυτοῦ οὐκ ἐλάλησα, ἀλλ' ὁ πέμψας με πατὴρ, αὐτός μοι ἐντολὴν ἔδωκε, τί εἴπω, καὶ λαλήσω· καὶ οἶδα ὅτι ἡ ἐντολὴ αὐτοῦ ζωὴ αἰώνιός ἐστιν· ἃ οὖν λαλῶ ἐγὼ, καθὼς εἴρηκέ μοι ὁ πατὴρ, οὕτω λαλῶ· τίς ἂν εἰς τοσαύτην ἐξέλθῃ μανίαν, ὥστε ἀφ' ἑαυτοῦ τολμῆσαι τὶ καὶ μέχρις ἐννοίας λαβεῖν, ὃς ὁδηγοῦ μὲν τοῦ ἁγίου καὶ ἀγαθοῦ πνεύματος χρείαν ἔχει, ἵνα κατευθυνθῇ εἰς τὴν ὁδὸν τῆς ἀληθείας, κατά τε νοῦν, καὶ λόγον, καὶ πρᾶξιν, τυφλὸς δὲ καὶ ἐν σκότει διάγει ἄνευ τοῦ ἡλίου τῆς δικαιοσύνης αὐτοῦ τοῦ κυρίου ἡμῶν Ἰησοῦ Χριστοῦ τοῦ φωτίζοντος, ὥσπερ ἀκτῖσι, ταῖς ἑαυτοῦ ἐντολαῖς; ἡ γὰρ ἐντολὴ κυρίου, φησὶ, τηλαυγὴς, φωτίζουσα ὀφθαλμούς. ὥσπερ δὲ τῶν ἐν ἡμῖν στρεφομένων πραγμάτων τὰ μέν ἐστιν ὑπὸ τῆς ἐντολῆς τοῦ Θεοῦ ἐν τῇ ἁγίᾳ γραφῇ διεσταλμένα, τὰ δὲ σεσιωπημένα· περὶ μὲν τῶν γεγραμμένων οὐδεμία ἐξουσία δέδοται καθόλου οὐδενὶ, οὔτε ποιῆσαί τι τῶν κεκωλυμένων, οὔτε παραλεῖψαί τι τῶν προστεταγμένων· τοῦ κυρίου ἅπαξ παραγγείλαντος, καὶ εἰπόντος· καὶ φυλάξῃ τὸ ῥῆμα ὃ ἐντέλλομαί σοι σήμερον·......περὶ δὲ τῶν σεσιωπημένων κανόνα ἡμῖν ἐξέθετο ὁ ἀπόστολος Παῦλος εἰπών· πάντα μοι ἔξεστιν, ἀλλ' οὐ πάντα συμφέρει. πάντα μοι ἔξεστιν, ἀλλ' οὐ πάντα οἰκοδομεῖ. Id. Regulæ Breviores. Interrogatio prima. Tom. II. pp. 623, 4.]

[4 Et nihil amplius quæramus nos qui aliquid de Deo scrutari volumus, sed quantum nobis evangelicus sermo tradit. Isychius, in Levit. Lib. v. cap. xvi. fol. 94. Ed. Basil. 1527.]

the apostle saith, 'He is not a Jew which is outward, &c.'), in like manner the very Jewry is Christianity, the hills are the scriptures of the apostles and prophets. And why doth he command all Christians at that time to resort to the scriptures? For in this time, since heresy hath prevailed in the church, there can be none other proof of true Christianity: neither can there be any other refuge for christian men (willing to know the truth of the right faith) but only unto the holy scriptures. Beforetime it was shewed by many other means, which was the true church of Christ, and which gentility: but now there is no way to know it. And why? For all those things, which pertain to Christ indeed, have the heretics in their schism: likewise churches, likewise the scriptures of God, likewise bishops, and other orders of clerks, and likewise baptism and the sacrament of thanksgiving, and (to conclude) Christ himself. Wherefore he that will know which is the true church of Christ in this so great a confusion of things being so like, how shall he know it but only by the scriptures? It was also known which was the true church of Christ by their manners, when the conversation of christian men (either of all or many) was holy, which was not among the heathen. But now christian men are become like, or worse than the gentiles or heretics: yea, and there is more continency found amongst them than amongst Christians. Therefore he that will know which is the true church of Christ, whereby shall he know it but only by the scriptures? The Lord therefore, knowing that so great a confusion of things should come in the latter time, commandeth that christian men, that be willing to know the right faith, should fly to none other things but only to the scriptures. For if they look upon any other thing but only the scriptures, they shall be offended and perish, not perceiving which is the true church; and so fall into the abominable desolation which standeth in the holy places of the church[5]."

An heavy saying, but, alas! too true.

The same in the Unperfect Work, Matth. 7. "Every preacher is a servant of the law, which may neither add anything above the law of his own mind, nor withdraw anything after his own understanding; but preach that thing only that is had in the law, as Salomon saith, 'Thou shalt add nothing to the word of God, nor take aught 25.
therefrom[6].'"

Preachers must neither add nor take aught from God's law.

The same of the Holy Ghost, tom. 3. "If you see any man saying that I have the Holy Ghost, and not speaking the gospel, but his own, that man speaketh of himself, and the Holy Ghost is not in him." And after: "If any of them therefore

They that boast themselves of the Holy Ghost, without scripture, be void of the Holy Ghost.

---

[[5] *Tunc cum videritis abominationem desolationis stantem in loco sancto.* Id est, cum videritis hæresim impiam, quæ est exercitus antichristi, stantem in locis sanctis ecclesiæ, in illo tempore qui in Judæa sunt fugiant ad montes: id est, qui sunt in Christianitate, conferant se ad scripturas. *Sicut enim verus Judæus est Christianus,* dicente apostolo,...sic vera Judæa Christianitas est.......Montes autem sunt scripturæ apostolorum aut prophetarum.....Et quare jubet in hoc tempore omnes Christianos conferre se ad scripturas? Quia in tempore hoc, ex quo obtinuit hæresis illas ecclesias, nulla probatio potest esse veræ Christianitatis, neque refugium potest esse Christianorum aliud, volentium cognoscere fidei veritatem, nisi scripturæ divinæ. Antea enim multis modis ostendebatur, quæ esset ecclesia Christi, et quæ gentilitas: nunc autem nullo modo cognoscitur volentibus cognoscere quæ sit vera ecclesia Christi, nisi tantummodo per scripturas. Quare? quia omnia hæc quæ sunt proprie Christi in veritate, habent et hæreses illæ in schismate: similiter ecclesias, similiter et ipsas scripturas divinas, similiter episcopos ceterosque ordines clericorum, similiter baptismum, similiter eucharistiam, et cetera omnia, denique ipsum Christum. Volens ergo quis cognoscere quæ sit vera ecclesia Christi, unde cognoscat in tantæ confusione similitudinis, nisi tantummodo per scripturas?......Item ex moribus ipsis prius intelligebatur ecclesia Christi, quando conversatio Christianorum, aut omnium, aut multorum, erat sancta, quæ apud impios non erat. Nunc autem aut tales, aut pejores facti sunt Christiani, quales sunt hæretici aut gentiles. Adhuc autem et major continentia apud illos invenitur, quamvis in schismate sunt, quam apud Christianos. Qui ergo vult cognoscere quæ sit vera ecclesia Christi, unde cognoscat, nisi tantummodo per scripturas? Sciens ergo Dominus tantam confusionem rerum in novissimis diebus esse futuram, ideo mandat, ut Christiani qui sunt in Christianitate, volentes firmitatem accipere fidei veræ, ad nullam rem fugiant nisi ad scripturas. Alioqui si alia respexerint, scandalizabuntur, et peribunt, non intelligentes quæ sit vera ecclesia; et per hoc incident in abominationem desolationis, quæ stat in sanctis ecclesiæ locis. Chrysostom. Opus Imperf. in Matthæum. in cap. xxiv. Hom. xlix. Tom. VI. col. cciv. Ed. Paris. 1718—38.]

[[6] Omnis doctor servus est legis, quia neque supra legem addere potest aliquid de suo sensu, neque subtrahere aliquid secundum proprium intellectum, sed hoc tantummodo prædicat, quod habetur in lege. Nec enim potest mens humana directare, id est extra rectum facere, scilicet perversum vel malum ostendere, quod sapientia divina dictavit. Sic enim ait Moses ac Salomon: Non addas verbis Dei, neque detrahas inde. Id. ibid. in cap. vii. Hom. xx. Tom. VI. col. xcix.]

which saith he hath the Holy Ghost, and speaketh anything of himself, and not forth of the gospel, say, Follow my counsel, believe him not[1]."

The same on the 7. of Matth. Hom. 19. Upon this text: "By their fruits ye shall know them." "The fruits of man is the confession of his faith, and the works of his conversation. If thou, therefore, shalt see a christian man, forthwith consider, if his confession agree with the scriptures, he is a true Christian: but if not, he is (as Christ said) false. For so John, when he wrote his epistle of the heretics, said not, If any come unto you, not having the name of Christ, 'bid him not God speed:' but, 'If any bring not this doctrine[2].'"

Heretics ought first to be convinced by the scriptures, and after by reason.

The same in the same place, the 22. chapt. and 42. Homily. "Let us first allege the authority of the scriptures to the false forgers, afterward let us shew them reasons: and to them that ask for any manner of purpose, first let us declare unto them the reason, and afterward the authority, that we may pacify them with reason, and stablish them with authority. For we ought to confute false interpreters, and instruct them that search[3]."

To preach any thing besides God's word is to sow sedition and heresy.

The same, upon the last of the Romans, upon this text: "I beseech you, brethren." "He saith, that dissensions and slanders, that is to say, heresies, are brought in of those, which bring any thing besides the doctrine and learning of the apostles[4]."

All things may be determined by the scripture.

The same, upon the latter epistle to Timothy, the third chapter. "There is nothing that cannot be determined by the scriptures, 'to reprove,' if it be to be reproved, that is to say, lies; 'to correct, and to teach in righteousness.' If it be needful (saith he) that any should be corrected or instructed, that is, to be made continent and sober unto righteousness, and to execute those things that be just; all that shall be given by the scripture, 'that the man of God may be perfect:' the amendment (saith he) is prepared by the scriptures, that nothing may be lacking to that man that walketh after God[5]."

The holy scripture containeth all things needful for our salvation.

The same, upon Matth. 22. cap. Hom. 4. "Whatsoever is required for our salvation is already contained in the holy scriptures. He that is ignorant, shall find there what he may learn; he that is stubborn, and a sinner, may find there scourges of the judgments to come, the which he may fear; he that is troubled, may find there
26. the joys and promises of everlasting life, through the beholding of the which he may be stirred to good works[6]."

The same, upon the 2. of the Thessalo. cap. 2. "All things be plain and clear in the scriptures; and what things soever be needful, be manifest there[7]."

---

[1 Ἐὰν ἴδητέ τινα λέγοντα, πνεῦμα ἅγιον ἔχω, καὶ μὴ λαλοῦντα τὰ εὐαγγελικὰ, ἀλλὰ τὰ ἴδια, ἀφ' ἑαυτοῦ λαλεῖ, καὶ οὐκ ἔστι πνεῦμα ἅγιον ἐν αὐτῷ.... ἐάν τις οὖν τῶν ὀνομαζόντων ἔχειν πνεῦμα λέγῃ τι ἀφ' ἑαυτοῦ, καὶ μὴ ἀπὸ τῶν εὐαγγελίων, μὴ πιστεύσατε. Id. De Spiritu Sancto. Cap. x. Tom. III. p. 808. This treatise is pronounced by the Benedictine editors to be spurious.]

[2 *Ex fructibus eorum cognoscetis eos.* Fructus enim hominis est confessio fidei ejus, et opera conversationis ipsius. Si ergo videris hominem christianum, statim considera, si confessio ejus conveniat cum scripturis, verus est Christianus: si autem non est quemadmodum Christus mandavit, falsus est. Sic enim et Joannes, cum de hæreticis scripsisset epistolam, non dixit, Si quis venerit ad vos non habens nomen Christi, nec ave ei dixeritis: sed, Si quis non attulerit istam doctrinam. Id. Opus Imperf. in Matthæum, in cap. vii. Hom. xix. Tom. VI. col. xciv.]

[3 Ut et nos calumniatoribus prius auctoritatem scripturæ proferamus, postea rationem reddamus. Interrogantibus autem quocumque proposito, prius rationem exponamus, postea auctoritatem; ut ratione quidem eos placemus, auctoritate confirmemus: quoniam calumniatores convincere oportet, interrogatores autem docere. Id. ibid. Hom. xlii. Tom. VI. col. clxxix, clxxx.]

[4 Ἡ δὲ διχοστασία πόθεν; ἀπὸ τῶν δογμάτων τῶν παρὰ τὴν διδαχὴν τῶν ἀποστόλων. Id. in Epist. ad Rom. Hom. xxxii. Tom. IX. p. 754.]

[5 Πᾶσα οὖν ἡ τοιαύτη θεόπνευστος. μηδὲν οὖν ἀμφίβαλλέ, φησι. καὶ ὠφέλιμος πρὸς διδασκαλίαν, πρὸς ἔλεγχον, πρὸς ἐπανόρθωσιν, ἵνα ἄρτιος ᾖ ὁ τοῦ Θεοῦ ἄνθρωπος, πρὸς πᾶν ἔργον ἀγαθὸν ἐξηρτισμένος. πρὸς διδασκαλίαν. ἵνα ἄρτιος ᾖ ὁ τοῦ Θεοῦ ἄνθρωπος. διὰ τοῦτό φησὶ, γέγονεν τῶν γραφῶν παράκλησις, ἵνα ἄρτιος ᾖ ὁ τοῦ Θεοῦ ἄνθρωπος, οὐκ ἄρα χωρὶς αὐτῆς ἄρτιον ἔνι γενέσθαι. Id. In 2 Epist. ad Timoth. cap. iii. Hom. ix. Tom. XI. p. 714.]

[6 Quidquid quæritur ad salutem, totum jam adimpletum est in scripturis. Qui ignarus est, inveniet ibi quod discat. Qui contumax est et peccator, inveniet ibi futuri judicii flagella, quæ timeat. Qui laborat, inveniet ibi glorias et promissiones vitæ perpetuæ, quas manducando amplius excitetur ad opus. Id. Opus Imp. in Matthæum, Hom. xli. in cap. xxii. Tom. VI. col. clxxiv.]

[7 Πάντα σαφῆ καὶ εὐθέα τὰ παρὰ ταῖς θείαις γραφαῖς· πάντα τὰ ἀναγκαῖα δῆλα. Id. in 2 Epist. ad Thessal. cap. ii. Hom. iv. Tom. XI. p. 528.]

The same, upon the 2. to Timo. cap. 3. "If there be any thing needful to be known, or not to be known, we shall learn it by the holy scriptures: if we shall need to reprove a falsehood, we shall fetch it from thence: if to be corrected, to be chastened, to be exhorted, or comforted, to be short, if aught lack that ought to be taught or learned, we shall also learn it out of the same scriptures[8]."

A preacher must speak nothing but out of God's mouth.

The same, Hom. 1. Titum. "Like as the beadle crieth openly to all them that be in the court, so do we preach openly; but on that condition, that we add nothing, but preach only that thing that we have heard. For the office of a crier is to speak out those things that be committed to him, and not to add, change, or take away any thing[9]."

Believe him not that speaketh without the scripture.

The same upon the later epistle to Timothy, cap. 3. "Therefore neither ought they to be believed at all, except they speak those things which be agreeable to the scriptures[10]."

He that believeth the gospel written, needeth believe no more.

The same, upon the 20. chap. of John, Hom. 89. "But why did not the apostles write all things? Chiefly, because of the multitude of them. Moreover, they did consider, that he which would not believe these, would not believe more: but he that believeth these, need no more to attain faith[11]."

The same, upon Genesis, the 12. Homily. "The holy scripture expoundeth itself, and suffereth not the hearer to err[12]."

Not man's wisdom, but the Holy Ghost, is the true expositor of the scripture.

The same, in the same book, Hom. 21. "Neither hath the scripture of God any need of man's wisdom, that it may be understand, but the revelation of the Holy Ghost: that, the true meaning being sucked thereout, great advantage may grow to us thereby[13]."

Nothing is of like authority with the holy scripture.

Hieronymus, in the prologue of the bible to Pauline. After he had recited the books of the New Testament and the Old, he saith: "I pray thee, dear brother, among these live, muse upon these, know nothing else, seek for none other thing[14]."

Again, upon the books of the Old and New Testament. "These writings be holy, these books be sound both in number and authority; there is none other to be compared to these; whatsoever is besides these may in no wise be received among these holy things."

God's word cutteth off all traditions apostolic, as they call them, which be beside the same word.

Again, upon the first chapter of Agge. "All other things which they seek out and invent at their own pleasure, without the authority and testimony of the scriptures (as though they were the traditions of the apostles), the sword of God cutteth off[15]."

We ought not to allow any man's doctrine, without God's word.

Again, in his little commentaries to the Galatians, upon this place: "Condescend
to no man: this persuasion is not of God, which hath called you:" thus he inter- 27.
preteth it: "Ye ought neither to consent to them, nor to me, without the word of God[16]."

---

[[8] Εἴ τι μαθεῖν, εἴ τι ἀγνοῆσαι χρὴ, ἐκεῖθεν εἰσόμεθα· εἰ ἐλέγξαι τὰ ψευδῆ, καὶ τοῦτο ἐκεῖθεν· εἰ ἐπανορθωθῆναι καὶ σωφρονισθῆναι. πρὸς παράκλησιν, πρὸς παραμυθίαν, φησὶ, πρὸς ἐπανόρθωσιν· τουτέστιν, εἴ τι λείπει, καὶ χρὴ προστεθῆναι. Id in 2 Epist. ad Timoth. cap. iii. Hom. ix. Tom. XI. p. 714.]

[[9] Ὥσπερ γὰρ ὁ κήρυξ πάντων παρόντων ἐν τῷ θεάτρῳ κηρύττει, οὕτω καὶ ἡμεῖς κηρύττομεν, ὥστε μηδὲν προσθεῖναι, ἀλλ' αὐτὰ ἃ ἠκούσαμεν εἰπεῖν. ἡ γὰρ τοῦ κήρυκος ἀρετὴ ἐν τῷ πᾶσιν εἰπεῖν ἐστὶ τὸ γεγονὸς, οὐκ ἐν τῷ προσθεῖναί τινα καὶ ἀφελεῖν. Id. In Epist. ad Titum. cap. i. Hom. i. Tom. XI. p. 732.]

[[10] These words are not found. Similar sentiments are in the end of Hom. viii. on 2 Timoth. Tom. XI. p. 713.]

[[11] Τίνος οὖν ἕνεκεν οὐ πάντα ἐπῆλθον; μάλιστα μὲν διὰ τὸ πλῆθος. ἔπειτα δὲ κἀκεῖνο ἐνενόουν, ὅτι ὁ μὴ πιστεύσας τοῖς εἰρημένοις οὐδὲ τοῖς πλείοσι προσέξει· ὁ δὲ ταῦτα δεξάμενος οὐδὲν δεήσεται ἑτέρου εἰς τὸν τῆς πίστεως λόγον. Id. In Joannem. cap. xx. Hom. lxxxvii. (al. lxxxvi.) Tom. VIII. p. 521.]

[[12] Καίτοι γε τῆς ἁγίας γραφῆς, ἐπειδὰν βούλεταί τι τοιοῦτον ἡμᾶς διδάσκειν, ἑαυτὴν ἑρμηνευούσης, καὶ οὐκ ἀφιείσης πλανᾶσθαι τὸν ἀκροατήν. Id. In Genes. cap. ii. Hom. xiii. (al. xii.) Tom. IV. p. 103.]

[[13] Οὐδὲ γὰρ σοφίας ἀνθρωπίνης δεῖται ἡ θεία γραφὴ πρὸς τὴν κατανόησιν τῶν γεγραμμένων, ἀλλὰ τῆς τοῦ πνεύματος ἀποκαλύψεως, ἵνα τὸν ἀληθῆ νοῦν τῶν ἐγκειμένων καταμαθόντες πολλὴν ἐκεῖθεν δεξώμεθα τὴν ὠφέλειαν. Id. In Genes. cap. iv. Hom. xxi. Tom. IV. p. 181.]

[[14] Oro te, frater carissime, inter hæc vivere, ista meditari, nihil aliud nosse, nihil quærere. Hieron. in Epist. ad Paulinum, de Studio divinæ scripturæ. Tom. III. p. 8. Ed. Francof. 1684.]

[[15] Sed et alia, quæ absque auctoritate et testimoniis scripturarum quasi traditione apostolica sponte reperiunt atque confingunt, percutit gladius Dei. Id. in Aggeum. cap. i. Tom. VI. p. 184.]

[[16] Nec illis, nec mihi, sine verbis Dei consentire debetis. Id. in Epist. ad Galat. cap. v. Tom. IX. p. 286.]

The apostles grounded all their doctrine upon the law and prophets.

Again, upon Matth. cap. 13. Upon this place: "Every learned scribe." "Whatsoever the apostles preached, they confirmed it by the oracles of the law and prophets[1]."

To build upon any doctor's saying, without scripture or reason agreeing to scripture, were to follow Pythagoras, rather than Christ.

The same, to Minerius and Alexander. "Not, according to Pythagoras' disciples, the opinion given sentence upon aforehand by the doctors, but the reason of the doctrine is to be weighed: but if any man, that is of a contrary sect, do murmur why I read their expositions unto whose doctrines I do not consent, let him know that I willingly hear this of the apostle, 'Prove all things, but cleave to that which is good;' and the words of our Saviour, saying, 'Be ye tried bankers;' and if any money be counterfeited, and have not the emperor's stamp, nor be current money, refuse it; but that that sheweth the face of Christ in the clear light, bestow it in the purse of your heart[2]."

The same, upon Matthew, 23d chap. "That which hath none authority of the scriptures may as easily be rejected as proved[3]."

The same, in the 98. Psal. "All that ever we speak we ought to prove it by the scriptures[4]."

[Be a man never so holy, and never so learned after the apostles, yet his words, without God's word, are of none authority[5].]

The same, in the 86. Psal. "The Lord shall speak in the scriptures of the people," &c. "And how shall he speak? Not with words, but with 'scriptures of those princes that were in it,' that is, of the apostles and evangelists. And mark what he saith, 'Of those princes that were in it,' and not 'which are.' So that (the apostles except) whatsoever shall be spoken afterward, let it be cut off, and have none authority. Be a man therefore never so holy, be he never so well learned, after the apostles he hath none authority: for the Lord speaketh in the scriptures, 'of those princes that were in it[6].'"

To teach that as needful to salvation, which Christ hath not taught, is damnable.

Ambrosius, of Virgins, Lib. 3. cap. 1. "We justly do condemn all new things which Christ hath not taught; for Christ is the way to the faithful. If therefore we ourselves preach any thing that Christ hath not taught, judge that abominable[7]."

The soul liveth only by the word of God.

The same, in the Psal. 118. "The word of God is the lively meat of our souls, with the which it is nourished, fed, and governed: neither is there any thing else that maketh a reasonable soul to live but the word of God[8]."

Nothing is to be added to the word of God, although it be for a good purpose.

28. The same, in his book of Paradise, chap. 12. "By that which Eva added to the word of God, ['Thou shalt not touch,' &c. we do learn how much this present lesson putteth us in remembrance that we ought to add nothing to the word of God[9],] yea, though it be for a good purpose. For if thou put to, or take away any thing,

---

[[1] Ut quicquid in evangelio prædicabant, legis et prophetarum vocibus comprobarent. Id. in Matthæum, cap. xiii. Tom. IX. p. 35.]

[[2] Nec juxta Pythagoræ discipulos præjudicata doctoris opinio, sed doctrinæ ratio ponderanda est. Si quis autem contrariæ factionis immurmurat, quare eorum explanationes legam, quorum dogmatibus non acquiesco; sciat me illud apostoli libenter audire: "Omnia probate, quod bonum est tenete;" [et Salvatoris verba dicentis: "Estote probati numularii,"] ut si quis nummus adulter est, et figuram Cæsaris non habet nec signatus est moneta publica, reprobetur. Qui autem Christi faciem claro præfert lumine, in cordis nostri marsupium recondatur. Id. Minerio et Alexandro. Tom. III. p. 128.]

[[3] Hoc quia de scripturis non habet auctoritatem, eadem facilitate contemnitur, qua probatur. Id. in Matth. cap. xxiii. Tom. IX. p. 57.]

[[4] Omne quod loquimur, debemus affirmare de scripturis sanctis. Id. in Psalmum xcviii. Tom. VIII. p. 118.]

[[5] This side-note is omitted in ed. 1582.]

[[6] [*Dominus narrabit*, &c.] Non dixit, qui sunt in ea, sed qui fuerunt in ea. Dominus narrabit: et quomodo narrabit? Non verbo, sed scriptura. In cujus scriptura? In populorum. Non sufficit in populorum, sed etiam principum dicit. Et quorum principum? Qui sunt in ea. Non dixit hoc, sed qui fuerunt in ea......Et principum, hoc est, apostolorum et evangelistarum: horum qui fuerunt in ea. Videte quid dicat: Qui fuerunt, non qui sunt: ut exceptis apostolis, quodcunque aliud postea dicetur, abscindatur; non habeat postea auctoritatem. Quamvis ergo sanctus sit aliquis post apostolos, quamvis disertus sit, non habet auctoritatem. Quoniam Dominus narrat in scriptura populorum et principum horum qui fuerunt in ea. Id. in Psalmum lxxxvi. Tom. VIII. p. 103.]

[[7] Nos enim nova omnia, quæ Christus non docuit, jure damnamus, quia fidelibus via Christus est. Si igitur Christus non docuit quod docemus, etiam nos id detestabile judicamus. Ambros. De Virginibus. Lib. III. cap. i. Tom. IV. p. 229. Ed. Colon. Agrip. 1616.]

[[8] Hæc est enim animæ nostræ vitalis substantia, qua alitur, pascitur, gubernatur. Nec quidquam aliud est quod vivere faciat rationabilem animam, quam alloquium Dei. Id. in Psalmum cxviii. (119) Octon. vii. Tom. II. p. 437.]

[[9] This passage is omitted in ed. 1582.]

it appeareth to be a transgression of the commandment: for there ought nothing to be added, although it seem good[10]."

The same, in the epistle to the Galatians, cap. 1. "Neither saith the apostle, if they preach contrary: but, 'if they preach any thing besides that that we have preached,' (that is, if they add any thing to it at all,) 'hold them accursed.' Neither do I except myself, if I put to any thing beside that which was preached afore[11]."

As well who preacheth beside the gospel, as against it, is accursed.

The same, in the same place. "He doth affirm the gospel, which he had preached unto them, to be so firm and true, that although it should chance themselves (that is to say, the apostles), being changed, to preach any other thing, he teacheth that they ought not to be heard[12]."

Even the apostles, preaching besides the gospel, are not to be believed.

Augustine, of the consent of the Evangelists. "He that sent the prophets before his incarnation, the same sent also his apostles after his ascension; yea, and by that manhood, which he took upon him, he is the head of all his disciples, which are members of his body: therefore, forasmuch as they wrote those things, which he shewed and taught them, it ought not to be said that he wrote them not, seeing that his members wrote that which they knew by their head teaching them. For whatsoever he would have us to read, both of his deeds and words, that commanded he them to write, as his hands of his body. Whosoever doth perceive this fellowship of unity, and agreement of members, ministering under one head in diverse offices, he shall none other ways take that that he readeth in the gospel, the disciples declaring it, than if he had seen the very hand of the Lord, which he bare in his own body, writing it[13]."

Christ made all to be written that he would we should read

We are as well bound to believe that which the apostles wrote, as though Christ had written it with his own hand.

The same, to Vincent, against the Donatists, the 6th tom. pa. 116, Epist. 48. "We therefore for this cause are certain and sure, that no man ought to withdraw himself from the communion of all men. And let none of us seek the church in our own righteousness, but in the holy scripture[14]."

The church is known by the scripture.

The same, to the Mandarens, Epi. 42. "All that ever our elders made mention of to be done towards mankind in times past, and delivered to us; all things also which we see and deliver to our posterity, which do appertain to getting and maintaining of true religion, the scripture of God did not pass with silence[15]."

All that concerneth true religion is contained in the scripture.

Again, to the brethren in the wilderness. "Read the holy scripture, wherein ye shall find fully what is to be followed, and what to be avoided[16]."

[The word written is enough for our salvation[17].]

The same, of nature and grace, lib. i. cap. 61. "I owe my consent to the canonical scriptures only, without any refusal[18]." 29.

---

[[10] Etenim quantum præsens lectio docet, discimus nihil vel cautionis gratia jungere nos debere mandato. Si quid enim vel addas vel detrahas, prævaricatio quædam videtur esse mandati.......Nihil igitur, vel quod bonum videtur, addendum est. Id. De Paradiso, cap. xii. Tom I. p. 62.]

[[11] Aut si forte diabolus angelum Dei se fingens, ut facile possit audiri, de cœlis appareret contra hæc prædicans, sciretur esse contrarium, et ut abominatio haberetur. Si ergo apostolos Christi, quorum tam præclara opinio in signis et prodigiis erat faciendis, et angelum de cœlo, quem possit spiritalis ratio commendare, aliter docentes quam ab apostolo Paulo edocti erant, anathematizari præcepit, &c. Id. in Epist. ad Galat. cap. i. Tom. III. p. 221.]

[[12] Nam tam firmum atque verum evangelium quod eis prædicaverat, asserit, ut etiam seipsos, id est apostolos, si immutati forte aliter prædicarent, non audiri doceret. Id. ibid. cap. i. Tom. III. p. 221.]

[[13] Proinde qui prophetas ante descensionem suam præmisit, ipse et apostolos post ascensionem suam misit. Omnibus autem discipulis suis per hominem quem assumpsit, tanquam membris sui corporis, caput est. Itaque cum illi scripserunt, quæ ille ostendit et dixit, nequaquam dicendum est quod ipse non scripserit: quandoquidem membra ejus id operata sunt, quod dictante capite cognoverunt. Quicquid enim ille de suis factis et dictis nos legere voluit, hoc scribendum illis tanquam suis manibus imperavit. Hoc unitatis consortium et in diversis officiis concordium membrorum sub uno capite ministerium, quisquis intellexerit, non aliter accipiet quod narrantibus discipulis Christi in evangelio legerit, quam si ipsam manum Domini, quam in proprio corpore gestabat, scribentem conspexerit. Augustin. De Consensu Evangelistarum. Lib. I. cap. xxxv. Tom. IV. p. 170. Ed. Paris. 1635.]

[[14] Nos autem ideo certi sumus, neminem se a communione omnium gentium juste seperare potuisse, quia non quisque nostrum in justitia sua, sed in scripturis divinis quærit ecclesiam. Id. Epist. xlviii. Vincentio contra Donatistas Tom. II. p. 68.]

[[15] Omnia quæ præteritis temporibus erga humanum genus majores nostri gesta esse meminerunt, nobisque tradiderunt; omnia etiam quæ nos videmus, et posteris tradimus, quæ tamen pertinent ad veram religionem quærendam et tenendam, divina scriptura non tacuit. Id. Epist. xlii. Mandaurensibus. Tom. II. p. 57.]

[[16] Legite sacram scripturam, in qua quid tenendum, et quid fugiendum sit, plene invenietis. Id. Sermones ad fratres in eremo. Serm. xxxviii. Tom. X. p. 734.]

[[17] Omitted in ed. 1582.]

[[18] Quia solis canonicis debeo sine ulla recusa-

The same, upon John, 49th Treatise, cap. 11. "Not all things that the Lord Jesus did are written, as the same evangelist witnesseth: for the Lord both did and said many things that are not written; but things were chosen out to be written, which seemed sufficient for the salvation of the believers[1]."

No man is bound to believe farther than the holy scriptures teach.

The same, against Faustus, lib. 23, cap. 9. "That which Faustus putteth forth upon the birth of Mary, that she had a certain priest to her father, of the tribe of Levi, named Joachim; because it is not canonical, it doth not bind me[2]."

The balance to try the truth is the holy scripture.

The same, of Baptism against the Donatists, lib. ii. cap. 6. "Let us not bring deceitful balances, wherein we may weigh what we will after our own pleasure, saying, 'this is heavy,' 'this is light;' but let us bring the divine balance of the holy scriptures, as of the treasures of the Lord, and in it let us weigh what is heavy; yea, let us not weigh, but rather acknowledge the things that are weighed of the Lord[3]."

They that sit on Moses' chair[4], and teach their own doctrine, are not to be believed.

Again, upon John, the 46th Treatise. "Sitting upon the chair of Moses, they teach the law of God: therefore God teacheth by them. But if they will teach their own, hear them not, do not after them: for truly such men search their own, but not those things which are of Jesus Christ[5]."

All evil is condemned by the scripture, and all good things are there found.

Again, Lib. 3. of the Christian Doctrine, cap. ult. "How much less the abundance of gold, silver, and clothing, which that people brought with them forth of Egypt, is in comparison of the riches which afterwards they had at Jerusalem, which, above all other, was shewed in king Salomon; so let all knowledge, which is in deed profitably gathered out of the books of the gentiles, be such, if it be compared to the knowledge of God's scriptures. For whatsoever man learneth without them, if it be evil, there it is condemned; if it be profitable, there it is found. And seeing then every man shall find all things there which he hath profitably learned other where; much more abundantly shall he find those things there, which can no where at all else be learned, but only in the marvellous deepness and wonderful humility of those scriptures[6]."

We may lawfully dissent from all doctrine except the scriptures only.

The same, in his book of Nature and Grace, the 16th chapt. "We may lawfully sometimes dissent from other learning; but to the catholic learning every man must give place, every man must subscribe, whether he be layman, priest, king, or emperor[7]."

30. The same, in his 2nd book of the Christian Doctrine, cap. 9. After that he hath numbered the canonical books, he saith thus: "In all these books they that fear God, and are tamed through godliness, do search the will of God. The first note of which labour and travail, as we said, is to know these books; and if as yet we cannot understand them, yet let us by reading get them in memory, or not to be altogether ignorant in them. Furthermore, those things which be plainly contained therein, whether they be precepts of living, or else of believing, are earnestly and diligently to be searched; which,

All things that concern faith, hope, love, and

tione consensum. Id. De Natura et Gratia contra Pelagianos. Lib. I. cap. lxi. Tom. VII. p. 322.]

[[1] Nam cum multa fecisset Dominus Jesus, non omnia scripta sunt: sicut idem ipse sanctus Joannes evangelista testatur, multa Dominum Christum et dixisse et fecisse quæ scripta non sunt. Electa sunt autem quæ scriberentur, quæ saluti credentium sufficere videbantur. Id. in Joannem. Tract. xlix. De cap. xi. Tom. IX. p. 146.]

[[2] Ac per hoc illud, quod de generatione Mariæ Faustus posuit, quod patrem habuerit ex tribu Levi sacerdotem quendam nomine Joachim, quia canonicum non est, non me constringit. Id. Contra Faustum, Lib. XXIII. cap. ix. Tom. VI. p. 188.]

[[3] Non afferamus stateras dolosas, ubi appendamus quod volumus, et quomodo volumus pro arbitrio nostro, dicentes, hoc grave, hoc leve est: sed afferamus divinam stateram de scripturis sanctis tanquam de thesauris Dominicis, et in illa quid sit gravius appendamns: imo non appendamus, sed a Domino appensa recognoscamus. Id. De Baptismo contra Donatistas. Lib. II. cap. vi. Tom. VII. p. 43.]

[[4] On Moses seat, Orig. ed.]

[[5] Sedendo enim [super] cathedram Moysi legem docent; ergo per illos Deus docet. Sua vero illi si velint docere, nolite audire, nolite facere: certe enim tales *sua quærunt, non quæ Jesu Christi.* Id. in Joannem. Tract. xlvi. De cap. x. Tom. IX. p. 139.]

[[6] Quantum autem minor est auri, argenti, vestisque copia, quam de Ægypto secum ille populus abstulit, in comparatione divitiarum, quas postea Hierosolymæ consecutus est, quæ maxime in Salomone rege ostenduntur; tanta fit cuncta scientia, quæ quidem est utilis collecta de libris gentium, si divinarum scripturarum scientiæ comparetur. Nam quicquid homo extra didicerit, si noxium est, ibi damnatur; si utile est, ibi invenitur. Et cum ibi quisquis invenerit omnia quæ utiliter alibi didicit; multo abundantius ibi inveniet ea quæ nusquam omnino alibi, sed in illarum tantummodo scripturarum mirabili altitudine et mirabili humilitate discuntur. Id. De Doctrina Christiana, Lib. II. cap. xlii. Tom. III. p. 20.]

[[7] The reference in the text appears to be erroneous.]

how many the more every man findeth, so much the more is he apt in his understanding. In these, therefore, which are evidently contained in the scripture, are found all things, which contain faith, manners of living, hope, and love[8]."

good manners, are contained in the scripture.

The same, of the Unity of the Church, cap. 3. "Let us not hear, 'I say,' 'Thou sayest;' but let us hear, 'Thus saith the Lord.' There are, out of doubt, the Lord's books, to the authority whereof we both consent, we both believe, we both serve. Let us search the church there; let us discuss our cause there[9]."

Not what we say, but what the Lord, that must be heard.

The church is known by the scriptures.

Again in his second book of Baptism, against the Donatists, cap. 3. "Who is he that knoweth not that the scripture canonical is so contained within his certain bounds[10] of the Old and New Testament, and is so to be preferred above all other writings[11] of bishops, that a man may not at all either doubt or dispute of it, whether any thing be true or right, that he is sure is written in it? but the letters of all other bishops, which are or shall be hereafter written, besides the canonical scriptures, already confirmed, may be reproved either by more grave authority of other bishops or learned men, and by the words of every man that is better seen in the matter[12]."

We may doubt of all men's doctrine, but not of holy scriptures.

Again, in his second book of the Merits and Forgiveness of Sins, cap. ult. Tom. vii. "Where disputation is had of a doubtful matter, if the certain and clear doctrine of the scriptures of God do not help it, man's reason ought to stay itself, nothing leaning to either part. For though I know not how to express every one of these things, yet I believe surely that the scriptures of God should be most plain herein, if a man might not be ignorant hereof without the loss of that salvation that is promised him[13]."

If God's scriptures cannot discuss a matter in doubt, let man never go about to discuss it.

Again, in his book of Pastors. "He appointed the hills of Israel, the authors of the scriptures of God; feed there, that you may feed safely. Whatsoever you hear out of that, let it savour well to you; whatsoever is besides that, refuse it, lest you wander into clouds. Get you to the hill[14] of the scriptures: there be the pleasures of your hearts; there is no noisome, hurtful, or venomous things, no inconvenient things; there be most plentiful pastures[15]."

Who feedeth with the scriptures, feedeth safely. Other, therefore, with unwritten verities feed untruly.

Again, of Christian Doctrine, lib. 2, cap. 9. "In these things that be plainly set 31.
forth in the scriptures are found all things that contain faith and manners of living, that is to wit, hope and charity. Then after a certain familiarity had with the speech of the scripture of God, we must go to expound and discuss those things that be dark, that (to give light to dark speeches) examples may be taken out of the more plain places,

In the scripture are all things necessary for faith and good life, which two suffice for salvation.

[8 In his omnibus libris timentes Deum et pietate mansueti quærunt voluntatem Dei. Cujus operis et laboris prima observatio est, ut diximus, nosse istos libros, et si nondum ad intellectum, legendo tamen vel mandare memoriæ, vel omnino incognitos non habere. Deinde illa quæ in eis aperte posita sunt, vel præcepta vivendi vel regulæ credendi, solertius diligentiusque investiganda sunt. Quæ tanto quisquis plura invenit, quanto est intelligentia capacior. In iis enim quæ aperte in scriptura posita sunt, inveniuntur illa omnia quæ continent fidem, moresque vivendi, spem scilicet atque caritatem. Id. De Doctrina Christiana. Lib. II. cap. ix. Tom. III. p. 12.]

[9 Sed, ut dicere cœperam, non audiamus, Hæc dico, hæc dicis; sed audiamus, Hæc dicit Dominus. Sunt certe libri Dominici, quorum auctoritati utrique consentimus, utrique credimus, utrique servimus: ibi quæramus ecclesiam, ibi discutiamus causam nostram. Id. De Unitate Ecclesiæ. cap. iii. Tom. VII. p. 142.]

[10 Certain bonds, Orig. ed.]

[11 All latter writings, Orig. ed.]

[12 Quis autem nesciat sanctam scripturam canonicam tam veteris quam novi testamenti certis suis terminis contineri, eamque omnibus posterioribus episcoporum literis ita præponi, ut de illa omnino dubitari et disceptari non possit, utrum verum vel utrum rectum sit, quicquid in ea scriptum constiterit; episcoporum autem literas, quæ post confirmatum canonem vel scriptæ sunt vel scribuntur, et per sermonem forte sapientiorem cujuslibet in ea re peritioris et per aliorum episcoporum graviorem authoritatem doctioremque prudentiam et per concilia licere reprehendi? Id. De Baptismo contra Donatistas, Lib. II. cap. iii. Tom. VII. p. 40.]

[13 Ubi enim de re obscurissima disputatur non adjuvantibus divinarum scripturarum certis clarisque documentis, cohibere se debet humana præsumptio, nihil faciens in partem alteram declinando. Etsi enim quodlibet horum, quemadmodum demonstrari et explicari possit, ignorem, illud tamen credo, quod etiam hinc divinorum eloquiorum clarissima auctoritas esset, si homo illud sine dispendio promissæ salutis ignorare non posset. Id. De peccatorum meritis et remissione, Lib. II. cap. xxxvi. Tom. VII. p. 304. Ib.]

[14 To the hills, Orig. ed.]

[15 Constituit montes Israel auctores scripturarum divinarum. Ibi pascite, ut secure pascatis. Quicquid inde audieritis, hoc vobis bene sapiat: quicquid extra est, respuite, ne erretis in nebula.... Colligite vos ad montes scripturæ sanctæ. Ibi sunt deliciæ cordis vestri, ibi nihil venenosum, nihil alienum; uberrima pascua sunt. Id. De Pastoribus, cap. xi. Tom. IX. p. 279.]

and some testimonies of places being certain may take away the doubt of the uncertain sentences[1]."

Again, of the Christian Doctrine, the 3 lib. cap. 26. "Dark places are to be expounded by plainer places. That is the surest way, to expound one scripture by another[2]."

Again, to Vincent the Donatist, Epist. 48. "This kind of learning (speaking of the old writers' doings) is not to be read with necessity of belief, but with liberty of judgment." And after: "There, that is, in the holy scriptures, it is not lawful to say, the author of this book perceived not the truth; but either that the book is false, or the interpreter hath erred, or thou understandest it not. But in the works of all them that come after, (which be contained in innumerable books, yet in no wise to be compared to the most holy excellency of the canonical scriptures,) although in some of them be found the same truth, yet the authority is far unlike. Therefore, if it fortune any thing in them to be thought to dissent from the truth, because they are not so understand as they be spoken, yet the reader or hearer hath his free judgment, so that either he may allow that that pleaseth him, or reject that which offendeth him. And therefore all such like (except they may be defended either by good reason, or by the canonical authority, that it may be proved that they are so in deed, or may be so, because either it is there disputed or declared), if it displease any man, or if he will not believe it, he is not to be blamed therefore[3]."

If any man's saying or writing cannot be proved by plain scripture, or good reason gathered of the same, a man may allow or refuse it, as him liketh.

The same, in the same place, Epist. 48. "Gather not, my brother, against so many, so clear, and so undoubted witnesses of the scriptures, sentences misunderstanded, out of
32. the writings of bishops, either of ours, or of Hilary, or Cyprian, bishop, and martyr of the church: for we must put a diversity betwixt this kind of writing and the canonical scriptures. For these are not so to be read, as though a witness might be alleged out of them, so that no man might think otherwise, if they fortune to judge otherwise than the truth requireth[4]."

The old writers are not of such authority but that we may deny them, if they dissent from the holy scriptures.

The same to Jerome. "I have learned to give this reverence and honour to those only writers which be now called canonical, that I dare be bold to believe that none of them did err any thing at all in writing. But if I find any thing in those scriptures that seemeth contrary to the truth, I doubt not but that either the book is false, or the interpreter did not attain the thing that was spoken, or else I understand it not. But all other authors, be they never so excellent both in virtue and learning, I do so read them, not that I think it true that they writ[5], because they thought so; but because they could persuade me either by other canonical scriptures, or by some probable reasons, a thing not altogether abhorring from the truth[6]."

We may not think all that the old fathers did write to be true.

---

[[1] In iis enim, quæ apertè in scriptura posita sunt, inveniuntur illa omnia quæ continent fidem moresque vivendi, spem scilicet atque charitatem:—Tum vero facta quadam familiaritate cum ipsa lingua divinarum scripturarum in ea quæ obscura sunt aperienda et discutienda pergendum est, ut ad obscuriores locutiones illustrandas de manifestioribus sumantur exempla, et quædam certarum sententiarum testimonia dubitationem de incertis auferant. Id. De Doctrina Christiana, Lib. II. cap. ix. Tom. III. p. 12.]

[[2] Ubi autem apertius ponuntur, ibi discendum est quomodo in locis intelligantur obscuris. Neque enim melius potest intelligi quod dictum est de Deo. Id. Lib. III. cap. xxvi. ibid. p. 25.]

[[3] The reference is erroneous; the passage is as follows:—Quod genus literarum non cum credendi necessitate, sed cum judicandi libertate legendum est. Ibi si quid velut absurdum moverit, non licet dicere, author hujus libri non tenuit veritatem: sed, aut codex mendosus est, aut interpres erravit, aut tu non intelligis. In opusculis autem posteriorum, quæ libris innumerabilibus continentur, sed nullo modo illi sacratissimæ canonicorum scripturarum excellentiæ coæquantur, etiam in quibuscunque eorum invenitur eadem veritas, longe tamen est impar authoritas: itaque in eis, si quæ forte propterea dissonare putantur à vero, quia non ut dicta sunt intelliguntur, tamen liberum ibi habet lector auditorve judicium, quo vel approbet quod placuerit, vel improbet quod offenderit: et ideo cuncta ejusmodi nisi vel certa ratione, vel ex illa canonica authoritate defendantur, ut demonstretur sive omnino ita esse, sive fieri potuisse, quod vel disputatum ibi est, vel narratum: si cui displicuerit, aut credere noluerit, non reprehenditur. Id. Contra Faustum, Lib. XI. cap. v. Tom. VI. pp. 104, 5.]

[[4] Noli ergo frater contra divina tam multa, tam clara, tam indubitata testimonia colligere velle calumnias ex episcoporum scriptis, sive nostrorum, sicut Hilarii, sive antequam pars Donati separaretur, ipsius unitatis, sicut Cypriani, et Agrippini: primo, quia hoc genus literarum ab authoritate canonis distinguendum est. Non enim sic leguntur, tanquam ita ex eis testimonium proferatur, ut contra sentire non liceat, sicubi forte aliter sapuerint quam veritas postulat. Id. Vincentio contra Donatistas, Tom. II. p. 70.]

[[5] That they wrote, Orig. ed.]

[[6] Ego enim fateor caritati tuæ, solis eis scripturarum libris, qui jam canonici appellantur, didici hunc timorem honoremque deferre, ut nullum eorum

The same against *Cresconium*, a grammarian, lib. ii. cap. 32. "I am not bound to his authority. For I do not account Cyprian's writings as canonical, but weigh them by the canonical scriptures; and that in them which agreeth with the canonical scriptures, I allow to his praise; but that that agreeth not, by his favour I refuse[7]."

All men's writings ought to be weighed by the canonical scriptures.

The same to Vincent Victor. "I cannot, nor ought not to deny, that like as in mine elders, so also in my so many books, be many things that by just judgment, without rashness, may be reproved[8]."

He confesseth many errors in his own books and others also.

The same, in the Prologue of his book of the Trinity. "Be not bound to my writings, as to the canonical scriptures: but if thou find any thing in them, which thou diddest not believe, straightway believe it; in these that thou art not sure of, except thou certainly understand it, believe it not certainly[9]."

Believe not his writings, except thou be sure of them by the scriptures.

The same to Fortunate, Epist. 198. "Neither ought we to allow the reasonings of any men, whatsoever they be, (although they be catholic and laudable men,) as the canonical scriptures; so that it shall not be lawful for us, saving the reverence that is due to those men, to reprove and refuse any thing in their writings, if it chance that they have judged otherwise than truth is; the same truth, by God's help, being understand either of other men, or of us. For I am even such an one in other men's writings as I would men should be in mine[10]."

We ought not to esteem man's writings further than they agree with the scriptures; but may refuse them at our pleasures.

The same, in the same place. "Let us seek no further than is written of God our
Saviour, lest a man would know more than the scriptures witness[11]." 33.

Cyril, lib. vi. upon Leviticus. "There be two offices of a bishop, to learn the scriptures of God, and by oft reading to digest the same, or else to teach the people; but let him teach those things, which he hath learned of God, and not of his own heart, or by man's understanding, but those things which the Holy Ghost teacheth[12]."

Understand the word written, for they that learn of it learn of God.

The same, in John, chap. vi. He saith, "By this we learn, that only Christ ought to be followed as a master, and we must cleave unto him only[13]."

The same, in John, chap. xx. "Not all things that the Lord did are written, but those things that the writers thought sufficient, as well to good manners as to doctrine; that we, shining with a constant faith, good works, and virtues, may come to the kingdom of heaven[14]."

All things pertaining to doctrine and good manners are in the word written, which is sufficient.

---

auctorem scribendo aliquid errasse firmissime credam. Ac si aliquid in eis offendero literis, quod videatur contrarium veritati: nihil aliud, quam vel mendosum esse codicem, vel interpretem non assequutum esse quod dictum est; vel me minime intellexisse, non ambigam. Alios autem ita lego, ut, quantalibet sanctitate doctrinaque præpolleant, non ideo verum putem, quia ipsi ita senserunt; sed quia mihi vel per illos auctores canonicos, vel probabili ratione, quod a vero non abhorreat, persuadere potuerunt. August. Epist. xix. (de Petro reprehenso a Paulo ad Hieronymum) Tom. II. p. 27. Ed. Paris. 1637.]

[7 Ego hujus epistolæ auctoritate non teneor, quia literas Cypriani non ut canonicas habeo, sed eas ex canonicis considero; et quod in eis divinarum scripturarum auctoritati congruit, cum laude ejus accipio; quod autem non congruit, cum pace ejus respuo. Id. contra Cresconium Grammaticum, Lib. II. cap. xxxii. Tom. VII. p. 177.]

[8 Neque enim negare debeo, sicut in ipsis moribus, ita multa esse in tam multis opusculis meis, quæ possint justo judicio et nulla temeritate culpari. Id. De Anima et ejus origine, Lib. IV. (ad Vincentium Victorem) cap. i. Tom. VII. p. 499.]

[9 Noli meis literis quasi scripturis canonicis inservire; sed in illis et quod non credebas cum inveneris incunctanter crede, in istis autem quod certum non habebas, nisi certum intellexeris, noli firmiter retinere. Id. Procemium in Lib. III. de Trinitate, Tom. III. p. 104.]

[10 Neque enim quorumlibet disputationes, quamvis catholicorum et laudatorum hominum, velut scripturas canonicas habere debemus, ut nobis non liceat salva honorificentia, quæ illis debetur hominibus, aliquid in eorum scriptis improbare atque respuere, si forte invenerimus quod aliter senserint quam veritas habet, divino adjutorio vel ab aliis intellecta vel a nobis. Talis ego sum in scriptis aliorum, tales volo esse intellectores meorum. Id. Fortunatiano, (de videndo Deo). Epist. cxi. Tom. II. p. 199.]

[11 De corpore autem spirituali pacatius et diligentius inquiramus, ne forte aliquid certum ac liquidum, si nobis hoc utile esse novit, secundum scripturas suas Deus dignetur demonstrare. Id. ibid.]

[12 Hæc duo sunt pontificis opera: ut a Deo discat legendo scripturas divinas et sæpius ruminando, aut populum doceat; sed illa doceat quæ ipse a Deo didicerit, non ex proprio corde, vel ex humano sensu, sed quæ Spiritus docet. Cyril. Alexand. In Levit. Lib. VI. col. 25. Ed. Paris. 1514.]

[13 Hinc etiam discimus unum solummodo Christum sequendum esse magistrum, illi soli inhærendum. Id. in Joannem, cap. vi. p. 384. Ed. Lutet. 1638.]

[14 Non igitur omnia quæ Dominus fecit conscripta sunt, sed quæ scribentes tam ad mores

Note this holy father's words, and print them in your hearts for ever.

Fulgence, in his sermon of the Confessors. "In the word of God is plenty for the strong man to eat; there is enough for the child to suck; there is also milk to drink, wherewith the tender infancy of the faithful may be nourished; and strong meat, wherewith the lusty youth of them that be perfect may receive the spiritual increasement of holy virtue. There provision is made for the salvation of all men whom the Lord doth vouchsafe to save. There is that that is agreeable to all ages; there is also that which is meet for all states. There we learn the commandments which we ought to do; there we know the rewards which we hope for[1]."

If preachers ought so, then so ought all others: for they all are prepared to come to one end by one ordinary rule.

Gregory, in Job, lib. xvi. cap. 28. "He that prepareth himself to the office of a true preacher, must needs fetch the foundation of his matters out of the holy scriptures; so that all that he saith he must reduce it to the first beginning of God's authority, and in that stay the effect of his sayings. For, as I have said many times afore, heretics, when they study to maintain their froward doctrine, surely they bring forth those things that are not contained in the holy scriptures[2]."

Theophylactus, upon this place of Paul, the last to the Romans, "I beseech you, brethren, mark them which cause division, and give occasion of evil, contrary to the doctrine which you have learned, and avoid them. For they that are such, serve not the Lord Jesus Christ, but their own bellies; and with sweet preachings and flattering words deceive the hearts of the innocents." Here saith Theophylactus, that "they bring in
34. divisions and occasions of evil, which bring forth any thing beside the doctrine and learning of the apostles[3]."

Damascenus, lib. i. cap. 1. "All that ever was delivered by the law, the prophets, the apostles, and the evangelists, we receive, acknowledge, and give reverence unto them, searching nothing besides them[4]."

The scriptures only are sufficient for matters of salvation[5].

Bruno, in the second to Timothy. "Doubtless the holy scriptures are able to instruct thee to salvation. For every scripture being inspired from God, that is to say, spiritually understand after the will of God, is profitable to teach them that be ignorant; to reprove, that is, to convince them that speak against the faith; to correct sinners, such as deny not themselves to be sinners; to instruct those that be yet rude and simple; to instruct, I say, in righteousness, that they may be made righteous by putting away their former instructions of infidelity, I say, that he may be so taught, that, as much as in the teacher lieth, he that is taught may be the perfect man of God; so perfect, that he may be instruct to do every good work[6]."

---

quam ad dogmata putarunt sufficere; ut recta fide et operibus ac virtute rutilantes, ad regnum cœlorum perveniamus. Id. in Joannem, cap. xxi. col. 220. Ed. Paris. 1508. This edition is quoted, since this reference made by the archbishop was undoubtedly extracted from it, and not from the Greek text of the author, which is more diffuse.]

[1 In quibus denuo mandatis, tanquam ditissimis ferculis, sic cœlestium deliciarum copia spiritalis exuberat, ut in verbo Dei abundet, quod perfectus comedat; abundet etiam, quod parvulus sugat. Ibi est enim simul et lacteus potus, quo tenera fidelium nutriatur infantia; et solidus cibus, quo robusta perfectorum juventus spiritalia sanctæ virtutis accipiat incrementa. Ibi prorsus ad salutem consulitur universis, quos Dominus salvare dignatur. Ibi est quod omni ætati congruat: ibi quod omni professioni conveniat. Ibi audimus præcepta quæ faciamus: ibi cognoscimus præmia quæ speremus. Fulgent. Sermo de Confessoribus, p. 649. Ed. Antverp. 1574.]

[2 Qui ad veræ prædicationis verba se præparat, necesse est ut causarum origines a sacris paginis sumat; ut omne quod loquitur, ad divinæ auctoritatis fundamentum revocet, atque in eo ædificium locutionis suæ firmet. Ut enim prædiximus, sæpe hæretici dum sua student perversa adstruere, ea proferunt quæ profecto in sacrorum librorum paginis non tenentur. Gregor. Papæ I. Op. (Moral. Lib. XVIII. in cap. xxxviii. beati Job.) Tom. I. col. 573. Ed. Paris. 1705.]

[3 Καὶ αἱ διχοστασίαι τοίνυν, καὶ τὰ σκάνδαλα, ἤγουν αἱ αἱρέσεις, ἐκ τῶν παρὰ τὴν ἀποστολικὴν διδαχὴν δογματιζόντων. Theoph. In Epist. ad Rom. Tom. II. p. 116. Ed. Venet. 1754.]

[4 Liber vero scripturæ est sacra pagina, legem, prophetas, et evangelium continens. In quibus divina revelatione nobis indultis manifesta traditur Dei cognitio, quid de eo tenere, quid sentire debeamus; ut quæ ibidem aperiuntur de Deo, inconcussa fide teneamus, et ultra illa temerarie quippiam astruere de ipso non tentemus. Damascen. Orthodoxæ fidei, Lib. I. p. 3. Ed. Basil. 1675.]

[5 Matter of salvation, Orig. ed.]

[6 Vere sacræ literæ possunt te instruere ad salutem: quia omnis scriptura inspirata divinitus, i. spiritualiter secundum Deum intellecta, utilis est ad docendum eos qui nesciunt; et ad arguendum, i. ad convincendum eos qui fidei contradicunt; et ad corripiendum peccantes, et se peccasse non abne-

Beda, in the 1st Epistle of Peter, chap. v. "If any man speak, let him speak as the words of God." "Fearing lest he say or command any thing besides the will of God, or besides that which is manifestly commanded in the holy scriptures, and be found as a false witness of God, or a committer of sacrilege, or a bringer in of any strange thing from the Lord's doctrine, or else leave out or pass over any thing that pleaseth God; seeing that Christ most plainly commandeth the preachers of the truth concerning them whom they had taught, saying, 'Teach them to keep all things that I have commanded you;' yea, even the same which he had commanded, and none other; and he commanded his preachers to command their hearers to keep, not some of these, but all[7]."

If any man speak, let him speak according to the word of God; except he will be called by these names here expressed.

Anselmus, bishop, in his book of Virginity, cap. xxiv. "God's law forbiddeth to follow the steps of the catholic, or universal faith, any more than the judgment of the canonical truth commandeth to believe. And all other apocryphal lies, the good policies of the best learned fathers have stablished in their decrees utterly to reject, and to banish them clean, as horrible thunderings of words[8]."

We may not believe the general faith, except the same agree with God's word.

Lyrane, upon the last chap. of the Proverbs. "Like as in a merchant's ship are carried divers things necessary for man's life, so in the scripture are contained all things needful to salvation[9]."

Thomas of Aquine. "The holy scripture is the rule of our faith, whereunto it is neither lawful to add, nor take any thing away. But the truth of our faith is contained in the holy scriptures diffusely and divers ways; in some places darkly; and to try out the truth of our faith by the scriptures, is required long study and exercise; to the which all they cannot come that need to know the truth of the faith, the more part whereof, being occupied with other business, cannot attend to study. And therefore it was needful out of the sentences of holy scripture to gather something into a short sum, which should be set forth for all men to believe; which is not added to the scriptures, but rather taken out of the scriptures[10]."

The truth of our faith is contained in the word written.

35.

Scotus, in the prologue of Sentences, quæst. 2. Question: "Whether knowledge above nature, sufficient for a man in this life, be sufficiently set forth in the holy scripture." The question is not, "Whether any things be true that are not written, or whether God, since the creation and redemption of the world, hath done or said any thing that is not written, and received of the church for the holy scripture;" but this is the question, "Whether the word of God written be sufficient for our salvation; or whether a christian man be bound to believe any thing that cannot be proved by the holy scripture." And this granted, that all things that may be gathered out of the scripture, and every thing that upon any truth granted may be proved by a good argument of the scripture,

---

gantes; et ad erudiendum eos qui adhuc rudes sunt et simplices, erudiendum dico in justitia, i. ad hoc ut justificentur exuendo rudimenta infidelitatis. Sic inquam erudiant ut, quantum in doctore est, sit ille qui eruditur perfectus homo Dei; perfectus ita ut sit instructus ad omne opus bonum faciendum. Brun. Carth. Patri. In 2 Tim. cap. iii. in fine. Ed. 1524.]

[7 *Si quis loquitur quasi sermones Dei.* Timens videlicet, ne præter voluntatem Dei, vel præter quod in scripturis sanctis evidenter præcipitur, vel dicat aliquid, vel imperet, et inveniatur tanquam falsus testis Dei, aut sacrilegus, vel introducens aliquid alienum a doctrina Domini, vel certe subrelinquens et præteriens aliquid eorum, quæ Deo placita sunt, cum ipse manifestissime prædicatoribus veritatis de his quos imbuerint præcipiat dicens: *Docentes eos servare omnia, quæcunque mandavi vobis.* Et ea enim, quæ ipse mandavit, non alia, et hæc non ex parte, sed omnia suis auditoribus observare tradere jubet. Bedæ Opera, Tom. IV. col. 710. Ed. Colon. Agrip. 1612.]

[8 The Editor has not succeeded in discovering the passage referred to.]

[9 Sicut enim in navi institoris portantur diversa vitæ humanæ necessaria; sic in scriptura continentur omnia necessaria ad salutem. Nico. de Lyra. In Prov. cap. xxxi. Pars III. p. 339. Ed. Basil. 1502.]

[10 Sacra enim scriptura est regula fidei, cui nec addere, nec subtrahere licet. Veritas fidei in sacra scriptura diffuse continetur et variis modis, et in quibusdam obscure, ita quod ad eliciendum fidei veritatem ex sacra scriptura requiritur longum studium et exercitium, ad quod non possunt pervenire omnes illi, quibus necessarium est cognoscere fidei veritatem; quorum plerique aliis negotiis occupati, studio vacare non possunt: et ideo fuit necessarium, ut ex sententiis sacræ scripturæ aliquid manifestum summarie colligeretur, quod proponeretur omnibus ad credendum: quod quidem non est additum sacræ scripturæ, sed potius ex sacra scriptura sumptum. Thomas Aquin. Secunda secundæ, Quæst. i. Art. ix. Tom. II. p. 5. Ed. Antverp. 1624.]

doth pertain to the holy scripture; this granted, I say, he concludeth, that "all things necessary for our salvation are fully contained in the holy scripture[1]."

¶ The school-authors call the stay of our faith, the truth shewed of God, and contained in the canon of the bible.

---

## THE THIRD CHAPTER.

36. *That the General Councils, without the Word of God, are not sufficient to make articles of our faith.*

They were gathered in the spirit of pride and envy, and not in the spirit of meekness and love.

EUSEBIUS, in his Ecclesiastical History, lib. i. cap. 8. [viii. 1.] "The head-rulers of the church, forgetting God's commandments, were inflamed one against another with contention, zeal, envy, pride, malice, and hatred; so that they thought rather that they occupied the room of tyrants than of priests. And also, forgetting christian humility and sincerity, they did celebrate the holy mysteries with unholy hands[2]."

Note these words diligently, and forget them not.

Gregory Nazianzen to Procopius. "Undoubtedly I think thus, if I must needs write the truth, that all assemblies of bishops are to be eschewed. For I never saw good end of any synod, that did not rather bring in evils, than put them away; for the lusts of strife and desire and of lordship reign there[3]."

Councils are not of such authority that whatsoever they decree must be holden for truth.

Augustine, in his second book and third chapter against the Donatists. "The councils, which are kept through every region or province, without all clokings, ought to give place to the general councils, which are made of all Christendom; yea, and the former general councils ought ofttimes to be reformed by the latter councils, if any thing in them do chance to err from the truth[4]."

The scripture must try all.

Augustine, against *Maximinum*, the bishop of the Arians, lib. iii. cap. 4. "But now neither ought I to allege the council of Nice, nor thou the council of Arimine, to take advantage thereby: for neither am I bound nor held by the authority of this, nor thou of that. Let matter with matter, cause with cause, or reason with reason, try the matter by the authority of scriptures, not proper witnesses to any of us, but indifferent witnesses for us both[5]."

Mark this.

Gerson. "We ought rather believe the saying of any teacher, armed with the canonical scripture, than the pope's determination[6]."

---

[[1] Quæstio ii. Utrum cognitio supernaturalis necessaria viatori sit sufficienter tradita in sacra scriptura: upon which the conclusion is, Quod sacra scriptura sufficienter continet doctrinam necessariam viatori.]

[[2] Οἵ τε δοκοῦντες ἡμῶν ποιμένες, τὸν τῆς θεοσεβείας θεσμὸν παρωσάμενοι, ταῖς πρὸς ἀλλήλους ἀνεφλέγοντο φιλονεικίαις· αὐτὰ δὴ ταῦτα μόνα, τὰς ἔριδας καὶ τὰς ἀπειλὰς τόν τε ζῆλον καὶ τὸ πρὸς ἀλλήλους ἔχθος καὶ μῖσος ἐπαύξοντες, οἷά τε τυραννίδας τὰς φιλαρχίας ἐκθύμως διεκδικοῦντες, τότε δὴ, κ. τ. ἑ. Euseb. Eccl. Hist. Lib. VIII. cap. i.]

[[3] Ἔχω μὲν οὕτως, εἰ δεῖ τἀληθὲς γράφειν, ὥστε πάντα σύλλογον φεύγειν ἐπισκόπων, ὅτι μηδεμιᾶς συνόδου τέλος εἶδον χρηστὸν, μηδὲ λύσιν κακῶν μᾶλλον ἐσχηκυίας ἢ προσθήκην· ἀεὶ γὰρ φιλονεικίαι καὶ φιλαρχίαι. Greg. Nazianz. Epist. cxxx. Procopio. Tom. II. p. 110. Ed. Paris. 1840.]

[[4] Et ipsa concilia, quæ per singulas regiones vel provincias fiunt, plenariorum conciliorum auctoritati, quæ fiunt ex universo orbe Christiano, sine ullis ambagibus cedere; ipsaque plenaria sæpe priora posterioribus emendari, cum aliquo experimento rerum aperitur quod clausum erat. Augustin. de Bapt. cont. Donat. Lib. II. cap. iii. Tom. VII. p. 42. Ed. Paris. 1635.]

[[5] Sed nunc nec ego Nicænum, nec tu debes Arimenense, tanquam præjudicaturus proferre concilium. Nec ego hujus auctoritate, nec tu illius detineris: scripturarum auctoritatibus, non quorumque propriis, sed utrisque communibus testibus, res cum re, causa cum causa, ratio cum ratione concertet. Id. Contra Maxim. Arrian. Epis. Lib. III. cap. xiv. Tom. VI. p. 306.]

[[6] Jungatur huic considerationi cum sua declaratione duplex veritas. Prima, staret quod aliquis simplex non auctorisatus, esset tam excellenter in sacris litteris eruditus, quod plus esset credendum in casu doctrinali suæ assertioni, quam papæ declarationi; constat enim plus esse credendum evangelio quam papæ: si doceat igitur talis eruditus veritatem aliquam in evangelio contineri, ubi et papa nesciret, vel ultro erraret; patet cujus præferendum sit judicium. Altera veritas, talis eruditus deberet in casu, si et dum celebraretur generale concilium, cui et ipse præsens esset, illi se opponere, si sentiret majorem partem ad oppositum evangelii malitia vel ignorantia declinare. Gerson. De Exam. Doctr. Pars i. Consid. v. Tom. I. col. ii. Ed. Antverp. 1706.]

The same. "More credit is to be given to a man that is singularly learned in the scripture, bringing forth catholic authority, than to the general council[7]." 37.

Read, ye papists, and be no longer ignorant.

Panormitan, in cap. "Significasti." "A simple layman, bringing forth the scriptures, is to be believed rather than a whole council. For a council may err, as it hath aforetimes erred[8]:" as did the council of Melchidense and Aquisgranum, of contracting of matrimony. The council of Constance, among other articles of John Hus and Hierome of Prague unjustly condemned, condemned also this article for heresy: That the two natures, that is, the divine[9] and humanity, be one Christ; which is a necessary article of our faith, expressed in the Creed of Athanasius, called *Quicunque vult;* where it is read, 'The right faith is, that we believe and confess that our Lord Jesus Christ, the Son of God, is God and man:' and a little after, 'Like as the reasonable soul and the flesh is one man, so God and man is one Christ.' The same is also decreed by the council of Nice and divers other catholic councils, and it is the doctrine of the church at this time. Finally, it may be proved by the express word of God: and yet these malicious clergy were not ashamed to condemn the same for an heresy.

Councils may and do err ofttimes.

Read the Psalm.

¶ Note here, gentle reader, unto what shameless and detestable heresies their popish, yea, antichristian general councils have fallen, of the which they boast so much that they cannot err, and whereupon chiefly they build all their errors and heresies. Moreover, the most part of the good laws and canons be in manner altogether abrogated, and nowhere kept: part whereof I shall express.

---

## CANONS OF THE APOSTLES AND COUNCILS NOT KEPT NOR USED. 38.

Canon 3.

"Let not a bishop, priest, or deacon, by any means put away his own wife under pretence of religion: but if he do, let him be excommunicated; and if he so continue, let him be deposed[10]."

Canon 4.

"Let no bishop, priest, or deacon, be received into another bishop's diocese, without a testimonial of his good behaviour: and when they have delivered their writings, let them be diligently examined if they be godly preachers[11]."

¶ If these two laws were throughly executed by indifferent judges, being no priests, the realm of England should not swarm so full of runagates, adulterous, and sodomical priests. For in Wales, for their cradle crowns paid to the ordinary, they kept their concubines or harlots openly; and in England many great beneficed men keep their harlots at rack and manger without any punishment, except it be by bribing of the ordinaries privily; and, all shame set aside, they have their own known bastards waiting upon them in sight of the whole world. But the poor purgatory priests, when they be taken in open advoutry, flee from east to west, from north to south, from diocese to diocese, and there be received without any letters testimonial at all; where they be taken for honest and chaste priests. But if the rich priests were deprived of all their promotions, so oft as they be known to be fornicators, (as they ought to be,) and the poor priests not received into any strange diocese without testimony of his honest demeanour from his former ordinary, you should scarcely find priests for every

---

[7 See note 6 on previous page.]

[8 Uni fideli privato, si meliorem scripturæ auctoritatem aut rationem habeat, plus credendum est, quam toti concilio—nam et concilium potest errare.—Panorm. (N. de Tudesch.) sup. Decretal. Lib. i. Tit. vi. Tom. I. fol. R. 2. Lib. Venet. Ed. Nur. et Basil. 1476-8.]

[9 The divinity and humanity, Orig. ed.]

[10 'Επίσκοπος, ἢ πρεσβύτερος, ἢ διάκονος τὴν ἑαυτοῦ γυναῖκα μὴ ἐκβαλλέτω προφάσει εὐλαβείας. 'Εὰν δὲ ἐκβάλλῃ, ἀφοριζέσθω· ἐπιμένων δὲ, καθαιρείσθω. Can. Apost. Can. v. Labbè et Cossart. Tom. I. col. 25. Ed. Paris. 1671.]

[11 Μηδένα τῶν ξένων ἐπισκόπων, ἢ πρεσβυτέρων, ἢ διακόνων ἄνευ συστατικῶν προσδέχεσθαι, καὶ ἐπιφερομένων αὐτῶν ἀνακρινέσθωσαν. Id. Can. xxii. Labbè et Cossart, Tom. I. col. 31. Ib. This Canon is given more fully, "ex interpretatione Dionysii exigui," in Latin, as follows (col. 50): "Nullus episcoporum peregrinorum, aut presbyterorum, aut diaconorum sine commendatitiis suscipiatur epistolis. Et cum scripta detulerint, discutiantur attentius, et ita suscipiantur, si prædicatores pietatis exstiterint." Id. Can. xxxiv. col. 50.]

third [1]benefice of England, and the priests themselves would be the first earnest suitors that they might have their lawful wives of their own. But as long as they be their own judges, (according to the old proverb, "One scabbed horse knappeth another,") what for favour and friendship, what for money and for slandering of their order, they wink one at another's faults, and help to cloke the same; insomuch that within my memory, which is above thirty years, and also by information of other, that be twenty years elder than I, I could never perceive or learn that any one priest under the pope's kingdom was ever punished for advoutry by his ordinary. And yet, not long ago, a petty canon of a cathedral church in England was accused[2], by three boys of the grammar-school, to the vice-dean or sub-dean of the same church; a man not unlike to a monk called Jodocus, of whom Erasmus maketh mention, that he were

O what a court is this, that in suspicion of heresy acquitteth no man, and in cause of adultery condemneth no priest, be his crime never so openly known!

39. worthy to walk openly with a bell and a cockscomb, if he were not set forth under the holy habit of a monk. But when he perceived that the said priest could not purge himself of the foresaid crime, he privily paid him his quarter's wages beforehand, and suffered him to depart without farther trial of the said crime: and now he jetteth in London, with side gown and sarcenet tippet, as good a virgin-priest as the best. If I should but briefly touch all the histories that I have known of the incontinency of priests, it would grow to a work thrice greater than all my whole book, and it would make some of the proudest of them to blush, if they be not past all shame: but I will not blot my good paper with so evil matter, although they be not ashamed openly to blot and stain their own good names with crimes worthy of such reproach and ignominy.

Canon 7.

"Let not any bishop, priest, or deacon, in any wise take upon him any secular business; but if he do, let him be excommunicated[3]."

¶ But now such shameless contemners they be of their own laws, which they so greatly extol and bind all other to keep, that they be hunters, falconers, stewards, surveyors, and receivers, to all great men, yea, and to the bishops themselves.

Canon 9.

"If any priest or deacon, or any other of the number of priesthood, do not receive at the communion, let him shew his cause: if it be reasonable, let him be pardoned; if not, let him be deprived from the communion[4]."

Canon 10.

"It is meet to put off from the communion all christian men which enter into the church, and hear the scriptures, but continue not in prayer until mass be done, nor receive there the holy communion, as disturbers of the quietness of the church[5]."

¶ By these two canons be subverted, and utterly overthrown, all private masses, where the priest only receiveth.

The council of Nice. Canon 6.

"Let the old custom continue still in Egypt, Lybia, and Pentapoli, that the bishop of Alexandrie have power over all these; forasmuch as the bishop of Rome hath a like custom. At Antioch also, and other provinces, let their honour be reserved to every church[6]."

The council of Nice. Canon 20.

"Because there be some that kneel at their prayers on the Sunday and in Whitsun-

40. week; be it therefore ordained by this holy council, that all men stand at their prayers; forsomuch as it is a convenient custom, fit to be kept in all churches[7]."

---

[1 Third be benefice, Ed. 1582.]

[2 Two words are omitted.]

[3 Ἐπίσκοπος, ἢ πρεσβύτερος, ἢ διάκονος κοσμικὰς φροντίδας μὴ ἀναλαμβανέτω· εἰ δὲ μὴ, καθαιρείσθω. Id. Can. vi. Labbè et Cossart. Tom. I. col. 25. Ib.]

[4 Εἴ τις ἐπίσκοπος, ἢ πρεσβύτερος, ἢ διάκονος, ἢ ἐκ τοῦ καταλόγου τοῦ ἱερατικοῦ, προσφορᾶς γενομένης μὴ μεταλάβοι, τὴν αἰτίαν εἰπάτω. Καὶ ἐὰν εὔλογος ᾖ, συγγνώμης τυγχανέτω· εἰ δὲ μὴ λέγει, ἀφοριζέσθω, &c. Id. Can. viii. Ib. Tom. I. col. 25.]

[5 Πάντας τοὺς εἰσιόντας πιστοὺς, καὶ τῶν γραφῶν ἀκούοντας, μὴ παραμένοντας δὲ τῇ προσευχῇ καὶ τῇ ἁγίᾳ μεταλήψει, ὡς ἀταξίαν ἐμποιοῦντας τῇ ἐκκλησίᾳ, ἀφορίζεσθαι χρή. Id. Can. ix. Ib. Tom. I. col. 27.]

[6 Τὰ ἀρχαῖα ἔθη κρατείτω, τὰ ἐν Αἰγύπτῳ καὶ Λιβύῃ καὶ Πενταπόλει, ὥστε τὸν Ἀλεξανδρείας ἐπίσκοπον πάντων τούτων ἔχειν τὴν ἐξουσίαν· ἐπειδὴ καὶ τῷ ἐν τῇ Ῥώμῃ ἐπισκόπῳ τοῦτο σύνηθές ἐστιν· ὁμοίως δὲ καὶ κατὰ τὴν Ἀντιόχειαν, καὶ ἐν ταῖς ἄλλαις ἐπαρχίαις, τὰ πρεσβεῖα σώζεσθαι ταῖς ἐκκλησίαις. Conc. Nicæn. Can. vi. Labbè et Cossart. Tom. II. col. 32. Lutet. Paris. 1671-2.]

[7 Ἐπειδή τινές εἰσιν ἐν τῇ κυριακῇ γόνυ κλίνοντες, καὶ ἐν ταῖς τῆς πεντηκοστῆς ἡμέραις, ὑπὲρ τοῦ πάντα ἐν πάσῃ παροικίᾳ ὁμοίως παραφυλάττεσθαι, ἑστῶτας ἔδοξε τῇ ἁγίᾳ συνόδῳ τὰς εὐχὰς ἀποδιδόναι Θεῷ. Id. Can. xx. Ib. Tom. II. col. 37.]

¶ But now Antichrist of Rome, contrary to this decree, hath extolled himself above his fellow-bishops, as God's vicar, yea, rather as God himself; and taketh upon him authority over kings and emperors, and sitteth in the temple of God, that is, in the consciences of men, and causeth his decrees to be more regarded than God's laws; yea, and for money he dispenseth with God's laws, and all other, giving men licence to break them.

"If any priest be found eating in a common alehouse, let him be excommunicated[8]." The council of Nice. Canon 6.

"If any man judge that a married priest ought not to offer, as it were for his marriage sake, and for that cause do abstain from his oblation, let him be excommunicated[9]." The council of Gangrense.

¶ But now married priests be excommunicated; and except they will forsake their lawful wives, they shall be burned therefore.

"Forasmuch as there are some which pray standing, both on the Sunday and in Whitsun-week, it is therefore ordained by this holy council, that because it is a convenient custom, and agreeable throughout all churches, that men should make their prayers to God standing[10]." Ibidem. Canon 7.

¶ This law is no where kept.

"Let no priest be made before thirty years, yea, though he be of an honest life; but let him tarry to the time appointed: for the Lord was baptized at thirty years, and then preached[11]." The council of Neocesaria.

¶ How this law is kept, the whole world may judge: for the cardinal of Loreyn was made about the twelfth year of his age; and pope Clement made two of his nephews cardinals, being very boys. And of late, in the pope's kingdom, children have been made archdeacons and deans of cathedral churches.

"No man may be received to baptism in Lent after two weeks[12]." The council of Laodicea.

"Bread ought not to be offered in Lent but in the Saturday and Sunday[13]." Ibidem.

¶ He speaketh of the bread of the holy communion. But who keepeth these laws?

"Laymen ought not to sing any made and commonly used songs in the church, nor read any book beside the canon; but only the canonical books of the new and old testament[14]." "Those books which ought to be read and received for authority, be those books which be divided from the books called Apocrypha, in the great bible. Unto the which Saint Cyprian, Hierome, Austin, with all the old writers, agree[15]." Ibidem. 41.

¶ But the third council of Carthage added to these the books of Wisdom, Ecclesiasticus, Tobie, Judith, Hester, and the books of the Machabees[16]; unto which latter council the papists cleave with tooth and nail, and thereupon stay their purgatory, praying to saints, with divers other errors and heresies, contrary to the elder and better councils. Hereby you may most easily perceive how shamefully their general councils have erred, as well in the judgment of the scriptures, as also in necessary articles of our faith and good manners. Yea, and the chiefest and oldest councils be (as Anacharsis said of the laws made by Solon for the Athenians) like to cobwebs, wherein small flies, gnats, and midges, be taken and devoured of the spiders; but great hornets and humble-bees fly through and break them, without any danger or hurt. And generally there is no laws regarded, kept, or maintained among them, but such as make (as they term them) *pro*

---

[[8] There is an error in the reference. But see Concil. Labb. et Cossart. Tom. II. p. 592. Tit. xxiii.]

[[9] *Εἴ τις διακρίνοιτο παρὰ πρεσβυτέρου γεγαμηκότος, ὡς μὴ χρῆναι λειτουργήσαντος αὐτοῦ προσφορᾶς μεταλαμβάνειν, ἀνάθεμα ἔστω.* Conc. Gangr. Can. iv. Tom. II. col. 419. Id.]

[[10] See preceding page, note 7.]

[[11] *Πρεσβύτερος πρὸ τῶν τριάκοντα ἐτῶν μὴ χειροτονείσθω, ἐὰν καὶ πάνυ ᾖ ὁ ἄνθρωπος ἄξιος, ἀλλὰ ἀποτηρείσθω. Ὁ γὰρ κύριος Ἰησοῦς Χριστὸς ἐν τῷ τριακοστῷ ἔτει ἐφωτίσθη, καὶ ἤρξατο διδάσκειν.* Concil. Neocæsarense, Can. xi. Ib. Tom. I. col. 1483.]

[[12] *με΄. Ὅτι οὐ δεῖ μετὰ δύο ἑβδομάδας τῆς τεσσαρακοστῆς δέχεσθαι εἰς τὸ φώτισμα.* Synodi Laodicenæ Canones, Can. xlv. Ib. Tom. I. col. 1503.]

[[13] *μθ΄. Ὅτι οὐ δεῖ τῇ τεσσαρακοστῇ ἄρτον προσφέρειν, εἰ μὴ ἐν σαββάτῳ καὶ κυριακῇ μόνον.* Can. xlix. Id. Tom. I. col. 1505.]

[[14] *νθ΄. Ὅτι οὐ δεῖ ἰδιωτικοὺς ψαλμοὺς λέγεσθαι ἐν τῇ ἐκκλησίᾳ, οὐδὲ ἀκανόνιστα βίβλια, αλλὰ μόνα τὰ κανονικὰ τῆς καινῆς καὶ παλαιᾶς διαθήκης.* Id. Can. lix. Tom. I. col. 1507.]

[[15] Vide Can. lx. Ib.]

[[16] Vide Canones Concilii Carthagin. iii. Can. xlvii. Id. Tom. II. col. 1177.]

Matt. xxiii. *pane lucrando*, that is, for their dignities, immunities, or liberties and profits. Wherefore the words of our Saviour Christ may be rightly verified of them: "They lay heavy and importable burthens on other men's shoulders, but will not once move them with their finger." For all their laws be but nets to take and kill the poor fishes, and to fill their own paunches.

---

## THE FOURTH CHAPTER.

42. *That nothing can be proved by oracles of angels touching religion*[1].

Gen. iii. SATAN, being changed into a serpent, deceived our first parents; and in them cast all mankind headlong into damnation.

1 Kings xxii. "I will go forth, and be a lying spirit in the mouth of all his prophets."

¶ Read the whole chapter.

Gal. i. "Though an angel from heaven preach any other gospel," &c.

2 Cor. xi. "Satan himself is changed into an angel of light."

Col. ii. "Let no man make you shoot at a wrong mark by the humbleness and holiness of angels."

[1 Tim. iv.] The same, chap. iv. "The Spirit speaketh evidently, that in the latter times some shall depart from the faith, and shall give heed unto spirits of error and devilish doctrine."

1 John iv. "Believe not every spirit, but prove the spirits, whether they are of God, or not."

Acts xvi. "A certain damsel, possessed with a spirit that prophesied, met us; which brought her master and mistress much vantage with prophesying. The same followed Paul and us, and cried, saying, These are the servants of the most High God, which shew unto us the way of salvation. And this did she many days: but Paul, not content, turned about, and said to the spirit, I command thee in the name of Jesu Christ, that thou come out of her. And he came out the same hour."

Cyprian, of the Simpleness of Prelates. "The enemy (after the words of the apostles[2]) changeth himself into an angel of light, and setteth forth his servants, as ministers of righteousness, affirming night for day, death for health, desperation under the colour of hope, false faith under the pretence of faith, antichrist under the name of Christ: so that whiles they counterfeit the like things, they make void the truth with subtlety. This, dearly-beloved brethren, cometh to pass by this means, that we resort not to the original of the truth, nor seek the head Christ, nor keep the doctrine of our heavenly Master[3]."

The devil deceiveth man, because he wandereth from the word written, and is not content therewith.

43.

[Spirits work no good, but evil[4].]

Cyprianus, in his fourth treatise of the Vanity of Idols. "Filthy spirits wandering abroad, being drowned in worldly vices, after they have shrunken from heavenly virtue through worldly corruption, being themselves destroyed, cease not to destroy other, and, being infect with evil, infect other with the same. These inspire the hearts of the prophets, ever lapping up lies with the truth; they trouble men's lives, disquiet their sleeps, drawing their members awry, hurt their health, provoke diseases, to force men to worshipping of them: and this is the remedy of them, when they cease to hurt. Neither have they any other study but to call men back from God, and turn them from the

[The devil's miracles are to work mischief[4].]

They hurt most of all when they cease from hurting.

---

[1 The *Confutation* here contains several authorities which are not to be found in Cranmer's Common-place Book at the British Museum, particularly the long quotation from Lactantius.]

[2 The apostle, Orig. ed.]

[3 (Blandiente adversario atque fallente,) qui secundum apostoli vocem transfigurat se velut angelum lucis, et ministros suos subornat velut ministros justitiæ, asserentes noctem pro die, interitum pro salute, desperationem sub obtentu spei, perfidiam sub prætextu fidei, antichristum sub vocabulo Christi; ut dum verisimilia mentiuntur, veritatem subtilitate frustrentur. Hoc eo fit, fratres dilectissimi, dum ad veritatis originem non reditur, nec caput quæritur, nec magistri cœlestis doctrina servatur. Cyprian, De Unit. Eccles. (*vulg.* de Simp. Præl.) p. 194. Ed. Paris. 1726.]

[4 These paragraphs are omitted in ed. 1582.]

perceiving of true religion to their superstition; and seeing they be in pain themselves, to seek those to be companions of their pain whom they have made, through their error, partakers of their sin[5]."

Lactantius, Institutionum, Lib. ii. cap. 15. "Corrupt and damned spirits stray over all the world, and seek for ease of their destruction through the destruction of men. They therefore fill all the world with snares, frauds, and errors; the which, because they be fine spirits, and cannot be perceived, convey themselves into men's bodies, and being secretly hid within the body, trouble health, bring sickness, fray men with dreams, vex men's minds with sweat, that through these harms they may force men to run to them for help. The cause of all which deceits is dark to them that be ignorant in the truth; for they think they profit when they cease from hurting which can do nothing but hurt. But they which have shrunken back from God's service, because they be enemies and transgressors of the truth, go about to challenge to themselves the name and honour of God: not because they desire any honour, (for what honour can the damned have?) nor that they should hurt God, who cannot be hurt; but to hurt men, whom they go about to draw away from the worship and knowledge of God's true majesty, lest they should attain immortality, which they have lost through their own malice. So they cover all with darkness, and compass the truth with clouds; so that they cannot know their Lord, nor their Father. And that they may easily allure men, they hide themselves in the churches, and are at hand in all sacrifices. Yea, many times they work miracles, through which men being astonied, do give to images the faith of the godhead. Hereof it cometh that a stone was cut in sunder with a razor by a sorcerer; and that Juno of Veia answered, that she would go to Rome; and that a ship followed the hand of Claudia; and that Juno being robbed, and Proserpina of Locrense, and Ceres of Milete, took vengeance of those that had committed sacrilege; and Hercules of Appius, and Jupiter of Atimus, and Minerva of Cæsar. Hereof also it cometh that a serpent delivered the city of Rome from the pestilence, being brought from Epidaure. But chiefly they deceive men in their oracles and answers, whose jugglings ungodly men cannot discern from the truth. Therefore they think that empires and victories, riches and lucky chances of things, are given of them; and to be short, ofttimes commonwealths to be delivered from present dangers at their beck, which dangers they both declared by their answer[6], and, being pacified with sacrifice, turned away. But all these be but deceits; for seeing they know before the disposition of God, because they were his ministers, they thrust themselves into these business[7], so that whatsoever things either be done or have been done of God, they might seem chiefly to do or have done it. And so oft as any goodness is coming at hand to any people or city, according to God's appointment, they promise that they will do it, either by miracles, dreams, or revelations, if churches, if honours, if sacrifices, be given to them: the which things being given, when that chanceth that needs must be, they get to themselves great worship. For this cause be temples vowed, for this cause be new images hallowed. And so oft as perils be at hand, for some foolish and light cause, they feign themselves angry, as Juno toward Varro. But these be the deceits of them, that lurking under the names of the dead, intend to plague them that be alive. Wherefore, whereas that danger that is at hand may be avoided, they would seem that they, being pacified, have turned it away. And if it cannot be eschewed, this they do, that it might appear to chance for the contempt of them. And so they purchase to themselves great authority and fear among men that know them not. Some men will say, Why doth God then suffer these things? neither doth he succour so evil errors? That evil

The devils vex both body and soul, to cause men to seek to them for help, and so to be worshipped as God.

Satan worketh miracles by images, and hereof springeth the worshipping of images.

44.

The devils speak in images as though they were gods.

Though devils prophesy truly of things to come, yet all is but deceit, to make men to worship them.

Satan, under pretence of dead men's souls, deceiveth them that live, and leadeth them into idolatry.

---

[5 Spiritus sunt insinceri et vagi, qui postea quam terrenis vitiis immersi sunt, et a vigore cœlesti terreno contagio receperunt, non desinunt perditi perdere, et depravati errorem pravitatis infundere. Hi afflatu suo vatum pectora inspirant, falsa veris semper involvunt; nam et falluntur et fallunt, vitam turbant, somnos inquietant, irrepentes etiam spiritus in corporibus occulte mentes terrent, membra distorquent, valetudinem frangunt, morbos lacessunt, ut ad cultum sui cogant. Hæc est de illis medela, cum illorum cessat injuria; nec aliud illis studium est quam a Deo homines avocare, et ad superstitionem sui ab intellectu veræ religionis avertere, et cum sint ipsi pœnales, quærere sibi ad pœnam comites quos ad crimen suum fecerint errore participes. Id. De Idolorum Vanitate, pp. 226, 7.]

[6 Answers, Orig. ed.]

[7 Businesses, Orig. ed.]

things may fight with good, that vices may be contrary to virtues, that he may have some whom he may punish, and some whom he may honour[1]."

Subtle Satan feigneth himself to be Christ, and worshipped as God.

45.

How shall we then know any certain truth by apparitions?

They that believe visions, often worship Satan for Christ.

Stapulensis, upon the 2nd Epistle to the Thessalonians, chap. ii. "Marvel not of counterfeit angels, and of the subtlety of Satan, resembling himself to Christ, seeing we read a like thing in the history of Heraclides, of a monk called Valent. The devil, saith he, changing himself into the likeness of our Saviour, came to him by night, with a company (as he feigned) of a thousand angels, holding burning lamps in their hands, and with a fiery chariot, in the which he feigned our Saviour to sit. Then one of them stept forth, and said thus unto him: 'Come forth out of thy cell now, and do nothing else but when thou seest him come affar off make haste to bow down thyself and worship him, and so straightway return again to thine own house.' Then he went forth out of his house, and believing that he had seen that godly offices of heavenly ministers, and all shining with fiery lamps, and Christ, as he thought, himself not past a furlong off, fell flat upon the ground, and worshipped him, whom he believed to be the Lord. See here how this fearful and foolish monk Valent, leaving very Christ, worshipped Christ's enemy, and, instead of the truth, a counterfeit antichrist and Satan[2]."

---

[[1] Hi, ut dico, spiritus contaminati ac perditi per omnem terram vagantur; et solatium perditionis suæ perdendis hominibus operantur. Itaque omnia insidiis, fraudibus, dolis, erroribus complent—qui quoniam sunt spiritus tenues, et incomprehensibiles, insinuant se corporibus hominum; et occulte in visceribus operti valetudinem vitiant, morbos citant; somniis animos terrent; mentes furoribus quatiunt; ut homines his malis cogant ad eorum auxilia decurrere. Quarum omnium fallaciarum ratio expertibus veritatis obscura est. Prodesse enim eos putant, cum nocere desinunt; qui nihil aliud possunt quam nocere.—Illi autem, qui desciverunt a Dei ministerio, quia sunt veritatis inimici, et prævaricatores Dei, nomen sibi et cultum deorum vendicare conantur: non quod ullum honorem desiderent, (quis enim honor perditis est?) nec ut Deo noceant, cui noceri non potest; sed ut hominibus, quos nituntur a cultura et notitia veræ majestatis avertere, ne immortalitatem adipisci possint, quam ipsi sua nequitia perdiderunt. Offundunt itaque tenebras, et veritatem caligine obducunt; ne Dominum, ne patrem suum norint. Et ut illiciant, facile in templis se occulunt, et sacrificiis omnibus præsto adsunt; eduntque sæpe prodigia, quibus obstupefacti homines, fidem commodent simulachris divinitatis ac numinis. Inde est, quod ab augure lapis novacula incisus est; et quod Juno Veiensis migrare se Romam velle respondit; quod Claudiæ manum navis secuta est; quod in sacrilegos et Juno nudata, et Locrensis Proserpina, et Ceres Milesia vindicavit; et Hercules de Appio, et Jupiter de Atinio, et Minerva de Cæsare. Hinc, quod serpens urbem Romam pestilentia liberavit Epidauro accersitus. In oraculis autem vel maxime fallunt, quorum præstigias profani a veritate intelligere non possunt: ideoque ab illis attribui putant et imperia, et victorias, et opes, et eventus prosperos rerum; denique ipsorum nutu sæpe rempublicam periculis imminentibus liberatam: quæ pericula et responsis denuntiaverunt, et sacrificiis placati averterunt. Sed omnia ista falaciæ sunt. Nam cum dispositiones Dei præsentiant, quippe qui ministri ejus fuerunt, interponunt se in his rebus; ut quæcunque a Deo vel facta sunt, vel fiunt, ipsi potissimum facere aut fecisse videantur. Et quoties alicui populo vel urbi secundum Dei statum boni quid impendet; illi se id facturos vel prodigiis, vel somniis, vel oraculis pollicentur; si sibi templa, si honores, si sacrificia tribuantur. Quibus datis, cum illud acciderit, quod necesse est, summam sibi pariunt venerationem. Hinc templa devoventur, et novæ imagines consecrantur.—Quoties autem pericula impendent; ob aliquam se ineptam et levem causam profitentur iratos; sicut Juno Varroni.—Sed illorum sunt isti lusus; qui sub nominibus mortuorum delitescentes, viventibus plagas tendunt. Itaque sive illud periculum, quod imminet, vitari potest, videri volunt id placati avertisse; sive non potest, id agunt ut propter illorum contemptum accidisse videatur. Ita sibi apud homines, qui eos nesciunt, auctoritatem ac timorem pariunt.—Dicet aliquis, Cur ergo Deus hæc fieri patitur? nec tam malis succurrit erroribus? Ut mala cum bonis pugnent; ut vitia sint adversa virtutibus; ut habeat alios quos puniat, alios quos honoret. Lactant. Lib. II. capp. 14, 15, 16, 17. pp. 138—143. Ed. Lugd. Batav. 1652.]

[[2] Non etiam mireris de fictitiis angelis et de simulato astutia Satanæ Christo, cum Valentini monacho ex historia Heraclidis simile accidisse agnoscatur. Dæmon (inquit) in effigiem salvatoris transfiguratus, nocte ad eum venit cum choro quodam mille (ut finxerat) angelorum, lampadas accensas tenentium, et cum flammea rota, in qua salvatorem sedere simulaverat, præcedente uno ex ipsis, eique ista dicente: Egredere igitur e cella tua nihilque aliud facias, nisi ut venientem eminus cernens, inclinans te, adorare festines, sic deinceps ad proprium habitaculum reversurus. Egressus igitur e cella sua, credensque se cernere divina mysterii cœlestis officia, cunctaque lampadum fulgore rutilantia, et ipsum Christum non ultra unius spacium stadii constitutum, protinus pronus in terra, et eum quem crederet dominum adoravit. Hæc Heraclides. Ecce quomodo, relicto vero Christo, timidus et insipiens Valens Christi adoravit adversarium, et pro veritate simulatum phantasma et ementitum simulachrum. J. Fabri Stapulens. Comment. in Epist. Pauli; in 2 Epist. Thess. cap. ii. fol. clv. Ed. Paris. 1531.]

## THE FIFTH CHAPTER.

*That apparitions of the dead be unsufficient to prove truth.*

Deut. xviii.

"When thou art come into the land which the Lord thy God giveth thee, see that thou follow not the abominations of those nations: let there not be found among you any one that maketh his son or daughter to go through the fire, or that useth witchcraft, or a chooser of days, and that regardeth the flying of fowls, or a sorcerer, or a charmer, or that counselleth with spirits, or a soothsayer, or that asketh the truth at them that be dead. For the Lord abhorreth all these: and for such abominations the Lord thy God doth cast them out before thee. But the Lord thy God hath not suffered thee so to do."

Isai. viii. Read the place.

"And if they say to you, Ask counsel at the soothsayers, witches, charmers, and conjurors; then make them this answer, Is there a people any where that asketh not counsel at his God? should men run unto the dead for the living? If any man want light, let him look upon the law and the testimony, whether they speak after this meaning." 46.

Luke xvi. Read the chapter.

"If they hear not Moses and the prophets, neither will they believe if one arise from death."

He laugheth their foolishness to scorn.

Lactantius, in his Institution[3], lib. ii. cap. 2. "The rude sort think that men's souls walk about the graves and relics of their bodies[4]."

The scripture ought to be believed rather than the testimony of the dead: for it is God's own word, and the other ofttimes the devil's.

Chrysostom in his fourth Homily of Lazarus. "That thou mayest know that the doctrines of the scriptures and prophets are of more force, than if they that be raised from death should tell any thing: consider this, that whosoever is dead, is a servant. But what the scriptures speak, the Lord himself speaketh: therefore, though a dead man arise, yea, although an angel come down from heaven, yet chiefly we ought to believe the scriptures. For he that is Master of angels, and Lord of the quick and the dead, made them. If dead men should come again from thence unto us, the devil might have brought to us false doctrines; and that very easily. For he might have shewed oftentimes ghosts, and have suborned[5] men that should counterfeit death and burial, and within a while after shew themselves as though they were raised again from death, and through them to persuade the people so beguiled whatsoever him list. For if now, when no such thing is done in deed, yet dreams seen of many men in their sleep, as though it were of them that are departed hence, have deceived, destroyed, and overthrown many men; much more it should have chanced, if the thing had been done in deed, and gotten credit in men's minds; that is to say, if many of the dead had returned again to life, that wicked devil would have wrought innumerable deceits, and brought much fraud into the life of men. And for that cause God hath shut up that way, neither doth he suffer any of the dead to come again hither, to tell what is done there; lest he by that means should bring in all his wiles and subtleties. For when there were prophets, he stirred up false prophets; when the apostles were, false apostles; when Christ appeared, he raised false Christs; when sound doctrine was brought in, he brought in corrupt doctrine, sowing cockle every where. But God, from whom nothing is hid, hath stopped his way to those snares, and he favouring us hath not suffered that any soul[6] at any time should come from thence hither, to tell what is there done to any men living, teaching us that we should rather believe the scriptures than all other things[7]."

The dead never return after the death to tell their state that be dead.

The scripture is to be believed above all things.

---

[3 Institutions, Orig. ed.]

[4 Quemadmodum vulgus existimat mortuorum animas circa tumulos et corporum suorum reliquias oberrare. Lactantius, Lib. II. cap. ii. p. 83.]

[5 Subornated, Orig. ed.]

[6 So corrected in the *errata* of Orig. ed. though ed. 1582 reads "son."]

[7 Ἵνα δὲ καὶ ἑτέρωθεν μάθῃς, ὅτι ἀξιοπιστότερα ἡ τῶν προφητῶν διδασκαλία τῆς τῶν ἀνισταμένων ἀπαγγελίας, ἐκεῖνο σκόπησον, ὅτι νεκρὸς μὲν ἅπας δοῦλός ἐστιν· ἃ δὲ αἱ γραφαὶ φθέγγονται, ταῦτα ὁ δεσπότης ἐφθέγξατο· ὥστε κἂν νεκρὸς ἀναστῇ, κἂν ἄγγελος ἐξ οὐρανοῦ καταβῇ, πάντων ἔστωσαν αἱ γραφαὶ ἀξιοπιστότεραι. ὁ γὰρ τῶν ἀγγέλων δεσπότης, καὶ τῶν νέκρων καὶ τῶν ζώντων κύριος, αὐτὸς ἐκείνας ἐνομοθέτησε. εἰ συνεχῶς ἔμελλον ἀνίστασθαι νεκροὶ, καὶ πονηρὰ ἂν εἰσήγαγε δόγματα ὁ διάβολος μετὰ πολλῆς τῆς εὐκολίας. εἴδωλα γὰρ ἐδύνατο δεικνύναι πολλάκις, ἢ καὶ παρασκευάζων τινὰς ὑποκρίνασθαι θάνατον καὶ κατ-

It is not the soul of the dead that saith, I am such a man's soul, but the devil counterfeiteth the dead to deceive the living: for souls departed the body cannot walk here on earth.

The same, in Matth. cap. viii. Homily ii. 9. "I will not deny but that men have been
47. killed of cursed charmers and sorcerers: but that dead men's souls work with them, how shall they make me believe that? Because thou hast heard dead men's souls many times cry, 'I am the soul of such a one.' Yea, but these words proceed out of the fraud and deceit of the devil. For it is not the dead man's soul that saith this, but the devil that feigneth this, that he may deceive the hearers. For these ought to be taken as old wives' fables, the words of liars, and fraybugs of children: neither can the soul, being departed from the body, walk in this earth. For the souls of the righteous are in the hand of God, and the souls of sinners are straight after their death carried away. Which is manifest by Lazarus and the rich man. The Lord saith also in another place: 'This day shall they fetch away thy soul.' The soul therefore, after it be departed from the body, cannot wander here amongst us. It may be proved by many scriptures, that the souls of the righteous cannot wander here after their death. For Stephen said, "Lord, receive my spirit." And Paul desired to be 'loosed from the body, and to be with Christ.' Of the patriarchs also the scripture saith, 'He was laid up with his fathers, he died in a good age.' And that the souls of sinners cannot tarry here with us, hearken to the rich man, what he saith: consider what he asketh, and obtaineth not. But if men's souls might be conversant here, he would have come as he desired, and have certified his brethren of the torments in hell. Of the which place of scripture it is manifest, that after the departure from the body the souls are carried into a certain place, from whence they cannot return at their pleasure, but look for that terrible day of judgment[1]."

Hierome in the 8. cap. of Jeremy [Isaiah]. "If you doubt of any thing (saith the prophet) know that it is written, that those nations, which the Lord shall scatter before thy face, shall hearken to dreams and soothsayers. But the Lord thy God hath commanded thee not so to do: but if you will know things that be doubtful, give yourselves rather to the testimonies of the law and the scriptures. But if your congregation will not search the word of the Lord, they shall not have the light of the truth, but shall wander in darkness of errors. You ought to know this, that every nation asketh counsel at their own gods, and inquireth of the dead for the health of the quick: but God hath given you the law for your help; so that you may say,

---

ορύττεσθαι, δεικνύναι πάλιν ὡς ἐκ νεκρῶν ἀναστάντες, καὶ δι' ἐκείνων ὅσα ἐβούλετο πιστεύεσθαι ταῖς τῶν ἀπατωμένων διανοίαις. εἰ γὰρ νῦν, οὐδενὸς ὄντος τοιούτου, ὄνειροι πολλάκις φανέντες ἐν τύποις τῶν ἀπελθόντων πολλοὺς ἠπάτησαν καὶ διέφθειραν· πολλῷ μᾶλλον, εἰ τοῦτο γεγενημένον ἦν καὶ κεκρατηκὸς ἐν ταῖς τῶν ἀνθρώπων διανοίαις, οἷον ὅτι πολλοὶ τῶν ἀπελθόντων ἐπανῆλθον πάλιν, μυρίοις ἂν ὁ μιαρὸς δαίμων ἐκεῖνος δόλοις ἔπλεξε, καὶ πολλὴν ἀπάτην εἰς τὸν βίον εἰσήγαγε. διὰ τοῦτο ἀπέκλεισε τὰς θύρας ὁ Θεὸς, καὶ οὐκ ἀφίησί τινα τῶν ἀπελθόντων ἐπανελθόντα εἰπεῖν τὰ ἐκεῖ, ἵνα μὴ λαβὼν ἀφορμὴν ἐντεῦθεν ἐκεῖνος τὰ παρ' ἑαυτοῦ πάντα εἰσαγάγῃ. καὶ γὰρ ὅτε προφῆται ἦσαν, ψευδοπροφήτας ἤγειρε, καὶ ὅτε ἀπόστολοι, ψευδαποστόλους, καὶ ὅτε Χριστὸς ἐφάνη, ψευδοχρίστους· καὶ ὅτε δόγματα εἰσηνέχθη ὑγιῆ, διεφθαρμένα εἰσήγαγε, καὶ ζιζανία πανταχοῦ διασπείρων. ἀλλ' ὁ Θεὸς ἅπαντα ταῦτα προειδὼς, ἀπετείχισεν αὐτῷ τὴν ἐπιβουλὴν ταύτην, καὶ φειδόμενος ἡμῖν, οὐ συνεχώρησεν ἐλθόντι τινί ποτε ἐκεῖθεν περὶ τῶν ἐκεῖ διαλεχθῆναι τοῖς ζῶσιν ἀνθρώποις, παιδεύων ἡμᾶς πάντων ἀξιοπιστοτέρας ἡγεῖσθαι τὰς θείας γραφάς. Chrysost. De Lazaro, Concio iv. cap. iii. Tom. I. pp. 755, 6. Ed. 1718–38.]

[1 Ego autem quod homines a scelestis aruspicibus atque magis occisi sint, non negabo. Quod vero immolatorum hominum animæ ipsis cooperentur, unde mihi persuadebitur? an quia ipsos dæmoniacos clamare nonnunquam audisti, Anima hujus ego sum? Verum hæc quoque oratio a fraude atque deceptione diabolica est. Non enim anima defuncti est quæ ista dicit, sed dæmon qui hæc audientes decipiat, fingit. Quare vetularum hæc verba temulentarum ducenda sunt, et puerorum terriculamenta. Nec enim potest anima a corpore separata in his regionibus errare. Justorum animæ enim in manu Dei sunt: peccatorum vero post hunc exitum continuo abducuntur, quod a Lazaro et divite planum efficitur. Sed alibi quoque Dominus ait, Hodie animam abs te repetent. Non igitur potest anima, cum a corpore abscesserit, apud nos hic errare. Multis e locis scripturæ comprobari potest, non errare hic post mortem justorum hominum animas. Nam et Stephanas ait: Suscipe spiritum meum. Et Paulus resolvi ac esse cum Christo desiderabat. De Patriarcha quoque scriptura dixit: Et appositus est ad patres suos, enutritus in senectute bona.—Quod vero nec peccatorum animæ hic commorari possint, divitem audias qui enixe eam rem petit, nihil tamen impetrat. Quod si possent animæ hominum hic conversari, venisset ipse ut cupiebat, et suos de tormentis inferni fecisset certiores: quo ex loco scripturæ illud etiam aperte patet, quod post exitum a corpore in locum quendam certum animæ deducuntur, unde redire sponte sua non possunt, sed terribilem illum judicii diem ibi exspectant. Chrysost. In Matth. cap. viii. Hom. xxix. Tom. II. cols. 270, 271. Ed. (Lat.) Basil. 1547.]

The soothsaying of the heathen, which deceive their worshippers, is not like ours, which is spoken out of the law without any cost[2]."

St Augustine also saith, that the spirit of Samuel, which the woman sorcerer raised to Saul, was not the soul of Samuel, but the devil which appeared in Samuel's likeness, for to deceive Saul: this doth he prove both by evident scriptures, and strong reasons[3]. 48.

---

## THE SIXTH CHAPTER.

*Neither are miracles able to prove our faith.*

"THE wise men and enchanters of Pharaoh turned their rods into serpents, and the waters of Egypt into blood; and made all the whole land to swarm with frogs, through their sorceries." Exod. vii. viii.

"If there arise among you a prophet, or a dreamer of dreams, and give thee a sign or a wonder, and that sign or wonder, which he hath said, come to pass, and then say, Let us go after strange gods, which thou hast not known, and let us serve them; hearken not unto the words of that prophet, or dreamer of dreams. For the Lord thy God tempteth thee, to wit whether ye love the Lord your God with all your hearts and all your souls." Deut. xiii.

"Behold, here am I, saith the Lord, against those prophets that dare prophesy lies, and deceive my people with their vanities and miracles, whom I never sent nor commanded." Jer. xxiii.

"Many shall say to me in those days, Lord, have we not prophesied in thy name? have we not cast out devils in thy name? And then it shall be answered them, I never knew you; depart from me, you children of iniquity." Matt. vii.

"An evil and froward generation seeketh a sign, and there shall no sign be given to them, but the sign of Jonas the prophet." Matt. xii.

"There shall arise false Christs and false prophets, and shall shew great miracles and wonders, insomuch that, if it were possible, even the very elect should be deceived: but take you heed, behold, I have shewed you all things before." Mark xiii. 49.

"The coming of that wicked one (meaning antichrist) shall be after the working of Satan, with all lying power, signs and wonders, and with all deceit of unrighteousness of them that shall perish, because they received not the love of the truth, that they might be saved. And therefore God shall send them strong delusions, that they might believe lies; that all they might be damned, which believed not the truth, but had pleasure in unrighteousness." 2 Thess. ii.

Simon Magus, an enchanter, by his wonders bewitched the Samaritans. Acts viii.

Elymas the sorcerer had of long time deceived the Antiochians. Read the stories. Acts xiii.

Irene, Lib. i. telleth of a certain judge[4], called Mark, which in the sacrament of thanksgiving wonderfully deceived the simple people. For he so changed the colour of wine, that it appeared utterly to be blood; and a little wine so increased through his juggling, that the chalice was filled, and ran over[5]. By this example ye may judge of the popish miracles.

---

[2 Si de aliquo, inquit, dubitatis, scitote scriptum: Gentes quas Dominus Deus tuus disperdet a facie tua, somnia audiunt et divinos; tibi autem non ita tradidit Dominus Deus tuus. Unde si vultis nosse quæ dubia sunt, magis vos legi et testimoniis tradite scripturarum. Quod si noluerit vestra congregatio verbum Domini quærere, non habebit lucem veritatis; sed versabitur in erroris tenebris. Hoc scire debetis, quod unaquæque gens proprios consulat Deos, et de virorum salute mortuos sciscitetur. Vobis autem in auxilium legem dedit Deus, ut possitis dicere: Non est talis ethnicorum divinatio, qui cultores suos sæpe decipiunt, sicut nostra, quæ absque ullo munere profertur ex lege. Hieron. Comment. in Esaiam. Lib. III. cap. viii. Tom. V. pp. 34, 5. Ed. Francof. 1684.]

[3 De Mirab. sacr. Scrip. Lib. II. cap. xi. Tom. III. p. 403. Ed. Paris. 1637.]

[4 A certain juggler, Orig. ed.]

[5 Irenæus, Adversus Hæreses, Lib. I. cap. ix. p. 57. Ed. Oxon. 1702.]

¶ By this juggling it is plain enough that those miracles, that be alleged of many men for the real presence in the sacrament of the altar, do not confirm their error, but be very delusions of the devil or of his juggling ministers.

[True christians work miracles profitable to the seers; but the wicked without profit at all[1].]

Chrysostom, in his 49. Homily, upon the 24. of Matth. "Aforetime it was known which were true christian men, and which false, by miracles: but how were the false known? Because they could not work such or like miracles as true christian men did; but they wrought vain things, making men to wonder, but bringing no profit at all. But the Christians did miracles which not only brought wonders, but also profit: and by these they were known, which were true Christians, and which false. But now working of miracles is utterly taken away. Yea, counterfeit miracles are rather found among them that be false Christians, as Peter declareth in Clement: "Antichrist shall have full power given him to work great miracles[2]."

God suffereth wicked men to work miracles, for the trial of the faithful.

The same, in his first oration against the Jews, upon this place of Deut. xiii. "If there arise among you a prophet, or a dreamer of dreams," &c. "That that he saith," saith Chrysostom, "is this: If any prophet say, I can raise a dead man, and give sight to a blind man, obey me, let us worship devils, let us do sacrifice to idols; moreover, if a man speak thus, that he can give the blind his sight, raise the dead, yea, though he do these things, believe him not. For the Lord, trying thee, suffereth him to do them, not that he knew not thy mind, but to give the occasion of trial whether thou love God in deed[3]."

50.

The faithful need no miracles; for signs are given to the unbelievers. 1 Cor. xiv.

The same, in John, cap. ii. in the end of the 22. Hom. "There be some doubtless now-a-days, that ask why men work no miracles now. If thou be faithful as thou oughtest to be, if thou love Christ as he should be loved, thou needest no miracles: for signs are given to unbelievers, and not to the faithful[4]."

Augustine, against Faustus the Manichee, Lib. 13. cap. 5. "The scriptures, that be stablished and set forth by so great authority, ye despise: miracles you work none; which though you did, yet we would beware of you, by the Lord instructing and teaching us, saying, 'There shall arise false Christs,' &c.[5]"

The same, Of the City of God, Lib. 20. cap. 19. "The presence of antichrist shall be after the working of Satan, with all lying powers," as afore. "For then shall Satan be let loose, and by him antichrist with all his power shall work marvellously, but lyingly: of the which miracles it was wont to be doubted, whether they be called lying signs and wonders, for this cause, that he shall deceive man's senses with visions, so that he seemeth to do the thing that he doeth not in deed; or else because the same, although they be true miracles, and not counterfeit, yet they draw men to believe that they cannot be done but by the power of God: whereas men know not the power of the devil; chiefly seeing that how great soever power he hath, he hath received it. For when fire fell down from heaven, and with one dash destroyed so great a family with so many herds of cattle of holy Job, and a sudden whirlwind, overthrowing his house, slew his children; these were no deceivable visions, but for

---

[1 This marginal note is omitted in Ed. 1582.]

[2 Item antea et per signa cognoscebantur, qui erant veri Christiani, et qui falsi. Quomodo? Falsi quidem aut non poterant facere, sicut veri Christiani: aut talia non poterant, qualia veri Christiani: sed faciebant vacua, admirationem quidem facientia, utilitatem autem nullam habentia: Christiani autem faciebant plena, non solum admirationem facientia, sed etiam omnem utilitatem habentia. Et per hæc cognoscebantur, qui erant veri Christiani, qui falsi. Nunc autem signorum operatio omnino levata est: magis autem et apud eos invenitur, qui falsi sunt Christiani, fieri facta. Sicut autem Petrus apud Clementem exponit, Antichristo etiam plenorum signorum faciendorum est danda potestas. Chrysost. Opus Imperfectum in Matt. Hom. xlix. ex cap. xxiv. Tom. VI. p. 205. Ed. Paris. 1718–38.]

Ο δὲ λέγει, τοιοῦτόν εστιν. ἐάν τις ἀναστῇ προφήτης, φησὶ, καὶ ποιήσῃ σημεῖον, ἢ νεκρὸν ἐγείρῃ, ἢ λεπρὸν καθάρῃ, ἢ πηρὸν ἰάσηται· καὶ, μετὰ τὸ ποιῆσαι τὸ σημεῖον, καλέσῃ σε εἰς ἀσέβειαν· μὴ πεισθῇς διὰ τὴν ἔκβασιν τοῦ σημείου. διὰ τί; πειράζει γάρ σε κύριος ὁ Θεός σου, ἰδεῖν, εἰ ἀγαπᾷς αὐτὸν ἐξ ὅλης τῆς καρδίας σου, καὶ ἐξ ὅλης τῆς ψυχῆς σου. Id. Adver. Judæos, Oratio i. Tom. I. p. 598.]

[4 Sunt sane et hac nostra ætate qui quærant, quare et nunc signa non fiunt? Si fidelis es, ut oportet; si Christum diligis, ut diligendus est, non indiges signis: signa enim incredulis dantur. Id. In Joannem, cap. ii. Hom. xxii. Tom. III. col. 119. Ed. (Lat.) Basil. 1547.]

[5 Scripturas tanta auctoritate firmatas commendatasque respuitis; miracula non facitis: quæ si feceritis, etiam ipsa in vobis caveremus, præstruente nos Domino et dicente, Exsurgent multi pseudochristi. August. cont. Faust. Manich. Lib. XIII. cap. v. Tom. VI. p. 118. Ed. Paris. 1637.]

every one of these it is said, They shall be beguiled with signs and wonders that shall deserve to be beguiled, 'forasmuch as they have not received the love of the truth, that they might be saved.' Neither did the apostle fear to say and add, 'God shall send them strong delusions, that they should believe lies.' For God doth send these things, because he suffereth the devil to do them: he indeed by his just judgment, although the devil doth[6] it of a wicked and malicious purpose[7]."

The same, Of the Unity of the Church, cap. 16. "Let them shew their church, if they can, not in the sayings and in the fame of the Africans, not in the determinations of their bishops, not in any man's reasonings, not in false signs and wonders (for against all this we be warned and armed by God's word), but in the things appointed in the law, spoken afore by the prophets, in the songs of the Psalms, in the voice of the Shepherd himself, and the preachings and painfulness of the evangelists, that is, in the authority of the books canonical: but not so that they may 51.
gather and rehearse those things that be spoken darkly and doubtfully and figuratively, which every man may understand as he list after his own mind. For such things cannot be understanded and expounded rightly, except those things that be very plainly spoken be perceived before with a constant faith. Let him not say, This is true, because I say it, or because my companion saith thus, or these my companions, or these our bishops, clerks, or laymen: or else, It is true, because such miracles did Donatus, Pontius, or whatsoever other: or else, because men pray at the tombs of our dead men, and be heard: or because these and these things chanced there: or that this brother of ours, or this sister of ours, saw such a vision; either waking, or sleeping, in his dream, saw such a vision or sight. Away with these. Either they be feignings of lying men, or the wonders of deceitful devils. For either they are not true that are spoken: or if any miracles be done among heretics, we ought the more to take heed of them, because that when the Lord had said there should come some that by working divers miracles should 'deceive, if it were possible, the very elect'; he added, and earnestly setting forth the thing, said, 'Behold, I have told you before.' Whereof the apostle, admonishing them, speaketh plainly, that 'in the latter times men should depart from the faith, giving heed to spirits of error, and doctrines of devils.' Furthermore, if any man be heard at the tombs of heretics, he receiveth, whether it be good or evil, not for the merit of the place, but for the merit[8] of his desire. For 'the Spirit of the Lord,' as it is written, 'filleth the whole world,' and the earnest ear heareth all things, and many be heard of God when he is angry, of whom the apostle saith, 'He had given them up to their hearts' desire.' And God to many, whom he favoureth, giveth not what they would, that he may give them that which is profitable: wherefore saith the same apostle of the sting of his flesh, the messenger of Satan, (which he said was given him to buffet him, lest he should be exalted above measure by the greatness of revelations,) 'For the which I prayed the Lord thrice that he would take it away from me; and he said unto me, My grace is sufficient for thee, for my strength is made perfect through weakness.' Do we not read that many men were heard of God himself in the high places of Jewry?

All doctrine ought to be tried by the canonical in plain sense, and not by words that be dark, doubtful, or figurative.

Miracles shewed at the tombs of saints prove no doctrine.

Visions seen either in dreams, or being awake, cannot make any doctrine.

Men be heard at the tombs of heretics, and yet is not their doctrine true.

---

[[6] The devil doeth it, Orig. ed.]

[[7] Præsentia quippe ejus (i.e. antichristi) erit, sicut dictum est, secundum operationem Satanæ in omni virtute, et signis, et prodigiis mendacii, et in omni seductione iniquitatis, his qui pereunt. Tunc enim solvetur Satanas, et per illum antichristum in omni sua virtute mirabiliter quidem, sed mendaciter operabitur. Quod solet ambigi, utrum propterea dicta sint signa et prodigia mendacii, quoniam mortales sensus per phantasmata decepturus est, ut quod non facit, facere videatur. An quia illa ipsa etiam si erunt vera prodigia, ad mendacium pertrahent credituros non ea potuisse nisi divinitus fieri, virtutem diaboli nescientes; maxime quando tantam quantam nunquam habuit, accipiet potestatem. Non enim quando de cœlo ignis cecidit, et tantam familiam cum tantis gregibus pecorum sancti Job uno impetu absumpsit, et turbo irruens, et domum dejiciens, filios ejus occidit, phantasmata fuerunt: quæ tamen fuerunt opera Satanæ, cui Deus dederat hanc potestatem. Propter quid horum ergo dicta sint prodigia et signa mendacii, tunc potius apparebit. Sed propter quodlibet horum dictum sit, Seducentur ejus signis, atque prodigiis, qui seduci merebuntur, pro eo quod dilectionem veritatis, inquit, non receperunt, ut salvi fierent. Nec dubitavit apostolus addere et dicere, Ideo mittet illis Deus operationem erroris, ut credant mendacio. Deus enim mittet, quia Deus diabolum facere ista permittet, justo ipsius judicio, quamvis faciat ille iniquo malignoque consilio.—August. De Civitate Dei. Lib. xx. cap. xix. Tom. V. p. 1373.]

[[8] For the rite, Ed. 1532.]

52. which high places nevertheless so displeased God, that kings which destroyed them not were blamed, and kings that destroyed them were praised. But this ought to be understand, that the desire of him that prayeth is more worthy or of more strength, than the place of prayer. But of false visions let them read what is written, both that Satan doth change himself into an angel of light, and that their dreams have deceived many men. Let them also hear what the heathen tell of their temples and gods, wonderfully either done or seen; and yet nevertheless the gods of the heathen be devils, but the Lord made the heavens. Therefore many men be heard and after many divers sorts, not only catholic Christians, but also Painims and Jews and heretics, given to divers errors and superstitions: doubtless they are heard either of deceitful spirits, which nevertheless do nothing except they be permitted of God highly and unspeakably judging what is meet to be given to every man, or else of God himself either for the punishment of malice, or the comfort of misery, or for the admonishment of eternal salvation. But to that eternal salvation cometh no man but he that hath the head Christ, yea, and no man can have the head Christ which is not in his body the church; which church, like as the Head itself, we must know in the canonical scriptures, and not to seek it in divers rumours and opinions of men, not in facts, sayings, and sights, &c. Let all this sort of them be chaff, and not give sentence aforehand against the wheat, if they be the church: but whether they be the church, let them shew none other ways but by the canonical books of the holy scriptures. For neither do we say that men ought to believe us, because we are in the catholic church of Christ, or because Optatus, bishop of Milivet, or Ambrose, bishop of Milane, or that innumerable other bishops of our congregation, do allow this doctrine that we keep; or because in churches of our companions it is preached; or else, because that through the whole world in those holy places, where our congregations resort, so many wonders, either of hearings or of healings, be done; so that bodies of martyrs, being hid so many years, (which, if they will ask, they may learn of many) were shewed to Ambrose; or that at those bodies a certain man, being many years blind, well known to the whole city of Milane, received his eyes and his sight; or because he being in a dream did see, or he being rapt in spirit did hear, either that he should not go to the part of the Donatists, or that they should depart[2] from their opinion. Whatsoever such things be done in the catholic church, the church is not therefore proved catholic, because these be done in it. The Lord Jesus himself, when he was risen from death, and offered his own body to be seen with the eyes and handled with the hands of his apostles, lest they
53. should then think themselves to be deceived, he rather judged that they ought to be stablished by the witnesses of the law, prophets, and Psalms, shewing those things to be fulfilled in him that were spoken so long before: so he set forth his church, bidding repentance and forgiveness of sins to be preached in his name through all nations, beginning at Jerusalem. That these things be written in the law and prophets, himself witnesseth: this is set out by word of mouth. These are the doctrines, these are the stays of our cause. We read written in the Acts of the Apostles of some faithful men, that 'they searched the scriptures whether they were so.' What scriptures, I pray you, but the canonical of the law and the prophets? To these are joined the Gospels, the Apostles' Epistles, the Acts of the Apostles, and the Apocalypsis of St John. Search all these, bring forth some plain thing, whereby you may declare that the church hath remained only in Africk: or that this, which the Lord saith shall come to pass, 'This gospel shall be preached to all the world, for a testimony to all nations,' shall be verified of Africk. But bring out somewhat that needeth none interpreter; whereby you may not be convinced that the things, which is spoken of another matter, you go about to wrest to your purpose[3]."

The devil worketh miracles in the temples and idols of the gentiles, although their religion be false and detestable.

[Men ought to prove themselves to be the true church by none other means, but by the scriptures only[1].]

[Neither miracles nor agreement of bishops in doctrine prove any thing in religion[1].]

---

[[1] These marginal notes are omitted in Ed. 1582.]

[[2] That he should depart, Orig. ed.]

[[3] Remotis ergo omnibus talibus, ecclesiam suam demonstrent, si possunt, non in sermonibus, et rumoribus Afrorum, non in conciliis episcoporum suorum, non in literis quorumlibet disputatorum, non in signis et prodigiis fallacibus, quia etiam contra ista verbo Domini præparati et cauti redditi sumus: sed in præscripto Legis, in Prophetarum prædictis, in Psalmorum cantibus, in ipsius Pastoris vocibus, in Evangelistarum prædicationibus et laboribus, hoc est, in omnibus canonicis sanctorum librorum auctoritatibus. Nec ita, ut ea colligant et commemorent, quæ obscure vel ambigue vel figu-

Chrysostom, of the Contrition of the Heart. "Christ promised not that he would reward at the latter day them that work signs and wonders, but them that keep his commandments, saying: 'Come, you blessed children of my Father, receive that kingdom which was prepared for you from the beginning of the world.' He said not, 'Because you did miracles;' but, 'Because I was hungry,' &c. He shall also call them blessed, not that wrought miracles, but the humble and meek in heart[4]."

Not miracle-workers, but the commandment-keepers, are called blessed of Christ.

---

rate dicta sunt, quæ quisque sicut voluerit, interpretetur secundum sensum suum. Talia enim recte intelligi exponique non possunt, nisi prius ea, quæ apertissime dicta sunt, firma fide teneantur.—Et sic ostendat, ut non dicat, Verum est, quia hoc ego dico, aut quia hoc dixit ille collega meus, aut illi collegæ mei, aut illi episcopi, vel clerici, vel laici nostri; aut ideo verum est, quia illa et illa mirabilia fecit Donatus vel Pontius, vel quilibet alius, aut quia homines ad memorias mortuorum nostrorum orant et exaudiuntur, aut quia illa et illa ibi contingunt, aut quia ille frater noster aut illa soror nostra tale visum vigilans vidit, vel tale visum dormiens somniavit. Removeantur ista vel figmenta mendacium hominum, vel portenta fallacium spirituum: aut enim non sunt vera quæ dicuntur, aut si hæreticorum aliqua mira facta sunt, magis cavere debemus! quod cum dixisset Dominus quosdam futuros esse fallaces, qui nonnulla signa faciendo etiam electos, si fieri posset, fallerent, adjecit vehementer commendans et ait, "Ecce prædixi vobis." Unde et apostolus admonens, "Spiritus," inquit, "manifeste dicit, quia in novissimis temporibus recedent quidam a fide, intendentes spiritibus seductoribus et doctrinis dæmoniorum." Porro si aliquis in hæreticorum memoriis orans exauditur, non pro merito loci, sed pro merito desiderii sui, recepit sive malum sive bonum. "Spiritus enim Domini," sicut scriptum est, "Replevit orbem terrarum." Et, "Auris zeli audit omnia." Et, "Multi Deo irato exaudiuntur." De qualibus dicit apostolus, "Tradidit illos Deus in concupiscentias cordis illorum." Et multis propitius Deus non tribuit quod volunt, ut quod utile est tribuat. Unde idem apostolus ait de stimulo carnis suæ, angelo Satanæ, quem sibi datum dicit a quo colaphizaretur, ne magnitudine revelationum extolleretur: "Propter quod ter Dominum rogavi, ut auferret eum a me. Et dixit mihi: Sufficit tibi gratia mea; nam virtus in infirmitate perficitur." Nonne legimus ab ipso Domino Deo nonnullos exauditos in excelsis montium Judeæ; quæ tamen excelsa ita displicebant Deo, ut reges qui ea non everterent, culparentur, et qui everterent, laudarentur? Unde intelligitur magis valere petentis affectum, quam petitionis locum. De visis autem fallacibus legant quæ scripta sunt, et quia "ipse Satanas transfigurat se tanquam angelum lucis," et quia multos seduxerunt somnia sua: audiant etiam quæ narrant pagani de templis et diis suis mirabiliter vel facta vel visa, et tamen "dii gentium dæmonia, Dominus autem cœlos fecit." Exaudiuntur ergo multi et multis modis, non solum Christiani catholici, sed et pagani, et Judæi hæretici, variis erroribus et superstitionibus dediti. Exaudiuntur autem vel ab spiritibus seductoribus, qui tamen nihil faciunt, nisi permittantur Deo sublimiter atque ineffabiliter judicante quid cuique tribuendum sit; vel ab ipso Deo, vel ad pœnam malitiæ, vel ad solatium miseriæ, vel ad monitionem quærendæ salutis æternæ. Ad ipsam vero salutem ac vitam æternam nemo pervenit, nisi qui habet caput Christum. Habere autem caput Christum nemo poterit, nisi qui in ejus corpore fuerit, quod est ecclesia; quam, sicut ipsum caput, in scripturis sanctis canonicis debemus agnoscere, non in variis hominum rumoribus et opinionibus, et factis, et dictis, et visis inquirere....Sit ista omnis turba palea eorum, nec frumentis præjudicet si ipsi ecclesiam tenent. Sed utrum ipsi ecclesiam teneant, non nisi de divinarum scripturarum canonicis libris ostendant: quia nec nos propterea dicimus nobis credi oportere quod in ecclesia Christi sumus, quia ipsam quam tenemus commendavit Milevitanus Optatus, vel Mediolanensis Ambrosius, vel alii innumerabiles nostræ communionis episcopi; aut quia nostrorum collegarum conciliis ipsa prædicata est; aut quia per totum orbem in locis sanctis, quæ frequentat nostra communio, tanta mirabilia vel exauditionum vel sanitatum fiunt, ita ut latentia per tot annos corpora martyrum, quod possunt a multis interrogantes audire, Ambrosio fuerint revelata, et ad ipsa corpora cæcus multorum annorum civitati Mediolanensi notissimus oculos lumenque receperit; aut quia ille somnium vidit, et ille spiritu assumptus audivit, sive ne iniret in partem Donati, sive ut recederet a parte Donati. Quæcunque talia in catholica fiunt, ideo sunt approbanda, quia in catholica fiunt; non ideo ipsa manifestatur catholica, quia hæc in ea fiunt. Ipse Dominus Jesus cum resurrexisset a mortuis, et discipulorum oculis videndum manibusque tangendum corpus suum offerret, ne quid tamen fallaciæ se pati arbitrarentur, magis eos testimoniis legis, et prophetarum, et psalmorum confirmandos esse judicavit, ostendens ea de se impleta, quæ fuerant tanto ante prædicta. Sic et ecclesiam suam commendavit dicens, "prædicari in nomine suo pœnitentiam et remissionem peccatorum per omnes gentes, incipientibus ab Hierusalem." Hoc in lege, et prophetis, et psalmis esse scriptum ipse testatus est, hoc ejus ore commendatum tenemus. Hæc sunt causæ nostræ documenta, hæc fundamenta, hæc firmamenta. Legimus in Actis Apostolorum dictum de quibusdam credentibus, quod "quotidie scrutarentur scripturas, an hæc ita se haberent." Quas utique scripturas, nisi canonicas legis et prophetarum? Huc accesserunt Evangelia, apostolicæ epistolæ, Actus Apostolorum, Apocalypsis Joannis. Scrutamini hæc omnia, et eruite aliquid manifestum, quo demonstretis ecclesiam vel in sola Africa remansisse, vel ex Africa futuram esse, ut impleatur quod Dominus dicit: "Prædicabitur hoc evangelium regni in universo orbe in testimonium omnibus gentibus, et tunc veniet finis." Sed aliquid proferte quod non egeat interprete, nec unde convincamini, quod de alia re dictum sit, et vos illud ad vestrum sensum detorquere conemini.—August. De Unit. Eccles. cap. xviii. xix. Tom. VII. pp. 154, 5. Ed. Paris. 1635.]

[4 Καὶ ὁ Χριστὸς δὲ κατὰ τὴν ἡμέραν ἐκείνην οὐ τοῖς τὰ σημεῖα ἐργασαμένοις ἁπλῶς τὰ ἔπαθλα δίδωσιν, ἀλλὰ τοῖς τὰ προστάγματα πεποιηκόσι τὰ αὐτοῦ. δεῦτε γάρ, φησιν, οἱ εὐλογημένοι τοῦ πατρός μου, κληρονομήσατε τὴν ἡτοιμασμένην ὑμῖν

To work miracles maketh no man holy; nor to work no miracles hindereth his holiness.

Cyril, in John, Lib. vii. cap. 13. "To work miracles maketh not a man one whit more holy, seeing that it is also common to evil men and abjects, as the Lord himself also witnesseth: 'Many shall say to me in that day,' &c. And, contrariwise, working of no miracles hindereth not a man's holiness. For John wrought neither sign nor miracle, and yet was this no derogation to his holiness; for among the children of women there was none greater than he[1]."

This would be put among the apparitions of the dead. Sathan counterfeiteth Moses.

Sabellic, upon the Life of Celestine, almost five hundred years after Christ: "The devil, taking upon him the person of Moses, shewed himself visibly in the sight of the Jews that dwelt at Candie, promising that he would bring them again into the land of promise, where Jerusalem standeth, dry-footed, the waters standing on either
54. side in manner of a wall, as when the children of Israel were brought out of the land of Egypt. Many of the Jews, rashly giving credit to these jugglings, and entering into the sea, were overwhelmed with the waves thereof, except a few, the which at last, being warned of their vanity, became Christians[2]."

## THE SEVENTH CHAPTER.

*Custom also is of no strength in this case of proving a religion.*

Exod. xxiii. "Follow not the multitude to do evil."

Levit. xviii. The Lord commanded the Israelites not to follow the customs of the Egyptians, nor the Canaanites. Read the chapter.

Ezek. xx. "Walk not in the statutes of your forefathers, and keep not their ordinances, and defile not yourselves with their idols."

2 Kings xvii. "Unto this day they keep their old customs; they fear not God, nor do after his customs, ordinances, and laws."

The same. "They did not hearken unto the Lord, but did after their old custom."

Jer. ix. "They followed the wickedness of their own hearts, and served strange gods, as their fathers taught them."

Tertullian, of Virginity, or Praises. "Custom, for the most part, taking his beginning either of ignorance or simplicity, in process of time waxeth strong by use: and so it is alleged against the truth. Whatsoever smelleth against the truth, that is heresy, yea, though it be old custom[3]."

Cyprian, unto Cæcilie, Lib. ii. Epist. 3. "There is no cause why, dear brother, that any man should think the custom of some men ought to be followed. If any man have thought that only water ought to be offered in the chalice, we must first ask, whom they
55. followed: and that Christ only ought to be heard, the Father witnesseth from heaven, saying: 'This is my well beloved Son, hear him.' Wherefore, if only Christ ought to be heard, we ought not to regard what any man afore us thought to be done, but what Christ, which is before, did first: neither ought we to follow the custom of man, but the truth of God[4]."

---

*βασιλείαν ἀπὸ καταβολῆς κόσμου· οὐχ ὅτι ἐθαυματουργήσατε· ἀλλ' ὅτι ἐπείνασα—καὶ ἐν τοῖς μακαρισμοῖς δὲ, οὐδαμοῦ τοὺς τὰ θαύματα ποιοῦντας τίθησιν, ἀλλὰ τοὺς βίον ἔχοντας ὀρθόν.* Chrysost. De Compunct. Cordis. Lib. I. cap. viii. Tom. I. pp. 136, 7. Ed. Paris. 1718—38.]

[1 Primum quia Joannes quidem nullum fecit signum, id est nullum miraculum ostendit, neque tamen id in aliquo derogat sanctitati ejus, quo inter natos mulierum non surrexit teste Salvatore major; nempe miracula operari nihil adjicit sanctitatis homini, cum malis et reprobis id competat, dicente Domino apud Mattheum, Multi dicent in illa die.—Quare e diverso, nulla signorum ostensio nihil detrahit homini sanctitatis.—Cyril. Alexandr. in Joannem. Lib. VII. cap. xiii. col. 45. Ed. Paris. 1508.]

[2 This is not found in Sabellicus, but is mentioned by Platina in his account of Pope Celestine I. as follows: Ferunt hoc tempore diabolum, personam Moysi indutum, multos Judæos decepisse, dum eos ex Creta in terram promissionis ad similitudinem historiæ veteris sicco pede per mare deducere pollicetur. Multi enim ex his, falsum Moysen secuti, in undis periere. Aiunt autem illos solos evasisse, qui tum Christum verum Deum credidere.—Plat. de Vit. Pontif. p. 57. Ed. Colon. Agrip. 1626.]

[3 Consuetudo, initium ab aliqua ignorantia vel simplicitate sortita, in usum per successionem corroboratur, et ita adversus veritatem vindicatur....Quodcunque adversus veritatem sapit, hoc erit hæresis, etiam vetus consuetudo. Tertull. De Virg. Veland. cap. i. pp. 172, 3. Ed. Paris. 1664.]

[4 Non est ergo, frater carissime, quod aliquis existimet sequendam esse quorundam consuetudinem, si qui in præteritum in calice dominico

The same to Julian, of the Baptizing of Heretics. "In vain do some men, when they be overcome with the truth, allege custom against us, as though custom were greater than the truth[5]." St Augustine hath the same[6].

The same to Pompus, against Steven's Epistle. "Custom without truth is an old error: for the which cause let us leave custom, and follow the truth[7]."

Chrysostom, upon Genesis xxix. Homily 59. "For if the counsel be good and profitable, yea, though it be not custom, keep it; but if it be hurtful and noisome, cast it away. For if we will be wise, and care for our salvation, we may leave off an evil custom, and bring in a good custom; and so shall we give no small occasion to them that come after us to change the same, and have the reward of those things that be done of them[8]."

Jerome, in his Preface to Job. "Old custom is of such force that vices, which many men themselves confess, please them through it[9]."

The same, Cap. 9. "Neither are the errors of our fathers, nor our elders to be followed, but the authority of the scriptures, and the commandments of God that teacheth us[10]."

Augustine, of one only Baptism, Lib. ii. Distinct. 8. cap. "When the truth is once known, let custom give place to the truth. For who doubteth but custom ought to give place to the manifest truth?[11]"

The same, in the same place. "Let no man prefer custom above truth and reason. For truth and reason do ever exclude custom[12]."

Gregorius to Guelmunde the bishop, 2 Distinct. *Si consuetudo.* "If thou chance to lay custom against me, thou must take heed what the Lord saith: 'I am the way, the truth, and the life.' He did not say, I am custom, but the truth[13]."

Nicolas the pope to Ignatius the reverend bishop, 8. Distinct. "An evil custom is no less to be avoided than an hurtful corruption: which except it be plucked up the sooner by the roots, it will be taken of the ungodly for a law[14]." 56.

---

aquam solam offerendam putaverunt. Quærendum est enim ipsi quem sint secuti.—Et quod Christus debeat solus audiri, Pater enim de cœlo contestatur dicens: "Hic est filius meus dilectissimus, in quo bene sensi; ipsum audite." Quare si solus Christus audiendus est, non debemus attendere quid alius ante nos faciendum esse putaverit; sed quid, qui ante omnes est, Christus prior fecerit. Neque enim hominis consuetudinem sequi oportet, sed Dei veritatem. Cyprian. ad Cæcil. de Sacram. Domin. cal. Epist. lxiii. p. 108. Ed. Paris. 1726. (Ed. Erasm. Lib. II. Epist. 3, as quoted in the text by the archbishop.)]

[5 Proinde frustra quidam qui ratione vincuntur consuetudinem nobis opponunt; quasi consuetudo major sit veritate. Id. ad Jubaian. de Bapt. Hæret. Epist. lxxiii. p. 133. Ed. Paris. 1726.]

[6 See below, note 11.]

[7 Nam consuetudo sine veritate vetustas erroris est. Propter quod relicto errore sequamur veritatem. Id. ad Pompei. contra Epist. Steph. de Hæret. Bapt. Epist. lxxiv. p. 141.]

[8 *Εἰ μὲν γὰρ καλόν ἐστι τὸ τῆς συμβουλῆς καὶ ἐπωφελὲς, κἂν μὴ συνήθεια ᾖ, γινέσθω· εἰ δὲ βλάβην ἔχον καὶ πολὺν τὸν ὄλεθρον τὸ νῦν παρ' ὑμῖν ἐπιτελούμενον, κἂν συνήθεια ᾖ, ἐγκοπτέσθω.—ἐὰν γὰρ βουλώμεθα νήφειν, καὶ πολλὴν τῆς ἑαυτῶν σωτηρίας ποιεῖσθαι τὴν φροντίδα, δυνησόμεθα καὶ τῆς κακῆς συνηθείας ἀποστῆναι, καὶ εἰς καλὴν συνήθειαν ἑαυτοὺς ἀγαγεῖν. καὶ οὕτω καὶ τοῖς μεθ' ἡμᾶς οὐ μικρὰν παρέξομεν ἀφορμὴν τοῦ τὰ αὐτὰ ζηλοῦν, καὶ τῶν ὑπ' ἐκείνων κατορθουμένων ἡμεῖς ληψόμεθα τὸν μισθόν.* Chrysost. in cap. xxix. Genes. Hom. lvi. Tom. IV. p. 540.]

[9 Tanta est enim vetustatis consuetudo, ut etiam confessa plerisque vitia placeant. Hieron. Præf. in Libr. Job. Alt. Tom. III. p. 17. Ed. Francof. 1684.]

[10 This passage is not found in the place referred to.]

[11 Itaque veritate manifestata cedat consuetudo veritati. Plane quis dubitet veritati manifestatæ debere consuetudinem cedere? August. De Bapt. contra Donatist. Lib. III. cap. vi. Tom. VII. p. 45. Ed. Paris. 1637. Gratian. Distinct. viii. Cap. iv. "Veritate manifestata." Tom. I. p. 6. Ed. Paris. 1687.]

[12 Nemo consuetudinem rationi et veritati præponat; quia consuetudinem ratio et veritas semper excludit. Id. ibid.]

[13 Si consuetudinem fortassis opponas, advertendum est, quod Dominus dicit: "Ego sum veritas et vita." Non dixit, Ego sum consuetudo, sed veritas. Gregor. Wimundo Aversano Episcopo. Id. ibid. Cap. v. "Si consuetudinem." Ibid.]

[14 Mala consuetudo, quæ non minus quam perniciosa corruptela vitanda est: nisi citius radicitus evellatur, in privilegiorum jus ab improbis assumitur. Nicol. Papa Hincmaro Remensi Archiepiscopo. Id. ibid. Cap. iii. "Mala consuetudo." Ibid.]

## THE EIGHTH CHAPTER.

### *Reasons against Unwritten Verities*[1].

The old testament was sufficient for the Jews; and why shall not both the new and old suffice us?

Christ and the apostles proved all their doctrines by the law and prophets. What an arrogancy is it then in us, to teach any thing which we can neither prove by the law, the prophets, the apostles, nor the evangelists!

The devil, when he tempted Christ, was not so far passed all shame to persuade any thing without the testimony of the scriptures, although he did (as his dear children the papists do) falsely allege them, wrest them from their true meaning to a contrary sense, and also cut off that which should make against him, or declare the true meaning of the scriptures.

This word, "unwritten verities," is a new term lately invented, and nowhere heard or read among the old writers: of which they could not have been ignorant, if there had been any such thing needful to salvation.

All contention which the old fathers had with heretics was for the scriptures: which heretics partly denied, as Marcion, Manichæus, and Faustus; partly they wrongly expounded: but for things which are not contained in the scriptures, they never accused any man of heresy.

If there were any word of God beside the scripture, we could never be certain of God's word; and if we be uncertain of God's word, the devil might bring in among us
57. a new word, a new doctrine, a new faith, a new church, a new god, yea, himself to be god, as he hath already done in the popish kingdom. For this is the foundation of antichrist's kingdom, to settle himself in God's temple, which is the heart and conscience of man, of him to be feared and worshipped, as though he were God himself.

If the church and the christian faith did not stay itself upon the word of God certain, as upon a sure and strong foundation, no man could know whether he had a right faith, and whether he were in the true church of Christ, or in the synagogue of Satan.

If we be bound to believe certain things delivered from the apostles by word of mouth only, without writing, as they would make us believe, (but what those things be, no man can tell,) it should hereof follow that we are bound to believe we wot not what.

---

[[1] The Reasons against Unwritten Verities are set forth in Cranmer's Common-place Book, in the British Museum, Royal MSS. 7. B. xi. p. 94. (Vid. Jenkyns' Remains of Archbp. Cranmer, Vol. IV. p. 215.) The following is quoted from Strype, Mem. Eccl. Vol. II. pp. 215, 16. Ed. Oxford, 1822.

"Reasons. *Idem.*

"If traditions apostolic have the force of God's word, so that every one is bound to the observation of them, the bishop of Rome hath a great advantage thereby to establish his primacy: not such a primacy as he hath lately usurped, but such a primacy as he hath had by prerogative from the beginning; that is to say, to be one of the four patriarchs of christendom, and the chief of all four. And the traditions be the chief authors, whereupon Pighius stayeth himself. And furthermore, if we admit traditions to be of such authority, it is to be feared that we must resort to the church of Rome to fetch there our traditions, as of the oldest and the mother church. Irenæus, *Ad hanc*, &c. Cyprian calls Rome *Petri cathedram et ecclesiam principalem.* Julius writing for Athanasius, &c. Melchiades, and other quotations he there mentioneth.

"The old testament was sufficient for the Jews: and is not both the old and the new sufficient for us?

"What things came by traditions from the apostles, no man can tell certainly: and if we be bound to receive them as articles of our faith, then is our faith uncertain. For we be bound to believe we know not what.

"Faith must needs be grounded upon God's word. For St Paul saith, *Fides ex auditu; auditus autem per verbum Dei. Omnis scriptura divinitus inspiratur.* This text St John Chrysostom, Theophylact, Thomas, with many other authors, both old and new, do expound plainly as the words be, that whatsoever truth is necessary to be taught for our salvation, or the contrary to be reproved; whatsoever is necessary for us to do, and what to forbear and not to do; all is completely contained in the scripture: so that a man thereby may be perfectly instructed unto all manner of goodness."]

Without faith it is not possible to please God; and faith cometh by hearing of God's word; *ergo*, where God's word lacketh, there can be no faith.

Almighty God, afore he gave to Moses the law written of the ten commandments, wherein he fully taught the true worshipping of him, as it were a preservative against a plague or a poison to come, gave them this notable lesson, worthy alway to be had in memory: "You shall add nothing to the words, &c.;" and again he oftentimes repeateth the same sentence both in the law and the prophets, in the gospels, and the epistles of the apostles. And because his people should never forget it, St John commandeth the same in the last words of all the new testament, threatening terrible plagues, that is, the loss of his everlasting joys of heaven, and the pain of eternal fire, to all them that either put to or take aught from the word of God.

---

## CHAPTER THE NINTH[2].

*Scriptures alleged by the Papists for Unwritten Verities, with answers to the same.* 58.

"WHERE two or three be gathered in my name, there am I in the midst of them." Matt. xviii.
But Christ cannot err, for he is the truth itself; *ergo*, they cannot err in their synods, Argument.
convocations, and general councils, being gathered together in his name.

Christ said, "When two or three be gathered in my name," &c.; and to be gathered Answer.
in his name, is in our assemblies to seek his only glory and not ours, to do all things by his prescript word. "For not every one that saith unto me, Lord, Lord, shall enter," Matt. vii.
&c.: as witches, charmers, necromancers, and conjurers, use their wicked arts all in the name of God and Christ, and yet is not Christ with them. For the seven sons of Acts xix.
Sceva, the chief priest of the Jews, went about to cast out evil spirits in the name of Jesus whom Paul preached; but yet Christ was not with them, but the wicked spirit, which wounded them, and drave them away naked. Moreover, all forgers of wills, counterfeiters of false instruments, and judges giving false sentences, in the ecclesiastical law, they begin with this glorious title, "In the name of God, Amen." Therefore sprang this old proverb, "In the name of God, beginneth all mischief." And yet Christ is with none of these, though they pretend to do all these things in his name. Christ saith also: "Many shall prophesy in my name, and cast out devils, and work miracles, Matt vii.
in my name; and then will I confess to them, that I never knew you." Read Eusebius and Athanasius, and you shall there see what pride, contention, hatred, malice, envy, and desire to bear rule, reigned in the councils of the clergy at those days, not much past four hundred years after Christ. What think you they would say if they saw our councils, where the Romish antichrist triumpheth? No doubt, that "though an angel from heaven preach any other," &c.

Here you will reply again, Christ saith, "Where two or three are gathered," &c. A replication.
Now in every council are not only two or three learned and godly men, but many; *ergo*, 59.
they cannot err.

I grant that in every general council be many good men which do not err, nor are Answer.
deceived; and yet it followeth not that the whole council cannot err. For in councils the more part is taken for the whole, and things be there determined and ordered, not by reason, learning, and authority of the word of God, but by stoutness, wilfulness, and consent of the more part. In those councils, where be mo evil and wicked men than good and godly, it cometh oftentimes to pass that, iniquity having the upper hand, the greater part overcometh the better; and yet the good men neither err, nor consent to these errors concluded by the wicked and the more part, but resist and speak against them to

---

[[2] The substance of the ninth and tenth chapters is in Cranmer's Common-place Book at the British Museum, but they are here much altered and enlarged. The subject of the sabbath in particular is treated at much greater length. Vid. Jenkyns' Remains of Archbp. Cranmer, Vol. IV. p. 217.]

the utmost of their power, not without great danger of their lives, yea, and sometimes it costeth them their lives indeed, as it is now daily seen.

The second argument. Matt. xxiii.

"The scribes and the Pharisees sit upon Moses' seat: whatsoever they bid you do, that do, but after their works do not; for they say, and do not." Here, they say, it appeareth plainly that Christ commandeth us to obey the heads of the church, how evil soever their lives be.

The first answer.

First, let them look well what manner men they make themselves, that is, scribes and Pharisees, the greatest enemies of God, persecutors and murderers of his prophets, of the apostles, and of Christ himself, and so antichrists.

The second answer.

Secondly, Moses' seat is not his office or authority, but his doctrine; and therefore saith St Augustine, that seat, which is his doctrine, suffereth them not to err: and in another place, They sitting in Moses' seat teach the law of God; therefore God teacheth by them. But if they will teach their own doctrine, believe them not; for such seek their own, and not Jesus Christ's: and Christ biddeth us beware of the leaven of the Pharisees; and then the disciples knew that he spake not of the leaven of bread, but of their doctrines, although they sat in Moses' seat, (if they will needs contend, the dignity or office of Moses to be Moses' seat,) and yet erred shamefully in their doctrine.

The fourth argument. Matt. xxviii.

" Behold, I am with you all the days unto the world's end." This promise was not made to the apostles only, (for they died shortly after Christ,) but to the church: *ergo*, the church cannot err.

Answer.

I beseech them to begin a little afore, and they shall plainly hear Christ himself unloose this knot. The words before are these in Mark: "Go and preach my gospel
60. to every creature;" and in Matthew: "Go and teach all people, baptizing them in the name of the Father, of the Son," &c.; "teaching them to observe all things whatsoever I have commanded you; and, lo, I will be with you unto the world's end." Here you may see this promise of Christ, " I will be with you," &c., is not absolute or universal, but given under a condition: that is, if you preach my gospel truly, if you baptize rightly, if you teach the baptized to do all things that I have commanded you, lo, then I will be with you unto the world's end. But if you teach any other gospel, or baptize otherwise, or bid them do any other thing, above that which I have commanded you, you have no promise of God, but the curse that Paul threateneth: " though we or an angel from heaven preach," &c.

The fifth argument. John xvi.

" I have yet many more things to say unto you, but you cannot bear them away now: howbeit when he is come, which is the Spirit of truth, he will lead you into all truth." Here you may see, say the enemies of God's truth, that Christ taught not all things himself, but left many things to be taught to the disciples by the Holy Ghost after his death.

Answer.

Christ said not, "I have many things to say, which I will not tell you now," but, " which you cannot bear now;" that is, you cannot perceive or understand them now: and thus Christ himself expoundeth these words: " The Comforter, which is the Holy Ghost, whom my Father will send in my name, he shall teach you all things, and put you in remembrance of all things that I have said unto you;" and no new or other things. For Christ saith plainly, that he himself had taught them all before, saying, "All things that I have heard of my Father have I opened unto you."

John xiv.

John xv.

Moreover, our Saviour in plain words sheweth what things those were that his disciples could not understand, although he many times told them the same before. "Behold," saith he, " we go up to Jerusalem, and all shall be fulfilled that are written by the prophets of the Son of man. For he shall be delivered to the Gentiles, and shall be mocked, and despitefully entreated, and spitted on; and when they have scourged him, they will put him to death; and the third day he will rise again: and they understood none of these things: for these sayings were hid from them, so that they perceived none of the things that were spoken:" although he spake to them in most plain terms. And the cause why they perceived not his so plain speech, was this: they were yet carnal, and understood the prophecies of Christ's kingdom carnally,
61. thinking that Christ should reign at Jerusalem like a mighty conqueror, and subdue all the Gentiles under the yoke of bondage to the Jews, so that the Jews should be lords and rulers over all the world for ever. And therefore James and John asked a

Luke xviii.

petition of Jesus by their mother, that they, "her two sons, might sit the one on his Matt. xx.
right hand, and the other on his left hand, in his kingdom:" and when he spake of his death, "Peter took him aside, and rebuked him, saying, Master, favour thyself; this Matt. xvi.
shall not happen unto thee." To whom Christ said: "Go after me, Satan." These be the things that the disciples could not then bear or understand, but thought that he had spoken some allegory, riddle, or dark speech unto them: but after his resurrection he opened their wits that they might understand the scriptures, and said unto them: "Thus it is written, and thus it behoved Christ to suffer." And to the two disciples going to Emmaus he expounded Moses, the prophets, and all the scriptures that were written of him. And after the ascension the Holy Ghost appeared to them in fiery tongues, and filled them with all knowledge, and they began to speak with sundry tongues, as the Holy Ghost gave them utterance; and then they understood the scriptures perfectly.

"Many other tokens did Jesus, which are not written in this book." Again: "There The sixth argument. John xxi.
are many other things that Jesus did, which, if they were written, I suppose the world should not be able to contain the books that should be written."

St John speaketh not here of faith and charity, but of miracles, the knowledge Answer.
whereof is not necessary for our salvation; as his words following do declare: "These are written, that you might believe that Jesus is Christ the Son of God, and in believing may have life in his name." And what is more required or desired of a Christian than to enjoy everlasting life? That ought to be our whole study and endeavour; to that end ought we to apply all our minds, words, and works, and prayers.

"Stand fast, brethren, and keep the ordinances that ye have learned, either by our The seventh argument. 2 Thess. ii.
preaching or by our epistle." Of these words they gather, that Paul taught divers things to the Thessalonians by word of mouth without writing, which nevertheless he commanded them to observe and do.

I grant that Paul taught many things by word of mouth, which he wrote not in his Answer.
epistles to the Thessalonians. But how shall they prove that the same things be neither written by him in any other of his epistles, nor in any other place of the holy bible? For what argument is this? It is not written in this place or to those persons; *ergo*, 61.
it is not written in the scripture at all. For the shortness of one epistle, or of one sermon, cannot sufficiently contain all things necessary for our salvation: and therefore be there so many books of the scripture, that whatso is omitted, and not spoken of in one place, or else darkly spoken of, might be written plainly in another place. And for this cause St Paul writeth to the Colossians, saying: "When this letter is read with you, cause it also to be read to the Laodiceans. And read you also the epistle written from Laodicea." And St Paul writeth of himself, "Such as we are in our 2 Cor. x.
absence by letters, such are we in deed being present." Moreover, Paul speaketh not here of doctrines of faith and charity, which ever continue without changing, adding, or minishing; but of certain traditions, observations, ceremonies, and outward rites and bodily exercises, which, as he saith, is little worth to God-ward, but to be used for comeliness, decent order, and uniformity in the church, and to avoid schism: which ceremonies every good man is bound to keep, lest he trouble the common order, and so break the order of charity in offending his weak brethren, so long as they be approved, received, and used by the heads and common consent. But they, and every one of such ceremonies as be neither sacraments, nor commandments of faith and charity, may be altered and changed, and other set in their places, or else utterly taken away by the authority of princes, and other their rulers and subjects in the church. Yea, also the traditions, made by the apostles in full council at Jerusalem, may be, and already are Acts xv.
taken away; as to abstain from things offered unto images, from blood and strangled, are nowhere kept. And this of Paul, that a man should neither pray nor preach capped, or with his head covered, is also clean abolished.

## THE TENTH CHAPTER.

63. *Doctors to the same purpose, with their answers*[1].

Argument. TERTULLIAN, of the Crown of a Soldier. He, reciting many traditions, as to renounce the devil, his pomp and his angels, afore baptism, to dip the children thrice in the font, to give it pap of honey and milk first thing after baptism, and not to wash it in a whole week after, to offer both at the day of the burial and birth, on the Sunday neither [2]to fast, nor to pray kneeling, nor also from Easter to Whitsuntide, crossing our foreheads, with divers such like, saith: "If thou require a law of these and other such disciplines, there can be no pretence of a law for them out of the scriptures. But thou shalt either perceive by thyself, or learn of some other that perceiveth it, that custom, being author, confirmer, conserver, and observer of faith, shall maintain and defend the cause of this tradition and custom of faith[3]."

Answer. By the scriptures before alleged it is evidently proved, that all things requisite for our salvation be set forth in the holy books of the bible, and that it is not lawful to put any thing thereto under pain of everlasting damnation. The same Tertullian also, as it is afore rehearsed[4], saith that "there is nothing else that ought to be believed after Christ's gospel once published." Yea, all the old authors, a thousand year after Christ, and likewise almost all the new, affirm the same, and would not have us credit their sayings without the proof of God's word.

Understand here as necessary to salvation.

Why should we then believe Tertullian against so plain scriptures, against the old fathers of the church, and also contrary to his own sayings? Yet here will I gently interpret him, so as he may both agree with the scriptures, with the old authors, and also with himself. Tertullian speaketh here not of doctrines of faith, hope, and charity,

---

[[1] "The following list of traditions is contained in the corresponding part of Cranmer's Commonplace Book at the British Museum." (Vid. Jenkyns' Remains of Archbp. Cranmer, Vol. IV. pp. 223, 4.)

"*Traditions not written recited by Tertullian.* That children should be christened but two times in the year, at Easter and Whitsuntide. That the bishops should christen them. That they that should be christened should be three times put in the water, the whole body. That by and by after they should eat milk and honey mixed together. That the whole week after they should not be washed. To offer yearly, the day of men's death, and of their birth. Upon the Sunday neither to fast, nor to kneel in prayer: and likewise from Easter to Whitsuntide. To make a cross upon our foreheads.

"*Traditions recited by Basilius.* Making a cross upon them that be christened. To turn our faces to the east, when we pray. Consecrating of oil and water in baptism, [and of him that is baptized.] Unction with oil. To put them that be baptized three times in the water. To renounce the devil and his angels in baptism.

"*Other authors rehearse a great number of traditions.* The fast of Lent. To fast Wednesday and Friday. Not to fast Saturday nor Sunday. That a bishop should be consecrated of two or three bishops, and priests of one. A bishop, priest, and deacon, shall not meddle with the business and care of worldly things; and if he do, let him be deposed. If a bishop give orders in another bishop's diocese without his licence, he shall be deposed, and also he that taketh orders of him. Giving of pax after mass. Consecrating of religious men. And a thousand mo traditions apostolic there be, if we give credence to St Denys, *De Ecclesiast. Hierarch.*, Ignatius, the Canons of the apostles, Ecclesiastica et Tripartita Historia, Cyprian, Tertullian, Irenæus, with other old ancient authors. And yet an infinite number mo we shall be constrained to receive, if we admit this rule, which St Augustine many times repeats, 'that whatsoever is universally observed, and not written in the scripture, nor ordained by general councils, is a tradition coming from the apostles: as, that bishops have authority to excommunicate all persons that be manifest and obstinate sinners; to admit or reject other bishops and curates presented by princes or patrons; to ordain ceremonies to be observed in the church; to make laws how to proceed in excommunication, and other laws ecclesiastical; and what punishment is to be given to offenders; and all people being within their jurisdiction, of what estate or condition soever they be, be bound to obey them." British Museum, Royal MSS. 7. B. xi. p. 92. Strype, Memorials, Vol. II. part i. pp. 214, 15, Ed. Oxford, 1822.]

[[2] To fast, neither to pray, Orig. ed.]

[[3] Harum et aliarum ejusmodi disciplinarum si legem expostules scripturarum, nullam invenies... Rationem traditioni et consuetudini et fidei patrocinaturam aut ipse perspicies, aut ab aliquo qui perspexerit disces: interim nonnullam esse credes, cui debeatur obsequium. Tertull. De Cor. p. 102. Ed. Lutet. Paris. 1664.]

[[4] Id. de Præscript. Hæret. cap. vi. p. 204. Vid. p. 22.]

but of traditions, outward gestures, rites and ceremonies, which be not necessary for our salvation, but be ordained for a decent order and conformity in the church; as is plainly shewed in the answer to St Paul in the epistle to the Thessalonians. And that he speaketh of such rites and ceremonies, it is evident. For all those that he rehearseth be mere ceremonies, and few of them kept at this day, which no man might have altered or abolished, if they had been necessarily to be kept under pain of damnation.

Argument. Cyprian to Pompeius, against Stephen's epistle. "It is of no less authority that the apostles delivered by the instruction of the Holy Ghost, than that which Christ himself delivered[5]."

Answer. Cyprian speaketh not here of traditions unwritten, but of such things as the apostles delivered in their writings, as the gospels and epistles; like as Paul saith: "I delivered you that I received of the Lord;" which thing he wrote to them. But if they will needs understand him of things delivered by the apostles without writing, then answer him as Tertullian.

Argument. Origen. "In observances of the church, there be divers things which all men must needs do, and yet the reason of them is unknown to all men." And he reciteth in many[6] the observances that Tertullian doth, and after he concludeth: "Who can certainly tell the cause of all these things?"

Answer. The answer made to Tertullian will serve Origen in this place[7].

Argument. Athanasius upon the second epistle to the Thessalonians, chap. ii. upon this place, *State et tenete*. "Hereby it is plain that Paul delivered many things without the scripture, not written in his epistles, but by word of mouth only. And these are worthy no less faith than the other: therefore I do judge the tradition of the church to be a thing worthy to be credited; so that if any thing be delivered by it, make no farther search[8]."

Chrysostomus, in the 2nd epistle to the Thessalonians, chap. ii.: "Stand fast, brethren, and keep the traditions," &c. "Hereof," saith Chrysostom, "it is plain that Paul delivered not all things in his epistles, but also many things without writing; and as well those as these are worthy of like faith. Wherefore we judge the tradition of the church worthy of credit: it is a tradition; search no farther[9]."

Argument. Epiphanius against Heresies, Lib. ii. tom. 1. Against those that call themselves apostles. 1 Cor. xi. xiv. xv. "We must," saith he, "use traditions, for all things cannot be perceived by the holy scripture. Wherefore the holy apostles have set forth unto us 65.
some things by the word of God, and some things by traditions, as the apostle saith: 'As I have delivered unto you, thus I teach;' and, 'Thus I have delivered in all churches;' and, 'Thus you remember by what means I have preached unto you, except you have believed in vain[10].'"

Answer. Answer these three authors like as Tertullian is answered, saving that they allege St Paul for their purpose, but clearly wrested from his true meaning, as it shall easily appear to every indifferent reader, that is not blinded of malice to resist the truth, as they may plainly perceive by the answer made to St Paul afore. And whereas they say, that things given by word of mouth are as well to be believed as those that be written; they

---

[5 Si ergo aut in evangelio præcipitur aut in apostolorum epistolis vel actibus continetur—observetur divina hæc et sancta traditio. Cyprian. Epist. lxxiv. ad Pompeium contr. epist. Stephani. p. 138. Ed. Paris. 1726.]

[6 In manner, Orig. ed.]

[7 Will serve Origen here, Orig. ed.]

[8 The passage cited is not from Athanasius, but Theophylact. Κἀντεῦθεν δῆλον ὅτι πολλὰ καὶ ἀγράφως διὰ λόγου, τουτέστι ζώσῃ φωνῇ, παρεδίδοσαν, οὐ μόνον δι' ἐπιστολῶν. ὁμοίως δὲ καὶ ταῦτα κἀκεῖνα ἀξιόπιστα. ὥστε καὶ τὴν παράδοσιν τῆς ἐκκλησίας ἀξιόπιστον ἡγούμεθα. παράδοσίς ἐστι· μηδὲν πλέον ζήτει.—Theoph. Comment. in Epist. II. ad Thessalon. cap. ii. v. 15. p. 730. Ed. Lond. 1636.]

[9 Ἐντεῦθεν δῆλον ὅτι οὐ πάντα δι' ἐπιστολῆς παρεδίδοσαν, ἀλλὰ πολλὰ καὶ ἀγράφως· ὁμοίως δε κἀκεῖνα καὶ ταῦτά ἐστιν ἀξιόπιστα. ὥστε καὶ τὴν παράδυσιν τῆς ἐκκλησίας ἀξιόπιστον ἡγώμεθα. παράδοσίς ἐστι· μηδὲν πλέον ζήτει. Chrysost. .n Epist. II. ad Thessal. cap. ii. Hom. iv. Tom. XI. p. 532. Ed. Paris. 1718-38.]

[10 Δεῖ δὲ καὶ παραδόσει κεχρῆσθαι· οὐ γὰρ πάντα ἀπὸ τῆς θείας γραφῆς δύναται λαμβάνεσθαι. διὸ τὰ μὲν ἐν γραφαῖς, τὰ δὲ ἐν παραδόσει παρέδωκαν οἱ ἅγιοι ἀπόστολοι· ὡς φησὶν ὁ ἅγιος ἀπόστολος, ὡς παρέδωκα ὑμῖν· καὶ ἄλλοτε, οὕτως διδάσκω, καὶ οὕτως παρέδωκα ἐν ταῖς ἐκκλησίαις. καὶ εἰ κατέχετε, ἐκτὸς εἰ μὴ εἰκῇ ἐπιστεύσατε. Epiphan. Adver. Hæres. Lib. II. Tom. I. p. 511. Ed. Colon. 1582.]

mean, that they are worthy of like credit with traditions written. For neither of both are of necessity to salvation, but may be changed and taken away by common consent, as it is afore said.

Argument. Basil, of the Holy Ghost, chap. 27. "Of those doctrines that are preached in the church, we have some delivered us by writing, and again some we have received by the traditions of the apostles in mystery, that is, in secret: both have like strength to godliness; neither doth any man speak against these, whatsoever he be, that hath but mean experience what the authority of the church is. For if we, like fools, go about to reject the customs of the church, which are not written, as things of small weight, we shall condemn those things that be needful for our salvation in the gospel. Yea, we shall rather cut short the true preaching of faith to bare name[1]." And he rehearseth like traditions as Tertullian did.

Jerome, against the Luciferians. "Although there were no authority of the scriptures at all, yet the consent of the whole world in this matter should have the force of a law. For many other things, which are observed in the church by tradition, have obtained the authority of a law written: as to dip the head thrice in baptism; and when they are christened, to give them first pap made of milk with honey, for a signification of their infancy; on the Sunday, and on Whitsun-week[2], not to kneel at their prayers[3]."

Augustine, upon the words of Basil. "Some of the ecclesiastical institutions we have received by writings; some, through traditions from the apostles, approved by succession; and some use hath allowed, being strengthened by custom. Unto all which like usage and like affections of godliness is due; of which who will doubt, though he have but
66. small experiences in the scriptures? For if we set our mind to regard lightly customs of the church, delivered us from our elders without the scriptures, it shall easily appear to them that look earnestly thereon, how great loss christian religion shall suffer[4]." And he reciteth the same that Jerome doth, with divers other.

Answer. These three authors, and all that make for the same purpose, be answered before in Tertullian. For not one of those things that they make mention of are necessary for our salvation: and many of them are now taken away; and the rest which yet remain, as to dip the child thrice wholly in the water, to hallow the water, oil, and cream, or to cross it in the forehead, are not of necessity to salvation. For John baptized in Jordan, and the chamberlain of the queen of Æthiopia was christened in the common stream, and children in danger of life are christened of the midwife, or some other woman, without any of these ceremonies: and yet they will not deny that all these baptisms be good, and allowed of God. In Spain also they dip the child but once, as it was decreed in the council of Tollet[5]. And I am sure they will not say that all the Spaniards so many years have wanted a thing necessary to salvation in their baptism. God also regardeth not our outward bodily gesture in our prayers; but he beholdeth the faith and earnest desire of the heart of him that prayeth, wheresoever he prayeth, and whatsoever his outward bodily gesture be.

Argument. The same against Cresconi, a grammarian, Lib. i. cap. 33, tom. 7. "Although we have no certain example of this matter in the canonical scripture, yet nevertheless the

---

[[1] Τῶν ἐν τῇ ἐκκλησίᾳ πεφυλαγμένων δογμάτων καὶ κηρυγμάτων, τὰ μὲν ἐκ τῆς ἐγγράφου διδασκαλίας ἔχομεν, τὰ δὲ ἐκ τῆς τῶν ἀποστόλων παραδόσεως διαδοθέντα ἡμῖν ἐν μυστηρίῳ παρεδεξάμεθα· ἅπερ ἀμφότερα τὴν αὐτὴν ἰσχὺν ἔχει πρὸς τὴν εὐσέβειαν· καὶ τούτοις οὐδεὶς ἀντερεῖ, ὅστίς γε κᾂν κατὰ μικρὸν γοῦν θεσμῶν ἐκκλησιαστικῶν πεπείραται. εἰ γὰρ ἐπιχειρήσομεν τὰ ἄγραφα τῶν ἐθῶν ὡς οὐ μεγάλην ἔχοντα τὴν δύναμιν παραιτεῖσθαι, λάθοιμεν ἂν εἰς αὐτὰ τὰ καίρια ζημιοῦντες τὸ εὐαγγέλιον· μᾶλλον δὲ εἰς ὄνομα ψιλὸν περιϊστῶντες τὸ κήρυγμα. Basil. De Spir. Sancto. cap. xxvii. Tom. II. p. 351. Ed. Paris. 1637.]

[[2] And all Whitsun-week, Orig. ed.]

[[3] Etiam si scripturæ auctoritas non subesset, totius orbis in hanc partem consensus instar præcepti obtineret. Nam et multa alia, quæ per traditionem in ecclesiis observantur, auctoritatem sibi scriptæ legis usurpaverunt: velut in lavacro ter caput mergitare; deinde egressos, lactis et mellis prægustare concordiam ad infantiæ significationem; die dominico et per omnem pentecosten nec de geniculis adorare. Hieron. Adver. Lucifer. Tom. II. p. 96. Ed. Francof. 1684.]

[[4] The "words of Basil" referred to in this brief comment are evidently those just quoted in note 1. The Editor has not discovered the comment itself in Augustine's writings.]

[[5] Conc. Tolet. IV. cap. vi. Labb. et Cossart. Tom. V. col. 1706, 7. Ed. Lutet. Paris. 1674.]

truth of the same scriptures in this matter is retained of us, when we do that the whole church[6] alloweth, which church the authority of the scriptures commend. And forasmuch as the holy scripture can deceive no man, whoso feareth to be deceived with any dark speaking of it, let him ask counsel at the church therein, which, without any doubt, the holy scripture doth shew[7]."

The answer is easy. Austin was more circumspect than to think that any doctrine Answer. might be proved by use and custom without the scripture. For baptism of infants he bringeth in this text: "Except a man be born again of water and the Holy Ghost, he cannot be my disciple." And because the Donatists, like as the anabaptists do now, wrest this to them that be of years of discretion, against this exposition he allegeth the manner of the church in christening of infants. By the which he proveth that the church hath alway taken this sentence, "Except a man be born again," to be spoken also of infants. What manner of argument should this be of Austin? The exposition of the scripture, and the use of the sacraments, may be judged by the custom used in the holy church alway; *ergo*, the church may make a new sacrament, and ordain any new article 67.
of our faith, without the scripture. By the sentences before cited of Austin himself it may be easily judged. I also grant, that every exposition of the scripture, whereinsoever the old, holy, and true church did agree, is necessary to be believed. But our controversy here is, whether any thing ought to be believed of necessity without the scripture.

The same against the epistle of Fundament, cap. v. tom. 6. "I would not believe Argument. the gospel, but that the authority of the church moveth me:" *ergo*, say they, whatsoever the church saith, we must needs believe them as well as the gospel[8].

This argument is naught: for the testimony of the church is but as a public office [Answer.] of a record; as the exchequer, the court of the rolls, the office of a recorder, or a register of all Christendom; in which office men may search and have, of the keepers of such offices, the true copies of such lands, or other moveables, as be due to them by the law. And yet may neither the registers, recorders, stewards of courts, or town-clerks, put to, or take away any thing from, the first original writings; no, nor the judge himself. But all things ought to be judged by those writings. So, likewise, we believe the holy canon of the bible, because that the primitive church of the apostles, and eldest writers, and next to their time, approved them in their register, that is, in their writings, which partly saw them, and partly heard them of the apostles. And more receive we not, because these old fathers of the first church testify in their books, that there was no more than these required to be believed as the scripture of God. And yet were these writings no less true, afore they were allowed by them, than since, Christ witnessing and saying, "I seek no witness of man."

Austin to Cassulane. "In these things, wherein the scripture of God hath determined Argument. nothing, the custom of the people, and our elders' ordinances, ought to be holden as a law; and the transgressors of the customs of the church are likewise to be punished, as the breakers of God's law. Of which things if thou wilt dispute, and reprove one custom by another, there shall arise an endless strife." He repeateth also this sentence many times: "That whatsoever is universally observed, and not written in the scripture, Answer.
nor ordained by general councils, is a tradition come from the apostles[9]." 68.

---

[6 We do that that the whole church, Orig. ed.]

[7 Proinde quamvis hujus rei certe de scripturis canonicis non proferatur exemplum, earumdem tamen scripturarum etiam in hac re a nobis tenetur veritas, cum hoc facimus quod universæ jam placuit ecclesiæ, quam ipsarum scripturarum commendat auctoritas: ut quoniam sancta scriptura fallere non potest, quisquis falli metuit hujus obscuritate quæstionis, eandem ecclesiam de illa consulat, quam sine ulla ambiguitate sancta scriptura demonstrat. August. Contra Crescon. Grammat. Lib. I. cap. xxxiii. Tom. VII. p. 168. Ed. Paris. 1637.]

[8 Ego vero evangelio non crederem, nisi me catholicæ ecclesiæ commoveret auctoritas. Id. Contr. Epist. Fund. Manich. cap. vi. Tom. VI. p. 46.]

[9 In his enim rebus, de quibus nihil certi statuit scriptura divina, mos populi Dei vel instituta majorum pro lege tenenda sunt. De quibus si disputare voluerimus, et ex aliorum consuetudine alios improbare, orietur interminata luctatio. Id. Casul. Epist. lxxxii. Tom. II. p. 143.]

Answer him as Tertullian. Yet of all[1] other authors he is most plain, that nothing is of necessity to salvation besides the scriptures of God. But let us grant for their pleasures, that those customs which they speak of be traditions apostolic, yet they be no longer nor other ways to be observed than the traditions apostolic written; which, as is before fully proved, may (and are already) be both changed, and clearly taken away. And as concerning custom, it is plainly proved, that it is not to be received against the scripture, truth, or reason.

Argument. They say, moreover, that the perpetual virginity of our lady is to be believed of necessity, as Cyprian, Chrysostom, Jerome, Ambrose, Austin, and all other speaking thereof say. But this is not found in the scripture; *ergo*, there is something to be believed that is not written in the scripture.

Answer. The minor, that is to say, that this is not written in the scripture, is false. For, first, none of the old authors that rehearse traditions of the apostles unwritten, make mention of the perpetual virginity of our lady to be one of them; but they rehearse only divers ceremonies, or bodily gestures, and such rites used in baptism, prayers, holydays, and fastings, which, as I have manifestly declared, are not necessary to salvation; but the most part of them are clean taken away, and the contrary commanded and used by the universal church. Moreover, all the said authors prove her perpetual virginity by this text of scripture: (Ezek. xliv.) "This door shall be still shut, and not opened for any man to go through it, but only for the Lord God of Israel; yea, he shall go through it, else shall it be shut still." For if these and such other fathers had not judged her perpetual virginity to have been written in the scriptures, they would never have judged it to have been a thing to be believed under pain of damnation. Saint Jerome also calleth Helvidium a rash and an ungodly man, because that he taught that our lady had other children by Joseph after Christ's birth; which doctrine he could not prove by the scriptures of God[2]. In like manner we call all them that preach any doctrine in the church, without the authority of God's word, both ungodly, rash, and wicked members of antichrist.

Argument. Yet they bring forth, to maintain their error, the baptism of infants, which, they say, is not contained in the scriptures: and yet this is to be observed upon pain of damnation of the said children. *Ergo*, there is something to be done, of necessity to our salvation, that is not contained in the scriptures.

Answer. O what a gap these men open both to the Donatists and to the anabaptists, that

69. deny the baptizing of infants! For, if it were not written in the word of God, no man ought to believe it, or use it: and so the Donatists' and anabaptists' doctrine were true, and ours false. But in deed the baptism of infants is proved by the plain scriptures. First, by the figure of the old law, which was circumcision. Infants in the old law were circumcised; *ergo*, in the new law they ought to be baptized. Again: infants pertain to God, as it is said to Abraham, (Gen. xvii.) "I will be thy God, and the God of thy seed after thee." (Matt. xix.) Christ saith also: "Suffer children to come to me; for of such is the kingdom of heaven." And again: "See that ye despise not one of these little ones: for their angels in heaven always behold the face of my Father which is in heaven: for (Luke xix.) the Son of man is come to save that which is lost." (1 Cor. vii.) And again, Paul saith, that "your children are holy now." By these, and many other plain words of scripture, it is evident that the baptism of infants is grounded upon the holy scriptures.

Argument. Furthermore, the church, say they, hath changed the sabbath-day into the Sunday, which sabbath was commanded by God, and never man found fault thereat. Seeing then that the church hath authority to change God's laws, much more it hath authority to make new laws necessary to salvation.

[Answer.] There be two parts of the sabbath-day: one is the outward bodily rest from all manner of labour and work; and this is mere ceremonial, and was taken away with other sacrifices and ceremonies by Christ at the preaching of the gospel. The other part

[1 And yet of all, Orig. ed.]

[2 Hieron. adv. Helvid. Tom. II. p. 7 et sqq. Tom. V. p. 162. Ed. Francof. 1684.]

of the sabbath-day is the inward rest, or ceasing from sin, from our own wills and lusts, and to do only God's will and commandments. Of this part speaketh the prophet Esay: "He that taketh heed that he unhallow not the sabbath-day, is he that keepeth himself that he do no evil; and they that hold greatly of the thing that pleaseth me, and keep my covenant, unto them will I give an everlasting name, that shall not perish." And moreover, the same prophet saith: "If thou turn thy feet from the sabbath, so that thou do not the thing which pleaseth thyself in my holy day, then shalt thou be called unto the pleasant, holy, and glorious sabbath of the Lord, where thou shalt be in honour; so that thou do not after thine own imaginations, neither seek thine own will, nor speak thine own words. Then shalt thou have thy pleasure in the Lord, which shall carry thee high above the earth, and feed thee with the heritage of Jacob thy father: for the Lord's own mouth hath spoken it." This spiritual sabbath, that is, to abstain 70.
from sin and to do good, are all men bound to keep all the days of their life, and not only on the sabbath-day. And this spiritual sabbath may no man alter nor change, no, not the whole church.

Isai. lvi.

Isai. lviii.

That the utter[3] observing of the sabbath is mere ceremonial, St Paul writeth plainly, as that the holy days of the new moon and of the sabbath-days are nothing but shadows of things to come[4].

And that the outward bodily rest is a mere ceremonial precept, St Austin also affirmeth, saying, that among all the ten commandments this only that is spoken of the sabbath is commanded figuratively; but all the other commandments we must observe plainly, as they be commanded, without any figure of speech[5].

To January, Epist. cxix. The bodily rest on the sabbath-day is figuratively to be kept.

Jerome also, to the Galatians, iv. according to the same, saith: "Lest the congregation of the people, without good order, should diminish the faith in Christ, therefore certain days were appointed, wherein we should come together; not that that day is holier than the other in which we come together, but that whatsoever day we assemble in there might arise greater joy by the sight of one of us to another.

"But he that will answer wittily to the question propounded, affirmeth all the days to be like, and not that Christ is crucified only on Good Friday, and riseth only on the Sunday; but that every day is the day of the Lord's resurrection, and we eat his flesh always. But fastings and comings together were ordained of wise men for them that give themselves rather to the world than to God; that cannot, yea, for them that will not, come there at all, there to make their sacrifice of prayers to God in the face of all the people[6]."

To the perfect Christian all days be like, and every day is Good Friday, every day is Easter-day, and we eat his flesh always.

Hereby you may easily perceive that the church hath not changed the special part of the sabbath, which is to cease from vice and sin; but the ceremonial part of the sabbath only, which was abrogate and taken away, with other ceremonies of Moses' law, by Christ, at the full preaching of the gospel: in place whereof the church hath ordained the Sunday for causes aforesaid[7].

---

[[3] i.e. outer.]

[[4] Coloss. ii. 16, 17.]

[[5] Ideoque inter omnia illa decem præcepta solum ibi quod de sabbato positum est, figurate observandum præcipitur,—cetera tamen ibi præcepta proprie, sicut præcepta sunt, sine ulla figurata significatione observamus. August. Januario. Epist. cxix. cap. xii. Tom. II. p. 217.]

[[6] Et ne inordinata congregatio populi fidem minueret in Christo, propterea dies aliqui constituti sunt, ut in unum omnes pariter veniremus. Non quo celebrior sit dies illa qua convenimus, sed quo quacumque die conveniendum sit, ex conspectu mutuo lætitia major oriatur. Qui vero oppositæ quæstioni acutius respondere conatur, illud affirmat, omnes dies æquales esse, nec per Parascevem tantum Christum crucifigi, et die dominica resurgere, sed semper sanctum resurrectionis esse diem, et semper eum carne vesci dominica. Jejunia autem et congregationes inter dies propter eos a viris prudentibus constitutos, qui magis seculo vacant quam Deo, nec possunt, imo nolunt toto in ecclesia vitæ suæ tempore congregari, et ante humanos actus Deo orationum suarum offerre sacrificium. Hieron. Lib. II. in Epist. ad Galat. cap. iv. Tom. IX. p. 142. Ed. Francof. 1684.]

[[7] "The following are some extracts from Cranmer's Common-place Book in the British Museum relating to the subject of this chapter.

*Novæ doctrinæ.*

Quod sacerdos sit qui non vivat ex doctrina verbi, sed ex missis quæ pro defunctis celebrantur.

Missa de scala cœli. Missa satisfactoria.

Indulgentiæ. Jubileus.

Communicatio sub una specie.

Satisfactio.

## THE ELEVENTH CHAPTER[1].

71. *The Papists' Objections, with answers unto them.*

Argument. THEY boast themselves[2], moreover, of the certainty of their doctrine, and prove it to be true by the long continuance thereof, and lucky prosperity of their kingdom; and their adversaries' doctrine to be false, by the persecutions, plagues, miseries, and afflictions, which they daily suffer for their doctrine's sake.

Answer. If the trial of true religion should rest upon antiquity of time, or upon worldly prosperity, then should the gentiles and pagans have a great advantage of us Christians, and their religion should be better than ours, by the testimonies of our own scriptures. For idolatry and worshipping of false gods, and their images, was used long before the law of God, written and given to Moses, in which errors and idolatry the heathen continue unto this day, in great prosperity and wealth, under most victorious emperors and princes: whereas the true church of Christ hath been most miserably afflicted from time to time; first under the Egyptians, after by the Philistines, Canaanites, Pharasites, &c.; then by the Babylonians, Assyrians, Medes, Persians, Syrians, and Romans, both subdued, conquered[3], and led away captives: and, last of all, by the Turk and the pope, the two horns of antichrist, the true church of Christ hath been most cruelly persecuted unto death, with prison, famine, water, fire, fagot, and sword, these seven or eight hundred years last past. Which Turk and pope, although they be mortal enemies one to the other, yet as Herod, Pilate, the bishops, scribes, and Pharisees, although they were utter foes each to other, conspired against innocent Christ, causeless condemning him to death on the cross; in like manner, I say, the pope and the Turk do fully agree in this one point, to persecute and murder Christ in his faithful members. For as the sun cannot be without his brightness, nor the fire without his heat; so cannot the true church of God be long without the cross of
72. persecution, as witnesseth St Paul: "All they that will live godly in Jesus Christ shall
Christ's badge. suffer persecution." And our Saviour Christ saith plainly, that his "kingdom is not of this world." For "if they persecute me," saith he, "they shall also persecute you." And Christ giveth not to his apostles earthly peace in this world, but peace and quietness of conscience, joined with persecution. For if the wicked persecuted Christ himself, shall they not also persecute his servants? And if they so handled Christ, being the lively tree, what think you they shall do to us his withered branches? And as the true church of Christ can never be long without persecution, in like manner can the false church of Satan and antichrist never cease from persecuting; as it appeareth throughout the histories of the whole bible. Of the tyranny and cruelty of antichrist in persecuting of Christ's true church, prophesied Daniel long before. Speaking of the

---

*In cæremoniis fere omnibus Judæos imitamur.*

Pro ephodo lineo habemus superpellicia.

Pro sacrificiis fecimus ex missa sacrificium, ne sacerdotes nostri non essent sacrifici.

Habemus et asyla pro locis refugii.

Habemus basilicas consecratas, cum altaribus, calicibus, vestibus, et reliquis utensilibus, ad divinum cultum pertinentibus.

Habemus etiam hæc omnia oleo peruncta.

Quin et sacerdotes ac reliqui ministri oleo imbuuntur, et consecrantur more Mosaico. De Consecratione, Dist. i. cap. i°. et iii°.

Non licet offerre nisi in loco consecrato. De Consecratione, Dist. ii. 'Sicut non alii,' quia scriptum est, *Vide ne offeras holocausta tua in omni loco quem videris, sed in omni loco quem elegerit Dominus Deus tuus.*

Festum dedicationis octo diebus celebramus, sicut Judæi. De Consecratione, Dist. i. 'Solemnitates.'

Quod autem octo diebus encænia sint celebranda, in libro regum (peracta dedicatione templi) reperies.

Habemus et velum atrii domus Domini, sicut Judæi. De consecratione, Dist. i. 'Nemo.'

Sicut solis sacerdotibus et Levitis licebat contrectare vasa sacra templi, ita et nunc. De Consecratione, Dist. i. 'In sancta.'

Nec in alios usus licet vestibus sacris frui, quam in sacros. De Consecratione, Dist. i. 'Vestimenta' et 'Ad nuptiarum.'" Royal MSS. 7. B. xi. p. 101. Vid. Jenkyns' Remains of Archbp. Cranmer, Vol. IV. p. 234.]

[1 It seems evident that the whole of this eleventh chapter could not proceed from the pen of the archbishop, if even any part of it was written by him. In several places there appear discrepancies of style, and there is reference made to a work which, according to the date, was not printed till after his death. The chapter is not found in the Commonplace Book in the British Museum.]

[2 Moreover they boast themselves, Orig. ed.]

[3 Conquest, Orig. ed.]

Dan. vii. The mark to know antichrist by is to prevail (by persecution) against God's elect saints.

Dan. viii. And the mark of the true Church is to be persecuted of antichrist.

empire and regiment of Rome: "The fourth beast," saith he, "shall be the fourth kingdom, which shall be greater than all other kingdoms: it shall devour, tread down, and destroy all other lands; he shall speak words against the Highest of all; he shall destroy the saints of the Most Highest, and think that he can change times and laws." And again, he saith of Antiochus, which was a figure of antichrist: "There shall arise a king unshamefaced of face; he shall be wise in dark speaking; he shall be mighty and strong, but not in his own strength; he shall destroy above measure, and all that he goeth about shall prosper in his hand: his heart shall be proud, he shall slay the strong and holy people, and through his craftiness falsehood shall prosper in his hand, and many one shall be put to death in his wealthiness; he shall stand up against the prince of princes, but he shall be slain without hand." Of the tyranny and prosperous success of antichrist in slaying of the saints of God, and the reward of them that be slain for the witness of God's truth, speaketh also St John, in the sixth chapter of his Apocalypse, under the opening of the four and five seals: and in the seventeenth chapter he lively setteth forth the pope in his own colours, under the person of the whore of Babylon being drunken with the blood of saints; pointing, as it were with his finger, who this whore of Babylon is, and the place where she shall reign, saying: "The woman which thou sawest is that great city which reigneth over the kings of the earth." Now what other city reigned at that time, or at any time since, over the christian kings of the earth, but only Rome? Whereof it followeth Rome to be the seat of antichrist, and the pope to be very antichrist himself. I 73.
could prove the same by many other scriptures, old writers, and strong reasons. But forasmuch as Rodulph Gualter hath written hereof a notable work in Latin, and now of Latin translated into English by I. O., I remit the reader to his book, wherein he may be fully satisfied hereof[4]. Of the prosperity and security that the false church hath in worldly pleasures, using the same with all greediness and voluptuousness of carnal lusts, with the wicked devices of tyranny against Christ and his true members, wherewith the ungodly daily persecute and murder God's elect for his truth, with the reward also of them that suffer for the same truth sake, it is most plainly written in the second and third chapters of the Book of Wisdom.

Read the places.

Read the chapters.

By these scriptures now rehearsed it appeareth most plainly, that worldly prosperity of the pope and his clergy prove not the truth of their doctrine; nor yet persecution of God's true preachers and other faithful people argueth their doctrine to be false. But if thou wilt needs know where the true church of Christ is, and where the false, and not to be deceived, herein take this for a plain and full answer, that wheresoever the word of God is truly preached, without addition of man's doctrines and traditions, and the sacraments duly ministered according to Christ's institution, there is the true church, the very spouse of God, Christ being the head thereof. But how many and who, of that number that hear the word of God and receive the sacraments, be God's elect church, and true members of Christ, is known to God only; "for the Lord knoweth who be his," and no man can tell of another man, whether he be worthy love or hatred, although their works seem never so holy and glorious afore men; so great a witch is hypocrisy.

Argument.

Last of all, to make all cock sure, and to maintain their idolatry beside, yea, and also contrary to the word of God, (as invocation and praying to saints, worshipping of images and relics, with pilgrimages and offerings, and the sacrifice of the mass for the quick and the dead, and pardons to deliver dead men's souls from purgatory, holy bread, holy water, ashes, palms, and such other baggage,) they allege revelations of angels, of our lady and other saints, and dead men's souls appearing to divers men and women, bidding them to cause certain masses, trentals[5], pilgrimages, and offering to images and relics of this and that saint, to be done for them, and they should be delivered from the fire of purgatory, where the pains be greater, say they, than man's wit can

[[4] The work referred to seems to be, Antichristus, id est, Homiliæ quinque, quibus Romanum Pontificem verum et magnum illum Antichristum esse probatur. Without date.—Antichrist, That is to saye: A true report that Antichrist is come, &c. Translated out of Latine into English, by J. O. (John Olde), Southwarke, 1556. See Herbert's Ames' Typog. Antiq. p. 1451.]

[[5] Trentals: services of thirty masses, said one on each of thirty different days for the soul of a person deceased.]

74. comprehend. And when such masses, pilgrimages, with offerings to such saints' relics and images, be done for them, they appear to the same persons again, saying, that by such means they be delivered out of purgatory into the eternal joys of heaven. They tell also of many wonders and strange miracles, to prove their doctrine, in all these aforesaid things, to be true. And because they have great profit and advantage thereby, they, "counting gains godliness," have filled all their books with such vanities and lies; of which some be so fond, and so directly against God's glory, that the most earnest papists (having either learning or wit) be ashamed of them; yea, and the pope himself hath clean put them out of God's service used in the church of Rome: and yet must we read them, believe them as necessary articles of our faith, or else burn therefore like heretics.

Answer. By the manifest and plain words of the scriptures, and the consent of the most ancient authors before written, it is evident, that neither the visions of angels, apparitions of the dead, nor miracles, nor all these together joined in one, are able or sufficient to make any one new article of our faith, or stablish any thing in religion, without the express words of God; because all such things (as is before proved) may be, yea, and have been, through God's permission, for our sins and unbelief's sake, done by the power of the devil himself, or feigned and counterfeited of his lively members, monks and friars, with other such hypocrites.

But what shall Satan need to tell oracles, use visions, shew apparitions, or work miracles now-a-days? What should he need to toil herein himself? or why should he not, like a gentleman, take his ease in his inn, seeing his subtle servants, monks, friars, nuns, and other pope-holy hypocrites, can and do counterfeit such things daily, and from their beginning hath done diligently? Part whereof I shall rehearse.

John Sleidane. About fourteen years past, at Orleance in France, the provost's wife died, willing to be buried at the Friars' in the same city, without pomp or other solemnity commonly used at burials. Wherefore the friars, fearing to lose a great prey, if this should be suffered to enter into the heads of the people, caused a young friar to speak in a vault in a woman's voice, many people hearing it, and said that she was the soul of the provost's wife, condemned in hell for contemning of the suffrages of the holy church, commanding also her body to be cast out of christian burial. But the provost so bolted out the matter, that the young friar confessed the place and the manner of his speaking; and all the friars were openly punished for that fault in the common market at Orleance[1].

75. But let us come home to our own realm of England. About thirty years past, in the borders of Wales, within a priory called Lymster, there was a young woman, called the holy maid of Lymster, which (as the fame was) lived only by angels' food, and was inclosed within a grate of iron; unto whom, certain days, when the prior of the place said mass, the third part of the host went, hanging in the air, (by miracle, as it seemed,) from the altar, where the prior massed, into the maid's mouth. Which thing brought the people into a great opinion of holiness in her, and caused great pilgrimage to be there used. But when the Lord of Burgavenny[2], with his brother Sir Edward Nevel, and divers other gentlemen and gentlewomen, came to try the truth hereof, they caused the door to be opened, and straightways the dogs fought for bones that were under her bed; whereupon they searching farther, found a privy door, whereby the prior might resort to her and she to him, at their pleasures. And then she confessed that she made, as it were, two fine threads of her own hairs singly tied together with fine knots; and then made a big hole with a bodkin through the corner of a quarter of the host, and fastened one end of the said hair to the corporas, where the said prior said mass, and the other end to her own bed wherein she lay, and tied the other hair fast to the quarter of the host, and wrapped the other end about her own finger. And when the prior had received his portion of the host, she wound up the thread, whereto the host was tied, upon her fingers, and so conveyed the host into her mouth. This both the prior and she confessed, and did open penance for the same[3].

---

[[1] Sleidan. De statu religionis et reipub. (A.D. 1534.) Book IX. pp. 175, 6. Ed. Francof. 1568.]

[[2] Burgavenny, i.e. Abergavenny. Vid. Works of Thomas Becon, Early Writings, pp. 61, n.; 87, n.; 307, n. Park. Soc. Ed. 1843.]

[[3] Sir Thomas More's Dialogues of Veneration and Worship of Images. Part I. Book I. cap. XIV. col. 25.]

To St Albans, about twenty-eight years past, came a maid, creeping upon her knees, and leaning upon two short staves, inquiring after St Alban's bones; affirming, that she should be made whole and go upright, so soon as she should come to the place where St Alban's bones were: in token whereof an angel had delivered her a key, whereby she should certainly know where his very bones were. And when she passed thus through the streets of St Alban's, creeping on her knees till she came to St Alban's shrine, after she had made her prayers devoutly there, she took out the key of her purse, which she said an angel had delivered to her; and then she stood upright, and opened the shrine with the said key, and then kneeled again to pray, and to give thanks to God and St Alban for her healing, and giving her strength to walk, which was born lame. And by and by the monks would have had it rung for a miracle; but some wiser men thought it meet to try the matter better, and to examine her farther, before they began[4] to ring a miracle openly. And upon her examination she said that she had been lame from her birth, declaring both her kindred and place
where she was born. Upon which confession she was committed to a nunnery called 76.
Sopwel, there to tarry until messengers, which they straightway sent forth, might return and testify the truth. And so she daily and holily visited St Alban's shrine. But the night before the return of the messengers she was conveyed away, and never heard of nor seen after. And the messengers declared to be lies all that ever she had said: for there was never none born lame, nor of her name, where she said she was born.

A strange thing it is to hear of the wonderful trances and visions of Mistress Anne Wentworth[5], of Suffolk, which told many men the secrets of their hearts, which they thought no man could have told, but God only. She cut stomachers in pieces, and made them whole again; and caused divers men that spake against her delusions to go stark mad. All which things were proved, and openly by her confessed, to be done by necromancy and the deceit of the devil.

Elizabeth Barton.

O devilish illusion!

But Elizabeth Barton[6], called the holy maid of Courtop Street in Kent, passed all others in devilish devices. For she could, when she list, feign herself to be in a trance, disfigure her face, draw her mouth awry toward the one ear, feigning that she was thus tormented of Satan for the sins of the people, and delivered from his power by our blessed lady of Courtop Street, and by her led into heaven, hell, and purgatory, and there saw all the joys and pains of those places; and took upon her to prophesy of things to come, and of the king's death. This instrument of the devil drew into her confederacy, both of heresy and treason, holy monks of the Charter House, obstinate (they would be called observant) friars of Greenwich, nice nuns of Sion, black monks (both of cowls and conditions) of Christ's Church and St Austin's of Canterbury, knights, squires, learned men, priests, and many other: of which sort (whether they were blinded by her, or else of their own mere malice and hypocrisy dissembled the matter) some, by due proof made against them, were justly condemned both of heresy and treason, and suffered with the said Elizabeth Barton, according to their demerits; and some, acknowledging their own offences, were delivered by the king's pardon. This wicked woman caused a letter to be made by a monk of St Austin's of Canterbury, in golden letters, feigning the same to be delivered to her by an angel from heaven. This monster was convented both before William Warham, archbishop of Canterbury, and Thomas Wolsey, cardinal and archbishop of York: who, either because that generation of the clergy hath alway defended idolatry and superstition,
or because she knew too much of their incontinency and other wickedness of living, 77.
(for she threatened them with eternal damnation, except they repented and amended their lives,) they clearly discharged her without finding of any fault in her at all. But when the matter came to be examined by Thomas Cranmer, archbishop of Canterbury,

Read more of her in her book set forth in print, and in Hall's Chronicle.

A letter forged as though it had come from heaven.

Bishops ever have been bolsterers of idolatry.

[4 Before they tempted, (i. e. attempted), Orig. ed.]

[5 Anne Wentworth, daughter of sir Roger Wentworth, of Ipswich, Suffolk. Vid. sir Thomas More's Dialogues, Of the Veneration and Worship of Images. Pt. I. Book I. chap. xvi. col. 27.]

[6 But yet Elizabeth Barton, Orig. ed. For an account of Elizabeth Barton, the maid of Kent, and her accomplices, vid. Hall's Chronicle: The 25th year of King Henry VIII.; fol. ccxviii. 2. Ed. 1548. Burnet, Hist. Reformat. Vol. I. p. 302 et sqq. Ed. Oxford. 1829. Strype, Eccl. Memorials, Vol. I. chap. xxv. p. 271 et sqq. Ed. Oxford 1822.]

and Thomas Cromwell, then master of the rolls, they so handled the matter, that they found out the whole nest of that conspiracy: wherein was disclosed the whole number of those confederates, their books of heresy and treason, the authors and writers of the same, and of the letter feigned to be sent from heaven. All whose detestable facts, as well of idolatry, heresy, and also of treason, were so wittily and learnedly by God's word convinced at Canterbury by Doctor Heath[1], now chancellor of England, (she being present and openly confessing the same,) and also by another learned man at Paul's cross, that the most part of them, which were before by her seduced, did then utterly abhor her shameless and abominable facts.

A notable miracle.

What a crafty point of legerdemain was played about the beginning of king Edward's reign by a priest; which, being at mass, pricked his own finger, and caused it to drop upon the host; persuading the people that the host bled of itself, by the miraculous working of God, for to make the world believe the body of Christ to be as really and naturally in the sacrament as he was born of the virgin Mary his mother! For the which heinous fact, proved against him and also by him confessed, he did open penance at Paul's cross.

I will rehearse one sermon, made in queen Mary's beginning, by a momish monk, and so leave off their vain and wicked lies. A new upstart preacher, being some time a monk of Christ's church in Canterbury, stept into the pulpit in St Paul's church, saying that the very body of Christ is really and naturally in the sacrament of the altar; yea, "By God's body is it," quoth he. And because that neither oath nor perjury can prove a good argument, he proved the same by three notable miracles: the first of an horse, refusing to eat wafers so long as their caky god was among them; the second, by the devil speaking in the likeness of an horse, being conjured of a priest by God's body to tell what he was; and the third, a maid of Northgate parish in Canterbury, who, he said, in pretence to wipe her mouth, kept the host in her handkercher; and when she came home, she put the same into a pot, close covered, and spitted in another pot; and after a few days she, looking in the one pot, found a little young pretty babe about a shaftmond long, and the other pot was full of gored blood.

Christ proved really in the host by two horses; the devil speaking in one of them.

78. Here is goodly pulpit matters to prove new articles of our faith! For if the priests that told the stories of the two horses, or the maid that said that the bread was turned into a little child, or the monk that preached these shameful blasphemies, or the devil himself, who is father of lies, could lie, speaking in the horse, or in any of them; then do all these foresaid miracles prove nothing his purpose. But, O merciful God, in what a miserable state were we thine afflicted members, if it were true, which they say, being both enemies to thee and to us also, for thy truth's sake! For we would not[2] only suffer extreme miseries, as loss of our goods, good names, and the company of our dear friends in our native country; but also burn as heretics in this world, if we came in their cruel handling, and also burn eternally in the unquenchable fire of hell, if their cruel curses might take effect. Wherefore we yield thee most hearty thanks, O Father of all mercies, and to thy Son Jesus Christ our Saviour, which hast promised, for his sake and in his name, thy kingdom of heaven to all them which suffer persecution for thy righteousness' sake.

How shall we then know true visions of angels from false, true apparitions and miracles from counterfeit, but by the scripture of God, which is the rule and true measure wherewith we must try all things? as St John saith: "Believe not every spirit, but prove them whether they be of God: for many false prophets are gone out into the world. Hereby is the Spirit of God known," saith he: "every spirit which confesseth that Jesus Christ is come in the flesh is of God," &c. Whosoever therefore saith, that there is any thing that pacifieth the wrath of God, or obtaineth his favour

[1 Nicholas Heath, successively bishop of Rochester and Worcester, under Henry VIII., was deprived under Edward VI.; but, under Mary, became Archbishop of York, and Lord chancellor, after the death of Gardiner in 1555, and therefore only about three months before the death of Cranmer, for whose execution he signed the warrant. Vid. Anderson's Annals of the English Bible. Vol. I. p. 374, n. 33. Burnet, Hist. of Reform. Vol. I. Part ii. p. 139, &c.]

[2 For we should not, Orig. ed.]

and forgiveness of sins, but only Christ's death and passion, he denieth Christ to be come a Saviour in the flesh. Wherefore these angels, saints, souls of the dead, and miracles, that allow worshipping of saints by invocation and praying to them, the sacrifice of the mass for the quick and the dead, worshipping of images, pilgrimages, offerings to holy relics, to forgive sins, or to deliver the dead out of purgatory, deny Christ to be come an only Saviour by his flesh. For they make all these to be saviours from purgatory, or, at the least, coadjutors to help him in that office of salvation, and delivering those souls from sin and the pains due for the same; and so they cannot be of God, but of antichrist.

Thus I have plainly, fully, and truly, without fraud of cloaking, or colour of rhetoric and dark speech, to blind the eyes of the simple people, answered to all that I remember, which the papists do or can allege, either by writing, preaching, or reasoning, for the defence of their unwritten verities, whereupon they build so many detestable idolatries and heresies. And the same answers, if they be aptly applied and placed by a discreet and witty reader, will suffice for the answer to all that they ever have 79.
or can bring forth for the maintaining of their unwritten and uncertain verities. And yet I will not be so much wedded to mine own wit or will, but that if they be able to answer so plainly and truly to the scriptures, authors, and reasons rehearsed by me, as I have done to theirs; and to prove their doctrine of unwritten verities by as plain consent both of scriptures, ancient doctors, and as pithy arguments, as I have done mine, and set it forth in print to the judgment of the whole world, as mine is; I shall not only acknowledge mine ignorance and error, but I shall gladly return into England, recant mine heresies, openly submitting myself to such discipline and correction as they shall think meet for mine offences. But if they refuse to answer my book by writing, and, using their old trade, burn both my book and the readers thereof, let them know they shall do nothing but cut off the head of Hydra. For for every heretic, as you call them, which you shall burn, will arise many faithful and constant Christians. For "except the grain or corn of wheat die, it remaineth alone; but if it die, it bringeth forth much fruit." Wherefore I most heartily beseech the Father of heaven, of his infinite mercy, (if you be not indurate in your hearts with that sin which is irremissible, and shall never be forgiven in this world nor in the world to come, and resist the Holy Ghost, impugning the truth of God of you known, and defending and maintaining wicked doctrines, which your consciences bear record to be idolatries and heresies,) that he will mollify your stony hearts, and give you fleshy hearts; yea, rather spiritual and godly hearts, to worship him truly in spirit, according to his godly will expressed in his holy word written. And I exhort all you which fear God and be desirous to save your own souls, to flee from this whore of Babylon, and from all her detestable idolatries and heresies, not building upon[3] the sure rock of God's infallible word written, but upon the quavemire[4] of unwritten verities; whereupon whatsoever is builded forthwith either sinketh or quite overthroweth. And stand thou fast, and stay thy faith, whereupon thou shalt build all thy works, upon the strong rock of God's word, written and contained within the old testament and the new; which is able sufficiently to instruct thee in all things needful to thy salvation, and to the attainment of the kingdom of heaven. To the which I beseech the Almighty Father of heaven, of his infinite mercy and goodness, and by the merits of his only Son, our Saviour and Redeemer, Jesus Christ, through his Holy Spirit in us, bring us all. Amen.

Which is Rome.

FINIS.

[[3] Builded upon, Orig. ed.]

[[4] Qualmire, Orig. ed.; i. e. quagmire.]

[A

## COLLECTION OF TENETS

EXTRACTED FROM

# THE CANON LAW,

SHEWING

### THE EXTRAVAGANT PRETENSIONS OF THE CHURCH OF ROME[1].]

C. C. C. C. CCCXL. p. 447. MSS. Stillingfleet. Lamb. Libr. 1107.

Burnet, Hist. of Reformat. Vol. I. Book III. Part ii. n. 27. pp. 391—398. Ed. Oxon. 1829.

*Dist.* 22. *Omnes*[2]. *De Major. et obedient.: Solitæ*[3]. *Extrav. De majorit. et obedient.: Unam sanctam*[4].

He that knowledgeth not himself to be under the bishop of Rome, and that the bishop of Rome is ordained by God to have primacy over all the world, is an heretic, and cannot be saved, nor is not of the flock of Christ.

*Dist.* 10[5]. *De sententia excommunicationis: Noverit*[6]. 25. *q.* 1: *Omne*[7].

Princes' laws, if they be against the canons and decrees of the bishop of Rome, be of no force nor strength.

*Dist.* 19.[8] 20.[9] 24. *q.* 1. *A recta; Memor; Quoties; Hæc est*[10]. 25. *q.* 1. *Generali; Violatores*[11].

All the decrees of the bishop of Rome ought to be kept perpetually of every man, without any repugnance, as God's word spoken by the mouth of Peter; and whosoever

[[1] In reference to these extracts from the Canon Law, Strype says: "And one of the first things wherein he (i. e. Cranmer) shewed his good service to the church was done in the parliament, in the latter end of this year, 1533. When the supremacy came under debate, and the usurped power of the bishop of Rome was propounded, then the old collections of the archbishop did him good service; for the chief, and in a manner the whole burden of this weighty cause was laid upon his shoulders." Strype, Memorials of Abp. Cranmer, Vol. I. p. 32. Ed. Oxon. 1840. Burnet places the passing of the act, "containing some former acts for revising the Canon Law," &c. in the year 1544, and says that "Cranmer pressed this often with great vehemence, and, to shew the necessity of it, drew out a short extract of some passages in the Canon Law," which he gives in "the Collection of Records." The text follows that of Burnet's History of the Reformation, but it is corrected in many places by the MS. in the Library of Corpus Christi College, Cambridge. Dr Jenkyns suggests that "the old collections," mentioned by Strype, are probably those which are still preserved at Lambeth under the title of Archbishop Cranmer's Collection of Laws, and that "they were formed, perhaps, while he resided at Cambridge, and consist of a large number of passages, extracted at length from the canon law, and followed by that short summary of some of its most remarkable doctrines which is here printed. They were doubtless of great use," he goes on to say, "in the discussions alluded to by Strype; but that was not the only nor the first occasion, in which they supplied the archbishop with arguments. He must have already availed himself of them, when, in stating to the king his unwillingness to accept the see of Canterbury, he 'disclosed therewithal the intolerable usurpation of the pope of Rome.' See his Examination before Brokes. And he frequently recurs to them in his subsequent writings, particularly in the Answer to the Devonshire Rebels, A. D. 1549, and in his long Letter to queen Mary, in September, A. D. 1555." See Dr Jenkyns' Remains of Abp. Cranmer, Vol. II. p. 1.]

[[2] Corpus Juris Canonici. Ed. Paris. 1687. Decret. i. Pars, Dist. 22. can. i. 'Omnes.' Tom. I. p. 29.]

[[3] Id. Decretal. Gregor. IX. Lib. I. Tit. xxxiii. De majorit. et obedient. cap. vi. 'Solitæ.' Tom. II. p. 59.]

[[4] Id. Extravag. Comm. Lib. I. Tit. viii. De majorit. et obedient. cap. i. 'Unam sanctam.' Tom. II. p. 394.]

[[5] Id. Decret. i. Pars, Dist. 10. Tom. I. p. 8.]

[[6] Id. Decretal. Gregor. IX. Lib. V. Tit. 39. De sentent. excommunicat. cap. xlix. 'Noverit.' Tom. II. p. 276.]

[[7] Id. Decret. ii. Pars, Causa xxv. Quæst. 1. can. viii. 'Omne.' Tom. I. p. 345.]

[[8] Id. Decret. i. Pars, Dist. 19. Tom. I. p. 23. et sqq.]

[[9] Id. ibid. Dist. 20. Tom. I. p. 26.]

[[10] Id. Decret. ii. Pars, Causa xxiv. Quæst. 1. can. ix. 'A recta.' can. x. 'Memor.' can. xii. 'Quoties.' can. xiv. 'Hæc est.' Tom. I. p. 332.]

[[11] Id. ibid. Causa xxv. Quæst. 1. cap. xi. 'Generali.' can. v. 'Violatores.' Tom. I. p. 345.]

doth not receive them, neither availeth them the catholic faith, nor the four evangelists; but they blaspheme the Holy Ghost, and shall have no forgiveness.

25. *q.* 1. *Generali* [12].

All kings, bishops, and nobles that allow [13] or suffer the bishop of Rome's decrees in any thing to be violate, be accursed, and for ever culpable before God, as transgressors of the catholic faith.

*Dist.* 21. *Quamvis* [14], *et* 24. *q.* 1. *A recta; Memor* [15].

The see of Rome hath neither spot nor wrinkle in it, nor cannot err.

25. *q.* 1. *Ideo* [16]. *De senten. et re judicata; Ad apostolicæ* [17]. *Li.* 6, *de jurejurando* [18].

The bishop of Rome is not bound to any decrees, but he may compel, as well the clergy as laymen, to receive his decrees and canon laws.

9. *q.* 3. *Ipsi* [19]*; Cuncta* [20]*; Nemo* [21]. 3. *q.* 6*: Dudum* [22]*; Aliorum* [23]. 17. *q.* 4*: Si quis* [24]. *De baptis. et ejus effectu. Majores* [25].

The bishop of Rome hath authority to judge all men, and specially to discern the articles of the faith, and that without any council, and may assoil them that the council hath damned; but no man hath authority to judge him, nor to meddle with any thing that he hath judged, neither emperor, king, people, nor the clergy: and it is not lawful for any man to dispute of his power.

*Gr. Duo sunt* [26]. 25. *q.* 6. *Alius; Nos sanctorum; Juratos* [27]. *In Clement. de hæreticis. Ut officium* [28].

The bishop of Rome may excommunicate emperors and princes, depose them from their states, and assoil their subjects from their oath of obedience to them, and so constrain them to rebellion.

*De major. et obedient. Solitæ* [29]. *Clement. de sententia et re judicata. Pastoralis* [30].

The emperor is the bishop of Rome's subject, and the bishop of Rome may revoke the emperor's sentence in temporal causes.

*De elect. et electi potestate. Venerabilem* [31].

It belongeth to the bishop of Rome to allow or disallow the emperor after he is elected; and he may translate the empire [32] from one region to another.

---

[12 Vid. supra, n. 11.]

[13 So it appears to be in the C. C. C. MS.: in Dr Jenkyns's edition it is printed *believe*.]

[14 Id. Decret. i. Pars, Dist. 21. can. iii. 'Quamvis.' Tom. I. p. 28.] [15 Vid. supra, n. 10.]

[16 Id. Decret. ii. Pars, Causa xxv. Quæst. 1. can. xvi. 'Ideo.' Tom. I. p. 346.]

[17 Id. Sexti Decretal. Lib. II. Tit. xiv. De senten. et re judicata. cap. ii. 'Ad apostolicæ.' Tom. II. p. 309.]

[18 Id. ibid. Lib. II. Tit. xi. Jurejurando. cap. i. 'Contingit.' Tom. II. p. 308.]

[19 Id. Decret. ii. Pars, Causa ix. Quæst. 3. can. xvi. 'Ipsi.' Tom. I. p. 210.]

[20 Id. ibid. can. xvii. xviii. 'Cuncta.' Tom. I. p. 211.]

[21 Id. ibid. can. xiii. 'Nemo.' Tom. I. p. 210.]

[22 Id. ibid. Causa iii. Quæst. 6. can. ix. 'Dudum.' Tom. I. p. 180.]

[23 Id. ibid. Causa ix. Quæst. 3. can. xiv. 'Aliorum.' Tom. I. p. 210.]

[24 Id. ibid. Causa xvii. Quæst. 4. can. xxii. 'Si quis.' Tom. I. p. 282.]

[25 Id. Decretal. Gregor. IX. Lib. III. De Baptismo et ejus effect. Tit. xlii. cap. iii. 'Majores.' Tom. II. p. 194.]

[26 Id. Decret. i. Pars, Dist. 96. can. 10. 'Duo sunt.' Tom. I. p. 118.]

[27 Id. Decret. ii. Pars, Causa xv. Quæst. 6. can. iii. 'Alius.' can. iv. 'Nos sanctorum.' can. v. 'Juratos.' Tom. I. p. 260.]

[28 Id. Sexti Decretal. Lib. v. Tit. ii. De hæret. cap. ii. 'Ut officium.' Tom. II. p. 332.]

[29 Vid. p. 68. n. 3.]

[30 Id. Clementin. Lib. II. Tit. xi. De sentent. et re judicat. cap. ii. 'Pastoralis.' Tom. II. p. 358.]

[31 Id. Decretal. Gregor. IX. Lib. I. Tit. vi. De elect. et electi potest. cap. xxxiv. 'Venerabilem.' Tom. II. p. 23.]

[32 C. C. C. MS. *emperor*.]

*De supplenda negligen. prælato. Grandi*[1].

The bishop of Rome may appoint coadjutors unto princes.

*Dist.* 17. *Synodum; Regula; Nec licuit; Multis; Concilia*[2]. *Dist.* 96. *Ubinam*[3].

There can be no council of bishops without the authority of the see of Rome; and the emperor ought not[4] to be present at the council, except when matters of faith be entreating, which belong universally to every man.

2. *q.* 6[5]. *Ad Romanum.*

Nothing may be done against him that appealeth unto Rome.

9. *q.* 3: *Aliorum*[6]. *Dist.* 40: *Si Papa*[7]. *Dist.* 96: *Satis*[8].

The bishop of Rome may be judged of none but of God only; for although he neither regard his own salvation, nor no man's else, but draw down with himself innumerable people by heaps unto hell; yet may no mortal man in this world presume to reprehend him. Forsomuch as he is called God, he may be judged of no man; for God may be judged of no man.

24. *q.* 5[9].

The bishop of Rome may open and shut heaven unto men.

*Dist.* 40. *Non nos*[10].

The see of Rome receiveth holy men, or else maketh them holy.

*De pœnitentia. Dist.* 1. *Serpens*[11].

He that maketh a lie to the bishop of Rome committeth sacrilege.

*De consecrat. Dist.* 1: *De locorum. Præcepta. Ecclesia*[12]. *De elect. et electi potestate. Fundamenta*[13].

To be senator, captain, patrician, governor, or officer of Rome, none shall be elected or pointed without the express licence and special consent of the see of Rome.

*De electione et electi potestate. Venerabilem*[14].

It appertaineth to the bishop of Rome to judge which oaths ought to be kept, and which not[15].

*De jurejurand. Si vero*[16]. 15. *q.* 6: *Auctoritatem*[17].

And he may absolve subjects from their oath of fidelity, and absolve from other oaths that ought to be kept.

[[1] Id. Sexti Decretal. Lib. I. Tit. viii. De supplenda negligen. prælat. cap. ii. 'Grandi.' Tom. II. p. 297.]

[[2] Id. Decret. i. Pars, Dist. 17. can. i. 'Synodum.' can. ii. 'Regula.' can. iv. 'Nec licuit.' can. v. 'Multis.' can. vi. 'Concilia.' Tom. I. pp. 20, 21.]

[[3] Id. ibid. Dist. 96. can. iv. 'Ubinam.' Tom. I. p. 118.]

[[4] *not* wanting in C. C. C. MS.]

[[5] Id. Decret. ii. Pars, Causa ii. Quæst. 6. can. vi. 'Ad Romanum.' Tom. I. p. 162.]

[[6] Vid. p. 69, n. 22.]

[[7] Id. Decret. i. Pars, Dist. 40. can. vi. 'Si Papa.' Tom. I. p. 53.]

[[8] Id. ibid. Dist. 96. can. vii. 'Satis.' Tom. I. p. 118.]

[[9] Id. Decret. ii. Pars, Causa xxiv. Quæst. 2. can. ii. 'Legatur.' Tom. I. p. 337.]

[[10] Id. Decret. i. Pars, Dist. 40. can. i. 'Non nos.' Tom. I. p. 53.]

[[11] Id. Decret. ii. Pars, Causa xxxiii. Quæst. 3. De Pœnit. Dist. 1. can. xlvii. 'Serpens.' Tom. I. p. 399.]

[[12] Id. Decret. iii. Pars. De consecrat. Dist. 1. can. iv. 'De locorum.' can. v. 'Præcepta.' can. viii. 'Ecclesia.' Tom. I. pp. 447, 8.]

[[13] Id. Sexti. Decretal. Lib. I. Tit. vi. De elect. et electi potestat. cap. xvii. 'Fundamenta.' Tom. II. p. 291.]

[[14] Vid. p. 69, n. 30.]

[[15] *And which not*, wanting in C. C. C. MS., as is also the whole of the following article.]

[[16] Id. Decretal. Gregor. IX. Lib. II. Tit. xxiv. De jurejurando. cap. viii. 'Si vero.' Tom. II. p. 107.]

[[17] Id. Decret. ii. Pars, Causa. xv. Quæst. 6. can. ii. 'Autoritatem.' Tom. I. p. 259.]

*De foro competent. Ex tenore*[18]. *De donat. inter virum et uxorem. De prudentia*[19]. *Qui filii sunt legitimi. Per venerabilem*[20]. *De elect. et electi potestate. Fundamenta*[21]. *Extravag. de majorit. et obedient. Unam sanctam*[22]. *De judiciis. Novit*[23].

The bishop of Rome is judge in temporal things, and hath two swords, spiritual and temporal.

[*Clement.*] *de hæreticis. Multorum*[24].

The bishop of Rome[25] may give authority to arrest men, and imprison them in manacles and fetters.

*Extrav. de consuetudine. Super gentes*[26].

The bishop of Rome may compel princes to receive his legates.

*De treuga et pace. Treugas*[27].

It belongeth also to him to appoint and command peace and truce to be observed and kept, or not.

*De præbend. et dig. Dilectus*[28]. *Et li.* 6: *Licet*[29].

The collation of all spiritual promotions appertain to the bishop of Rome.

*De excessibus prælatorum. Sicut unire*[30].

The bishop of Rome may unite bishopricks together, and put one under another at his pleasure.

*Lib.* 6. *De pœnis. Felicis*[31].

In the chapter *Felicis*, *lib.* 6. *de pœnis*, is the most partial and unreasonable decree, made by Bonifacius VIII. that ever was read or heard, against them that be adversaries to any cardinal of Rome, or to any clerk, or religious man of the bishop of Rome's family.

*Dist.* 28. *Consulendum*[32]. *Dist.* 96. *Si imperator*[33]. 11. *q.* 1. *Quod clericus. Nemo; Nullus; Clericum*[34], *&c. et q.* 2. *Quod vero*[35]. *De sentent. excommunication. Si*

[[18] Id. Decretal. Gregor. IX. Lib. II. Tit. ii. De foro compet. cap. xi. 'Ex tenore.' Tom. II. p. 75.]

[[19] Id. ibid. Lib. IV. Tit. xx. De donat. inter virum et uxorem, &c. cap. iii. 'De prudentia.' Tom. II. p. 222.]

[[20] Id. ibid. Lib. IV. Tit. xvii. Qui filii sint legit. cap. xiii. 'Per venerabilem.' Tom. II. p. 219.]

[[21] Vid. p. 70. n. 12.] [[22] Vid. p. 68. n. 4.]

[[23] Id. Decretal. Gregor. IX. Lib. II. Tit. i. De judiciis. cap. xiii. 'Novit ille.' Tom. II. p. 72.]

[[24] Id. Clementin. Lib. v. Tit. iii. De hæret. cap. i. 'Multorum.' Tom. II. p. 369.]

[[25] *Rome's judge*, C. C. C. MS.]

[[26] Id. Extrav. Comm. Lib. I. Tit. i. De consuetud. cap. i. 'Super gentes.' Tom. II. p. 391.]

[[27] Id. Decretal. Gregor. IX. Lib. I. Tit. xxxiv. De treuga et pace. cap. i. 'Treugas.' Tom. II. p. 61.]

[[28] Id. ibid. Lib. III. Tit. v. De præbend. et dignitat. cap. xxvii. 'Dilectus.' Tom. II. p. 141.]

[[29] Id. Sexti Decretal. Lib. III. Tit. iv. cap. ii. Licet.' Tom. II. p. 313.]

[[30] Id. Decretal. Gregor. IX. Lib. v. Tit. xxxi. De excess. prælat. cap. viii. 'Sicut unire.' Tom. II. p. 256.]

[[31] Id. Sexti Decretal. Lib. v. Tit. ix. De pœnis. cap. v. 'Felicis.' Tom. II. p. 338.]

[[32] Id. Decret. I. Pars, Dist. xxviii. can. xvii. 'Consulendum.' Tom. I. p. 39.]

[[33] Id. ibid. Dist. 96. can. xi. 'Si imperator.' Tom. I. pp. 118, 19.]

[[34] Id. Decret. ii. Pars, Causa xi. Quæst. i. 'Quod clericus.' can. i. 'Nemo.' can. ii. 'Nullus.' can. iii. 'Clericum.' Tom. I. p. 216.]

[[35] Id. ibid. Quæst. ii. 'Quod vero.' Tom. I. p. 221.]

*judex*[1]. 2. *q.* 5: *Si quis*[2]. *De foro competent.: Nullus*[3]; *Si quis*[4]; *Ex transmissa*[5]. *De foro compet. in li.* 6. *Seculares*[6].

Laymen may not be judges to any of the clergy, nor compel them to pay their undoubted debts, but the bishops only must be their judges.

*De foro competent. Cum sit*[7]; *Licet*[8].

Rectors of churches may convent[9] such as do them wrong, whither[9] they will, before a spiritual judge, or a temporal.

*Ibidem. Ex parte; Dilecti*[10].

A layman being spoiled may convent his adversaries before a spiritual judge, whether the lord of the feod[11] consent thereto or not.

*Ibidem. Significasti*[12]: *et* 11. *q.* 1. *Placuit*[13].

A layman may commit his cause to a spiritual judge; but one of the clergy may not commit his cause to a temporal judge without the consent of the bishop.

*Ne clerici vel monachi. Secundum*[14].

Laymen may have no benefices to farm.

*De sententia excommunicationis. Noverit*[15]. *Extrav. de pœnitentiis et remiss. Etsi*[16].

All they that make or write any statutes contrary to the liberties of the church, and all princes, rulers, and counsellors, where such statutes be made, or such customs observed, and all the judges and other that put the same in execution; and where such statutes and customs have been made and observed of old time, all they that put them not out of their books, be excommunicate, and that so grievously, that they cannot be assoiled but only by the bishop of Rome.

*De immunitate ecclesiæ. Non minus; Adversus; Quia*[17]; *Quum*[18]. *et in* 6. *Clericis*[19].

The clergy to the relief of any common necessity can nothing confer without the consent of the bishop of Rome: nor it is not lawful for any layman to lay any imposition of taxes, subsidies, or any charges upon the clergy.

*Dist.* 97. *Hoc capitulo*[20]; *et* 63. *Nullus, et quæ sequuntur*[21]. *Et* 96. *Illud; et Bene quidem*[22]. *De rebus eccles. non alien. Cum laicis*[23].

Laymen may not meddle with elections of the clergy, nor with any other thing that belongeth unto them.

---

[1 Id. Sexti Decretal. Lib. v. Tit. xi. De sentent. excommunicat. cap. xii. 'Si judex.' Tom. II. p. 341.]

[2 Id. Decreti. ii. Pars, Causa ii. Quæst. 5. can. iv. 'Si quis.' Tom. I. p. 158.]

[3 Id. Decretal. Gregor. IX. Lib. II. Tit. ii. De foro compet. cap. ii. 'Nullus.' Tom. II. p. 74.]

[4 Id. ibid. cap. i. 'Si quis.' Ibid.]

[5 Id. ibid. cap. vi. 'Ex transmissa.' Ibid.]

[6 Id. Sexti Decretal. Lib. II. Tit. ii. De foro compet. cap. ii. 'Seculares.' Tom. II. p. 306.]

[7 Id. Decretal. Gregor. IX. Lib. II. Tit. ii. De foro compet. cap. viii. 'Cum sit.' Tom. II. p. 74.]

[8 Id. ibid. cap. x. 'Licet.' Tom. II. p. 75.]

[9 *convict, whether*, C. C. C. MS.]

[10 Id. ibid. cap. xv. 'Ex parte.' Ibid. cap. xvii. 'Dilecti.' Tom. II. p. 76.]

[11 i. e. Fee, tenure. C. C. C. MS. reads *fee*.]

[12 Id. ibid. cap. xviii. 'Significasti.' Tom. II. p. 76.]

[13 Id. Decret. ii. Pars, Causa xi. Quæst. 1. can. xi. 'Placuit.' Tom. I. p. 217.]

[14 Id Decretal. Gregor. IX. Lib. III. Tit. i. Ne clerici vel monachi. cap. vi. 'Secundum.' Tom. II. p. 199.]

[15 Vid. p. 68. n. 6.]

[16 Id. Extravag. Commun. Lib. v. Tit. ix. De pœnitent. et remiss. cap. iii. 'Etsi.' Tom. II. p. 423.]

[17 Id. Decretal. Gregor. IX. Lib. III. Tit. xlix. De immunitate eccles. cap. iv. 'Non minus.' cap. vii. 'Adversus.' cap. viii. 'Quia.' Tom. II. pp. 197, 8. Et Sexti Decretal. Lib. III. Tit. xxiii. cap. i. Tom. II. p. 327.]

[18 Id. ibid. Lib. III. Tit. xlix. cap. v. 'Cum.' Tom. II. p. 198.]

[19 Id. Sexti Decretal. Lib. III. Tit. xxiii. De immunit. eccles. &c. cap. iii. 'Clericis.' Tom. II. p. 327.]

[20 Id. Decret. i. Pars, Dist. 97. 'Hoc capitulo.' Tom. I. p. 120.]

[21 Id. ibid. Dist. 63. can. i. 'Nullus.' Tom. I. p. 83.]

[22 Id. ibid. Dist. 96. 'Illud.' can. i. 'Bene quidem.' Tom. I. p. 117.]

[23 Id. Decretal. Gregor. IX. Lib. III. Tit. xiii. De rebus eccl. aliend. cap. xii. 'Cum laicis.' Tom. II. p. 153.]

*De jurejurando. Nimis*[24].

The clergy ought to give no oath of fidelity to their temporal governors, except they have temporalities of them.

*Dist.* 96. *Bene quidem*[25]. 12. *q.* 2. *Apostolicos*[26]; *Quisquis*[27].

The goods of the church may in no wise be alienated, but whosoever receiveth or buyeth of them, is bound to restitution; and if the church have any ground which is little or nothing worth, yet it shall not be given to the prince; and if the prince would needs buy it, the sale shall be void and of no strength.

12. *q.* 2. *Non liceat*[28].

It is not lawful for the bishop of Rome to alienate or mortgage any lands of the church for any manner of necessity, except it be houses in cities, which be very chargeable to support and maintain.

*Dist.* 96. *Quis*[29]; *Nunquam*[30]. 2. *q.* 7. *Accusatio*[31]. 11. *q.* 1. *Continua; Nullus; Testimonium; Relatum; Experientiæ; Si quisquam; Si quæ; Sicut; Statuimus; Nullus; De persona; Si quis*[32].

Princes ought to obey the bishops, and the decrees of the church, and to submit their heads unto the bishops, and not to be judges over the bishops; for the bishops ought to be forborne, and to be judged of no laymen.

*De major. et obedient. Solitæ*[33].

Kings and princes ought not to set bishops beneath them, but reverently to rise against them, and assign them an honourable seat by them.

11. *q.* 1. *Quæcumque*[34]; *Relatum; Si quæ*[35]; *Omnes; Volumus; Placuit*[36].

All manner of causes, whatsoever they be, spiritual or temporal, ought to be determined and judged by the spiritualty.

*Ibidem. Omnes*[37].

No judge ought to refuse the witnesses of one bishop, although he be but alone.

*De hæreticis. Ad abolendam*[38]. *Et in Clementinis. Ut officium*[39].

Whosoever teacheth or thinketh of the sacraments otherwise than the see of Rome doth teach and observe, and all they that the same see doth judge heretics, be excommunicate. And the bishop of Rome may compel by an oath all rulers and other people

---

[[24] Id. ibid. Lib. II. Tit. xxiv. De jurejurando. cap. xxx. 'Nimis.' Tom. II. p. 111.]

[[25] Vid. p. 72. n. 22.]

[[26] Id. Decret. ii. Pars, Causa xii. Quæst. 2. can. xiii. 'Apostolicos.' Tom. I. p. 237.]

[[27] Id. ibid. can. xix. 'Quisquis.' Tom. I. p. 238.]

[[28] Id. ibid. can. xx. 'Non liceat.' Ibid.]

[[29] Id. Decret. i. Pars, Dist. 96. can. ix. 'Quis.' Tom. I. p. 118.]

[[30] Id. ibid. can. xii. 'Numquam.' Tom. I. p. 119.]

[[31] Id. Decret. ii. Pars, Causa ii. Quæst. 7. can. xv. 'Accusatio.' Tom. I. p. 168.]

[[32] Id. ibid. Causa xi. Quæst. 1. can. v. 'Continua.' can. vi. 'Nullus.' can. ix. 'Testimonium.' can. xiv. 'Relatum.' can. xv. 'Experientiæ.' can. xvi. 'Si quisquam.' can. xxvi. 'Si quæ.' can. xxx. 'Sicut.' can. xxxi. 'Statuimus.' can. xxxiii. 'Nullus.' can. xxxviii. 'De persona.' can. xlv. 'Si quis.' Tom. I. pp. 216—220.]

[[33] Vid. p. 68. n. 3. p. 69. n. 28.]

[[34] Id. Decret. ii. Pars, Causa. xi. Quæst. i. can. vii. 'Quæcumque.' Tom. I. p. 216.]

[[35] 'Relatum;' 'Si quæ.' Vid. supra. n. 32.]

[[36] Id. Decret. ii. Pars, Causa xi. can. xxxvi. 'Omnes.' can. xxxvii. 'Volumus.' can. xliii. 'Placuit.' Tom. I. pp. 219, 20.]

[[37] 'Omnes.' Vid. supra. n. 36.]

[[38] Id. Decretal. Gregor. IX. Lib. v. Tit. vii. De hæret. cap. ix. 'Ad abolendam.' Tom. II. p. 238.]

[[39] Id. Sexti Decretal. Lib. v. Tit. ii. De hæret. cap. xi. 'Ut officium.' Tom. II. p. 332.]

to observe, and cause to be observed, whatsoever the see of Rome shall ordain concerning heresy, and the fautors thereof; and who will not obey, he may deprive them of their dignities.

*Clement. de reliq. et venerat. sanctorum. Si Dominum*[1]. *Extravag. de reliq. et venerat. sanctorum. Cum præ excelsa*[2]. *De pœnitent. et remiss. Antiquorum. et Clemen. Unigenitus; Quemadmodum*[3].

We obtain remission of sin by observing of certain [feasts, and certain][4] pilgrimages in the jubilee, and other prescribed times, by virtue of the bishop of Rome's pardons.

*De pœnitentiis et remissionibus extravag. ca.* 5. *Et si dominici*[5].

Whosoever offendeth the liberties of the church, or doth violate any interdiction that cometh from Rome, or conspireth against the person or state of the bishop of Rome or his see; or by any ways offendeth, disobeyeth or rebelleth against the said bishop or see; or that killeth a priest, or offendeth personally against a bishop or other prelate; or invadeth, spoileth, withholdeth, or wasteth lands belonging to the church of Rome, or to any other church immediately subjected to the same; or whosoever invadeth any pilgrims that go to Rome, or any suitors to the court of Rome, or that let the devolution of causes unto that court, or that put any new charges or impositions real or personal upon any church or ecclesiastical person; and generally, all other that offend in the causes contained in the bull[6] which is usually published by the bishops of Rome upon Maundy Thursday; all these can be assoiled by no priest, bishop, archbishop, nor by none other, but only by the bishop of Rome, [or by his express licence][4].

24. *q.* 3: *Si quis*[7].

Robbing of the clergy, and poor men, appertaineth unto the judgment of the bishops.

23. *q.* 5. *Excommunicatorum*[8].

He is [no][4] manslayer which slayeth a man which is excommunicate.

*Dist.* 63. *Tibi Domino*[9]. *De sententia excommunicationis. Si judex*[10].

Here may be added[11] to the most tyrannical and abominable oaths which the bishop of Rome exacts of the emperors; *in Clement. de jurejurando. Romani*[12]. *Dist.* 63. *Tibi domino*[13].

*De consecrat. Dist.* 1. *Sicut*[14].

It is better not to consecrate, than to consecrate in a place not hallowed.

*De consecrat. Dist.* 5: *De his; Manus: Ut jejuni*[15].

Confirmation, if it be ministered by any other than a bishop, is of no value, nor is no sacrament of the church: also confirmation is more to be had in reverence than baptism; and no man by baptism can be a christian man without confirmation.

---

[[1] Id. Clementin. Lib. III. Tit. xvi. De reliq. et venerat. sanct. cap. i. 'Si Dominum.' Tom. II. p. 367.]

[[2] Id. Extravag. Comm. Lib. III. Tit. xii. De reliq. et venerat. sanct. cap. i. 'Cum præ excelsa.' Tom. II. p. 414.]

[[3] Id. ibid. Lib. v. Tit. ix. De pœnit. et remiss. cap. i. 'Antiquorum.' cap. ii. 'Unigenitus.' cap. iv. 'Quemadmodum.' Tom. II. pp. 423, 4.]

[[4] Wanting in the C. C. C. MS.]

[[5] Id. ibid. cap. v. 'Et si dominici.' Ibid.]

[[6] The bull, 'In cœna Domini.']

[[7] Id. Decret. ii. Pars, Causa xxiv. Quæst. iii. can. xxi. 'Si quis.' Tom. I. p. 341.]

[[8] Id. ibid. Causa xxiii. Quæst. v. can. xlvii. 'Excommunicatorem.' Tom. I. p. 324.]

[[9] Id. Decret. i. Pars, Dist. 63 can. xxxii. 'Tibi domino.' (Constitutio Othonis. An. 960. in Germania). Tom. I. p. 87.]

[[10] Id. Sexti Decretal. Lib. v. Tit. xi. De sentent. excommanicat. cap. xii. 'Si judex.' Tom. II. p. 341.]

[[11] In the C. C. C. MS. is a mark of abbreviation, perhaps intended for *adverted* or *alluded*.]

[[12] Id. Clementin. Lib. II. Tit. ix. De jurejurando. cap. i. 'Romani.' Tom. II. pp. 356, 7.]

[[13] Vid. supra. n. 7.]

[[14] Id. Decret. iii. Pars. De consecrat. Dist. 1. can. xi. 'Sicut.' Tom. I. p. 448.]

[[15] Id. ibid. Dist. 5. can. iii. 'De his.' can. iv. 'Manus.' can. vi. 'Ut jejuni.' Tom. I. p. 483.]

*De pœnitent. Dist. 1. Multiplex*[16].

A penitent man can have no remission of his sins, but by supplication of the priest.

[17] The bishop of Rome allegeth falsely to maintain his usurped power these scriptures following, with many other:

In the chapter *Unam sanctam*[18], he abuseth to that purpose this text, *Pasce oves meas;* and this also, *Unum est ovile et unus pastor;* and, *Ecce duo gladii hic;* et, *Converte gladium tuum in vaginam;* et, *Quæcunque sunt, a Deo ordinatæ sunt;* et, *Ecce constitui te hodie super gentes et regna;* et, *Spiritualis homo judicat omnia, ipse autem a nemine judicatur;* et, *Quodcunque ligaveris super terram, &c.;* et, *In principio creavit Deus cœlum et terram.* John xxi. 15–17. John x. 16. Luke xxii. 38. Matt. xxvi. 52. Rom. xiii. 1. Jer. i. 10. 1 Cor. ii. 15. Matt. xvi. 19. Gen. i. 1.

In the chapter *Solitæ*[19], *De major. et obed.*, he abuseth this text, *Subditi estote omni humanæ creaturæ propter Deum, sive regi tanquam præcellenti, sive ducibus, &c.;* also this text, *Ecce constitui te super gentes et regna, &c.;* also this, *Fecit Deus duo luminaria magna in firmamento cœli, luminare majus, &c.;* also, *Pasce oves meas;* et, *Quodcunque ligaveris super terram, &c.* 1 Pet. ii. 13. Jer. i. 10. Gen. i. 16. John xxi. 15. Matt. xvi. 19.

In the chapter *Per venerabilem*[20], *Qui filii sunt legit.*, he abuseth and false corrupteth this text, *Si difficile et ambiguum apud te judicium esse perspexeris inter sanguinem et sanguinem, &c.*, leaving out these words, *secundum legem Dei:* also he abuseth this text, *Nescitis quoniam angelos judicabimus? quanto magis secularia!* Deut. xvii. 8. 1 Cor. vi. 3.

---

[[16] Id. Decret. ii. Pars, Causa xxxiii. Quæst. iii. De penitent. Dist. 1. can. xlix. 'Multiplex.' Tom. I. p. 399.]

[[17] "These remarks on the papal abuses of scripture follow the extracts in the original manuscript at Lambeth, but are not printed by Burnet. The latter part of them is in Cranmer's own handwriting." Jenkyns' Remains of Abp. Cranmer, Vol. II. p. 9.]

[[18] Vid. p. 68. n. 4.]

[[19] Ibid. n. 3. et p. 69. n. 28.]

[[20] Vid. p. 71. n. 18.]

# [SUBSTANCE OF A SPEECH

DELIVERED BY

# CRANMER,

## ABOUT THE YEAR 1534, ON THE AUTHORITY OF THE POPE, AND OF GENERAL COUNCILS[1].]

---

Burnet, Hist. of Reformat. Vol. I. p. 353. Ed. Oxon. 1829.

"I HAVE seen a long speech of Cranmer's, written by one of his secretaries. It was spoken soon after the parliament had passed the acts[2] formerly mentioned, for it relates to them as lately done: it was delivered either in the house of lords, the upper house of convocation, or at the council-board; but I rather think it was in the house of lords, for it begins, "My lords." The matter of it does so much concern the business of reformation, that I know the reader will expect I should set down the heads of it. It appears he had been ordered to inform the house about these things. The preamble of his speech runs upon this conceit:"

That as rich men, flying from their enemies, carry away all they can with them, and what they cannot take away they either hide or destroy it; so the court of Rome had destroyed so many ancient writings, and hid the rest, having carefully preserved every thing that was of advantage to them, that it was not easy to discover what they had so artificially concealed: therefore in the canon law some honest truths were yet to be found, but so mislaid, that they are not placed where one might expect them; but are to be met with in some other chapters, where one would least look for them. And many more things, said by the ancients of the see of Rome and against their authority, were lost, as appears by the fragments yet remaining. He shewed that many of the ancients called every thing which they thought well done, "of divine institution," by a large extent of the phrase; in which sense the passages of many fathers, that magnified the see of Rome, were to be understood.

Then he shewed for what end general councils were called; to declare the faith, and reform errors: not that ever any council was truly general, for even at Nice there were no bishops almost but out of Egypt, Asia, and Greece; but they were called general, because the emperor summoned them, and all Christendom did agree to their definitions, which he proved by several authorities: therefore, though there were many more bishops in the council of Arimini, than at Nice or Constantinople, yet the one was not received as a general council, and the others were: so that it was not the number nor authority of the bishops, but the matter of their decisions, which made them be received with so general a submission.

As for the head of the council: St Peter and St James had the chief direction of the council of the apostles, but there were no contests then about headship. Christ named no head; which could be no more called a defect in him, than it was one in God, that had named no head to govern the world. Yet the church found it convenient to have one over them; so archbishops were set over provinces. And though St Peter had been head of the apostles, yet as it is not certain that he was ever in Rome, so it does not appear that he had his headship for Rome's sake, or that he left it there; but he was made head for his faith, and not for the dignity of any see: therefore

---

[[1] A copy of this speech is said by Burnet to exist among bishop Stillingfleet's manuscripts. But those which are now in the library at Lambeth do not contain it. "Neither can it be discovered in Marsh's library at Dublin, where some of the bishop's books are preserved." See Dr Jenkyns' Remains of Abp. Cranmer, Vol. II. p. 11.]

[[2] "For declaring the king's supremacy, for confirming the oath of succession, for granting the first-fruits and tenths to the king, for appointing suffragan bishops; all passed in the session of November and December, 1534." Dr Jenkyns.]

the bishops of Rome could pretend to nothing from him, but as they followed his faith; and Liberius, and some other bishops there, had been condemned for heresy; and if, according to St James, faith be to be tried by works, the lives of the popes for several ages gave shrewd presumptions that their faith was not good. And though it were granted that such a power was given to the see of Rome, yet by many instances he shewed that positive precepts, in a matter of that nature, were not for ever obligatory. And therefore Gerson wrote a book, *De Auferibilitate Papæ:* so that if a pope with the cardinals be corrupted, they ought to be tried by a general council, and submit to it. St Peter gave an account of his baptizing Cornelius, when he was questioned about it. So Damasus, Sixtus, and Leo, purged themselves of some scandals.

Then he shewed how corrupt the present pope was, both in his person and government, for which he was abhorred even by some of his cardinals, as himself had heard and seen at Rome. It is true, there was no law to proceed against a vicious pope, for it was a thing not foreseen, and thought scarcely possible; but new diseases required new remedies: and if a pope that is a heretic may be judged in a council, the same reason would hold against a simoniacal, covetous, and impious pope, who was salt that had lost its savour. And by several authorities he proved, that every man who lives so, is thereby out of the communion of the church; and that, as the preeminence of the see of Rome flowed only from the laws of men, so there was now good cause to repeal these: for the pope, as was said in the council of Basil, was only vicar of the church, and not of Christ; so he was accountable to the church. The council of Constance, and the divines of Paris, had, according to the doctrine of the ancient church, declared the pope to be subject to a general council, which many popes in former ages had confessed. And all that the pope can claim, even by the canon law, is, only to call and preside in a general council; but not to overrule it, or have a negative vote in it.

The power of councils did not extend to princes, dominions, or secular matters, but only to points of faith, which they were to declare; and to condemn heretics: nor were their decrees laws, till they were enacted by princes. Upon this he enlarged much, to shew that though a council did proceed against a king, (with which they then threatened the king,) that their sentence was of no force, as being without their sphere. The determination of councils ought to be well considered and examined by the scriptures; and in matters indifferent men ought to be left to their freedom. He taxed the severity of Victor's proceedings against the churches of the East about the day of Easter: and concluded, that, as a member of the body is not cut off, except a gangrene comes in it; so no part of the church ought to be cut off, but upon a great and inevitable cause. And he very largely shewed, with what moderation and charity the church should proceed even against those that held errors. And the standard of the council's definitions should only be taken from the scriptures, and not from men's traditions.

He said, some general councils had been rejected by others; and it was a tender point, how much ought to be deferred to a council: some decrees of councils were not at all obeyed. The divines of Paris held, that a council could not make a new article of faith, that was not in the scriptures. And as all God's promises to the people of Israel had this condition implied within them, If they kept his commandments; so he thought the promises to the christian church had this condition in them, If they kept the faith. Therefore he had much doubting in himself as to general councils; and he thought that only the word of God was the rule of faith, which ought to take place in all controversies of religion. The scriptures were called canonical, as being the only rule of the faith of Christians; and these, by appointment of the ancient council, were only to be read in the churches. The fathers SS. Ambrose, Jerome, and Austin, did in many things differ from one another; but always appealed to the scriptures, as the common and certain standard. And he cited some remarkable passage out of St Austin, to shew what difference he put between the scriptures and all the other writings even of the best and holiest fathers. But when all the fathers agreed in the exposition of any place of scripture, he acknowledged he looked on that as flowing from the Spirit of God; and it was a most dangerous thing to be wise in our own conceit: therefore he thought councils ought to found their decisions on the word of God, and those expositions of it that had been agreed on by the doctors of the church.

Then he discoursed very largely what a person a judge ought to be: he must not be partial, nor a judge in his own cause, nor so much as sit on the bench when it is tried, lest his presence should overawe others. Things also done upon a common error cannot bind, when the error upon which they were done comes to be discovered; and all human laws ought to be changed, when a public visible inconvenience follows them. From which he concluded, that the pope, being a party, and having already passed his sentence, in things which ought to be examined by a general council, could not be a judge, nor sit in it. Princes also, who, upon a common mistake, thinking the pope head of the church, had sworn to him, finding that this was done upon a false ground, may pull their neck out of his yoke, as every man may make his escape out of the hands of a robber. And the court of Rome was so corrupt, that a pope, though he meant well, as Hadrian[1] did, yet could never bring any good design to an issue; the cardinals and the rest of that court being so engaged to maintain their corruptions.

---

[[1] i.e. Adrian. VI. A.D. 1522 to Sept. 1523. Vid. Mosheim's Eccl. Hist. Vol. III. p. 584. Ed. Lond. 1845.]

## [A SPEECH

### DELIVERED AT AN ASSEMBLY OF BISHOPS, 1536[2].]

It beseemeth not men of learning and gravity to make much babbling and brawling about bare words, so that we agree in the very substance and effect of the matter. For to brawl about words is the property of sophisters and such as mean deceit and subtilty, which delight in the debate and dissension of the world, and in the miserable state of the church; and not of them which should seek the glory of Christ, and should study for the unity and quietness of the church. There be weighty controversies now moved and put forth, not of ceremonies and light things, but of the true understanding and of the right difference of the law and of the gospel; of the manner and way how sins be forgiven; of comforting doubtful and wavering consciences, by what means they may be certified that they please God, seeing they feel the strength of the law accusing them of sin; of the true use of the sacraments, whether the outward work of them doth justify man, or whether we receive our justification by faith. Item, which be the good works, and the true service and honour which pleaseth God: and whether the choice of meats, the difference of garments, the vows of monks and priests, and other traditions which have no word of God to confirm them, whether these, I say, be right good works, and such as make a perfect christian man, or no. Item, whether vain service, and false honouring of God, and man's traditions, do bind men's consciences, or no. Finally, whether the ceremony of confirmation, of orders, and of annealing, and such other (which cannot be proved to be institute of Christ, nor have any word in them to certify us of remission of sins,) ought to be called sacraments, and to be compared with baptism and the supper of the Lord, or no. Foxe, p. 1182. Ed. 1583.

These be no light matters, but even the principal points of our christian religion. Wherefore we contend not about words and titles, but about high and earnest matters. Christ saith, "Blessed be the peace-makers, for they shall be called the sons of God." Matt. v. And Paul, writing unto Timothy, commanded bishops to avoid brawling and contention about words, which be profitable to nothing but unto the subversion and destruction of the hearers; and monisheth him specially, that he should resist with the scriptures, when any man disputeth with him of the faith: and he addeth a cause, whereas he saith: "Doing this thou shalt preserve both thyself, and also them which hear thee." 1 Tim. iv. Now if ye will follow these counsellors, Christ and Paul, all contention and brawling about words must be set apart, and ye must stablish a godly and a perfect unity and concord out of the scripture. Wherefore in this disputation we must first agree of the number of sacraments, and what a sacrament doth signify in the holy scripture; and when we call baptism and the supper of the Lord sacraments of the gospel, what we mean thereby. I know right well that St Ambrose and other authors call the washing of the disciples' feet, and other things, sacraments; which I am sure you yourselves would not suffer to be numbered among the other sacraments.

[[2] This speech is printed from Foxe's Acts and Monuments, and was delivered by Cranmer at an assembly of bishops, appointed by Henry VIII. to "determine those things which pertained unto religion." The whole of the discussion is related in Foxe, and an abridged statement of it is given in Burnet, Hist. Reformat. (Vol. I. p. 429. et sqq. Ed. Oxon. 1829.) Crumwell presided as vicar-general; and those who took part in favour of the reform of abuses, were, besides the president, Cranmer, Fox, bishop of Hereford, and "one Alexander Alesse, a Scotchman, much esteemed for his learning and piety, whom Cranmer entertained at Lambeth," and whom Crumwell brought with him to give his opinion respecting the sacraments. Stokesley, bishop of London, replied to him, attempting to maintain the opposite argument. The articles of 1536, about religion, resulted from this discussion. See Foxe's Acts and Monuments, pp. 1181—1183. Ed. 1583.]

SOME

# QUERIES CONCERNING CONFIRMATION,

WITH THE ANSWERS WHICH WERE GIVEN TO THEM BY

# CRANMER[1].

---

## THE JUDGMENT OF CRANMER, ARCHBISHOP OF CANTERBURY.

Cotton Lib. Cleop. E. v. fol. 83. Strype, Eccl. Memor. App. Vol. I. n. 88. Ed. Oxon. 1822. Burnet, Hist. of Reformat. Addend. Vol. I. n. 3. Ed. Oxon. 1822.

Whether confirmation be instituted by Christ?

*Respon.* There is no place in scripture that declareth this sacrament to be institute of Christ.

First, for the places alleged for the same be no institutions, but acts and deeds of the apostles.

Second, these acts were done by a special gift given to the apostles for the confirmation of God's word at that time.

Thirdly, the said special gift doth not now remain with the successors of the apostles.

What is the external sign?

The church useth *chrisma* for the exterior sign, but the scripture maketh no mention thereof.

What is the efficacy of this sacrament?

The bishop, in the name of the church, doth invocate the Holy Ghost to give strength and constancy, with other spiritual gifts, unto the person confirmed; so that the efficacy of this sacrament is of such value as is the prayer of the bishop made in the name of the church.

*Hæc respondeo, salvo semper eruditiorum et ecclesiæ orthodoxæ judicio.*

---

[[1] Burnet says this paper was written with Cranmer's hand. Hist. of Reformat. Vol. I. Pt. II. p. 479. Strype, however, states, "This is writ (i.e. Hæc respondeo, &c.) with the archbishop's own hand; the rest above is the hand of his secretary." Eccl. Mem. Vol. I. Pt. II. pp. 349, 50.]

# INJUNCTIONS

GIVEN BY

# THOMAS ARCHBISHOP OF CANTERBURY

## TO THE PARSONS, VICARS, AND OTHER CURATES, IN HIS VISITATION KEPT (SEDE VACANTE[2]) WITHIN THE DIOCESE OF HEREFORD, ANNO DOMINI 1538.

---

### I.

First; That ye and every one of you shall, with all your diligence and faithful obedience, observe, and cause to be observed, all and singular the king's highness' injunctions, by his grace's commissaries given in such places as they in times past have visited.

Regist. Cranm. fol. 96. b. fol. 97. Burnet, Hist. of Reformat. Append. Vol. I. Book III. n. 12. pp. 285,6. Ed. Oxon. 1829.

### II.

*Item;* That ye and every one of you shall have, by the first day of August next coming, as well a whole bible in Latin and English, or at the least a new testament of both the same languages, as the copies of the king's highness' injunctions.

### III.

*Item;* That ye shall every day study one chapter of the said bible, or new testament, conferring the Latin and English together, and to begin at the first part of the book, and so to continue until the end of the same.

### IV.

*Item;* That ye, nor none of you, shall discourage any layman from the reading of the bible in Latin or English, but encourage them to it, admonishing them that they so read it, for reformation of their own life and knowledge of their duty; and that they be not bold or presumptuous in judging of matters afore they have perfect knowledge.

### V.

*Item;* That ye, both in your preaching and secret confession, and all other works and doings, shall excite and move your parishioners unto such works as are commanded expressly of God, for the which God shall demand of them a strait reckoning; and all other works which men do of their own will or devotion, to teach your parishioners, that they are not to be so highly esteemed as the other; and that for the not doing of them God will not ask any account.

---

[2 "Fox, bishop of Hereford, died May 8, 1538. Boner was elected to succeed him Nov. 27 of the same year. In the interval Cranmer deputed Hugh Coren, prebendary of Hereford, to visit the diocese, and promulgate these Injunctions. Boner was translated to London before consecration, and the see of Hereford was not permanently filled till Skyp was elected, Oct. 24, 1539. On his death, in 1552, the custody of the spiritualities was again committed to Hugh Coren, then dean, in conjunction with Richard Cheney, archdeacon. Strype, Mem. of Abp. Cranmer, Vol. I. pp. 70, 268. Ed. Oxford, 1840. Nicolas, Synopsis of the Peerage." Jenkyns' Remains of Abp. Cranmer, Vol. II. p. 19.]

VI.

*Item;* That ye, nor none of you, suffer no friar or religious man to have any cure or service within your churches or cures, except they be lawfully dispensed withal, or licensed by the ordinary.

VII.

*Item;* That ye and every one of you do not admit any young man or woman to receive the sacrament of the altar, which never received it before, until that he or she openly in the church, after mass, or evening song, upon the holy-day, do recite in the vulgar tongue the *Pater Noster*, the Creed, and the Ten Commandments.

VIII.

*Item;* That ye and every one of you shall two times in a quarter declare to your parishioners the band of matrimony, and what great danger it is to all men that useth their bodies but with such persons as they lawfully may by the law of God. And to exhort in the said times your parishioners, that they make no privy contracts, as they will avoid the extreme pain of the laws used within the king's realm by his grace's authority.

# CORRECTIONS

OF THE

# INSTITUTION OF A CHRISTIAN MAN,

BY

# HENRY VIII.[1]

## WITH ARCHBISHOP CRANMER'S ANNOTATIONS.

[It is to be observed that the passages in small Roman type are extracted from the *Institution*, &c.; the marginal remarks in Italic are the Corrections proposed by Henry VIII. applying to the passages in the text marked by *. The Annotations of Cranmer are in larger type, connected with the King's Corrections by the numerals added to the latter and prefixed to the former; and they are here placed so as to follow immediately after the passages they notice.]

*The Institution of a Christian Man*, pp. 30, 1. (edit. Oxf. 1825.) I believe also and profess, that this God and this Father is almighty, that is to say, that his power and might excelleth incomparably all the other powers in heaven and earth: and that all other powers, which be in heaven, earth, or hell, be nothing as of themselves, but have all their might, force, and strength of him only, and be all subject unto his power, and be ruled and governed[a] *thereby,* and cannot resist or let the same[b].

[a] *by his ordinate power.* i.
[b] *but by his grace.* ii.

### *Annotations upon the King's book*[2].

C. C. C. C. MSS. CIV. p. 241.

I believe in God, the Father Almighty, Maker of heaven and earth.
And in Jesu Christ his only Son our Lord:
Which was conceived by the Holy Ghost, born of the Virgin Mary:
He suffered under Pontius Pilate, and was crucified, died, and was buried, and descended into hell:
The third day he arose again from death:
He ascended into heaven, and sitteth upon the right hand of God:
From thence he shall come to judge both quick and dead.
I believe in the Holy Ghost:
And that there is an holy catholic church:
A communion of saints, remission of sins:
And that there shall be resurrection of the body:
And life everlasting. Amen.

This *Credo* I have translated as nigh as I can conveniently, word for word, according to the Latin.

[[1] Dr Jenkyns has printed these Corrections (Vol. II. p. 21. et sqq.) "as a necessary introduction to Cranmer's Annotations upon them," and states that "they are taken from a copy of the Institution formerly belonging to Rawlinson, and now in the Bodleian library," as well as that Rawlinson believed them to have been written by Cranmer; but that Lewis of Margate, in a letter still preserved, clearly proved, that, supposing the Annotations on the King's Book, attributed to the archbishop, to be genuine, these Corrections, instead of being those which he made, must be those on which he commented; and that he further expressed his opinion, that Rawlinson's copy of The Institution was the identical Book on which Cranmer drew up his remarks. Dr Jenkyns thinks that in this conjecture he seems to have gone too far. "The probability is," he says, "that these are Henry VIII.'s rough memoranda, which were afterwards transcribed fairly, and submitted, with some additions, to Cranmer's judgment. They are written chiefly by the King's own hand, and it would seem in his own copy; for on the inside of the cover appears this order: 'The king's commandment is that I should not be had out of the privy chamber.'" They are here printed from Dr Jenkyns' Remains of Cranmer, with most of his notes; but they are differently arranged, so as to present the whole at one view to the reader. They have been collated with the copy in the Bodleian Library, and also corrected by it.]

[[2] The Annotations are printed from the C. C. C. MSS. The title only is in Cranmer's hand, the Annotations themselves being a copy by a secretary. Extracts were printed by Strype, Mem. of Abp. Cranmer, p. 137, and Appendix, Num. xxxi. p. 757, and the whole in the "Fathers of the English Church:" but the editor of the latter work, as well as Strype, supposed them to refer to the "Necessary Doctrine," generally known as the "King's Book," while the "Institution" was called the "Bishops' Book." There is some doubt respecting the time when they were written, Lewis stating them to have appeared in 1538, and Strype, in 1542, but the former date seems the more probable.]

i. "By his ordinate power." This word "ordinate power" obscureth the sentence in the understanding of them that be simple and unlearned; and among the learned it gendereth contention and disputation, rather than it any thing edifieth. Therefore meseemeth it better and more plain as it is in the print; or else to say, "By his ordinance." For the scripture speaketh simply and plainly: *Potestati ejus quis resistit?* And, *Omnia quæcunque voluit fecit.*

ii. "But by his grace." It seemeth these words were better out; for God giveth not his grace to let his own power and ordinance.

*Inst.* pp. 31, 2. And I believe also and profess, that among his other creatures he did create and make me, and did give unto me this my soul, my life, my body, with all the members that I have, great and small, and all the wit, reason, knowledge, and understanding that I have; and finally, all the other outward substance, possessions, and things that I have or can have in this world[c].

And I believe also and profess, that he is my very God, my Lord, and my Father, and that I am his servant and his own son by adoption and grace, and[d] *the right inheritor* of his kingdom; and that it proceedeth and cometh of his mere goodness only, without all my desert, that I am in this life preserved and kept from dangers and perils[e], and that I am sustained, nourished, fed[f], clothed, and that I have health, tranquillity, rest, peace, *or any[g]* other thing necessary for this corporal life[h]. I knowledge also and confess, that he *suffereth[i]* and causeth the sun, the moon, the stars, the day, the night, the air, the fire, the water, the land, the sea, the fowls, the fishes, the beasts, and all the fruits of the earth, to serve me for my profit and my necessity.

And in like manner I confess and knowledge, that all bodily sickness and adversity, which do fortune unto me in this world, *[k] be sent unto me by his hand and his visitation, and that he punisheth me not* to destroy me, but only to save me, and to reduce me again by penance unto the right way of his laws and his religion.

[c] *only by his sufferance.* iii.
[d] *as long as I persevere in his precepts and laws, one of the right inheritors.* iv.
[e] *by his grace and mercy.* v.
[f] *and.*
[g] *and all.*
[h] *by his ordinance.* vi.
[i] *ordained.* vii.
[k] *be sometime suffered by him, and sometime sent by his visitation, and that when he punisheth me he doth not punish.* viii.

iii. "Only by his sufferance." This word "sufferance" diminisheth the goodness of God, and agreeth not with the three verbs to whom it is referred, *create*, *make*, and *give*; for these three verbs import more than sufferance; and all the things that be here spoken of, be good and none of them evil, and therefore we may undoubtedly say, that we have them of God's gift, and by his liberal benefit.

iv. "As long as I persevere in his precepts and laws, one of the right inheritors of his kingdom." This book speaketh of the pure christian faith unfeigned, which is without colour, as well in heart, as in mouth. He that hath this faith, converteth from his sin, repenteth him, that he like *filius prodigus* vainly consumed his will, reason, wits, and other goods, which he received of the mere benefit of his heavenly Father, to his said Father's displeasure; and applieth himself wholly to please him again, and trusteth assuredly, that for Christ's sake he will and doth remit his sin, withdraweth his indignation, delivereth him from hell, from the power of the infernal spirits, taketh him to his mercy, and maketh him his own son and his own heir: and he hath also the very christian hope, that after this life he shall reign ever with Christ in his kingdom. For St Paul saith: *Si filii sumus, et hæredes; hæredes quidem Dei, cohæredes autem Christi.*

This is the very pure christian faith and hope, which every good christian man ought to profess, believe, and trust, and to say of himself, even as Job said: *Scio quod Redemptor meus vivit, et in novissimo die terra surrecturus sum, et rursum circumdabor pelle mea, et in carne mea videbo Deum salvatorem meum, quem visurus sum ego ipse, et non alius. Reposita est hæc spes mea in sinu meo.*

And as for the other faith, that the good shall arise unto glory, and the evil unto pain; or that those which "persevere in God's precepts and laws, so long as they so do, they be the right inheritors of his kingdom;" this is not the commendation of a christian man's faith, but a most certain proposition, which also the devils believe most certainly, and yet they shall never have their sins forgiven by this faith, nor be inheritors of God's kingdom; because they lack the very christian faith, not trusting to the goodness and mercy of God for their own offences; but they hate God, envy his glory, and be utterly in desperation.

For the more large declaration of the pure christian faith, it is to be considered, that there is a general faith, which all that be christian, as well good as evil, have: as, to believe that God is, that he is the Maker and Creator of all things, and that Christ is the Saviour and Redeemer of the world, and for his sake all penitent sinners have remission of their sins; and that there shall be a general resurrection at the end of this mortal world, at the which Christ shall judge all the good to joy without end, and the evil to pain without end; with such other like things. And all these things even the devils also believe, and tremble for fear and grievousness of God's indignation and torments, which they endure and ever shall do. But they have not the right christian faith, that their own sins by Christ's redemption be pardoned and forgiven, that themselves by Christ be delivered from God's wrath, and be made his beloved children and heirs of his kingdom to come.

The other faith hath all devils and wicked christian people, that be his members: but this pure christian faith have none, but those that truly belong to Christ, and be the very members of his body, and endeavour themselves to persevere in his precepts and laws; although many pretend to have the said pure faith, which nevertheless have it not, but only in their mouths. For as there is a love in the mouth, and a love in the heart, even so there is a faith in mouth and a faith in heart. Examine every man, if he trust in God and love God above all things; and in words he will answer, yea: but examine every man's acts and deeds, and surely in a great number their acts and deeds condemn their words. For they walk after their own wills and pleasures, and not after God's commandments. And Christ himself saith: *Qui diligit me, mandata mea servat;* and St John saith: *Qui dicit se nosse Deum, et mandata ejus non custodit, mendax est.*

And therefore all those that bridle not their own appetites, but follow them, and accomplish the will of their own carnal minds, they trust in God and love God no further than the lips. And if they persuade themselves that they trust in God, and love God in their hearts, and be of any estimation before God, then be they much deceived, and, as St Paul saith, "They deceive their own hearts." Our own flesh and carnal mind is contrary to the Spirit and motion of God; and "they," saith St Paul, "that belong unto Christ, do crucify their flesh with the affections and lusts thereof." And contrary, he saith, they that follow the works of the flesh "shall not inherit the kingdom of God."

These be very notable and fearful sentences unto all such as be not repentant, but live after their own wills and not after God's will, neither have the right faith nor love unto God, nor shall be inheritors of his kingdom. And though Christ hath paid a sufficient ransom for all the sins in the world, and is a sufficient Redeemer and Saviour of all the world, yet shall they have no part thereof; for they belong not unto Christ; and Christ utterly refuseth them for his, which have faith and love only in their mouth, and have not the same engraven in their hearts, and expressed in their acts and deeds.

St James assimileth him, that hath this faith only in his mouth, unto a man that pitieth his naked or hungry brother, and biddeth him go warm him or fill his belly; and yet will give him neither clothes nor meat, wherewith he may warm him or feed his hungriness. What availeth this mercy spoken only with the tongue, when he sheweth no mercy in deed, in relieving his brother's necessity? But St James saith, "So say, so do;" for he shall not receive mercy of God that speaketh mercifully, except he hath the same in his heart to do it in deed. For the mercy that is not in the heart, dieth even in the mouth, and he shall have judgment without mercy that showeth not mercy in deed, how mercifully that ever he speak. And as the body is but dead that lacketh a soul, even so is that faith but dead that is but in the mouth, and doth not enter effectuously into the heart, and work accordingly.

What love soever the son pretendeth unto his father, or the servant unto his master, yet surely all that love is but coloured and feigned, if they be not glad to accomplish the will and commandments of their father and master, and very loath and sorry to transgress any part thereof. Likewise, how can the son persuade with himself that his father loveth him, favoureth him, and will do all good for him, and at length make him his heir, if he love not his father, nor be sorry to offend his father, but, like an unnatural and disobedient child, is ready to follow his own sensual mind, and to rebel against his father and all his precepts? It is not possible that such a son should have a sure trust of his father's benignity, gracious goodness, and fatherly love towards him, unless it come either of the ignorance or else the iniquity of his father; so that he either dissemble with his father, and trust that his father knoweth not of his folly, disobedience and rebellion; or else that he know that his father be so evil himself, that he favoureth ill-doers, and delighteth in the iniquity of his son, and loveth him never the worse for his vicious living. But to God (who knoweth all things, even before they be done, and knoweth all men's hearts even to the bottom better than they do themselves, and who also can favour no iniquity or malice of sin, but hateth it and the doers of the same,) cannot be ascribed any ignorance or evilness. Therefore, let no man deceive his own mind; for no man surely can have the right faith and sure trust of God's favour towards him, and persuade with himself that God is his benign and loving Father, and taketh him for his well-beloved son and heir, except he love God in his heart, and have a willing and glad mind, and a delight to do all things that may please God, and a very great repentance and sorrow that ever he did any thing that should offend and displease so loving a Father, whose goodness he can never account.

And as sure as it is, that God loveth and favoureth them that be thus minded; even as certain it is, that God hateth all those wicked children that love not him, and that be otherwise minded, that follow their own will, and rebel against his will: so that all such, what faith or love soever they pretend and say they have toward God, it is but in the lips and words only, and not in the heart altereth the whole man from all evil unto all good. Even as treacle kept only in the mouth doth not remedy poison in the whole body; but the treacle must enter down into the body, and then it altereth the whole body, and expelleth all venom and poison: in like manner, he whose profession of his faith is only in his mouth, altereth not his evil life, is not forgiven his sin, is not delivered from hell nor from the power of devils, is not made the son of God; but he continueth still in the poison of sin, in the wrath and indignation of God, and in the damnation of the wicked in hell.

But, if the profession of our faith of the remission of our own sins enter within us into the deepness of our hearts, then it must needs kindle a warm fire of love in our hearts towards God, and towards all other for the love of God,—a fervent mind to seek and procure God's honour, will, and pleasure in all things,—a good will and mind to help every man and to do good unto them, so far as our might, wisdom, learning, counsel, health, strength, and all other gifts which we have received of God, will extend,—and, *in summa*, a firm intent and purpose to do all that is good, and leave all that is evil. This is the very right, pure, perfect, lively, christian, hearty, and justifying "faith, which worketh by love," as St Paul saith, and suffereth no venom or poison of sin to remain within the heart, *fide Deus purificans corda*, (Acts xv.), but gendereth in the heart an hatred to sin, and maketh the sinner clean a new man. And this is the faith which every christian man ought to profess in his creed, and of this faith runneth all our paraphrasis upon the same. For, as for the other feigned, pretended, hypocritical, and adulterate faith in the mouth, it is but only a painted visor before men; but before God it is hollow within, dead, rotten, and nothing worth.

This being declared, in my judgment it shall not be necessary to interline or insert in many places, where we protest our pure christian faith, these words or sentences, that be newly added, namely, "I being in will to follow God's precepts;" "I rejecting in my will and heart the devil and his works;" "I willing to return to God;" "If I continue not in sin;" "If I continue a christian life;" "If I follow Christ's precepts;" "We living well;" "If we order and conform our wills in this world to his precepts;" "If we join our wills to his godly motions;" and such other like sentences or clauses conditional, which to the right faith need not to be added: for without these conditions is no right faith. And these sentences, methinks, come not in aptly in some places, as they be brought in, but rather interrupt and let the right course and phrase of the paraphrasis, and obscure the same rather than make it clear. In this part I have spoken the more largely, because I do refer unto this fourth note all other places like to the same matter appertaining.

v. "By his grace and mercy." This obscureth the sentence, and is superfluous: for it is sufficiently expressed by the former words, that is to say, "by his mere goodness only."

vi. "By his ordinance." This also obscureth the sense, and is superfluous.

vii. "Ordained." The preter tense may not conveniently be joined with the present tense.

viii. "Sometime be suffered by him, and sometime sent by his visitation. And that when he punisheth me he doth not punish." The sentence, as it is printed, runneth more evenly, and is very comfortable to every good man in all sickness and adversities, to take all such things to be of God's hand by his visitation. For as of meat, drink, clothing, and such like, which other men prepare for us or give unto us, we say, as we ought indeed to say, that we have all of God's hand, although other men or creatures be God's ministers therein; even so ought we to take all sickness and adversity in this world with all humility and gladness, as the rod of Almighty God, whereby he justly and lovingly scourgeth and punisheth us for our correction and reformation; yea, although it be sent unto us from him by ministration of wicked angels or men, as it shall appear more at length in the Annotation lxxiii.

*Inst.* p. 33. And sith he is my Father[l], I am assured that, for the fatherly love and pity which he hath and beareth unto me, he will not only care for me, but he will be also continually present with me by his grace and favour.

[l] *as afore.* ix.

ix. "As afore." These words do let and interrupt the course of the paraphrasis; and if they should be put in this place, there must be added more, viz. "as before is said."

*Inst.* pp. 34—36. And I believe also and profess, that Jesu Christ is not only Jesus and Lord to me and to all men that believe in him, but also that he is my Jesus, my God, and my Lord[m]. For whereas of my nature I was born in sin, and in the indignation and displeasure of God, and was the very child of wrath, condemned to everlasting death, subject and thrall to the power of the devil and sin, having all the principal parts or portions of my soul, as my reason and understanding, and my free-will, and all the other powers of my soul and body, not only so destituted and deprived of the gifts of God, wherewith they were first endued, but also so blinded, corrupted, and poisoned with error, ignorance, and carnal concupiscence, that neither my said powers could exercise the natural function and office for the which they were ordained by God at the first creation[n], nor I by them could do or think any thing which might be acceptable to God, but was utterly dead to God and all godly things, and utterly unable and insufficient of mine own self to observe the least part of God's commandments, and utterly inclined and ready to run headlong into all kinds of sin and mischief; I believe, I say, that I being in this case, Jesu Christ, by suffering of most painful and shameful death upon the cross, and by shedding of his most precious blood, and by that glorious victory which he had, when he descending into hell, and there overcoming both the devil and death, rose again the third day from death to life, and so ascended into heaven, hath now pacified his Father's indignation towards me, and hath reconciled me again into his favour, and that he hath loosed and delivered me from the yoke and tyranny of death, of the devil, and of sin, and hath made me so free from them, that they shall not finally hurt or annoy me, and that he hath poured out plentifully his Holy Spirit and his graces upon me, specially faith, to illumine and direct my reason and judgment, and charity, to direct my will and affections towards God, whereby I[o] am so perfectly restored to the light and knowledge of God, to the spiritual fear and dread of God, and unto the love of him and mine neighbour, that with his grace I am now ready to obey, and able to fulfil and accomplish his will and commandments. Besides all this, he hath brought and delivered me from darkness and blindness to light, from death to life, and from sin to justice; and he hath taken me into his protection, and made me as his own peculiar possession; and he hath planted and grafted me into his own body, and made me a member of the same, and he hath communicated and made me participant of his justice, his power, his life, his felicity, and of all his goods; so that now I may boldly say and believe, as indeed I do perfectly believe, that by his passion, his death, his blood, and his conquering of death, of sin, and of the devil by his resurrection and ascension, he hath made a sufficient expiation or propitiation towards God, that is to say, a sufficient satisfaction and recompence as well for my original sin, as also for all the actual sins that ever I have committed[p]; and that I am so clearly rid from all the guilt of my said offences, and from the everlasting pain due for the same, that neither sin, nor death, nor hell shall be able, or have any power, to hurt me or to let me[q], but that after this transitory life I shall ascend into heaven, there to reign with my Saviour Christ perpetually in glory and felicity.

[m] *I being Christian, and in will to follow his precepts.* x.

[n] *and shall continue as long as the world lasteth.* xi.

[o] *rejecting in my will and heart the devil and his works.* xii.

[p] *before my reconciliation.* xiii.

[q] *for them.*

All which things considered, I may worthily call him my Jesus, that is to say, my Saviour, and my Christ, that is to say, mine anointed King and Priest, and my Lord, that is to say, my Redeemer and Governor. For he hath done and fulfilled the very office both of a Priest, and of a King, and of a Lord: of a Priest, in that he hath offered up his blessed body and blood, in the altar of the cross, for the satisfaction of my sins; and of a King and Lord, in that he hath, like a most mighty conqueror, overcome and utterly oppressed his enemies, (which were also mine enemies,) and hath spoiled them of the possession of mankind[r], which they won before by fraud and deceit, by lying and blasphemy, and hath brought us now into his possession and dominion, to reign over us in mercy and love, like a most loving Lord and Governor.

[r] *willing to return to him.* xiv.

Finally, I believe assuredly, and also profess, that this redemption and justification of mankind could not have been wrought nor brought to pass by any other means in the world, but by the means of this Jesu Christ, God's only Son; and that never man could yet, nor never shall be able to come unto God the Father, or to believe in him, or to attain his favour, by his own wit or reason, or by his own science and learning, or by any his own works, or by whatsoever may be named in heaven or in earth, but[s] *by the faith* in the name and power of Jesu Christ, and by the gifts and graces of his Holy Spirit. And therefore, sith he is my Jesu Christ and my Lord, I will put my whole trust and confidence in him, and will have the self-same faith and affiance in him in all points which I have in God the

[s] *by his grace first called, and then by the faith.* xv.

Father. And I will knowledge him for my only Lord, and will obey all his commandments during my life, without any grudging. And I am sure that while he is my Lord and Governor, and I under his protection[t], neither sin, neither the devil, nor yet death, nor hell, can do me any hurt.

[t] *which I am void of whiles I continue in sin.* xvi.

x. "I being christian, and in will to follow his precepts." He that hath the true faith in heart is christian, and in will to follow his precepts; ut supra ad iv. Annotationem.

xi. "And shall continue as long as the world lasteth." This maketh the sentence very dark and ambiguous, to what noun the verb "continue" is referred; whether to the powers, or to the function and office. And I cannot perceive any manner of consideration why those words should be put in that place.

xii. "Rejecting in my will and heart the devil and his works." His heart is not replenished with a right faith, which in will and heart rejecteth not the devil and his works; ut supra ad iv.

xiii. "Before my reconciliation." These words be superfluous; for the true faithful heart is already reconciled: and the place can no otherwise be understand but of sins committed before reconciliation; for immediately before be written these words, "for all actual sins that ever I have committed:" which words cannot be extended to them which I shall commit hereafter.

xiv. "Willing to return to him." It is good to speak of our redemption after the fashion of the scripture, which useth ever to say, that Christ hath spoiled the devils, and redeemed the world, without this or any like addition: *Ipse*, saith the scripture, *spoliavit principatus et potestates;* et, *Passus est pro peccatis nostris, non solum autem nostris, sed et totius mundi.* And thus the scripture speaketh, to set forth only the glory of our redemption by Christ. And he that hath the pure faith is not only willing, but also indeed returneth to Christ; ut supra ad iv.

xv. "By his grace first called, and then by the faith." Calling for God's grace precedeth not faith; but, contrary, faith must needs precede our invocation of God, as St Paul saith: *Quomodo invocabunt in quem non crediderunt?*

xvi. "Which I am void of, if I continue in sin." These words may stand, but they were sufficiently expressed before by these words: "while he is my Lord and Governor, and I under his protection."

*Inst.* pp. 37, 8. And I believe also, that this child Jesu Christ was not only thus conceived without sin, but also that he was born in like manner of his said most blessed mother; and that she, both in the conception, and also in the birth and nativity of this her child, *and ever after,* retained still her virginity pure and immaculate, and as clear without blot, as she was at the time that she was first born[u].

[u] [1] *and ever after also, as we verily believe.*

And I believe, that this conception and nativity of our said Saviour was ordained to be thus pure, holy, and undefiled, to the intent that all filthiness and malediction, wherewith the conception and birth of me, and of all other men that ever were sith Adam, or shall be, and all the filthiness and malice of the sins *of the whole world,[x]* as well original as actual, should thereby be purified, purged, and made clean[y].

[x] *of all the christian people of the world.*

[y] *as soon as they reconcile themselves by his grace after their fall.*

*Inst.* pp. 38, 9. [2] And I believe, that our Saviour Jesu Christ, being thus most falsely and wrongfully accused, and brought before the said judge, was at length in public and open judgment condemned, by the sentence of the said judge, to be nailed unto a cross, and to be hanged upon the same, to the intent he should so suffer that kind of death, which among the Jews was ever most abhorred and detested, and accounted to be the most shameful and cursed of all others.

And I believe, that after this sentence and judgment thus pronounced and given contrary to all justice and equity, the Jews did take this innocent Jesu Christ our Saviour, and first of all binding him fast to a pillar, and pressing with great violence a crown of thorn upon his head, they did not only most spitefully mock him, and scorn him, but they also most cruelly scourged, tormented, and afflicted him, and finally they crucified him, that is to say, they nailed him through hands and feet unto a cross, and so hanged him up upon the same, on a certain hill called Calvary.

*And I believe that this innocent Jesu Christ our Saviour was grievously scourged by the commandment of Pilate, and had a crown of thorn put upon his head by the soldiers, and was by them not only most spitefully mocked and scorned, but also most cruelly tormented and afflicted. And after this he was at the last in public and open judgement condemned by the sentence of the said judge to be crucified, to the intent he should suffer that kind of death, which among the Jews was evermore most abhorred and detested, and accounted to be the most shameful and cursed of all other. And so according to the said sentence the soldiers crucified him, that is to say, they nailed him through hands and feet unto a cross, and hanged him upon the same, on a certain hill called Calvary.*

And I believe also and profess, that he hanged there upon the same cross between two thieves, *which were malefactors,* until he was dead, *and his soul departed from his body:* and that after he was thus dead, one Joseph ab Arimathea, being one of Christ's disciples, *and certain other devout men and women,

[[1] See Necessary Doctrine, p. 232, Ed. Oxford, 1825.] [[2] Ibid. p. 233.]

which also believed in Christ,* obtained licence of the said judge to take down this blessed body of our Saviour Jesu Christ from the said cross: *and that when they had so done, they[z]* wrapped and folded the same body in a clean sindone, and so laid it and buried it in a new grave or sepulchre, which the said Joseph had made of stone, wherein there was never man buried before.

[z] *And that done, he with another of Christ's disciples called Nicodemus*[3].

*Inst.* p. 40. And I believe that by this passion and death of our Saviour Jesu Christ[a], not only my corporal death is so destroyed that it shall never have power to hurt me, but rather it is made wholesome and profitable unto me; but also that all my sins, and the sins also of all them that do believe in him and follow him, be mortified and dead, that is to say, all the guilt and offence thereof, and also the damnation and pain due for the same, is clearly extincted, abolished, and washed away, so that the same shall not afterward be imputed or inflicted unto me.

[a] *I doing my duty.* xvii.

xvii. "I doing my duty." We may not say that we do our duty. Nevertheless he hath not the right faith in his heart, that hath not a good heart and will to do his duty; ut supra ad iv. But no man doth do all his duty, for then he needeth not to have any faith for the remission of his sins. Therefore this particle following "that all my sins be washed away."

### **The sense and interpretation of the fifth Article*[4].*

*Inst.* pp. 40—42. *I believe assuredly with my heart, and with my mouth I do profess, that this our Saviour Jesu Christ, after he was thus dead upon the cross, he descended immediately in his soul down into hell, leaving his most blessed body here in earth, and that at his coming thither, by the incomparable might and force of his Godhead, he entered into hell.*

*And I believe assuredly that this our Saviour Jesu Christ, after he was thus crucified, dead upon the cross, and buried, descended with his soul into hell, leaving his blessed body in sepulture here in earth, and loosed the pains and sorrows thereof, wherewith it was not possible that he should be holden*[5].

And like as that mighty man, of whom St Luke speaketh, which entering into the house of another strong man, first overcame him, and bound him hand and foot, and afterward spoiling him of all his armour and strength, wherein he trusted, took also away from him all the goods and substance he had; and like as strong Samson slew the mighty lion, and took out of his mouth the sweet honey: even so our Saviour Jesu Christ *at his said entry into hell, first he* conquered and oppressed both the devil and hell, and also death itself, whereunto all mankind was condemned, *and so bound them fast, that is to say, restrained the power and tyranny which they had before, and exercised over all mankind, that they never had sith that time, nor never shall have, any power finally to hurt or annoy any of them* that do faithfully believe in Jesu Christ; *and afterward he spoiled hell, and delivered and brought with him from thence all the souls of those righteous and good men, which from the fall of Adam died in the favour of God, and in the faith and belief of this our Saviour Jesu Christ, which was then to come. And I believe that by this descending of our Saviour Jesu Christ into hell, not only his elect people, which were holden there as captives, were delivered from thence; but also that the sentence and judgment* of the malediction and of eternal damnation (which God himself most rightfully pronounced upon Adam and all his posterity, and so consequently upon me) was clearly dissolved, satisfied, released, and discharged, and that the devil and hell both have utterly lost and be deprived of all the right, claim, and interest which they might have pretended to have had in me by the authority of that sentence, or by reason of any sin that ever I had or have committed, be it original or actual: and that the devil, with all his power, craft, subtilty, and malice, is now subdued and made captive, not only unto me, but also unto all the other faithful people and right believers in Jesu Christ that ever was or shall be *sith the time of Christ's said descending into hell:* and that our Saviour Jesu Christ hath also, by this his passion, and this his descending into hell, paid *my[b]* ransom, *and[c] hath merited and deserved*, that neither my soul, neither the souls of any such as be right believers in Christ, shall come therein, or shall finally be encumbered with any title or accusation that the devil can object against us, or lay unto our charge[d].

Luke xi.

Judges xiv.

*in simili, though their powers be not comparable to his.* xviii.

*and so conquered it, that finally he bereaved the devil and hell of all their power to hurt any of them.*

*and I believe, that not only by this his sufferance of passion, death, and descent into hell, he did deliver his elect people from the captivity and thraldom of the devil, but also that the sentence and judgment.*

[b] *our.*

[c] *so.*

[d] *If we so die.* xix.

xviii. "*In simili*, though their powers be not comparable to his." *In simili* is superfluous; for the same is before spoken in English, "even so:" also the rest is not true; for we may compare God's power and acts unto his creature *in similitudine*, but not *in æqualitate.*

xix. "If we so die." This condition taketh away the right belief of a faithful man: for the faithful man trusteth surely in God's goodness, that he will give him grace so to die. So that it pertaineth as well to our faith, that we should so die, as that we should be saved; ut supra ad iv.

[[3] See Nec. Doctr. p. 233.]

[[4] In The Institution, the fifth article of the Creed comprises the descent into hell and the resurrection. Henry VIII. adds the descent into hell to the fourth article, and places the resurrection alone in the fifth. This division is adopted both in Cranmer's Annotations and The Necessary Doctrine.]

[[5] See Nec. Doctr. p. 234.]

*Inst.* pp. 42, 3. And I believe assuredly, that by *this descending of Christ into hell, and* this his resurrection again from death to life, Christ hath merited and deserved for me and all true and faithful christian men, *not only that our souls shall never come into hell, but also* that we shall here in this life be perfectly justified in the sight and acceptation of God, and shall have such grace, might, and power given unto us by him, that we shall be made able thereby to subdue, to mortify, and to extinguish our old Adam, and all our carnal and fleshly concupiscences, in such sort, that sin shall never[e] *afterward* reign in our mortal bodies, but that we shall be wholly delivered from the kingdom of sin, and from spiritual death, and shall be resuscitated and regenerated into the new life of the Spirit and grace.

[e] *finally*

And whereas I and all other christian men should have been the most miserable of all other creatures in the world, and should have died like heathens and pagans, without all hope of everlasting life, or of rising again after our death, if Christ our head and Saviour had not risen again to life after his death; I believe and trust now assuredly, that by the virtue and efficacy of this[f] *descending of Christ into hell, and of his* resurrection again *from death to life*, not only our corporal death and all the afflictions which we may sustain in this world shall not annoy us, but shall rather turn unto our profit, and be as entries and occasions of our greater glory; but also that we[g] shall after our corporal death be preserved from the captivity of hell, and shall be made partakers of Christ's resurrection.

[f] *his passion, death, and*

[g] *continuing a Christian's life.* xx.

xx. "Continuing a Christian's life." These words be superfluous, for continuance of a Christian's life pertaineth unto a pure faith; ut supra ad iv.

*Inst.* p. 45. And I believe, that according thereunto our Saviour Jesu Christ is of his own goodness not only more ready always than any other creature *in the world* is, to help me by his mediation and intercession; but also that whensoever I do invocate and call upon him in right faith and hope with full intent and purpose to amend and return from my naughty life, *he presenteth and exhibiteth unto the sight of his Father his most blessed body, as it was wounded, crucified, and offered up in sacrifice for the redemption of mankind, and so from time to time maketh continual request and intercession unto God his Father for the remission of all* my sins, and for my reconciliation unto his favour.

*he being present always in the sight of his Father exhibiteth from time to time, and maketh continual request and intercession unto him for the remission of all*

*Inst.* pp. 49, 50. Neither it is possible for any man to come unto the Father by Christ, that is to say, to be reconciled into the favour of God, and to be made and adopted into the number of his children, or to obtain any part of that incomparable treasure which our Saviour Jesu Christ, by his nativity, his passion, his death, his resurrection, and his ascension, hath merited for mankind, unless this Holy Spirit shall first illumine and inspire[h] into his heart the right knowledge and faith of Christ[i], with due contrition and penance for his sins, and shall also afterward instruct him, govern him, aid him, direct him, and endue him with such special gifts and graces, as shall be requisite and necessary to that end and purpose.

[h] *by grace*

[i] [1] *man adhibiting his will thereto.* xxi.

And I believe also assuredly, that this Holy Spirit of God is of his own nature full of all goodness and benignity, or rather that he is goodness itself: forasmuch as he is the only Ghost or Spirit, which with the Father by Christ instilloth and infoundeth into the hearts of mortal men (after they be once purified from sin by[k] faith, and delivered from the power of the Devil) divers and manifold most noble and excellent gifts and graces; as, the[l] gift of holy fear and dread of God; the gift of fervent love and charity towards God and our neighbour; the gift of spiritual wisdom and understanding; the gift of[m] *free-will and desire,* and also of very fortitude and strength to contemn this world, to subdue and mortify all carnal concupiscence, and to walk in the ways of God; the gift of perseverance to continue in the same; the gift of pity and mercy, of patience and benignity, of science and cunning, of prophesying, of curing and healing, and of all other virtues necessary for christian men to have, either for the attaining of their own salvation, or for the edifying and profit of their neighbours. All and singular which gifts and graces I knowledge and profess that they proceed from this Holy Spirit, and that they be given, conferred, and distributed unto us mortal men here in earth, at his own godly will, arbitre, and dispensation, and that no man can purchase or obtain, ne yet receive, retain, or use any one of them, without the special operation of this Holy Spirit. *And although he giveth not nor dispenseth the same equally and unto every man in like; yet he giveth always some portion thereof unto all persons which be accepted in the sight of God, and that not only freely, and without all their deservings, but also in such plenty and measure, as unto his godly knowledge is thought to be most beneficial and expedient.*

[k] *right*

[l] *the gift of calling by many ways the sinner from sin, and such other.* xxii.

[m] *counsel, and the gift of free-will and desire to follow the same*[2],

*Which will not let: and was left with us therefore to remember us of our duty, if we willingly and wilfully reject not the same his illuminations and good motions. And yet he giveth not nor dispenseth the same equally and unto every man in like; but he divideth them peculiarly and specially to every member of his mystical body the church, as is most necessary for the whole body, and in such plenty and measure as unto his godly will and knowledge is thought to be most beneficial and expedient for the same. All which things he doth of his mere mercy and goodness, freely and without all our deserving*[3].

xxi. "Man adhibiting his will thereto." This interrupteth the phrase of speech; and man's will is most amply and fully contained in the words next immediately following, "contrition and penance."

xxii. "The gift of calling by many ways the sinner from sin, and such other."

---

[1 See Nec. Doctr. p. 242.] [2 See Nec. Doctr. ibid.] [3 See Nec. Doctr. ibid.]

Calling is no gift of God in us, as all the other following, but the operation of God toward us.

*Inst.* p. 53. All the prayers, good works, and merits, yea, and all the gifts, graces, and goods which be conferred, done, or wrought in or *unto this whole body, or any member of the same, shall be applied unto every one of them, and shall redound commonly unto the benefit of them all.*

*unto any member of Christ's mystical body, shall be applied and redound commonly unto the benefit of the whole, to the edifying and increase of Christ's church. And likewise all gifts, graces, and goods which be conferred unto the whole body, shall be applied and redound unto the commodity and profit of every one of the members of the same.* xxiii.

xxiii. "Any member of Christ's mystical body, &c." This particle, I confess, I never well understood, neither as it was by us made, nor as it is now corrected; but I consented thereto only because there is no evil doctrine therein contained, as far as I perceive and discern.

*Inst.* pp. 53, 4. Although God doth ofttimes suffer not only sin, error, and iniquity so to abound here in the world, and the congregation of the wicked to exercise such tyranny, cruelty, and persecution over this holy church, and the members of the same, that it might seem the said church to be utterly oppressed and extinguished, but also suffereth many and sundry of the members of the same holy church to fall out from this body for a season, and to commit many grievous and horrible offences and crimes, for the which they deserve to be precided and excluded for a season[n] from the communion of this holy church; yet I believe assuredly, that God will never utterly abject this holy church, nor any of the members thereof, but that the same doth and shall perpetually continue and endure here in this world[o], and that God shall at all times (yea, when persecution is greatest and most fervent) be present with his Holy Spirit in the same church, and preserve it all holy and undefiled, and shall keep, ratify, and hold sure all his promises made unto the same church or congregation: and finally, that all such members as be fallen out from the same by sin, shall at length rise again by penance, and shall be restored and united again unto the same holy body[p].

[n] *that is to say, till by repentance and penance they return.*

[o] [4] *if fault be not in themselves.* xxiv.

[p] *if wilfully and obstinately they withstand not his calling.* xxv.

xxiv. "If fault be not in themselves." This article speaketh only of the elect, in whom finally no fault shall be, but they shall perpetually continue and endure.

xxv. "If wilfully and obstinately they withstand not his calling." Likewise the elect shall not wilfully and obstinately withstand God's calling[5].

*Inst.* pp. 54, 5. And I believe that this holy church is catholic, that is to say, that it cannot be coarcted or restrained within the limits or bonds of any one town, city, province, region, or country; but that it is dispersed and spread universally throughout all the whole world: insomuch that in what part soever of the world, be it in Africa, Asia, or Europe, there may be found any number of people, of what sort, state, or condition soever they be, which do believe in one God the Father, Creator of all things, and in one Lord Jesu Christ his Son, and in one Holy Ghost, and do also profess and have all one faith, one hope, and one charity, according as is prescribed in holy scripture, and do all consent in the true interpretation of the same scripture, and in the right use of the sacraments of Christ; we may boldly pronounce and say, that there is this holy church, the very espouse and body of Christ, the very kingdom of Christ, and the very temple of God.

And *I[q] believe that these* particular churches, in what place of the world soever they be congregated, be the very parts, portions, or members of this catholic and universal church.

[q] *that all.* xxvi.

xxvi. "And that all particular churches." This word "these" must needs remain, and not be put out: and it were better to say, "and that all these particular churches;" for if there be any particular church, out of the number of the elect, it is no number [member?] of this universal holy church.

*Inst.* p. 58. And I believe, that I being united and *corporated*[r] as a living member into this catholic church, (as undoubtedly I trust that I am,)[s] not only Christ himself, being Head of this body, and the infinite treasure of all goodness*[t], and all the holy saints and members of the same body do* and shall necessarily help me, love me, pray for me, care for me, weigh on my side, comfort me, and assist me in all my necessities here in this world[u]; but also that I shall be made partaker of the fruit, benefit, and treasure of Christ's most blessed life and his bitter passion, and of all the holy life, passions, and patience, and of all the prayers and other good works of faith and charity, which have been or shall be done or sustained by any[x] and every one of all those faithful and righteous people, which ever have been or shall be members of this catholic church.

[r] *incorporated*

[s] *and so continuing.* xxvii.

[t] *doth*

[u] *according to his promise;*

[x] *of the holy saints*

And I believe that in this catholic church I, and all the lively and quick members of the same, shall continually and from time to time, so long as we shall live here on earth[y], obtain remission and forgiveness of all our sins, as well original as actual, by the merits

[y] *following Christ's precepts, or when we fall repent our fault.* xxviii.

---

[4 See Nec. Doctr. p. 244.] [5 See Nec. Doctr. ibid.]

[z] *shall the more plenteously attain the same*

of Christ's blood and his passion, and[z] by the virtue and efficacy of Christ's sacraments, instituted by him for that purpose, so oft as we shall worthily receive the same.

And like as it is not in the power of any man to dispense, minister, or distribute any part of that nutriment which he receiveth in at his mouth unto any member which either is mortified and dead in his body, or that is cut off from the same; even so I believe assuredly, that neither Christ's blood, nor his sacraments, nor any of the graces of the Holy Ghost, nor any good work in the world, do or can any thing profit to remission and forgiveness of sin, or salvation unto any person, which is in very deed out of the catholic church, as long as he shall so stand, and continue out of the same[a].

[a] *obstinately and without repentance.* xxix.

xxvii. "And so continuing." Continuance is comprehended in faith; for if I believe not that I shall continue in the holy catholic church, I cannot believe that I shall have any benefit by Christ; ut supra ad iv.

xxviii. "Following Christ's steps, or when we fall repent our fault." The elect, of whom is here spoken, will follow Christ's precepts, and rise again when they fall; and the right faith cannot be without following of Christ's precepts, and repentance after falling. See the fourth annotation. Therefore in my judgment it were better to say thus: "The elect shall follow Christ's precepts, or when they fall, they shall repent and rise again, and obtain remission," &c.

xxix. "Obstinately and without repentance." These words need not; for without obstinacy, and lack of repentance, no man is out of the catholic church.

*Inst.* p. 67. In the fifth article it is to be noted, that therein is included and contained the grounds and foundations of the greatest part of all the mysteries of our catholic faith: insomuch that St Paul saith, that whosoever believeth in his heart that God the Father did resuscitate and raise up his Son Christ from death to life, he shall be saved. And in another place he saith[b], that whosoever believeth not that Christ is risen from death to life, [c]*it is not possible his sins should be remitted.*

[b] *to this effect,*

[c] *remaineth still in sin, and so dying cannot be saved.*

*There is nothing that can in all adversity and trouble be more joyful and comfortable unto us than the belief of this article, that Christ rose again from death to life, and that we shall also do the same. The faith and belief of this (we living well[1],)* xxx. *is our victory and triumph over the Devil, hell, and death, and the only remedy to put away the horror and fear of them; forasmuch as hereby we be assured, that as death could not hold Christ, even so it cannot hold us which are by a christian faith the very members and body of Christ, but that we shall rise from death and live again[2], if we order and conform our will in this world to his precepts.* xxxi. *And the only hope hereof maketh us, that we regard not persecutions nor adversities in this world which we sustain for Christ's sake, because we be assured to have a better and a more glorious life after this, as St Paul writeth unto the Corinthians, saying, "If we christian men that live in persecution, and contempt of the world, had no hope of other life than this that is present, then were we the most miserable of all men. But now Christ is risen again from death, and hath declared thereby, that there is a life after this life which all christian men hope to come to." According hereto saith St Austen, All the hope of our faith standeth in this point, that we shall rise again. This made St Paul to wish to be dissolved, and be with Christ. Of this article the epistles of St Paul and the New Testament be full. To the Romans he writeth: "Christ rose again for our justification." To Timothy he saith: "Remember that Jesus Christ is risen again from death." The apostles, beside other names pertaining to their office, be especially called the witnesses of Christ's resurrection. The which resurrection as it was by many and sundry apparitions and other infallible arguments declared and proved unto them, so they did in all places and at all times open and inculcate the same, as a principal and a chief article of Christ's doctrine: wherein should depend and rest the great comfort and solace of all true and faithful believers in Christ.*

*Inst.* pp. 67, 8. *It is also to be noted in this article, that the victory and conquest which Christ had over death, hell, and the Devil himself, with all their power and tyranny, besides that it proceeded of the infinite mercy and goodness of God towards us, it was also founded upon very justice. For surely like as the sin of man and his disobedience was the only mean and cause, wherefore God ordained and suffered that death and the Devil should have and occupy such dominion and tyranny over all mankind as they had; even so was it contrary to the will and ordinance of God, that death, hell, or the Devil should have or exercise any power or authority where as no sin reigned: insomuch that if man had never sinned, he should never have died, but should have been immortal; nor never should have descended into hell, but should ever have had the superiority over the Devil, death, and hell, and should have had them always subdued unto him. And therefore, sith the Devil himself did perfectly know that our Saviour Jesu Christ expressed in all his life most exact and most perfect obedience unto the laws and will of God, and so fulfilled and satisfied the same in every point to the uttermost, that there could never be found untruth or deceit in his mouth, nor any spot or blot of filthiness or impurity in any part of all his living; and yet that notwithstanding, (knowing him to be a very natural man,) laboured, procured, and caused the Jews to kill this innocent Christ, and to put him unto most sharp and bitter death, contrary to all equity and justice, and all to the intent that he might, after his said death, have Christ with him down into hell, as one of his captives, and so there to exercise his tyranny upon him, like as he had done over all other men from the beginning of the world until that time; no doubt but the Devil, in this doing, did extreme and manifest wrong, and utterly exceeded the limits of the power given unto him. And therefore God, considering this high presumption and malice of the Devil, and this intolerable abuse of his said power, did send his only-begotten Son down into hell, there to condemn the Devil of this extreme iniquity, and to conquer, to spoil, and deprive him, not only of the possession of all the souls of the righteous men, which by his craft and subtilty he had before reduced and brought under his dominion; but also restrained him of the power and authority which he by death and hell had over mankind. All which things Christ did not by the might of his godly power only, but for and upon this just and reasonable cause given unto him on the behalf of the Devil, which for the causes aforesaid most worthily deserved to be served so.*

[[1] See Nec. Doctr. p. 235.] [[2] See Nec. Doctr. ibid.]

xxx. "We living well." The right faith requireth good living; but yet our triumph and victory over the devil, hell, and death, standeth not in our well living, but in Jesus Christ; to whom whensoever we convert in heart and mind, we have the triumph and victory of the Devil and sin, notwithstanding our evil life before. See the fourth annotation.

xxxi. "If we order and conform our will in this world to his precepts." Whether we order our will to his precepts or not, we shall rise from death to life, but not to the glorious life. And yet to the glorious life also we shall rise, though we have not in all things conformed our will to God's will, but have repugned to his will, so that we be repentant and amend, as David, Peter, and Paul did. And the true faithful man endeavoureth himself to conform his will to God's will in all things, and to walk right forth in all his precepts. And where by infirmity he chanceth to take a fall, he lieth not still, but by God's help riseth again. And his trust is so much in God, that he doubteth not in God's goodness toward him, but that, if by fragility and weakness he fall again, God will not suffer him so to lie still, but put his hand to him and help him up again, and so at the last he will take him up from death unto the life of glory everlasting[3].

*Inst.* pp. 69, 70. Notwithstanding, if any of you shall fortune to commit any * deadly * sin, yet let him consider and remember, that Jesu Christ, which fulfilled all justice for us, and by the sacrificing and offering up of his precious blood [d] * made due satisfaction and propitiation * unto God his Father, not only for all our sins, but also for the sins of all the world, is now our continual and perpetual advocate, our patron and defender before the throne of his Father, and maketh continual intercession and prayer for the remission of all our sins.

[d] *became and made himself our redeemer, saviour, and intercessor.* xxxii.

xxxii. "Became, and made himself our redeemer, saviour, and intercessor." "Satisfaction," which is put out, meseemeth in any wise should stand still, to take away the root, ground, and fountain of all the chief errors, whereby the bishop of Rome corrupted the pure foundation of christian faith and doctrine. For upon this satisfaction did he build his sticks, hay, and straw, satisfactory masses, trentals, *scala cœli*, foundations of chantries, monasteries, pardons, and a thousand other abuses, to satisfy the covetousness of him and his; and yet for their covetousness there never could be found any satisfaction, that is to say, any thing that could satisfy it.

*Inst.* p. 70. Thirdly, it is to be noted, that although it be said in this article that Christ is our only mediator and intercessor [e], yet thereby is not excluded the * intercession [f] * of the holy saints [g] which be now in heaven, or hereafter shall be; neither yet the * intercession [h] * of the ministers of Christ's church, or of any the holy members of the same, which be living here in this world. But we must know for certain, that all the [i] members of Christ's church, whether they be departed this life, or yet living here in the world, be all knit and united together in perfect charity, and each doth care and pray for other continually unto [k] * Almighty God *, and that Christ, being head of the same body, is advocate and intercessor for them all [l], like as it is more at large declared in the tenth article of this Creed.

[e] *to his Father.*
[f] *mediation and prayers.*
[g] *to Christ.* xxxiii.
[h] *mediation and prayers.*
[i] *true and perfect.*
[k] *Christ.*
[l] *to his Father.*

xxxiii. "Mediation and prayers of holy saints to Christ." Because that St Paul saith, that "there is but one mediator between God and man, and that is Christ Jesus," which doctors expound to be understand of mediation by redemption, not of mediation by prayer; therefore I think it better to say, "mediation by prayer of holy saints[4]," putting "by" in the stead of "and." And the same is spoken twice. It is written there also, that "the members of Christ should be mediators by prayer one for another only unto Christ:" which is not true; for, as St Paul saith in divers places, by Christ we have also access unto the Father. And Christ in all places teacheth us to pray unto the Father, *Pater noster;* et, *Adorabitis Patrem in spiritu et veritate;* et, *Flecto genua mea ad Patrem.*

*Inst.* p. 74. Like as Christ is the author, the mean, and the very highway to come unto God the Father, so is this Holy Spirit the very conductor, the guide, the director, and the governor, to bring us into the same highway, and to minister unto us not only * alacrity and * strength to walk and run therein, but also perseverance to continue in the same, until we shall come unto our journey's end [m].

[m] *if we accept the same, and join our will to his godly motions.*

---

[[3] See Nec. Doctr. p. 235.]
[[4] Cranmer's amendment was adopted in the Nec. Doctr. p. 237.]

*Ibid.* Thirdly, that it is also the peculiar function or office of this Holy Spirit, (after[n] we be inspired, and perfectly instructed in the said knowledge,) first to purge and purify our hearts by *this* faith and knowledge from the malice and filthiness of sin, and afterward to stir, inflame, and ravish our hearts, and to make us able gladly and thankfully to embrace and receive the said benefits, and so to keep them, to use them, and to dispose them to our own wealth, and to the edifying and profit of our neighbours[o]; and finally, to comfort us, and to be unto us in manner as a certain pledge or an earnest-penny, to assure and warrant us, by true and infallible tokens, that we[p] be in the favour of God, and his own children by grace and adoption, and the right inheritors of heaven.

[n] *baptism by us received, and that.*

[o] *that we may attain in the end the place by all true christian folk to be desired.*

[p] *applying our will to his motions.* xxxiv.

xxxiv. "Applying our will to his motions." Our faith and trust that we be in God's favour and his own children hangeth not of our own merits and applying of our will to his motions: for, insomuch as many times the good men do the contrary, that were the ready way unto desperation. Therefore if any thing should be here added, it were good, in mine opinion, to say thus: "that we, which be renovate by the same Spirit, and do convert our lives from following our own carnal wills and pleasures, and repenting us that we have followed the same, and now apply our minds to follow the will of that Holy Spirit, be in the favour of God." &c.

*Inst.* p. 78. Although the lively members of this militant church be subject to the infirmities of their flesh, and fall ofttimes into error and sin, as was said before; yet they always in scripture be called holy, as well because they be sanctified in the blood of Christ, and professing in their baptism to believe in God, and to forsake the devil and all his works, they be consecrated and dedicated unto Christ; as also for that they be from time to time purged[q] by the word of God, and by faith, hope, and charity, and by the exercise of other virtues; and finally, shall be endued with such grace of the Holy Ghost, that they shall be clearly sanctified and purified from all filthiness, and shall be made the glorious espouse of Christ, shining in all cleanness, without having any spot or wrinkle, or any other thing worthy to be reprehended.

[q] *by penance,*

*Inst.* pp. 80, 1. To the attaining of which faith, it is also to be noted, that Christ hath instituted and ordained in the world but only two means and instruments, whereof the one is the ministration of his word, and the other is the administration of his sacraments instituted by him; so that it is not possible[r] to attain this faith, but by one or both of these two means, as shall be hereafter declared.

[r] *commonly*

*xxxv.*[1] "Which in spiritual cure are committed to them." It is small difference between "cure" and "charge," but that the one is plain English, and the other is deducted out of the Latin. And as for the diversity between these two sayings, "they are committed to them in cure or charge," and "they be committed to their cure or charge," is no more, I suppose, than is between these two, "it is committed to me in custody," and, "it is committed to my custody;" which I reckon to be all one.

*Inst.* pp. 83, 4. God prohibited that any matrimony should be made between the father and the daughter, the mother and the son, the brother and the sister, and between[s] divers other persons, being in certain degrees of consanguinity and affinity: which laws of prohibition in marriage, although they were not by express words of God declared at the first institution of matrimony, ne yet at this second repetition of the same, made unto Noe; yet undoubtedly God [t]*had engraved and enprinted* the same laws in the heart of man at his first creation. [u]*And forasmuch as in long continuance and process of time* the natural light and knowledge of man was almost by sin and malice extincted, or at the least so corrupted and obscured in the most part of men, that they could not perceive and judge what things were of their own nature naughty and detestable in the sight of God, ne yet how far that natural honesty and reverence which we owe unto such persons as be near of blood, or of near alliance unto us, was extended; *God[x]* commanded his prophet Moses to promulgate and to declare by his word unto the people of Israel the said laws of prohibition of matrimony in certain degrees of consanguinity and affinity, which be specially mentioned in the book of Leviticus.

[s] *The rest of the degrees prohibited are necessarily to be expressed here also.* xxxvi.

[t] *did engrave and emprint.*

[u] [2] *which soon after blinded to sin, and not preserving the natural light, so ran in darkness by long continuance and process of time: whereby*

[x] *which God perceiving and willing man to return from darkness*

xxxvi. "Nota, that the rest of the degrees prohibited are necessary to be expressed also." All the degrees prohibited, in my judgment, may be best expressed in these general words: that no man may marry his mother, nor mother-in-law, and so upward in *linea recta;* daughter, nor daughter-in-law, and so downward in *linea recta;* sister, nor sister-in-law; aunt, nor aunt-in-law; niece, nor niece-in-law.

[[1] Where the number of the Annotations is thus printed, the expression criticised is not to be found in the Bodleian copy of Hen. VIII.'s Corrections.]

[[2] See Nec. Doctr. p. 270, and Letter to Crumwell, 7 Sept. 1536.]

*Inst.* p. 93. It is offered unto all men, as well infants as such as have the use of reason, that by baptism they shall have remission of all their sins, the grace and favour of God, and everlasting life, according to the saying of Christ, Whosoever believeth and is baptized shall be saved[y].

[y] *they dying in that grace which by the sacrament of baptism is conferred to them, and not by sin alter the same.* xxxvii.

xxxvii. "They dying in the grace, which by the sacrament of baptism is conferred unto them, and not by sin alter the same." It is better speech to say, "If they die," &c. And these words come in such place immediately after Christ's words, that they seem to be Christ's own words, which they be not; therefore it were better to put them next after these words, which be in the line before, viz. "everlasting life[3]."

*Inst.* p. 96. Like as such men, which after baptism do fall again into sin, if they do not penance in this life, shall undoubtedly be damned; even so whensoever the same men shall convert themselves from their naughty life, and[z] do such penance for the same as Christ requireth of them, they shall without doubt attain remission of their sins, and shall be saved.

[z] *having time and space*

*Inst.* p. 97. The penitent must conceive certain hope and faith that God will forgive him his sins, and repute him justified, and of the number of his elect children, not[a] for the worthiness of any merit or work done by the penitent, but[b] for the only merits of the blood and passion of our Saviour Jesus Christ.

[a] *only*
[b] *chiefly.* xxxviii.

xxxviii. "Only, chiefly." These two words may not be put in this place in any wise: for they signify that our election and justification cometh partly of our merits, though chiefly it cometh of the goodness of God. But certain it is, that our election cometh only and wholly of the benefit and grace of God, for the merits of Christ's passion, and for no part of our merits and good works: as St Paul disputeth and proveth at length in the epistle to the Romans and Galatians, and divers other places, saying, *Si ex operibus, non ex gratia; si ex gratia, non ex operibus.*

*Inst.* p. 98. *Item,* That the people may in no wise contemn this auricular confession, which is made unto the ministers of the church; but that they ought to repute the same as a very expedient and necessary mean, *whereby they may require and ask this absolution at the priest's hands,* at such time as they shall find their consciences grieved with mortal sin, and have occasion so to do[c], to the intent they may thereby attain certain comfort and consolation of their consciences. xxxix.

[c] *whereby they may require and ask this absolution at the priest's hands,*

xxxix. "To the intent that they may thereby attain certain comfort and consolation of their consciences." Although these words make the sentences not very perfect in English, yet they may stand: but I like it better as it is in the print.

*Inst.* pp. 98, 9. As touching the third part of penance, we think it convenient that all bishops and preachers shall instruct and teach the people committed unto their spiritual charge, that although Christ and his death be the sufficient oblation, [d]sacrifice, *satisfaction, and recompence,* for the which God the Father forgiveth and remitteth to all sinners not only their sins, but also eternal pain due for the same; *yet[e] all men truly* penitent, contrite, and confessed, *must needs also* bring forth the fruits of penance, that is to say, prayer, fasting, and almsdeed, with much mourning and lamenting for their sins before committed. And they must also make restitution or satisfaction in will *and deed* to their neighbours, in such things as they have done them wrong and injury in[f]. And finally, they must do all other good works of mercy and charity, and express their obedient will in the executing and fulfilling of God's commandment outwardly, when time, power, and occasion shall be ministered unto them, or else they shall never be saved. For this is the express precept and commandment of God, Do you the worthy fruits of penance. And St Paul saith, Like as in times past you have given and applied yourselves, and all the members of your bodies, to all filthy living and wickedness, continually increasing in the same; in like manner you be now bound, and must give and apply yourselves wholly to justice, increasing continually in purity and cleanness of life. And in another place he saith, I chastise and subdue my carnal body, and the affections of the same, and make them obedient unto the spirit.

[d] *and*
[e] *yet christian people which daily fall cannot enjoy the benefit of the same, except they be truly*
[f] *and also in deed, if they be able.* xl.

*Item,* That these precepts and works of charity be necessary works to our salvation; and God necessarily requireth that every penitent man shall perform the same, whensoever time, power, and occasion shall be ministered unto him so to do.

xl. "And also in deed, if they be able, though they put themselves to pain." This is well added; and yet there might be said more amply, "how painful soever it be unto them:" for there is no perfect contrition, where is not also a good will to make restitution according to all possible power[4].

[[3] See Nec. Doctr. p. 2[illegible].]    [[4] Ibid. p. 260.]

Item, *That though by baptism and faith we become the children of Christ, yet we living in this vale of misery, and continuing in the same, shall by penance and other good works of the same be made meet and apt and assured to receive the virtue of Christ's passion* (xli.), *which is our everlasting life, and also by them we*[1]

*Item*, That by penance, and such good works of the same, we shall not only obtain everlasting life, but also we shall deserve remission or mitigation of the present pains and afflictions, which we sustain here in this world.

xli. "Be made meet, apt, and assured, to receive the virtue of Christ's passion." The penitent person, as soon as he repenteth from the bottom of his heart, for Christ's sake only he is made partaker of Christ's passion, and good works follow thereof; but they be not the cause thereof. And if we should esteem our works so highly, we should glory against Christ.

*Inst.* pp. 100, 1. As touching the sacrament of the altar, we think it convenient, that all bishops and preachers shall instruct and teach the people committed unto their spiritual charge, that they ought and must constantly believe, that under the form and figure of bread and wine, which we there presently do see and perceive by outward senses[2], is verily, substantially, and really contained and comprehended the very selfsame body and blood of our Saviour Jesu Christ, which was born of the Virgin Mary, and suffered upon the cross for our redemption: and that under the same form and figure of bread and wine the very selfsame body and blood of Christ is corporally, really, and in the very same substance exhibited, distributed, and received unto and of all them which receive the said sacrament: and that *therefore[g]* the said sacrament is to be used with all due reverence and honour; and that every man ought first to prove and examine himself, and *religiously[h]* to try and search his own conscience, before he shall receive the same, according to the saying of St Paul, Whosoever eateth this body of Christ unworthily, or drinketh of this blood of Christ unworthily, shall be guilty of the very body and blood of Christ: wherefore let every man first prove himself, and so let him eat of this bread, and drink of this drink[i]. For whosoever eateth it or drinketh it unworthily, he eateth it and drinketh it to his own damnation; * because he putteth no difference between the very body of Christ and other kinds of meat.*

[g] *further*

[h] *straitly*

1 Cor. xi.

[i] *that he may do it worthily and to his salvation.*

*xlii.* "We living as we ought to do." Who liveth as he ought to do? Who ever kept so his journey that he never fell? And the penitent knowledgeth that he hath lived otherwise than he ought to do. And the words next immediately following declare the same, sc. "that we shall attain remission of our sins," &c. He that hath sinned hath lived otherwise than he ought to do. And ten or twelve lines together need good interpretation; for they seem to attribute unto the words of consecration all things whatsoever we have of Christ, and ought to attribute unto him, or to any of God's words contained in the holy scripture.

## *The Sacrament of Orders.*

*Inst.* pp. 101, 2. As touching the sacrament of * holy * orders, we think it convenient, that all bishops and preachers shall instruct and teach the people committed unto their spiritual charge, first, how that Christ and his apostles did institute and ordain in the new testament, that besides the civil powers and governance of kings and princes (which is called *potestas gladii*, the power of the sword) there should also be continually in the church militant certain * other * ministers or officers, which[k] should have special[l] * power, authority, and commission,* under Christ, [m]* to preach and teach the word of God unto his people; to dispense and administer the sacraments of God unto them, and by the same to confer and give the graces of the Holy Ghost; to consecrate the blessed body of Christ in the sacrament of the altar; to loose and absoyle from sin all persons which be duly penitent and sorry for the same; to bind and to excommunicate such as be guilty in manifest crimes and sins[n], and will not amend their defaults; to order and consecrate others in the same room, order, and office, whereunto they be called and admitted themselves; and finally,* to feed Christ's people, like good pastors and rectors, (as the apostle calleth them,) with their wholesome doctrine[o]; and by their continual exhortations and admonitions to reduce them from sin and iniquity, so much as in them lieth, and to bring them unto the perfect knowledge, the perfect love and dread of God, and unto the perfect charity of their neighbours.

[k] *being chosen as the apostles were, and living ad normam Scripturæ*[3],

[l] *cure, authority, power, and administration, given by God unto them.*

[m] *as hereafter followeth, first that they (being according to the laws of every region elect and constitute) have cure of soul, authority to preach and teach the word of God, and*

[n] *expressed in scripture.*

[o] *clean living and good example;*

---

[[1] This correction is written on the fly leaf at the end of the volume; but it appears from its purport, and from the number prefixed to Cranmer's Annotation on it, to belong to this place. It was probably intended to be substituted for, "*Item*, that by penance...also we."]

[[2] In the original copy the words from "they ought" to "senses," are erased, and in the margin is written,—"and in many things God's works be wondrous."]

[[3] These corrections are written in so confused a manner in the original, that they have been arranged in great measure by conjecture. Henry VIII. was evidently much dissatisfied with this article 'Of Orders;' for the marks of his pen occur in all parts of it, and he has frequently expressed his disapprobation of particular passages by the word *nihil.* It was probably re-written before it was submitted to Cranmer; for he here refers, not, as usual, to the number of the leaf in the printed book, but to "fo. script." i.e. to a manuscript leaf inserted. As might be expected from the king's objections, the article is very much altered in The Necessary Doctrine. See that Formulary, p. 278.]

*Item*, That this office, this ministration, this power and authority, [p]* is no tyrannical power, having no * certain laws or limits within the which it ought to be contained, [q]* nor yet none absolute power; but it is a moderate power, subject, determined, and restrained unto those certain ends and limits, for the which the same was appointed by God's ordinance; which, as was said before, is only to administer and distribute unto the members of Christ's mystical body spiritual and everlasting things, that is to say, the pure and heavenly doctrine of Christ's gospel, and the graces conferred in his sacraments; and further to do and execute such other things appertaining unto their office, as were before rehearsed.

[p] *to loose and absolve all persons that sin according to the scriptures, to bind and excommunicate, to consecrate sacraments* (xliii.), *and to administer the same with conferring and giving the gifts of the Holy Ghost have*

[q] *and*

xliii. "To consecrate sacraments." Consecration is called only of the sacrament of the altar: therefore it is more plain to say thus: "to consecrate the body of Christ, and to minister the sacraments[4]."

*Inst.* pp. 102, 3. [r]* And that they should also not cease from the execution of their said office, until all the said members were not only reduced and brought unto the unity of the faith, and the knowledge of the Son of God; but also that they were come unto a perfect state and full age therein, that is to say, until they were so established and confirmed in the same, that they could no more afterward be wavering therein, and be* led or carried like children into any contrary doctrine or opinion, by the craft and subtile persuasion of the false pastors and teachers, which go about by craft to bring them into erroneous opinions: but that they should constantly follow the true doctrine of Christ's gospel, growing and increasing continually by charity unto a perfect member of that body, whereof Christ is the [s]* very * head.

[r] *And that they should be so vigilant upon their flock, that they should not suffer them to be*

[s] *only*

*xliv.* "As heretofore be rehearsed." It appeareth to me to be in vain, after a particular recitation, to add this general, "and such other," and then to restrain the general only to the particulars before expressed. For what availeth it to say "such other," when it is meant of none other than before is expressed?

*xlv.* "And the head thereby fully pleased." I can perceive no good cause why these words should be put in this place; for they come in very strangely.

*Inst.* p. 104. Thirdly, because the said [t]* power* and office, or * function,* hath annexed unto it assured promises of excellent and inestimable things[u].

[t] *order*

[u] *the occupiers thereof being such as afore.*

*Inst.* pp. 104, 5. *Item*, That this office, this power, and authority, was committed and given by Christ and his apostles unto certain persons only, that is to say, unto priests or bishops, whom they did elect, call, and admit thereunto by their prayer and imposition of their hands.

*Note, that there were no kings christian under whom they did dwell.*

* Second,* we think it [x] convenient, that all bishops and preachers shall instruct and teach the people committed unto their spiritual charge, that the sacrament of orders may worthily be called a sacrament, * because it is a holy rite or ceremony instituted by Christ and his apostles in the new testament, and doth consist of two part, like as the other sacraments of the church do, that is to say, of a spiritual and an invisible grace, and also of an outward and a visible sign. The invisible gift or grace conferred in this sacrament is nothing else but the power, the office, and the authority before mentioned. The visible and outward sign is the prayer and imposition of the bishop's hands upon the person which receiveth the said gift or grace. And [y]* to the intent the church of Christ should never be destituted of such ministers, as should have and execute the [z] said power * of the keys,* it was also ordained and commanded by the apostles, that the same sacrament should be applied and administered by the bishop from time to time unto such other persons as had the qualities necessarily required thereunto; which said qualities the apostles did also very diligently describe, as it appeareth evidently in the third chapter of the first Epistle of St Paul to Timothy, and the first chapter of his Epistle unto Titus[a].

[x] *also*

[y] *and that it was institute*

[z] *former*

[a] *Quare non hic exprimuntur?*

*Inst.* pp. 108, 9. And [b]* in this part also two things be * to be noted. * The first is,* that all punishment which priests or bishops may, by the authority of the gospel, inflict or put to any person, is by word only, and not by any violence or constraint corporal. [c]* The second is,* that although priests and bishops have the power and jurisdiction to excommunicate, as is aforesaid, yet they be not bound so precisely by any commandment of God, but that they ought and may attemper, moderate, or forbear the execution of their said jurisdiction in that part at all times, whensoever they shall perceive and think that by doing the contrary they should not cure or help the offenders, or else give such occasion of further trouble and unquietness in the church, that the peace and tranquillity thereof might thereby be impeached, troubled, or otherwise interrupted or broken.

[d]* The second point, wherein consisteth* the jurisdiction committed unto priests and bishops by the authority of God's law, is to approve and admit such persons as (being nominated, elected, and presented unto them to exercise the office and room of preaching the gospel, and of ministering the sacraments, and to have the cure of jurisdiction over these certain people within this parish or within this diocese) shall be thought unto them meet and worthy to exercise the same; and to reject and

[b] *farther it is*

[c] *also*

[d] *Farther*

[[4] See Nec. Doctr. p. 278.]

repel from the said room such as they shall judge to be unmeet therefore. And in this part we must know and understand, that the said presentation and nomination * is of man's ordinance, and * appertaineth unto the founders and patrons, or other persons, according to the laws and ordinances of men provided for the same[e].

[e] *in every region.*

*Inst.* p. 110. * The third point, wherein consisteth the jurisdiction committed unto priests and bishops by the authority of God's law, is to make and ordain *[f] certain rules or canons, [g]* concerning* holy days, fasting days, the manner and ceremonies to be used in [h]the ministration of the sacraments, the manner of singing the psalms and spiritual hymns, (as St Paul calleth them,) the diversity of degrees among the ministers, and the form and manner of their ornaments, and finally concerning such other rites, ceremonies, and observances as do tend and conduce to the preservation of quietness and decent order to be had and used among the people when they shall be assembled together in the temple[i]. For sith that scripture commandeth that all Christian people should at certain times assemble themselves, and convene together in some public or open place, there to invocate and call upon the name of God, there to hear his will and his word by * our * preachers, there to receive the sacraments, there to give laud and praise to God in psalmody, in prayers, in meditations, and in reading; and finally, with all humility and reverent order, to magnify, extol, and set forth the honour of God with all our possible power; and forasmuch also as great trouble, unquietness, and tumult might arise among the multitude so assembled, in case there were no certain rules, ordinances, and ceremonies prescribed unto them, whereby they should be contained in quietness, and not suffered to do every man after his own fashion or appetite; [k]* it belongeth unto the jurisdiction of priests or bishops to * make certain rules or canons concerning all these things, and for the causes aforesaid.

[f] *Moreover concerning.*
[g] *establishing*
[h] *the church in*
[i] *: it is thought convenient that the clergy of every region should labour and be vigilant in them, and foresee that by them there should not be induced idolatry, superstitiousness, or any detriment to Christ's honour or his church, and then they be reputed most meet to have authority to both institute and publish the same, the king and his people giving their assent thereto.*
[k] *it is therefore thought requisite and right necessary that the clergy should*

*Inst.* p. 111. Although the whole jurisdiction appertaining (as is aforesaid) unto priests and bishops be committed unto them in general words, (as it appeareth by divers places of scripture, and specially in the 20th chapter of the Acts[l], where the apostle saith, Take diligent heed to yourselves, and to all your whole flock, among whom the Holy Ghost hath set, ordained, and made you bishops, to rule and govern the church of God;) yet there is also a particular order, form, and manner requisite to the due execution of the same, according to the saying of St Paul, Look that all things be done in the church seemly and in a decent order[m].

[l] *Here is cure spoken of, and not jurisdiction or power.*
[m] *videlicet, as far as you have power in.*

*Inst.* p. 114. * The second thing to be noted is, that like as it is the will and commandment of God that priests and bishops should, in the execution of all those things which appertain unto their jurisdiction by the authority of the gospel, (as is aforesaid,) attemper their doings and proceedings with all charity and mildness, and should foresee by their singular wisdom that they pronounce no sentence, nor prescribe or make any constitution or ordinance which may in any wise be prejudicial or hurtful unto their flock, but such as undoubtedly do tend as well to the good preservation and increase of Christ's true religion, as also of Christian charity and tranquillity to be had among them; even so and in like manner[n] * all the people being under their[o] cure, and within the limits of their said jurisdiction, * (of what estate or condition soever they be,) be also bound by the law of God, and by the order and bond of charity,* humbly[p] * to * obey them, and * to[p] * fulfil all their said precepts and ordinances, duly and rightfully made by the authority of [q]their said jurisdiction; specially being the same ones received by the common consent of the people, and authorised by the laws of the christian princes.

[n] *Also it is thought convenient that*
[o] *spiritual*
[p] *should*
[q] *Scripture and*

*Inst.* p. 116. Finally, being thus declared, not only what is the virtue and efficacy, with the whole institution and use of the sacrament of * holy * orders, but also in what things consisteth the power and jurisdiction of priests and bishops, and unto what limits the same is extended * by the authority of the gospel, and also what is added thereunto by the grants and sufferances, or permission of kings and princes: * we[r] think it convenient, that all * bishops and * preachers shall instruct and teach the people committed unto[s] their spiritual charge, that whereas certain men do imagine and affirm that Christ should give unto the bishop of Rome power and authority, not only to be head and governor of all priests and bishops in Christ's church, but also to have and occupy the whole monarchy of the world in his hands, and that he may thereby lawfully depose kings and princes from their realms, dominions, and seigniories, and so transfer and give the same to such persons as him liketh; that is utterly false and untrue: for Christ never gave unto St Peter, or unto any of the apostles, or their successors, any such authority.

[r] *bishops*
[s] *our and*

*Inst.* pp. 120, 1. Moreover the truth is, that God constituted and ordained the authority of christian kings and princes to be the most high and supreme above all other powers and offices[t] in the regiment and governance of [u]* his * people; and committed unto them, as unto the chief heads of their commonwealths, the cure and oversight of all the people which be within their realms and dominions, without any exception.

[t] *in this world*
[u] *their*

*Inst.* p. 121. We must think and believe that God hath constituted and made christian kings and princes to be as the chief heads and overlookers over the said priests and bishops, to cause them to administer their office and power committed unto them purely and sincerely; and in case they shall be negligent in any part thereof[x], to cause them to supply and repair the same again[y]. And God hath also commanded the said priests and bishops to obey, with all humbleness and reverence, all the laws made by the said princes, being not contrary to the laws of God, whatsoever they be; and that not only *propter iram*, but also *propter conscientiam*.

[x] *or will not diligently execute the same,*
[y] *or else to put other in their place.*

*Inst.* pp. 123, 4. Second, that although it be not expressed in scripture, that the said apostles had then any new commandment of Christ to anoint such as they had healed with oil; yet, forasmuch as the holy apostle St James, endued with the holy Spirit of Christ, prescribed a certain rule or doctrine, and gave in manner a commandment, that whensoever any person should fortune to fall sick, [z]*he should* call or send for the priests or ancients of the church, and cause them to pray over him, anointing him with oil in the name of our Lord; [a]* and further added hereunto, as an assured promise, that by the said prayer of the priests and the sick person, made in right faith and confidence in God, the sick man should be restored unto his health, and God should set him on foot again, and if he were in sin, his sins should be forgiven him;* it shall therefore be very necessary and expedient that all true christian people do use and observe this manner of anoiling of sick persons with due reverence and honour, as it is prescribed by the holy apostle St James.

[z] *and*

[a] *that then they should minister the same* (xlvi.) *to him or them so calling for it:*

xlvi. "That then they minister the same." The commandment requireth first, that the sick man should call for the priests, and that they, being called, should pray over him. And the promise made of the prayer in time of anointing is stricken out, which chiefly ought to be known[1].

*Inst.* pp. 124-6. And to the intent the same should be had in more honour and veneration, the said holy fathers willed and taught, that all christian men should repute and account the said manner of anoiling among the other sacraments of the church, *forasmuch as it is a visible sign of an invisible grace: whereof the visible sign is the anoiling with oil in the name of God; which oil (for the natural properties belonging unto the same) is a very convenient thing to signify and figure the great mercy and grace of God, and the spiritual light, joy, comfort, and gladness which God poureth out upon all faithful people calling upon him by the inward unction of the Holy Ghost: and the grace conferred in this sacrament is the relief and recovery of the disease and sickness wherewith the sick person is then diseased and troubled, and also the remission of his sins, if he be then in sin. This grace we be assured to obtain by the virtue and efficacy of the faithful and fervent prayer used in the ministration of this sacrament of anoiling, according to the saying of St James before rehearsed, and also according to the sundry promises made by Christ unto the faithful prayer of his church; as when Christ saith, Whatsoever ye shall ask and pray my Father to give unto you in my name, it shall be granted unto you. For the better understanding whereof, two things be here specially to be noted. The first is, that St James calleth here the prayer to be used in the time of this inunction the prayer of faith: whereby he meaneth, that this prayer ought to be made in that right faith, trust, and confidence, which we ought to have in God, to obtain the effect of our petitions made in the ministration of this sacrament; and that it ought to contain nothing but that shall stand with the pleasure, the honour, and glory of God; and that when we direct our prayers unto God for any bodily health or relief, or for any other temporal commodity, we ought always to temper our said prayer with this condition, that is to say, if it shall so stand with God's will and his pleasure; and that we ought to say, as Christ said in his prayer unto his Father, Father, if it shall please thee, I am content to die and suffer this shameful and cruel death of the cross: thy will be fulfilled herein: let not my will and desire be followed, but let thy will and disposition be fulfilled, whereunto I wholly commit myself.*

[b]* The second thing to be noted is, that* to the attaining of the said grace, (xlvii.) conferred in this sacrament of extreme unction, it is expedient *also* that the sick person himself shall knowledge his offences towards God and his neighbour, and ask forgiveness of them for the same; and likewise forgive all them that have offended him in word or deed: and so being in perfect love and charity, to pray himself (as he may) with faithful heart, and full hope and confidence in God, for the remission of his sins, and restoring unto his bodily health, if it shall so stand with God's pleasure.

[b] *Also*

xlvii. "Also to the attaining of the said grace." The said grace mentioned of before, and the virtue of the prayer also whereby the same grace is given, be both stricken out.

*Inst.* pp. 128, 9. Thus being declared the virtue and efficacy of all the seven sacraments, we think it convenient, that all bishops and preachers shall instruct and teach the people committed to their spiritual charge, that although the sacraments *of matrimony,* of confirmation, of *holy* orders, and of extreme unction, have been of long time past received and approved by the common consent of the catholic church, to have the name and dignity of sacraments, as indeed they be well worthy to have; (forasmuch as they be holy and godly signs, whereby, and by the prayer of the minister, be not only signified and represented, but also given and conferred some certain and special gifts of the Holy Ghost, necessary for christian men to have for one godly purpose or other, like as it hath been before declared;) yet there is a difference in dignity and necessity between them and the other *three [c]* sacraments, that is to say, the sacraments of baptism [d], of penance, (xlviii.) and of the altar; and that for divers causes. First, because these *four* sacraments[2] be instituted of Christ, to be as certain instruments or remedies necessary for our salvation and the attaining of everlasting life. Second, because [e]*they* be also commanded by Christ to be ministered and received in their outward visible signs. Thirdly, because they have annexed and conjoined unto their said visible signs such spiritual graces, as whereby our sins be remitted and forgiven, and we be perfectly renewed, regenerated, purified, justified, and made the very members of Christ's mystical body, so oft as we worthily and duly receive the same.

[c] *four*

[d] *matrimony,*

[e] *that most of them*

xlviii. "Of matrimony, of baptism, and of penance." The causes there assigned

[1 Nec. Doctr. p. 290.] [2 Three Sacraments. Inst. Ed. Oxon. 1825.]

may not be well applied to matrimony; that it should be, as the other were, by the manifest institution of Christ: or, that it is of necessity to salvation: or, that thereby we should have the forgiveness of sins, renovation of life, and justification, &c.[1]

*The Ten Commandments.*

[*Inst.* p. 130.] 1. THOU shalt[f] have[g] *none other* gods but me[h].

2. Thou shalt not make to thyself any graven thing, ne any similitude of any thing that is in heaven above, or in earth beneath, nor in the water under the earth[i]. *Thou shalt not* bow down to them, *ne[k] worship them.*

3. Thou shalt not take the name of thy Lord God in vain.

4. Remember that thou do sanctify and keep holy thy sabbath day.

5. Honour thy father and mother.

6. Thou shalt not kill.

7. Thou shalt not commit adultery.

8. Thou shalt not steal.

9. Thou shalt not bear false witness against thy neighbour.

10. Thou shalt not desire thy neighbour's house, his wife, his servant, his maid, his ox, his ass, ne any other thing that is his[l].

[f] *not*
[g] *nor repute any other God, or*
[h] *Jesu Christ,* xlix.
[i] *to the intent to*
[k] *or honour them as God or Gods.* l.
[l] *wrongfully or unjustly.* li.

xlix. "But me Jesus Christ." It is not the use of scripture to attribute to one person of the Trinity peculiarly that thing which doth express the three persons in one deity. And we must not repute for God only Jesus Christ, but also the Father and the Holy Ghost. And here be set forth the ten commandments, as they were written by God in the two tables. And it seemeth better to read these commandments, taken out of the scripture, even as they be there written, without any addition, than that we should alter the words of scripture, and specially of God's own commandments[2].

l. "Or honour them as God or Gods." We may not thus add to the words of scripture, but set them out first plainly and surely, even as they be, and after expound and declare them[3].

li. "Wrongfully or unjustly." To this I say as to the next before[4].

*Inst.* p. 131. To have God is not to have him as we have other outward things, as clothes upon our back, or treasure in our chests; nor also to name him with our mouth[m], or to worship him with kneeling, or other such gestures[n]: but to have him our God is to conceive him in our hearts, to cleave fast and surely unto him with heart and mind, to put all our trust and confidence in him, to set all our thought and care upon him, and to hang wholly of him, taking him to be infinitely good and merciful unto us.

[m] *outwardly*
[n] *only*

*Inst.* p. 133. *And so do they, that by superstition repute (lii.) some days good, some dismal or infortunate; or think it a thing unlucky to meet in a morning with certain kind of beasts, or with men of certain professions. For such superstitious folk infame the creatures of God.*

*Item,* That they be of the same sort, which by lots, *astrology,* divination, chattering of birds, *physiognomy,* and looking of men's hands, or other unlawful and superstitious crafts, take upon them certainly to tell, determine, and judge beforehand of men's acts and fortunes, which be to come afterward.

lii. "They that by superstition repute." Whereas the same is stricken out, it seemeth more necessary to remain, forsomuch as the common people do in nothing more superstitiously. Likewise of astrology, and specially physiognomy[5].

*Inst.* pp. 134-36. The second commandment Moses declareth at good length in the book of Deuteronomy, where he speaketh in this manner: "In the day when our Lord spake to you in Horeb from the midst of the fire, you heard the voice, and the sound of his words, but you saw no form or similitude, lest peradventure you should have been thereby deceived, and should have made to yourself an engraved similitude or image of man or woman, or a similitude of any manner beast upon earth, or of fowl under heaven, or of any beast that creepeth upon the earth, or of fishes that tarry in the water under the earth; and lest peradventure lifting up your eyes to heaven, and there seeing the sun, and the moon, and the stars of heaven, you should by error be deceived, and bow down to them, and worship them, which the Lord hath created to serve all people under heaven[o]."

[o] *and not to be honoured as God.* liii.

liii. "And not be honoured as God." All the long sentence before, whereunto these words be added, is the very words of God in Deuteronomy, which would be recited sincerely without any addition. And the images ought to have no manner of honour, neither such honour as is due unto God, nor such as is due unto his reasonable creatures. And the same words "as God" be added in another place in the same side of the leaf, and not well, as I surely think.

---

[[1] See Nec. Doctr. p. 293.] [[2] Ibid. p. 295.] [[3] Ibid.] [[4] Ibid.] [[5] Ibid. p. 298.]

By these words we be utterly forbidden to make or to have any similitude or image, to the intent to bow down to it, or to worship it. And therefore we think it convenient, that all bishops and preachers shall instruct and teach the people committed to their spiritual charge, first, that God in his substance cannot by any similitude or image be represented or expressed; for no wit ne understanding can comprehend his substance: and that the fathers of the church, considering the dulness of man's wit, and partly yielding to the custom of gentility, (which before their coming unto the faith of Christ had certain representations of their false gods,) suffered the picture or similitude of the Father of heaven to be had and set up in churches; not that he is any such thing as we in that image do behold, (for he is no corporal ne bodily substance,) but only to put us in remembrance that there is a Father in heaven, and that he is a distinct person from the Son and the Holy Ghost; * which thing nevertheless, if the common people would duly conceive of the heavenly Father without any bodily representation, it were more seemly for christian people to be without all such images of the Father, than to have any of them.* (liv.)

Second, that although all images, be they engraven, painted, or wrought in arras, or in any other wise made, be so prohibited that they may neither be bowed down unto ne worshipped[p], (forasmuch as they be the works of man's hand only,) yet they be not so prohibited, but that they may be had and set up [q]* in churches,* so it be for none other purpose but only to the intent that we (in beholding and looking upon them, as in certain books, and seeing represented in them the manifold examples of virtues, which were in the saints, represented by the said images) may the rather be provoked, kindled, and stirred to yield thanks to our Lord, and to praise him in his said saints, and to remember and lament our sins and offences, and to pray God that we may have grace to follow their goodness and holy living. As for an example. The image of our Saviour, as an open book, hangeth on the cross in the rood, or is painted in cloths, walls, or windows, to the intent that beside the examples of virtues which we may learn at Christ, we may be also many ways provoked to remember his painful and cruel passion, and also to consider ourselves, when we behold the said image, and to condemn and abhor our sin, which was the cause of his so cruel death, and thereby to profess that we will no more sin: and furthermore, considering what high charity was in him that would die for us his enemies, and what great dangers we have escaped, and what high benefits we receive by his redemption, we may be provoked in all our distresses and troubles to run for comfort unto him. All these lessons, with many more, * we may learn in this book of the rood, if we will entirely and earnestly look upon it.* And as the life of our Saviour Christ is represented by this image, even so the lives of the holy saints which followed him be represented unto us by their images. And therefore the said images may well be set up in churches, to be as books for unlearned people, to learn therein examples of humility, charity, patience, temperance, contempt of the world, the flesh, and the devil, and to learn example of all other virtues, and for the other causes above rehearsed. For which causes only images [r]* be to* be set in the churches, and not for any honour to be done unto them. For although we use to cense the said images, and to kneel before them, and to offer unto them, and to kiss their feet, and such other things; yet we must know and understand, that such things be not nor ought to be done to the images self, but only to God, and in his honour, or in the honour of the holy saint or saints which be represented by the said images.

[p] *as God,*

[q] *both in churches and out of churches,*

[s] *be brought to our remembrance by the book of the rood, if we being first well instruct and taught what is represented and meant thereby, do diligently behold and look upon it.*

[r] *may*

liv. "Which thing nevertheless, if the common people." I marvel why these words should be stricken out, seeing that it is contrary to the scripture to have any such images of the Father of heaven, as St Austin saith, and they be suffered only for the infirmity of the people, as we have declared. St Austin saith, in his book "De fide et Symbolo," cap. 7. "*Tale [enim] simulacrum Deo nefas est Christiano in templo collocare*[7]." And likewise he and many of the most ancient authors do say in many other places[8].

*Inst.* p. 138. The right use of the name of God, and the outward honour of the same, standeth chiefly in these things following, that is to say, in the constant confession of his name, in the right invocation of the same, in giving of due thanks unto God, as well in prosperity as in adversity, [s]*and in the preaching and teaching of* his word.

[s] *and in avowing and sticking to*

*Inst.* p. 139. And we[t] must also preach the word of God truly and purely, and set forth the name of God unto other, and reprove all false and erroneous doctrine and heresies. For although priests and bishops only be specially called and deputed as public ministers of God's word, yet every christian man is bound particularly[u] to teach[x] his family, and such as be under his governance within his house, when time and place requireth[y].

[t] *priests and bishops.* lv.

[u] *according to his vocation and knowledge*

[x] *and order*

[y] *so that as much as in them lieth, they suffer not open sin to be used in their rule and family, but virtue to be exercised instead of it.*

lv. "Priests and bishops." If these words be added, then this sentence joineth not well with the sentence following. And if any man be offended with this word "preach," then if it be put out, and this word "teach" put in the stead thereof after this sort, "and we must also teach," then do both the sentences run in a good composition together, so that no man can be offended[9].

---

[[6] Nec. Doctr. p. 300.]

[[7] August. De fide et symb. cap. vii. Tom. III. p. 63. Ed. Paris. 1636.]

[[8] See Nec. Doctr. p. 299.]

[[9] Ibid. p. 303.]

*Inst.* p. 140. *Item,* That they also do take the name of God in vain, which swear to do that thing which they intended not to do; or swear to forbear that which they intended not to forbear; or swear to do any thing, which to do is unlawful; or swear to leave undone any thing, which to omit or leave undone [z] * is unlawful.* And such as so swear to do things unlawful, not only offend in such swearing, but also they much more offend, if they perform the thing that they do swear.

[z] *is not right nor reasonable.*

*Item,* That they also break this commandment, which swear to do or to observe any thing which to do and observe they know not whether it be lawful or unlawful; or that make any oath contrary to their lawful oath or promise made before, so long as their former oath or promise standeth in strength [a].

[a] *and toucheth not their prince.* lvi.

*Ibid.* Priests and ministers of Christ's church do also break this commandment, if, in the administration of the sacraments, they yield not the whole efficacy, virtue, and grace thereof to our Lord, as the very author of the same; but ascribe the said efficacy, virtue, and grace, or any part thereof, to themselves: or if any of them do use any [b] of the sacraments to any conjurations, or any other strange practice, contrary to that holy use for the which they be ordained.

[b] *words longing to the consecration.* * lvi.

lvi. "And toucheth not their prince." Methinketh this clause need not to be added, or rather, that it is not true; for a latter oath may be made touching the prince, contrary to the former lawful oath, and yet good: as when the first by the king's laws continueth no longer in his strength[1].

*lvi.[2] "Words belonging to the consecration." We say not "the words of the consecration" of any of the sacraments, saving only of the sacrament of the altar.

*Inst.* p. 141. Nevertheless, to pray to saints to be intercessors with us and for us to our Lord for our suits which we make to him, and for such things as we can obtain of none but of him, [c] *so that we make no invocation of them,* is lawful, and allowed by the catholic church.

[c] *so that we esteem not nor worship them not, as givers of those gifts, but as intercessors for those same*[3],

*Inst.* p. 142. Notwithstanding it is not necessary to alter [d] the common speech which is used, nor there is any error therein; so that the sentence or meaning thereof be well and truly understanded, that is to say, that the said altars and churches be not dedicated to any saint, but to God only, and of the saints but a memorial, to put us in remembrance of them, that we may follow their example and living.

[d] *the right understanding or meaning that ought to be conceived of.* lvii.

lvii. "The right understanding." In the book it is evident that it was reasoned, whether it were necessary to alter the common speech which is used, and seemeth not to agree with the truth of God's word, as it is there confessed it doth not, except it be better understand than it appeareth to sound. And that it is meant of the alteration of the speech, the words following do shew; sc. "that is used, nor is there any error therein, so that the sentence and meaning thereof be well and truly understand:" now these words, "therein and thereof," cannot be referred to that is added, for then the sentence were thus: "There is no error in the right understanding and meaning, &c. so that the sentence of the right understanding and meaning be well understanded."

*Inst.* pp. 142, 3. As St. Austin saith, All the other nine commandments be moral commandments, and belonged not only to the Jews, and all the other people of the world, in the time of the old testament, but also [e] to all christian people in the new testament. But this precept of sabbath, as concerning rest from bodily labour the seventh day, pertained only unto the Jews in the old testament, before the coming of Christ, and [f] not to us christian people in the new testament[4].

[e] *belong now*

[f] *pertaineth*

*Inst.* p. 143. Make thy will to be wrought in us, that from our own corrupt will we may rest and cease. And for this purpose God hath ordained [g] * that we should * fast, watch, and labour; to the end that by these [h] * remedies * we might mortify and kill the evil and sensual desires of the flesh, and attain this spiritual rest and quietness, which is signified and figured in this commandment.

[g] *these that follow, as remedies, that is to say,*

[h] *and such others*

*Inst.* p. 145. And they that can read may be well occupied upon the holy day, if they read unto other [i] such good works which may be unto them instead of a sermon. For all things that edify man's soul in our Lord God be good and wholesome sermons.

[i] *such as they have care of.* lviii.

---

[[1] See Nec. Doctr. p. 304.]

[[2] Two Annotations are numbered (lvi.) in the original manuscript. Though probably a mistake, it has been retained to avoid confusion in reference.]

[[3] See Nec. Doctr. p. 305.]

[[4] The following is perhaps the passage intended: Cetera tamen ibi præcepta proprie, sicut præcepta sunt, sine ulla figurata significatione observamus....Observare tamen diem sabbati non ad literam jubemur, secundum otium ab opere corporali, sicut observant Judæi: et ipsa eorum observatio quia ita præcepta est, nisi aliam quandam spiritalem requiem significet, ridenda judicata. August. Epist. cxix. ad Januar. cap. xii. Tom. II. p. 217. Ed. Paris. 1635.]

lviii. "Such as they have charge of." The words of the print import no more, but that those which can read may be well occupied to read good works to others which cannot read; and then if these words should be added, "such as they have charge of," it might seem that no man were well occupied to read good works, but the father to the children, the master to his servants, the parson to his own parishioners, and such like. But I think surely, that he that can read may be well occupied, if he read some part of scripture unto all them which cannot read; not as taking the office of a priest or bishop upon him, except he be called thereunto, but of charity moved, as he shall see necessity, time, and opportunity. Whereof St Paul saith, *Verbum Christi habitet in vobis abundanter in omni sapientia; docete et monete vos in vicem*[5].

*Ibid.* For notwithstanding all that is afore spoken, it is not meant but that in time of necessity we may upon the holy day give ourselves to labour[k], as for saving of our corn and cattle, when it is in danger, or likely to be destroyed, if remedy be not had in time.

[k] *so that we neglect not mass and even-song.* lix.

lix. "So that we neglect not mass and even-song." As well there might be added, "matins." And so it signifieth, that whatsoever necessity happeneth upon the holy day, we must so apply ourselves to such urgent business, that mass, matins, and even-song, may not be omitted; and yet matins and even-song be wholly of man's tradition and ordinance, and mass also almost altogether, as it is now used; and these things were not understand in this commandment, which were made and ordained sithence the commandments were given. And the law in his most rigour doth permit otherwise, namely, to the husbandman, cooks, bakers, mariners, fishers, and such other, which, laying aside all such service, must take the time as it cometh[6].

*Inst.* pp. 145, 6. Against this commandment generally do offend all they, which will not cease and rest from their own carnal wills and pleasure, that God may work in them after his pleasure and will.

*Item,* All they, which, having no lawful impediment, do not give themselves upon the holy day to hear the word of God, to remember the benefits of God, to give thanks for the same, to pray, and to exercise such other holy works as be appointed for the same; but (as commonly is used) pass the time either in idleness, in gluttony, in riot, or in plays, or other vain and idle pastime[l].

[l] *do break this commandment.*

*Inst.* p. 147. Therefore concerning such ceremonies of the church[m], we think it convenient, that all bishops and preachers shall instruct and teach the people committed unto their spiritual charge, that although the said ceremonies have no power to remit sin, yet they be very expedient things to stir and cause us to lift up our minds unto God, and to put us in continual remembrance of those spiritual things which be signified by them.

[m] [7] *as have been instituted by our forefathers not repugnant to Christ's laws,*

[*Inst.* pp. 147, 8.] Therefore they be not to be contemned and cast away, but be to be used and continued as things good and laudable for the purposes abovesaid[n].

[n] *so long as it shall be seen to the head rulers and chief ministers of the church or churches convenient to have them observed and kept*[8].

## *The declaration of the fifth Commandment.*

[*Inst.* p. 148.] As touching the fifth Commandment, we think it convenient, that all bishops and preachers shall instruct and teach the people committed to their spiritual charge, first, that by this word *father* is understanded here, not only the natural father and mother which did carnally beget us and brought us up, but also * the spiritual father, (lx.) by whom we be spiritually regenerated and nourished in Christ; and * all other governors and rulers, under whom we be nourished and brought up, or ordered and guided. *And although this commandment make express mention only of the children or inferiors to their parents and superiors, yet in the same is also understanded and comprised the office and duty of the parents and superiors again unto their children and inferiors.*

lx. "Also the spiritual father, by whom." Methinketh this might well remain, that the preachers of God's word might be the better esteemed and had in reputation: neither should it be so done without example of good authority to be followed, seeing that St Paul looked so to be reputed of the Corinthians, yea, and rebuked them as unkind children, in that they had more regard of other which were but their schoolmasters, than of him which was their father, that is, did first beget them unto Christ by preaching the word of God unto them: as he saith, 1 Cor. iv. *Si decem millia pædagogorum habeatis in Christo, at non multos patres. Nam in Christo Jesu per evangelium ego vos genui.* And now also they that preaching the word of God do

[[5] See Nec. Doctr. p. 308.] [[6] Ibid. p. 309.] [[7] Ibid. p. 310.] [[8] Ibid. p. 311.]

teach us in our youth the principles of our faith, seem to supply the same room, and may be right well called our spiritual fathers[1].

Deut. xxi. *Inst.* p. 149. *And, if any man have a stubborn (lxi.) and a disobedient son, which will not hear the voice of his father and mother, and for correction will not amend and follow them; then shall his father and mother take him, and bring him to the judges of the city, and say, This our son is stubborn and disobedient, and despiseth our monitions, and is a rioter and a drunkard. Then shall all the people stone him to death; and thou shalt put away the evil from thee, that all Israel may hear thereof, and be

Luke xi. [o] *for* afraid. And* [o] in the book of Exody it is * also * written, He that striketh his father or mother, he shall be put to death.

lxi. "If any man have a stubborn," &c. Of all the precepts there rehearsed, none ought rather to stand than this; for none of them doth express so largely the form of the punishment of an inobedient child, and for what offences against the father he should in such wise be punished, than this doth which is stricken out[2].

*Inst.* pp. 151, 2. All bishops and preachers shall instruct and teach the people committed unto their spiritual charge, that all christian men be bound to exhibit[p] *and do unto them, which under God be* their spiritual fathers and parents[q] *of their souls, the like and the selfsame honour, which (as is aforesaid) children of duty do owe unto their natural fathers.

[p] *a certain reverence and credit unto.* lxii.
[q] *which hath charge of their souls, and to understand and believe that they be*

*Item,* That these spiritual fathers be* appointed by God to minister his sacraments unto them, *to bring them up, and* to feed them with the word of God, [r] *and to teach them* his gospel and scripture, *and by the same to govern,* to conduct, and *to* lead them in the straight way to the Father in heaven everlasting.

[r] *and by*

*Item,* That our Saviour Christ, in the gospel, maketh mention as well of the obedience as also of the corporal sustenance which all christian people do owe unto their spiritual fathers. Of the obedience he saith, That whosoever receiveth you receiveth me. And in another place he saith, He that heareth you heareth me; and he that despiseth you despiseth me. *And in another place he saith, Whatsoever they bid you do, do it.* And St Paul saith, Obey your prelates, and give place unto them: for they[s] have much charge and care for your souls, as they which must give an account therefore, that they may do it with joy and not with grief; that is to say, that they may gladly and with much comfort do their cure and charge, when they do perceive that the people be obedient to their teaching: like as on the contrariwise they have little joy or pleasure to do it, when they find the people disobedient and repugnant[t].

[s] *ought and should*
[t] *and yet nevertheless they be bound to it.*

And for the sustenance of their living, which is comprised in this word *honour,* (as before is declared,) Christ saith in the gospel, The workman is worthy his wages. And St Paul saith, Who goeth on warfare upon his own stipend? And who planteth the vine, and eateth no part of the fruit? And who feedeth the flock, and eateth no part of the milk? And after followeth, Even so hath the Lord ordained, that they which preach the gospel should live of the gospel. And therefore in another place it is written, Priests or ancients that rule well be worthy of double honour, specially they that labour in the ministration of the word of God, and his doctrine. In which place the apostle meaneth by *double honour,* not only the reverence which is due unto the spiritual fathers, (as is aforesaid,) but also that all christian people be bound to minister, find, and give unto their spiritual fathers sufficiency of all things necessary and requisite, as well for their sustenance and finding, as for the quiet and commodious exercising and executing of their said office[u].

[u] *if they have it none other way.*

Fourthly, we think it convenient, that all bishops and preachers shall instruct and teach the people committed unto their spiritual charge, that this commandment also containeth the honour and obedience which subjects owe unto their princes, and also the office of princes towards their subjects. For scripture taketh princes to be, as it were, fathers and nourices to their subjects. And by scripture it appeareth, that it appertaineth unto the office of princes to see that the right religion and true doctrine of Christ may be maintained and taught; and that their subjects may be well ruled and governed by good and just laws; *and to provide and care for them, (lxiii.) that all things necessary for them may be plenteous;* and that the people and common weal may increase; and to defend them from oppression and invasion, as well within the realm as without[x]; and to see that justice be ministered unto them indifferently; and to hear[y] benignly all their complaints; and to shew towards them (although they[z] offend) fatherly pity.

[x] *they aiding him thereto;*
[y] *or cause to be heard*
[z] *ignorantly*

lxii. "A certain reverence and credit thereto," &c. It seemeth that St Paul required as much obsequy as was to be shewed to the natural father, in the place above mentioned, and rather it may seem to reason, that more should be shewed; forsomuch as the regeneration, which is towards God and to everlasting life, far passeth the first generation, which is to a damnable state and endless punishment[3].

lxiii. "To provide and care for them." It may right well appear that St Paul affirmeth this point, specially to be required in all such as have governance over other, in these words that he saith, Rom. xii. *Qui præest in solicitudine præsit*[4].

[[1] Cranmer's attempt to preserve the paragraph failed. Nec. Doctr. p. 311.]
[[2] See Nec. Doctr. p. 312.]
[[3] Ibid. p. 318.]
[[4] Cranmer preserved the substance of this clause. Nec. Doctr. p. 315.]

*Inst.* p. 158. No man may kill, or use such bodily coercion, but only princes, and they which have authority from princes. Ne the said * princes[a], ne * any for them, may do the same, but by and according to the just order of their laws[b].

[a] *inferior rulers, or.* lxiv.
[b] *and ordinances.*

lxiv. "Inferior rulers." Princes must also do all things with justice, which otherwise cannot be known, than by their laws and ordinances institute for the ministration thereof: and when princes give pardons, placards, protections, and licences, contrary to the common order of their laws, yet that also is done by the law, so that it be never done against justice and equity between party and party. And moreover it is not amply spoken that the inferior rulers should do nothing, but by the order of their laws: for the laws be not theirs, but the princes, instead of whom they do minister the same justice, that he would do himself by the common order of his laws, if it should happen him to take the judgment thereof in his own hands[5].

*Inst.* p. 163. They also that do nourish, stir up, and provoke themselves or any other to carnal lusts and pleasures of the body, [c]* by uncleanly and wanton words, tales, songs, sights,* touchings, * gay and wanton apparel, and lascivious decking of themselves,* or any such other wanton behaviour and enticement; * and also all those which procure any such act, or that minister house, licence, or place thereto; * and all counsellors, helpers, and consenters to the same, do grievously offend God, and do transgress this commandment[d].

[c] *by uncleanly sights and wanton words.* lxv.
[d] *in procuring of the same.* lxvi.

Likewise, all they that avoid not the causes hereof so much as they conveniently may, as [e]* surfeiting, sloth, (lxvii.) idleness, immoderate sleep,* and company of such (both men and women) as be unchaste and evil disposed, be guilty of the transgression of this commandment[f].

[e] *use of idleness,*
[f] *if thereby they be provoked thereto, or cause others.* lxviii.

lxv. "And wanton words." I think that wanton tales, unclean songs, and lascivious apparel, need to be spoken of as much as any thing else, being so much used as it is, contrary to God's word; which commandeth us in this wise, "Let not filthy communication come from your mouth." Ephes. iv. And as touching the prohibition of lascivious apparel, namely of women, it appeareth, 1 Tim. ii. and 1 Pet. iii.[6]

lxvi. "In procuring of the same." The whole sentence shall yet be more perfect, if it be said, "in maintenance of the same;" for they that be only consenters to such evil be not also procurers, albeit they be maintainers.

lxvii. "As surfeiting, sloth." It seemeth much better expressed before, because the chief and special causes of unchaste living were rehearsed more at large.

lxviii. "If thereby they be provoked." Whether they be or not provoked, they that wittingly doth accompany with such, although they keep themselves chaste, yet forsomuch as they seem to be fautors of them, they be guilty of the transgression of this commandment: for that is, even as St Paul saith, to communicate with the unfruitful works of darkness, and not to reprove them. Ephes. v. To the avoiding whereof, he would us so much to eschew the company of them that be evil, that we should neither eat nor drink with them, 1 Cor. v.

*Inst.* p. 172. They chiefly be transgressors of this commandment, which, by deliberation and full consent, cast their minds and studies to accomplish the concupiscence and desire which they have to obtain and get another man's wife, child, servant, house, land, corn, cattle, or any thing or goods that be his[g].

[g] *without due recompence.* lxix.

And they also be transgressors of this commandment, which by envy be sorry of their neighbour's wealth and prosperity, or be glad of their sorrow, hinderance, or adversity; and also all they which do not set their minds and studies to preserve, maintain, and defend unto their neighbours (as much as lieth in them) their wives, children, servants, houses, lands, goods, and all that is theirs. For (as before is declared) this commandment not only forbiddeth us to desire[h] from our neighbour any thing which is his, but by the same we be also commanded gladly to wish and will unto him that he may quietly possess and enjoy all that God hath sent him, be it never so great abundance. And this mind we ought to bear unto every man by this commandment, not only if they be our friends and lovers, but also if they be our enemies and adversaries.

[h] *unlawfully*

lxix. "Without due recompence." This addition agreeth not well with the coveting of another man's wife, wherein is no recompensation; and in the other things,

---

[[5] See Nec. Doctr. p. 322.]
[[6] In this and the three following objections Cranmer succeeded. Nec. Doctr. p. 326.]

although recompensation be made, yet the commandment nevertheless is transgressed and broken[1].

lxx. "Here follow certain notes." All the notes[2] after the commandments be clean put out, which be very good, and contain many things necessary and expedient to be known: as, the threatenings of God to the transgressors, and the promises to the observers of the same; a most brief and short content of every commandment; a declaration of the love of God and of our neighbour, what it is, and how therein all the ten commandments be comprised; the causes why the ten commandments be necessary to be known; and the transition from the ten commandments unto the *Paternoster*. And none of these things, meseemeth, were good to be left out.

*Inst.* p. 178. 1. Our Father that art in heaven, thy name be hallowed.
2. Thy kingdom come unto us.
3. Thy will be done *and fulfilled* in earth, as it is in heaven.
4. Give us this day our daily bread.
5. And forgive us our trespasses, as we forgive them that trespass against us.
i *And suffer not us to be led.* lxxi. 6. i* And lead us not* into temptation.
7. But deliver us from the evil. Amen.

lxxi. "Suffer not us to be led." Christ taught us thus to pray, "Lead us not into temptation." And we should not alter any word in the scripture, which wholly is ministered unto us by the Ghost of God, 2 Pet. i., although it shall appear to us in many places to signify much absurdity: but first, the scripture must be set out in God's own words, and if there be any ambiguity, absurdity, or scruple, after it would be declared, according to the true sense thereof[3].

*Inst.* p. 182. Fifthly, that in these words, *Our Father*, is signified, that we ought to believe, *not only* that Almighty God is the common Father of all christian people, and equally and indifferently regardeth the rich and the poor, the free and the bond, the lord and the subject; k*but* also that all christian people l be Christ's own brethren, and the very co-inheritors and compartioners with him in the kingdom of heaven; and finally, that all christian men be brethren together, and have all one Father, which is m God Almighty.

k *touching the soul, and.* lxxii.
l *endeavouring themselves to live according to his precepts*
m *our*

lxxii. "Touching the soul." Christ testifieth that all that be elect shall of God be equally and indifferently regarded of him in every condition, concerning not only the soul but also the body: so that, considering the state whereunto he hath called them, he provideth meat, drink, and clothing for them, Matt. vi.: yea, and that every hair of their head is in reputation under God, and in his preservation, Matt. x., Luke xii. And although he provide more abundantly for the lords and rich men, than he doth for the subjects and poor folks, yet he no more accepteth and regardeth the rich with their riches, than he doth the poor with their poverty: but every man, as his heart is joined and affied to God, so he is accepted and regarded of God, whether he be rich or poor, free or bond.

*Inst.* pp. 182, 3. Sixthly, by these words, *which art in heaven*, we be taught, that we ought to have, *not only* an inward desire and a great care and study to come to that place where our heavenly Father is, n*but also an inward sorrow and grief that we be so long kept from* the presence of our heavenly Father, *and be subject here unto so manifold cures and thoughts, to so many troubles and misery, and to so many and so grievous perils and dangers of the world, of sin, and of the devil.* For like as a loving child is ever desirous to be where his father is, *and if his father shall depart to any place, he will lament and be sorry, unless he may go with him, and in his absence he will mourn, and at his return he will be joyful;* even so ought we desire ever to be with our heavenly Father; and to o*see* that our conversation be all withdrawn from the world, the flesh, and the devil, and be set in heaven and heavenly things, as St Paul saith.

n *and much to covet*
o *endeavour ourselves*

*Inst.* pp. 184, 5. For the devil (undoubtedly) is king over all the children of pride, that is to say, over all them that be sinners, rebels, and disobedient unto God p.

p *as long as they so continue.*

*Inst.* p. 186. Make us *that we impute not to the devil or evil men,* when any adversity chanceth unto us; *but* that we may attribute all unto *thy godly will*q, and give thee thanks therefore, which dost ordain all such things for our weal and benefit.

q *our desert.* lxxiii.

[1 This addition was struck out according to Cranmer's wish. Nec. Doctr. p. 333.]

[2 Notwithstanding Cranmer's remonstrance, these notes were all omitted in The Necessary Doctrine.]

[3 See Nec. Doctr. p. 178.]

lxxiii. "To our desert." [4]Verily, although we ever deserve as much punishment as is laid upon us, and much more, yet no part of that is afflict unto us by the will of God; yea, and as touching [us,] which are so taken into his favour that through Christ we be made his children, though it seem never so grievous, it is done of his most beneficial and fatherly good-will, that he beareth towards us, which chasteth, as St Paul saith, all those that he loveth. So that of right faith we should believe, that all punishments, tribulations, and persecution, be of the sending of God; notwithstanding that to our judgment they shall seem many times and often to come only of the devil, or the wickedness of his ministers.

As when to the holy man Job, the example of all patience, so many mischances happened together;—the Sabees stole his oxen and asses; the fire, coming from above, brent up his sheep; the Chaldees drove away his camels; the hurtling wind overthrew his son's house, wherewith all his children were slain,—who would not have thought, but that all this had come only of the devil, and of thieves and robbers, and that he had been so far out of God's favour, that the devil had then his full power over him? But he, being constant in the faith of God, and knowing certainly that for all this God did bear his favour towards him, wist that all this came from him, and that the devil had no power to do any such things, saving that God would even the same. He said not, the devil owed me shame; or, these wicked thieves have wrought me this woe; but referred all to God, and did acknowledge that it was wrought all at his pleasure. Whose ensample all we that be the faithful people should follow, as Austin testifieth, saying: *Cuicunque aliquid accidit, dicat, Dominus dedit, Dominus abstulit. Non enim dixit Job, Dominus dedit, diabolus abstulit. Intendat ergo caritas vestra ne forte dicatis, Hæc mihi diabolus fecit: prorsus ad Deum flagellum tuum refer, quia nec diabolus aliquid fecit, nisi ille permittat qui desuper habet potestatem ad pœnam vel ad disciplinam.* In Psalm. xxxi. and xxxii.[5]

Likewise, when Samei did curse king David, and said, "Come forth, thou blood-supper, Baal's man, usurper of another man's kingdom: God hath acquitted thee, and given thy kingdom to Absalom thy son; behold, thou art wrapt in mischief, as thou wast desirous of blood-shedding:" who would have thought other, but that this malediction had come to so blessed a prince even from the devil? But this chosen person of God, king David, knowing and believing that God had not withdrawn his favour from him, wist it was much otherwise; and said unto Abisai, who for this railing and cursing of the king would have cut off Samei's head, "Suffer him to curse, for the Lord hath commanded him to curse:" and after it followeth, "Suffer him to curse, according to the precept of the Lord. It may hap, that God would thus look upon mine affliction, and give me goodness for the cursing this day." In this it is evident that David denied [not] this grievous temptation to come of God, at his will and commandment, all for the best, and to the provocation of the greater favour of God, in case for his sake which sent it he could suffer it patiently. He ascribeth this to the will of God and to his power, without whom Pilate could not have given sentence of condemnation against Christ, as the gospel testifieth.

We then should evermore, when any adversity cometh, knowledge therein God's power, and think it is also of his sending; as Austin in divers places giveth us counsel, saying: *Quicquid acciderit justo, voluntati divinæ deputat, non potestati inimici. Sævire iste potest ut feriat; ferire autem, si ille noluerit, non potest.* In Psalm. xxxvi. And again he saith, *Quantum diabolus accipit potestatis, tantum ego patior; non ergo ab illo patior, sed ab eo qui potestatem dedit.* In Psalm. ciii.[6]

*Ibid.* For the better understanding of this third petition, we think it convenient, that all bishops and preachers shall instruct and teach the people committed unto their spiritual charge, how that by the occasion and ever sith the disobedience and sin of our first father Adam the will of man hath been so corrupted with

[4 See Nec. Doctr. p. 341.]

[5 August. in Psalm. xxxi. Tom. VIII. p. 82. Ed. Paris. 1635.—Ideo bene eruditus ipse Job non ait, Dominus dedit et diabolus abstulit: sed, "Dominus dedit et Dominus abstulit." Id. in Psalm. xxxii. Tom. VIII. p. 88.]

[6 Id. in Psalm. xxxvi. et ciii. Tom. VIII. pp. 116, 497.]

r *as only of ourselves.* lxxiv.

original sin, that we be all[r] utterly inclined to disobey the will and precepts of God, and so to love ourselves and our own wills, that without a special grace and a singular inspiration of God, we cannot heartily love neither God nor man, but in respect to ourselves, as we may have benefit and commodity by them.

lxxiv. "As only of ourself." It need not to be added, for it followeth by and by after, "Without a special grace and a singular inspiration of God;" which is all one with this, "As only of ourself." And if these words be added to signify, that by the common influence of grace given generally we have inclination to obey the will and precepts of God; so much the Pelagians will grant unto us. And then also it will not agree with that followeth, that without a special grace and singular inspiration we cannot love God nor man, but in respect to ourselves. And moreover when [we] have received the special grace and singular inspiration of God, and even the Holy Ghost himself, yet our own carnal inclination is still unto evil, as St Paul saith: *Caro pugnat adversus spiritum, et spiritus adversus carnem.* Et, *Condelector lege Dei secundum interiorem hominem; habeo autem aliam legem in membris meis repugnantem legi mentis meæ, et captivantem me in lege peccati, quæ est in membris meis*[1].

*Inst.* p. 187. Like as corn, though it be never so clean winnowed and purged from chaff, yet if it be sown, the young seed is full of chaff again, until it be winnowed and made clean: even so be the children born full of chaff and corruption of original sin, until that by baptism [s]*in the blood* of our Saviour Jesu Christ they be washed and purged, as their parents were.

s *grace and mercy*

*Inst.* pp. 188, 9. And to them, to whom thou dost vouchsafe to give more than their own portion necessary for their[t] vocation and degree, give thy grace, *that they may be thy diligent and true dispensators and stewards,* to distribute that they have over and above that is necessary, considering their estate and degree, to them that have need of it. For so, good Lord, thou dost provide for thy poor people that have nothing, by them which have of thy gift sufficient to relieve themselves and other[u]. And give also thy grace to us, that we have not too much solicitude and care for these transitory and unstable things; but that our hearts may be fixed in things which be eternal, and in thy kingdom, which is everlasting. And yet moreover, good Lord, not only give us our necessaries, but also conserve that thou dost give us, and cause that it may come to our use, and by us to the poor people, for whom by us thou hast provided. Give us grace, that we may be fed and nourished with all the life of Christ, that is to say, both his words and works; and that they may be to us an effectual example and spectacle of all virtues. Grant that all they that preach thy word may profitably and godly preach *thee[x] and thy Son Jesu Christ* through all the world; and that all we which hear thy word preached may so be fed therewith, that not only we may outwardly receive the same, but also digest it within our hearts; and that it may so work and feed every part of us, that it may appear in all the acts and deeds of our life.

t *wife and family.* lxxv.

u *But one thing herein is to be noted, that there be many folk which had lever live by the graffle of bekyng sloughtfully*[2] *than other work or labour for their living: truly, these be none of them of whom before we spoke of; for we think it right necessary that such should be compelled by one means or other to serve the world with their bodily labour, thinking it small charity to bestow otherwise alms on them.*

x *it to the honour of thee and thy Son Jesu Christ.*

lxxv. "Wife and family." These words make the sentence very obscure, and no perfect English, and they be put of no necessity, for they be contained sufficiently in the words following immediately, viz. "Necessary for their vocation and degree;" which no man, I think, will take otherwise than such a portion, as is enough, not only for himself, but also for his wife and family and other which appertain to his charge and provision.

*Inst.* p. 191. As the husbandman tilleth and soweth his ground, weedeth it, and keepeth it from destroying, and yet he prayeth to God for the increase, and putteth all his trust in him to send him more or less at his pleasure; even so, besides our own diligence, policy, labour, and travail, we must also pray daily to God to send us sufficient; and we must take thankfully at his hands all that is sent; and be no further careful,[y] but put our whole confidence and trust in him.

y *than needeth.*

*Inst.* p. 192. But seek you first the kingdom of God and his righteousness, and then God shall cast all these things unto you[z].

z *and teach you the ways justly and truly to live.* lxxvi.

These be the words of Christ, full of good and comfortable lessons, that we should not care ne set our hearts too much upon these worldly things, ne care so much for to-morrow, that we shall seem to mistrust our Lord; *and that we should sequester this care from us, and seek for the kingdom of God, and employ ourselves wholly to the getting thereof: and then he maketh a comfortable promise that we shall not lack things necessary for us.*

*And also here is a thing greatly to be noted in comfort of the true labouring man: for surely, be he craftsman, be he labourer, [he] doing truly his office whereto he is called, shall attain salvation as surely as any other creature, and they that do contrary shall be in jeopardy of damnation.* lxxvii.

---

[1 See Nec. Doctr. p. 340.]

[2 "The craft of begging slothfully" seems to be the subject of Henry VIII.'s animadversion here; but as there is some doubt respecting the words, the orthography of the original manuscript has been preserved.]

lxxvi. "And teach us the ways justly and truly to live." We may not add in such wise to the scripture, as no man that can read it can judge other, but that it is some part of the promise made there by Christ. For besides that the text will give it, also it followeth immediately: "These be the words of Christ." Now we may not so boldly make promises of God's behalf. *Si enim verum sit illud Pauli, Hominis testamentum, ubi semel probatum sit, nemo rejicit, aut addit ei aliquid; quanto magis testimoniis et testamento Dei altissimi nihil est addendum vel detrahendum!*[3]

lxxvii. "Also here is a thing greatly to be noted." This is a good saying, but it seemeth not spoken in his place; for in the words of Christ, whereof is here spoken, is no mention made of the true labouring man, or that he should be certain of his salvation[4].

[*Inst.* pp. 192, 3.] Fourthly, that by this bread, which our Saviour teacheth us to ask in this petition, is principally meant the word of God, which is the spiritual bread that feedeth the soul. For as the body is nourished, brought up, groweth, and feedeth with bread and meat; so needeth the soul, even from our youth, to be nourished and brought up with the word of God, and to be fed * daily * (lxxviii.) with it. And like as the body will faint and decay, if it be not from time to time relieved and refreshed with bodily sustenance; even so the soul waxeth feeble and weak towards God, unless the same be * continually * cherished, refreshed, and kept up with the word of God, according to the saying of Christ, A man liveth not with meat only, but by every word that proceedeth from the mouth of God.

lxxviii. "Daily." The scripture would, that those that be the blessed sort of God, should at all times and at all hours call to remembrance the comfortable words of God. *Ut meditetur*, as David saith, *in lege Domini die ac nocte.* Like as God also requireth by manifest commandment, where as Moses in his behalf said these words: "That now here I command thee, print them in thy heart, tell them to thy children, muse of them sitting in thy house, walking in thy journey, lying down and uprising: clasp them in thy hand for a memorial, make them to stir before thine eyes, and write them in the posts and doors of thy house." Deut. vi. This commandment of God requireth that at all times and in all places we should be mindful of his words, yea, daily and hourly[5]."

*Inst.* p. 193. Our heavenly Father, [a] * lo, * we wretched sinners, knowledging and confessing * unto thee, our most merciful Father, * the great and manifold sins wherewith our conscience is continually cumbered, and having none other refuge but unto thy mercy, * we most humbly beseech thee, * [b] comfort our conscience both now and in the hour of our death, which is * now * abashed and ashamed to look upon our sin and iniquity.

[a] *we most humbly beseech thee, that*
[b] *that thou wouldest.*

*Inst.* p. 194. Judge us not after the accusation of the devil, and our [c] * wretched * consciences, neither hear the voice of our enemies, which accuse us day and night before thee. But like as we forgive [d] them heartily which trespass against us, even so we beseech thee forgive us the manifold sins, whereby from our youth we have provoked thy displeasure and wrath against us, and daily do provoke it, by doing that is evil, and omitting that is good. And so wash [e] our sins daily more and more.

[c] *weak*
[d] *ought to.* lxxix.
[e] *away*

[*Inst.* pp. 194, 5.] We cannot otherwise trust or look for any forgiveness or remission of our trespasses at thy hands, unless we shall, according to thy commandment, [f] forgive all them [g] that have trespassed in any wise against us.

[f] *do that lieth in us to*
[g] *in heart*

For the better understanding of this fifth petition, we think it convenient, that all bishops and preachers shall instruct and teach the people * committed [h] unto their spiritual charge, * that no man ought to glory in himself, as though he were innocent, and without sin; but rather that every good christian man (without exception) ought to knowledge himself to be a sinner, and that he hath need to ask forgiveness of God for his sins, and to require him of his mercy. For doubtless he daily committeth sin, which is commanded daily to ask remission of his sins. And St John saith in his Epistle, If we say that we be without sin, we deceive ourselves, and truth is not in us.

[h] *which in spiritual cure are committed to them,*

Second, that [i] * God will not * forgive us our sins, [k] * but upon condition that we shall likewise * forgive all them which trespass against us; [l] * and that not in tongue only, but also in our hearts. And that this is a certain sure law and decree

[i] *by this prayer and petition we desire God to*
[k] *like as we*
[l] *and that it is Christ's in-*

---

[[3] See Nec. Doctr. p. 344.]

[[4] This "good saying" kept its place, Nec. Doctr. p. 344.]

[[5] "Daily" was omitted in spite of Cranmer. Nec. Doctr. p. 345.]

*tent and mind to have us do so, appeareth in many places of scripture.* of God, Christ declareth in sundry places of the gospel.* For, first, by express words Christ saith, If you forgive men their offences done against you, your heavenly Father will forgive you your offences. *And if you will not forgive them that offend you, be you assured your Father will not forgive you your offences.*

lxxix. "[1] Ought to forgive." Christ taught us not here in this petition to pray unto our Father, that he should forgive us, as we "ought" to forgive other: meaning thereby, that unless we forgive other in "deed," our prayer is frustrate and made in vain. And to certify us, that he meant so thereby, immediately after the *Pater-noster*, to leave us out of all doubt what he meant by this petition, he saith: *Si dimiseritis hominibus peccata eorum, Pater vester cœlestis dimittet vobis peccata vestra. Si autem non dimiseritis hominibus, nec Pater vester dimittet vobis peccata vestra*[2].

*Inst.* pp. 196-8. Thus it appeareth plainly, that if we will be forgiven, if we will escape everlasting damnation, we must [m]* heartily forgive those which have trespassed and offended against us. No man can offend us so much as we offend God; and yet he is alway ready to forgive us. What ingratitude is it then, what hardness of heart, what cruelness is in us, if we for his sake will not forgive one another! There is none offence great that man doth to man, if it be compared to our offences against God.* And therefore we may be well accounted to have little respect and consideration unto our own benefit, if we will not remit and forgive small faults done unto us, that we may have pardon and forgiveness of so many thousands of great offences which we have committed against God. And if any peradventure will think it to be a hard thing to suffer and forgive his enemy, which in word and deed hath done him many displeasures; let him consider again, how many hard storms our Saviour Christ suffered and abode for us. What were we, when he gave his most precious life and blood for us, but horrible sinners, and his enemies? How meekly took he for our sake all rebukes, mocks, binding, beating, crowning with thorn, and the most opprobrious death! (lxxx.) * Why do we boast us to be christian men, if we care not for Christ, of whom we be so named, if we endeavour not ourselves to take example at him? We be not worthy to have the name of the members, if we follow not the Head. And if any will say that his enemy is not worthy to be forgiven, let him consider and think that no more is he worthy to have forgiveness of God. And by what equity or justice can we require that God should be merciful unto us, if we will shew no mercy, but extremity, unto our neighbour and brother? Is it a great matter for one sinner to forgive another, seeing that Christ forgave them that crucified him? And although thy enemy be not worthy to be forgiven, yet we be worthy to forgive: and Christ is worthy, that for his sake we should forgive.* But surely it is above our frail and corrupt nature to love our enemies that do hate us, and to forgive them that do hurt and offend us. Thus to do is a greater grace than can come of ourselves. Therefore our Saviour Christ teacheth us to ask this heavenly gift of our heavenly Father, that we may forgive our enemies, and that he will forgive us our trespasses, even so as we forgive them that trespass against us.

*[m] eradicate and take away all rancour, malice, and will to revenge out of our heart, and commit the punishment of the offenders (being contrary to God or the princes' laws) to the order of justice*[3].

Thirdly, that to forgive our brother his default is to pray to our Lord that he will forgive him, and will not impute his offence to him; and to wish to him the same grace and glory that we desire unto ourselves; [n]* and in no case to annoy him, but* when occasion shall come, to help him, as we be bound to help our christian brother.

*[n] and*

* Fourthly, that none enemy can wish or desire more hurt unto us than we desire unto our own selves, when we offer unto God this fifth petition, if we will not remit and forgive our displeasure unto them which offend us. For what enemy was ever so malicious, or so far from all grace and humanity, that would desire and daily pray to God to send unto his enemy eternal damnation, and that God should withdraw his mercy from him for ever? And surely in this petition we ask continually these things of God for ourselves, if we will be merciless towards our enemies, and will not forgive them their trespasses. For none otherwise we do ask forgiveness of God, but upon this condition, that we shall forgive them which trespass against us. And in case we do not fulfil this condition, then we pray unto God that he shall never shew mercy unto us, nor never forgive us our sins, but suffer us to be damned perpetually.*

lxxx. "Why do we boast us to be christian men? Why these words should be stricken out I cannot tell, seeing that St Paul, as concerning our imitation of Christ even in the same point, speaketh the same words in effect, saying, "Forgive you one another, if any of you have a grief against another; as the Lord hath forgiven you, even so do you." Col. iii. And as touching that reason that followeth, which

---

[[1] The opinions of Henry VIII. which induced him to propose an alteration, seem to have been similar to those whom Latimer speaks of, "who, when they said this petition, perceived that they asked of God forgiveness, like as they themselves forgive their neighbours; and again perceiving themselves so unapt to forgive their neighbours' faults, came to that point, that they would not say this prayer at all; but took our Lady's Psalter in hand, and such fooleries; thinking they might then do unto their neighbour a foul turn with a better conscience, than if they should say this petition." Latimer, Sixth Sermon on the Lord's Prayer, pp. 425, 6. Park. Soc. Ed. 1844.]

[[2] See Nec. Doctr. pp. 346, 7.]

[[3] Ibid. p. 347.]

is also stricken out, that is, that we may not think to have forgiveness of God, if we should shew extremity to our neighbour, the scripture testifieth that to look for that, it were unreasonable; saying, *Qui vindicari vult, a Domino inveniet vindictam, et peccata illius servans servabit. Dimitte proximo tuo nocenti te, et tunc deprecanti tibi peccata solventur. Homo homini reservat iram, et a Deo quærit medelam? In hominem similem sibi non habet misericordiam, et de peccatis suis deprecatur? Ipse, dum caro sit, reservat iram, et propitiationem petit a Deo? Quis orabit pro delictis illius*[4]? Prov. [Ecclus.] xxviii.

*lxxxi.* "And[5] in case that he which hath committed the offence," &c. This remission that is required by Christ, nothing toucheth debts that ought to be paid, nor yet goods and lands unjustly withholden, that ought to be restored; but the displeasure and malice of the heart of him that injury is done unto, and an appetite to be revenged of such displeasures as be done unto him. For he that suffereth injury should be sorry in his heart, that his brother should use himself contrary to the laws and ordinances of God or of his prince: he should pray for his amendment, and not of his private power render evil for evil, nor take the sword to avenge his own quarrel; but commit the whole punishment of the trespass unto God and to his ministers, whom he hath ordained for that intent.

So doth the scripture command us, saying, "Say thou not, I will acquit this evil; but tarry the Lord, and he shall help thee." Prov. xx. Likewise St Paul saith: "Dearly beloved, avenge not yourselves one of another, but give place unto displeasure: for it is written, Leave the revenging unto me, and I will acquit it, saith the Lord." Rom. xii. Where God biddeth us to reserve the vengeance unto him, it is not meant that the superior powers and their ministers should not meddle therewith; but that we should preserve our hearts clear from all vengeful appetites, and that we should not enterprise any part of God's office and judgment; but commit it unto them which be God's ministers in that behalf, as the prince is, and they that be substitute of him. For as St Paul saith, *Dei minister est ultor ad iram.* Rom. xiii. So that referring it to them, we refer it even to the judgment of God, which they by his authority do exercise to us: as Josophat, giving commandment to the judges, said, *Videte quid facitis; non enim hominis exercetis judicium, sed Domini.* 2 Chron. xix.

Now, these things well considered, these two may stand both well together; that we, as private persons, may forgive all such as have trespassed against us, with all our heart; and yet that the public ministers of God may see a redress of the same trespasses that we have forgiven. For my forgiveness concerneth only mine own person, but I cannot forgive the punishment and correction that by God's ordinance is to be ministered by the superior powers: for insomuch as the same trespass which I do forgive, may be to the maintenance of vice, not only of the offender, but also of other taking evil example thereby, it lieth not in me to forgive the same. For so should I enterprise in the office of others, which by the ordinance of God be deputed to the same. Yea, and that such justice may be ministered to the abolishment of vice and sin, I may, yea and rather, as the cause shall require, I am bound to make relation to the superior powers of the enormities and trespasses done to me and other, and, being sorry that I should have cause so to do, seek upon the reformation of such evil-doers, not as desirous of vengeance, but of the amendment of their life. And yet I may not the more cruelly persecute the matter, because the offence is peradventure done towards me; but I ought to handle it as if it were done to any other only, for the zeal of the extirpation of sin, the maintenance of justice and quietness, which may right well stand with the ferventness of charity, as scripture testifieth: *Non oderis fratrem tuum in corde tuo, sed publice argue eum, ne habeas super illo peccatum.* Levit. xix.

That this may stand with charity, and also the forgiveness that Christ requires of every one of us, for and yet in this doing I must forgive him with all my heart; for as much as lieth in me, I must be sorry that sin should have so much ruled in

[4 See Nec. Doctr. p. 348.]
[5 Though this clause is not found in the Corrections, it appears in the Necessary Doctrine, p. 349.]

him; I must pray to God to give him repentance for his misdeeds; I must desire God, that for Christ's sake he will not impute the sin unto him, being truly repentant, and so to strengthen him in grace, that he fall not again so dangerously. I think I were no true christian man, if I would not thus do. And what other thing is this, than, for as much as lieth in me, with all my heart to remit the trespass? But I may by the laws require all that is due unto me by right. And as for the punishment and correction, it is not my part to enterprise therein: but that only belongeth to the superior powers, to whom, if the grievousness of the cause shall require, by God's commandment which willeth us to take away the evil from amongst us, we ought to shew the offences and complain thereof. For he would not that we should take away the evil but after a just and lawful mean, which is only by the ordinance of God to shew the same to the superior powers, that they may take an order in it according to God's judgment and justice.

In this matter I have written much more than needeth, and nothing disallowing the three leaves added to the printed book, for I like them very well; saving that the first side is not perfect English nor much material, and therefore I think it were good to leave out the beginning of the first side, and to begin at the last end thereof, at this particle, "It is expedient that all bishops and preachers shall instruct," &c. And where the fourth note is stricken out, I think it might well remain; for it is very good, and not repugnant to any thing written in the three leaves: and the three leaves would very conveniently and aptly follow the fourth note[1].

*lxxxii.* "Though our doings be never so good and consonant to equity." He that is justified knowledgeth humbly his offences and sins, saying, as the publican did, *Deus, propitius esto mihi peccatori;* and, as David also said, *Lava me ab iniquitate mea, quia malum coram te feci; et, Iniquitates meæ supergressæ sunt caput meum.* And he confesseth that before his justification his doings were naught, nor consonant unto equity; and therefore this parenthesis cometh not well in this place.

*lxxxiii.* "For the first offence of our father Adam." No man shall be damned for the offences of Adam, but for his own proper offences, either actual or original; which original sin every man hath of his own, and is born in it, although it come from Adam.

[o] *us so strong with thy fortitude,*

*Inst.* p. 198. Make [o] that we may resist and fight against all temptation.

[p] *signification of the word,*

[q] *by Christ.*

*Inst.* pp. 209, 10. As touching the [p] *order* and cause of our justification, we think it convenient, that all bishops and preachers shall instruct and teach the people committed unto their spiritual charge, that this word *justification* signifieth remission of our sins, and our acceptation or reconciliation into the grace and favour of God [q], *that is to say, our perfect renovation in Christ.*

[r] *Item, That the chief and first mean whereby sinners attain the same justification,* (lxxxiv.) *was only by the great zeal and love which that Christ bare and beareth to us, undeserved on our behalf; for by his passion and death we attain our redemption and justification: wherefore he most worthily is to be of us honoured, and esteemed our sole redeemer and justifier.*

[r] *Item,* That sinners attain this justification by contrition and faith, joined with charity, after such sort and manner as is before mentioned and declared in the sacrament of penance. Not as though our contrition or faith, or any works proceeding thereof, can worthily merit or deserve to attain the said justification. For the only mercy and grace of the Father, promised freely unto us for his Son's sake Jesu Christ, and the merits of his blood and passion, be the only sufficient and worthy causes thereof. And yet that notwithstanding, to the attaining of the same justification, God requireth to be in us not only inward contrition, perfect faith and charity, certain hope and confidence, with all other spiritual graces and motions, which, as was said before, must necessarily concur in remission of our sins, that is to say, our justification; but also he requireth and commandeth us that, after we be justified, we must also have good works of charity and obedience towards God, in the observing and fulfilling outwardly of his laws and commandments. For although acceptation to everlasting life be conjoined with justification, yet our good works be necessarily required to the attaining of everlasting life. And we, being justified, be necessarily bound, and it is our necessary duty, to do good works, according to the saying of St Paul, We be bound not to live according to the flesh and to fleshly appetites; for if we live so, we shall undoubtedly be damned. And contrary, if we will mortify the deeds of our flesh, and live according to the Spirit, we shall

---

[[1] The fourth note was struck out notwithstanding Cranmer's representations. Pp. 348, 9, of the Necessary Doctrine probably contain what was written on the three leaves here spoken of. Perhaps the paragraph from "And finally...to...neighbour" may be that which Cranmer thought not "much material." The remainder agrees perfectly with his Annotation, but is more concisely expressed. In the 349th page occur the very words "And in case," &c. with which he commences his remarks.]

**be saved. For whosoever be led by the Spirit of God, they be the children of God. And Christ saith, If you will come to heaven, keep the commandments. And St Paul, speaking of evil works, saith, Whosoever commit sinful deeds shall never come to heaven. Wherefore all good christian people must understand and believe certainly, that God necessarily requireth of us to do good works commanded by him, and that not only outward and civil works, but also the inward spiritual motions and graces of the Holy Ghost, that is to say, to dread and fear God; to love God; to have firm confidence and trust in God; to invocate and call upon God; to have patience in all adversities; to hate sin; and to have certain purpose and will not to sin again; and such other like motions and virtues. For Christ saith, We must not only do outward civil good works, but we must also have these foresaid inward spiritual motions, consenting and agreeable to the law of God.**

lxxxiv. "The principal mean whereby all sinners attain this justification." This sentence importeth, that the favour and love of the Father of heaven towards us is the mean whereby we come to his favour and love; and so should one thing be a mean to itself. And it is not the use of scripture to call any other the mean or mediator for us, but only Jesus Christ, by whom our access is to the Father; so that it is a strange thing to attribute unto the Father this word "mean," but his love was the original and beginning of our salvation.

*lxxxv.* "And then to be contrite." It were better to say "and to be contrite," putting out "then."

*lxxxvi.* "Having assured hope and confidence in Christ's mercy, willing to enter into the perfect faith." He that hath assured hope and confidence in Christ's mercy, hath already entered into a perfect faith, and not only hath a will to enter into it. For perfect faith is nothing else but assured hope and confidence in Christ's mercy: and after it followeth, that he shall enter into perfect faith by undoubted trust in God, in his words and promise, which also be both one thing: for these three be all one, "perfect faith,"—"assured hope and confidence in Christ's mercy,"—and "undoubted trust in God, in his words and promises."

And, for a further declaration, to know how we obtain our justification, it is expedient to consider, first, how naughty and sinful we are all, that be of Adam's kindred; and contrariwise, what mercifulness is in God, which to all faithful and penitent sinners pardoneth all their offences for Christ's sake. Of these two things no man is lightly ignorant that ever hath heard of the fall of Adam, which was to the infection of all his posterity; and again, of the inexplicable mercy of our heavenly Father, which sent his only-begotten Son to suffer his most grievous passion for us, and shed his most precious blood, the price of our redemption. But it is greatly to be wished and desired, that as all christian men do know the same, so that every man might knowledge and undoubtedly believe the same to be true and verified, even upon himself; so that both he may humble himself to God and knowledge himself a miserable sinner not worthy to be called his son; and yet surely trust, that to him being repentant God's mercy is ready to forgive. And he that seeth not these two things verified in himself, can take no manner of emolument and profit by knowledging and believing these things to be verified in others. But we cannot satisfy our minds [and] settle our conscience that these things are true, saving that we do evidently see that God's word so teacheth us.

The commandments of God lay our faults before our eyes, which putteth us in fear and dread, and maketh us see the wrath of God against our sins, as St Paul saith, *Per legem agnitio peccati, et, Lex iram operatur*, and maketh us sorry and repentant, that ever we should come into the displeasure of God and the captivity of the devil. The gracious and benign promises of God by the mediation of Christ sheweth us, (and that to our great relief and comfort,) whensoever we be repentant, and return fully to God in our hearts, that we have forgiveness of our sins, be reconciled to God, and accepted, and reputed just and righteous in his sight, only by his grace and mercy, which he doth grant and give unto us for his dearly-beloved Son's sake, Jesus Christ; who paid a sufficient ransom for our sins; whose blood doth wash away the same; whose bitter and grievous passion is the only pacifying oblation, that putteth away from us the wrath of God his Father; whose sanctified body offered on the cross is the only sacrifice of sweet and pleasant savour, as St Paul saith; that is to say, of such sweetness and pleasantness to the Father, that for the same he accepteth and reputeth of like sweetness all them that the same offering doth serve for.

These benefits of God, with innumerable other, whosoever expendeth, and well pondereth in his heart, and thereby conceiveth a firm trust and feeling of God's mercy, whereof springeth in his heart a warm love and fervent heat of zeal towards God, it is not possible but that he shall fall to work, and be ready to the performance of all such works as he knoweth to be acceptable unto God. And these works only which follow our justification, do please God; forsomuch as they proceed from an heart endued with pure faith and love to God. But the works which we do before our justification, be not allowed and accepted before God, although they appear never so good and glorious in the sight of man. For after our justification only begin we to work as the law of God requireth. Then we shall do all good works willingly, although not so exactly as the law requireth, by mean of infirmity of the flesh. Nevertheless, by the merit and benefit of Christ, we being sorry that we cannot do all things no more exquisitely and duly, all our works shall be accepted and taken of God, as most exquisite, pure, and perfect.

Now they that think they may come to justification by performance of the law, by their own deeds and merits, or by any other mean than is above rehearsed, they go from Christ, they renounce his grace: *Evacuati estis a Christo*, saith St Paul, Gal. v., *quicunque in lege justificamini, a gratia excidistis.* They be not partakers of the justice that he hath procured, or the merciful benefits that be given by him. For St Paul saith a general rule for all them that will seek such by-paths to obtain justification: those, saith he, which will not knowledge the justness or righteousness which cometh by God, but go about to advance their own righteousness, shall never come to that righteousness which we have by God; which is the righteousness of Christ: by whom only all the saints in heaven, and all other that have been saved, have been reputed righteous, and justified. So that to Christ our only Saviour and Redeemer, on whose righteousness both their and our justification both depend, is to be transcribed all the glory thereof.

# [QUESTIONS[1] AND ANSWERS

CONCERNING

## THE SACRAMENTS AND THE APPOINTMENT AND POWER OF BISHOPS AND PRIESTS.]

---

1. What a sacrament is by the scripture? Cott. Libr. Cleop. E. v. fol. 53. Stillingfleet MSS. Lamb. Libr. 1108. fol. 69.

The scripture sheweth not what a sacrament is: nevertheless, where in the Latin text we have *sacramentum*, there in the Greek we have *mysterium;* and so by the scripture *sacramentum* may be called *mysterium, id est, res occulta sive arcana.*

2. What a sacrament is by the ancient authors?

The ancient authors call a sacrament *sacræ rei signum*, or *visibile verbum, symbolumque, atque pactio qua sumus constricti.*

3. How many sacraments there be by the scriptures?

The scripture sheweth not how many sacraments there be; but *incarnatio Christi* and *matrimonium* be called in the scripture *mysteria*, and therefore we may call them by the scripture *sacramenta*. But one *sacramentum* the scripture maketh mention of, which is hard to be revealed fully, (as would to God it were!) and that is, *mysterium iniquitatis*, or *mysterium meretricis magnæ et bestiæ.*

4. How many sacraments there be by ancient authors?

By the ancient authors there be many sacraments more than seven; for all the figures which signified Christ to come, or testify that he is come, be called sacraments, as all the figures of the old law, and the new law; *eucharistia, baptismus, pascha, dies Dominicus, lotio pedum, signum crucis, chrisma, matrimonium, ordo, sabbatum, impositio manuum, oleum, consecratio olei, lac, mel, aqua, vinum, sal, ignis, cineres, adapertio aurium, vestis candida*, and all the parables of Christ, with the prophecies of the Apocalypse, and such other, be called by the doctors *sacramenta.*

5. Whether this word sacrament be, and ought to be, attributed to the seven only? And whether the seven sacraments be found in any of the old authors, or not?

I know no cause why this word "sacrament" should be attributed to the seven only: for the old authors never prescribe any certain number of sacraments, nor in all their books I never read these two words joined together, viz. *septem sacramenta.*

6. Whether the determinate number of seven sacraments be a doctrine, either of the scripture, or of the old authors, and so to be taught?

The determinate number of seven sacraments is no doctrine of the scripture, nor of the old authors.

7. What is found in scripture of the matter, nature, effect, and virtue of such as we call the seven sacraments; so as although the name be not there, yet whether the thing be in scripture or no? and in what wise spoken of?

I find not in the scripture, the matter, nature, and effect of all those which we

---

[[1] The above questions and answers are printed verbatim as they stand in the Cott. Libr. Cleop. MSS. E. v. f. 53, preserved in the British Museum. Another copy is found amongst the Stillingfleet MSS. in the Lambeth palace library; and they have been also printed by Burnet and by Collier. Answers were given to these questions by other divines, amongst which are those of Thirlby, who is called "elect of Westminster," which fixes their date between Sept. 17 and Dec. 29, 1540. The questions, "believed to have been proposed to commissioners appointed in that year to draw up a declaration of the christian doctrine," have been attributed to Henry VIII.; but Strype supposes that he was instigated by Cranmer in the matter, which supposition is confirmed by draughts of some of them in the archbishop's handwriting being still found in the Lambeth MSS. 1108. fol. 1. Vid. Burnet's Hist. of Reformat. Vol. I. pp. 578-82. App. Vol. I. b. iii. No. 21. pp. 314-67. Vol. III. p. 294. App. Vol. III. b. iii. No. 69, 70, 71. pp. 223-30. Ed. Oxon. 1829. Collier, Eccles. Hist. Vol. V. pp. 97, 8. App. No. 49. Vol. IX. pp. 175-214. Ed. Lond. 1840-41. Strype's Memorials of Abp. Cranmer, Vol. I. pp. 110, 11. and App. No. 27 and 28. Vol. II. pp. 744-8. Ed. Oxon. 1840. Todd's Life of Cranmer, Vol. I. p. 299, et sqq. Jenkyns' Remains of Abp. Cranmer, Vol. II. p. 98.]

call the seven sacraments, but only of certain of them: as of baptism, in which we be regenerated and pardoned of our sin by the blood of Christ.

Of *eucharistia*, in which we be concorporated unto Christ, and made lively members of his body, nourished and fed to the everlasting life, if we receive it as we ought to do; and else it is to us rather death than life.

Of penance also I find in the scripture, whereby sinners after baptism, returning wholly unto God, be accepted again unto his favour and mercy. But the scripture speaketh not of penance, as we call it a sacrament, consisting in three parts, contrition, confession, and satisfaction; but the scripture taketh penance for a pure conversion of a sinner in heart and mind from his sins unto God, making no mention of private confession of all deadly sins to a priest, nor of ecclesiastical satisfaction to be enjoined by him.

Of matrimony also I find very much in scripture, and among other things, that it is a mean whereby God doth use the infirmity of our concupiscence to the setting forth of his glory, and increase of the world, thereby sanctifying the act of carnal commixtion between the man and the wife to that use; yea, although one party be an infidel: and in this matrimony is also a promise of salvation, if the parents bring up their children in the faith, love, and fear of God.

Of the matter, nature, and effect of the other three, that is to say, confirmation, order, and extreme unction, I read nothing in the scripture, as they be taken for sacraments.

8. Whether confirmation, *cum chrismate*, of them that be baptized, be found in scripture?

Of confirmation with chrism, without which it is counted no sacrament, there is no manner of mention in the scripture.

9. Whether the apostles lacking a higher power, as in not having a christian king among them, made bishops by that necessity, or by authority given them by God?

All christian princes have committed unto them immediately of God the whole cure of all their subjects, as well concerning the administration of God's word for the cure of souls, as concerning the ministration of things political and civil governance. And in both these ministrations they must have sundry ministers under them, to supply that which is appointed to their several offices.

The civil ministers under the king's majesty in this realm of England, be those whom it shall please his highness for the time to put in authority under him: as for example, the lord chancellor, lord treasurer, lord great master, lord privy seal, lord admiral, mayors, sheriffs, &c.

The ministers of God's word under his majesty be the bishops, parsons, vicars, and such other priests as be appointed by his highness to that ministration: as for example, the bishop of Canterbury, the bishop of Duresme, the bishop of Winchester, the parson of Winwick, &c. All the said officers and ministers, as well of the one sort as of the other, be appointed, assigned, and elected in every place, by the laws and orders of kings and princes.

In the admission of many of these officers be divers comely ceremonies and solemnities used, which be not of necessity, but only for a good order and seemly fashion: for if such offices and ministrations were committed without such solemnity, they were nevertheless truly committed. And there is no more promise of God, that grace is given in the committing of the ecclesiastical office, than it is in the committing of the civil office.

In the apostles' time, when there was no christian princes, by whose authority ministers of God's word might be appointed, nor sins by the sword corrected, there was no remedy then for the correction of vice, or appointing of ministers, but only the consent of christian multitude among themselves, by an uniform consent to follow the advice and persuasion of such persons whom God had most endued with the spirit of counsel and wisdom. And at that time, forasmuch as the christian people had no sword nor governor amongst them, they were constrained of necessity to take such curates and priests as either they knew themselves to be meet thereunto, or else as were commended unto them by other that were so replete with the Spirit of God, with such knowledge in the profession of Christ, such wisdom, such conversation and counsel, that they ought even of very conscience to give credit unto them, and to accept such as by them were presented: and so sometime the apostles, and other, unto whom God had given abundantly his Spirit, sent or appointed ministers of God's word; sometime the people did choose such as they thought meet thereunto; and when any were appointed or sent by the apostles or other, the people of their own voluntary will with thanks did accept them; not for the supremity, impery, or dominion that the apostles had over them to command, as their princes or masters; but as good people, ready to obey the advice of good counsellors, and to accept any thing that was necessary for their edification and benefit.

10. Whether bishops or priests were first? and if the priests were first, then the priest made the bishop?

The bishops and priests were at one time, and were not two things, but both one office in the beginning of Christ's religion.

11. Whether a bishop hath authority to make a priest by the scripture, or no? and whether any other, but only a bishop, may make a priest?

A bishop may make a priest by the scripture, and so may princes and governors also, and that by the authority of God committed to them, and the people also by their election: for as we read that bishops have done it, so christian emperors and princes usually have done it; and the people, before christian princes were, commonly did elect their bishops and priests.

12. Whether in the new Testament be required any consecration of a bishop and priest, or only appointing to the office be sufficient?

In the new Testament, he that is appointed to be a bishop or a priest, needeth no consecration by the scripture; for election or appointing thereto is sufficient.

13. Whether (if it befortuned a prince christian-learned to conquer certain dominions of infidels, having none but temporal-learned men with him) it be defended by God's law, that he and they should preach and teach the word of God there, or no? and also make and constitute priests, or no?

It is not against God's law, but contrary, they ought indeed so to do; and there be histories that witnesseth, that some christian princes, and other laymen unconsecrate, have done the same.

14. Whether it be forfended by God's law, that (if it so fortuned that all the bishops and priests of a region were dead, and that the word of God should remain there unpreached, the sacrament of baptism and others unministered,) that the king of that region should make bishops and priests to supply the same, or no?

It is not forbidden by God's law.

15. Whether a man be bound by authority of this scripture, "*Quorum remiseritis*," and such like, to confess his secret deadly sins to a priest if he may have him, or no?

A man is not bound by the authority of this scripture, "*Quorum remiseritis*," and such like, to confess his secret deadly sins to a priest, although he may have him.

16. Whether a bishop or a priest may excommunicate, and for what crimes? and whether they only may excommunicate by God's law?

A bishop or a priest by the scripture is neither commanded nor forbidden to excommunicate, but where the laws of any region giveth him authority to excommunicate, there they ought to use the same in such crimes as the laws have such authority in; and where the laws of the region forbiddeth them, there they have none authority at all: and they that be no priests may also excommunicate, if the law allow them thereunto.

17. Whether unction of the sick with oil to remit venial sins, as it is now used, be spoken of in the scripture, or in any ancient author?

Unction of the sick with oil to remit venial sins, as it is now used, is not spoken of in the scripture, nor in any ancient author.

This is mine opinion and sentence at present, which nevertheless I do not temerariously define, but refer the judgment thereof wholly unto your majesty.

*T. Cantuarien.* This is mine opinion and sentence at this present, which I do not temerariously define, and do remit the judgment thereof wholly unto your majesty[1].

---

[[1] This passage, with the signature of the archbishop, is in his own hand-writing, both in the Cotton and Stillingfleet MSS.]

A

# PROLOGUE OR PREFACE

MADE BY

THE MOST REVEREND FATHER IN GOD,

## THOMAS, ARCHBISHOP OF CANTERBURY,

METROPOLITAN AND PRIMATE OF ENGLAND[1].

---

Cranmer's Bible, 1540.

FOR two sundry sorts of people, it seemeth much necessary that something be said in the entry of this book, by the way of a preface or prologue; whereby hereafter it may be both the better accepted of them which hitherto could not well bear it, and also the better used of them which heretofore have misused it. For truly some there are that be too slow, and need the spur: some other seem too quick, and need more of the bridle: some lose their game by short shooting, some by overshooting: some walk too much on the left hand, some too much on the right. In the former sort be all they that refuse to read, or to hear read the scripture in the vulgar tongues; much worse they that also let or discourage the other from the reading or hearing thereof. In the latter sort be they, which by their inordinate reading, undiscreet speaking, contentious disputing, or otherwise, by their licentious living, slander and hinder the word of God most of all other, whereof they would seem to be greatest furtherers. These two sorts, albeit they be most far unlike the one to the other, yet they both deserve in effect like reproach. Neither can I well tell whether of them I may judge the more offender, him that doth obstinately refuse so godly and goodly knowledge, or him that so ungodly and so ungoodly doth abuse the same.

And as touching the former, I would marvel much that any man should be so mad as to refuse in darkness light; in hunger, food; in cold, fire: for the word of God is light; *lucerna pedibus meis verbum tuum:* food; *non in solo pane vivit homo, sed in omni verbo Dei:* fire; *ignem veni mittere in terram, et quid volo, nisi ut ardeat?* I would marvel (I say) at this, save that I consider how much custom and usage may do. So that if there were a people, as some write, *De Cimmeriis*, which never saw the sun by reason that they be situated far toward the north pole, and be inclosed and overshadowed with high mountains; it is credible and like enough that if, by the power and will of God, the mountains should sink down and give place, that the light of the sun might have entrance to them, at the first some of them would be offended therewith. And the old proverb affirmeth, that after tillage of corn was first found, many delighted more to feed of mast and acorns, wherewith they had been accustomed, than to eat bread made of good corn. Such is the nature of custom[2], that it causeth us to bear all things well and easily, wherewith we have been accustomed, and to be offended with all things thereunto

Psal. cxix. Matt. iv. Luke xii.

---

[[1] This prologue is not found in the edition of the bible, which was issued A. D. 1539, and which is commonly attributed to the archbishop. The prologue was prepared by Cranmer during this year, and submitted by him for Henry VIII.'s approbation through Crumwell, to whom he had also sent it for his approval; but it was not issued till the April of the following year, when it was prefixed to the great bible appointed to be read in churches, which is properly called Cranmer's bible. Nine editions in folio of this bible were from time to time published, containing the prologue, but all differing in orthography. The version here given is transcribed from the vellum copy (large folio), as being most accurate, preserved in the British Museum, which once belonged to Henry VIII., the gift to him of "Anthony Marler, of London, haberdasher." The various readings of other (paper) copies have been also noted, and the marginal references added, which are not found in the vellum copy, but are copied from another edition in the British Museum, bearing on the title the date of 1540, and on the last page 1541. See Anderson's Annals of the English Bible, Vol. II. pp. 86, 7, 130. et sqq. Ed. Lond. 1845. Cranmer's Letter to Crumwell, 14 Nov. 1539. Lewis's History of English Bibles. Cotton's List of Editions.]

[[2] Other copies read, manner and custom.]

contrary. And therefore I can well think them worthy pardon, which at the coming abroad of scripture doubted and drew back. But such as will persist still in their wilfulness, I must needs judge, not only foolish, froward, and obstinate, but also peevish, perverse, and indurate.

And yet, if the matter should be tried by custom, we might also allege custom for the reading of the scripture in the vulgar tongues, and prescribe the more ancient custom. For it is not much above one hundred years ago, since scripture hath not been accustomed to be read in the vulgar tongues within this realm; and many hundred years before that it was translated and read in the Saxons' tongue, which at that time was our mother's tongue: whereof there remaineth yet divers copies found lately in old abbeys, of such antique manners of writing and speaking, that few men now been able to read and understand them. And when this language waxed old and out of common usage, because folk should not lack the fruit of reading, it was again translated in[3] the newer language. Whereof yet also many copies remain and be daily found.

But now to let pass custom, and to weigh, as wise men ever should, the thing in his own nature: let us here discuss, what availeth scripture to be had and read of the lay and vulgar people. And to this question I intend here to say nothing but that was spoken and written by the noble doctor and most moral divine, St John Chrysostom, in his third sermon *De Lazaro:* albeit I will be something shorter, and gather the matter into fewer words and less room than he doth there, because I would not be tedious. He exhorteth there his audience, that every man should read by himself at home in the mean days and time, between sermon and sermon, to the intent they might both more profoundly fix in their minds and memories that he had said before upon such texts, whereupon he had already preached; and also that they might have their minds the more ready and better prepared to receive and perceive that which he should say from thenceforth in his sermons, upon such texts as he had not yet declared and preached upon: therefore saith he there: "My common usage is to give you warning before, what matter I intend after to entreat upon, that you yourselves, in the mean days, may take the book in hand, read, weigh, and perceive the sum and effect of the matter, and mark what hath been declared, and what remaineth yet to be declared: so that thereby your mind may be the more furnished, to hear the rest that shall be said. And that I exhort you," saith he, "and ever have and will exhort you, that ye (not only here in the church) give ear to that that is said by the preacher, but that also, when ye be at home in your houses, ye apply yourselves from time to time to the reading of holy[4] scriptures: which thing also I never linn[5] to beat into the ears of them that been my familiars, and with whom I have private acquaintance and conversation. Let no man make excuse and say," saith he, "'I am busied about matters of the commonwealth;' 'I bear this office or that;' 'I am a craftsman, I must apply mine occupation;' 'I have a wife, my children must be fed, my household must I provide for:' briefly, 'I am a man of the world, it is not for me to read the scriptures, that belongeth to them that hath bidden the world farewell, which live in solitariness and contemplation, that hath been[6] brought up and continually nosylled[7] in learning and religion.'"

St Chrysostom.

To this answering, "What sayest thou, man?" saith he: "Is it not for thee to study and to read the scripture, because thou art encumbered and distract with cures and business? So much the more it is behoveful for thee to have defence of scriptures, how much thou art the more distressed in worldly dangers. They that be free and far from trouble and intermeddling of worldly things, liveth in safeguard, and tranquillity, and in the calm, or within a sure haven. Thou art in the midst of the sea of worldly wickedness, and therefore thou needest the more of ghostly succour and comfort: they sit far from the strokes of battle, and far out of gunshot, and therefore they be but seldom wounded: thou that standest in the forefront of the host and nighest to thine enemies, must needs take now and then many strokes, and be grievously wounded. And therefore

[[3] Other copies read, into.]
[[4] Of the holy, other copies.]
[[5] Linn, i. e. cease.]
[[6] Other copies read, and have been.]
[[7] Nosylled, i. e. nussled, nurtured.]

thou hast more need to have thy remedies and medicines at hand. Thy wife provoketh thee to anger, thy child giveth thee occasion to take sorrow and pensiveness, thine enemies lieth in wait for thee, thy friend (as thou takest him) sometime envieth thee, thy neighbour misreporteth thee, or pricketh quarrels against thee, thy mate or partner undermineth thee, thy lord judge or justice threateneth thee, poverty is painful unto thee, the loss of thy dear and well-beloved causeth thee to mourn; prosperity exalteth thee, adversity bringeth thee low. Briefly, so divers and so manifold occasions of cares, tribulations, and temptations besetteth thee and besiegeth thee round about. Where canst thou have armour or fortress against thine assaults? Where canst thou have salve[1] for thy sores, but of holy scripture? Thy flesh must needs be prone and subject to fleshly lusts, which daily walkest and art conversant amongst[2] women, seest their beauties set forth to the eye, hearest their nice and wanton words, smellest their balm, civit, and musk, with other like provocations and stirrings, except thou hast in a readiness wherewith to suppress and avoid them, which cannot elsewhere be had, but only out of the holy scriptures. Let us read and seek all remedies that we can, and all shall be little enough. How shall we then do, if we suffer and take daily wounds, and when we have done, will sit still and search for no medicines? Dost thou not mark and consider how the smith, mason, or carpenter, or any other handy-craftsman, what need soever he be in, what other shift soever he make, he will not sell nor lay to pledge the tools of his occupation; for then how should he work his feat, or get a living thereby? Of like mind and affection ought we to be towards holy scripture; for as mallets, hammers, saws, chisels, axes, and hatchets, be the tools of their occupation, so been[3] the books of the prophets and apostles, and all holy writ inspired by the Holy Ghost, the instruments of our salvation. Wherefore, let us not stick to buy and provide us the bible, that is to say, the books of holy scripture. And let us think that to be a better jewel in our house than either gold or silver. For like as thieves been loth to assault an house where they know to be good armour and artillery; so wheresoever these holy and ghostly books been occupied, there neither the devil nor none of his angels dare come near. And they that occupy them been in much safeguard, and having great[4] consolation, and been the readier unto all goodness, the slower to all evil[5]; and if they have done any thing amiss, anon, even by the sight of the books, their consciences been admonished, and they waxen sorry and ashamed of the fact.

"Peradventure they will say unto me, How and if we understand not that we read that is contained in the books? What then? Suppose thou understand not the deep and profound mysteries of scripture; yet can it not be, but that much fruit and holiness must come and grow unto thee by the reading: for it cannot be that thou shouldest be ignorant in all things alike. For the Holy Ghost hath so ordered and attempered the scriptures, that in them as well publicans, fishers, and shepherds may find their edification, as great doctors their erudition: for those books were not made to vain-glory, like as were the writings of the Gentile philosophers and rhetoricians, to the intent the makers should be had in admiration for their high styles and obscure manner of writing[6], whereof nothing can be understand without a master or an expositor. But the apostles and prophets wrote their books so that their special intent and purpose might be understanded[7] and perceived of every reader, which was nothing but the edification or amendment of the life of them that readeth or heareth it. Who is that reading[8] or hearing read in the gospel, 'Blessed are they that been meek, blessed are they that been merciful, blessed are they that been of clean heart,' and such other like places, can perceive nothing, except he have a master to teach him what it meaneth? Likewise the signs and miracles with all other histories of the doings of Christ or his apostles, who is there of so simple wit and capacity, but he may be able to perceive and understand them? These be but excuses and cloaks for the rain, and coverings of their own idle slothfulness. 'I cannot understand it.' What marvel? How shouldest thou understand, if thou wilt not read nor look upon it? Take the books into thine hands, read the whole story, and that

[[1] Other copies read, salves.]
[[2] Among.]
[[3] So be.]
[[4] And have a great.]
[[5] Slower of all evil.]
[[6] Obscure manner and writing.]
[[7] Understand.]
[[8] Who is it, that hearing.]

thou understandest keep it well in memory; that thou understandest not, read it again and again: if thou can neither so come by it, counsel with some other that is better learned. Go to thy curate and preacher; shew thyself to be desirous to know and learn: and I doubt not but God, seeing thy diligence and readiness (if no man else teach thee,) will himself vouchsafe with his holy Spirit to illuminate thee, and to open unto thee that which was locked from thee.

"Remember the eunuchus of Candace, queen of Ethiopy, which, albeit he was a man of a wild and barbarous country, and one occupied with worldly cures and businesses, yet riding in his chariot, he was reading the scripture. Now consider, if this man passing in his journey, was so diligent as to read the scripture, what thinkest thou of like was he wont to do sitting at home? Again, he that letted[9] not to read, albeit he did not understand, what did he then, trowest thou, after that, when he had learned and gotten understanding? For, that thou may well[10] know that he understood not what he read, hearken what Philip there saith unto him: 'Understandest thou what thou readest?' And he, nothing ashamed to confess his ignorance, answereth, 'How should I understand, having no body to shew me the way?' Lo! when he lacked one to shew him the way and to expound to him the scriptures, yet did he read; and therefore God the rather provided for him a guide of the way, that taught him to understand it. God perceived his willing and toward mind; and therefore he sent him a teacher by and bye. Therefore let no man be negligent about his own health and salvation: though thou have not Philip always when thou wouldest, the Holy Ghost, which then moved and stirred up Philip, will be ready and not to fail thee if thou do thy diligence accordingly. All these things been written for us to our edification[11] and amendment, which be born towards the latter end of the world. The reading of scriptures is a great and strong bulwark or fortress against sin; the ignorance of the same is the greater ruin and destruction of them that will not know it. That is the thing that bringeth in heresies[12], that is it that causeth all corrupt and perverse living, that it is[13] that bringeth all things out of good order[14]."

Hitherto, all that I have said, I have taken and gathered out of the foresaid sermon of this holy doctor, St John Chrysostom. Now if I should in like manner bring forth what the self-same doctor speaketh in other places, and what other doctors and writers say concerning the same purpose, I might seem to you to write another bible rather than to make a preface to the bible. Wherefore, in few words to comprehend the largeness and utility of the scripture, how it containeth fruitful instruction and erudition for every man; if any things[15] be necessary to be learned, of the holy scripture we may learn it. If falsehood shall be reproved, thereof we may gather wherewithal. If any thing be to be corrected and amended, if there need any exhortation or consolation, of the scripture we may well learn. In the scriptures be the fat pastures of the soul; therein is no venomous meat, no unwholesome thing; they be the very dainty and pure feeding. He that is ignorant, shall find there what he should learn. He that is a perverse sinner, shall there find his damnation to make him to tremble for fear. He that laboureth to serve God, shall find there his glory, and the promissions of eternal life, exhorting him more diligently to labour. Herein may princes learn how to govern their subjects; subjects obedience, love and dread to their princes: husbands, how they should behave them unto their wives; how to educate their children and servants: and contrary the wives, children, and servants may know their duty to their husbands, parents and masters. Here may all manner of persons, men, women, young, old, learned, unlearned, rich, poor, priests, laymen, lords, ladies, officers, tenants, and mean men, virgins, wives, widows, lawyers, merchants, artificers, husbandmen, and all manner of persons, of what estate or condition soever they be, may in this book learn all things what they ought to believe, what they ought to do, and what they should not do, as well concerning Almighty God, as also concerning themselves and all other. Briefly, to the reading of the scripture none can be enemy, but that either be so sick that they love not to hear of any medicine, or else that be so ignorant that they know not scripture to be the most healthful medicine.

The conclusion.

[[9] Letteth not, other copies.]
[[10] Thou mayest well.]
[[11] Written unto us for our edification.]
[[12] Heresy.]
[[13] That is it.]
[[14] Chrysost. De Lazaro. Concio iii. Tom. I. pp. 737-740. ed. Paris. 1718-38.]
[[15] Other copies read, any thing.]

Therefore, as touching this former part, I will here conclude and take it as a conclusion sufficiently determined and approved[1], that it is convenient and good the scripture to be read of all sorts and kinds of people, and in the vulgar tongue, without further allegations and probations for the same; which shall not need, since that this one place of John Chrysostom is enough and sufficient to persuade all them that be not frowardly and perversely set in their own wilful opinion; specially now that the king's highness, being supreme head next under Christ of this church of England, hath approved with his royal assent the setting forth hereof, which only to all true and obedient subjects ought to be a sufficient reason for the allowance of the same, without farther delay, reclamation, or resistance, although there were no preface nor other reason herein expressed.

The king's highness hath allow the scripture as necessary for us.

There is nothing but it may be abused.

Therefore now to come to the second and latter part of my purpose. There is nothing[2] so good in this world, but it may be abused, and turned from fruitful and wholesome to hurtful and noisome. What is there above better than the sun, the moon, the stars? Yet was there that took occasion by the great beauty and virtue of them to dishonour God, and to defile themselves with idolatry, giving the honour of the living God and Creator of all things to such things as he had created. What is there here beneath better than fire, water, meats, drinks, metals of gold, silver, iron, and steel? Yet we see daily great harm and much mischief done by every one of these, as well for lack of wisdom and providence of them that suffer evil, as by the malice of them that worketh the evil. Thus to them that be evil of themselves every thing setteth forward and increaseth their evil, be it of his own nature a thing never so good; like as contrarily, to them that studieth and endeavoureth themselves to goodness, every thing prevaileth them, and profiteth unto good, be it of his own nature a thing never so bad. As St Paul saith: *His qui diligant Deum, omnia cooperantur in bonum:* even as out of most venomous worms is made triacle, the most sovereign medicine for the preservation of man's health in time of danger. Wherefore I would advise you all, that cometh to the reading or hearing of this book, which is the word of God, the most precious jewel, and most holy relic that remaineth upon earth, that ye bring with you the fear of God, and that ye do it with all due reverence, and use your knowledge thereof, not to vainglory of frivolous disputation, but to the honour of God, increase of virtue, and edification both of yourselves and other.

St Gregory Nazianzene.

And to the intent that my words may be the more regarded, I will use in this part the authority of St Gregory Nazianzene, like as in the other I did of St John Chrysostom. It appeareth that in his time there were some (as I fear me, there been also now at these days a great number) which were idle babblers and talkers of the scripture out of season and all good order, and without any increase of virtue or example of good living. To them he writeth all his first book, *De Theologia:* whereof[3] I shall briefly gather the whole effect, and recite it here unto you. "There been some," saith he, "whose not only ears and tongues, but also their fists, been whetted and ready bent all to contention and unprofitable disputation; whom I would wish, as they been vehement and earnest to reason the matter with tongue, so they were also ready and practive to do good deeds. But forasmuch as they, subverting the order of all godliness, have respect only to this thing, how they may bind and loose subtle questions, so that now every market-place, every alehouse and tavern, every feast-house, briefly, every company of men, every assembly of women, is filled with such talk; since the matter is so," saith he, "and that our faith and holy religion of Christ beginneth to wax nothing else, but as it were a sophistry or a talking-craft, I can no less do but say something thereunto. It is not fit," saith he, "for every man to dispute the high questions of divinity, neither is it to be done at all times, neither in every audience must we discuss every doubt: but we must know when, to whom, and how far we ought to enter into such matters.

"First, it is not for every man, but it is for such as be of exact and exquisite judgments, and such as have spent their time before in study and contemplation; and such as before have cleansed themselves as well in soul as body, or at the least, endeavoured

[1 Sufficiently determine and appoint, other copies.] [2 Here is nothing.] [3 Wherefore.]

themselves to be made clean. For it is dangerous," saith he, "for the unclean to touch that thing that is most clean; like as the sore eye taketh harm by looking upon the sun.

"Secondarily, not at all times, but when we be reposed and at rest from all outward dregs and trouble, and when that our heads be not[4] encumbered with other worldly and wandering imaginations: as if a man should mingle balm and dirt together. For he that shall judge and determine such matters and doubts of scriptures, must take his time when he may apply his wits thereunto, that he may thereby the better see and discern what is truth.

"Thirdly, where, and in what audience? There and among those that been studious to learn, 'and not among such as have pleasure to trifle with such matters as with other things of pastime, which repute for their chief delicates the disputation of high questions, to shew their wits, learning and eloquence in reasoning of high matters.

"Fourthly, it is to be considered how far to wade in such matters of difficulty. No further," saith he, "but as every man's own capacity will serve him; and again, no further than the weakness or intelligence of the other audience may bear. For like as too great noise hurteth the ear, too much meat hurteth a man's body[5], too heavy burdens hurteth the bearers of them, too much rain doth more hurt than good to the ground; briefly, in all things too much is noyous; even so weak wits and weak consciences may soon be oppressed with over-hard questions. I say not this to dissuade men from the knowledge of God, and reading or studying of the scripture. For I say, that it is as necessary for the life of man's soul, as for the body to breathe. And if it were possible so to live, I would think it good for a man to spend all his life in that, and to do no other thing[6]. I commend the law which biddeth to meditate and study the scriptures always, both night and day, and sermons and preachings to be made both morning, noon, and eventide; and God to be lauded and blessed in all times, to bedward, from bed, in our journeys, and all our other works. I forbid not to read, but I forbid to reason. Neither forbid I to reason so far as is good and godly. But I allow not that is done out of season, and out of measure and good order. A man may eat too much of honey[7], be it never so sweet, and there is time for every thing; and that thing that is good is not good, if it be ungodly done: even as a flower in winter is out of season, and as a woman's apparel becometh not a man, neither contrarily, the man's the woman; neither is weeping convenient at a bridal, neither laughing at burial[8]. Now if we can observe and keep that is comely and timely in all other things, shall not we then the rather[9] do the same in the holy scriptures? Let us not run forth as it were wild horse[10], that can suffer neither bridle in their mouths, nor sitter on their backs. Let us keep us in our bounds, and neither let us go too far on the one side, lest we return into Egypt, neither too far over the other, lest we be carried away to Babylon. Let us not sing the song of our Lord in a strange land; that is to say, let us not dispute the word of God at all adventures, as well where it is not to be reasoned as where it is, and as well in the ears of them that be not fit therefore as of them that be. If we can in no wise forbear but that we must needs dispute, let us forbear thus much at the least, to do it out of time and place convenient. And let us entreat of those things which be holy holily; and upon those things that been mystical, mystically; and not to utter the divine mysteries in the ears unworthy to hear them: but let us know what is comely as well in our silence and talking, as in our garments' wearing, in our feeding, in our gesture, in our goings, and in all our other behaving. This contention and debate about scriptures and doubts thereof (specially when such as pretend to be the favourers and students thereof cannot agree within themselves) doth most hurt to ourselves, and to the furthering of the cause and quarrels that we would have furthered above all other things. And we in this," saith he, "be not unlike to them that, being mad,

[4 Been not, other copies.]
[5 The man's body, heavy burdens.]
[6 No other song.]
[7 Too much honey.]
[8 At a burial.]
[9 We then rather.]
[10 Wild horses.]

set their own houses on fire, and that slay their own children, or beat their own parents. I marvel much," saith he, "to recount whereof cometh all this desire of vain-glory, whereof cometh all this tongue-itch, that we have so much delight to talk and clatter? And wherein is our communication? Not in the commendations of virtuous and good deeds of hospitality, of love between christian brother and brother, of love between man and wife, of virginity and chastity, and of alms towards the poor; not in psalms and godly songs, not in lamenting for our sins, not in repressing the affections of the body, not in prayers to God. We talk of scripture, but in the meantime we subdue not our flesh by fasting, waking, and weeping; we make not this life a meditation of death; we do not strive to be lords of our appetites[1] and affections; we go not about to pull down our proud and high minds, to abate our fumish and rancorous stomachs, to restrain our lusts and bodily delectations, our undiscrete sorrows, our lascivious mirth, our inordinate looking, our insatiable hearing of vanities, our speaking without measure, our inconvenient thoughts, and briefly, to reform our life and manners. But all our holiness consisteth in talking. And we pardon each other from all good living, so that we may stick fast together in argumentation; as though there were no mo ways to heaven, but this alone, the way of speculation and knowledge (as they take it); but in very deed it is rather the way of superfluous contention and sophistication[2]."

Hitherto have I recited the mind of Gregory Nazianzene in that book which I spake of before. The same author saith also in another place, that "the learning of a christian man ought to begin of the fear of God, to end in matters of high speculation; and not contrarily to begin with speculation, and to end in fear. For speculation," saith he, "either high cunning and knowledge, if it be not stayed with the bridle of fear to offend God, is dangerous and enough to tumble a man headlong down the hill. Therefore," saith he, "the fear of God must be the first beginning, and as it were an A. B. C., or an introduction to all them that shall enter to the very true and most fruitful knowledge of holy scriptures. Where as is the fear of God, there is," saith he, "the keeping of the commandments, there is the cleansing of the flesh, which flesh is a cloud before the soul's eye, and suffereth it not purely to see the beam of the heavenly light. Where as is the cleansing of the flesh, there is the illumination of the Holy Ghost, the end of all our desires, and the very light whereby the verity of scriptures is seen and perceived[3]." This is the mind and almost the words of Gregory Nazianzene, doctor of the Greek church, of whom St Jerome saith, that unto his time the Latin church had no writer able to be compared and to make an even match with him[4].

Therefore to conclude this latter part, every man that cometh to the reading of this holy book ought to bring with him first and foremost this fear of Almighty God, and then next a firm and stable purpose to reform his own self according thereunto; and so to continue, proceed, and prosper from time to time, shewing himself to be a sober and fruitful hearer and learner. Which if he do, he shall prove at the length well able to teach, though not with his mouth, yet with his living and good example, which is sure the most lively and most effectuous[5] form and manner of teaching. He that otherwise intermeddleth with this book, let him be assured that once he shall make account therefore, when he shall have said to him, as it is written in the prophet David, *Peccatori dicit Deus*, &c.: "Unto the ungodly said God, Why dost thou preach my laws, and takest my testament in thy mouth? Whereas thou hatest to be reformed, and hast been partakers with advoutrers. Thou hast let thy mouth speak wickedness, and with thy tongue thou hast set forth deceit. Thou

---

[[1] Lords over our appetites, other copies.]

[[2] Greg. Nazianz. Orat. xxvii. Theol. I. adver. Eunomian. Tom. I. p. 487, et sqq. Ed. Paris. 1778-1840.]

[[3] Id. Orat. xxxix. In sancta lumina. Tom. I. pp. 681, 2.]

[[4] Numquid in illa epistola Gregorium virum eloquentissimum non potui nominare? Quis apud Latinos par sui est? Quo ego magistro glorior et exulto. Hieron. Apol. adv. Ruffin. Lib. I. Tom. II. p. 137. Ed. Francof. 1684.]

[[5] Other copies read, and effectuous.]

sattest and spakest against thy brother; and hast slandered thine own mother's son. These things hast thou done, and I held my tongue, and thou thoughtest (wickedly) that I am even such a one as thyself. But I will reprove thee, and set before thee the things that thou hast done. O consider this, ye that forget God; lest I pluck you away, and there be none to deliver you. Whoso offereth me thanks and praise, he honoureth me; and to him that ordereth his conversation right will I shew the salvation of God."

God save the King[6].

---

[[6] The volume containing "A list of some of the early printed books in the Archiepiscopal Library at Lambeth," Lond. 1843, contains some interesting notices of fragments occupying the place of fly leaves and end papers in volumes with which they had no connexion. Among them is the following. The Rev. S. R. Maitland, the librarian, says:

"Two leaves, each containing the PROLOGUE TO CRANMER'S BIBLE on one side, and the usual matter on the other side." One of these is the prologue to the edition of December 1541, and requires no description; but the other is, as far as I can find, unique. Mr Lea Wilson, whose magnificent collection of bibles contains (as a very small part of its treasures) twelve copies exhibiting every variety of Cranmer's Bible, and who has spared neither pains nor expense in making himself fully acquainted with the details of the subject, informs me that he had never before seen it. I am indebted to the same gentleman for the suggestion, that these two leaves so differing from each other, and both found together in the binding of one volume, that volume being a Salisbury Breviary, printed by Francis Regnault, at Paris, in 1535, agrees with the notion, supported by other evidence, that this bible was printed in France. Certainly the large black letter of this prologue, and of the Breviary, are as like as can be imagined. Under these circumstances, it seems worth while to reprint this prologue in something like the form in which it stands, premising that it is all in black letter, and that the initial F. is not, as in some copies of the prologue, a Roman letter, but the same flourishing capital as appears in the edition of December, 1541. It should I presume be headed, 'A prologue expressynge what is *meant by certaine sygnes and tokens that we have set in the Byble*;' but what was probably the first line has been cut off, and only what is here in *italics* remains. The Prologue itself is as follows:—"

FIRST where as often tymes ye shall fynde a smal letter in the text, it sygnifieth that so moch as in (sic) the small letter doth abounde & is more in the common translaciō in Latyne then is founde ether in the Hebrue or in y^e Greke. Moreouer where as ye finde this sygne o+ it betokeneth a dyuersite & difference of readyng betwene the Hebrues and the Chaldees in the same place, whych diuersytes of readynges we were purposed to haue set forth perticularly vnto you. But for so moch as they are very large and tedyous, & thys volume is very great and houge allready, we haue therfore left thē out. We haue also (as ye maye se) added many handes both in the mergent of this volume and also in the text, vpon the whyche we purposed to haue made in the ende of the Byble (in a table by themselues) certen annotaciōs: but for so moch as yet there hath not bene suffycyent tyme mynistred to the Kynges mooste honorable councell, for the ouersyght and correcion of the sayde annotacions, we do therfore omyt them, tyll theyr more conuenyent leysoure. Doynge nowe no more but beseake the, moost gentle reader, that when thou commest at soch a place where a hande doth stande (or any other where, in the Byble) and thou canst not attayne to the meanynge & true knowledge of that sentence, then do not rashly presume to make any pryuate interpretacyon thereof: but submytte thy self to the iudgement of those that are learned.

God saue the Kynge.

[THE

# ARCHBISHOP'S SPEECH

AT THE

## CORONATION OF EDWARD VI., FEB. 20, 1547.[1]]

---

Foxes and Firebrands, Part ii. pp. 2—9. Strype, Memorials of Abp. Cranmer, Vol. i. pp. 205-7. Ed. Oxon. 1840.

MOST dread and royal sovereign: The promises your highness hath made here at your coronation, to forsake the devil and all his works, are not to be taken in the bishop of Rome's sense, when you commit any thing distasteful to that see, to hit your majesty in the teeth; as pope Paul the third, late bishop of Rome, sent to your royal father, saying, "Didst thou not promise, at our permission of thy coronation, to forsake the devil and all his works, and dost thou turn to heresy[2]? For the breach of this thy promise, knowest thou not, that 'tis in our power to dispose of the sword[3] and sceptre to whom we please?" We, your majesty's clergy, do humbly conceive, that this promise reacheth not at your highness' sword, spiritual or temporal, or in the least at your highness swaying the sceptre of this your dominion, as you and your predecessors have had them from God. Neither could your ancestors lawfully resign up their crowns to the bishop of Rome or to his legates[4], according to their ancient oaths then taken upon that ceremony.

The bishops of Canterbury for the most part have crowned your predecessors, and anointed them kings of this land: yet it was not in their power to receive or reject them, neither did it give them authority to prescribe them conditions to take or to leave their crowns; although the bishops of Rome would encroach upon your predecessors by his bishops' act and oil[5], that in the end they might possess those bishops with an interest to dispose of their crowns at their pleasure. But the wiser sort will look to their claws and clip them.

The solemn rites of coronation have their ends and utility, yet neither direct force or necessity: they be good admonitions to put kings in mind of their duty to God, but no increasement of their dignity. For they be God's anointed, not in respect of the oil which the bishop useth, but in consideration of their power which is ordained, of the sword which is authorised, of their persons which are elected by God[6], and endued with the gifts of his Spirit for the better ruling and guiding of his people. The oil, if added, is but a ceremony; if it be wanting, that king is yet a perfect monarch notwithstanding, and God's anointed, as well as if he was inoiled. Now for the person or bishop that doth anoint a king, it is proper to be done by the chiefest; but if they cannot, or will not, any bishop may perform this ceremony.

To condition with monarchs upon these ceremonies, the bishop of Rome (or other bishops owning his supremacy) hath no authority, but he may faithfully declare what God requires at the hands of kings and rulers; that is, religion and virtue. Therefore not from the bishop of Rome, but as a messenger from my Saviour Jesus Christ, I shall most humbly admonish your royal majesty, what things your highness is to perform.

---

[1 Strype asserts, that "at this coronation, (Edw. VI.) there was no sermon, but that was supplied by an excellent speech, which was made by the archbishop," and that "it was found among the inestimable collections of archbishop Usher." Dr Jenkyns was unable to meet with the original, search having been made in vain for it in Dublin, (Vol. II. p. 118, *n.*) A farther search for it has also been made for the present edition, but equally without success. It is here printed from the second part of "Foxes and Firebrands," published by Robert Warre, (Ed. Dublin, 1682, pp. 2—9.) who says that "the collections in this second part are most of them either out of the memorials of that great minister of state, the lord Cecil, or from the testimonies of persons that are still living." Part I. To the reader, A. 4.]

[2 Run to heresy, Strype.]

[3 That it is in our power to dispose of thy sword, Ibid.]

[4 Or his legates, Ibid.]

[5 By their act and oil, Ibid.]

[6 Elected of God, Ibid.]

Your majesty is God's vice-gerent and Christ's vicar within your own dominions, and to see, with your predecessor Josiah[7], God truly worshipped, and idolatry destroyed, the tyranny of the bishops of Rome banished from your subjects, and images removed. These acts be signs of a second Josiah[7], who reformed the church of God in his days. You are to reward virtue, to revenge sin, to justify the innocent, to relieve the poor, to procure peace, to repress violence, and to execute justice throughout your realms. For precedents[8], on those kings who performed not these things, the old law shews how the Lord revenged his quarrel; and on those kings who fulfilled these things, he poured forth his blessings in abundance. For example, it is written of Josiah in the book of the Kings thus: "Like unto him there was no king before him that turned[9] to the Lord with all his heart, according to all the law of Moses, neither after him arose there any like him." This was to that prince a perpetual fame of dignity, to remain to the end of days.

Being bound by my function to lay these things before your royal highness, the one as a reward, if you fulfil; the other as a judgment from God, if you neglect them; yet I openly declare before the living God, and before these nobles of the land, that I have no commission to denounce your majesty deprived, if your highness miss in part, or in whole, of these performances, much less to draw up indentures between God and your majesty, or to say you forfeit your crown with a clause, for the bishop of Rome, as have been done by your majesty's predecessors, king John, and his son Henry of this land. The Almighty God of his mercy let the light of his countenance shine upon your majesty, grant you a prosperous and happy reign, defend you and save you; and let your subjects say,

Amen!

God save the king.

---

[7 Josias, Ibid.] [8 Presidents, F. and F.] [9 There was no king, that turned, Ibid.]

# HOMILY OF SALVATION[1]

BECAUSE all men be sinners and offenders against God, and breakers of his law and commandments, therefore can no man by his own acts, works, and deeds[2] (seem they never so good) be justified and made righteous before God; but every man of necessity is constrained to seek for another righteousness, or justification, to be received at God's own hands, that is to say, the remission, pardon[3], and forgiveness of his sins and trespasses in such things as he hath offended. And this justification or righteousness, which we so receive by God's mercy[4] and Christ's merits, embraced by faith, is taken, accepted, and allowed of God for our perfect and full justification.

For the more full understanding hereof, it is our parts and duty ever to remember the great mercy of God, how that (all the world being wrapped in sin by breaking of the law) God sent his only Son our Saviour Christ into this world, to fulfil the law for us; and by shedding of his most precious blood, to make a sacrifice and satisfaction, or (as it may be called) amends, to his Father for our sins[5], to assuage his wrath and indignation conceived against us for the same. Insomuch that infants, being baptized, and dying in their infancy, are by this sacrifice washed from their sins, brought to God's favour, and made his children, and inheritors of his kingdom of heaven. And they which actually do[6] sin after their baptism, when they convert and turn again[7] to God unfeignedly, they are likewise washed by this sacrifice from their sins, in such sort, that there remaineth not any spot of sin that shall be imputed to their damnation. This is that justification, or righteousness, which St Paul speaketh of, when he saith: "No man is justified by the works of the law, but freely by faith in Jesus Christ." And again he saith: "We believe in Christ Jesu, that we be justified freely by the faith of Christ, and not by the works of the law, because that no man shall be justified by the works of the law."

The efficacy of Christ's passion and oblation.

Rom. iii. [Gal. ii.]

---

[[1] The three homilies, "Of Salvation," "Of the true, lively, and christian Faith," and "Of Good Works," have generally been attributed to Cranmer. Gardener, in his letter to protector Somerset, several times ascribes that of "Salvation" to him. Vid. Foxe's Acts and Monuments, 1st Ed. Lond. 1563, pp. 742, 5,803. Of this homily, and the other two, Todd says: "But more extensive declarations of doctrine had now been formed, entitled Homilies. They are in number twelve. Of these at least three, if not a fourth, appear to have been written by Cranmer himself. If internal evidence had been wanting in support of this belief, the authority of nearly contemporary assertion exists. John Woolton, the nephew of the celebrated Alexander Nowell, was the author of several theological works in the reign of Elizabeth. He became bishop of Exeter. Not long before he was advanced to the prelacy, he published, in 1576, the Christian Manual, in which he says, (Chr. Man. Sign. c. iii.) 'What we teach and think of good works, those homilies written in our English tongue of Salvation, Faith, and Works, by that light and martyr of Christ's church, Cranmer, archbishop of Canterbury, do plain testify and declare; which are built upon so sure a foundation, that no sycophant can deface them, nor sophister confute them, while the world shall endure.' Dr Wordsworth is of opinion that Cranmer wrote also the homily of the Misery of Mankind, Eccl. Biogr. iii. 505. I should rather attribute to his pen that against the Fear of Death, there being among the fragments of his composition, given by Strype, part of a discourse on this subject." Todd's Life of Cranmer, Vol. II. pp. 10, 11. Ed. Lond. 1831.—But the homily of the Misery of Mankind, ascribed by Dr Wordsworth to Cranmer, appears in "Homilies set forth by the right reverend father in God, Edmunde (Bonner), bishop of London," Ed. Lond. (Cawode) 1555. with the name of Harpesfield at the end, thus: Jo. Harpesfield sacræ theologiæ professor. Arch. London.—Vid. also, Strype's Memorials of Abp. Cranmer, Vol. I. pp. 213, 14. 249. Ed. Oxon. 1840. Eccl. Memorials, Vol. I. pp. 533-5. Ed. Oxon. 1822. Annals of the Reformation, Vol. I. pp. 498, 9. Ed. Oxon. 1824. Burnet, Hist. of Reformat. Vol. III. p. 358. Ed. Oxon. 1829.—The text of this reprint follows that of Grafton's edition, "imprinted at London, the last day of July, 1547," and has been collated with that of Whitchurch, Aug. 20, 1547, Jugge and Cawood, 1560, and with a small 12mo. copy, (Cawood) 1562. The Ed. 1547, referred to throughout the notes, is that of Whitchurch, 1547.]

[[2] Deed, Ed. 1560.]

[[3] Remission and pardon, omitted in Eds. 1560, 62.]

[[4] Of God's mercy, Ed. 1560.]

[[5] For our sin, Ed. 1547.]

[[6] Which in act or deed do sin, Eds. 1560, 62.]

[[7] When they turn again, Ibid.]

And although this justification be free unto us, yet it cometh not so freely to us[8], that there is no ransom paid therefore at all.

But here may man's reason be astonied, reasoning after this fashion: If a ransom be paid for our redemption, then it is not[9] given us freely. For a prisoner that payeth his ransom is not let go freely; for if he go freely, then he goeth without ransom: for what is it else to go freely, than to be set at liberty without payment of ransom? This reason is satisfied by the great wisdom of God in this mystery of our redemption, who hath so tempered his justice and mercy together, that he would neither by his justice condemn us unto the perpetual captivity[10] of the devil, and his prison of hell, remediless for ever, without mercy; nor by his mercy deliver us clearly, without justice, or payment of a just ransom; but with his endless mercy he joined his most upright and equal justice. His great mercy he shewed unto us in delivering us from our former captivity, without requiring of any ransom to be paid, or amends to be made upon our parts; which thing by us had been impossible to be done. And whereas it lay not in us that to do, he provided a ransom for us; that was the most precious body and blood of his most dear and best beloved son Jesu Christ, who, besides his ransom[11], fulfilled the law for us perfectly. And so the justice of God and his mercy did embrace together, and fulfilled the mystery of our redemption. And of this justice and mercy of God knit together speaketh St Paul in the third chapter to the Romans: "All have offended, and have need of the glory of God, justified[12] freely by his grace, by redemption which is in Jesu Christ, whom God hath set forth to us[13] for a reconciler and peace-maker, through faith in his blood, to shew his righteousness." And in the tenth chapter: "Christ is the end of the law unto righteousness to every man that believeth." And in the eighth chapter: "That which was impossible by the law, inasmuch as it was weak by the flesh, God sending his own Son in the similitude of sinful flesh, by sin damned sin in the flesh; that the righteousness of the law might be fulfilled in us, which walk not after the flesh, but after the Spirit."

Objection.

An answer.

Rom. iii.

Rom. x.

Rom. viii.

In these foresaid places the apostle toucheth specially three things, which must concur and go together[14] in our justification: upon God's part, his great mercy and grace; upon Christ's part, justice, that is, the satisfaction of God's justice, or price of our redemption, by the offering of his body and shedding of his blood, with fulfilling of the law perfectly and throughly; and upon our part, true and lively faith in the merits of Jesu Christ, which yet is not ours, but by God's working in us. So that in our justification is not only God's mercy and grace, but also his justice, which the apostle calleth the justice of God; and it consisteth in paying our ransom, and fulfilling of the law: and so the grace of God doth not exclude the justice of God in our justification, but only excludeth the justice of man[15], that is to say, the justice of our works, as to be merits of deserving our justification. And therefore St Paul declareth here nothing upon the behalf of man concerning his justification, but only a true and lively faith; which nevertheless is the gift of God, and not man's only work without God.

Three things must go together in our justification.

And yet that faith doth not exclude[16] repentance, hope, love, dread, and the fear of God, to be joined with faith in every man that is justified; but it excludeth them[17] from the office of justifying: so that although they be all present together in him that is justified, yet they justify not altogether. Nor that faith also[18] doth not exclude[19] the justice of our good works, necessarily to be done afterward of duty towards God, (for we are most bounden to serve God in doing good deeds, commanded by him in his holy scripture, all the days of our life;) but it excludeth them, so that we may not do them to this intent, to be made good by doing of them. For all the good works that we can do be unperfect, and therefore not able to deserve our justi-

How is it to be understand, that faith justifieth without works.

[8 Unto us, Eds. 1560, 62.]
[9 Then is it not, Ibid.]
[10 Everlasting captivity, Ibid.]
[11 Besides this ransom, Ibid.]
[12 But are justified, Ibid.]
[13 Unto us, Ed. 1562.]
[14 Which must go together, Eds. 1560, 62.]
[15 Doth not shut out the justice, but only shutteth out the justice of man, Ibid.]
[16 Doth not shut out, Ibid.]
[17 It shutteth them out, Ibid.]
[18 The faith were, Ed. 1560.]
[19 Doth not shut out, Ed. 1560, 2.]

fication: but our justification doth come freely by the mere mercy of God, and of so great and free mercy, that whereas all the world was not able of theirselves to pay any part towards their ransom, it pleased our heavenly Father, of his infinite mercy, without any our desert or deserving, to prepare for us the most precious jewels of Christ's body and blood, whereby our ransom might be fully paid, the law fulfilled, and his justice fully satisfied. So that Christ is now the righteousness of all them that truly do believe in him. He for them paid their ransom by his death: he for them fulfilled the law in his life: so that now in him, and by him, every true christian man may be called a fulfiller of the law; forasmuch as that which their infirmity lacketh, Christ's justice hath supplied.

[1] *The Second Part of the Sermon of Salvation.*

Ye have heard of whom all men ought to seek their justification and righteousness, and how also this righteousness cometh unto men by Christ's death and merits: ye heard also that three things are required to the obtaining of our righteousness; that is, God's mercy, Christ's justice, and a true and lively faith, out of the which faith springeth good works.

Before[2] was declared at large that no man can be justified by his own good works, because that no man[3] fulfilleth the law, according to the full request of the law. And

Gal. iii. St Paul, in his epistle to the Galatians, proveth the same, saying thus: "If there had been any law given which could have justified, verily righteousness should have been

Gal. ii. by the law." And again he saith: "If righteousness be by the law, then Christ died

Gal. v. in vain." And again he saith: "You that are justified by the law[4] are fallen away

Ephes. ii. from grace." And furthermore he writeth to the Ephesians on this wise: "By grace are ye saved through faith, and that not of yourselves, for it is the gift of God, and not of works, lest any man should glory." And, to be short, the sum of all Paul's disputation is this, that if justice come of works, then it cometh not of grace; and if it come of grace, then it cometh not of works. And to this end tendeth all the

Acts x. prophets, as St Peter saith in the tenth of the Acts: "Of Christ all the prophets," saith St Peter, "do witness, that through his name all they that believe in him shall receive the remission of sins."

Faith only justifieth, is the doctrine of old doctors.

And after this wise to be justified, only by this true and lively faith in Christ, speaketh all the old and ancient authors, both Greeks and Latins; of whom I will specially rehearse three, Hilary, Basil, and Ambrose. St Hilary saith these words plainly in the ninth canon upon Matthew: "Faith only justifieth[5]." And St Basil, a Greek author, writeth thus: ["This is a perfect and a whole glorying in God, when a man doth not boast himself for his own justice, but knoweth himself certainly to be unworthy of true justice, but to be justified by only faith in Christ.[6]] This is a perfect and a whole rejoicing in God, when a man advanceth not himself for his own righteousness, but knowledgeth himself to lack true justice and righteousness, and to be justified by

Phil. iii. the only faith in Christ[7]." "And Paul," saith he, "doth glory in the contempt of his own righteousness, and that he looketh for his righteousness[8] of God by faith."

These be the very words of St Basil. And St Ambrose, a Latin author, saith these words: "This is the ordinance of God, that he which believeth[9] in Christ should be saved without works, by faith only, freely receiving remission of his sins[10]." Consider diligently these words: "without works," "by faith only," "freely we receive remission of our sins." What can be spoken more plainly than to say, that freely,

---

[[1] This passage is inserted from the Eds. 1560, 1562, and is not found in the earlier copies, which were not broken by divisions.]

[[2] Also before, Eds. 1560, 62.]

[[3] Works, that no man, Ibid.]

[[4] Justified in the law, Ed. 1547.]

[[5] Fides enim sola justificat.—Hilar. Comment. in Matthæum. Can. viii. col. 500, Ed. Paris. 1531.]

[[6] This passage is omitted in Ed. (Grafton) 1547.]

[[7] Αὕτη γὰρ δὴ ἡ τελεία καὶ ὁλόκληρος καύχησις ἐν Θεῷ, ὅτι μήτε ἐπὶ δικαιοσύνῃ τις ἐπαίρεται τῇ ἑαυτοῦ, ἀλλ' ἔγνω μὲν ἐνδεῆ ὄντα ἑαυτὸν δικαιοσύνης ἀληθοῦς, πίστει δὲ μόνῃ τῇ εἰς Χριστὸν δεδικαιωμένον. καὶ καυχᾶται Παῦλος ἐπὶ τῷ καταφρονῆσαι τῆς ἑαυτοῦ δικαιοσύνης, ζητεῖν δὲ τὴν διὰ Χριστοῦ.—Basil. Hom. xxii. De humilitate. Tom. I. p. 473, Ed. Paris. 1538.]

[[8] For the righteousness, Eds. 1560, 62.]

[[9] That they which believe, Ed. 1560. That he which believe, Ed. 1562.]

[[10] Quia hoc constitutum est a Deo, ut qui credit in Christum, salvus sit sine opere, sola fide gratis accipiens remissionem peccatorum.—Ambros. in Epist. 1 ad Corinth. Cap. i. v. 4. Tom. III. p. 161. Ed. Colon. Agrip. 1616.]

without works, by faith only, we obtain remission of our sins? These and other like sentences, that we be justified by faith only, freely, and without works, we do read ofttimes in the most best and ancient writers: as, beside Hilary, Basil, and St Ambrose, before rehearsed, we read the same in Origen, St Chrysostom, St Cyprian, St Augustine, Prosper, Œcumenius, Photius, Bernardus, Anselm, and many other authors, Greek and Latin[11].

Nevertheless, this sentence, that we be justified by faith only, is not so meant of them, that the said justifying faith is alone in man, without true repentance, hope, charity, dread, and the fear of God, at any time or season. Nor when they say, that we be justified freely, they mean not that we should or might afterward be idle, and that nothing should be required on our parts afterward. Neither they mean not so to be justified without our good works, that we should do no good works at all; like as shall be more expressed at large hereafter. But this proposition[12], that we be justified by faith only, freely, and without works, is spoken for to take away clearly all merit of our works, as being insufficient to deserve[13] our justification at God's hands, and thereby most plainly to express the weakness of man, and the goodness of God; the great infirmity of ourselves, and the might and power of God; the imperfectness of our own works, and the most abundant grace of our Saviour Christ; and thereby wholly to ascribe[14] the merit and deserving of our justification unto Christ only, and his most precious blood-shedding. This faith the holy scripture teacheth; this is the strong rock and foundation of christian religion; this doctrine all old and ancient authors of Christ's church do approve; this doctrine advanceth and setteth forth the true glory of Christ, and suppresseth[15] the vain-glory of man; this whosoever denieth is not to be reputed for[16] a true christian man, nor for[17] a setter-forth of Christ's glory, but for an adversary of Christ and his gospel, and for a setter-forth of men's vain-glory.

Faith alone, how it is to be understand.

The profit of the doctrine of faith only justifieth.

What they be that impugn the doctrine of faith only justifieth.

And although this doctrine be never so true (as it is most true indeed), that we be justified freely, without all merit of our own good works (as St Paul doth express it), and freely, by this lively and perfect faith in Christ only, as the ancient authors use to speak it; yet this true doctrine must be also truly understand, and most plainly declared, lest carnal men should take unjustly occasion thereby to live carnally after the appetite and will of the world, the flesh, and the devil. And because no man should err by mistaking of this doctrine[18], I shall plainly and shortly so declare the right understanding of the same, that no man shall justly think that he may thereby take any occasion of carnal liberty to follow the desires of the flesh, or that thereby any kind of sin shall be committed, or any ungodly living the more used.

A declaration of this doctrine: faith without works justifieth.

First, you shall understand, that in our justification by Christ it is not all one thing, the office of God unto man, and the office of man unto God. Justification is not the office of man, but of God: for man cannot justify himself by his own works[19], neither in part, nor in the whole; for that were the greatest arrogancy and presumption of man that antichrist could erect against God[20], to affirm that a man might by his own works take away and purge his own sins, and so justify himself. But justification[21] is the office of God only, and is not a thing which we render unto him, but which we receive of him; not which we give to him, but which we take of him, by his free mercy, and by the only merits of his most dearly-beloved Son, our only Redeemer, Saviour, and Justifier, Jesus Christ. So that the true understanding of this doctrine, we be justified freely by faith without works, or that we be justified by faith in Christ only, is not, that this our own act to believe in Christ, or this our faith in Christ, which is within us, doth justify us, and merit our justification[22] unto

Justification is the office of God only.

[11 Many of the passages on this subject from these writers will be found in Cranmer's Notes on Justification.]

[12 But this saying, Eds. 1560, 62.]

[13 As being unable to deserve, Ibid.]

[14 And therefore wholly, Ibid. And thereby wholly for to ascribe, Ed. 1547.]

[15 And beateth down, Eds. 1560, 62.]

[16 Is not to be counted for, Ibid.]

[17 Not for, Ibid.]

[18 Of this true doctrine, Ed. 1547.]

[19 Cannot make himself righteous by his own works, Ed. 1560, 62.]

[20 Could set up against God, Ibid.]

[21 But in justification, Ibid.]

[22 And deserve our justification, Ibid.]

us (for that were to count ourselves to be justified by some act or virtue that is within ourselves): but the true understanding and meaning thereof is, that although we hear God's word, and believe it; although we have faith, hope, charity, repentance, dread, and fear of God within us, and do never so many good works thereunto; yet we must renounce the merit of all our said virtues, of faith, hope, charity, and all our other virtues and good deeds, which we either have done, shall do, or can do, as things that be far too weak and insufficient and unperfect, to deserve remission of our sins, and our justification; and therefore we must trust only in God's mercy, and in that sacrifice which our High Priest and Saviour Christ Jesus, the Son of God, once offered for us upon the cross, to obtain thereby God's grace and remission, as well of our original sin in baptism, as of all actual sin committed by us after our baptism, if we truly repent, and convert unfeignedly[1] to him again. So that, as St John Baptist, although he were never so virtuous and godly a man, yet in this matter of forgiving of sin he did put the people from him, and appointed them unto Christ, saying thus unto them, "Behold, yonder is the Lamb of God, which taketh away the sins of the world:" even so, as great and as godly a virtue as the lively faith is, yet it putteth us from itself, and remitteth or appointeth us unto Christ, for to have only by him remission of our sins, or justification. So that our faith in Christ (as it were) saith unto us thus: It is not I that take away your sins, but it is Christ only; and to him only I send you for that purpose, renouncing therein[2] all your good virtues, words, thoughts, and works, and only putting your trust in Christ.

John i.

### [3] *The Third Part of the Sermon of Salvation.*

It hath been manifestly declared unto you, that no man can fulfil the law of God, and therefore by the law all men are condemned: whereupon it followed necessarily, that some other thing should be required for our salvation than the law; and that is a true and a lively faith in Christ, bringing forth good works, and a life according to God's commandments. And also you heard the ancient authors' minds of this saying, Faith in Christ only justifieth man, so plainly declared, that you see the very true meaning of this proposition, or saying, &c.

Thus you do see that the very true sense of this proposition, We be justified by faith in Christ only, according to the meaning of the old ancient authors, is this: We put our faith in Christ, that we be justified by him only, that we be justified by God's free mercy, and the merits of our Saviour Christ only, and by no virtue or good work of our own that is in us, or that we can be able to have or to do, for to deserve the same, Christ himself only being the cause meritorious thereof.

Here you perceive many words to be used to avoid contention in words with them that delighteth[4] to brawl about words, and also to shew the true meaning, to avoid evil taking and misunderstanding; and yet peradventure all will not serve with them that be contentious, but contenders will ever forge matter of contention[5], even when they have none occasion thereto. Notwithstanding, such be the less to be passed upon, so that the rest may profit, which will be more desirous to know the truth, than (when it is plain enough) to contend about it, and with contentions and captious cavillations to obscure and darken it.

Truth it is, that our own works doth not[6] justify us, to speak properly of our justification; that is to say, our works do not merit or deserve remission of our sins, and make us, of unjust, just before God; but God of his mere mercy, through the only merits and deservings[7] of his Son Jesus Christ, doth justify us. Nevertheless, because faith doth directly send us to Christ for remission of our sins, and that by faith given us of God we embrace the promise of God's mercy and of the remission of our sins, (which thing none other of our virtues or works properly doth,) therefore scripture useth to say, that faith without works doth justify. And forasmuch that it is all one sentence in effect, to say, faith without works, and only faith, doth justify us; therefore the old

---

[[1] And turn unfeignedly, Ed. 1560, 62.]
[[2] Forsaking therein, Ibid.]
[[3] Inserted from Eds. 1560, 62. Vid. p 130, *n*. 1.]
[[4] That delight, Ed. 1560, 62.]
[[5] Matters of contention, Ed. 1560.]
[[6] Works do not, Eds. 1560, 62.]
[[7] Only merits or deserving, Ed. 1547. Only mercies and deservings, Ed. 1560.]

ancient fathers of the church from time to time have uttered our justification with this speech, Only faith justifieth us; meaning none other thing than St Paul meant, when he said, Faith without works justifieth us. And because all this is brought to pass through the only merits and deservings of our Saviour Christ, and not through our merits, or through the merit of any virtue that we have within us, or of any work that cometh from us; therefore, in that respect of merit and deserving, we renounce, as it were[8], altogether again faith, works, and all other virtues. For our own imperfection is so great, through the corruption of original sin, that all is imperfect that is within us; faith, charity, hope, dread, thoughts, words, and works; and therefore not apt to merit and deserve any part of our justification for us. And this form of speaking we use[9], in the humbling of ourselves to God, and to give all the glory to our Saviour Christ, which is best worthy to have it.

Here you have heard the office of God in our justification, and how we receive it of him freely, by his mercy, without our deserts, through true and lively faith. Now you shall hear the office and duty of a christian man unto God, what we ought on our part to render unto God again for his great mercy and goodness. Our office is, not to pass the time of this present life[10] unfruitfully and idly, after that we are baptized or justified, not caring how few good works we do, to the glory of God, and profit of our neighbours: much less it is our office[11], after that we be once made Christ's members, to live contrary to the same; making ourselves members of the devil, walking after his enticements, and after the suggestions of the world and the flesh, whereby we know that we do serve the world and the devil, and not God. For that faith which bringeth forth (without repentance) either evil works, or no good works, is not a right, pure, and lively faith, but a dead, devilish, counterfeit, and feigned faith, as St Paul and St James call it. For even the devils know and believe that Christ was born of a virgin; that he fasted forty days and forty nights without meat and drink; that he wrought all kind of miracles, declaring himself very God[12]: they believe also that Christ for our sakes suffered most painful death, to redeem us from eternal death[13], and that he rose again from death the third day: they believe that he ascended into heaven, and that he sitteth on the right hand of the Father[14], and at the last end of this world shall come again, and judge both the quick and the dead. These articles of our faith the devils believe, and so they believe all things that be written in the new and old Testament to be true: and yet for all this faith they be but devils, remaining still in their damnable estate, lacking the very true christian faith.

They that preach faith only justifieth, do not teach carnal liberty, or that we should do no good works.

The devils have faith, but not the true faith.

For the right and true christian faith is, not only to believe that holy scripture and all the foresaid articles of our faith are true, but also to have a sure trust and confidence in God's merciful promises, to be saved from everlasting damnation by Christ: whereof doth follow a loving heart to obey his commandments. And this true christian faith neither any devil hath, nor yet any man, which in the outward profession of his mouth, and in his outward receiving of the sacraments, in coming to the church, and in all other outward appearances, seemeth to be a christian man, and yet in his living and deeds sheweth the contrary. For how can a man have this true faith, this sure trust and confidence in God, that by the merits of Christ his sins be remitted[15], and he reconciled to the favour of God, and to be partaker of the kingdom of heaven by Christ, when he liveth ungodly, and denieth Christ in his deeds? Surely no such ungodly man can have this faith and trust in God. For as they know Christ to be the only Saviour of the world, so they know also that wicked men shall not possess the kingdom[16] of God. They know that God "hateth unrighteousness;" that he will "destroy all those that speak untruly;" that those that have done good works (which cannot be done without a lively faith in Christ) "shall come forth into the resurrection of life, and those that have done evil shall

What is the true and justifying faith.

They that continue in evil living have not true faith.

Psal. v.

[8 We forsake (as it were), Eds. 1560, 62.]
[9 Use we, Ibid.]
[10 Ed. 1547 (Grafton) reads, "his present life," probably a misprint.]
[11 Less is it our office, Eds. 1560, 62.]
[12 Himself to be very God, Ed. 1562.]
[13 From everlasting death, Eds. 1560, 62.]
[14 Hand of God the Father, Ed. 1562.]
[15 Be forgiven, Eds. 1560, 62.]
[16 Shall not enjoy the kingdom, Ibid.]

come unto resurrection[1] of judgment." And very well they know[2] also, that "to them that be contentious, and to them that will not be obedient unto the truth, but will obey unrighteousness, shall come indignation, wrath, and affliction," &c.

Therefore, to conclude, considering the infinite benefits of God, shewed and exhibited unto us[3] mercifully without our deserts, who hath not only created us of nothing, and from a piece of vile clay of his infinite goodness hath exalted us, as touching our soul, unto his own similitude and likeness; but also, whereas we were condemned to hell and death eternal[4], hath given his own natural Son, being God eternal, immortal, and equal unto himself in power and glory, to be incarnated, and to take our mortal nature upon him, with the infirmities of the same, and in the same nature to suffer most shameful and painful death for our offences, to the intent to justify us and to restore us to life everlasting; so making us also his dear beloved children, brethren unto his only Son our Saviour Christ, and inheritors for ever with him of his eternal kingdom of heaven: these great and merciful benefits of God, if they be well considered, do neither minister unto us occasion to be idle, and to live without doing any good works, neither yet stirreth us by any means to do evil things; but contrariwise, if we be not desperate persons, and our hearts harder than stones, they move us to render ourselves unto God wholly, with all our will, hearts, might, and power, to serve him in all good deeds, obeying his commandments during our lives, to seek in all things his glory and honour, not our sensual pleasures and vain-glory; evermore dreading willingly to offend such a merciful God and loving Redeemer, in word, thought, or deed. And the said benefits of God, deeply considered, do move us[5] for his sake also to be ever ready to give ourselves to our neighbours, and, as much as lieth in us, to study with all our endeavour to do good to every man. These be the fruits of the true faith, to do good, as much as lieth in us, to every man, and, above all things, and in all things, to advance the glory of God, of whom only we have our sanctification, justification, salvation, and redemption. To whom be ever glory, praise, and honour, world without end.
Amen.

---

[[1] Into resurrection, Ed. 1562.]
[[2] Judgment: very well they know, Eds. 1560, 62.]
[[3] And given unto us, Ibid.]
[[4] And death everlasting, Ibid.]
[[5] Deeply considered, move us, Ibid.]

# A SHORT DECLARATION

OF THE

# TRUE, LIVELY, AND CHRISTIAN FAITH.

---

THE first entry unto God[6], good christian people, is through faith, whereby (as it is declared in the last sermon) we be justified before God. And lest any man should be deceived for lack of right understanding thereof[7], it is diligently to be noted, that faith is taken in the scripture two manner of ways. There is one faith, which in scripture is called a dead faith, which bringeth forth no good works, but is idle, barren, and unfruitful. And this faith by the holy apostle St James is compared to the faith of devils, which believe God to be true and just, and tremble for fear; yet they do nothing well, but all evil. And such a manner of faith have the wicked and naughty christian people, "which confess God," as St Paul saith, "in their mouth, but deny him in their deeds, being abominable, and without the right faith, and in all good works[8] reprovable." And this faith is a persuasion and belief in man's heart, whereby he knoweth that there is a God, and assenteth unto all truth of God's most holy word, contained in holy scripture: so that it consisteth only in believing of the word[9] of God, that it is true. And this is not properly called faith. But as he that readeth Cæsar's Commentaries, believing the same to be true, hath thereby a knowledge of Cæsar's life and noble acts[10], because he believeth the history of Cæsar; yet it is not properly said, that he believeth in Cæsar, of whom he looketh for no help nor benefit: even so, he that believeth that all that is spoken of God in the bible is true, and yet liveth so ungodly, that he cannot look to enjoy the promises and benefits of God; although it may be said that such a man hath a faith and belief to the words of God, yet it is not properly said that he believeth in God, or hath such a faith and trust in God, whereby he may surely look for grace, mercy, and eternal life[11] at God's hand, but rather for indignation and punishment, according to the merits of his wicked life. For, as it is written in a book, intituled to be of Didymus Alexandrinus: "Forasmuch as faith without works is dead, it is not now faith, as a dead man is not a man[12]." This dead faith therefore is not that sure and substantial faith, which saveth sinners.

Faith.

A dead faith.

James ii.

Tit. i.

Another faith there is in scripture, which is not, as the foresaid faith, idle, unfruitful, and dead, but "worketh by charity," as St Paul declareth (Gal. v.); which, as the other vain faith is called a dead faith, so may this be called a quick or lively faith. And this is not only the common belief of the articles of our faith, but it is also a sure trust[14] and confidence of the mercy of God through our Lord Jesus Christ, and a steadfast hope of all good things to be received at God's hand; and that, although we through infirmity, or temptation of our ghostly enemy, do fall from him by sin, yet if we return again unto him by true repentance, that he will forgive and forget our offences for his Son's sake, our Saviour Jesus Christ, and will make us inheritors with him of his everlasting kingdom; and that in the mean time, until that kingdom come, he will be our protector and defender in all perils and dangers, whatsoever do chance: and that, though sometime he doth send us sharp adversity, yet that evermore he will be a loving father unto us, correcting us for our sin, but not withdrawing his mercy finally from us, if we trust in him, and commit ourselves wholly to him[15], hang only upon him, and call upon him,

A lively faith.
Gal. v.[13]

---

[6 The first coming unto God, Eds. 1560, 62.]
[7 Understanding hereof, Ed. 1547.]
[8 To all good works, Eds. 1560, 62.]
[9 In believing in the word, Ibid.]
[10 Notable acts, Ibid.]
[11 And everlasting life, Eds. 1560, 62.]
[12 Notandum scilicet quia cum fides mortua sit præter opera, jam neque fides est: nam neque homo mortuus homo est. Didym. Alex. Enarr. in Epist. Jacob. cap. ii. in Biblioth. Patr. Tom. VIII. p. 127. Par. 1610.]
[13 Omitted in Ed. 1547.]
[14 A true trust, Ed. 1560.]
[15 Wholly unto him, Eds. 1560, 62.]

ready to obey and serve him. This is the true, lively, and unfeigned christian faith, and is not in the mouth and outward profession only, but it liveth and stirreth inwardly in the heart. And this faith is not without hope and trust in God, nor without the love of God and of our neighbours, nor without the fear of God, nor without the desire to hear God's word, and to follow the same, in eschewing evil and doing gladly all good works.

Heb. xi.[1] This faith, as St Paul describeth it, is the "sure ground and foundation of the benefits which we ought to look for, and trust to receive of God; a certificate and sure expectation of them, although they yet sensibly appear not unto us." And after he saith: "He that cometh to God must believe both that he is, and that he is a merciful rewarder of well-doers." And nothing commendeth good men unto God so much as this assured faith and trust in him.

Heb. xi.

Three things are to be noted of faith.

Of this faith three things are specially to be noted. First, that this faith doth not lie dead in the heart, but is lively and fruitful in bringing forth good works. Second, that without it can no good works be done, that shall be acceptable and pleasant to God. Third, what manner of good works they be that this faith doth bring forth.

Faith is full of good works.

For the first, as the light cannot be hid, but will shew forth itself at one place or other; so a true faith cannot be kept secret, but, when occasion is offered, it will break out, and shew itself by good works. And as the living body of a man ever exerciseth such things as belongeth to a natural and living body, for nourishment and preservation of the same, as it hath need, opportunity, and occasion; even so the soul, that hath a lively faith in it, will be doing alway some good work, which shall declare that it is living, and will not be unoccupied. Therefore, when men hear in the scriptures so high commendations of faith, that it maketh us to please God, to live with God, and to be the children of God; if then they phantasy that they be set at liberty from doing all good works, and may live as they list[2], they trifle with God, and deceive themselves. And it is a manifest token that they be far from having the true and lively faith, and also far from knowledge what true faith meaneth. For the very sure and lively christian faith is, not only to believe all things of God which are contained in holy scripture; but also is an earnest trust and confidence in God, that he doth regard us, and hath cure of us, as the father of the child[3] whom he doth love, and that he will be merciful unto us for his only Son's sake, and that we have our Saviour Christ our perpetual advocate and priest, in whose only merits, oblation, and suffering, we do trust that our offences be continually washed and purged, whensoever we, repenting truly, do return to him with our whole heart, steadfastly determining with ourselves, through his grace, to obey and serve him in keeping his commandments, and never to turn back again to sin. Such is the true faith that the scripture doth so much commend; the which, when it seeth and considereth what God hath done for us, is also moved, through continual assistance of the Spirit of God, to serve and please him, to keep his favour, to fear his displeasure, to continue his obedient children, shewing thankfulness again by observing his commandments[4], and that freely, for true love chiefly, and not for dread of punishment or love of temporal reward; considering how clearly, without our deservings, we have received his mercy and pardon freely.

This true faith will shew forth itself, and cannot long be idle: for, as it is written,

Habak. ii. "The just man doth live by his faith." He neither sleepeth, nor is idle, when he should

Jer. xvii. wake and be well occupied. And God by his prophet Jeremy saith, that "he is a happy and blessed man which hath faith and confidence in God. For he is like a tree set by the water-side, that spreadeth his roots abroad toward the moisture, and feareth not heat when it cometh; his leaf will be green, and will not cease to bring forth his fruit:" even so faithful men, putting away all fear of adversity, will shew forth the fruit of their good works, as occasion is offered to do them.

---

[[1] Omitted in Ed. 1547.]

[[2] Live as they lust, Eds. 1547, 60, 62.]

[[3] And that he is careful over us, as the father is of the child, Eds. 1560, 62.]

[[4] By observing or keeping his commandments, Ibid.]

### [5] *The Second Part of the Sermon of Faith.*

Ye have heard in the first part of this sermon, that there be two kinds of faith: a dead and an unfruitful faith, and a faith lively, that worketh by charity: the first to be unprofitable, the second necessary for the obtaining of our salvation; the which faith hath charity always joined unto it, and is fruitful, bringing forth all good works. Now as concerning the same matter, you shall hear what followeth.

The wise man saith: "He that believeth in God will hearken unto his commandments." Ecclus. xxxii. For if we do not shew ourselves faithful in our conversation, the faith which we pretend to have is but a feigned faith; because the true christian faith is manifestly shewed by good living, and not by words only, as St Augustine saith: "Good living cannot be separated from true faith, which worketh by love[6]." Lib. de fide et Oper. ii. And St Chrysostom saith: "Faith of itself is full of good works: as soon as a man doth believe, he shall be garnished with them[7]." Serm. de lege et fide.

How plentiful this faith is of good works, and how it maketh the work of one man more acceptable to God than of another, St Paul teacheth at large in the eleventh chapter to the Hebrews, Heb. xi. saying, that faith made the oblation of Abel better than the oblation of Cain. Gen. iv.[8] This made Noe to build the ark. Gen. vi.[8] This made Abraham to forsake his country, and all his friends, and to go into a far country, there to dwell among strangers. Ecclus. xliv.[8] Gen. xi.[8] So did also Isaac and Jacob, depending only of the help and trust that they had in God. And when they came to the country which God promised them, they would build no cities, towns, nor houses; but lived like strangers in tents, that might every day be removed. Their trust was so much in God, that they set but little by any worldly thing; for that God had prepared for them better dwelling-places in heaven, of his own foundation and building. This faith made Abraham ready at God's commandment to offer his own son and heir Isaac, Gen. xxii.[8] Ecclus. xliv.[8] whom he loved so well, and by whom he was promised to have innumerable issue, among the which one should be born, in whom all nations should be blessed; trusting so much in God, that though he were slain, yet that God was able by his omnipotent power to raise him from death, and perform his promise. He mistrusted not the promise of God, although unto his reason every thing seemed contrary. He believed verily that God would not forsake him in dearth and famine that was in the country. And in all other dangers that he was brought unto, he trusted ever that God would be his God and his protector, whatsoever he saw to the contrary. This faith wrought so in the heart of Moses, that he refused to be taken for king Pharaoh his daughter's son, Exod. ii.[8] and to have great inheritance in Egypt; thinking it better with the people of God to have affliction and sorrow, than with naughty men in sin to live pleasantly for a time. By faith he cared not for the threatening of king Pharaoh: for his trust was so in God, that he passed not of the felicity of this world, but looked for the reward to come in heaven; setting his heart upon the invisible God, as if he had seen him ever present before his eyes. By faith the children of Israel passed through the Red Sea. Exod. xiv.[8] By faith the walls of Jericho fell down without stroke, Josh. vi.[8] and many other wonderful miracles have been wrought. In all good men that heretofore have been, faith hath brought forth their good works, and obtained the promises of God. Faith hath stopped the lions' mouths: Dan. vi. faith hath quenched the force of fire: Dan. iii. faith hath escaped the sword's edges: faith hath given weak men strength, victory in battle, overthrown the armies of infidels, raised the dead to life: faith hath made good men to take adversity in good part: some have been mocked and whipped, bound and cast in prison; some have lost all their goods, and lived in great poverty; some have wandered in mountains[9], hills, and wilderness; some have been racked, some slain, some stoned, some sawn, some rent in pieces, some headed, some brent without mercy, and would not be delivered, because they looked to rise again to a better state.

---

[[5] Inserted from Eds. 1560, 62. Vid. pp. 130, 132.]

[[6] Apertissime scriptura testatur, nihil prodesse fidem, nisi eam quam definivit apostolus, id est, *quæ per dilectionem operatur*; sine operibus autem salvare non posse.—August. De Fid. et Op. cap. xvi. Tom. IV. p. 31. Ed. Paris. 1635.]

[[7] Igitur quam primum credideris, simul et operibus ornatus ëris: non quod desint opera, sed per seipsam fides plena est operibus bonis.—Chrysost. Sermo de Fide, et Lege naturæ, et Sancto Spiritu. Tom. II. col. 901. Ed. (Lat.) Basil. 1547.]

[[8] Omitted in Ed. 1547.]

[[9] Some have wandered mountains, Ibid.]

All these fathers, martyrs, and other holy men, whom St Paul spake of, had their faith surely fixed in God, when all the world was against them. They did not only know God to be Lord[1], maker, and governor of all men in the world; but also they had a special confidence and trust that he was and would be their God, their comforter, aider, helper, maintainer, and defender. This is the christian faith, which these holy men had, and we also ought to have. And although they were not named christian men, yet was it a christian faith that they had; for they looked for all benefits of God the Father through the merits of his Son Jesu Christ, as we now do. This difference is between them and us; for they looked when Christ should come, and we be in the time when he is come. Therefore saith St Augustine: "The time is altered, but not the faith[2]." For we have both one faith in one Christ. The same Holy Ghost also that we have, had they, saith St Paul. For as the Holy Ghost doth teach us to trust in God, and to call upon him as our Father, so did he teach them to say, as it is written: "Thou, Lord, art our Father and Redeemer; and thy name is without beginning, and everlasting." God gave them then grace to be his children, as he doth us now. But now, by the coming of our Saviour Christ, we have received more abundantly the Spirit of God in our hearts, whereby we may conceive a greater faith, and a surer trust, than many of them had. But in effect they and we be all one: we have the same faith that they had in God, and they the same that we have. And St Paul so much extolleth their faith, because we should no less, but rather more, give ourselves wholly unto Christ both in profession and living, now when Christ is come, than the old fathers did before his coming. And by all the declaration of St Paul it is evident, that the true, lively, and christian faith is no dead, vain, or unfruitful thing, but a thing of perfect virtue, of wonderful[3] operation and strength[4], bringing forth all good motions and good works.

In Joan. Tra. xlv. — 2 Cor. iv. — Isai. lxiii.

All holy scripture agreeably beareth witness, that a true lively faith in Christ doth bring forth good works; and therefore every man must examine himself[5] diligently, to know whether he have the same true lively faith in his heart unfeignedly, or not; which he shall know by the fruits thereof. Many that professed the faith of Christ were in this error, that they thought they knew God and believed in him, when in their life they declared to the contrary: which error St John in his first Epistle confuting, writeth in this wise: "Hereby we are certified that we know God, if we observe his commandments. He that saith he knoweth God, and observeth not his commandments, is a liar, and the truth is not in him." And again he saith: "Whosoever sinneth doth not see God, nor know him: let no man deceive you, well-beloved children." And moreover he saith: "Hereby we know that we be of the truth, and so we shall persuade our hearts before him. For if our own hearts reprove us, God is above our hearts, and knoweth all things. Well-beloved, if our hearts reprove us not, then have we confidence in God, and shall have of him whatsoever we ask, because we keep his commandments, and do those things that please him." And yet further he saith: "Every man that believeth that Jesus is Christ is born of God; and we know that whosoever is born of God doth not sin: but the generation of God purgeth him, and the devil doth not touch him." And finally he concludeth, and, shewing the cause why he wrote this Epistle, saith: "For this cause have I written unto you, that you may know that you have everlasting life, which do believe in the Son of God." And in his third Epistle he confirmeth the whole matter of faith and works in few words, saying: "He that doth well is of God; and he that doth evil knoweth not God."

1 John ii. — 1 John iii. — 1 John iii. — 1 John v. — 1 John v. — 3 John.

And as St John saith, that the lively[6] knowledge and faith of God bringeth forth good works; so saith he likewise of hope and charity, that they cannot stand with evil living. Of hope he writeth thus: "We know that when God shall appear, we shall be like unto him; for we shall see him even as he is. And whosoever hath this hope in him doth purify himself, like as God is pure." And of charity he saith these words: "He that

1 John iii. — 1 John ii.

[1 God to be the Lord, Eds. 1560, 62.]

[2 Tempora variata sunt, non fides.—August. In Evang. Joan. Tract. xlv. De cap. x. Tom. IX. p. 136. Ed. Paris. 1635.]

[3 And wonderful, Ed. 1562.]

[4 Operation or working, and strength, Eds. 1560, 62.]

[5 Must, and examine and try himself, Ibid.]

[6 That as the lively, Eds. 1560, 62.]

doth keep God's word or commandment, in him is truly the perfect love of God." And again he saith: "This is the love of God, that we should keep his commandments." 1 John v. And St John wrote not this as a subtle proposition[7] devised of his own phantasy, but as a most certain and necessary truth, taught unto him by Christ himself, the eternal and infallible Verity, who in many places doth most clearly affirm, that faith, hope, and charity cannot consist[8] without good and godly works. Of faith he saith: "He that 1 John v. John iii. believeth in the Son hath everlasting life; but he that believeth not in the Son shall not see that life, but the wrath of God remaineth upon him." And the same he confirmeth with a double oath, saying: "Forsooth and forsooth, I say unto you, he that believeth in John vi. me hath everlasting life." Now, forasmuch as he that believeth in Christ hath everlasting life, it must needs consequently follow, that he that hath this faith must have also good works, and be studious to observe God's commandments obediently. For to them that have evil works, and lead their life in disobedience and transgression of God's commandments[9], without repentance, pertaineth not everlasting life, but everlasting death, as Christ himself saith: "They that do well shall go into life eternal; but they that do evil shall Matt. xxv. go into the eternal fire." And again he saith[10]: "I am the first letter and the last, the Rev. xxi. beginning and the ending. To him that is athirst I will give of the well of the water of life freely. He that hath the victory shall have all things, and I will be his God, and he shall be my son: but they that be fearful, mistrusting God and lacking faith, they that be cursed people, and murderers, and fornicators, and sorcerers, and idolaters, and all liars, shall have their portion in the lake that burneth with fire and brimstone, which is the second death." And as Christ undoubtedly affirmeth, that true faith bringeth forth Charity bringeth forth good works. good works, so doth he say likewise of charity: "Whosoever hath my commandments, and keepeth them, that is he that loveth me." And after he saith: "He that loveth me John xiv. will keep my word, and he that loveth me not keepeth not my words." And as the love of God is tried by good works, so is the fear of God also, as the wise man[11] saith: Ecclus. i. "The dread of God putteth away sin." And also he saith: "He that feareth God will Ecclus. xv. do good works."

### [12] *The Third Part of the Sermon of Faith.*

You have heard in the second part of this sermon, that no man should think that he hath that lively faith which scripture commandeth, when he liveth not obediently to God's laws. For all good works spring out of that faith. And also it hath been declared unto you by examples, that faith maketh men steadfast, quiet, and patient in all affliction. Now as concerning the same matter, you shall hear what followeth.

A man may soon deceive himself, and think in his own phantasy that he by faith knoweth God, loveth him, feareth him, and belongeth to him, when in very deed he doth nothing less. For the trial of all these things is a very godly and christian life. He that feeleth his heart set to seek God's honour, and studieth to know the will and commandments of God, and to conform himself[13] thereunto, and leadeth not his life after the desire of his own flesh to serve the devil by sin, but setteth his mind to serve God, for God's own sake[14], and for his sake also to love all his neighbours, whether they be friends or adversaries, doing good to every man, as opportunity serveth, and willingly hurting no man; such a man may well rejoice in God, perceiving by the trade of his life that he unfeignedly hath the right knowledge of God, a lively faith, a constant hope, a true and unfeigned love and fear of God. But he that casteth away the yoke of God's commandments from his neck, and giveth himself to live without true repentance, after his own sensual mind and pleasure, not regarding to know God's word, and much less to live according thereunto; such a man clearly deceiveth himself, and seeth not his own heart, if he thinketh that he either knoweth God, loveth

[7 A subtle saying, Eds. 1560, 62.]
[8 Cannot consist or stand, Ibid.]
[9 Transgression or breaking of God's commandments, Ibid.]
[10 Again he saith, Ed. 1547.]
[11 Of God: as the wise, Ed. 1547.]
[12 Inserted from Eds. 1560, 62. Vid. pp. 130, 132, 137.]
[13 And to frame himself, Eds. 1560, 62.]
[14 For his own sake, 1547.]

him, feareth him, or trusteth in him. Some peradventure phantasy in themselves that they belong to God, although they live in sin, and so they come to the church, and shew themselves as God's dear children: but St John saith plainly: "If we say that we have any company with God, and walk in darkness, we do lie." Other do vainly think that they know and love God, although they pass not of his commandments[1]: but St John saith clearly: "He that saith, I know God, and keepeth not his commandments, he is a liar." Some falsely persuade themselves that they love God, when they hate their neighbours: but St John saith manifestly: "If any man say, I love God, and yet hateth his brother, he is a liar." "He that saith that he is in the light, and hateth his brother, he is still in darkness. He that loveth his brother dwelleth in the light; but he that hateth his brother is in darkness, and walketh in darkness, and knoweth not whither he goeth; for darkness hath blinded his eyes." And moreover he saith: "Hereby we manifestly know the children of God from the children of the devil: he that doth not righteously is not the child of God, nor he that hateth his brother."

1 John i.

1 John ii.

1 John iv.

1 John ii.

1 John iii.

Deceive not yourselves therefore, thinking that you have faith in God, or that you love God, or do trust in him, or do fear him, when you live in sin; for then your ungodly and sinful life declareth the contrary, whatsoever ye say or think. It pertaineth to a christian man to have this true christian faith, and to try himself whether he hath it or no, and to know what belongeth to it, and how it doth work in him. It is not the world that we can trust to: the world, and all that is therein, is but vanity. It is God that must be our defence and protection against all temptations of wickedness and sin, errors, superstition, idolatry, and all evil. If all the world were on our side, and God against us, what could the world avail us? Therefore let us set our whole faith and trust in God, and neither the world, the devil, nor all the power of them, shall prevail against us. Let us therefore, good christian people, try and examine our faith, what it is: let us not flatter ourselves, but look upon our works, and so judge of our faith what it is. Christ himself speaketh of this matter, and saith: "The tree is known by the fruit." Therefore let us do good works, and thereby declare our faith to be the lively christian faith. Let us by such virtues as ought to spring out of faith shew our election to be sure and stable, as St Peter teacheth: "Endeavour yourselves to make your calling and election certain by good works." And also he saith: "Minister or declare in your faith virtue, in virtue knowledge, in knowledge temperance, in temperance patience; again, in patience godliness, in godliness brotherly charity, in brotherly charity love." So shall we shew indeed that we have the very lively christian faith, and may so both certify our conscience the better that we be in the right faith, and also by these means confirm other men.

Luke vi.

2 Pet. i.

2 Pet. i.

If these fruits do not follow, we do but mock with God, deceive ourselves, and also other men. Well may we bear the name of christian men, but we do lack the true faith that doth belong thereunto. For true faith doth ever bring forth good works, as St James saith: "Shew me thy faith by thy deeds." Thy deeds and works must be an open testimonial of thy faith: otherwise thy faith, being without good works, is but the devils' faith, the faith of the wicked, a phantasy of faith, and not a true christian faith. And like as the devils and evil people be nothing the better for their counterfeit faith, but it is unto them the more cause of damnation; so they that be christened, and have received knowledge of God and of Christ's merits, and yet of a set purpose do live idly, without good works, thinking the name of a naked faith to be either sufficient for them; or else, setting their minds upon vain pleasures of this world, do live in sin[2], without repentance, not uttering the fruits that do belong to such an high profession; upon such presumptuous persons and wilful sinners must needs remain the great vengeance of God, and eternal punishment in hell, prepared for the devil and wicked livers[3].

James ii.

Therefore, as you profess the name of Christ, good christian people, let no such

[1 Of the commandments, Eds. 1560, 62.]
[2 Liveth in sin, Ed. 1547.]
[3 For the unjust and wicked livers, Ed. 1560.]

phantasy and imagination of faith at any time beguile you; but be sure of your faith, try it by your living, look upon the fruits that cometh of it, mark the increase of love and charity by it towards God[4] and your neighbour, and so shall you perceive it to be a true lively faith. If you feel and perceive such a faith in you, rejoice in it, and be diligent to maintain it, and keep it still in you; let it be daily increasing, and more and more be well working, and so shall you be sure that you shall please God by this faith; and at the length, as other faithful men have done before, so shall you[5], when his will is, come to him, and receive "the end and final reward of your faith," as St Peter nameth it, "the salvation of your souls:" the which God grant us, that hath promised the same unto his faithful! To whom be all honour and glory, world without end. Amen. 1 Pet. i.

---

# AN HOMILY OR SERMON

OF

# GOOD WORKS ANNEXED UNTO FAITH.

In the last sermon was declared unto you what the lively and true faith of a christian man is; that it causeth not a man to be idle, but to be occupied in bringing forth good works, as occasion serveth.

No good work can be done without faith. John xv.

Now, by God's grace, shall be declared the second thing that before was noted of faith, that without it can no good work be done acceptable and pleasant[6] unto God. "For as a branch cannot bear fruit of itself," saith our Saviour Christ, "except it abide in the vine, so cannot you except you abide in me. I am the vine, and you be the branches: he that abideth in me, and I in him, he bringeth forth much fruit: for without me you can do nothing." And St Paul proveth that Enoch had faith, because he pleased God: "For without faith," saith he, "it is not possible to please God." And again, to the Romans he saith: "Whatsoever work is done without faith, it is sin." Faith giveth life to the soul; and they be as much dead to God that lack faith, as they be to the world whose bodies lack souls. Without faith all that is done of us is but dead before God, although the work seem never so gay and glorious before man. Even as a picture graven or painted is but a dead representation of the thing itself, and is without life, or any manner of moving; so be the works of all unfaithful persons before God. They do appear to be lively works, and indeed they be but dead, not availing to the eternal life[7]. They be but shadows and shews of lively and good things, and not good and lively things indeed; for true faith doth give life to the works[8], and out of such faith come good works, that be very good works indeed; and without it no work is good before God. Heb. xi. Rom. xiv.

In Præf. Psal. xxxi.

As saith St Augustine: "We must set no good works before faith, nor think that before faith a man may do any good work; for such works, although they seem unto men to be praise-worthy, yet indeed they be but vain, and not allowed before God. They be as the course of a horse that runneth out of the way, which taketh great labour, but to no purpose. Let no man, therefore," saith he, "reckon upon his good

[4 Toward God, Ed. 1547.]
[5 So shall ye, Ed. 1547.]
[6 Accepted and pleasant, Ed. 1560.]
[7 To the everlasting life, Ed. 1563, 62.]
[8 To the work, Ed. 1547.]

works before his faith; where as faith was not, good works were not. The intent," saith he, "maketh the good works; but faith must guide and order the intent of man[1]." And Christ saith: "If thine eye be naught, thy whole body is full of darkness." "The eye doth signify the intent," saith St Augustine, "wherewith a man doth a thing; so that he which doth not his good works with a godly intent, and a true faith that worketh by love, the whole body beside, that is to say, all the whole number of his works, is dark, and there is no light in it[2]." For good deeds be not measured by the facts themselves, and so dissevered from vices[3], but by the ends and intents for the which they be done. If a heathen man clothe the naked, feed the hungry, and do such other like works; yet because he doth them not in faith for the honour and love of God, they be but dead, vain, and fruitless works to him. Faith it is that doth commend the work to God: "for," as St Augustine saith, "whether thou wilt or no, that work that cometh not of faith is naught[4];" where the faith of Christ is not the foundation, there is no good work, what building soever we make. "There is one work, in the which be all good works, that is, faith which worketh by charity[5]:" if thou have it, thou hast the ground of all good works; for the virtues of strength, wisdom, temperance, and justice, be all referred unto this same faith. Without this faith we have not them, but only the names and shadows of them, as St Augustine saith: "All the life of them that lack the true faith is sin; and nothing is good without him that is the author of goodness: where he is not, there is but feigned virtue, although it be in the best works[6]." And St Augustine, declaring this verse of the psalm, "The turtle hath found a nest where she may keep her young birds," saith, that Jews, heretics, and pagans do good works: they clothe the naked, feed the poor, and do other good works of mercy; but because they be not done in the true faith, therefore the birds be lost[7]. But if they remain in faith, then faith is the nest and safeguard of their birds; that is to say, safeguard of their good works, that the reward of them be not utterly lost.

Matt. vi.

In Præf. Psal. xxxi.

And this matter (which St Augustine at large in many books disputeth) St Ambrose concludeth in few words, saying: "He that by nature would withstand vice, either by natural will or reason, he doth in vain garnish the time of this life, and attaineth not the very true virtues; for without the worshipping of the true God that which seemeth to be virtue is vice[8]."

De Vocat. Gent. Lib. I. cap. iii.

And yet most plainly to this purpose writeth St John Chrysostom in this wise: "You shall find many which have not the true faith, and be not of the flock of

In Serm. de Fide, Lege, et Spiritu Sanct.

[1 Debemus nulla opera præponere fidei: id est, ut ante fidem quisquam dicatur bene operatus. Ea enim ipsa opera quæ dicuntur ante fidem, quamvis videantur hominibus laudabilia, inania sunt. Ita mihi videntur esse, ut magnæ vires et cursus celerrimus præter iram. Nemo ergo computet bona opera sua ante fidem: ubi fides non erat, bonum opus non erat. Bonum enim opus intentio facit, intentionem fides diriget.—August. in Psalm. xxxi. Tom. VIII. p. 76. Ed. Paris 1635.]

[2 Oculum ergo hic accipere debemus ipsam intentionem, qua facimus quicquid facimus.—Id. de Serm. Dom. in Monte Lib. II. cap. xiii. Tom. IV. p. 352. Et hunc oculum agnosce intentionem, qua facit quisque quod facit; et per hoc disce eum, qui non facit opera bona intentione fidei bonæ, hoc est ejus quæ per dilectionem operatur, totum quasi corpus, quod illis, velut membris, operibus constat, tenebrosum esse, hoc est, plenum nigredine peccatorum.—Id. contra Julian. Pelagian. Lib. IV. Tom. VII. p. 406.]

[3 So discerned from vices, Eds. 1560, 62.]

[4 Omne enim, velis nolis, quod non ex fide, peccatum est.—August. contra Julian. Pelagian. Lib. IV. Tom. VII. p. 406.]

[5 Opus ergo unum est, in quo sunt omnia, fides quæ per dilectionem operatur.—Id. in Psalm. lxxxix. Tom. VIII. p. 408.]

[6 Omnis infidelium vita peccatum est, et nihil est bonum sine summo bono. Ubi enim deest agnitio æternæ et incommutabilis veritatis, falsa virtus est, etiam in optimis moribus.—Prosper. Lib. sentent. ex August. cvi. p. 558. Ed. Paris. 1711.]

[7 Quanti videntur præter ecclesiam bona operari! Quam multi etiam pagani pascunt esurientem, vestiunt nudum, suscipiunt hospitem, visitant ægrotum, consolantur inclusum! Quam multi hæc faciunt!—Quam multa multi hæretici non in ecclesia operantur, non in nido pullos ponunt! Conculcabuntur et conterentur; non servabuntur, non custodientur.—August. in Psalm. lxxxiii. Tom. VIII. p. 375. Ed. Paris. 1635.]

[8 Quia etsi fuit qui naturali intellectu conatus sit vitiis reluctari, hujus tantum temporis vitam steriliter ordinavit, ad veras autem virtutes æternamque beatitudinem non profecit. Sine cultu enim veri Dei, etiam quod virtus videtur esse, peccatum est.—Ambros. De Vocat. Gent. Lib. I. cap. iii. Tom. IV. p. 245. Ed. Colon. Agrip. 1616. This treatise is asserted by the Benedictines, Erasmus, and others, to be spurious. Prosper was probably the author.—Vid. Riveti Critica Sacra. p. 289. Ed. Genevæ, 1626. Coci Censura Patrum, pp. 259, 60. Ed. Helmes, 1683.]

Christ, and yet (as it appeareth) they flourish in good works of mercy: you shall find them full of pity[9], compassion, and given to justice; and yet for all that they have no fruit of their works, because the chief work lacketh. For when the Jews asked of Christ what they should do to work good works, he answered: 'This is the work of God, to believe in him whom he sent:' so that he called faith[10] the work of God. And as soon as a man hath faith, anon he shall flourish in good works; for faith of itself is full of good works, and nothing is good without faith." And for a similitude, he saith, that "they which glister and shine in good works without faith in God, be like dead men, which have goodly and precious tombs, and yet it availeth them nothing. Faith may not be naked without works, for then it is no true faith; and when it is adjoined to works, yet it is above the works. For as men, that be very men indeed, first have life, and after be nourished; so must our faith in Christ go before, and after be nourished with good works. And life may be without nourishment, but nourishment cannot be without life. A man must needs be nourished by good works, but first he must have faith. He that doth good deeds, yet without faith, he hath not life[11]. I can shew a man that by faith without works lived, and came to heaven; but without faith never man had life. The thief that was hanged when Christ suffered, did believe only, and the most merciful God did justify him. And because no man shall object[12], that he lacked time to do good works, for else he would have done them; truth it is, and I will not contend therein: but this I will surely affirm, that faith only saved him. If he had lived, and not regarded faith and the works thereof, he should have lost his salvation again. But this is the effect that I say, that faith by itself saved him, but works by themselves never justified any man[13]." Here ye have heard the mind of St Chrysostom, whereby you may perceive, that neither faith is without works, (having opportunity thereto,) nor works can avail to eternal life without faith.

John vi.

### [14] *The Second Part of the Sermon of Good Works.*

Of three things which were in the former sermon specially noted of lively faith, two be declared unto you. The first was that faith is never idle without good works, when occasion serveth: the second, that good works acceptable to God, cannot be done without faith.

Now to proceed[15] to the third part, (which in the former sermon was noted of faith,) that is to say, what manner of works they be which spring out of true faith, and lead

What works they are that spring of faith.

---

[[9] Full of piety, Eds. 1560, 62.]

[[10] He calleth faith, Ed. 1547.]

[[11] Hath no life, Eds. 1560, 62.]

[[12] Shall say again, Ibid.]

[[13] Offendes equidem multos, qui quamvis sermonem veritatis non acceperint, et foris sint, operibus tamen pietatis, ut apparet, sunt conspicui. Invenies viros misericordes, compatientes, justitiæ vacantes; sed nullos facientes fructus operum, quia nescierunt opus veritatis.—Enimvero cum olim Judæi dicerent Domino, 'Quid faciemus, ut operemur opera Dei?' respondit eis: 'Hoc est opus Dei, ut credatis in eum, quem misit ille.' Vides quomodo fidem opus vocavit? Igitur quamprimum credideris, simul et operibus ornatus eris: non quod desint opera, sed per seipsam fides plena est operibus bonis.—Nihil enim extra fidem bonum. Et ut quadam verbi similitudine utar, fratres, similes mihi videntur, qui operibus bonis florent, et Deum pietatis ignorant, reliquiis mortuorum pulchre quidem indutis, sensum autem pulchrorum non habentibus. Quæ enim utilitas animæ mortuæ, Deo quidem mortuæ fide et ratione, bonis autem operibus vestitæ? —Non oportet quidem nudam ab operibus esse fidem, ut ne vituperetur. Veruntamen sublimior est fides quam opera. Sicut enim hominibus, qui hominis nomen merentur, opus est primum, ut præcedat vita, et sic enutriantur; conservat enim vitam nostram alimentum: ita necessarium, ut præcedat vitam nostram spes in Christum, quæ postea pascenda bonis operibus. Conceditur vivere quempiam qui non nutritur: non conceditur autem nutriri aliquem non viventem.—Ita et opus quidem habet anima, ut operibus alatur. Ante opera tamen fides primum inducenda est. Eum qui operatur opera justitiæ, sine fide non possum probare vivum fuisse. Fidelem autem absque operibus possum monstrare et vixisse, et regnum cœlorum assecutum. Nullus sine fide vitam habuit, latro autem credidit duntaxat, et justificatus est a misericordissimo Deo. Atque hic ne mihi dixeris, defuisse ei tempus, quo juste viveret, et honesta faceret opera. Neque enim de hoc contenderim ego, sed illud unum asseveraverim, quod sola fides per se salvum fecerit. Nam si super vixisset, fideique et operum fuisset negligens, a salute excidisset. Hoc autem nunc quæritur, et agitur, quod et fides per seipsam salvum fecerit: opera autem per se nullos unquam operarios justificarunt.—Chrysost. Serm. de Fide, et Lege naturæ, et Sancto Spiritu. Tom. II. col. 902, 3. Ed. (Lat.) Basil. 1547.]

[[14] Inserted from Eds. 560, 62, Vid. pp. 130, 132, 137, 139.]

[[15] Now to go forth to the third part, that is, what manner, &c. Ibid.]

faithful men unto eternal life[1]: this cannot be known so well, as by our Saviour Christ himself, who was asked of a certain great man the same question: "What works shall I do," said a prince, "to come to everlasting life?" To whom Jesus answered: "If thou wilt come to the eternal life[2], keep the commandments." But the prince, not satisfied herewith, asked farther: "Which commandments?" The scribes and Pharisees had made so many of their own laws and traditions, to bring men to heaven, beside God's commandments, that this man was in doubt whether he should come to heaven by those laws and traditions, or by the laws of God[3]; and therefore he asked Christ which commandments he meant. Whereunto Christ made him a plain answer, rehearsing the commandments of God, saying: "Thou shalt not kill, thou shalt not commit adultery, thou shalt not steal, thou shalt not bear false witness, honour thy father and mother," and, "Love thy neighbour[4] as thyself." By which words Christ declared that the laws of God be the very way that do lead to eternal life[5], and not the traditions and laws of men. So that this is to be taked[6] for a most true lesson taught by Christ's own mouth, that the works of the moral commandments[7] of God be the very true works of faith, which lead to the blessed life to come.

Matt. xix.

Matt. xix.

Matt. xix.

The works that lead to heaven be the works of God's commandments.

But the blindness and malice of man, even from the beginning, hath ever been ready to fall from God's commandments: as Adam the first man, having but one commandment, that he should not eat of the fruit forbidden, notwithstanding God's commandment, he gave credit unto the woman, seduced by the subtle persuasion of the serpent, and so followed his own will, and left God's commandment. And ever since that time all his succession[9] hath been so blinded through original sin, that they have been ever ready to decline from[10] God and his law, and to invent a new way unto salvation, by works of their own device: so much, that almost all the world, forsaking the true honour of the only eternal, living God, wandered about their own[11] phantasies, worshipping some the sun, the moon, the stars; some, Jupiter, Juno, Diana, Saturnus, Apollo, Neptunus, Ceres, Bacchus, and other dead men and women: some, therewith not satisfied, worshipped divers kinds of beasts, birds, fish, fowl, and serpents; every region, town, and house, in manner[12] being divided, and setting up images of such things as they liked, and worshipping the same. Such was the rudeness of the people after they fell to their own phantasies, and left the eternal living God and his commandments, that they devised innumerable images and gods. In which error and blindness they did remain, until such time as Almighty God, pitying the blindness of man, sent his true prophet Moses into the world, to reprehend this extreme madness[13], and to teach the people to know the only living God, and his true honour and worship. But the corrupt inclination of man was so much given to follow his own phantasies, and (as you would say) to favour his own bird that he brought up himself, that all the admonitions, exhortations, benefits, and threatenings of God could not keep him from such his inventions. For notwithstanding all the benefits of God, shewed unto the people of Israel, yet when Moses went up into the mountain, to speak with Almighty God, he had tarried there but a few days, when the people began to invent new gods. And, as it came into their heads[15], they made a calf of gold, and kneeled down and worshipped it. And after that they followed the Moabites, and worshipped Beelphegor, the Moabites' god. Read the book of Judges, the books of the Kings, and the Prophets; and there you shall find, how inconstant the people[16] were, how full of inventions, and more ready to run after their own phantasies than God's most holy commandments. There shall you read of Baal, Moloch, Chamos, Mechom, Baalpeor, Astaroth, Bel the dragon, Priapus, the brasen serpent, the twelve signs, and many other; unto whose

Man, from his first falling from God's commandments, hath ever been ready to do the like, and to devise[8] works of his own phantasy to please God withal.

The devices and idolatry of the Gentiles.

The devices and idolatries of the Gentiles[14].

[[1] Unto everlasting life, Ibid.]
[[2] To the everlasting life, Ibid.]
[[3] By the law of God, Ed. 1560.]
[[4] Thy neighbours, Ibid.]
[[5] To everlasting life, Ed. 1560, 62.]
[[6] To be taken, Ibid. and Ed. 1547.]
[[7] Of the mortal commandments, Ed. 1560.]
[[8] And doth devise, Ibid.]
[[9] All that came of him, Ed. 1560, 62.]
[[10] To fall from, Ibid.]
[[11] About in their own, Ed. 1547.]
[[12] In a manner, Ibid.]
[[13] To reprove and rebuke this extreme madness, Eds. 1560, 62.]
[[14] Of the Israelites, Ed. 1560.]
[[15] In their heads, Eds. 1560, 62.]
[[16] How unsteadfast, Ibid.]

images the people with great devotion invented pilgrimages, preciously decking and censing them, kneeling down and offering to them, thinking that an high merit before God, and to be esteemed above the precepts and commandments of God. And where at that time God commanded no sacrifice to be made, but in Jerusalem only, they did clean contrary, making altars and sacrifices every where, in hills, in woods, and in houses, not regarding God's commandments, but esteeming their own phantasies and devotion to be better than them[17]. And the error hereof was so spread abroad, that not only the unlearned people, but also the priests and teachers of the people, partly by glory and avarice[18] were corrupted, and partly by ignorance blindly seduced with[19] the same abominations: so much, that king Achab having but only Helias a true teacher and minister of God, there were eight hundred and fifty priests, that persuaded him to honour Baal, and to do sacrifice in the woods or groves. And so continued that horrible error, until the three noble kings, as Josaphat, Ezechias, and Josias, God's elect ministers, destroyed the same clearly, and reduced the people[20] from such their feigned inventions unto the very commandments of God: for the which thing their immortal reward and glory doth and shall remain with God for ever.

Religions and sects among the Jews.

And beside the foresaid inventions, the inclination of man to have his own holy devotions devised new sects and religions, called Pharisees, Sadducees, and Scribes, with many holy and godly traditions and ordinances, (as it seemed by the outward appearance and goodly glistering[21] of the works,) but in very deed all tending to idolatry, superstition, and hypocrisy, their hearts within being full of malice, pride, covetousness, and all iniquity[22]. Against which sects, and their pretensed holiness, Christ cried out more vehemently than he did against any other persons, saying and often repeating these words: "Woe be to you, scribes and Pharisees, ye hypocrites! for you make clean the vessel without, but within you be full of ravine and filthiness: thou blind Pharisee and hypocrite, first make the inward part clean." For, notwithstanding all the goodly traditions and outward shews[23] of good works, devised of their own imagination, whereby they appeared to the world most religious and holy of all men; yet Christ, who saw their hearts, knew that they were inwardly, in the sight of God, most unholy, most abominable, and farthest from God of all men. Therefore said he unto them: "Hypocrites, the prophet Esay spake full truly of you, when he said, This people honour me with their lips, but their heart is far from me: they worship me in vain, that teach doctrines and commandments of men: for you leave the commandments of God to keep your own traditions."

Matt. xxiii.

Matt. xv. Isai. xix.

Man's laws must be observed and kept, but not as God's laws.

And though Christ said, "They worshipped God in vain that teach doctrines and commandments of men," yet he meant not thereby to overthrow all men's commandments; for he himself was ever obedient to the princes and their laws, made for good order and governance of the people: but he reproved the laws and traditions made by the scribes and Pharisees, which were not made only for good order of the people, (as the civil laws were,) but they were so highly extolled, that[24] they were made to be a right and sincere worshipping[25] of God, as they had been equal with God's laws, or above them: for many of God's laws could not be kept, but were fain to give place unto them. This arrogancy God detested, that man should so advance his laws to make them equal with God's laws, wherein the true honouring and right worshipping of God standeth, and to make his laws for them to be omitted[26]. God hath appointed his laws, whereby his pleasure is to be honoured. His pleasure is also, that all man's laws, being not contrary to his laws, shall be obeyed and kept, as good and necessary for every commonweal, but not as things wherein principally his honour resteth. And all civil and man's laws either be or should be made, to induce men the better to observe God's laws[27], that consequently[28] God should be the better honoured by them.

[17 Better than they, Ibid.]
[18 By glory and covetousness, Ibid.]
[19 Blindly deceived with, Ibid.]
[20 And brought again the people, Ibid.]
[21 And godly glistering, Ed. 1562.]
[22 And all wickedness, Eds. 1560, 62.]
[23 Outward shew, Ed. 1547.]
[24 Were set up so high, that, Eds. 1560, 62.]
[25 And pure worshipping, Ibid.]
[26 To be left off, Ibid.]
[27 Made to bring in men the better to keep God's laws, Ibid.]
[28 Consequently, or followingly, Ibid.]

Howbeit, the scribes and Pharisees were not content that their laws should be no higher esteemed than other positive and civil laws, nor would not have them called by the name of other temporal laws, but called them holy and godly traditions, and would have them esteemed, not only for a right and true worshipping of God, (as God's laws be indeed,) but also to be the most high honouring of God, to the which the commandments of God should give place. And for this cause did Christ so vehemently speak against them, saying, Your traditions, which men esteem so high, be abomination before God: for commonly of such traditions followeth the transgression[1] of God's commandments, and a more devotion in the observing of such things, and a greater conscience in breaking of them, than of the commandments of God; as the scribes and Pharisees so superstitiously and scrupulously kept the sabbath, that they were offended with Christ because he healed sick men, and with his apostles, because they, being sore hungry, gathered the ears of corn to eat upon that day. And because his disciples washed not their hands so often as the traditions required, the scribes and Pharisees quarrelled with Christ, saying: "Why do thy disciples break the traditions of the seniors?" But Christ objected against them[2], that they, for to observe their own[3] traditions, did teach men to break the very commandments of God. For they taught the people such a devotion, that they offered their goods into the treasure-house of the temple, under the pretence of God's honour, leaving their fathers and mothers, to whom they were chiefly bound, unholpen: and so they brake the commandments of God, to keep their own traditions. They esteemed more an oath made by the gold or oblation in the temple, than an oath made in the name of God himself, or of the temple. They were more studious to pay their tithes of small things, than to do the greater things commanded of God, as works of mercy, or to do justice, or to deal sincerely, uprightly, and faithfully with God and man: "These," saith Christ, "ought to be done, and the other not omitted[4]." And, to be short, they were of so blind judgment, that they stumbled at a straw, and leaped over a block. They would, as it were, nicely take a fly out of their cup, and drink down a whole camel: and therefore Christ called them "blind guides," warning his disciples from time to time to eschew their doctrine. For although they seemed to the world to be most perfect men, both in living and teaching; yet was their life but hypocrisy, and their doctrine but sour leaven, mixt[5] with superstition, idolatry, and preposterous[6] judgment; setting up the traditions and ordinances of man in the stead of God's commandments.

Holy traditions were esteemed as God's laws.

Luke xvi.

Holiness of man's device is commonly occasion that God is offended.

Matt. xii.

Matt. xv.

Matt. xxiii.

## [7] *The Third Part of the Sermon of Good Works.*

That all men might rightly judge of good works, it hath been declared in the second part of this Sermon, what kind of good works they be that God would have his people to walk in, namely, such as he hath commanded in his holy scripture, and not such works as men have studied out of[8] their own brain, of a blind zeal and devotion, without the word of God. And by mistaking the nature of good works man hath most highly displeased God, and hath gone from his will and commandment.

Thus have you heard how much the world, from the beginning until Christ's time, was ever ready to fall from the commandments of God, and to seek other means to honour and serve him, after a devotion imagined of their own[9] heads; and how they extolled their own traditions[10] as high or above God's commandments: which hath happened also in our times, (the more it is to be lamented,) no less than it did among the Jews, and that by the corruption, or at the least by the negligence, of them that chiefly ought to have preferred God's commandments[11], and to have preserved the sincere and

[1 The transgression or breaking of, Ibid.]
[2 But Christ laid to their charge, Ibid.]
[3 For to keep their own, Ibid.]
[4 The other not left undone, Ibid.]
[5 Leaven, mingled with, Ed. 1560.]
[6 And overwart, Ed. 1560, And overthart, Ed. 1562.]
[7 Inserted from Eds. 1560, 62. Vid. pp. 130, 132, 137, 139, 144.]
[8 Have imagined out of, Ed. 1562.]
[9 A devotion found out of their own, Eds. 1560, 62.]
[10 And how they did set up their own traditions, Ibid.]
[11 Ed. 1560 omits the words "to have preferred God's commandments."]

heavenly[12] doctrine left by Christ. What man having any judgment or learning, joined with a true zeal unto God, doth not see and lament to have entered into Christ's religion such false doctrine, superstition, idolatry, hypocrisy, and other enormities and abuses, so as by little and little, through the sour leaven thereof, the sweet bread of God's holy word hath been much hindered and laid apart? Never had the Jews in their most blindness so many pilgrimages unto images, nor used so much kneeling, kissing, and censing of them, as hath been used in our time. Sects and feigned religions were neither the forty part so many among the Jews, nor more superstitiously and ungodly abused than of late days they have been among us: which sects and religions had so many hypocritical works in their state of religion, as they arrogantly named it, that their lamps, as they said, ran always over, able to satisfy, not only for their own sins, but also for all other their benefactors, brother, and sisters of their religion[13], as most ungodly and craftily they had persuaded the multitude of ignorant people; keeping in divers places, as it were, marts or markets of merits, being full of their holy relics, images, shrines, and works of supererogation ready[14] to be sold. And all things which they had were called holy; holy cowls, holy girdles, holy pardoned beads[15], holy shoes, holy rules, and all full of holiness. And what thing can be more foolish, more superstitious, or ungodly, than that men, women, and children, should wear a friar's coat to deliver them from agues or pestilence; or when they die, or when they be buried, cause it to be cast upon them, in hope thereby to be saved? Which superstition, although (thanks be to God!) it hath been little used in this realm; yet in divers other realms it hath been and yet is used among many, both learned and unlearned.

Sects and religions amongst christian men.

But, to pass over the innumerable superstitiousness that hath been in strange apparel, in silence, in dormitory, in cloister, in chapter, in choice of meats and in drinks, and in such like things; let us consider what enormities and abuses have been in the three chief principal points, which they called the three essentials of religion, that is to say, obedience, chastity, and wilful poverty.

First, under pretence of obedience[16] to their father in religion, (which obedience they made themselves,) they were exempted, by their rules[17] and canons, from the obedience of their natural father and mother, and from the obedience of emperor and king, and all temporal power, whom of very duty by God's laws they were bound to obey. And so the profession of their obedience not due was a renunciation of their[18] due obedience. And how their profession of chastity was observed, it is more honesty to pass over in silence, and let the world judge of that which is well known, than with unchaste words, by expressing of their unchaste life, to offend chaste and godly ears. And as for their wilful poverty, it was such, that when in possessions, jewels, plate, and riches, they were equal or above merchants, gentlemen, barons, earls, and dukes; yet by this subtle sophistical term, *Proprium in communi*[19], they deluded the world[20], persuading that, notwithstanding all their possessions and riches, yet they observed their vow, and were in wilful poverty. But for all their riches, they might neither help[21] father nor mother, nor other that were indeed very needy and poor, without the licence of their father abbot, prior, or warden. And yet they might take of every man, but they might not give aught to any man, no, not to them whom the laws of God bound them to help. And so, through their traditions and rules, the laws of God could bear no rule with them. And therefore of them might be most truly said that which Christ spake unto the Pharisees: "You break the commandments of God by your traditions; you honour God with your lips, but your hearts be far from him." And the longer prayers they used by day and by night, under pretence of[22] such holiness, to get the favour of widows and other simple folks, that they might sing trentals and service for their husbands and friends, and admit them into their suffrages[23], the more truly is verified of them the saying of Christ:

The three chief vows of religion.

Matt. xv.

[12 The pure and heavenly, Eds. 1560, 62.]
[13 Sisters of religion, Ibid.]
[14 Of overflowing abundance, ready, Ibid.]
[15 Holy pardons, beads, Ibid.]
[16 Under pretence, or colour of obedience, Ibid.]
[17 Were made free by their rules, Ibid.]
[18 A forsaking of their, Ibid.]
[19 Eds. 1560, 62, add, "that is to say, proper in common."]
[20 They mocked the world, Ibid.]
[21 Might never help, Ed. 1560.]
[22 Under pretence or colour of, Eds. 1560, 62.]
[23 And admit or receive them into their prayers, Ibid.]

Matt xxiii. "Woe be to you, scribes Pharisees, hypocrites! for you devour widows' houses, under colour of long prayers; therefore your damnation shall be the greater. Woe be to you, scribes and Pharisees, hypocrites! for you go about by sea and by land to make mo novices and new brethren; and when they be admitted of your sect[1], you make them the children of hell worse than yourselves be."

Honour be to God, who did put light in the heart of his faithful and true minister of most famous memory, king Henry the eighth, and gave him the knowledge of his word, and an earnest affection to seek his glory, and to put away all such superstitious and pharisaical sects by antichrist invented, and set up against the true word[2] of God, and glory of his most blessed name, as he gave the like spirit unto the most noble and famous princes, Josaphat, Josias, and Ezechias. God grant all us, the king's highness'[3] faithful and true subjects, to feed of the sweet and savoury bread of God's own word, and, as Christ commanded, to eschew all our pharisaical and papistical leaven of man's feigned religion; which, although it were before God most abominable, and contrary to God's commandments and Christ's pure religion, yet it was extolled to be[4] a most godly life and highest state of perfection; as though a man might be more godly and more perfect by keeping the rules, traditions, and professions of men, than by keeping the holy commandments of God.

Other devices and superstitions.

And briefly to pass over the ungodly and counterfeit religions, let us rehearse some other kinds of papistical superstitions and abuses; as of beads, of lady psalters, and rosaries, of fifteen Oos, of St Barnard's verses, of St Agathe's letters[5], of purgatory, of masses satisfactory, of stations and jubilees, of feigned relics, of hallowed beads, bells, bread, water, palms, candles, fire, and such other[6]; of superstitious fastings, of fraternities, of pardons, with such like merchandise, which were so esteemed and abused to the great prejudice of God's glory and commandments, that they were made most high and most holy things, whereby to attain to the eternal life[7], or remission of sin. Yea also, vain inventions, unfruitful ceremonies, and ungodly laws, decrees, and councils of Rome, were in such wise advanced, that nothing was thought comparable in authority, wisdom, learning, and godliness unto them: so that the laws of Rome, as they said, were to be received of all men as the four evangelists; to the which all laws of princes must give place. And the laws of God also partly were omitted[8] and less esteemed, that the said laws, decrees, and councils, with their traditions and ceremonies, might be more duly observed, and had in greater reverence. Thus was the people, through ignorance, so blinded with the goodly shew and appearance of those things, that they thought the observing of them to be a more holiness, a more perfect service and honouring of God, and more pleasing to God, than the keeping of God's commandments. Such hath been the corrupt inclination of man, ever superstitiously given to make new honouring of God of his own head, and then to have more affection and devotion to observe that[9], than to search out God's holy commandments, and to keep them; and furthermore, to take God's commandments for men's commandments, and men's commandments for God's commandments, yea, and for the highest and most perfect and holy of all God's commandments. And so was all confused, that scant well-learned men, and but a small number of them, knew, or at the least would know, and durst affirm the truth, to separate[10] God's commandments from the commandments of men: whereupon did grow much error, superstition, idolatry, vain religion, preposterous judgment[11], great contention, with all ungodly living.

Decrees and decretals.

An exhortation to the keeping of God's commandments.

Wherefore, as you have any zeal to the right and pure honouring of God; as you have any regard to your own souls, and to the life that is to come, which is both without pain and without end, apply yourselves chiefly above all thing to read and to hear God's

---

[1 When they be let in and received of the sect, Ibid.]

[2 Again the true word, Ed. 1560.]

[3 The queen's highness', Eds. 1560, 62, in reference to Elizabeth, in whose reign these editions were published.]

[4 It was praised to be, Ibid.]

[5 Vid. Pilkington's Works, pp. 177, 536, 563. Park. Soc. Ed. 1842.]

[6 Vid. Cardwell's Documentary Annals, Vol. I. pp. 37, 8, note. "The archbishop's letter," Ed. Oxon. 1829.]

[7 To the everlasting life, Ibid.]

[8 Were left off, Ibid.]

[9 To keep that, Ibid.]

[10 To separate or sever, Ibid.]

[11 Overwhart judgment, Ed. 1560. Overthwart, Ed. 1562.]

word; mark diligently therein what his will is you shall do, and with all your endeavour apply yourselves to follow the same. First, you must have an assured faith in God, and give yourselves wholly unto him, love him in prosperity and adversity, and dread to offend him evermore. Then, for his sake, love all men, friends and foes, because they be his creation and image, and redeemed by Christ as ye are. Cast in your minds how you may do good unto all men, unto your powers, and hurt no man. Obey all your superiors and governors, serve your masters faithfully and diligently, as well in their absence as in their presence, not for dread of punishment only, but for conscience sake, knowing that you are bound so to do by God's commandments. Disobey not your fathers and mothers, but honour them, help them, and please them to your power. Oppress not, kill not, beat not, neither slander nor hate any man: but love all men, speak well of all men, help and succour every man as you may, yea, even your enemies that hate you, that speak evil of you, and that do hurt you. Take no man's goods, nor covet your neighbour's goods wrongfully, but content yourselves with that which ye get truly, and also bestow your own goods charitably, as need and case requireth. Flee all idolatry, witchcraft, and perjury; commit no manner of adultery, fornication, nor other unchasteness, in will nor in deed, with any other man's wife, widow, maid, or otherwise.

A brief rehearsal of God's commandments.

And travailing continually during your life thus in the observing the commandments[12] of God, (wherein consisteth the pure[13], principal, and direct honour of God, and which, wrought in faith[14], God hath ordained to be the right trade and path-way unto heaven;) you shall not fail, as Christ hath promised, to come to that blessed and eternal life[15], where you shall live in glory and joy with God for ever. To whom be laud, honour, and impery, for ever and ever. Amen.

---

[[12] In keeping the commandments, Eds. 1560, 62.]

[[13] Wherein standeth the pure, Ibid.]

[[14] And which God, Ed. 1547.]

[[15] And everlasting life, Ibid.]

# QUESTIONS[1]

## PUT CONCERNING SOME ABUSES OF THE MASS:

WITH

# THE ANSWERS[2]

## THAT WERE MADE BY MANY BISHOPS AND DIVINES TO THEM.

---

*Quest.* 1.

Stillingfleet MSS Lambeth Libr. 1108. fol. 6. Ed. Oxon. 1829. Burnet's Hist. of Reformat. Vol. ii. App. B. 1. No. 25. pp. 192—210. Ed. Oxon. 1829.

WHETHER the sacrament of the altar was instituted to be received of one man for another, or to be received of every man for himself?

The sacrament of the altar was not instituted to be received of one man for another, but to be received by every man for himself.

*Quest.* 2.

Whether the receiving of the said sacrament of one man doth avail and profit any other?

The receiving of the said sacrament by one man doth avail and profit only him that receiveth the same.

*Quest.* 3.

What is the oblation and sacrifice of Christ in the mass?

The oblation and sacrifice of Christ in the mass is not so called, because Christ indeed is there offered and sacrificed by the priest and the people, (for that was done but once by himself upon the cross;) but it is so called, because it is a memory and representation of that very true sacrifice and immolation which before was made upon the cross.

*Quest.* 4.

Wherein consisteth the mass by Christ's institution?

The mass, by Christ's institution, consisteth in those things which be set forth in the Evangelists: Matt. xxvi. Mark xiv. Luke xxii. 1 Cor. x. and xi.

---

[[1] Of these queries Collier says: "The latter end of this winter (1547, 8) a committee of divines were commanded by the king to draw up an order for administering the holy Eucharist in English under both kinds, pursuant to the late act of Parliament.—These prelates and divines, before they came to a resolution concerning the form for the administration in both kinds, considered the present practice of the church, and broke the question into several divisions. And here it was settled, that every one in the commission should give his answer in writing." Collier's Eccl. Hist. Vol. V. p. 246, Ed. Lond. 1840, 1. But he adds, "Whether these questions were debated before the late statute, for communicating under both kinds, is somewhat uncertain, &c." Id. p. 254. Dr Jenkyns supposes he was not aware of the uncertainty being removed by the last of the further questions, p. 153, which, he says, "was obviously written subsequently to the statute to which Collier alludes. The parliament which passed this act being prorogued on the 24th of December, 1547, and the new order of communion compiled in consequence, and to which the present deliberations were preparatory, appeared under the sanction of a royal proclamation on the 8th of March following."—Vid. Foxe's Acts and Monuments, p. 1299, Ed. Lond. 1583. Burnet's Hist. of Reformation, Vol. II. p. 126. Strype's Mem. of Abp. Cranmer, Vol. I. p. 224, 5. Ed. Oxon. 1840. Eccl. Memorials, Vol. II. pp. 96—99. Ed. Oxon. 1822. Todd's Life of Abp. Cranmer, Vol. II. p. 19. Jenkyns' Remains of Abp. Cranmer, Vol. II. p. 178.]

[[2] A manuscript containing many of these answers is preserved at Lambeth. Jenkyns.]

*Quest.* 5.

What time the accustomed order began first in the church, that the priest alone should receive the sacrament?

I think the use, that the priest alone did receive the sacrament without the people, began not within six or seven hundred years after Christ.

*Quest.* 6.

Whether it be convenient that the same custom continue still within this realm?

I think it more agreeable to the scripture and primitive church, that the first usage should be restored again, that the people should receive the sacrament with the priest.

*Quest.* 7.

Whether it be convenient that masses satisfactory should continue, that is to say, priests hired to sing for souls departed?

I think it not convenient that satisfactory masses should continue.

*Quest.* 8.

Whether the gospel ought to be taught at the time of the mass, to the understanding of the people being present?

I think it very convenient, that the gospel, concerning the death of Christ and our redemption, should be taught to the people in the mass.

*Quest.* 9.

Whether in the mass it were convenient to use such speech as the people may understand?

I think it convenient to use the vulgar tongue in the mass, except in certain secret mysteries, whereof I doubt.

*Quest.* 10.

When the reservation of the sacrament and the hanging up of the same first began?

The reservation of the sacrament began, I think, six or seven hundred years after Christ: the hanging up, I think, began of late time.

# SOME QUESTIONS, WITH ANSWERS

MADE TO THEM BY THE

# BISHOPS OF WORCESTER[1], CHICHESTER[2], AND HEREFORD[3].

Stillingfleet MSS. Lamb. Libr. 1108. fol. 40. Burnet's Hist. of Reformat. Vol. ii. App. B. i. No. 25. pp. 210–212. Ed. Oxon. 1829. Strype's Mem. of Abp. Cranmer, Vol. i. pp. 224, 5. Ed. Oxon. 1840.

*The Question.*

WHAT or wherein John's fasting, giving alms, being baptized, or receiving the sacrament of thanks in England, doth profit and avail Thomas dwelling in Italy, and not knowing what John in England doth?

*The Answer*[4].

The distance of place doth not let nor hinder the spiritual communion which is between one and another; so that John and Thomas, wheresoever they be, far and sundry, or near together, being both lively members of Christ, receive either of other's goodness some commodity; although to limit what or wherein, is unsearchable, and only pertaineth to the knowledge of God.

*The Question.*

Whether the said acts in John do profit them that be in heaven, and wherein?

*The Answer.*

*Gaudium est in cœlo super uno peccatore pœnitentiam agente, &c.*

*The Question.*

Worcester. Chichester. Hereford.

Whether it lieth in the said John to defraud any member of Christ's body of the benefit of his fasting, alms-deeds, baptism, or receiving of the sacrament, and to apply the same benefit to one person more than to another?

*The Answer.*

Charity defraudeth no man of any such benefit that might come to him; and it lieth in God only to apply the same, and not in any man, otherwise than by desire and prayer; but the better the man is, the more available his prayer is to them for whom he especially prayeth.

*The Question.*

What thing is the presentation of the body and blood of Christ in the mass, which you call the oblation and sacrifice of Christ? and wherein standeth it, in act, gesture, or words? and in what act, gesture, or words?

*The Answer.*

The presentation, &c. standeth in such words, prayers, supplications, and actions, as the priest useth at the mass, having the body and blood of Christ there present in the sacrament.

*The Question.*

Is there any rite or prayer not expressed in the scripture which Christ used, or commanded at the first institution of the mass, which we be now bound to use; and what the same be?

*The Answer.*

That Christ used rites and prayers at the institution and distribution of the sacrament, the scripture declareth: but what rites and prayers they were, we know not; but I think that[5] we ought to use such rites and prayers as the catholic church hath, and doth uniformly observe.

---

[[1] Nicholas Heath. Vide p. 66, n. 1.]

[[2] George Day.]

[[3] John Skyp.]

[[4] "This paper is all in Bonner's hand, with whom these three bishops agreed." Vid. Strype's Corrections of Burnet's Hist. of Reformat. Vol. III. Part II. p. 521.]

[[5] Dr Jenkyns omits the word "that."]

*The Question.*

Whether in the primitive church there were any priests that lived by saying of mass, matins, and even-song, and praying for souls only? And whether any such state of priesthood be allowed in the scripture, or be meet to be allowed now?

*The Answer.*

There were priests in the primitive church which preached not, but exercised themselves in prayer for the quick and the dead, and other spiritual ministrations in the church, and accustomably used common prayers both morning and evening; and such state of priesthood is not against the scripture.

*The Question.*

For what cause it were not expedient nor convenient to have the whole mass in English?[6]

*The Answer.*

This question is answered by Dionyse and Basil *De Spiritu Sancto;* and also an uniformity of all churches in that thing is to be kept.

## [*Further Questions*[7] *in reply to the above Answers.*]

If you cannot tell what or wherein the acts of John can profit Thomas, being so far distant from him, that he can never hear of him; why do you then affirm that to be true, which you cannot tell how, nor wherein it can be true?

Stillingfleet MSS. Lamb. Libr. 1108. fol. 44. Burnet's Hist. of Reformat. Vol. iii. part ii. App. (Strype's corrections,) pp. 549—50.

Whether our prayers for all the souls departed do profit the apostles, prophets, and martyrs?

Whether they know all the acts of every man here in earth; and if not, how do they rejoice of those good acts which they know not?

Whether our evil deeds do them hurt, as our good deeds profit them?

Whether the presentation of the body and blood of Christ in the mass do stand in all the words and actions that the priest useth in the mass? [And if not, then in which of them it standeth?

Whether we may change those rites and ceremonies of the mass,][8] which now we do use?

Whereby is it known that in the primitive church were priests which preached not?

Why may we not as well alter the mass into the English tongue, or alter the ceremonies of the same, as we alter the communion to be under both kinds, which in other churches is uniformly ministered to the people under one kind, seeing that the uniformity of all churches requireth not more the uniformity in one than in the other?

---

[6 Another copy of the above Questions, corrected by Cranmer, is found in the Lambeth MSS., "written by a clerk," to which are added the two following of the original questions, as well as another, to which no reply has yet been found extant.

*Question.*

"What time did the honouring of the same first begin, and by whom, and what proofs there is thereof?" Vid. p. 151, Quest. 10.]

*Question.*

"What time did the use of reserving the Sacrament first begin, and by whom?"

*Question.*

"What time began the use to hang up the same in the Church, and by whom?"

[7 Burnet has not given these queries, which are printed from the Lambeth MSS., and are called by Strype "a reply by Cranmer." Burnet's Hist. of Reformat. Vol. III. Part II. p. 549.]

[8 Strype omits this passage, which is found both in the Lambeth MSS. and in Burnet.]

# ARTICLES

## TO BE INQUIRED OF IN THE VISITATIONS TO BE HAD WITHIN THE DIOCESE OF CANTERBURY, IN THE SECOND YEAR OF THE REIGN OF OUR DREAD SOVEREIGN LORD, EDWARD THE SIXTH, BY THE GRACE OF GOD KING OF ENGLAND, FRANCE, AND IRELAND, DEFENDER OF THE FAITH, AND IN EARTH OF THE CHURCH OF ENGLAND, AND ALSO OF IRELAND, THE SUPREME HEAD[1].

---

Wilkins, Concilia, Vol. iv. pp. 23—26. Ed. Lond. 1737. Sparrow's Collection of Articles, &c. pp. 25—33. Ed. Lond. 1684.

First, whether parsons, vicars, and curates, and every of them, have purely and sincerely, without colour or dissimulation, four times in the year at the least, preached against the usurped power, pretended authority and jurisdiction of the bishop of Rome.

*Item*, Whether they have preached and declared likewise four times in the year at the least, that the king's majesty's power, authority, and pre-eminence, within his realms and dominions, is the highest power under God.

*Item*, Whether any person hath by writing, cyphering, preaching or teaching, deed or act, obstinately holden and stand with to extol, set forth, maintain, or defend the authority, jurisdiction, or power of the bishop of Rome or of his see heretofore claimed and usurped, or by any pretence, obstinately or maliciously invented any thing for the extolling of the same, or any part thereof.

*Item*, Whether in their common prayers they use not the collects made for the king, and make not special mention of his majesty's name in the same.

*Item*, Whether they do not every Sunday and holyday, with the collects of the English procession, say the prayer set forth by the king's majesty for peace between England and Scotland[2].

---

[[1] These articles are printed from Wilkins' Concilia, and have been collated with Sparrow's Collection of Articles, &c. Both Strype and Burnet assert that they were issued at Cranmer's Visitation, A. D. 1548. Vid. Strype's Mem. of Abp. Cranmer, Vol. I. p. 259, Ed. Oxon. 1840. Burnet's Hist. of Reformat. Vol. II. p. 211. Ed. Oxon. 1829. Cardwell's Documentary Annals, Vol. I. pp. 41—51. Vid. Injunctions to the Dean and Chapter of Canterbury, No. 2, p. 162. Yet Strype, (Vol. II. p. 613, 14) also says, "The articles whereof (king Edward VIth's Visitation) were drawn up by the archbishop, and preserved to us in Bishop Sparrow's Collections." They were printed by Grafton, Ed. Lond. 1548. Vid. Ames' Typogr. Antiq. Ed. Dibdin. Vol. III. p. 458, who mentions, (p. 467, *n.*) Abp. Cranmer's Articles of Visitation in the Diocese of Norwich, a copy of which has not yet been discovered.]

[[2] "A prayer for victory and peace was sent to the archbishop with an order from the privy council for its use, 6th May, 1548. Wilkins' Concilia, Vol. IV. p. 26. Strype's Mem. of Abp. Cranmer, Vol. I. p. 253, and Eccl. Mem. Vol. II. Part I. p. 166. Ed. Oxon. 1822. The following prayer is found in the State Paper Office. Dr Jenkyns suggests that it "may probably be that which was then set forth;" and that "it was perhaps composed by Cranmer himself."

*The Common Prayer.*

Most merciful God, the granter of all peace and quietness, the giver of all good gifts, the defender of all nations, who hast willed all men to be accounted as our neighbours, and commanded us to love them as ourselves, and not to hate our enemies, but rather to wish them, yea, and also to do them, good if we can: bow down thy holy and merciful eyes upon us, and look upon the small portion of earth, which professeth thy holy name and thy Son Jesu Christ. Give to all us desire of peace, unity, and quietness, and a speedy wearisomeness of all war, hostility, and enmity to all them that be our enemies; that we and they may, in one heart and charitable agreement, praise thy most holy name, and reform our lives to thy godly commandments. And especially have an eye to this small isle of Britain. And that which was begun by thy great and infinite mercy and love to the unity and concord of both the nations, that the Scottish men and we might for ever live hereafter in one love and amity, knit into one nation, by the most happy and godly marriage of the king's majesty our sovereign lord, and the young Scottish queen; whereunto promises and agreements hath been heretofore most firmly made by human order: grant, O Lord, that the same might go forward, and that our sons' sons, and all our posterity hereafter, may feel the benefit and commodity of thy great gift of unity, granted in our days. Confound all those that worketh against it: let not their counsel prevail: diminish their strength: lay thy sword of punishment upon them that interrupteth this godly peace; or rather convert their hearts to the better way, and make them embrace that unity and peace, which shall be most for thy glory, and the profit of both the realms.

*Item*, Whether they have not removed, taken away, and utterly extincted and destroyed in their churches, chapels, and houses, all images, all shrines, coverings of shrines, all tables, candlesticks, trindals or rolls of war, pictures, paintings, and all other monuments of feigned miracles, pilgrimages, idolatry, and superstition, so that there remain no memory of the same in walls, glass windows, or elsewhere.

*Item*, Whether they have exhorted, moved, and stirred their parishioners to do the like in every of their houses.

*Item*, Whether they have declared to their parishioners the articles concerning the abrogation of certain superfluous holydays, and done their endeavour to persuade the said parishioners to keep and observe the same articles inviolably; and whether any of those abrogate days have been kept as holydays, and by whose occasion they were so kept.

*Item*, Whether they have diligently, duly, and reverently ministered the sacraments in their cures.

*Item*, Whether they have preached, or caused to be preached, purely and sincerely the word of God, in every of their cures, every quarter of the year, once at the least, exhorting their parishioners to works commanded[3] by the scripture, and not to works devised by men's phantasies besides scripture, as wearing or praying upon beads, or such like.

*Item*, Whether they suffer any torches, candles, tapers, or any other lights to be in your churches, but only two lights upon the high altar.

*Item*, Whether they have not every holyday, when they have no sermon, immediately after the gospel, openly, plainly, and distinctly recited to their parishioners in the pulpit, the *Paternoster*, the Creed, and the Ten Commandments in English.

*Item*, Whether every Lent, they examine such persons as come to confession to them, whether they can recite the *Paternoster*, the Articles of our Faith, and the Ten Commandments in English.

*Item*, Whether they have charged fathers and mothers, masters and governors of youth, to bring them up in some virtuous study and occupation.

*Item*, Whether such beneficed men, as be lawfully absent from their benefices, do leave their cure to a rude and unlearned person, and not an honest, well-learned, and expert curate, which can and will teach you wholesome doctrine.

*Item*, Whether, in every cure they have, they have provided one book of the whole bible of the largest volume in English, and the Paraphrasis of Erasmus also in English upon the gospels, and set up the same in some convenient place in the church, where their parishioners may most commodiously resort to the same.

*Item*, Whether they have discouraged any person from reading of any part of the bible, either in Latin or English, but rather comforted and exhorted every person to read the same, as the very lively word of God, and the special food of man's soul.

---

Put away from us all war and hostility, and if we be driven thereto, hold thy holy and strong power and defence over us: be our garrison, our shield, and buckler. And seeing we seek but a perpetual amity and concord, and performance of quietness promised in thy name, pursue the same with us, and send thy holy angels to be our aiders; that either none at all, or else so little loss and effusion of christian blood as can, be made thereby. Look not, O Lord, upon our sins, or the sins of our enemies, what they deserve; but have regard to thy most plenteous and abundant mercy, which passeth all thy works, being so infinite and marvellous. Do this, O Lord, for thy Son's sake, Jesu Christ.

"The same topic," adds Dr Jenkyns, "was introduced also into the bidding prayer before the sermon. The following form is printed by Strype, Eccl. Mem. Vol. II. Part I. p. 73, from some manuscript additions attributed to Cranmer, in a Book of Articles and Injunctions then in the possession of N. Battely."

Ye shall also make your hearty and effectual prayer to Almighty God for the peace of all Christian regions, and especially, that the most joyful and perpetual peace and unity of this realm and Scotland may shortly be profited* and brought to pass, by the most godly and happy marriage of the king's majesty and the young queen of Scotland: and that it would please Almighty God to aid with strength, wisdom, and power, and with his holy defence, all those which favour and set forward the same, and vanquish and confound all those which labour and study to the lett and interruption of so godly a quiet and unity, whereof these two realms should take such a benefit and profit: for these and all other, &c. Vid. Jenkyns' Remains of Abp. Cranmer, Vol. II. pp. 186, 7.]

[[3] To words commanded. Sparrow.]

[* perfected. Jenkyns.]

*Item*, Whether parsons, vicars, curates, and other priests, be common haunters and resorters to taverns or ale-houses, giving themselves to drinking, rioting, or playing at unlawful games, and do not occupy themselves in the reading or hearing of some part of holy scripture, or in some other godly exercise.

*Item*, Whether they have admitted any man to preach in their cures not being lawfully licensed thereunto, or have refused or denied such to preach as have been licensed accordingly.

*Item*, Whether they which have heretofore declared to their parishioners anything to the extolling or setting forth of pilgrimages, relics, or images, or lighting of candles, kissing, kneeling, decking of the same images, or any such superstition, have not openly recanted and reproved the same.

*Item*, Whether they have one book or register safely kept, wherein they write the day of every wedding, christening, and burying.

*Item*, Whether they have exhorted the people to obedience to the king's majesty and his ministers, and to charity and love one to another.

*Item*, Whether they have admonished their parishioners, that they ought not to presume to receive the sacrament of the body and blood of Christ, before they can perfectly rehearse the *Paternoster*, the Articles of the Faith, and the Ten Commandments in English.

*Item*, Whether they have declared, and to their wits and power have persuaded the people, that the manner and kind of fasting in Lent, and other days in the year, is but a mere positive law; and that therefore all persons, having just cause of sickness, or other necessity, or being licensed by the king's majesty, may moderately eat all kind of meats without grudge or scruple of conscience.

*Item*, Whether they be resident upon their benefices, and keep hospitality, or no; and if they be absent, or keep no hospitality, whether they do make due distributions among the poor parishioners, or not.

*Item*, Whether parsons, vicars, clerks, and other beneficed men, having yearly to dispend an hundred pound, do not find competently one scholar in the university of Cambridge or Oxford, or some grammar-school; and for as many hundred pounds as every of them may dispend, so many scholars likewise to be found by them; and what be their names that they so find.

*Item*, Whether proprietaries, parsons, vicars, and clerks, having churches, chapels, or mansions, do keep their chancels, rectories, vicarages, and all other houses appertaining to them, in due reparations.

*Item*, Whether they have counselled or moved their parishioners rather to pray in a tongue not known, than in English, or to put their trust in a prescribed number of prayers, as in saying over a number of beads, or other like.

*Item*, Whether they have read the king's majesty's Injunctions[1] every quarter of the year, the first holyday of the same quarter.

*Item*, Whether the parsons, vicars, curates, and other priests, being under the degree of a bachelor of divinity, have of their own the new Testament both in Latin and English, and the Paraphrase of Erasmus upon the same.

*Item*, Whether within every church he that ministereth hath read or caused to be read the epistle and gospel in English, and not in Latin, either in the pulpit or some other meet place, so as the people may hear the same.

*Item*, Whether every Sunday and holyday at matins they have read or caused to be read plainly and distinctly, in the said place, one chapter of the new Testament in English, immediately after the lessons, and at even-song after *Magnificat* one chapter of the old Testament.

*Item*, Whether they have not at matins omitted three lessons, when nine should have been read in the church, and at even-song the responds with all the memories.

*Item*, Whether they have declared to their parishioners, that St Mark's day and the evens of the abrogate holydays should not be fasted.

[[1] Vid. Wilkins' Concilia, Vol. IV. pp. 3—8; and Sparrow's Collection of Articles, pp. 1—13, and the Appendix to this Volume.]

*Item*, Whether they have the procession-book in English, and have said or sung the said litany in any other place but upon their knees in the midst of their church; and whether they use any other procession, or omit the said litany at any time, or say it or sing it in such sort as the people cannot understand the same.

*Item*, Whether they have put out of their church-books this word "*Papa*," and the name and service of Thomas Becket, and prayers having rubrics containing pardons or indulgences, and all other superstitious legends and prayers.

*Item*, Whether they bid not the beads according to the order appointed by the king's majesty.

*Item*, Whether they have opened and declared unto you the true use of ceremonies, that is to say, that they be no workers nor works of salvation, but only outward signs and tokens, to put us in remembrance of things of higher perfection.

*Item*, Whether they have taught and declared to their parishioners, that they may with a safe and quiet conscience in the time of harvest labour upon the holy and festival days; and if superstitiously they abstain from working upon those days, that then they do grievously offend and displease God.

*Item*, Whether they have admitted any person to the communion, being openly known to be out of charity with their neighbours.

*Item*, Whether the deans, archdeacons, masters of hospitals, and prebendaries, have preached by themselves personally twice every year at the least.

*Item*, Whether they have provided and have a strong chest for the poor men's box, and set and fastened the same near to their high altar[2].

*Item*, Whether they have diligently called upon, exhorted, and moved their parishioners, and specially when they make their testaments, to give to the said poor men's box, and to bestow that upon the poor chest, which they were wont to bestow upon pardons, pilgrimages, trentals, masses satisfactory, decking of images, offering of candles, giving to friars, and upon other like blind devotions.

*Item*, Whether they have denied to visit the sick, or bury the dead being brought to the church.

*Item*, Whether they have bought their benefices, or come to them by fraud or deceit.

*Item*, Whether they have every Sunday, when the people be most gathered, read one of the homilies in order as they stand in the book set forth by the king's majesty.

*Item*, Whether they do not omit prime and hours, when they have any sermon or homily.

*Item*, Whether they have said or sung any mass, in any oratory, chapel, or any man's house, not being hallowed.

*Item*, Whether they have given open monition to their parishioners that they should not wear beads, nor pray upon them.

*Item*, Whether they have moved their parishioners, lying upon their death-beds, or at any other time, to bestow any part of their substance upon trentals, masses satisfactory, or any such blind devotions.

*Item*, Whether they take any trentals or other masses satisfactory to say or sing for the quick or the dead.

*Item*, Whether they have given open monition to their parishioners to detect and present to their ordinary all adulterers and fornicators, and such men as have two wives living, and such women as have two husbands living, within their parishes.

*Item*, Whether they have not monished their parishioners openly, that they should not sell, give, nor otherwise alienate any of their churches' goods.

*Item*, Whether they or any of them do keep more benefices and other ecclesiastical promotions than they ought to do, not having sufficient licence and dispensations thereunto, and how many they be, and their names.

*Item*, Whether they minister the communion any other ways than only after such form and manner as is set forth by the king's majesty in the book of the communion.

*Item*, Whether they hallowed and delivered to the people any candles upon candlemas-day, and ashes upon Ash-Wednesday, or any palms upon Palm-Sunday last past.

[2 To the high altar. Sparrow.]

*Item*, Whether they had upon Good-Friday last past the sepulchres with their lights, having the sacrament therein.

*Item*, Whether they upon Easter-even last past hallowed the font, fire, or paschal, or had any paschal set up, or burning in their churches.

*Item*, Whether your parsons and vicars have admitted any curates to serve their cures, which were not first examined and allowed either by my lord of Canterbury, master archdeacon, or their officers.

*Item*, Whether you know any person within your parish or elsewhere, that is a letter of the word of God to be read in English or sincerely preached, or of the execution of the king's majesty's Injunctions, or other his majesty's proceedings in matters of religion.

*Item*, Whether every parish have provided a chest with two locks and keys for the book[1] of wedding, christening, and burying.

*Item*, Whether in the time of the litany or any other common prayer, in the time of the sermon or homily, and when the priest readeth the scripture to the parishioners, any person have departed out of the church without a just and necessary cause.

*Item*, Whether any bells have been knolled or rung at the time of the premises.

*Item*, Whether any person hath abused the ceremonies, as in casting holy water upon his bed, or bearing about him holy bread, St John's Gospel, ringing of holy bells, or keeping of private holydays, as tailors, bakers, brewers, smiths, shoemakers, and such other.

*Item*, Whether the money coming and rising of any cattle, or other moveable stocks of the church, and money given or bequeathed to the finding of torches, lights, tapers, or lamps, (not paid out of any lands,) have not been employed to the poor men's chest.

*Item*, Who hath the said stocks and money in their hands, and what be their names.

*Item*, Whether any undiscreet persons do uncharitably contemn and abuse priests and ministers of the church.

*Item*, Whether they that understand not the Latin do pray upon any primer but the English primer, set forth by the king's majesty's authority; and whether they that understand Latin do use any other than the Latin primer, set forth by like authority.

*Item*, Whether there be any other grammar taught in any other school within this diocese than that which is set forth by the king's majesty.

*Item*, Whether any person keep their church holyday and the dedication-day any otherwise, or at any other time, than is appointed by the king's majesty.

*Item*, Whether the service in the church be done at due and convenient hours.

*Item*, Whether any have used to commune, jangle, and talk in the church, in the time of the common prayer, reading of the homily, preaching, reading or declaring of the scripture.

*Item*, Whether any have wilfully maintained and defended any heresies, errors, or false opinions, contrary to the faith of Christ and holy scripture.

*Item*, Whether any be common drunkards, swearers, or blasphemers of the name of God.

*Item*, Whether any have committed adultery, fornication, or incest, or be common bawds, and receivers of such evil persons, or vehemently suspected of any of the premises.

*Item*, Whether any be brawlers, slanderers, chiders, scolders, and sowers of discord between one person and another.

*Item*, Whether you know any that use charms, sorcery, enchantments, witchcraft, soothsaying, or any like craft invented by the devil.

*Item*, Whether the churches, pulpits, and other necessaries appertaining to the same, be sufficiently repaired.

*Item*, Whether you know any that, in contempt of your own parish church, do resort to any other church.

*Item*, Whether any inn-holders or alehouse-keepers do use commonly to sell meat and drink in the time of common prayer, preaching, or reading of the homilies or scripture.

*Item*, Whether you know any to be married within the degrees prohibited by the

---

[[1] And for the book. Sparrow.]

laws of God, or that be separated or divorced without a just cause, allowed by the law of God, and whether any such have married again.

*Item*, Whether you know any to have made privy contracts of matrimony, not calling two or more thereunto.

*Item*, Whether they have married solemnly, the banns not first lawfully asked.

*Item*, Whether you know any executors or administrators of dead men's goods, which do not bestow such of the said goods as were given and bequeathed, or appointed to be distributed among the poor people, repairing of highways, finding of poor scholars, or marrying of poor maids, or such other like charitable deeds.

*Item*, Whether any do contemn married priests, and, for that they be married, will not receive the communion or other sacraments at their hands.

*Item*, Whether you know any that keep in their houses undefaced any abused or feigned images, any tables, pictures, paintings, or other monuments of feigned miracles, pilgrimages, idolatry, or superstition.

---

# ARTICLES OF INQUIRY

AT THE

## VISITATION OF THE CATHEDRAL CHURCH OF CANTERBURY, 1550[2].

---

1550, 10 *Septembris, Visitation in the Chapter-house by my lord Archbishop, and Articles there ministered to be answered unto.* Harl. MSS. 7044. p. 284. Copy by Baker from Bp. Gunning's MSS.

WHETHER any of this church is a privy or an apert setter forth of the bishop of Rome his authority, or is a maintainer of heresy, superstition, idolatry, or anything repugnant or derogatory to the holy scripture, or the king's majesty's proceedings in matters of religion.

*Item*, Whether any of this church do keep or observe, diligently and inviolably, without colour or fraud, the book called the Common Prayer, according to the rules of the same, and the statute of parliament authorising the same book, and whether you use any other ceremonies at the communion or other divine service than is mentioned or allowed in the same book.

*Item*, Whether any inhabiter within my diocese of Canterbury have been admitted to the communion within this church, except such as be of the same church[3].

*Item*, Whether the sermons by foundation or statutes of this church or otherwise lawfully assigned have been made by the dean, prebendaries, or preachers of the same, at the times and places appointed therefore.

*Item*, Whether any prebendary, petty canon, or vicar of this church is beneficed beside the same, how many every one of them have, what be their names, and what their clear yearly value.

*Item*, Whether such distributions as should be made to the poor, either here, or at

---

[[2] These Articles and the Injunctions which follow, though found in different collections, manifestly belong to the same Visitation. The Articles were issued on the 10th of Sept. 1550. On the receipt of the answer to them, the Injunctions were given on the 29th of the ensuing October.

The chronological order has in this instance been departed from for the sake of keeping together documents of the same character. If it had been followed strictly, these two papers would have been placed after the work on the Lord's Supper. Jenkyns.]

[[3] See the sixth of the Injunctions to the Dean and Chapter of Canterbury, p. 162.]

the benefices appropriated to this church, or elsewhere, by the appropriations, ordinances, and statutes of this church, have been done accordingly, or no.

*Item*, Whether the grammar-school be diligently and duly kept, and the schoolmaster, being learned in the Greek and Latin tongue, and usher, do resort and continue at the same in due times and convenient hours, and whether the scholars do profit in learning, or no.

*Item*, Whether the just number of scholars and ministers of this church be continually maintained in the same, as they ought to be by the foundation and statutes thereof, and whether any have been admitted to any scholarship but such as have been destitute of all help of friends.

*Item*, Whether any of this church have taken any gifts in money or otherwise, for the preferment of any person to any petty canonship, scholarship, or any other office or room within the said church.

*Item*, Whether there be any incorrigible, troublesome makebates, or otherwise disobedient to the dean of this church, or other their superiors.

*Item*, Whether any be more absent from the church than by the ordinances and statutes of the same they may or ought to be.

*Item*, Whether the foundation of this church or statutes, or any portion of the same, be by any colourable ways or means wrested, or derogated, or made void and of no force.

*Item*, Where, when, and to whom the books of the Latin service were delivered, and how many, and whether any of them were sold, and by whom, or doth remain still in the hands and custody of any of this church.

*Item*, Whether any of the petty canons, vicars, and ministers of this church be a carder, dicer, rioter, fighter, brawler, swearer, or drunkard.

*Item*, Whether they do occupy themselves out of service-time and meals in some virtuous exercise and learning.

*Item*, Whether there be any strife, rancour, malice, or debate, between any of this church; and if any be, between whom it is, and for what cause.

*Item*, Whether any have committed adultery, fornication, or incest, or be vehemently suspected of the premises.

*Item*, Whether the prebendaries and other of this church, which are bound to be resident, do keep hospitality, and specially for the poor, and the ministers of this church.

*Item*, Whether they do come to the church so much as they ought to do.

*Item*, Whether the correction of faults by clerks, choristers, vergers, ringers, and other ministers, be made and done accordingly.

*Item*, What are the whole and yearly revenues of this church, and what portion of the same is assigned for the poor, and mending of highways, or other deeds of charity, and on whom it hath been bestowed.

*Item*, Whether lands, goods, moveables, or chattels, appertaining to this church, is sold or otherwise alienated; to whom, and for how much.

*Item*, What treasure they have in store to supply all necessaries and chances that may be incident unto this church.

*Item*, Whether the treasure of this church and jewels be well and diligently kept by just indented inventory.

*Item*, Whether this church, every prebendary's house, and other buildings within the said church, and the lands, tenements, and rectories belonging to the said church, be duly surveyed and kept in good reparation.

*Item*, Whether the common seal of this church is safely kept, according to the foundation or other ordinances of the same.

*Item*, Whether there is a perfect register kept of all leases, fees, and offices, granted or confirmed by the church.

*Item*, Whether every year once there is a perfect and full account made of all and singular the revenues and other profits, in anywise to this church belonging.

*Item*, Whether any within this church have been or is a hinderer of the word of God, either for reading or preaching of the same, or a notorious slanderer of the preachers thereof.

*Item*, Whether those of this church, which may dispend in benefices and other promotions ecclesiastical an hundred pounds, do give competent exhibition to one scholar at one of the universities of Cambridge or Oxford, and so for so many hundred pounds as he may dispend, do find so many scholars, and what be their names[1].

*Item*, Whether any use commonly to be absent from the sermons made within this church.

*Item*, Whether there be a library within this church, and in the same St Augustine's works, Basil, Gregory Nazianzene, Hierome, Ambrose, Chrysostome, Cyprian, Theophylact, Erasmus, and other good authors and works.

*Item*, Whether you have every day some part of holy scripture read in English at your table, at the time of your meals.

*Item*, Whether there be two bibles of the largest volume in English in some meet and convenient place in the body of this church.

*Item*, Whether there be any lecture of divinity within this said church.

*Item*, Whether ye know any other thing more than these worthy of reformation.

*Item*, Whether the dean, prebendaries, preachers, schoolmaster, usher, petty canons, and other ministers of this church, have taken a corporal oath to observe and keep all and singular the statutes of this church, so much as concerns them, or any of them.

*Item*, What was done with the images lately in this church, and whether any doth remain not defaced and utterly extincted, and in whose custody and keeping they be.

---

# INJUNCTIONS

TO THE

## DEAN AND CHAPTER OF CANTERBURY, 1550[2].

---

*Injunctions given by me Thomas, Archbishop of Canterbury, Primate of all England and Metropolitan, to the dean, prebendaries, preachers, and other ministers and officers of the metropolitan and cathedral church of Canterbury, the 29th day of October, in the fourth year of the reign of our sovereign lord Edward the VIth, by the grace of God king of England, France, and Ireland, defender of the faith, and in earth next under Christ of the Church of England, and also of Ireland, the supreme head.*

*First*, They and every of them shall inviolably observe, fulfil, and keep all and singular the king's majesty's Injunctions, devised as well for the said church as for other metropolitical and cathedral churches of this realm. C. C. C. C. MSS. cxx. p. 68. Copy.

*Item*, That they keep mine injunctions[3] given within my diocese of Canterbury and peculiars, inasmuch as they shall concern the clergy of the same, except such as can in no wise be executed within the said church.

*Item*, That the prebendaries and other ministers of the said church, shall sit in the chapter-house at the sermons made there, and no where else.

---

[[1] See the preceding Articles, No. 26, and Letter to Crumwell, 29 Nov. 1539. Jenkyns.]

[[2] See note 2, p. 159.]

[[3] "It is clear from hence, that besides Edw. VI.'s Injunctions Cranmer had issued some of his own. Articles of Inquiry at his Visitation, 1548, are printed by Sparrow and Wilkins, and will be found above, p. 154; but neither of these collectors makes any mention of his Injunctions." Jenkyns.]

*Item*, That every prebendary of the said church shall preach, or cause to be preached, two sermons at the least yearly in the parish churches appropriated to the said church, being within my said diocese of Canterbury.

*Item*, That every preacher of the said church, not being beneficed within my said diocese, and resident upon the same, shall be resident yearly in the said church by the space of six months at the least: and that always there be three of the said preachers within my said diocese of Canterbury.

*Item*[1], That no inhabiter within my said diocese of Canterbury shall be admitted to the communion within the said church, without the expressed consent of the parson, vicar, or curate, where he or she dwelleth, first obtained and had; except wayfaring persons, or necessity doth otherwise require.

*Item*, That hereafter there be no selling nor changing of prebendaries' houses, but that every one shall be contented with that house, which immediately before was his predecessor's.

*Item*, That the schoolmaster of the grammar-school do daily hear the scholars of the higher form to repeat their ordinary lessons. And the usher of the same to hear daily the scholars of the lower form to parse their ordinary lessons.

*Item*, That no women do accustomably lie within the precinct of the said church, but such as have their husbands with them, or that be servants.

*Item*, That all back doors into the city out of any prebendary's house or others shall be clearly shut up.

*Item*, That every petty canon and vicar of this church do personally receive the communion in his own course, except sickness or other necessity do let.

*Item*, That no sale be hereafter made of any goods belonging to the said church without the consent of the dean and chapter.

---

[[1] See third Article of Visitation above, p. 159.]

# ANSWERS

TO THE

# FIFTEEN ARTICLES OF THE REBELS, DEVON, ANNO 1549[2].

---

WHEN I first read your request, O ignorant men of Devonshire and Cornwall, straightways came to my mind a request, which James and John made unto Christ; to whom Christ answered: "You ask you wot not what." Even so thought I of you, as soon as ever I heard your articles, that you were deceived by some crafty papist[3], which devised those articles for you, to make you ask you wist not what. MSS. C. C. C. C. cii. p. 337. Strype, Mem. of Abp. Cranmer, App. No. 40. Vol. ii. pp. 799—839. Ed. Oxon. 1840. Todd, Life of Abp. Cranmer, Vol. ii. p. 76—139. Ed. Lond. 1831.

As for the devisers of your articles, if they understand them, I may not call them ignorant persons, but, as they be indeed, most rank papists, and wilful traitors and adversaries both to God and to our sovereign lord the king, and to the whole realm. But I cannot be persuaded so to think of you, that in your hearts willingly you be papists and traitors; but that those that be such have craftily seduced you, being simple and unlearned people, to ask you wot not what.

Wherefore my duty unto God, and the pity that I have of your ignorance, move me now at this time to open plainly and particularly your own articles unto you, that you may understand them, and no longer be deceived.

In your first article you require, that all the general councils and holy decrees of our forefathers may be observed and kept, and whosoever shall againsay them to be holden as heretics.

This you all ask; but what you ask, I dare say[4], very few or none of you understand. For how many of you, I pray you, do know certainly which be called the general councils[5] and holy decrees of the fathers, and what is in them contained? The holy decrees, as they call them, be nothing else but the laws and ordinances of the bishop of Rome: whereof the most part be made for his own advancement, glory, and lucre, and to make him and his clergy governors of the whole world, and to be exempted from all princes' laws, and to do what they list. And would you ask, if you knew what you asked, that we should put away the laws of our own realm, and be governed by the bishop of Rome's laws? If you mean this, then be you traitors to the king, and enemies

---

[2 "The commons this year brake out into a dangerous rebellion; and though they were once or twice appeased, and scattered in some places, yet they made insurrections in others: and chiefly in Devon, where they were very formidable for their numbers. The reason they pretended was double. The one was, the oppression of the gentry in inclosing of their commons from them: the other, the laying aside the old religion; which, because it was old, and the way their forefathers worshipped God, they were very fond of. The lord Russel, lord privy seal, who was sent against them, offering to receive their complaints, the rebels sent them to him, drawn up under fifteen articles: as before they had sent their demands in seven articles, and a protestation that they were the king's, body and goods. In answer to which the king sent a message to them, that may be seen in Foxe. They sent also a supplication to the king, to the which an answer was made by the king's learned council. To the fifteen articles the archbishop drew up an excellent answer at good length." The archbishop wrote this answer "after the rout at Exeter given them by the lord Russel, and the taking prisoners divers of their captains and priests, and between the condemnation and execution of Humphrey Arundel, and Bray, mayor of Bodmin." Strype's Mem. of Abp. Cranmer, Vol. I. pp. 264, 5. Ed. Oxon. 1840. The text follows that of Strype, but has been collated for this edition with the C. C. C. C. MS. of which the different readings are given in the notes. Vid. Foxe's Acts and Monuments, p. 1305 et seqq. Lond. 1583. Burnet's Hist. of Reformat. Vol. II. pp. 237—242. Oxon. 1829. Holinshed's Chronicles, Vol. III. p. 1002. In the C. C. C. C. MS. it is headed "Against the Articles of the Devonshire men."] Anno 1549.

[3 Papists, MS. C. C. C. C.]

[4 I dare boldly say, Ibid.]

[5 Vid. Speech on the Authority of the Pope and of General Councils, p. 76 et sqq.]

to your own realm: and if you mean it not, consider what persons they be, and how they have deceived you, that make you ask you wot not what.

And as for the general councils, you say you will have them all kept: but you be not so destitute of all reason, that you would have spoken such words, if you had known what you had said. For a great number of the councils repugn one against another. How should they then be all kept, when one is contrary to another, and the keeping of one is the breaking of another? And among your own articles you say, you will have divers things observed, which be not only contrary to the general councils, but also contrary to the law[1] of this realm, and also to God's laws[2], as it shall be plainly declared when we come to the articles.

And all reason is contrary that you should have asked such things, if you had known what you had asked. I have this opinion of the great number of you, that you would fain walk in the right way, if you could find it. And forasmuch as I perceive that wicked and false guides, under pretence to bring you to the high way, have brought you clean out of it, my good-will shall be, seeing you so far wandering out of the way, and so blindfolded with evil persuasions, that you cannot see where you go, to open your eyes that you may see, and to set you again into the right way. And when your eyes be so opened that you may see, and the right way shewed unto you, wherein you should walk; then if you will still wink, and not see, and run headlong in error, and not come to the right way, you may[3] no longer be called simple and ignorant people, but perverse, froward, and wicked papists and traitors, enemies to God and your own realm.

But now I will come to your articles particularly, opening every one of them by himself, that you may see the bowels thereof, and what is contained in the same; that when you shall understand the whole, you may judge whether you knew before what you asked, or you were deceived by subtle and wily papistical traitors.

YOUR FIRST ARTICLE IS THIS:

"*We will have all the general councils, and holy decrees of our forefathers, observed, kept, and performed: and whosoever shall againsay them, we hold them as heretics.*"

First, to begin with the manner of your phrase. Is this the fashion of subjects to speak unto their prince, "We will have?" Was this manner of speech at any time used of the subjects to their prince since the beginning of the world? Have not all true subjects ever used to their sovereign lord[4] this form of speaking, "Most humbly beseecheth your faithful and obedient subjects?" Although the papists have abused your ignorance in propounding such articles, which you understand not, yet you should not have suffered yourselves so much to be led by the nose and bridled by them, that you should clearly forget your duty of allegiance unto your sovereign lord, saying unto him, "This we will have;" and that saying with armour upon your backs and swords in your hands. Would any of you that be householders be content that your servants should come upon you with harness unto their backs[5], and swords in their hands, and say unto you, "This we will have?" If then you would abhor and detest this in your servants towards yourselves, how can you allow your fact? With what conscience can you, being but subjects, do to your king that thing which you would condemn in your servants towards yourselves? But answer me this: Be you subjects or no? If you be subjects, then I admonish you, as St Paul taught Titus, saying: "Warn them to be subject to princes and rulers, obeying them at a word." But tell me again: Pertaineth this to subjection and obedience to say, "This we will have?" St Peter saith: "Be subject unto kings, as unto chief heads[6], and to other rulers sent by them. For so is the will of God." God's will is, that you should be ruled by your princes. But whether is this to be ruled by your king, or to rule your king, to say, "Thus we will have the realm governed?" Your servants be by the scripture commanded, as they fear God, to be

[1 Laws of this realm, C. C. C. C. MS.]
[2 To God's law, Ibid.]
[3 Then you may, Ibid.]
[4 Sovereign lord and king, Ibid.]
[5 Be contented, that your servants should come unto you, with harness upon their backs, Ibid.]
[6 As chief heads, Ibid.]

obedient to their masters, whether their masters be good or evil. And can you think it meet and lawful[7] for you to disobey your undoubted king, being a prince most innocent, most godly, and most careful for your surety[8] and wealth? If any thing can declare disobedience, what can declare it more, than subjects to come with force of arms to their natural king and prince, and say, "This we will have?"

But now, leaving your rude and unhandsome manner[9] of speech to your most sovereign lord, I will come to the point, and join with you in the effect of your first article. You say, you will have all the holy decrees observed and kept. But do you know what they be? The holy decrees, as I told you before, be called the bishop of Rome's ordinances and laws: which how holy and godly soever they be called, they be indeed so wicked, so ungodly, so full of tyranny, and so partial, that since the beginning of the world were never devised or invented the like. I shall rehearse a certain of them, [whereby you may judge of the rest, to the intent][10] that yourselves may see how holy they be, and may say your minds, whether you would have them kept or no. And at the hearing of them, if you shall not think them meet to be kept here in this realm, then you may see how they deceived you, that moved you to ask this article. And if you like them, and would have them kept, after you know what they be, then I say assuredly, that you be not only wicked papists, but also heretics, and most heinous traitors to the king and this his realm. And yet how an absolute papist varieth from an heretic or traitor, I know not; but that a papist is also both a heretic and a traitor withal.

One decree saith, that "whosoever doth not acknowledge himself[11] to be under the obedience of the bishop of Rome, is an heretic[12]." Now answer me to this question, Whether be you under the obedience of the bishop of Rome, or not? If you say that you be under his obedience, then be you traitors by the laws of this realm; and if you deny it, then be you heretics by this decree. And shift is there none to save you from treason, but to renounce this decree, that commandeth you to be under the bishop of Rome; and so to confess, contrary to your own first article, that all decrees are not to be kept.

Yet a great many other decrees be as evil[13], and worse than this. One saith, that "all princes' laws which be against a decree[14] of the bishop of Rome, be void and of no strength[15]." Another decree saith, that "all the decrees of the bishop of Rome ought for ever to be kept of all men, as God's word[15]." Another decree there is, that "whosoever receiveth not the laws of the bishop of Rome, availeth neither[16] him the catholic faith, nor the four evangelists. For his sin[17] shall never be forgiven[15]." Yet is there a worse and more detestable decree, that "all kings and princes that suffer the bishop of Rome's decrees to be broken in any point, are to be taken as infidels[18]." Another is there also, "that the bishop of Rome is bound to no manner of decrees, but he may constrain all other persons, both spiritual and temporal, to receive all his decrees and canons[18]." Another is yet more devilish than any before rehearsed, that "although the bishop of Rome neither regard his own salvation, nor no man's else, but put down with himself headlong innumerable people by heaps unto hell, yet may no mortal man presume to reprove him therefore[18]." But what should I tarry, and make you weary in rehearsing a number[19]? For a thousand other like canons and decrees there be to the advancement of the bishop of Rome his usurped power and authority.

I cannot think of you, that you be so far from all godliness, from all wit and discretion, that you would have these decrees observed within this realm, which be so blasphemous to God, so injurious to all princes and realms, and so far from all equity and reason. But here you may easily perceive, what wily foxes you met withal, which persuaded you to arm yourselves, to make sedition in your own country, to stand against

---

[7 Meet or lawful, Ibid.]
[8 So MS. C. C. C. C. Strype reads "sorrow."]
[9 Unseemly manner, MS. C. C. C. C.]
[10 This clause is inserted from the C. C. C. C. MS.]
[11 Doth not knowledge himself, Ibid.]
[12 Vid. Collection of Tenets from the Canon Law, p. 68.]
[13 Be as ill, MS. C. C. C. C.]
[14 Any decree, Ibid.]
[15 Vid. p. 68.]
[16 Neither availeth, MS. C. C. C. C.]
[17 For his sins, Ibid.]
[18 Vid. Collection of Tenets from the Canon Law, pp. 69, 70, &c. and Letter to Queen Mary, Sept. 1555.]
[19 In rehearsing a number of laws, MS. C. C. C. C.]

your princes and the laws of your realm, for such articles as you understand not[1], and to ask you wist not what. For I dare say for you, that the subtle papists, when they moved you to stand in this article, "that all the holy decrees should be observed," they shewed you nothing of these decrees, that they were taken for holy decrees: for if they had, they knew right well that you would never have consented unto this article; but would have taken them for traitors, that first moved you thereto.

For now shall I shew you, what miserable case you should bring yourselves unto, if the king's majesty should assent unto this first article[2], "that all the decrees should be kept and observed." For among other partial decrees made in the favour of the clergy, this is one: "That none of the clergy shall be called, or sued before any temporal judge, for any manner of cause, either for debt, suit of lands, felony, murder, or for any other cause or crime; nor shall have any other judge, but his bishop only[3]." Another is: "That a spiritual man may sue a temporal man before a temporal or spiritual judge[4] at his pleasure; but a temporal man cannot sue a spiritual, but only before his ordinary[3]." I cannot deny, but these been good[5] and beneficial laws for the liberty of the clergy. But for your own part[6], I suppose you do not think it any indifferent law[7], that a priest shall sue you where he list, with the licence of his ordinary; and you shall sue him for no manner of cause, but only before his own ordinary[8]; or if a priest had slain one of your sons or brethren, that you should have no remedy against him, but only before the bishop[8]. What mean those[9] papistical priests, that stirred you to ask and will such decrees and laws to be observed in this realm, but covertly and craftily to bring you under their subjection; and that you yourselves, ignorantly asking you wist not what, should put your own heads under their girdles?

For surely, if you had known these decrees, when you consented to this article, you would have torn the article in pieces, and they that moved you[10] thereto also. For these decrees be not only partial, and against all equity and reason, made only for the favour of the clergy, and the suppression of the laity; but also they be, and ever have been, clearly contrary to the laws and customs of this realm. And yet by this article you will have the old ancient laws and customs of this realm (which have ever been used in all kings' times hitherto) to be void and to cease, and these decrees to come in their place, and be observed of all men, and againsaid of no man: for whosoever speaketh against them, you will hold them for heretics. And in so saying, look what sentence to give[11] of yourselves. Although your article say it, yet I am sure you be not so much enemies to your own realm, that you would have the old ancient laws and customs of this realm (for the defence whereof all the noble kings of this realm have so valiantly and so justly stand against the bishops of Rome) now to be taken away, and give place unto Romish decrees. And then by your own article you hold and condemn yourselves to be heretics.

How be you bewitched by these false papists? Why do you suffer them thus to abuse you by their subtlety, to make you condemn yourselves of heresy? Why do you not send them unto the king's majesty, like errant traitors, as indeed they be, saying unto him, "Most mighty prince, and most dread sovereign lord, we present here unto you most heinous traitors against your majesty and realm, and greatest dissemblers and false deceivers of us, your simple and ignorant people, and yet in our own hearts[12] your true and faithful subjects. We have erred, we have grievously offended your majesty, but by ignorance, being so seduced and provoked by the crafty persuasions of these most heinous traitors, that we wist not what we did. But pardon us, sovereign lord, have pity upon our simplicity and ignorance; and these abominable traitors punish according to their deservings. Have mercy, most merciful prince, of us, your poor flock, which were ignorantly led out of the way; and strike with the sword those malicious guides, that purposely would have led us to our utter destruction."

---

[[1] Understood not, C. C. C. C. MS.]
[[2] Would assent unto this your first article, Ibid.]
[[3] Vid. Collection of Tenets from the Canon Law, p. 72.]
[[4] A spiritual or temporal judge, MS. C. C. C. C.]
[[5] But these be good, Ibid.]
[[6] But for your own parts, Ibid.]
[[7] An indifferent law, Ibid.]
[[8] The bishops, Ibid.]
[[9] What meant then those, Ibid.]
[[10] And them that moved you, Ibid.]
[[11] You give, Ibid.]
[[12] Yet in our hearts, Ibid.]

If you did thus, then would you do[13] the parts of true, faithful, and loyal subjects[14], and should declare to the world, that all that you have hitherto done was done by error and ignorance. And I would nothing doubt of the king's majesty his clemency and mercy towards you.

But yet, to the intent that you may further know how unreasonable your first article is, I will yet rehearse another sort of the holy laws and decrees. One is: "That no layman may have a benefice to farm[15]." Another is: "That none of the clergy may give any thing to the relief of the commonweal and necessity of their own realm, without the consent of the bishop of Rome[15]." Another is: "That no layman may meddle with election or any other thing, that pertaineth unto any of the clergy[16]." Another is: "That none of the clergy ought to give any oath of fidelity to their princes, except they have temporal lands of them[17]." Another is: "That princes ought to obey the bishops and the decrees of the church, and to submit their heads unto their bishops, and not to be judges over the bishops[18]." Another is this: "Whosoever offendeth the liberties of the church, or doth break any interdiction that cometh from Rome, or conspireth against the person or estate of the bishop or see of Rome, or by any ways offendeth, disobeyeth, or rebelleth against the same bishop or see, or that killeth a priest, or offendeth personally against a bishop or other prelate, or invadeth, spoileth, withholdeth, or wasteth lands belonging to the church of Rome, or to any other church immediately subject unto Rome; or whosoever invadeth any pilgrims that go to Rome, or any suitors to the court of Rome, or that let the devolution of causes unto that court, or that put any new charges or impositions, real or personal, upon a church[19] or ecclesiastical person; and generally, all others that offend[20] in the cases contained in the bull, which is usually published by the bishops of Rome upon Maundy Thursday; all these can be assoiled by no priest, bishop, archbishop, nor by none other, but only by the bishop of Rome, or by his express licence[21]." These, with an infinite number of like sort, be the *godly* and *holy* decrees which you long so sore for, and so much desire.

Now would I know, whether you think that these decrees were made for the common wealth of all realms, or only for the private weal of the bishop of Rome, and of his bishops and clergy; and whether you like and long for these laws; or now, at the hearing of them, your longing is done? If you like them, well: for my part I would you had them practised among you for a while, (so that the rest of the realm were not troubled, neither with you nor with your decrees,) until you repented yourselves of your foolish demands. I think within a year you would kneel on your knees to the king's majesty, desiring him to take from your necks the yokes and altars which you had made for yourselves.

But to conclude the sum of the first article[22] in few words: it is nothing else but a clear subversion of the whole state and laws of this realm; and to make this realm to be wholly governed by Romish laws, and to crown the idol and antichrist of Rome king of this realm, and to make our most undoubted and natural king his vile subject and slave. Oh! what was in your minds to ask such a thing, and so presumptuously to say, that you *will* have it? I trust there be not in you so much malice and devilishness, as the article containeth, but that you were craftily subornate by subtle papists to ask and demand you wist not what.

If you had asked, that the word of God might be duly observed and kept every where within this realm, and whosoever would gainsay[23] God's word, to be holden as a heretic; if you had[24] declared yourselves to be godly men; all that be godly[25] would have commended and furthered your request. But forasmuch as you ask Romish canons and decrees to be observed and kept here in England, and whosoever shall againsay them, to be holden as heretics, there is neither godly nor truly English man, that will allow you, or consent to your articles. But clean contrary to your articles, a great number of godly

---

[13 Should you do, Ibid.]
[14 Loving subjects, Ibid.]
[15 Vid. Collection of Tenets from the Canon Law, p. 72.]
[16 Ibid.]
[17 Ibid. p. 73.]
[18 Ibid.]
[19 Upon any church, MS. C. C. C. C.]
[20 All other that offend, Ibid.]
[21 Vid. Collection of Tenets, &c. p. 74.]
[22 Of your first article, MS. C. C. C. C.]
[23 Againsay, Ibid.]
[24 Heretic; you had &c., Ibid.]
[25 And all that be godly, Ibid.]

persons within this realm, for the very love that they have to God, that his name may be glorified above all things, be daily humble suitors to the king's majesty, that he, following the steps of his father, will study and travail to weed out of this his realm all popish decrees, laws, and canons, and whatsoever else is contrary to God's word; and that the speakers against God's word may be taken (as they be indeed) for heretics. And is any of you so far from reason, that he thinketh the king's majesty ought to hearken to you, that by force and stubbornness[1] say, you will have Romish laws and decrees kept in this realm, and to turn his ears from them that with all humility be suitors for God's word?

But now will I come to your other articles, wherein I will be brief, forasmuch as in the first I have been long and tedious.

### YOUR SECOND ARTICLE IS THIS:

"*We will have the law of our sovereign lord king Henry VIII.*[2] *concerning the Six Articles*[3] *to be used again, as in his time they were.*"

Letting pass your rude style, nothing becoming subjects to say, "You will have:" First, I examine you of the cause of your wilful will, wherefore you will have these six articles; which never were laws in no region but this; nor in this realm also, until the 31st year of king Henry VIII[2]; and in some things[4] so enforced by the evil counsel of certain papists, against the truth, and common judgment both of divines and lawyers, that if the king's majesty himself had not come personally into the parliament house, those laws had never passed. And yet within a year or little more the same most noble prince was fain to temper his said laws[5], and moderate them in divers points: so that the statute of Six Articles continued in his force little above the space of one year. Is this then so great a matter to make these uproars, and to arise against the whole realm? Will you take away the present laws of this realm, (which be and ever have been the laws of all other countries also,) and set up new laws, which never were but in this realm only, and were here in force not fully thirteen months? And how chanceth it, that you be so earnest in this article, which is directly contrary to your first article, but you know not[6] what neither of the articles meaneth, but be persuaded by perverse papists to ask you wot not what? But now here is the repugnance of the two articles[7]: by your first you will have all general councils and decrees observed and kept; and by your second article you will have the Six Articles used again. Then let us compare the general councils and decrees with the Six Articles; and you shall see them agree as well together as black and white.

First, it is contained in the canons of the apostles[8], that a priest under no pretence of holiness may put away his wife; and, if he do, he shall be excommunicated: and the

---

[[1] Force and stoutness, C. C. C. C. MS.]

[[2] Henry VIII. the most noble prince of famous memory, Ibid.]

[[3] The following are the six articles, which were "resolved by the convocation the old popish way," and enacted by the parliament, under the title, "An act for abolishing diversities of opinions." Cranmer and other divines argued boldly against them, but unsuccessfully.

First.—That in the sacrament of the altar, after the consecration, there remain no substance of bread and wine, but under these forms the natural body and blood of Christ were present.

Secondly.—That communion in both kinds was not necessary to salvation to all persons by the law of God; but that both the flesh and blood of Christ were together in each of the kinds.

Thirdly.—That priests, after the order of priesthood, might not marry by the law of God.

Fourthly.—That vows of chastity ought to be observed by the law of God.

Fifthly.—That the use of private masses ought to be continued; which as it was agreeable to God's law, so men received great benefit by them.

Sixthly.—That auricular confession was expedient and necessary, and ought to be retained in the church. Vid. Burnet's Hist. of Reformat. Vol. I. pp. 518, 19. Ed. Oxon. 1829. Collier's Eccl. Hist. Vol. V. p. 38. Ed. Lond. 1840, 1. Strype's Eccl. Mem. Vol. I. Part I. pp. 542, 3. Ed. Oxon. 1822.]

[[4] And then in some things, MS. C. C. C. C.]

[[5] The said laws, Ibid.]

[[6] But that you know not, Ibid.]

[[7] But now hear the repugnance of your two articles, Ibid.]

[[8] Ἐπίσκοπος, ἢ πρεσβύτερος, ἢ διάκονος, τὴν αὐτοῦ γυναῖκα μὴ ἐκβαλλέτω προφάσει εὐλαβείας· ἐὰν δὲ ἐκβάλλῃ, ἀφοριζέσθω. Canon. Apostol. can. vi. Labb. et Cossart. Tom. I. col. 26. Ed. Lutet. Paris. 1671.]

Six Articles say, that if a priest put not away his wife, he shall be taken for a felon. If he keep her not still, he must be excommunicate by the canon of the apostles: and if he keep her still, he must suffer death by the Six Articles. You be cunning men, if you can set these two together. Also the council of Nice, which was the chief of all the general councils, and was celebrated more than twelve hundred years past, decreed clean directly contrary to the Six Articles. For where the Six Articles command all priests to be separate from their wives, Nicene council determined clean contrary, that they should not be separated, confessing such copulation to be holy and godly[9]. And the council Gangrense, which was about the same time, so much allowed the marriage of priests, that they accursed them[10] that would abstain from the ministration[11] of priests, because they were married[12]. These councils vary so far from the Six Articles, that either you must put the general councils out of your book, or else the Six Articles.

Likewise concerning private masses, the law of Six Articles far differeth from the canon of the apostles, and from the councils Nicene and Antioch, as shall be declared in the next article.

Other things there be divers also in the Six Articles, which cannot stand with sundry old canons, decrees, and councils: so that if you will stand to the canons, decrees, and councils, you must of force be constrained utterly to put out of your book your second article, which requireth the usage of the Six Articles. But now for shortness of time I will come to your third article, which is this:

## THE THIRD ARTICLE.

"*We will have the mass in Latin, as was before, and celebrated by the priest, without any man or woman communicating with him.*"

Forasmuch as there is nothing with you but "will," let your will be conferred with reason and God's word; and then you shall see how far your will differeth from them both. First, as touching the Latin masses, whatsoever the priest saith in the old masses, whether he pray and ask any thing of God, or give thanks to God, or make the true profession of the faith, or whatsoever he doth besides[13], all he doth in your persons and in your names; and you answer unto that which he saith, sometime *Amen*, sometime *Et cum spiritu tuo*, and sometime other things, as the matter serveth. For all the whole that is done should be the act of the people[14] and pertain to the people, as well as to the priest. And standeth it with reason, that the priest should speak for you, and in your name, and you answer him again in your own person; and yet you understand never a word, neither what he saith, nor what you say yourselves? The priest prayeth to God for you, and you answer *Amen*, you wot not whereto. Is there any reason herein? Will you not understand what the priest prayeth for you, what thanks he giveth for you, what he asketh for you? Will you neither understand what he saith, nor let your hearts understand what your own tongues answer? Then must you needs confess yourselves to be such people as Christ spake of, when he said, "These people honour me with their lips, but their hearts be far from me." Had you rather be like pies or parrots, that be taught to speak, and yet understand not one word what they say, than be true christian men, that pray unto God in heart and in faith? The priest is your proctor and attorney,

---

[9 Ἐν δὲ τῷ περὶ τούτου βουλεύεσθαι, τοῖς μὲν ἄλλοις ἐδόκει νόμους ἐπεισάγειν, ἐπισκόπους καὶ πρεσβυτέρους, διακόνους τε καὶ ὑποδιακόνους μὴ συγκαθεύδειν ταῖς γαμεταῖς, ἃς πρὶν ἱερᾶσθαι ἠγάγοντο. ἀναστὰς δὲ Παφνούτιος ὁ ὁμολογητὴς ἀντεῖπε· τίμιον δὲ τὸν γάμον ἀποκαλῶν, σωφροσύνην δὲ τὴν πρὸς τὰς ἰδίας γυναῖκας συνουσίαν, συνεβούλευσε τῇ συνόδῳ μὴ τοιοῦτον θέσθαι νόμον· χαλεπὸν γὰρ εἶναι τὸ πρᾶγμα φέρειν· ἴσως δὲ καὶ αὐτοῖς καὶ ταῖς τούτων γαμεταῖς τοῦ μὴ σωφρονεῖν αἰτία γενήσεται......ἐπήνεσε δὲ καὶ ἡ σύνοδος τὴν βουλὴν, καὶ περὶ τούτου οὐδὲν ἐνομοθέτησεν. Sozomen. Eccl. Hist. Lib. I. cap. xxiii. Vid. Todd's Life of Abp. Cranmer, Vol. I. p. 267, Ed. Lond. 1831.]

[10 Accursed all them, MS. C. C. C. C.]

[11 From the administration, Ibid.]

[12 α΄. Εἴ τις τὸν γάμον μέμφοιτο, καὶ τὴν καθεύδουσαν μετὰ τοῦ ἀνδρὸς αὐτῆς, οὖσαν πιστὴν καὶ εὐλαβῆ, βδελύσσοιτο ἢ μέμφοιτο, ὡς ἂν μὴ δυναμένην εἰς βασιλείαν εἰσελθεῖν, ἀνάθεμα ἔστω. Concil. Gangren. circa A.D. 324. Labb. et Cossart. Tom. II. col. 415.]

[13 He doth beside, MS. C. C. C. C.]

[14 Action of the people, Ibid.]

to plead your cause, and to speak for you all; and had you rather not know than know what he saith for you? I have heard suitors murmur at the bar, because their attornies have pleaded their cases in the French tongue, which they understood not. Why then be you offended, that the priests, which plead[1] your cause before God, should speak such language as you may understand? If you were before the king's highness, and should choose one to speak for you all, I am sure you would not choose one that should speak Greek or Hebrew, French or Italian; no, nor one that should speak Latin neither. But you would be glad to provide such one as should speak your own language, and speak so loud, that you might both hear him, and understand him; that you might allow or disallow that that he said in your names. Why do you then refuse to do the like unto God? When the priest desireth any thing of God[2] for you, or giveth thanks for you, how can you in your heart confirm his sayings, when you know not one word what he saith? For the heart is not moved with words that be not understand.

But if reason will not persuade you, I will prove what God's word will do unto you. St Paul, in the first epistle to the Corinthians[3], saith, that whosoever shall speak to the people in the church to their edification, must speak such language as the people may understand; or else he willeth him to hold his peace, and speak softly to himself and to God. For he which speaketh[4] a strange language which the people understand not, doth not edify them, as St Paul saith. And he giveth an example of the trumpet in the field, which when it giveth such a sound that the soldier understandeth, it availeth much[5]: for every soldier thereby knoweth what to do. But if such a blast be blown as no man understandeth, then the blast is utterly in vain: for no man knoweth thereby, whether the horsemen shall make them ready, or leap upon horseback, or go to their standard; or whether the footmen shall make them ready, or set themselves in array, or set upon the enemy, or retire to the standard. Even so should the priests be God's trump in his church: so that if he blow such a certain blast that the people may understand, they be much edified thereby; but if he give such a sound as is to the people unknown, it is clearly in vain, saith St Paul: for he speaks to the air[6]; but no man is the better or edified thereby, nor knoweth what he should do by that he heareth. Furthermore, in the same place St Paul saith, that if a man giveth thanks to God in a language to the people unknown, how can they say *Amen* to that they understand not? He doth well in giving thanks to God; but that nothing availeth or edifieth the people, that know not what he saith. And St Paul in one brief sentence concludeth his whole disputation of that matter, saying: "I had rather have five words spoken in the church to the instruction and edifying of the people, than ten thousand in a language unknown, that edifieth not." And for this purpose allegeth[7] the prophet Esay, who saith, that "God will speak to his people in other tongues, and in other languages;" meaning thereby, that he would speak to every country in their own language. So have the Greeks the mass in the Greek tongue, the Syrians in the Syry tongue, the Armenians in their tongue, and the Indians in their own tongue. And be you so much addict to the Romish tongue, (which is the Latin tongue,) that you will have your mass in none other language but the Romish language? Christ himself used among the Jews the Jews' language, and willed his apostles to do the like in every country wheresoever they came. And be you such enemies to your own country, that you will not suffer us to laud God, to thank him, and to use his sacraments in our own tongue; but will enforce us contrary[8], as well to all reason, as to the word of God?

So many as be godly[9], or have reason, will be satisfied with this. But the mere papist will be satisfied with nothing. Wherefore I will no longer tarry to satisfy them that never will be satisfied, but will proceed to the second part of this article, wherein you say that you will have neither men nor women[10] communicate with the priest. Alas, good simple souls! how be you blinded with the papists! How contrary be your articles

[1 Which pleadeth, C. C. C. C. MS.]
[2 Desireth of God any thing, Ibid.]
[3 To the Corinthes, Ibid.]
[4 For he that speaketh, Ibid.]
[5 That the soldiers understand, then it availeth much, Ibid.]
[6 For he speaketh to the air, Ibid.]
[7 This purpose S. Paul allegeth, Ibid.]
[8 Will enforce things contrary, Ibid.]
[9 As either be godly, Ibid.]
[10 Man nor woman, Ibid.]

one to another! You say in your first article, that you will have all general councils and decrees observed, and now you go from them yourselves. You say, you will have nobody to communicate with the priest. Hear then, what divers canons, decrees, and general councils say clean against you. There is one decree which saith thus: "When the consecration is done, let all the people receive the communion, except they will be put out of the church[11]." And in the canons of the apostles, in the eighth chapter, is contained, "That whensoever there is any mass or communion, if any bishop, priest, deacon, or any other of the clergy, being there present, do not communicate, except he can shew some reasonable cause to the contrary, he shall be put out of the communion, as one that giveth occasion to the people to think evil of the ministers[12]." And in the ninth chapter of the same canons of the apostles, and in the general council held at Antioch, is thus written: "That all christian people that come into the church, and hear the holy scriptures read, and after will not tarry to pray, and to receive the holy communion with the rest of the people, but for some misordering of themselves will abstain therefrom, let them be put out of the church, until by humble knowledging of their fault, and by the fruits of penance, and prayers, they obtain pardon and forgiveness[13]." And the council Nicene also sheweth the order, how men should sit in receiving the communion, and who should receive first[14]. All these decrees and general councils utterly condemn your third article, wherein you will, that the priest shall receive the communion alone, without any man or woman communicating with him. And the whole church of Christ also, both Greeks and Latins, many hundred years after Christ and the apostles[15], do also condemn this your article; which ever received the communion in flocks and numbers together, and not the priest alone.

And besides this[16], the very words of the mass (as it is called) shew plainly, that it was ordained not only for the priest, but for other also to communicate with the priest. For in the very canon, which they so much extol, and which is so holy that no man may know what it is, (and therefore is read so softly that no man can hear it,) in that same canon, I say, is a prayer containing this; that "not only the priest, but also as many beside as communicate with him, may be fulfilled with grace and heavenly benediction[17]." How agreeth this prayer with your article, wherein you say, that neither man nor woman shall communicate with the priest? In another place also of the said canon, the priest prayeth for himself, and "for all that receive the

---

[11 Peracta consecratione omnes communicent, qui noluerint ecclesiasticis carere liminibus. Sic enim et apostoli statuerunt, et sancta Romana tenet ecclesia. Corpus Juris Canon. Ed. Paris. 1687. Decreti Pars III. De Consecrat. Dist. II. can. x. Tom. I. p. 453.]

[12 ή. Εἴτις ἐπίσκοπος, ἢ πρεσβύτερος, ἢ διάκονος, ἢ ἐκ τοῦ καταλόγου ἱερατικοῦ, προσφορᾶς γενομένης μὴ μεταλάβοι, τὴν αἰτίαν εἰπάτω· καὶ ἐὰν ᾖ εὔλογος, συγγνώμης τυγχανέτω. εἰ δὲ μὴ λέγει, ἀφοριζέσθω, ὡς αἴτιος βλάβης γενόμενος τῷ λαῷ, καὶ ὑπόνοιαν ποιήσας κατὰ τοῦ προσενέγκαντος. Canon. Apostol. can. viii. Labb. et Cossart. Tom. I. col. 26—28.]

[13 θ'. Πάντας τοὺς εἰσιόντας πιστοὺς, καὶ τῶν γραφῶν ἀκούοντας, μὴ παραμένοντας δὲ τῇ προσευχῇ καὶ τῇ ἁγίᾳ μεταλήψει, ὡς ἀταξίαν ἐμποιοῦντας τῇ ἐκκλησίᾳ, ἀφορίζεσθαι χρή. Ibid. can. ix. col. 29. Πάντας τοὺς εἰσιόντας εἰς τὴν ἐκκλησίαν τοῦ Θεοῦ, καὶ τῶν ἱερῶν γραφῶν ἀκούοντας, μὴ κοινωνοῦντας δὲ εὐχῆς ἅμα τῷ λαῷ, ἢ ἀποστρεφομένους τὴν μετάληψιν τῆς εὐχαριστίας κατά τινα ἀταξίαν, τούτους ἀποβλήτους γίνεσθαι τῆς ἐκκλησίας, ἕως ἂν ἐξομολογησάμενοι καὶ δείξαντες καρποὺς μετανοίας, καὶ παρακαλέσαντες, τυχεῖν δυνηθῶσι συγγνώμης. Concil. Antioch. I. A. D. 340. can. ii. Ibid. Tom. II. col. 561.]

[14 ιή. Ἦλθεν εἰς τὴν ἁγίαν καὶ μεγάλην σύνοδον, ὅτι ἔν τισι τόποις καὶ πόλεσι τοῖς πρεσβυτέροις τὴν εὐχαριστίαν οἱ διάκονοι διδόασιν· ὅπερ οὔτε ὁ κανὼν οὔτε ἡ συνηθεία παρέδωκε, τοὺς ἐξουσίαν μὴ ἔχοντας προσφέρειν τοῖς προσφέρουσι διδόναι τὸ σῶμα τοῦ Χριστοῦ. κἀκεῖνο δὲ ἐγνωρίσθη, ὅτι ἤδη τινὲς τῶν διακόνων καὶ πρὸ τῶν ἐπισκόπων τῆς εὐχαριστίας ἅπτονται. ταῦτα μὲν οὖν ἅπαντα περιῃρήσθω· καὶ ἐμμενέτωσαν οἱ διάκονοι τοῖς ἰδίοις μέτροις, εἰδότες ὅτι τοῦ μὲν ἐπισκόπου ὑπηρέται εἰσι, τῶν δὲ πρεσβυτέρων ἐλάττους τυγχάνουσι· λαμβανέτωσαν δὲ κατὰ τὴν τάξιν τὴν εὐχαριστίαν μετὰ τοὺς πρεσβυτέρους, ἢ τοῦ ἐπισκόπου διδόντος αὐτοῖς ἢ τοῦ πρεσβυτέρου. ἀλλὰ μηδὲ καθῆσθαι ἐν μέσῳ τῶν πρεσβυτέρων ἐξέστω τοῖς διακόνοις· παρὰ κανόνα γὰρ καὶ παρὰ τάξιν ἔστι τὸ γινόμενον. εἰ δέ τις μὴ θέλοι πειθαρχεῖν καὶ μετὰ τούτους τοὺς ὅρους, πεπαύσθω τῆς διακονίας. Concil. Nicæn. can. xviii. Ibid. Tom. II. col. 37.]

[15 His apostles, MS. C. C. C. C.]

[16 Beside this, Ibid.]

[17 Supplices te rogamus, omnipotens Deus: jube hæc perferri per manus sancti angeli tui in sublime altare tuum, in conspectu divinæ majestatis tuæ: ut quotquot ex hac altaris participatione sacrosanctum Filii tui corpus et sanguinem sumpserimus, omni benedictione cœlesti et gratia repleamur, per eundem Christum Dominum nostrum. Amen. Canon Missæ, Missale Sarisbur. fol. cxxxii. Ed. 1533. Missale Rom. p. 238. Ed. Mechlin. 1840.]

communion with him, that it may be a preparation for them unto everlasting life[1]." Which prayer were but a very fond prayer, and a very mocking with God, if nobody should communicate with the priest. And the communion concludes with two prayers made in the name of the priest and them that communicate with him, wherein they pray thus: "O Lord, that thing which we have taken in our mouth, let us take it also with pure minds[2], that this communion may purge us from our sins, and make us partakers of heavenly remedy[3]." And beside all this, there be an infinite sort of post-communions in the mass-books; which all do evidently shew, that in the masses the people did communicate with the priest.

And although I would exhort every good christian man often to receive the holy communion, yet I do not recite all these things to the intent, that I would in this corrupt world, when men live so ungodly as they do, that the old canons should be restored again, which command[4] every man present to receive the communion with the priest: which canons, if they were now used, I fear that many would receive it unworthily. But I speak them to condemn your article, which would have nobody, neither man nor woman, to be communicated with the priest: which your article condemneth the old decrees, canons, and general councils, condemneth all the old primitive church, all the old ancient holy doctors and martyrs, and all the forms and manner of masses that ever were made, both new and old. Therefore eat again this article, if you will not be condemned of the whole world, and of yourselves also by your first article; wherein you will all decrees and general councils to be observed. But forasmuch as I have been so tedious[5] in this article, I will endeavour myself to be shorter in the next.

YOUR FOURTH ARTICLE IS THIS:

"*We will have the sacrament hang over the high altar, and there to be worshipped, as it was wont to be; and they which will not thereto consent, we will have them die like heretics against the holy catholic faith.*"

What say you, O ignorant people in things pertaining to God? Is this the holy catholic faith, that the sacrament should be hanged over the altar and worshipped? and be they heretics that will not consent thereto? I pray you, who made this faith? Any other but the bishops of Rome? and that more than a thousand years after the faith of Christ[6] was full and perfect! Innocent III. about 1215 years after Christ, did ordain that the sacrament and chrism should be kept under lock and key[7]. But yet no motion[8] is made of hanging the sacrament over the high altar, nor of the worshipping of it. After him came Honorius III. and he added further, commanding that the sacrament should be devoutly kept in a clean place, and sealed, and that the priest[9] should often teach the people reverendly[10] to bow down to the host, when it was lifted up in the mass time, and when the priest should carry it to the sick folks[11]. And

---

[[1] Hæc sacrosancta commixtio corporis et sanguinis Domini nostri Jesu Christi fiat mihi omnibusque sumentibus salus mentis et corporis, et ad vitam æternam promerendam et capescendam præparatio salutaris, per eundem ipsum Dominum nostrum. Amen. Missale Sarisbur. fol. cxxxiv.]

[[2] With pure mind, MS. C. C. C. C.]

[[3] Quod ore sumpsimus, Domine, pura mente capiamus: et de munere temporali fiat nobis remedium sempiternum. Missale Sarisbur. fol. cxxxiii. 2. Missale Rom. p. 244.]

[[4] Which commanded, MS. C. C. C. C.]

[[5] I have been too tedious, Ibid.]

[[6] After Christ's faith, Ibid.]

[[7] Statuimus, et in cunctis ecclesiis chrisma et eucharistia sub fideli custodia clavibus adhibitis conserventur; ne possit ad illa temeraria manus extendi, ad aliqua horribilia vel nefaria exercenda. Corpus Juris Canon. Ed. Paris. 1687. Decretal. Gregor. IX. Lib. III. Tit. xliv. cap. i. Tom. II. p. 196.]

[[8] No mention, MS. C. C. C. C.]

[[9] That the priests, Ibid.]

[[10] Reverently, Ibid.]

[[11] Ne propter incuriam sacerdotum divina indignatio gravius exardescat, districte præcipiendo mandamus, quatenus a sacerdotibus eucharistia in loco singulari mundo et signato semper honorifice collocata, devote ac fideliter conservetur. Sacerdos vero frequenter doceat plebem suam, ut cum in celebratione missarum elevatur hostia salutaris, se reverenter inclinet, idem faciens cum eam defert presbyter ad infirmum. Corpus Juris Canon. Decretal. Gregor. IX. Lib. III. Tit. xli. cap. x. Tom. II. p. 193.]

although this Honorius[12] added the worshipping of the sacrament, yet he made no mention of the hanging thereof over the high altar, as your article proporteth[13]. Nor how long after, or by what means, that came first up into this realm, I think no man can tell. And in Italy it is not yet used until this day. And in the beginning of the church it was not only not used to be hanged up, but also it was utterly forbid to be kept.

And will you have all them that will not consent to your article, to die like heretics that hold against the catholic faith? Were the apostles and evangelists heretics? Were the martyrs and confessors heretics? Were all the old doctors of the church heretics? Were all christian people heretics, until within three or four hundred years last past, that the bishops of Rome taught them what they should do and believe? All they before rehearsed neither hanged the sacrament over the altar, neither worshipped it, nor not one of them all spake any one word, either of the hanging up, or worshipping of the sacrament. Marry, they speak very much of the worshipping of Christ himself, sitting in heaven at the right hand of his Father. And no man doth duly receive the sacrament, except he so, after that manner, do worship Christ, whom he spiritually receiveth, spiritually feedeth and nourisheth upon, and by whom spiritually he liveth, and continueth that life that is towards God. And this the sacrament teacheth us.

Now to knit up this article shortly. Here is the issue of this matter: that you must either condemn of heresy the apostles, martyrs, confessors, doctors, and all the holy church of Christ, until the time of Innocentius and Honorius, because they hanged not the sacrament over the altar to be worshipped; or else you must be condemned yourselves by your own article, to die like heretics against the holy catholic faith. Now to your fifth article.

### YOUR FIFTH ARTICLE IS THIS:

"*We will have the sacrament of the altar but at Easter delivered to the lay-people; and then but in one kind.*"

Methinks you be like a man that were brought up in a dark dungeon, that never saw light, nor knew nothing that is abroad in the world. And if a friend of his, pitying his ignorance and state, would bring him out of his dungeon, that he might see the light and come to knowledge, he, being from his youth used to darkness, could not abide the light, but would wilfully shut his eyes, and be offended both with the light, and with his friend also. A most godly prince of famous memory, king Henry VIII. our late sovereign lord, pitying to see his subjects many years so brought up in darkness and ignorance of God by the erroneous doctrine and superstitions[14] of the bishop of Rome, with the counsel of all his nobles and learned men, studied by all means, and that to his no little danger and charges, to bring you out of your said ignorance and darkness unto the true light and knowledge of God's word. And our most dread sovereign lord that now is, succeeding his father, as well in this godly intent, as in his realms and dominions, hath with no less care and diligence studied to perform his father's godly intent and purpose. And you, like men that wilfully shut[15] their own eyes, refuse to receive the light, saying you will remain[16] in your darkness. Or rather you be like men that be so far wandered out of the right way, that they can never come to it again without good and expert guides: and yet when the guides would tell them the truth, they would not be ordered by them, but would say unto them, We will have and follow our own ways.

And that you may understand how far you be wandered from the right way in this one article, wherein you will have the sacrament of the altar delivered to the lay-people but once in the year, and then but under one kind; be you assured, that

---

[[12] This Innocentius, MS. C. C. C. C. Strype has here corrected the C. C. C. C. MS.]

[[13] Your article purporteth, Ibid.]

[[14] Doctrines and traditions, Ibid.]

[[15] That wilfully shutteth, Ibid.]

[[16] Saying that you will still remain, Ibid.]

there was never such law nor such request made among christian people until this day. What injury do you to many godly persons, which would devoutly receive it many times, and you command the priest to deliver it them but at Easter! All learned men and godly[1] have exhorted christian people (although they have not commanded them) often to receive the communion. And in the apostles' time the people at Jerusalem received it every day, as it appears[2] by the manifest word of the scripture[3]. And after, they received it in some places every day; in some places four times in the week; in some three times; some twice; commonly[4] everywhere at the least once in the week. In the beginning, when men were most godly and most fervent in the Holy Spirit, then they received the communion daily. But when the Spirit of God began to be more cold in men's hearts, and they waxed more worldly than godly, then their desire was not so hot to receive the communion as it was before. And ever from time to time, as the world waxed more wicked, the more the people withdrew themselves from the holy communion. For it is so holy a thing, and the threatenings of God be so sore against them that come thereto unworthily, that an ungodly man abhorreth it, and not without cause dare in no wise approach thereunto. But to them that live godly it is the greatest comfort that in this world can be imagined. And the more godly a man is, the more sweetness and spiritual pleasure and desire he shall have often to receive it. And will you be so ungodly to command the priest that he shall not deliver it to him but at Easter, and then but only in one kind? when Christ ordained both the kinds, as well for the laymen as for the priests; and that to be eaten and drunken at all times.

What enemies be you to all laymen, and to yourselves also, to refuse[5] to drink of Christ's cup, which he commanded all men to drink upon, saying, "Take and divide this among you;" and, "Drink ye all[6] of it!"

But what need any more be brought for the reproving of this article, than your own first article, where you will have kept all decrees and councils? Now in the decrees, *De Consecrat.* Di. 2, there is one decree that commandeth all men to receive the communion at the least thrice in the year, at Easter, Whitsuntide, and Christmas[7]. Another commandeth every man to receive the same upon Shere-Thursday[8]. The council Agathense saith, that all laymen which receive not the communion at Christmas, Easter, Whitsuntide, shall not be taken for catholics[9]: and the decree[10] of Gelasius[11], that the receiving under one kind is great sacrilege. Then by your first article you do not only condemn this your fifth article, but also you shew yourselves not to be catholics, except you receive the communion at the least three times in the year, and that under both the kinds, which is clean repugnant to this article. And yet I pray God you may receive it worthily once in your life: which you shall never do, except you wonderfully repent this your misbehaviour; and all your life-time study to amend and redress that you have now offended. Now to your sixth article.

---

[[1] All learned and godly men, C. C. C. C. MS.]

[[2] As it appeareth, Ibid.]

[[3] Words of the scripture, Ibid.]

[[4] And commonly, Ibid.]

[[5] Also that refuse, Ibid.]

[[6] Drink you all, Ibid.]

[[7] Etsi non frequentius, saltem in anno ter laici homines communicent (nisi forte quis majoribus quibuslibet criminibus impediatur), in Pascha videlicet, et Pentecoste, et Natali Domino. Corpus Juris Canon. Ed. Paris. 1687, Decreti Pars iii. De Consecrat. Dist. ii. can. xvi. Tom. I. p. 455.]

[[8] In cœna Domini a quibusdam perceptio eucharistiæ negligitur: quæ quoniam in eadem die ab omnibus fidelibus (exceptis iis, quibus pro gravibus criminibus inhibitum est) percipienda sit, ecclesiasticus usus demonstrat: cum etiam pœnitentes eadem die ad percipienda corporis et sanguinis dominici sacramenta reconcilientur. Id. ibid. can. xvii. Ibid.

Shere-Thursday: the Thursday before Easter, formerly so called. See Dr Wordsworth's Eccl. Biogr. Vol. I. p. 295; and Nares' Glossary under the phrase. Todd's Life of Cranmer, Vol. II. p. 105.]

[[9] Seculares, qui in Natali Domini, Pascha, et Pentecoste non communicaverint, catholici non credantur, nec inter catholicos habeantur. Id. ibid. can. xix. (ex Concil. Agathen.) A.D. 506. Ibid. Vid. Labb. et Cossart. Tom. IV. col. 1386. Ed. Lutet. Paris. 1670.]

[[10] Decree of Gelasius saith, MS. C. C. C. C.]

[[11] Comperimus autem, quod quidam sumpta tantummodo corporis sacri portione a calice sacri cruoris abstineant. Qui proculdubio (quoniam nescio qua superstitione docentur adstringi) aut integra sacramenta percipiant, aut ab integris arceantur: quia divisio unius ejusdemque mysterii sine grandi sacrilegio non potest provenire. Corpus Juris Canon. Decreti Pars iii. De Consecrat. Dist. ii. can. xii. Tom. I. pp. 454, 5.]

YOUR SIXTH ARTICLE IS THIS:

"*We will that our curates shall minister the sacrament of baptism at all times, as well in the week-day as on the holy-day.*"

Who letteth your ministers to baptize your children every day, if any cause of necessity so do require? But commonly it is more convenient, that baptism should not be ministered but upon the holy-day, when the most number of people be together; as well for that the whole church[12] there present may rejoice together of the receiving of new members of Christ into the same church, as also, that all men being present may remember, and the better know, what they promised themselves by their godfathers and godmothers in their own baptism; and be the more earnestly stirred in their hearts to perform the same; and also may all together pray for them that be baptized, that they may have grace to perform their profession. St Gregory Nazianzene, as great a clerk as ever was in Christ's church, and master to St Hierome, counselled, that children should not be christened until they came to three years of age or thereabout, except they were in danger of life[13]. And it was thought sufficient to our forefathers to be done two times in the year, at Easter and Whitsuntide; as it appeareth by divers of their councils and decrees[14], which forbid baptism to be ministered at any other time than Easter and Whitsuntide, except in case of necessity. And there remained lately divers signs and tokens thereof. For every Easter and Whitsun-even, until this time, the fonts were hallowed in every church, and many collects and other prayers were read for them that were baptized. But alas! in vain[15], and as it were a mocking with God: for at those times, except it were by chance, none were baptized, but all were baptized before[16]. For as vigils, otherwise called watchings, remained in the calendars upon certain saints' evens, because in old times the people watched all those nights[17]; and Vigilantius, because he speaketh against[18] these watchings, was condemned of heresy[19]; but now these many years those vigils remained in vain in the books, for no man did watch: even so until this day the order and form of christening was read and kept every year at Easter and Whitsuntide, but none was then christened. Wherein it appeareth, how far we be swerved from our forefathers.

And, to conclude this article shortly, if you will needs have baptism ministered no

---

[12 The whole church of Christ, Ibid.]

[13 Περὶ δὲ τῶν ἄλλων δίδωμι γνώμην, τὴν τριετίαν ἀναμείναντες, ἢ μικρὸν ἐντὸς τούτου, ἢ ὑπὲρ τοῦτο,......οὕτως ἁγιάζειν καὶ ψυχὰς καὶ σώματα τῷ μεγάλῳ μυστηρίῳ τῆς τελειώσεως. Gregor. Nazianz. Orat. xl. in Sanctum Baptismum. Tom. I. p. 658. Ed. Paris. 1630.]

[14 Non ratione auctoritatis alicujus, sed sola temeritate præsumitur, ut passim ac libere natalitiis Christi, apparatione, necnon et apostolorum seu martyrum festivitatibus, innumeræ, ut asseris, plebes baptismi mysterium consequantur: cum hoc sibi privilegium et apud nos et apud omnes ecclesias dominicum specialiter Pascha defendat cum sua Pentecoste. Corpus Juris Canon. Ed. Paris. 1687. Decreti Pars iii. De Consecrat. Dist. ii. can. xi. Tom. I. p. 469.—Duo tempora, id est, Pascha et Pentecoste, ad baptizandum a Romano pontifice legitime sunt præfixa. Unde, quia manifestime patet baptizandis in ecclesia electis hæc duo tempora, de quibus locuti sumus, esse legitima; dilectionem vestram monemus, ut nullos alios dies huic observantiæ misceatis. Id. ibid. can. xii. Ibid.—Proprie in morte crucifixi et in resurrectione ex mortuis potentia baptismi novam creaturam condidit, ex veteri: ut in renascentibus et mors Christi operetur, et vita,......ut appareret ex hujus doctrinæ spiritu regenerandis filiis hominum et in Dei filios adoptandis illum diem esse, et illud tempus electum, in quo per similitudinem formamque mysterii ea, quæ geruntur in membris, his, quæ in ipso sunt capite gesta, congruerunt. § 2.—De catechumenis baptizandis id statutum est, ut in Paschæ solennitate vel Pentecostes, quanto majoris celebritatis major celebritas est, tanto magis ad baptizandum veniant: ceteris solennitatibus infirmi tantummodo debeant baptizari, quibus quocumque tempore convenit baptismum non negari. Id. ibid. can. xv. Ibid.—Si qui necessitate mortis, ægritudinis, obsidionis, persecutionis, et naufragii urgentur, omni tempore debeant baptizari. Id. ibid. can. xvi. Ibid.—Venerabilis baptismi sacramentum non nisi in festivitate Paschali et Pentecostes tradere præsumat episcopus, exceptis iis, quibus, urgente mortis periculo, talibus oportet, ne in æternum pereant, remediis subveniri. Id. ibid. can. xvii. Ibid. pp. 469, 70.]

[15 But all was in vain, MS. C. C. C. C.]

[16 For none were baptized at those times, except it were by chance, but all were baptized before, Ibid.]

[17 See Bingham's Antiquities of the Christian Church, Book XIII. chap. ix. sect. IV. Vol. IV. pp. 357—363. Ed. Lond. 1840.]

[18 He spake against, MS. C. C. C. C.]

[19 Vid. Hieron. adv. Vigilant. Epist. lx. Tom. II. pp. 83—87. Ed. Francof. 1684. Bayle's Dictionary, Vol. IX. pp. 713—16. Ed. Lond. 1739.]

more at one time than another, then must you needs renounce your first article; which willeth the councils and decrees of the forefathers to be observed and kept. And this briefly sufficeth for the sixth article.

YOUR SEVENTH ARTICLE IS THIS:

"*We will have holy bread and holy water every Sunday*[1], *palms and ashes at the times accustomed; images to be set up again in every church; and all other ancient old ceremonies used heretofore by our mother holy church.*"

Oh! superstition and idolatry, how they prevail among you. The very true heavenly bread of life, the food of[2] everlasting life, offered unto you in the sacrament of the holy communion, you refuse to eat, but only at Easter. And the cup of the most holy blood, wherewith you were redeemed and washed from your sins, you refuse utterly to drink of at any time. And yet in the stead of these you will eat often of the unsavoury and poisoned bread of the bishop of Rome, and drink of his stinking puddles, which he nameth holy bread and holy water. Consider, O ignorant people, the authors and intents of the makers of them both. The water of baptism, and the holy bread and wine of the holy communion, none other person did ordain, but Christ himself. The other, that is called holy bread, holy water, holy ashes, holy palms[3], and all other like ceremonies[4] ordained the bishops of Rome; adversaries to Christ, and therefore rightly called antichrist[5]. And Christ ordained his bread, and his wine[6], and his water, to our great comfort, to instruct us and teach us what things we have only by him. But antichrist on the other side hath set up his superstitions, under the name of holiness, to none other intent, but as the devil seeketh all means to draw us from Christ, so doth antichrist advance his holy superstitions, to the intent that we should take him in the stead of Christ, and believe that we have by him such things as we have only by Christ; that is to say, spiritual food, remission of our sins, and salvation.

First, our Saviour Christ ordained the water of baptism to signify unto us, that as that water washeth our bodies outwardly, so be we spiritually within washed by Christ from all our sins. And as the water[7] is called water of regeneration, or new birth, so it declareth unto us, that through Christ we be born anew, and begin a new life towards God; and that Christ is the beginning of this new life. And as the body that is new born, although it have life within it, yet can it not continue [without meat and drink; even so can we not continue][8] in the spiritual life towards God, except we be continually nourished with spiritual food: and that spiritual food is Christ also. For as he is the first beginning of our spiritual life, so is he the continuance and ending thereof. And for this cause did Christ ordain in the holy communion to be eaten bread, and drunken wine, that we should surely believe, that as our bodies be fed with bread and wine in these holy mysteries, so be we out of doubt that our souls be fed spiritually with the lively food of Christ's body and blood; whereby we have remission of our sins and salvation[9]. But the bishop of Rome invented new devices of his own making, and by them promised remission of sins and salvation, that he might be set up and honoured for a saviour equal to Christ; and so to be esteemed above all creatures, and to sit in the temple of God, that is to say, in the church of Christ, as he were God.

And to bring this to pass he hath horribly abused holy scriptures, altering them to his purpose, in the stead of Christ's most holy blood putting in his holy water:

---

[1 Holy water made every Sunday, MS. C.C.C.C.]

[2 Heavenly bread, the food, &c. Ibid.]

[3 Vid. p. 148. n. 6.]

[4 And all such other like, MS. C. C. C. C.]

[5 Called antichrists, Ibid.]

[6 His bread, his wine, Ibid.]

[7 As that water, Ibid.]

[8 The passage within brackets is supplied from the C. C. C. C. MS.]

[9 "But my meaning is, that the force, the grace, the virtue, and benefit of Christ's body that was crucified for us, and of his blood that was shed for us, be really and effectually present with all them that duly receive the sacraments: but all this I understand of his spiritual presence." Vid. Preface to the Reader, Ed. 1551. Cranmer's Answer to Winchester, Vol. I. p. 3, Park. Soc. Ed.]

as it appeareth evidently in this sentence of St Paul written in the ninth chapter of the Hebrews[10]: "If the blood of oxen and goats," saith St Paul, "and the ashes of a young cow purified the unclean, as touching the purifying of the flesh, how much more the blood of Christ, which through the eternal Spirit offered himself without[11] spot unto God, shall purge your consciences from dead works for to serve the living God! And for this cause he is the Mediator of the new covenant[12]." Consider well this sentence of Paul, and you shall find two purifyings, one of the body, and another of the soul or conscience. You shall find also two mediators: one was the priest of Moses' law, and the other is Christ. The priests of the old law, with the blood of oxen and goats, and other their sacrifices, purged only the bodies of them that were defiled; but the soul or conscience they could not help. But our Saviour Christ by his own blood purged both body and soul. And for that cause he, and none other, is the Mediator of the new covenant[12]. But the bishop of Rome, to make himself also a mediator with Christ, hath taken upon him to purify the soul and conscience with holy water, holy salt, and other his holy creatures of his own devising, to the intolerable injury of Christ's blood, which only hath the effect[13]. And to bring this to pass, he hath most shamefully changed the words of the scripture, and wrested them to his purpose; some words putting out, and also in the stead of Christ's blood putting in his own holy water and salt. For whereas St Paul saith, "If the blood of oxen and goats and the ashes of a cow purified the unclean, as touching the purifying of the flesh:" here the bishop of Rome leaveth out these words, "as touching the purifying of the flesh." And where St Paul, extolling the effects of Christ's blood in comparison of the blood of oxen and goats, saith, "How much more the blood of Christ, which through the eternal Spirit offered himself, being without spot, unto God, shall purge your consciences:" here the bishop of Rome, extolling his water and salt, puts[14] out Christ's blood, and in the place thereof puts his[15] holy water and salt; saying, "How much more water, which is sprinkled with salt and hallowed with godly prayers, shall sanctify and purify the people[16]!" O intolerable blasphemy against the most precious blood of Christ! O shameless audacity and boldness, so to corrupt and pervert God's holy word! If he by his holy water presume to purify our souls, as Christ did by his blood, what is that else but to make himself equal, and another mediator with Christ? And what is it to tread under foot[17] the Son of God, and to make the blood of the new testament, whereby he was sanctified[18], like other common things, and to dishonour the Spirit of grace, if this be not? And yet, not contented with this blaspheming the blood[19] of Christ, he preferreth his holy creatures far above the blood of Christ, promising by them many benefits which by the blood of Christ be not promised. For in the same place he promiseth by his holy ceremonies to take away from us dearth and scarcity of all worldly things, and to multiply and increase us with the same; also to defend us from the assaults of the devil, and all his deceits, and to give us health both of body and soul. But all men see him so shamefully to lie in these worldly things, that no man that wise is will trust him in the rest. Nor no man that is godly will desire such things to remain still, which so much have deceived simple people, and dishonoured God, and been contumelious to the blood of Christ.

But now to your images, which, you say, you will have set up again in every church. What moved you to require this article, but only ignorance? For if you had known the laws of God, and the use of godly religion, as well before the incarnation

[10 To the Hebrews, MS. C. C. C. C.]
[11 Himself being without spot, Ibid.]
[12 Of the new testament, Ibid.]
[13 That effect, Ibid.]
[14 Putteth out, Ibid.]
[15 Putteth his, Ibid.]
[16 Aquam sale aspersam populis benedicimus, ut ea cuncti aspersi sanctificentur et purificentur; quod et omnibus sacerdotibus faciendum esse mandamus: nam si cinis vitulæ aspersus populum sanctificabat, atque mundabat, s. a venialibus; multo magis aqua sale aspersa divinisque precibus sacrata populum sanctificat, atque mundat a venialibus. Durandi Rational. Divin. Offic. Lib. IV. c. 4. p. 63. Ven. 1609.]
[17 To tread under his foot, MS. C. C. C. C.]
[18 Whereby we be sanctified, Ibid.]
[19 Blaspheming of the blood, Ibid.]

of Christ, as four or five hundred years next after, and by whom images were first brought into Christ's church, and how much idolatry was every where committed by the means of the same; it could not have been that ever you would have desired this article, except you had more affection to idolatry than to true religion. For Almighty God among the ten commandments rehearsed this for the second, as one of the chief: "Thou shalt not make to thyself any graven image, nor the likeness of any thing that is in heaven above, or in the earth beneath, or in the water[1] under the earth. Thou shalt not bow down to them, nor worship them." This commandment was diligently kept in the old Testament, so long as the people pleased God. For in their tabernacle was not one image, less nor more, that the people might see: although upon the propitiatory were two cherubims[2] of gold by the commandment of God; and that was in such a place as the people never came near, nor saw[3]. But when the people, forgetting this commandment, began to make them images, and to set them up in the place of adoration, by and by they provoked God's indignation against them, and were grievously punished therefore.

The church of Christ likewise in the new Testament, for the space of four or five hundred years after Christ's ascension, utterly refused to have images in the church, a place of adoration; as it may plainly appear[4] by all the old ancient authors that lived and wrote in that time: insomuch[5] that above four hundred years after Christ, when some superstitious and ignorant people in some places began to bring painted images, not into the church, but to the church-doors, the great clerk Epiphanius, bishop at Cyprus, finding such a painted image of Christ, or some other saint, hanging at the church-door in a town called Anablatha, he cut it in pieces, saying, that "it was against the authority of scripture that in the church of Christ should hang the image of a man." And the same Epiphanius wrote unto the bishop of Jerusalem, that he should command the priests, that in no wise they should suffer such images to be hanged in the church of Christ, which were contrary to our religion[6].

But peradventure you will marvel, and ask me the question, how it was brought to pass, that of late years all churches were so full of images, and so much offering and pilgrimages done unto them, if it were against the commandment of God, against the usage of all godly people in the old Testament, and also against the custom of Christ's church in the new Testament, so long as it was pure and holy, and kept from idolatry? Who was able to bring this to effect, contrary both to God's express commandment, and the custom of all godly people from the beginning of the world until four or five hundred years after Christ? No man surely could have wrought this thing so much contrary to God, but antichrist himself, that is to say, the bishop of Rome; to whom God hath given great power to work great wonders, to bring into error those that will not believe the truth. But by what means did he compass this matter? By such means as were most meet[7] for himself, and as he hath commonly practised in all other matters; that is to say, by sedition and murder, by confederacies and persecutions, by raising the son against the father, the children against their mother, and the subjects against their rulers; by deposing of emperors and princes, and murdering of learned men, saints and martyrs. For thus he wrought against the

---

[[1] Nor in the water, MS. C. C. C. C.]

[[2] Were set two cherubims, Ibid.]

[[3] Never came, nor saw them, Ibid.]

[[4] The word "appear" is put in the C. C. C. C. MS. evidently by another hand.]

[[5] So much, MS. C. C. C. C.]

[[6] Præterea quod audivi quosdam murmurare contra me, quia quando simul pergebamus ad sanctum locum, qui vocatur Bethel, ut ibi collectam tecum ex more ecclesiastico facerem, et venissem ad villam, quæ dicitur Anablatha, vidissemque ibi præteriens lucernam ardentem, et interrogassem, quis locus esset, didicissemque esse ecclesiam, et intrassem ut orarem; inveni ibi velum pendens in foribus ejusdem ecclesiæ tinctum atque depictum, et habens imaginem, quasi Christi, vel sancti cujusdam: non enim satis memini, cujus imago fuerit. Cum ergo hoc vidissem, in ecclesia Christi contra auctoritatem scripturarum hominis pendere imaginem, scidi illud, et magis dedi consilium custodibus ejusdem loci, ut pauperem mortuum eo absolverent et efferrent......Nunc autem nisi quod potui reperire, et precor ut jubeas presbyteros ejusdem loci deinceps præcipere, in ecclesia Christi ejusmodi vela, quæ contra religionem nostram veniunt, non appendi. Epiphan. Epist. ad Joan. Episc. Hier. Tom. II. p. 317. Ed. Colon. 1682. Vid. Bingham's Antiquities of the Christian Church, Vol. II. Book VIII. chap. viii. Sect. VI.]

[[7] As was most meet, MS. C. C. C. C.]

emperor[8] of the east parties from Gregory II. his time until Gregory III.[9]; who at length, after this condition[10] had endured above five hundred years, in a council held at Lyons, by feigned promises persuaded the emperor of the east to condescend to his purpose, as well to receive images into the churches, as to other his requests. But nevertheless the bishop of Rome failed of his purpose. For yet to this day the christian men in the east do not allow images to stand in their churches; neither the Greeks, nor the Armenians, nor the Indians, nor none[11] other christian men. And, that more is, search all the world[12] throughout, of what religion soever they be, whether they be Jews, Turks, Saracens, Tartaries, or christian people, and you shall not find an image in none of their churches, but that was brought in by the bishop of Rome, and where the bishop of Rome is, or within these forty years was, taken for the head of the church and Christ's vicar in earth.

And at the beginning the bishops of Rome, to cloak their idolatry, pretended to have images set up only for a remembrance to laymen, and to be, as it were, laymen's books. But after, they defined plainly that these should be[13] worshipped. And so it increased at length, that images were kneeled unto, offered unto, prayed unto, sought unto, incensed and pilgrimages done unto them, and all manner of superstition and idolatry that could be devised. Almighty God knoweth our corrupt nature better than we do ourselves. He knoweth well the inclinations of man[14], how much he is given to worship creatures and the works of his own hands; and specially fond women, which commonly follow superstition rather than true religion. And therefore he utterly forbad the people the use of graven images, specially in places dedicated to the honour of God, knowing assuredly that of the having would follow the worshipping of them.

Now (thanks be to God!) in this realm we be clearly delivered from that kind of idolatry, which most highly offended God, and we do according to the council Elebertine, which ordained that no images should be in churches[15]. And this council is so ancient, that is was about the same year that Nicene council was. What should then move you to ask again your images in the church, being not only against God's commandments, and the use of God's church evermore since the beginning of the world, when it was pure from idolatry, but also being chargeable to the realm, and great occasion of heinous idolatry, but that some papistical and covetous priests have persuaded you hereto? which care neither for God's honour[16], nor your damnation, so that they may have any commodity or profit thereby.

I have been very long in this article, and yet the matter is so large that it requireth much more to be spoken therein, which for shortness of time I am constrained to leave until a more occasion; and to come to your eighth article.

### YOUR EIGHTH ARTICLE IS THIS:

"*We will not receive the new service, because it is but like a Christmas game; but we will have our old service of matins, mass, even-song, and procession in Latin, as it was before. And so we the Cornish men, whereof certain of us understand no English, utterly refuse this new English.*"

As concerning the having of the service in the Latin tongue, is sufficiently spoken of in the answer to your third article. But I would gladly know the reason why the Cornish men[17] refuse utterly the new English, as you call it, because certain of you understand it not; and yet you will have the service in Latin, which almost none of you understand. If this be a sufficient cause for Cornwall to refuse the English service, because some of you[18] understand none English, a much greater cause have they, both

[8 Against the empire, Ibid.]

[9 Gregory II. May 18, A. D. 715, to Feb. 20, A. D. 732. Gregory III. March 18, A. D. 732, to Nov. 27, A. D. 741. Vid. Mosheim's Eccl. Hist. Vol. II. Part II. chap. iii. § 11. pp. 154, 5, and 673. Ed. Lond. 1845.]

[10 This contention, MS. C. C. C. C.]

[11 Nor nor none, Ibid.]

[12 Search the all world, Ibid.]

[13 That they should be, Ibid.]

[14 Inclination of man, Ibid.]

[15 Placuit picturas in ecclesia esse non debere, ne quod colitur et adoratur, in parietibus depingatur. Concil. Eliberit. A. D. 305, cap. XXXVI. Labb. et Cossart. Tom. I. col. 974. Ed. Lutet. Paris. 1671.]

[16 God's dishonour, MS. C. C. C. C.]

[17 Why you Cornish men, Ibid.]

[18 Some of them, Ibid.]

of Cornwall and Devonshire, to refuse utterly the late service[1]; forasmuch as fewer of them know the Latin tongue than they of Cornwall[2] the English tongue. But where you say that you will have the old service, because the new is "like a Christmas game," you declare yourselves what spirit you be led withal, or rather what spirit leadeth them that persuaded you[3] that the word of God is but like a Christmas game. It is more like a game and a fond play to be laughed at of all men, to hear the priest speak aloud to the people in Latin, and the people listen with their ears[4] to hear; and some walking up and down in the church, some saying other[5] prayers in Latin, and none understandeth other. Neither the priest nor his parish[6] wot what they say. And many times the thing that the priest saith in Latin is so fond of itself, that it is more like a play than a godly prayer.

But in the English service appointed to be read there is[7] nothing else but the eternal word of God: the new and the old Testament is read, that hath power[8] to save your souls; which, as St Paul saith, "is the power of God to the salvation of all that believe;" the clear light to our eyes, without the which we cannot see; and a lantern unto our feet[9], without which we should stumble in darkness. It is in itself the wisdom of God, and yet "to the Jews it is a stumblingblock, and to the Gentiles it is but foolishness: but to such as be called of God, whether they be Jews or Gentiles, it is the power of God, and the wisdom of God." Then unto you if it be but foolishness and a Christmas game, you may discern yourselves what miserable state you be in, and how far you be from God. For St Paul saith plainly, that the word of God is foolishness only to them that perish; but to them that shall be saved it is God's might and power. To some it is a lively savour unto life, and to some it is a deadly savour unto death. If it be to you but a Christmas game, it is then a savour of death unto death. And surely persuade yourselves that you be not led with the Spirit of God, so long as the word of God savoureth no better unto you[10], but seemeth unto you[11] a Christmas pastime, and foolishness. And therefore the old service pleaseth you better: which in many things is so foolish and so ungodly, that it seems rather[12] to be old wives' tales and lies than to sound to any godliness. The devil is a liar, and the author of lies; and they may think themselves governed rather of his spirit, than of God, when lies delight more than God's most true word.

But this I judge rather of your leaders than of yourselves, who by ignorance be carried away by others[13], you wot not whither. For when the service was in the Latin tongue, which you understood not, they might read to you truth or fables[14], godly or ungodly things, as they pleased; but you[15] could not judge that you understood not. And what was the cause[16] why St Paul would have such languages spoken in the church as that people[17] might understand? that they might learn and be edified thereby, and judge of that which should be spoken, whether it were according to God's word or not.

But forasmuch as you understand not[18] the old Latin service, I shall rehearse some things in English that were wont[19] to be read in Latin, that when you understand them, you may judge them whether they seem to be true tales, or fables; and whether they or God's word seem to be more like plays and Christmas games. "The devil entered into a certain person, in whose mouth St Martin put his finger; and because the devil could not get out at his mouth, the man blew him[20] out behind." This is one of the tales that was wont to be read in the Latin service, that you will needs have again. As though the devil had a body, and that so crass that he could not pass out by the small pores of the flesh, but must needs have a wide hole to go out at. Is this

[1 The Latin service, MS. C. C. C. C.]
[2 Them of Cornwall, Ibid.]
[3 Persuaded to you, Ibid.]
[4 Listen to some, Ibid.]
[5 Some in the church, saying other, Ibid.]
[6 Nor the parish, Ibid.]
[7 Is there, Ibid.]
[8 Old Testament, the word that hath, Ibid.]
[9 To our feet, Ibid.]
[10 No better to you, Ibid.]
[11 Seemeth to you, Ibid.]
[12 Seemeth rather, Ibid.]
[13 By other, Ibid.]
[14 Truths or fables, Ibid.]
[15 For you, Ibid.]
[16 And that was the cause, Ibid.]
[17 As the people, Ibid.]
[18 You understood not, Ibid.]
[19 Which were wont, Ibid.]
[20 Three words are omitted.]

a grave and godly matter to be read in the church, or rather a foolish Christmas tale, or an old wives' fable, worthy to be laughed at and scorned of every man that hath either wit or godly judgment? Yet more foolish, erroneous, and superstitious things be read in the feasts of St Blase, St Valentine, St Margaret, St Peter, of the Visitation of Our Lady, and the Conception, of the Transfiguration of Christ, and in the feast of Corpus Christi, and a great number mo: whereof some be most vain fables, some very superstitious, some directly against God's word, and the laws of this realm; and all together be full of error and superstition. But as Christ commonly excused the simple people because of their ignorance, and justly condemned the scribes and Pharisees, which by their crafty persuasions led the people out of the right way; so I think not you so much to be blamed as those Pharisees and papistical priests, which, abusing your simplicity, caused you to ask you wist not what, desiring rather to drink of the dregs of corrupt error, which you knew not, than of the pure and sweet wine of God's word, which you may and ought to understand. But now have I sufficiently spoke[21] of your eighth article: I will go forward unto the ninth.

YOUR NINTH ARTICLE IS THIS:

"*We will have every preacher in his sermon, and every priest at the mass*[22]*, pray specially by name for the souls in purgatory, as our forefathers did.*"

To reason with you by learning, which be unlearned, it were but folly: therefore I will convince your article with very reason. First, tell me, I pray, if you can[23], whether there be a purgatory or no; and where, or what it is. And if you cannot tell, then I may tell you that you ask you wot not what. The scripture maketh mention of two places where the dead be received after this life, of heaven and of hell; but of purgatory is not one word spoken. Purgatory was wont to be called a fire as hot as hell, but not so long during. But now the defenders of purgatory within this realm be ashamed so to say: nevertheless they say it is a third place; but where or what it is, they confess themselves they cannot tell. And of God's word they have nothing to shew, neither where it is, nor what it is, nor that it is. But all is feigned of their own brains[24], without authority of scripture.

I would ask of them then, wherefore it is, and to what use it serveth? For if it be to no use, then it is a thing frustrate and in vain. Mary, say they, it is a place of punishment, whereby they be purged from their sins, that depart out of this life not fully purged before. I cannot tell whether this saying be more foolish[25], or more contumelious to Christ. For what can be more foolish than to say, that pains can wash sins out of the soul? I do not deny but that corrections and punishments[26] in this life is a calling of men to repentance and amendment, and so to be purged by the blood of Christ. But correction without repentance can nothing avail; and they that be dead be past the time of repentance; and so no correction or torments in purgatory can avail them. And what a contumely[27] and injury is this to Christ, to affirm that all have not[28] full and perfect purgation by his blood, that die in his faith! Is not all our trust in the blood of Christ, that we be cleansed, purged, and washed thereby? And will you have us now to forsake our faith in Christ, and bring us to the pope's purgatory to be washed therein; thinking that Christ's blood is an imperfect lee or soap that washeth not clean? If he shall die without mercy that treadeth Christ's blood under his feet, what is treading of his blood under our feet, if this be not? But if according to the catholic faith, which the holy scripture teacheth, and the prophets, apostles, and martyrs confirmed with their blood, all the faithful that die in the Lord be pardoned of all their offences by Christ, and their sins be clearly sponged and washed away by his blood; shall they after be cast into another strong and grievous prison of purgatory, there to be punished again for

[21 Sufficiently be spoken, MS. C. C. C. C.]
[22 At his mass, Ibid.]
[23 I pray you, if you can, Ibid.]
[24 Their own brain, Ibid.]
[25 Be more foolishness, Ibid.]
[26 But correction and punishment, Ibid.]
[27 And how great a contumely, Ibid.]
[28 All they have not, Ibid.]

that which was pardoned before? God hath promised by his word, that the souls of the just[1] be in God's hand, and no pain shall touch them: and again he saith, "Blessed be they that die in the Lord. For the Spirit of God saith, that from henceforth they shall rest from their pains." And Christ himself saith: "He that believeth in him that sent me, hath everlasting life, and shall not come to judgment, but shall pass from death unto life." And is God no truer of his promises[2] but to punish that which he promiseth to pardon? Consider the matter by your own cases. If the king's majesty should pardon your offences, and after would cast you into prison, would you think that he had well observed his promise? For what is to pardon your offences, but to pardon the punishment for the same? If the king would punish[3] you, would you take that for a pardon? Would you not allege your pardon, and say that you ought not to be punished? Who can then, that hath but a crumb of reason in his head, imagine of God that he will after our death punish those things that he pardoned in our life-time?

Truth it is that scripture maketh mention of paradise and Abraham's bosom after this life; but those be places of joy and consolation, not of pains and torments. But yet I know what subtle sophisters use to mutter in men's ears to deceive them withal. David, say they[4], with many other, were pardoned of their offences, and yet were they sore punished after for the same of God; and some of them so long as they lived. Well, be it it were so. Yet after their lives they were not punished in purgatory therefore: but the end of their lives was the end of their punishment. And likewise it is of original sin after baptism, which although it be pardoned, yet after-pains[5] thereof continue so long as we live. But this punishment in this life-time[6] is not to revenge our original sin, which is pardoned in baptism, but to make us humble, penitent, obedient to God, fearful to offend, to know ourselves, and ever to stand in fear and awe; as, if a father that hath beaten a wilful child for his faults should hang the rod continually at the child's girdle, it should be no small pain and grief to the child, ever hanging by his side: and yet the father doth it not to beat the child for that which is past and forgiven; but to make him beware hereafter that he offend not again, and to be gentle, tractable, obedient, and loath to do any thing amiss. But after this life there is no such cause of punishment; where no rod nor whip can force any man to go any faster or farther, being already at the end of his journey. Likewise a master that hath an unthrifty servant, which out of his master's sight doth nothing but riot and disorder himself, if he forgive his servant, and for the love he beareth to him, and the desire he hath to see him corrected and reformed, he will command him never to be out of his sight, this command[7], although indeed it be a great pain to the servant, yet the master doth it not to punish those faults, which before he had pardoued and forgiven, but to keep him in stay, that he fall no mo to like disorder. But these examples and cases of punishment here in this life can in no wise be wrested and drawn to the life to come; and so in no wise can serve for purgatory.

And furthermore, seeing that the scriptures so often and so diligently teach us, almost in every place, to relieve all them that be in necessity, to feed the hungry, to clothe the naked, to visit the sick and the prisoner[8], to comfort the sorrowful, and so to all others[9] that have need of our help; and the same in no place make mention[10] either of such pains in purgatory, or what comfort we may do them; it is certain that the same is feigned for lucre, and not grounded upon God's word. For else the scripture in some place would have told us plainly what case they stood in that be in purgatory, and what relief and help we might do unto them. But forasmuch[11] as God's words speaketh not one word of neither of them both, my counsel shall be, that you keep not the bishop of Rome's decrees that you may come to purgatory, but keep God's laws that you may come to heaven: or else I promise you assuredly that you shall never escape hell. Now to your next article.

---

[[1] Of the Jews, Strype.]
[[2] Of his promise, MS. C. C. C. C.]
[[3] Pardon, Strype.]
[[4] David, they say, MS. C. C. C. C.]
[[5] Yet certain pains, Ibid.]
[[6] In our life-time, Ibid.]
[[7] This commandment, Ibid.]
[[8] The prisoners, Ibid.]
[[9] To all other, Ibid.]
[[10] In no place maketh mention, Ibid.]
[[11] So MS. C. C. C. C.—Strype, But as for such.]

YOUR TENTH ARTICLE IS THIS:

"*We will have the bible, and all books of scripture in English, to be called in again. For we be informed that otherwise the clergy shall not of long time confound the heretics.*"

Alas! it grieveth me to hear your articles; and much I rue and lament your ignorance; praying God most earnestly once to lighten your eyes that you my see the truth[12]. What christian heart would not be grieved to see you so ignorant, (for willingly and wilfully, I trust, you do it not,) that you refuse Christ, and join yourselves with antichrist? You refuse the holy bible and all holy scriptures so much, that you will have them called in again; and the bishop of Rome's decrees you will have advanced and observed. I may well say to you as Christ said to Peter, "Turn back again, for you savour not godly things." As many of you as understand no Latin cannot know God's word but in English, except it be the Cornish men, which cannot understand likewise none but their own speech. Then you must be content to have it in English, which you know, or else you must confess that you refuse utterly the knowledge thereof. And wherefore did the Holy Ghost come down [among the apostles[13]] in fiery tongues, and gave them knowledge of all languages, but that all nations might hear, speak, and learn God's word in their mother-tongue? And can you name me any Christians in all the world[14], but they have, and ever had[15], God's word in their own tongue? And the Jews, to whom God gave his scriptures in the Hebrew tongue, after their long captivity among the Chaldees, so that mo of them knew the Chaldee rather than the Hebrew[16] tongue, they caused the scripture to be turned into the Chaldee tongue, that they might understand it: which until this day is called Targum. And Ptolemy, king of Egypt, caused sixty [seventy] of the greatest clerks that might be gotten to translate the scripture out of Hebrew into Greek. And until this day the Greeks have it in the Greek tongue, the Latins in the Latin tongue, and all other nations in their own tongue. And will you have God farther from us than from all other countries; that he shall speak to every man in his own language that he understandeth and was born in, and to us shall speak a strange language that we understand not? And will you that all other realms shall laud God in their own speech, and we shall say to him we know not what?

Although you savour so little of godliness that you list not to read his word yourselves, you ought not to be so malicious and envious to let them that be more godly, and would gladly read it to their comfort and edification. And if there be an English heretic, how will you have him confuted but in English? and whereby else but by God's word? Then it followeth, that to confute English heretics we must needs have God's word in English, as all other nations have it in their own native language. St Paul to the Ephesians teacheth all men, as well laymen as priests, to arm themselves, and to fight against all adversaries with God's word; without the which we cannot be able to prevail, neither against subtle heretics, puissant devils, this deceitful world, nor our own sinful flesh. And therefore, until God's word came to light, the bishop of Rome, under the prince of darkness, reigned quietly in the world, and his heresies were received and allowed for the true catholic faith. And it can none otherwise be but that heresies must reign where the light of God's word driveth not away our darkness.

YOUR ELEVENTH ARTICLE IS THIS:

"*We will have Dr Moreman and Dr Crispin*[17]*, which hold our opinions, to be safely sent unto us; and to them we require the king's majesty to give some certain livings, to preach among us our catholic faith.*"

---

[[12] See his truth, MS. C. C. C. C.]

[[13] In C. C. C. C. MS. but not in Strype.]

[[14] Any christian nation in all the world, Ibid.]

[[15] And ever have had, Ibid.]

[[16] The Chaldee than the Hebrew, Ibid.]

[[17] "Of Crispin," Strype says, "I find little, but

If you be of Moreman's and Crispin's faith, I like you much the worse. For "like lettuce, like lips." And to declare you plainly the qualities of Crispin and Moreman, and how unmeet men they be to be your teachers, they be persons very ignorant in God's word, and yet thereto very wilful, crafty, and full of dissimulation. For if they were profoundly learned, and of sincere judgments, as they be not, they might be godly teachers of you. Or if they were not *toto* wilful, and standing wholly in their own conceits, they might learn and be taught of others[1]. But now they be so wilful that they will not learn, and so ignorant that they cannot teach, and so full of craft and hypocrisy that they be able to deceive you all, and to lead you into error after themselves. So that if you ask them, you ask your own poison. Now if a man were in such a sickness that he longed for poison, (as many diseases desire things most noyful unto them,) yet it were not the part of a good physician to give it unto them. No more is it the office of a most godly prince to give you such teachers (although you long never so sore for them) as he knoweth would corrupt you, feeding you rather with sour and unwholesome leaven of Romish pharisaical doctrine, than with the sweet, pure, and wholesome bread of God's heavenly word. And where you would have God's word in English destroyed, and Crispin and Moreman delivered unto you, you do even as the people of the Jews did; which cried out that Christ might be crucified, and that Barabbas, the strong thief, might be delivered unto them.

YOUR TWELFTH ARTICLE IS THIS:

*"We think it very meet, because the lord cardinal Pole is of the king's blood[2], that he should not[3] only have his pardon, but also be sent for to Rome, and promoted to be of the king's council."*

In this article I will answer no more but this: If ever any cardinal or legate were beneficial unto this realm, we may have some hope of some other to follow his steps: but if all that ever were in this realm were pernicious and hurtful unto the same, I know not why we should be with child to long for any mo. For by the experience of them that have been heretofore, we may conjecture of them that be to come. And I fear me that cardinal Pole would follow rather the whole race of the rest, than to begin a better of himself. Surely I have read a book of his making[4], which whosoever shall read, if he have a true heart to our late sovereign lord king Henry VIII, or to this realm, he will judge cardinal Pole neither worthy to dwell in this realm, nor yet to live. For he doth

---

that he was once proctor of the university of Oxon, and doctor of the faculty of physic, and of Oriel college. Moreman was beneficed in Cornwall in king Henry's time, and seemed to go along with that king in his steps of reformation, and was observed to be the first that taught his parishioners the creed, the Lord's prayer, and the ten commandments in English; yet shewing himself in the next king's reign a zealot for the old superstitions. Hence we perceive the reason why the archbishop charged him to be a man full of craft and hypocrisy. In queen Mary's time he was for his popish merits preferred to be dean of Exeter, and was coadjutor to the bishop (Voisey) of that diocese." Vid. Strype's Mem. of Abp. Cranmer, Vol. I. p. 265, 6. Ed. Oxon. 1840. "But it may be doubted whether Strype has not confused Richard and Edmund Crispin, both of Oriel college, and both proctors of the university of Oxford." Vid. Dr Jenkyns' Remains of Abp. Cranmer, Vol. IV. p. 238. Moreman was engaged in the disputation in the convocation-house about the real presence, on the day of the third session, Oct. 23, 1553. Vid. Foxe's Acts and Monuments, p. 1411. Ed. Lond. 1583. Burnet's Hist. of Reformat. Vol. II. pp. 529, 532, Ed. Oxon. 1829.]

[1 Of other, C. C. C. C. MS.]

[2 "He was of the blood royal, and cousin-germain to the king, (Henry VIII.) by both the houses of York and Lancaster, being by his mother descended from the duke of Clarence, brother to king Edward IV.;" and was "educated with princely munificence by him." Vid. Collier's Eccl. Hist. Vol. IV. p. 389. Ed. Lond. 1840, 41. Burnet's Hist. of Reformat. Vol. I. p. 444.]

[3 Blood, should not, MS. C. C. C. C.]

[4 The book is entitled by Strype and Collier, "De Unione Ecclesiastica," by Burnet, "De Unitate Ecclesiastica," and was written against Henry's divorce from Queen Katherine, and his assuming the supremacy. It was completed in March, 1535, but not published till twelve months afterwards. Vid. Collier and Burnet, ut supra; and Strype's Memorials of Abp. Cranmer, Vol. I. pp. 63, 4. Todd's Life of Abp. Cranmer, Vol. II. p. 132. Ed. Lond. 1831.]

extend all his wits and eloquence in that book to persuade the bishop of Rome, the emperor, the French king, and all other princes, to invade this realm by force. And sure I am, that if you have him, you must have the bishop of Rome also: for the cardinal cannot be a subject, but where the other is his head. This sufficeth briefly to this article.

YOUR THIRTEENTH ARTICLE IS THIS:

"*We will that no gentleman shall have any mo servants than one to wait upon him, except he may dispend one hundred mark land. And for every hundred mark we think it reasonable he should have a man.*"

Yet have you not foreseen one thing, you wise disposers of the commonwealth. For if a gentleman of an hundred mark land[5] (who by your order must have but one servant, except he might spend two hundred marks) should send that one servant to London, you have not provided who shall wait upon him until his servant come home again. Nor you have not provided where every gentleman may have one servant that can do all things necessary for him. I fear me the most part of you that devised this article, (whom I take to be loiterers and idle unthrifts,) if you should serve a gentleman, he should be fain to do all things himself, for any thing that you could or would do for him. But one thing methink very strange: for where much complaint is made of divers gentlemen, because they keep not houses, you provide by your order that no gentleman shall keep house, but all shall sojourn with other men. For who can keep an household with one servant, or with two servants, after the rate of two hundred marks, or with three, after the rate of three hundred, and so upward? For here, it seems[6], you be very desirous to make gentlemen rich: for after this proportion every gentleman may lay up clearly in his coffers at the least the one half of his yearly revenue, and much more.

But it was not for good mind that you bare to the gentlemen, that you devised this article; but it appeareth plainly that you devised it to diminish their strength, and to take away their friends, that you might command gentlemen at your pleasures. But you be much deceived in your account. For although by your appointment they lacked household servants, yet shall they not lack tenants and farmers: which, if they do their duties, will be as assured to their lords as their own household servants. For of those lands, which they have or hold of their lords, they have their whole livings for themselves, their wives, children, and servants. And for all these they attend their own business, and wait not upon their lords but when they be called thereto. But the household servant, leaving all his own business, waiteth daily and continually upon his master's service; and for the same hath no more but meat and drink and apparel for himself only: so that all tenants and farmers, which know their duties, and be kind to their lords, will die and live with them, no less than their own household servants. Therefore I would wish you to put this phantasy out of your heads, and this article out of your book, as well for the unreasonableness as for the ungodliness thereof.

For was it ever seen in any country since the world began, that the commons did appoint the nobles and gentlemen the number of their servants? Standeth it with any reason to turn upside down[7] the good order of the whole world, that is every where, and ever hath been, that is to say, the commoners to be governed by the nobles, and the servants by their masters? Will you now have[8] the subjects to govern their king, the villains to rule the gentlemen, and the servants their masters? If men would suffer this, God will not; but will take vengeance of all them that will break his order, as he did of Dathan and Abiram: although for a time he be a God of much sufferance, and hideth his indignation under his mercy, that the evil of themselves may repent, and see their own folly.

---

[[5] Of an hundred pounds land, MS. C.C.C.C.]
[[6] But here it seemeth, Ibid.]
[[7] To turn upso down, Ibid.]
[[8] Will you have now, Ibid.]

YOUR FOURTEENTH ARTICLE IS THIS:

"*We will that the half part of the abbey-lands and chantry-lands in every man's possession, however he came by them, be given again to two places, where two of the chief abbeys were*[1] *within every county; where such half part shall be taken out, and there to be established a place for devout persons, which shall pray for the king and the commonwealth. And to the same we will have all the alms of the church-box given for these seven years.*"

At the beginning you pretended that you meant nothing against the king's majesty, but now you open yourselves plainly to the world that you go about to pluck the crown from his head; and, against all justice and equity, not only to take from him such lands as be annexed unto his crown, and be parcel of the same, but also against all right and reason to take from all other men such lands as they came to by most just title, by gift, by sale, by exchange, or otherwise. There is no respect nor difference had amongst you, whether they came to them by right or by wrong. Be you so blind that you cannot see how justly you proceed to take the sword in your hands against your prince, and to dispossess just inheritors without any cause? Christ would not take upon him to judge the right and title of lands between two brethren; and you arrogantly presume not only to judge, but unjustly to take away all men's right titles; yea, even from the king himself. And do you not tremble for fear that the vengeance of God shall fall upon you, before you have grace to repent? And yet you, not contented with this your rebellion, would have your shameful act celebrated with a perpetual memory, as it were to boast and glory of your iniquity. For, in memory of your fact, you would have stablished in every county two places to pray for the king and the commonwealth: whereby your abominable behaviour at this present may never be forgotten, but be remembered unto the world's end; that when the king's majesty was in wars both with Scotland and France, you, under pretence of the commonwealth, rebelled, and made so great sedition against him within his own realm, as never before was heard of. And therefore you must be prayed for for ever, in every county of this realm.

It were more fit for you[2] to make humble supplication upon your knees to the king's majesty, desiring him not only to forgive you this fault, but also that the same may never be put in chronicle nor writing; and that neither shew nor mention may remain to your posterity, that ever subjects were so unkind to their prince, and so ungracious towards God, that, contrary to God's word, they should so use[3] themselves against their sovereign lord and king. And this I assure you of, that if all the whole world should pray for you until doomsday, their prayers should no more avail you than they should avail the devils in hell, if they prayed for them, unless you be so penitent and sorry for your disobedience, that you will ever after, so long as you live, study to redub[4] and recompense the same with all true and faithful obedience, not only yourselves, but also procuring all other, so much as lieth in you; and so much detesting such uproars and seditions, that if you see any man towards any such things, you will to your power resist him, and open him unto such governors and rulers as may straightway[5] repress the same. As for your last article, thanks be to God, it needeth not to be answered, which is this.

YOUR LAST ARTICLE IS THIS:

"*For the particular griefs of our country, we will have them so ordered, as Humphry Arundel and Henry Bray, the king's mayor of Bodman, shall inform the king's majesty, if they may have safe conduct under the king's great seal to pass and repass with an herald of arms*[6]."

---

[[1] Abbeys was, C. C. C. C. MS.]
[[2] More meet for you, Ibid.]
[[3] Would so use, Ibid.]
[[4] Redub: repair, or make amends for.]
[[5] As may straightways, C. C. C. C. MS.]
[[6] "Humphry Arundel, the leader of the ten thousand Devonshire rebels, was of good family, and governor of St Michael's Mount. He was sent

Who ever heard such arrogancy in subjects, to require and will of their princes, that their own particular causes may be ordered, neither according to reason, nor the laws of this realm, but according to the information of two most heinous traitors? Was it ever heard before this time, that an information should be a judgment, although the informer were of never so great credit? and will you have suffice the information of two villainous papistical traitors? You will deprive the king of his lands[7] pertaining to his crown, and other men of their just possessions and inheritance, and judge your own causes as you list yourselves. And what can you be called then but most wicked judges, and most errant traitors? except only ignorance or force may excuse you; that either you were constrained by your captains[8] against your wills, or deceived by blind priests and other crafty persuaders, to ask you wist not what. How much then ought you to detest and abhor such men hereafter, and to beware of all such like, so long as you live; and to give most humble and hearty thanks unto God, who hath made an end of this article, and brought Arundel and Bray to that they have deserved; that is, perpetual shame, confusion, and death! Yet I beseech God so to extend his grace unto them, that they may die well which have lived ill. Amen.

---

to London after being for some time confined at Exeter, and there executed. Bray was mayor of Bodmin, in Cornwall." Dr Jenkyns (Remains of Abp. Cranmer, Vol. II. p. 244) remarks that "attempts, it is said, were made to exculpate the mayor of Bodmin, on the ground of his having been forced into the insurrection against his will. As if this defence had been successful, Sir Anthony Kingston, provost-marshal of the army, appointed a day for dining with him. Having been 'right heartily welcomed,' he after dinner expressed a wish to see a pair of gallows, which he had desired his host to erect. On coming thither and beholding them, he said to the mayor, 'Think you, master mayor, that they be strong enough?' 'Yea, sir,' quoth he, 'that they are.' 'Well then,' said Sir Anthony, 'get you even up unto them, for they are provided for you.' The mayor, greatly abashed herewith, said, 'I trust you mean no such thing to me.' 'Sir,' said he, 'there is no remedy; ye have been a busy rebel, and therefore this is appointed for your reward.' And so without respite or stay there was the mayor hanged. But Boyer, and not Bray, is the name given by Holinshed to this victim of Kingston's cruel pleasantry. It may therefore be doubted whether he is correctly described as mayor of Bodmin. The story perhaps may apply to another person named Boyer, who is said by Strype to have suffered death among the rebel leaders." See Strype's Eccl. Mem. Vol. II. Part I. p. 281. Ed. Oxon. 1822. Holinshed's Chronicles, Vol. III. pp. 1006, 1026.]

[7 Of the lands, C. C. C. C. MS.]

[8 "Of whom the chief gentlemen captains were, Humfrey Arundell, Esquire, governor of the mount, James Rosogan, John Rosogan, John Payne, Thomas Underhil, John Soleman, William Segar. Of priests which were principal stirrers, and some of them governors of the camps, and after executed, were to the number of eight, whose names were Rob. Bochim, John Tompson, Roger Barret, John Wolcocke, Wil. Asa, James Mourton, John Barow, Rich. Benet; besides a multitude of other popish priests, which to the same faction were adjoined. The number of the whole rebellion, speaking with the least, mounted little less than to the sum of ten thousand stout traitors." Foxe's Acts and Monuments, p. 1305. Ed. Lond. 1583. "Their names were Arundel, Pomeroy, Coffin, Winslade, Rosogan, Holmes, Bury, Underhil, Soleman, Segar, Boyer, Lee, two mayors, Pain, Maunder, Ashridge, Thompson, Baret, Bocham, Wolcock, Alsa, Morton, Welsh, Barrow, Benet; which last-recited nine were priests." See Strype's Eccl. Mem. Vol. II. Part I. p. 281.]

# [THE ARCHBISHOP'S NOTES

## FOR A HOMILY AGAINST REBELLION[1].]

---

*Sentences of the Scripture against Sedition.*

C.C.C.C. MSS. cii. pp. 529—534. Strype's Mem. of Abp. Cranmer, Vol. ii. App. No. 41. pp. 840—2. Ed. Oxon. 1840.

1 Cor. iii. *Cum sit inter vos zelus et contentio, nonne carnales estis, et sicut homines ambulatis?*

1 Cor. vi. *Quare non magis injuriam accipitis? Quare non magis fraudem patimini?*

Jac. iii. *Si zelum amarum habetis, et contentiones sint in cordibus vestris, &c. non est ista sapientia desursum descendens a Patre luminum, sed terrena, animalis, diabolica. Ubi enim zelus et contentio, ibi inconstantia et omne opus malum*[2], *&c.* [*Quæ autem desursum est sapientia, primum quidem pudica est, deinde pacifica, modesta, suadibilis, &c. Fructus autem justitiæ in pace seminatur facientibus pacem.*][3]

Jac. iv. *Unde bella et lites inter vos*[4]*? Nonne ex concupiscentiis vestris, quæ militant in membris vestris?*

*How God hath plagued sedition in time past.*

Numb. xvi.[5] Dathan and Abiram, for their sedition against Moses and Aaron, did miserably perish by God's just judgment, the earth opening and swallowing them down quick.

2 Reg. [Samuel] xv. and xviii. Absalom, moving sedition against David, did miserably perish likewise.

2 Reg. [Samuel] xx. Seba for his sedition against David lost his head.

3 Reg. [1 Kings] i. and ii. Adonias also for his sedition against Solomon was slain.

Acts viii. Judas and Theudas for their sedition were justly slain.

Acts xxi. An Egyptian likewise, which moved the people of Israel to sedition, received that he deserved.

Tumults in England. Jack Cade. Jack Straw.

In Germany for their sedition were slain almost in one month about two hundred thousand.

The sword by God's word pertaineth not to subjects, but only to magistrates.

Though the magistrates be evil, and very tyrants against the commonwealth, and enemies to Christ's religion; yet the subjects must obey in all worldly things, as the Christians do under the Turk, and ought so to do, so long as he commandeth them not do against God.

How ungodly then it is[6] for our subjects to take the sword, where there reigneth a most christian prince, most desirous to reform all griefs!

---

[[1] "The archbishop procured sermons to be made against the rebellion;" one was made by Peter Martyr, and another written by M. Bucer against the sedition; and "an office of fasting was composed for this rebellion, which, being allayed in the west, grew more formidable in Norfolk and Yorkshire. For I find a prayer composed by the archbishop, with these words preceding: 'The exhortation to penance, or the supplication may end with this or some other like prayer.' And then the prayer followeth*......After this follow some rude draughts, written by archbishop Cranmer's own hand, for the composing, as I suppose, of an homily or homilies to be used for the office aforesaid." Strype's Mem. of Cranmer, Vol. I. pp. 266, 8, 9.]

[[2] Opus pravum, C. C. C. C. MS.]

[[3] This passage is not in Strype.]

[[4] In vobis, C. C. C. C. MS.]

[[5] Num. 18. Strype.]

[[6] Ungodly is it then, C. C. C. C. MS.]

* Vid. end of Sermon concerning time of Rebellion, p. 202.

Subjects ought to make humble suit to their prince for reformation of all injuries, and not to come with force.

The sword of the subjects at this present cometh not of God, nor for the commonweal of the realm; but of the devil, and destroyeth the commonweal.

First, For that it is against the word of God.

Secondly, For that they raise so many lies; whereof the devil is ever the author. *Quia mendax est et pater ejus.*

Thirdly, For that they spoil and rob men, and command every man to come to them, and to send to them what they please.

Fourthly, For that they let the harvest, which is the chief sustentation of our life, and God of his goodness hath sent it abundantly; and they by their folly do cause it to be lost and abandoned.

Fifthly, For that they be led by rage and fury, without reason; have no respect[7] neither of the king's authority[8]; nor of the papists in the west country; nor of our affairs in France, nor Scotland; which by their sedition is so much hindered, that there could not be imagined so great a damage to the realm.

Sixthly, That they give commandments in the king's name, and in pain of death, having none authority so to do.

Ever against God the devil hath raised sedition.

As appeareth by the sedition of Dathan and Abiram; and all the murmurations of the children of Israel against Moses and Aaron.

Also, of the conspiracy[9] against Zorobabel in the re-edifying of the temple.

Also, against Christ and his apostles, in sundry parts of the world.

Also, in Germany lately, and now among us. For the devil can abide no right reformation in religion.

Civil war is the greatest scourge that can be, and most certain argument of God's indignation against us for our ingratitude; that we either will not receive his true word, or that they which receive the same dishonour God in their living, when they pretend to honour him with their mouths. Which ingratitude and contumely God can in no wise bear at our hands.

The remedies to avert God's indignation from us is to receive his word, and to live according thereunto, returning unto God with prayer and penance. Or else surely more grievous affliction shall follow, if more grievous may be than civil war among ourselves.

The chief authors of all these tumults be idle and naughty people, which nothing have, nor nothing or little will labour to have; that will riot in expending, but not labour in getting.

And these tumults first were excitated by the papists and others which came from the western camp, to the intent, that by sowing division among ourselves we should not be able to impeach them[10].

---

[[7] Having no respect, Ibid.]
[[8] King's minority, Ibid.]
[[9] Of the conspiracies, Ibid.]
[[10] The allusion is probably to the rebellion at Wymondham, in Norfolk, and Norwich, headed by Ket, the tanner. Vid. Burnet's Hist. of Reformat. Vol. II. pp. 242, 3. Ed. Oxon. 1829.]

# A SERMON

## CONCERNING THE TIME OF REBELLION[1].

C.C.C.C. MSS. cii. pp. 409—499.

THE common sorrow of this present time[2], dearly beloved brethren in Christ, if I should be more led thereby, than by reason and zeal to my country, would move me rather to hold my peace, than to speak. For the great evils, which we now suffer at this present time, are to be bewailed with tears and silence, rather than with words. And hereunto I might allege for me the example of Job, who when he came to his extreme misery, he lying upon a dunghill, and three of his friends sitting upon the ground by him, for the space of seven days for great sorrow not one of them opened his mouth to speak a word to another. If then the miserable state of Job, like a most hard and sharp bit, stopped his mouth from speaking, and the lamentable case of their friend stayed those three men, being of speech most eloquent, that they could not utter their words; surely it seemeth that I have a much more cause to be still and hold my peace. For there was the piteous lamentation of no mo but of one man, or one household, and that only concerning temporal and worldly substance; but we have cause to bewail a whole realm, and that most noble, which lately being in that state, that all other realms envied our wealth and feared our force, is now so troubled, so vexed, so tossed and deformed, (and that by sedition among ourselves, of such as be members of the same,) that nothing is left unattempted to the utter ruin and subversion thereof. And besides this, the eternal punishment of God threateneth sore as well the authorers and procurers of these seditions, as all other that join themselves unto them. So that we be constrained day and night to bewail the decay, not only of a worldly kingdom and most noble realm, but also the eternal damnation of innumerable souls.

These reasons perchance might move some men to be quiet and hold their peace; but me they do not so much move, which know right well that our common sorrow and lamentable state cannot be remedied with silence, nor good counsel can be given with holding my peace. Now therefore, in this common sorrow, I know nothing that is more able to suage our griefs, and to comfort our heaviness, than is the word of God. For as the sun many times with his beams driveth away great thick and dark clouds, and stayeth great storms of winds; so doth the light of God's word stay men's minds, bringing them from

[[1] Dr Jenkyns supposes that, "although this sermon has been placed among Cranmer's works, his claim to it is not indisputable." It is here printed from the C. C. C. C. MS. written by a secretary, but corrected throughout by the archbishop; respecting which the following memorandum at the commencement of the MS. has been left by archbishop Parker: "Hic sermo prius descriptus Latine a Petro Martyre." The Latin sermons referred to are found in the same collection, CCCXL, Articles 4 and 6. The English sermon is founded on the two in Latin by P. Martyr, but is not a translation of them, sentences being omitted and new matter added. They contain "descriptions of the disturbed state of the country, and of the angry feelings existing between the gentry and the lower orders." Both the Latin and English sermons contain the same topics and examples as the rough notes of the archbishop*. Dr Jenkyns conjectures that "Cranmer placed these brief notes in the hands of P. Martyr, to be expanded into a regular homily; and that afterwards, from the materials thus prepared in Latin, he drew up the English sermon which follows." It is probably the same "which Burnet says was preached by Cranmer on a fast-day at court, and which he saw at C. C. C. C. under the archbishop's own hand, being the only sermon of his that he ever saw." He was undoubtedly mistaken with respect to the hand-writing, and he gives no authority for the rest of his statement, which the expressions of the concluding prayer somewhat corroborate. Strype appears to think a "fast-day was appointed on account of the insurrections, that the archbishop directed sermons on the occasion to be composed for the curates to read to the people, and that this was one of them which was printed for common use." See note, p. 188. Strype's Mem. of Abp. Cranmer, Vol. I. pp. 266—8. Burnet's Hist. of Reformat. Vol. II. Part I. p. 242, and Part II. pp. 239—41. App. B. i. No. 36. Jenkyns' Remains of Abp. Cranmer, Vol. II. p. 248.]

[[2] This sermon was probably directed against the Norfolk rebellion headed by Ket. Vid. p. 189. n. 10.]

* Vid. p. 188.

trouble to quietness, from darkness to brightness, from heaviness and desperation to gladness, joy, and comfort. Wherefore I most humbly beseech Almighty God to grant me by his Spirit, that out of holy scripture I may plainly set out before your eyes the principal causes of all these tumults and seditions: for if the causes be once known, it shall be the more easy to provide remedy therefore.

The general cause of all these commotions is sin, and under christian profession unchristian living. But there be also certain special causes, of the which some pertain both to the high and lower sort, as well to the governors as to the common people; some appertain only to the people; and some again only to the governors and rulers. [3]And of them I will first begin to speak.

Prima causa[4]. Remissness of correction in the governors.

The governors and rulers be ordained of God (as St Paul declareth in his epistle to the Romans) for this intent and purpose, that they should be God's officers and ministers here in earth, to encourage and advance them that be good, and to rebuke and correct those that be evil.

But herein, O good Lord, be merciful unto us; for we have been too remiss in punishing offenders, and many things we have winked at. We have suffered perjury, blasphemy, and adultery, slandering and lying, gluttony and drunkenness, vagabonds and idle persons, either lightly punished, or else not punished at all; either thinking this clemency for the time expedient for the commonwealth, or else not duly weighing how grievous those offences be in the sight of God. And whilst we lacked this right judgment of God's wrath against sin, lo! suddenly cometh upon us this scourge of sedition, the rod of God's wrath, to teach us how sore God hateth all wickedness, and is displeased with his ministers that wink thereat. For except we be duller than stocks and stones, we must needs feel that this plague is the grievous scourge of God for our offences, that we have suffered too much them that have offended against his most holy name. We have dissimuled the matter, we have been cold in God's cause, and have rather winked at than punished the contempt both of God and his laws.

And this surely is one great cause, wherefore we suffer worthily this plague of God. Heli suffered his children too much, and was too soft in chastising of them, when they sinned against God; but that his softness was the destruction of him, his children, and of a great number also of the people of Israel. David, because in time he did not correct his three sons Amon, Absolon, and Adonias, he lost them all three, and was in great danger to be destroyed by them himself. And if the perils of this most chosen king of God do little move us, let us call to our remembrance, I pray you, the plague of God against the whole tribe of Benjamin, because they let pass unpunished the abominable abusing of the Levite's wife; whereof followed that the whole tribe of Benjamin was almost utterly destroyed; for there was slain of them above twenty-five thousand, and there was left alive of the whole tribe no mo but six hundred. Consider, I pray you, by this example, how certain and present destruction cometh to commonweals, because offenders against God are unpunished. And whensoever the magistrates be slack in doing their office herein[5], let them look for none other but that the plague of God shall fall in their necks for the same. Which thing not only the foresaid examples, but also experiences within ourselves, doth plainly teach us. For whensoever any member of our body is diseased or sore, if we suffer it long to continue and fester, do we not see that at length it doth infect the whole body, and in process of time utterly corrupteth the same? But for what purpose, brethren, do I speak so much of this matter? Verily, for none other intent, but that when we know one of the causes of these evils, we may duly repent and amend the same.

But peradventure some will say, If the governors offend because they do not justly

---

[[3] "Ac ne videar potentioribus *nostroque* ordini æquior esse quum par sit, ab eo sermonem auspicabor," &c. Pet. Mart. "This clause is favourable to the supposition, that the sermon was prepared, at least in the first instance, for the archbishop's own use." See p. 190. *n.* 1. Jenkyns' Remains of Abp. Cranmer. Vol. II. p. 250.]

[[4] The marginal notes are in the archbishop's hand-writing.]

[[5] "When the magistrate by negligence or preposterous pity will not punish for sin, then God striketh, as ye may see by the universal flood, by the fire in Sodom and Gomorre." Bp. Hooper, Sermon III. upon Jonas, p. 484, Park. Soc. Ed. 1843.]

punish offenders, what doth that pertain to us the common people, which have not offended? Let them repent that have offended; let them be sorry for their slackness in punishment, and more sharply correct from henceforth such as by their horrible offences provoke God's indignation against us all. Nay, not so, my friends; let no men charge the governors, and excuse themselves: we have offended God both high and low; we have deserved this plague at God's hands, and much more. Therefore let every man search his own conscience, and (like as Daniel did) let every man confess and bewail as well his own sins, as the sins of the heads and rulers. And let every man for his own part correct and amend himself, forasmuch as he knoweth that our offences be the causes not only of private, but also of public and common calamities.

Secunda Causa. Avaritia.

Now the time requireth to declare another cause of our sedition, which is the greedy desire and, as it were, worshipping of riches, wherewith both the high and low sort being too much blinded have brought our realm to this point. And surely nothing more hath caused great and puissant armies, realms, and empires to be overthrown, than hath done the insatiable covetousness of worldly goods. For hereby, as by a most strong poison, whole realms many times have come to ruin, which seemed else to have endured for ever: sundry commonwealths, which before were conserved in unity, have by incurable disorder been divided and separated into many parts. This manner of vice, if it be unseemly unto any other people, to them surely that profess Christ it is utterly shameful and detestable; which above all nations should be the true esteemers and lovers of pure godly things which be eternal and immortal, and ought to seek for right judgment and estimation of things only at their own profession. For as many of us as be truly called Christians of Christ, do confess that we be redeemed by him, not through the vain and uncertain riches of this world, but through the strong and perfect obedience whereby he submitted himself unto his Father, to be obedient even unto the death of the cross. Worldly-wise men esteem worldly riches and wealth above all other things; but the wisdom of God esteemeth obedience above all things, that is to say, that a man should submit his will to God's will, that he should not desire to use any thing in this world, no, not his own life, but as it shall please God and be to his glory; and to be content with that state, place, and degree, that God, the Author of all good things, hath called him unto. With this sacrifice of obedience Christ did reconcile us unto his Father, humbling himself to his Father's will even to the death of the cross; and he hath commanded all them that profess to be his disciples to follow this his example.

But, alas! how far be all they from this rule and example, which come with force of arms in the king's majesty's realm without his licence and authority, mustering themselves in unlawful assemblies and tumults, to the disorder and disquietness of the whole realm, and of a greedy and covetous mind to spoil and rob and take from others; or they also, which through covetousness of joining land to land, and inclosures to inclosures, have wronged and oppressed a great multitude of the king's faithful subjects! I speak of both these sorts of people together, because both of them be diseased with a like sickness. But are they so ignorant in godly religion, that they know not that God is the distributor and giver of the goods of the world? And if they know this, why then do they go about to get goods of this world by unlawful means, contrary to God's will and commandment? Wherein what other thing else do they than forsake their master Christ, and yield themselves unto Satan, worshipping him for their God, because he promiseth to give them the lands and goods of this world? But, Almighty God, I beseech thee, open the eyes of these blind persons, that they may once see and perceive that the true riches of christian men be not gold, silver, or great possessions, but those things which neither "the eye hath seen, nor the ear hath heard, nor man's heart can comprehend." Is it not a great wonder that the devil should so rob these men of their wits, that either oppress the poor, or stir these commotions, that they do forget death? For if they did call to their remembrance that death every day and hour hangeth over their heads, they would not be so greedy of worldly goods, that for the same they would either do injury to their neighbour, or confound all things upsy down with seditious uproars and unquietness; seeing that of all the goods in this world they shall carry with them when they die not the value of one farthing. No; he that dieth in the displeasure of God, were he never so rich, shall not in the world to come be able to buy one drop of water to quench the flames of everlasting fire, wherewith he shall be tormented in hell. We came naked into this world, and naked we shall depart hence again.

What madness is it then so to labour and toil both day and night, yea, to adventure both body and soul, for these things that be so transitory; which we be sure we shall not possess after this life, and be unsure whether we shall keep them so long or no? For we see by common experience, that many which have had great possessions and riches, are suddenly by divers chances brought to great lack and extreme poverty. For the which cause St Paul doth teach us, that we ought not to "put our confidence in riches which are uncertain and unstable;" for riches be like an untrusty servant, which runneth from his master when he has most need of him. The wretched man, saith the prophet David, "doth hoard up great treasures, but he cannot tell for whom." We see by daily experience that men be so mad, when they once give themselves to covetousness, that they less esteem the loss of their honesty, commonwealth, liberty, religion, yea, of God himself and everlasting life, than the loss of their riches.

Against them that pretend that they rose to relieve the poor and the common-wealth.

But here methinketh I hear some of these unlawful assemblers mutter and say, "Sir, it is truth that you have said; covetousness is it that undoeth all this realm, and this was the cause of our assemblies, to have the covetousness of the rich men and gentlemen reformed, and that the poor might be provided for." But to this I answer on this wise: That gentlemen were never poorer than they be at this present, for the more part. And in what case soever the gentlemen be in, yet who gave subjects authority to levy armies in a king's realm without his leave and consent? Or when had ever any such commotion good success, or came to good end? Who did ever see the feet and legs divide themselves from the head and other superior parts? Doth it then become the lower sort of the people to flock together against their heads and rulers? and specially now at this time in the king's majesty's tender age, when we be round about environed with other enemies; outward with Scots and Frenchmen, and among ourselves with subtle papists, who have persuaded the simple and ignorant Devonshire men, under pretence and colour of religion, to withstand all godly reformation. Shall we now destroy our realm, and make it a prey to our adversaries? Remember the fable of Æsop, that when the frog and the mouse did fight together, the puttock came, and snatched them up both. What greater pleasure can we do to the Scots and Frenchmen, than to be at variance within ourselves, and so make our realm a prey for them? What joy is this to the bishop of Rome, to hear that the blood of Englishmen (for the which he hath so long thirsted) is now like to be shed by their own brethren and countrymen! But let us be joined together like members of one body, and then we shall have less need to fear our foreign enemy. It is an easy thing to break a whole fagot, when every stick is loosed from another; but it is hard to break the fagot, when it is fast bound together.

Subditis non licet accipere gladium.

A tempore.

Non est plebis abusus reformare.

But peradventure some will say: The gentlemen have done the commons great wrong, and things must needs be redressed. But is this the way, I pray you, to reform that is amiss, to redress one injury with another? Is it the office of subjects, to take upon them the reformation of the commonwealth, without the commandment of common authority? To whom hath God given the ordering and reformation of realms? To kings or to subjects? Hearken, and fear the saying of Christ: "He that taketh the sword shall perish with the sword." To take the sword, is to draw the sword without authority of the prince. For God in his scriptures expressly forbiddeth all private revenging, and hath made this order in commonweals, that there should be kings and governors, to whom he hath willed all men to be subject and obedient. Those he hath ordained to be common revengers, correctors, and reformers of all common and private things that be amiss. And he hath forbidden all private persons to presume to take any such thing upon them, because he would not that his godly order should be broken or troubled of any man. Christ refused to divide the inheritance between two brethren, because he would not intermeddle with that office unto the which he was not sent of his Father. How presumptuous then be they that enterprise to be judges in the limits and bands of lands, not being called thereunto, neither having any commission to do it? Among the Israelites, when they had entered into the land of Canaan, none durst be so bold as to usurp unto himself either house, city, or land; but they tarried till Josue their governor had divided the same, and every man was contented with his appointment. And why then do not our people patiently tarry, till our Josue, that is the king's majesty, and his council do make just reformations, as they intend to do; but will take upon themselves to be reformers and judges of their own causes, and so by uproars and tumults hinder the most godly purposes and proceedings of him and his council?

Paupertatis prætextu non debet tumultuari populus.

But poverty, they say, constrained them to do as they have done. So might the thief say, that poverty constraineth him to rob, if that would excuse him. But this is no sufficient cause of their disobedience. For our Saviour Christ was so poor that he saith of himself, "Foxes have buries, and birds of the air have nests; but the Son of man hath no place where he may lay his head." And Peter also forsook all that he had, and followed Christ's poverty. And yet they both paid quietly tribute to Cæsar. And we read not that they made any business, or gathered numbers of people together to stir a commotion, crying, as heaven and earth should go together, that it was not justly ordered that they which were most godly had no possessions, and yet were compelled to pay tribute to Cæsar. They said no such words, but paid their tribute without murmuring or grudging. They to whom God hath sent poverty in goods, let them also be poor and humble in spirit, and then be they blessed in heaven, howsoever they be here in earth. Christ himself saith, "Blessed are the poor in spirit, for theirs is the kingdom of heaven." For no poverty can move such men to do anything against God's commandments, or to disquiet the commonwealth.

This sedition doth not relieve but increase poverty.

But although they pretend that poverty constraineth them thus to do, be they so blind that they cannot see that this sedition doth not remedy, but increase their poverty? Be their eyes so hard shut in their heads, that they cannot see what evil they have done to their own commonwealth, what victuals they have consumed, how they have hindered the harvest upon the ground which God sent them to be their living the next year? and so they destroy their own livings themselves. They nothing consider how many men they have undone, how many they have spoiled and robbed, how many children they have caused to be fatherless, and wives to be widows. And what be they the better therefore? What have they gotten thereby, but only loaded themselves with the burden of the spoil and robbery of other men, whom they be never able to satisfy? And yet they may be assured that God will be satisfied of them for their evil doings, even unto the uttermost farthing.

And although their offences be as great as may be thought, thus to consume and annoy their own country, their own friends and neighbours, yet the mercy of God is never consumed to them that will repent and amend. Wherefore let us pray God for them, that he will give them eyes to see, and ears to hear, and hearts to understand their own misdemeanour and folly.

Quales sunt hujus seditionis præcipui auctores.

But the great part of them that be the chief stirrers in these insurrections be ruffians and sturdy idle fellows, which be the causes of their own poverty, commonly resorting to tippling and to alehouses, much drinking and little working, much spending and little getting; and yet will they be clad gorgeously, fare daintiously, and lie softly, which, neither caring for God nor man, seek now nothing else, but to get something by spoil and robbing of other men. These fellows make all this hurly-burly in every place, and when the rage of the people is quieted in one place, then they run to another, never quiet themselves, nor ceasing to disquiet other, until at length they hope to come to their prey. Happy is that place where none such be, and in great danger be they where many such be. This realm had never so many; and that evidently appeareth at this present time.

Otiosis nebulonibus nihil est dandum.

All the holy scripture exhorteth to pity and compassion upon the poor, and to help them; but such poor as be oppressed with children or other necessary charges, or by fire, water, or other chance, come to poverty, or for age, sickness, or other causes, be not able to labour: but to such as be poor by their own folly, that be able to labour and will not, the scripture commandeth in no wise to aid them or help them, but chargeth utterly all men to abhor them. But these men, repugning against God, gape at nothing else, but unjustly and by force to take from other men that which God hath given unto them by their just labour.

And yet they pretend that they mean nothing else but a reformation of things that be amiss; and they complain much of rich men and gentlemen, saying, that they take the commons from the poor, that they raise the prices of all manner of things, that they rule the poverty, and oppress them at their pleasure. Thus they excuse their own outrageous presumption by charging the gentlemen. But whilst they look so earnestly at other men's faults, they do not see their own. They speak much against Achab, that took from Naboth his vineyard; but they follow not the example of Naboth, who would rather lose his vineyard, than he would make any commotion or tumult among the people. They make exclamations against Achab, and yet follow him rather than the patience of Naboth. We never read that any just man, which is praised in the scripture, did take sword in his hand as against his prince or nobility, although he suffered never so much wrong or oppression. And yet now they accuse the gentlemen of taking of commons, which take from the gentlemen both the common and proper. They charge the rich men that they enhance the prices; but in this unseemly commotion they take from the rich man what they list without any price. They say that the gentlemen rule the poor and oppress them at their pleasure. But they so say that be out of all rule and order, and rule the gentlemen as pleaseth them, except they will have their goods spoiled, their houses brent, and further be in danger of their lives[1]. They say, gentlemen have ruled aforetime, and they will rule now another while[2]. A goodly realm shall that be, that shall be ruled by them that never had experience to govern, nor cannot rule themselves. A prentice must learn seven years before he can be a good merchant: no less time were required to be a good governor.

Quod sit falsa horum nebulonum querela.

Quod miserum esset regnum, si ab iis nebulonibus gubernaretur.

But if God were so offended with our realm, and by our ingratitude and wickedness were so much provoked to indignation against us, that he would make them governors and rulers over us, O Lord, what a realm should this be! What fruit should we see of their governance? What end or measure would be of their covetousness? What justice should be looked for at their hands, if they were rulers, which now, being but private persons, without law or justice take from every man at their pleasure? How would they temper themselves being in authority, that now without authority be ruled by their own affections, without the fear of God, or respect to reason or honesty! It is a common and a true saying, that authority sheweth what every man is; and a gentleman will ever shew himself a gentleman, and a villain a villain. We see daily by experience that a gentleman in authority hath a respect to his reputation and worship; but a villain called to office and authority commonly regardeth neither God, worship, nor honesty, but to catch what he can by right or by wrong: for unto him all is fish that cometh to the net.

And yet it is reported, that there be many among these unlawful assemblies that pretend knowledge of the gospel, and will needs be called gospellers; as though the gospel were the cause of disobedience, sedition, and carnal liberality, and the destruction of those policies, kingdoms, and commonweals, where it is received. But if they will be true gospellers, let them then be obedient, meek, patient in adversity and long-suffering, and in no wise rebel against the laws and magistrates. These lessons are taught in the gospel, both by evident scriptures, and also by the examples of Christ and his apostles. Christ

Quod sunt impii qui in his sceleribus prætexunt evangelium.

[1 "As for the other malcontents, the other rabble of Norfolk rebels, thus he proceeded to argue with them: Ye pretend a commonwealth. How amend ye it? By killing of gentlemen, by spoiling of gentlemen, by imprisoning of gentlemen? A marvellous tanned commonwealth. Why should ye thus hate them? For their riches or for their rule? Rule they never took so much in hand as ye do now ......In countries some must rule, some must obey, every man may not bear like stroke; for every man is not like wise. And they that have seen most, and be best able to bear it, and of just dealing beside, be most fit to rule......If riches offend you, because ye wish the like, then think that to be no commonwealth, but envy to the commonwealth. Envy it is to appair another man's estate, without the amendment of your own. And to have no gentlemen, because ye be none yourselves, is to bring down an estate, and to mend none. Would ye have all alike rich? That is the overthrow of labour, and utter decay of work in this realm," &c. Sir John Cheke, *The Hurt of Sedition.* "Cheke's treatise is precisely of the same date with this sermon, and throws much light on it. It will be found in Holinshed, Vol. III. p. 1042. See also Strype's Life of Cheke, ch. iii. sect. II."—Jenkyns.]

[2 "Some crieth, Pluck down inclosures and parks; some for their commons; others pretend the religion; *a number would rule another while*, and direct things as gentlemen have done: and indeed all have conceived a wonderful hate against gentlemen, and taketh them all as their enemies. The ruffians among them, and the soldiers, which be the chief doers, look for spoil. So that it seemeth no other thing but a plague and a fury among the vilest and worst sort of men." A Letter from Protector Somerset to Sir Philip Hobby, concerning the rebellions at home. Burnet, Hist of Reformat. Vol. II. App. B. i. No. 36, pp. 239—40. Ed. Oxon. 1829, quoted by Dr Jenkyns.]

himself was poor, and pronounceth himself them to be blessed that patiently suffer poverty; the apostles forsook all that they had, and followed Christ; the prophets oftentimes refused great riches offered unto them: and can they say that they have the spirit of the prophets and the apostles, which, having no possessions of their own, go about by force, violence, and sedition, to get other men's? No; this spirit is not of Christ, but of the devil; and such a spirit, as among the Romans Catiline, Cethegus, and Manlius were inspired withal; and here in England, Jack Straw, Jack Cade the blacksmith, Captain Aske, and divers other rebels, who have suffered just punishment after their deserving.

And although here I seem only to speak against these unlawful assemblers, yet I cannot allow those, but I must needs threaten everlasting damnation unto them, whether they be gentlemen or whatsoever they be, which never cease to purchase and join house to house, and land to land, as though they alone ought to possess and inhabit the earth. For to such Esay the prophet threateneth everlasting woe and the curse of God, except they repent and amend their lives in time. But yet their fault excuseth not those, which without the commandment of the king and his laws have taken harness upon their backs, and refused to lay it down when they were by the king's authority commanded so to do. What other reward can I promise to them, than the anger and vengeance of God, which they shall feel both in this life and in the life to come, both sorer and sorer than they look for, except they acknowledge their fault, and amend by time?

Multo deteriores sunt rebelles et seditiosi quam avari.

But let us now compare these two destructions of the commonweal together, the covetous men, which (as they say) do inclose and possess unjustly the commons, and these mutineers, which rashly and without all reason will be both the hearers, judgers, and reformers of their own causes; and, that is most unjustice of all and against all man's law and God's law, this they will do, the other parties neither heard nor called, and thereunto they take the king's power upon them, the authority of the magistrate, and the sword, which they never had by no law. Which of these two is the greater injury? which is the more intolerable robbery? which is the more pernicious confusion? Is this a remedy to their griefs? is this to bring in justice? I am sure themselves, being quiet from their furor and rage, cannot so think. Foolishness is not healed by madness, theft is not amended with spoil aud ravine; neither is the commonwealth stayed or made strong by the breach of laws, orders, and states. Wherefore let both parties lay away this so furious and excessive desire of vain and worldly things, which, as we have now learned by experience, and as the apostle saith, "is the root of all evils."

Odium nebulonum in nobiles et divites.

But now I will go further to speak somewhat of the great hatred which divers of these seditious persons do bear against the gentlemen; which hatred in many is so outrageous, that they desire nothing more than the spoil, ruin, and destruction of them that be rich and wealthy; for this thing many of them do cry and openly profess. Oh a goodly purpose, and benefit to the realm! this declareth what spirit they be led withal. If these devilish spirits might have their wills, what destruction should hang over this realm! what miserable state should this commonweal come unto! This noble realm, which yet is feared of all nations, should then be a prey to all nations, to the Frenchmen, to the Scots, and to every realm that would spoil them; and among ourselves should be such confusion, that every man should spoil other, if he were stronger. For take away gentlemen and rulers, and straightway all other falleth clearly away, and followeth barbarical confusion. Oh! how far be these men from all fear of God! for God commandeth all inferiors most readily to obey their superiors; but these, more like beasts than men, bend themselves clearly against God, not only to disobey, but also to destroy, their superiors which God hath appointed over them. The scripture saith, "He that hateth his brother is a murderer" before God: but these men not only mortally hate, but also threaten the destruction not only of one man, but of one whole state, and that, next the king's majesty, the chief state of the whole realm.

Against them that refuse the king's pardon.

And not only this, but, that which is more wonderful and to be lamented, part of them do despise and openly refuse the king's majesty's pardon[1]. He is loath to

[1 "Pardon was proclaimed in Norwich by a herald on the 31st of July, ineffectually, Ket the leader declaring, that he needed no pardon, having 'done nothing but that belonged to the duty of a

shed his subjects' blood, although they be unworthy the name of his subjects; but they seek to shed the blood of them which have hitherto defended their blood from shedding. He, like a merciful prince, is loath to cut off the members of his body, although many of them are so rotten and corrupt, that, if they might, they would infect the whole body. And what madness is it, that diseased members refuse to be anointed with the most soft and gentle ointment of his majesty's mercy! He is as careful of their health and life as it were possible if they were his children; although by these seditions and uproars he hath been more grievously offended, than the gentlemen have offended them, with whom they be angry. For the gentlemen, in case those things be true wherewith they be charged, yet they have only done wrong to the poor commons in their inclosures and such like matters. But by these seditions the majesty of a most high and godly king is hurt and wronged, forsomuch as they take upon them his office, and as it were pulleth the sword out of his hands. For he is ordained of God to have the hearing and decision of such causes, and to have the administration and distribution of these worldly goods; but they in their rage do in a manner pull him out of his throne and chair of estate, and cast him down to the ground, who is here in earth God's vicar and chief minister, and of whom only next unto God dependeth all the wealth and felicity of this realm; as it would soon appear, if he were missing, which God forbid, and all the realm should bewail. Verily, when I consider with myself their unjust desire in revenging, and the king's majesty's gentleness in suffering and pardoning, methink I see the accustomed order of things to be clean turned and changed upside down: for Solomon saith, "A king's anger is like the roaring of a lion." But their sovereign lord doth not roar against them, (which notwithstanding have grievously offended and provoked his anger,) but rather doth fawn upon them, and use them gently. Contrariwise they, which ought to be as gentle and meek as lambs, whose part it were either to hold their peace and not open their mouths, or else to speak very mildly and lowly, do now roar and make outcries like most cruel lions: the which thing how justly they do it, God's vengeance (except they take heed) will speedily declare.

Gravius peccarunt isti seditiosi in regem et regnum, quam quæ conqueruntur illi de nobilibus.

One thing there is, which after all I think necessary to be added hereunto, and that in mine opinion is the head and beginning of all these tribulations. For the gospel of God now set forth to the whole realm is of many so hated, that it is reject, refused, reviled, and blasphemed; and by those which have received the same, and would be counted to be great favourers thereof, yet it sustaineth much injury and reproach, and by their occasion is ill spoken of. For the great number of them, pretending a zeal thereto in their lips, and not in their hearts, counterfeiting godliness in name, but not in deed, live after their own pleasure, like epicures, and so ungodly as though there were no God. And what is it that St Paul calleth the having of God's truth in unrighteousness, if this be not it? These, having more knowledge of God than they had before, and receiving a taste of the heavenly gifts, notwithstanding retain their old vices in their corrupt manners and dissolute conversation, being nothing amended, but rather paired[2]. Which thing being in this case, what other thing should we look for than the severe and terrible judgment of God, to make us an example to all them that abuse his word, (sith by repentance we will not be amended, nor by the pure word of God be healed,) that thereby all men may learn how abominable it is before God, his name to be so dishonoured, and the doctrine of the gospel so lightly esteemed? The heathen poet[3] could not wink at such men, but with his pen rubbed them on the gall, which, pretending holiness, so dissolutely did live. And shall God's judgment leave them unpunished, which, always having in their mouth "the gospel, the gospel," reasoning of it, bragging of it, yet in their conversation live after the world, the flesh, and the devil? which, as St Paul wrote unto Titus, "confessing God with their mouth, deny him with their deeds?"

Præcipua causa omnium malorum est contemptus aut abusus evangelii.

---

true subject.' The rebels were defeated, and Ket taken on the 27th of August. This sermon was probably delivered in the interval. Holinshed, Vol. III. p. 1032—1039."—Jenkyns, Remains of Abp. Cranmer, Vol. II. p. 262.]

[[2] Paired: impaired, made worse.]

[[3] Juvenal, Sat. II. 3. Qui Curios simulant, et Bacchanalia vivunt.]

But such as rejoice and brag in such things, utterly deceive themselves. Whoso listeth to read the histories of the heathen people and greatest idolaters, he shall not find among them all any region, people, or nation that was so scourged by God, so oft brought into servitude, so oft carried into captivity, with so divers, strange, and many calamities oppressed, as were the children of Israel. And yet they bragged and gloried that none other nation but they only had the law of God, their rites and ceremonies of God, God's promises and his testaments. And so it was indeed: nevertheless St Paul, writing to the Romans, doth most sore rebuke and reprove them, saying: "Thou art called a Jew, and dost trust in the law, and makest thy boast of God, and knowest his will, and allowest the things that be best, and are informed by the law, and thinkest that thou art a guide to the blind, a light to them that are in darkness, a teacher of them that be ignorant, a doctor to them that be unlearned, which hast the true form and knowledge of the truth by the law. But yet thou which teachest another teachest not thyself; thou preachest that a man should not steal, yet thou stealest; thou sayest that a man should not commit adultery, but thou breakest wedlock. Thou abhorrest images, and yet thou dost commit idolatry by honouring of them. Thou that makest thy boast of the law, through breaking of the law dishonourest God: for the name of God is ill spoken of among the heathen by your means."

Thus the apostle St Paul charging the Jews, chargeth us also, which with our mouths say that we have received the word of God, and yet our conversation is contrary and ungodly. Why then do we marvel, if we suffer these punishments for our dissimulation and hypocrisy? For God useth first to begin and correct his own family: then if he should suffer this amongst us unpunished, should not he be thought to approve sin, to be a favourer of the wicked, and the God of unthrifts and lewd people?

The church of God, most dearly beloved brethren, ought not to be reputed and taken as a common place, whereunto men resort only to gaze and to hear, either for their solace or for their pastime. But whatsoever is there declared of the word of God, that should we devoutly receive, and so earnestly print in our minds, that we should both believe it as most certain truth, and most diligently endeavour ourselves to express the same in our manners and living. If we receive and repute the gospel as a thing most true and godly, why do we not live according to the same? If we count it as fables and trifles, why do we take upon us to give such credit and authority unto it? To what purpose tendeth such dissimulation and hypocrisy? If we take it for a Canterbury tale, why do we not refuse it? why do we not laugh it out of place, and whistle at it? why do we with words approve it, with conscience receive and allow it, give credit unto it, repute and take it as a thing most true, wholesome, and godly, and in our living clearly reject it? Brethren, God will not be mocked: for this cause did God so severely and grievously punish the Jews above all other nations. And sith our cause is the like and the same, the selfsame ire and displeasure of God is now provoked and kindled against us.

The empire of Rome never appeared to be in worse case, or in a more troublous and unquiet state, than when Christ's religion was preached and received among them. Whereupon arose neither few nor small complaints of the heathen, ascribing all these adversities unto the receiving of the gospel and the religion of Christ. To whom the godly and learned fathers and martyrs made answer, that it was not long of Christ's doctrine and religion, which teach things most virtuous and godly, that such calamities did ensue; but it was long of the corrupt execution and negligent observation of the same religion. For our Lord did say, The servant which knoweth his master's commandment, and doth it not, shall be sorer punished, than he which knoweth not his master's will, and offendeth by ignorance: whereby it is evident, as the word of God (if it be godly received, and with all the heart embraced) is most comfortable, of most efficacy, strength and virtue; so otherwise, if it be trodden under foot, rejected, and despised, or craftily under the cloke of dissimulation and hypocrisy received, it is a compendious and a short way unto destruction, it is an instrument whereby the punishment and displeasure of God is both augmented and also more speedily and sooner brought upon us, as we have most justly deserved.

If we will consider the histories of the books of the Kings, we shall no time find mo prophets among the people of Israel, nor the light of the word of God more spread abroad every where, than it was a little before the captivity and destruction of the same by the Babylonians. A man would think that even at that same time God had set up a school of holy scriptures and doctrine: then were the heavenly prophets in all places and to all men declared. But because so great knowledge of God and of his doctrine no good fruits did follow, but daily their living and conversation went backward and became worse, the said miserable destruction and captivity did ensue. And yet a worse captivity and misery fell upon the same people, when most perfect knowledge of God was offered unto them by the coming of Christ, what time the Lord Jesus Christ himself did preach there, his apostles did preach there, yea, many other disciples, evangelists, and doctors did preach there; whose preachings and doctrines when they would not receive, nor fruitfully and condignly accomplish and execute, then sprang up so many dissensions, tumults, and commotions, that at the last they were brought unto utter subversion and destruction in the time of Vespasian and Titus.

Of the chances of the Germans, which in a manner have suffered the same, because it is so lately done, I need not much to speak[1]. It is yet before our eyes and in present memory, so that it needeth no declaration in word.

These things before rehearsed have I for this intent and purpose spoken, that we should acknowledge and repute all these seditions and troubles, which we now suffer, to be the very plague of God for the rejecting or ungodly abusing of his most holy word, and to provoke and entice every man to true and fruitful repentance and to receive the gospel, (which now by God's mercy and the good zeal of the king's majesty and his council is every where set abroad,) not feignedly and faintly as many have done, nor stubbornly and contemptuously to reject it and forsake it, as many other do now-a-days, not knowing what it is, but thankfully to take and embrace it at God's hands, and with all humbleness and reverence to follow and use the same to God's glory and our benefit.

Ye have heard now, as I suppose, the chief and principal causes of these tumultuations. Now shall I shew you by examples of times past, what plagues of God remaineth for them that stir up seditions, unless they repent in time, and cease from their shameful and ungodly enterprises.

The children of Israel in the desert did oftentimes seditiously use themselves against Moses, but always did follow great plagues of death: so that this was the end of it, that six hundred and twenty thousand which came out of Egypt all died and were slain, and no mo came to the land of Canaan but two persons only. How miserably Core, Dathan, and Abiron perished, making of sedition, the holy bible manifestly and at large declareth. Mary[2] seditiously used herself against her brother Moyses; and was she not suddenly stricken with a leprosy, of the which she had perished, if Moyses for her had not made intercession to God? Absolon against his father king David was seditious; but was not he miserably hanged by the hair in a wood by the punishment of God? Seba and Adonias for their sedition, lost they not both their lives? In the rebellion made against Nabucodonozor in the time of the prophet Hieremy, which instantly dissuaded them from their fury, they little regarding his admonition went down unto Egypt, where at the last they were all destroyed. Did not the tribe of Ephrata make a commotion against Jephthe their judge, but were they not all miserably slain therefore?

*Quomodo Deus semper affligere solebat seditiosos.*

If I would recite and add hereunto all the histories of the heathen, which declare the miserable end of seditious persons and rebellions, I should be more prolix and tedious than this present time doth suffer. Wherefore I shall think it sufficient for this time to bring unto your remembrance the great destruction of the rude and homely

[[1] The archbishop alludes here probably to the war in Germany, A.D. 1525, in which the rustics were defeated, and Muncer their leader slain. Vid. Sleidan, De Statu religionis; Lib. v. p. 86. Ed. Francof. 1568.]

[[2] Miriam. Numb. xii.]

people, which not many years ago chanced to rise in Germany, by and by after that the word of God began there to shine and flourish, of the which were slain within the time of three months above an hundred thousand persons[1]. And what followed further thereof? Great dearth of victual, great hunger and penury.

The remedy of all our plagues is only penance.

But methinks that I have not done my office and duty, until I have shewed also the remedies to appease God's wrath, and to avoid his plagues. And to shew you the sum in few words, the only help and remedy is repentance: for other medicine and preservative can I give you none by God's word, but that which Christ did preach and declare unto the world, and which also his faithful messenger, John the Baptist, coming before to prepare his ways, did also teach, saying, "Repent you and amend, and the kingdom of heaven shall come unto you." And on this wise did our Lord Jesus Christ instruct his disciples, to whom he gave commandment specially to preach repentance and remission of sins, when he sent them forth into all the world to preach in his name. The effect of sin is to put us away from God, the very well-spring of all goodness; but by penance we return again to him from whom we were gone and departed by sin; that as we went from God, and ran after worldly things, being inflamed with insatiable desires thereof, so by penance we return from worldly creatures unto God the Creator of all things. And what mutation and change can be more comfortable or more to be desired than this? By repentance we be sorry for those things which greatly pleased us before; we forsake those things which we much made of before, not without great contempt of God, and violation of his most holy laws.

Effectus peccati. Effectus pœnitentiæ.

Wherefore sith repentance doth bring so many benefits, that thereby we be returned unto God, that we be altered into a better mind, that we bewail those things which we before unjustly loved; who doth not manifestly perceive that it is the only refuge and anchor of our health and salvation? And for this cause is penance so much commended unto us, both of Christ himself, and of St John, and of Christ's apostles.

Cur Deus differt statim punire delinquentes.

And why doth God forbear and so long defer to make punishment upon sin? Surely, because he would have us to repent and amend. And why doth he many times strike so sore at length those that continue in evil doings? Because that with the rod he would constrain to repent and amend such as by gentleness and long-suffering wax worse and worse. If God did not tarry for us, looking for our repentance and amendment, we should have perished by God's righteous judgment long before this time. If God by and by should have punished offences, we should not have had Peter among the apostles, the church should have lacked that elect vessel Paul, yea, we all long ago had been destroyed. And if God should have suffered us any longer, being so evil as we were, peradventure we should have forgotten God, and died without repentance.

Cur tandem gravius animadvertit.

Wherefore that thing that God so much desireth of us, and hath provoked unto, first by long-suffering, and now by sore punishing, that is true and godly repentance. Let us consider well in our minds, how many ways God doth call and allure sinners to penance. Our first parents Adam and Eve, after they had transgressed God's commandment, he called them unto him, he rebuked them, he sharply punished them, to endure again to repentance. And after, when all things in the earth were corrupted by the sins of man, God commanded Nohe to build an ark, to save him and all that were righteous, that only the wicked might be drowned throughout all the world. And for what purpose was the ark so long in making, but for a long preaching and warning of the world to repent and amend? How oft is it read in the book of Judges, that the children of Israel were given over unto the hands of heathen princes, that they should be punished by them, and by punishment repent and amend! It is an extreme impiety and madness to think that God is cruel and delighteth in the punishment of his people, but for their amendment. For so did the Marcionists and the Manichees blaspheme God, which for this purpose did accuse him of cruelty and unmercifulness, that thereby they might take away all credit from the old Testament. But we do acknowledge that God did therein shew his great mercy, that the Israelites,

[[1] See note, p. 199.]

admonished by afflictions, whom no speaking nor writing could move, might by repentance return again to God. Also the great slaughter, that the other tribes of Israel suffered of the tribe of Benjamin, came of none other cause, but that they being converted by penance might at the last obtain the victory.

Furthermore, the prophets sent of God did most earnestly persuade all men to repentance. The godly king David was no otherwise healed than by repentance. And the prophet Hely was sent to Achab king of Israel to call him to repentance. And by the same Manasses king of Judah did obtain remission. By the selfsame repentance did his father Ezechias obtain prolongation of his life. The king of Nineve, with all his people, by the means of repentance had God merciful unto them. The great king Nabucodonozor, after that he had repented, recovered not only his former state, being changed from a beast to a man, but also was restored to his empire and kingdom, which before he had lost. By the same means did Peter obtain remission of his abjuration and denial of Christ. By the same Paul of a persecutor became an apostle. Mary Magdalene, at the feet of the Lord, taking repentance was absolved and remitted. And the thief on the cross by this same remedy obtained salvation. This did the apostles persuade unto them that received their preaching, as it appeareth in the Acts of the Apostles. This did Peter propound unto Simon Magus. This did Paul commend unto the Corinthians, and almost to all other to whomsoever he wrote, and did both often and diligently beat it into men's heads. This we must receive as the first part of the gospel. This God requireth of all offenders, if they will be reconciled unto him. Wherefore now let us repent while we have time; for the axe is laid ready at the root of the tree to fell it down. If we will harden our hearts, and will not now be repentant of our misdoings, God will surely strike us clean out of his book.

Hitherto ye have heard of the profit and commodity of repentance: now shall ye hear what it is, and of what parts it consisteth. And to declare it plainly and grossly unto you, it is a sorrow conceived for sins committed, with hope and trust to obtain remission by Christ, with a firm and effectual purpose of amendment, and to alter all things that hath been done amiss. Pœnitentia quid sit.

I have described unto you this heavenly medicine; which if we use, God hath promised by his prophet, that "if our sins were so red as scarlet, they shall be made as white as snow." But God's word hath thus much prevailed among us, that in the stead of sorrow for our sin is crept in a great looseness of living without repentance: in the stead of hope and trust of remission of our sins is come in a great boldness to sin without the fear of God: instead of amendment of our lives I see daily every thing waxeth worse and worse. So that it is much to be afraid, that God will take away from us his vineyard, and bestow it to other husbandmen which will till it better, that it shall bring forth fruit in due season. We be come to the point almost that Hieremy spake of, when he said: "The people spake not that was right, no man would repent him so much of his sin that he would once say, What have I done? Every man ran after his own way, as a horse runneth headlong in battle; they have committed abominable mischief, and yet be they nothing ashamed, nor know the way to be abashed."

These words of Hieremy may well be spoken of us this present time. But let us repent in time without further delay. For we have enough and overmuch already provoked God's wrath and indignation against us. Wherefore let us pray and fall down and lament before the Lord our Maker; for "he is the Lord our God, and we are the people of his pasture and the sheep of his fold. To-day if we hear his voice, let us not harden our hearts, as the people did in the desert:" for of continuance in evil living there is none other end to be looked for than eternal damnation; but of repentance and perfect conversion unto God the end is perpetual salvation and everlasting life. And if we do not repent in time, at the last we shall be compelled to hear this terrible voice of damnation: "Go, ye wicked, into everlasting fire, which is prepared for the devil and those that be his." Then there shall be no remedy; then no intercession shall serve; then it shall be too late to come to repentance. Let us rather repent and turn in time, and make intercession unto the Lord by his Son Jesus

Christ. Let us lament for our sins, and call for God's mercy, that when Christ shall come at the last day, we may hear these words of him: "Come to me, you that be blessed of my Father, and take possession of the kingdom which my Father hath prepared for you."

And now with this humble prayer let us make an end:

O Lord, whose goodness far exceedeth our naughtiness, and whose mercy passeth all measure, we confess thy judgment to be most just, and that we worthily have deserved this rod wherewith thou hast now beaten us. We have offended the Lord God: we have lived wickedly: we have gone out of the way: we have not heard thy prophets which thou hast sent unto us to teach us thy word, nor have done as thou hast commanded us: wherefore we be most worthy to suffer all these plagues. Thou hast done justly, and we be worthy to be confounded. But we provoke unto thy goodness; we appeal unto thy mercy; we humble ourselves; we knowledge our faults. We turn to thee, O Lord, with our whole hearts, in praying, in fasting, in lamenting and sorrowing for our offences. Have mercy upon us, cast us not away according to our deserts; but hear us, and deliver us with speed, and call us to thee again according to thy mercy; that we, with one consent, and one mind, may evermore glorify thee, world without end[1].

*Amen.*

---

[1 "There are two copies of this prayer in the C. C. C. C. MS. One is placed at the end of the sermon: the other, which is a draft corrected by Cranmer, stands by itself, bearing the title described by Strype, Cranmer, Vol. I. p. 269. Ed. Oxon."—Jenkyns.]

# [NOTES ON JUSTIFICATION,

WITH

## AUTHORITIES FROM SCRIPTURE, THE FATHERS, AND THE SCHOOLMEN[2].]

---

AUGUSTINUS, *De fide ad Petrum.* "Fundamentum est *Christus Jesus, id est,... Christi fides,...* scilicet ...quæ per dilectionem operatur,... per quam Christus habitat in cordibus,... quæ neminem perire sinit[3]." Stillingfleet MSS. Lambeth Library. 1108. f. 58.

THOMAS. "Fides...et spes attingunt...Deum secundum quod ex ipso provenit nobis vel cognitio veri vel adeptio boni; sed caritas attingit...Deum, ut in ipso sistat, *non ut ex eo aliquid nobis proveniat*[4]."

AUGUSTINUS *et* ALIPIUS *Bonifacio, Epist.* 106.

"Quis nos .... ab illa perditionis massa .... discernit, nisi qui venit quærere et salvare quod perierat? Unde apostolus interrogat, dicens, 'Quis enim te discernit?' Ubi si dixerit homo, 'Fides mea,' 'voluntas mea,' 'bonum opus meum;' respondetur ei: 'Quid .... habes quod non accepisti?'" &c.

"Si aliquid boni operatur homo, ut gratiam mereatur, non ei merces imputatur secundum gratiam, sed secundum debitum. Si autem credat in eum qui justificat impium, ut deputetur fides ejus ad justitiam, ('Justus enim ex fide vivit,') *profecto antequam gratia justificetur, id est, justus efficiatur, impius quid est nisi impius?* Quem si debitum sequeretur, quid ejus merito nisi supplicium redderetur?"

"Si quis autum dixerit, *quod gratiam bene operandi fides mereatur,* negare non possumus, imo vero gratissime confitemur."

"*Ipsa est justitia ex fide, qua credimus nos justificari, hoc est, justos fieri, gratia Dei per Jesum Christum Dominum nostrum,* ut inveniamur in illo non habentes nostram justitiam quæ ex lege est, sed eam quæ est per fidem Christi. *Quæ est ex Deo justitia in fide? Utique in fide qua credimus nobis justitiam divinitus dari, non a nobis in nobis nostris viribus fieri.*"

"Justificati .... gratis per gratiam ipsius, ne fides ipsa superba sit. Nec dicat sibi, Si ex fide, quomodo gratis? *Quod enim fides meretur, cur non potius redditur quam donatur?* Non dicat ista homo fidelis; quia cum dixerit, 'Ut merear justificationem habeo fidem;' respondetur ei: 'Quid habes quod non accepisti?' Cum ergo fides impetrat justificationem, (sicut unicuique Deus partitus est etiam ipsius mensuram fidei,) non gratiam Dei aliquid meriti præcedit humani, sed ipsa gratia meretur augeri, ut aucta mereatur perfici, comitante non ducente, pedissequa non prævia voluntate[6]." *Fides non meretur justificationem*[5].

AUGUSTINUS, *Enchirid.* ca. 3. "Quæris .... quonam modo sit colendus Deus? Hic si respondero, *fide, spe, caritate,* colendum Deum; profecto dicturus es, brevius hoc dictum esse quam velis: ac deinde petiturus, ea tibi breviter explicari, *quæ ad singula tria ista pertineant, quid credendum scilicet, quid sperandum, quid amandum sit*[7]."

Et ca. 8. "Fides est et malarum rerum et bonarum, et periturarum rerum[8] et præsentium et futurarum, .... et suarum rerum .... et alienarum..... Spes autem non nisi bonarum rerum est, nec nisi futurarum, et ad eum pertinentium qui earum spem gerere perhibetur. Quæ cum ita sint, propter has causas *distinguenda erit fides a spe, sicut vocabulo, ita et rationabili differentia.....* Jam de amore quid dicam, sine quo fides nihil prodest? Spes vero sine amore esse non potest....... 'Demones credunt et contremiscunt,' nec tamen sperant vel amant: .... propter quod .... Paulus fidem quæ per dilectionem operatur approbat atque commendat, quæ utique sine spe esse non potest. Proinde nec amor sine spe est, nec sine amore spes, neque utrumque sine fide[9]."

CYRILLUS, *In Joh.* lib. x. ca. 16. "'Sicut palmes non potest ferre fructum a semet ipso, nisi manserit in vite; sic nec vos, nisi in me manseritis.' Manifestius jam ex hoc loco discimus *sincera fide palmites justos viti fideles fieri.* Sed non est minoris curæ, jugiter per caritatem, id est, mandati servationem, Christo

---

[[2] The following "notes on Justification" are printed from MSS. in the Lambeth Library, which formerly belonged to Archbishop Stillingfleet, and which are in Archbishop Cranmer's hand-writing, except where otherwise noted. The passages printed in italic type are underscored in the MSS. in red ink, (Dr Jenkyns conjectures,) "by Cranmer himself." Vid. Jenkyns' Remains of Abp. Cranmer, Vol. II. p. 121, and Burnet's Hist. of Reformat. Vol. II. pp. 576, 7. Ed. Oxon. 1829.]

[[3] August. De Fid. et Op. cap. xvi. Tom. IV. p. 31. Ed. Paris. 1635; where *utique* for *scilicet*, *permittit* for *sinit;* and the whole passage is greatly compressed in the quotation.]

[[4] Thom. Aquin. Summ. Theolog. Secund. Secundæ. q. xxiii. Art. VI. Conclus. Tom. II. p. 69. Antverp. 1569.]

[[5] The side note is inserted in the margin with red ink in the archbishop's hand-writing.]

[[6] August. et Alip. Bonifacio, Epist. cvi. Tom. II. pp. 181, 2; where, *si autem credit in eum,* and *quæ ex Deo est justitia, in fide utique est; qua credimus.* The Benedictine editors call this Epist. clxxxvi. Alyp. et August. ad Paulinum.]

[[7] Id. Enchirid. ad Laurent. cap. ii. iii. Tom. III. p. 66.]

[[8] *Rerum* is omitted by Dr Jenkyns, Vol. II. p. 135.]

[[9] August. Enchirid. ad Laurent. cap. viii. p. 67, where *est itaque fides et malarum.*]

inhærere..... *Non igitur sufficit ad perfectionem* (id est, ad sanctificationem, quæ per Christum in spiritu est) *in numero palmitum recipi, sed oportet ardenti caritate atque continuo immaculate Christum sequi*[1]."

THOMAS. *Ad Hebr.* x.[2] lect. 4. "Justitia duplex est. Una, quo ad humanum judicium, Rom. x. 'Ignorantes Dei justitiam et suam quærentes statuere,' &c. Alia, quo ad divinum, Luc. i. 'Erant ambo justi ante Deum.....' *Illud autem per quod homo justificatur apud Deum est fides.* Rom. iii. 'Justitia Dei per fidem Jesu Christi.' *Cujus ratio est: quia per hoc est homo justus,* per quod ordinatur ad Deum. *Illud autem per quod primo . . . ordinatur in Deum est fides.* Et ideo dicit, 'Justus meus... ex fide vivit.' Nec solum justitia per fidem, sed etiam per fidem justificatus vivit. Sicut enim per animam vivit corpus, ita anima per Deum. Unde, *sicut per illud per quod primo unitur anima corpori, vivit corpus: ita per id per quod primo unitur Deus animæ, vivit anima. Hoc autem est fides.....* Gal. ii. 'Quantum nunc vivo, .... in fide vivo Filii Dei.' Fides autem si non est formata caritate, mortua est, et ideo non vivificat animam sine caritate. Gal. v. 'Fides quæ per dilectionem operatur.' 1 Joh. iii. 'Nos scimus quod translati sumus de morte ad vitam, quum diligimus fratres[3].'"

HUGO DE STO. VICTORE, to. 3. *Summa Sententiarum* tract. I. ca. 2. "De fide tanquam fundamento omnium bonorum spes et caritas oriuntur, quia nihil potest sperari vel speratum amari, nisi prius credatur. *Licet simul sint tempore, et non prius fides .... quam spes et caritas; tamen in causa fides præcedit spem et caritatem*[4]."

AMBROSIUS. Rom. x. "'Finis legis Christus ad salutem omni credenti:'.... hoc dicit, *quia perfectionem legis habet, qui credit in Christum.* Cum enim nullus justificaretur ex lege (quia nemo implebat legem nisi qui speraret in promisso Christo), *fides posita est, quæ crederet perfectionem legis, ut omnibus prætermissis fides satisfaceret pro tota lege et prophetis*[5]."

THOMAS. 1 Cor. xiii. "De fide, spe, et caritate dicitur, Ecclus. ii. 'Qui timetis Deum, *credite in illum,*' *quantum ad fidem.* 'Qui timetis Deum, *sperate in illum,*' *quantum ad spem.* 'Qui timetis Deum, *diligite eum,*' *quantum ad caritatem.* Tria ergo ista manent nunc[6]."

MAGISTER SENTENTIARUM, *li.* ii. *Di.* 23.

"Fides est virtus, qua creduntur quæ non videntur[7]."

*Di.* 26.

"Spes est virtus, qua spiritualia et æterna bona sperantur[8]."

*Di.* 27.

"Caritas est dilectio, qua diligitur Deus propter se, et proximus propter Deum vel in Deo[9]."

AUGUSTINUS.

"Fides est credere quod non vides[10]."

DORBELLUS, *li.* iii. *di.* 23.

"Fides acquisita præcedit caritatem, .... sed fides infusa non infunditur sine caritate[11]."

*Di.* 26.

"Respectu actus desiderandi est aliqua virtus theologica. Sed illa non potest esse fides nec caritas, quia est spes. Probatio minoris:.... Quia omnis actus fidei est credere, nullum autem desiderare est credere;.... et caritas est suprema virtus affectiva, et per consequens supremus amor habitualis; amor autem amicitiæ, quo volumus Deum esse in se bonum, est simpliciter perfectior amore concupiscentiæ, quo desideramus Deum esse bonum nostrum: ergo caritas, quæ inclinat ad amandum Deum amore amicitiæ, est alia virtus ab illa quæ inclinat ad desiderandum nobis bonum infinitum."

*Eadem di.*

"Credere me justum finaliter esse salvandum non est nisi fides applicata ad quoddam particulare: sed desiderare istud est actus spei. Et sic certitudo sperantis non est actus spei, sed præcedit ipsum[12]."

*Di.* 27.

"Ad diligendum Deum super omnia est aliqua virtus theologica inclinans; hæc autem caritas est. Et distinguitur a spe, quod actus ejus non est concupiscere amanti bonum, in quantum est commodum amantis, sed tendere in objectum secundum se, etiam si per impossibile circumscriberetur commoditas amantis."

Et mox. "Licet posset poni amicitia quædam acquisita ex actibus dilectionis divinæ inclinans ad Deum

---

[[1] Cyril. Alex. in Joan. Lib. x. cap. xvi. Ed. (Lat.) Paris. 1508, where *facere fructum, ex hoc loco dicimus, palmites insertos viti.* The Greek will be found, Cyril. Op. Tom. IV. p. 874. Ed. Lutet. Paris. 1638.]

[[2] The chapter is omitted by Dr Jenkyns.]

[[3] Thom. Aquin. Op. in Epist. ad Heb. cap. x. Lect. IV. Tom. XVI. fol. 421, 2. Ed. Venet. 1593, where *Erant autem* is read for *erant ambo,* and *apud Deum,—ordinatur apud Deum,—vivit —Quod autem nunc,—caritatem, fratres,* are omitted.]

[[4] Hugo de S. Vict. Summa Sentent. Tract. i. cap. ii. Tom. III. p. 298. Ed. Mogunt. 1617.]

[[5] Ambros. In Epist. ad Rom. cap. x. Tom. III. p. 145. Ed. Colon. Agrip. 1616, where *in promissum Christum, quæ traderet.*—This treatise is considered spurious, and has been attributed to Hilary the deacon.]

[[6] Thom. Aquin. Op. in 1 Epist. ad Cor. cap. xiii. Lect. iv. Tom. XVI. fol. 82, 2.]

[[7] Pet. Lombard. Magist. Sentent. Lib. III. Dist. xxiii. p. 287, (2.) Ed. Colon. Agrip. 1566.]

[[8] Id. ibid. Dist. xxvi. p. 293, (2.) where, *est autem spes virtus.*]

[[9] Id. ibid. Dist. xxvii. p. 294, (2.)]

[[10] Quid est enim fides nisi, &c.—August. In Joan. Evang. cap. viii. Tractat. xl. Tom. IX. p. 124.]

[[11] Fides autem ista præcedit caritatem, et per consequens est acquisita; quia infusa non infunditur sine caritate.—Nicol. de Orbellis in Sentent. Exposit. Sent. III. Dist. xxiii. fol. xix. Ed. Paris. 1498.]

[[12] Id. ibid. Dist. xxvi. foll. xxii., xxiii.]

diligendum, tamen actus dilectionis non elicitur ita intensus mediante tali habitu, sicut mediante caritate a Deo infusa, per quam etiam acceptatur a Deo humana operatio[13]."

*Di.* 31.

"Habitus caritatis manebit in patria, quod ibi erit actus ad quem inclinat, sed diligendi Deum in se[14]."

St Paul saith that we be justified freely by faith without works, because no man should glory in his works. Stillingfleet MSS. Lambeth Library. 1108. f. 69.

Ephes. ii. "Gratia salvi facti estis per fidem, idque non ex vobis; Dei donum est: non ex operibus, *ne quis glorietur*."

Titus iii. "Apparuit gratia Dei Salvatoris nostri, non ex operibus justitiæ quæ fecimus nos, sed secundum suam misericordiam salvos nos fecit."

Rom. iii. "Omnes peccaverunt, et egent gloria Dei, justificati gratis gratia ipsius per redemptionem quæ est in Christo Jesu." Et mox. "*Ubi est ergo gloriatio tua? Exclusa est.* Per quam legem? Operum? Non, *sed per legem fidei.* Arbitramur enim fide justificari, &c. *Si Abraham ex operibus justificatus est, habet gloriationem,* sed non apud Deum."

Gal. iii. "Si data esset lex, quæ posset vivificare, vere ex lege esset justitia. Sed conclusit scriptura omnia sub peccatum, ut promissio ex fide Jesu Christi daretur credentibus."

[Gal.] v. "Evacuati estis a Christo, quicunque in lege justificamini; a gratia cecidistis. Nos autem Spiritu ex fide spem justitiæ exspectamus."

1 Cor. i. "Videte vocationem vestram, fratres, quia non multi sapientes secundum carnem, non multi potentes, non multi nobiles; sed quæ stulta sunt mundi elegit Deus, &c. *ut non glorietur omnis caro coram ipso.*"

"Christus factus est nobis sapientia a Deo, justitiaque et sanctificatio et redemptio, *ut, quemadmodum scriptum est, qui gloriatur in Domino glorietur.*"

Gal. vi. "Mihi absit gloriari, nisi in cruce Domini nostri Jesu Christi."

ORIGENES.

"Audi quid dicat apostolus: 'Mihi .... absit gloriari, nisi in cruce Domini nostri Jesu Christi.'.... *Vides apostolum non gloriantem super justitia sua,* neque super castitate, neque super sapientia, *neque super ceteris virtutibus vel actibus suis;* sed apertissime pronunciantem et dicentem, 'Qui gloriatur in Domino glorietur.'" Et mox: "Quis .... vel justitia sua gloriabitur, cum audiat Deum per prophetam dicentem, 'Omnis justitia vestra sicut pannus mulieris menstruatæ?' Sola igitur justa gloriatio est in fide crucis Christi[15]."

BASILIUS.

"Dicit apostolus quod 'Christus nobis factus est sapientia a Deo, *justitiaque et sanctificatio et redemptio,* ut, quemadmodum scriptum est, *qui gloriatur in Domino glorietur.*' Hæc enim est perfecta ac integra gloriatio in Deo, quum *neque ob justitiam suam quis se jactet,* sed novit quidem seipsum veræ justitiæ indignum esse, sola autem fide in Christum justificatur. Et *gloriatur Paulus ob justitiæ suæ contemptum,* et quia quærit per Christum justitiam ex Deo in fide[16]."

HIERONYMUS.

"Convertentem impium per solam fidem justificat Deus, non per opera bona quæ non habuit. Alioquin per impietatis opera fuerat puniendus[17]."

THEODORETUS.

"'Ego sum qui deleo iniquitates tuas propter me, et peccatorum tuorum non recordabor.' *Nec enim ullis operibus, sed per solam fidem mystica bona consecuti sunt*[18]."

AUGUSTINUS.

"Si gratia est, gratis datur. Quid est 'gratis datur?'...... Nihil boni fecisti, et datur tibi remissio peccatorum. Attenduntur opera tua, et inveniuntur omnia mala. Si quod debetur istis operibus, Deus redderet, utique damnaret..... Non .... reddit Deus debitam pœnam, sed donat indebitam gratiam[19].

Nec quod recti sunt corde, sed .... ut recti sint corde, prætendit justitiam suam qua justificat impium." *De Spiritu et Litera*, ca. 7[20].

AMBROSIUS.

"*Ideo nemo glorietur in operibus, quod nemo factis suis justificatur;* sed qui justus est, donatum habet[21]."

*Idem.* "Manifeste beati sunt, quibus sine labore aut opere aliquo remittuntur iniquitates et peccata teguntur, nulla ab eis requisita pœnitentiæ opera, nisi tantum ut credant[22]."

---

[[13] Id. Dist. xxvii. fol. xxiii., where *hujusmodi operatio* for *humana.*]

[[14] Id. Dist. xxxi. fol. xxvi.]

[[15] Origen. Comment. in Epist. ad Rom. Lib. III. Tom. IV. p. 517. Ed. Paris. 1733—59.]

[[16] Basil. Hom. xxii. De Humilitat. Tom. I. p. 473. Ed. Paris. 1638.]

[[17] Hieron. In Epist. ad Rom. cap. iv. Tom. IX. p. 220. Ed. Francof. 1684.]

[[18] Theodoret. Serm. vii. De sacrificiis. Tom. IV. p. 587. Ed. Lutet. Paris. 1642.]

[[19] August. In Psalm. xxxi. Præfat. Tom. VIII. p. 77.]

[[20] Id. De Spiritu et Litera, ad Marcell. cap. vii. Tom. III. p. 307.]

[[21] Ambros. Epist. xli. Lib. VI. Tom. V. p. 143. Ed. Colon. Agrip. 1616, where *quia nemo factis.*]

[[22] Id. Comm. in Epist. ad Rom. cap. iv. Tom. III. p. 124.]

*Idem.* "Convenit .... ut creatura *in solo nomine Domini Creatoris consequatur salutem, hoc est, per fidem*[1]."

LOMBARDUS.

"'*Ubi est gloriatio tua*'? .... *Sola fide sine operibus præcedentibus fit homo justus*[2]."

BRUNO.

"*Vere per fidem excluditur gloriatio* [*tua*]; *nam fides sola justificat sine omni opere legis*[3]."

PROSPER, *De Gratia et Lib. Arb.*

"Qui credunt, Dei aguntur Spiritu: qui non credunt, libero avertuntur arbitrio. Conversio ergo nostra ad Deum non ex nobis, sed ex Deo est, sicut apostolus dicit: 'Gratia salvi facti estis per fidem, et hoc non ex vobis, sed donum Dei est, et *non ex operibus, ne quis glorietur.*'"

Et mox: "Non juste agebat homo, et aucta est justitia ejus. Nec ad Deum gradiebatur, et confirmatus est cursus ejus. Nec diligebat Deum, et inflammata est caritas ejus. Sed *cum esset sine fide ac proinde impius, accepit Spiritum Dei et factus est justus.*"

Et mox: "*Gratia igitur Dei quoscunque justificat,* non ex bonis meliores, sed *ex malis bonos fecit,* postea per profectum ex bonis factura meliores[4]."

CHRYSOSTOMUS. Rom. iii.

"Dicens Paulus, '*Exclusa est gloriatio,*' *simul etiam ostendit quomodo sit exclusa.* Quomodo igitur exclusa est? inquit; 'Per quam legem? Operum? Nequaquam, sed *per legem fidei.*' .... Quæ vero ista fidei lex est? *Per gratiam videlicet salvari*[5]."

Meaning thereby to exclude the merit and dignity of all works and virtues, as insufficient to deserve remission of sin, and to ascribe the same only to Christ.

Rom. iv. "Ideo ex fide ut secundum gratiam."

ORIGENES, BASILIUS, HIERONYMUS, AUGUSTINUS, THEODORETUS, AMBROSIUS — supra.
CHRYSOSTOMUS postea.

AMBROSIUS.

"Dignitatem et meritum non facit nisi fides[6]."

AUGUSTINUS.

"Opera bona sequuntur justificatum, non præcedunt justificandum[7]."

"*Per gratiam justificatur homo gratis, id est, nullis suorum operum præcedentibus meritis.* Alioquin gratia jam non est gratia." *De Spiritu et Lit.* ca. 10[7].

"*Nihilque aliud velit intelligi in eo quod dicit gratis, nisi quod justificationem opera non præcedunt.*" *De Spiritu et Lit.* [ca.] 26[8].

"Per fidem impetratio gratiæ contra peccatum, per gratiam sanatio animæ a vitio peccati, per animæ sanitatem libertas arbitrii," &c. *De Spiritu et Lit.* ca. 30[9].

BERNARDUS.

"*Non est quo gratia intret, ubi jam meritum occupavit.* .... Deest gratiæ quicunque meritis deputat. .... *Gratia me reddit justificatum gratis,* et sic liberatum a servitute peccati[10]."

BRUNO.

"Fides credentis reputatur ei ad justitiam, quod justificatur *sine omni merito* per solam fidem[11]."

CHRYSOSTOMUS.

"Non ex benefactis, nec laboribus, nec pensatore, sed sola gratia justificavit genus nostrum. Quod et Paulus declarans dicit, 'Nunc autem absque lege justitia Dei manifestata est.' Justitia autem Dei per fidem Jesu Christi, non per ullum sudorem aut dolorem[12]."

---

[[1] Id. In Epist. ad Rom. cap. ix. Tom. III. p. 144, where *ut in solo nomine Domini et conditoris consequatur salutem creatura.*]

[[2] Pet. Lombard. Magist. in Paul. Epistt. Collectan. ad Rom. cap. iii. foll. 17, 8. Ed. Paris. 1537.]

[[3] Brunon. Exposit. in Pauli Epistt. Ad Rom. iv. fol. xi. Ed. Paris. 1509.]

[[4] Prosper. Ad Rufin. cap. vi. 7. col. 92, Ed. Paris. 1711, where *non enim juste agebat et,* and *spiritum fidei.*—Ibid. cap. ix. 10. col. 93, where *bonos facit.*]

[[5] Chrysost. in Epist. ad Rom. Hom. vii. cap. iii. Tom. IX. p. 487. Ed. Paris. 1718—38.]

[[6] Ambros. in Epist. ad Rom. cap. iii. Tom. III. p. 124. Ed. Colon. Agrip. 1616.]

[[7] August. De Spiritu et Litera, ad Marcell. cap. x. Tom. III. p. 308. Ed. Paris. 1635, where *per ipsam quippe justificatur gratis.*]

[[8] Id. ibid. cap. xxvi. p. 314, where *nisi quia.*]

[[9] Id. ibid. cap. xxx. p. 316.]

[[10] Bernard. in Cantica, Serm. lxvii. Tom. I. col. 1504. Ed. Paris. 1690.]

[[11] Brunon. Exposit. ad Roman. iv. fol. xii.]

[[12] Chrysost. Adv. Judæos, Orat. vii. Tom. I. p. 665.]

*Idem.* "Ne tuæ confidas pœnitentiæ; tua namque pœnitentia tanta nequit peccata delere[13]."

"*Si sola foret pænitentia, jure timeres:* sed postquam cum pœnitentia commiscetur Dei misericordia, confide,... quia tuam vicit nequitiam[14]."

GENNADIUS.

"*Gratis, hoc est, absque bonis operibus* salvus factus es, ut nihil contuleris præter fidem. Justificatus autem *gratis justificaris, et a tergo venis post gloriam et beneficium Dei.* Egent gloria Dei, hoc est, a tergo veniunt, et non præoccupaverunt glorificare Deum. Ideo omnes qui crediderunt in Christum, gratis justificantur, credere tamen coimportantes[15]."

LOMBARDUS.

"Per .... fidem justificatur impius, ut *deinde* ipsa fides incipiat per dilectionem operari. *Ea enim sola bona opera dicenda sunt, quæ fiunt per dilectionem Dei.* Ipsa enim dilectio opus fidei dicitur[16]."

ERASMUS.

"His qui pure simpliciterque Christo fidunt, hoc præstat fides, ut pro justis habeantur, *nulla legis observatæ commendatione,* sed solius fidei[17]."

AUGUSTINUS.

"*Quomodo ergo justificabitur homo per fidem sine operibus?* Responderet ipse apostolus, *Propterea* hoc dixi tibi, O homo, *ne quasi de operibus tuis præsumere videreris, et merito operum tuorum* accepisse fidei gratiam[18]."

PROSPER, *in Psalm.* cii.

"Retributiones Dei *non secundum merita* humana sunt factæ. Nam damnatio peccatoribus debebatur, sed gratia præstita est malis, et salus perditis."

Et mox: "Ostendit per quos gradus gratiæ anima humana salvetur. '*Qui propitius sit,*' inquit, '*omnibus iniquitatibus tuis.*' *Non ait, omnibus virtutibus tuis, quæ utique nullæ ei inessent, nisi fieret remissio peccatorum.* Quæ ne rursus exsurgant, 'Sanat,' inquit, 'omnes languores tuos[19].'

CHRYSOSTOMUS. Rom. iii.

"Cujusnam gratia omnia fecit lex? Quatenus justum redderet hominem. Verum illud præstare lex non potuit: 'Omnes enim,' inquit, 'peccaverunt.' Adveniens vero fides illud præstitit. *Quam primum enim homo credidit, confestim simul justificatus est*[20]."

ANSELMUS. Rom. iv.

"Non ideo apostolus dicit, 'Arbitramur hominem justificari per fidem,' uti, si quis crediderit, non ad eum pertineat bene operari; sed *ideo* potius, ut *nemo putet meritis priorum bonorum operum se pervenisse ad donum justificationis quæ est in fide.* .... Nam *justificatus per fidem, quomodo potest nisi juste deinceps operari? quamvis nihil antea juste operatus ad fidei justificationem pervenerit.* .... Sequuntur enim opera justificatum, non præcedunt justificandum."

*Idem.* "Manifestum est Jacobum loqui de operibus quæ fidem subsequuntur. Paulus sine præcedentibus operibus dixit hominem sola fide justificari. *Nemo enim fidem suis præcedentibus meritis habere potest,* et *ideo* qui per fidem gratis sibi datam justificatur, non in se sed in Domino glorietur[21]."

When St Paul said, "We be justified freely by faith without works," he meant of all manner of works of the law, as well of the Ten Commandments, as of ceremonials and judicials.

Rom. iii. "Ex operibus legis non justificabitur omnis caro. Nam per legem agnitio peccati. Legem ergo destruimus per fidem? Absit, sed legem stabilimus."

Rom. ii. "Si præputium justificationes legis servaverit, nonne præputium illius pro circumcisione imputabitur? Et judicabit quod est ex natura præputium (si legem servaverit) te qui per literam et circumcisionem transgressor es legis."

"Qui prædicas non furandum, furaris: qui dicis non mœchandum, mœcharis: qui abominaris idola, sacrilegium facis: qui in lege gloriaris, per prævaricationem legis Deum inhonoras."

"Circumcisio quidem prodest, si legem observes. Si autem prævaricator legis sis, circumcisio tua præputium facta est."

Rom. iv. "Lex iram operatur; ubi enim non est lex, nec prævaricatio."

Rom. v. "Peccatum non imputatur, cum non est lex."

"Lex subintravit, ut abundaret delictum."

---

[[13] Id. De Pœnit. Hom. viii. Tom. II. p. 341.]

[[14] Id. ibid.]

[[15] The passage has not been found. It does not appear what work of his is here intended.]

[[16] Pet. Lombard. Magist. Sentent. Lib. III. Dist. xxiii. p. 288. Ed. Colon. Agrip. 1566.]

[[17] Erasm. In Epist. ad Rom. cap. iv. Tom. VII. col. 788, Ed. Lugd. Bat. 1703—6, where *pure simpliciterque fidunt illi...his... fides non præstat.*]

[[18] August. In Psalm. xxxi. Præfat. Tom. VIII. p. 77. Ed. Paris. 1635, where *respondet, hoc tibi dixi,* and *te accepisse.*]

[[19] Prosper. in Psalm. cii. col. 379. Ed. Paris. 1711.]

[[20] Chrysost. in Epist. ad Rom. Hom. vii. Tom. IX. p. 488.]

[[21] Anselm. in Pauli Epistt. Enarrat. In Roman. iv. pp. 25, 26. Ed. Colon. 1545. But these commentaries are supposed to have been written by Herv. Natalis. See Coci Censura Patrum. p. 433, 4. Ed. Helmes. 1683.

In the Lambeth MSS. this extract from Anselm appears to be in another hand than that of the archbishop.]

Rom. vii. "Peccatum non cognovi, nisi per legem. Nam et concupiscentiam non novissem, nisi lex dixisset, Non concupisces. Lex quidem sancta, et mandatum sanctum et justum et bonum. Quod ergo bonum est, mihi factum est mors? Absit.——Scimus enim quod lex spiritualis est, ego autem carnalis.—— Invenio igitur legem volenti mihi facere bonum, quum mihi malum adjacet. Condelector enim legi Dei secundum interiorem hominem."

Rom. viii. "De peccato damnavit peccatum in carne, ut justificatio legis impleretur in nobis."

Rom. ix. "Israel persequens legem justitiæ in legem justitiæ non pervenit. Propter quid? Quia non ex fide, sed tanquam ex operibus legis."

2 Cor. iii. "Litera occidit, spiritus autem vivificat."

Gal. ii. "Si per legem est justitia, ergo Christus gratis mortuus est."

[Gal.] iii. "Si data esset lex, quæ posset justificare, vere ex lege esset justitia."

Ephes. ii. "Gratia salvi facti estis per fidem, idque non ex vobis."

Philippen. iii. "Secundum justitiam quæ est in lege factus irreprehensibilis.——Omnia reputavi stercora esse, ut Christum lucrifaciam, et reperiar in illo non habens meam justitiam quæ est ex lege, sed illam quæ est ex fide Christi."

Tit. iii. "Apparuit gratia Dei Salvatoris nostri, non ex operibus justitiæ quæ fecimus nos, sed secundum suam misericordiam salvos nos fecit."

The same meant divers ancient authors, as well Greeks as Latins, when they said, "We be justified by only faith, or faith alone."

ORIGENES supra.

HIERONYMUS.

"'Ex operibus legis non justificabitur omnis caro.' Quod ne de lege Mosi tantum dictum putes, et non de omnibus mandatis, (quæ uno legis nomine continentur,) idem apostolus scribit dicens, 'Consentio legi Dei' &c.[1]"

GENNADIUS.

"*Gratis servaris, hoc est, sine operibus virtutum, aut officiis rectis et perfectis*[2]."

THEODORETUS, AMBROSIUS, CHRYSOSTOMUS, BERNARDUS } supra.

AUGUSTINUS, *De Spiritu et Litera*, ca. 8, 13, 14, 29[3]. Et, *Ad Simplicianum*, q. 2.

THOMAS.

"'Arbitramur justificari hominem ex fide sine operibus legis.' Non ... solum *sine operibus cæremonialibus* (quæ gratiam non conferebant, sed solum significabant), *sed etiam sine operibus moralium præceptorum, sed illud ad, &c.* Tit. iii. 'Non ex operibus justitiæ[4].'"

*Idem.* "Moralium præceptorum legitimus usus est, ut homo attribuat eis quod in eis continetur. 'Data est lex ut cognoscatur peccatum.'...Non est ergo in eis spes justificationis, sed in sola fide. Rom. iii. 'Arbitramur justificari hominem per fidem sine operibus legis[5].'"

AUGUSTINUS, *De Spiritu et Lit.* ca. 4.

"Doctrina...illa, qua mandatum accepimus continenter recteque vivendi, litera est occidens, nisi adsit vivificans Spiritus[6]."

St James meant of justification in another sense, when he said, "A man is justified by works, and not by faith only." For he spake of such a justification which is a declaration, continuation, and increase of that justification which St Paul spake of before.

Jac. ii. "Si fidem quis dicat se habere, opera autem non habeat, &c.[7]"

"Ostende mihi fidem tuam ex operibus tuis, et ego ostendam tibi fidem meam ex operibus meis."

"Abraham pater noster nonne ex operibus justificatus est, cum immolaret filium suum super altare?"

1 Mac. ii. "Abraham in tentatione nonne inventus est fidelis?"

Gen. xxii. "Tentavit Deus Abraham."

Apoc. [xxii.] "Qui justus est, justificetur adhuc."

BEDA.

"Credere in Deum soli novere qui diligunt Deum, qui non solo nomine fiunt Christiani, sed et factis et vita."

---

[1 Hieron. Ad Ctesiph. Epist. xliii. Tom. II. p. 172. Ed. Francof. 1684, where *consentio enim.*]

[2 See the preceding page, note 15.]

[3 August. Tom. III. pp. 307, 9, 10, 16.]

[4 Thom. Aquin. Op. Venet. 1593. Ad. Rom. cap. iii. Tom. XVI. fol. 13, 2, where *secundum illud ad Tit. iii.* Dr Jenkyns has omitted the words *sed illud ad, &c.*, and inserted the following, *quæ fecimus——nos fecit*, which are not found in the Lambeth MSS. Vid. Jenkyns' Remains of Abp. Cranmer, Vol. II. p. 128.]

[5 Id. in 1 Tim. i. Tom. XVI. fol. 175, 1. where *Horum legitimus.*]

[6 August. De Spiritu et Litera, ad Marcell. Tom. III. p. 305.]

[7 Dr Jenkyns has added the following words: *numquid poterit fides salvare eum?* Vol. II. p. 128.]

Et mox. "Cum [Jacobus] bona opera commemorat Abrahæ, quæ ejus fidem comitata sunt, satis ostendit Paulum apostolum non ita per Abraham docere justificari hominem per fidem sine operibus, ut, si quis crediderit, non ad eum pertineat bene operari; sed ad hoc potius, ut nemo arbitretur meritis priorum bonorum operum *se pervenisse ad donum justificationis*, quæ est in fide [8].

Unde apostolus Paulus dicit posse hominem sine operibus, scilicet præcedentibus, *justificari per fidem.* Nam justificatus per fidem quomodo potest nisi *juste operari* [9] ?"

*Glossa ordinaria.*

"Probavit [apostolus,] eos qui opera non habent, veram fidem non habere.... Quod Abraham per fidem sine operibus justificatus dicitur, de operibus quæ præcedebant intelligitur; quia per opera quæ fecit insons non fuit, sed sola fide. Hic de operibus agitur quæ fidem sequuntur, per quæ *amplius justificatur,* cum jam per fidem *fuisset justus*.... [Heb. xi.] 'Fide Abraham obtulit filium suum, cum tentaretur.' Hæc oblatio fuit opus et testimonium fidei et justitiæ [10]."

HUGO CARDINALIS.

"Apostolus loquitur ad Rom. de operibus præcedentibus fidem, quibus non Abraham nec alius justificatus est: hic vero est sermo de operibus sequentibus fidem; *quæ dicuntur justificare,* tum quod justificationem jam habitam per fidem infusam *notificant,* tum quod eam *perficiunt et conservant.* Et tunc res fieri dicitur, quando perficitur, vel quum innotescit [11]."

Et mox: "[Abraham per fidem fuit justificatus;] opera autem fidem perficiunt, notificant, augmentant, et confirmant [12]."

LYRA.

"'Et suppleta est scriptura dicens, Credidit Abraham Deo, et imputatum est ei ad justitiam'...Ex oblatione Isaac scriptura illa dicitur esse suppleta, in quantum per hoc magnitudo fidei Abrahæ fuit aliis declarata [13]."

PROSPER, *De Vita contemplativa*, Li. iii. ca. 21.

"Fides—quæ est justitiæ fundamentum, quam nulla bona opera præcedunt, et ex *qua* omnia—procedunt, ipsa nos a peccatis omnibus purgat, mentes nostras illuminat, Deo reconciliat [14]," &c.

*Idem, in Libro Sententiarum ex Augustino:* "Sicut duo sunt officia medicinæ, unum quo sanatur infirmitas, aliud quo custoditur sanitas; ita duo sunt dona gratiæ, unum quod aufert carnis cupiditatem, aliud quod facit animi perseverari virtutem [15]."

*Idem, eodem,* ca. 7. et in *Psal.* ciii. "Caritas Dei et proximi propria et specialis virtus est piorum atque sanctorum, cum ceteræ virtutes et bonis et malis possunt esse communes [16]."

This proposition, that we be justified by Christ only and not by our good works, is a very true and necessary doctrine of St Paul and other the apostles and prophets, taught by them to set forth thereby the glory of Christ, and mercy of God by Christ.

1 Timo. ii. "Unus Deus, unus Mediator Dei et hominum."

Rom. xi. "Si ex gratia, non ex operibus; alioqui gratia jam non est gratia."

"Si ex operibus, jam non est gratia."

1 Cor. i. "Ut non glorietur omnis caro," sed, "qui gloriatur, in Domino glorietur."

Gal. iii. "Abrahæ dictæ sunt promissiones et semini ejus. Non dicit seminibus, sed quasi in uno, et semini tuo, qui est Christus."

Although all that be justified must of necessity have charity as well as faith, yet neither faith nor charity be the worthiness and merits of our justification, but that is to be ascribed only to our Saviour Christ, which was offered upon the cross for our sins, and rose again for our justification.

Tit. iii. "Non ex operibus justitiæ quæ fecimus nos, sed secundum suam misericordiam salvos nos fecit."

Daniel. ix. "Non in justificationibus nostris prosternimus preces ante faciem tuam, sed in miserationibus tuis multis."

ANSELM. Rom. iii.

"Ne fides ipsa superbire incipiat et dicat: Si ex fide, quomodo gratis? Quod enim fides meretur, potius redditur quam datur. Sed *si quis dixerit, Ut merear justificationem, habeo fidem; respondetur ei, 'Quid habes quod non accepisti* [17] *?'* "

THOMAS fo. sequenti.

[[8] Ven. Bed. In Epist. Jacob. Tom. V. p. 942. Ed. Basil. 1563.]

[[9] Id. ibid.]

[[10] Bib. cum Gloss. Ord. et Expos. N. de Lyra, Pars VI. fol. 212, 3. In Jac. cap. ii. Ed. Basil. 1502, where *justus*, *Isaac*, and *est opus.*]

[[11] Hug. de S. Charo. Epist. Jacob. cap. ii. Tom. VII. fol. 316, Ed. Col. Agrip. 1621, where *tunc quia*, *tum quia*, and *quando innotescit.*]

[[12] Id. ibid., where *opera enim*, and *consummant.*]

[[13] Nic. de Lyra, ubi supr.]

[[14] Prosper. Append. Op. de Vit. Contempl. Lib. III. cap. xxi. col. 73. Ed. Paris. 1711.]

[[15] Id. Lib. Sentent. ex August. CXXXI. col. 561.]

[[16] Id. in Psalm. ciii. col. 383.]

[[17] Anselm. in Rom. iii. p. 24.]

Yet nevertheless, because *by faith we know God's mercy* and grace promised by his word, (and that freely for Christ's death and passion sake,) and *believe the same*, and, being truly penitent, we by faith *receive the same*, and so excluding all glory from ourselves, we do by faith *transcribe the whole glory of our justification to the merits of Christ only*, (which properly is not the nature and office of charity;) therefore to set forth the same, it is said of faith in ancient writers, "we be justified only by faith," or, "by faith alone," and in St Paul, "we be justified by faith freely without works."

Rom. iv. "Ideo ex fide, ut secundum gratiam."

Gal. iii. "Christus nos redemit ex maledicto legis, factus pro nobis maledictus: ut in gentes benedictio Dei fieret in Christo Jesu, ut promissionem Spiritus acciperemus per fidem."

Acts x. "Huic omnes prophetæ testimonium perhibent, remissionem peccatorum accipere per nomen ejus omnes qui credunt in eum."

[Acts] xiii. "Notum sit vobis, viri fratres, quod per hunc vobis remissio peccatorum annunciatur, et ab omnibus a quibus non potuistis in lege Mosis justificari, in hoc omnis qui credit justificatur."

AUGUSTINUS.

"His qui gratiam (quam commendat apostolus *et percipit fides Christi*) putatis esse naturam, verissime dicit: '*Si ex natura justitia, ergo gratis Christus mortuus est*[1].'"

PROSPER.

"Si aliqui consequi hoc per gratiam confitentur, et *id non accepit nisi fides;* quæ accepta non est, in ipsa est meritum: cui non donum datur, sed meritum redditur[2]."

AMBROSIUS.

'Per fidem ... prædicationis Jesu Christi agnoscitur donum dudum promissum a Deo, *vel sumitur*[3]."

THEODORETUS in folio 1° præcedente[4].

HISICHIUS.

"Miseratus .... Deus humanum genus, cum illud ad explenda legis opera infirmatum vidisset, jam non ex operibus salvari, sed per gratiam, hominem voluit. Gratia vero ex misericordia atque compassione præbetur, *et fide comprehenditur sola*, 'non ex operibus,' ut Paulus dicit, nam 'gratia jam non erit gratia[5].'"

BERNARDUS.

"Oleum misericordiæ non reponit *nisi in vasa fidei*[6]."

THOMAS.

"Fides hominis imputatur ad justitiam, ... *non quidem ita, quod per fidem justitiam mereatur, sed quod ipsum credere est primus actus justitiæ, quam Deus in eo operatur.* Ex eo enim quod credit in Deum justificantem, justificationi ejus subjicit se, et sic *recipit effectum*[7]."

MAGISTER SENTENTIARUM.

"Per ... fidem justificatur impius, .. . ut *deinde* ipsa fides incipiat per dilectionem operari. Ea enim sola bona opera dicenda sunt, quæ fiunt per dilectionem Dei. *Ipsa enim dilectio opus fidei dicitur*[8]."

*Antididagma.*

"*Per fidem* (qua absque dubitatione firmiter confidimus nobis, qui veram peccatorum pœnitentiam habemus, peccata nostra propter Christum esse dimissa) *justificamur tanquam per causam susceptivam*[9]."

AUGUSTINUS, *De Spiritu et Lit.*

"Per legem fidei quisque *cognoscit*, si quis bene vivit, Dei gratiam se habere, et ut perficiatur in dilectionem justitiæ non se aliunde consecuturum. Quæ cogitatio pium facit, quia pietas est vera sapientia[10]."

*Contra Julianum.* "Ex fide autem justitiam *ideo* dicit esse ex Deo, quia Deus 'unicuique partitur mensuram fidei,' *et ad fidem pertinet credere*, quod 'Deus in nobis operetur et velle[11],'" &c.

"Fides habetur, quod aliquanto post dicit, *quum* '*omnis qui invocaverit nomen Domini salvus erit:*' ad quam salutem pertinet, ut opera nulla sint, et justitia nobis ex Deo sit[12]."

---

[[1] Eis qui gratiam, quam commendat et percipit fides Christi, putant esse naturam, verissime dicitur: Si per naturam justitia est, ergo, &c.—(Gennadii) De Eccles. Dogm. cap. xlviii.]

[[2] Prosper. Resp. ad Excerpt. Gen. Dub. ix. where *aliquid conferri homini*, and *debitum redditur.*]

[[3] Ambros. Comm. in Epist. ad Rom. cap. iii. Tom. V. p. 187. Basil. 1567.]

[[4] Vid. p. 205.]

[[5] Isych. In Levit. Lib. IV. cap. xiv. fol. 81. (1.) Ed. Basil. 1527, where *salvare.*]

[[6] Bernard. In Annunt. Domin. Serm. iii. Tom. I. col. 169, Ed. Paris. 1586, where *vase fiduciæ ponis.*]

[[7] Thom. Aquin. Comm. in Paul. Epist. Ed. Venet. 1593. Ad Rom. cap. iv. fol. 14, 1, where *Credenti autem in eum qui justificat impium, computabitur hæc ejus fides ad justitiam*, &c.]

[[8] Pet. Lomb. in Paul. Epistt. Collectan. ad Rom. cap. iv. fol. 18, F. et ad Gal. cap. v. fol. 157, E. Ed. Paris 1537.]

[[9] This passage has not been found.]

[[10] August. Lib. De Spiritu et Litera, capp. x. xi. 17, 8. Tom. III. p. 308, Ed. Paris. 1635, where *si quid* and *Dei gratia.*]

[[11] Id. Op. Imperf. contr. Julian. Lib. II. 158. Tom. X. col. 1016. Ed. Paris. 1679—1709, where *in nobis Deus.*]

[[12] Id. ibid. Lib. I. cap. cxli. Tom. X. col. 955, where *fides enim habet, quoniam omnis, opera bona et*, and *Deo sint.*]

*Idem.* "Fides in nobis, Christus in nobis. Quid enim aliud dicit apostolus, 'habitare Christum in cordibus nostris per fidem?' Ergo *fides tua de Christo, Christus est in corde tuo*[13]."

Et *In Psalm.* cxviii. "In lege... factorum est Dei jubentis justitia; in lege autem fidei subvenientis misericordia[14]."

ORIGENES. Rom. iv.

"Jam sane considerabis, sic ut de fide dictum est, quod reputatum est ei ad justitiam, ita de aliis virtutibus dici possit," &c.

Et mox: "Quod autem dicit, 'Ei vero qui operatur,' &c. videtur ostendere, *quasi in fide quidem gratia sit justificantis, in opere vero justitia tribuentis*[15]."

Et longe infra super hunc locum, 'Ideo ex fide, ut secundum gratiam.' "In superioribus, inquit, distinctionem dedit mercedis et gratiæ, dicens mercedem rem debitam esse, gratiam autem nullius esse debiti, sed benevolentiæ beneficium. Et *in præsenti ergo loco ostendere volens, Deum hæreditatem promissionum non ex debito, sed ex gratia dare, dicit quia hæreditas a Deo his qui credunt, non ex mercedis debito, sed fidei munere concedatur.* Sicut enim (ut exempli gratia dixerim) hoc quod subsistimus non potest intelligi, quasi ex operis nostri mercede subsistamus, sed evidenter Dei munus est quod sumus, et gratia Conditoris, qui esse nos voluit; ita, etsi hæreditatem promissionum Dei capiamus, divinæ gratiæ est, non alicujus debiti aut operis merces[16]."

AUGUSTINUS.

"Medicina enim animæ vulnerum, et *una propitiatio* pro delictis omnibus, est credere in Christum[17]."

"Credentibus *sufficit fides* ad justificationem[18]."

"'Credidit Abraham Deo, et reputatum est illi ad justitiam, et amicus Dei appellatus est.' Quod credidit Deo, intus in corde, *in sola fide est*[19]."

"Ipsa justitia est ex fide, qua credimus nos justificari, hoc est, justos fieri, gratia Dei per Jesum Christum Dominum nostrum[20]."

*'Ne quis glorietur.'*

AUGUSTINUS.

"Non hoc *ideo* dicit, quod opera bona pia cogitatione facta frustrentur (cum Deus reddat cuique secundum opera ejus, sitque gloria Dei operanti bonum,) sed quod opera ex gratia, non ex operibus gratia[21]."

THOMAS. Ephes. ii.

"'Justificati .... per gratiam ipsius.' Idem enim est salvari et justificari."

"Subdit .... rationem *quare* Deus salvat homines per fidem absque meritis præcedentibus: ut ne quis glorietur in seipso, sed tota gloria in Deum referatur. .... 1 Cor. i. 'Ut non glorietur omnis caro in conspectu ejus[22].'"

AMBROSIUS. Ephes. ii.

"Verum est, quod omnis gratiarum actio salutis nostræ ad Deum referenda est, qui misericordiam suam nobis præstat, ut revocaret errantes ad vitam, non quærentes rectum iter. *Ideoque non est* gloriandum nobis in nobis ipsis, sed in Deo; qui nos regeneravit nativitate cœlesti per fidem Christi[23]."

HIERONYMUS. Ephes. ii.

"Hoc autem totum *propterea* [dixit,] ne quis glorietur a semet ipso et non a Deo se esse salvatum[24]."

*'Ideo ex fide ut secundum gratiam.'*

THEOPHYLACTUS. Rom. iv.

"Quia lex iram operatur, *propterea ex fide* dicitur justificari Abrahamus ac hæres constitui, ut secundum gratiam omnia fiant[25]."

ŒCUMENIUS.

"Per legem, inquit, non confirmantur promissiones, quod secundum modum aliquem impediuntur. Quomodo? Quia lex iram operatur, eo quod non observatur: nemo enim illam poterat implere. Unde autem ira, quomodo hæreditas? Quomodo hæreditatem accipiet, qui irritavit? Quomodo venient promissiones? Fides, inquit, gratiam inducit Dei; existente autem gratia, veniunt et implentur promissiones[26]."

---

[[13] Id. in Joan. Evang. cap. xi. Tractat. xlix. 19. Tom. IX. p. 149. Ed. Paris. 1635, where *ait apostolus*, and *per fidem in cordibus vestris.*]

[[14] Id. in Psalm. cxviii. Concio x. Tom. VIII. p. 552.]

[[15] Origen. in Epist. ad Rom. Lib. iv. 1. Tom. IV. p. 522, Ed. Paris. 1733-59, where *quod reputata, ita ut de aliis, justitia retribuentis, rem debiti esse, sed per gratiam dare, ut exempli causa.*]

[[16] Id. ibid. 5. p. 528.]

[[17] August. Op. Serm. cxliii. De Verb. Evang. Joh. xvi. Tom. V. col. 690, Ed. Paris. 1679—1709, where *medicina omnium*, and *delictis hominum.*]

[[18] Id. Ad Paulin. Epist. Tom. II. col. 666.]

[[19] Id. Serm. ii. 9. Tom. V. col. 9; where *credidit enim Abraham.*]

[[20] Id. ad Paulin. Epist. clxxxvi. 8. Tom. II. col. 666. where *ipsa est justitia.*]

[[21] Id. ibid. 4. col. 665, where *hoc utique totum ideo.... Non quia bona opera frustrantur, cum Deus reddat unicuique secundum opera ejus, sitque gloria...omni operanti bonum; sed quia opera ex gratia, non ex operibus gratia.*]

[[22] Thom. Aquin. Op. In Epist. ad Ephes. cap. ii. Lect. iii. Tom. XVI. pp. 138, 9. where 1 *Cor. ii.*]

[[23] Ambros. in Epist. ad Ephes. cap. ii. Tom. III. p. 235. Ed. Colon. Agrip. 1616, where *quia omnes.*]

[[24] Hieron. in Ephes. cap. ii. Tom. IX. p. 169. Ed. Francof. 1684.]

[[25] Theophylact. in Epist. ad Rom. cap. iv. Tom. II. p. 33. Ed. Venet. 1754—63.]

[[26] Œcumen. in Epist. ad Rom. Comm. cap. v. Tom. I. pp. 253, 4. Ed. Paris. 1630—31.]

# [EXAMINATION AT OXFORD BEFORE BROKES,

## SEPTEMBER, 1555[1].]

[Foxe's Act and Monuments, pp 1872—81, ed. Lond. 1583.]

[AFTER the disputations done and finished in Oxford between the doctors of both universities and the three worthy bishops, Dr Cranmer, Ridley, and Latimer, ye heard then how sentence condemnatory immediately upon the same was ministered against them by Dr Weston and other of the university: whereby they were judged to be heretics, and so committed to the mayor and sheriffs of Oxford. But forasmuch as the sentence given them[2] was void in law, (for at that time the authority of the pope was not yet received into the land,) therefore was a new commission sent from Rome, and a new process framed for the conviction of these reverend and godly-learned men aforesaid. In which commission, first was doctor James Brokes, bishop of Gloucester, the pope's subdelegate[3], with doctor Martin and doctor Story, commissioners in the king and queen's behalf, for the execution of the same.... *Imprimis*, here is to be understand, that the coming down[4] of the foresaid commissioners, which was upon Thursday, the 12. of September, anno 1555, in the church of St Mary, and in the east end of the said church, at the high altar, was erected a solemn scaffold for bishop Brokes aforesaid, representing the pope's person, ten foot high. The seat was made that he might sit under the sacrament of the altar. And on the right hand of the pope's delegate, beneath him, sat doctor Martin, and on the left hand sat doctor Story, the king and queen's commissioners, which were both doctors of the civil law.... And anon one of the proctors for the pope, or else his doctor, called, "Thomas, archbishop of Canterbury, appear here, and make answer to that shall be laid to thy charge: that is to say, for blasphemy, incontinency, and heresy: and make an answer here to the bishop of Gloucester, representing the pope's person."

Dr Brokes, Dr Martin, Dr Story, commissioners against the archbishop.

The order of setting and placing the commissioners.

* * * * * * *

When doctor Martin had ended his oration, the archbishop beginneth, as here followeth.

*Cranmer:*—"Shall I then make my answer?"

*Martin:*—"As you think good; no man shall let you."

And here the archbishop, kneeling down on both knees towards the west, said first the Lord's prayer. Then rising up, he reciteth the articles of the creed. Which done, he entereth with his protestation, in form as followeth.]

### *The Faith and Profession of doctor Cranmer, archbishop of Canterbury before the Commissioners[5].*

The profession or protestation of Dr Cranmer before the commissioners.

This I do profess as touching my faith, and make my protestation, which I desire you to note. I will never consent that the bishop of Rome shall have any jurisdiction within this realm.

*Story:*—Take a note thereof.

*Martin:*—Mark, M. Cranmer, how you answer for yourself. You refuse and deny him, by whose laws ye yet do remain in life, being otherwise attainted of high treason[6], and but a dead man by the laws of this realm.

*Cranmer:*—I protest before God I was no traitor; but indeed I confessed more at my arraignment than was true.

*Martin:*—That is not to be reasoned at this present. You know ye were con-

[1 The examination of Archbishop Cranmer is printed from Foxe's Acts and Monuments, pp. 1872—1881. Ed. Lond. 1583. The "Processus contra Cranmerum," which contains the official report of the examination, sent by Brokes to Cardinal James de Puteo, will be found in the Appendix. See Cranmer's second Letter to Queen Mary, Sept. 1555. Burnet's Hist. of Reformat. Vol. II. p. 664. et seq. Ed. Oxon. 1829.]

[2 Other editions read, "Given against them."]

[3 Subdelegate to the Cardinal de Puteo, who is called in the Processus cont. Cranm. "Judex ac Commissarius a sanctissimo domino nostro papa specialiter deputatus." Strype's Mem. of Abp. Cranmer. Todd's Addenda, No. 2. Vol. II. p. 1069. Ed. Oxon. 1840.]

[4 Other editions read, "that at the coming down."]

[5 Vid. the Archbishop's letters to queen Mary, and to a Lawyer, Sept. 1555, and his Appeal to a General Council, infra p. 224.]

[6 Vid. the Archbishop's letters to queen Mary, Sept. 1555. Foxe's Acts and Monuments, p. 1871. Ed. Lond. 1583. Burnet's Hist. of Reformat. Vol. II. p. 664, et seqq. Strype's Mem. of Abp. Cranmer, Vol. II. p. 459. Ed. Oxon. 1840.]

demned for a traitor, and *res judicata pro veritate accipitur.* But proceed to your matter.

*Cranmer:*—I will never consent to the bishop of Rome; for then should I give myself to the devil: for I have made an oath to the king, and I must obey the king by God's laws. By the scripture the king is chief, and no foreign person in his own realm above him. There is no subject but to a king. I am a subject, I owe my fidelity to the crown. The pope is contrary to the crown. I cannot obey both: for no man can serve two masters at once, as you in the beginning of your oration declared by the sword and the keys, attributing the keys to the pope, and the sword to the king. But I say the king hath both. Therefore he that is subject to Rome and the laws of Rome, he is perjured; for the pope's and the judge's laws are contrary, they are uncertain and confounded.

Causes alleged why Dr Cranmer cannot receive the pope.

The laws of this realm and the pope's contrary.

A priest indebted, by the laws of the realm shall be sued before a temporal judge; by the pope's laws, contrary[7].

The pope doth the king injury, in that he hath his power from the pope. The king is head in his own realm: but the pope claimeth all bishops, priests, curates, &c. So the pope in every realm hath a realm.

Again, by the laws of Rome the benefice must be given by the bishop; by the laws of the realm the patron giveth the benefice. Herein the laws be as contrary as fire and water.

No man can by the laws of Rome proceed in a *præmunire;* and so is the law of the realm expelled, and the king standeth accursed in maintaining his own laws. Therefore, in consideration that the king and queen take their power of him, as though God should give it to them, there is no true subject, unless he be abrogate, seeing the crown is holden of him, being out of the realm.

The bishop of Rome is contrary to God, and injurious to his laws: for God commanded all men to be diligent in the knowledge of his law; and therefore hath appointed one holy-day in the week at the least, for the people to come to the church, and hear the word of God expounded unto them, and that they might the better understand it, to hear it in their mother tongue, which they know. The pope doth contrary: for he willeth the service to be had in the Latin tongue, which they do not understand. God would have it to be perceived: the pope will not. When the priest giveth thanks, God would that the people should do so too, and God will them to confess all together: the pope will not.

The pope's proceedings contrary to God.

Now as concerning the sacrament, I have taught no false doctrine of the sacrament of the altar: for if it can be proved by any doctor above a thousand years after Christ, that Christ's body is there really, I will give over. My book was made seven years ago, and no man hath brought any authors against it. I believe, that whoso eateth and drinketh that sacrament, Christ is within them, whole Christ, his nativity, passion, resurrection, and ascension, but not that corporally that sitteth in heaven.

The real presence is not to be proved by any doctor above a thousand years after Christ.

Now Christ commanded all to drink of the cup: the pope taketh it away from the laymen: and yet one saith, that if Christ had died for the devil, that he should drink thereof.

Christ biddeth us to obey the king, *etiam dyscolo* [δυσκόλῳ]: the bishop of Rome biddeth us to obey him. Therefore, unless he be antichrist, I cannot tell what to make of him. Wherefore if I should obey him, I cannot obey Christ.

He is like the devil in his doings, for the devil said to Christ: "If thou wilt fall down and worship me, I will give thee all the kingdoms of the world." Thus he took upon him to give that which was not his own. Even so the bishop of Rome giveth princes their crowns, being none of his own: for where princes either by election, either by succession, either by inheritage[8] obtain their crown, he saith, that they should have it from him.

The pope likened to the devil, and wherein.

Christ saith, that antichrist shall be. And who shall he be? Forsooth, he that advanceth himself above all other creatures. Now if there be none already that hath

The pope proved antichrist.

[[7] Vid. Collection of Tenets from the Canon Law, p. 72, *nn.* 12, 13.]

[[8] Other editions read, "by inheritance."]

advanced himself after such sort besides the pope, then in the mean time let him be antichrist.

*Story:*—Pleaseth it you to make an end?

*Cranmer:*—For he will be the vicar of Christ, he will dispense with the old and new Testament also, yea, and with apostasy.

Now I have declared why I cannot with my conscience obey the pope. I speak not this for hatred I bear to him that now supplieth the room, for I know him not. I pray God give him grace not to follow his ancestors. Neither say I this for my defence, but to declare my conscience, for the zeal that I bear to God's word, trodden under foot by the bishop of Rome. I cast fear apart; for Christ said to his apostles, that in the latter days they should suffer much sorrow, and be put to death for his name's sake: "Fear them not," saith he, "but fear him, which, when he hath killed the body, hath power to cast the soul into fire everlasting." Also Christ saith, that

Matt. xvi. "he that will live shall die, and he that loseth his life for my name's sake, he shall

Mark viii. find it again." Moreover he said: "Confess me before men, and be not afraid; for if you do so, I will stand with you: if you shrink from me, I will shrink from you." This is a comfortable and a terrible saying: this maketh me to set all fear apart. I say therefore, the bishop of Rome treadeth under foot God's laws and the king's.

The pope's laws against the laws of this realm.

The pope would give bishopricks; so would the king. But at the last the king gat the upper hand; and so are all bishops perjured, first to the pope, and then to the king.

The crown hath nothing to do with the clergy. For if a clerk come before a judge, the judge shall make process against him, but not to execute any laws. For if the judge should put him to execution, then is the king accursed in maintaining his own laws. And therefore say I, that he is neither true to God, neither to the king, that first received the pope. But I shall heartily pray for such councillors as may inform her the truth; for the king and queen, if they be well informed, will do well."

*Martin:*—As you understand then, if they maintain the supremacy of Rome, they cannot maintain England too."

To be called universal head is a mark of antichrist. Gregory.

*Cranmer:*—I require you to declare to the king and queen what I have said, and how their oaths do stand with the realm and the pope. St Gregory saith, 'He that taketh upon him to be head of the universal church, is worse than the antichrist[1].' If any man can shew me that it is not against God's word to hold his stirrup, when he taketh his horse, and kiss his feet, (as kings do,) then will I kiss his feet also.

The bishop of Gloucester charged with perjury.

And you, for your part, my lord, are perjured; for now ye sit judge for the pope, and yet did you receive your bishoprick of the king[2]. You have taken an oath to be adversary to this realm[3]; for the pope's laws are contrary to the laws of the realm.

*Gloucester:*—You were the cause that I did forsake the pope, and did swear that he ought not to be supreme head, and gave it to king Henry the eighth, that he ought to be it; and this you made me to do.

Warham, archbishop, gave up first the supremacy to the king.

*Cranmer:*—To this I answer, you report me ill, and say not the truth, and I will prove it here before you all[4]. The truth is, that my predecessor, bishop Warham,

---

[[1] Ego autem fidenter dico, quia quisquis se universalem sacerdotem vocat, vel vocari desiderat, in elatione sua antichristum præcurrit, quia superbiendo se præponit.—Gregor. Magni Papæ I. Op. Lib. VII. Indict. 15. Epist. xxxiii. Ad Maur. August. Tom.. II. col. 881. Ed. Paris. 1705.]

[[2] "Ant. Wood's account of Brokes is, that he was Fellow of C. C. C. and B. A. 1531; D.D. 1546; Master of Balliol, 1547; Bishop of Gloucester, on the deprivation of Hoper, April 1, 1554. This is inconsistent with the statement here attributed to Cranmer, both on the point of his doctor's degree, and his appointment to a bishoprick; but it is *not* inconsistent either with 'the more full answer of the archbishop,' printed below, or with his letter to the queen (Sept. 1555), or with Brokes's official report. It must therefore be concluded that this narrative is, as Foxe suspected, not to be trusted. See Wood, Athenæ, Vol. I. p. 314. Ed. Bliss." Jenkyns' Remains of Abp. Cranmer, Vol. IV. p. 87, *n*. h.]

[[3] Other editions read, "to the realm."]

[[4] "Archbishop Parker gives the following account of the first admission of the king's supremacy by the clergy: 'Clerus Anglicanus, qui Cardinali [Wolseio] ut Romani pontificis legato obtemperabant, ob admissam receptamque papæ potestatem actione de *præmunire* teneri putabatur: cujus vi proscribi et cum bonis atque membris adjudicari regi debuit, nisi rex misertus esset. Itaque.... consilium iniit clerus de tam dira pœna redimenda. ... At rex, qui solus regnare, nec divisum et dis-

gave the supremacy to king Henry the eighth, and said that he ought to have it before the bishop of Rome, and that God's word would bear him[5]. And upon the same was there sent to both the universities, Oxford and Cambridge, to know what the word of God would do touching the supremacy; and it was reasoned upon and argued at length. So at the last both the universities agreed, and set to their seals, and sent it to king Henry the eighth to the court, that he ought to be supreme head, and not the pope. Whereupon you were then doctor of divinity at that time, and your consent was thereunto, as by your hand doth appear. Therefore you misreport me, that I was the cause of your falling away from the pope, but it was yourself. All this was in bishop Warham's time, and whilst he was alive; so that it was three quarters of a year after, ere ever I had the bishoprick of Canterbury in my hands, and before I might do any thing. So that here ye have reported of me that which ye cannot prove, which is evil done.

Both the universities subscribed to the king's supremacy before Cranmer was archbishop.

*Gloucester:*—We come to examine you, and you, methink, examine us.

* * * * * * * *

*Talk between doctor Martin and the archbishop.*

*Martin:*—Master Cranmer, ye have told here a long glorious tale, pretending some matter of conscience in appearance, but in verity you have no conscience at all. You say that you have sworn once to king Henry the eighth against the pope's jurisdiction, and therefore you may never forswear the same; and so ye make a great matter of conscience in the breach of the said oath. Here will I ask you a question or two. What if ye made an oath to an harlot, to live with her in continual adultery, ought you to keep it?

Talk between Dr Martin and the archbishop.

*Cranmer:*—I think no.

Unadvised oaths are not to be kept.

*Martin:*—What if you did swear never to lend a poor man one penny, ought you to keep it?

*Cranmer:*—I think not.

*Martin:*—Herod did swear whatsoever his harlot asked of him he would give her, and he gave her John Baptist's head. Did he well in keeping his oath?

*Cranmer:*—I think not.

*Martin:*—Jephthe, one of the judges of Israel, did swear unto God, that if he would give him victory over his enemies, he would offer unto God the first soul that came forth of his house. It happened that his own daughter came first, and he slew her to save his oath. Did he well?

Jephthe's oath.

*Cranmer:*—I think not.

---

pertitum de clero et populo suo gubernando cum papa officium amplius gerere voluit, non alia conditione hac oblata pecunia redimere clerum voluit, quam si se solum suum totiusque populi proxime ac secundum Christum protectorem *supremumque Caput* in ea synodo agnoscerent. Hujus consilii Cranmerus et Cromwellus clam auctores fuisse existimabantur. Clerus animo toto jam obstupuit; nondum enim quid sibi hic novus vellet titulus, aut quorsum tenderet, prospexit. Sed nasuti quidam olfecerunt rei exitum; inter quos fuisse Warhamum archiepiscopum, ex his quæ mox dicemus, verisimile est. Magnæ res; deliberatum diu; procrastinationes et prorogationes crebræ; disputatum sæpius. Tandem archiepiscopus, cum exquisivisset præsulum de ea re sententias, ac plerique siluissent, 'Qui tacet,' inquit, 'consentire videtur:' responsumque illico fuit: 'Ergo tacemus omnes.' Verum postea, cum neque tutum neque e gravitate synodi fore cernerent sic illudere regi, frequentes ierunt in sententiam his verbis conceptam: 'Ecclesiæ et cleri Anglicani singularum protectorem, supremum dominum, et, quantum per Christi leges licet, etiam supremum caput, regiam majestatem agnoscimus.' (See Parker, Ant. Eccles. Brit. Warham; Wilkins' Concilia, Tom. III. p. 725; Burnet's Hist. of Reformat. Vol. I. p. 227. This resolution was voted on the 11th Feb. 1531. But the title of Supreme Head was not given to the king by Act of Parliament till 1534; (Stat. 26 Hen. VIII. cap. i.) Nor does it appear to have been acknowledged by the universities before that year. Wilkins, ibid. pp. 771, 775; Burnet's Hist. of Reformat. Vol. III. App. b. ii. No. 27, p. 72; State Papers, Vol. I. p. 425.) Yet Cranmer's words, as here reported, imply, that it had been formally approved by them during the primacy of Warham. This is another reason, in addition to those given in a preceding note, for suspecting the accuracy of this account of the examination."—Jenkyns' Remains of Abp. Cranmer, Vol. IV. p. 88.]

[[5] Vid. Todd's Life of Abp. Cranmer, Vol. I. p. 69. Ed. Lond. 1831.]

*Martin:*—So saith St Ambrose, *De Officiis: Miserabilis necessitas, quæ solvitur parricidio*[1]; id est, "It is a miserable necessity which is paid with parricide." Then, master Cranmer, you can no less confess by the premises, but that you ought not to have conscience of every oath, but if it be just, lawful, and advisedly taken.

*Cranmer:*—So was that oath.

*Martin:*—That is not so. For first it was unjust, for it tended to the taking away of another man's right. It was not lawful, for the laws of God and the church were against it. Besides, it was not voluntary; for every man and woman were compelled to take it.

*Cranmer:*—It pleaseth you to say so.

The archbishop, being sworn to the king, ought not to swear to the pope.

*Martin:*—Let all the world be judge. But, sir, you that pretend to have such a conscience to break an oath; I pray you, did you never swear, and break the same?

*Cranmer:*—I remember not.

*Martin:*—I will help your memory. Did you never swear obedience to the see of Rome?

*Cranmer:*—Indeed I did once swear unto the same.

*Martin:*—Yea, that you did twice[2], as appeareth by records and writings here ready to be shewed.

The archbishop sworn first to the pope by protestation.

*Cranmer:*—But I remember I saved all by protestation that I made by the counsel of the best learned men I could get at that time[3].

*Martin:*—Hearken, good people, what this man saith. He made a protestation one day to keep never a whit of that which he would swear the next day. Was this the part of a christian man? If a christian man would bargain with a Turk, and before he maketh his bargain, solemnly before witness readeth in his paper that he holdeth secretly in hand[4], or peradventure protesteth before one or two, that he mindeth not to perform whatsoever he shall promise to the Turk; I say, if a christian man would serve a Turk[5] in this manner, that the christian man were worse than the Turk. What would you then say to this man, that made a solemn oath and promise unto God and his church, and made a protestation before quite contrary?

*Cranmer:*—That which I did, I did by the best learned men's advice I could get at that time.

Dr Martin would prove the archbishop perjured in for swearing his oath made to the pope.

*Martin:*—I protest before all the learned men here, that there is no learning will save your perjury herein; for there be two rules of the civil law clean contrary against you: (and so brought forth his rules; which being done, he proceeded further.) But will you have the truth of the matter? King Henry the eighth even then meant the lamentable change which after you see came to pass: and to further his pitiful proceedings, from the divorcement of his most lawful wife to the detestable departing from the blessed unity of Christ's church, this man made the foresaid protestation, and, on the other side, he letted not to make two solemn oaths quite contrary: and why? for otherwise, by the laws and canons of this realm, he could not aspire to the archbishoprick of Canterbury.

Dr Cranmer unwilling to be made archbishop.

*Cranmer:*—I protest before you all, there was never man came more unwillingly to a bishoprick than I did to that: insomuch that when king Henry did send for [me] in post, that I should come over, I prolonged my journey by seven weeks at the least, thinking that he would be forgetful of me in the mean time[6].

---

[[1] Ambros. De Officiis, Lib. III. cap. xii. Tom. IV. p. 38. Colon. Agrip. 1616.]

[[2] Dr Jenkyns supposes that the oaths here referred to were the two which Cranmer took at his consecration, and were all that Martin meant.—Remains of Abp. Cranmer, Vol. IV. p. 91.]

[[3] See Strype's Mem. of Abp. Cranmer, Vol. I. pp. 27, 28. Ed. Oxon. 1840; Hallam's Constit. Hist. 8vo. Vol. I. p. 135, note; Todd's Life of Abp. Cranmer, Vol. I. p. 58.]

[[4] Other editions read, "in his hand."]

[[5] Other editions read, "should serve a Turk."]

[[6] Dr Jenkyns remarks hereon, that "this assertion has been questioned, but without sufficient reason. (See Lingard, Vol. VI. p. 251; Todd's Life of Abp. Cranmer, Vol. I. p. 50.) Warham died on the 23d of Aug. 1532. The precise date of Cranmer's return from the continent is not known. Strype indeed states, that Cranmer was in England and present at the marriage of Anne Boleyn, on the 14th of November. He may possibly have been then in England; but neither was Anne Boleyn married on that day, nor was Cranmer present on the occasion. See his letter to Hawkyns. It is certain that on the 20th of October, he was still in Germany, at Villach; and the letter which he wrote from that place contains no allusion to his coming home. Nor were the bulls for his promotion applied for at Rome till the end of January, 1533." Jenkyns' Remains of Abp. Cranmer, Vol. IV. p. 92, *n*.]

*Martin*:—You declare well by the way that the king took you to be a man of good conscience, who could not find within all his realm any man that would set forth his strange attempts, but was enforced to send for you in post to come out of Germany. What may we conjecture hereby, but that there was a compact between you, being then queen Anne's chaplain, and the king: "Give me the archbishoprick of Canterbury, and I will give you licence to live in adultery?"

False slander of Dr Martin.

*Cranmer*:—You say not true.

*Martin*:—Let your protestation, joined with the rest of your talk, give judgment. *Hinc prima mali labes.* Of that your execrable perjury, and his coloured and too shamefully suffered adultery, came heresy and all mischief to this realm.

And thus have I spoken as touching your conscience[7] you make for breaking your heretical oath made to the king. But to break your former oath, made at two sundry times both to God and his church, you have no conscience at all. And now to answer another part of your oration, wherein you bring in God's word, that you have it on your side, and no man else, and that the pope hath devised a new scripture, contrary to the scriptures of God; ye play herein as the Pharisees did, which cried always, *Verbum Domini, verbum Domini*, 'The word of the Lord, the word of the Lord,' when they meant nothing so. This bettereth not your cause, because you have God's word for you; for so Basilides[8] and Photinus the heretics said that they had God's word to maintain their heresy. So Nestorius, so Macedonius, so Pelagius, and, briefly, all the heretics that ever were, pretended that they had God's word for them; yea, and so the devil, being the father of heresies, alleged God's word for him, saying, *Scriptum est*, It is written.' So said he to Christ, *Mitte te deorsum*, 'Cast thyself backward[9];' which you applied most falsely against the pope. But if you mark the devil's language well, it agreed with your proceedings most truly. For, *Mitte te deorsum*, 'Cast thyself downward,' said he; and so taught you to cast all things downward. Down with the sacrament! down with the mass! down with the altars! down with the arms of Christ, and up with a lion and a dog! down with the abbeys! down with the chauntries! down with hospitals and colleges! down with fasting and prayer! yea, down with all that good and godly is! All your proceedings and preachings tended to no other, but to fulfil the devil's request, *Mitte te deorsum.* And therefore tell not us that you have God's word. For God hath given us by his word a mark to know that your teaching proceeded not of God, but of the devil, and that your doctrine came not of Christ, but of antichrist. For Christ said[10] there should come against his church *lupi rapaces*, id est, 'ravening wolves;' and *pseudo-apostoli*, id est, 'false apostles.' But how should we know them? Christ teacheth us, saying, *Ex fructibus eorum cognoscetis eos;* id est, 'By their fruits ye shall know them.' Why, what be their fruits? St Paul declareth: *Post carnem in concupiscentia et immunditia ambulant: potestatem contemnunt*, &c.: i. e. 'After the flesh they walk in concupiscence and uncleanness; they contemn *potestates*.' Again, *In diebus novissimis erunt periculosa tempora, erunt seipsos amantes, cupidi, elati, immorigeri parentibus, proditores*, &c.: i.e. 'In the latter days there shall be perilous times: then shall there be men loving themselves, covetous, proud, disobedient to parents, treason-workers.' Whether these be not the fruits of your gospel, I refer me to this worshipful audience: whether the said gospel began not with perjury, proceeded with adultery, was maintained with heresy, and ended in conspiracy.

Nay, the Pharisees cried not *Verbum Domini*, but *Templum Domini*, as the papists do now against the protestants.

So did king Ezechias and Josias down with monuments of idolatry, and are commended.

Another false slander of Dr Martin.

Whether these be the fruits of the gospellers or of the papists more, let the conversation of them both give judgment.

Now, sir, two points more I marked in your raging discourse that you made here: the one against the holy sacrament; the other against the pope's jurisdiction and the authority of the see apostolic.

Touching the first, ye say you have God's word with you, yea, and all the doctors. I would here ask but one question of you, whether God's word be contrary to itself, and whether the doctors teach doctrine contrary to themselves, or no? For you, master Cranmer, have taught in this high sacrament of the altar three contrary doctrines, and yet you pretended in every one *verbum Domini.*

Doctrine of the sacrament.

---

[[7] Other editions read, "touching the conscience."]

[[8] Other editions read, "for Basilides."]

[[9] Other editions read, "Cast thyself downward."]

[[10] Other editions read, "Christ foresaid."]

*Cranmer:*—Nay, I taught but two contrary doctrines in the same[1].

*Martin:*—What doctrine taught you when you condemned Lambert the sacramentary, in the king's presence in Whitehall?[2]

So was St Augustine first a Pagan, then a Manichee, and then a Catholic.

*Cranmer:*—I maintained then the papists' doctrine.

*Martin:*—That is to say, the catholic and universal doctrine of Christ's church. And how when king Henry died? Did you not translate Justus Jonas's book?[3]

*Cranmer:*—I did so.

*Martin:*—Then there you defended another doctrine touching the sacrament, by the same token that you sent to Lynne your printer; that whereas in the first print there was an affirmative, that is to say, Christ's body really in the sacrament, you sent then to your printer to put in a 'not,' whereby it came miraculously to pass, that Christ's body was clean conveyed out of the sacrament[4].

*Cranmer:*—I remember there were two printers of my said book; but where the same 'not' was put in, I cannot tell.

*Martin:*—Then from a Lutheran ye became a Zwinglian, which is the vilest heresy of all in the high mystery of the sacrament; and for the same heresy you did help to burn Lambert the sacramentary, which you now call the catholic faith and God's word.

Dr Cranmer first won to the knowledge of the sacrament by bishop Ridley.

*Cranmer:*—I grant that then I believed otherwise than I do now; and so I did, until my lord of London, doctor Ridley, did confer with me, and by sundry persuasions and authorities of doctors drew me quite from my opinion[5].

---

[[1] Vid. Jenkyns' Remains of Abp. Cranmer, Vol. IV. p. 95, where is found the following note: "Dr Wordsworth seems to think this declaration decisive against the common belief, that Cranmer at one time held the Lutheran tenets on the eucharist. Yet such an opinion seems to have been entertained, not only by Foxe, to whom Dr W. traces it, but by the archbishop's contemporaries in general. (See [Dr J.'s] Preface.) It is therefore scarcely to be surrendered on the authority of a conversation, which, there is reason to suppose, has not been reported accurately. As far indeed as it rested on the translation of Justus Jonas' Catechism, it must be admitted to be without foundation: for Cranmer repeatedly declared, that the doctrine there taught, though it had been misunderstood, was none other than that which was maintained in the Defence. But the following extract from his Answer to Smythe's Preface leaves a strong impression, that in his passage from transubstantiation to the tenets of the Church of England, he had paused at the Real Presence according to the Lutheran sense. Smythe, he says, 'understood not the matter—no more than he understood my book of the Catechism; and therefore reporteth untruly of me, that I in that book did set forth the real presence of Christ's body in the sacrament. Unto which false report I have answered in my fourth book, the eighth chapter. But this I confess of myself, that not long before I wrote the said Catechism, I was in that error of the real presence, as I was many years past in divers other errors; as of transubstantiation, of the sacrifice propitiatory of the priests in the mass, of pilgrimages, purgatory, pardons, and many other superstitions and errors that came from Rome.... But after it had pleased God to shew unto me, by his holy word, a more perfect knowledge of his Son Jesus Christ, from time to time, as I grew in knowledge of him, by little and little I put away my former ignorance.'"—See Writings of Abp. Cranmer on the Sacrament, Vol. I. pp. 190, 226, 7; (Answer to Smythe's Preface), p. 374, Park. Soc. Ed.; Wordsworth's Eccl. Biogr. Vol. III. p. 550; Preface to Cranmer's Catechism, p. 18. Ed. Oxon. 1829; Boner's attack on Cranmer; Foxe's Acts and Monuments pp. 1312, 1317. Ed. Lond. 1683.]

[[2] "John Nicholson, alias Lambert, burnt for denying the corporal presence, A.D. 1538, was not condemned by Cranmer, but by the king in person, Crumwell reading the sentence. Before his sentence was passed, there was a disputation, opened by a speech from Sampson, bishop of Chichester. The king himself disputed against Lambert's first position, and then he commanded Thomas Cranmer, Archbishop of Canterbury, to refute him." Jenkyns. —Vid. Foxe's Acts and Monuments, pp. 1122, et seqq.; Strype's Mem. of Abp. Cranmer, Vol. I. pp. 92—94. Ed. Oxon. 1840.]

[[3] The book commonly called "Cranmer's Catechism," translated under his direction from a catechism compiled in Latin by Justus Jonas. See Preface to Cranmer's Catechism, ed. Oxford, 1829; Todd's Life of Cranmer, Vol. II. p. 45.]

[[4] "This catechism was printed first, by the archbishop's order, about the time of king Henry's death, or soon after. In a second edition the word 'not' was inserted in a certain place of the book, to alter the doctrine of the real presence, which was asserted in the first edition. This Dr Martin... threw in his dish at his examination in Oxford. But the archbishop professed his ignorance concerning the foisting of that word."—Strype's Mem. of Abp. Cranmer, Vol. II. p. 569. The word "not" has not been found in any copy extant.—Vid. Jenkyns' Remains of Abp. Cranmer, Vol. IV. p. 97.]

[[5] Ne quis autem putet, hunc sanctum Dei martyrem ad asserendam hanc de cœna Dominica explicationem . . . vel temere vel factiose descendisse; neutiquam id te latere velim, pie lector, hunc virum, post multam scripturarum pervestigationem, ex unius beati martyris Ridlei episcopi Londinensis institutione sero tandem (nimirum anno 1546) in eam quam hic tuetur sententiam adductum esse.—Preface to Embd. Ed. of the Defence of the Sacrament, Vol. I. Appendix, pp. 2, 6. Park. Soc. Ed.]

*Martin*:—Now, sir, as touching the last part of your oration, you denied that the pope's holiness was supreme head of the church of Christ. Supremacy of the pope.

*Cranmer*:—I did so.

*Martin*:—Who say you then is supreme head?

*Cranmer*:—Christ.

*Martin*:—But whom hath Christ left here in earth his vicar and head of his church?

*Cranmer*:—Nobody.

*Martin*:—Ah! why told you not king Henry this, when you made him supreme head? and now nobody is. This is treason against his own person, as you then made him.

*Cranmer*:—I mean not but every king in his own realm and dominion is supreme head, and so was he supreme head of the church of Christ in England. King Henry was not supreme head but only of his own realm. The pope will be universal head over all.

*Martin*:—Is this always true? and was it ever so in Christ's church?

*Cranmer*:—It was so.

*Martin*:—Then what say you by Nero? He was the mightiest prince of the earth, after Christ was ascended. Was he head of Christ's church?

*Cranmer*:—Nero was Peter's head.

*Martin*:—I ask, whether Nero was head of the church, or no? If he were not, it is false that you said before, that all princes be, and ever were, heads of the church within their realms.

*Cranmer*:—Nay, it is true, for Nero was head of the church, that is, in worldly respect of the temporal bodies of men, of whom the church consisteth; for so he beheaded Peter and the apostles. And the Turk too is head of the church of Turkey.

*Martin*:—Then he that beheaded the heads of the church, and crucified the apostles, was head of Christ's church; and he that was never member of the church, is head of the church, by your new found understanding of God's word.

* * * * * * * * *

*Interrogatories objected to the archbishop, with his Answers annexed to the same*[6].

1. *Interrog.* First was objected, that he, the foresaid Thomas Cranmer, being yet free, and before he entered into holy orders, married one Joan, surnamed black, or brown, dwelling at the sign of the Dolphin, in Cambridge[7]. Interrogatories laid against the archbishop.

*Answ.* Whereunto he answered, that whether she was called black or brown he knew not; but that he married there one Joan, that he granted. The first marriage of the archbishop.

2. *Interrog.* That, after the death of the foresaid wife, he entered into holy orders, and after that was made archbishop by the pope.

*Answ.* He received (he said) a certain bull of the pope, which he delivered unto the king, and was archbishop by him.

3. *Interrog.* Item, that he, being in holy orders, married another woman, as his second wife, named Anne; and so was twice married[8]. The second marriage of the archbishop.

*Answ.* To this he granted.

4. *Interrog.* Item, in the time of king Henry the eighth he kept the said wife secretly, and had children by her[9].

*Answ.* Hereunto he also granted; affirming that it was better for him to have his own, than to do like other priests, holding and keeping other men's wives.

---

[[6] See the *Processus contra Cranmerum* in the Appendix.]

[[7] "And so being Master of Arts and Fellow of the same college, [Jesus college,] it chanced him to marry a gentleman's daughter: by means whereof he lost and gave over his fellowship there, and became the reader in Buckingham college [now Magdalene;] and for that he would with more diligence apply that his office of reading, he placed his said wife in an inn, called the Dolphin, in Cambridge, the wife of the house being of affinity unto her." Foxe's Acts and Monuments, p. 1860. Upon the death of his wife he was re-elected Fellow of Jesus. Todd's Life of Abp. Cranmer, Vol. I. p. 8.]

[[8] He married the niece of Osiander, during his embassy in Germany, about the beginning of the year 1532. Strype's Mem. of Abp. Cranmer, Vol. I. p. 15; Todd's Life of Abp. Cranmer, Vol. I. p. 39.]

[[9] Thomas and Margaret, who survived the archbishop, and were restored in blood A. D. 1563, and Anne, who died before his death. Vid. Genealogical Table in Vol. I. of Todd's Life of Abp. Cranmer.]

5. *Interrog.* Item, in the time of king Edward he brought out the said his wife[1] openly, affirming and professing publicly the same to be his wife.

*Answ.* He denied not but he so did, and lawfully might do the same, forasmuch as the laws of the realm did so permit him.

6. *Interrog.* Item, that he shamed not openly to glory himself to have had his wife in secret many years.

*Answ.* And though he so did, (he said,) there was no cause why he should be ashamed thereof.

The archbishop charged with his doctrine and books.

7. *Interrog.* Item, that the said Thomas Cranmer, falling afterward into the deep bottom of errors, did fly and refuse the authority of the church; did hold and follow the heresy concerning the sacrament of the altar; and also did compile and caused to be set abroad divers books.

*Answ.* Whereunto, when the names of the books were recited to him, he denied not such books which he was the author of[2]. As touching the treatise of Peter Martyr upon the sacrament, he denied that he ever saw it before it was abroad, yet did approve and well like of the same. As for the Catechism[3], the book of Articles, with the other book against Winchester, he granted the same to be his doings.

8. *Interrog.* Item, that he compelled many, against their wills, to subscribe to the same articles.

*Answ.* He exhorted (he said) such as were willing to subscribe: but against their wills he compelled none[4].

9. *Interrog.* Item, forsomuch as he surceased not to perpetrate enorme and inordinate crimes, he was therefore cast into the Tower, and from thence was brought to Oxford, at what time it was commonly thought that the parliament there should be holden.

*Answ.* To this he said, that he knew no such enorme and inordinate crimes that ever he committed.

10. *Interrog.* Item, that in the said city of Oxford he did openly maintain his heresy, and there was convicted upon the same.

*Answ.* He defended (he said) there the cause of the sacrament; but to be convicted[5] in the same, that he denied.

11. *Interrog.* Item, when he persevered still in the same, he was by the public censure of the university pronounced an heretic, and his books to be heretical.

*Answ.* That he was so denounced, he denied not; but that he was an heretic, or his books heretical, that he denied.

12. *Interrog.* Item, that he was and is notoriously infamed with the note of schism, as who not only himself receded from the catholic church and see of Rome, but also moved the king and subjects of this realm to the same.

*Answ.* As touching the receding, that he well granted; but that receding or departing (said he) was only from the see of Rome, and had in it no matter of any schism.

---

[[1] Other editions read, "the said wife."]

[[2] Dr Jenkyns, (Remains of Abp. Cranmer, Vol. IV. p. 101, 2) says: "There is some confusion respecting the books here mentioned, even between the different parts of the official report; a Discourse of the Lord's Supper, &c. being named in Cranmer's answer, which does not appear in the corresponding article of accusation. Peter Martyr printed two works on the Eucharist in 1549, one entitled Disputatio de Eucharistiæ sacramento habita in celeberr. Universitate Oxoniæ, &c.; the other, Tractatio de sacramento Eucharistiæ habita publice Oxonii, &c. The Disputation was published at the request of Cranmer and of the royal commissioners before whom it was held. 'Quid enim negare ausim,' says he in an address to the reader, 'Reverssimo Archiepisc. Cantuariensi, cui plane omnia debeo? quidve regiis visitatoribus, qui hisce disputationibus non solum interfuerunt, sed præfuerunt? Damus itaque tibi hanc disputationem, cui ad majorem evidentiam, Tractationem de eadem re adjecimus.' To the Tractatio was prefixed a long epistle dedicatory to Cranmer. Both were translated into English; the latter by Nic. Udall, under the title, A Discourse or Traictise of Petur Martyr Vermilla, &c. See Wood, Athenæ Oxon. Vol. I. p. 329. Ed. Bliss; Strype's Eccl. Mem. Vol. II. p. 306. Ed. Oxon. 1822; Ames' Typograph. Antiq. Ed. Dibdin, Vol. IV. p. 314; Pet. Martyr, De Eucharist. pp. 614, 662. Ed. 1562."]

[[3] i.e. the Short Catechism added to the Articles of 1552.—Vid. Disputations at Oxford, Vol. I. p. 422, *n.* 2; Park. Soc. Ed.; Jenkyns' Remains of Abp. Cranmer, Vol. IV. pp. 65, *n.* u. 102, *n.* f.]

[[4] The witnesses for the most part were silent on this article, and those who gave evidence spoke only from report. Vid. *Process. cont. Cranm.* Appendix.]

[[5] Other editions read, "But that he was convicted."]

13. *Interrog.* Item, that he had been twice sworn to the pope.—And withal Dr Martin brought out the instrument of the public notary[6], wherein was contained his protestation made when he should be consecrated, asking if he had any thing else protested. The archbishop sworn to the pope by protestation.

*Answ.* Whereunto he answered, that he did nothing but by the laws of the realm.

14. *Interrog.* Item, that he, the said archbishop of Canterbury, did not only offend in the premises, but also in taking upon him the authority of the see of Rome, in that, without leave or licence from the said see, he consecrated bishops and priests.

*Answ.* He granted that he did execute such things as were wont to be referred to the pope, at what time it was permitted to him by the public laws and determination of the realm.

15. *Interrog.* Item, that when the whole realm had subscribed to the authority of the pope, he only still persisted in his error.

*Answ.* That he did not admit the pope's authority, he confessed to be true: but that he erred in the same, that he denied.

16. *Interrog.* Item, that all and singular the premises be true.

*Answ.* That likewise he granted, excepting those things whereunto he had now answered.

* * * * * *

### *A more full Answer of the archbishop of Canterbury to the first Oration of bishop Brokes.*

[When the bishop had thus ended his tale, my lord of Canterbury, desiring licence to speak, which was gently granted him by the bishop, made answer to this effect:]

My lord, I do not acknowledge this session of yours, nor yet you as my lawful judge; neither would I have appeared here this day before you, but that I was brought hither as a prisoner. And therefore I openly here renounce you for my judge, protesting that my meaning is not to make any answers as in a lawful judgment, (for then would I be silent,) but only for that I am bound in conscience to answer every man of that hope which I have in Jesus Christ, by the counsel of St Peter, and lest by my silence many of those which are weak here present might be offended. And so I desire that my answers may be accepted as *extrajudicialia*.

[And when he had ended his protestation, he began thus[7]:]

My lord, you have very learnedly and eloquently in your oration put me in remembrance of many things touching myself, wherein I do not mean to spend the time in answering of them. I acknowledge God's goodness to me in all his gifts, and thank him as heartily for this state wherein I find myself now, as ever I did for the time of my prosperity; and it is not the loss of my promotions that grieveth me. The greatest grief I have at this time is, and one of the greatest that ever I had in all my life, to see the king and queen's majesties, by their proctors, here to become my accusers, and that in their own realm and country, before a foreign power. If I have transgressed the laws of the land, their majesties have sufficient authority and power, both from God and by the ordinance of this realm, to punish me; whereunto I both have, and at all times shall be content to submit myself. A more full answer of the archbishop to bishop Brokes's oration. Queen Mary accuseth the archbishop for taking her own part against a foreign power.

Alas! what hath the pope to do in England? whose jurisdiction is so far different from the jurisdiction of this realm, that it is impossible to be true to the one and true to the other. The laws also are so diverse, that whosoever sweareth to both, must needs incur perjury to the one. Which as oft as I remember, even for the love that I bear to her grace, I cannot but be heartily sorry to think upon it, how that her highness, the day of her coronation, at which time she took a solemn oath to observe all the laws and liberties of this realm of England, at the same time also took an oath to the bishop of Rome, and promised to maintain that see. The state of England being so repugnant to the supremacy of the pope, it was impossible but she must needs be forsworn in the one. Wherein if her grace had been faithfully advertised by her council, then surely she would never have done it. The laws of the realm and of the pope are contrary. No man can be true both to the realm and to the pope together.

[6 Vid. Disputations at Oxford, Vol. I. pp. 394, 5, 423.]

[7 This passage is found only in the first edition of Foxe's Acts and Monuments. Ed. 1563, p. 1481.]

The contrariety between the laws of this realm and of the pope described.

The laws of this realm are, that the king of England is the supreme and sole governor of all his countries and dominions; and that he holdeth his crown and sceptre of himself, by the ancient laws, customs, and descents of the kings of the realm, and of none other. The pope saith, that all emperors and kings hold their crowns and regalities of him, and that he may depose them when he list: which is high treason for any man to affirm and think, being born within the king's dominions.

The laws of England are, that all bishops and priests, offending in cases of felony or treason, are to be judged and tried by the laws and customs of the realm. The pope's laws are, that the secular power cannot judge the spiritual power, and that they are not under their jurisdiction: which robbeth the king of the one part of his people.

Kings and princes cannot use their own laws in their dominions for the pope.

The laws also of England are, that whosoever hindereth the execution or proceeding of the laws of England, for any other foreign laws, ecclesiastical or temporal, incurreth the danger of a *præmunire*. The pope's laws are, that whosoever hindereth the proceedings or executions of his laws, for any other laws of any other king or country, both the prince himself, his council, all his officers, scribes, clerks, and whosoever give consent or aid to the making or executing of any such laws, stand accursed. A heavy case, (if his curse were any thing worth,) that the king and queen cannot use their own laws, but they and all theirs must stand accursed!—These things and many more examples he alleged, which (he said) stirred him that he could not give his consent to the receiving of such an enemy into the realm, so subverting the dignity and ancient liberties of the same.

Cause why the archbishop would not admit the pope.

And as for the matter of heresy and schism wherewith he was charged, he protested and called God to witness, that he knew none that he maintained. But if that were an heresy, to deny the pope's authority, and the religion which the see of Rome hath published to the world these latter years, then all the ancient fathers of the primitive church, the apostles, and Christ himself, taught heresy: and he desired all them present to bear him witness, that he took the traditions and religion of that usurping prelate to be most erroneous, false, and against the doctrine of the whole scripture; which he had oftentimes well proved by writing, and the author of the same to be very antichrist, so often preached of by the apostles and prophets, in whom did most evidently concur all signs and tokens whereby he was painted out to the world[2] to be known.

The pope's religion most erroneous.

All marks of antichrist most concur in the pope[1].

The pope's pride and tyranny.

For it was most evident that he had advanced himself above all emperors and kings of the world, whom he affirmeth to hold their estates and empires of him, as of their chief, and to be at his commandment, to depose and erect at his good will and pleasure; and that the stories make mention of his intolerable and insolent pride and tyranny, used over them in such sort, as no king would have used to his christian subjects, nor yet a good master to his servants; setting his feet on the emperor's neck, affirming that to be verified in him which was spoken only of our Saviour Jesus Christ, in these words, *Super aspidem et basiliscum ambulabis, et conculcabis leonem et draconem.* Other some had he made to hold his stirrups[3]; others he had displaced and removed from their empires and seats royal: and not content herewithal, more insolent than Lucifer, hath occupied[4] not only the highest place in this world, above kings and princes, but hath further presumed to sit in the seat of Almighty God, which only he reserved to himself, which is the conscience of man; and to keep the possession thereof, he hath promised forgiveness of sins *totiens quotiens.*

[Psal. xci. 13.]

Marks of antichrist.

He hath brought in gods of his own framing, and invented a new religion, full of gain and lucre, quite contrary to the doctrine of the holy scripture, only for the maintaining of his kingdom, displacing Christ from his glory, and holding his people in a miserable servitude of blindness, to the loss of a great number of souls, which God at the latter day shall exact at his hand: boasting many times in his canons and decrees, that he can dispense *contra Petrum, contra Paulum, contra vetus et novum Testamentum;* and

The pope dispenseth against the new and old Testament.

---

[[1] Other editions read, "Antichrist must concur in the pope."]

[[2] Other editions read, "whereby he was pointed out to the world."]

[[3] Other editions read, "his stirrup."]

[[4] Other editions read, "he hath occupied."]

that he, *plenitudine potestatis, tantum potest quantum Deus:* that is, "Against Peter, against Paul, against the old and new Testament; and of the fulness of power may do as much as God." O Lord, who ever heard such blasphemy? If there be any man that can advance himself above him, let him be judged antichrist.

This enemy of God and of our redemption is so evidently painted out in the scriptures, by such manifest signs and tokens, which all so clearly appear in him, that, except a man will shut up his eyes and heart against the light, he cannot but know him: and therefore, for my part, I will never give my consent to the receiving of him into this church of England. And you, my lord, and the rest that sit here in commission, consider well and examine your own consciences: you have sworn against him; you are learned, and can judge of the truth. I pray God you be not wilfully blind. As for me, I have herein discharged mine own conscience toward the world, and I will write also my mind to her grace, touching this matter[5].

* * * * * * * * *

[After this, ye heard also, how they proceeded to examine him of divers articles, whereof the chief was, that at the time of his creating archbishop of Canterbury, he was sworn to the pope, and had his institution and induction from him, and promised to maintain then the authority of that see; and therefore was perjured: wherefore he should rather stick to his first oath, and return to his old fold again, than to continue obstinately in an oath forced in the time of schism.]

To that he answered, saving his protestation, (which term he used before all his answers,) that at such time as archbishop Warham died, he was ambassador in Germany for the king, who sent for him thereupon home, and having intelligence by some of his friends (who were near about the king) how he meant to bestow the same bishoprick upon him, and therefore counselled him in that case to make haste home, he, feeling in himself a great inability to such a promotion, and very sorry to leave his study, and especially considering by what means he must have it, which was clean against his conscience, which he could not utter without great peril and danger, devised an excuse to the king of matter of great importance, for the which his longer abode there should be most necessary, thinking by that means, in his absence, that the king would have bestowed it upon some other, and so remained there, by that device, one half year after the king had written for him to come home. But after that no such matter fell out as he seemed to make suspicion of, the king sent for him again: who, after his return, understanding still the archbishoprick to be reserved for him, made means by divers of his best friends to shift it off, desiring rather some smaller living, that he might more quietly follow his book.

His answer to their articles. How Cranmer was made archbishop against his will.

To be brief, when the king himself spake with him, declaring his full intention[6], for his service sake, and for the good opinion he conceived of him, was to bestow that dignity upon him; after long disabling of himself, perceiving he could by no persuasions alter the king's determination, he brake frankly his conscience with him, most humbly craving first his grace's pardon for that he should declare unto his highness. Which obtained, he declared, that if he accepted the office, then he must receive it at the pope's hand; which he neither would nor could do, for that his highness was only the supreme governor of this church of England, as well in causes ecclesiastical as temporal, and that the full right and donation of all manner of bishopricks and benefices, as well as of any other temporal dignities and promotions, appertained to his grace, and not to any other foreign authority, whatsoever it was: and therefore, if he might serve God in that vocation[7], him, and his country, seeing it was his pleasure so to have it, he would accept it and receive it of his majesty, and of none other stranger, who had no authority within this realm, neither in any such gift, nor in any other thing. Whereat the king, said he, staying a while and musing, asked me, how I was able to prove it. At which time I alleged many texts out of the scriptures, and the fathers also, approving the supreme and highest authority of kings in their realms and dominions, disclosing therewithal the intolerable usurpation of the pope of Rome.

Dr Cranmer denied that he took the archbishoprick at the pope's hands. Cranmer's answer to king Henry, refusing to be archbishop.

First breaking of the matter of the pope's supremacy to king Henry.

[5 Vid. Letters to Queen Mary, Sept. 1555.]

[6 Other editions read, "declaring that his full intention."]

[7 Other editions read, "if he might in that vocation serve God."]

Cranmer sworn to the pope under protestation. Cranmer, in swearing to the pope, did nothing without advice of the best learned in this realm.

Afterwards it pleased his highness (quoth the archbishop) many and sundry times to talk with me of it; and perceiving that I could not be brought to acknowledge the authority of the bishop of Rome, the king himself called doctor Oliver and other civil lawyers[1], and devised with them how he might bestow it upon me, enforcing me nothing against my conscience. Who thereupon informed him, that I might do it by the way of protestation, and so one to be sent to Rome, who might take the oath, and do every thing in my name. Which when I understood, I said he should do it *super animam suam:* and I indeed *bona fide* made my protestation, that I did not acknowledge his authority any further than as it agreed with the express word of God, and that it might be lawful for me at all times to speak against him, and to impugn his errors, when time and occasion should serve me. And this my protestation did I cause to be enrolled, and there I think it remaineth.

* * * * * * * * *

Because there was offence taken at this word 'supreme head,' it was declared in the queen's style to be supreme governor.

After this, doctor Martin demanded of him, who was supreme head of the church of England? "Marry," quoth my lord of Canterbury, "Christ is the head of this member, as he is of the whole body of the universal church." "Why," quoth doctor Martin, "you made king Henry the eighth supreme head of the church." "Yea," said the archbishop, "of all the people of England, as well ecclesiastical as temporal." "And not of the church?" said Martin. "No," said he, "for Christ is only head of his church, and of the faith and religion of the same. The king is head and governor of his people, which are the visible church." "What!" quoth Martin; "you never durst tell the king so." "Yes, that I durst," quoth he, "and did, in the publication of his style, wherein he was named supreme head of the church; there was never other thing meant."

# [APPEAL AT HIS DEGRADATION

Foxe's Acts and Monuments, pp. 1881—1884. Ed. Lond. 1583.

## BEFORE DOCTOR THURLBY AND DOCTOR BONER COMING WITH A NEW COMMISSION TO SIT UPON THE ARCHBISHOP THE 14TH DAY OF FEBRUARY[2].]

*The tenor of the Appeal of the archbishop of Canterbury from the Pope to the next General Council[3].*

Challenge or appeal of the archbishop from the pope to a general council.

IN the name of the Father, and of the Son, and of the Holy Ghost.

First, my plain protestation made, that I intend to speak nothing against one holy, catholic, and apostolical church, or the authority thereof, (the which authority I have in great reverence, and to whom my mind is in all things to obey,) and if any thing peradventure, either by slipperiness of tongue, or by indignation of abuses, or else by the

[1 Vid. Strype's Mem. of Abp. Cranmer, Vol. I. p. 24. Ed. Oxon. 1840.]

[2 "Cranmer received a citation on the 7th of September, 1555, to appear at Rome within eighty days. Such appearance was of course impossible, as he was closely imprisoned at Oxford. But the cause proceeded, as if his absence had been voluntary. Being pronounced contumacious, he was sentenced by the pope to be degraded and delivered over to the secular magistrate." Jenkyns.]

[3 Dr Jenkyns suggests that Cranmer was probably assisted by a lawyer in drawing up this appeal. Vol. IV. p. 121. See also the Letter to a Lawyer.]

provocation of mine adversaries, be spoken or done otherwise than well, or not with such reverence as becometh me, I am most ready to amend it.

Although the bishop of Rome (whom they call pope) beareth the room of Christ in earth, and hath authority of God, yet by that power or authority he is not become unsinnable, neither hath he received that power to destroy, but to edify the congregation. Therefore, if he shall command any thing that is not right to be done, he ought to take it patiently and in good part, in case he be not therein obeyed. And he must not be obeyed, if he command any thing against the precepts of God: no, rather he may lawfully be resisted, even as Paul withstood Peter. And if he be aided[4] by help of princes, deceived perchance by false suggestion, or with evil counsel, cannot be resisted, but the remedies of withstanding him be taken away; there is nevertheless one remedy of appealing, (which no prince can take away,) uttered by the very law of nature: forsomuch as it is a certain defence, which is meet for every body by the law of God, of nature, and of man.

The pope not unsinnable. The pope hath no power to destruction, but to edify.

Remedy of appealing standeth with the law of God and nature.

And whereas the laws do permit a man to appeal, not only from the griefs and injuries done, but also from such as shall be done hereafter, or threatened to be done, insomuch that the inferior cannot make laws of not appealing to a superior power; and since it is openly enough confessed, that a holy general council, lawfully gathered together in the Holy Ghost, and representing the holy catholic church, is above the pope, especially in matters concerning faith, that he cannot make decrees that men shall not appeal from him to a general council: therefore I, Thomas Cranmer, archbishop of Canterbury, or in time past ruler of the metropolitical church[5] of Canterbury, doctor in divinity, do say and publish before you, the public notary and witnesses here present, with mind and intent to challenge and appeal from the persons and griefs underneath written, and to proffer myself in place and time convenient and meet, to prove the articles that follow. And I openly confess, that I would lawfully have published them before this day, if I might have had either liberty to come abroad myself, or licence of a notary and witnesses. But further than I am able to do, I know well, is not required of the laws.

The inferior cannot forbid to appeal to the superior.

A general council is superior to the pope.

1. First, I say and publish, that James, by the mercy of God priest, called cardinal of the pit[6], and of the title of our lady in the way of the church of Rome, judge and commissary specially deputed of our most holy lord the pope, (as he affirmed,) caused me to be cited to Rome, there to appear eighty days[7] after the citation served on me, to make answer to certain articles touching the peril of my state and life. And whereas I was kept in prison with most strait ward, so that I could in no wise be suffered to go to Rome, nor to come out of prison, and in so grievous causes concerning state and life no man is bound to send a proctor; and, though I would never so fain send my proctor, yet by reason of poverty I am not able, (for all that ever I had, wherewith I should bear my proctor's costs and charges, is quite taken from me;) nevertheless the most reverend cardinal aforesaid doth sore threaten me, that whether I shall appear or not, he will nevertheless yet proceed in judgment against me. Wherein I feel myself so grieved, that nothing can be imagined more mischievous or further from reason.

The causes why he doth appeal. The first cause.

The archbishop cited to appear at Rome, when he was fast in prison that he could not come.

Note with what justice and sincerity this catholic church doth proceed.

2. Secondly, the reverend father James Brokes, by the mercy of God bishop of Gloucester, judge and under-deputy (as he affirmed) of the most reverend cardinal, caused me to be cited at Oxford, (where I was then kept in prison,) to answer to certain articles concerning the danger of my state and life. And when I, being unlearned and ignorant in the laws, desired counsel of the learned in the law, that thing was most unrighteously denied me, contrary to the equity of all laws both of God and man. Wherein again I feel me most wrongfully grieved.

The second cause.

The archbishop denied to have counsel of the law.

3. And when I refused the said bishop of Gloucester to be my judge, for most just causes, which I then declared; he nevertheless went on still, and made process against me, contrary to the rule of the laws of appealing, which say, "A judge

The third cause.

The papists proceed contrary to law.

[4 Other editions read, "if he being aided."]
[5 Metropolical church, Ed. 1583.]
[6 Vide Proceedings before Brokes, p. 212, n. 3.]
[7 Other editions read, "fourscore days."]

that is refused ought not to proceed in the cause, but to leave off." And when he had required of me answers to certain articles, I refused to make him any answer: I said I would yet gladly make answer to the most renowned king's and queen's deputies or attornies then present, with this condition notwithstanding, that mine answer should be extrajudicial; and that was permitted me. And with this my protestation made and admitted, I made answer, but mine answer was sudden and unprovided for; and therefore I desired to have a copy of mine answers, that I might put to, take away, change, and amend them: and this was also permitted me. Nevertheless, contrary to his promise made unto me, no respect had to my protestation, nor licence given to amend mine answer, the said reverend father, bishop of Gloucester, (as I hear,) commanded mine answers to be enacted contrary to the equity of the law. In which thing again I feel me much grieved.

The papists contrary to their promise.

The fourth cause. Causes moving the archbishop why he could not admit the pope's authority.

4. Furthermore, I could not, for many causes, admit the bishop of Rome's usurped authority in this realm, nor consent to it: first, my solemn oath letting me, which I made in the time of king Henry the eighth, of most famous memory[1], according to the laws of England. Secondly, because I knew the authority of the bishop of Rome, which he usurpeth, to be against the crown, customs, and laws of this realm of England; insomuch that neither the king can be crowned in this realm without the most grievous crime of perjury, nor may bishops enjoy their bishopricks, nor judgments be used[2] according to the laws and customs of this realm, except by the bishop of Rome's authority be accursed both the king and queen, the judges, writers, and executers of the laws and customs, with all that consent to them. Finally, the whole realm shall be accursed.

The pope's authority cannot be admitted in this realm without perjury.

The fifth cause. Inconvenience to this realm in receiving the pope's authority.

5. Moreover, that heinous and usurped authority of the bishop of Rome, through reservations of the bishopricks, provisions, annuates, dispensations, pardons, appellations, bulls, and other cursed merchandise of Rome, was wont exceedingly to spoil and consume the riches and substance of this realm; all which things[3] should follow again by recognising and receiving of that usurped authority, unto the unmeasurable loss of this realm.

The sixth cause.

6. Finally, it is most evident, by that usurped authority, not only the crown of England to be under yoke, the laws and customs of this realm to be thrown down and trodden under foot; but also the most holy decrees of councils, together with the precepts both of the gospel and of God.

When in times past, the Sun of righteousness being risen in the world, christian religion by the preaching of the apostles began to be spread very far abroad and to flourish, insomuch that their sound went out into all the world; innumerable people, which walked in darkness, saw a great light; God's glory, every where published, did flourish; the only cark and care of the ministers of the church was purely and sincerely to preach Christ, the people, to embrace and follow Christ's doctrine. Then the church of Rome, as it were lady of the world, both was, and also was counted worthily, the mother of other churches; forasmuch as then she first begat to Christ, nourished with the food of pure doctrine, did help them with their riches, succoured the oppressed, and was a sanctuary for the miserable, she rejoiced with them that rejoiced, and wept with them that wept. Then, by the examples of the bishops of Rome, riches were despised, worldly glory and pomp was trodden under foot, pleasures and riot nothing regarded. Then this frail and uncertain life, being full of all miseries, was laughed to scorn, whiles, through the example of Romish martyrs, men did every where press forward to the life to come. But afterward, the ungraciousness[4] of damnable ambition never satisfied, avarice, and the horrible enormity of vices, had corrupted and taken the see of Rome; there followed every where almost the deformities of all churches, growing out of kind, into the manners of the church, their mother, leaving their former innocency and purity, and slipping into foul and heinous usages.

The primitive state of the church of Rome sincere and pure.

The church of Rome, how and where it began to alter. Deformities of the church of Rome infecting all other churches.

---

[1 In the time of most famous memory of king Henry the eighth, Ed. 1583.]

[2 Other editions read, "judgments to be used."]

[3 Which all things, Ed. 1583.]

[4 Other editions read, "afterward when the ungraciousness."]

For the foresaid and many other griefs and abuses, (which I intend to prove, and do proffer myself in time convenient to prove hereafter,) since reformation of the above-mentioned abuses is not to be looked for of the bishop of Rome; neither can I hope, by reason of his wicked abuses and usurped authority, to have him an equal judge in his own cause; therefore I do challenge and appeal in these writings from the pope, having no good counsel, and from the above-named pretences, commissions, and judges, from their citations, processes, and from all other things that have or shall follow thereupon, and from every one of them, and from all their sentences, censures, pains, and punishments of cursing, suspension, and interdicting, and from all others whatsoever their denouncings and declarations (as they pretend) of schism, of heresy, adultery, deprivation, degrading[5], by them or by any of them in any manner wise attempted, done, and set forward, to be attempted, to be done, and to be set forward hereafter, (saving always their honours and reverences,) as unequal and unrighteous, more tyrannical[6] and violent, and from every grief to come, which shall happen to me, as well for myself as for all and every one that cleaveth to me, or will hereafter be on my side, unto a free general council, that shall hereafter lawfully be, and in a sure place, to the which place I, or a proctor deputed by me, may freely and with safety come, and to him or them to whom a man may by the law, privilege, custom, or otherwise challenge and appeal.

*The bishop of Rome no equal judge in his own cause.*

*Appellation from the pope to a general council.*

And I desire the first, the second, and the third time, instantly, more instantly, and most instantly, that I may have "messengers," if there be any man that will and can give me them. And I make open promise of prosecuting this mine appellation, by the way of disannulling, abuse, inequality, and unrighteousness, or otherwise as I shall be better able; choice and liberty reserved to me, to put to, diminish, change, correct, and interpret my sayings, and to reform all things after a better fashion, saving always to me every other benefit of the law, and to them that either be or will be on my part.

*i. e. Letters of protection and defence.*

And touching my doctrine of the sacrament, and other my doctrine, of what kind soever it be, I protest that it was never my mind to write, speak, or understand any thing contrary to the most holy word of God, or else against the holy catholic church of Christ; but purely and simply to imitate and teach those things only, which I had learned of the sacred scripture, and of the holy catholic church of Christ from the beginning, and also according to the exposition of the most holy and learned fathers and martyrs of the church.

*Defence of his doctrine.*

And if any thing hath peradventure chanced otherwise than I thought, I may err; but heretic I cannot be, forasmuch as I am ready in all things to follow the judgment of the most sacred word of God and of the holy catholic church, desiring none other thing than meekly and gently to be taught, if any where (which God forbid!) I have swerved from the truth.

*The archbishop no heretic, and why.*

And I protest and openly confess, that in all my doctrine and preaching, both of the sacrament and of other my doctrine, whatsoever it be, not only I mean and judge those things as the catholic church and the most holy fathers of old, with one accord, have meant and judged; but also I would gladly use the same words that they used, and not use any other words, but to set my hand to all and singular their speeches, phrases, ways, and forms of speech, which they do use in their treatises upon the sacrament, and to keep still their interpretation. But in this thing I only am accused for an heretic, because I allow not the doctrine lately brought in of the sacrament, and because I consent not to words not accustomed in scripture, and unknown to the ancient fathers, but newly invented and brought in by men, and belonging to the destruction of souls, and overthrowing of the pure and old religion. Given, &c.

*He protesteth himself to be catholic.*

*New terms of the sacrament brought in by the pope, unknown to the scripture and old doctors.*

This appeal being put up to the bishop of Ely, he said, "My lord, our commission is to proceed against you *omni appellatione remota*, and therefore we cannot admit it."

[5 Disgrading, Ed. 1583.]

[6 Other editions read, "most tyrannical."]

"Why," (quoth he,) "then you do me the more wrong; for my case is not as every private man's case. The matter is between the pope and me *immediate*, and none otherwise: and I think no man ought to be a judge in his own cause."

Talk between Dr Thurlby and the archbishop about the appeal.

"Well," (quoth Ely,) "if it may be admitted, it shall;" and so received it of him. And then began he to persuade earnestly with the archbishop to consider his state, and to weigh it well, while there was time to do him good, promising to become a suitor to the king and queen for him: and so protested his great love and friendship that had been between them, heartily weeping, so that for a time he could not go on with his tale. After, going forward, he earnestly affirmed, that if it had not been the king and queen's commandment, whom he could not deny, else no worldly commodity should have made him to have done it; concluding that to be one of the sorrowfulest things that ever happened unto him. The archbishop gently, seeming to comfort him, said, he was very well content withal: and so proceeded they to his degradation. . . .[1]

Thurlby weeping for the archbishop.

[[1] The account which follows in Foxe of the Prayer, Exhortation and Confession of Dr Cranmer before his death, will be found in the first volume of this edition, pp. xxiii—xxix.]

# LETTERS[2]

OF

# ARCHBISHOP CRANMER.

## I. TO THE RIGHT HONOURABLE, AND MY SINGULAR GOOD LORD, MY LORD OF WILTSHIRE[3].

[4]It may please your lordship to be advertised, that the king his grace, my lady your wife, my lady Anne your daughter, be in good health, whereof thanks be to God.

Lansdowne MS. 115. fol. i. Original, holograph, British Museum. Strype's Mem. of Abp. Cranmer, Vol. II. App. No. I. pp. 675—679. Ed. Oxon. 1840.

As concerning the king his cause, master Raynolde Poole hath written a book[5] much contrary to the king his purpose, with such wit, that it appeareth that he might be for his wisdom of the council to the king his grace; and of such eloquence, that if it were set forth and known to the common people, I suppose it were not possible to persuade them to the contrary. The principal intent whereof is, that the king his grace should be content to commit his great cause to the judgment of the pope: wherein meseemeth he lacketh much judgment. But he suadeth that with such goodly eloquence, both of words and sentence, that he were like to persuade many: but me he persuadeth in that point nothing at all. But in many other things he satisfieth me very well. The sum whereof I shall shortly rehearse.

First, he sheweth the cause wherefore he had never pleasure to intromit himself in this cause, and that was the trouble which was like to ensue to this realm thereof by diversity of titles; whereof what hurt might come, we have had example in our fathers' days by the titles of Lancaster and York. And whereas God hath given many noble gifts unto the king his grace, as well of body and mind, as also of fortune; yet this exceedeth all other, that in him all titles do meet and come together, and this realm is restored to tranquillity and peace: so oweth he to provide, that this land fall not again to the foresaid misery and trouble; which may come as well by the people within this realm, (which think surely that they have an heir lawful already, with whom they all be well content, and would be sorry to have any other, and it would be hard to persuade them to take any other, leaving her,) as also by the emperor, which is a man of so great power, the queen being his aunt, the princess his niece, whom he so much doth and ever hath favoured.

---

[[2] The Letters of Abp. Cranmer have been collated with and corrected by the original MSS., as far as has been practicable, for this edition: where they have not been found, a note is made to that effect.]

[[3] Thomas Boleyn, father of queen Anne Boleyn, was created earl of Wiltshire, Dec. 8, 1529.]

[[4] Dr Jenkyns considers, that this letter was probably written in June, 1531, whilst Cranmer was in England, after his return from Rome, where, as ambassador, he had presented his book on the divorce to the pope, and previously to his departure to Germany on his mission to the emperor. He was probably residing at this time with the Boleyn family, as had been the case before he accompanied the earl to Italy. See Todd's Life of Abp. Cranmer, Vol. I. p. 30, where some errors of Strype respecting this letter are corrected. Jenkyns's Remains of Abp. Cranmer, Vol. I. p. 1.]

[[5] The book which Pole some years afterwards declared he had delivered to Henry VIII. "with secretness." Vid. Burnet's Hist. of the Reformat. Vol. III. Pt. II. Appendix. Book III. No. 51. pp. 159—163. Ed. Oxon. 1829. Beccatelli, who wrote the life of cardinal Pole, and other authors, having made no reference to this book, led Anthony à Wood to doubt whether it had ever been written. Vid. Athenæ Oxon. Vol. I. col. 293. Ed. Bliss. Lond. 1813—20. Phillips (Life of Reginald Pole, p. 66—68. Ed. Oxon. 1764) says that Pole first declared his opinion on the divorce to Henry VIII. personally, and afterwards, to soften the king's displeasure, "sent his reasons in writing, with an assurance, which he knew would be acceptable, that the purport of the letter had been communicated to nobody."]

And where he heard reasons for the king his party, that he was moved of God his law, which doth straitly forbid, and that with many great threats, that no man shall marry his brother his wife: and as for the people, that longeth not to their judgment, and yet it is to be thought that they will be content, when they shall know that the ancient doctors of the church, and the determinations of so many great universities be of the king his sentence: and as concerning the emperor, if he be so unrightful that he will maintain an unjust cause, yet God will never fail them that stand upon his party, and for any thing will not transgress his commandments: and beside that, we shall not lack the aid of the French king, which partly for the league which he hath made with us, and partly for the displeasure and old grudge which he beareth toward the emperor, would be glad to have occasion to be avenged: these reasons he bringeth for the king's party against his own opinion.

To which he maketh answer in this manner. First, as touching the law of God, he thinketh that if the king were pleased to take the contrary part, he might as well justify that, and have as good ground of the scripture therefore, as for that part which he now taketh. And yet if he thought the king's party never so just, and that this his marriage were undoubtedly against God's pleasure, then he could not deny but it should be well done for the king to refuse this marriage, and to take another wife: but that he should be a doer therein, and a setter forward thereof, he could never find in his heart. And yet he granteth that he hath no good reason therefore, but only affection[1] which he beareth and of duty oweth unto the king's person. For in so doing he should not only weaken, yea and utterly take away the princess' title, but also he must needs accuse the most and chief part of all the king's life hitherto, which hath been so infortunate to live more than twenty years in a matrimony so shameful, so abominable, so bestial and against nature, (if it be so as the books which do defend the king's party do say,) that the abomination thereof is naturally written and graven in every man's heart, so that none excusation can be made by ignorance; and thus to accuse the noble nature of the king's grace, and to take away the title of his succession, he could never find in his heart, were [the] king's cause never so good; which he doth knowledge to be only affection.

Now as concerning the people, he thinketh not possible to satisfy them by learning or preaching; but as they now do begin to hate priests, this shall make them rather to hate much more both learned men and also the name of learning, and bring them in abomination of every man. For what loving men toward their prince would gladly hear, that either their prince should be so infortunate, to live so many years in matrimony so abominable; or that they should be taken and counted so bestial, to approve and take for lawful, and that so many years, a matrimony so unlawful and so much against nature, that every man in his heart naturally doth abhor it? and, that is more, when they hear this matrimony dispraised and spoken against, neither by their own minds, nor by reasons that be made against this matrimony, can they be persuaded to grudge against the matrimony; but for any thing they do grudge against the divorce, wherein the people should shew themselves no men but beasts. And that the people should be persuaded hereto, he cannot think it.

And as for the authority of the universities, he thinketh and sayeth that many times they be led by affections, which is well known to every man, and wisheth that they never did err in their determinations. Then he sheweth with how great difficulty the universities were brought to the king's party. And moreover against the authority of the universities he setteth the authority of the king's grace['s] father and his council, the queen's father and his council, and the pope and his council.

Then he cometh again to the pope, and the emperor, and French king. And first the pope, how much he is adversary unto the king's purpose, he hath shewed divers tokens already, and not without a cause: for if he should consent to the king's purpose, he must needs do against his predecessors, and also restrain his own power more than it hath been in time past, which rather he would be glad to extend; and moreover he

[[1] Therefore, only affection. Strype.]

should set great sedition in many realms, as in Portugal, of which king the emperor hath married one sister, and the duke of Savoy the other. Then he extolleth the power of the emperor, and diminish[eth] the aid of the French king toward us, saying, that the emperor, without drawing of any sword, but only by forbidding the course of merchandise into Flanders and Spain, may put this realm into great damage and ruin. And what if he will thereto draw his sword, wherein is so much power, which, being of much less power than he is now, subdued the pope and the French king? And as for the Frenchmen, [they] never used to keep league with us but for their own advantage, and we can never find in our hearts to trust them. And yet if now contrary to their old nature they keep their league, yet our nation shall think themselves in miserable condition, if they shall be compelled to trust upon their aid, which always have been our mortal enemies, and never we loved them, nor they us. And if the Frenchmen have any suspicion that this new matrimony shall not continue, then we shall have no succour of them, but upon such conditions as shall be intolerable to this realm. And if they, following their old nature and custom, then do break league with us, then we shall look for none other, but that England shall be a prey between the emperor and them. After all this he cometh to the point to save the king's honour, saying, that the king standeth even upon the brink of the water, and yet he may save all his honour; but if he put forth his foot but one step forward, all his honour is drowned. And the means which he hath devised to save the king's honour is this[2].

The rest of this matter I must leave to shew your lordship by mouth when I speak with you, which I purpose, God willing, shall be to-morrow, if the king's grace let me not. Now the bearer maketh such haste that I can write no more, but that I hear no word from my benefice, nor master Russell['s] servant is not yet returned again, whereof I do not a little marvel. The king and my lady Anne rode yesterday to Windsor, and this night they be looked for again at Hampton Court: God be their guide, and preserve your lordship to his most pleasure. From Hampton Court this xiii. day of June, [1531.][3]

Your most humble beadman,

THOMAS CRANMAR[4].

---

## II. TO KING HENRY VIII.[5]

PLEASETH it your highness to understand, that at my last solicitation unto Monsieur Grandeveile[6] for an answer of the contract of merchandise between the merchants of your grace's realm, and the merchants of the emperor's Low Countries, the said Monsieur Grandeveile shewed me, that forsomuch as the diet concerning the said contract was lately held in Flaundres, where the queen of Hungary[7] is governatrice, the emperor thought good to do nothing therein without her advice, but to make answer by her rather than by me. Wherefore it may please your grace no further to look for answer of me herein, but of the queen, unto whom the whole answer is committed.

Printed from Strype's Mem. of Abp. Cranmer, App. Vol. II. p. 679. Ed. Oxon. 1840. No. II. from Sir W. Hickes's MSS.

---

[2 As has been observed by Strype and Mr Todd, the beginning of the letter shews, that the means devised were, for the king to be "content to commit his great cause to the judgment of the pope." Vid. Jenkyns' Remains of Abp. Cranmer, Vol. I. p. 5, *n.* d.]

[3 Vid. Todd's Life of Abp. Cranmer, Vol. I. p. 30.]

[4 So spelled in this single instance, the only one in which it is written with the archbishop's own hand.]

[5 This and the following letter are reports from Cranmer whilst he was at the court of the emperor Charles V. as sole ambassador, to which office he was appointed by a commission with instructions, Jan. 24, 1531-2, "wherein he was styled Consiliarius Regius et ad Cæsarem orator." Vid. Strype's Mem. of Abp. Cranmer, Vol. I. p. 14. Ed. Oxon. 1840. Also Seckendorf, Comment. de Lutheran. Lib. III. sect. 7. § xvi. Add. p. 41. Ed. Francof. et Lips. 1692.]

[6 Cranmer had divers conferences with M. Grandeville, at Regensburgh. Strype's Mem. of Abp. Cranmer, Vol. I. p. 16. Ed. Oxon. 1840.]

[7 "Mary, the sister of Charles V., queen dowager of Hungary, and governess of the Netherlands." Jenkyns.]

Moreover, when the said Monsieur Grandeveile inquired of me, if I had any answer of the aid and subsidy which the emperor desired of your grace, I reported unto him fully your grace's answer, according unto mine instructions sent unto me by your grace's servant, William Paget. Which answer he desired me to deliver him in writing, that he might refer the same truly unto the emperor; and so I did. Nevertheless the emperor, now at his departing[1], hath had such importune business, that Monsieur Grandeveile assigned me to repair unto the emperor again at Lyntz; for there, he said, I shall have an answer again in writing. The French ambassador and I with all diligence do make preparation to furnish ourselves of wagons, horses, ships, tents, and other things necessary to our voyage; but it will be at the least eight or ten days before we can be ready to depart hence. Yet we trust to be at Lyntz before the emperor; for he will tarry by the way at Passaw ten or twelve days.

As for the Turk, he resideth still in Hungary in the same place environed upon all parts, whereof I wrote unto your highness in my last letters. And the emperor departed from Abagh toward Vienna the second day of this month by land, not coming by this town; but the same day the king Ferdinando[2] departed from this town by water, and at Passaw, fourteen miles hence, they shall meet, and so pass forth unto Lyntz, which is the midway from hence unto Vienna. And there the emperor will tarry to counsel what he will do[3]: and there all the ambassadors shall know his pleasure, as Monsieur Grandeveile shewed me.

I have sent herewith unto your grace the copy of the emperor's proclamation[4] concerning a general council, and a reformation to be had in Germany for the controversies of the faith. Also I have sent the tax of all the states of the empire, how many soldiers every man is limited unto for the aid against the Turk. Wherein your grace may perceive, that the greatest prince in Germany (only the duke of Burgundy and Austry except) is not appointed above 120 horsemen and 554 footmen. Thus our Lord evermore have your highness in his preservation and governance. From Regenspurgh, the iv. day of September, [1532.]

Your grace's most humble subject, chaplain, and beadman,

THOMAS CRANMER.

## III. TO KING HENRY VIII.[5]

Cotton MS. Vitellius, B. XXI. fol. 79. Original holograph. Imperator. 20 Octob. 1532. British Museum.

PLEASETH it your highness to understand, that [the emperor hath made] such speed in his journey toward Spayne, that [he hath travelled] two hundredth English miles from Vienna, and is [now at a] town called Villach, but six Dutch miles from Italy, [from whence, if] possible, he intendeth to pass the seas into Spayne bef[ore Chri]stmas[6]. But in his passage through Italy he will speak [with the] pope, with whom, among other matters, I suppose he will tr[eat of] a general council to be had this next year to come, accordi[ng] to his promise unto the princes of Almayne at this last di[et][7]. And I do think that he will not forget to make mention u[nto

[1 Viz. to take the command of the combined forces against the Turks. Vid. Letter III. infra.]

[2 Ferdinand was brother of Charles V. and his successor in the empire.]

[3 Vid. Sleidan, De Statu Religionis et Reipub. Book VIII. p. 167. Ed. Francof. 1568.]

[4 Dr Jenkyns concludes that this was "the edict of August 3rd, 1532; by which the emperor, on the conclusion of the treaty of Nuremberg, announced a general peace in Germany until the meeting of a general, christian, and free council. The protestants on their part engaged to assist the emperor against the Turks." Vid. Seckendorf, Comment. Hist. Apol. de Lutheran, Lib. III. sect. 4. § ix. p. 25. Ed. Francof. et Lips. 1692. (12); Robertson's Life of Charles V. Vol. III. p. 57. Ed. Lond. 1787.]

[5 This letter being injured by fire, Dr Jenkyns has supplied some of the deficiencies by conjecture. Vid. Remains of Abp. Cranmer, Vol. I. p. 8.]

[6 He did not land in Spain till April 22, 1533. Vid. Robertson's Life of Charles V. Vol. III. p. 63.]

[7 See note 4 supra.]

the] pope of your grace's great cause; wherein I humbly beseech your highness that I may be instructed of your pleasure what I shall do. Because the said meeting should not much empech the emperor's long [journey] into Spayne, he hath directed letters unto the pope, to meet him [at] some place in his way toward Genua. What place that shall be, is not yet known, as Monsieur Grandeveile informed me, but I shall certify your grace as soon as I shall have sure knowledge thereof. But I fear that the emperor will depart thence, before my letters shall may come unto your grace's hands: and if not, I beseech your grace of instructions, what I shall entreat with your grace's ambassadors unto the pope's holiness[8], if we meet together, as I suppose we shall.

As touching the emperor's army of Italians and Spaniards that came out of Italy, in their coming to Vienna by Isprugh, Passaw, Lyntz, and other places adjoining to the waters of Enus and Danubius, they have done great damage unto all the countries that they have passed by, as I wrote unto your highness in my last letters, dated the second day of this month; but now, in returning again into Italy by another way through Austria, Stiria, and Carinthia, the Italians have done much more harm. For eight thousand of them[9], which were conducted hither *per comitem Sancti Secundi, Martionem Colump... comitem Philippum Tornierum, et Jo. Baptista Castoldum*, for indignation that the emperor would not prosecute the Turk, and for lack of payment of their wages, departed from the emperor and from their captains, and chose captain among themselves, and went before the emperor, spoiling and robbing all the countries of Austria, Stiria, and Carinthia, more than two hundredth English miles in length, as well churches as other houses, not leaving monstral nor the sacrament. And the men of arms that come with the emperor, and other that follow the court, do con[sume] all that the other left, in such sort, that I, following two days after the emperor from Vienna, found in no town that was unwalled man, woman, nor child, meat, drink, nor bedding; but, thanked be God! I found straw, hay, and corn, for my horses to eat, and for myself and my servant to lie in, but the people were all fled into [the] mountains for fear.

The said Italians not only robbed the towns, but also ravished the [wo]men, and beat the men, and slew many. And yet cometh after the emperor [the] captain called Fabricius Maromaus[10] with his band about three thousand, who brenneth up all the towns which before were but spoiled, as I am informed by two of my servants which I left at Vienna, the one sick, and the other to keep him: and they told me that all the towns by the way, so far as Fabricius Maromaus hath gone, be clean brent up, so much that not one house is standing, except in such strong holds as they could not attain unto. And yet one walled town they have entered into and spoiled, which the other that went before durst not attempt to assault; the name of it is Newmarkes, and a servant of mine was present, when they brake the gates and slew the porters. Of this sacking and brenning is like to ensue great penury and default of all victuals, and specially of corn; forsomuch as the corn here is brent up, whereupon the people should live this year, and sow their land against the next year. Thus is this country miserably oppressed of all parties, but much more by them that came to defend this country, than it was by the Turks.

*So that hitherto I can see no great fruit that hath succeeded of this puissant army assembled against the Turk. For it hath alienated the minds of the Almains from the Italians and Spaniards much more than ever they were before. And moreover, as far as I can understand, it hath not a little diminished the minds, as well of the*

---

[[8] "Sir Edward Karne, Dr Bennet, and sir Thomas Elyot, were Henry VIII.'s ambassadors with the pope at this time. In consequence of queen Catharine's appeal, an advocation of the divorce cause to Rome had been granted; and it was now pressed by her party that the king should appear there by proxy. Henry refused, and was labouring to procure a commission to try the question in England." Vid. Jenkyns' Remains of Abp. Cranmer, Vol. I. p. 9, who refers to Burnet's Hist. of the Reformat. Vol. I. p. 242. Ed. Oxon. 1829. Strype's Eccl. Mem. Vol. I. p. 341. Ed. Oxon. 1822; Mem. of Abp. Cranmer, Vol. I. p. 13. Ed. Oxon. 1840; and State Papers, Vol. I. pp. 336, 346, 347.

[[9] Vid. Knolles' Hist. of the Turks, p. 625. Ed. Lond. 1638.]

[[10] Discontent at the appointment of Fabricius Maramaldus to the command was one of the causes of the mutiny. Id. p. 623.]

*Italians as Almains, towards the emperor, because that he so shortly hath dissolved the said army that came to him with so good courages, and he hath not prosecuted the said enterprise against the Turk throughout all Hungary and Greece, according to their expectation; but now the men of arms be much displeased, [and many of them do say openly, that they will never return at his calling hereafter]*[1].

And now the husbandmen of this country be in such a tumultuation for the loss of their goods and the brenning of their houses, that they muster together upon the mountains, and with guns and stones do slay many of the emperor's people. And in divers places they come down from the mountains in the night, and do slay all the small companies that they may find sleeping. And many times they come down in the day in good companies, and rob carriages that do follow the court, and slay as many as will withstand them: so much that they have slain many gentlemen of the court; and yesterday they slew three or four gentlemen of Burgon, for whose death the emperor is right pensive. But the boors put no difference between one man and another, for all that go with the emperor be to them Italians and Spaniards. They have also slain the ambassador of Mantua, as the constant fame hath been here continually these three days. And the legate de Medices[2], at a town six miles hence called St Vite, was taken prison[er, but was released] by favour of the emperor's letters; but after in another place [they would have] slain him, if he had not escaped with good horses; [they slew] one of his men of arms with an arquebuse, and took Mon...... whom your grace knoweth right well, and he had been sl[ain by the stroke of] an halberd, if the stroke had not light short: nevertheless [his clothes] upon his breast were cut down with the stroke unto the bare [flesh]; and afterwards they led him into the mountains almost two days, and [would] have slain him, if one man had not been his friend. And [since] is word brought, that four of the said legate's carriages be robbed, [which] came after the emperor; and every day we hear of much murder and [rob]bing done by the boors. And yet all these dangers, than[ked be God,] I have escaped; but these two days to come I shall be [in] more jeopardy of the boors, than I was at any time yet: nevertheless, he that conducted me safely hither, I trust he will likewise conduct me into Italy and Spain, and afterward to England again.

*Don Ferdinando is not much beloved in these parts, neither of the princes that be adjoining to them, nor also of his own subjects. And this wasting of this country is*

---

[[1] The passages in Italics were written in cypher in the original, but have been decyphered in the margin: those within brackets have been supplied by Dr Jenkyns.

"The protestants, as a testimony of their gratitude to the emperor, exerted themselves with extraordinary zeal, and brought into the field forces that exceeded in number the quota imposed on them: the catholics imitating their example, one of the greatest and best appointed armies that had ever been levied in Germany assembled near Vienna. Being joined by a body of Spanish and Italian veterans under the Marquis dal Guasto, by some heavy-armed cavalry from the Low Countries, and by the troops which Ferdinand had raised in Bohemia, Austria, and his other territories, it amounted in all to ninety thousand disciplined foot, and thirty thousand horse, besides a prodigious swarm of irregulars. Of this vast army, worthy the first prince in Christendom, the emperor took the command in person; and mankind waited in suspense the issue of a decisive battle between the two greatest monarchs in the world. But each of them dreading the other's power and good fortune, they both conducted their operations with such excessive caution, that a campaign, for which such immense preparations had been made, ended without any memorable event. Solyman, finding it impossible to gain ground upon an enemy always attentive and on his guard, marched back to Constantinople towards the end of autumn." Robertson's Life of Charles V. Vol. III. pp. 58, 9, quoted in Remains of Cranmer. Cranmer appears to have given a more full account of this transaction than any other writer. "Sed taxant hic Cæsarem scriptores Hungari, et cum iis Pallavicinus, Lib. III. cap. xi. sect. 1, quod in Hispaniam ad uxorem, prolis generandæ cupidus, Ferdinando fratre deserto, festinasset. Magna autem culpæ pars pontifici tribuenda est. Hujus enim copiæ, cum reliquias belli in Pannonia persequi debuissent, seditione facta, Italiam repetierunt, hostiliter in ditione Austriaca incendiis grassatæ, sic vindicare se dictitantes quæ Germani in Italia (sub Borbonio scilicet et Franspegio) patrassent." Seckendorf, Comment. Hist. Apol. de Lutheran. Lib. III. sect. 6. § xi. p. 30.]

[[2] The emperor ordered both the legate, cardinal Hippolytus de Medici, and Pietro Maria Rosso, to whom the mutiny was ascribed, to be arrested, but he speedily set the cardinal at liberty with many apologies, and soon afterwards released Rosso also. Dr Jenkyns suggests that Cranmer's account may be suspected to be a different version of the same transaction. Guicciardini, Istor. D'Italia. Vol. X. Lib. XX. p. 165. Ed. Milan. 1803.]

*like to augment the murmur of the people against him; whereupon many men do fear an insurrection to follow very shortly, whereunto this commotion of the commons is a very preparative.* Deus omnia vertat in gloriam suam: *for hereof might follow such inconvenience as in many years after should be irrep[arable].*

Here hath appeared two hours before daylight every morning since the fifth or sixth day of this month a blazing star, called *cometa*, straight in the east, casting his beam upward, partly inclined toward the south, much whiter in colour than was the other that appeared the last year. And moreover many persons here do affirm, that they have seen above the moon a blue cross, which mine host in a city called Indiburs and all his household did see, as they shewed me. Other do say, that they have seen an horse-head flaming, other have seen a flaming sword. But of these other impressions I cannot assure your grace; for I saw no mo but the comet, which I saw within these two days[3]. What strange things these tokens do signify to come hereafter, God knoweth: for they do not lightly appear, but against some great mutation; and it hath not be seen (as I suppose) that so ma[ny] comets have appeared in so short time.

. . . . . . . . . na is a great infection of the plague, whereof is dead many of the em[peror's] household, and among other is dead Waldesius, a Spaniard, the em[peror's] chief secretary, and was in his singular favour. He was well learned in the Latin tongue, and partly in the Greek; and whensoever the emperor would have any thing well and exactly done in the Latin tongue, it was ever put to Waldesius; and I suppose that he made the draught of the answer of the emperor, which I sent unto your grace inclosed with my last letters.

In my journey I passed through the place where was the first battle against the fourteen thousand Turks that came to Ens, though many say they were but eight thousand. In which battle were captains of our party, Cassiander, born in Croatia, and two Turks which have been long time servants unto king Ferdinando; one is called Bacrespal, and the other Turk Waylande. But the Turks durst not abide for fear of duke Frederick, which was very near with six thousand horsemen and a great number of footmen. By the high way, as I rode almost two English miles, lay many dead men and horses, part of Christian, and part of Turks. But the great number were Turks. But to mine estimation, as much as I could view the ground, there was not slain upon both parties two thousand men. But after in another place were slain about two thousand Turks of the same band, and they slew again two or three thousand Spaniards arquebusiers at the same time, and took divers prisoners, whom they carried with them into Hungary. Beside that, from their first entering into Austria and Stiria until their returning into Hungary again, they slew in one place and other above fifteen or sixteen thousand christian men, and took many prisoners, and escaped themselves all but three or four thousand[4], which were slain as I have above written. This is the voice of this country, which I have now written unto your grace; but Monsieur Grandeveile shewed me otherwise, that all the said Turks were slain except two or three hundredth, as I wrote unto your grace in my last letters. Now I have signified unto your grace both the saying of Monsieur Grandeveile, and also the voice of this country, permitting unto your grace's wisdom the judgment of both.

---

[3 "This was the end of those wonderful preparations made by the two great monarchs, Solyman and Charles V., in the year 1532, which held the world in great suspense, with the fearful expectation of some marvellous alteration; and so much the more, for that at the same time appeared a great blazing star for the space of fifteen days." Vid. Knolles' Hist. of the Turks, p. 626.—Per Septembrem et Octobrem visus hoc tempore cometa fuit ante solis ortum. Sleidan, De statu Religionis et Reipub. Book VIII. p. 168. Ed. Francof. 1568.]

[4 Solymannus...prædatum emittit ad quindecim equitum millia, duce Casono. Is Lincium usque supra Viennam excurrit, et longe lateque devastatis agris, nullum immanitatis genus prætermittit. Cum vero pedem referret, in nostros equites, qui fuerant emissi, ut rapinis et populationibus illum prohiberent, incidit, et diversis locis ad internecionem prope concisus, tandem et ipse occumbit. Sleidan, De statu Religionis et Reipub. Book VIII. p. 167. Ed. Francof. 1668. Knolles (p. 622) asserts that this destruction befel a division of eight thousand men only, under Cason, and that the remainder escaped with little loss to Solyman. Dr Jenkyns appears to think that Knolles has followed "the voice of the country," Sleidan the statement of Granvelle. Vid. Remains of Abp. Cranmer, Vol. I. p. 14, *n.* c.]

This same day a doctor, chaplain to the bishop of Saltzburg, shewed me that the Turk prepareth another army; but I can hear no good ground thereof to give credence unto as yet: as soon as I can inquire the truth, I shall certify your grace thereof.

The king Ferdinando hitherto hath accompanied the emperor, and shortly he shall depart unto Isbrugh, where the queen is. And because that I must follow the emperor, I thought it good to salute him before his departure from the emperor, and to offer him my service, and to understand if he would any thing command me unto your grace; who [commended] him unto your highness, and said that forsomuch as the emperor [made your highness] participant of all the news here, it should not require [any other] news sent but only this, that the emperor and he have recei[ved letters from] sundry parts according in one thing, that Andrew Doria h[ad capti]vate and taken from the Turk Modona and Corona in Morea[1], [with an]other strong hold, whereof he remembered not the name. But [because] that hitherto they have no letters thereof from Andrew Doria himself, they will not yet give firm credence thereto.

Moreover the emperor hath sent for the duke William of Bavaria to come to him, that before his departing out of Almayne he may conclu[de] peace between the king Ferdinando and the duke of Bavaria, lest that after his departing more inconven[iences] may fall than hath been heretofore.

The duke Dalby an Hispaniard came hither to help the emperor in his wars, and this same day is word come, that his brother's carriages, six mulettes, and fourteen horses be taken by the boors, and two of his servants slain, and the rest fled away. And this is done in the way which, by the grace of God, I must ride to-morrow.

As concerning the duke Frederick[2], the French ambassador advised me not to speak with him in the camp, for that should gender a suspicion unto the emperor; and after that the emperor had dissolved his army, duke Frederick incontinent departed with his band of the empire toward his own dominion by Regenspurg; so that I, going with the emperor another way, cou[ld] not speak with duke Frederick, to understand if he had any communication with the emperor in your grace's cause. But the French ambassador, (which, coming to Vienna by the water of Danubius, left his horses at Passaw, almost two hundredth English miles from Vienna,) was compelled to leave the emperor, and in wagons to ride to his horses the same way that duke Frederick went. And he promised me to speak to duke Frederick in your grace's cause, and to bring me an answer, which as soon as he cometh I shall send unto your grace. And thus Almighty God have your highness evermore in his preservation and governance! From Villach, the xxty day of October, [1532.]

Your highness

. . . . . chaplain and[3]

---

[[1] Doria [Auria] ravaged the coasts of Peloponnesus, and took Coron, Patras, and Rhium, but not Modon. Knolles' Hist. of the Turks, pp. 626, 7.]

[[2] This duke Frederick was probably John Frederick, duke of Saxony, who had lately succeeded the elector John, with whom Cranmer, having left Ratisbon incognito, had a private conference. Vid. Seckendorf, Comment. Hist. Apol. Lib. III. sect. 7. § xvi. p. 41, Add.; Strype's Mem. of Abp. Cranmer, Vol. I. pp. 18, 19. Ed. Oxon. 1840.]

[[3] The signature is destroyed by fire.]

## IV. TO CRUMWELL.

Cotton MS. Vespasian. F. XIII. fol. 75. Original holograph. British Museum.

MASTER Crumwell, in my right hearty wise I commend me to you; and likewise pray you to be good master unto mine old acquainted lover and friend master Newman this bearer, in such his suits as he at this time shall have unto you. And albeit I have diverse suits and causes of mine own to be made and moved unto you at our next meeting, which I have many times forgotten when I have been personally with you; yet I am so much beholding to the said Mr Newman for many considerations and respects, that I am thus bold to write unto you in his favour at this time, leaving mine own causes apart until our next meeting, or some other good opportunity of time, praying you to be as good unto him in the same, as ye shall be sure to have me ready at all times to shew you any pleasure that shall lie in me. At Chanon Rowe in Westminster, the viiith day of February, [1533.]

Your own assured and very loving good friend,

THOMAS ELECT OF CANT.[4]

---

## V. TO KING HENRY VIII.

State Paper Office. Domestic Letters, Vol. II fol. 144. Original holograph. Harl. MS. 6148. fol. 2. British Museum Copy. Todd, Introduction to Cranmer's Defence, p. xlvi.

PLEASE it your highness, that where your grace's great cause of matrimony is (as it is thought) through all Christianity divulgated, and in the mouths of the rude and ignorant common people of this your grace's realm so talked of, that few of them do fear to report and say, thereof is likelihood hereafter to ensue great inconvenience, danger, and peril to this your grace's realm, and much uncertainty of succession; by which things the said ignorant people be not a little offended: and forasmuch as it hath pleased Almighty God, and your grace of your abundant goodness to me shewed, to call me (albeit a poor wretch and much unworthy) unto this high and chargeable office of primate and archbishop in this your grace's realm, wherein I beseech Almighty God to grant me his grace so to use and demean myself, as may be standing with his pleasure and the discharge of my conscience, and to the weal of this your grace's realm: and considering also the obloquy and bruit, which daily doth spring and increase, of the clergy of this realm, and specially of the heads and presidents of the same, because they in this behalf do not foresee and provide such convenient remedies, as might expel and put out of doubt all such inconveniences, perils, and dangers, as the said rude and ignorant people do speak and talk to be imminent: I, your most humble orator and beadman, am, in consideration of the premises, urgently constrained at this time most humbly to beseech your most noble grace, that where the office and duty of the archbishop of Canterbury, by your and your progenitors' sufferance and grants, is to direct, order, judge, and determine causes spiritual in this your grace's realm; and because I would be right loth, and also it shall not become me, forasmuch as your grace is my prince and sovereign, to enterprise any part of my office in the said weighty cause touching your highness, without your gr[illegible]'s favour and licence obtained in that behalf: it may please, therefore, your most [illegible] majesty (considerations had to the premises, and to my most bounden duty toward[illegible]ness, your realm, succession, and posterity, and for the exoneration of my consc[illegible]rds Almighty God) to license me, according to mine office and duty, to proceed to the examination, final determination, and judgment in the said great cause touching your

---

[[4] Eleven bulls, the last which were received in the reign of Henry VIII., were sent by the pope, Clement VII., for Cranmer's promotion to the archbishoprick of Canterbury. The first eight bear date Feb. 21, the ninth Feb. 22, the tenth and eleventh, March 2, 1533. Henry VIII. had applied for them to the pope at the end of the preceding January, though a statute had been passed against procuring more bulls from Rome, in order that he might not begin the breach till forced to it by Clement VII. The consecration of Cranmer by the bishops of Lincoln, Exeter, and St Asaph, took place on March 30, 1533. Vid. Burnet's Hist. of Reformat. Vol. I. pp. 259, 60. Ed. Oxon. 1829; Strype's Mem. of Abp. Cranmer, Vol. I. pp. 26, 7. Ed. Oxon. 1840.]

highness: eftsoons, as prostrate at the feet of your majesty, beseeching the same to pardon me of these my bold and rude letters, and the same to accept and take in good sense and part as I do mean; which, calling our Lord to record, is only for the zeal that I have to the causes aforesaid, and for none other intent and purpose. From my manor at Lambith, the 11th day of April, in the first year of my consecration[1], [1533.]

Your highness' most humble beadsman and chaplain,

THOMAS CANTUAR.

*To the king's highness, from the Archbishop of Cant. at Lambyth, the xi. day of April, the xxv. year of your reign.*

State Paper Office. Ibid. fol. 143. Original holograph.

"Please it your highness, that where your grace's great cause of matrimony is, as it is thought, through all Christianity divulgated, and in the mouths of the rude and ignorant common people of this your grace's realm so talked of, that few of them do fear to report and say, that thereof is likelihood hereafter to ensue great inconvenience, danger, and peril to this your grace's realm, and much uncertainty if the said cause of matrimony should be suffered still to continue in question, undecided; and also reducing to your remembrance the great blame that hath been arrected to the clergy of this our realm, and specially to the heads and presidents of the same, because they have not hitherto studied and travailed for remedies to exclude and put out of doubt such uncertainty, inconveniences, perils, and dangers; being moved in your conscience by reason of the premises to endeavour yourself as far as you may, by reason of your said office of primacy, to set some direction and end in the said cause of matrimony, according to the pleasure of Almighty God. And thereupon ye duly recognising, that it becometh you not, being our subject, to enterprise any part of your said office, in so great and weighty cause pertaining to us, being your prince and sovereign, without our licence obtained so to do; and therefore, in your most humble wise ye supply unto us, in your said letters, to grant unto you our licence to proceed to the examination and final determination of the said cause, in exoneration of your conscience towards God, and for the satisfying of your bounden duty towards us, our realm, succession and posterity, in avoiding of the said inconveniences; and, finally, in the end of your said letters, ye beseech us to pardon your boldness and rude writing in that behalf, and to take the same in good sense and part, as you do mean, calling God to your record, that only for the zeal that ye have to the premises, ye have written your said letters, and for none other intent, cause, or purpose. My lord, where you write in the last part of your said letters, whereunto we make you first answer, that ye be moved only by the zeal that ye have to justice, and for the exoneration of your conscience against God, to write as you do unto us; we cannot of reason be discontented therewith, but condignly praise you therein. And for that we perceive that ye have such a good mind and fervent zeal to do justice according to your office, for the quieting of our realm, and for the excluding of such dangers and perils as be in your said letters mentioned; and also for putting our succession and posterity out of question, doubt, and uncertainty; we cannot but much commend and laud your good and virtuous intended purpose on that behalf. In consideration whereof, albeit we, being your king and sovereign, do recognise no superior in earth, but only God, and not being subject to the laws of any other earthly creature; yet, because ye be under us, by God's calling and ours, the

---

[[1] "This letter is wholly in the archbishop's hand-writing; and it is not a little singular, that another letter of the same date, and nearly of the same tenor, likewise written by the archbishop himself, is preserved in the State Paper office. They both bear the marks of having been folded and sealed, and of having been received by the king. It is so difficult to conjecture why they were both written, and why they differed from each other, that the second is subjoined." Note to State Papers, Vol. I. p. 391. This Letter is thus endorsed, either in Paget's or Wriothesley's hand-writing, most probably by the latter: "Letters from the Bishop of Canterbury, monitory to the king's highness, with others written in the time of his process, and the copy of the sentence subscribed by two notaries." The first of these letters is that which was entered by Cranmer's secretary in his book of copies, Harl. MSS. 6148.

The following answer of Henry VIII. to Abp. Cranmer, granting him licence to proceed to the final determination of his cause of matrimony, may be seen in the State Papers, Vol. I. Part II. p. 392, from which it is here inserted.

King Henry VIII.'s letter to archbishop Cranmer, authorising him to give a final determination concerning the marriage between the king and Catharine of Spain.

Ex Biblioth. R. Harley. Armig. April, A.D. 1533.

Most Reverend Father, &c., we greet you well. Doing you to understand, that the 12th day of this month of April we receive letters from you, dated at Lambeth the 11 day of the same month, in which letters ye writ, that, forasmuch as our great cause of matrimony, which has long depended in question, is divulgated (as it is thought) throughout all Christente, and it is communed of the mouths of no small number of our people; and that many of them fear not to say and report, that thereof is likelihood hereafter to ensue great inconveniences, dangers, and perils to this realm, and much uncertainty to our succession, whereby our said people is seen to be not a little offended: whereupon ye, whom God and we have ordained archbishop of Canterbury, and primate of all this our realm of England, to whose office it hath been, and is, appertaining, by the sufferance of us and our progenitors, as ye write yourself both justly and truly, to order, judge, and determine mere spiritual causes within this our realm, having due consideration to the said inconveniences, dangers, perils, and incertainty,

of succession; by which things the said ignorant people be not a little offended: and forasmuch as it hath pleased Almighty God, and your grace of your abundant goodness to me shewed, to call me, albeit a poor wretch and much unworthy, unto this high and chargeable office of primate and archbishop in this your grace's realm, wherein I beseech Almighty God to grant me his grace so to use and demean myself, as may be standing with his pleasure, and the discharge of my conscience, and to the weal of this your grace's said realm: and considering also the obloquy and bruit, which daily doth spring and increase, of the clergy of this realm, and specially of the heads and presidents of the same, because they in this behalf do not foresee and provide convenient remedies, as might expel and put out of doubt all such inconveniences, perils and dangers, as the said rude and ignorant people do speak and talk to be imminent: I, your most humble orator and beadman, am, in consideration of the premises, urgently constrained at this time most humbly to beseech your most noble grace, that where my office and duty is, by your and your predecessors' sufferance and grants, to direct and order causes spiritual in this your grace's realm, according to the laws of God and holy church, and for relief of all manner griefs and infirmities of the people, God's subjects and yours, happening in the said spiritual causes, to provide such remedy as shall be thought most convenient for their help and relief in that behalf; and because I would be right loth, and also it shall not become me, forasmuch as your grace is my prince and sovereign, to enterprise any part of my office in the said weighty cause without your grace's favour obtained, and pleasure therein first known: it may please the same to ascertain me of your grace's pleasure in the premises, to the intent that, the same known, I may proceed, for my discharge afore God, to the execution of my said office and duty, according to his calling and yours: beseeching your highness most humbly upon my knees, to pardon me of these my bold and rude letters, and the same to accept and take in good sense and part. From my manor at Lamhith, the 11th day of April, in the first year of my consecration.

"Your highness' most humble beadsman and chaplain,

"Thomas Cantuar."

"*To the king's highness, from the Bishop of Cantor. at Lambythe, the xi. day of April, the xxv. year of your reign.*"

## VI. TO CRUMWELL.

Right worshipful Mr Crumwell, in my hearty manner I commend me to you; likewise praying you to have in good remembrance mine old suit for the receipt of Mr Benet's advowson of the benefice of Barnake[2], that the same may be delivered to my hands and custody, to the use of my friend[3] for whom I have thus long sued; and that it may please you, in case ye have not already spoken to master Benet's factor in that behalf, to send this bearer my secretary, or some trusty servant of yours, with your letters or token, and with the same letters which ye have received from Mr Benet for the grant of the same advowson, to receive the same in your name. I am informed that the incumbent is very sick, and in great danger and peril of life; which thing moveth me to be the more importune in calling upon you in the premises, praying you to continue your good mind and favour in this and in all other my suits unto you hereafter, for which, and all other your kindness heretofore shewed, ye shall have me your own assured always during my life. At Lamhith, the 21 day of April.

State Paper Office. Miscellaneous Letters. Temp. Hen. VIII. 3rd Series, Vol. IX.

Your own assured,

Thomas Cantuar.

*To the right worshipful and my very loving friend Mr Crumwell, one of the king's grace's most honourable council.*

most principal minister of our spiritual jurisdiction, within this our realm, who we think assuredly is so in the fear of God, and love towards the observance of his laws, to the which laws we as a christian king have always heretofore, and shall ever most obediently submit ourself, will not therefore refuse (our pre-eminence and authority to us and our successors, in this behalf, nevertheless saved) your humble request, offer, and towardness; that is, to mean to make an end, according to the will and pleasure of Almighty God, in our said great cause of matrimony, which hath so long depended undetermined, to our great and grievous inquietness and burthen of our conscience. Wherefore we, inclining to your humble petition, by these our letters sealed with our seal, and signed with our sign manual, do license you to proceed in the said cause, and to the examination and final determination of the same; not doubting but that ye will have God and the justice of the said cause only before your eyes, and not to regard any earthly or worldly affection therein. For assuredly, the thing that we most covet in this world is to proceed, in all our acts and doings, as may be most acceptable to the pleasure of Almighty God, our Creator, and to the wealth, honour of us, our succession and posterity, and the surety of our realm, and subjects within the same.]

[2 Barnack in Northamptonshire, near Stamford.]

[3 Apparently Newman. Dr Jenkyns' Remains of Abp. Cranmer, Vol. I. p. 17, n. m.]

## VII. TO THE ABBOT OF ST AUGUSTIN'S, CANTERBURY[1].

Harl. MS. 6148. fol. 22. British Museum. Copy.

BROTHER abbot, in my right hearty wise I commend me to you: likewise praying you to give credence to this bearer my servant in such requests and suits as he shall have with you touching my behalf, and the same to ponder and tender with effect, according to such special trust and confidence as I have in you; for so doing ye shall be sure to have me at all times as ready to shew unto you as much pleasure, when ye shall the same desire of me. At my manor in Mortlaque, xxviii<sup>ti</sup> day of April.

*To my brother abbot of St Augstyn's,*
*besides Canterbury.*

---

## VIII. TO THE ABBOT OF WESTMINSTER[2].

Harl. MS. 6148. fol. 22. British Museum. Copy.

IN my right hearty wise I commend me unto you, &c. And where it is so, as I am credibly informed, that at this season there is a place or room of a vicar void within the college[3] of St Marteyns, in the city of London, by the death of one master Framton, late incumbent there, (where also you are dean,) and as I understand as yet not appointed or named to any person: in consideration whereof, and forasmuch as now it lieth in you by reason of your deanery to do pleasure therein; I heartily require you to shew your lawful favour herein, in preferment of this said room, unto this bearer sir John Smythe, one of the same college; that forasmuch as he being both of honest conversation and good name, thereby may have the more furtherance in this behalf before another stranger, not being your friend and acquaintance, and in thus so doing you shall deserve of me like commodity. And thus fare you well. From our manor of Mortelacke, the ivth day of May.

---

## IX. TO CRUMWELL.

State Paper Office. Miscellaneous Letters. Original holograph. Temp. Hen. VIII. 3rd Series, Vol. IX.

RIGHT worshipful Mr Crumwell, in my right hearty manner I commend me to you: advertising you that I have received your letters, by which ye write that the prior of St Gregorie's in Canterbury is willing to resign his room and office there; wherefore your desire is, that I shall take and accept such a person to the same room as ye shall name unto me, promising to provide one, that not only for his discretion, good learning, and religious life, but also for many other his commendable merits and qualities, shall be right apt and meet to supply the said room.

---

[1 John Sturvey, alias Essex, abbot of St Augustin's, Canterbury, from 1523 to the dissolution. Willis' Hist. of Abbeys, Vol. I. p. 54. Ed. Lond. 1718.]

[2 "William Boston, according to his oath in Rymer, or Benson, according to his will, was the last abbot, and the first dean of Westminster. Some estimate may be formed of his character from his memorable argument on the oath of succession. When sir Thomas More pleaded his conscience for refusing it, he was told by the pliant abbot, that he 'might see his conscience was erroneous, since the great council of the realm was of another mind; and therefore he ought to change his conscience.' With this laxity of principle, it excites no surprise that under Henry VIII. he acquiesced in the dissolution of the monastery, and under Edward VI. in the spoliation of the chapter. By his conduct on the latter occasion, says Heylyn, he 'saved the deanery, but lost himself; for calling to remembrance, that formerly he had been a means to surrender the abbey, and was now forced on the necessity of dilapidating the estate of the deanery, he fell into a great disquiet of mind, which brought him to his death within a few months after.' Burnet's Hist. of Reformat. Vol. I. p. 316; Willis' Hist. of Abbeys, Vol. I. p 207; Heylyn, Eccles. Restaur. Edw. VI. p. 61. Ed. Lond. 1674." Jenkyns' Remains of Abp. Cranmer, Vol. I. pp. 18, 19.]

[3 The college of St Martin le Grand, within Aldersgate, granted by Henry VII. to the abbot and convent of Westminster. Newcourt's Repertorium, Vol. I. p. 424. Ed. Lond. 1708.]

Master Crumwell, as touching this behalf, or any other thing wherein I may lawfully shew you any pleasure, ye shall be as well assured of the same as ye would be willing to desire it of me. But the truth is, that in my mind I am entirely resolved to prefer to the same office, and all such other when the same shall be void, some such one person as was professed in the same house, *et sic de eodem gremio,* if any such shall be found apt and meet in the same house for it; for as long as there may be had some one meet for that room in the same house, I do think it much inconvenient for many considerations to provide a stranger to be head and ruler there. If there be none so apt and meet in the said house for the said office as the law will require, then I will be glad to provide the most meetest that can be found in any other place, of the same rule, habit, and religion, of whose sufficiency and ability I ought, if I do my office and duty, to have good experience and knowledge myself, afore that I will admit or prefer him: and forasmuch as I do not know the person whom ye would prefer to this office, and to the intent also that I may inquire of his learning, living, and of other his good qualities, I pray you that I may be ascertained of his name, and of the place where he doth demore[4]; and that done, I will hereafter in this behalf make you such further answer as I trust ye shall be pleased withal: albeit the bringer of your letters and bearer hereof shewed me, that ye did write your said letters for him and in his favour; which thing, I assure you, moveth me to take longer respite in this behalf. Ye do know what ambition and desire of promotion is in men of the church, and what indirect means they do use and have used to obtain their purpose; which their unreasonable desires and appetites I do trust that ye will be more ready to oppress and extinguish, than to favour or further the same; and I remit to your wisdom and judgment, what an unreasonable thing it is for a man to labour for his own promotion spiritual. At Mortlake, the vith day of May.

Your own assured,

THOMAS CANTUAR.

*To the right worshipful and my very loving friend master Crumwell, of the king's grace's most honourable council.*

---

## X. TO KING HENRY VIII.

PLEASE it your highness to be advertised, that I have received your grace's most honourable letters, bearing date at your grace's manor of Grenewich, the 11th day of this present month of May, and do right well perceive the contents of the same. Signifying to your highness, that where, upon Saturday last passed, the noble lady Catharine was, for her non-appearance the same day afore me, and upon such certificate as the mandatary only made unto me upon his oath, pronounced *contumax;* I have, this present Monday, upon such depositions as have been made and taken afore me, by Mr Briane, Gage, and Vaux, my fellows, your grace's servants, of and upon such words and sayings as were spoken by the said noble lady, in the time of the execution and serving of my monition, pronounced her *vere et manifeste contumacem,* so that she is (as the counsel informed me) precluded from farther monition to appear; by reason whereof I shall make more acceleration and expedition in my process than I thought I should, and I have declared my farther mind in this behalf to Mr Brian, to whom I humbly beseech your grace to give credence. At Dunstable, the 12th day of this present month of May, [1533.]

State Paper Office. Domestic Letters, Vol. II. fol. 145. Original.

Your highness' most humble beadman and chaplain,

THOMAS CANTUAR.

*To the king's highness, from the Bishop of Canter. at Dunstable, the xii. day of May, the xxv. year of your reign.*

[[4] Demore: sojourn, dwell. Lat. *demoror.*]

## XI. TO KING HENRY VIII.

State Paper Office. Domestic Letters, Vol. II. fol. 146. Original holograph.

PLEASE it your highness to be advertised, that your grace's great matter is now brought to a final sentence, to be given upon Friday now next ensuing. And because every day in the next week[1] shall be ferial, except Friday and Saturday, therefore I cannot assign any shorter time *ad audiendam sententiam*, than in the said Friday: at which time I trust so to endeavour myself further in this behalf, as shall become me to do, to the pleasure of Almighty God, and the mere truth of the matter. From Dunstable, the 17th of May, [1533.]

Your highness' most humble beadsman and chaplain,

THOMAS CANTUAR.

*To the king's highness, from the Bishop of Cant. at Dunstable, the xvii. day of May, the xxv. year of your reign.*

---

## XII. TO CRUMWELL.

Cott. MSS. Otho. C. x. fol. 166. Original holograph. British Museum.

[2]RIGHT worshipful master Crumwell, in my right hearty w[*ise*] I commend me to you: and likewise I thank you for your two [*letters*] and good advertisement by the same, which I trust I have h[*itherto*] satisfied, according to such trust and expectation as the king'[*s*] highness hath in me; for where I never yet went about to [*injure*] willingly any man living, I would be loth now to begin [*with*] my prince, and defraud him of his trust in me. And therefore [*I*] have used all the expedition that I might conveniently use in th[*e king's*] behalf, and have brought the matter to a final sentence, to [*be*] given upon Friday next ensuing. Because every day in t[*he*] next week shall be ferial, except Friday and Saturday, therefo[*re I*] cannot assign any shorter time *ad audiendam sententiam*, than ... Friday: at which time I trust so to endeavour myself furthe[*r in*] this behalf, as shall become me to do, to the pleasure of Almigh[*ty God,*] and the mere truth of the matter. Furthermore I pray y[*ou to*] think no unkindness in me, for that I have not hitherto [*advertised*] you of such process as I have made in this matter[3]; for I [*assure*] you I have not hitherto written unto the queen's grace,... neither to no man living, but only to the king's highness. [*For*] divers considerations I do think it right expedient, that [*the matter*] and the process of the same be kept secret for a time; [*therefore*] I pray you to make no relation thereof, as I know w[*ell you*] will not. For if the noble lady Catherine should, by the [*bruit of*] this matter in the mouths of the inhabitants of the [country, or] by her friends or counsel hearing of this bruit, be [moved, stirred,] counselled, or persuaded, to appear afore me in the ti[me, or afore] the time of sentence, I should be thereby greatly staye[d and let] in the process, and the king's grace's counsel here pre[sent shall be] much uncertain what shall be then further done the[rein. For a] great bruit and voice of the people in this behalf [might perchance] move her to do that thing herein, which peradventure [she would] not do, if she shall hear little of it. And therefore I [pray you] to speak as little of this matter as ye may, and to [move the] king's

---

[[1] "This is stated in a note to the State Papers to have been the week preceding Whitsunday; but it will be seen by the letter to Hawkyns, No. XIV. (p. 244) that it was the second week before Whitsunday, or Rogation week; for Cranmer there says, that 'he gave final sentence the morrow after Ascension-day.' And in that week, according to his remark, every day before Friday was ferial; Monday, Tuesday, Wednesday, the three Rogation days, being fasts, and Ascension-day or Holy Thursday being a festival." Jenkyns' Remains of Abp. Cranmer, Vol. I. p. 24.]

[[2] This letter has been much injured by fire. Several of the defects in the latter part of it are filled up from an extract printed by Heylyn, Eccles. Restaur. Qu. Mary, p. 177. Ed. Lond. 1674. Some others are supplied from Dr Jenkyns' conjectures, and are printed in Italic type.]

[[3] "Crumwell, however, was not ignorant of the proceedings, having received an account of them from Bedyll, one of 'the counsellors in the law for the king's part,' in a letter dated the 12th of May. It is there stated, that 'my lord of Canterbury handleth himself very well, and very uprightly, without any evident cause of suspicion to be noted in him by the counsel of the lady Katerine, if she had had any present there.' State Papers, Vol. I. p. 395." Id. ibid. p. 25.]

highness in like wise so to do, for the conside[rations above] recited. And this my opinion in this behalf not[*withstanding, I*] do refer all and singular the premises to the king's [*pleasure*] and judgment. From Dunstaple, the xviith d[*ay of May*] [1533.]

Your assur...........

THOM...........[4]

## XIII. TO KING HENRY VIII.

State Paper Office. Domestic Letters, Vol. II. fol. 147. Original holograph.

PLEASE it your highness to be advertised, that this 23[d] day of this present month of May, I have given sentence in your grace's great and weighty cause; the copy[5] whereof I have sent unto your highness by this bearer, Richard Watkyns. And

[4 The remainder of the signature is destroyed by fire.]

[5 *The sentence of divorce.*

Harl. MSS. 6148. fol. 2. British Museum. Copy.

An. 25 H. 8.

In an Inspeximus, Rot. Pat. 25 Reg. Pt. 2[1].

Anno incarnationis millesimo quingentesimo tricesimo tertio, indictione sexta, Clementis papæ decimo, mensis Maii vicesimo tertio, in ecclesia conventuali monasterii Sancti Petri Dunstabliæ, ordinis Sancti Augustini Lincoln. Dioces. nostri Cantuariensis provinciæ.

In Dei nomine, Amen. Nos Thomas, permissione divina, Cantuariensis Archiepiscopus, totius Angliæ primas, et apostolicæ sedis legatus, in quadam causa inquisitionis de et super viribus matrimonii, inter illustrissimum et potentissimum principem et dominum nostrum Henricum octavum, Dei gratia Angliæ et Franciæ regem, fidei defensorem, et dominum Hiberniæ, ac serenissimam dominam Catharinam, nobilis memoriæ Ferdinandi Hispaniarum regis filiam, contracti et consummati, quæ coram nobis in judicio ex officio nostro mero aliquamdiu vertebatur, et adhuc vertitur, et pendet indecisa, rite et legitime procedentes, visis primitus per nos et diligenter inspectis articulis sive capitulis in dicta causa objectis et ministratis, una cum responsis eis ex parte dicti illustrissimi et potentissimi principis Henrici octavi factis et redditis, visisque et similiter per nos inspectis plurimorum nobilium et aliorum testium fide dignorum dictis et depositionibus in eadem causa habitis et factis, visisque præterea et similiter per nos inspectis, quam plurium[2], fere totius Christiani orbis principalium academiarum censuris seu conclusionibus magistralibus, etiam tam theologorum quam jurisperitorum responsis et opinionibus, utriusque denique provinciæ Anglicanæ conciliorum provincialium assertionibus et affirmationibus, aliisque salutaribus monitis et doctrinis super dicto matrimonio desuper respective habitis et factis; visisque ulterius, et pari modo per nos inspectis, tractatibus seu fœderibus[3] pacis et amicitiæ inter perennis famæ Henricum septimum nuper regem Angliæ, et dictum nobilis memoriæ Ferdinandum nuper regem Hispaniæ desuper initis et factis; visis quoque peramplius, et diligenter per nos inspectis, omnibus et singulis actis, actitatis, literis, processibus, instrumentis, scripturis, munimentis, rebusque aliis universis in dicta causa quomodolibet gestis et factis, ac his omnibus et singulis per nos visis et inspectis, atque a nobis cum diligentia et maturitate ponderatis et recensitis, servatisque ulterius per nos in hac parte de jure servandis, nec non partibus prædictis, videlicet præfato illustrissimo et potentissimo principe Henrico octavo per ejus procuratorem idoneum coram nobis in dicta causa legitime comparante, dicta vero serenissima domina Catharina per contumaciam absente, cujus absentia divina repleatur præsentia; de consilio jurisperitorum et theologorum, cum quibus in hac parte communicavimus, ad sententiam nostram definitivam sive finale decretum nostrum in dicta causa ferendam sive ferendum sic duximus procedendum, et procedimus in hunc modum. Quia per acta, infactitata, deducta, proposita, exhibita, et allegata, probata pariter et confessata, articulataque, capitulata, partis responsa, testium depositiones, et dicta instrumenta, munimenta, literas, scripturas, censuras, conclusiones magistrales, opiniones, consilia, assertiones, affirmationes, tractatus et fœdera pacis, processus, res alias, et cetera præmissa coram nobis in dicta causa respective habita, gesta, facta, exhibita, et producta; nec non ex eisdem, et diversis aliis ex causis et considerationibus, argumentisque, et probationum generibus variis, et multiplicibus validis quidem et efficacibus, quibus animum nostrum in hac parte ad plenum informavimus, plene et evidenter invenimus et comperimus dictum matrimonium inter præfatos illustrissimum et potentissimum principem et dominum nostrum Henricum octavum, ac serenissimam dominam Catharinam, ut præmittitur, contractum et consummatum nullum et omnino invalidum fuisse et esse, ac divino jure prohibente contractum et consummatum extitisse: idcirco nos Thomas archiepiscopus primas et legatus antedictus, Christi nomine primitus invocato, ac solum Deum præ oculis nostris habentes, pro nullitate et invaliditate dicti matrimonii pronunciamus, decernimus, et declaramus, ipsumque prætensum matrimonium fuisse et esse nullum et invalidum, ac divino jure prohibente contractum et consummatum, nulliusque valoris aut momenti esse, sed viribus et firmitate juris caruisse et carere, præfatoque illustrissimo et potentissimo principi Henrico octavo, et serenissimæ dominæ Catharinæ non licere in eodem prætenso matrimonio remanere, etiam pronunciamus, decernimus et declaramus; ipsosque illustrissimum et potentissimum principem Henricum octavum, ac serenissimam dominam Catharinam, quatenus de facto et non de jure dictum prætensum matrimonium ad invicem contraxerunt et consummarunt, ab invicem separamus et divorciamus, atque sic divorciatos et seperatos, nec non ab omni vinculo matrimoniali respectu dicti prætensi matrimonii liberos et immunes fuisse et esse, pronunciamus, decernimus, et declaramus, per hanc nostram sententiam definitivam, sive hoc nostrum finale decretum, quam sive quod ferimus et promulgamus in his scriptis. In quorum promissorum fidem et testimonium, has literas nostras testimoniales, sive præsens publicum sententiæ vel decreti instrumentum,

[1 This is found in Burnet.] [2 Quam plurimum. Ibid.] [3 Pactis seu fœderibus. Ibid.]

where I was by the letters of Mr Thurlesby, your grace's chaplain, advertised of your grace's pleasure, that I should cause your grace's counsel to conceive a procuracy concerning the second matrimony, I have sent the said letters unto them, and required them to do according to the tenor thereof: most humbly beseeching your highness, that I may know your grace's further pleasure concerning the same matrimony, as soon as your grace with your council shall be perfectly resolved therein. For the time of the coronation[1] is so instant and so near at hand, that the matter requireth good expedition to be had in the same. And thus our Lord have your highness evermore in his blessed tuition and governance. From Dunstable, the 23[d] day of May, [1533.]

Your highness' most humble chaplain and beadsman,

THOMAS CANTUAR.

*To the king's highness, from the Archbishop of Cant. at Dunstable, the xxiii. day of May.*

---

## XIV. TO ARCHDEACON HAWKYNS[2].

Harl. MSS. 6148. fol. 23. British Museum. Copy. Archæologia, Vol. XVIII. p. 78. Ellis, Orig. Letters, first series, Lett. cxiv. Vol. II. pp. 33, 4. Ed. Lond. 1824. Todd's Life of Abp. Cranmer, Vol. I. p. 80.

IN my most hearty wise I commend me unto you, and even so would be right glad to hear of your welfare, &c. These be to advertise you, that inasmuch as you now and then take some pains in writing unto me, I would be loth you should think your labour utterly lost and forgotten for lack of writing again: therefore, and because I reckon you be some deal desirous of such news as hath been here with us of late in the king's grace's matters, I intend to inform you a part thereof, according to the tenor and purport used in that behalf.

And first, as touching the final determination and concluding of the matter of divorce between my lady Katherine and the king's grace, which said matter, after the convocation in that behalf had determined and agreed according to the former consent of the universities, it was thought convenient by the king and his learned counsel, that I should repair unto Dunstable, which is within four miles unto Ampthill, where the said lady Katherine keepeth her house, and there to call her before me to hear the final sentence in the said matter. Notwithstanding, she would not at all obey thereunto; for when she was by doctor Lee cited to appear by a day, she utterly refused the same, saying, that inasmuch as her cause was before the pope, she would have none other judge; and therefore would not take me for her judge.

Nevertheless the viiith day of May, according to the said appointment, I came unto Dunstable, my lord of Lincoln[3] being assistant unto me, and my lord of Wynchester[4], doctor Bell, Dr Claybroke, Dr Trygonnell, Dr Hewis, Dr Olyver, Dr Brytten, Mr Bedell[5], with divers other learned in the law, being counsellors in the law for the king's part: and so there at our coming kept a court for the appearance of the said lady Katherine, where were examined certain witness which testified that she was lawfully

---

exinde fieri ac per notarios publicos subscriptos, scribas et actuarios nostros in ea parte specialiter assumptos, scribi et signari, nostrique sigilli appensione jussimus et fecimus communiri.

"He likewise passed judgment (confirming the king's marriage with queen Ann) at Lambeth, May 28, 1533, which is in the same Inspeximus." The sentence of divorce here follows Rymer's Fœdera, Vol. XIV. p. 462—4, and has been collated with Kennet's Hist. of England, Vol. II. Lord Herbert's Life of Henry VIII. pp. 163, 4, and with Burnet's Hist. of Reformat. Vol. I. Pt. I. App. Book II. No. xlvii. pp. 190—192. Ed. Oxon. 1829, the readings of which differ in places, but not materially.]

[[1] The coronation took place on Whitsunday, the 1st of June. Burnet's Hist. of Reformat. Vol. I. p. 266.]

[[2] "Nicholas Hawkyns, archdeacon of Ely, succeeded Cranmer as ambassador to the emperor Charles V." Jenkyns.]

[[3] John Longland, the king's confessor.]

[[4] Stephen Gardiner.]

[[5] Vid. p. 242, n. 3. "Thomas Bedyl, who was clerk of the council, a learned man, and much made use of by Crumwell." Strype's Eccles. Mem. Vol. I. p. 299. Ed. Oxon. 1822.]

cited and called to appear, whom for fault of appearance was declared *contumax;* proceeding in the said cause against her *in pœnam contumaciæ*[6], as the process of the law thereunto belongeth; which continued fifteen days after our coming thither. And the morrow after Ascension-day I gave final sentence therein, how that it was indispensable for the pope to license any such marriages.

This done, and after our rejourneying home again, the king's highness prepared all things convenient for the coronation of the queen[7], which also was after such a manner as followeth.

The Thursday next before the feast of Pentecost, the king and the queen being at Grenewich, all the crafts of London thereunto well appointed, in several barges decked after the most gorgeous and sumptuous manner, with divers pageants thereunto belonging, repaired and waited all together upon the mayor of London; and so well furnished came all unto Grenewich, where they tarried and waited for the queen's coming to her barge: which so done, they brought her unto the Tower, trumpets, shambes, and other divers instruments all the ways playing and making great melody, which, as is reported, was so comely done as never was like in any time nigh to our remembrance.

Coronation of Qu. Ann.

And so her grace came to the Tower on Thursday at night, about five of the clock, where also was such a peal of guns as hath not been heard like a great while before. And the same night, and Friday all day, the king and queen tarried there; and on Friday at night the king's grace made eighteen knights of the Bath, whose creation was not alonely so strange to hear of, as also their garments stranger to behold or look on, which said knights the next day, which was Saturday, rid before the queen's grace throughout the city of London towards Westminster palace, over and besides the most part of the nobles of the realm, which like accompanied her grace throughout the said city; she sitting in her hair upon a horse litter, richly apparelled[8], and four knights of the five ports bearing a canopy over her head. And after her came four rich chariots, one of them empty, and three other furnished with divers ancient old ladies; and after them came a great train of other ladies and gentlewomen: which said progress, from the beginning to the ending, extended half a mile in length by estimation, or thereabout. To whom also, as she came along the city, was shewed many costly pageants, with divers other encomies spoken of children to her. [Wine also running at certain conduits plentifully[9].] And so proceeding throughout the streets, passed forth unto Westminster-hall, where was a certain banquet prepared for her; which done, she was conveyed out of the backside of the palace into a barge, and so unto York-place, where the king's grace was before her coming: for this you must ever presuppose, that his grace came always before her secretly in a barge, as well from Grenewich to the Tower, as from the Tower to York-place.

Now then on Sunday was the coronation, which also was of such a manner. In the morning there assemble[d] with me at Westminster church the bishop of York[10], the bishop of London[11], the bishop of Winchester[12], the bishop of Lincoln[13], the bishop of Bath[14], and the bishop of St Asse[15]; the abbot of Westminster[16], with ten or twelve more abbots; which all revestred ourselves in our pontificalibus, and so furnished, with our crosses and crosiers, proceeded out of the abbey in a procession unto Westminster-hall, where we received the queen apparelled in a robe of purple velvet, and all the ladies and gentlewomen in robes and gowns of scarlet, according to the manner used before time in such business: and so her grace sustained of each side with two bishops, the bishop of London and the bishop of Winchester, came forth

---

[6 Corrected by Mr Todd for *contumaciam.*]

[7 For the details of the coronation of Anne Boleyn, vid. Stow's Annals, p. 562, et sqq. Ed. London, 1615.]

[8 "She had on a kirtle of white cloth of tissue, and a mantle of the same furred with ermine, her hair hanging down: but on her head she had a coif with a circlet about it full of rich stones." id. ibid.]

[9 This passage is omitted by Dr Jenkyns.]

[10 Edward Lee.]

[11 John Stokesley.]

[12 Stephen Gardiner.]

[13 John Longland.]

[14 John Clerk.]

[15 Henry Standish.]

[16 William Benson or Boston. Vid. p. 240. n. 2.]

in procession unto the church of Westminster, she in her hair, my lord of Suffolk bearing before her the crown, and two other lords bearing also before her a sceptre and a white rod, and so entered up into the high altar, where divers ceremonies used about her, I did set the crown on her head, and then was sung *Te Deum*, &c. And after that was sung a solemn mass: all which while her grace sat crowned upon a scaffold, which was made between the high altar and the choir in Westminster church; which mass and ceremonies done and finished, all the assembly of noblemen brought her into Westminster-hall again, where was kept a great solemn feast all that day; the good order thereof were too long to write at this time to you. But now, sir, you may not imagine that this coronation was before her marriage; for she was married much about St Paul's day[1] last, as the condition thereof doth well appear, by reason she is now somewhat big with child. Notwithstanding it hath been reported throughout a great part of the realm that I married her; which was plainly false, for I myself knew not thereof a fortnight after it was done. And many other things be also reported of me, which be mere lies and tales.

Other news have we none notable, but that one Fryth[2], which was in the Tower in prison, was appointed by the king's grace to be examined before me, my lord of London, my lord of Winchester, my lord of Suffolk, my lord Chancellor[3], and my lord of Wiltshire; whose opinion was so notably erroneous, that we could not dispatch him, but was fain to leave him to the determination of his ordinary, which is the bishop of London. His said opinion is of such nature, that he thought it not necessary to be believed as an article of our faith, that there is the very corporal presence of Christ within the host and sacrament of the altar, and holdeth of this point most after the opinion of Œcolampadius. And surely I myself sent for him three or four times to persuade him to leave that his imagination; but for all that we could do therein, he would not apply to any counsel: notwithstanding now he is at a final end with all examinations, for my lord of London hath given sentence and delivered him to the secular power, where he looketh every day to go unto the fire[4]. And there is also condemned with him one Andrewe, a tailor of London, for the said selfsame opinion.

[5]If you have not heard of our ambassadors lately gone over, you shall understand that my lord of Northfolk, my lord of Rocheforde, master Paulet, Sir Francis Bryan, Sir Antony Browne, &c., Dr Gooderyche, D. Aldryche, and D. Thrylbey, be gone unto France to the French king[6]. And, as I suppose, they go from him to the pope unto . . . . . .[7].

Further you shall understand, that there is many here which wish you to succeed

---

[[1] Sir Henry Ellis observes, that this part of Abp. Cranmer's letter settles two facts which have been much disputed: one, that Anne Boleyn was married on St Paul's day, the 25th of January; the other, that Cranmer was not present on the occasion. Stow (p. 543) gives the correct date, but Hollinshed (Chronicles, Vol. III. p. 929. Ed. Lond. 1587) and Hall (Chronicles, fol. ccix. 2. Ed. Lond. 1548) state it incorrectly to have been St Erkenwald's day, Nov. 14, 1532.]

[[2] John Frith, the associate and friend of Tyndale, the translator of the Bible, was the first Englishman, after Wycliffe, who wrote against the Romish doctrine of the sacrament of the Lord's supper, and was opposed by sir Thomas More. For a full account of his opinions, imprisonment, examination, and death, vid. Anderson's Annals of the English Bible, Vol. I. pp. 339—377. Ed. Lond. 1845. Vid. also Burnet's Hist. of Reformat. Vol. I. pp. 338—345. Foxe's Acts and Monuments, pp. 1031—36. Ed. Lond. 1583; and App. Vol. III. pp. 989—992. Ed. Lond. 1631.]

[[3] Sir Thomas Audeley.]

[[4] Both Frith and Andrew Hewet were burnt in Smithfield on the 4th of July, 1533. Foxe's Acts and Monuments, p. 1036. Burnet, (Hist. of Reformat. Vol. I. p. 344), following Hall and Stow, places their execution in 1534, but Foxe's date, as observed by Dr Jenkyns, is strongly supported by this letter.]

[[5] This latter part of the letter is omitted, both by Mr Todd and by sir Henry Ellis.]

[[6] "The king understanding that the pope, the emperor, and the French king, should meet at Nice in June following, he appointed the duke of Norfolk," ... "to go in ambassage to the French king, and both to accompany him to Nice, and also to commune with the pope there concerning his stay in the king's divorce." Stow's Annals, p. 562.]

[[7] The interview between the pope (Clement VII.) and the French king (Francis I.) was at Marseilles in October, where the marriage was made up between the Duke of Orleance (afterwards Henry II.) and Katherine de Medici. Burnet's Hist. of Reformat. Vol. I. pp. 271, 2. Ed. Oxon. 1829.]

your uncle[8]; notwithstanding I would you should not think the contrary, but that there be a great sort which would it should not come to pass: nevertheless you be neither the nearer ne further off through such idle communication.

Finally, I here send unto you a bill for the bank of four ducats de largo, which sum I would you should not take it up before you have need thereof, and therefore I send it for your commodity and necessity; for it is none of the king's grace's money, nor his said grace knoweth nothing thereof, but alonely of my benevolence to serve your purpose, in case, as I said, you should lack the same. And thus fare ye well. From my manor of Croydon, the xvii. day of June, [1533.]

---

## XV. TO THE MAYOR OF CAMBRIDGE AND HIS BRETHREN.

In my right hearty wise I commend me unto you, and to each of you. And where of late I wrote unto you in the favour of one of mine ally, called Humfrye Stockewith, concerning his liberty in absenting himself from the offices of your town, the reasonable causes whereof I declared unto you in my other letters to you directed in that behalf, and since that time I have no understanding ne certification of your minds in that behalf: in consideration whereof, and forasmuch as I am some deal desirous to be advertised of your towardness therein, I heartily desire you to send me word by this bearer in writing, what you intend to do concerning the same. And if I herein may perceive any kindness in you for the obtaining of my request, I will at all times be ready to shew you like pleasure. And thus fare you well. From my manor of Croydon, the xxv. day of June.

Harl. MSS. 6148. f. 22, b. Copy.

*To Master Mayor of Cambridge and his brethren.*

---

## XVI. TO THE MASTER[9] OF JESUS COLLEGE[10], CAMBRIDGE.

In my right hearty wise I commend [me] unto you, &c. And so certifying you that I send you here a buck to be bestowed amonges your company within your college. And forasmuch as you have more store of money, and also less need than I at this season, therefore I bequeath a noble of your purse towards the baking and seasoning of him. And whensoever I have so much money before hand as I am now behind hand, I shall repay you your noble again. And thus fare you well. From my manor of Croydon, the xxvi. day of June[11].

Harl. MSS. 6148. f. 22, b Copy. Todd's Life of Abp. Cranmer, Vol. II. pp 295, 6.

*To the Master of Jesus College in Cantabrige.*

---

[8 "On the death of Dr West, bishop of Ely, his nephew and godson, Dr Nicholas Hawkins, archdeacon of Ely, at that time the king's ambassador in foreign parts, was designed to succeed him; but he dying before his consecration could be effected, the king granted his licence to the prior and convent, dated March 6, 1534, to choose themselves a bishop; who immediately elected in their chapter-house, the seventeenth of the same month, Thomas Goodrich." Chalmers, Biogr. Dict. art. Goodrich. Vol. XVI. p. 99.]

[9 Wm. Capon. Vid. Le Neve, Fasti. p. 431. Ed. Lond. 1716.]

[10 Cranmer (about 1510, or 1511,) was elected fellow of Jesus College. He married when he had not attained the age of twenty-three, and before he had been admitted into holy orders. In about a year after his marriage his wife died. Such was his character, and such the regard of his former college for him, that he was immediately restored to the fellowship he had forfeited.—Todd's Life of Abp. Cranmer, Vol. I. pp. 3, 4, 8.]

[11 This letter is placed by Mr Todd under the year 1552. Dr Jenkyns says he gives no conclusive reason for his arrangement; and that the book of copies from which it is taken, may be fairly assumed from the known dates of some of its contents to have been wholly written before 1536. Vid. Remains of Abp. Cranmer, Vol. I. p. 34.]

## XVII. TO ———

Harl. MSS. 6148. f. 22, b. Copy.

Right hearty and well-beloved, I commend me unto you, &c. letting you to understand, that by the great suit and instance of my special friends I have overcharged my house with servants. Wherefore I desire you, that your son W. may be with you at home unto such time as my business be something overpast. I can put none of my servants from me but such as have some friends to take unto, for else I think they should be greatly hindered thereby; therefore I intend to put none away but such as be my friends' children. For lether I had be bold of my own friends than of strangers, by reason that strangers will peradventure take it more displeasantly and unkindly, than I am sure my own friends will. Surely and unfeignedly I do like your son singularly well, and therefore I intend to send for him, God willing, again, as shortly as I may conveniently. Moreover, I have spoken with doctor Elyston in your favour, and he hath taken day with me to St James' day next, to the intent he may be sure what the Chapel of St Marget is worth by the year: that done, I trust that matter will come to good effect, and that ye need not to doubt therein by God's grace; and thus fare ye well. From my manor of Croydon, the xxvi$^{ti}$ day of June.

---

## XVIII. TO THE BISHOP OF LINCOLN[1].

Harl. MSS. 6148. f. 21, b. Copy.

My very loving lord, I commend me heartily to you. So it is that my servant John Creke, this bearer, is in good hope of a preferment in the University of Oxforthe, by means of special good friends which do and would earnestly labour for him, as he shall declare unto you: wherein I pray you, my lord, right heartily, that he may for my sake have your favour and assistance; which when it shall lie in me, I would surely requite and recompense, God willing; who keep and preserve you! From Croydon, the vth day of July.

*To my lord of Lincoln.*

---

## XIX. TO BALTHASOR.

Harl. MSS. 6148. f. 26. Copy.

In my right hearty wise I commend me unto you. And where it is so, that one of my chaplains, named master Witwell[2], by reason of a certain disease lying and being within his knee, is now under your cure for the remedy of the same; and, as I am credibly informed, [it] is so inveterately congealed, that it is not like easily and in short time to be dissolved, notwithstanding I understand you have declared hitherto as well kindness as diligence to him in that behalf; wherefore I heartily thank you for your said pains; requiring to continue your good towardness therein as you have begun, and so to use all such lawful expedition herein as may conveniently be devised, to the intent he may be the sooner released of this his pain. And in so doing I shall be ready to shew you always such pleasure as lieth in me to do, when you shall the same require. And thus fare you well. From my manor of Croydon, the vth day of July.

*To master Balthasor, surgeon unto the king's highness.*

---

[[1] John Longland, bishop of Lincoln, succeeded archbishop Warham as chancellor of the University of Oxford in 1532. Wood's Fasti Oxon. p. 90. Ed. Bliss. Lond. 1813-20.]

[[2] Probably John Whitwel, the archbishop's almoner and chaplain. Strype's Mem. of Abp. Cranmer, Vol. I. pp. 251, 256. Ed. Oxon. 1840.]

## XX. TO THE BISHOP OF LINCOLN[3].

In my right hearty wise I commend me unto you, &c. And where there is a matter of variance between the warden of All Souls' College within the university of Oxford, and this bearer, sir W. A. priest, for the interest of a chauntry lying and being within your diocese, from which he is expelled, as he saith, unjustly: in consideration thereof, and forasmuch as all such variances begun without my diocese, by the statute[4] I cannot call them before me; having also in consideration the great cost and vexation whereby the parties should be put to coming unto me so far: I heartily pray you therefore, you being within three or four miles thereunto, to take some pains to set the parties at a unity and peace therein, according to right and conscience. And in thus doing, I will be as ready to shew you like pleasure at all times. And thus fare you well. From my manor of Croydon, the viiith day of July. Harl. MSS. 6148. f. 26. Copy.

*To my lord of Lincoln.*

## XXI. TO POTTKYNS.

Master Pottkyns, I greet you well, &c. And where there is a collation of a benefice now in my hands through the death of one sir Richarde Baylis, priest of the college of Mallying, according as you may be further instruct by this letter herein inclosed, the place and room whereof I intend to dispose, I will therefore, that you send unto me a collation thereof; and that your said collation have a window expedient to set what name[5] I will therein. And thus fare you well, &c. [1533.] Harl. MSS. 6148. f. 26, b. Copy.

## XXII. TO HIS CHANCELLOR.

Master Chancellor, I greet you well. And where I sent unto you for the process of a variance between Pery[6] and Benbowe, supposing you had taken and examined the witness thereof, which I understand is not as yet done: in consideration thereof, I will that you forthwith examine the said witness, to the intent their depositions may be joined unto your said process, and then sent again therewithal unto [me]. Thus fare you well. From Croydon, the viiith day of July, &c. Harl. MSS. 6148. f. 26. b. Copy.

## XXIII. TO ———

In my right hearty wise I commend me unto you. And where I understand, that through the virtue of a certain commission to you directed, you have liberty and authority to examine and finish a matter in controversy of land between one A. B. of the one party, and my loving friend C. D. of the other, father unto my trusty and wellbeloved servant this bearer: in consideration thereof, and forasmuch as this said variance hath so long depended undetermined, not without great damage, and vexation of the said A. B.; I heartily desire you, that at this mine instance, if you can conveniently at this time use such Harl. MSS. 6148. f. 26, b. Copy.

[3 Vid. p. 248. n. 1.]

[4 Dr Jenkyns thinks this was probably the statute 24 Hen. VIII. c. 12, for restraint of appeals to Rome; by which it was enacted, that appeals should thenceforth be made "from the archdeacon or his official, if the matter be there begun, to the bishop diocesan of the said see, if in case any of the parties be grieved;" and if it be commenced before the bishop diocesan, to the archbishop of the province. Statutes of the Realm. Vid. Remains of Abp. Cranmer, Vol. I. p. 36.]

[5 The name inserted was Stephen Padley, who succeeded Richard Bayley the 9th of July, 1533. Cranmer's Register, fol. 340, a.]

[6 Vid. Letters, No. XXVIII. p. 252. No. XXXIII. p. 253.]

expedition herein, that thereby he may know now to what determination he shall stand unto, which, after so many delays past, should now be unto him singular pleasure to know: exhorting you furthermore to shew unto him your lawful favour in his right, and, so doing, I will be as ready at all times, &c.

## XXIV. WARRANT FOR VENISON.

Harl. MSS. 6148. f. 77, b. Copy.

We will and command you to bring, or cause to be brought, into our larder, to the use of our household within our manor of Otford, against the xxii[ti] day of this present month, one buck of season, to be taken out of our parks of Slyndon[1] within your office, any restraint or commandment had or made to the contrary heretofore thereof in any wise notwithstanding, and that you fail not as ye tender our favour. And these our letters shall be your sufficient warrant and discharge in this behalf. Given under our signet at our manor of Otford, the xviii[ti] day of the month of July, in the xxv. year of the reign of, &c. and the first year of our consecration. [1533.]

## XXV. TO KYNGESTON.

Harl. MSS. 6148. f. 27. Copy.

Cousin Kyngeston[2], in my right hearty wise I commend me to you: doing you to understand that I have received your letters, and do perceive the contents of the same. And where ye write, that your son Antony had small speed afore me, marvelling why I did use the old process, whereby you do think that the whole matter is frustrate and destroyed, and your son also: ye may be well assured, that I did pursue the said old process for none other intent, than for the information of my conscience only. And albeit I did thus use it, yet I was never minded to reduce the same in my sentence. And as I did therein, so would or should every good judge have done, if he would do his office and duty with equity. Ye do know well, that at the first beginning I sent for the same, and used it for my information. If I had not, or would not so have done, I might right well have been noted negligent, as not willing to know the truth. And I should have done otherwise than ever any judge did hitherto, or ever will do hereafter. And it is pity that ever I had been judge, if I would not have sought all means to be right informed. And when I took new depositions of other witness, I did it for none other intent but upon your son's words; supposing and trusting that he could have brought such witness as may have countervailed the first sixteen witness brought by you, which cometh now to none effect; nor, as all the learned men in the law that were then present with me at that time, as well the Dean of the Arches as also both his counsel and her's, did then plainly say, it is not possible to bring any witness that should countervail the first sixteen witness, unless the said sixteen could be rejected as not honest men, and not indifferent to depose in the cause; which thing although Dorothy Harp do say that she can do, nevertheless I do not think it. And to be plain with you, as far as I do see yet in the matter, I am at my wits' end to give you counsel in it; for by my faith, if I could imagine any good counsel in the same, I would be no less glad to give it you, than you would be to take it. But in my judgment, all the learned men of England cannot give

[1 In Sussex, near Arundel.]

[2 Dr Jenkyns conjectures that this may have been sir William Kingston, commander of the guard sent to conduct Wolsey to the king, and constable of the Tower at the time of Anne Boleyn's imprisonment there: (see Ellis, Original Letters, 1st ser. Vol. II. p. 53. Ed. Lond. 1824) and that Anthony his son may have been the sir Anthony Kingston, who, as provost-marshal of the western army in 1549, was more distinguished for the readiness of his wit than for his humanity. See an instance of his cruelty in Cranmer's Answer to the fifteen Articles of the Rebels of Devon, supra pp. 186, 7, *n.* 6.]

you counsel, except you take the other way of your son's impotency; and yet I think that will not serve neither. And where you write, that the setting forth of the first process and witness was only your act for three causes special in your letters expressed: I do think verily, that if those witness examined, knowing the truth, do conceal the truth, and depose otherwise than truth, surely they be much to be blamed and worthy great punishment; and then they, and you that brought them forth, have lost your son, and not I. And contrariwise, if they knowing the truth have deposed nothing but truth, and as they do know, then the matter must stand as it may stand with equity, and ye to be contented therewith. Wherein you shall be well assured to have me upright and just, without any manner of inclination to any party otherwise than justice will suffer; but so far as equity and justice will permit, I shall be glad to incline to your desire, and specially seeing that it is the desire of the other party also. But meseemeth for this time, that if your son and his wife would both set apart their wilful minds, and agree together as man and wife, it should be great comfort to them and all their friends, and to the pleasure of God. And if they will continue in their folly still, except I can see some better cause why they should not be man and wife than I do see yet, I shall never consent, that he shall live in adultery with another woman, and she with another man. For if he were my son, I had rather that he begged all his life than to live in adultery; and so I think you had also. And thus our Lord preserve you! From my manor of Otford the xix. day of July.

## XXVI. TO CERTAIN CURATES.

Harl. MSS. 6148. f. 28. Copy.

FORASMUCH as I am credibly informed by the churchwardens of the parish of Malling, how that their church is so far in decay, that the said parish of itself is not able to repair the same again without great help of their well-disposed neighbours; by reason whereof they have instantly desired of me [to] write to your parish in their behalf: I will therefore, that ye at a convenient time exhort and move your parishioners to give their aid and help unto them therein; inasmuch as in so doing it will be both a right charitable deed, and also a very good occasion whereby your said parish may require of them such like commodity when you shall need (as they do) likewise the same. Willing you also to desire two of the most honest men of your said parish, to take the pains in gathering and preserving of that which shall be given in this behalf. And thus fare you well. From my manor of Otford, the xix. day of July.

*To certain Curates.*

## XXVII. TO THE ABBOT OF WESTMINSTER[3].

Harl. MSS. 6148. f. 28. Copy.

BROTHER Abbott, in my right hearty wise I commend me unto you, &c. And where and forasmuch as ye were contented to promise unto me the next room that should chance hereafter to be void, among the beadmen in the foundation[4] of that noble prince of perpetual memory, king Henry the VIIth, for one John Fyssher, whom I do much tender in that behalf; I heartily desire you therefore not to forget your said promise, but that ye will remember the same, even as you would be remembered of me at such time as it lieth in me to shew you any pleasure hereafter. And thus fare you well. From my manor of Otford, the xix. day of July.

*To my brother Abbot of Westminster.*

[[3] Vid. Letter VIII. p. 240.]

[[4] Vid. the oath of William Boston, abbot of Westminster. Rymer's Fœdera, Vol. XIV. pp. 459-62.]

## XXVIII. TO HIS CHANCELLOR.

Harl. MSS. 6148. f. 28. Copy.

Mr Chancellor, I greet you well. I will that you send unto me all the process of the judges delegatory, with the depositions of such witness as I wrote of late to you of to be examined concerning the matter of variance of matrimony between Thomas Perry and Jane Benbowe, which if you have accordingly done, then to warn the parties to appear before me on Monday next coming. And thus fare you well, &c.

---

## XXIX. TO CRUMWELL.

Harl. MSS. 6148 f. 28, b. Copy.

In my right hearty wise I commend me unto you. And where the prior of the friar preachers of Bristol sueth unto me for a licence to preach, yet am I loth to grant the same, unless I might have some sure information by one of the council how he is discharged of his business before them: in consideration hereof I heartily desire you to advertise me by this bearer, in what case he standeth, and whether he be after such a sort and manner discharged, so that it be meet for me to give him my said licence to preach through my province. And thus fare ye well. From my manor of Otford, the xix. day of July.

Over this, I most heartily desire you at this mine instance to further all that in you is this said bearer, my servant, touching his preferment to the room of the esquire bedell of arts at Oxford, which is now in the king's grace's hands to give to whom he will at his pleasure, forasmuch as the said university hath without his grace's assent and licence admitted one by way of resignation to the said room, (their[1] statutes and liberties as well then as now being in the king's hands,) which admittance, as I am informed, is frustrate, if it would so please his grace to consider the same; therefore gladly would I that my said servant were preferred thereunto before another, considering how it would be to him an apt room, and also a good living therewithal. Wherefore, eftsoons I pray you to shew unto him your lawful favour in this behalf, whereby you shall not alonely bind him to be your daily beadman, but also be sure of me to shew you any pleasure that I can therefore. And thus fare you well. From my manor of Otford, the xix. day of July.

*To my especial friend, master Cromwell.*

---

## XXX. TO THE PRIORESS OF ST SEPULCHRE'S, CANTERBURY.

Harl. MSS. 6148. f. 28, b. Copy.

Sister prioress, in my hearty wise I commend me unto you. And so likewise will that you do repair unto me to my manor of Otford, and bring with you your nun[2] which was some time at Courteupstrete, against Wednesday next coming: and that ye fail not herein in any wise. Thus fare you well. From our manor of Otford, &c. [1533.]

*To the Prioress.*

---

[1 "After these troubles followed others of greater moment between the university and town, concerning divers liberties and privileges, the report of which coming to the king's hearing, instructions were sent down from him to make a surrender of their liberties." In pursuance of these instructions the university surrendered their privileges both regal and papal. "Soon after, or about that time, the burgesses surrendered up their chiefest privileges, (though not all, as from several complaints is apparent,) together with an obligation, whereby they stood bound to abide the word or decision of the king. After he had retained them some time in his hands, (the places in the university disposal, which fell in that time, being bestowed by him on those he thought fit, as particularly a bedell's place,) he at length (after several articles had been put up against each other in that time, which for brevity I omit) confirmed all the ancient privileges and liberties of the university, and commanded all his subjects, particularly the mayor and burghers of Oxford, to observe, keep, and in no wise infringe them." Wood's Annals, A.D. 1532.]

[2 Elizabeth Barton. Vid. Confutation of Unwritten Verities, p. 65.]

## XXXI. TO LORD ABERGAVENNY[3].

In my right hearty wise I commend me unto your lordship, &c. And where I am informed by divers of my tenants of Mayfield[4], that there be certain ancient franchises and liberties thereunto belonging, which hitherto hath been always quietly maintained by my predecessors; notwithstanding, as they do again report, there is one William Smythe hath enterprised to infringe the said liberties, in serving of a *supplicavit* to one John Kydder tenant there: in consideration thereof, I heartily desire you, forasmuch as I am myself ignorant of such liberties, that you will execute and provide such condign punishment for the offender herein as law and conscience will suffer you thereunto, so that this poor man may have some redress thereby. Requiring you furthermore henceforward to redress all such offences within my said liberties, upon like informations, according to your discreet and politic wisdom in that behalf, as you shall think most necessary from time to time. And in thus doing you shall not alonely do unto me singular pleasure, but also thereby be sure of me to shew at all times that pleasure I may. Thus fare you well. From my manor of Otford, the xix. day of July. Harl. MSS. 6148. f. 29. Copy.

*To mine especial friend my lord of Burgavenny.*

---

## XXXII. TO THE DEAN OF THE ARCHES.

Mr Dean, I greet you well. And where I am informed by one James Bulstrode, that he hath divers witness, which could make manifest depositions concerning the matter of variance in matrimony between him and one Edwardes, whose said witness as yet you have not examined, ne will not, as he reporteth, unless you have some knowledge from me therein: I will therefore, in case it be not repugnant or prejudicial to the course of the law, that you take all manner of depositions, as well for the one part as for the other, to the intent the knowledge of the truth may the more openly appear in this behalf. And thus fare you well. From my manor of Otford, the xxi. day of July. Harl. MSS. 6148. f. 29. Copy.

---

## XXXIII. TO THE DEAN OF THE ARCHES.

Mr Dean, I greet you well. And where as well the matter in controversy between Thomas Perry and one Benbowe, as also the matter between James Bulstrode and one Edwardes, stand undetermined, the parties with importune suit always calling unto me thereupon, and the term almost now at an end: i[n] consideration thereof, and forasmuch as I am not assured what day is most convenient to appoint the said parties to be here before me, having your assistance therewithal; I will therefore, that ye appoint both day and time in that behalf, willing you further to warn Doctor Townsende to be here with you, so that he may still continue with me in the vacation time. And further, that you appoint either party to bring with them their learned counsel, to the intent we make the more speed therein. Over this I advertise you, that where you desire to know my Harl. MSS. 6148. f. 29. b. Copy.

---

[[3] Vid. p. 64, *n.* 2.]

[[4] "Accordingly I find, in the forementioned manuscript book of sales of kings' lands, that Thomas, archbishop of Canterbury, did, in the first year of king Edward VI., partly by purchase, and partly by exchange of other lands, procure divers lands of the king. He obtained the rectory of Whalley, Blackbourn, and Rochdale, in the county of Lancaster, lately belonging to the monastery or abbey of Whalley in the same county; and divers other lands and tenements in the counties of Lancaster, Surrey, London, Bangor. And this partly in consideration of king Henry VIII. his promise, and in performance of his will; and partly in exchange for the manor and park of Mayfield in the county of Sussex, and divers other lands and tenements in the counties of Middlesex, Hertford, Kent, Buckingham, and York." Strype's Mem. of Abp. Cranmer, Vol. I. p. 403. Ed. Oxon. 1840.]

mind, whether you shall make privy Mr Chancellor and Pottkyns in the matter which you wrote to me of; my mind is in that behalf, that you shall shew nothing to them thereof, but keep the same to yourself until your next resort unto me, when you shall know further of my mind therein. And thus fare you well. From my manor of Otford, the xxii. day of July.

---

## XXXIV. TO DR BELL.

Harl. MSS. 6148. f. 33. Copy.

I HEARTILY commend me unto you: and forasmuch as ye heretofore promised me that I should have a determinate answer of you, as touching the taking to farm of your benefice beside Southwell called Normanton for a kinsman of mine, and that the time which ye appointed to give the same is now past: I desire you therefore, that ye without any further delay will send me now by my servant, this bearer, a final answer in this behalf. And where ye before made a stop herein, because of your promise which ye made to master Basset, I assure you, he hath assigned and remitted unto me his interest and title in the same, like as I shall plainly shew you by his letters, what time soever ye shall require to see them. Thus fare ye well. From my manor of Otford, the xxii[ti] day of July.

*To master Dr Bell be this delivered.*

---

## XXXV. TO DR BELL.

Harl. MSS. 6148. f. 33. Copy.

IN my right hearty wise I commend me unto you. And even so thank you for your benevolent kindness, which for my sake ye have shewed unto this bearer my kinsman, requiring you hereunto, as ye have begun so to proceed with the same, in all such his matters and affairs as he shall have hereafter to do with you. And forasmuch as ye be so good to grant unto him a lease of your benefice, I require you as in that behalf to let him enjoy it as shortly as you may conveniently, trusting also that you will thereunto extend and enlarge your conscience, for granting sufficient years therein. And look what pleasure or commodity on my behalf I can do for you, ye may be sure of me to accomplish the same from time to time, &c.

*To the same.*

---

## XXXVI. TO DR CLAYBROKE AND DR BASSETT.

Harl. MSS. 6148. f. 33. Copy.

I HEARTILY commend me unto you: likewise thanking you for this bearer my kinsman, to whom as I understand you be especial friend, in such matters and causes as he hath to do with you, requiring you also in my name and behalf to give condign thanks unto the vicars chorals at Southwell for the same. And if I may do unto you or them any pleasure, ye shall always have me ready to that lieth in me the best I can, &c.

*To doctor Claybroke and doctor Bassett.*

---

## XXXVII. TO THE DUCHESS OF NORFOLK[1].

Harl. MSS. 6148. f. 30. Copy.

MADAM, in my most hearty wise I commend me unto your ladyship: and so certify you, that I have received your letter concerning the permutation of the benefice of

---

[[1] "Probably the duchess dowager, who was afterwards attainted of misprision of treason, for concealing the misconduct of her granddaughter, Catharine Howard." Vid. Jenkyns' Remains of Abp. Cranmer, Vol. I. p. 47, and Burnet's Hist. of Reformat. Vol. I. p. 626 Ed. Oxon. 1829.]

Cheving unto your chaplain, Mr Molinex, wherein I was ever minded to satisfy your desire so much as in me was; but forsomuch as the said Mr Baschirche[2] changed his mind, and that he hath resigned the said benefice unto another man[3], your ladyship's further request now is, to have the next grant of the said benefice of Cheving, when it shall be by any manner way void, promising therefore the resignation of a benefice of the king's patronage, named Curremalet in Somersetshire, to whomsoever I shall name the same. Truly I am right well contented to apply unto your mind therein, although this said benefice of Cheving is well worth forty marks, which is much more than the eighteen pounds. And where you wrote, that after so many times sent to know my mind herein, as yet you have no word thereof: surely I commanded my servant Creke to inform you after what condition the said benefice was resigned; as knoweth Almighty Jesus, who I beseech to preserve your good ladyship. From my manor of Otford, the xxiii. day of July, [1533.]

*To the right honourable and my very good lady the duchess of Northfolk.*

---

## XXXVIII. TO LORD ARUNDEL.

In my right hearty wise I commend me unto your good lordship, &c. And where I am credibly informed of a certain composition concluded between my predecessors and yours, concerning the game and other liberties in the forest of Arundell, for the number of thirteen bucks or stags in summer, and for so many does or hinds in winter, which (as is more plainly specified) are yearly due unto the archbishop of Canterbury's larder, within his manor of Slyndon[4]; in consideration hereof, and forasmuch as the store of my other parks and games are now, by reason of this last vacation, utterly wasted and decayed, whereby I am at this season destitute of venison, both for myself and my friends; and so am thereby also now constrained more effectually to require of you this my said duty herein; I most heartily desire your lordship, that I may have these my said bucks or stags at your pleasure at this time. And hereafter when my game is better increased and replenished, I shall be as glad again to accomplish your requests in such like matters from time to time, &c. Harl. MSS. 6148. f. 30. Copy.

*To my very singular good lord, my lord of Arundell.*

---

## XXXIX. THE DUKE OF NORFOLK TO CRANMER.

My lord, in my right hearty manner I commend me unto you: signifying unto the same that the king's pleasure is, that ye do send unto me, with all speed and celerity, all such books and writings as ye have in your custody, sealed or subscribed with the hands of learned men, for the justifying of his highness' great cause; and that with the said books and writings ye do send also all such manner process in form authentic, as hath been made by you touching his grace's said cause. From Grenwich, the vth[5] day of September, [1533.] Harl. MSS. 6148. f. 30, b. Copy.

Yours, T. Norfolke.

*To my lord of Canterbury his grace.*

---

[[2] Probably sir Thomas Baschurche, a priest, sometime secretary to archbishop Warham.]

[[3] Viz. Richard Astall, collated to Chevening the 15th of Oct. 1533. Vid. Cranmer's Register.]

[[4] Vid. Letter XXIV. p. 250. *n*. 1.]

[[5] The court of Henry VIII. was at this time at Greenwich, where the accouchment of Anne Boleyn was expected. The documents referred to above were probably considered necessary to establish the validity of his marriage with Anne Boleyn, and consequently the legitimacy of her child.]

## XL. TO THE DUKE OF NORFOLK.

Harl. MSS. 6148. f. 30, b. Copy.

My lord, in my right hearty manner I commend me unto your good lordship: certifying the same, that this present Sunday[1] I have caused to be delivered unto master Cromewell all such books and writings as have come to my hands concerning the king's grace's great cause, according to the said Mr Cromewell's request, made unto me therein in his said grace's behalf. And as for all manner process had and made in the said matter, they be remaining in the hands of my chancellor, to be reduced in authentic form according to the order of the law for such a process. And for this intent I have sent one of my secretaries to bring them unto you with all celerity he can. [1533.]

*To my lord of Norfolk his grace.*

---

## XLI. TO ROSELL[2].

Harl. MSS. 6148. f. 31. Copy.

Brother Rosell, in my right hearty wise I commend me unto you, and in like wise to my sister your bedfellow, &c. And where I understand that your son is very apt to learn and given to his book, I will advise you therefore that ye suffer not him to lose his time; but either that ye set him forth to school at Southwell, or else send him hither unto me, that at the least between us he utterly lose not his youth, &c. Further, I pray you, have me commended unto your father and mother. And thus fare ye well. From my manor of Otford, &c.

---

## XLII. TO HIS CHANCELLOR.

Harl. MSS. 6148. f. 31. Copy.

Master Chancellor, I commend me unto you: and so will that, according to the due form and manner of my licence in that behalf, you do admit into the arches this bringer, Mr doctor Cave, a civilian, in as ample manner and condition as shall be most convenient both for his state and degree therein. And thus fare you well, &c.

*To master chancellor.*

---

## XLIII. TO THE DEAN OF THE ARCHES.

Harl. MSS. 6148. f. 31. Copy.

Master dean, I commend me unto you, &c., signifying the same, that inasmuch as I have admitted this bearer, Mr doctor Cave, for one of the arches, I will that you in like condition and effect do consider and take the same from time to time accordingly, &c.

*To master dean.*

---

## XLIV. TO DR TRYGONELL.

Harl. MSS. 6148. f. 31. Copy.

In my right hearty wise I commend me unto you, &c., and so in like manner require the same to go unto my lord chancellor[3], and that in my name, not alonely to desire his lordship to shew his lawful favour unto master Hutton, of London, grocer, in

---

[[1] Sept. 7th, 1533, on which day queen Anne Boleyn was delivered of her daughter Elizabeth. Burnet's Hist. of Reformat. Vol. I. p. 264. Ed. Oxon. 1829.]

[[2] Dorothy, sister of the archbishop, was married to Harold Rosell, Esq. of Radcliffe on Trent, in Nottinghamshire. Strype's Mem. of Abp. Cranmer, Vol. II. p. 602. Ed. Oxon. 1840. Todd's Life of Abp. Cranmer, Genealogy of the archbishop's family.]

[[3] Sir Thomas Audeley. Vid. Letter XIV. p. 246. *n.* 3.]

his matter which I wrote unto you of before, but also ye will so instruct and ripe him therein, that he need not, for lack of information, be doubtful in that behalf; and in thus doing I will be as ready to shew unto you like pleasure when you shall require the same. Thus fare you well, &c.

*To Mr doctor Trygonell.*

---

## XLV. TO BROWGH.

I COMMEND me unto you, &c. For certain causes [moving] me reasonably hereunto, I charge you to be with me at Otford upon Saturday next ensuing. At your coming you shall know more of my mind. From my manor of Otford, &c. Harl. MSS. 6148. f. 31. Copy

*To master Browgh.*

---

## XLVI. TO JOHN FLEMYNG.

I DO commend me unto you, &c. and so will, for divers considerations me moving hereunto, that ye do repair immediately after the sight hereof unto me, at my manor of Otford, or where by chance I shall be else. At which time you shall know further of my mind in such matters as I have to do with you. From my manor of Otford, the xviith day of September. Harl. MSS. 6148. f. 29, b. Copy.

*To sir John Flemyng, curate of St Nicolas parish in Bristoll.*

---

## XLVII. TO CRUMWELL.

RIGHT worshipful master Crumwell, in my hearty wise I commend me to you: and where I am credibly informed of a matter afore my lord chancellor depending, between John Broke, plaintiff of the one party, and Richarde Mares and other, defendants of the other, wherein hath been used marvellous delays by the means of contrary parts and their counsel, I pray you to be for my sake good master unto the said Broke, and to such as be of his counsel in the furtherance of his right; and also to speak effectuously in your own name to my lord chancellor to make a speedy end in this matter. For this doing ye shall have me at all times ready to shew such pleasure as shall lie in me; and I pray you to remember my kinsman, John Padley, sanctuary man in Westminster. From Otford, the xxiiith day of September. State Paper Office. Miscellaneous Letters. Temp. Hen. VIII. Third series. Vol. IX. Original Holograph.

Your assured,

THOMAS CANTUAR.

*To the right worshipful and my very loving friend master Crumwell, one of the king's grace's most honourable council.*

---

## XLVIII. TO ———

IN my right hearty wise I commend me unto you, &c. And where I am credibly informed that this bearer, my well beloved servant[4], A. B. hath a full grant of Mr A[5]. Harl. MSS. 6149. f. 31, b. Copy.

---

[[4] Thomas Abberforde.]

[[5] Richard Astall, parson of Chevening. Vid. Letter XXXVII. p. 255.]

to be the farmer of his parsonage with you; and forasmuch as my said servant, intending for his most surety and profit to abide thereupon, supposeth by reason he is destitute of a convenient mansion for that behalf, that he cannot more expediently bestow himself and his household, if he might thereunto obtain your favour, than with you: in consideration hereof, and forasmuch as your vacant houses be now most apt for him that shall be farmer of the said parsonage, I heartily require you to owe unto him your lawful favour herein, and that the rather at this mine instance, which I were loth you should consider, in case I thought it should not be more for your commodity in this your solace, than his profit. From my manor of Otford, the ii^de^ day of October.

*To the parson*[1] *of Che[vening].*

## XLIX. TO THE PRIORESS AND CONVENT OF WILTON.

Harl. MSS. 6148. f. 31, b. Copy.

In my right hearty wise I commend me unto you: and where I am advertised by your authentic letters unto me, addressed by this bearer, sir Robert F., how desirous ye are, for the zeal ye bear unto the good order of your religion, to have an election[2] of an abbess, whereunto by those your said letters you move and also require of me aid concerning the same: this is to signify unto you hereby, that inasmuch as I perceive, that this your suit doth as well proceed of your mere and own free wills, without provocation of other men's suits, as of the love and zeal ye bear unto your said religion, I will, (the king's grace's pleasure know[n] therein,) do that lieth in me to do; and owe unto you my lawful favour from time to time, &c.

*To my well beloved sister and sisters the prioress and convent of the monastery of Wilton.*

## L. TO ———

Harl. MSS. 6148. f. 31, b. Copy.

Wellbeloved, I greet you well, &c. your supplication by this bearer I have received, whereby I perceive your griefs, which to redress some part after your mind (the king's grace's pleasure known therein) I shall be as glad to do and accomplish, as any that hath been in such a room as God now hath called me unto. From my manor of Otford, the vth day of October, &c.

## LI. TO GRESHAM.

Harl. MSS. 6148. f. 32. Copy.

Master Gresham[3], I heartily commend me unto you: thanking you for your credit unto master Gerves for me; and also for your letter, where I am now more ascertained of my day, which I understand is past, than I was before; by reason whereof I am not even now in a very readiness to accomplish your mind herein; notwithstanding wherefore

[1 Dr Jenkyns suggests that there seems to be an error here, since the parson is spoken of in the letter as a third person. Remains of Abp. Cranmer, Vol. I. p. 53.]

[2 Henry VIII. and Wolsey had a dispute respecting the appointment of an abbess of Wilton, the latter having successfully supported Isabella Jordayn, the prioress, in opposition to the wishes of Henry and Anne Boleyn. The convent had been badly regulated, and was much in need of being reformed, which several of the nuns resisted. In the present instance Cecil Bodenham appears to have been successful; who, when the convent was afterwards dissolved, was pensioned with the prioress and thirty-one nuns. Vid. State Papers, Vol. I. p. 313, et sqq.; Harl. MSS. Vol. III. p. 58; Willis' Hist. of Abbeys, Vol. II. App. p. 29.]

[3 Dr Jenkyns thinks this may have been either Sir Richard the father, or Sir John the uncle, of the celebrated Sir Thomas Gresham, who were both opulent merchants in the city of London. Remains of Abp. Cranmer, Vol. I. p. 54.]

I trust you shall be in no danger, for shortly I will send to the said master Gerves to require of him a little respite unto my next audit at Lambeth, which will not be long unto, and then I trust to satisfy him, and be glad to do for you as great pleasure by the grace of God, &c. From Otford the vith day of October.

## LII. TO LORD ROCHFORD[4].

My lord, in my right hearty wise I commend me unto your good lordship: and where this bringer P. M. sueth unto me to write unto you in his favour, that you would be so good lord unto him, as to move my lord of Northfolke at your request to prefer the same to my lord of Richmonde's[5] service to the room of a secretary, which, as I perceive, is now void: in consideration hereof, and forasmuch that at your request I took his brother[6] to my service, whose diligence and fidelity I do now much esteem, I heartily require your lordship to tender this his said suit; and that the rather at this my request ye do therein the more effectually, as your discreet wisdom in that behalf doth think best for his furtherance: for I myself have this confidence in him, that by reason he is brother unto my said servant, he will do no less diligent service unto my said lord of Richmond than his brother doth now unto me; as knoweth God, who preserve you, my good lord Rocheford. From my manor of Otford the vith day of October, &c. Harl. MSS. 6148. f. 32. Copy.

*To my very singular good lord, my lord of Rocheforde, &c.*

## LIII. TO COLLMAN[7].

Master Collman, I commend me unto you, &c. praying you, as my trust and fidelity is in the same, to proceed in making of a sale in Buchurste of such woods as shall be thought most best by your discretion for my profit, according to such informations as my officers made unto you at their last being at Canterbury; and in thus doing you shall at this time do me pleasure. And for your further surety herein, this my writing shall be a sufficient warrant for you at all times in this behalf, &c. vii. day of October. Harl. MSS. 6148. f. 30, b. Copy.

*To Mr Collman at Canterbury.*

## LIV. TO HIS CHANCELLOR.

Master chancellor, I greet you well. And forasmuch as I am credibly informed that the nomination of a vicar unto the vicarage of Withbroke in the diocese of Coventry and Lichfield belongeth unto me in the vacation of the bishop there[8], which said nomination I have given unto the prior of Coventry, [I will that] ye do dispatch the said prior according to your form devised by the law in that behalf, and as you shall think most convenient, &c. Harl. MSS. 6148. f. 32. Copy.

*To master chancellor.*

[4 Brother of Anne Boleyn.]

[5 Henry Fitzroy, a natural son of Henry VIII.]

[6 Probably Rafe Morice, the archbishop's secretary, in whom he had great confidence. Vid. Strype's Mem. of Abp. Cranmer, Vol. I. pp. 97, 176, 394; Vol. II. pp. 611, 1054. Ed. Oxon. 1840.]

[7 John Colman was, in 1535, the archbishop's bailiff for Wyngham and its dependencies. Valor. Eccles.]

[8 Geoffrey Blythe, bishop of Coventry and Lichfield, died the latter end of 1533. Rowland Lee, his successor, was elected the 10th of Jan. 1534, consecrated the 19th of April, and the temporalities restored to him the 6th of May following. Le Neve, Fasti. p. 125. Ed. Lond. 1716. See below, Letter LXXXII.]

## LV. TO THE CURATE OF SUNDRIDGE.

Harl. MSS. 6148. f. 32, b. Copy.

I COMMEND me unto you, &c. And where I am advertised by this bringer, John Pers, that for lack of a banns asking you defer the same from solemnizing of his matrimony, the default whereof he reporteth was [in] one, who in his absence for him should have given money to the clerk for the intimation thereof: I will therefore that you make no further lets or impediments herein, advertising the same, that forasmuch as in considering the premises there appeareth in his behalf no coven or deceit, I am content at this time to dispense with him. From Otford, &c.

*To the curate of Sunriche.*

---

## LVI. TO THE PRIOR OF CHRIST'S CHURCH, CANTERBURY.

Harl. MSS. 6148. f. 32, b. Copy.

BROTHER prior, in my right hearty wise I commend me unto you: heartily thanking you for your good and kind token which I have received by your brothern and mine, not deserved as yet; nevertheless you should have done me much more greater pleasure, if you had lent it me full of gold, not for any pleasure or delectation that I have in the thing, but for the contentation of such as I am indebted and dangered unto; which I assure you hath grieved me more of late, than any worldly thing hath done a great season: in this I am bold to shew you my necessity, thinking of good congruence I might in such lawful necessity be more bolder of you, and you likewise of me, than to attempt or prove any foreign friends. Wherefore, trusting in your benevolence and of all my brethren for the premises, I shall so recompense the same again, according as ye shall be well contented and pleased withal. Thus fare ye well.

*To my brother the prior of Christ's Church in Canterbury.*

---

## LVII. TO THE PARSON OF CHEVENING[1].

Harl. MSS. 6148. f. 32, b. & 33. Copy.

MASTER Astall, I commend me unto you. And where you were contented that I should have the farm[2] of your parsonage of Chevening for one of my servants, which then I minded unto my servant Abberforde, supposing you would not have exacted of him, ne charged the same further for the yearly rent and revenues thereof, than was wont to be paid; yet, that notwithstanding, as I am informed, ye be not contented and agreeable to take xvi$^{li}$. yearly therefore of him, which, as I hear say, is xl$^{s}$. more than was accustomed to be paid before master Milles had raised the same; but thereunto also you would have him stand charged, over and besides the xvi$^{li}$. with iiii$^{li}$. more, which amounteth every year to the sum of xx$^{li}$: sir, I much marvel that you will desire thus far to exceed, in this uncertain world, from the accustomed rent thereof; I had thought you would rather have minished the old exaction than now to increase the same. I trust, therefore, you will not so hardly regard my first request herein; but am sure, after the most simple manner, ye will accomplish your said promise to me in this behalf. For in case my friend cannot somewhat likely have a living thereby, I had rather he were without it than have it. And what ye intend to do herein, I require you to send me an answer thereof by this bringer. Thus fare you well. From my manor of Otford the viii. day of October.

*To the new parson of Chevenyng, Mr A.*

---

[[1] Vid. Letters XXXVII. XLVIII. pp. 255, 258.]

[[2] It was a common practice in the times of the archbishop to farm benefices, which was distinct from fee farming, which was afterwards introduced as a permanent commutation.]

## LVIII. TO DR DOWNES[3].

In my right hearty wise I commend me unto you: and forasmuch as heretofore I had a promise made unto me by doctor[4] Bennett, (whose soul God pardon,) for the farm of his prebend in Southwell, for a kinsman of mine named John Thorpe; which said promise I doubted not herein should have taken good effect in case death had not prevented the same: in consideration hereof, and inasmuch as by the death of the said doctor Benett, the collation of it belongeth unto my lord your master[5], I heartily pray you, that if it be yours or any of my lord's chaplains, ye will be so good unto my said kinsman as to grant him, at this my request, to have the farm thereof, doing as other reasonably will do. And this if you can bring to pass to succeed accordingly, I will be both bound for the payment of the money thereof, and also shew unto you and yours like pleasure, &c. ix. day of October. Harl. MSS. 6148. f. 33, b. Copy.

*To Mr doctor Downes.*

---

## LIX. TO A PARK-KEEPER.

I commend me unto you: and where upon certain communication had with this bearer, Master Roger Herman, I have assigned unto the same vi. loads of wood, to be delivered out of that my park called Corell's Wood, within that your office; I will and command you therefore, that you suffer him to carry the same, when he shall require it to be delivered and appointed unto him, of such waste wood as shall be meet for fuel, to the intent the timber or young spring be not wasted thereby. And for your surety herein this my letter shall be unto you a sufficient warrant and discharge. The x. day. Harl. MSS. 6148. f. 33, b. Copy.

*To the keeper of my parks, called Corell's Wood.*

---

## LX. TO THE DEAN OF THE ARCHES.

Master Dean, I greet you well. And where you advise me (upon the suit of Edwardes[6] unto you) to grant a new commission to the same, for the examination of certain witness, you know very well how aforetime I granted both parties to have commissions in that behalf, at which season the said Edwardes regarded it not. And now forasmuch (by all likelihood) as he, perceiving what the other witness hath deposed, would hereby find some way to delay and prolong the matter; Sir, herein I signify unto you, that I am nothing willing thereunto: for on this manner of granting commissions we shall spend another year in waste, and be no more nearer the matter than we be now. And where you write unto me that master Bedell[7] hath such business, that he cannot intend to examine the witness concerning the matter in variance between the abbot of Tiltey[8] and my lord of London's chaplain, and so thereby you stay in making out the commission; I will that you appoint master Trygonell to be jointly with Mr Doctor Oliver, instead of Mr Bedell, in the said commission. The xi. day. Harl. MSS. 6148. f. 33, b. & 34. Copy.

*To the dean of the Arches.*

---

[[3] Chancellor of the church of York, and one of the divines employed in compiling The Institution of a Christian Man.]

[[4] Dr William Benett succeeded Gardiner, A.D. 1529, as Henry VIII.'s ambassador at Rome, and died abroad in the autumn, A.D. 1533. Burnet's Hist. of Reformat. Vol. III. p. 158. Ed. Oxon. 1840; State Papers, Vol. I. p. 337.]

[[5] The archbishop of York.]

[[6] Vid. Letters XXXII. XXXIII. p. 253.]

[[7] Vid. Letter XIV. p. 241, n. 5.]

[[8] An abbey of white monks in Essex, near Dunmow. Tanner's Notit. Monast. Essex. xlii. Tiltey. Ed. Lond. 1787.]

## LXI. TO STAPLETON.

Harl. MSS. 6148. f. 34. Copy.

In my right hearty wise I commend me unto you: signifying to the same, that I am right glad to hear such good report of you as I do, as well in that ye be so effectuously minded and given to see your pastoral cure discharged by your continual preaching and teaching, as also in confirming the same by your good conversation, example of living, and charitable behaviour towards your neighbours; whereunto I exhort you in Christ's behalf to go forward and proceed, as ye have hitherto right well begun. And where also I am advertised, that by your both good provision, and provident wisdom, there is a free school maintained with you for the virtuous bringing up of youth; I heartily require you, inasmuch as with this bearer I send now unto you my sister's son, named Thomas Rosell[1], apt (as I suppose) to learning, that ye will at this my attemptation and request do so much as to see him ordered and instruct in such doctrine as shall be convenient both for his age and capacity. And for those your pains in so doing I will always be ready to shew unto you like pleasure. Thus fare you well. From my manor of Otford, the xiith day of October.

*To master Stapleton, parson of Byngham.*

---

## LXII. TO ROSELL.

Harl. MSS. 6148 f. 34. Copy.

Brother, I right heartily commend me unto you, and in like wise unto my sister your bedfellow, &c. And where of late I wrote to you, that ye should send your son to school unto Southwell, supposing at that time that those parties had been clear from sickness, so it is as I am now advertised that they die there. In consideration thereof, and forasmuch as I am credibly informed that master Stapleton, parson of Bingham, hath by his provision set up a free school in his parish, of whose good name and conversation I hear much report worthy of commendation and praise; I will therefore advise you that forthwith you send your said son thither unto school, to the intent the said master Stapleton may have the governance of him, to whom I have written a letter in that behalf. The xii. day [of October].

*To my right well-beloved brother, Mr Rosell.*

POSTSCRIPTA.

Harl MSS. 6148. f. 34, b. Copy.

I commend me unto you, and where I am uncertified of the deliverance of a letter sent to you, and dated the xth day of this present month, the intent and purport whereof was, that (for divers causes reasonably me moving,) you should repair unto me at Otford, which now inasmuch as I am in doubt of the deliverance thereof, [I] will eftsoons that you with all speed and celerity at the sight hereof do accomplish that my said intent. And at your coming you shall know further of my mind in this behalf. From my manor of Otford[2].

---

## LXIII. TO CRUMWELL.

State Paper Office. Miscellaneous Letters. Temp. Hen. VIII. Third series. Vol. IX. Original Holograph

Right worshipful master Crumwell, in my right hearty wise I commend me to you: and likewise pray you to have my friend Mr Newman[3] in your good remembrance for Mr Benett's advowsonage, so that it may please you to call the same out

---

[[1] Vid. Letter XLI. p. 256.]

[[2] This postscript stands here in the original MSS. Dr Jenkyns thinking it out of its place has inserted it after the Letter to Browgh (supra, p. 257), supposing that it must clearly have followed some such summons as is contained in that letter. Remains of Abp. Cranmer, Vol. I. p. 51.]

[[3] Vid. Letters IV. LX. LXXVII. CLIII. pp. 237, 261, 269, 309.]

of Mr Benett's kinsman's hands, and to send the same unto me by my secretary, this bearer, whom I do send unto you purposely at this time for that matter. And at such time as I may shew you any pleasure, I pray you to be as bold upon me. From my manor at Otford, the xviith day of October.

Your own assured

THOMAS CANTUAR.

*To the Right worshipful and my very loving friend Mr Crumwell, of the king's grace's most honourable council.*

---

## LXIV. TO THE BISHOP OF HEREFORD[4].

IN my right hearty wise I commend me unto you, &c. And forasmuch as I understand, by a supplication to me delivered by this bearer, the parson of ——, that heretofore, through the procuration of one Mr Robert ap David Lloyd, your receiver, the same hath persuaded divers of this complaintiff's parish, not alonely to withdraw their tithes and oblations, but thereunto by the said David Lloyd's sinister and misreport to you caused his benefice to be sequestrate, and the sequestration thereof committed to certain temporal men; amonges whom one named Howell Abowan, after he had received the fruits thereof, did so waste and consume them, that when the sequestration was relaxed, and this said complaintiff restored again, he could not, ne yet cannot obtain of the said Abowan any restitution of his said fruits; and where also after that time you made a final determination between this complaintiff and his parishioners concerning the said tithes and other misorders, which for a certain time was well observed and took right good effect, whereupon it was thought that all things should have grown to a quietness; yet now, that notwithstanding, the said David Lloyd hath (as this complaintiff reporteth) renewed the said variance, whereby as well his tithes is now withdrawn again, contrary to your former determination, as also ——— denied him for the reformation thereof, against all right and equity: in consideration of the premises, and inasmuch as you in your diocese ought, before all other, to see justice ministered, I exhort you, and thereunto require the same, the rather at this my instance and request, to see your foresaid determination concerning these matters of variance to be executed with justice; for this complaintiff requireth of you none other favour in this behalf, but according to your determination he may enjoy the effect thereof. And surely loth were I to take on me the redressing of any such griefs within your diocese, unless for fault of justice I must be constrained thereunto: but herein I doubt not that your discretion and wisdom will suffer any such enormities to be unreformed, when the verity and truth of them shall be patified and made open unto you. Thus fare you well. From my manor of Otford the xviii. day of October.

Harl. MSS. 6148. f. 34, b. British Museum. Copy.

*To the bishop of Harwarde.*

---

## LXV. TO PALLGRAVE[5].

I DO commend me unto you: signifying to the same, that inasmuch as you write unto me, as well for the agreement of the fruits of your benefice of St Dunston's

Harl. MSS 6148. f. 35. Copy.

---

[4 Charles Booth, who died May 5, A.D. 1535, and was succeeded by Edward Fox, a friend of the archbishop. Vid. Strype's Mem. of Abp. Cranmer, Vol. I. p. 53. Ed. Oxon. 1840; Le Neve's Fasti. pp. 110, 11. Ed. Lond. 1716.]

[5 John Pawlesgrave was instituted to the rectory of St Dunstan's, the 3rd of October, 1533. Newcourt, Repertorium, Vol. I. p. 334. Ed. Lond. 1708.]

concerning the last quarter in the vacation time, as also for the oblations offered there upon your church holiday, I will that you, for a final determination herein, do resort unto Pottekyns, to know your end, to whom I have committed the ordering of all such matters belonging unto me: for you may right well consider, that I am neither skilled herein, nor that it is convenient for me to meddle in such causes; and yet not doubting but that mine officer will minister justice unto all parties accordingly. And where you say also, that you are not able to pay further out of hand so much money, but thereunto requireth days of payment for the same: Sir, as touching that, I suppose you may better bear your necessity than I may mine, considering both my great charges hitherto, and how I am thereby at this season compelled to prove all the friends that I can make, for the satisfying of such sums as be now due to be paid; and yet I think not the contrary but that I shall lack much for the accomplishment of the same. Therefore I reckon you will rather endanger yourself to your friends than now to require any such commodity of me, being so far behind hand.

*To master Pallgrave, parson of St Dounston's*
*in the East at London.*

## LXVI. TO LORD CHANCELLOR AUDELEY.

Harl. MSS. 6148. f. 35. Copy.

In my right hearty wise I commend me unto your good lordship, &c. And where I am advertised by this bearer, doctor Maye, my vicar-general within the diocese of Ely[1], that by reason that doctor Clyff[2] and other keepeth away from him the records and registers belonging unto his office, he cannot in divers matters and causes minister justice accordingly; and forasmuch also as there is none other convenient way or means, neither by the course of the law spiritual nor temporal, for the obtaining of them, as I am in this behalf informed; I heartily require your good lordship, that you will at this mine instance cause a sergeant of arms to call the parties which have the custody of the said registers before you, to the intent they may shew reasonable causes why they ought not to deliver them: and in thus doing you shall both help to aid justice, and do also unto me singular pleasure, which to recompense I will be at all times ready and glad. This said bringer can further instruct your lordship in this, to whom I pray you to give credence. Thus fare you well. From my manor at Otford, the xxiiiith day of October.

*To my Lord Chancellor.*

## LXVII. TO ——

Harl. MSS. 6148. f. 35. Copy.

I greet you well. And where this bearer, my friend master Chesewryght, one of the king's chaplains, hath the benefice of Wisbeche given unto him, within the diocese of Ely, whose suit unto me is for the agreement of the fruits thereof now

[[1] Nic. West, bishop of Ely, died April 28th, A.D. 1533, whom Thomas Goodrich succeeded, having been elected March 17th, and consecrated April 19th, A.D. 1534. Le Neve's Fasti. Dr May, as the archbishop's vicar-general, seems to have governed the diocese in the interval. There were two Doctors May, brothers, and both eminent men. Dr William May, who is probably the person here mentioned, visited the diocese of Norwich as Cranmer's commissary A.D. 1534, was one of the divines engaged in drawing up the "Institution of a Christian Man," became dean of St Paul's, A.D. 1554, was deprived under Mary, and in the reign of Elizabeth was restored to his deanery, and afterwards nominated to the archbishoprick of York, but died before his consecration. Strype's Mem. of Abp. Cranmer, Vol. I. pp. 41, 77, 209; Annals of Reformat. Vol. I. part v. pp. 75, 230, 287, 306. Ed. Oxon. 1824; Life of Abp. Parker, Vol. I. pp. 128, 171, 2. Ed. Oxon. 1821; Life of Abp. Grindal, p. 56. Dr John May was master of Catharine Hall, Cambridge, and A.D. 1577 bishop of Carlisle. Strype's Life of Abp. Parker, Vol. I. p. 177; Annals of Reformat. Vol. II. Part II. pp. 52, 3. Ed. Oxon. 1840.]

[[2] Probably Dr Cliff, chanter of York and dean of Chester.]

in the vacation time, I will, that inasmuch as I can little skill in that behalf, that you, with master Pottkyns, order the matter according to your discretions with favour. And thus fare you well, &c.

---

## LXVIII. TO HIS CHANCELLOR.

MASTER Chancellor, I greet you well. And forasmuch as this bringer, the vicar of Milton, complaineth and findeth himself aggrieved, as well for that he is overcharged for the king's subsidy[3], as also for an acre of glebe land withholden from him; which injuries the abbot of St Austin's[4] doth enforce him to sustain, both contrary to an ancient composition, and also the act of the parliament favouring him in that behalf: I will that you, in consideration hereof, examine his said composition, and thereupon send me word how you think the matter standeth, to the intent I may see a redress in that behalf. Harl. MSS. 6148. f. 35, b. Copy.

---

## LXIX. TO ——

MY especial good lord, I most heartily commend me unto your lordship. Your loving letter by your servant I have received, whereby I perceive your request therein; which to accomplish I would be as glad as any man living, if it might stand both with my ordinary power and my honesty withal: for I fear me I have gone and proceeded so far already by way of promise herein, that conveniently I cannot fulfil your desire in that behalf, whereof I am right sorry; and yet notwithstanding I will promise you to do that I may therein, as it shall be well known to you hereafter. Harl. MSS. 6148. f. 36. Copy.

---

## LXX. TO ——

IN my right hearty wise I commend me unto you. And where I am advertised by master dean of Lincoln's[5] letters of your toward mind that you bear unto my kinsman and servant Henry Bingham[6], for his preferment unto the office of the auditorship of the church of Lincoln, now being in your hands and disposition; to whom, as I understand, in that behalf ye could be right well content to declare your convenient favour, in case you had not made a former grant unto a kinsman of your own; which notwithstanding, as I do again perceive, your mind is to entreat your said kinsman to relinquish his interest therein: Sir, for this your gentle and favourable behaviour hitherto towards my said kinsman, I heartily give unto you condign thanks therefore; requiring the same, that now, the rather at this mine instance and request, ye will as well on your behalf as also for the obtaining the good will of your said kinsman, accomplish your intended purpose herein; and in so doing I shall be at all times ready to acquit and recompense the same accordingly. Harl. MSS. 6148. f. 36. Copy.

---

[3 Probably the subsidy granted by Convocation A. D. 1523, consisting of the half of all spiritual benefices, to be levied in five years. Vid. Wilkins' Concilia, Vol. III. p. 699. Ed. Lond. 1737.]

[4 John Sturvey, alias Essex, abbot of St Augustin's, Canterbury.]

[5 George Heneage succeeded to the deanery of Lincoln 1528, and died 1548. Le Neve's Fasti. p. 146. Ed. Lond. 1716. The James Mallet, mentioned by Dr Jenkyns, was not dean, but precentor.]

[6 Probably the Bingham who is mentioned in the articles preferred against the archbishop, A. D. 1543, as having married Cranmer's sister whilst her former husband was living. Vid. Strype's Mem. of Abp. Cranmer, Vol. I. p. 168. Ed. Oxon. 1840.]

## LXXI. TO ———

Harl. MSS. 6148. f. 36. Copy.

In my right hearty wise I commend me unto you. And where I am advertised by my servant Jefere Eton, that you by your deed obligatory did stand bound in x[li]. to one Thomas Eton his brother, late deceased, to pay to him lxvi[s]. viii[d]. yearly, unto such time that he were advanced to some spiritual promotion of the clear value of viii[li]. by the year, over and above all charges and reprises; which said Thomas Eton then afterward for a time exercised the room of the officialship in Exeter; whereupon you denied the payment of the said pension or annuity, contrary to the right and order of the temporal law, as I am informed by learned counsel: therefore and inasmuch as my said servant, now being sole executor unto his brother, must accomplish and perform his testament, I require you, and that the rather at this mine instance and request, that ye will either now pay unto the same all such sums of money, which in the name of a pension or annuity were heretofore due unto the said Thomas Eton his brother, or else to conclude some reasonable agreement with him therefore, to the intent he need not any further attempt the law in this behalf.

## LXXII. THE EARL OF ESSEX[1] TO CRANMER.

Harl. MSS. 6148. f. 36, b. Copy.

My very good lord, in my right hearty manner I commend me unto your grace; and where it hath pleased you to write unto me in favour of one Richard Stansby, that is to admit him favourably to his declaration against a bill of complaint offered to me against him, so that if he were found faultless of such things as be surmised in the said complaint, he might with my favour enjoy such as conscience would require; or else, if he be found faulty, that then upon his submission I would weigh the matter with some charitable favour, the sooner at your request: my Lord, so it is, that there is no such complaint offered to me against the said Richard Stansby, wherefore I might accomplish your said request. But the said Stansby was of late my baily, and also my copyholder of certain lands in Bilston, in Suffolk, for the favour that of long time I did bear unto him, until that now of late, at my court holden at Bilston foresaid, as well his dissimulate and cloaked untruth in misusing of his office both as against me and my tenants there, as his misdemeaning of his copyhold against the customs used within the said manor, was by the whole homage presented. Wherefore I have seized into my hands his said copyhold, according to right, conscience, and custom, and have also deprived him of his office, intending never hereafter to bear him no such favour, that he shall have any thing of me more than right and conscience shall require; praying your grace so to be contented therewith, nothing doubting the same, if your grace knew the said misdemeanours. And what pleasure I may shew to any other person at your request hereafter, I shall be glad to do the same, as our Lord knoweth; who have you in his blessed tuition. The xiii. day of October.

*By my lord of Essex.*

## LXXIII. TO THE EARL OF ESSEX.

Harl. MSS. 6148. f. 36, b. & 37. Copy.

In my right hearty wise I commend me unto your good lordship. These be to advertise you, that I have received your letters dated at Stansted the xiii. day of October. Whereby I perceive that you intend not to do any wrong to Richard Stansby, not-

[[1] Henry Bouchier, "in whom that line (i. e. of the earldom of Essex) was extinct, who had been a severe persecutor, falling from his horse, and breaking his neck, died without being able to speak one word." The earldom of Essex was afterwards given to Crumwell, with all that fell to the crown by reason of the former earl dying without heirs. Burnet's Hist. of Reformat. Vol. III. p. 276. Ed. Oxon. 1829.]

withstanding any complaint or presentment made against him, which is my very trust, and the rather at my request. Wherefore eftsoons I will desire you to be so good lord unto him, that two well learned men and indifferent may have the hearing of all matters, that your lordship is informed that he hath misordered himself against you. And so be it, that the said Stansby by any such misdemeanour hath not forfeit any of his land or copyhold, then I trust your lordship will be contented that he may enjoy his lands and copyhold according to right and conscience. And if the said two indifferent learned men shall reasonably think that he hath misordered himself in any point, the same Richard Stansby shall humbly require you to be his good lord, and shall to his small power make such amends for his offences, as shall be by the said two learned men thought reasonable. Trusting that in this his age ye will the rather be good lord unto him, and have herein the less regard to his negligence. Which to recompense I doubt not but that you shall have now no less good service of him, than ever you had of the same heretofore; and of my behalf such pleasure and commodity as you shall at any time require of me accordingly[2].

*An answer to the same by my lord.*

---

## LXXIV. TO CERTAIN GENTLEMEN IN HERTFORDSHIRE.

IN my right hearty wise I commend me unto you. And where this bringer, Thomas Wiggynton, one of my tenants of Tring, hath offered unto me a supplication concerning such injuries and wrongs as he is compelled to sustain, by reason that certain unadvised persons, whose names are comprised in the said supplication, hath unjustly, as he reporteth, both slandered and spoiled him of his goods and good name; and by cause it is against reason to give credence to one party, the other parties not heard; and also, forasmuch as the matter also being in a place so far distant from me, that I cannot call the parties and witness before me without their intolerable charges: I require you, forasmuch as you being as well justices of the peace as also dwelling nigh there, to whom

Harl. MSS. 6148. f. 39. Copy.

---

[[2] The earl of Essex, not having paid attention to this or any other letters, at length provoked the following peremptory order from Henry VIII.

Harl. MSS. 6148. f. 37, b.

"*By the King.*

"*To our right trusty and right wellbeloved cousin and counsellor, the earl of Essex.*

"Right trusty and right wellbeloved cousin, we greet you well. And where upon complaint made unto us by our subject Richard Stansby for putting him out of certain copyholds, lands, and tenements, in your town of Bylston, which he and his ancestors have holden of you and your ancestors many years, it was thought by our council upon the examination of the matter to be reasonable, that our said subject should be restored to the possession of the said customary lands and tenements, paying his rents and services to you for the same, as hath been accustomed, till such time as the cause of seizure thereof were examined by our said council, and an order therein taken as to justice and equity should appertain; and that afterward our right trusty and right wellbeloved counsellor, sir Thomas Audeley, knight, our chancellor of England, and other of our counsellors, have directed unto you their several loving letters, advertising you of the mind of the residue of our council in the premises, and advising you rather of yourself, upon the humble suit of our said subject, to restore him accordingly, than it should be done by any order of compulsion; which notwithstanding, ye, neither following their wholesome admonitions, nor yet the mind and order of our said council, will not in any wise [be] answerable to the same, but have lately sent to the lands and grounds in variance certain persons unknown; which being there assembled have forcibly kept the possession of the same, intending to cast out the goods of our said subject therein; being to the evil example of other, in case it should be suffered, as we be informed; whereof we do not a little marvel: We let you to wit, that forasmuch as it belongeth unto us to minister right justice and equity to every of our subjects, and willing the order and decrees of our council to be firmly obeyed and observed without violation, do signify unto you the premises; and not doubting that ye, being of such authority and one of our council, will conform yourself to observe and ensue such orders as is or shall be taken by our said council, without giving evil examples to other persons, or otherwise to give us occasion to compel you; which of necessity we must do, if after such proceeding ye thus attempt us; seeing it standeth not with good congruence nor our prerogative, that the process and orders made by us and our council, or by our writs in causes of justice, should be resisted by any of our subjects, by colour of any manner liberty or franchise. And therefore we will and command you to take good respect to yourself in this behalf, and to follow the orders of our council therein, as ye will answer unto us at your peril in that behalf, and as you tender our pleasure. Yeven under our signet, at our manor of Westminster the xxvi. day of March."]

the administration of justice the rather belongeth, that you will take the pains to peruse this said supplication, and thereto to see such justice ministered, as shall be thought convenient according to law and good conscience, to the intent this poor man need not any further to complain unto me or any other for the same.

*To certain gentlemen in Hartefordshire.*

---

## LXXV. TO THE ARCHDEACON OF CANTERBURY[1].

Harl. MSS. 6148. f. 39, b. Copy.

Master archdeacon, in my right hearty wise I commend me unto you. And where I am informed by my servant John Creake[2], that the farm of your parsonage of Hayes is already, or else shortly like to be void, I heartily require you, at this mine instance, that you will grant to him the preferment thereof, whensoever the same shall next happen to be void, he finding you sufficient sureties for the payment thereof, and thereto giving you as much as any other reasonably will give. And what you intend to do herein, I require you to advertise me by this bearer, or as shortly as you may conveniently. And if there be any pleasure that I may do for you again, you may be sure to be bold of me accordingly.

*To the archdeacon of Canterbury.*

---

## LXXVI. TO BONER[3].

Cotton MSS. Cleop. E. vi. f. 234. b. Original. Burnet's Hist. of Reformat. App. Vol. III. Book ii. No. 24. p. 62. Ed. Oxon. 1829.

In my right hearty manner I commend me to you. So it is, (as ye know right well,) I stand in dread, lest our holy father the pope do intend to make some manner of prejudicial process against me and my church. And therefore, having probable conjectures thereof, I have provoked[4] from his holiness to the general council, according as the king's highness[5] and his council have advised me to do: which my provocation[6] and a procuracy under my seal I do send unto you herewith, desiring you right heartily to have me commended to my lord of Winchester[7]; and with his advice and counsel to intimate the said provocation, after the best manner that his lordship and you shall think most expedient for me. I am the bolder thus to write unto you, because the king's highness

---

[[1] William Warham, the nephew of archbishop Warham, who parted with the archdeaconry of Canterbury, and the provostship of Wingham by cession (March, A.D. 1534) in favour of Edmund Cranmer, brother of the archbishop, and had a pension of £60 per annum allowed him, during his life, from the archdeaconry, and £20 per annum out of Wingham, by his successor. Strype's Mem. of Abp. Cranmer, Vol. I. p. 24. Ed. Oxon. 1840; Le Neve's Fasti. p. 13.]

[[2] Vid. Letters XVIII. XXXVII. pp. 246, 255.]

[[3] "I find moreover, that the archbishop of Canterbury at this time, suspecting the pope would proceed against him, by the advice of our king made his appeal also to the council; which he desired our agents to intimate to the pope. The success whereof yet doth not appear in our records." Kennet's Hist. of England, Vol. II.; Lord Herbert's Life of Henry VIII. p. 170. Boner was at this time Henry VIII.'s agent to pope Clement VII., and "had made his appeal from the pope to the next general council lawfully called." By the king and council's advice, Cranmer "soon after did the same; sending his appeal with his proxy, under his seal, to Boner, desiring him, together with Gardiner, to consult together, and to intimate his appeal in the best manner they could think expedient for him." Strype's Mem. of Abp. Cranmer, Vol. I. p. 31. Burnet says that Cranmer sent the instrument with a warrant to execute it to Crumwell, that it might be sent to the bishop of Winchester, to get it to be intimated to the pope in the best manner that could be thought of;" but he gives no authority for his assertion. Burnet's Hist. of Reformat. Vol. III. p. 160. It is not probable that the archbishop's appeal was ever presented, since Boner, in a lengthy letter to Henry VIII., dated Nov. 13th, nine days previously to that of the archbishop above, states that the pope had gone towards Rome from Marseilles, Nov. 12th, and that he was leaving for Lyons, Nov. 13th, the day on which his letter is dated, probably with a view to his return home. Vid. Boner's letter to the king, in Burnet's Hist. of Reformat. Vol. III. Part II. App. Book II. No. 23. pp. 49-62.]

[[4] I have appealed, Strype.]

[[5] As his highness, Ibid.]

[[6] Which my appeal, Ibid.]

[[7] Stephen Gardiner, at this time at Marseilles as ambassador from Henry VIII. to Francis I.]

commanded[8] me thus to do, (as ye shall I trust further perceive by his grace's letters[9],) nothing doubting in your goodness, but at this mine own desire ye will be contented to take this pains, though his highness shall percase forget to write unto you therein: which your pains and kindness if it shall lie in me in time to come to recompense, I will not forget it, with God's grace; who preserve you as myself. From Lambeth, the xxiid day[10] of November, [1533].

THOMAS CANTUAR.

## LXXVII. TO CRUMWELL.

State Paper Office. Miscellaneous Letters. Temp. Hen. VIII. Third series. Vol. IX. Original Holograph.

RIGHT worshipful master Crumwell. I commend me heartily to you, likewise praying you to continue good master to my friend of old acquaintance, Mr Newman[11], this bearer, to whom, albeit I have been a tedious suitor unto you a long time, upon such comfortable promise as ye first made unto me for him, I eftsoons pray you now to make such resolute and comfortable answer therein, as I do trust to receive from you in the same: for seeing this was the first suit that ever I made unto you, wherein, after that ye had answer from doctor Benet[12], ye promised me that I should have my desire, and that I should not mistrust the matter; it would grieve me that the same should now take none effect, seeing the matter doth now rest in your goodness and benevolence. As long as ye were only mediator for me in it to him that had the thing, ye did ever give me good hope and comfort in it; and therefore I do now trust verily, that, seeing the same thing is come to your own hands and disposition at your pleasure, ye will now be as good in it, as ye were when ye were mediator for the same. The truth is, that my friend aforesaid was born in the same paroche, which thing moveth him to be the more desirous of it, and me to be the more importune upon you for him; for albeit I have offered unto him the expectation and advowsonage of some one promotion of my collation, of as good value as is the value of the same thing that I do desire of you, I assure you he hath refused the same, and desired me (as a man much affectionate to his native country) to continue suitor unto you in this behalf: so that he regardeth that benefice much better than my said overture[13]. And therefore I pray you, good Mr Crumwell, stay not with me now in this matter, seeing I have sued so long for the same, and ever have had comfortable promise in it. And by these my letters I do faithfully promise you, that ye shall have, when ye will, as good a benefice of my gift for the same, as that is; and so should ye have had and shall have, and as much other pleasure as I may at any time shew unto you, or to any friend of yours for your sake, though I had never written or spoken in this matter. When ye shall have cause to prove me, ye shall be assured to find me conformable to this my promise, God willing; who ever keep you. From Otford the 26th day of November.

Your own assured

THOMAS CANTUAR.

*To the right worshipful and my very loving friend master Crumwell, of the king's grace's most honourable council.*

---

[8 Commandeth me this to do, Strype.]
[9 By his grace's letter, Ibid.]
[10 xxviith day, Ibid.]
[11 Vid. Letters IV. LX. CLIII. pp. 237, 261, 309.]
[12 Vid. Letter LVIII. p. 261.]
[13 "If, as may be conjectured from Letter V., the benefice coveted by Newman was Barnack, Cranmer seems to have failed in his application: for Robert Benett, probably a relative of Dr W. Benett to whom the advowson appears to have belonged, was rector there in 1535. Valor Eccles." Jenkyns' Remains of Abp. Cranmer, Vol. I. p. 73.]

## LXXVIII. TO CRUMWELL.

State Paper Office. Miscellaneous Letters. Temp. Hen. VIII. Third series. Vol. IX. Original. Todd's Life of Cranmer, Vol. I. p. 99.

RIGHT worshipful master Crumwell, in my right hearty manner I commend me to you. So it is, that I lately received certain letters from my friend doctor Goderic[1], by whom I do perceive, that ye have not only spoken to the king's highness for the loan of a thousand marks to my use, whose pleasure is (as the same master Goderic writeth) that I shall receive of you at this time five hundred pounds and no more; but also have practised with my lord of Wiltshire and other, which at this time do claim many duties of me: for which your kindness I do heartily thank you, praying you to cause the same five hundred pounds to be delivered to my secretary Thomas Berthlet, this bearer, which shall deliver unto you an obligation for the payment thereof, at such day as is expressed in the same; which obligation (in case the same be not made according to your mind) I will be glad to reform, and seal unto you a new accordingly as ye shall require a new to be made, and will send the same unto you with speed. From Otford, the 26th day of November.

Your own assured,

THOMAS CANTUAR.

*To the right worshipful and my very loving friend master Crumwell, of the king's grace's most honourable council.*

---

## LXXIX. TO LORD ABERGAVENNY[2].

Harl. MSS. 6148. f. 40. British Museum. Copy.

MY very special good lord, I commend me heartily unto your lordship: signifying to the same, that my servant John Creke hath advertised me of your loving mind towards me, how willing you be to accompany me at Canterbury[3], wherefore I give unto you most hearty thanks. Nevertheless I will not at this season put you to any pains in this behalf. Notwithstanding, if your lordship [do send me some venison, and especially a red deer or two,][4] against Tuesday next, you should do unto me herein singular pleasure, which to requite I would be always ready, God willing; who keep and preserve your good lordship. From my manor of Otford, the xxvii. of November.

*To my lord of Burgaveny.*

---

## LXXX. TO THE ABBOT OF WESTMINSTER[5].

Harl. MSS. 6148. f. 39, b. Copy.

BROTHER abbot, in my right hearty wise I commend me unto you. And where, of your benevolence, ye promised unto me the next room which should chance to be void amonges the beadmen of the foundation of king Henry the Eighth[6] for one William Fyssher[6]; so it is, as I am credibly informed, that there is now one of the said rooms void and in your disposition. I heartily require you therefore, that the said John F. may be preferred thereunto, according to your aforesaid promise. And in so doing I will be at all times ready to requite the same accordingly, God willing; who keep you, &c. The xxix. day of November.

*To my brother abbot, the abbot of Westminster.*

---

[1 Probably Dr Thomas Goodrich, afterwards bishop of Ely and lord chancellor. Vid. p. 247, n. 8.]

[2 "In October or November (A. D. 1533), the archbishop went down to Canterbury, in order to a visitation. The third day of December he received the pontifical seat in the monastry of the holy Trinity." Strype's Mem. of Abp. Cranmer, Vol. I. p. 30. Ed. Oxon. 1840.]

[3 Dr Jenkyns suggests that "lord Abergavenny, who held an office under him, had probably offered to attend him on the occasion." Remains of Abp. Cranmer, Vol. I. p. 75.]

4 [The passage within brackets is substituted in the margin of the copy, for "if your lordship might spare me a red deer or two," which stands otherwise unaltered in the MS.]

[5 William Boston or Benson. Vid. Letter VIII. p. 240.]

[6 By mistake apparently for Henry VII. and *John* Fyssher. Vid. Letter XXVII. p. 251.]

## LXXXI. TO KING HENRY VIII.

PLEASETH it your most noble grace to understand, that the feigned revelations and illusions of the false nun[7] of St Sepulchre's here at Canterbury, and the other matters contained in them, now after that they have been opened and declared to the people[8], be had in great abomination and detestation unto them. And as far as I can perceive or learn, all your grace's people here be as glad as any men may be, that the said false and forged matters be come to light. And as concerning the prior[9] and convent of my church, (whom I have diligently examined,) I find them as conformable and reformable as any number with whom I have communed any time. And I see them greatly sorrow and lament, that any of their congregation[10] should order himself so, that such word and slander should grow of this occasion, or that thereby occasion should be given to your grace to take displeasure against the whole company, amonges whom few in comparison of their great number appear to be knowing or consenting to the said false revelations or illusions; and almost only such as were doctor Bokkynge's novices, men of young years, and of less knowledge and experience. The prior of my church, a man of great simplicity, and void of malice, as far as I can judge, hath been touched with this matter; but I cannot understand that he hath reported it to any other, but only to my predecessor, then being his ordinary and your grace's counsellor. Which prior and his brethren, the saddest and seniors of the house, with all the other young sort, considering the matter sounding to your grace's displeasure, which they regard as greatly as they do any thing else in this world, (as far as I can judge,) be greatly discomforted, dismayed, and sad, and have desired me very instantly to be a mediator for them to your most noble majesty, to be gracious and merciful unto them, offering of their free wills (besides their fervent prayers for your noble estate long and prosperously to endure) to do some pleasure unto your highness after their power, to attain your gracious favour, mercy, and pardon. And I suppose they will desire me to offer unto your grace for a pleasure, ii. or iii. c$^{li}$. Wherein I dare nothing do, unless your grace's pleasure be to me first known; assuring your grace, that as far as I can understand by any means that I can devise, that besides the ornaments of the church and some plate that the prior and some officers hath, this monastery is not aforehand, but in debt divers ways. In consideration whereof and of their good minds, I most humbly beseech your highness to be gracious and merciful unto them, the rather for my poor intercession; and that they may have some comfortable word or letter from your grace, for their comfortation in this their great pensiveness and dolour. Thus our Lord have your grace evermore in his preservation and governance. From my place at Canterburye, the xiii. day of December. [1533.]

Harl. MSS. 6148. f. 3. Copy.

---

## LXXXII. TO CRUMWELL.

RIGHT worshipful Mr Crumwell, in my right hearty wise I commend me unto you: doing you to understand, that I have received by John Anthony, this bearer, such letters as ye directed to my lord elect of Chester[11], and to Mr Bedill[12]; by which I do

State Paper Office. Miscellaneous Letters. Temp. Hen. VIII. Third series. Vol. IX. Original Holograph.

---

[7 Vid. Confutation of Unwritten Verities, pp. 65, 6.]

[8 A portion of an address to the people on this imposture, with corrections in Cranmer's handwriting, is preserved in the Public Record Office, Tractat. Theol. et Polit. Vol. VII. A. 1. 13, pp. 37, et seq. Dr Jenkyns supposes that it may perhaps be part of the above-mentioned discourse by Hethe, which the archbishop probably thought proper to submit to the inspection of Crumwell. Vid. Remains of Abp. Cranmer, Vol. I. p. 76.]

[9 Thomas Goldwell, who at the dissolution of Christ's Church, Canterbury, had been prior twenty-three years. Somner's Antiquities of Canterbury, by Battely, Part III. p. 116. Ed. Lond. 1703.]

[10 Dr Edward Bockyng, the chief author of Elizabeth Barton's dissimulation, and her confessor, and John Dering, who made and composed the books of her revelations, were both monks of Christ's Church, Canterbury. Strype's Eccl. Mem. Vol. I. Part I. p. 278. Ed. Oxon. 1822; Mem. of Abp. Cranmer, Vol. I. p. 30.]

[11 Dr Rowland Lee, bishop of Lichfield; but the two sees being then incorporated, the bishops of Lichfield were sometimes called bishops of Chester. See the next Letter, p. 274.]

[12 Vid. Letters XII. XIV. pp. 242, 244.]

perceive, that it is the king's grace's pleasure that my said lord elect and master Bedyll, which departed from Canterbury afore the receipt of your said letters, should leave the parson of Aldington[1], Dering the monk, and father Laurence[2] behind them in ward and safe keeping, but not as men at liberty. But forasmuch as this bearer sheweth me, that it was your mind that the said persons should be put to liberty in their own houses upon sufficient surety, I do now stand in doubt, whether I may commit them to ward and safe keeping according to your said letters, or else put them at liberty in their own houses upon sufficient surety, according to such word as the said Anthony brought unto me; whom I do remit unto you at this time with these my letters to ascertain you of the premises, and to bring from you such letters as shall please you to direct unto me of your resolute mind in this behalf. The said three persons shall in the mean time remain in ward and safe keeping, until I may know your mind in this matter. The parson of Aldington and the monk Dering were this Tuesday at night delivered unto me at my manor at Forde, and the other is not yet come unto me. From my manor at Forde, the xvi. day of December. [1533.]

Your assured,

THOMAS CANTUAR.

*To the right worshipful and my very loving friend Mr Crumwell, of the king's grace's most honourable council.*

---

## LXXXIII. TO ARCHDEACON HAWKYNS.

Harl. MSS. 6148. ff. 38,39. British Museum. Copy. Todd's Life of Abp. Cranmer, Vol. I. p. 89.

MASTER archdeacon, i[n] my right hearty wise I commend me unto you. These be to ascertain you of such news as be here now in fame amonges us in England. And first ye shall understand, that at Canterbury within my diocese, about eight years past, there was wrought a great miracle in a maid by the power of God and our lady, named our lady of Courteupstret; by reason of the which miracle there is stablished a great pilgrimage, and ever since many devout people hath sought to that devout foresaid lady of Courte of Strett.

The miracle was this: the maid was taken with a grievous and a continual sickness, and induring her said sickness she had divers and many trances, speaking of many high and godly things; telling also wondrously, by the power of the Holy Ghost as it was thought, things done and said in other places, where as neither she was herself, nor yet heard no report thereof. She had also in her trances many strange visions and revelations, as of heaven, hell, and purgatory, and of the state of certain souls departed[3]; and amonges all other visions one was, that [she] should be conveyed to our lady of Courte of Strett, where she was promised to be healed of her sickness, and that Almighty God should work wonders in her; and when she was brought thither and laid before the image of our lady, her face was wonderfully disfigured, her tongue hanging out, and her eyes being in a manner plucked out and laid upon her cheeks, and so greatly disordered. Then was

---

[[1] "Richard Master. He was very instrumental in bringing Elizabeth Barton into notice, Aldington being the place where at the commencement of the imposture she was living as a maid-servant." Jenkyns.]

[[2] "Thomas Lawrence, being register to the archdeacon of Canterbury, at the instance of Edw. Bockyng wrote a great book of the false and feigned miracles and revelations of the said Elizabeth, in a fair hand, ready to be a copy to the printer." Stat. 25 Hen. VIII. c. 12. "She sent her revelation [to the pope,] by Silvester Darius and by one John Anthony Pulleon, the pope's ambassadors in England; betwixt the which nun and Silvester Darius was interpreter this old man, one Lawrence of Canterbury, scribe to the archdeacon of Canterbury." MS. Public Record Office, Tractat. Theol. et Polit. Vol. VII. A. 1. 13.]

[[3] For instance: "that my lord cardinal came to his death before God would have had him by the space of fifteen years, and therefore Almighty God hath given no sentence upon him, but will defer it till those years be expired, which it was the will of God he should have lived in the world." MSS. ibid. In another of her revelations she described, "that since she died, she saw the disputations of the devils for his [Wolsey's] soul; and how she was three times lift up, and could not see him, neither in heaven, hell, nor purgatory; and at the last where she saw him; and how by her penance he was brought unto heaven." Vid. Strype's Eccl. Mem. Vol. I. Part I. p. 273. Ed. Oxon. 1822.]

there heard a voice speaking within her belly, as it had been in a tun; her lips not greatly moving; she all that while continuing by the space of three hours and more in a trance: the which voice, when it told any thing of the joys of heaven, it spake so sweetly and so heavenly, that every man was ravished with the hearing thereof; and contrary, when it told any thing of hell, it spake so horribly and terribly, that it put the hearers in a great fear. It spake also many things for the confirmation of pilgrimages and trentals, hearing of masses, and confession, and many such other things. And after she had lain there a long time, she came to herself again, and was perfectly whole [4]; and so this miracle was finished and solemnly rung, and a book written of all the whole story thereof, and put into print, which ever since that time hath been commonly sold and gone abroad amongst all people. After this miracle done, she had a commandment from God in a vision, as she said, to profess herself a nun. And so she was professed, and hath so continued, in a nunnery at Canterbury, called St Sepulchre's, ever since.

And then she chose a monk of Christ's Church, a doctor in divinity [5], to be ghostly father, whose counsel she hath used and evermore followed in all her doing: and evermore since from time to time hath had almost every week, or at the furthest every fortnight, new visions and revelations; and she hath had oftentimes trances and raptures, by reason whereof, and also of the great perfectness that was thought to be in her, divers and many as well great men of the realm as mean men, and many learned men, but specially divers and many religious men, had great confidence in her, and often resorted unto her and communed with her, to the intent they might by her know the will of God; and chiefly concerning the king's marriage [6], the great heresies and schisms within the realm, and the taking away the liberties of the church; for in these three points standeth the great number of her visions, which were so many, that her ghostly father could scantly write them in three or four quires of paper. And surely I think, that she did marvellously stop the going forward of the king's marriage by the reason of her visions, which she said was of God, persuading them that came unto her how highly God was displeased therewith, and what vengeance Almighty God would take upon all the favourers thereof; insomuch that she wrote letters to the pope, calling upon him in God's behalf to stop and let the said marriage, and to use his high and heavenly power therein, as he would avoid the great stroke of God, which then hanged ready over his head, if he did the contrary. She had also communication with my lord Cardinal and with my lord of Canterbury, my predecessor, in the matter; and [in] mine opinion, with her feigned visions and godly threatenings, she stayed them very much in the matter.

She had also secret knowledge of divers other things, and then she feigned that she had knowledge thereof from God; insomuch that she conceived letters and sent

---

[4 "After mass she kneeled afore the image of our lady of Court of Street, and said then she was made perfectly whole, where she was perfectly whole afore she came thither, as she hath plainly and openly confessed afore divers of the king's grace's council." MS. Public Record Office, Tractat. Theol. et Polit. Vol. VII. A. 1. 13.]

[5 Edward Bockyng. "He informed the said archbishop [Warham,] that a voice had spoken in her in one of her trances, that it was the pleasure of God that he should be her ghostly father." MS. ibid.]

[6 "For all the time of her abode at Aldington, she meddled not with the king's grace's marriage.... But after that she had been at Canterbury a while, and had heard this said Dr Bockyng rail and jest like a frantic person against the king's grace his purposed marriage, against his acts of parliament, and against the maintenance of heresies within this realm, declaring and blustering out his cankered malice to the said Elizabeth in the said matters,... then soon after she began to feign herself to have visions and revelations from God, and said that God commanded her to say to the late cardinal, and also to the said late archbishop of Canterbury, that if they married, or furthered the king's grace to be married to the queen that now is, they both should be utterly destroyed. And so she shewed them under such manner, that it appeared by their acts and deeds that they gave confidence to her: for the said archbishop had, afore her coming to him, provoked from the pope to the general council, intending to proceed in the king's grace's matter of matrimony and divorce, seeing his grace could have none indifferent justice shewed him in other places. And the said cardinal was as well minded and bent to go forth in the king's grace's said cause of matrimony and divorce as any man living, according to the law of God and the law of nature, till he was perverted by this nun, and induced to believe, that if he proceeded in the same, God would sore strike him." MS. ibid.]

them forth, making divers people believe that those letters were written in heaven[1], and sent from thence to earthly creatures. Now about Midsummer last, I, hearing of these matters, sent for this holy maid, to examine her[2]; and from me she was had to master Cromewell, to be further examined there. And now she hath confessed all, and uttered the very truth, which is this: that she never had vision in all her life, but all that ever she said was feigned of her own imagination, only to satisfy the minds of them the which resorted unto her, and to obtain worldly praise: by reason of the which her confession many and divers, both religious men and other, be now in trouble, forasmuch as they consented to her mischievous and feigned visions, which contained much perilous sedition and also treason, and would not utter it, but rather further the same to their power.

She said that the king should not continue king a month after that he were married; and within six months after God would strike the realm with such a plague as never was seen, and then the king should be destroyed. She took upon her also to shew the condition and state of souls departed, as of my lord Cardinal[3], my late lord of Canterbury, with divers other. To shew you the whole story of all the matter, it were too long to write in two or three letters; you shall know further thereof at your coming home.

As touching the bishopricks that be void, ye shall understand, that doctor Salcott, the abbot of Hydde, is elect bishop of Bangor, doctor Lee, the lawyer, is elect bishop of Chester[4]. There is as yet none elect bishop of Ely: you shall know at your coming home who shall be[5]. The parliament is not holden this term, but is prorogued to the xv. day of January. The queen's grace was brought [to bed] about the xiii. or xiv.[6] day of September of a princess. I myself was godfather, the old duchess of Northfolke and my lady marquess Dorset were godmothers. The duke of Richmonde[7] hath married my lady Mary, the duke of Northfolke's daughter. From Lamethe, the xx. day of December, A°. xxv. Reg. [1533.]

---

## LXXXIV. TO A PRIOR.

Harl. MSS. 6148. f. 40. Copy.

BROTHER Prior, I do right heartily commend me unto you. And so likewise desire the same, that at this mine instance ye will grant unto me the next admission of a student unto the university of Oxford, when any such of your company shall hereafter happen to be permitted thereunto. And for the same I will be ready to do unto [you] as great a pleasure. From my manor of Ford, the xxv. day of December.

---

[[1] Mary Magdalen was said to have given her a letter that was written in heaven in characters of gold: "which is as false as God is true: for by much inquisition Mary Magdalen is found out, and is turned into a monk of St Augustin's in this town, named Hawkeherste, which hath confessed the writing thereof, and the limning of these golden words *Jehus Maria*, which be written above the letter." MS. ibid.]

[[2] Vid. Letter XXX. p. 252.]

[[3] Vid. p. 272. *n.* 3.]

[[4] "There sate but one bishop here [at Chester] before 1541, viz. Peter, [consecrated 1067,] who continued bishop but about twenty years; yet several of his successors in the see denominated themselves bishops of Chester instead of Litchfield." Willis' Survey of Cathedrals, Vol. I. p. 318. Ed. Lond. 1727—30. So also Le Neve's Fasti, pp. 122, 341. Ed. Lond. 1716. Stow however says, "Dr Rowland Lee, that married the king to queen Anne, was made bishop of Chester, then bishop of Coventry and Litchfield, and president of Wales." Annals, p. 562. Ed. Lond. 1631. His election to the see of Litchfield and Coventry took place the 10th of January, 1534. Le Neve's Fasti, p. 125.]

[[5] See Letter XIV. p. 247, *n.* 8.]

[[6] This date is incorrect, the princess Elizabeth having been born on Sunday, September 7th. An official note from queen Anne Boleyn to lord Cobham, announcing the event, still preserved in the Harleian collection, and printed in the State Papers, proves the fact. See also Holinshed's Chronicles, Vol. II. p. 935. Ed. Lond. 1587.]

[[7] Henry Fitzroy, an illegitimate son of Henry VIII., who was at this time fourteen years old.]

## LXXXV. TO HIS CHANCELLOR AND DEAN OF THE ARCHES.

I COMMEND me unto you. And whereas the commissary[8] of my jurisdiction in Calice writeth unto me as well concerning my visitation there, as also for mine advice in an unlawful matrimony now depending before him; wherein it seemeth, that he hath further proceeded in that behalf than peradventure he ought, as you may partly conjecture by this his letter herein inclosed: I require you therefore, that inasmuch as these matters before specified are more largely declared in his said letter, that you, according to the effect of them, with all celerity do send me your advice what is most expedient to be done, touching the ready expedition hereof. Thus fare you well. From my manor of Ford, the xxvii. day of December. Harl. MSS. 6148. f. 40. Copy.

*To my Chancellor and Dean of the Arches.*

---

## LXXXVI. TO THE ABBOT OF READING[9].

BROTHER abbot, I commend me unto you. And whereas I am credibly informed, that through the death of Dr Benet (whose soul God pardon!) there is the collation of a benefice called Aston, in Hartfordshire, in your hands and disposition; which, forasmuch as the same standeth very commodiously for a friend of mine, I heartily require you that at this time you will give unto me the collation thereof, not doubting but that I shall exhibit and promote such a personage thereunto, as you shall hereafter think the same well bestowed. And I for my part will be ready at all times to shew unto you like pleasure accordingly. Harl. MSS. 6148. f. 40. Copy.

---

## LXXXVII. TO ——

I COMMEND me unto you. And where I do right well perceive by a testament now before me of one Thomas Broune, late poticary of the town of Bristow, that he, amongst other legacies comprised therein, hath bequeathed and given a certain garden lying and being in C. Street to my loving friend David Hutton; which said garden ye (in the name and title of Marget your wife, late wife and executrix to the said Thomas Broune) do retain and occupy, not alonely contrary to the intent of his said will, but also against good right and conscience denieth unto the said David the just possession thereof: I do require you, and thereto likewise exhort you, for a more quietness herein, that ye, according to the delegation of the said testament, from henceforth do not interrupt, let, or hinder the said David lawfully requiring or seeking his interest in the said garden; to the intent that you, in your so doing, may both accomplish justice, and also avoid thereby farther inconvenience that may ensue on your behalf, if he, in attempting the law against you, do attain unto the same; whereunto you shall enforce him, if you persist in denying his just claim thereunto. And where also the said Thomas Broune bequeathed xx$^{li.}$ towards the marriage of a certain maid named Ales B., as likewise amongst the legacies of the said testament more evidently it doth appear; which sum of money the said David Hutton delivered unto you, to the intent that you should in the mean season have the occupying of the same; so it is, as I am informed, that ye be not now willing to depart from it, and in a man- Harl. MSS. 6148. f. 40, b. Copy.

---

[8 Sir John Butler. Vid. Strype's Mem. of Abp. Cranmer, Vol. I. pp. 125, 6. Ed. Oxon. 1840.]

[9 "There is no authority in the manuscript for this address, but there can be little doubt of its being correct: for the manor and church of Aston were given by Adelia, queen to King Henry I., to the abbot and monks of Reading, and continued in their possession till the general dissolution. Chauncy's Antiq. of Hertfordshire, p. 350. Ed. Lond. 1700." Jenkyns.]

ner denieth the receipt thereof. Therefore eftsoons I desire you, to the intent so charitable a deed be not hindered, nor the young woman defrauded of her right, that the said xx^li. may be delivered unto the said David Hutton, that thereby he, according both to his office, trust, and fidelity to him committed, may as well foresee the performance of the said legacy, as also provide for the safe custody of the same sum against such time it may be due to be paid.

---

## LXXXVIII. TO CRUMWELL.[1]

State Paper Office, Miscellaneous Letters. Temp. Hen. VIII. Third series. Vol. IX. Original holograph. Todd's Life of Cranmer, Vol. I. p. 148.

In my right hearty manner I commend me unto you: certifying you, that to accomplish the king's commandment I shall send unto you Mr Heth[2] to-morrow, which for his learning, wisdom, discretion, and sincere mind towards his prince, I know no man in my judgment more meet to serve the king's highness' purpose: yet for many other considerations I know no man more unable to appoint himself to the king's honour than he; for he lacketh apparel, horses, plate, money, and all things convenient for such a journey; he hath also no benefice, nor no promotion towards the bearing of his charges. And as you know I am in great necessity, and not able to help him, in all these things I know no remedy, unless it please the king's highness to furnish him of all things necessary to his voyage, and moreover to allow him such a diet, whereof alone he may maintain his room and office to the king's honour. Wherein I beseech you to persuade the king's highness in my name, adding thereunto all the help that you may do also. And as for his acquaintance with the king's great cause, I know no man in England can defend it better than he. Nevertheless I pray you send him again to me, that we may confer it together once again, before he depart hence. Thus our Lord have you in his preservation! From my manor at Otford the 5th day of January.

Your own assured

Thomas Cantuar.

*To mine especial and singular good friend, Master Cromewell.*

---

[[1] The following are Dr Jenkyns' remarks upon this letter; (Remains of Abp. Cranmer, Vol. I. p. 86.) "Mr Todd considers this letter to refer to an embassy from England to the German princes assembled at Smalcald in Dec. 1535, in which Heath was associated with Fox, bishop of Hereford, and Dr Barnes. (Life of Cranmer, Vol. I. p. 147.) But the object of that mission was the formation of a protestant league against the pope, rather than the defence of the king's marriage to Anne Boleyn; which was manifestly the 'great cause' now to be maintained. The letter seems also to have been addressed to Crumwell before he was secretary of state; and if so, must have been written in January, 1534. (See State Papers, Vol. I. p. 425, note.) And it is clear from the language of Letter CLII. that Heath filled some diplomatic situation on the continent before June 1535. He may perhaps have succeeded archdeacon Hawkyns at the court of the emperor Charles V. early in 1534; or he may have been sent to a meeting of the German reformers held at Nuremberg in May of the same year; (when, according to Seckendorf, an attempt was made on the part of Hen. VIII. to obtain their approbation of his divorce;) or he may have been employed on both these services. Upon the whole, the most probable date of the letter appears to be 1534." Vid. Letter XIV. p. 247. *n.* 8. Seckendorf, Comment. de Lutheran et Reformat. pp. 75, 111. Ed. Francof. et Lips. 1692. Lib. III. § xxvi. (8.) and § xxxix. Add. (d) and (e).]

[[2] Vid. Confutation of unwritten Verities, p. 66. Under Elizabeth, "Heath lived, after a little trouble, quietly and nobly in his own lordship of Cobham, situate in Surrey. He was always honourably esteemed by the queen, and sometimes had the honour to be visited by her majesty." Strype's Annals, Vol. I. p. 212. Ed. Oxon. 1824. Melancthon, who became acquainted with him at the conferences at Smalcald, thus speaks of him: "Unus Nicolaus Hethus Archidiaconus humanitate et literis excellit inter hospites nostros. Ceteri ἄγευστοι ἡμετέρας φιλοσοφίας καὶ γλυκύτητος, nostræ philosophiæ et dulcedinis incapaces; ideo conversationem eorum fugio, quantum possum." Seckendorf, Comment. de Lutheran. et Reformat. Lib. III. § xxxix. Add. (e.) p. 111. See also Wood's Athen. Oxon. Vol. I. col. 603, 4. Ed. Lond. 1691. Fuller's Church Hist. Vol. IV. Book VIII. Sect. ii. § 19. p. 191. Ed. Oxon. 1815.]

## LXXXIX. TO CRUMWELL.

State Paper Office, Miscellaneous Letters. Temp. Hen. VIII. Third series. Vol. IX. Original holograph.

RIGHT worshipful master Crumwell, in my hearty manner I commend me to you. So it is that at my late being at Ford, it was brought to my notice and knowledge, that the monk Dering[3] hath lately compiled and made (sithens the first time that Mr Henry Golde[4] came to be examined before me) a certain treaty *de Duplice Spiritu*, in which mention is made, as well for the defence of the nun's revelations, as for the soluting of my reasons made unto the said Golde. Whereupon I have diligently examined the said Dering, which hath confessed that he hath made such a book, but he will in no wise be known where it is, saying that he hath burned the same. That notwithstanding, I have caused him to write the whole effect (as he saith it is) of the same book, the copy whereof I have sent unto you sealed, which is a very minute thing, in respect of the same book which was first made, as it is thought. And therefore I pray you to take the pains to examine the said Golde, and such other of his adherents, as ye shall think most meet to be examined in this matter; whether he or they, or any of them do know of any such book, or have seen or heard of any such or not; and at your convenient leisure to ascertain me of his and their sayings in this behalf, and of all such other comperts as you shall by the same your examination try and search out. For the person, by whom I came to the knowledge hereof, hath informed me, that the book was delivered unto the said Golde, and that he thinketh that Golde hath it still in his custody: wherefore I do think it very expedient that some good and politic mean be made for the trial and search of the verity in the premises betimes, without tract or delay, praying you that it may be so. From Otford, the 6th day of January, [1534.]

Your own assured ever

THOMAS CANTUAR.

*To the right worshipful and his very loving friend Mr Crumwell, of the king's grace's most honourable council.*

---

## XC. TO JOHN BUTLER[5].

Harl. MSS. 6148. f. 18. British Museum. Copy.

I COMMEND me to you: willing you that ye shall nothing do touching my visitation in those parties at Calice, until ye shall farther know of my mind therein; but such diligent inquisition as shall lie in you to make for the trial and truth of the matrimony between Frauneeis Hastynges and his pretended wife, I will that ye shall use and make; and especially to learn and know, how and for what cause the first matrimony between Davison and the said pretended wife of Hastynges was dissolved, and of the premises to ascertain me, with as good speed as ye may therein conveniently use. This done, ye shall afterwards know farther of my mind touching the same. Albeit in the mean time, if Davison be dwelling or commorant within my jurisdiction there, ye shall call and convent him and the other two personages afore you; and first examine the former contract: which done, ye shall much the sooner come to the verity and truth of the second. But in case the said Davison be in England, or in any place out of my jurisdiction, I will then that, upon knowledge had of the certainty where he is, ye shall either write your letters to the ordinary there, and to him intimate the very fact and merit of the same matter, (as far as ye do know in it,) and to desire him in my name to examine the said Davison herein, and to transmit unto you the copies of the same examination for your information and instruction in that behalf; or else shall advertise and advise the said

---

[3 Vid. Letter LXXXII. p. 272.]

[4 "Henry Golde took upon him to be interpreter between Elizabeth Barton, and one of the pope's orators, named Anthonye Pullyon."..."And the said Henry Gold over this, actually travelled and made relation thereof to the lady Katharyne, princess dowager, to animate her to make commotion in this realm against our sovereign lord." Stat. 25 Hen. VIII. cap. 12.]

[5 Vid. Letter LXXXV. p. 275.]

Frauncis Hastynges and his pretended wife to be contented that the matter may be examined where the said Davison doth dwell. And in this behalf I require you to use such diligence and industry as shall beseem you to use, as well for the due trial and truth in the premises, as for your certificate unto me in the same. From Otford, the xiiith day of the month of January.

*To master Butler, my Commissary at Calice.*

---

## XCI. TO THE RECTOR OF PETWORTH.

Harl. MSS. 6148. f. 42. Copy.

In my right hearty wise I commend me unto you. So it is, as I am informed, that one John Bower[1], now farmer of your parsonage of Petewourth, doth therein enjoy a lease of yours, which by reason when it shall happen to be expired, the same much doubteth, lest that at the end and term of the same he be clearly avoided thereof, by some other suit, to his no little both damage and hinderance, being now so furnished and settled therein: I require you at this my instance, ye will not alonely renew to him his said lease from time to time, but also to suffer to continue therein all such covenants as hath been hitherto observed between you. And in thus doing I will shew unto you like pleasure, when you shall reasonably require the same. From Lameth the viiith day of February.

---

## XCII. TO ———

Harl. MSS. 6148. f. 42. Copy.

I commend me unto you. And where it is so, that through a controversy, lately begun between you and divers of your parochinars, for certain tithe which you now challenge of them by the course of the law, and so thereby constrained, they have sued unto me for a more quiet end in that behalf: my pleasure is therefore, that you stay your said suit in attempting the law any further against them, until such time that I myself being in those parts may hear the due examination hereof; which I suppose will not be prejudicial either to you or them, but rather most quiet for all parties at length. From Lameheth, the viii. day of February.

---

## XCIII. TO THE PRIORESS OF STANFELD[2].

Harl. MSS. 6148. f. 42. Copy.

Sister prioress, I do right heartily commend me unto you. Where it is so that the vicar of Quadring is contented, for the love and favour he beareth unto this bearer, master Nicholas Robertes, my old acquaintance, to resign unto the same his vicarage, if so that he might obtain your good will thereunto: these shall be therefore heartily to desire and require you, that he may herein obtain your convenient favour, and that the rather at this instance and request. And if there be any like pleasure that I may do for you, I will be always ready to accomplish your requests accordingly. The xiiii. day of February.

---

## XCIV. TO THE PARSON OF CHEVENING[3].

Harl. MSS. 6148. f. 42. Copy.

I commend me unto you. And where it is so that one Asleyne Durmeryght, wife unto John Durmeryght, of your parish of Chevening, hath complained to me of the

---

[[1] John Bowyar was seneschal of the rectory lands of Petworth, and Thomas Maundvyld was rector. Vid. Valor Ecclesiasticus, 1535.]

[[2] Stanfeld in Lincolnshire, a Benedictine nunnery. The church of Quadring in the same county was appropriated to it in the reign of Richard II. Tanner's Not. Monast. Lincoln. lxxi. Stanfeld. Ed. Lond. 1787.]

[[3] R. Astall. Vid. Letter LVII. p. 260.]

unjust and uncharitable demeanour of her said husband, for his unreasonable and oft beating and cruel threatening of her, as in that behalf somewhat I perceive like to be true, by reason both parties hath been examined with me: I will therefore that you from henceforward see that there be a reformation had between them; and that when any such breaches hereafter shall happen in this behalf, according to your both duty and discretion, ye set a charitable end between them: and if he or she do refuse to apply unto your such directions, as you shall think convenient at any time, ye then do advertise me thereof accordingly. From Croydon, &c.

*To the parson of Chevenyng.*

---

## XCV. TO THE BISHOP OF ROCHESTER[4].

My lord, in my right hearty wise I commend me unto you: and so likewise desire the same, that whereas one master Devenyshe[5], master of art and my kinsman, is very desirous (for his better information and knowledge in divinity) to continue his study and learning at the university, to be so good lord unto him at this mine instance and request, that the same may obtain your convenient favour to be admitted one of the fellows of St John's college in Cambridge, amongst whom (as I am advertised) there is now a room void and at your disposition: whereunto if your lordship do admit him, I doubt nothing at all but that you shall like the man every day better than other; for verily I think he lacketh not of those qualities which should become any honest man to have, over and besides the gift of nature wherewith God hath above the common rate endued him, as I trust the master of the college, this bearer, can more expressly ascertain your said lordship in that behalf. And if there be any like pleasure that I may shew unto you therefore, I will be at all times ready to accomplish the same to my power; as knoweth our Lord, who keep your good lordship in health. From, &c.

Harl. MSS. 6148. f. 42, b. Copy.

*To my lord of Rochester.*

---

## XCVI. TO THE WARDEN[6] OF ALL SOULS' COLLEGE, OXFORD.

Master warden, in my right hearty wise I commend me unto you. And where at your last being with me at Lameheth I desired your good will in a farm of yours, the name whereof at that time I could not readily call unto my remembrance; so it is, as I am advertised, that the same is named Les Wydon in Northamptonshire[7]: which forasmuch as the years and term thereof shall be shortly expired, I heartily require you, that at this mine instance and request ye will, as effectually as you may, move the rest of your company to accomplish this my said suit, so that by yours and their agreement I may obtain the next lease that shall be granted in that behalf for a special friend of mine, paying in every condition as much as any other reasonably will give for the same; for the which I will at all times be ready to shew both to you and them like pleasure accordingly, &c.

Harl. MSS. 6148. f. 42, b. Copy.

*To the warden of All Souls' college in Oxford.*

---

[4 This letter was probably written to John Fisher, bishop of Rochester, aad chancellor of the university of Cambridge, early in 1534, before his imprisonment for refusing to take the oath of succession. He had been confessor to Margaret, mother of Hen. VII. and is supposed to have suggested to her the foundation of St John's and Christ's colleges.]

[5 Perhaps William Devenish, afterwards prebendary of Canterbury, who, having married, was deprived under queen Mary. Le Neve's Fasti, p. 17. Ed. Lond. 1716.]

[6 Roger Stokeley; elected the 10th of March 1533, resigned in 1536. Wood's History of Oxford. Vol. III. p. 269. Ed. (Gutch.) Oxon. 1786.]

[7 Lois Weedon, near Towcester.]

## XCVII. TO THE INHABITANTS OF HADLEIGH.

Harl. MSS. 6148. f. 1. Copy.

In my right hearty wise I commend me unto you. And sorry I am to hear there is lack of charity, and also be many grudges amongst you, you all being christian men, which should be of such charity and unity as if ye were but one body. And to the intent ye should be so, and that ye should the rather be induced to concord, and specially against this good time[1], I have desired this bearer, master Hughe Vaghan, to take the pain to come unto you now with these my letters, and to exhort you all in my name and on my behalf, and most specially in the name of our Lord, that you and every of you put away such grudges[2] as ye have one against another, and become lovers together as children of God ought to do: (for whosoever is out of charity, do what he will, it is not acceptable in the sight of God; and how can he love God that hateth his christian brother, which is the creature of God?) so to continue in charity here in this world together as the sons of one Father, our Lord in heaven, that ye may be beloved of him after in heaven.

And where sir Thomas Ros[3], your curate, hath been before me for these words, which (as it is surmised) he spake in the pulpit there, here following: "A man's goods spent for his soul after his death prevaileth him not:" forasmuch as I am credibly informed that no small number of you which were present at that sermon when these words were spoken, (as it is pretended,) doth affirm that he said not so, but these: "That a man's goods, given out of charity, and so the child of damnation, spent after his death shall not prevail his soul:" and forasmuch as I understand that your said curate, as soon as he heard that such matters was surmised against him by such as have not been his friends and favourers heretofore, (as I am also credibly informed,) went into the pulpit and declared, that he neither said, neither meant those words but of such as died out of charity and was buried in hell, as the rich glutton was in the gospel, of which he treated when those words were spoken, and also to the intent that the more charity should continue among you:

I have sent the said curate to you again, desiring you which have not been his friends heretofore to leave your grudges, and you all to accept him favourably, the rather for this my writing. Not intending hereby, but if you or any of you shall have just cause against him hereafter, [you] shall and may prosecute the same according to justice; for it is not mine intent in any wise hereby to let justice, if it be justly prosecuted without great and probable suspicion of malice and calumnious accusation. And if any of you shall have at any time hereafter any just cause to sue afore me, ye shall be sure of such favour as I may lawfully shew unto you. At Lameth, the xx[ti]. day of March.

*To my well-beloved the inhabitants of*
*Hadleghe.*

---

[1 i.e. the season of Easter.]

[2 For a narrative of the disturbances at Hadleigh, vid. "the story of Thomas Rose," Foxe's Acts and Monuments, pp. 2082, et sqq. Ed. Lond. 1583.]

[3 Sir Thomas Rose was arrested A.D. 1533, by the sergeant at arms at the instigation of Walter and John Clerke, by whom he was charged with having been "privy of the burning of the rood of Dover court," but he was set at liberty by archbishop Cranmer's means; "but yet so, that he was bounden not to come within twenty miles of Hadleigh. After this he came to London, and there preached the gospel half a year, till Hadleigh men, hearing thereof, laboured to have him to Hadleigh again; and indeed by means of Sir John Rainford, knight, obtained at the archbishop's house to have him thither. Howbeit, by means one was placed in the cure at Hadleigh, he could not enjoy his office again there, but went to Stratford three miles off, and there continued in preaching the word three years; till at length the adversaries procured an inhibition from the bishop of Norwich, to put him to silence."—Foxe's Acts and Monuments, p. 2083. Ed. Lond. 1583. Strype's Mem. of Abp. Cranmer, Vol. I. pp. 395, 6. Ed. Oxon. 1840. Sir Thomas Rose was afterwards recommended by Abp. Cranmer in a letter to Cecil, dated 25th August, 1552, (q. v.) with others as a fit person for an Irish archbishoprick.]

## XCVIII. TO THE ARCHBISHOP OF YORK[4].

Harl. MSS. 6148. f. 21. b. Copy.

MY lord, in my right hearty wise I commend me unto you. And where at the[5] last day of the late convocation kept at Paul's in London, many questions and doubts were

---

[[4] Edward Lee.]

[[5] i.e. The 31st of March 1534. "The general sentence was a solemn curse to be denounced by the curates to their parishes once a quarter: wherein a great number of persons were wont to be accursed; and a large share of these execrations were framed to fall upon those that infringed the privileges and immunities of holy church, or that deprived it of any of its rights or dues."—Strype's Eccl. Mem. Vol. I. p. 253, Part. ii. No. xlvi. pp. 188—193. Ed. Oxon. 1822. Wilkins' Concilia, Vol. III. pp. 760, 70. Ed. Lond. 1737. Wake's State of the Church, p. 479. Ed. Lond. 1703. The following is the form used on these occasions.

*The general sentence, or curse: used to be read to the people four times in the year. Taken out of the Festival, printed by Wynkyn de Worde,* 1532:—

The Festival.

GOOD men and women, I do you to understand, that we that have the cure of your souls been commanded of our ordinaries, and by the constitutions and the law of holy church, to shew to you four times in the year, in each quarter of the year once, when the people is most plenary in holy church, the articles of the sentence of cursing: so that none for our default, neither man nor woman, fall therein; and if any be fallen therein, that he may through the help of Almighty God, and all holy church, with shrift and penance making good for his sin, rise up and him amend. Wherefore I do you to understand, that cursing is such vengeance-taking, that it departeth a man from the bliss of heaven, from housel, shrift, and all the sacraments of holy church, and betake him to the devil, and to the pains of hell, the which shall endure perpetually without end, but if he have grace of our Lord him to amend. But therefore see that no man or woman say, that I curse them; for it longeth not to me, but for to shew the points and the articles of the sentence of cursing. For I do you well to wit, that whoso doth against any of these points, that I shall shew you, he is accursed in the deed doing, of the pope, archbishop, bishop, and of all holy church: and that God Almighty give you grace for to keep you out of cursing, listen and hear, and I shall, through the help of God, Father Almighty, to you then tell and shew.

By the authority of God, the Son, and the Holy Ghost, and his glorious mother and maiden, our lady Saint Mary: and the blessed apostles Peter, and Paul, and all the apostles, martyrs, confessors, and virgins, and all the hallows of God, I denounce and shew for accursed all those that the franchise of holy church break or distrouble, or are against the state of holy church, or thereto assent with deed or counsel. And also all those that deprive holy church of any right to make of holy church any lay fee, that is hallowed or sanctified. And also all those that withhold the rights of holy church, that is to say, offerings, tithes, rents, or freedoms of holy church, let or distrouble, or break: that is to say, if any man flee to church, or churchyard, whoso him outdraw, and all those that thereto procure or assent. And all those that purchaseth letters of any lord's court, wherefore letting is made in christian court, that process of right may not be determined or ended. And all those that the peace of the land distrouble. And all those that blood draw of man or of woman in violence, or in villany make to be drawn, in church or in churchyard, wherefore the church or the churchyard is interdicted or suspended. And all those that be against the right of our sovereign lord the king. And all those that war sustain against the king wrongfully. And all those that are common robbers, revers, or manslayers, but it be in themselves defending. And all those that be against the great charter of the king that is confirmed of the court of Rome. And all those that false witness bear wrongfully: namely in cause of matrimony, in what court soever it be or out of court. And all those that false witness bring forth in right of matrimony, for to distrouble man or woman; or for to disherit any man of lands or tenements, or any other cattle. And all false advocates, that for meed put forth any false exceptions, or quarrels, through the which the right of matrimony is foredone, or any other manner of right instead of judgment. And all those that for meed or favour maliciously man or woman bringeth out of their good fame into wicked; or make them for to lose their worldly goods or honour, or them put wrongfully to their purgation, of the which was no fame nor renown known before that time. And also all those that maliciously, and through cawtel or guile, distrouble, letteth, or gainsayeth the right presentment of our mother holy church militant here in earth, thereas the very patron should be present; and all that thereto procure with word or deed, or with false conquest, or with other power. And all those that maliciously despise the commandment of the king, or take a cursed man from the time that he hath lain in cursing forty days, and will seek for no remedy. And all those, that prisoners distrouble with false judgment, or false inquest; and all those, that their deliverance purchase against the right of holy church. And all those that take meed for to distrouble peace, there love should be, and charity, or strife maintain with words or deeds, or till they have yielded again their meed, that they take of them, they may never be assailed; and all those that hold houses, manors, granges of parsons, vicars, or of any other man of holy church against their will. And all those that any manner of moveable good, or unmoveable, away bear with strength, or wrongfully away draw or waste: of the which cursing they may not be assoiled, till they have made satisfaction unto whom the wrong is done. And all those that any manner of goods with violence or malice bear out of holy church sted or abbey, or house of religion, which that therein is laid or done for warandyse or succour, or for to be kept: and all those which that thereto procure or assent. And all those that them maintain or sustain. And all those that have laid hand on priest or clerk with malice, but it be by himself defending. And all those that give counsel to Saracenes, or help them against Christendom. And all those that their chil-

moved of the reading and declaration of the general sentence commonly used at four terms of the year; and after much communication and debatements of great arguments and reasons therein made and had, it was at the last, by the counsels of our whole house, condescended and agreed, that the reading of the same general sentence should be for a time suspended and stayed, until some other direction may be therein further taken and provided, (which, as I suppose, cannot be conveniently done before the next assembly of bishops and prelates of my province the next convocation;) and that I should by my letters speedily advertise your lordship of the premises, to the intent it may please you to cause general monitions to be made within your province, that the said general sentence be no more read or declared until some other direction may be further taken therein: I therefore pray you, my lord, that, forasmuch as it shall be meet and convenient that one conformity be used in your province and mine, specially touching the said general sentence, that the declaration and reading of the same may be respited, until some other direction may be hereafter further taken in that behalf. And how ye shall be minded therein, I pray you that I may be ascertained by your letters as soon as you may. [1534.]

---

dren wrongfully father wittingly, or their children witting any other man with malice. And all those that vary or slay their generations, or their children destroy with drinks, or with any other craft. And all those that make false money, or thereto be assenting. And all those that good money clip or shear, them to advantage to deceive any man with. And all those that false the pope's bull, or counterfeit the king's seal. And all those that buy or sell with false measures or false weights: that is to say, to buy with one and to sell with another. And all those that false the king's standard themself witting. And all those that any testament distrouble, or thereto procure with word or with deed, wherefore the deed's will is not fulfilled. And all those that forswear them upon the holy dome, willing and witting, for meed or for hate, for to do any man or woman to lose their worldly goods or honour. And all robbers or revers, openly or privily, by day or by night, or any man's good steal, wherefore they were worthy for to have judgment. And all those that withhold any man's good, that have been spired thrice in holy church themself witting. And all those that distrouble the peace of holy church, or of the land, and all the king's felons. And all those that them maintain. And all false conspirators, and all false forswearers in assizes, or in any other court. And all those that any false plaints put forth against the franchise of holy church, or of the king, or of the realm. And all those offerings that are offered in holy church or in churchyard or chapel, or in oratory, or in any other stead within the province of Canterbury, withholden, or put away in any other place against the will of the parson or vicar, or their attorney in the parish that it is offered in. And all those that their goods away give for dread of death, in fraud of holy church, or to forbear their debts paying. And all those that such gifts take, or thereto help or counsel. And all those that let prelates or ordinaries for to hold consistory, session, or chapters, for to inquire of sins, and of excess, in good amendment of man's soul. And all witches, and all that on them believe. And all heretics that believe not in the sacrament of the altar, that is God's own body in flesh and blood in form of bread, and other sacraments that toucheth help of man's soul. And all jugglers and usurers: that is to say, that if any man or woman lend they cattle to man or woman for any advantage to take by covenant more or less than their own: and if there be any such found in town or city, the city or the town should be interdicted by the old law, and neither do their mass, nor sacrament ministered, till he were out thereof. And all that withhold tithes, or withdraw their tithes wittingly or maliciously, to the harm of holy church; or tithes let to be given of all the goods which they be commanded, and ordained to be given by the law of holy church, that is to say, of all fruits of herds, corns, herbs, the ware, fruits of trees, of all manner of beasts that are newing, of wool, lamb, and cheese, in time of the year of swans, geese, doves, ducks, of bees, honey, wax, of hay, as often as it is neweth, of flax, of hemp, of wind-mills, or all manner of mills, of all manner of merchandise of chaffering men and of men of craft. And all those that maliciously or wittingly any of these things, or any other withhold, the which ought to be given to holy church by God's law, to the harm of holy church, and all that thereto procure in word or in deed.

*Modus fulminandi sententiam.*

Prælatus alba indutus cum ceteris sacerdotibus in ecclesia existentibus, cruce erecta, candelis accensis, stans in pulpito, pronunciet verba quæ sequuntur:

Ex auctoritate Dei Patris Omnipotentis et beatæ Mariæ virginis et omnium sanctorum, excommunicamus, anathematizamus, et diabolo commendamus, omnes supra dictos malefactores, ut excommunicati sint, anathematizati, et diabolo commendati: maledicti sint in villis, in campis, in viis, in semitis, in domibus, extra domos, et in omnibus aliis locis, stando, sedendo, jacendo, surgendo, ambulando, currendo, vigilando, dormiendo, comedendo, bibendo, et aliud opus faciendo; et illos a luminibus et omnibus bonis ecclesiæ sequestramus, et diabolo damnamus, et in pœnis inferni animas eorum extinguamus, sicut extinguitur ista candela; nisi resipiscant et ad satisfactionem veniant.

Finita sententia, extinguat lumen ad terrorem, pulsantibus campanis.]

## XCIX. TO ——[1].

....I therefore will you to cause general monitions to be made within the diocese of Sarum, that the said general sentence may be no more read or declared, until some other direction may be further taken as aforesaid; and that ye ascertain me as soon as ye may conveniently, with speed, of your doings in the premises. From Croydon, the iv. day of April. [1534.] Harl. MSS. 6148. f. 21. b. Copy.

## C. TO A BISHOP.

*The copy of an Inhibition sent by my lord of Canterbury unto other for seditious preaching begun in Easter week*[2] *concerning the king's grace's marriage, in Anno Regni xxv°. H. VIII.* [1534.][3]

In my right hearty wise I commend me unto you: letting you wit, that forasmuch as it hath come to my knowledge, that divers persons at this present time, under the pretence of preaching to the people the word of God, which is the word of charity, unity, and concord, do minister unto their audience matter of contention, slander, debate, and murmur, as well concerning the true catholic doctrine of Christ's church, as also other public matters, nothing meet ne convenient for their audience; and I therefore, calling unto me my right well-beloved brothers in God, the bishops of London[4], Winchester[5], and Lincoln[6], have, for speedy remedy hereof, devised and agreed with my said brothers, that an inhibition should be incontinently sent forth from every one of us in our diocese, to forbid all such as have already licence to preach by any letter heretofore granted unto them, to preach from henceforth by virtue and authority of any such letters, but that they shall resort to every of us in our diocese to obtain new letters and licence concerning the same: and also all curates authorised by the law to preach in their own parish churches shall, if they be disposed to preach, first resort unto us in like manner; so as at such time as they shall repair to us or our officers for any such licence, injunction shall be made unto them to have regard and respect in their preaching to the Constitution Provincial, in the title there *De Hæreticis*, in the first chapter, that is to say, that they shall temper their matter *secundum subjectum auditorum;* and in no wise to touch or intermeddle themselves to preach or teach any such thing that might slander or bring in doubt and opinion the catholic and received doctrine of Christ's church, or speak of such matters as touch the prince, his laws, or succession; considering that thereupon can ensue no edification in the people, but rather occasion of talking and rumour to their great hurt and damage, and the danger and perils of their bodies and souls: Wherefore, in consideration of the premises, I require you and pray you to follow the said order, as well sending forth speedy monition or inhibition, as also in giving instruction of such your curates as intend to preach, and other such as ye shall Harl. MSS. 6148. f. 20. Copy.

[1 Dr Jenkyns says of this letter, that Strype supposes it was addressed to the bishop of Sarum: but in April 1534, which from the reference to the resolution respecting the General Sentence is clearly its date, there was no bishop of that see; Cardinal Campegio having been recently deprived by act of parliament, and his successor, Nicholas Shaxton, not being yet elected; and that it must therefore have been written to some one who administered the diocese during the vacancy.—Remains of Abp. Cranmer, Vol. I. p. 97. *n*. d.]

[2 The Easter-day of 25 Hen. VIII. was the 5th of April, 1534. Ibid.]

[3 "After the archbishop's sentence against queen Katharine and confirmation of queen Ann's marriage," A. D. 1533, "he forbad all preaching throughout his diocese, and warned the rest of the bishops throughout England to do the same,...but only for a time".... "it being thought convenient that preaching at this juncture should be restrained, because now the matter of sermons chiefly consisted in tossing about the king's marriage with the lady Anne, and condemning so publicly and boldly his doings against queen Katharine; the priests being set on work by her friends and faction."—Strype's Mem. of Abp. Cranmer, Vol. I. p. 30. Ed. Oxon. 1840. The preaching friars were invariably on the side of queen Katharine. Vid. Strype's Eccl. Mem. Vol. I. p. 357. Ed. Oxon. 1822.]

[4 John Stokesley.]

[5 Stephen Gardiner.]

[6 John Longland.]

afterward admit by yourself or by your trusty officers, as is afore written, having such respect to the execution hereof, as will satisfy the duty of your office in the sight of God and man[1]. Whereunto ye will, I doubt not, have such regard at all time as becometh you. Thus, my lord, most heartily fare you well. At my manor of Lameth.

## CI. TO THE PRIORESS OF STANFELD.

Harl. MSS. 6148. f. 19. Copy.

SISTER prioress, in my right hearty wise I commend me unto you, and likewise to the other my sisters of your convent. And where, at my request and instance to you made in my other letters[2] in the favour of my friend Mr N. R. for his preferment to the vicarage of Quadring, ye, according to the effect and tenor thereof, have accomplished the same, as now in that behalf I am advertised by your letters dated the first day of April; I give unto you most hearty and condign thanks therefore, trusting the said Mr Roberts, according to my letters to him addressed for the same, will in such manner be conformable and agreeable to all ordinances and customs as hath been heretofore used by his predecessors for the quietness of you and your house, that ye shall have cause to be glad to have preferred him for my sake. The which if I perceive to happen in him the contrary, surely he shall both lose my favour and be in danger of my displeasure therefore: and you notwithstanding to be sure of me to requite and recompense this your gratuity and gentle behaviour accordingly. From Lamehe.

*To the prioress of Stanfeld.*

## CII. TO N. ROBERTS.

Harl. MSS. 6148. f. 19. Copy.

I COMMEND me unto you. And where at my request and instance the prioress and convent of Stanfeld hath given to you the presentation of Quadring, as according to their letters to me addressed in that behalf I am credibly informed, wherein they have desired me also to exhort you to be content with the same, observing such laudable customs as the late incumbent and other his predecessors hath done, without further trouble, vexation, or unquietness to them or their house; these shall be therefore likewise to admonish you herein, (as ye tender my favour and will avoid my displeasure,) that according to this their reasonable request you do so endeavour yourself from time to time to accomplish the same, that they have not just cause to repent hereafter of this their benevolence declared unto you, which to happen would be unto me great displeasure, but much more your hinderance in so doing, &c.

## CIII. TO THE PRIORESS OF SHEPPEY.

Harl. MSS. 6148. f. 39. b. Copy.

SISTER prioress, I greet you well. And forasmuch as I understand by my servant Thomas Abberforde, that the farm of your parsonage of Gillyngham is shortly like to be void, of which (as he reporteth) you aforetime promised him the next avoidance; I require you, that now, the rather of this mine instance, ye will let him have the preferment thereunto, he finding you sufficient sureties for the payment thereof. And what you intend to do in this behalf I require you to advertise me by my secretary, whom I send unto you for that intent. And if you will accomplish mine request herein, I will at all time be as good unto you in other matters, wherein you shall have to do with me.

[[1] The order for the regulation of preaching, issued in June, 1534, will be found in the Appendix.]

[[2] See Letter XCIII. p. 278.]

## CIV. TO THE PRIORESS OF SHEPPEY.

SISTER prioress, I commend me unto you. Where heretofore I wrote unto you my letters in the favour of my servant T. Abberforde, for the lease of your farm at Gillyngham, whereof ye have aforetime (as I am credibly informed) made unto him a promise, as honest witness examined by mine officers in that matter have affirmed; I pray you that ye will now at his coming to you, not alonely finish and accomplish your said former promise, but also for my sake to shew him such other favour therein, as ye may shew lawfully; whereby ye shall minister unto me right good cause and occasion to tender as much your desire another time, when ye shall any thing reasonably desire of me. And how ye shall be minded herein, I pray you that I may be ascertained by your letters at the return of my servant. And where my said servant hath further informed me, that ye, at his last being with you to know your mind to my former letters, answered him that ye would right gladly satisfy my request herein, if I would affirm and say that ye may thus do justly without any dishonesty; I assure you I do not see how ye may better save and conserve your honesty in this matter, than to accomplish your promise in the same made, whereof is good record and testimony. And if you will otherwise do, ye should by so doing cumber your conscience and dishonest yourself much. And albeit I do trust verily........[3]

Harl. MSS. 6148. f. 19. b. Copy.

*To the prioress of Sheppey.*

---

## CV. TO CRUMWELL.

RIGHT worshipful master Crumwell, after most hearty commendations, &c. I doubt not but you do right well remember, that my lord of Rochester and master More[4] were contented to be sworn to the Act of the king's succession[5], but not to the preamble

Cott. MSS. Cleop. E. vi. f. 181. Original holograph. British Museum. Harl. MSS. 283. f. 120. Copy. Strype's Mem. of Abp. Cranmer, App. No. xi. Vol. II. pp. 693, 4. Ed. Oxon. 1840.

---

[3 The copy of this letter was left unfinished.]

[4 Fisher, Bishop of Rochester, and Sir Thomas More, refused to take the preamble of the oath of succession before Cranmer and other commissioners, April, 13, 1534. Strype's Mem. of Abp. Cranmer, Vol. I. pp. 36—8; Burnet's Reformat. Vol. I. p. 315. Ed. Oxon. 1829.]

[5 Stat. 25. Hen. VIII. cap. 22. in the Statute Book, 34. in the Record, 26. in the Journal. The following is the substance of the preamble of the act.—"The distractions that had been in England about the succession to the crown, which had occasioned the effusion of much blood, with many other mischiefs, all which flowed from the want of a clear decision of the true title, from which the popes had usurped a power of investing such as pleased them in other princes' kingdoms, and princes had often maintained such donations for their other ends; therefore, to avoid the like inconveniencies, the king's former marriage with the princess Katharine is judged contrary to the laws of God, and void, and of no effect; and the sentence passed by the Archbishop of Canterbury, annulling it, is confirmed, and the lady Katharine is thenceforth to be reputed only princess dowager, and not queen, and the marriage with queen Ann is established and confirmed: and marriages within the degrees prohibited by Moses (which are enumerated in the statute) are declared to be unlawful, according to the judgment of the convocations of this realm, and of the most famous universities, and learned men abroad, any dispensations to the contrary notwithstanding, which are also declared null, since contrary to the laws of God; and all that were married within these degrees are appointed to be divorced, and the children begotten in such marriages were declared illegitimate: and all the issue that should be between the king and the present queen is declared lawful, and the crown was to descend on his issue male by her, or any other wife; or in default of issue male, to the issue female by the queen; and in default of any such, to the right heirs of the king's highness for ever; and any that after the first of May should maliciously divulge any thing to the slander of the king's marriage, or of the issue begotten in it, were to be adjudged for misprision of treason, and to suffer imprisonment at the king's will, and forfeit all their goods and chattels to him; and if the queen outlived the king, she is declared regent till the issue by her were of age, if a son, eighteen, and if a daughter sixteen years of age; and all the king's subjects were to swear that they would maintain the contents of this act; and whoever, being required, did refuse it, was to be judged guilty of misprision of treason, and punished accordingly."—The oath, it seems, was likewise agreed on in the house of lords; for the form of it is set down in their Journal as follows:—"Ye shall swear to bear faith, truth, and obedience alonely to the king's majesty, and to his heirs of his body, of his most dear and entirely beloved lawful wife queen Ann begotten and to be begotten. And further, to the heirs of our said sovereign lord according to the limitation in the statute made for surety of his succession in the

of the same. What was the cause of their refusal thereof I am uncertain, and they would by no means express the same. Nevertheless it must needs be either the diminution of the authority of the bishop of Rome, or else the reprobation of the king's first pretensed matrimony. But if they do obstinately persist in their opinions of the preamble, yet meseemeth it should not be refused, if they will be sworn to the very act of succession; so that they will be sworn to maintain the same against all powers and potentates. For hereby shall be a great occasion to satisfy the princess dowager and the lady Mary, which do think they should damn their souls, if they should abandon and relinquish their estates. And not only it should stop the mouths of them, but also of the emperor, and other their friends, if they give as much credence to my lord of Rochester and master More, speaking or doing against them, as they hitherto have done and thought that all other should have done, when they spake and did with them. And peradventure it should be a good quietation to many other within this realm, if such men should say, that the succession, comprised within the said act, is good and according to God's laws: for then I think there is not one within this realm, that would once reclaim against it. And whereas divers persons, either of a wilfulness will not, or of an indurate and invertible conscience cannot, alter from their opinions of the king's first pretensed marriage, (wherein they have once said their minds, and percase have a persuasion in their heads, that if they should now vary therefrom, their fame and estimation were distained for ever,) or else of the authority of the bishop of Rome; yet if all the realm with one accord would apprehend the said succession, in my judgment it is a thing to be amplected and embraced. Which thing, although I trust surely in God that it shall be brought to pass, yet hereunto might not a little avail the consent and oaths of these two persons, the bishop of Rochester and master More, with their adherents, or rather confederates. And if the king's pleasure so were, their said oaths might be suppressed, but when and where his highness might take some commodity by the publishing of the same. Thus our Lord have you ever in his conservation. From my manor at Croydon, the xvii. day of April.

Your own assured ever,

THOMAS CANTUAR.

---

## CVI. TO CRUMWELL.

State Paper Office, Miscellaneous Letters. Temp. Hen. VIII. Third series. Vol. IX. Original holograph.

IN my most hearty wise I commend me unto you. And so likewise desire you to be good master unto this bearer, Robert Markeham, whom, for the good qualities I know in him, I heartily desire you in all his such suits and causes as the same hath now before you, to shew unto him your lawful favour, and that the rather at this mine instance. And what pleasure I may shew unto you for the same, ye shall be sure thereof accordingly. Thus our Lord preserve you. From Croydon, the xxvi[ti] day of April.

Your own assured,

THOMAS CANTUAR.

*To my especial and singular good friend,*
*Mr Crumwell.*

---

crown of this realm mentioned and contained, and not to any other within this realm, nor foreign authority or potentate. And in case any oath be made, or hath been made by you, to any person or persons, that then ye to repute the same as vain and annihilate. And that to your cunning, wit, and uttermost of your power, without guile, fraud, or other undue means, ye shall observe, keep, maintain, and defend the said act of succession, and all the whole effects and contents thereof, and all other acts and statutes made in confirmation, or for execution of the same, or of any thing therein contained. And this ye shall do against all manner of persons, of what estate, dignity, degree, or condition soever they be; and in no wise to do or attempt, nor to your power suffer to be done or attempted, directly or indirectly, any thing or things, privily or apartly, to the let, hinderance, damage, or derogation thereof, or of any part of the same, by any manner of means, or for any manner of pretence. So help you God, and all saints, and the holy evangelists."—Burnet's Hist. of Reformat. Vol. I. pp. 294—297.]

## CVII. TO CRUMWELL.

RIGHT worshipful Mr Crumwell, in my right hearty wise I commend me unto you. Likewise praying you to have in your good remembrance such suit as I heretofore, as well by mouth as writing, made unto you for my kinsman Henry Hatfilde, surveyor of my lands. So it is that, by agreement lately taken between him and the prebendar[ies] of Southwell, he shall exchange certain lands of his for certain lands in mortmain belonging to the said prebendaries. And amongst other things of the said agreement it is condescended, that the same my kinsman shall procure the said lands, which the said prebendaries shall have of him, to be mortmained by a certain day, for the same lands which he shall have of the said prebendaries out of mortmain. Wherefore I heartily pray you, that my said kinsman may have your favourable expedition as soon as it may be: for surely, unless the same lands which the said prebendaries shall have of my said kinsman may be mortmained afore the day shall be expired, the said agreement shall stand void, and much inquietness shall continue in these parties, as have continued already there this hundred years; whereof hath grown great occasion of manslaughter divers times, as well to my said kinsman's grandfather of his father's side, as to his grandfather of his mother's side, and to divers other: and it is to be feared, unless this agreement take effect now, that the same variance shall continue still, which God forbid. Wherefore I pray you to be his good master for the expedition of his suit, as my special trust is in you.

State Paper Office, Miscellaneous Letters. Temp. Hen. VIII. Third series. Vol. IX. Original.

Mr Roodd hath also been with me at Croydon, and there hath subscribed the book of the king's grace's succession, and also the conclusion "*quod Romanus Episcopus non habet majorem auctoritatem a Deo sibi collatam in hoc regno Angliæ quam quivis alius externus episcopus;*" and hath promised me, that he will at all times hereafter so conform himself as shall be always to the king's grace's contentation, and that he will at no time hereafter preach in any doubtful case, but that he will first counsel with me therein. Wherefore, if it may stand with the king's grace's pleasure, I would that he might have licence again to preach; wherein I pray you to know the king's grace's pleasure. From Croydon the 28th day of April[1].

Your assured ever,

THOMAS CANTUAR.

*To the right worshipful and my very loving friend, master Crumwell, of the king's grace's most honourable council.*

---

## CVIII. TO ———

IN my most hearty wise I commend me unto you. And forasmuch as I [am] credibly informed by this bearer, John Hutton, that the same hath a certain suit unto you; to whom for many considerations, as my friend, I owe as special favour as to any man else of his like state and degree; I heartily require you therefore, that he may for my sake obtain your lawful favour in such his said suits and requests, as in that behalf at this time shall be by him declared unto you: for the which, when it shall lie in me, I will likewise be ready to requite and recompense the same unto you accordingly.

Harl. MSS. 6148. f. 43. British Museum. Copy.

---

[[1] Dr Jenkyns thinks that "the mention of subscribing the book of the king's succession, proves that this letter could not have been written earlier than 1534. Yet Crumwell," he says, "is not addressed as secretary, though he was appointed to that office before the 12th of April of this year. See Note to State Papers, Vol. I. p. 425." He therefore supposes that in this case the evidence for the date derived from the address clearly fails; and has therefore disregarded it, as he has done in some other letters, where, in his opinion, there are reasons, though not so conclusive as in the present instance, for suspecting it. Remains of Abp. Cranmer, Vol. I. p. 104. *n.* q.]

## CIX. TO ———

Harl. MSS. 6148. f. 43. Copy.

In my hearty wise I commend me unto you. And so likewise desire you to be good to this bearer A. B. my friend, in all those his suits and requests as he hath now to do with you. He is the man whom for many considerations I do much favour, and would the best that lieth in me his preferment. Wherefore I heartily require you, at this mine instance the rather, to tender his said pursuits, and shew unto him such your lawful favour in this behalf as you would use towards me, in case I myself had the same now to practise with you.

## CX. TO ———

Harl. MSS. 6148. f. 43. Copy.

I commend me unto you. And where this bearer, Richard S., hath complained unto me, how that ye withhold from him an Enchiridion[1] in English, supposing the same to be of no good authority or privilege; I will that, forasmuch as the king and his council doth indifferently permit the said book to be read of all and singular his subjects, ye, without any farther let or perturbation to the said Richard, do either deliver unto him his said book, or else that ye repair unto me immediately after the sight hereof, to declare unto me some cause why you should thus detain from him the said Enchiridion, and so manifestly deny the authority of the same.

*For inhibiting of Enchiridion.*

## CXI. TO THE VICAR OF CHARING.

Harl. MSS. 6148. f. 43. Copy.

I commend me unto you, &c. And where I am advertised by this bearer, W. S., that ye have a suit against him in my commissary's court at Canterbury for a matter of defamation, the circumstances whereof he hath declared unto me; so it is that I perceive, as well by his behaviour as by his sorrowful words, that he is right repentant in misusing any such slanderous reports towards you, and so hath sued unto me for to instance you in like wise not to pursue any farther herein, to his no little damage and undoing, but charitably to remit his offence, and that the rather at this my request. I therefore advise you and also require you to be contented herewith, considering he is so willing to submit himself to you accordingly. Whereunto I do exhort you, for divers considerations, to cease all rigorous suit in the law, specially in this cumbrous time, and to receive him friendly unto you, forgiving all displeasure and grudges hitherto past; as according to the rule of charity ye be bound one to another. Which end no doubt shall both please greatly Almighty God, and also be very meritorious to you in accomplishing the same.

*To the Vicar of Charyng.*

## CXII. TO DR COCKS[2], HIS CHANCELLOR.

Harl. MSS. 6148. f. 43. b. Copy.

In my right hearty wise I commend me unto you. And whereas the bearer hereof hath been suspended, and, as he thinketh, further process made against him for a suit

[1 This might have been Tyndale's translation of Erasmus' Enchiridion Militis Christiani. Vid. Jortin's Life of Erasmus, Vol. II. p. 178. Ed. 1758—60. Ames, Typogr. Antiq. Dibdin, Vol. II. p. 235. Ed. Lond. 1810—19.]

[2 John Cocks, the Archbishop's Auditor of the Audience, and Vicar-General in spirituals. The archbishop left the discovery of mischief intended against him by his enemies, (A. D. 1543) to Cocks and Hussey; "but being secret favourers of the papists, they handled the matter so, that nothing would be disclosed and espied, but every thing colorably was hid."—Strype, Mem. of Abp. Cranmer, Vol. I. pp. 27, 130, 170, 172.]

of certain tithe that you demand of him before my commissary at Canterbury; and, as he reporteth unto me, hath been always conformable to agree with your deputies and farmer at Egerton, for such his duties as hath been customably required of him and other aforetime, until now of late, for certain things as meseemeth of small value, hath been sued at the law, whereby so constrained by rigour of the same, he sueth unto me for a more quiet and charitable end in this behalf: I therefore advise you and thereunto exhort you, considering such towardness in him, that, specially in this cumbrous world, ye do entreat and handle as well him as other your parishioners and neighbours after some other more charitable means, avoiding as much as in you is the obloquy of such enormities, wherewith the whole clergy is daily reproached and slandered; and rather that some charitable end should now seem to come of you, than he thus to be enforced to seek for the same.

*To doctor Cokes, my chancellor.*

---

## CXIII. TO ———

I COMMEND me unto you. And where at the late parliament there was a bill promoted into the parliament house concerning certain exactions of tithes within Rumney marsh[3] and other certain grounds, as I now remember, by cause that, as in the said bill was pretended, the inhabitants there do pay not only tithes for all things that do renew there, but also over and besides the same do pay iii*d.* for every acre, contrary to all law, reason, and conscience; which said bill I restrained at that [time], promising to see a reformation in the same: I will therefore, inasmuch as ye partly know the very circumstances hereof, that accordingly ye do farther so ensearch the verity herein, that thereby, against such time as I shall have the examination thereof, ye may make me ready and ripe in that behalf; and that herein you do your endeavour with all speed and celerity. First day of May. [1534.]

Harl. MSS. 6148. f. 43. b. Copy.

---

## CXIV. TO A PREACHER AT PAUL'S CROSS.

I COMMEND me unto you. Signifying to the same, that I do not a little marvel why you should leave a note with John Blag my grocer in writing, to preach at Paul's Cross on the third Sunday after Trinity Sunday; when, contrary to the same, at your own request to me made, you desired that ye might be there the first Sunday after Trinity Sunday, whereunto ye were accordingly appointed and named. And therefore I will, that ye in any condition fail not to be at the Cross on the said first Sunday, whatsoever other appointment or determination ye have made with yourself to the contrary, according to such expectation, trust, and confidence as I have in you for the accomplishment of the same. And of your mind in this behalf I will that you send me word by this bearer, to the intent I may thereby be in full surety hereof. At Croydon, the vi. day of May.

*To one that was appointed to preach*
*at Paul's Cross.*

Harl. MSS. 6148. f. 45. b. & 46. Copy.

---

## CXV. TO CRUMWELL.

RIGHT worshipful master Crumwell, I desire you, at this my instance, to be good master to sir Edward Mowll, priest, bearer hereof, and favourably to tender his suit

State Paper Office. Miscellaneous Letters. Temp. Hen. VIII. Third series. Vol. IX. Original.

[3 "A bill concerning tithes in Romney Marsh, having been brought up from the commons, was read the first time in the house of lords the 24th of March, 1534, and then appears to have been dropped."—Lords' Journals; Jenkyns' Remains of Abp. Cranmer, Vol. I. p. 107, *n.* u.]

which he shall make unto you. He was chaplain to Dr Benet[1] at the time of his decease, and continued with him in service as long as he was the king's ambassador in Italy. The said chaplain hath lain sick at Pyemount, at Susa, by the space of six months; by reason whereof he is so far in debt, that he is like all his life to be in danger of his creditors, and to live in great poverty, unless some provision, by mean of spiritual promotion or otherwise by your good industry and counsel, be made for him, whereby he may be relieved, and in process of time able to satisfy his creditors. Wherefore, inasmuch as the man hath incurred many adversities, partly by sickness and chiefly by the loss of his special good master, Dr Benet, and is also a very honest man and worthy of better fortune; I do heartily require you, at this my instance, to be as good master to him as you may conveniently, and you shall bind me for this and other your manifold kindness exhibit unto me, to do you such pleasure as shall lie in my power. Written at my house at Croydon the seventh day of May, [1534.]

Your assured ever,

THOMAS CANTUAR.

*To the right worshipful master Cromwell be this letter delivered.*

---

## CXVI. TO ———

Harl. MSS. 6148. f. 18. British Museum. Copy.

MY Lord, in my most hearty wise I commend me unto you, &c. So it is, that I am credibly informed and certified by this bearer, sir Thomas Donkester, subprior of Neweshham[2], that my suffragan, late abbot of the same house, is departed out of this miserable world, of whose soul Jesus have mercy; and forasmuch as the said late suffragan in his life so favour[ed] this bearer, and oftentimes so commended him unto me, that he (as I perceived) intended to have preferred him to be his successor in that room and office in the said house, (as ye, I suppose, do know right well); and because likewise I of mine own knowledge and experience can record and testify of his good life, providence, and other right commendable qualities meet for an head and ruler of that house, in whom heretofore the chief order, administration, provision, and husbandry of the same have only consist: I therefore right heartily pray you to be good lord unto him for my sake, and accepting these my letters in like stead and effect as though I had written the same unto you for myself in such a like matter; and to bear towards him your favour and assistance for his preferment to the said abbacy and office, as I may, for your goodness therein, be in your danger, which I would right thankfully requite, whensoever it shall lie in me to shew to you pleasure for yourself or for your friend; trusting now, at this mine attemptation, ye will do that you may for the acceleration of the election, under such both expedition and condition, that this my friend shall obtain thereby the benefit thereof accordingly.

And albeit I may, if I would, obtain the king's grace's favourable letters, and the queen's grace's also, for the furtherances and accomplishment of this request; yet forasmuch as I do well know that it consisteth in you to shew me this pleasure, without further suit, I therefore do make this request only to you, praying the same to be as good and favourable herein for this man my friend, as ye promised me to have been to my said suffragan in the other matter. And think [not], my lord, but that I (if God grant me life) will so thankfully remember and recompense your favour and gratuity herein, (if it shall please you the same to shew unto me,) as ye shall have good cause to rejoice thus to have done for me: which thing, if ye intend to satisfy my request, must be speedily done with all celerity, lest, by delay taken therein, ye may be stayed and restrained from that pleasure and liberty to do for your friend, which you may do in case ye so will;

---

[[1] Vid. Letter LVIII. p. 261.]

[[2] A monastery of Premonstratensians in Lincolnshire, the first of that order established in England, which maintained, at the dissolution, an abbot and eleven canons. Tanner's Notit. Monast. Lincoln. lvi. Ed. Camb. 1787.]

eftsoons praying you to have the premises in your good remembrance, and no less to esteem the same than ye would in case I had so spoken the same unto you in my own personage. From my manor at, &c.

## CXVII. TO THE CONVENT OF NEWESHAM[3].

In my right hearty wise I commend me unto you, and likewise to everich of you. And where it hath pleased Almighty God to call your father and abbot, which was my suffragan, to his mercy, by whose decease ye be now destitute of a governor and ruler: I therefore pray you, and every one of you, to bear your favours and good minds to my friend of old acquaintance sir Thomas Donkester, your brother and prior, that he, by your favourable means and assistance, may be preferred to that vacant room for my sake afore any other: which thing if you can be contented to do at this mine instance, ye shall be well assured to have me to be hereafter not alonely a right special friend to you and your house, to the most of my power, at such time as I may shew any gratuity and pleasure again for his sake, but also shall have such succour and comfort of him at all times hereafter, as ye shall have cause to be glad to have preferred him for my sake. Thus fare you well. From my manor at Lameheth, the xviii. day of May. Harl. MSS. 6148. f. 18. b. Copy.

*To the Convent.*

## CXVIII. TO ———[4]

My lord, in my most hearty wise I commend me unto your good lordship. And whereas I am credibly informed, that at your commandment one sir Thomas Mownteforde, priest, is committed to the Fleet for certain words (as is reported) by him spoken against me, which now he utterly refuseth, and thereto offereth himself to prove the contrary in that behalf by divers that were there present when the said words should have been spoken of me: I most heartily desire your lordship, at this mine instance and request, ye will discharge him for [the] time of this his trouble and vexation: for surely of all sorts of men I am daily informed that priests report the worse of me; and therefore so to be reported of a priest it should very little grieve me, although he had confessed it; much less now would I then this his trouble for the same, he himself reporting the contrary. Wherefore eftsoons I require you to be good lord unto him herein, and that the rather at this mine instance. Harl. MSS. 6148. f. 44. Copy.

Furthermore, touching my commission to take oaths of the king's subjects for his highness' succession[5], I am by your last letters well instructed, saving that I know not how I shall order them that cannot subscribe by writing: hitherto I have caused one of my secretaries to subscr[ib]e for such persons, and made them to write their shepe mark, or some other mark, as they can ..... scribble. Now would I know, whether I shall, instead of subscription, take their seals.

Also, where you have sent forth commissions to justices of peace to take the same oath, I pray you send me word, whether you have given them commission to take oaths as well of priests as of other. And if so, then I trust my labours be abbreviate, for in a short time the oaths (hereby) shall be take[n] through all England; which seemeth to me very expedient so to be; trusting this expedition shall discharge your

[3 See the preceding Letter.]

[4 Dr Jenkyns offers the following observations upon this letter:—"Strype, in his manuscript copy of this letter (Lands. MSS. 1045.) supposes it to have been addressed to Crumwell. But the questions respecting the oath of succession prove its date to be 1534, when Crumwell had attained no higher rank than that of secretary of state. It is not unlikely that it was written to the Lord Chancellor Audeley, who was one of the commissioners appointed to tender the oath." He founds this opinion upon the statement of Strype, that secretary Crumwell was one of the king's commissioners. Mem. of Abp. Cranmer, Vol. I. p. 36. Ed. Oxon. 1840.]

[5 See Letter CV.]

lordship, me, and other of much travail in this behalf: but yet I would gladly know who shall take the oaths at the religious of Syon[1], which is specially to be observed, and also the charter houses, and observants, and other religious exempt. I beseech your good lordship, that I may have answers herein by writing with all celerity.

---

## CXIX. TO ARCHDEACON THIRLBY[2].

Harl. MSS. 6148. f. 45. Copy.

MASTER archdeacon, I commend me unto you: signifying to you, that I have received your letters with a billet[3] from the king's highness in them inclosed, whereby, amongst other things I perceive your ambitious mind in seeking your own glory and advancement of your name, and that unjustly without your deserts, in that you desire to have me confess by writing your diligence, laying to my charge, that heretofore I have been a testimony of your negligence. If you have hitherto been accounted negligent, there is nothing (as meseemeth) as yet commenced and done on your behalf, whereby you do not declare yourself in deed the same man that I spake in word; although ye have changed the kind of negligence, from a slow negligence to a rash negligence: for so negligently you have run of heed in this matter, that you have advertised me never a word of those things which I desire to know the king's pleasure in.

For there be three places specially noted in the said bill, one in the margin of the first leaf, another in the third, where be divers words to be inserted within the process, of the which I would you should know his gracious pleasure, whether he would allow those words there or no. The third place is on the second side in the fourteenth line, whereof I would have known likewise if the king's grace would have left out "miracles," which all the bishops do think good to be left out. And for the same purpose the selfsame place in the book of parchment is void.

Of the king's grace's advertisement in these three points I would you had declared your diligence. But for to obtain the said bill of his grace, the premises never the more declared, was rather after mine opinion a rash negligence, than worthy to be reputed and taken for any manner of diligence. And therefore according to your

[[1] Dr Jenkyns gives the following note from the State Papers, Vol. I. p. 422, extracted from a long and interesting letter from Bedyll to Crumwell, dated the 28th of August, 1534; in which he laments "the foolishness and obstinacy of divers religious men, so addicted to the bishop of Rome and his usurped power, that they contemn all counsel, and likewise the jeopardy of their bodies and souls, and the suppression of their houses." Nine of the friars of Sion, he says, as soon as the preacher began to declare the king's title of supreme head, "departed from the sermon, contrary to the rule of their religion, to the great slander of all the audience. ...And it is doubted that some of them will attempt to escape out of their cloister; and if they so did, so men should never hear tidings of them, neither know where they became, it were no great loss." He states, however, "that the confessor there, and some other of the wisest of his brethren, the abbess and all her religious sisters, like good, wise, and faithful ladies to our sovereign lord, be well contented with the king's grace's said title;" and that there was good likelihood that the Carthusians of London "would be brought to good conformity according to their duty." But these hopes, at least in part, were disappointed. See Strype, Memorials, Vol. I. pp. 195, 277. Vid. Remains of Abp. Cranmer, Vol. I. p. 113. *n.* e. Burnet and Strype state that the nuns and friars of Sion, with several others of the religious orders, offered great opposition to the reformation and to the proceedings adopted by Henry VIII., and that many of them also gave credence to the sayings of Elizabeth Barton, called the holy maid of Kent. Vid. Confutation of unwritten Verities, pp. 65, 66, also Letters LXXXI. CXLIII. pp. 271, 303. Strype's Eccl. Mem. Vol. I. pp. 299, 300, 427. Ed. Oxon. 1822. Burnet's Hist. of Reformat. Vol. I. pp. 366, 336, 704. Ed. Oxon. 1829.]

[[2] Thirlby succeeded Hawkyns in the archdeaconry of Ely, 1534. Le Neve's Fasti, p. 74. Ed. Lond. 1716.]

[[3] Mr Todd places this "billet," or letter, as written A. D. 1536, and as applicable to the articles of that year. Life of Abp. Cranmer, Vol. I. 159—161. Dr Jenkyns suggests that it may have been the "order for preaching and bidding of the beads in all sermons," issued, according to Strype, (Mem. of Abp. Cranmer, Vol. I. p. 35. Ed. Oxon. 1840.) in June, 1534, which he gives in his Appendix, No. iii. Remains of Abp. Cranmer, Vol. IV. p. 252, and evidently thinks, as the copy-book from which the letter is taken seems to contain no articles of so late a date, and as in that case also Shaxton, who was consecrated the 11th of April, 1535, would probably have been styled "my lord of Sarum," that the authority of Strype is preferable to that of Todd. Remains of Abp. Cranmer, Vol. I. p. 113, *n.* g.]

deserts, where you were in time past esteemed but negligent in delaying, now you shall obtain a more ample name, and be called also negligent by imprudency and precipitation in your most expedition. Notwithstanding, forasmuch as you would fain obtain some other better name, to prove again your diligence I have sent the said billet again to you, to the intent, when ye shall know [the] king's pleasure in the premises, ye may advertise me thereof, after such manner as in that behalf ye may deserve to have your name changed, and not augmented, as it is now. And where I wrote not to you before so amply as I do now, is not to be imputed to my negligence, but to yours, by cause you did not consult with doctor Shaxton[4], or doctor Buttes[5], fully in this matter. Nor yet I have not instructed you by these letters all things, but some you must learn by mouth of doctor Shaxton, who knoweth all my whole mind herein.

And where you write, that the king's grace supposeth that I have these articles in parchment, subscribed with hands of the council; surely at what time I was last at Lambeth, master Crumwell sent to me for it in the king's name, and since as yet I hear nothing thereof. Wherefore I think it convenient that you inquire thereof, by cause it may be forthcoming, and not required of me, where it is not as it is thought to be.

Furthermore, ye may shew master vice-chancellor[6] of Cambridge, that I have lost his bill of Paul's Cross, and therefore I look for him these holydays to bring me another, not doubting but that you will bear him company; at which your resort we shall commune of the preferment of your diligence; and if you lack horse, you shall have of me, at such time as you shall appoint by this bearer. Thus fare you well. From Croydon, the xxiv. day of May.

*To doctor Thrylby, archdeacon of Ely.*

---

## CXX. TO THE RECORDER OF LONDON.

Master recorder, in my right hearty wise I commend me unto you. And where heretofore I wrote unto my lord mayor of London, in the favour and preferment of one mistress Pachette, widow, for a house belonging unto the chamber of London, which gladly she desireth to hold and occupy for her commodity and ease, in case she might the same attain with favour of my said lord and his brethren; and forasmuch as I am credibly informed, that by reason of such your good testimony, discretion, and wisdom, wherein ye be in credit with my said lord and his brethren, in such matters and affairs as passeth from them by their grants: I most heartily require you therefore, the rather at this mine instance and request, ye will bear towards the said mistress Pachette such your favour and assistance for her preferment towards the said house, as I may for your benevolence herein be in your danger for the same, in the accomplishing your like requests of me either for yourself or for your friends. Thus fare you well. From Croydon, the xxv. day of May.

Harl. MSS. 6148. f. 44. Copy.

*To master Baker, recorder of London.*

---

[[4] Shaxton was taken by Anne Boleyn to be her chaplain and almoner, having been preferred with Latimer to the former office by Crumwell, A.D. 1534, and was soon after promoted by her to the bishoprick of Salisbury, April 11, 1535, (Vid. supra, *n.* 3.) to which he had been elected Feb. 22, 1535. Latimer was consecrated bishop of Worcester in September of the same year. Vid. Letter CLII. p. 309. Burnet's Hist. of Reformat. Vol. I. p. 347. Strype's Eccl. Mem. Vol. III. Part I. p. 570.]

[[5] Dr Butts was one of the physicians to Henry VIII., and shewed many acts of kindness to Abp. Cranmer. Burnet's Hist. of Reformat. Vol. I. pp. 561, 687.]

[[6] John Craiford, "gladiator melior quam Procancellarius." Fuller's History of Cambridge, p. 159. Ed. Lond. 1840.]

## CXXI. TO THE DUCHESS OF NORFOLK.

Harl. MSS. 6148. f. 44. b. & 45. Copy.

My most singular good lady, in my most hearty wise I commend me unto your ladyship. And where your servant and mine ally, Thomas Cade, hath obtained a certain office in Calice to the value of v*id.* a day, which would be both for his preferment and commodity, in case he might enjoy the same without check, and that he is contented to supply and discharge all manner usages and customs to the said office belonging by his sufficient deputy, as herein divers and many doth likewise use the same manner there; in consideration hereof, the said Thomas intending to sue unto the king's highness for a licence to be had in that behalf, hath made a supplication unto his said grace for the obtaining of the same, the which I myself would gladly have promoted for him, unless of late I had not been very importune unto his highness for sundry matters concerning myself, whereby even now I am the more unapt to sue in this behalf: I most heartily desire your good ladyship, therefore, (for this time,) at this mine instance and request, you will cause some of your special friends nigh about the king's highness to promote this his said suit, according to the supplication made in that behalf; wherein your good ladyship shall deserve of me such pleasure as I may, and bind him both to owe unto you such his fidelity and service as he can, and also to be your daily beadsman for the same. Thus our Lord long preserve your good ladyship, to his most pleasure and your heart's ease.

*To the right honourable and mine especial good lady, my lady duchess of Northfolke.*

---

## CXXII. TO CRUMWELL[1].

State Paper Office. Miscellaneous Letters. Temp. Hen. VIII. Third series. Vol. IX. Original.

Right worshipful master Crumwell, in my right hearty wise I commend me to you. So it is, that upon Tuesday next ensuing I intend (God willing) to be at Rochester in my visitation, where if ye have any special matters to be inquired of, I will be glad to do my endeavour in the same, in case it may please you to advertise me thereof at this side Sunday next ensuing. Furthermore, I heartily thank you for your favours and goodness shewed to my secretary, Jamys Barnarde, this bearer, in such his suits as he hath lately had unto you, for the reformation of such persons as lately committed robbery upon his father; and likewise pray you to continue the same unto him, and specially to take further pains to examine in your own personage the said misdoers and offenders; whereby I trust (if it shall please you so to do) many things yet concealed and kept secret shall manifestly appear unto you by their own confession: for if they once look you in the face, they shall have no power to conceal any thing from you. From Croydon, the third day of June.

Your own assured ever,

Thomas Cantuar.

---

## CXXIII. TO CRUMWELL.

State Paper Office. Ibid. Original.

Right worshipful master Crumwell, in my right hearty wise I commend me to you. So it is, that this bearer, which is master of my mint at Canterbury, hath divers times informed me, that the provost of the king's grace's mint in the tower will not suffer him to have for his wages and money such coiners of the tower as is lawful for him to have by the king's grace's grant under his grace's great seal; because the same provost, as I am informed, endeavoureth, as much as in him lieth, to discourage the merchants to have any access or resort to my said mint, for lack of speedy coinage. And albeit the

[[1] This letter and the next are endorsed, "My Lord of Canterbury," but by what hand is uncertain.]

said master of my mint may, by the king's grace's said grant, take in all places, as well exempt as not exempt, such workmen and as many of them as he would have; yet he would (if it may stand with your favour and pleasure) have none other but such as do belong unto the said tower, because they be men of true dealing and of good honesty. Wherefore I pray you to be good master unto him, and for my sake to speak unto the said provost, that he may have for his wages at all times such persons of the said tower and as many of them to work with him, as he shall hereafter desire. For unless it may please you thus to do, my said mint[2] and master of the same shall be unoccupied; which thing the said provost, as far as I can perceive, doth most covet and desire. From Croydon, the 6th day of June.

Your own ever assured,

THOMAS CANTUAR.

*To the right worshipful and my very loving friend master Crumwell, of the king's grace's most honourable council.*

## CXXIV. TO CRUMWELL[3].

RIGHT worshipful master Crumwell, in my right hearty wise I commend me to you: likewise thanking you for your favours borne to my cousin Molyneux, in his cause which a long time hath depended in the Chancery; which your favour I pray you to continue likewise as you have begun; wherein in my opinion ye do take the just part, and for so doing shall merit and deserve thanks of God. From Croydon, the viith day of June. State Paper Office. Ibid. Original.

Your own ever assured,

THOMAS CANTUAR.

*To the right worshipful and my very loving friend master Crumwell, of the king's grace's most honourable council.*

## CXXV. TO CRUMWELL.

RIGHT worshipful master Crumwell, in my right hearty wise I commend me to you. So it is, that the provincial of the friars Austyns hath of late constituted and ordained one friar Olyver, prior of the black friars in Cambridge, which is not only a man of very small learning, sinister behaviour, ill qualities, and of suspected conversation of living, (as by the letters of divers well learned personages of the said university, whereof I have sent you one, I have been credibly informed;) but is also the very same man which of all other most indiscreetly preached against the king's grace's great cause, and most defended the authority of the bishop of Rome, and of all men most unapt to bear any rule in so noble a university, by whom also a great number of the best learned in the same is much offended: wherefore I pray you to be a mean, that he may be amoved from that office, and that Dr Hilsey[4] or some other worshipful man may have it. There State Paper Office. Ibid. Original.

[[2] "Amongst the places where king John in his letters makes mention of mints kept in England, Canterbury is one, and had been so, I suppose, for many ages. King Athelstane appointing out the places for mints, and the number of minters throughout the kingdom, begins with Canterbury, to which he allowed seven minters: a greater number than to any other place in the kingdom, except London, which was allowed to have eight. Of these seven, four were for the king, two for the archbishop, and the seventh for the abbot of St Augustin's......When or how the archbishop lost or left off his mintage here, I do no where find." Somner's Antiq. of Canterbury, p. 123, Ed. Lond. 1640. "The privilege was lost in the reign of Stephen." Jenkyns' Remains of Abp. Cranmer, Vol. I. p. 118, *n.* 1.]

[[3] This letter is endorsed, "Canterbury," and the next, (CXXV.) "My Lord of Canterbury," in the same hand as Letters CXXII. and CXXIII.]

[[4] "John Hilsey, a friar of the order of preachers, first of Bristol, afterwards of Oxford, was consecrated bishop of Rochester, (Oct. A.D. 1535) next

be in the same house of the black friars men of good study, living, learning, and judgment; and pity it were but that they should have such a head and ruler as is of like qualities. And I delivered unto you about Easter last passed, or else afore, a certain billet containing such matter as the same friar Olyver preached in the last Lent; which bill if ye had remembered, I doubt not but that ye would have provided for the same friar afore this time; albeit (if it may please you now to remember him) there is no time yet lost, but that the same may be renewed again. From Croydon, the viith day of June.

Your own ever assured,

*To the right worshipful and my very loving friend master Crumwell, of the king's grace's most honourable council.*

---

## CXXVI. TO CRUMWELL[1].

MSS. State Paper Office. Ibid. Original.

Right worshipful Mr Crumwell, in my right hearty wise I commend me to you. And where the county Palantyne[2] amonges all other pleasures doth much esteem the pastime of hunting with great greyhounds, and specially with great mastiffs, which in those parties be had in great price and value: these therefore be to pray you to advertise the king's highness to send unto the said county a couple or two of great greyhounds, and as many of great mastiffs: the same shall be as well accepted to him as though it had pleased his grace to have sent him a precious jewel or reward; which thing shall be no great charge to his grace, and yet nevertheless shall be highly esteemed with the receiver of the same. And therefore I pray you to have this thing in your special remembrance, when ye shall have convenient time. From Otford, the xth day of June.

Your own ever assured,

Thomas Cantuar.

*To the right worshipful and my very loving friend master Crumwell, of the king's grace's most honourable council.*

---

## CXXVII. TO LATYMER.

Harl. MSS. 6148. f. 41. British Museum. Copy.

In my right hearty wise I commend me unto you. And where that in April last past, upon certain urgent grounds and causes reasonably thereto moving, both I, and other the bishops within my province, caused an inhibition[3] to be had for preaching in every of our dioceses, specially to the intent that the malignity of divers preachers might not have place in the minds of the common people; which intending then as well to hinder the king's grace's just cause of matrimony, as also to deprave the acts and statutes made by the parliament[4], it did appear that in their sermons they rather preached sedition than edification; whereupon it was amonges us concluded, that from thenceforward no bishop, ne bishop's officer, should license any to preach without special injunction in that behalf first to them declared in such manner, that is to wit, that all such as shall take on them

---

after John Fisher, executed for treason." He "was a learned man, and a great assistant to archbishop Cranmer, and died A. D. 1538." Strype's Cranmer, p. 37. Dr Jenkyns adds, "It does not appear that he obtained the appointment to which he was now recommended; but he afterwards became prior of the Dominicans in London." Remains of Abp. Cranmer, Vol. I. pp. 119, 20.]

[1 This letter is endorsed, "My Lord of Canterbury," but in a different hand from the endorsement of the former letters.]

[2 Lewis the Pacific, elector palatine.]

[3 See Letter C. p. 283.]

[4 Dr Jenkyns thinks that Cranmer probably here alludes to the acts "For the submission of the clergy to the king's majesty," "For restraining the payment of annates," "For the exoneration from exactions paid to the see of Rome," "For the establishment of the king's succession," all passed in the early part of 1534. Remains of Abp. Cranmer, Vol. I. p. 121, *n*. p.]

the office of preaching should neither preach any thing which might seem prejudicial to the said matrimony, whereby the king's issue might come into question and doubt amongst the vulgar people, nor likewise reprehend in their sermons any such ordinances, acts, or statutes, heretofore made, or by the said high court of parliament hereafter to be ordained: Therefore, inasmuch as at your instance and request I have licensed divers to preach within my province, to whom I have neither given such injunctions accordingly as is before specified, nor yet (though I minded so to do) conveniently I could not without their intolerable charges and expenses in resorting so far unto me for the same; I will that you for my discharge herein, in my name and for my behalf, do take upon you the administration of these said injunctions for all such as hath already had or hereafter shall have my said licence to preach at your said request and instance. Wherein I would ye were right circumspect that they may be well observed, or else to send me such my licences again, of whom ye doubt for the observation hereof. Thus fare you well. [1534.]

*To master Latymer, parson of Weste Kynton, in Wiltshire.*

---

## CXXVIII. TO CRUMWELL.

Right worshipful master secretary, in my right hearty wise I commend me to you. So it is, I intend to prefer my servant John Brice, this bearer, to the king's grace's service, if I may the same obtain for him; but I being discouraged thus to do, because of late I heard you reprove him very sore, for causes you then moving and yet unknown unto me; being also very loath to do or attempt any thing concerning his said preferment, unless it may first please you to stand good master unto him; [I] am moved of very charity and pity to desire you to be good master unto him, and for my sake (remitting all old matters and occasions of displeasure) to bear towards him your favour and good will, the rather at this my instance; without which he recogniseth neither to be able to enjoy the said preferment quietly in case it were granted, neither yet by any other promotion to joy of himself. Wherefore I heartily pray you, good master secretary, to be good unto him, and in this matter to make unto me or to him such comfortable answer as may satisfy my expectation, and quiet his mind: assuring you, that I have many times noted such pensiveness in him, conceived by your said reproving words, as I do think him very penitent and sorrowful for your displeasure towards him. And therefore I pray you to forgive and pardon him, as he may be your daily beadsman. From Knoll, the 26. day of December.

State Paper Office. Miscellaneous Letters. Temp. Hen. VIII. Third series. Vol. IX. Original.

Your own ever assured,

Thomas Cantuar.

*To the right worshipful and my very loving friend, master secretary to the king's highness.*

---

## CXXIX. TO CRUMWELL.

Right worshipful master secretary, I commend me heartily to you. And these be to desire you to be good master unto my servant Nevell, this bearer, which hath been a suitor long time, to his great loss, hinderance, and utter undoing, in the matter of Wilton Abbey, unless your charitable favour may be to him shewed. And as far as I can perceive, the matter again him surmised was done of malice and of no just cause: wherefore I am the more desirous to write unto you in his favour, trusting that you will be the better unto him at this my desire; and that he may have your favourable letters unto the abbess[5] there, whereby he may be restored unto his office according to his

State Paper Office. Ibid. Original.

---

[[5] Cecil Bodenham. See Letter XLIX. p. 258.]

patent, without any further suit in the law. And he shall be at all times ready to stand to all such order as please you to take therein. From Knoll, 15th day of January.

Your own ever assured,

THOMAS CANTUAR.

*To the worshipful and my very loving friend master secretary to the king's grace.*

---

## CXXX. TO CRUMWELL.

State Paper Office. Ibid. Original.

RIGHT worshipful master secretary, I commend me heartily to you: likewise praying you to have in your good remembrance the contents of such my letters, as I of late sent unto you, for the king's grace's letters to be obtained and directed to the lord deputy of Calice, and other his grace's counsellors there, in the favour of two such chaplains of mine, as I intend to send thither with all speed to preach the word of God; whom I would have sent thither before this time, if I might have had the said letters, for which this bearer doth only repair unto you for expedition therein, whom I pray you to dispatch as soon as ye may. From Knoll, the 22. day of January.

Your own assured ever,

THOMAS CANTUAR.

*To the worshipful and my very loving friend master Crumwell, secretary to the king's most noble grace.*

---

## CXXXI. TO LORD LISLE.

State Paper Office, Lisle Papers, Vol. II. No. 79.

AFTER due recommendations unto your lordship, this shall be to give unto you hearty thanks for this bearer, Mr Hoore[1], your chaplain, whom at this time I have sent unto you to be a preacher this time of Lent within the town of Calice, beseeching you, as you have ever been good lord unto him, so to continue. Over this that I may be most heartily commended unto my good lady your wife, with thanks unto her for the said Mr Hoore. Thus, my lord, right heartily fare you well. At Croydon the 4th day of February.

Your assured,

THOMAS CANTUAR.

*To my very loving lord, my lord Lisle, lord deputy of the town of Calice.*

---

[[1] Arthur Plantagenet, natural son of king Edward IV. having married Elizabeth (widow of Edmund Dudley, so well known with his colleague Richard Empson as the rapacious minister of Henry VIII.) daughter and heiress of Edward Grey, third viscount De L'Isle, of Kingston L'Isle, co. Berks, was created, in 1533, lord viscount De L'Isle. He served on board the fleet, was afterwards ambassador to the king of France, and in 24 Henry VIII. (A.D. 1533) was constituted lieutenant of Calais. Sometime after, incurring suspicion of being privy to a plot to deliver up the garrison to the French, he was recalled and committed to the tower of London: but his innocence appearing manifest upon investigation, the king not only gave immediate orders for his release, but sent him a diamond ring and a most gracious message; which made such impression upon the sensitive nobleman, that he died the night following, March 3, 1541, of excessive joy. His lordship was knight of the most noble order of the garter. Vid. Buswell's Knights of the Garter, Burke's Peerages extinct, dormant and in abeyance; Sir Harris Nicholas' Synopsis of the Peerage of England. Art. De Lisle.

This and several letters, which will follow, have never been before printed, and have been found amongst the Lisle papers, preserved in the State Paper office. It is difficult to determine the date of this letter, but it seems probable that it may have been written in the year 1535, from the archbishop's signature, as well as from reference to the subject in the previous letter. There are two letters from Hore, in the eleventh volume of the Lisle papers, signed Ri. Hore, to lady Lisle, but neither throws any light on the above.]

## CXXXII. TO ———

In my right hearty wise I commend me unto you. And whereas I understand, that the prior of the charter house within the isle of Axholme hath a certain suit unto you, I heartily desire you, ye will, the rather at this my request, shew unto him your convenient favour in all such his affairs and suits as he now hath with you. And for to recompense the same, I will be ready at all times to shew unto you like pleasure accordingly. Harl. MSS. 6148. f. 40. b. British Museum. Copy.

## CXXXIII. TO ———

In my right hearty manner I commend me unto you. And whereas you have always heretofore exhibited and shewed favourable and special friend unto your poor tenant Jackson, and now of late, for that the said Jackson being oppressed with poverty and by divers casualties fallen into decay, is grown much in your debt, ye have distrained the goods of the said Jackson, and made reenter again into your farm, which is not alonely to the utter destruction and undoing of the said poor man, but also great let and hinderance to you in the obtaining a full satisfaction and payment of your duty: this shall be heartily to desire and pray you, that at the contemplation of these my letters ye will be contented not alonely to give and grant unto the said Jackson, (finding you sufficient sureties, as well for the payment of your yearly rent, as also for the payment of five pounds yearly over and above the said yearly rent, until the arrearages be fully satisfied and paid,) according to the tenor of the old lease, the occupying of his farm for the terms of xxiv. years, but also permit and suffer him to have now at Candlemas the sale of his corn, and other profits which be risen of the said farm; and thus shall you not alonely do for me a right singular pleasure and gratuity, which I would be glad to requite hereafter at all times accordingly, but also bind the poor man, his wife, and children to pray for you during their lives. And thus fare you well. Harl. MSS. 6148. f. 47. b. & 48. Copy.

## CXXXIV. TO ———

Wellbeloved, I commend me heartily unto you all. Likewise praying you to be good masters unto John Jackson your farmer, that he may have a new lease of your farm for xxiv. years, to him and his assigns, according to the tenor of your former lease in all points and clauses. And for such debts as he oweth unto you, he shall and will find sufficient sureties to pay you at days, after the rate of five pounds a year, until the same whole debts be fully contented and paid, over and above the yearly rent for the farm. If it may please you thus to do for my sake, the poor man shall not alonely pray for you, but find such surety as well for the payment of the old debts as for the yearly farm, as shall be a good mean to you for the recovery of all that which is owing; and how ye shall be minded herein, I pray you ascertain me by your letters. From Lambeth. Harl. MSS. 6148. f. 47. b. Copy.

## CXXXV. TO A PRIOR.

Brother prior, in my right hearty wise I commend me unto you. And where this bearer, Thomas Hogeson, my servant, hath certain business and affairs to be done in those your parties, I require you for my sake that, if he shall need of your favour herein, he may have recourse unto you for the same; for the which at all times I will be ready to requite it unto you. Harl. MSS. 6148. f. 49. Copy.

## CXXXVI. TO ———

Harl. MSS. 6148. f. 49. Copy.

In my right hearty wise I commend me unto you: likewise desiring you for my sake, that you will bear such your favour unto this bearer, Tho. H. my servant, as thereby he may the rather bring to pass such his business and affairs, as at this time he hath to do in your parties; and for the same I will be ready at any time to shew you like pleasure accordingly.

## CXXXVII. TO ———

Harl. MSS. 6148. f. 49. b. Copy.

I commend me unto you. And where certain of your parochians were lately afore me at Knoll for certain crimes and causes, as ye do know, and to some of them I have enjoined certain penance, as by a book inclosed within these my letters you shall at large perceive; I therefore will and require you, that upon Sunday, which shall be the last day of February[1], ye see that the said persons do their penance penitently, according to the purport of the said book, and that you certify me duly thereof by this bearer my servant, of whom ye shall receive a monition for all such persons as can and will gainsay to the purgation of John Manyng, assigned to be made according to the contents of the said monition. Wherein in all other the premises I will that you do your diligent endeavour as shall beseem you. [1535.]

## CXXXVIII. TO CRUMWELL.

State Paper Office. Miscellaneous Letters. Temp. Hen. VIII. Third series. Vol. IX. Original.
Harl. MSS. 6148. f. 49. b. Copy.

Right worshipful master secretary, I commend me heartily to you. And where for the honesty and good service of my servant Thomas Barthelet[2] I do tender his preferment, and cannot, as I would gladly, do for him unless he were disposed to be a secular, which, as I perceive, he intendeth not; I therefore, minding to do for him otherwise by my friends as I may, being also now, as oftentimes heretofore, bold upon you to desire you to supply my necessities when I cannot compass the same myself, do by these my letters commend and present him unto you, with no less good heart and mind than ye presented him unto me, praying you heartily to accept him to your service at my hand, and for my sake to set him to such beneficial exercise as ye shall think meet for him, as he and his may pray for you: wherein I trust he shall do such service as shall always be acceptable, and to the contentation of your mind. And how ye shall be minded herein, I pray you to declare to the bearer hereof. From Knoll, the first day of March.

Your own ever assured,

Thomas Cantuar.

*To the right worshipful and my very loving friend, master secretary to the king's highness.*

## CXXXIX. TO CRUMWELL.

State Paper Office. Miscellaneous. Letters. Temp. Hen. VIII. Third series. Vol. IX. Original.

Right worshipful master secretary, in most hearty wise I commend me unto you. And as I understand ye have sent for Dr Benger[3] of Wingham, so it is, that yesterday,

[[1] As Sunday fell on the last day of February in 1535, Dr Jenkyns therefore assumes it to be the year in which this letter was written. Nicolas' Notitia Historica. Remains of Abp. Cranmer, Vol. I. p. 129.]

[[2] See Letter LXXVIII.]

[[3] Under the prosecutions, which subsequently took place upon the Six Articles, Dr Benger was sent to the tower; and he is probably the person to whom the archbishop refers. Vid. Burnet's Hist. of Reformat. Vol. III. p. 269, Ed. Oxon. 1829.]

the 13th day of March, I received a letter from my brother, the archdeacon of Canterbury[4], concerning the said doctor Benger, which I thought expedient to send unto you with speed: the words of the letter were these:

"Upon St Matthew's even last past the said doctor Benger, being at my table, affirmed the authority of the bishop of Rome; and after many arguments and reasons he said, 'These new laws may be suffered for a season, but in time to come it will cost broken heads, and set men together by the ears:' and then I said, 'Master doctor, take heed what you say, for I am sworn to the king's grace, and neither may nor will conceal any thing contrary to his majesty:' who answered again, and said, 'I mean not here, but somewhere else out of this realm.'"

These words the archdeacon writeth, but who was else present and heard the same he writeth not: wherefore I have sent unto him for the whole process of their communication to be sent in writing, with the seals of them that were present.

This day my lord of Wilshire, my lord of Burgavenny, and my lord Cobham, were with me at Knoll, to counsel together of the king's commissions concerning the subsidy[5], directed unto us with many other; and we have appointed the Tuesday after Palm Sunday for all the commissioners to meet at Maidstone, at nine of the clock in the morning. And forasmuch as the same persons be in another commission, concerning the valuation of the tenth and first-fruits of the clergy, except eight that be altered, I have therefore sent for those eight to be also at Maidstone the same time appointed, that under one journey we may finish two labours: and because that ye be in both the commissions, I pray you that I may know your pleasure, whether ye will be there, as I suppose ye cannot; or else, if you have any thing to advertise us of, that you would have done there. Thus our Lord preserve you. At Knoll, the 14th day of March. [1535.]

Your own assured ever,

THOMAS CANTUAR.

*To the right worshipful and my very special friend, master secretary.*

## DEPOSITIONS AGAINST DR BENGER.

State Paper Office. Ibid.

Jhus. 1535.

*Testymonye or wytnesse upon certen wordes spoken by Doctor Benger to Mr Provost of Wyngham.*

Syr Thomas Shellmore, Curate of Wyngham, testefyeth that Doctor Benger sayed that with as good reason he myght denye the authoritye of Paule and of all scrypture as we myght the authoryte of the Pope of Rome.

Per me Thomam Shellmorum, prædictum.

Edward Lacy, master Provostes servant, wytnesseth the same.

Wylliam Nores testefyeth that Doctor Benger sayed that the Pope hath authority to make lawes. And when it was answered that it was agaynst the law of God so to doo, he sayed furthermore that this new lernyng had set men togyther by the eares allredy, and though it wer suffered for a season, yet in tyme commyng it wolld set men togyther by the eares and cause broken heads; but he, reproved for so saying of Mr Provost, qualefyed his wordes sayeng, I mene not here but some where elles; and admonished of his othe, sayed, he knew it well inowgh. Moreover he sayed that by what authorytie we denyed the Pope, by the same authoryte he wolld denye the Scripture, and saye that Chryst is not yet borne, sayeng that he wolld abyde by the same.

Mr Attfelld wytnessethe that Doctor Benger sayed that this new learnyng wyll sett men togyther by the eares.

*Thomas Lawney's Deposition.*

These be the wordys of Doctyr Benger in mastyr Archedeacon's howse. He cam in to the parlor sodenly, where in I with certayne other wear; and as son as he cam in he began to pyke a mater, no man sayynge any thynge to hym, takynge hys purpose apon a fyer that was ther, and thus began: "Thys fyer, Mastyrs, ys goode for to rost, and to seythe, and to warme, but not to burne no men, Sir Thomas, I trow," sayd he:

---

[[4] Edmund Cranmer, archdeacon of Canterbury, and provost of Wingham. See Letter LXXV. p. 268, *n.* 1.]

[[5] The act for the subsidy, (26 Hen. VIII. c. 19,) and the act for the valuation of the tenths, &c. (26 Hen. VIII. c. 3.) were both passed in the session which began the 3rd of Nov. 1534. See Statutes of the Realm. Strype's Eccl. Mem. Vol. I. p. 325, et sqq. Ed Oxon. 1822. Burnet's Hist. of Reformat. Vol. I. p. 320.]

and I sayd agen, "Whom wolde you have burnt?" and he sayd, "I wolde have al thys new lernyd men burnt." And one that stode by, a merchant man, whom I am not vere well aqueyntyd with, sayd, "Whom thynke you new lernyd men? they that speakythe agenst the Poope or any other?" And the Doctyr sayd, "They wer no good men that wold speake agenst hym." And I then sayd, "Take heade, master Doctyr, what ye say, for ye are bounde by your othe to speake agenst hym." And he sayd he was sworne to the Chyrche. "Ye," sayd I, "ye are sworn to the Chyrche, but yt ys the Chyrche of Inglonde and not of Rome." And he sayde agayne he wolde nevyr speake agenst the Chyrche off Rome whyle he lyvyd, "nor no mor wold any good man," sayd he. And thus partyd in a fume.

Per me Thomas Lawney.

Also Frear Brencheley aftyr many raylynge wordys in hys sermone sayd, "Mastyrs, take heade, we have now adayse many new lawyse, I trow we shall have a newe God schortely," sayde he. Also the next preachynge after cam a Doctyr of the monkys of Cantyrbere ther prayynge for the kynge, but namyde hym not Head of the Chyrche; and after thys browt in a story of a kynge whyche by covetusnes reservyd godys to hymselfe that he toke frome certayne transgresorse, wherfor he lost hys kyngdom and nevyr recoveryd yt agene: and thus left yt ondeclaryd; by the which many gether opynyon that he ment yt by the kyng, to move the commonse to insurrectyon. From the whyche help us. Amen.

## CXL. TO ———

Harl. MSS. 6148. f. 50. British Museum. Copy.

SISTER, in my right hearty wise I commend me unto you: signifying to you, that I have appointed one mistress Creke[1] to come to you within these three or four days, late wife unto one of my servants deceased. And forasmuch as she was left very bare, and in great necessity and need, void now of all aid, succour, and friendship, and also hitherto brought up both wealthily and after an honest sort and manner, and so the rather unmeet either to serve or labour for her living; I am minded to see her to have both an honest living, and honestly bestowed: wherefore I require you, that with all favour you will entreat and entertain her when she shall resort unto you, and I myself will see you contented for her board. Over this, you must be content to forbear your chaplain Mr Rix. My lord of Wilteshere, notwithstanding my many persuasions to the contrary, is so importunate for him, that he will not have no nay; insomuch that his mind is, that he come to-morrow sennight, which is Tuesday, unto Maidstone, and so thence to depart with him home for altogethers. I pray you therefore that you will discharge him against the same day, so that he shall not need to rejourney again to you.

## CXLI. TO MR RIX.

Harl. MSS. 6148. f. 50. b. Copy.

I COMMEND me to you. These be to signify to you, that my lord of Wilteshere is fully determined, notwithstanding any manner suit or insinuation to the contrary, to have you abide with him in his household; insomuch that he willed me on Passion Sunday last to send you word, that you fail not to meet with him at Maidstone on Tuesday come sennight, from whence you must depart with him; and therefore against that time see that you be in such a readiness, as you need not rejourney again, but to accomplish his mind and pleasure with all your endeavour accordingly.

## CXLII. TO CRUMWELL.

State Paper Office. Miscellaneous Letters. Temp. Hen. VIII. Third series. Vol. IX. Original.

RIGHT worshipful, in my most hearty wise I commend me to you. And whereas I am informed, that upon suit to you made you have of late directed your letters to the

[1 This might have been the widow of John Creke, who was servant to the archbishop. Letters XVIII. p. 248, XXXVII. p 255, LXXV. p. 268, LXXX. p. 270.]

master and fellows of Jesus college[2] of Cambridge, moving them, forasmuch as you were informed that certain seditious persons should trouble the quiet possession of a farmer of theirs, lately having interest in a certain farm belonging to the said college, to signify to you their names, to the intent you might see a reformation in that behalf: I most heartily require you, that in this matter you will suspend your judgment, and repel all manner information and suit made to you herein, until such time that I myself shall farther commune with you for the same; which, God willing, I intend shall be shortly, as well to have communication with you of St Stephen's, as also to do my duty to the king's highness and the queen, whom of long I have not seen. Thus our Lord long preserve you in health! At Otford, the 6th day of April.

Your own ever assured,

Thomas Cantuar.

*To my singular and especial good friend, master secretary.*

---

## CXLIII. TO CRUMWELL.

Right worshipful, in my most hearty wise I commend me unto you. And whereas I understand, that amongst other persons attainted of high treason the prior of Axholme, named Webster, and master Raynold of Syon[3], be judged according to the law, for offending against the late act[4] of parliament made for the suppressing of the usurped power of the bishop of Rome; surely I do much marvel of them both, specially of Mr Raynold, having such sight in scriptures and doctors, and also of the other, which promised me that he would never meddle for the defence of that opinion; much pitying me that such men should suffer with so ignorant judgments, and if there be none other offence laid against them than this one, it will be much more for the conversion of all the fautors hereof, after mine opinion, that their consciences may be clearly averted from the same by communication of sincere doctrine, and so they to publish it likewise to the world, than by the justice of the law to suffer in such ignorance. And if it would please the king's highness to send them unto me, I suppose I could do very much with them in this behalf. Now whether this mine advertisement shall make as well for our sovereign lord the king's safeguard, and the weal of this his realm, as this justice, I remit it to your discretion and wisdom. Thus our Lord preserve you in health! At Otford, the xxx. day of April. [1535.]

State Paper Office Ibid. Original.

Your own ever assured,

Thomas Cantuar.

*To my very singular and especial friend, master secretary.*

---

[2 Vid. Letter XVI. p. 247.]

[3 For an account of Augustine Webster, prior of the Charter House in the isle of Axholme, Richard Raynold, a monk of Sion, John Houghton, prior of the Charter House, London, Robert Lawrence, prior of Beauvale, and John Haile, vicar of Thistleworth, who were condemned for treason, April 29, 1535; Vid. Strype's Eccl. Mem. Vol. I. p. 302 et sqq. Burnet's Hist. of Reformat. Vol. I. p. 704. Stow's Annals, p. 570, Ed. Lond. 1615.]

[4 "The statute 28 Hen. VIII. c. 10, for 'the extirpation of the bishop of Rome's authority,' was not passed till 1536. The act therefore to which Cranmer here alludes must be 26 Hen. VIII. c. 13, 'For the expositions of certain treasons;' by which it was made treason to 'practise to deprive the king of the dignity, title, or name of his royal estate.' As one of his titles by a former statute, 26 Hen. VIII. c. 1, was 'supreme head,' all who denied his supremacy were indictable for treason. See Statutes of the Realm. The ordinary report among the common people was, that these men had combined together to kill the king." Jenkyns' Remains of Abp. Cranmer, Vol. I. p. 134, *n*. g.]

## CXLIV. TO CRUMWELL.

MSS. State Paper Office. Crumwell's Correspondence. Original.

Right worshipful, in my most hearty wise I commend me unto you. And whereas I understand by this bearer, that you hitherto hath borne unto the same your favour; it will like you now, the rather for my sake, both to continue the same, and also to shew him your more ample favour in such things as now he hath to do with you, for I suppose the man intendeth well; and in so doing I will be always ready to accomplish your like requests. Thus our Lord preserve you in health! At Otford, the 6th day of May.

Your own ever assured,

Thomas Cantuar.

*To the right worshipful and my very singular good friend, master secretary.*

---

## CXLV. TO CRUMWELL.

Cott. MSS. Cleop. F. I. f. 260. British Museum. Original. Burn. Ref. App. Vol. III. b. iii. No. 37, pp. 120—123. Strype's Mem. of Abp. Cranmer, App. No. xiv. Vol. II. pp. 701—704.

Right worshipful, in my most hearty wise I commend me unto you: most heartily thanking you, for that you have signified unto me, by my chaplain master Champion, the complaint of the bishop of Winchester unto the king's highness in two things concerning my visitation[1]. The one is, that in my style I am written, "Totius Angliæ Primas," to the derogation and prejudice of the king's high power and authority, being supreme head of the church. The other is, that his diocese not past five years agone was visited by my predecessor, and must from henceforth pay the tenth part of the spiritualties, according to the act granted in the last session of this parliament[2]; wherefore he thinketh, that his diocese should not be charged with my visitation at this time.

First, as concerning my style, wherein I am named "Totius Angliæ Primas," I suppose, that to make his cause good, (which else in deed were naught,) he doth mix it with the king's cause, (as ye know the man lacketh neither learning in the law, neither witty invention, ne craft to set forth his matters to the best,) that he might appear not to maintain his own cause, but the king's; against whose highness, he knoweth right well, that I will maintain no cause, but give place, and lay both my cause and myself at my prince's feet. But to be plain what I think of the bishop of Winchester, I cannot persuade with myself that he so much tendereth the king's cause as he doth his own, that I should not visit him: and that appeareth by the very time. For if he cast no farther but the defence of the king's grace's authority, or if he intended that at all, why moved he not the matter, before he received my monition for my visitation; which was within four miles of Winchester delivered unto him the 20th day of April last, as he came up to the court? Moreover, I do not a little marvel, why he should now find fault, rather than he did before[3], when he took the bishop of Rome as chief head: for though the bishop of Rome was taken for supreme head, notwithstanding that, he had a great number of primates under him; and by having his primates under him his supreme authority was not less esteemed, but much the more. Why then may not the king's highness, being supreme head, have primates under him, without any diminishing, but with the augmenting, of his said supreme authority? And of this I doubt not at all, but that the bishop of Winchester knoweth as well as any man living, that in case this said style or title, had been in any point impediment or hinderance to the bishop

---

[[1] Vid. Strype's Mem. of Abp. Cranmer, p. 46, Ed. Oxon. 1840. Burnet's Hist. of Reformat. Vol. III. p. 200.]

[[2] Stat. 26 Hen. VIII. c. 3. Session of Parliament. See Letter CXXXIX. p. 301. *n.* 5.]

[[3] "The archbishop of Canterbury's title was also in convocation ordered to be altered: instead of the title of 'legate of the apostolic see,' he was to be designed 'metropolitan, and primate.' This last was one of his ancient titles." Burnet's Hist. of Reformat. Vol. III. p. 199. The proceedings of the convocation are given in Wilkins' Concilia, Vol. III. p. 769.]

of Rome's usurped authority, it would not have so long been unreformed as it hath been. For I doubt not but all the bishops of England would ever gladly have had the archbishop's both authority and title taken away[4], that they might have been equal together: which well appeareth by the many contentions against the archbishops for jurisdiction in the court of Rome; which had been easily brought to pass, if the bishops of Rome had thought the archbishop's titles and styles to be any derogation to their supreme authority.

All this notwithstanding, if the bishops of this realm pass no more of their names, styles, and titles, than I do of mine, the king's highness shall soon order the matter between us all. And if I saw that my style were against the king's authority, (whereunto I am specially sworn,) I would sue myself unto his grace, that I might leave it; and so would have done before this time. For I pray God never be merciful unto me at the general judgment, if I perceive in my heart that I set more by any title, name, or style that I write, than I do by the paring of an apple, farther than it shall be to the setting forth of God's word and will. Yet I will not utterly excuse me herein; for God must be judge, who knoweth the bottom of my heart, and so do not I myself: but I speak for so much as I do feel in my heart; for many evil affections lie lurking there, and will not lightly be espied. But yet I would not gladly leave any just thing at the pleasure and suit of the bishop of Winchester, he being none otherwise affectionate unto me than he is. Even at the beginning first of Christ's[5] profession, Diotrephes desired *gerere primatum in ecclesia*, as saith St John in his last epistle: and since, he hath had more successors than all the apostles had, of whom have come all these glorious titles, styles, and pomps into the church. But I would that I, and all my brethren the bishops, would leave all our styles, and write the style of our offices, calling ourselves *apostolos Jesu Christi:* so that we took not upon us the name vainly, but were so even indeed; so that we might order our diocese in such sort, that neither paper, parchment, lead, nor wax, but the very christian conversation of the people might be the letters and seals of our offices, as the Corinthians were unto Paul, to whom he said: *Literæ nostræ et signa apostolatus nostri vos estis.*

Now for the second. Where the bishop of Winchester allegeth the visitation of my predecessor, and the tenth part now to be paid to the king; truth it is, that my predecessor visited the diocese of Winchester after the decease of my lord cardinal[6], as he did all other dioceses, *sede vacante;* but else I think it was not visited by none of my predecessors this forty years. And notwithstanding that, he himself, not considering their charges at that time, charged them with a new visitation within less than half a year after; and that against all right, as doctor Incent hath reported to my chancellor; the clergy at that time[7] paying to the king half of their benefices in five years, which is the tenth part every year, as they paid before, and have paid since, and shall pay still for ever by the last act. But I am very glad that he hath now some compassion of his diocese, although at that time he had very small, when he did visit them the same year that my predecessor did visit. And also other bishops, whose course is to visit this year, keep their visitation, where I did visit the last year, notwithstanding the tenth part to be paid to the king's grace. Howbeit I do not so in Winchester diocese; for it is now the third year since that diocese was visited by any man, so that he hath the least cause to complain of any bishop, for it is longer since his diocese was visited than the other. Therefore where he layeth, to aggravate the matter, the charges of the late act granted, it is no more against me, than against all other bishops that do visit this year, nor maketh no more against me this year, than it made against me the last year, and shall do every year hereafter. For if they were true men, in accompting and paying the king's subsidy, they are no more charged by this new act than they were for the space of ten years past,

[4 And the title taken away. Burnet.]

[5 Beginning of Christ's. Strype.]

[6 Cardinal [Wolsey]. Strype.]

[7 "The convocation of 1523 granted to the king mediam partem 'valoris omnium fructuum, &c.......intra quinque annos levandam.' But the act contained a protestation, that this grant was new and unusual, occasioned by their special regard for his majesty, and not to be drawn into a precedent." Wilkins' Concilia, Vol. III. p. 699. Jenkyns' Remains of Cranmer, Vol. I. p. 138, *n.* e.]

and shall be charged ever hereafter. And thus to conclude; if my said lord of Winchester's objections should be allowed this year, he might by such arguments both disallow all manner visitations that hath be done these ten years past, and that ever shall be done hereafter. Now I pray you, good master secretary, of your advice, whether I shall need to write unto the king's highness herein. And thus our Lord have you ever in his preservation! At Otford, the xii. day of May. [1535.]

Your own ever assured,

THOMAS CANTUAR.

---

## CXLVI. TO CRUMWELL.

State Paper Office. Miscellaneous Letters. Temp. Hen. VIII. Third series. Vol. IX. Original.

MASTER secretary, in most hearty wise I commend me unto you: and so send unto you here inclosed such thing as were noticed unto me this present Tuesday[1], which I cannot (observing my fidelity) keep undisclosed. Wherefore I require you to open the same unto the king's highness, to the intent his grace's pleasure may be known herein. And as touching sir John[2], the parish priest of Wytesham, he is in prison at Maidstone until such time as I shall hear word from you what shall be done in this behalf. Thus our Lord preserve you in prosperity! At Otford, the xxv. day of May. [1535.]

Your assured ever,

THOMAS CANTUAR.

*To the right worshipful and my singular good friend, master secretary.*

---

## CXLVII. TO CRUMWELL.

State Paper Office. Ibid. Original.

RIGHT worshipful, in my most hearty wise I commend me unto you. And whereas this bearer, Mr Roode of Grayes Inn, hath a certain suit for title of land depending in the chancery[3], wherein he hath divers that beareth against him; I desire you to be so good and favourable unto him at this my request and instance, that he may have right with expedition; wherein you shall do a right good deed, and have my hearty thanks for the same. Thus our Lord preserve [you]. At Otford, the xxvii. day of May. [1535.]

Your own assured ever,

THOMAS CANTUAR.

*To my singular and especial friend, Mr Secretary.*

---

## CXLVIII. TO CRUMWELL[4].

Cott. MSS. Cleop. E. VI. f 233. b. British Museum. Original.

RIGHT worshipful master secretary, in my right hearty wise I commend me to you. These shall be to advertise you, that this fourth day of June I have received the king's

---

[1 "The 25th of May, 1535, fell on a Tuesday, and thus determines the date of this letter." Jenkyns' Cranmer, Vol. I. p. 139, *n.* m.]

[2 John Hastings was parson of Wyttrisham near Tenterden in 1535. Valor. Eccles.]

[3 "If this letter is rightly placed in 1535, Crumwell was now master of the rolls, having succeeded Dr Taylor in that office in Oct. 1534. He resigned it on being appointed lord privy seal, the 2nd of July 1536." Jenkyns' Remains of Abp. Cranmer, Vol. I. p. 140, *n.* o.]

[4 "As the bishops had subscribed to the king's supremacy the last year, so the king now required them, by his letters, to publish and declare as much in their own cathedral churches, and to set forth the king's title of 'supreme head, under God, of the Church of England;' and to see the people in their respective dioceses effectually instructed in this point by the clergy in their parishes. These letters bear date in the beginning of June this year. Which, with a declaration to be read to the people, were sent by Crumwell to all the archbishops and bishops." Strype's Eccl. Mem. Vol. I. p. 285, Ed. Oxon. 1822.]

grace's most honourable letters, bearing date from Grenewiche, the third of the same, concerning such effects as be therein expressed, touching the speedy and diligent declaration and setting forth of the king's grace's title and style of supreme head in earth, immediately under God, of the Church of England, at such times and in all such places, as be in the same the king's most honourable letters at length limited and assigned. Wherein I intend (God willing) to satisfy the king's grace's express commandment in every point to the most of my power, according to my bounden duty, as speedily as I may, praying you to advertise me by this bearer, or otherwise as you shall think good, of your mind and resolution touching such doubts, as the same shall open unto you on my behalf, concerning some of the contents of the king's grace's said letters. Thus our Lord have you in his tuition! At Lambeth, the fourth day of June. [1535.]

Your assured ever,

THOMAS CANTUARIEN.

---

## CXLIX. TO CRUMWELL.

State Paper Office. Miscellaneous Letters. Temp. Hen. VIII. Third series. Vol. IX. Original.

RIGHT worshipful, in my right hearty wise I commend me to you. And so here send unto you as well the priest, which in reading of the act[5] concerning the tenth part of the spiritualty bid avengeance on the king, and all those that assented to the making of that act; as also the woman which said, that since this new queen was made, there was never so much pilling and polling in this realm, asking avengeance also upon her. Thus fare you well. At Lambeth, the 7th day of June. [1535.]

Your own assured ever,

THOMAS CANTUAR.

*To the right worshipful and my very singular and especial friend, master secretary.*

---

## CL. TO CRUMWELL.

State Paper Office. Ibid. Original.

RIGHT worshipful master secretary, in my most hearty wise I commend me unto you. And where I have sued unto the king's highness, and obtained of the same his grace's letters unto the mayor of London, in the favour of a servant of mine named James Arnold, for his preferment unto the room of the swordbearership of London, when it shall happen next to be vacant; I most heartily desire you, (insomuch as my said servant hath in the parties beyond the seas taken great pains, both with me, Mr Aliote[6], and with master Hethe[7] in the king's service,) that you will not alonely be good master unto him, in the despatching of the king's grace's said letters, but also at this my request and instance, to write your favourable letters unto my said lord mayor of London[8], for the better furtherance of his suit. Wherein ye shall not alonely shew unto me singular pleasure, but also bind my said servant thereby, to be both at your

---

[[5] "The act meant seems to be Stat. 26 Hen. VIII. c. 3, for giving the first-fruits and tenths to the king, which was passed in the session beginning the 3rd of Nov. 1534. If so, this letter must have been written in 1535, and not, as Mr Todd places it, in 1534." (Life of Cranmer, Vol. I. p. 109.) Jenkyns' Remains of Cranmer, Vol. I. p. 141, *n*. g.]

[[6] Probably Sir Thomas Elyot, one of the ambassadors to the pope, A. D. 1532. See Letter CLXXXI. p. 332; Strype's Eccl. Mem. Vol. I. p. 222, &c.]

[[7] See Letter LXXXVIII. p. 276.]

[[8] See Letter CLXXXI. p. 332; "from which it appears that the person applied to was Sir John Champneis, lord mayor, A. D. 1534. Nothing seems to be recorded of him, excepting that 'he builded in his house an high tower of brick, the first that ever I heard of in any private man's house, to overlook his neighbours in this city. But this delight of his eye was punished with blindness some years before his death.'" Stow's Survey of London, pp. 137, 581, Ed. Lond. 1615.]

commandment, and also to pray for your long prosperity. Thus our Lord have you in his preservation! At Otford, the last day of June. [1535.]

Your own assured,

THOMAS CANTUAR.

*To the right worshipful and my singular good friend, master secretary.*

---

## CLI. TO ———[1]

Harl. MSS. 6148. f. 41. British Museum. Copy.

I COMMEND me unto you, &c. These be to certify you of the king's pleasure, how that his grace is contented that ye shall be admitted to preach on all the Wednesdays of this next Lent before him. Whereupon I thought it very expedient, for divers considerations reasonably me moving thereto, to admonish you of certain things in no wise to be neglect and omitted on your behalf in time of your preaching; which to observe and follow according to mine advice hereafter to you prescribed, shall at the length redound to your no little laud and praise.

First, therefore, take this order, (if ye will,) reading over the book ye take for your purpose some processes of scripture, the gospel, pistill, or any other part of scripture in the bible, and the same to expound and declare according to the pure sense and meaning thereof: wherein, above all things, it will be most convenient, that ye do not at all persuade for the defence of your own causes and matters lately in controversy[2]; but that ye rather do seem utterly [to pass over] those your accusations, than now in that place any sparkle or suspicion of grudge should appear to remain in you for the same. This done, that likewise ye be very circumspect to overpass and omit all manner speech, either apertly or suspiciously sounding against any special man's facts, acts, manners, or sayings, to the intent your audience have none occasion thereby namely to slander your adversaries; which would seem to many that you were void of charity, and so much the more unworthy to occupy that room. Nevertheless, if such occasion be given by the word of God, let none offence or superstition be unreprehended, specially if it be generally spoken, without affection.

Furthermore, I would ye should so study to comprehend your matters, that in any condition you stand no longer in the pulpit than an hour, or an hour and an half at the most; for by long expense of time the king and the queen shall peradventure wax so weary at the beginning, that they shall have small delight to continue throughout with you to the end. Therefore let the effect of the premises take no place in your mind, specially before this circumspect audience, to the intent that you in so doing need not to have any other declaration hereafter against the misreports of your adversaries. And for your further instruction in this behalf, I would ye should the sooner come up to London, here to prepare all things in a readiness, according to such expectation as is had in you.

*To the same.*

---

[[1] This letter has no address affixed, but as it follows in the MSS. the letter to Latimer, CXXVII. p. 296, it was most probably addressed to him.]

[[2] "During this parliament [A. D. 1534], every Sunday at Paul's Cross preached a bishop, declaring the pope not to be supreme head of the church. Also in other places of the realm great troubles were raised about preaching, namely at Bristow, where master Latimer preached, and there preached against him one Hobberton and Dr Powell, so that there was great part-takings on both sides: insomuch that divers priests and other set up bills against the mayor, and against master Latimer; but the mayor (permitting laymen to preach) caused divers priests to be apprehended and cast into Newgate, with bolts upon them, and divers other ran away and lost their livings, rather than come to the mayor's handling." Stow's Annals, p. 570, Ed. Lond. 1615. Vid. Strype's Eccl. Mem. Vol. I. p. 245, Ed. Oxon. 1822, who places these events as occurring A. D. 1533; also Letters of Latimer. Foxe's Acts and Monuments, p. 1741, Ed. 1583. "Also Wilkins' Concilia, Vol. III. p. 760, for Stokesley's inhibition of master Hugh Latymer from preaching within the diocese of London, dated the 2nd of October, 1533."]

## CLII. TO THE DEAN OF THE CHAPEL ROYAL.

Master dean, in my right hearty wise I commend me unto you. And whereas master Latymer, a man of singular learning, virtuous example of living, and sincere preaching the word of God, hath lately been endangered, and suffered great obloquy[3]; and also I myself, for justly licensing him to preach within the precincts and limits of my province, have been likewise misreported; I intending evermore the furtherance of the truth and the pure dispensation of the word of God, in consideration of my discharge, declaration of master Latymer, and satisfaction of such misreporters, have most humbly desired and sued unto the king's highness, to grant unto the said master Latymer licence to preach before his grace all the Wednesdays of this next Lent ensuing. Therefore these shall be to desire and require you, upon the king's pleasure thus known, for to discharge the assignment already appointed, or hereafter to be, to any person in that behalf, and require him (if any such be) to be contented with the same; for I, upon the king's pleasure thus willing, have already admonished the said master Latymer to provide therefore. Harl. MSS. 6148. f. 41. b. Copy.

Furthermore, these shall be heartily to desire you also, that my old acquainted friend, master Shaxton[4], the queen's grace's almoner, may be assigned likewise to preach the third Sunday in Lent before the king's grace; and that you will forthwith, upon the sight hereof, ascertain me in your letters by this bearer, accordingly to the king's grace's said pleasure and my request. For thus doing you shall have me ready to accomplish condignly your requests, and shew unto you like pleasure from time to time. At Otford, the ixth day of July[5].

## CLIII. TO CRUMWELL.

Right worshipful, in most hearty wise I commend me unto you. And forasmuch as at my late request you were content to accept Mr Newman[6] into your service; I here send him unto you now, for his further advertisement of your pleasure in that behalf, not doubting but that you shall be sure both to have of him a right honest and faithful servant, and also no less diligent service. And therefore I beseech you, and that the rather at this mine instance, to be his special good master. Thus heartily fare you well. At Lambeth, the 12th day of July. State Paper Office. Miscellaneous Letters. Temp. Hen. VIII. Third series. Vol. IX. Original.

Your own assured ever,

T. Cantuarien.

*To the right worshipful and my singular good friend, master secretary.*

## CLIV. TO CRUMWELL.

Right worshipful master secretary, most heartily I have me commended unto you: and by this bearer I have sent you herewith inclosed two letters, one superscribed unto my lord of Wiltshire, and the other unto me; which letters I have sent with expedition unto you, because they concern as well you as words of treason unto the king, which State Paper Office. Ibid. Original holograph.

[3 See Letter CLI. p. 308.]

[4 See Letter CXIX. p. 293.]

[5 Dr Jenkyns thinks that this may be a clerical error for January, and in arranging this and the preceding letter he has preferred Stow's date of the controversy at Bristol to that of Strype; but he says the point is exceedingly doubtful, for if Strype is correct, these two letters were probably written in January 1534. Remains of Abp. Cranmer, Vol. I. pp. 125, 6.]

[6 Vid. Letters IV., LXIII., LXXVII. pp. 237, 263, 269.]

treason I pray you to detect unto the king's highness, which I am most sure you would do, although I required you to the contrary. Moreover I understand the priory of Worcester shall be shortly void; which if it so be, I pray you be good master unto Mr Holbech[1], doctor of divinity, of the house of Crowlande, or else to Dane Richard Gorton, bachelor of divinity, of the house of Burton-upon-Trent. And if the priorship of Worcester shall not be vacant, yet I pray you be good master unto these two, when you shall find places meet for them; for I know no religious men in England of that habit, that be of better learning, judgment, conversation, and all qualities meet for an head and master of an house. Thus our Lord have you ever in his preservation. From Otford, upon the day of the assumption of our lady. [15 Aug. 1535.]

Your own ever assured,

T. Cantuarien.

*To mine especial good friend, master secretary unto the king's highness.*

## CLV. TO CRUMWELL.

State Paper Office. Ibid. Original. Todd's Life of Cranmer, Vol. I. p. 137.

Right worshipful, in my most hearty wise I commend me unto you. And whereas among other of the king's dominions, within this his realm, there is no part (in my opinion) that more needeth good instruction of the word of God, or aid of learned curates to be resident, than doth the town and marches of Calice, considering specially, not alonely the great ignorance and blindness as well of the heads now resident there, as of the common and vulgar people, in the doctrine and knowledge of scripture, but also having respect unto the universal concourse of aliens and strangers, which daily diverteth and resorteth thither; I think that it will no less be a charitable and godly deed than a singular commodity for this realm, to have in those parties at the least two learned persons planted and settled there by the king's authority in some honest living, whose sincerity in conversation of living and teaching shall shortly (no doubt) clearly extinct and extirpate all manner of hypocrisy, false faith, and blindness of God and his word, wherein now the inhabitants there be altogether wrapt, to the no little slander (I fear me) of this realm, and prejudice of the good and laudable acts[2] lately conceived by the king's grace and his high court of parliament; which thing to reform lieth much in you, in case you will but move the king's highness (forasmuch as the collations of the benefices there belongeth unto his grace) to give them, as they fall, unto such men as be both able and willing to do God and his grace acceptable service in discharging of their cures.

In consideration hereof, and inasmuch as I am advertised that the parsonage of St Peter's besides Calice is like shortly to be void, and in the king's grace's disposition, I beseech you either to obtain the same for master Garret[3], whose learning and conversation is known to be right good and honest, or else for some other as is so able and willing to discharge the same as he is. Wherein I assure you that you shall

[[1] Henry Holbech, called sometimes Henry Rands of Holbech in Lincolnshire, was a "true favourer of the gospel, and made much use of in the reforming and settling of the church." Strype's Eccl. Mem. Vol. II. p. ii. pp. 167, 8, Ed. Oxon. 1822. He was appointed prior of Worcester, March 13, 1536; suffragan bishop of Bristol, March 24, 1538; dean of Worcester, January 18, 1540; bishop of Rochester, May 3, 1544, and bishop of Lincoln, August 9, 1547. Vid. Willis' Hist. of Abbeys, Vol. I. p. 311. Ed. Lond. 1718. Le Neve's Fasti, pp. 141, 250. Ed. Lond. 1716.]

[[2] These were probably the acts which were passed against the authority of the pope, in the sessions of January and of November 1534. Vid. Letters CXXVII. CXLIII. CXLVIII. CXLIX. pp. 296, 303, 307. Burnet's Hist. of Reformat. Vol. I. pp. 291, 318, Ed. Oxon. 1829.]

[[3] Thomas Garret, or Garrerd, was persecuted and burnt at Smithfield with Barnes, and Hierome, vicar of Stepney, for heresy: they had been amongst the earliest converts to Luther's doctrine, and were prosecuted under the act of the Six Articles. Three papists, Powell, Fatherstone, and Abell were executed at the same time and day, and in the same place, for denying the king's supremacy. Vid. Foxe's Acts and Monuments, pp. 1194—1201. Ed. Lond. 1583; Burnet's Hist. of Reformat. Vol. I. p. 590.]

accomplish a right meritorious deed before God, and deserve condign thanks hereafter of your prince for promoting of so great a commodity for his realm.

And whereas I am informed, that the curate of St Mary's within Calice intendeth to make suit unto you for the said benefice; I pray you not to regard his suit, for I know that he is nothing meet for that room, specially in this world of reformation.

Over this I beseech you to be good master unto this bearer, Henry Turney[4]; for, as I perceive, his matters be so grievously taken and borne against him, that without your only aid and help he is like to lose his living. Surely I do much marvel of his uncharitable handling, if it be none other than it is reported. Wherefore if you can try out the truth, and find him not so culpable as it is pretended, you shall do a right good deed for many considerations to restore him to his room and living again. Thus our Lord have you in his blessed tuition! At Otford, the viiith day of October. [1535.]

[5]I have written to the queen's grace to obtain the gift of two the first benefices that shall fall within the marches of Calice. I pray you commune with the queen's grace therein, and help thereunto.

Your own ever assured,

T. Cantuarien.

*To the right worshipful and my singular good friend, Mr Secretary.*

## CLVI. TO CRUMWELL.

Right worshipful, in my most hearty wise I commend me unto you. And whereas this bearer informeth me, that you are advertised how that I should complain of him unto the king's council for his preaching; surely I do not a little marvel that you will think in me such lightness to complain of him, by whom I know no fault. This is true, that when I was at the court, there were some persons which complained unto me of him, to whom I gave less credence, by cause that afore time I heard good report of him by many honest, sober, and discreet men; which thing made me say these words unto the complainers: "That forsomuch as I heard divers times so many of both parties, some laud and some dispraise him, I could not tell to whom to give credence." And now again, since I came unto Kent, I have had complaints of him by divers, and of them that should seem honest and credible; and nevertheless divers other very honest men and of good judgments, which both heard and understood him, doth report contrary, testifying that he is nothing culpable of the things laid against him: wherefore, the matter standing in this controversy, I am enforced rather to believe them which report well by him than the other; for in mine opinion the other commonly be such persons as little regard the promoting of the gospel, but be rather papistical and superstitious. I therefore require you, for nothing that either hath been reported unto me of him, or for any thing that the uncertain fame hath conceived without due proof of him, you will thereby withdraw your favour from him; for if you should do so, it should be a great discourage for learned men which favoureth the truth, to take any pains on them in setting forth of the same; whose labours and endeavours were never more need to be had and esteemed than now at this season. Thus our Lord have you in his tuition! At Wingham, 12. day of October. [1535.]

State Paper Office. Ibid. Original.

Your assured ever,

T. Cantuarien.

*To mine especial and singular friend, master secretary.*

[[4] Henry Tourney was a sufferer in the persecutions at Calais, against heretics, with Damplip and others, and was sent to England, where he was confined till the death of Crumwell. Vid. Foxe's Acts and Monuments, pp. 1223, 1227, 8.]

[[5] The postscript is in the Archbishop's hand.]

## CLVII. TO CRUMWELL.

State Paper Office. Ibid. Original.

Right worshipful, in my most hearty wise I commend me unto you. And whereas the priors of Davyngton did hold of the bishops of Canterbury for the time being thirty-five acres of wood, parcel of Okenfold wood, and nineteen acres of land in Davyngton aforesaid, and eight acres in Tenam, within the county of Kent; which, by reason that the said house is dissolved[1], ought of right to escheat to me, as in the right of the see of Canterbury, as this bearer shall declare unto you more at large; I therefore right heartily desire you, that the said parcels may not be put ne specified within the office to be found for the king, so that by your lawful favour in this behalf I may the better come to the trial of my right: wherein you shall bind me to shew unto you such pleasure as lieth in me to do accordingly. Thus our Lord have you in his tuition! At Ford, the 17. day of October. [1535.]

Your assured ever,

T. Cantuarien.

*To the right worshipful and my singular good friend, master secretary.*

---

## CLVIII. TO CRUMWELL.

State Paper Office. Ibid. Original.

Right worshipful master secretary, in my right hearty wise I commend me unto you: even so praying you to be good master for my sake unto doctor Thornidon, warden of the manors of Christ Church in Canterbury, and to the cellerar of the same. And first, as touching my suit for the said warden of the manors; I beseech you heartily that he may continue in the said office, like as you have granted unto the warden of the manors of St Swythin in Winchester.

And as concerning the said cellerar, which I assure you is a right honest man, and of such dexterity and wisdom, as none is like unto him in that house, to whom at your request I gave the office of the cellerarship; I beseech you therefore, at my request, to grant him some liberty[2] to be taken at some times in the said office for continuance of his health: for surely he is corpulent, full of gross humours, and much sickly; and if he should still continue within the house, where is no manner walk at all or good air, his life should not only be abridged, but the said monastery should also lack many commodities, which daily do grow and increase by his policy and wisdom by his provision abroad; for he is the only jewel and housewife of that house[3]. Wherefore, good Mr Secretary, I beseech you to tender my suit, as well concerning

---

[[1] Vid. Letter CLX. p. 313.]

[[2] In the General Injunctions issued by Crumwell, A. D. 1535, "on the king's highness behalf in all monasteries and other houses, or whatsoever order or religion they be," it was enjoined "that no monk or brother of this monastery by any means go forth of the precinct of the same." Burnet's Hist. of Reformat. App. Vol. I. Part. II. Book iii. No. 2. p. 218.]

[[3] "Of this hall and the provision for the same and the ordering thereof, the chief care and oversight was entrusted to the cellerar, one of the four great obedientiarii (or officers) of the monastery;.... the sacrista, camerarius, and thesaurarius being the other three...... The cellerar, no doubt, was a great man in the college .....The office was indeed so exceeding great and troublesome, that, like as the prior had his sub-prior, .... so had this our cellerar his sub-cellerarius to assist him and bear a share with him, (and surely need enough,) in the managing of this burthensome office and weighty province.... He had a large part of principal housing allotted him, all contiguous to the convent hall and kitchen, (the sphere wherein he chiefly moved,) namely, his hall and his lodgings, as they were called. His hall, that which is now the archbishop's for the keeping of his temporal courts.... His lodgings lay on the west side or quarter of the cloister, into which it had a double door, having in the windows the name, coat of arms, and rebus or name device of Richard Dering the monk, one of them that conspired with the Holy Maid of Kent in Henry VIII's days, and saluted Tyburn for his pains, who in his time was cellerar to the church." Somner's Antiquities of Canterbury, pp. 201, 3, 4, 5. Ed. Lond. 1640. "John Cross was cellerar at the dissolution." Jenkyns' Remains of Abp. Cranmer, Vol. I. p. 149, n. c.]

the doctor as the said cellerar, as I may deserve it unto you. And thus fare ye heartily well. At Forde, the 26th day of October. [1535.]

Your own assured ever,

T. Cantuarien.

*To the right worshipful and my singular good friend, Master Crumwell.*

---

## CLIX. TO CRUMWELL.

Right worshipful, in my right hearty wise I commend me unto you. These be to desire you to be good master unto this bearer, Henry Turney[4]. For notwithstanding your other two favourable letters in his behalf, he is never the better regarded: wherefore if you be not otherwise his only aid and help, so that he may by your means obtain the king's grace's letters according to the tenor herein inclosed, or in such like manner, he is like to be utterly cast away; which for many considerations in mine opinion would (specially in this corrupt world) be no good precedent in setting forth of the truth. I therefore pray you to continue good master unto him, as you have hitherto done; wherein you shall do a charitable deed worthy to be rewarded of God; who preserve you in long health! At Dover, the 27 day of October. [1535.] State Paper Office. Ibid. Original.

Your assured ever,

T. Cantuarien.

*To the right worshipful and my singular good friend, Mr Secretary.*

---

## CLX. TO CRUMWELL.

After most hearty commendations: this shall be to advertise you, that lately I received a letter from you, whereby I understand that you have been advertised, that I, pretending title to certain woods in Okenfold and to certain lands in Denham lately belonging to the house of Davyngton[5], and my brother[6] in like manner to the benefice sometime impropried to the same, have lately by our friends and servants stayed the verdict that should have been given by the inquest charged for the king upon the same. State Paper Office. Ibid. Original.

First, as touching my brother; of whomsoever you had the same information, it is utterly untrue; for he stayed no verdict that should[7] [have been] given for the king by the inquest, nor yet made [claim] unto any tithes to the inquest: but he said to Antony Ager your servant privately, that he thought it was his right to have the tithes, and desired him to inform you of the truth. Nevertheless, Antony Ager carried the tithes away, without any let or interruption on my brother's behalf. Notwithstanding, my brother trusteth that you will be so good unto him as to suffer him to have the tithes, if it be his right, according to the tenor of your letter.

And as touching mine own self, I never went about to stay the verdict, but

---

[[4] Vid. Letter CLV. p. 311.]

[[5] "Davington or Daunton, a benedictine nunnery near Feversham, was deserted from the poverty of the house, and escheated to the crown 'tanquam locum profanum et dissolutum,' 27 Hen. VIII. i. e. between April 1535 and April 1536. This letter therefore was written in Nov. 1535. The priory with its property was granted 35 Hen. VIII. to Sir Thomas Cheney. Hasted's History of Kent, Vol. II. p. 726." Ed. Canter. 1778—99. Vid. Letter CLVII. p. 312. Jenkyns' Remains of Abp. Cranmer, Vol. I. p. 150, *n. g.*]

[[6] Vid. Letter LXXV. p. 268.]

[[7] This letter is here torn, and it is defaced in other places from damp.]

would have been as glad that the quest should have passed according to their consciences, as they would themselves. Only, being informed by every man that I heard speak, which were of learning and experience, that I had a just title, I made my claim, and caused the quest to be informed of my title, neither staying the true verdict, (as you were informed,) nor by any means procuring that the quest should otherwise do than their consciences should judge right. And where you do write unto me very friendly, that you would be sorry it should come to the king's highness's knowledge that I should weigh in any matter against him, I would you saw the very bottom of my heart herein; for I trust that I have so conceived justice into my heart, that I shall not for so small a matter, nor yet for any other worldly thing, be it never so great, weigh in any wise contrary to right against the poorest subject within the king's highness's realm. And I am assured the king's grace's mind is, not to do wrong unto any subject he hath; and if I knew that it were his grace's pleasure to have my title in the said lands, I would be more desirous to give it unto his highness, than he can be to have it. But forsomuch as I know not but his grace would that I should have it, if my title be good, I must needs make my claim and declare my title; else I must lose it, be it never so just.

The bishop of Worcester[1] lately wrote unto me in your name, that I looked upon the king's business through my fingers, doing nothing in that matter wherefore we were sent for unto Winchester[2]; and I marvel not that you do so think, which knoweth not what I have done. For first, the day before we took our leave of the king's highness to depart home, I drew certain articles touching the bishop of Rome, to give only occasion unto preachers that had no great exercise in that matter, what they might say, and what titles they might study for to declare. They that have excellent learning cannot lack matter abundant of their own inventions; but such as be of mean learning, have need of some matter to be ministered unto them, whereof they may take occasion to search their books. There is not one article of those which I have drawn [but would supp]editate sufficient occasion for a whole sermon, and some of them .... will minister matter sufficient for four or five sermons, if that [they] be searched to the bottom. Moreover at the same day I wrote certain doubts to be moved in the council; and because the council sat no more before our departure, my labour therein came to none effect, saving that I delivered a copy of my articles to certain of the bishops that were then present, thinking it good that they should procure them to be preached within their dioceses; which I, with all my chaplains, be doing here in my diocese with all diligence: a copy of the which, as well articles as doubts, I have herewith sent unto you, to the intent that if you think it good, you may add other and take away what you please, or else make other articles all new; so that when they shall be devised exactly and with all diligence, you may cause them to be sent into every diocese, to be preached throughout all the whole realm. And when the articles shall be with all deliberation absolved, if they were then read once or more every quarter in every parish church throughout the realm by the bishop's authority, I think it should do as much good to persuade the people as many sermons.

Thus fare you well, good Mr Secretary; and where at our last being together you willed me to prove your friendship towards me, which I never doubted of, yet I heartily pray you to declare part of it in my friend Hutton, for whom whatsoever you shall do, I shall impute it done unto myself. I would no more desire, but that he were so well acquainted with you as he is with me, and that you knew him as

---

[[1] Hugh Latimer, consecrated bishop of Worcester, Sept. A.D. 1535.]

[[2] "The king, resolving to vindicate his own right of supremacy against the encroachments of popes in his dominions, especially now the Parliament had restored it to him, being at Winchester, sent for his bishops thither about Michaelmas, ordering them to go down to their respective dioceses, and there in their own persons to preach up the regal authority, and to explain to the people the reason of excluding the pope from all jurisdiction in these realms." Strype's Mem. of Abp. Cranmer, p. 42. Ed. Oxon. 1840. In Letter CLXXVII. pp. 326, et sqq., addressed by the archbishop to Henry VIII. dated August 26, 1536, he makes especial mention of his own sermons against the authority of the bishop of Rome.]

I do. Again fare you well, and Almighty God long preserve you to his gospel, and the wealth of our prince and his realm! At Ford, the 2d day of November. [1535.]

Your own ever assured,

T. CANTUARIEN.

[3]Read further.

I thank you heartily for that you be so good master unto Dr Peter[4], as I am informed that you be. I was fully minded that he should have been the dean of mine arches, which yet he shall have, if you think it good, and that he may therewith serve you in that room whereunto you have appointed him. Herein I pray you that I may be advertised of your mind by this bearer; for if it be your pleasure, I shall make him dean before the next term. I know no man so meet for it.

*To the right worshipful and my singular friend, master secretary.*

---

## CLXI. TO CRUMWELL.

RIGHT worshipful, in my most hearty wise I commend me unto you. And albeit that many times heretofore I have been fully purposed and minded most effectually and earnestly to write unto you in the favour of this bearer, my friend Sir John Markham, touching his business and suits now depending before my Lord Chancellor; yet inasmuch as he hath always testified unto me that you were much better unto him than he could wish or desire, I have deferred the same hitherto, right heartily desiring and praying you, as you have always been his special good master and friend, so you will, the rather at this my request, continue; and specially now touching this his suit before my lord chancellor, so that by your favourable word he may be the more indifferently heard, and have the sooner an end in the same: for I assure you he is the gentleman, whom, amongst all other, I never knew none that hath ordered himself so uprightly in quietness amongs his neighbours within his country, as he hath ever done, or that is universally better beloved, saving that he is only hated of him whom no man can favour or love. I therefore eftsoons beseech you to help that he be discharged of this his unquiet vexation and trouble, none otherways but as it shall seem to you just so to do; wherein you shall not alonely shew unto me no small pleasure, but also be sure to do for a right honest gentleman. Thus our Lord preserve you. At Ford, the iii. day of November. [1535.]

State Paper Office. Ibid. Original.

[5]I have known the good conversation and indifferency of Sir John Markham in his country above thirty years, and that causeth me the bolder to write in his favour; for else I love not to intermeddle myself in other men's causes. Also Sir William

---

[3 The postscript is in the archbishop's hand.]

[4 This was Sir William Petre, a master of chancery, whom Crumwell appointed to visit the monasteries with Leighton, Legh, and Loudon as his deputies, Oct. 1535, and who with Cranmer and others had been appointed to draw up a bill for the enactment of the Six Articles (A.D. 1539), which was not adopted. He was a great friend of the archbishop, was made secretary of state, and in conjunction with the queen, Cranmer, lord Wriothesley, (the newly appointed lord chancellor,) and the earl of Hartford, had the government of the kingdom entrusted to him by the king, when he departed for France, A.D. 1544. In 1545 he was sent as ambassador to Germany. He was also one of the privy council appointed by Henry VIIIth's will to assist his executors, and afterwards became a member of Edward VIth's privy council. He signed Edward VIth's limitation of the crown, as well as the letter to Mary, acquainting her that the lady Jane Grey had been proclaimed "sovereign according to the ancient laws of the land;" but with the other members of the council afterwards declared for queen Mary, and, A.D. 1556, was appointed one of the select committee for regulating the affairs of the kingdom during the absence of Philip, queen Mary's husband, and became one of queen Elizabeth's first privy councillors. Vid. Strype's Mem. of Abp. Cranmer, Vol. I. p. 50; Burnet's Hist. of Reformat. Vol. I. pp. 517, 663; Vol. II. pp. 7, 36, 471, 478-9, 752; Vol. III. pp. 317, 490, Part II. pp. 281, 342. Ed. Oxon. 1829.]

[5 The postscript is in the archbishop's hand.]

Meryngc hath desired me to write unto you in his favour, whose letter[1] I have sent unto you, commending his cause also unto you; for I know his impotency this five or six years. Meseemeth it is a strange thing that the king's justices of peace should be handled as the adversaries of these men pretend, unless some manifest and evident cause were against them. I am informed that the baily of Newark boasteth, that Sir John Markham shall be committed unto ward before he make his answer.

Your assured ever,

T. Cantuarien.

*To mine especial good friend, master secretary, this be delivered.*

---

## CLXII. TO LORD LISLE[2].

State Paper Office. Lisle Papers, Vol. 11. No. 90.

After my right hearty commendations to your lordship. This shall be to yield unto the same my hearty thanks for your pains taken with my loving friend Sir Edward Kyngisley in provision of such wines as are sent unto Canterbury for me against this time; wherein you have shewed unto me no small pleasure: requiring your lordship of your like assistance in the provision of the rest, for the which I have written my mind unto the said Sir Edward Kyngisley. And if there be any pleasure here that I may shew unto you or any of yours, I pray you to be as bold of me; beseeching you, my lord, that I may be heartily commended unto my lady your wife. Thus, my lord, most heartily fare you well. At Croydon, the 17th day of November. [1535.]

Your lordship's

T. Cantuarien.

*To my very loving lord, my lord deputy of Calais.*

---

[1 The following is a copy of Sir W. Meryngc's letter:

State Paper Office. Miscellaneous Letters. Temp. Hen. VIII. Third series. Vol. IX. Copy.

"Most reverend and honourable father in God and my most singular good lord, in my most humble and lowliest manner I recommend me unto your good lordship: most humbly beseeching your grace to be good and gracious lord to me now; for so it is, that my lord the bishop of Lincoln [John Longland] and his ungracious servant Foster, his baily of Newark, hath delivered me a subpœna, to appear in the chancery quindena Michelis next coming, upon pain of an c^li^.; and God knoweth, if I should lose all the land and goods that I have in the world, I may neither ride nor go but with two staves like two crutches: and farther do I not labour, but in my poor house to my chapel and to my garden; and when I go in my wagon to Newark to do my duty in serving the king's most noble grace at his sessions there; and God he knoweth what pain that is to me. I suppose, of my conscience, no poor wretch in this world doth labour with such pain as I do; and now to have a subpœna, to answer unto such matters as I never offended in, nor never gave cause unto the bishop of Lincoln, nor unto Foster his baily, nor never did them any manner of displeasure, but that I did my duty in serving the king's most noble grace at his sessions, without that at ever I did or caused thing to be done there contrary to the king's laws; and that if I should die this hour, I would take it death as I would answer before God. Thus, my own most singular good lord, I beseech your lordship to be good and gracious lord to me, and to shew my lord chancellor and master secretary what case I am in, and to require them to be good lord and master to me, and to the poor town of Newark, which without your and their good lordships and mastership the poor town of Newark is and shall be utterly destroyed and undone for ever; for such bribery and such polling as is there, is not within any town in England this day. And if they can prove that ever I did to Foster, or caused to be done, contrary to the king's laws, then let me be punished to the example of all others. Thus I can no more, but to my little power I am and ever shall be during my life natural your true beadman, as knoweth the Holy Trinity, who ever preserve your good lordship. From Morynge, the 6th day of October, by the hand of your old beadman, William Morynge.

"*To his most reverend and honourable father in God, and my most singular good lord, my lord archbishop of Canterbury's good grace.*"]

[2 This letter has never been before printed: the date is doubtful, but upon examination of the other letters of the archbishop, it seems probable that it was written in this year.]

## CLXIII. TO CRUMWELL.

State Paper Office. Miscellaneous Letters. Temp. Hen. VIII. Third Series. Vol. IX. Original.

Right worshipful, in my most hearty wise I commend me unto you. These shall be to signify unto you, that at my being at Christ's church in Canterbury this last week, I was desired to interpretate one article of the late injunctions, giving in the king's grace's visitation, which concerneth the dimission, as well of such as were professed under twenty years of age, as also other that be now under twenty-four. And although the words be so plain, that (in mine opinion) there needeth no interpretation, yet forasmuch as doubts be made therein, I will not take upon me to make any exposition herein but such as you shall make, by whose authority the injunctions were given.

The article is this[3]: "Item, quod nullus deinceps permittatur profiteri regularem observantiam, aut vestem suscipere religionis per confratres hujus domus gestari solitam, nisi vicesimum suæ ætatis annum compleverit. Et si qui jam sub vicesimo anno completo in veste hujusmodi intra hanc domum jam inducti sunt, et si qui alii sub vicesimo quarto anno existentes discedere velint, illam quamprimum se exuant; et magister hujus domus suo sumptu vestibus secularibus et honestis ad præsens ornet, et ad amicos suos clariores cum viaticis competentibus transmittendos curet."

The first doubt is this, whether such persons only shall be dimissed of their religion as were professed under twenty year of age, and be now under twenty-four; or else both they that be now under twenty-four, though they were professed after twenty, and also they that were professed under twenty, though they be now above twenty-four. The second doubt is, where the prior is commanded to apparel those that shall be dimissed in secular habits, and to send them unto their chief friends upon his proper costs and charges; whether he shall take from them their wages, and such money and stuff as they have given them by their friends, or spared of their wages, or that he shall take all manner of things from them, and send them to their friends with only their apparel and necessary expenses. Whatsoever interpretation you shall give hereunto, I shall see it put in execution, desiring you that I may be certified of your mind by this bearer. Thus our Lord preserve you in health. At Canterbury, the 18th day of November. [1535.]

Your assured ever,

T. Cantuarien.

*To the right worshipful and my special friend, master secretary.*

---

## CLXIV. TO CRUMWELL.

State Paper Office. Ibid. Original holograph.

After most hearty commendations: this shall be to signify unto you, that my servant Kylligrewe shewed me that your mind was, I should send unto you one of my servants whom I trusted as myself, by whom you might communicate unto me your mind in certain things which you have to say unto me. And to satisfy your mind herein I have sent unto you my chaplain, master Champion[4], who hath a head able to receive all that you put into it; and he is of that trust, that whatsoever you

---

[[3] The only article which appears in the "General injunctions to be given on the king's highness's behalf in all monasteries and other houses," printed by Burnet, (Hist. of Reformat. Vol. I. Part II. pp. 217—223,) from Cotton MSS. Cleop. E. 4. fol. 21, now preserved in the British Museum, is the following: "Also, that no man be suffered to profess, or to wear the habit of religion in this house, ere he be twenty-four years of age complete; and that they entice nor allure no man with suasions and blandishments to take the religion upon him." (p. 222.) At the end of the injunctions is the following passage: "Other spiritual injunctions may be added by the visitor, as the place and nature of the comperts shall require after his discretion." The original word is "jurisdictions," which Burnet suggests is evidently meant for "injunctions."]

[[4] Vid. Letter CXLV. p. 304.]

shall say unto him, you may impute it said only unto myself. By him also I have sent letters to be delivered unto the king's highness by you or by him, as you shall think good. Thus Almighty God have you alway in his preservation! From Ford, the 22nd day of November. [1535.]

Your assured ever,

T. CANTUARIEN.

*To mine especial good friend, master Crumwell, chief secretary unto the king's highness.*

---

## CLXV. TO LORD LISLE[1].

MSS. State Paper Office. Lisle Papers, Vol. II. No. 77.

MY very good lord, in my most hearty wise I commend me unto your lordship. And where that upon credible report I understand that there is one Thomas King now abiding in the town of Calice, which heretofore was married unto one Elynour Saygrave, whose company and conversation he hath left, and liveth now incontinently with another woman, denying his former marriage; and to the intent that his both offence and ungodly example be not unto other an occasion of evil, I have sent unto my commissary commanding him to see them both punished according to the law. Wherein I desire you, my lord, to be assistant unto him in this behalf, so that by your favour and aid the same may be more earnestly accomplished as justice shall require therein. Over this I beseech you, my lord, (inasmuch as I hear say that there is good provision of wines with you,) that you will send me word if it be so, and then to help me therein when I shall send to your lordship for the same; wherein you shall do unto me a singular pleasure. Thus, my lord, right heartily fare you well, beseeching your lordship to have me most heartily commended unto my good lady: I am her own for her goodness shewed unto my chaplains. At Ford, the 20th day of December. [1535.]

Your own assured,

T. CANTUARIEN.

*To my very singular good lord, my lord Lisle, lord deputy of Calice.*

---

## CLXVI. TO CRUMWELL.

Cott. MSS. Vespasian, F. XIII. fol. 79. b. British Museum. Original.

RIGHT worshipful, in my right hearty manner I commend me unto you: likewise thanking you for the good favour which ye bear to this bearer doctor Mallet[2], my chaplain, declaring your benevolence to him in his preferment unto the mastership of Mychel House[3] in Cambridge; for the which your goodness, as I well perceive, he is right sorry that he is not of ability partly to recompense the same: howbeit I beseech

---

[[1] This letter has never before been printed: the date is not easily to be determined, but as the archbishop was at Ford, Nov. 22, it may have followed in that year.]

[[2] Francis Mallet was the successor of Nicholas Wilson, in the mastership of Michael-house, Cambridge, A.D. 1533. He was twice Vice-chancellor of this university, and was chaplain to the princess Mary: he was indicted for saying mass in the reign of Edward VI., and sent to the tower: Parker, afterwards archbishop of Canterbury, being "spoiled" of the deanery of Lincoln, May 21, A.D. 1554, it was conferred upon Mallet by queen Mary, who intended to have made him bishop of Salisbury. He subscribed, by proxy, as a member of convocation, the articles of A.D. 1562. Vid. Fuller's Hist. of Cambridge, pp. 169, 70. Ed. Lond. 1840. Strype's Eccl. Mem. Vol. II. Part I. pp. 46, 447, 452; Vol. III. Part II. p. 136. Ed. Oxon. 1822. Annals, Vol. I. Part I. p. 490; Vol. IV. p. 613. Life of Abp. Parker, Vol. I. p. 65. Lamb's Hist. Account of XXXIX. Articles, p. 21.]

[[3] A.D. 1546, Hen. VIII. "seized Michael-house into his hands, .... and King's-hall, the best landed foundation in the university. Also he took Fistewick's-hostle, (a house unendowed.) .... Of these three he compounded one fair college, dedicating it to the holy and undivided Trinity, and endowing it with plentiful revenues." Fuller's Hist. of Cambridge, pp. 173, 4.]

you therein to accept his good mind and heart, which I know he beareth to you unfeignedly, reknowledging thankfully your favourable mind declared effectuously to his preferment.

And where it is appointed by the king's grace's visitation[4], that he should bring up to you or yours all manner statutes, muniments, and writings, that appertaineth unto his college and to the foundation thereof, before Candlemas next; I pray you, inasmuch as I have occupied him here in preaching within my diocese all this quarter last past, and have appointed him to preach at Paul's Cross the Sunday immediately before Candlemas, that you will give him liberty till a fortnight after Candlemas-day. And by that time he shall be ready to accomplish his injunction in that behalf. Over this, I heartily desire you to be so good unto him, as to hear him and favour his reasonable request, in a matter concerning not only his college but also the quietness of the whole university; which thing if you stay not, he fears shall turn both to the hinderance of that good order which he hath already set in his own house, and also to the disquietness of the university. Thus heartily fare ye well. At Knolle, the xviiith day of Januarii. [1536.]

Your own assured ever,

T. Cantuarien.

---

## CLXVII. TO KING HENRY VIII.

Public RecordOffice. Ancient State Papers of the Treasury of the Receipt of the Exchequer. Royal Letters, Vol. I. "B. 3. 3." Original.

Please it your most noble grace to be advertised, that upon Friday last passed one called John Milles of Chevenyng opened a book in the church, wherein he found this schedule which I send now unto your grace herein inclosed, in the which is written "*Rex tanquam Tyrannus opprimit populum suum.*" Then the said John Milles called two or three of his neighbours unto him, and consulted whose hand the said writing should be of, but they could not divine who did write it: howbeit they suspect one Sir Thomas Baschurche[5], priest, sometime secretary unto the bishop of Canterbury my predecessor, whom I suppose your grace doth know. This same day in the morning the said Sir Thomas of his own mind came unto the foresaid John Milles, and confessed the same schedule to be of his making and writing.

Here I have shewed unto your grace the said Sir Thomas' fact and his confession, according as by mine allegiance and oath I am bounden. If it please the same to hear also some of his qualities, I shall inform your grace, partly as I know, and partly as I am informed.

At April next coming it shall be three years since the said Sir Thomas fell into despair, and thereby into a sickness, so that he was in peril of death. Of his sickness within a quarter of a year after he recovered; but of his despair he never yet recovered, but saith he is assured that he shall be perpetually damned. My chaplains and divers other learned men have reasoned with him, but no man can bring him in other opinion, but that he, like unto Esau, was created unto damnation; and hath divers times and sundry ways attempted to kill himself, but by diligent looking unto he hath hitherto been preserved. A little before Christmas last, as I am credibly informed by honest men of the same parish, a priest deceived him of twenty nobles, and ever since he hath been much worse than ever he was before; so that upon St Thomas' day in Christmas he had almost hanged himself with his own tippet, and

---

[4 Dr Legh, or Lee, who had been appointed with Leighton and Loudon to visit the monasteries by Crumwell, was at Cambridge, Oct. 22, 1535. "In obedience to Dr Legh's injunctions, the whole university before Candlemas-day next ensuing surrendered to the king all their charters, donations, statutes, popes' bulls, and papistical muniments, with an exact rental of their lands, and inventory of their goods. The Vice-chancellor and senior proctor went up to London and delivered them to secretary Crumwell, chancellor of the university." In his custody "the records slept well-nigh a whole year," when "it was thought fit to restore them again, without the loss of a shoe-latchet." Fuller's Hist. of Cambridge, pp. 166, 7, 169. Vid. Burnet's Hist. of Reformat. Vol. I. p. 369.]

[5 Vid. Letter XXXVII. p. 255.]

said to certain persons the same day, as soon as high mass was done, he would proclaim your grace a traitor, which nevertheless he did not. And within this ten or twelve days he had almost slain himself with a pen-knife. And this same day in the morning when he confessed the foresaid schedule to be made and written by him, John Milles said unto him, that he supposed your grace would pardon his offence, considering what case he was in. Then he in a rage said, "If I cannot be rid this way, I shall be rid another way."

Now have I declared unto your grace as well the fact, as the state and condition of the said Sir Thomas Baschurche, that your grace may order him after your most gracious pleasure, whereof I beseech your grace that I may be ascertained by this bearer my chaplain.

I was purposed this week according to my duties to have waited upon your grace; but I am so vexed with a catarrh and a rheum in my head, that not only it should be dangerous unto me, but also noisome unto your grace by reason of extreme coughing and excreations which I cannot eschew. As soon as I shall be delivered hereof, I shall attend upon your highness, by the grace of Almighty God; who ever have your most noble grace in his most blessed tuition and guidance. From Knoll, the xviith day of January. [1536.]

Your grace's most humble
beadsman and chaplain,

*Unto the king's most noble grace.* T. CANTUARIEN.

---

## CLXVIII. TO LORD LISLE[1].

State Paper Office. Lisle Papers, Vol. II. No. 75.

MY very loving lord, in my right hearty wise I commend me unto your lordship. And so, according to your desire and request, I send here unto you your own man, master Hoore, whom, forasmuch as the last Lent you liked so well, I have appointed again to preach with you, now accompanied with a very honest, discreet, and well learned man, named master Nycols; beseeching your lordship with the rest of the council, to aid and assist them in the doctrine of the gospel, and in the promoting of the truth; wherein no doubt you shall not alonely do acceptable service unto God, worthy to be condignly rewarded, but also deserve of our prince thanks for the same. Over this I pray you, my lord, to have me most heartily commended unto my good lady. Thus, my lord, heartily fare you well. At Lambeth, the 4th day of March. [1536.]

Your ever assured,

T. CANTUARIEN.

*To my very loving lord, my lord Lyle, lord deputy of the town of Calice.*

---

## CLXIX. TO LORD LISLE.

State Paper Office. Lisle Papers, Vol. II. No. 74.

RIGHT worshipful and my very loving lord, in my right hearty wise I commend me to your lordship; likewise thanking the same for the good cheer which ye made to my suffragan at his late being with you in these parts. So it is that a poor widow, of the town of Calise, named Elizabeth Beston, have offered unto me her supplication, which I send unto you herein inclosed; whereby she complaineth of injury done unto her (as she pretendeth) by one William, Berdiseley of the same town. Forasmuch as it is meritorious to help and succour poor widows and such other as be comfortless and oppressed with injury, I therefore pray your lordship to take some pains to hear the same matter, and the same so to order as your lordship shall think to stand with equity and justice, and with the true meaning of a certain will and

[[1] This and the following letter have not appeared in any previous collection.]

testament which she shall exhibit and shew unto you for the proof and trial of her claim and interest, as she pretendeth. For thus doing she shall pray for you. And as these be further to desire you to move, monish, and advertise my commissary there to do his duty and office at such times as ye shall see him remiss or negligent in the same, (albeit I have good confidence that he will diligently attend thereunto, and in the same minister justice indifferently;) so in like wise I pray you to aid and assist him in all his lawful and sincere proceedings, specially at such times as he shall fear to do justice for displeasure of worshipful and noble personages. From Lamhith, the 16th day of March. [1536.]

Your own assured,

T. CANTUAR.

*To the right worshipful and my very loving lord, my lord Lisle, deputy of Calise.*

---

## CLXX. TO CRUMWELL.

RIGHT worshipful, in my most hearty wise I commend me unto you: and, as one that is bold many times to trouble you with suits both for myself and my friends, which naturally, yea, and by the law of God, I am bound to do, in my right heartiest wise desire you to be so good master unto this bearer my brother-in-law[2], who is now the clerk of my kitchen, and for whom I spake unto you yesterday at the court, as to get him the farm or lease of the priory of Shelford, or of some other house of religion in Nottinghamshire, where his native country is, which now are by the act of Parliament suppressed[3]; and he shall find the king's grace sufficient sureties for the payment of the rents and revenues thereto belonging. Thus right heartily fare you well. At Lambeth, the 25 day of March. [1536].

State Paper Office. Miscellaneous letters. Temp. Hen. VIII. Third Series. Vol. IX.

[4]I pray you let not this suit be prejudicial to my servant Francis Basset, who would gladly be your servant, but that I may also continue a suitor unto you for him.

Your own assured ever,

T. CANTUARIEN.

*To the right worshipful master secretary unto the king's highness.*

---

## CLXXI. TO CRUMWELL.

RIGHT worshipful, in my right hearty wise I commend me unto you. These shall be to desire you to give credence unto this bearer Mr Champion[5], my chaplain, touching such things as he shall open and declare unto you; and that you will signify unto me by him part of your mind in that behalf. Thus heartily fare you well. At Lambeth, the 29 day of March. [1536.]

State Paper Office. Ibid. Original.

Your own ever assured,

T. CANTUARIEN.

*To the right honourable and my singular good friend, master secretary.*

---

[[2] Probably, as Dr Jenkyns suggests, the Harold Rosell addressed in Letter XLI.]

[[3] The great business of this session (Feb. 1536) was, the suppressing the lesser monasteries ..... "whereupon it was enacted, that all houses, which might spend yearly £200. or within it, should be suppressed, and their revenues converted to better uses," &c. Burnet's Hist. of Reformat. Vol. I. pp. 388, 9. Ed. Oxon. 1829. The priory of Shelford came under this act, which possessed the annual income of £151. 14*s*. Vid. Speed's History of Great Britain, Catalogue of Religious Houses, p. 1085. 2. Ed. Lond. 1632. Vid. Tanner's Notit. Monast. Nottinghamshire. XVII. Shelford. Ed. Camb. 1787.]

[[4] The postscript is in the archbishop's hand.]

[[5] Vid. Letters CXLV CLXIV. pp. 304, 317.]

## CLXXII. TO CRUMWELL.

State Paper Office. Ibid Original holograph.

ALAS, master secretary! you forget master Smyth[1] of the exchequer, who is near consumed with thought and pensiveness: even pity moveth me to rue the man, if I could, for his son's sake chiefly, and also for his own. I would give a great part of that I have to help him; and where I cannot myself, I make all my friends for him: so importune I am upon my friends from my friend his cause, I suppose more than I would be for mine own, or ever was: ruth and importunity of my friend maketh me so vehement against mine own nature. I have sent this bearer only to wait upon you until you have an answer of the king, and to put you in continual remembrance; for much business maketh you to forget many things, and yet I wonder that you remember so many things as you do. I was ever hitherto cold, but now I am in a heat with the cause of religion, which goeth all contrary to mine expectation, if it be as the fame goeth; wherein I would wonder fain break my mind unto you, and if you please, I will come to such place as you shall appoint for the same purpose. Thus he that made you ever keep you! From Knoll, the 22 day of April. [1536.]

Your own assured ever,

T. CANTUARIEN.

*To my very loving friend, Mr Secretary.*

---

## CLXXIII. TO LORD LISLE[2].

State Paper Office. Lisle Papers. Vol. II. No. 76.

MY Lord, in my most hearty wise I commend me to you, and in like wise to my good lady your wife, thanking you both for the well and gentle entreating of my chaplains[3] which of late were with you at Calice. And where you wrote unto me, that you have been noted a papist by some of my house (as you be informed), and that unworthily, inasmuch as you have every where spoken against the acts and living of the pope, and thereby the less have deserved to be accounted his fautour; my lord, it is not the person of the bishop of Rome, which usurpeth the name of the pope, that is so much to be detested, but the very papacy and the see of Rome, which hath by their laws suppressed Christ, and set up the bishop of that see as a God of this world. And where the word of God was adversary and against his authority, pomp, covetousness, idolatry, and superstitious doctrine, he spying this became adversary unto the word of God, falsifying it, extorting it out of the true sense, and (as much as he might) suppressing it by policy, craft, bye-laws and doctrines, contrary to the word of God, by power of himself and aid of other princes, and by divers other ways and means. And this is the chief thing to be detested in that see, that it hath brought the professors of Christ into such an ignorance of Christ. And besides this he hath consumed and wasted innumerable goods of all Christendom for the maintenance of that estate, to the intolerable impoverishment of all christian realms. Which said dominion and power, with other corrupt doctrines by them invented, is the thing rather to be abhorred than the person; yea, and the person also, if he prosecute to

---

[[1] "This may perhaps have been John Smith, father of the celebrated Sir Thomas Smith, who about this time was distinguishing himself by his lectures on Greek at Cambridge. See Strype's Life of Smith." Jenkyns' Remains of Abp. Cranmer, Vol. I. p. 162, *n*. d.]

[[2] This Letter has not appeared in any previous collection.]

[[3] Hore and Nycols were sent as Lent preachers, March 4, [A. D. 1536.] In that year Easter fell on the 16th April, and Ash Wednesday on the 1st March; and this letter was evidently forwarded on their return. In the preceding year, 1535, Easter fell on 28th March, and Hore was dispatched over to Calais a month earlier. The year in which this letter was sent to Lord Lisle was therefore, in all probability, 1536. Vid. Letters CXXXI. CLXVIII. pp. 293, 320.]

maintain the same. Therefore, albeit that some peradventure have partly suspected you to have favoured this his said usurped power by ignorance; yet nevertheless, inasmuch as I perceive that both you, of your gentle nature and the great towardness of that your good lady, be so inclined to promote the word of God, that shall from henceforth enforce me from time to time to stand in this behalf for your defence, as well to the king's highness and his most honourable council, as to other; requiring your lordship, as you do now favour the word of God, so to persevere to the end; whereby you shall not alonely deserve of God immortal reward for the same, but also be sure of me to do unto you such pleasure as I may. And as touching my commissary, I require you to be his good lord: he is the man of whom I never heard evil word spoken by you; I trust you shall both find him a plain and an honest man. Over this I give unto your lordship most hearty thanks for the pains which you have taken in my cousin Barton's cause. If there be any causes whereby I may take such pains for you or yours, I will be at all times ready to accomplish the same. And thus to make an end, I pray you to have me most heartily commended unto my good lady. Thus our Lord preserve you both in prosperity. At Otford, the 28 day of April. [1536.]

Your loving friend,

(Signed) THOMAS CANTUAR.

*To my very singular good lord and my especial friend my lord Lyall, deputy of our sovereign lord the king in the town of Calice.*

---

## CLXXIV. TO KING HENRY VIII.[4]

PLEASETH it your most noble grace to be advertised, that at your grace's commandment by Mr Secretary his letters written in your grace's name, I came to Lamehith yesterday, and do there remain to know your grace's further pleasure. And forsomuch as without your grace's commandment I dare not, contrary to the contents of the said letters, presume to come unto your grace's presence; nevertheless, of my most bounden duty, I can do no less than most humbly to desire your grace, by your great wisdom and by the assistance of God's help, somewhat to suppress the deep sorrows of your grace's heart, and to take all adversities of God's hand both patiently and thankfully.

Cott. MSS. Otho. C. x. f. 226. Original holograph. British Museum.

Burnet's Hist. of Reformat. Vol. I. p. 402, Ed. Oxon. 1829.

Todd's Life of Abp. Cranmer, Vol. I. p 154.

I cannot deny but your grace hath great causes many ways of lamentable heaviness; and also, that in the wrongful estimation of the world your grace's honour of every part is so highly touched, (whether the things that commonly be spoken of be true, or not,) that I remember not that ever Almighty God sent unto your grace any like occasion to try your grace's constancy throughout, whether your highness can be content to take of God's hand as well things displeasant as pleasant. And if he find in your noble heart such an obedience unto his will, that your grace, without murmuration and overmuch heaviness, do accept all adversities, not less thanking him than when all things succeeded after your grace's will and pleasure, nor less procuring his glory and honour; then I suppose your grace did never thing more acceptable unto him, since your first governance of this your realm: and moreover, your grace shall give unto him occasion to multiply and increase his graces and benefits unto your highness, as he did unto his most faithful servant Job; unto whom, after his

[4 "For the circumstances under which this letter was written, and for some of the discordant judgments which have been passed on it, see Burnet's Hist. of Reformat. Vol. I. p. 402; Lingard, Hist. of Engl. Vol. VI. p. 319. 8vo.; Turner, Modern Hist. of Engl. Vol. II. pp. 436, 442, 8vo.: Mackintosh, Hist. of Engl. in Lardner's Cabinet Cyclopædia, Vol. II. p. 194." Jenkyns.—The original letter is much injured by fire: the sentences wanting are supplied from Burnet.]

great calamities and heaviness, for his obedient heart and willing acceptation of God's scourge and rod, "addidit ei Dominus cuncta duplicia."

And if it be true, that is openly reported of the queen's grace; if men had a right estimation of things, they should not esteem any part of your grace's honour to be touched thereby, but her honour only to be clearly disparaged. And I am in such a perplexity, that my mind is clean amazed; for I never had better opinion in woman, than I had in her; which maketh me to think, that she should not be culpable. And again, I think your highness would not have gone so far, except she had surely been culpable. Now I think that your grace best knoweth, that next unto your grace I was most bound unto her of all creatures living. Wherefore I most humbly beseech your grace to suffer me in that, which both God's law, nature, and also her kindness, bindeth me unto; that is, that I may with your grace's favour wish and pray for her, that she may declare herself inculpable and innocent. And if she be found culpable, considering your grace's goodness towards her, and from what condition your grace of your only mere goodness took her and set the crown upon her head; I repute him not your grace's faithful servant and subject, nor true unto the realm, that would not desire the offence without mercy to be punished to the example of all other. And as I loved her not a little for the love which I judged her to bear towards God and his gospel; so, if she be proved culpable, there is not one that loveth God and his gospel that ever will favour her, but must hate her above all other; and the more they favour the gospel, the more they will hate her: for then there was never creature in our time that so much slandered the gospel; and God hath sent her this punishment, for that she feignedly hath professed his gospel in her mouth, and not in heart and deed.

And though she have offended so, that she hath deserved never to be reconciled unto your grace's favour; yet Almighty God hath manifoldly declared his goodness towards your grace, and never offended you. But your grace, I am sure, knowledgeth that you have offended him. Wherefore I trust that your grace will bear no less entire favour unto the truth of the gospel, than you did before; forsomuch as your grace's favour to the gospel was not led by affection unto her, but by zeal unto the truth. And thus I beseech Almighty God, whose gospel he hath ordained your grace to be defender of, ever to preserve your grace from all evil, and give you at the end the promise of his gospel. From Lambeth, the third day of May. [1536.]

After I had written this letter unto you grace, my lord chancellor, my lord of Oxford, my lord of Sussex, and my lord chamberlain of your grace's house, sent for me to come unto the star-chamber; and there declared unto me such things as your grace's pleasure was they should make me privy unto. For the which I am most bounden unto your grace. And what communication we had together, I doubt not but they will make the true report thereof unto your grace. I am exceeding sorry that such faults can be proved by the queen, as I heard of their relation. But I am, and ever shall be, your faithful subject.

Your grace's most humble subject
and chaplain,
T. Cantuariensis.

---

## CLXXV. TO LORD LISLE[1].

State Paper Office. Lisle Papers. Vol. II. No. 78.

My very singular good lord, in my most hearty wise I commend me unto your lordship. This be to signify unto the same, that I am very much beholding to your lordship, for that it liked you to send this bearer your servant by me in his recourse to Calice. And as now I have nothing unto your said lordship, saving that I may be most heartily commended unto my good lady, to whom eftsoons, as also to you, I give condign thanks for the well entreating of my chaplains at their late being at Calice. And if there be any pleasure in these parties, wherein I may do any thing

[1] This letter has not appeared in any previous collection.]

for you, from time to time, I will be ready to accomplish the same. Thus our Lord preserve you both in prosperity. At Otford, the 8 day of May. [1536.]

Your lordship's assured,

THOMAS CANTUAR.

*To my very singular good lord, my lord Lyle, deputy unto our sovereign lord the king at the town of Calice.*

## CLXXVI. TO CRUMWELL.

MY very singular good lord, in my most hearty wise I commend me unto your lordship. And whereas the bearer hereof, Mr Hambleton[2], upon no consideration else (as I understand) is put from his lands and possession in Scotland, but for that he favoureth the truth of God's word; and is, besides his birth[3], a man of right good living and honest conversation, and of gentill behaviour, by whom the word of God in this his exile hath no slander, but is the rather to be had in price and esteemed of other, considering that he so willingly hath borne his adversity: these shall be to desire you, my lord, to be a mediator unto the king's highness for him, that, being of this good judgment, he may have of his grace some competent living for his degree. Which, in mine opinion, shall not only be a good and an acceptable deed unto God, but also much redound to the king's grace's honour, so to consider the necessity of a gentleman for God's quarrel; and besides this, your lordship for your part cannot be unrewarded of God for the same. Thus Almighty God have your good lordship in his blessed tuition. At Aldington[4], the 9th day of August. [1536.]

State Paper Office. Miscellaneous Letters. Temp. Hen. VIII. Third Series. Vol. IX. Original. Todd's Life of Cranmer, Vol. I. p. 150.

Your own ever assured,

T. CANTUARIEN.

*To the right honourable and my singular good lord, my lord privy seal.*

## CLXXVII. TO KING HENRY VIII[5].

PLEASETH it your grace to be advertised, that where, as well by your grace's special

Cott. MSS. Cleop. E. vi. f. 232. Original holograph. British Museum. Strype's Mem. of Abp. Cranmer, App. No. 13, Vol. II. pp. 696—701. Ed. Oxon. 1840

[2 Probably James Hamilton, brother of Patrick Hamilton the first martyr of the reformation in Scotland, [A.D 1527.] Foxe gives a narrative of the execution of Patrick Hamilton at St Andrew's, A.D. 1528. Acts and Monuments, pp. 973, et seq. Ed. Lond. 1583. . . . "James Hamilton was accused as one that maintained the opinion of master Patrick his brother. To whom the king gave counsel to depart, and not to appear; for in case he appeared, he could not help him, because the bishops had persuaded him that the cause of heresy did in no wise appertain unto him. And so James fled, and was condemned as an heretic, and all his goods and lands confiscate, and disposed unto others." Ibid. p. 982.]

[3 "This allusion to Mr Hambleton's birth, agrees well with the supposition that he was the James Hamilton mentioned in the foregoing note, who . . . . was nearly related to the king of Scotland." Jenkyns' Remains of Abp. Cranmer, Vol. I p. 166.]

[4 Strype gives a list of the several manors, &c. exchanged by Henry VIII., "as he found them dispersed in Philpot's book of Kent;" amongst which Aldington (near Ashford) is named, "where was a seat for the archbishop, a park, and a chase for deer, called Aldington Frith." Strype's Mem. of Abp. Cranmer, Vol. I. pp. 404, 5. Ed. Oxon. 1840.]

[5 Dr Jenkyns has fixed the date of this letter. A.D. 1536, and gives the following note to establish his opinion:—"Some writers have named 1534 as the date of this letter. Strype (Mem. of Abp. Cranmer, p. 32) and Mr Todd (Life of Cranmer, Vol. I. p. 110) fix 1535. But the Michaelmas mentioned in the first sentence, as might be supposed from the context, and as is proved beyond question by Letter CLX. (pp. 313, 14, of this edition,) was the Michaelmas of 1535; and the letter therefore must have been written in 1536. There can also be no doubt respecting the time, when the king sent his order to the bishops to preach against the papal supremacy; for this order is here positively stated to have been dated the third of

letters, dated the third day of June[1] in the xxviith year of your grace's most noble reign, as also by mouth in Winchester at Michaelmas last past[2], your grace commanded all the prelates of your realm, that they with all acceleration and expedition should do their diligence every one in his diocese, fully to persuade your people of the bishop of Rome his authority, that it is but a false and unjust usurpation, and that your grace, of very right and by God's law, is the supreme head of this church of England, next immediately unto God; I, to accomplish your grace's commandment, incontinent upon my return from Winchester, (knowing that all the country about Otford and Knoll, where my most abode was, were sufficiently instructed in those matters already,) came up into these parts of East Kent, only by preaching to persuade the people in the said two articles: and in mine own church at Canterbury, because I was informed that that town in those two points was least persuaded of all my diocese, I preached there two sermons myself; and, as it then chanced, Dr Leighton was present at my first sermon, being then your grace's visitor[3]. Of whom, if it so please your grace, you may hear the report, what I preached.

The scope and effect of both my sermons stood in three things. First, I declared that the bishop of Rome was not God's vicar in earth, as he was taken: and although it was so taught these three or four hundreth years, yet it was done by means of the bishop of Rome, who compelled men by oaths so to teach, to the maintenance of his authority, contrary to God's word. And here I declared by what means and craft the bishops of Rome obtained such usurped authority.

Second, because the see of Rome was called "sancta sedes Romana," and the bishop was called "sanctissimus papa;" and men's consciences peradventure could not be quiet to be separated from so holy a place, and from God's most holy vicar; I shewed the people that this thing ought nothing to move them, for it was but a holiness in name; for indeed there was no such holiness at Rome. And hereupon I took occasion to declare the glory and pomp of Rome, the covetousness, the unchaste living, and the maintenance of all vices.

Third, I spake against the bishop of Rome his laws; which he calleth "divinas leges," and "sacros canones," and maketh them equal with God's law. And here I declared that many of his laws were contrary to God's laws. And some of them which were good and laudable, yet they were not of such holiness as he would make them; that is, to be taken as God's laws, or to have remission of sins by observing of them. And here I said, that so many of his laws as were good, men ought not to contemn and despise them, and wilfully to break them; for those that be good your grace had received as laws of your realm, until such time as others should be made. And therefore as laws of your realm they must be observed, and not contemned.

And here I spake as well of the ceremonies of the church as of the foresaid laws; that they ought neither to be rejected or despised, nor yet to be observed with this opinion, that they of themselves make men holy, or that they remit sin. For seeing that our sins be remitted by the death of our Saviour Christ Jesus, I said it was too much injury to Christ to impute the remission of our sins to any laws or ceremonies of man's making: nor the laws and ceremonies of the church at their first making were ordained for that intent. But as the common laws of your grace's realm be not made to remit sin, nor no man doth observe them for that intent, but for a common commo-

---

June, 27 Hen. VIII. i.e. 1535. Yet both of the above-named writers, together with Wilkins, have supposed a proclamation of the 9th of June, which refers to it, to have been issued in 1534. Strype's Mem. Eccl. Vol. I. p. 168. (Vol. I. p. 259. Ed. Oxon. 1822.) Todd's Life of Cranmer, Vol. I. p. 110. Wilkins' Concilia, Vol. III. p. 772. This is the more extraordinary, as a document of the 25th of June, of a similar character, printed by Burnet, contains in itself evidence of its date in an allusion to the deaths of bishop Fisher and Sir Thomas More, who suffered on the 22d of June, 1535. See Burnet, Hist. of Reformat. Vol. III. p. 188, and Append. Book ii. No. 32." (Vol. III. Part II. p. 100. Ed. Oxon. 1829.)]

[1 Vid. Letter CXLVIII. pp. 306, 7.]

[2 Vid. Letter CLX. p. 314, *n.* 2.]

[3 "This again confirms the dates given above; for it was in Oct. 1535, that Leighton was first employed as visitor of monasteries. Burnet's Hist. of Reformat. Vol. I. p. 369." Jenkyns' Remains of Abp. Cranmer, Vol. I. p. 168, *n.* n.]

dity, and for a good order and quietness to be observed among your subjects; even so were the laws and ceremonies first instituted in the church for a good order, and remembrances of many good things, but not for remission of our sins. And though it be good to observe them well for that intent they were first ordained; yet it is not good, but a contumely unto Christ, to observe them with this opinion, that they remit sin; or that the very bare observation of them in itself is a holiness before God: although they be remembrances of many holy things, or a disposition unto goodness. And even so do the laws of your grace's realm dispose men unto justice, to peace, and other true and perfect holiness. Wherefore I did conclude for a general rule, that the people ought to observe them, as they do the laws of your grace's realm, and with no more opinion of holiness, or remission of sin, than the other common laws of your grace's realm.

Though my two sermons were long, yet I have written briefly unto your highness the sum of them both. And I was informed by sundry reports, that the people were glad that they heard so much as they did; until such time as the prior of the black friars[4] at Canterbury preached a sermon, as it was thought and reported, clean contrary unto all the three things which I had preached before.

For as touching the first part, where I had preached against the erroneous doctrine of the bishop of Rome his power; which error was, that by God's law he should be God's vicar here in earth; the prior would not name the bishop of Rome, but under colour spake generally, that the church of Christ never erred.

And as touching the second part, where I spake of the vices of the bishops of Rome and their see; the prior said that he would not slander the bishops of Rome. And he said openly to me in a good audience, that he knew no vices by none of the bishops of Rome. And he said also openly, that I preached uncharitably, when I said that these many years I had daily prayed unto God that I might see the power of Rome destroyed; and that I thanked God that I had now seen it in this realm. And yet in my sermon I declared the cause wherefore I so prayed. For I said, that I perceived the see of Rome work so many things contrary to God's honour and the wealth of this realm, and I saw no hope of amendment so long as that see reigned over us; and for this cause only I had prayed unto God continually, that we might be separated from that see; and for no private malice or displeasure that I had either to the bishop[5] or see of Rome. But this seemed an uncharitable prayer to the said prior, that the power of Rome should be destroyed.

And as for the third part, where I preached against the laws of the bishop of Rome; that they ought not to be taken as God's laws, nor to be esteemed so highly as he would have them; the prior, craftily leaving out the name of the bishop of Rome, preached, that the laws of the church be equal with God's laws. These things he preached, as it is proved both by sufficient witness and also by his own confession.

I leave the judgment hereof unto your grace and to your council, whether this were a defence of the bishop of Rome, or not. And I only, according to my bounden duty, have reported the truth of the fact. But in mine opinion, if he had spoken nothing else, yet whosoever saith that the church never erred, maintaineth the bishop of Rome his power. For if that were not erroneous that was taught of his power, That he is Christ's vicar in earth, and by God's law head of all the world, spiritual and temporal; and that all people must believe that "de necessitate salutis;" and that whosoever doeth any thing against the see of Rome is an heretic; and that he hath authority also in purgatory; with such other many false things, which were taught in times past to be articles of our faith: if these things were not erroneous, yea, and

---

[[4] They were called "dominican, black, preaching friars: preaching, because they were the only preachers of all the friars; black, because of their habit, which was a black cope and cowl over a white coat; dominican, because St Dominic was their founder." Somner's Antiq. of Cant. p. 106, Ed. Lond. 1640.]

[[5] To the bishops, Strype.]

errors in the faith, then must needs your grace's laws be erroneous, that pronounce the bishop of Rome to be of no more power by God's law than other bishops, and them to be traitors that defend the contrary. This is certain, that whosoever saith that the church never erred, must either deny that the church ever taught any such errors[1] of the bishop of Rome his power, and then they speak against that which all the world knoweth, and all books written of that matter these three or four hundreth years do testify; or else they must say, that the said errors be none errors, but truths. And then it is both treason and heresy.

At my first examination of him, which was before Christmas, he said, that he preached not against me, nor that I had preached any thing amiss. But now he saith, that I preached amiss in very many things, and that he purposely preached against me[2]; and this he reporteth openly: by which words I am marvellously slandered in these parts. And for this cause I beseech your grace, that I may not have the judgment of the cause, forsomuch as he taketh me for a party; but that your grace would commit the hearing hereof unto my lord privy seal, or else to associate unto me some other person at your grace's pleasure, that we may hear the case jointly together.

If this man, who hath so highly offended your grace, and preached against me openly, being ordinary and metropolitan of this province; and that in such matters as concern the authority, misliving, and the laws of the bishop of Rome; and that also within mine own church; if he, I say, be not looked upon, I leave unto your grace's prudence to expend, what example this may be unto others with like colour to maintain the bishop of Rome his authority; and also, of what estimation I shall be reputed hereafter, and what credence shall be given unto my preaching, whatsoever I shall say hereafter.

I beseech your grace to pardon me of my long and tedious writing; for I could not otherwise set the matter forth plain. And I most heartily thank your grace for the stag which your grace sent unto me from Windsor forest: which, if your grace knew for how many causes it was welcome unto me, and how many ways it did me service, I am sure you would think it much the better bestowed. Thus our Lord have your highness always in his preservation and governance. From Ford, the xxvi. day of August, [1536.]

Your grace's most humble chaplain and beadsman,

T. CANTUARIEN.

---

## CLXXVIII. TO CRUMWELL.

Cott. MSS. Cleop. E. v. f. 102. Original. British Museum. Strype's Mem. of Abp. Cranmer, Vol. I. pp. 65—67. Ed. Oxon. 1840.

My very singular good lord, in my most hearty wise I commend me to your lordship[3]. And whereas your lordship writeth to me in the favour of this bearer, Massey, an old servant to the king's highness, that, being contracted to his sister's daughter of his late wife deceased, he might enjoy the benefit of a dispensation in that behalf; specially, considering it is none of the cases of prohibition contained in the statute[4]; surely, my lord, I would gladly accomplish your request herein, if the

---

[1 Any such error, Strype.]

[2 Dr Jenkyns supposes that "this change may have arisen from the execution of Anne Boleyn in the preceding May, which tended greatly to raise the spirits of the popish party. It would seem however from Letter CLXVIII, (Letter CLXXII. p. 322 of this edition,) that they had been gaining ground before that event." Remains of Abp. Cranmer, Vol. I. pp. 171, 2. *n.* p.]

[3 Unto your lordship, Strype.]

[4 Stat. 28 Hen. VIII. cap 7. "'For the establishment of the succession of the imperial crown of this realm.' It was passed a few months before, on the king's marriage to Jane Seymour. The prohibited degrees were expressed in it in nearly the same terms as in the former act of succession, 25 Hen. VIII. c. 22, but were extended to cases of carnal knowledge." Jenkyns' Remains of Abp. Cranmer, Vol. I. p. 173, *n.* r.—"Indeed in these times there were great irregularities about marriage in the realm, many being incestuous and unlawful; which caused the parliament, two or three years

word of God would permit the same. And where you require me, that if I think this licence may not be granted by the law of God, then I should write unto you the reasons and authorities that move me so to think; that upon the declaration[5] unto the king's highness, you may confer thereupon with some other learned men, and so advertise me of the king's farther resolution[6] in the same accordingly; for shortness of time, I shall shew you one reason, which is this: by the law of God many persons be prohibited, which be not expressed, but be understand by like prohibitions in equal degree. As St Ambrose saith[7], that the niece is forbid by the law of God, although it be not expressed in Leviticus that the uncle shall not marry his niece. But where the nephew is forbid there, that he shall not marry his aunt, by the same is understand that the niece shall not be married unto her uncle. Likewise, as the daughter is not there plainly expressed, yet where the same is forbid[8] to marry his mother, it is understand that the daughter may not be married to her father, by cause they be of like degree. Even so it is in this case and many other; for where it is there expressed that the nephew shall not marry his uncle's wife, it must needs be understand that the niece shall not be married unto the aunt's husband, by cause that all is one equality of degree. And although I could allege many reasons and authorities mo for this purpose, yet I trust this one reason shall satisfy all that be learned and of judgment.

And as touching the act of parliament concerning the degrees prohibited by God's law, they be not so plainly set forth as I would they were. Wherein I somewhat spake my mind at the making of the said[9], but it was not then accepted. I required then, that there might be expressed mother, and mother-in-law, daughter, and daughter-in-law; and so in further degrees directly upward and downward, *in linea recta;* also sister and sister-in-law, aunt and aunt-in-law, niece and niece-in-law. And this limitation, in my judgment, should have contained all the degrees[10] prohibited by God's law, expressed and not expressed[11]: and should have satisfied this man, and such other, which would marry their nieces-in-law.

My lord[12], I have no news to send you from these parties, but I much long to hear such news as be occurrent with you[13]. And therefore, if you have any good news, I pray you to send me some. Thus, my lord, right heartily fare you well. At Ford, the viith day of September. [1536.]

Your lordship's own,

T. Cantuarien.

---

past, viz. 1533, in one of their acts, to publish a table of degrees, wherein it was prohibited by God's law to marry. But the act did not cure this evil; many thought to bear themselves out in their illegal contracts, by getting dispensations from the archbishop; which created him much trouble by his denying to grant them. There was one Massy, a courtier, who had contracted himself to his deceased wife's niece: which needing a dispensation, the party got the lord Crumwell to write to the archbishop in his behalf; especially because it was thought to be none of the cases of prohibition contained in the act. But such was the integrity of the archbishop, that he refused to do any thing he thought not allowable, though it were upon the persuasion of the greatest men and best friends he had." Strype's Mem. of Abp. Cranmer, Vol. I. p. 65.]

[5 Upon declaration. Strype.]

[6 Advertise me the king's. Ibid.]

[7 Ambros. Epist. Lib. vi. Epist. xlviii. Paterno. Vol. V. pp. 150, 1. Ed. Colon. Agrip. 1616.]

[8 The son is forbid. Strype.]

[9 The said law. Ibid.]

[10 Would have contained all degrees. Ibid.]

[11 "Nota, that the rest of the degrees prohibited are necessary to be expressed also. All the degrees prohibited, in my judgment, may be best expressed in these general words: that no man may marry his mother, nor mother-in-law, and so upward in *linea recta;* daughter, nor daughter-in-law, and so downward in *linea recta;* sister, nor sister-in-law; aunt, nor aunt-in-law; niece, nor niece-in-law."—Abp. Cranmer's Annotations, upon Henry VIIIths Corrections of the Institution of a Christian Man, Annot. xxxvi. p. 94, supra.]

[12 Strype omits, "my lord."]

[13 Concurrent with you. Strype.]

## CLXXIX. TO CRUMWELL.

State Paper Office. Miscellaneous. Temp. Hen. VIII. Third series. Vol. IX. Original.

My singular good lord, in my most hearty wise I commend me unto your lordship. And whereas I perceive that your lordship, not without urgent and godly considerations, hath suppressed already divers friars' houses, and bestowed them upon honest men, as I am informed, which your godly proceeding I trust shall as well extend unto Canterbury as in other places, to the intent that the irreligious religion there may be extincted with other; and forasmuch as the gray friars [1] in Canterbury lieth very commodiously for this bearer Thomas Cobham, brother unto my lord Cobham, and my servant [2], specially by cause the same is not only in his native country, but also nigh unto his friends: these shall be to beseech your lordship to be so good lord unto him as to help him unto the said house of the gray friars; for having already some land of his own, he shall be the more able to maintain the house in an honest state. And in thus doing, your lordship shall both do for the preferment of an honest man, and also make him more able to do the king's grace service, and your lordship such pleasure as shall lie in him during his life. Thus, my lord, right heartily fare you well. At Lambeth, the vth day of October. [1536.]

Your own ever assured,

T. Cantuarien.

*To my very singular good lord, my lord privy seal.*

---

## CLXXX. TO KING HENRY VIII [3].

Harl. MSS. 787, f. 18. British Museum. Copy. Ellis' Original Letters, second series, No. cxiii. Vol. II. pp. 65—68. Todd's Life of Abp. Cranmer, Vol. I. p. 96

Pleaseth it your grace to be advertised, that I have received news out of Rome, from one named John Bianket, a Bononois born, some time my servant, and now servant unto the cardinal [4] which was late bishop of Worcester, and more privy with him of all secrets than any other about him. And among other things thus he writeth:

---

[1 The following note is given by Dr Jenkyns respecting "the gray friars at Canterbury," the references of which have been examined and amended: "Hasted states that the house of the gray friars in Canterbury was suppressed in 1534; yet this letter, being addressed to Crumwell as lord privy seal, could not have been written earlier than 1536. Hasted probably may not have attended to the division of the gray friars, or Franciscans, into the observants and conventuals. The observants, as Stow relates, were put down in August 1534, and Augustine friars set in their places for the time; but the conventuals do not then appear to have been disturbed. On the contrary, Parkinson, in his Antiquities of English Franciscans, asserts, that 'many of the observants were thrust into the houses of the conventuals for a time;' and in some instances perhaps the latter may have been substituted for the former. The act 27 Hen. VIII. cap. 28, for the suppression of the smaller religious houses in general, was passed in the parliament which met on the 4th of Feb. 1536; but it does not seem to have been carried into execution immediately, and 1539 is mentioned as the year, when 'all the Franciscan convents in the nation were taken into the king's hands, and the friars turned out of doors to shift for themselves.'" See Hasted's Hist. of Kent, Vol. IV. pp. 446, 7; Ed. Cant. 1778-99. Stow's Annals, p. 570. Ed Lond. 1615. Parkinson's Collectan. Anglo-Minorit. p. 233. Ed. Lond. 1726.]

[2 Thomas, brother of Lord Cobham, married Susan Cranmer, daughter of John Cranmer, of Aslacton, brother of the archbishop, by Margaret, daughter of John Fitzwilliams of Spotboro', his second wife. She afterwards married Anthony Vaughan, son of Sir Hugh Vaughan. Vid. Genealogical Table, Todd's Life of Abp. Cranmer. This application in his behalf must have been unsuccessful, as the site of the gray friars was afterwards granted to Thomas Spilman, 31 Hen. VIII. [A. D. 1539.] Hasted's Hist. of Kent, Vol. IV. p. 447.]

[3 Mr Todd has assigned this letter to 1533; Sir H. Ellis has not given any date to it, "but has placed it among papers of 1535." Dr Jenkyns thinks, "the historical events which it mentions, sufficiently prove it to have been written in 1536." Remains of Abp. Cranmer, Vol. I. pp. 175, 6, *n.* x.]

[4 "There passed [A. D. 1531] a private act for depriving the bishops of Salisbury and Worcester; who were cardinal Campegio and Jerome de Ghinucci: the former deserved greater severities at the king's hand; but the latter seems to have served him faithfully, and was recommended both by the king and the French king, about a year before, to a cardinal's hat." Burnet's Hist. of Reformat. Vol. I. p. 301. Ed. Oxon. 1829.]

"The pope has called hither many prelates for matters concerning the council[5], among whom is Mr Raynold Pole made much of and much set by, and received of the pope himself very gladly. And because the saying is, that the king hath sent for him home into England, and desired him, and promised him also great things if he would come, or at the least if that he would not go to Rome[6]; he now is come hither, not regarding the king's desire, promise, nor threats. And here men do esteem and think surely that the pope will make him cardinal, and now he hath given him lodgings for himself within the palace, and will have him near him.

"And among those great men that be here for this matter, the selfsame Raynold Pole is here truly most esteemed and most set by of all. And doubtless they be all[7] singular fellows, and such as ever absented themselves from the court, desiring to live holily; as the bishop of Verona, the bishop of Chiete, the archbishop of Salerne, the bishop of Carpentras, otherwise called Sadoletus, and many other that now be here, for... to consult these matters of the council; the which I cannot see how it can go forward, as long as the matters of war kindled between the princes are unquenched, without whom it is like that it cannot go forward. Nevertheless there be sent messengers to intimate the council through Christendom, leaving you apart, to whom they will intimate it there in writing and in citations. Friar Denis, which wrote on the king's side, being now general of the religion, cometh as ambassador from the pope towards the king of Scots.

"The emperor[8] is now in Genoa, and many princes, specially the duke of Florence[9], go to see him, and to shew themselves glad that he has arrived there safe and in good health; which chanced but to few gentlemen, which be almost all sick[10].

"There is entreaty made for peace all that may be, and it seemeth that the Frenchmen have good hope therein: for they have left off war, and have no more men in Italy now but Guido Rangone his men, and those of Turin; which as yet they hold, with certain other castles. And the pope is fervent and hot in entreating of this peace[11]."

---

[[5] "Paul III.... first made a promise, in 1535, that he would assemble a council at Mantua; and afterwards, A. D. 1536, he actually proclaimed one by letters despatched through all provinces of the Roman world." Mosheim's Eccl. Hist. Book IV. Cent. XVI. Sect. 1. §. 9. Vol. III. p. 145. Ed. Lond. 1845. Previously to the meeting of the council, he assembled at Rome "persons of known abilities to concert means of facilitating a happy issue to so necessary and arduous an undertaking." Phillips' Life of Reginald Pole, p. 153. Ed. Lond. 1767.]

[[6] "Reginald, in obedience to Paul III's orders, was now set out from Venice in his way to Rome, when a courier from England overtook him at Verona. The news of his journey had already reached the king's ears, and the courier came furnished with every argument to disconcert it. Lord Crumwell expressed himself by nothing but threats and invectives; Tunstal renewed his objections to the papal authority: but the other letters...were eloquent indeed, being from the countess of Salisbury, his mother, and his brother lord Montague; in which they entreated him, by all the ties of duty and affection, to desist from a step which was so displeasing to the king." Id. pp. 155, 6.]

[[7] Dr Jenkyns says, (Remains of Abp. Cranmer, Vol. I. p. 174), that these were doubtless the same distinguished men, who, on the prorogation of the council, were directed by the pope to digest a plan of reformation. They were nine in number. "Pole was in the thirty-sixth year of his age, and the youngest of all the associates... : and though they were men of the first character for learning and probity, yet he was the directing mind that guided the whole; and alone drew up the plan of reformation, the substance of which had been the joint labours of them all; and when it was printed some years after, it appeared in his name, without any mention of his colleagues." Id. p. 159. The names of the commissioners and an abstract of their plan may be seen in Sleidan, (De statu Religionis et reipub.) Book XII. p. 233. English Ed. Lond. 1689.]

[8] [Charles V. went to Genoa on his return from his disastrous campaign in Provence. "As he could not bear to expose himself to the scorn of the Italians after such a sad reverse of fortune, he embarked directly for Spain," i.e. in November, 1536. Robertson's Hist. of Charles V. Vol. II. p. 404. Ed. Lond. 1769.]

[[9] Alexander de Medici, who was assassinated in the beginning of 1537 by his nearest kinsman, Lorenzo. Id. pp. 415, 6.]

[[10] Charles V. "had lost one half of his troops by disease or by famine." Id. p. 403.]

[[11] "The pope....made it his business to procure a cessation [of arms] in Italy and in other places.... First therefore the truce was agreed upon for a certain term; when that was expired, it was continued for another; till at last a peace was made....Now the pope's design in reconciling these princes, was to persuade them to join their forces against his mortal enemy the king of England, and against the Lutherans." Sleidan, (De statu Religionis et reipub.) Book XI. p. 239. This peace, or rather truce for ten years between Charles and Francis, was concluded in June 1538. Id. Book XII. p. 244.]

Here have I written the very words of the letter, as I did translate them out of Italian into English, as near as I could, word for word; which I can do no less than signify unto your highness, forsomuch as there be some things concerning the general council and Mr Raynold Pole, whereof I thought it my duty to give notice unto your grace. And thus I beseech the mighty Lord of lords to strengthen and preserve your grace ever, and to resist and suppress all your highness's adversaries with your rebel and untrue subjects[1]. At Knoll, the 18th day of November. [1536.]

Your grace's most humble chaplain and beadsman,

T. CANTUARIEN.

*To the king's highness.*

## CLXXXI. TO CRUMWELL.

State Paper Office. Miscellaneous Letters. Temp. Hen. VIII. Vol. IX. Original.

MY very singular good lord, in my most hearty wise I commend me unto your lordship. And whereas your lordship was so good lord unto James Arnold, my servant, this bearer, as to direct (besides the king's gracious letters) your favourable letters unto sir John Champenes, knight, then lord mayor of London, and to his brethren, in the preferment of my said servant to the room and office of the sword-bearer of London[2], when it should chance next to be void; by means whereof there was a record in writing made of their grant unto my said servant; and forsomuch as I now understand that the sword-bearer is in danger of death, and not like to escape: these shall be to beseech your lordship, in case need so require, to direct your favourable letters unto the mayor and aldermen that now be, putting them in rememberance of their former grant made by reason of the king's grace's letters and your lordship's unto my said servant; so that he may, without further molestation or suit, enjoy that room, if it chance to be now void. And surely, my lord, I am more desirous to seek his preferment, because he hath sustained no small pains in journeys beyond the seas with me, with the bishop of Harforth[3], Mr Eliot[4], and with Mr Hethe[5], in the king's affairs; beseeching your lordship therefore the rather to be his good lord in this behalf. Thus, my lord, right heartily fare you well. At Ford, the ivth day of January. [1537.]

Your own ever assured,

THOMAS CANTUARIEN.

*To the right honourable and my singular good lord, my lord privy seal.*

## CLXXXII. TO CRUMWELL.

State Paper Office. Miscellaneous Letters, Temp. Hen. VIII. Third Series. Vol. IX. Original.

MY very especial and singular good lord, these shall be to signify unto your good lordship, that I have sent unto you by Richard Nevell my servant, the bringer hereof,

[1 Alluding to the rebellion in Yorkshire under Aske, which was still raging in Nov. 1536. Vid. Kennett's Hist. of England, Lord Herbert's Life of Hen. VIII. Vol. II. p. 205. Ed. Lond. 1706; and State Papers, Vol. I. p. 511, &c.]

[2 Vid. Letter CL. p. 307.]

[3 Edward Fox, bishop of Hereford, was sent by Henry VIII. as ambassador to the pope with Gardiner, A.D. 1527, respecting his divorce from queen Catharine, and in Dec. 1535, he was again sent with Hethe and Barnes to the princes assembled at Smalcald, where he remained after the others returned home in January, A.D. 1531, the king having left further negociation of matters to him alone. He was accused of having made the matter of the king's "inclination to the evangelical doctrine more than it was," in order to influence the judgment of the German divines concerning the divorce. Strype's Eccl. Mem. Vol. I. pp. 136, 348, 354, 5. Ed. Oxon. 1822. Seckendorf, Comment. Hist. Apol. de Lutheran. Lib. III, Sect. 13. § 39, Add. p. 111. Ed. Francof. et Lips. 1692. Vid. Letter LXXXVIII. p. 276, n. 1.]

[4 See Letter CL. p. 307, n. 6.]

[5 See Letters LXXXVIII. CL. pp. 276, 307.]

xx[li]. for your fee of this year, desiring your good lordship, in all such affairs and business as I have to you at this time, as well for Mortlake[6] as other things, that you give credence unto him, which knoweth my whole mind herein. And so Almighty God preserve your good lordship. From Ford, the xvth day of January. [1537.]

Your own ever assured,

T. Cantuarien.

*To my especial and singular good lord, my lord privy seal.*

---

## CLXXXIII. TO CRUMWELL.

My very singular good lord, in my most hearty manner I commend me unto your lordship. And whereas I received a letter from you, wherein you will me to send sir Hugh Payne unto you after his appearance, whom ye are informed that I acited to appear before me; your lordship shall understand, that the said sir Hugh Payne was curate of Hadley in the county of Suffolk, of my peculiar jurisdiction, and for his erroneous and seditious preaching there he was detected to me: upon which detection I sent for him; and in the mean space, while he stood in examination, I commanded him, before doctor Revet, parson of Hadley, that he should not preach within my diocese or peculiars; which my commandment he disobediently contemning, did both preach at Hadley and also at London in my peculiars there. And in his examination had before me concerning those things wherein he was detected, he was proved openly perjured. And that he there erroneously preached, a taste of his teaching your lordship shall perceive. He taught openly in the pulpit there, that one paternoster, said by the injunction of a priest, was worth a million paternosters said of a man's mere voluntary mind: by this you may soon savour what judgment this man is of, and how sincerely he would instruct the people. At the last he, seeing these things proved against him, submitted himself to my correction. And whereas I might by justice have pronounced him perjured, and farther have proceeded against him for his erroneous preaching, I enjoined to him but certain penance, and not so much as he deserved; which he did receive, and swear by the holy evangelists to accomplish the same. And therein again he was forsworn and did it not, but fled into the said county of Suffolk again, and became a parish priest and a preacher at Stoke Nayland, where he is (as I am informed) as well liked as he was at Hadley. I hearing that he was there, caused him to be cited to appear before me; which thing he did not: whereupon I did excommunicate him, and so now for his contumacy he standeth excommunicate. And if he come unto me, I will send him unto your lordship; but in the mean space these my letters are to desire your lordship that you will put with me your helping hand to see him punished: for although many of the observants[7] were wolves in sheep's skins, yet in my opinion he ought to give place to none of them in dissimulation, hypocrisy, flattery, and all other qualities of the wolfish Pharisees.

State Paper Office. Ibid. Original.

Furthermore I send unto your lordship herewithal a letter directed to me by a monk of Christ's church in Canterbury, named Dan John Walkeham, concerning certain detections. Upon which letter this day I have examined Dan Stephen Gyles and Dan John Stone, monks; and I have sent for Dan Thomas Becket to examine him to-morrow. And as for John Stone, I have committed him to ward: beseeching your

---

[6 "The archiepiscopal possessions at Mortlake were assured to Crumwell by an act of parliament passed in 1536, entitled 'An Act concerning an exchange of lands between the king's highness, the archbishop of Canterbury, and Thomas Crumwell, Esq. the king's chief secretary.' Stat. 28 Hen. VIII. cap. 50." Jenkyns' Remains of Abp. Cranmer, Vol. I. p. 180, *n.* q.]

[7 Vid. Letters CXVIII. CXLIII. CLXXIX. pp. 291, 303, 330.]

lordship that I may know with expedition the king's grace's pleasure concerning the ordering of these persons[1].

Over this I have received letters directed both unto your lordship and to me from Turney[2] of Calice; and because our letters concern divers matters, I have sent you mine also, thinking it good that your lordship know the contents thereof. Thus, my lord, right heartily fare you well. At Ford, the 28th day of January. [1537.]

Your own ever assured,

T. CANTUARIEN.

*To the right honourable and my singular good lord, my lord privy seal.*

---

## CLXXXIV. TO CRUMWELL.

State Paper Office. Ibid. Original. Todd's Life of Abp. Cranmer, Vol. I. p. 172.

MY very singular good lord, in my most hearty manner I commend me unto your lordship. And where you require me to advertise you, what farther knowledge I have concerning the misdemeanor of such monks of Christ's church as of late were detected unto you[3], as yet I know no more than I wrote to you of, saving that the observation of the king's injunctions is not regarded; for when any of the convent will move to have any of the said injunctions observed, by and by the prior saith that he hath a dispensation for it: insomuch that, amongst other things, on St Blase day[4] last past, the prior commanded that the relics should be set forth as they were wont to be, and thereof sent word to the convent unto the chapter-house, that it was the king's pleasure so to be done, which is contrary to the injunctions[5] given. But forasmuch as I was uncertain whether he be thus dispensed withal for such things or no, I thought it good to advertise your lordship thereof. Besides this you shall understand, that there is one, named Dan Robert Antoney, a subcellerar of Christ's church, for fear of examination is gone his ways; who left a letter to the prior behind him, the tenor whereof you shall perceive by the copy of this letter herein inclosed.

Further you shall receive herewithal a letter sent to me from Calice, concerning an oath to be had there for the extirpation of the bishop of Rome's power and authority according to the act[6] of parliament: by which said letter your lordship shall perceive more in that behalf.

Also I have in durance with me a French priest of Calice, of whom I wrote to your lordship, and with him I have received an English book, which my commissary[7], with other soldiers of the town, in reprehending such corrupt sayings as are therein contained, sustained much reproof and displeasure: the notable places therein this bearer my servant can inform you. If your lordship be minded to have the priest, I will send him unto you. He is surely a simple man, without all knowledge of learning; and therefore I think that he hath spoken nothing of malice or purpose, but of ignorance. And forasmuch as he is the French king's subject, and served there for no purpose else but to be a gardener, in mine opinion it will be well done that he be sent unto Calice

---

[[1] Vid. Letter CLXXXIV. infra.]

[[2] Vid. Letters CLV. CLIX. pp. 311, 313, &c.; Foxe's Acts and Monuments, p. 1223. Ed. Lond. 1583; Stat. 32 Hen. VIII. cap. 49.]

[[3] Vid. Letter CLXXXIII. supra.]

[[4] Feb. 3rd.]

[[5] "Item, That they shall not shew no relics or feigned miracles for increase of lucre, but that they exhort pilgrims and strangers to give that to the poor that they thought to offer to their images or relics." Burnet's Hist. of Reformat. Book III. No. 2, Vol. I. Part II. p. 222. "To the intent that all superstition and hypocrisy, crept into divers men's hearts, may vanish away, they shall not set forth or extol any images, relics, or miracles, for any superstition or lucre." Id. Injunctions to the Clergy of the Realm. Vol. I. Part II. Book III. No. 7, p. 252. Ed. Oxon. 1829.]

[[6] Stat. 28 Hen. VIII. cap. 10.]

[[7] Sir John Butler. Vid. Foxe's Acts and Monuments, p. 1234. Ed. Lond. 1583.]

again, and so banished the town, and sent home unto his natural country. Thus, my lord, right heartily fare you well. At Ford, the xvi. day of February. [1537.]

Your own ever assured,

T. Cantuarien.

*To my very singular good lord, my lord privy seal.*

---

## CLXXXV. TO CRUMWELL.

State Paper Office. Ibid. Original.

My very singular good lord, in most hearty wise I commend me unto your lordship. And whereas this bearer, Mr Hambleton[8], shewed unto your lordship certain letters which he received from Rome, and your lordship willed him that he should in no wise agree unto them, promising him to move the king's highness to give him some living here in England; these shall be therefore to desire your lordship to be so beneficial unto him, (and the rather at this my instant request,) to move the king's highness to give him somewhat to live on here in England, until it please God to send the true light of his gospel into his country, and unto such time as he may more quietly enjoy his own. And in so doing your lordship shall do a very good deed to further him, being a right honest man and destitute of friends, and bind him during his life to owe unto your lordship his service and prayer. Furthermore I desire your lordship, as shortly as you can conveniently, to give unto the said Mr Hambleton an answer of the king's pleasure in the same, so that he may know whereunto to trust. Thus I pray God long to preserve your lordship in health to his pleasure. From Ford, the 28th day of February. [1537.]

Your own ever assured,

T. Cantuarien.

*To my very singular good lord, my lord privy seal.*

---

## CLXXXVI. TO CRUMWELL.

State Paper Office. Ibid. Original.

After most hearty commendations unto your lordship; these be to advertise the same, that this bearer moveth me of the weight of certain plate, wherein should be much profit unto the king's highness, as he saith: which matter neither I do well understand, nor it appertaineth unto mine office: wherefore I have sent him unto your good lordship; unto whom, if you please, he will shew the whole effect of his mind; which known, you may do as you shall think good. Thus our Lord have you in his most blessed preservation. From my manor of Lamehyth, the xiii. day of March. [1537.]

Your lordship's assured,

T. Cantuarien.

*To my singular good lord, my lord privy seal.*

---

## CLXXXVII. TO CRUMWELL.

State Paper Office. Ibid. Original holograph.

My very singular good lord, after most hearty recommendations unto your good lordship: this shall be to desire and heartily to pray you, that my lord Cobham[9]

---

[[8] Vid. Letter CLXXVI. p. 325.]

[[9] George Brooke, Lord Cobham, deputy of Calais "for a period extending from A.D. 1544 to 1550 (as appears from his papers), but no date is found of his appointment." The Chronicle of Calais, p. xxxviii. n. §. Camd. Soc. Ed. Strype's Eccl. Mem. Vol. II. Part I. p. 319. Ed. Oxon. 1822. Letter CLXXIX. p. 330, n. 4.]

may be put in the commission[1], not concerning Canterbury, but only for Rochester, because he lieth within three or four miles of Rochester. I know no benefit that can come to my lord thereby, but only that I think it should be a pleasure for him, and to me surely your lordship shall do a very great pleasure therein: wherefore I entirely beseech your lordship to put him in the said commission. And thus Almighty God have your lordship ever in his preservation. From Croydon, this last day of March. [1537.]

Your own assured ever,

T. Cantuarien.

*To my very good lord, my lord Crumwel, lord privy seal.*

---

## CLXXXVIII. TO CRUMWELL.

State Paper Office. Ibid. Original.

After most hearty commendations unto your lordship: whereas within the diocese of Norwich there is one named M. Gounthorp, parson of Wetyng, whom of long time, above twenty years past, I have known not only for a great clerk, but also of such singular judgment, sobriety, and conversation of living, that in all those qualities I have known very few like unto him; and yet, this notwithstanding, (as I am informed,) he cannot in that diocese be accepted ne allowed, as he ought to be, by reason that one named Dale (whom also I knew in Cambridge, without all learning and discretion, now chaplain unto the bishop of Norwich[2]) preacheth not only against the said master Gounthorp, but also (as it is reported) publisheth no good doctrine himself; and, forasmuch as I know the said Mr Gounthorp to be a very meet personage to preach unto the people in this time, and of such soberness and discretion, that he is not like to be author of any discord or dissension; and forasmuch also that he the bishop of Norwich doth approve none to preach in his diocese that be of right judgment, as I do hear reported of credible persons: these shall be to desire and pray you, my lord, to be so good unto the said Mr Gounthorp, at this my request, as to grant him as well the king's licence to preach within this realm, as also that he may from time to time have recourse unto your lordship for your favourable aid and assistance in his right, in case the said Dale promote causes against him before the bishop of Norwich. I know also three or four grave men and substantially learned within Norwich diocese, and of very good conversation, to whom if your lordship would give the king's licence, I doubt not but you should do a deed very acceptable unto God. For it were great pity that the diocese of Norwich should not be continued in the right knowledge of God, which is begun amongst them. Thus, my lord, right heartily fare you well. At Lambeth, the 26th day of May. [1537.]

Your lordship's own assured,

T. Cantuarien.

*To my very singular good lord, my lord privy seal.*

---

[[1] "Probably the commission for the collection of the subsidy to the king." Jenkyns' Remains of Abp. Cranmer, Vol. I. p. 185, *n.* f.]

[[2] William Rugge, alias Reps, was elected bishop of Norwich the 31st of May and consecrated in June, A. D. 1536. He subsequently gave his support, A. D. 1539, to the carrying of the act of the Six Articles; dissented from the act for allowing the communion in both kinds to the laity; to that for permitting the clergy to marry, and from that for confirming the new Liturgy, and was prevailed upon to resign his bishoprick in favour of Thirlby of Westminster, A. D. 1549. Strype's Mem. of Abp. Cranmer, Vol. I. pp. 71, 274. Vol. II. p. 743. Ed. Oxon. 1840. Burnet's Hist. of Reformat. Vol. I. p. 173. Vol. II. pp. 84, 183, 192, 309. Vol. III. p. 272. Ed. Oxon. 1829.]

## CLXXXIX. TO CRUMWELL.

State Paper Office. Ibid. Original.

My very singular good lord, in most hearty wise I commend me unto you. And whereas my suit hath been unto you for my friend Henry Stoketh to have a lease of the demesne lands of the Charter-house in the Isle of Axholme, I have sent my servant, this bearer, to put your lordship in remembrance of the same, desiring you heartily to move the king's highness in the said suit, so that he may have it either by lease, or else that he may purchase the said demesne lands, according as other have done; and in so doing your lordship shall do unto me a very singular pleasure; as knoweth Almighty God, who have your good lordship in his tuition. At Lambeth, the 20th of July. [1537.]

Your own ever assured,

T. Cantuarien.

*To my singular good lord, my lord privy seal.*

---

## CXC. TO CRUMWELL.

Cott. MSS. Cleop. E. v. fol. 52. Original. British Museum.

After most hearty commendations unto your lordship: these shall be to signify unto you, that I, with other bishops and learned men here assembled by the king's commandment, have almost made an end of our determinations[3]: for we have already

---

[[3] "These 'determinations' were published shortly afterwards under the title of 'The Institution of a Christian Man.' See preface to the reprint of it at Oxford in 1825, and the works there referred to. See also in the State Papers some interesting letters respecting it, addressed to Crumwell by bishops Fox and Latymer, two of the commissioners employed in its compilation. It appears from these, that there was great difficulty in coming to an agreement. Latymer prays God, 'that when it is done, it will be well and sufficiently done, so that we shall not need to have any more such doings; for verily, for my part, I had lever be poor parson of poor Kynton again, than to continue thus bishop of Worcester; not for any thing that I have had to do therein, or can do; but yet forsooth it is a troublous thing to agree upon a doctrine in things of such controversy, with judgments of such diversity, every man, I trust, meaning well, and yet not all meaning one way. But I doubt not but now in the end we shall agree both one with another, and all with the truth, though some will then marvel.' And bishop Fox also says, with reference probably to the heat of their debates, that they 'wanted much Crumwell's presence.' Cranmer and Fox are represented to have taken the lead in the discussions; and the latter, when the book was completed, undertook to superintend the printing of it. 'This day,' says Latymer, 'we had finished, I trow, the rest of our book, if my lord of Hereford had not been diseased; to whom surely we owe great thanks for his great diligence in all our proceedings. Upon Monday I think it will be done altogether, and then my lord of Canterbury will send it unto your lordship with all speed: to whom also, if any thing be praiseworthy, *bona pars laudis optimo jure debetur*.'—When their determinations were thus concluded, an important question arose respecting the authority by which they should be issued. And accordingly Fox beseeches Crumwell 'to know the king's pleasure for the prefaces which shall be put unto the said book, and whether his highness will that the book shall go forth in his name, according to such device as I once moved unto your lordship, or in the name of the bishops.' State Papers, Vol. I. pp. 556, 562, 565. Fox's 'device' perhaps may have been, that the commissioners should send a letter to the king, reporting their proceedings, and praying for his majesty's sanction; that the king should return a gracious answer, complying with their request; and that both these documents should be printed by way of introduction to the new book. Such a letter from the commissioners was actually prefixed to The Institution; and a minute of an answer from the king is preserved in the Public Record Office, Theological Tracts, Vol. IX. p. 73; though it does not seem to have been noticed by the historians. In this he informs the prelates, that although he had not had time to overlook their work, he trusted to them for its being according to scripture; that he permitted it to be printed, and commanded all who had care of souls to read a portion of it every Sunday and holy day for three years, and to preach conformably thereto. But it would appear that, cautiously as this reply was worded, Hen. VIII. did not choose to commit himself by its publication; for The Institution came out with no other preface than the above-named letter of the prelates, and with no farther claim to royal authority, than was implied by its issuing from the press of the king's printer. It rested therefore on very different grounds from the Articles of Religion which preceded, and the 'Necessary Doctrine' which followed it. For both of these formularies of faith were first approved in convocation, and were then provided with a preface by the king, and declared in the title-page to be set forth by his authority. Thus it was not a distinction without a difference, that The Institution was called the bishops', and the Necessary Doctrine the King's Book.—This statement has been given at some length, because, if correct, it will solve some difficulties in the subsequent letters, and because there are several conflicting accounts of the matter in our ecclesiastical writers." Jenkyns.]

subscribed unto the declarations of the Paternoster and the Ave Maria, the creed and the ten commandments; and there remaineth no more but certain notes of the creed, unto the which we be agreed to subscribe on Monday next: which all, when they shall be subscribed, I pray you that I may know your mind and pleasure, whether I shall send them incontinently unto you, or leave them in my lord of Herteforde's hands, to be delivered by him when he cometh next unto the court: beseeching you, my lord, to be intercessor unto the king's highness for us all, that we may have his grace's licence to depart for this time, until his grace's further pleasure be known; for they die almost every where in London, Westminster, and in Lambeth they die at my gate even at the next house to me[1]. I would fain see the king's highness at my departing, but I fear me that I shall not, by cause that I shall come from this smoky air; yet I would gladly know the king's pleasure herein.

Also, where you granted unto me licence to visit my diocese this year, I beseech you that I may have your letters to doctor Peter[2], to put that in my commission.

Moreover I beseech your lordship not to forget to be a suitor for me unto the king's highness concerning mine exchange, and especially for the remission of such debts as are yet behind unpaid, which I owe unto his grace[3]. Thus, my lord, right heartily fare you well. At Lambeth, the xxi. day of July. [1537.]

Over this, I pray you shew unto me your advice, how I shall order in my said visitation such persons as hath transgressed the king's grace's injunctions[4].

Your own ever assured,

T. CANTUARIEN.

[5]I beseech your lordship to send me word whether I shall examine the vicar of Croyden in this presence of the bishops and other learned men of our assembly, or otherwise how I shall order him.

State Paper Office. Miscellaneous Letters. Temp. Hen. VIII. Third Series. Vol. IX.

[Examination of Roland Philipps, 28 and 29 July, A.D. 1537.][6]

*Examinatio D. Rolandi Philipps coram Domino Archiepiscopo Cantuarien. vicesimo octavo die mensis Julii anno supradicto.*

3. *Item interrogatur*, Whome he knoweth fallen into this errour, that thai truste to be savid by faith and baptisme, and have lefte all good workes, and how long it is syns the people fell into that errour. *Respondet*, that he knoweth no speciall person that is in that errour, butt yt is abowt 2 yeres agoo syns the people cam into that errour.

*Item*, what good warkes the people have left. *Respondet*, that thei have lefte prayer, fasting, and almes dedes.

*Item*, whether he knowe any persons that doth evil warkes, and leave all good warkes, which thinke thay do well therin, and that thei may do soo withoute perill of dampnation. *Respondet*, that he cannott knowe that.

*Item*, those people that leave all good workes and do evill workes, whether he thinketh thei do it bycause of this erronius opinion, that thei thinke thei may do so; or thei do it of fraylnes or maliciousnes, knowyng thei ought not so to doo, and yet do it. *Respondet*, that he knoweth not whether any man do it of that erronious opinion or no.

5. *Item*, whether Esay and the angell preached the gospell, holly sincere, dilucide, and precise. *Respondet negative;* for thei preached it inchoative, but not holly.

*Item*, whether the evangelistes wrote the gospell holly, sincere, dilucide, and precise. *Respondet*, that thei wrote the gospel holly, but not syncere, dilucide, and precise.

*Item*, whither the Appostells likewise wrote the gospell holly, syncere, dilucide, and precise. *Respondet*, that the Apostells wrote not the gospell.

*Item*, whether the churche hath the gospell holly, syncere, dilucide, and precise. *Respondet*, that none of the evangelistes alone wrote the gospell, but all together did.

---

[1 "Sir, we be here not without all peril, for beside too, two hath died of my keeper's folks, out of my gate-house, three be yet there with raw sores; and even now master Nevell cometh and telleth me, that my under cook is fallen sick, and like to be of the plague." Vid. Bp. Latimer to Crumwell; Letter XCVI. part ii. State Papers, p. 563.]

[2 Vid. Letter CLX. p. 315; Strype's Mem. of Abp. Cranmer, p. 79. Ed. Oxon. 1840.]

[3 Vid. Letters LXXVIII. CXCIX. pp. 270, 348.]

[4 These were the injunctions given by authority of the king's highness to the clergy of this realm, printed by Burnet, Hist. of Reformat. Vol. I. Part II. Book III. No. 7, pp. 250—56. Ed. Oxon. Vid. Strype's Eccl. Mem. Vol. I. pp. 494, et seqq. Ed. Oxon. 1822. Wilkins' Concilia, Vol. I. p. 813.]

[5 The postscript is in the archbishop's hand.]

[6 Dr Jenkyns has given some heads of this examination, but it is here printed entire from the MSS. in the State Paper Office.]

*Item*, whether hymself ever preached the gospell holly, syncere, dilucide, and precise. *Respondet*, never in all his liffe.

7. *Item*, whether the Apostells preachyd to the gentilles that which the evangelistes wrote. *Respondet*, that the evangelistes wrote that that apostelles hadd preached.

8. *Item*, whome he hath harde say that thei wold not have the olde Testament meddeld withall, for it was but figures and shadowes; and likewise condempne all seculer sciences. *Respondet*, that he knoweth no particuler persons.

9. *Item*, whome he ment by the catholike churche, whan he said that the catholike churche shall never erre in thinges that be necessary for salvation. *Respondet*, that he mente the universall multitude of christen people, as well laymen as the clargie, subjects as rulers.

*Vicesimo nono die Julii.*

10. *Item*, whome he knoweth to have taken this wourde *syncere* to be put only to exclude all maner of myxtion of sciences, storyes and similitudes. *Respondet*, that it hath ben so taken both lately and 20 yeres agoo, then by Mr Sheffeld and divers other officers of London, lately he hereth in a multitude, but he knoweth no certen person. And moreover he saith, that I sent it furth, and why shuld I send it furth, excepte it were to make some restraynte?

11. *Item*, whome he knoweth that, after the comission was sent furth, have respersid thair sermondes with lyes, detractions, and perverse judgementes. *Respondet*, that thei lyed whan thei said the truthe hath be kepte from the people, and thei have ben mystaught thes 5 or 6 hundred yeres; and whan thei say that the people wurship stockes and stones; and thei respersid thair sermons with perverse judgements whan thei slandered other men, and said they preachede for promotions and vayne glorie.

12. *Item*, whome he hath harde say of manny's traditions which cam originally of scripture and of the revelation of the Father, or the doctrine of the Sonne, or by instincte of the Holy Gooste, that thei be but manny's traditions. *Respondet*, that the most parte of theym that have preachyd at London this 2 yeres.

15. *Item*, whether he thinketh that men have been ledde in any darkenes or errour this many yeres by erronious doctrines, instructions, and abuses of the clergie. *Respondet*, that thei have not be ledde in any darkenes or errour, as concernyng the faith, but have be tawght as cam from the fete of the Apostells.

28 *Julii.*

17. *Item*, What people he knoweth that take the warkes of the commandementes of Godd as actes voluntary, good, and honest, but not necessary. *Respondet*, that he knoweth none in especiall.

18. *Item*, whome he knoweth to be of this opinion, that faith which justifieth of necessitie bryngeth furth good warkes, and whether he be of the same opinion or noo? *Respondet*, that Barons[7], Crome[8], Champion[9], and many other soo have preached, and he is not of that opinion hymself.

19. *Item*, whome he knoweth that doth exclude all bodely observance as fryvol and vayne, all ceremoneys of religion, and all vocall prayer, calling it lippe labour. *Respondet*, the Bisshop of Wurceiter[10] and Doctour Crome have so done; for it folowith of thair wordes, *Adorabitis Patrem in spiritu.*

20. *Item*, whom he knoweth that in masse do use to clappe thair finger apon thair lipps and say never a worde. *Respondet*, that he hath sene many so doo, but he can name none, but some greate men in the courte do soo, as he hath harde reported.

21. *Item*, what preistes he knoweth whiche bifore the aulter, goyng to masse, close thair lipps and so do revest theym and speke not one wourde. *Respondet*, that he hath sene some do so in Powles, but he cannot name theym, nor he never spake to theym.

22. *Item*, whome he knoweth that do dampe all syngyng and redyng and organ-playing. *Respondet*, specially the Scottish fryre Maydewell.

29 *Julii.*

23. *Item*, whether tythes and offerynges be deu unto the clergie by Goddes lawe. *Respondet*, that he will not answer unto it, for it towchith not his sermonde.

*Item*, whither by their wourdes, *Exhibeatis corpora vestra hostiam sanctam, &c.*, thei do so exclude offeryng of candells and ymages and other like thinges, as thinges that may not be done, or as thinges that by this texte be not commanded to be done. *Respondet*, that he cannot tell whiche thei mente; but he knowith that the people toke it to exclude theym as thinges that ought not to be done.

*Item*, whether it be expedient to seperate Goddes commandementes from thinges not commanded, or nott? *Respondet*, that it is expedient.

28 *Julii.*

24. *Item*, whome he harde saye, that thei knew not what the materiall churches servid for, but to kepe men from the rayne, or to by and sell in. *Respondet*, that one said so the same mornyng that he preachid, whome he knoweth nott.

---

[[7] For an account of Dr Robert Barnes, vid. Burnet's Hist. of Reformat. Vol. I. p. 590, et sqq. Ed. Oxon. 1829.]

[[8] Dr Edward Crome was much esteemed by Cranmer, and was recommended by him to Henry VIII. for the deanery of Canterbury, to which office, however, he was not elected, Dr Nicholas Wotton being appointed instead of him. Vid. Strype's Eccl. Mem. Vol. III. pp. 157, et seqq. Ed. Oxon. 1822. Burnet's Hist. of Reformat. Vol. III. p. 287. Le Neve's Fasti, p. 10. Ed. Lond. 1716.]

[[9] Probably Cranmer's chaplain, by whom Crumwell certified to him in this year (A. D. 1535) of Gardiner's opposition to the proposed visitation of his diocese. Vid. Strype's Mem. of Abp. Cranmer, Vol. I. p. 46. Ed. Oxon. 1840. Vid. Letters CXLV. CLXIV. CLXX. pp. 304, 317, 322.]

[[10] The bishop of Worcester, Latimer.]

26. *Item,* whome he knoweth that hath said, that we should not pray, bycause Godd knoweth our thoughtes all redy. *Respondet,* that he harde none say soo, nor knowe none that so said.

27. *Item,* whome he knoweth that in thair sermondes praying for theym that be departid, craftely ment of theym that be separated from Godd by synne, and not of the deade. *Respondet,* that he knoweth none.

30. *Item,* whether he thinketh it convenient and necessary to teache the people the difference betwen Goddes lawes and mannys lawes; betwene those thinges that be commanded of Godde, and thos whiche be but only mannys traditions and ordinances. *Respondet affirmative,* that he thinketh it necessary.

31. *Item,* whither all thinges determyned by the Counsailes ar to be receyvid and bilevid, and it should be sufficient for us to fynde that it was there determyned; for that should be our shotte ancre. *Respondet,* that it is true in thinges concernyng our faithe.

29 *Julii.*

*Item,* whether that Esay and the angell preachid the gospell holly, syncere, lucide and precise. *Respondet,* thei preached the gospell incoative, but not holly, syncere, lucide, and precise.

*Item,* whither the Evangelistes wrote the gospell holly, syncere, dilucide, and precise. *Respondet,* that thei wrote it not holly, *quod multa alia fecit Jesus quæ non sunt scripta;* nor *lucide,* that is to say, to every mannys capacite. But they wrote it sincere, *ut ex Deo coram Deo et in Christo;* and precise, *absque admixtione alicujus contrarii.*

*Item,* whither the Appostells wrote the gospell holly, syncere, dilucide, and precise. *Respondet,* that thei wrote not the gospell, but thei amongest them all did preache it syncere, lucide, and precise, but not holly, *quod multa alia fecit Jesus quæ non sunt scripta;* but thei preachid holly so much as came to us of the evangelistes' writyng, but none of them alone could do it all.

*Item,* whither the Churche hath the gospell holly, syncere, dilucide, and precise. *Respondet,* that the Churche hath not the gospell holly, but so moche as the evangelistes wrote of it.

*Item,* whither he himself ever preached it holly, syncerly, dilucide, and precise. *Respondet,* that parte whiche he preachid he ever preachid it holly, leaving no difficultie for the people to stomble at; also syncere, he trusteth, dilucide and precise[1].

---

## CXCI. TO CRUMWELL.

State Paper Office. Original.

After hearty commendations unto your lordship; this is to advertise the same, that the bearer hereof, Mr Tybbold, one that hath exercised his study in Almayn these two or three years past, brought from Capito[2] and Monsterus[3] both letters and books to the king's highness; and if his grace's pleasure be to reward them for their pains and good hearts which they bear unto his said grace, this man that brought the said letters shall very conveniently do the king good service in that behalf: for he is going thitherward now again, and is a very honest man, and both loved and trusted of the learned men in those parties; with whom if it please your lordship to commune, he can well inform you of the state of that country. Wherefore not only in this, but also for his passport, I beseech you to be his good lord, so that he may have your favourable letters unto the ports for his passage and safe conduct. Thus our Lord have your lordship in his tuition! At Lambeth, the xxii. day of July. [1537.]

Your lordship's assured,

T. Cantuarien.

*To my very singular good lord,*
*my lord privy seal.*

---

## CXCII. TO WOLFGANG CAPITO[4].

Ex Archivis Eccles. Tuincens. ex Autogr. Cranmeri in MSS. Scrinii Eccles. Argentorat. Vol. II. p. 28. Original.

Libellum tuum[5], amice Capito, regiæ majestati, cui tu inscripseras, ipse manu mea porrexi. Accepit, ut mihi sane visus est, gratanter et libenter. Submonui quoque ut labores tuos respiceret. Annuit se visurum; nec multo post tempore dominum Crum-

[1 These interesting interrogatories were probably drawn up by Cranmer himself. They are in the handwriting of his clerk. The numbers, not being consecutive, probably refer to similar numbers or points of the sermon in question.]

[2 Vid. the following letter.]

[3 Sebastian Munster, a distinguished Hebrew scholar, at this time resident at Basle.]

[4 This letter is printed without place or date. Dr Jenkyns has assigned the letter to A.D. 1537, which date is here followed.]

[5 "Responsum de Missa, Matrimonio, et jure magistratus in religione, 11 Martii, 1537, Henrico VIII. inscriptum. A Capitone recognitum Rihelius excudit Argentorati 1540. V. Gesnerum in Biblioth." Note of Mr Solomon Hess, by whom the Zurich MS. was copied.]

wellum, privati sigilli custodem, qui ab intimis consiliis regis est, quique in his conficiendis quæ hactenus circa religionis et cleri reformationem facta et transacta sunt plus unus omnibus fecit, Harfordensis[6] et ego, cum apud illum una essemus, una eum rogavimus, ut regiam majestatem iterum tui admoneret. Fecit, et tibi pro munere centum coronati deputantur, quos jussit et harum latorem secum delaturum.

Scire adhuc desideras, ecquid munus tuum gratum fuerit? Age dicam, non quæ ipse scio vera esse, sed quæ ab aliis, qui in aula nuperius quam ego fuerunt, accepi. Solet rex (ut est acerrimus et ad omnia vigilantissimus) libros hujusmodi sibi oblatos, præsertim quos ipse non sustinet legere, suorum alicui tradere legendos, a quo ipse postea discat, quid in illis contentum fuerit: deinde resumptos eosdem alteri cuipiam, qui sit a priore diversissimi judicii, obtrudit examinandos. Ita cum ab ipsis omnia expiscatus fuerit, et quid laudent, quidve vituperent, sciverit ac satis expenderit, tum demum et ipse suam de eisdem palam profert sententiam. Sic et cum libello tuo actum fuisse intelligo; quodque, cum in illo multa valde approbaverit, fuerint etiam nonnulla, quæ nullo pacto concoquere neque comprobare potuerit. Suspicor ea esse, quæ de missa adjunxeras. Habes quantum hactenus ego de libello illo potui vel præsens audire et cernere, vel absens ex aliorum relationibus excerpere atque colligere.

De me hoc tibi persuadeto, te amo ex animo venerorque, et dignum judico cui ob insignem eruditionem cum pari morum probitate conjunctam omnes boni bene faciant. Atque utinam voluntati meæ erga te propensæ facultas responderet! Tunc profecto, mi Capito, sentires, quanti te facio. Interim te rogo, ut hoc munusculum a me boni consulas, parum [parvum] quidem si ad merita tua respiciatur, sed profecto non contemnendum, si vel animus meus dantis, vel sumtus necessarii et multiplices, quibus propemodum vel supra facultates oneror, rite considerentur. Quod superest, oro, ut hunc amicum meum Thomam Tybaldum, qui hasce ad te perfert, mea causa, quantum potes, foveas et adjuves. Vale.

T. Cantuarien.

[TRANSLATION.]

The treatise, my friend Capito, which you had dedicated to the king's majesty, I presented to him with my own hand. He received it, as I thought, with pleasure and satisfaction. I also hinted to him that he should recompense your labours, and he promised to see to it. Not long after, when the bishop of Hereford and I were together in company with the Lord Crumwell, the keeper of the privy seal, who is one of the privy councillors, and who has himself done more than all others in whatever has hitherto been effected respecting the reformation of religion and of the clergy, we united in requesting him to put his majesty again in mind of you, which he has done, and a hundred crowns are assigned to you as a present, which he has ordered the bearer of this letter to take with him. Do you still desire to know whether your offering was acceptable? Well, I will state, not what I myself know to be the fact, but what I have heard from others who have been at court more recently than myself. The king, who is a most acute and vigilant observer, is wont to hand over books of this kind that have been presented to him, and those especially which he has not the patience to read himself, to one of his lords in waiting for perusal, from whom he may afterwards learn their contents. He then takes them back, and presently gives them to be examined by some one else, of an entirely opposite way of thinking to the former party. Thus, when he has made himself master of their opinions, and sufficiently ascertained both what they commend and what they find fault with, he at length openly declares his own judgment respecting the same points. And this, I understand, he has done with respect to your book. And while he was much pleased with many things in it, there were also some things which he could by no means digest or approve. I suspect they were the statements you made concerning the mass. You now have every thing respecting that book which I have been able either to hear and see in person, or to gather and collect, when absent, from the report of others. As to myself, be assured of this, that I love and reverence you from my heart, and regard you as one who, by reason of your remarkable erudition united to an equal integrity of manners, is deserving of the friendly offices of all good men. And I wish that my ability corresponded with my inclination to serve you; for you should then perceive, my Capito, how greatly I esteem you. I request you in the mean time to take in good part from me this trifling present, small indeed, if regard be had to your deserts, but yet not to be despised, if you duly consider, either the feelings of the giver, or the necessary and manifold expenses by which I am almost burdened beyond my strength. In fine, I request you to favour and assist for my sake, as far as you can, this my friend Thomas Tybald, who is the bearer of this letter. Farewell.

T. Cantuar.

[6 Edward Fox, bishop of Hereford, A.D. 1535. He died A.D. 1538.]

## CXCIII. TO JOACHIM VADIAN[1].

Archiv. Eccles. Tigurin. Original. Duditthius, Oration. et Opuscul. Colomesius, Epist. Claror. Virorum, No. 36. Strype's Mem. of Abp. Cranmer, Vol. II. App. No. 25. pp. 740–743. Ed. Oxon. 1840.

TANDEM a negotiis consiliisque publicis missionem vel verius respirationem nactus, et inter ceteros doctos viros, quorum epistolis responsa jam diu debueram, tibi quoque, Vadiane, vir illustris doctissimeque, nunc demum vertente anno respondere incipiens, (utpote cujus literas superiore hyeme acceperim, una cum munere literario; quod genus quidem soleo vel inter pretiosissima numerare,) illud imprimis mecum reputare pudibundus occœpi vererique, ne forte suspicionem aut etiam opinionem mihi aliquam sinistram apud animum tuum silentio meo tam diuturno contraxerim; quia sciam apud vulgus hominum fieri plerumque solere, cum hospes hospitem salutat, ut in primo maxime aditu responsum solicite exspectent: quod si differatur, superbiam aliquam vel neglectum sui, vel, ut minimum, oblivionem intervenire suspicantur; qualemque in primo illo accessu invenere, talem in universam reliquam vitam erga se fore præjudicant. Cum qui cito respondet, libenter et gratanter id facere judicatur, eumque proinde humanum, facilem, gratumque interpretantur; contra, qui tarde, fastuosus, difficilis, et incivilibus ac inamœnis moribus præditus existimatur. Usque adeo bis facit quod cito facit, quicquid quis cito facit. Verum ego de tua neutiquam vulgari prudentia et humanitate meliora mihi polliceor, confidoque te hanc meam non spontaneam tarditatem aut cessationem, sed necessariam dilationem benigne accepturum, eamque non tam moribus quam negotiis meis imputaturum: quæ qualia et quanta fuerint, puto rumores ad vos usque jampridem pertulisse, et ego de eisdem nonnihil ad Grynæum meum, imo nostrum, scripsi; cum quo pro amicitiæ jure omnia tibi communia futura esse non ambigo. Ad illum igitur te remitto, siquid hac re offenderis, qui me tibi reddat excusatiorem.

Tuam erga me voluntatem et promptitudinem animi ad contrahendam mecum sanctiorem necessitudinem in literis tuis perspicio, et libens amplector osculorque. Virum enim dignum te judico, quem ego propter eximiam eruditionem, qua me quoque adjutum profecisse neutiquam dissimulavero, et propter morum probitatem, multorum gravissimorum virorum testimoniis comprobatam, omni amore, favore, ac veneratione prosequar. Veruntamen ut animi mei sensum (sicuti inter bonos viros fieri oportet) ingenue tibi profitear, argumentum quod tractas in sex illis libris[2], quos mihi dono dederas, in totum mihi displicet; vellemque vigilias tuas tantas felicius collocasses, et mecum jucundæ amicitiæ melioribus, aut certe minus improbatis, auspiciis fuisses usus. Nam ego nisi certiora afferri video, quam hactenus videre potui, sententiæ illius vestræ nec patronus nec astipulator esse volo. Et plane mihi vel ex eo maxime persuasum est, causam esse non bonam, quod eam viri tam ingeniosi, tam diserti, tamque omnibus artibus et disciplinis instructi, non videamini satis valide tueri ac sustinere. Vidi pleraque omnia, quæ vel ab Œcolampadio vel a Zuinglio scripta sunt et edita, didicique omnium hominum omnia cum delectu esse legenda. Et fortasse illud D. Hieronymi de Origene elogium in illos quoque non absurde aliquis detorserit, "Ubi bene, nemo melius," &c. Nosti enim quod sequitur. Quatenus quidem papisticos et sophisticos errores et abusus indicare, convincere, corrigereque sunt conati, laudo et approbo. Atque utinam intra fines illos constitissent, neque fruges una cum zizaniis conculcassent, hoc est, veterum doctorum primorumque in ecclesia Christi scriptorum auctoritatem una violassent! Nam ut ingenia vestra quantumcunque versaveritis, mihi tamen certe nunquam approbaveritis, nec cuiquam, opinor, æquo lectori, veteres illos auctores in hac controversia pro vestra facere sententia. Fuistis nimirum in investigandis erroribus plus satis curiosi; et dum omnia purgare studetis, illic quoque errorem subesse putavistis, ubi nullus fuit. Quando

---

[[1] Joachim Vadian was born at St Gall, Switzerland, A. D. 1484, and was celebrated as a scholar and mathematician.]

[[2] "There was one Joachim Vadianus, a learned man of St Gall in Helvetia, and an acquaintance of the archbishop's. He had framed a treatise, intituled, "Aphorisms upon the consideration of the Eucharist," in six books; which were intended to prove no corporal presence." Strype's Mem. of Abp. Cranmer, Vol. I. p. 94. Ed. Oxon. 1840. Cranmer held this doctrine till A. D. 1546, "when by more mature and calm deliberation, and considering the point with less prejudice, and the sense of the fathers more closely, in conference with Dr Ridley, afterwards bishop of Rochester, and his fellow-martyr, he at last quitted and freed himself from the fetters of that unsound doctrine." Zurich Letters, 3rd Series, Letter VII. p. 13. Park. Soc. Ed.]

hic certe, si error est, jam inde a primordio ecclesiæ ab ipsis patribus et viris apostolicis nobis fuit propinatus. Quod quis pius sustinuerit vel audire, nedum credere? ut nequid interim dicam, quod bonus Dominus noster unice dilectam sponsam suam nunquam in tam pudenda cæcitate tamdiu dereliquisset. Quamobrem quum hæc, quam tenemus, catholica fides de vera presentia corporis tam apertis ac manifestis scripturis fuerit ecclesiæ ab initio promulgata, et eadem postea per primos ecclesiasticos scriptores fidelium auribus tam clare tamque studiose commendata; ne, quæso, ne mihi pergatis eam tam bene radicatam et suffultam velle amplius convellere aut subruere. Satis jam, satis tentatum est hactenus. Et nisi super firmam petram fuisset firmiter ædificata, jamdudum cum magnæ ruinæ fragore cecidisset. Dici non potest, quantum hæc tam cruenta controversia, cum per universum orbem Christianum, tum maxime apud nos, bene currenti verbo evangelii obstiterit. Vobis ipsis affert ingens periculum, et ceteris omnibus præbet non dicendum offendiculum. Quocirca, si me audietis, hortor et suadeo, imo vos oro, obsecro, et visceribus Jesu Christi obtestor et adjuro, uti concordiam procedere et coire sinatis; in illam confirmandam totis viribus incumbatis; pacemque Dei tandem, quæ superat omnem sensum, ecclesiis permittatis, ut evangelicam doctrinam unam, sanam, puram, et cum primitivæ ecclesiæ disciplina consonam, junctis viribus quam maxime propagemus. Facile vel Turcas ad evangelii nostri obedientiam converterimus, modo intra nosmetipsos consentiamus, et pia quadam conjuratione conspiremus. At si ad hunc modum pergimus ad invicem contendere et commordere, timendum erit, ne (quod dicens abominor), juxta comminationem apostolicam, ad invicem consumamur.

Habes, optime Vadiane, meam de tota controversia illa neutiquam fictam sententiam, una cum admonitione libera ac fideli. Cui si obtemperaveris, non modo inter amicos, sed etiam vel inter amicissimos mihi nomen tuum ascripsero. Bene vale. [1537.]

T. Cantuariens.

*Illustri et erudito viro Joachimo Vadiano, consuli apud sanctum Gallum in Helvetia.*

[TRANSLATION.]

Having obtained a release, or rather a respite, from public affairs and deliberations, and beginning, illustrious and most learned Vadian, at the turn of the year, to reply to you among my other learned correspondents, to whose letters I had long been owing an answer, (to you, I say, as having received your letter last winter, together with a literary present, which kind of presents I always regard as of the greatest value,) I first begin to consider with myself, and entertain some apprehension, lest by my so long protracted silence I may have given occasion in your mind to some suspicion or opinion not altogether favourable to me: for I know that it is usual among the generality of mankind, that when one person sends his commendations to another, he anxiously expects an acknowledgment of them by the very first opportunity. And if this be delayed, he will suspect that it has been owing to pride, or neglect, or at least forgetfulness; and will conclude beforehand that the party will continue such through the whole of his life, as he has been found to be upon a first introduction. Whereas the person who sends a speedy reply, is judged to have done so from kind and friendly motives, and is therefore regarded as courteous, accessible, and grateful; he on the other hand, who is tardy in his acknowledgments, is considered hard of access, and a person of rude and disagreeable manners. So true it is, that whatever a man does quickly, and without delay, he may be said to do twice over. But I promise myself a far better reception from your more than ordinary discretion and courtesy, and am confident that you will take in good part this my involuntary tardiness or delay, and not ascribe it so much to my manners as to my engagements. The nature and importance of these has, I think, long since been made known to you by report; and I have written something respecting them to our common friend Grynæus, who will, I doubt not, as the rights of friendship require, make you acquainted with every circumstance. To him therefore I refer you, in case you are offended with me in this matter, as to one who will render me more excusable in your eyes. I perceive in your letter, and readily accept and embrace, your good-will towards me, and inclination to cultivate a more intimate friendship with me. For I consider you as one who, by reason of your extraordinary erudition, (by which I shall not scruple to acknowledge that I have myself derived benefit,) and of your probity of morals, confirmed by the testimony of many most excellent persons, is worthy of being regarded by me with all love, favour, and respect. Nevertheless, if I may candidly express my sentiments, (as ought to be the case between good men,) the subject you treat of in those six books which you sent me as a present, is altogether displeasing to me; and I could wish you had bestowed your labours to better purpose, and commenced an agreeable friendship with myself under better or, at least, more approved auspices. For, unless I see stronger evidence brought forward than I have yet been able to see, I desire neither to be the patron nor the approver of the opinion maintained by you. And I am plainly convinced, and from this circumstance especially, that the cause is not a good one, because you who are so shrewd, so eloquent, and so perfectly accomplished in all arts and learning, do not seem to defend and support it with sufficient validity. I have seen almost every thing that has been written and published either by Œcolampadius or Zuinglius, and I have come to the conclusion that the writings of every man must be read with discrimination. And perhaps one might apply to these men, and not without reason, the remark of Jerome respecting Origen, that where they wrote well, nobody wrote better, &c.: you know what follows. As far indeed as they have endeavoured to point out, confute, and correct papistical and sophistical errors and abuses, I commend and approve them. And I wish that they had confined themselves within those limits, and not trodden down the wheat together with the tares; that is, had not at the same time done violence to the authority of the ancient doctors and chief writers in the church of Christ. For how much soever you may exercise your ingenuity, you will certainly never convince me, nor, I think, any unprejudiced reader, that those ancient authors are on your side in this controversy. You have been, in fact, more than enough inquisitive in your investigation of errors; and while you are endeavouring to purify every thing, you have fancied error to lurk in places where none existed. And this error, most certainly, if error it be, has been handed down to us by the fathers themselves, and men of apostolical character, from the very beginning of the church. And what godly man could endure to hear this, much less to believe it? Not to mention in the mean time, that our gracious Lord would never have left his beloved spouse in such lamentable blindness for so long a period. Wherefore, since this catholic faith which we hold respecting the real presence has been declared to the church from the beginning by such evident and manifest passages of scripture, and the same has also been subsequently commended to the ears of the faithful with so much clearness and diligence by the first ecclesiastical writers; do not, I pray, persist in wishing any longer to carp at or subvert a doctrine so well grounded and supported. You have sufficiently made the attempt already. And unless it had been firmly founded upon a solid rock, it would long since have fallen with the crash of a mighty ruin. It cannot be told, how greatly this so bloody controversy has impeded the full course of the gospel both throughout the whole christian world, and especially among ourselves. It brings very great danger to yourselves, and occasions to all others a stumbling-block greater than I can express. Wherefore, if you will listen to me, I exhort and advise you, yea, I beg, beseech, and implore and adjure you in the bowels of Jesus Christ, to agree and unite in a christian concord, to exert your whole strength in establishing it, and at length to afford to the churches the peace of God which passeth all understanding, so that we may, with united strength, extend as widely as possible one sound, pure, evangelical doctrine, conformable to the discipline of the primitive church. We should easily convert even the Turks to the obedience of our gospel, if only we would agree among ourselves, and unite together in some holy confederacy. But if we go on in this way "to bite and devour each other," there will be reason to fear, lest (what I abhor the mention of), according to the warning of the apostle, we "be consumed one of another."

You have, worthy Vadian, my true and genuine opinion respecting that entire controversy, together with a free and faithful admonition. To which if you will pay attention, I shall enrol your name not only among my friends, but among my best friends. Farewell. [1537.][1]

T. CANTUAR.

## CXCIV. TO CRUMWELL.

State Paper Office. Miscellaneous Letters. Temp. Hen. VIII. Third Series. Vol. IX. Original. State Papers, Vol. I. part ii. No. xciv. pp. 561, 2. Todd's Life of Abp. Cranmer, Vol. I. p. 211.

MY especial good lord, after most hearty commendations unto your lordship; these shall be to signify unto the same, that you shall receive by the bringer thereof a bible[2] in English, both of a new translation and of a new print, dedicated unto the king's majesty, as farther appeareth by a pistle unto his grace in the beginning of the book, which in mine opinion is very well done, and therefore I pray your lordship to read the same. And as for the translation, so far as I have read thereof, I like it better than any other translation heretofore made; yet not doubting but that there may and will be found some fault therein, as you know no man ever did or can do so well, but it may be from time to time amended. And forasmuch as the book is dedicated unto the king's grace, and also great pains and labour taken in setting forth of the same; I pray you, my lord, that you will exhibit the book unto the king's highness, and to obtain of his grace, if you can, a licence that the same may be sold and read of every person, without danger of any act, proclamation, or ordinance heretofore granted to the contrary, until such time that we the bishops shall set forth a better translation, which I think will not be till a day after doomsday[3]. And if you continue to take such pains for the setting forth of God's word, as you do, although in the mean season you suffer some snubs, and many slanders, lies, and reproaches for the same, yet one day he will requite altogether. And the same word (as St John saith) which shall judge every man at the

[[1] This date is assigned by Colomesius.]

[[2] "The bible, which is the Holy Scripture: in which are contained the Old and New Testament, truly and purely translated into English, by Thomas Matthew. MDXXXVII." For an account of this translation, vid. Anderson's Annals of the English Bible, Vol. I. pp. 375—387. Ed. Lond. 1845.]

[[3] Vid. Strype's Mem. of Abp. Cranmer, Vol. I. pp. 48, 9. Ed. Oxon. 1840: and Lewis' Hist. of Translations of the Bible, p. 115. Ed. Lond. 1818.]

last day, must needs shew favour to them that now do favour it. Thus, my lord, right heartily fare you well. At Ford, the ivth day of August. [1537.]

Your assured ever,

T. Cantuarien.

*To the right honourable and my especial good lord, my lord privy seal.*

---

## CXCV. TO CRUMWELL.

After most hearty commendations unto your lordship: whereas the same writeth unto me to stay a suit which should be made unto me for the induction of a certain person in St Quintune's in Spelake[4], in the marches of Calais, upon an advowson granted of the same; surely, my lord, as yet there is no such suit made unto me: howbeit, if any suit be made, I shall, according to your mind, stay the same, and likewise incontinently send unto mine officers that they on their behalf do the same accordingly. Thus, my lord, right heartily fare you well. At Canterbury, the 5th day of August. [1537.]

State Paper Office. Ibid. Original.

Your lordship's own,

T. Cantuarien.

*To my very singular good lord, my lord privy seal.*

---

## CXCVI. TO CRUMWELL.

My singular good lord, in my right hearty wise I commend me unto your lordship. These shall be to yield unto the same my most hearty thanks for your good advertisement unto the king's majesty touching the tenor of my letters, which I sent to you by sir Edward Ryngsley, knight[5]. And as touching your commendation of the said sir Edward, with your effectious request for my favour to be declared towards him in such things as he may have to do with me, I am right glad that you have conceived so good opinion of him; and for my part, though my ability be but small, he shall have such commodity and pleasure as I may do for him. Howbeit I shall desire your lordship so to extend your goodness towards him, that thereby he may have some preferment now in the alteration of these religious houses; wherein surely you shall not only much animate the man to do the king's majesty his most faithful service, but also bind him to be at your commandment. Thus, my lord, right heartily fare you well. At Ford, the viiith day of August. [1537.]

State Paper Office. Ibid. Original.

Your assured ever,

T. Cantuarien.

*To my very singular good lord, my lord privy seal.*

---

## CXCVII. TO CRUMWELL.

My very singular good lord, in my most hearty wise I commend me unto your lordship. And whereas I understand that your lordship, at my request, hath not only exhibited the bible which I sent unto you,[6], to the king's majesty, but also hath obtained of his grace, that the same shall be allowed by his authority to be bought and read within this realm; my lord, for this your pain[7], taken in this behalf, I give unto you my most hearty thanks[8]: assuring your lordship, for the contentation of my mind, you

Cotton MSS. Cleop. E. v. f. 329. b. British Museum. Original. Strype's Mem. of Abp. Cranmer, Vol. I. p. 82. Ed. Oxon. 1840.

---

[4 Vid. Letter CCI. p. 349.]

[5 There is a Sir Edw. Ringleis mentioned by Foxe, as "controller of the town of Calais, an office of no small charge, though he knew not a B from a battledore, nor ever a letter of the book." Foxe's Acts and Monuments, p. 1227. Ed. Lond. 1583.]

[6 Vid. Letter CXCIV.]

[7 This your pains. Strype.]

[8 I give you my most hearty thanks. Ibid.]

have shewed me more pleasure herein, than if you had given me a thousand pound; and I doubt not but that hereby such fruit of good knowledge shall ensue, that it shall well appear hereafter, what high and acceptable service you have done unto God and the king: which shall so much redound to your honour, that, besides God's reward, you shall obtain perpetual memory for the same within this realm. And as for me, you may reckon me your bondman for the same[1]. And I dare be bold to say, so may ye do my lord of Wurceiter[2]. Thus, my lord, right heartily fare ye well. At Ford, the xiiith day of August. [1537.]

Your own bondman ever,

T. Cantuarien.

---

## CXCVIII. TO CRUMWELL.

Cotton MSS. Cleop. E. v. f. 292. Original. Strype's Mem. of Abp. Cranmer, p. 83. and Appendix, No. xix. Vol. II. pp. 728, 9.

My very singular and especial good lord, in my most hearty wise I commend me to your lordship. These shall be to give you most hearty thanks that any heart can think, and that in the name of them all which favoureth God's word[3], for your diligence at this time in procuring the king's highness to set forth the said God's word and his gospel by his grace's authority[4]. For the which act, not only the king's majesty, but also you

[[1] The words "for the same" are inserted in the archbishop's hand.]

[[2] Hugh Latimer.]

[[3] Which favour God's word. Strype.]

[[4] For a full account of the bringing over, and setting forth this copy of the bible, vid. Anderson's Annals of the English Bible, Vol. I. pp. 576, et seqq.

The following letter was sent by Grafton, the printer, to Crumwell, Aug. 28, 1537, the very day on which Cranmer wrote this letter.

Cotton MSS. Cleop. E. v. f. 330. British Museum. Original. Strype's Mem. of Abp. Cranmer, Vol. I. pp. 84, 5.

"Most humbly beseeching your lordship to understand, that according to your request, I have sent your lordship six bibles; which gladly I would have brought myself, but because of the sickness that remaineth in the city; and therefore I have sent them by my servant, which this day came out of Flanders. Requiring your lordship, if I may be so bold as to desire you, to accept them as my simple gift, given to you for those most godly pains, for which the heavenly Father is bound, even of his justice, to reward you with the everlasting kingdom of God. For your lordship's moving our most gracious prince to the allowance and licensing of such a work, hath wrought such an act worthy of praise, as never was mentioned in any chronicle in this realm; and, as my lord of Canterbury said, the tidings thereof did him more good than the gift of £1000: yet certain there are which believe not that it pleased the king's grace to license it to go forth. Wherefore if your lordship's pleasure were such, that we might have it licensed under your privy seal, it should be a defence at this present and in time to come for all enemies and adversaries of the same. And forasmuch as this request is for the maintenance of the Lord's word, which is to maintain the Lord himself, I fear not but that your lordship will be earnest therein. And I am assured, that my lords of Canterbury, Worcester, and Salisbury*, will give your lordship such thanks as in them lieth. And sure ye may be, that the heavenly Lord will reward you for the establishing of his glorious truth. And what your lordship's pleasure is in this request, if it may please your lordship to inform my servant, I, and all that love God heartily, are bound to pray for your preservation all the days of our life. At London the xxviii[th] day of this present month of August, 1537.

"Your orator while he liveth,

"Richard Grafton, Grocer."†

*To the honorable lord privy seal.*

In the injunctions given by the authority of the king's highness to the clergy of his realm, it is commanded, "that every parson or proprietary of any parish-church within this realm shall .... provide a book of the whole bible, both in Latin and English, and lay the same in the quire for every man that will to look and read therein, and shall discourage no man from reading of any part of the bible either Latin or English, but rather comfort, exhort, and admonish every man to read the same, as the very word of God, the spiritual food of man's soul, &c." Vid. Foxe's Acts and Monuments, p. 1095. Ed. Lond. 1583. Burnet's Hist. of Reformat. Vol. I. Part. I. Appendix, Book III. No. vii. p. 254. Ed. Oxon. 1829. Collier's Eccl. Hist. Vol. IV. p. 373. Ed. Lond. 1840-41. This injunction is, however, not found in Cranmer's Register, in Wilkins' Concilia, and the folio ed. of Burnet's Hist. of Reformat., and has probably been inserted "incautiously from a draft, which was afterwards altered." (Jenkyns.)

In the Injunctions exhibited (Sept.) 1538, it is pronounced: "Item,—That ye shall provide on this side the feast of next coming, one book of the whole bible of the largest volume in English, and the same set up in some convenient place within the said church that ye have cure of, where as your parishioners may most commodiously resort to the same and read it." Foxe's Acts and Monuments, p. 1096. Burnet's Hist. of Reformat. Vol. I. Append. B. iii. No. 11, p. 279. "This month of September, [A. D. 1538,] Thomas Crumwell, lord privy seal, vicegerent to the king's highness, sent forth injunctions to all bishops and curates through the realm, charging them to see that in every parish-church the bible of the largest volume printed in English were placed for all men to read in." Stow's Annals, p. 574. Ed. Lond. 1615.]

[* i. e. Cranmer, Latimer, and Shaxton.]

[† "Grafton was a member of the Grocer's Company in London."]

shall have a perpetual laud and memory of all them that be now, or hereafter shall be, God's faithful people and the favourers of his word. And this deed you shall hear of at the great day, when all things shall be opened and made manifest. For our Saviour Christ saith in the said gospel, that whosoever shrinketh from him and his word, and is abashed to profess and set it forth before men in this world, he will refuse him at that day; and contrary, whosoever constantly doth profess him and his word, and studieth to set that forward in this world, Christ will declare the same at the last day before his Father and all his angels, and take upon him the defence of those men.

These shall be farther to advertise[5] your lordship, that since my last coming from London into Kent, I have found the people of my diocese very obstinately given to observe and keep with solemnity the holidays lately abrogated[6]. Whereupon I have punished divers of the offenders; and to divers I have given gentle monition to amend. But inasmuch as by examination I have perceived that the people were partly animated thereunto by their curates, I have given strait commandment and injunction unto all the parsons and vicars within my diocese, upon pain of deprivation of their benefices, that they shall not only, on their behalf, cause the said holidays so abrogated from time to time not to be observed within their cures; but also shall from henceforth present to me such persons of their parishes, as will practise in word or deed contrary to that ordinance or any other, which is or hereafter shall be set forth by the king's grace's authority, for the redress or ordering of the doctrine or ceremony of this church of England. So that now I suppose, through this means, all disobedience and contempt of the king's grace's said acts[7] and ordinances in this behalf shall be clearly avoided in my diocese hereafter: not doubting also, but if every bishop in this realm had commandment to do the same in their dioceses, it would avoid both much disobedience and contention in this said realm. I would fain that all the envy and grudge of the people in this matter should be put from the king and his council; and that we, which be ordinaries, should take it upon us: or else I fear lest a grudge against the prince and his council, in such causes of religion, should gender in many of the people's hearts a faint subjection and obedience.

But, my lord, if in the court you do keep such holidays and fasting days as be abrogated, when shall we persuade the people to cease from keeping of them? For the king's own house shall be an example unto all the realm to break his own ordinances[8].

Over this, whereas your lordship hath twice written for this poor man, William Gronnowe[9], the bearer hereof, to my lord deputy of Calice, for him to be restored to his room; as far as I understand, it prevailed nothing at all; for so he can get none answer of my lord deputy: so that the poor man despaireth that your request shall do him any good. If your lordship would be so good to him, as to obtain a bill, signed by the king's grace, to the treasurers and controllers of Calice for the time being, commanding them to pay to the said W. Gronnowe his accustomed wages yearly, and to none other, your lordship should not only not further trouble my lord deputy any more, but also do a right meritorious deed. For if the poor man be put thus from his living, he were but utterly undone. Thus, my lord, right heartily fare you well. At Ford, the xxviii. day of August. [1537.]

Your lordship's own ever,

T. CANTUARIENS.

---

[5 Shall be to advertise. Strype.]

[6 The holidays were abrogated by an act of convocation. Vid. Letter of Hen. VIII. to the bishops; Wilkins' Concilia, Vol. III. p. 823. Vid. also Mandatum Archiepisc. Cantuar. de non celebrandis Festis diebus, in Appendix.]

[7 King's grace's acts. Strype.]

[8 This [viz. the whole paragraph] was writ with the archbishop's own hand. All the rest of the letter was his secretaries'. Strype.]

[9 Vid. Letter CCVI. p. 356.]

## CXCIX. TO CRUMWELL.

State Paper Office. Miscellaneous Letters. Temp. Hen. VIII. Third series. Vol. IX. Original.

My very special good lord, in my right hearty wise I commend me unto you. Likewise thanking you for your loving and kind answer which you sent me by my servant Nevell, and especially for your good mind towards me concerning my debts[1] to the king's highness, which of all other things lieth most nigh unto my stomach; trusting, for the declaration of this your gentle heart towards me, not to be forgotten on my behalf hereafter, as it shall lie in my power. And as concerning such lands of mine as the king's highness is minded to have by exchange at Maidestone and Otford[2]; forsomuch as I am the man that hath small experience in such causes, and have no mistrust at all in my prince in that behalf, I wholly commit unto you to do therein for me as by you shall be thought expedient, not doubting but that you foresee as much for my commodity, as you would that I should do for you in such a like matter.

As touching the prior of the black Friars in Canterbury[3], I have written nothing to you of him but that I will justify. And whereas I understand, that the *Custos Rotulorum* within Nottinghamshire is depart this miserable life, this shall be to desire and pray you, that you will write your favourable letters unto my lord chancellor for the preferment of a friend of mine there, named Antony Nevell, who is a man of right good wisdom, experience, and discretion, and useth himself very indifferently[4] in the country.

Over this you shall understand that I have received from the king's highness three letters concerning the collection of the subsidy[5]; one for Canterbury, and one for the shire, and the third for Rochester; with the which I have received but one commission, which is alonely for Canterbury town. Wherefore I pray you that the other two commissions may be sent, or else to signify unto me to whom they are delivered. I have sent unto my commissary[6] at Calice to withdraw his process against Mr Chamberleyn, and therefore he not to doubt in that matter. Thus, my lord, right heartily fare you well. At Ford, the xxxi. day of August. [1537.]

Your own ever assured,

T. CANTUARIEN.

*To my very singular good lord, my, lord privy seal.*

---

## CC. TO POTKYNS[7].

Wilkins' Concilia, Vol. III. p. 827, Excerpt. Heylyn, Actor. Convocat.

I COMMEND me unto you. And whereas I have received the king's most honourable letters[8] concerning the speedy declaration of his grace's pleasure, for the abolishing of certain holidays named in the late act of convocation, whereof the transumpt I send you herewithal; my mind is therefore, that you cause, with all expedition, the king's pleasure in this behalf to be published unto all the clergy within the deaneries of my

[1 Vid Letters LXXVIII. CXC. pp. 270, 338.]

[2 The indenture for effecting the exchange bears date Nov. 30, 29 Hen. VIII. i.e. 1537. Hasted's Hist. of Kent, Vol. I. p. 322. Ed. Cant. 1742—99. A full account of the archbishop's houses at Maidstone, Otford, and Knoll, will be found, Ib. Vol. I. pp. 323, 338, and Vol. III. p. 624. "My lord, minded to have retained Knol unto himself, said, 'That it was too small a house for his majesty.' 'Marry,' said the king, 'I had rather have it than this house,' meaning Otford, 'for it standeth on a better soil. This house standeth low and is rheumatic, like unto Croydon, where I could never be without sickness. And as for Knol, it standeth on a sound, perfect, wholesome ground: and if I should make abode here, as I do surely mind to do now and then, I will live at Knol, and most of my house shall live at Otford.' And so by this means both those houses were delivered up to the king's hands." Strype's Mem. of Abp. Cranmer, Vol. II. p. 625. Ed. Oxon. 1840.]

[3 Vid. Letter CLXXV. p. 326.]

[4 indifferently, i. e. fairly, justly.]

[5 Vid. Letters CXXXIX. CLXXXVII. pp. 301, 336, *n.* 1.]

[6 John Butler.]

[7 The archbishop's register.]

[8 Dr Jenkyns thinks this letter belongs to A. D. 1536, and has reference to the king's letter, (vid. Letter CXCVIII. p. 347, *n.* 6), the date of which he assigns as being probably Aug. 11, 1536. The supposed date of the letter fixed by Wilkins is here followed, as it also is in Dr Jenkyns, Vol. I. p. 202.]

peculiars, to the intent that the said act of convocation may from henceforth be put in due exercise, according to the purport and effect of the same. Thus fare you well. At Ford, the 16th day of September. [1537.]

T. Cantuarien.

---

## CCI. TO CRUMWELL.

My very singular and especial good lord, in my most hearty wise I commend me to your lordship. These shall be to give to your lordship right hearty thanks for this bearer, Thomas Wakefeld, my servant; for, as I understand, you have been many ways his special good lord; beseeching you of continuance towards him. And albeit your lordship wrote unto me of late to stay such suit[9] as should be made to me concerning the institution of the parsonage of St Quintyne of Spellacke[10] within the marches of Calice, which I have hitherto accomplished accordingly; yet I shall nevertheless beseech your lordship, forsomuch as I perceive that this my said servant is, by virtue of the king's advowson, presented thereunto, to be no less his good lord in this his suit than you have hitherto been, and that the rather at this mine instant request, so that having right thereunto, he may enjoy the same with your favour: and that upon your lordship's pleasure known in this behalf, he may have a token from you unto my chancellor for his institution; for the which you shall bind him to do unto your lordship his both daily prayer and service, and me to requite the same if it lie in my power. Thus, my lord, right heartily fare you well. At Ford, the xx. day of September. [1537.]

State Paper Office. Miscellaneous Letters. Temp. Hen. VIII. Third Series. Vol. IX. Original.

Your own assured,

T. Cantuarien.

*To the right honourable and my singular good lord, my lord privy seal.*

---

## CCII. TO A JUSTICE[11].

In my right hearty wise I commend me to you. And whereas divers times heretofore, of mere love and favour, which in my heart I bear to you unfeignedly, I have moved, exhorted, and in as much as in me was, allured you to alter your judgment, minding to bring you to favour the word of God and the knowledge thereof, to the intent that by your good ensample the king's subjects within my diocese might the rather be obedient and willing to conceive and apply themselves to the observation of such ordinances, as by the king's majesty and his learned counsel in the laws of God should from time to time be set forth and published, concerning as well the abolishment and extirpation of superstition, as also of the bishop of Rome's erroneous doctrine, which in many points within this realm still sticketh in men's hearts; this notwithstanding, (as far as I many ways perceive,) my said exhortation and good intent towards you taketh little effect; which thing I assure you is no little grief to me. But inasmuch

Public Record Office. Tractat. Theol. et Polit. Vol. II. pp. 171—174. A. I. 8. Original.

---

[9 Vid. Letter CXCV. p. 345.]

[10 Cranmer admitted Robert Palmere to the church of the parish Sti. Quintini de Spellache within the marches of Calais, vacant by the death of John Hayburne, Oct. 2, 1537. Vid. Cranmer's Register, fol. 362, b.]

[11 The letters between Cranmer and the Kentish justice are in the hand of a secretary, and Dr Jenkyns conjectures that they were prepared for the information of Crumwell. Remains of Abp. Cranmer, Vol. I. p. 201, *n.* y. They bear the following endorsements: "The copie l're of exhortacōn, wt. alsoo an answer to the same, from Rayneham." Also by a later hand, "I thinke this was betwixt Cranmer and Fissher." Fisher was, however, executed June 22, A.D. 1535. In Morice's "Letter sent to sir Wm. Butts, and sir Anthony Deny, defending the cause of M. Rich. Turner, preacher, against the papists," he makes mention of sir John Baker, sir Christopher Hales, and sir Thomas Moile, knights, as Kentish "justices, such as then favoured their cause and faction, [i. e. the papists',] and such as are no small fools." Foxe's Acts and Monuments, p. 1869. Ed. Lond. 1683. If the name of Fisher be incorrect in the endorsement, it is difficult to discover who might have been intended.]

as it is better for me in time, after a friendly fashion, to be plain with you, than so long to forbear that both you and I may repent our dallying, if the king (or rather God) shall by opportunity see just cause to punish our overmuch untowardness; I will at this time open fully my mind to you, and eftsoons exhort you either to be in such opinion and faith as is by the word of God and the king's ordinances prescribed and set forth to his people without colour; or else I cannot see the contrary but of necessity I must be constrained to complain to the king's majesty of you in that behalf, which I were very loth to do, and it is contrary to my mind and usage hitherto; nevertheless, if you overmuch constrain me, I will not fail to do it.

For I am fully persuaded that it will little avail me, either by myself or by such as I shall substitute, to preach within my diocese the word of God or the king's ordinance, you and yours being reputed and known, both of the commons and gentlemen of the shire, of a contrary opinion to me. In something myself (besides the common fame that I hear of you) I have experience of your judgment, that you take not indifferently such things as of late years hath been set forth by the authority of the word of God: and besides this, it is known to many, that you let, in as much as in you is, the people in my diocese to exercise themselves in the knowledge of God's laws; but that from time to time you promote them to all trouble and vexation[1], without any discerning good knowledge from manifest error, so that (as it is thought) you rather thereby intend to extinguish the whole knowledge of God, than to have him by his word known and glorified. I pray you, what other ways was there at any time invented better to maintain, continue, or uphold the bishop of Rome's usurped authority and other superstitiousness, than to banish and suppress the word of God and the knowledge thereof specially from the simple and common people, and to restrain the same to the knowledge of a certain few persons? yea, this thing hath been universally the only decay of our faith. And why then may not men think of you to be a special favourer covertly of his authority, when you bear the people such a hatred for favouring of God's word, which word hath uttered unto all the world his crafty inventions?

Surely you so handle yourself in this thing, that it is not only known to the people that you hate God's word, but also that you cannot abide any reformation or alteration of abuses in the church, or amongst the people; uttering your words and communication in such wise, that every thing that is set forth contrary to the late custom used by the authority of Rome must seem to you and yours new learning and erroneous. And again, if any ceremony or ordinance of the church be but brought to his first sense and meaning, and cut away from superstition, by and by it is blasted abroad under your authority and by such as appertaineth to you, that all old fashions are restored again, spite of this new doctrine and new preachers; and so declared and communed of, that the people daily conceiveth great murmuration both against the ordinances, against the king's majesty, his council, and against me and all other that by our preaching declareth such abuses and superstition as hath been hitherto brought from Rome, which would restore God his honour, obedience to the prince, and peace and tranquillity to the realm.

And to the intent that you shall perceive that these things be not feigned ne imagined without cause, you shall understand, that (besides the common and vulgar fame touching the premises) certain of your servants and family lately, since this new book of the clergy's determination came forth by the king's grace's commandment[2], hath not only misreported the said book in divers and many things, (as I am informed,) but also hath spoken such words or like in effect as hereafter ensueth, that is to say to move divers by these words, "I am sorry for you, and I can do no less than shew unto you that thing that I know to be true, and that the king's book willeth; for of truth it alloweth all the old fashion, and putteth all the knaves of the new learning to silence, so that now they dare not speak one word,"—willing them to leave the teachers of the New Testament, for they be but knaves, cobblers, and

[[1] Vid. Letter CCXXIII. p. 367.]
[[2] i.e. The Institution of a Christian Man. Vid. Letter CXC. p. 337.]

such other abominable heretics; further saying, that "my master and divers other could have favoured you much better, saving that you smelled of the new learning." If these, and such like words, be not both contentious and seditious, I know not what may be cause of sedition in this matter. For surely I think that those which begun the rebellion in Lincolnshire[3] had no better occasion to turn the people's hearts against their prince, than such manner of communication as is used here by your maintenance, or at the least trusting to your defence. Which thing much grieveth me, yea, it pitieth me not a little, to think that you, having so kind and loving a sovereign lord as the king's grace is to you, of whom you have received no small benefits, but over that of his great goodness hath called you to so high estimation as to be reputed one of his council, should thus slenderly regard his godly intent in the reformation of doctrine within this his realm, that by your comfort the vulgar people conceiveth hatred towards such things as by the prince's commandment are set forth. It is every where within Kent spoken and murmured, that the people dare not apply themselves to read God's word, for fear of your threats at sizes and sessions.

And whereas your servants report that all things are restored by this new book to their old use, both of ceremonies, pilgrimages, purgatory, and such other, calling those that of late hath preached of the abuses of them, false knaves and men worthy of no credence: truly you and your servants be so blinded, that you call old that is new, and new that is old; and of malice, as it appeareth, you will not learn of them that can tell you, what is new and what is old. But in very deed the people be restored by this book to their old good usages, although they be not restored to their late abused usages; for the old usage was in the primitive church, and nigh thereunto when the church was most purest, nothing less so to phantasy of ceremonies, pilgrimage, purgatory, saints, images, works, and such like, as hath these three or four hundred years been corruptly taught. And if men will indifferently read these late declarations, they shall well perceive, that purgatory, pilgrimages, praying to saints, images, holy bread, holy water, holy days, merits, works, ceremony, and such other, be not restored to their late accustomed abuses; but shall evidently perceive that the word of God hath gotten the upper hand of them all, and hath set them in their right use and estimation; although it be otherwise reported by them that would fain have the people maintained in sedition, and continue in blindness and in disobedience.

Wherefore in mine opinion, if you mind and intend that the hearts of the people should be given to the law of God and their prince, it appertaineth as well to you as to me to open to the people, in time and place convenient, how much they are bound to give God eternal thanks, laud, and praise, that in their time it hath pleased his goodness thus manifestly to shew himself by his word to them, whereby they may perceive in what error, superstition, and blindness they were led in of late years; and that they have no less cause to give him thanks, in that he hath sent us so good and virtuous a prince, as to cause these things to be made open to them both by his word, and otherwise by declaration of learned men: and not thus to bear in hand and glory, that in all things the people must do as they did before, and whatsoever hath been preached by these new preachers are mere heresies: so that in thus reporting bringeth in a grudge and hatred no small number of people one against another.

And surely if it were not for the favour I bear to you, I would call before me such of your servants and other that appertain to you, and proceed against them as against heretics, if they will maintain either pilgrimage, purgatory, images, or saints, merits or works, as they have been heretofore by many both taught and used, by the space of two or three hundred years, for all their brag; and therefore let them look more wisely upon this new book than so to report of it. Howbeit, I trust your wisdom and discretion is such, that you will see your family and retinue so ordered,

[3 "The first rising was in Lincolnshire, in the beginning of October," (A.D. 1536.) Vid. Burnet's Hist. of Reformat. Vol. I. p. 456. Ed. Oxon. 1829.]

that they may be agreeable to such things as are truly set forth for the preservation of the common opinion and religion within this realm. And trusting also, that both on your part, and on theirs likewise, quietness amongst the people may be observed, and love towards our prince engendered; to the furtherance whereof every man in his state is bound both of duty and of conscience.

---

## CCIII. A JUSTICE TO CRANMER.

Public Record Office. Tractat. Theol. et Polit. Vol. II. pp. 174—176. A. I. 8. Original.

In right humble manner I recommend me unto your lordship: ascertaining you, that yesterday I received your letters at Mynster in the Isle of Thanet, written at Ford the 2nd day of this month, thinking continually before my receipt thereof, that your lordship had been much more my good lord than I may well now perceive that ye be. And even as, before your lordship knew me or any part of my conversation, ye judged me to be a man that favoured not the word of God; so, notwithstanding your often favourable acceptation of me into your presence heretofore, and hearing of mine answer thereunto directly made unto you, your lordship, without cause, persevereth in that opinion, (in manner) as if ye had so tried me; and for answer hereto I pray you, my lord, pardon me of my plainness ensuing.

I let you know reverently, that I love God and his most blessed word, believe in him, dread him, confess him, and am as obedient to him and to his laws as ye be, and as a true Christian oweth to be. Wherefore, as in that point, your judgment doth me wrong. Also, my lord, I trust verily in God, and doubt it nothing, but that if ye do your duty to God as a good christian prelate, (which I pray God give you grace to do,) and also your duty to the king's majesty on your behalf as appertaineth to your honour, as I have ever intended to do, have done, and will do continually to my feeble power, neither of us shall have cause to repent our dealing, neither rebukeful untowardness shall be seen to be in either of us. And, my lord, I have not used to colour or dissemble, to advance or extol any thing which the king's highness hath set forth to his people; and if ye know that I have, do your duty by complaint, as ye threat me by your letters: and I trust that little honour shall ensue to you by your complaint, being grounded upon so little truth.

And as touching the preaching of your lordship and of your substitutes, ye cannot truly accuse me to have impugned against the same. And as for the experience which your lordship hath of my judgment, that I take not indifferently such things as of late hath been set forth by the authority of the word of God, I am ready to answer to your knowledge and experience therein, whensoever I shall be called. Also I say expressly, that neither ye nor any other knoweth, nor can prove, that I have let any people of your diocese to exercise themselves in the knowledge of God's laws, neither hath promoted any such to trouble or vexation. And I dare well say, that none honest man thinketh, that I rather intend to extinguish the whole or any part of the knowledge of God, than to have him by his word known and glorified. But your lordship, being prone to hear the tongues of false liars your explorators, thus listeth by their false reports to touch me with your letters.

And as to the false traitors in Lincolnshire, which ye ascribe to be adherents to the bishop of Rome, and subsequently ye parify me unto them; my lord, I think ye shew thereby your good will and charity toward me to be but little: for I let your lordship know, that I am as true a subject to the king as ye be, and no papist, nor set any more by the bishop of Rome, or his traditions or usurpations, than I think he setteth by you. And untruly ye conclude thereupon, that I bear the people hatred for favouring of God's word, affirming that I so handle myself that it is not unknown to the people, that I hate God's word; and also that I cannot abide any reformation or alteration of abuses in the church or among the people: which matter it seemeth, by your letters, that your lordship hath gathered by my words and communications brought unto you by the false tongues before rehearsed; and yet ye give faith and credit unto them as though ye had heard or seen me to shew myself. I marvel much of that your light credence therein, not hearing me which am a party to be called thereunto: which lightness of credence doth not well in so great a prelate as your lordship is. After this your lordship imputeth much default in me, that by mine authority and by such as appertain to me, ceremonies or ordinances of the church cut away from superstition is blasted to be restitution of all old fashions, spite of this new doctrine and new preachers; whereupon your lordship, by your letters, doth express specially many great offences committed against the ordinances to the king's majesty, his council, and yourself; and for approbation thereof ye rehearse divers misdemeanours committed by certain of my servants, sythe that the book, which ye call the clergy's determinations, hath come forth by the king's commandment. My lord, I have none authority but of the king's majesty, and I trust I know how to use that according to his grace's pleasure and laws, and will not let so to do, how many soever espies ye set to look upon me. And of the said book I have spoken openly in the last sessions, at Canterbury and elsewhere, so that my words were manifest, and I will abide by them; and let my servants answer to theirs: for, my lord, ye shall find me to be no seditious nor contentious person, nor ye can prove me to be a maintainer of communication sounding or extending to any such abominable effect as ye write of, nor that any person hath had or conceived any occasion to trust to any defence in such wicked matter. And it is not honourable to you so to write, unless that ye can prove it, (as I am sure ye cannot.)

And as touching the benefits by me received by the king's highness, your lordship needeth not to put me in remembrance of them; for I should shew too much ingrate and unnatural disposition in me, if I should not recognise that I have received of his grace's benignity and liberality an hundred-fold more good and goodness than ever I shall be able to deserve or recompense unto his grace, as your lordship and many other have done semblably, which I perfectly and well knew before that I knew your lordship; and therefore have alway considered that my duty is to pray to Almighty God daily for preservation of his most royal estate, and with my body and all that I have to serve him unto my life's end.

And as for my threats at assizes and sessions, *ego palam locutus sum;* and am sure that I neither offended God, my sovereign lord, nor my own conscience therein, in such wise as ye write. And as to my blindness in reading the said new book, of truth I am so blind, that when I read in it, it seemeth to me that it is so full and perfect of itself, that there needeth none other doctor or clerk to be expositor thereof: wherefore I and all other the king's true and unlearned subjects be much bound to pray for his grace, that hath set forth among us such a noble and comfortable work for the advancement of christian faith and true doctrine.

And, my lord, if ye have matter or cause sufficient to convent before you any of my servants, or other that appertain to me, and to proceed against them as against heretics, I pray you let not the favour or love that ye pretend to bear to me be the let thereof; for your lordship giveth me now little cause to trust unto it; and therefore I may think mine own poor heart being set in affection toward you, next unto my sovereign lord, to have had a weary journey. God preserve your lordship! Written at Sandwich this Wednesday morning, the 3rd day of October, an°. 29. [1537.]

---

## CCIV. TO A JUSTICE.

Public Record Office Tractat. Theol. et Polit. Vol. II. pp 177—180. A. 1. 8. Original.

After hearty commendations; these shall be to signify unto you, that I have received your letters dated at Sandwich the third day of this present month of October, answering to my late letters to you directed the second day of the said month; the contents and circumstances whereof I have thoroughly pondered and considered: by which I perceive that you cannot well bear the exhortation of your friend in such things as of duty appertaineth one to admonish another; as specially it becometh every man without respect to do, when the thing toucheth God's quarrel and the prince's: for you make an answer unto my said letters with such comparisons, and so clearly avoiding yourself from every conjecture and reason objected, that you would seem to be out of suspicion of all together: which thing if you could persuade unto me to be true, I would gladly abide both reproach for writing so unadvisedly, and also make you a large amends, so that the most part of my diocese could likewise believe the same as well as I. Howbeit I am twice sorry to find you in this taking; once, by cause you set so light by your friend's honest admonition; again, by cause you be of that courage, rather to be content to be evil spoken of by many that dare not once tell you a word to your face, but in murmuration all behind your back, than to abide your friend's plain, simple, and loving monition, which telleth you what other men heareth, talketh, and judgeth of you.

And now to come somewhat to touch your letter particularly, you shall right well understand that you are much deceived, to think that I withdraw my good mind, or that at any time, either now or heretofore, I have not loved you in my heart, but (as it were) dissembled with you all this while. And inasmuch as you say that I judged you, before I knew you, not to be a favourer of God's word, and so doth persist in that opinion, in manner as if I had so tried you: in that you may perceive that there was a fame of you in this behalf before I knew you; which declareth that neither I nor none of mine hath invented any such things against you of late; and therefore, the fame not yet quenched made me to write my mind so plainly to you as I did. As for the profession of your religion, that you love God and his most blessed word, believe in him, dread him, &c. I did never doubt in that behalf at all, but that you had a fervent zeal to him, saving that it may be doubtful whether that zeal were according to knowledge, or no: specially considering that in your sessions and elsewhere you be not so diligent nor circumspect to open and set forth things requisite of necessity to our salvation, (as the point of our justification by Christ's passion only, the difference between faith and works, works of mercy to be done before voluntary works, the obedience towards our prince by the authority of the word of God, and such other concerning the stiff opinion of the people in alteration of ordinances and laws in the church, as holidays, fasting days, &c.,) as you be in the declaration and setting forth of mere voluntary things, of the which we have no ground ne foundation of scripture. The abuses of which voluntary things have been so nourished in the church, that the estimation of them hath put out of place, or at the least greatly obscured and hindered, the very articles of our faith, and such things as of necessity and upon pain of damnation we are bound both to believe and do; yet notwithstanding must they be at sessions and elsewhere in letes[1] restored to their old use,

[1 This word, "letes," i. e. "court leets," is omitted by Dr Jenkyns.]

without any mention made of the abuses, and without any word mentioned of things necessary for our salvation. Methink God and the king hath wrong, in thus declaring the worst, and speaking never a word of the best: God first, by cause his commandment is not preferred; and then the king, by cause [he] hath caused great labours and pains to be taken to discern the one from the other; the best to be worthiest esteemed, and the other to have their degree and right use, the abuses cut away. And yet the matter is so handled, and every thing restored to his old use by your declaration, as I am credibly informed, that no abuse is found, and that it seemeth that the king and his council are worthy of no laud and praise at all for their great pains, expenses, and labours; and the people nevertheless led in blindness.

Surely therefore I do not impute this to you, as doing it of malice or of purpose, but rather for lack of some knowledge, in not discerning sincerely things commanded by God and by his word from things ordained by man and grounded upon mere devotion, without any foundation and ground of the word of God: which manner of discerning these two things, no doubt, these many years hath not been greatly regarded, pondered, ne weighed, but rather wittingly let slip, by cause that without controlment of the word of God men might build whatsoever they list for their own glory, commodity, advantage, and lucre. These things shall you evidently espy, if you advisedly ponder these late and last determinations of the clergy[1]: and I marvel that you do not perceive this in reading the same, seeing that, as you say, they be so plain they need no declaration.

As touching that you lay to my charge in sundry places of your letters, that I am light of credence and prone to hear false liars my explorators, thinking that I go about to set spies for you; I trust in your conscience you do not think so as you have written, for hitherto I have not so handled myself, neither to you ne to none other; at the least I dare say that I am out of common fame thereof. If you have of me no better estimation for my friendly admonition, I may think that you have borne little good mind to me hitherto, thus suddenly to lay to my charge that [of] which no man living (besides you) can accuse me of suspicion, much less of proof. And do you think that I am so ready, at the informations of light persons, to write so earnestly to such a one as you be, both of experience and wisdom in no small estimation, not having both manifest conjectures, proofs some, and vulgar fame sufficient, to inform me thereunto? Surely, notwithstanding your imagination in this behalf, I may not wink at such things as be by common fame and great likelihood opened to me, specially when the matter tendeth to disquietness, murmur, or disobedience. For if I had intended so to undermine you, (as you pretend I do,) you may trust me, surely, that I would never have opened so plainly to you my mind as I have done, but have declared and proved my grief so to the king's grace and his council, not doubting but that I should rather have thereby had laud and praise than any dishonour, mine intent thoroughly known to the king's majesty in that behalf.

And where you say, that I parify you to the false traitors in Lincolnshire, thinking thereby to shew my good-will and charity towards you to be but little, and so thereupon you declare your true obedience to the king's majesty; sir, although you have uncharitably received my letter, and gathered upon me in this point more than can be proved justly, yet did I not intend herein to break charity with you, or to bear you any worse will, in declaring mine opinion, what I thought your servants' words and such other might prove to, leaving for example that such like words was the ground and foundation of the rebellion lately conceived in Lincolnshire. And to be plain with you, I am sorry to perceive how ready you be to ascribe that to yourself, which was only laid to your servants, for such words as I suppose I can justly prove against them. And therefore when I write this parification (as you call it) of the rebels of Lincolnshire, I nothing thought less than to compare any man hereabout to them: only I shewed what seditious words might do here, as it did there; for I think that if such monitions had been in time there sent to wise men, it would never have come to so great a ruffle as it did. And I do assure you, (by cause the pacifying of seditiousness as much appertaineth to you as to me,) I had

[[1] The Institution of a Christian Man. Vid. Letters CXC. CCII. pp. 337, 350.]

thought when I wrote that my said letter to you, you would rather have required of me the names of your servants, the time and place, and to whom those words were spoken, than thus, by taking to yourself the defence of your said servants, impute that the matter was specially rehearsed against you.

As touching many other things at large in your letter, of your hatred towards the people for favouring of the word of God, of your interpreting new and old fashions, of your open speaking at sessions, or elsewhere, both of the new book and of other things, and of your threats there; forsomuch as you allege this text, *Ego palam locutus sum*, I think in very deed that your open speaking hath engendered much grudge amongst the people, and also putteth your own servants in this courage and comfort, thus without discretion to babble and talk such slanderous and seditious words as they do.

And therefore, to make an end, I require you not to take my monition to the worst, but as you would accept the monition of him that loveth you better than he that dare not tell you his mind according to his conscience. And as for that that I have done hitherto by my letters, you have no cause why you should take it but after a charitable manner, considering that it is our private and secret communication. And if you cannot thus take it, then I remit the judgment of my letters to the king and his council, and to the report of such as shall be called before them for the same. And now, where upon occasion of my other letter you wish to me that God should give me grace to do my office, truly I can no less do than thank you therefore, requiring you (as you shall from time to time see cause why) that you will both earnestly and plainly admonish me of such things as you shall think in your conscience worthy of reformation. And I trust I shall not only better accept your admonitions than you have done mine, but shall in my heart also yield unto you condign thanks for the same.

---

## CCV. A JUSTICE TO CRANMER.

AFTER due reverence as appertaineth to your lordship remembered; it may please you to know that yesterday before noon I received your second letters, whereby I perceive that your lordship calleth your former letters to me directed, which I received at Mynster in Thanett, "a friendly exhortation." And ye allege that I cannot bear the same: which allegation it seemeth ye make because of certain comparisons comprised in mine answer to your lordship thereunto made. My lord, ye may be assured that your said former letters distempered not me in such wise, that I forgat wherein I made my comparison; for they be such as I may well make, and eftsoons hereby I affirm them. And as to your lordship's friendly exhortation, albeit that ye be an high prelate and percase deeply seen in divinity, and I a man but meanly learned in morality, I despair not so much in myself as to think, that I cannot discern between a friendly exhortation or admonition, and a captious impetition or dangerous commination. And where your lordship offereth to abide reproach, or to make me amends, in case that I could persuade unto you mine Irreite[2] to be true, as I have heretofore written, I will not desire any of those to be had; but I will make recompence to myself by being ware of your lordship hereafter. And, my lord, I know well that honest men of this shire be not in such fear of me, as to forbear to speak to me presently as they think, nor use to detract me, as ye write.

Public Record Office. Tractat. Theol. et Polit. Vol. II. pp. 180—182. A. 1. 8. Original.

And where your lordship, touching the particulars of mine answer to your said former letters, writeth, that your judgment conceived of me before ye knew me, in that I favoured not the word of God, and your perseverance in the same argueth that there was a fame of me in that behalf before ye knew me; it seemeth to be but a weak argument, and thereto I say and I think verily, that ye never knew nor heard of any such fame, but that ye invented that objection against me for another cause, which I well remember. For when I came first to your presence, which was at Otford, and moved you therein, ye justified not that your judgment by any fame thereof being upon me, but advised me to apply study of scripture; which hitherto I durst never enterprise, for doubt that I should, with little learning and less discretion, take upon me high knowledge, as I see many do now-a-days.

And such things as ye impute default in me for matters not set forth in sessions, which be requisite for our salvation; those things be more pertinent to the office and part of a standing preacher in a pulpit, than to a sitting justiciar in a temporal session of peace: and what your lordship meaneth by voluntary things set forth in sessions, which ye allege have greatly obscured our faith and such things as we be bound to believe and do upon pain of damnation, I know not; and I never heard the king's courts of sessions so defamed as your lordship doth with your pen, writing that the worst been there declared, and of the best never a word spoken. Thus your lordship taketh opinion by the reports of the tongues of such false persons as I have written of to your lordship before; and in the process of this matter it may be reasonably

[[2] This word is omitted by Dr Jenkyns. It is here printed as it stands in the MS.; but it is either a mistake, or at least the meaning of it is doubtful.]

gathered upon the writing to me, that a session of the king's laws cannot be laudably kept, unless there be in manner a sermon of divinity clerkly made therein. Whereunto ye add great lack of discretion in men between things commanded by God and by his word, and things ordained by man and grounded of mere devotion, without any foundation or ground of the word of God. I suppose that few men have so little discretion as to think, that liberal things proceeding but of devotion be to be done or practised, and the commandment of God to be omitted: albeit I doubt not but that Almighty God accepteth to his pleasure good things done which proceed of mere devotion, though that the thing be not expressly commanded to be done by the word of God; or else all foundations of ecclesiastical things and other like perpetuities be of little reputation.

Also your lordship marvelleth that I do not perceive things which ye write of, in reading the last determinations of the clergy, because I say they be so plain that they need no declaration; and I marvel more that ye so marvel, ere that ye know or hear mine intelligence in them. And most heartily I beseech your lordship to let me know your manifest conjectures, proofs, and vulgar fame which ye write of; whereupon ye have grounded, or reasonably may ground yourself to impeach me by your former letters as ye have done; for till your lordship so letteth me know by some reasonable mean, I cannot think but that ye have dealt hardly with me and uncharitably. And let the openers to you of those things, and such other as ye may not wink at, be known; and I doubt not but that they shall be seen to be such persons as I have written of, and thereby also ye shall know me better than ye do. And hithereto, I am sure, that I have been as vigilant to things tending to disquietness, murmur, or disobedience, as any poor man of my degree in this shire, and have detested them as much: and because that it seemeth that divers of my servants offended your lordship in speaking of some words, I pray you send for them, and upon due proof thereof made, use them according to their demerits.

And where I have written, *ego palam locutus sum,* let the hearers testify, and I am ready to make answer; and beseech Almighty God to grant me grace never to have more dangerous matter to answer unto than that: and I doubt not but that I have so borne myself hitherto, and trust in God to do hereafter, that I shall not need to dread the complaint of your lordship nor of any other; and so finally I intend truly to serve God and the king during my poor life, as well as God will give me grace, and so to live in good tranquillity and little care of evil tongues, what ears or eyes soever be bent against me. And so also I pray God your lordship may do. Written at Raynham, the first Sunday of this month of October. [Oct. 7, A. D. 1537.]

---

## CCVI. TO CRUMWELL.

State Paper Office. Miscellaneous Letters. Temp. Hen. VIII. Third series. Vol. IX. Original.

My very singular good lord, after most hearty commendations unto your lordship; these shall be to signify unto the same, that you shall receive news by this bearer Mr Hethe[1], which of late I have received out of Germany from Osiander; requiring you, my lord, to give further credence unto this said bearer touching such things as he shall declare unto you.

And albeit that I have written to your lordship so many times in the favour of that poor man, William Gronnowe[2], to be restored unto his room at Calice, that I am at my wit's end farther how to behave myself to do him good by my suit, considering that your letters, three times already directed in his favour, prevaileth nothing at all; yet once again, having in respect both his importune suit, and also his extreme poverty, or rather undoing, I shall beseech your lordship, (inasmuch as you have thus far attempted in his behalf,) that you will not now leave off your good intent towards him; for if you do, surely I do not only count the man undone, but also take that this his extreme handling shall be a great hinderance to the advancement of God's word: and I beseech you procure, that there may be one of the council of Caleis that earnestly favoureth the furtherance thereof. Thus, my lord, right heartily fare you well. At Ford, the 9th day of October. [1537.]

Your own assured ever,

T. CANTUARIEN.

*To the right honourable and my singular good lord, my lord privy seal.*

---

[[1] Vid. Letters LXXXVIII. CL. pp. 276, 307. Seckendorf, Comment. Hist. Apol. de Lutheran. Lib. III. Sect. 13. § xxxix. Add. p. 111, and Sect. 16. § lxvi. Add. (b) p. 180. Ed. Francof. et Lips. 1692.]

[[2] Vid. Letter CXCVIII. p. 347.]

## CCVII. TO DR SNEDE, VICAR OF RYE.

State Paper Office. Ibid.

I COMMEND me unto you. And whereas I understand that (by reason of bloodshed lately committed within your church by William Guston upon one Robert a Wood) you be in doubt whether that you may lawfully celebrate divine service there: I do signify unto you that, upon due examination of the manner and circumstance thereof, I do find therein no lawful impediment whereby you may have cause to abstain from your said divine service, but that you may exercise the same as it hath been heretofore accustomed; which I will and command you to do, this said chance notwithstanding. Thus fare you well. At Ford, the 11 day of November. [1537.]

T. CANTUARIEN[3].

*To my wellbeloved doctor Snede, vicar of Rye, and in his absence to the curate there.*

## CCVIII. TO CRUMWELL.

State Paper Office. Ibid. Original.

MY singular good lord, I heartily commend me unto you. And whereas my trusty servant master Towker, my physician, being a man of good learning and conversation, hath exercised the office of a physician of long continuance with the prior and convent of Christ's church, in Canterbury, and had the fees, profits, and commodities belonging to the same; the which said office, by the custom of the house, hath always been esteemed a perpetuity, and the prior promised me at Christmas last, that my said servant should have a patent thereof during his life; the which his former promise the prior nothing regarding sithen that time will now in no wise condescend that my said servant shall have any patent of the said office: wherefore, in consideration of the good service he hath done to the said prior and convent at all times, I beseech your good lordship to direct your letters to the said prior and convent, requiring them without further delay to seal and deliver the said letters patents; whereby ye shall not only do a very good deed, but also bind my said servant to be your daily beadman, and with his poor service to be at all times at your lordship's commandment. And thus heartily fare you well. From Lamehithe, the xith day of this month of November. [1537.]

Your own assured ever,

T. CANTUARIEN.

*To the right honourable and my singular good lord, my lord privy seal.*

## CCIX. TO CRUMWELL.

State Paper Office. Ibid. Original.

MY very singular good lord, in my most hearty wise I commend me unto your lordship. And where I have written unto the wardens of the goldsmiths, requiring them to take a view of the pix belonging unto the mint at Canterbury[4], as well for my discharge as to the intent the king's highness may be the more substantially served in his coins there; the said wardens hath sent me word, that they would gladly take pains in that behalf, so that they may have commandment from one of the council besides me; for so in times past they have accomplished my predecessors' request herein, and not else, (as they say:) these shall be therefore to beseech your lordship to assign this bill herein inclosed, to the intent that the master and con-

[[3] This letter has not been printed in any former collection of the archbishop's letters.]
[[4] Vid. Letter CXXIII. p. 295, *n.* 1.]

troller of the said mint, being now in the town at my commandment, may the sooner have expedition in the premises. Thus, my lord, right heartily fare you well. At Lambeth, the ivth day of December. [1537.]

Your own assured ever,

T. CANTUARIEN.

*To my very singular good lord, my lord privy seal.*

---

## CCX. TO CRUMWELL.

State Paper Office. Ibid. Original.

MY very singular good lord, in my most hearty wise I commend me unto your lordship. These shall be to signify unto the same, that at my late being at the court, forsomuch as I failed of you there, I attempted alone to be a suitor unto the king's majesty for my loving friend sir John Markham[1], knight, declaring unto his grace not only the old and continual service which the said sir John Markeham did first unto his grace's grandame[2], and since to his said grace ever since his coronation, being in all the wars which the king hath had since his most gracious reign, except he had wars in divers places at one time, and then he was ever in one of them, which from time to time hath been great charge unto him: moreover I declared unto his highness, how the said sir John, of long season, hath unfeignedly favoured the truth of God's word; and so upon these my persuasions I besought his grace to be good in a suit which your lordship and I should make for the said sir John, whereof I referred the relation unto your lordship: and I found the king's grace very well minded towards the said sir John; wherefore I nothing doubt, but if it will please your lordship this present time earnestly to set forward the said suit, the king's grace is well inclined to hear it; so that I trust you shall easily obtain the same, which I beseech you to do at this my request, and this gentleman shall be ever bound to do you service. And yet one thing I did forget to say unto his highness, which is this, that the said sir John Markham hath been no great craver unto his grace; for this is the first thing that ever he asked of his grace. Wherefore, my lord, considering the matter is thus far opened and wholly committed unto you, I shall desire you to promote the same with expedition, and that the rather at this mine instant request: wherein surely you shall not only do for the preferment of a faithful and honest gentleman[3], but thereby bind me to be at your lordship's commandment. Thus, my lord, right heartily fare you well. At Lambeth, the vith day of December. [1537.]

Your lordship's own ever,

T. CANTUARIEN.

*To my very singular good lord, my lord privy seal.*

---

## CCXI. TO CRUMWELL.

State Paper Office. Ibid. Original. State Papers, Vol. I. Part II. Let. cv. pp. 574, 5. Todd's Life of Abp. Cranmer, Vol. I. p. 184.

MY very singular good lord, after most hearty commendations; this shall be to signify unto your lordship, that I have received both your letters, and the book[4] also lately by us devised, and now overseen and corrected by the king's majesty; which book, according to his grace's pleasure, (all other business laid apart,) I shall with all possible expedition peruse and oversee within this sevennight, or fortnight at the

[1 Vid. Letter CLXI. p. 315.]

[2 The lady Margaret, countess of Richmond.]

[3 The site of the Premonstratensian Abbey of Neubo or Newboth, in Lincolnshire, was granted to sir John Markham, 29 Hen. VIII. Tanner's Notitia Monast. Lincoln. lv. Neubo. Ed. Camb. 1787.]

[4 i.e. The Institution of a Christian Man. Vid. Letters CXC. CCII. CCXII. pp. 337, 350, 359.]

uttermost, and thereof advertise his majesty, by your lordship, of my judgment and opinion in such places as are in the same book by his grace corrected.

And as touching your farther advertisement of the king's most gracious pleasure to be resolved in the case of matrimony between the late duke of Richmond[5] and my lord of Norfolk's daughter, wherein his highness willeth me to call my doctors unto me, and to propone the same case amongst them, whether such marriage be matrimony or no; I assure your lordship, that, without farther convocation of doctors, I am fully persuaded that such marriages as be in lawful age contracted *per verba de præsenti* are matrimony before God. And the same case is (as I remember) plainly opened and declared in the king's grace's book of his own cause of matrimony[6]. Howbeit, I shall eftsoons consult herein with such learned men as at this time be with me present, and send unto your lordship our resolution in the same. And if his grace will have me further to consult therein, then I must send for other learned men, or else come to London myself. Thus Almighty God have your lordship in his tuition! At Ford, the 14th day of January. [1538.]

Your own ever assured,

T. Cantuarien.

*To my very singular good lord, my lord privy seal.*

---

## CCXII. TO CRUMWELL[7].

My very singular good lord, after most hearty commendations unto your lordship; these shall be to advertise the same, that as concerning the book lately devised by me and other bishops of this realm, which you sent unto me corrected by the king's highness, your lordship shall receive the same again by this bearer the pursuivant, with certain annotations of mine own concerning the same: wherein I trust the king's highness will pardon my presumption, that I have been so scrupulous, and as it were a picker of quarrels to his grace's book, making a great matter of every light fault, or rather where no fault is at all; which I do only for this intent, that because the book now shall be set forth by his grace's censure and judgment, I would have nothing therein that Momus could reprehend: and yet I refer all mine annotations again to his grace's most exact judgment; and I have ordered my annotations so by numbers, that his grace may readily turn to every place, and in the lower margin of this book, next to the binding, he may find the numbers which shall direct him to the words whereupon I make the annotations: and all those his grace's castigations which I have made none annotation upon, I like them very well; and in divers places also

Cotton MSS. Cleop. E. v. f. 101. British Museum. Original.

---

[[5] Vid. Letter LXXXIII. p. 273, *n*. 6. Henry Fitzroy, duke of Richmond, died July 22, A.D. 1536, when about seventeen years of age. Stow's Annals, p. 572. Ed. Lond. 1615. Note to State Papers, Vol. I. p. 321.]

[[6] This was probably "the determinations of the moste famous and mooste excellent Universities of Italy and Fraunce, that it is so unlefule for a man to marie his brother's wyfe, that the pope hath no power to dispence therewith;" published by Berthelet, Nov. A.D. 1530; Ames' Typ. Antiq. Vol. III. p. 275. Ed. Lond. 1810—19. Strype's Mem. of Abp. Cranmer, Vol. I. p. 74. Ed. Oxon. 1840. Of the books written for the king's cause Burnet says: "But all these, and many more, were summed up in a short book, and printed first in Latin, then in English, with the determination of the universities before it," of which he also gives an abstract. Vid. Hist. of Reformat. Vol. I. pp. 195, et sqq. Ed. Oxon. 1829.]

[[7] Dr Jenkyns (Remains of Abp. Cranmer, Vol. I. p. 227,) fixes the date of this and the preceding letter, A.D. 1538, because Cranmer, with the other bishops had almost completed in July, 1537, their determinations "upon the preparation of the Institution of a Christian Man," (Vid. Letter CXC. p. 337.) which is spoken of in this letter as "the book lately devised," which could scarcely place the letter earlier than A.D. 1538. The allusion to the duke of Richmond's marriage in the former letter leads to the inference, that it was written soon after his death, which took place July 22, A.D. 1536, and would scarcely make it later than that year. Todd and Strype, however, fix the date as A.D. 1537. Vid. Todd's Life of Abp. Cranmer, Vol. I. pp. 184, 5; Strype's Mem. of Abp. Cranmer, Vol. I. pp. 73, et sqq. Ed. Oxon. 1840.]

I have made annotations, which places nevertheless I mislike not, as it shall appear by the same annotations[1].

And as touching the punishment of those evil persons, which have in these parties set forth seditious bruits[2] of the king's majesty, one of them upon Wednesday last was ordered at Canterbury according to the king's grace's commandment, and another shall suffer the same to-morrow at Sandwich, and the other shall be served accordingly.

And as for the case of marriage wherein your lordship first required to know, whether marriage contracted and solemnisated in lawful age, "per verba de præsenti," and without carnal copulation, be matrimony before God or no; and now you require farther to know, whether such matrimony be consummate or no; and what the woman may thereupon demand by the law civil after the death of her husband[3]: to the first part I answer, that I and my doctors that are now with me are of this opinion, that this matrimony contracted, "per verba de præsenti," is perfect matrimony before God, but not utterly consummated (as this term is commonly used amongst the school divines and lawyers) but by carnal copulation. And as for the demand of the woman by the law civil, I will therein profess mine ignorance; and I have no learned men here with me in the said civil law, but only doctor Barbare[4], who in this matter saith he cannot pronounce his mind, except he had books here, and the company of learned men of the said faculty to consult withal. And I marvel that the votes of the civil lawyers be required herein, seeing that all manner of causes of dower be judged within this realm by the common laws of the same; and there be plenty of well learned men in the civil law at London, which undoubtedly can certify the king's majesty of the truth herein, as much as appertaineth unto that law[5]. Thus, my lord, right heartily fare you well. At Ford, the xxvth day of January. [1538.]

Your lordship's own assured,

T. CANTUARIEN.

---

[[1] Vid. Corrections of "The Institution of a Christian Man," by Henry VIII. and Abp. Cranmer's Annotations, p. 83, &c. supra.]

[[2] Vid. Strype's Mem. of Abp. Cranmer, p. 90.]

[[3] The words "after the death of her husband" are inserted in the archbishop's hand.]

[[4] Dr John Barber was the archbishop's "official of his court of Canterbury," whom he "retained with him in his household for expedition of matters in suit before him, being his officer, and as a counsellor to him in the law when need required." He was, however, discovered by the archbishop to have acted treacherously during the conspiracies of the bishop of Winchester and others against him, A.D. 1543. Strype's Mem. of Abp. Cranmer, pp. 131, 173. Ed. Oxon. 1840.]

[[5] The following letter was written by Mary, widow of Henry, duke of Richmond, to the duke of Norfolk, her father, respecting her suit to the king for her maintenance.

Cotton MSS. Vespasian. F. xiii. f. 75. British Museum. Original.

"And though I am in doubt how your grace shall take it, that I should thus daily trouble you with my own letters, yet I trust your grace will consider how this matter troubleth me most of any other, and mine is the part both to speak and sue, if I had not such a good intercessor to the king's majesty in my behalf as your grace is, whereof as yet provideth no effect but words, which maketh me think the king's highness is not ascertained of my whole widowful and right therein; for if he were, he is so just a prince, so gracious, and of such equity, that I am sure he would never suffer the justice of his laws to be denied to me the unworthy desolate widow of his late son, that never yet was denied to the poorest gentlewoman in this realm. And if it would please ye, as ofttimes I have humbly desired your grace to give me leave to come up and sue mine own cause, being no wise too good to be in person an humble suitor to his majesty; I do not doubt but upon the sight thereof his highness should be moved to have compassion on me, considering that he himself alone made the marriage, and to think that it shall be much his majesty's honour to grant me that that his laws give me to maintain me with, the desolate widow of his late son, in the degree that his majesty hath called me to; yet nevertheless putting my whole matter into your grace's hands and my lord privy seal's, who (as ye write) hath promised to be good lord therein, most humbly desiring your blessing I bid your grace farewell, from Kengygael this Wednesday.

"By your humble dowther,

"MARY RICHMOND.

"*To my very good lord and father the duke of Norfolk, this be delivered.*"

This letter has also been printed in Ellis' Original Letters, 2nd Series, Letter CXX. Vol. II. pp. 83—85; State Papers, Vol. I. pp. 576-578.

In a letter by Sadleyr to Crumwell, dated July 14, [1538,] preserved in the State Paper Office, (Miscell. Letters, Temp. Hen. VIII. 2nd Series, Vol. XXXVII.) he says: "These shall be to advertise you, that the king's highness hath commanded me to signify unto you, on his grace's behalf, that my lord of Norfolk, taking an opportunity to meet with his highness, the same day that his grace removed from Westminster to Hampton Court, amongst other, thanked most humbly his majesty for his daughter, the duchess of Richmond, and so not only made a suit and motion unto his majesty touching his said daughter's jointure, as your lord-

## CCXIII. TO CRUMWELL.

My very singular good lord, in my most hearty wise I commend me to your lordship. And whereas this last year I became a suitor for this bearer, John Culpeper, unto the king's majesty, requiring his grace to accept into his service the said Culpeper, and farther, to be so gracious lord unto him, as in time convenient to make him one of the grooms of his privy chamber; his grace most benignly tendering my suit and request at that time not only accepted him into the room of a gentleman waiter, but thereunto also said, that he would see for him upon convenient opportunity: now my lord, these shall be most heartily to desire and pray you to be so good lord unto the said John Culpeper, as to renew my suit unto the king's majesty for him at such time as any alteration shall be made within the king's grace's privy chamber, not doubting at all, but that he shall not only do unto the king's highness his most true and faithful service, but also be at your lordship's commandment during his life. Thus our Lord have your good lordship in his most blessed tuition! At Ford, the xxviiith day of January. [1538.]

State Paper Office. Miscellaneous Letters. Temp. Hen. VIII. Third series. Vol. IX. Original.

Your own ever assured,

Thomas Cantuarien.

*To the right honourable and my singular good lord, my lord privy seal.*

## CCXIV. TO CRUMWELL.

My very singular good lord, in my most hearty wise I commend me unto your lordship. And where of late[6] I wrote unto you, how that one of those seditions persons which here spread false bruits of the king's highness, was punished at Canterbury: this shall be to certify your lordship, that another of them was likewise punished at Sandwich, as this bearer Sir Edward Ryngisley[7], knight, can more at large inform your lordship of the manner thereof; for he was present at Sandwich to see all things executed according to the king's commandment: and he was also very diligent always in examination of divers persons to see the matters tried out, so that no man could be more willing and ready to satisfy the king's commandment. To whom I beseech your lordship for his pains taken in this behalf to give unto him your hearty thanks, which will be unto him (I dare well say) no small courage and pleasure: and as for the priest not yet punished, this day, with the assistance of Mr Sheriff and this said bearer, we have appointed him to be punished at Asheforth the next market-day. Thus, my lord, right heartily fare you well. At Ford, the 29th day of January. [1538.]

State Paper Office. Ibid. Original.

Your own assured ever,

T. Cantuarien.

*To my very singular good lord, my lord privy seal[7].*

## CCXV. TO CRUMWELL.

My very singular good lord, in my most hearty wise I commend me to your lordship. And whereas the benefice of Sutton Magna, within the county of Essex, of the

State Paper Office. Ibid. Original.

ship hath since had knowledge from his grace by Mr Wryothesley, but also made a further overture for the marriage of his said daughter." This letter goes on to state that the duke of Norfolk named two persons to the king, whom he approved, as husbands for his daughter, "to whom his heart most inclined;" one of whom was sir Thomas Seymour, who afterwards married queen Catherine Parr. The name of the other was forgotten by the king: but the duke does not appear to have succeeded in uniting his daughter to either of these persons. State Papers, Vol. I. Part II. pp. 576-578.]

[6 Vid. Letter CCXII. p. 360.]

[7 Vid. Letter CXCVI. p. 345.]

patronage of Margaret Wyate, widow, and George Coverte, *alternis vicibus*, being void this last year, came in controversy of the law, which of them should present the incumbent, so that either of them presented one to the said benefice; the said Margaret Wyate presenting sir John Gylderde of Rayley, in the county of Essex, a man, as I am credibly informed, both for his literature, good judgment, and honest conversation, worthy of commendation and preferment; and the said George Coverte presenting one sir Heugh Payne[1], late observant, whom I knew neither to be of good learning nor judgment, but a seditious person, and I suppose your lordship knew the same: of the which two persons so presented, the bishop of London[2], notwithstanding that the matter was then in controversy, and not favouring so much the learning and judgment of the said sir John of Rayly as he did sir Heugh Payne's, gave the institution unto the said sir Heugh Payne[3], leaving the patroness in suit at the common law for the same; which said suit hath ever since continued, until now that at this time the said sir Heugh Payne, being in the Marshalsea for his demerits, is departed: and now, forasmuch as the said Margery Wyate, pretending the maintenance not only of her just title unto the said benefice, but also the discharging of her conscience in the same, hath once again presented the said sir John of Rayley, being very loth that the benefice should be bestowed upon such as afore time have been drowned in superstitious religion, as partly she feareth that one Roche, late observant, will promote himself thereunto as much as in him lieth: these shall be therefore to beseech your lordship, in consideration of her godly mind in this behalf, and to the intent that the said bishop of London may with better will accept the said sir John of Rayley, to direct your letters in his favour unto the said bishop of London, requiring him to induct the said sir John without farther interruption; forasmuch as the said Coverte can claim no more at the most, but to present once against the said Mistress Wyate twice; and therefore it seemeth to me, that he can have no colour of interest in the said benefice at this time[4], sir Heugh Payne dying in possession, who was by him last presented. And in thus doing your lordship shall do for the advancement of God's word, which I think is but easily set forward in Essex. Thus, my lord, right heartily fare you well. At Ford, the viith day of February, [1538.]

Your own assured ever,

T. CANTUARIEN.

*To the right honourable and my singular good lord, my lord privy seal.*

---

## CCXVI. TO CRUMWELL.

State Paper Office. Ibid. Original. Todd's Life of Abp. Cranmer, Vol. I. p. 205.

My very singular good lord, in my most hearty wise I commend me unto your lordship. And whereas divers times I have been desirous and minded to sue unto the king's majesty for some preferment for John Wakefelde, gentleman, controller of my household, a man of good judgment and affection towards God's word, which I have known him for the space of these twelve years always ready to promote in his country, not rashly nor seditiously, but gently and soberly, so that his own country could neither greatly hate him nor love him; they could not hate him for his kindness and gentleness, being ready to do every man good as much as in his power was; and yet they could not heartily love him, by cause he ever commended the knowledge of God's word, studied in himself diligently, and exhorted them unto the same, and spake many times against the abusions of the clergy, for which he had all the hate that most of the clergy could procure against him: and partly for his sincere mind which he beareth

---

[1 Vid. Letter CLXXXIII. p. 333.]

[2 Stokesley.]

[3 Hugh Payne was appointed to the rectory of Sutton Magna, Nov. 23, A.D. 1536. Newcourt's Repertorium, Vol. II. p. 567. Ed. Lond. 1708-10.]

[4 It appears that notwithstanding Cranmer's efforts Covert appointed Thomas Roche to the living, Feb. 10, 1538.]

towards God's word, partly for his true and faithful heart which he hath borne towards his prince and such things as from time to time his highness hath set forth, and specially in this last commotion in the north parties, forsomuch as he so unfeignedly declared his true and faithful allegiance unto the king's highness, refusing the confederacy of the lord Darcy and other being gathered together unto the castle of Pomfrete, which lord Darcy[5] had trained him thither, (as further your lordship shall perceive by the said lord Darcy's letters herein inclosed,) and yet that notwithstanding, after that my said controller by communication had with the said lord Darcy had perceived that there was no towardness of fidelity in him, he withdrew himself out of the said castle, to his great jeopardy and loss of all his goods, which at that time were specially spoiled, because he was so unobedient unto their minds; for the which spoil of his goods he hath been partly recompensed by my lord of Norfolk, but not in comparison to his loss: I say therefore, for this cause of his vexation and other the premises, I was many times minded to sue for his preferment, saving that hitherto I saw nothing meet for his commodity. And now forasmuch as I am informed that the priory of Pomfrete[6] shall be surrendered unto the king's grace's hands, and that both the situation and the demesne lands of that house lieth very commodiously for him, specially in the town where he dwelleth: these shall be to beseech your lordship to be so good lord unto him, as to be a mean unto the king's majesty that he may have the preferment of the said priory with the demesnes in farm, doing in that behalf as any other will do for the king's grace's advantage. It is for no man so meet as for him, and I think there will be but small suit for it, by reason that the lands are valued to the uttermost, and not only lieth in tillage, saving certain pasture for the maintenance of the tilth, but also no common pasture ne woods belonging to the same; for the which cause also my said controller would not sue, saving that it lieth so nigh unto him: beseeching your lordship, that if hereafter he espy any better thing in the country, that he may have your favour therein; and I doubt not in this his small preferment but that his neighbours shall perceive, that the king's majesty doth not forget those that bear his grace their true hearts and fidelity. If your lordship would be so good as to shew these my letters unto the king's majesty, declaring the considerations thereof, I trust his highness will tender my suit, if it were a greater matter: for his highness will gladly help his faithful subjects, if his grace have information of them; and except his grace be informed of them, he cannot help the trusty subjects he hath. Thus, my lord, most heartily fare you well. At Ford, the 28th of February. [1538.]

Your own ever to command,

T. Cantuarien.

*To the right honourable and my singular good lord, my lord privy seal.*

---

## CCXVII. TO ———[7].

After most hearty commendations to your lordship: forasmuch as I am informed, that your lordship intendeth to depose the prior of the Charter House within the Isle of Axholme[8], this shall be to desire you to permit the said prior still to continue in

MSS. Cotton, Cleop. E. iv. f. 212, British Museum. Original.

---

[[5] Lord Darcy was executed on Tower-hill, June 20, A.D. 1537, for taking part in the Lincolnshire insurrection, which was denominated by the rebels the "pilgrimage of grace." It broke out at Louth, Monday, Oct. 2, 1536, on the day that the ecclesiastical commissioners were to hold their visitation in that place. The original documents referring to this insurrection are preserved in the State Paper Office.]

[[6] A priory of dominicans or black friars at Pontefract, surrendered November 26, A.D. 1538, (Burnet's Hist. of Reformat. Vol. I. Part II. Appendix. Book III. No. 3. p. 230. Ed. Oxon. 1829.) It was granted, 36 Hen. VIII., to W. Clifford and Mich. Wildbore. Tanner's Notitia Monast. Yorkshire. xcvi. Pontefract. Ed. Camb. 1787.]

[[7] The address of this letter is wanting. It was in all probability written to Crumwell.]

[[8] In Lincolnshire.]

his room; for I am about, through the help of such friends as I have in those parties, to procure that the said prior shall willingly resign the same into the king's hands. Thus Almighty God preserve your lordship! From Ford, the viith day of March. [1538.]

Your own assured ever,

T. CANTUARIEN.

---

## CCXVIII. TO CRUMWELL.

State Paper Office. Miscellaneous Letters. Temp. Hen. VIII. Third Series. Vol. IX. Original.

MY very singular good lord, I heartily commend me unto you; and thank you in like manner for your pains taken with my folk and my letters divers and many times; and now I am driven to desire you to take further pains. So it is, that one Symone Cornethwaite, dwelling with my lord Russell, did sue a cause of matrimony in the Arches against one Anne Barker, daughter to William Barker of Cheswicke, and brought the mother, and divers other witness, with the confession of the maid, to justify his intent; and then the maid was sequestered, lest any violence should be used towards her, unto the house of master Vaghan in Chepe side; and in very deed, at the special request of my lord of Sussex, I heard the matter myself one day at Lamebethe, and thought it necessary that the maid should continue still in sequestration till the matter were tried. And this suit depending, one William Bridges, brother to sir John Bridges[1], took out the maid from the sequestration, and married her before day without any banns asked, or any licence or dispensation obtained, and in the time forbidden[2], within three days afore Christenmas last, and hath ever since lien by her, and keeps her in a secret corner in master Ambrose Barker's house; and she is declared accurst for violating of the sequestration, and is so denounced at Poule's Cross, and at divers other places, and so hath continued forty days: and this notwithstanding, he keeps her still, more like a rebellion than an obedient subject to the laws and good order of this realm; and swears great oaths, that he will keep her in spite of any man. Now my desire is, for the zeal I do know that you bear unto justice and the evitation of notorious sin, it may please you to send for the said Willian Bridges by privy seal or otherwise, commanding him to bring the woman with him: and then you to sequester her to some honest indifferent house, till the matter be tried whose wife she is; and otherwise to correct him for his misdemeanour in this behalf, as shall be thought good to your lordship. In which doing I doubt not but you shall please God highly; and cause other to beware of such misdemeanour in the king's realm. As knows our Lord, who preserve you as myself. Amen. At Ford, the 14th day of March. [1538.]

Your own ever assured,

T. CANTUARIEN.

*To my very singular good lord, my lord privy seal, these be given.*

---

## CCXIX. TO CRUMWELL.

State Paper Office. Ibid. Original.

MY very singular good lord, in most hearty wise I commend me unto your lordship. And whereas there is suit made unto me for one sir William Chevenay, parson of Kyng-

---

[[1] This was probably sir John Bridges, "created lord Chandois" by queen Mary, April 8, A.D. 1554, "for the more honourable reception of the prince of Spain." Strype's Eccl. Mem. Vol. III. p. 86. Ed. Oxon. 1822.]

[[2] "The times forbidden to matrimony by old canons, and by the custom of England, were from Advent Sunday till a week after Epiphany; from Septuagesima Sunday till a week after Easter; and from Ascension-day till Trinity Sunday. Comber. Quando clauditur tempus nuptiarum, et quando aperitur, nota in his versibus sequentibus:

'Aspiciens veterem, circum, qua, quis, benedicta.
'Conjugium vetat Adventus, Hilariusque relaxat.
'Septuagena vetat, octavum Pasche relaxat.'
Missale ad usum Sarum. 1529."

Jenkyns' Remains of Abp. Cranmer. Vol. I. pp 236, 7, *n.* m.]

ston besides Canterbury, which being a very impotent man, above fourscore years of age, and also blind, is not able in his own person to discharge his cure, and would very gladly have licence to abide with his friends and kinsfolks, and would find an honest priest in the meantime to discharge his cure; forasmuch as he is not able, besides the finding of the priest, to keep house of the same, the benefice being of so small value, as I am credibly informed that it is: these shall be, therefore, to desire you to be good lord unto the said parson in this his suit unto your lordship, that he may be discharged of the act concerning residence[3], if it may be. And he shall pray during his life, which is not like to pass one year, for the preservation of your good lordship. Thus right heartily fare you well. From Canterbury, the 16th of March. [1538.]

Your own assured ever,

T. Cantuarien.

*To my very singular good lord, my lord privy seal.*

---

## CCXX. TO CRUMWELL.

State Paper Office. Ibid. Original.

My very singular good lord, in my most hearty manner I commend me unto your lordship: and where I am informed, that one Sandwich,[4] a monk of Christ's church in Canterbury, and warden of Canterbury college in Oxforth[5], doth sue for the preferment of the prior's office in the said house of Canterbury; these my letters are most effectuously to desire your lordship, if any such alteration be, to bear your favour and aid to the warden of the manors of the said house, a man of right honest behaviour, clean living, good learning, good judgment, without superstition, very tractable, and as ready to set forward his prince's causes, as no man more of his coat; and in that house, in mine opinion, there is no meeter man. I am moved to write to your lordship in this behalf, inasmuch as I consider what a great commodity I shall have, if such one be promoted to the said office, that is a right honest man and of his qualities; and I insure your lordship the said room requireth such one; as knoweth God, who ever preserve you. From Canterbury, the 17th day of March. [1538.]

Your own ever assured,

T. Cantuarien.

*To my very singular good lord, my lord privy seal.*

---

## CCXXI. TO CRUMWELL.

State Paper Office. Ibid. Original.

My very singular good lord, in my most hearty wise I commend me unto your lordship; signifying to the same, that according to the effect and purport of your letters to me directed concerning friar Forest, the bishop of Wurceiter and I will be to-morrow with your lordship, to know farther of your pleasure in that behalf. For if we should proceed against him according to the order of the law, there must be articles devised beforehand, which must be ministered unto him; and therefore it will be very well done,

---

[3 Stat. 21 Hen. VIII. c. 13.]

[4 At the period of the dissolution of Christ's Church, Canterbury, William Gardiner, alias Sandwich, who was afterwards a prebendary of Canterbury, and canon of Christ's Church, Oxford, a violent enemy of the Reformation, and of the archbishop, was warden of the college. Vid. Somner's Antiq. of Canterbury, p. 127. Ed. Battely, Lond. 1703.]

[5 Canterbury College in Oxford, A. D. 1538, was under the jurisdiction of the Benedictine priory of Christ Church, Canterbury, and was "an habitation chiefly for the student monks of Canterbury." It was granted A. D. 1541, to the dean and chapter of Canterbury, but A. D. 1547, it was transferred to the new foundation, consisting of the dean and chapter, "and is now part of Christ Church College," Oxford. Tanner's Notit. Monast. xxiii. 8. Oxford. Ed. Camb. 1787.]

that one draw them against our meeting[1]. Thus, my lord, right heartily fare you well. At Lambeth, the 6th day of April. [1538.]

Your own assured ever,

T. CANTUARIEN.

*To my very singular good lord, my lord privy seal.*

## CCXXII. TO CRUMWELL.

State Paper Office. Ibid. Original.

My very singular good Lord, in my right hearty wise I commend me unto you. And whereas my servant Fraunces Bassett, this bearer, was, by the mean of your good lordship, put in possession of the granges of Musden and Caldon, and is dispossessed by the earl of Shrewsbury that now is, to his great hurt and hinderance, forasmuch as he is not able to contend with him in the law; these therefore shall be to desire your lordship to sign these letters inclosed, directed unto the said earl in his behalf, or to alter them if any thing mislike you, or else to direct such other letters to him as may stand most with your lordship's pleasure in the preferment of this bearer, which only hath and must depend upon your goodness; whom I am the more bold to name your kinsman, by cause I would the said earl should more earnestly tender your lordship his letters and request. And thus I pray God long to preserve your lordship in health. From Croydon, the viiith day of April. [1538.]

Your own assured ever,

T. CANTUARIEN.

*To my very singular good lord, my lord privy seal.*

## CCXXIII. TO CRUMWELL.

State Paper Office. Ibid. Original. Todd's Life of Abp. Cranmer, Vol. I. p. 198.

My very singular good lord; forasmuch as this bearer, your trusty chaplain, Mr Malet, at this his return towards London from Ford, where as I left him, according to your lordship's assignment, occupied in the affairs of our church service[2], and now at

[[1] "Dr John Forest, a friar observant, was apprehended, for that in secret confession he had declared to many the king's subjects, that the king was not supreme head of the church, whereas before he had been sworn to the same supremacy. Upon this point he was examined, and answered, that he took this oath with his outward man, but his inward man never consented thereunto: then being further accused of divers heretical opinions, he submitted himself to the punishment of the church, but having more liberty than before, to talk with whom he would, when his abjuration was sent him to read, he utterly refused it. Whereupon he was condemned, and afterward on a pair of new gallows set up for that purpose in Smithfield, he was hanged by the middle and armpits quick, and under the gallows was made a fire, wherewith he was burnt and consumed, on the 22nd day of May, [A.D. 1538.]"—"Also a pulpit was there set, in the which M. Hugh Latymer, bishop of Worcester, preached a sermon, confuting the friar's errors, and moving him to repentance," but all availed not. Stow's Annals, p. 574. Ed. Lond. 1615. Vid. also Foxe's Acts and Monuments, p. 1100. Ed. Lond. 1583.]

[[2] Dr Jenkyns thinks it possible that the preparation of the church service upon which Dr Malet was engaged, might have been an amended breviary, which was printed A.D. 1541, and 1544, entituled: Portiforium secundum usum Sarum, noviter impressum et a plurimis purgatum mendis, in quo nomen Romano pontifici falso ascriptum omittitur, una cum aliis quæ christianissimi nostri regis statuto repugnant. Excusum Londini. per R. Grafton et E. Whitchurch, 1541, per Edvardum Whytechurch, cum privilegio ad imprimendum solum; in which "the alterations were too inconsiderable to satisfy the reformers, and much more sweeping changes seem to have been in contemplation, when, on Cranmer's announcement of the king's pleasure, it was ordered by the convocation in 1543, that 'the examination and correction of the service books should be committed to the bishops of Sarum and Ely, [Salcot and Goodrich,] taking to each of them three of the lower house, such as should be appointed for that purpose: but this the lower house released.'" Although the bishops of Salisbury and Ely were not hearty in the prosecution of the work allotted to them, Cranmer mentions "in the minute of the king's majesty's letters to be addressed to the archbishop of Canterbury," appended to his letter to Henry VIII., dated Jan. 24, [A.D. 1546.] that the king with himself had appointed the bishops of Worcester, [Hethe,] and Chichester, [Day,] "with other chaplains and learned men to peruse certain books of service;" and there is every probability, from the following

the writing up of so much as he had to do, came by me here at Croden to know my further pleasure and commandment in that behalf; I shall beseech you, my lord, that after his duty done in seeing your lordship, he may repair unto me again with speed, for further furtherance and final finishing of that we have begun. For I like his diligence and pains in this business, and his honest humanity declared in my house for this season of his being therein so well, that I can be bold so to commend him to your lordship, that I shall with all my heart beseech the same to declare your goodness and favour to him by helping his small and poor living. I know he hath very little growing towards the supporting of his necessaries; which is much pity, his good qualities, right judgment in learning, and discreet wisdom considered. Thus fare your good lordship heartily well. From Croden, the 11th of April. [1538.]

Your own assured ever,

T. CANTUARIEN.

*To the right honourable and my very good lord, my lord privy seal.*

---

## CCXXIV. TO CRUMWELL[3].

MY lord, in my most hearty wise I commend me unto your lordship. This shall be to desire you to be good lord unto certain men of Smarden and Pluckeley in Kent, whose names shall be delivered unto your lordship herewithal, which are indicted for unlawful assemblies at the last sessions at Canterbury, and (as they report unto me) of none occasion or ground else, but for by cause they are accounted fauters of the new doctrine, as they call it; beseeching your lordship therefore, that if it cannot be duly proved that they are worthy thus to be indicted, they may be released of this their indictment. For if the king's subjects within this realm which favour God's word, shall be unjustly vexed at sessions[4], it will be no marvel though much sedition be daily engendered within this realm. Wherefore I pray you, my lord, that some remedy may in time be devised for the redress of such indictments. Thus, my lord, right heartily fare you well. At Lambeth, the 29th day of April. [1538.]

State Paper Office. Ibid. Original.

Your own assured,

T. CANTUARIEN.

*To the right honourable and my singular good lord, my lord privy seal.*

---

## CCXXV. TO CRUMWELL.

MY lord, in my most hearty wise I commend me unto you. And whereas I moved you to write in the favour of sir Thomas Lawney[5] unto young Mr Parre, for the resigna-

State Paper Office. Ibid. Original.

---

quotation from the petition of Edward VIth's first convocation, that it was in the end completed: "Whereas by the commandment of king Henry VIII., certain prelates and other learned men were appointed to alter the service of the church, and to devise other convenient and useful order therein, who according to the same appointment did make certain books, as they be informed; their request is, that the said books may be seen and perused by them, for a better expedition of Divine service to be set forth accordingly." Vid. Collier's Eccl. Hist. Vol. V. p. 106. Ed. Lond. 1840—41; Strype's Eccl. Mem. Vol. I. p. 580. Ed. Oxon. 1822; Ames' Typog. Antiq. Vol. III. pp. 449, 485. Ed. Lond. 1810—19. Jenkyns' Remains of Abp. Cranmer, Vol. I. pp. 241, 2.]

[3 Within the folds of this letter a paper is pasted, written in the same hand as the letter, to this effect: "Persons indicted within the county of Kent. *Pluckley:* Henry Harte, John Stanstrete. *Smarden:* Gervis Golde, John Hynkesell, Thomas Baker, Richarde Lucke."]

[4 Amongst the presentments at a visitation held by the archbishop, about the month of September, A.D. 1540, was a Vincent Ingeam, (a justice of peace), who had "commanded on Easter-Monday, 38° of the king, that no man should read, or hear the bible read, upon pain of imprisonment, and cast two into prison, the one for speaking against him therein, and the other for shewing him the king's injunctions concerning the same." Strype's Mem. of Abp. Cranmer, Vol. I. pp. 143, 4. Ed. Oxon. 1840; Vid. Letters CCII. &c. pp. 349—356.]

[5 "This Lawney was a witty man, and chaplain to the old duke of Norfolk, and had been one of the scholars placed by the cardinal in his new

tion[1] of the vicarage of Royden in Essex, belonging unto his chaplain; I have sent unto your lordship letters devised for that purpose, beseeching you, my lord, to assign them if you like the draught of them, or else that they may be amended according to your mind. In accomplishing whereof you shall prefer a right honest man, worthy to have a much better thing than this is. Thus, my lord, right heartily fare you well. At Lambeth, the first day of May. [1538.]

Your own assured,

T. CANTUARIEN.

*To my very singular good lord, my lord privy seal.*

---

## CCXXVI. TO CRUMWELL.

State Paper Office. Ibid. Original.

MY lord, in my hearty wise I commend me unto your lordship. And whereas this bearer, my friend and kinsman, hath certain suits before you, I pray you, my lord, that ye will be so good lord unto him in these his suits, if it may be, that he may have a short end of them, according to justice and equity, with your reasonable favour, and the rather at this my request and instance; wherein ye shall both shew unto me singular pleasure, and bind him to be your daily beadsman. Thus, my lord, right heartily fare you well. From my manor of Lambhyth, the 2nd day of May. [1538.]

Your lordship's assured,

T. CANTUARIEN.

*To my very singular good lord, my lord privy seal.*

---

## CCXXVII. TO CRUMWELL.

State Paper Office. Ibid. Original.

MY very singular good lord, after most hearty recommendations: so it is, as I am informed, that there is an office founden before the late excheator of the county of Lincoln, after the death of one Thomas Tamworth; in the which office, amongs other things, it is founden, that the said Thomas Tamworth should be seized and die seized of one mese and fifty-eight acres of land and pasture, lying in a town called Leeke, in the said county of Lincoln; which lands, as I am credibly informed, is the true inheritance of this poor gentleman John Tamworth, this bearer; and he that is heir of the said Thomas Tamworth is now the king's ward, and was in the custody of sir William Musgrave, knight, and dame Elizabeth his wife, by the king's letters patents to the said dame Elizabeth made; who having the custody of the same ward, by colour of the said office so founden, both against the due order of law and good conscience, hath, since the death of the said Thomas Tamworth, not only taken the profits of the said mese and fifty-eight acres of land, but also of forty acres more of other lands lying in the said town, in the said office not contained, which also is the inheritance of this poor gentleman; and forasmuch as his counsel doth inform him, that he can have no traverse to the said office during the minority of the said John Tamworth, son and heir of the said Thomas Tamworth; therefore for restitution of the other lands in the said office not comprised, he hath sued to the master of the king's wards, who, upon his long suit, did direct a commission to certain worshipful gentlemen of the said county of Lincoln, to inquire of the truth of the premises; who, by authority of the said commission, hath sitten and inquired by the oath of twelve men duly of the same, and which twelve men have given their verdict to the said commissioners, and put thereunto their several seals; and, as I am informed, there is so

---

college at Oxon: where he was chaplain of the house, and prisoner there with Frith. In the time of the six articles he was a minister in Kent, placed there, I suppose, by the archbishop." Strype's Mem. of Abp. Cranmer, Vol. I. p. 49.]

[1 Osias le Moyne held the vicarage from March A.D. 1523 to his death, A.D. 1541, so that it is certain the resignation referred to by the archbishop did not take place. Newcourt's Repertorium, Vol. II. p. 503. Ed. Lond. 1708.]

much affection in Thomas Browne, one of the said commissioners, (who, by the consent of other his fellows, had the commission delivered unto him to make certificate thereof at the day of return specified in the said commission,) that as yet he hath made no certificate of the same, saying it is the commandment of some of your lordship's counsel, that he shall keep it out and make no certificate, which is great hinderance and cost to this poor gentleman, and loss of his inheritance: wherefore I beseech your good lordship to give in commandment to the said Thomas Browne, who hath the custody of the said commission, to make certificate thereof to the master of the king's wards; either else that the matter may be heard by your counsel, and, upon certificate thereof made to your lordship, such direction and order may be taken in the same, as shall stand with the king's laws, right, and good conscience; and you shall bind this gentleman during his life to do you such service as may lie in him for to do. Thus Almighty God long preserve your lordship in honour! From my manor of Croydon, the xxixth of May. [1538.]

Your own assured ever,

T. CANTUARIEN.

[2]The said John Tamworth is a near kinsman of mine; wherefore I pray you be good lord unto him.

*To my singular good lord, my lord privy seal.*

---

## CCXXVIII. TO CRUMWELL[3].

AFTER my most hearty commendations unto your good lordship: these shall be to signify unto the same, that this bearer, John Robynson, is one of my lord of Wiltshire servants, for whom I spake unto your lordship to accept into your service, beseeching your lordship, inasmuch as he daily giveth attendance to know your pleasure herein, that you will be his good lord in this his suit, and I trust that he shall do unto you his true and faithful service; and as for his honesty and other qualities, I doubt not but that the experience of my lord of Wiltshire's service is a sufficient testimony for him in that behalf. Thus, my lord, most heartily fare you well. At Lambeth, the vth day of June. [1538.] State Paper Office. Ibid. Original.

Your own assured ever,

T. CANTUARIEN.

*To my very singular good lord, my lord privy seal.*

---

## CCXXIX. TO CRUMWELL.

MY singular good lord, after most hearty wise I commend me unto your good lordship, signifying unto you, that about a twelve months past, as I was in my journey towards the king's highness, I lodged at my house in Croydon; where certain of my chaplains by chance went into the church there, and as they looked in certain books, they found the names of bishops of Rome not put out according unto the king's commandment[4]: wherefore I sent for all the priests of the church, and their books State Paper Office. Ibid. Original.

---

[2 This paragraph is in the archbishop's hand.]

[3 This letter seems to have been written on the breaking up of the earl of Wiltshire's establishment by his death in 1538. Jenkyns' Remains of Abp. Cranmer, Vol. I. p. 246. *n.* y.]

[4 The following is the letter against the pope's authority here referred to:

HENRY R.

TRUSTY and right welbeloved, we grete you well. And wher as heretofore, as ye know, both upon most just and vertuouse fundations, grownded upon the lawes of Almighty God and holly scripture, and also by the deliberate advice, consultation, consent, and agreement, as well of the bishops and clergie, as by the nobles and comons temporall of this our realme, assembled in our high court of parliament, and by auctoritie of the same, the abuses of the bishop of Rome his auctoritie and jurisdiction, of

also, and shewed them the place where such names were, and also commanded them that they shculd amend their said books; and I discharged the parish priest of his

---

longe time usurped against us, have been not only utterly extirped, abolished and secluded; but also the same our nobles and comons, both of the clergie and temporaltie, by another severall acte and upon like fundation, for the publique weale of this our realme, have united, knyt and annexed to us and the corone imperiall of this our realme, the title, dignitie, and stile of supreme hed in earthe, immediatly under God, of the church of England, as undoubtedly evermore we have been: which things also the said bishops and clergie, particularly in their convocations, have holly and entierly consented, recognised, ratified, confermed and approved autentiquely in writing, both by their speciall othes, profession and wryting, under their signes and seales; so utterly renouncyng all other othes, obedience and jurisdiction, either of the said bishop of Rome, or of any other potentate: we late you witt, that perpendyng and consideryng the charge and commission in this behalf geven unto us by Almighty God, together with the great quietnes, rest and tranquillite, that hereby may ensue to our faithful subjects, both in their consciences, and other wise to the pleasure of Almighty God, in case the said bishops and clergie of this our realme should sincerely, truly and faithfully sett forth, declare and preache unto our said subjects the very true word of God, and without all maner color, dissimulation, hipocrisie, manifest, publishe and declare the great and innumerable enormities and abuses, which the said bishop of Rome, as well in title and stile, as also in auctoritie and jurisdiction, of long tyme unlawfully and injustly hath usurped upon us, our progenitors, and all other Christen princes, [we] have not only addressed our letters generall to all and every the same bishops, straitly chargyng and commanding them, not only in their proper persons, to declare, teach and preach unto the people, the true, mere and sincere word of God, and how the said title, stile, and jurisdiction of supreme hed apperteyneth unto us, our corone and dignitie royall; and to gyve like warnyng, monition and charge, to all abbots, priors, deanes, arche deacons, provosts, parsons, vicars, curats, scole masters, and all other ecclesiastical persons within their dioces, to do the semblable in their churches, every Sunday and solem feast, and also in their scoles; and to cause all maner of prayers, orisons, rubrics and canons in masse books, and all other books used in churches, wherin the said bishop is named, utterly to be abolished, eradicate, and rased out in such wise, as the said bishop of Rome, his name and memorie for evermore (except to his contumelly and reproche) may be extinct, suppressed and obscured; but also to the justices of our peace, that they, in every place within the precint of their commissions, do make and cause to be made diligent serche wayse, and especially, whedder the said bishops and clergie do truly and sincerly, without any maner cloke or dissimulation, execute and accomplish their said charge to them commytted in this behalf; and to satisfie us and our councill of such of them that should omytt or leave undone any parte of the premisses, or ells in the execution therof should coldely or fainedly use any maner of synister addition, interpretation or cloke, as more plainly is expressed in our said letters. We, considering the great good and furderaunce, that ye may do in these matters in the parties about you, and specially at your being at sises and sessions; in the declaration of the premisses, have thought it good, necessary and expedient, to write these our letters unto you; whom we esteem to be of such singuler zeale and affection towards the glory of Almighty God, and of so faithfull and loving harte towards us, as ye woll not only, with all your wisdome, diligences and labours, accomplish all such things, as might be to the preferment and setting forward of Godes worde, and the amplification, defence and maintenance of our said interests, right, title, stile, jurisdiction and auctoritie, apperteyning unto us, our dignitie, prerogative, and corone imperiall of this our realme, woll and desire you, and nevertheless straitely charge and command you, that laying aparte all vain affections, respects, and carnal considerations, and setting before your eyes the mirror of truth, the glorie of God, the right and dignitie of your soveraigne lord; thus sounding to the inestimable unitie and commoditie both of your self, and all other our loving and faithfull subjects, ye do not only make diligent search within the precinct of your commission and auctoritie, whether the said bishops and clergie do truly, sincerely, as before, preach, teach, and declare to the people the premisses, according to their duties, but also at your said setting in sises and sessions ye do persuade, shewe, and declare unto the same people the very tenor, effect, and purpose of the premisses in such wise, as the said bishops and clergie may the better, not only do thereby, and execute their said dueties, but that also the parents and rulers of families may declare, teache, and informe their children and servants in the specialties of the same, to the utter extirpacion of the said bishop's usurped authority, name, and jurisdiction; for ever shewyng and declarying also to the people at your said sessions the treasons traymerously commytted against us and our lawes, by the late bishop of Rochestre, and sir Thomas Moore, knight, who thereby, and by diverse secrete practises of their maliciouse mynds against us intended, to semynate, engender, and brede amongs our people and subjects most mischievous and sediciouse opynyon, not only to their own confusion, but also of diverse others who lately have condignely suffered execution according to their demerites, and in such wise dilating the same with persuacions to the same our people, as they may be the better fixed, established, and satisfied in the truth, and consequently, that all our faythfull and true subjects may therby detest and abhore in their harts and deeds, the most recreant and traiterouse abuses and behaveours of the said maliciouse malefactors as they be most worthy, and fynding any defaulte, negligence, or dissimulacion in any manner of person, or persons, not doyng his duetie in this partie, ye immediately do advertise us and our counsel of the defaulte, manner, and facion of the same; lating you witt, that considering the greate moment, weight, and importance of this matter, as wherupon dependeth the unity, rest, and quietnes of this our realme, yf ye should contrary to your dueties, and our expectations and trust, neglect, be slake, or omytte to doe diligently your dueties in the true performance and excecucion of our mynde, pleasure,

service at the same time. Now, if it please your good lordship, it chanced in these holidays the dean of the arches to say mass with a book belonging to one of the chantry priests of the said church; which book is nothing amended since that time of my being there, and yet then I myself shewed the places in the same book, and the said chantry priest promised to put them out: and whether this be a maintenance of the bishop of Rome his authority or no, I will not determine, but remit the matter wholly to your good lordship; yet in the mean season I have called him before me, and have taken certain honest men, which be bound that he shall be ready at all times to come before any of the king's council, there to make answer unto all such things as shall be laid to his charge concerning the same. I desire your good lordship that I may have an answer by this bearer, what I shall do herein; and I desire Almighty God to have your good lordship continually in his preservation. From my manor of Croydon, the 12. day of June. [1538.]

Your own ever assured,

T. Cantuarien.

*To my singular good lord, my lord privy seal.*

---

## CCXXX. TO CRUMWELL.

After most hearty commendations to your good lordship: these be to certify you, that I will not fail, God willing, to meet you at London to-morrow, accordingly as I perceive by your letters it is the king's pleasure. And forasmuch as I have no manner of stuff nor provision at Lamehyth as now, so that I am not in no wise provided to receive the ambassadors[1] thither as to-morrow; therefore I beseech you to appoint some other place where we may have conference with them, and to send me word by this bearer as well of the time as of the place, where and when ye will appoint me to meet with them; and at our meeting I shall be right glad to have your counsel, what provision is meet that I make for them, which I shall be right glad to do to my power: as knoweth our Lord God, who long preserve you to his pleasure! At my manor of Croydon, the xiiith day of June. [1538.]

State Paper Office. Ibid. Original.

Your own assured ever,

T. Cantuarien.

*The bishop of Canterbury to my L. P. S.*

---

## CCXXXI. TO CRUMWELL.

My very singular good Lord, after my most hearty commendations: these shall be to signify unto your lordship, that as yesterday Franciscus[2], the duke of Saxon's chancellor, was in hand with me and the bishop of Chichester very instantly, to

State Paper Office. Ibid. Original. Todd's Life of Abp. Cranmer. Vol. I. p. 262.

---

and commandment as before, or wolde halte or stumble at any person, or specialtie of the same, be ye assured that we, like a prince of justice, well so punish and correct your default and negligence thereyn, as it shall be an example to all others, how contrary to their allegeance, othes and dueties, they do frustrate, deceive, and disobey the just and lawfull commandment of their soveraign lord, in such things as by the true hartie and faithfull execucion whereof, they shall not only prefer the honour and glory of God, and sett forth the majesty and imperial dignitie of their soveraign lorde, but allso importe and bringe an inestimable unitie, concorde, and tranquillitie of the publique, and common state of this realme, whereunto both by the lawes of God and nature and man they be utterly obliged and bounden: and therefore fail ye not most effectually, ernestly, and entierly to see the premisses done and executed upon paine of your allegeance, and as ye woll advoyde our high indignacion and displeasure, at your uttermost perills: given under our signet at our manor besids Westminster, the xxvth day of June. Burnet's Hist. of Reformat. Vol. III. Part II. App. Book ii. No. 32, p. 100. Ed. Oxon. 1829. Wilkins' Concilia, Vol. III. p. 772. et sqq.]

[[1] Probably the German protestants' ambassadors, who arrived in England in May, 1538. Todd's Life of Cranmer, Vol. I. p. 249, 50. Vid. Letters CCXXXVII. CCXXXIX. pp. 377, 379.]

[[2] "Franciscus Burcardus, (Burckhardt,) vice-chancellor to the elector of Saxony, was at the head of the German embassy." Vid. Letters CCXXXVII.

have Atkynson's penance altered from Paul's unto the parish-church of the said Atkynson: whereunto we made him this answer, that forasmuch as that error of the sacrament of the altar was so greatly spread abroad in this realm, and daily increasing more and more, we thought it needful, for the suppressing thereof, most specially to have him do his penance at Paul's, where the most people might be present, and thereby, in seeing him punished, to be ware of like offence; declaring farther unto him, that it lay not in us to alter that penance to any other place, by cause we were but commissaries appointed by your lordship; and therefore, without your advice and consent, we could not grant unto him any thing in this behalf. He then, perceiving that we nothing did incline unto his request, answered and said, that if any person coming from the king of England unto the duke his master should require a greater request than this was, it should be granted unto him; alleging that the bishop of Hereforde[1] asked of his master one that was condemned to death, and he was liberally delivered unto him. Howbeit, said he, I do not require such a thing, but only that this Atkynson his penance may be altered from one place unto another. Then I promised him that I would consult with your lordship therein as this day, touching his request. Wherefore I beseech your lordship to advertise me by this bearer, what answer I shall make unto him in this behalf. Thus Almighty God preserve your good lordship! At Lambeth, the 22nd day of June. [1538.]

Your own ever assured,

T. CANTUARIEN.

[2]My lord, I pray you have in your good remembrance sir Edward Ryngelay[3].

*To my very singular good lord, my lord privy seal.*

---

## CCXXXII. TO CRUMWELL.

State Paper Office. Ibid. Original.

AFTER my most hearty commendations unto your good lordship; these shall be to beseech the same to direct your letters unto my commissary at Calise, giving him power and authority to take away as well such images[4] now being within the priory of the black Friars at Calise, to whom any pilgrimage appertaineth, as all other images of like estimation within my jurisdiction there. And whereas my said commissary hath written unto me concerning this bearer, Adam Damplippe[5], desiring to have certain requests accomplished, as farther shall appear unto your lordship by his letter herein inclosed; I right heartily desire you, my lord, so to tender the said requests, that this said bearer may return again thither, and there to proceed with quietness as he

---

CCXXXIX. pp. 377, 379. Seckendorf, Comment. Hist. Apol. de Lutheran. Lib. III. Sect. 16. §. lxvi. x. p. 180. Ed. Francof. et Lips. 1692.]

[1 Edward Fox. Vid. Seckendorf, Comment. Hist. Apol. de Lutheran. Lib. III. Sect. 13. §. xxxix. Add. p. 111.]

[2 This paragraph is in the archbishop's hand.]

[3 Vid. Letters CXCVI. CCXIV. pp. 345, 361.]

[4 "Besides this, to the intent that all superstition and hypocrisy, crept into divers men's hearts, may vanish away, they shall not set forth or extol any images, relics, or miracles, for any superstition or lucre." Injunctions given by authority of the king's highness to the clergy of the realm, A. D. 1536. This was a positive command to remove the images. But a more forcible injunction is found to that effect in those to the clergy by Crumwell, Sept. A. D. 1538: "Item, that such feigned miracles as ye know in any of your cures to be so abused with pilgrimages, or offerings of any thing made thereunto, ye shall, for avoiding of that most detestable offence of idolatry, forthwith take down, and [without] delay, &c." This injunction not having been issued at the date of this letter, it required such a special authority from Crumwell to remove the images as that which is here asked for. Burnet's Hist. of Reformat. Vol. I. part ii. Appendix. Book III. Nos. vii. and xi. pp. 250, 281. Stow's Annals, p. 574. Ed. Lond. 1615.]

[5 For a full account of the persecutions at Calais, in which George Bucker, alias Adam Damplip, was concerned, vid. Foxe's Acts and Monuments, p. 1223. et seq. Ed. Lond. 1583. Vid. also Stat. 32 Hen. VIII. cap. 49; Letters CCXXIX. CCXXX.; Strype's Mem. of Abp. Cranmer, pp. 96, 7; Todd's Life of Abp. Cranmer, Vol. I. p. 174, et seq.; Part of "a Letter from the deputy of Calais and others, touching the examination of one Damplip and Stevens, touching cardinal Poole," anno 30 Hen. VIII. Harl. MSS. 283, f. 89. Original. British Museum.]

hath begun; assuring your lordship, that he is of right good knowledge and judgment as far as I can perceive by him: and therefore, if it would please your lordship to direct your favourable letters unto the council there in his behalf, you should do a right meritorious deed; and surely I will myself write to like effect, but I know your letters shall be much more esteemed and accepted than mine. In accomplishing whereof you shall deserve of Almighty God condign thanks for the same. Thus our Lord have your good lordship in his blessed tuition! At Lambeth, the 24th day of July. [1538.]

Your own ever assured,

T. CANTUARIEN.

*To the right honourable and my singular good lord, my lord privy seal.*

[The following is the letter above referred to:

JOHN BUTLER, COMMISSARY AT CALAIS, TO CRANMER.]

IN most humble wise please it your grace to be advertised, that Adam Damlippe, bearer hereof, is purposely come over to declare his mind unto your grace. For it is perceived that certain, which favour nothing the truth, would gladly hinder him, if it were in their power, that he should neither teach nor preach the word of God; as in their large writing, not only against him, but also against other persons; which their writing will not be justified no more than was their false suggestion, saying, that there was in Cales which openly and manifestly did deny Christ. Their saying is now, that here are certain which deny Christ to be put in the sacrament of the altar. I trust they shall take little honour of their so writing. This bearer will declare more unto your grace. I will not write what I have seen, but I marvel that men will write of malice; saving that they utter what they are from within forth. God send them a better spirit! State Paper Office. Ibid. Original.

Humbly requiring your grace to be good and gracious lord unto this bearer, Adam Damplippe, and that he may shortly return to Cales again with your grace's favourable letters, and my lord privy seal's, if it be possible they may be obtained of his lordship, to be curate of our lady's church in Cales; and that the council here may assist him in reading and preaching the true word of God; for by his long absence the poor commonalty, which is very desirous to hear him, shall have great hinderance.

Your grace might do a right meritorious deed to aid the prior of the friars hence; for I assure your grace he doth much harm here, and that secretly. God send him grace to turn unto the truth, as he promised to do in Lent last past, knowledging himself to be in the wrong: saying to be sorry that he had so long erred from the truth. Further to advertise your grace, that I have declared to the prior that his third article is not lowable; and he answered me again, that whosoever did say the contrary of his third article is an heretic, and will so prove him Those words spake he to me upon Sunday, the 21st of this month, in the presence of one Richard Bennet, alderman of Cales. And as touching the other two articles, the said Adam and the prior do agree in their sayings. God send light where darkness is. Thus Jesus preserve your grace in health! From Cales, the 22nd day of July. [1538.]

Your humble servant,

JOHN BUTLARE[6].

*To my lord of Canterbury's good grace.*

## CCXXXIII. TO CRUMWELL.

MY very singular good lord, in my most hearty wise I commend me unto your lordship. And whereas I wrote unto you about this time[7] twelvemonth of one Robert Antony, subcellerar of Christ's church in Canterbury, declaring how that he was run away, and had left a very suspicious letter in his chamber unto the prior of the house, the copy of which letter I sent at that time unto you, if your lordship can call it unto your remembrance: so it is, that the said Robert Antony, being all this year forth out of this realm without the king's grace's licence, and, as I am informed, at Rome, and is now come home unto Christ's church again; and, since his coming (as I hear say by such persons as both favoureth God's word and the king's majesty there) the prior hath called a chapter, and hath admitted him again into the convent, as he was before; which in mine opinion is not well done, unless he had been first State Paper Office. Ibid Original.

[6 For an account of John Butlar, the writer of this letter, vid. Foxe's Acts and Monuments, pp. 1055, 1226; Strype's Mem. of Abp. Cranmer, Vol. I. p. 125. "An expression in his letter is of great use in fixing the date of these proceedings, respecting which there is much confusion in Foxe and Strype. He speaks of Sunday the 21st of July. He wrote therefore in 1538; for in that year the 21st of July fell on a Sunday." Jenkyns' Remains of Cranmer, Vol. I. p. 252.]

[7 Vid. Letters CLXXXIII. CLXXXIV. pp. 333, 4.]

examined by some of the council, where he hath been, and upon what occasion he so departed. Therefore, as a thing appertaining unto my duty towards my sovereign lord, I thought it expedient to advertise you thereof, to the intent his highness may have knowledge of the same: and of this I am sure, that I had letters from a scholar beyond the seas, which met him in a company going to Rome-ward; but whether he hath been there or no, I am not sure.

Besides this, my lord, I beseech you to be good lord unto my servant Nevell, this bearer, concerning his suit unto you for his farm at Bowghton under the Blayne, which he had of the abbot and convent of Feversham[1]. The truth is, that at the feast of Easter last past, or thereabout, he was a suitor for the same unto the abbot and his convent: notwithstanding, they could not agree, for certain considerations which he can declare unto your lordship; insomuch that tendering his preferment to the same, I both spake to your lordship, and obtained your favourable letters unto the said abbot and convent in that behalf, by means only whereof he had a lease of the same under the convent seal for a term of fifty-one years; and so since the feast of St John Baptist last past, he hath occupied and been in possession thereof, until now (as I am informed) that by information of such as of late were the king's commissioners, the king's grace's commandment by you is, that he should be dispossessed, unto such time as his grace's farther pleasure be known: which will be no little to his loss and hinderance, except your goodness be extended unto him in this behalf; assuring your lordship, beside his hinderance herein, it is a great disquietness unto me to perceive my servant and officer, which hath not only done me good service in my household, but also [hath been] very towards and ready at all times to apply such business as hath been committed unto me by the king's majesty, as in the last commotion and otherways, should thus suddenly be expelled for so small advantage. Howbeit, considering that he obtained this thing only by your lordship's letters and favour, I trust you will be no less good lord unto him now, than you have been heretofore; and if by your wisdom and discretion it shall be thought good to reform any thing in his said lease, I doubt not but that he will abide your lordship's direction in that behalf. But to have him clearly excluded, it were too much extremity, considering that he came to the same by his open and honest suit. Thus, my lord, as well in this suit as in all other, both for myself and mine, I have no refuge but only unto your lordship, which to recompense I shall never be able as my mind would give me; beseeching your lordship in this suit that you will be so good lord unto him, as to maintain him in this his just cause. Thus, my lord, right heartily fare you well. At Lambeth, the iiid day of August. [1538.]

Your own ever assured,

T. CANTUARIEN.

*To the right honourable and my very special good lord, my lord privy seal.*

---

## CCXXXIV. TO CRUMWELL.

State Paper Office. Ibid. Original.

MY very singular good lord, after most hearty commendations unto your lordship; I likewise thank the same for your goodness toward the bringer hereof, William Swerder[2], desiring you to continue the same. I have intended, as I shewed you when

---

[[1] The abbey of Feversham was surrendered to Henry VIII., July 8, A. D. 1538, by whom it was granted to sir Thomas Cheyney on March 16, A. D. 1540. Vid. Lewis's Hist. of Feversham Abbey, pp. 29, 22. Ed. Lond. 1627. Tanner's Notitia Monast. Kent. xxiv. Feversham. Ed. Camb. 1787. The date of this letter is assumed to be A. D. 1538, by Dr Jenkyns, from the probability of its having been written soon after the abbey came into the king's possession; and on similar grounds he was led to fix Letters CLXXVII. CLXXVIII. (Letters CLXXXIII. CLXXXIV. of this edition, pp. 333, 4.) to the year 1537. Remains of Abp. Cranmer, Vol. I. p. 254. n. 1.]

[[2] This might have been the William Swerder, master of Eastbridge Hospital, Canterbury, mentioned by Abp. Parker in his statutes for that hospital, as "nuper magistri hospitali prædict." Strype's Life of Abp. Parker, Appendix. No. lviii. Vol. III. p. 174. Ed. Oxon. 1821.]

I spake with you last, to send him into France or Italy, except you be otherwise minded to set him forward, as truly I would be right glad it might please you so to do; and therefore I have sent him unto you, that he should inform your lordship of his mind, desiring you to be good lord unto him for his passport.

Also I heartily require your lordship to be good lord unto master Statham, and mistress Statham, my lord of Worcester[3] his nurse, as touching the suit that the bishop of Worcester had unto you for them; and although I doubt not but that your lordship will be good unto them, yet I pray you that my suit and request be not without place, but that for my sake you will be much the better unto them.

Moreover, I beseech you most heartily to remember master Hutton, now absent in Flanders[4], and having none to trust unto and that is able to help him but only your lordship. If you could make him an abbot or a prior, and his wife an abbess or a prioress, he were bound unto you, as he is nevertheless most bound unto you of all men: but if you would help him to such a perfection, I dare undertake for him that he shall keep a better religion than was kept there before, though you appoint him unto the best house of religion in England. Thus Almighty God long preserve your lordship. At Lambeth, the third day of August. [1538.]

These houses of religion be in master Hutton's country[5], Combe Abbey, Merevale, Eytun, and Polysworth. I beseech your lordship to remember him with one of these in special, or any other in general.

Your own assured ever,

T. CANTUARIEN.

*To the right honourable and my singular good lord, my lord privy seal.*

---

## CCXXXV. TO CRUMWELL.

MY very singular good lord, after my most hearty commendations unto your lordship: these shall be to advertise the same, that I have sent for Robert Antony[6], late cellerar of Christ's church in Canterbury; and when he cometh, I shall order him according to your instruction and advice, and so to get out of him what I can, concerning his progress to Rome-ward, and the same to send unto you with expedition. State Paper Office. Ibid. Original.

As concerning Adam Damplip of Calice[7], he utterly denieth that ever he taught or said that the very body and blood of Christ was not presently in the sacrament of the altar, and confesseth the same to be there really; but he saith, that the controversy between him and the prior was, by cause he confuted the opinion of the transubstantiation, and therein I think he taught but the truth[8]. Howbeit there came

---

[3 Hugh Latymer.]

[4 It appears that John Hutton was employed as an agent in the Netherlands A. D. 1538, having been sent over to negociate a marriage between the duchess of Milan and Henry VIII. Kennet's Hist. of England; Lord Herbert's Life of Henry VIII. Vol. II. p. 214. Ed. Lond. 1706. He merely opened the negociations for the marriage, which Wryothesley and Vaughan were commissioned to conclude: he died Sept. 5, A. D. 1538. Several letters from Hutton to Henry VIII. and Crumwell are found in the Cotton MSS. Galba, B. x. f. 329, 333, 335, and Vespasian, C. xiii. f. 340. British Museum. In A.D. 1542, Hutton was king's servant, and governor of the adventurers in Flanders, as appears by a letter from the "council of London to Henry VIII." by a minute endorsed from Stepney, which letter is preserved in the Cotton MSS. Galba, B. x. f. 342. British Museum; and the date of which is fixed by the correspondence of the commissioners appointed to enter into negociations with Mons. Chapuys, the imperial ambassador, at Stepney, May 1542, preserved in the German Correspondence in the State Paper Office. Vid. State Papers, Vol. I. p. 741.]

[5 Viz. in Warwickshire.]

[6 Vid. Letter CCXXXIII. p. 373.]

[7 Vid. Letter CCXXXII. p. 372.]

[8 The following event is probably that here referred to by the archbishop. "There came a commission from the king to the lord deputy (De Lisle), M. Grendfield, Sir John Butler, commissary, the king's mason and smith, with others, that they should search whether there were......three hosts lying upon a marble stone, besprinkled with blood; and if they found it not so, that immediately it should be plucked down; and so it was. For in searching thereof, as they brake up a stone in the corner of the tomb, they, instead of the three hosts, found soldered in the cross of marble lying under the sepulchre three plain white counters, which they had painted like unto hosts, and a bone that is in the tip of a sheep's tail. All which trumpery Damlip shewed unto the people the next day following, which was Sunday, out of the pulpit, and after that they were sent by the lord deputy to the

in two friars against him, to testify that he had denied the presence of the body and blood to be in the sacrament; which when he perceived, straightways he withdrew himself, and since that time no man can tell where he is become; for which I am very sorry, by cause that I think that he is rather fled, suspecting the rigour of the law, than the defence of his own cause. In consideration hereof, and to the intent that the people of Calice may be quiet and satisfied in this matter, I have appointed two of my chaplains[1] to go thither and preach incontinently: nevertheless it is thought that they shall do little good there, if the said prior return home again; for whatsoever hath been done heretofore, either by my chaplains or by other, in setting forth of the word of God there, no man hath hindered the matter so much as this prior, nor no superstition more maintained than by this prior; which I perceive to be true, both by the report of my chaplains heretofore, and of other men of credence. I have herewith sent unto your lordship two letters, which shall something inform you of the prior's subtlety and craft, praying your lordship that in any wise he come not at Calice any more to tarry, but either that the house may be suppressed, or else that an honest and a learned man may be appointed in his room; and forasmuch as the prior is here now, I pray you, my lord, that I may have your authority by your letter, to command him that he return not again to Calice.

And where in my last letters I prayed your lordship to remember Mr Hutton, that he might be made an abbot or a prior, which I doubt not that your lordship will effectiously attempt with the king's majesty; yet forsomuch as his presence with the king might, as I suppose, work something therein, meseemeth it were very good if he might come home for a little time to see the king's grace, which I beseech your lordship may be brought to pass, if you can by any means. Thus, my lord, right heartily fare you well. At Lambeth, the xvth day of August. [1538.]

Your own ever assured,

T. Cantuarien.

*To the right honourable and my very singular good lord, my lord privy seal.*

---

## CCXXXVI. TO CRUMWELL.

State Paper Office. Ibid. Original.

After due commendations unto your lordship: so it is, that I have received also your letters concerning the prior[2] of the friars at Calice, with letters from your lordship unto my lord deputy[3], which I sent unto him incontinently; and reading the copy

---

king. Notwithstanding the devil stirred up a Dove ......the prior of the White Friars, who with Sir Gregory Buttol, chaplain to the lord Lisle, began to bark against him. Yet after the said Adam had in three or four sermons confuted the said friar's erroneous doctrines of transubstantiation, and of the propitiatory sacrifice of the mass, the said friar outwardly seemed to give place, ceasing openly to inveigh, and secretly practised to peach him by letters sent unto the clergy here in England; so that within eight or ten days after the said Damlip was sent for to appear before the bishop of Canterbury, with whom was assistant Stephen Gardiner, bishop of Winchester, D. Sampson, bishop of Chichester, and divers others, before whom he most constantly affirmed and defended the doctrine which he had taught, in such sort answering, confuting, and soluting the objections, as his adversaries, yea, even among other the learned, godly, and blessed martyr Cranmer, then yet but a Lutheran, marvelled at it, and said plainly that the scripture knew no such term as transubstantiation." Foxe's Acts and Monuments, p. 1224. Ed. Lond. 1583.]

[1 "Whereupon, during yet the days of the lord Crumwell, were sent over doctor Champion, doctor of divinity, and Mr Garret who after was burned, two godly and learned men, to preach and instruct the people, and to confute all pernicious errors, who in effect preached and maintained the same true doctrine which Adam Damlip had before set forth; and by reason thereof they left the town at their departure very quiet, and greatly purged of the slander that had run on it." Id. ibid. Oct. 8, A. D. 1535, the archbishop had asked Crumwell for "the parsonage of St Peter's besides Calais, like shortly to be void, and in the king's grace's disposition, for master Garrett." Vid. Letter CLV. p. 310. Vid. also Letters CXLV. CLXIV. CLXXI. pp. 304, 317, 321.]

[2 Vid. Letters CCXXXII. CCXXXV. pp. 372, 375.]

[3 Arthur Plantagenet, created lord De Lisle, April, A. D. 1523, and appointed governor of Calais, June 2. A. D. 1533, was recalled by a letter from the king, (British Museum, Cotton. MSS. Calig. E. IV. f. 34, Original,) dated April 17, the 31st year of

of the same, I could not but much allow them, considering how frankly and freely you do admonish him and provoke him, as well to favour God's word, as also to the right administration of his room and office. And as for the prior, according to your advertisement, I have him in safe custody, and so shall keep him until your return into these parties; and I doubt not but there will be matter enough for his deprivation. Thus Almighty God have your lordship in his blessed tuition. At Lambeth, the xviiith day of August. [1538.]

[4]I beseech your lordship to remember Mr Hutton, that by your means he may have some occasion to come over into England.

Your own ever assured,

T. Cantuarien.

*To the right honourable and my singular good lord, my lord privy seal.*

---

## CCXXXVII. TO CRUMWELL.

My very singular and especial good lord, after my most hearty commendations unto your lordship; these shall be to signify unto the same, that according to your letters to me addressed the 15th day of this present month, I sent for the orators of Germany[5], and required them in the king's grace's behalf, so gentilly as I could, to demore here until his highness coming nearer into these parties: whereat they were somewhat astonied, saying, that at the king's request they would be very well content to tarry during his pleasure, not only a month or two, but a year or two, if they were at their own liberty; but forasmuch as they had been so long from their princes, and had not all this season any letters from them, it was not to be doubted but that they were daily looked for at home, and therefore they durst not tarry, unless the king's highness would make their excuse of their long abode here unto their princes; and yet therein they would give me no determinate answer by no means that time, but they would consult together and make me an answer the next day after. And the next day they were fully determined to depart within eight days; nevertheless after long reasoning, upon hope that their tarrying should grow unto some good success concerning the points of their commission, which I much put them in

State Paper Office. Ibid. Original. State Papers, Vol. I. pt. ii. Lett. CIX. pp. 579, 80. Todd's Life of Abp. Cranmer, Vol. I. p. 250.

---

his reign, [A. D. 1539,] on account of Henry's suspicions that he favoured the Poles and the Roman catholic party; for although he "officially professed himself an opponent of the Romish doctrines, he and his lady were suspected of favouring them." He was also accused of "want of management in his affairs, so that, for the sake of obtaining money, he was often compelled to put offices to sale, which should have been bestowed upon merit, and which thus often fell into the hands of improper persons." He was included, "as a matter of courtesy," amongst the commissioners who were sent over to Calais, March 1540, "to examine into the state of the laws of religion" there, who arrived on the 16th of that month; from whose investigations it was proved that "the town had been very carelessly kept," and that lord De Lisle "had communicated with the pope and cardinal Pole, and that he had presented Damplip with 5s., to whom lady De Lisle had also given 15s.....On the pretext that the presence of the commissioners in Calais afforded him a proper opportunity for a visit to the king," he went over to England in obedience to the letter of recall, and "immediately on his arrival was sent prisoner to the tower." He was not publicly tried for the offences alleged against him, and died suddenly, as stated supra, Letter CXXXI. *n.* 1, p. 298. Vid. The Chronicle of Calais, pp. 32, 44, 186, 7. Camden Soc. Ed. Lond. 1846.]

[4 This paragraph is in the archbishop's hand.]

[5 i. e. Francis Burgart, vice-chancellor to the elector of Saxony, (vid. Letter CCXXXI. p. 371.) George a Boyneburgh, doctor of laws, and Frederic Myconius, superintendent of the church of Gotha. Henry VIII. "fearing least the German princes might comply with the emperor upon some terms for the sake of peace and quietness, and being also jealous that after the return of their ambassadors they did not presently write to him," as well as "minding to have some of their learned men to be sent over for further disputation, because he was willing, if possible, to bring the German protestants over from some of their articles in the Augustine confession,......sent two agents, Christopher Mount and Thomas Paynil, to the princes......desiring to know the conditions they proceeded upon." John Frederic, elector of Saxony, and Philip, landgrave of Hesse, sent over the above-named persons as ambassadors and three others; but the object of their embassy "came to nothing." Strype's Eccl. Mem. Vol. I. pp. 522, 3, 529. Ed. Oxon. 1822. Burnet's Hist. of Reformat. Vol. I. Part II. Addenda, No. vii. 493—517. Ed. Oxon. 1829. Seckendorf, Comment. Hist. Apol. De Lutheran. Lib. III. Sect. 17. §. lxvi. p. 180. and Ad. i. Sect. 19. §. lxxiii. Ad. ii. (f). p. 225, 6. Ed. Francof. et Lips. 1792.]

hope of on your behalf, they condescended and were very well contented to tarry for a month, so that they should be no longer detained; but that after the said month should be expired, they might take their leave, and so depart without farther tract of time, trusting that the king's majesty would write unto their princes for their excuse in thus long tarrying: besides this they require in the mean time, while they tarry here, that we may entreat of the abuses, and put the same articles in writing, as we have done the others[1]; which thing I promised them: nevertheless I would gladly have the king's grace's pleasure and commandment therein, whereby we shall the sooner finish the matter[2].

Farther, by cause that I have in great suspect that St Thomas of Canterbury his blood, in Christ's church in Canterbury, is but a feigned thing[3] and made of some red ochre or of such like matter; I beseech your lordship that Doctor Lee[4] and Doctor Barbor[5], my chaplains, may have the king's commission to try and examine that and all other like things there. Thus, my lord, right heartily fare you well, praying you to give farther credence unto this bearer. At Lambeth, the 18th day of August. [1538.]

Your own ever assured,

T. CANTUARIEN.

*To the right honourable and my very singular good lord, my lord privy seal.*

---

## CCXXXVIII. TO SIR THOMAS WRIOTHESLEY[6].

State Paper Office. Ibid. Original.

MR WRYSLEY[7], in my right hearty wise I commend me to you. And whereas I have written to my lord privy seal heretofore, that upon some occasion his lordship

---

[1 Vid. "A book containing divers articles, De Unitate Dei, et Trinitate Personarum, De Peccato Originali," &c. in the Appendix, which were probably the articles that were agreed to. Vid. also "Frederichus Mychonius, ad D. Thomam Crumwellium," (Cotton MSS. Cleopat. E. V. f. 227. Original. British Museum) printed by Strype, Eccl. Mem. Vol. I. Part II. No. xcv. pp. 384, 5. Ed. Oxon. 1829, and Letter CCXXXI. p. 371.]

[2 It appears by Cranmer's letter (CCXXXIX.) p. 379, that the delay arose from the king's having taken the answer into his own hands. State Papers, Vol. I. Part. II. p. 580.]

[3 "As for shrines, copses, and reliquiaries of saints, so called, although the most were nothing less, forasmuch as his highness hath found other idolatry or detestable superstition used thereabouts, and perceived for the most part they were feigned things; as the blood of Christ, so called, in some place, was but a piece of red silk, inclosed in a piece of thick glass of crystalline; in another place, oil, coloured of 'sanguinis draconis,'......and other innumerable illusions, superstitions and apparent deceits......His majesty......hath caused the same to be taken away, and the abusive pieces thereof to be brent, the doubtful to be set and hidden honestly away for fear of idolatry." Collier's Eccl. Hist. Appendix, Vol. IX. pp. 170, 1. Ed. Lond. 1840-41. "The shrine of Thomas Becket [Sept. A.D. 1538] in the priory of Christ Church was likewise taken to the king's use. This shrine was builded about a man's height, all of stone, then upward of timber plain, within the which was a chest of iron, containing the bones of Thomas Becket, skull and all, with the wound of his death, and the piece cut out of his skull laid in the same wound. These bones (by commandment of the lord Crumwell) were then and there burnt.—The spoil of which shrine in gold and precious stones filled two great chests, such as six or seven strong men could do no more than convey one of them at once out of the church." Stowe's Annals, p. 575, Ed. Lond. 1516. A proclamation, still preserved, (Cotton. MSS. Titus, B. i. British Museum) was issued, "chiefly concerning Becket," at Westminster, Nov. 16, 30 Hen. VIII. [A.D. 1538] declaring that there appeared "nothing in his life and exterior conversation whereby he should be called a saint, but rather esteemed to have been a rebel and traitor to his prince," and that from henceforth he should "not be esteemed, named, reputed, nor called a saint;...and that his images and pictures, through the whole realm, should be put down and avoided out of all churches, chapels, and other places; and that......the days used to be festivals in his name should not be observed," &c. Vid. Burnet's Hist. of Reformat. Vol. III. Part II. Appendix, Book iii. No. 62. pp. 206, 7. Ed. Oxon. 1829. Also Kennet's Hist. of England. Lord Herbert's Life of Hen. VIII. Vol. II. p. 215. Ed. Lond. 1706.]

[4 This was probably doctor Leigh, Cranmer's commissary, [A.D. 1543.] Vid. Strype's Mem. of Abp. Cranmer, Vol. I. pp. 167, 172. Ed. Oxon. 1840.]

[5 Vid. Letter CCXII. p. 360.]

[6 This letter has not been printed in any former collection of the archbishop's letters.]

[7 i.e. Wriothesley, afterwards Sir Thomas Wriothesley.]

would send for Mr Hutton[8], to the intent that he might, by his presence, prefer himself in obtaining of the king's majesty some honest living appertaining to these abbeys; these shall be to desire you to put my said lord privy seal in remembrance to send for him, so that upon some occasion he may come unto the king's majesty for his preferment in this behalf. If there were here as good store of news as you have in the court, I would send you some; but here is none worthy of writing. Thus heartily fare you well. At Lambeth, the 18th day of August. [1538.]

Your loving friend,

T. CANTUARIEN.

*To my very loving friend, Mr Wrysley, esquire.*

---

## CCXXXIX. TO CRUMWELL.

Cotton MSS. Cleop. E. v. f. 212. Original. British Museum. Burnet, Ref. Vol. III. App. B. iii. No. 48.

MY very singular good lord, in my most hearty wise I commend me unto your lordship. And where that the orators of Germany, when they granted to tarry one month, required that we should go forth in their book and entreat of the abuses, so that the same might be set forth in writing as the other articles are[9]; I have since effectiously moved the bishops thereto, but they have made me this answer: that they know that the king's grace hath taken upon himself to answer the said orators in that behalf, and thereof a book is already devised by the king's majesty[10]; and therefore they will not meddle with the abuses, lest they should write therein contrary to that the king shall write. Wherefore they have required me to entreat now of the sacraments of matrimony, orders, confirmation, and extreme unction[11]; wherein they know certainly that the Germans will not agree with us, except it be in matrimony only: so that I perceive that the bishops seek only an occasion to break the concord; assuring your lordship that nothing shall be done, unless the king's grace's special commandment be unto us therein directed. For they manifestly see that they cannot defend the abuses, and yet they would in no wise grant unto them.

Farther, as concerning the orators of Germany, I am advertised that they are very evil lodged where they be; for besides the multitude of rats daily and nightly running in their chambers, which is no small disquietness, the kitchen standeth directly against their parlour where they daily dine and sup, and by reason thereof the house savoureth so ill, that it offendeth all men that come into it[12]. Therefore if your lordship do but offer them a more commodious house to demore in, I doubt not but that they will accept that offer most thankfully, albeit I am sure that they will not remove for this time.

And whereas of late I did put your lordship in remembrance for the suppression of the abbey of Tudberye[13]; now I beseech your lordship, not only that commissioners may be sent unto that house, but also in like wise unto the abbey of Rocester[14], or

---

[[8] Hutton died 5 Sept. A. D. 1538. Vid. Letter CCXXXIV. p. 375, *n.* 4.]

[[9] Vid. Letter CCXXXVII. p. 377.]

[[10] The letter written by the German ambassadors to the king, against the taking away of the chalice, and against private masses, and the celibacy of the clergy, &c. and the king's answer, which was drawn up by Tunstall, are still preserved amongst the Cotton. MSS. Cleop. E. v. fol. 173, 215, Original, in the British Museum. They are also printed in Burnet's Hist. of Reformat. Vol. I. Part II. Addenda, pp. 493—538. Ed. Oxon. 1829.]

[[11] These four Roman catholic sacraments found no place in the Augsburgh confession; but those of baptism, the Lord's supper, and penance, were retained. Vid. Sylloge Confessionum, Ed. Oxon. 1827.]

[[12] Sumptus illius legationis magnus tunc visus est Protestantium proceribus, splendide tamen vixerant legati et liberalem mensam exhibuerant.—Seckendorf, Comment. Hist. Apol. de Lutheran. Lib. III. Sect. 16, §. lxvi. (9). p. 180. Ed. Francof. et Lips. 1792.]

[[13] A Benedictine priory in Staffordshire, surrendered 30 Hen. VIII., and the site granted (6 Edw. VI.) to Sir William Cavendish. Tanner's Notitia Monast. Stafford. xxx. Tutbury. Ed. Camb. 1787.]

[[14] A Benedictine abbey in Staffordshire, whose annual revenues amounted to £111. 11*s.* 7*d.*, was suppressed (30 Hen. VIII.), the site granted (31 Hen. VIII.) to Richard Trentham. Tanner's Notitia Monast. Stafford. xxi. Roucester. Burnet's Hist. of Reformat. Vol. I. Part II. Appendix. Book iii. p. 227.]

Crockesdon[1]: beseeching your lordship to be good lord unto this bearer Francis Basset, my servant, for his preferment unto a lease of one of the said houses; not doubting but you shall prefer a right honest man, who at all times shall be able to do the king's grace right good service in those parties, and also be at your lordship's commandment during his life. Thus Almighty God have your good lordship in his blessed tuition! At Lambeth, the xxiiid day of August. [1538.]

Your own ever assured,

T. Cantuarien.

---

## CCXL. TO CRUMWELL.

State Paper Office. Ibid. Original.

My very singular good lord, after most hearty recommendations to your lordship; I desire you to be good lord to this bearer, an old acquaintance of mine in Cambridge, a man of good learning in divers kinds of letters, but specially in the Latin tongue, in the which he hath obtained excellent knowledge by long exercise of reading eloquent authors, and also of teaching, both in the university, and now in Ludlow, where he was born. His purpose is, for causes moving his conscience, (which he hath opened to me, and will also to your lordship,) to renounce his priesthood; whereby he feareth (the rawness and ignorance of the people is such in those parties) that he should lose his salary whereof he should live, except he have your lordship's help. Wherefore I beseech your lordship to write for him your letters to the warden of the guild there and his brethren, which hath the collation of the said school, that he may continue in his room and be schoolmaster still, notwithstanding that he left the office of priesthood; which was no furtherance, but rather an impediment to him in the applying of his scholars. There is no foundation nor ordinance, as he sheweth me, that the schoolmaster thereof should be a priest. And I beseech you to be good lord unto him in any farther suit, which he shall have unto your lordship. Thus Almighty God long preserve your lordship! At Lambeth, the xxvth day of August. [1538.]

Your own ever assured,

T. Cantuarien.

*To my very singular good lord, my lord privy seal.*

---

## CCXLI. TO CRUMWELL.

State Paper Office. Ibid. Original.

My very singular good lord, in my most hearty wise I commend me unto your lordship. And whereas I am credibly informed that Mr Parker, brother unto the abbot of Gloucester, is departed, who amongs other his promotions had the deanery of a college named Tameworth college[2], within the county of Stafford, being of the king's grace's collation: these shall be most heartily to desire your lordship, (inasmuch as that country is destitute of learned men and preachers,) that you will have in remembrance Doctor Barons[3] unto the king's majesty, for his preferment thereunto.

---

[[1] "The [Cistercian] monastery of Crokesden, or Croxden, in Staffordshire, 'had an abbot and twelve monks, whose yearly revenues were, 26 Hen. VIII., £103. 6*s*. 7*d*. Speed.' Though this was one of the lesser abbeys, and so should have been dissolved by 27 Hen. VIII. yet the king was pleased to continue this house, which finally surrendered, 30 Hen. VIII. The site was granted (36 Hen. VIII.) to Jeffry Foljamb." Tanner's Notitia Monast. Stafford. vii. viii. Crokesden. Burnet, Hist. of Reformat. Ibid.]

[[2] A college for a dean and six prebendaries. Vid. Tanner's Notitia Monast. Stafford. xxvii. Tamworth.]

[[3] Probably Dr Barnes, "who had been amongst the earliest converts to Luther's doctrines; whom Fox, bishop of Hereford, being at Smalcald, in the year 1536, sent over to England, where he was received and kindly entertained by Crumwell, and well used by the king, by whose means the correspondence with the Germans was chiefly kept up: for he was often sent over to the courts of several princes. But in particular he had the misfortune to be first employed in the project of the king's marriage with Ann of Cleves; for that giving the king so little satisfaction, all who were the main promoters of it fell in disgrace upon it." He also controverted against a sermon preached by Gardiner at

Your lordship knoweth full well, that hitherto he hath had very small preferment for such pains and travail as he most willingly hath sustained in the king's affairs from time to time. Howbeit, I doubt not but the king's grace and your lordship doth perceive such fidelity and towardness in the man, that he hath deserved a greater living than this promotion, which is esteemed unto me but at the clear yearly value of xx$^{li.}$ or thereabouts; beseeching your lordship eftsoons to be his good lord in this behalf, and that the rather at this mine instant request. Thus, my lord, right heartily fare you well. At Lambeth, the xxviiith day of August. [1538.]

Your own ever assured,

T. Cantuarien.

*To the right honourable and my singular good lord, my lord privy seal.*

---

## CCXLII. TO CRUMWELL.

State Paper Office. Ibid. Original.

My singular good lord, after my most hearty commendations; these shall be to beseech your lordship to direct your letters unto Mr Vawghan, willing him to send home into England Mistress Hutton[4], so that she may come from thence without danger of the law, bringing with her only her apparel; and the rest of the goods to be kept there, until your lordship's farther pleasure be known in that behalf. Thus, my lord, most heartily fare you well. At Lambeth, the second day of October. [1538.]

Your own ever assured,

T. Cantuarien.

*To my very singular good lord, my lord privy seal.*

---

## CCXLIII. TO CRUMWELL.

State Paper Office. Ibid. Original.

My singular good lord, in my most hearty wise I commend me to your lordship. And where of late[5] I wrote unto your lordship in the behalf of Mistress Hutton; these shall be eftsoons to beseech you, my lord, to direct your letters unto Mr Vawghan, willing him so to see her discharged from those parties where she is now, that she may come home incontinently into England, without danger of the law, bringing with her all such apparel as appertaineth unto her and to her chamber: and as for the other stuff, there to remain, until your lordship's farther pleasure be known in that behalf. Thus, my lord, right heartily fare you well.

Your own ever assured,

T. Cantuarien.

*To my very singular good lord, my lord privy seal.*

---

## CCXLIV. TO CRUMWELL.

State Paper Office. Ibid. Original.

After my most hearty commendations unto your good lordship; these shall be to signify unto you, that a scholar of Oxford hath uttered unto me certain things, which, forasmuch as they appertain unto the king's majesty, I send them unto your lordship herein inclosed[6], to be examined by you: and if your lordship require farther information in this behalf, I think the said scholar can partly instruct you therein.

---

Paul's Cross, upon "justification and other points," and made reflections upon his person, "alluding to a Gardener's setting ill plants in a garden," for which he was questioned, as well as for his doctrines. He was burnt, with Garret and Jerome, for his opinions, A.D. 1540. Vid. Burnet's Hist. of Reformat. Vol. I. pp. 590, et sqq.; also above, p. 339, with *n*. 7.]

[4 Vid. Letters CCXXXIV. CCXXXV. CCXXXVI. CCXLIII. pp. 375, 376, 377, 381.]

[5 See the preceding Letter.]

[6 The inclosure here referred to is appended after this letter.]

Thus, my lord, most heartily fare you well. At Lambeth, the 8th day of October. [1538.]

[1]My lord, I beseech you to be good lord unto M. Bul, parson of Northflete, whom I have known many years to be a man of good learning, judgment, soberness, and a very quiet man, whatsoever report is made of him to the contrary.

Your own ever assured,
T. Cantuarien.

*To my very singular good lord, my lord privy seal.*

"JESUS.

"As concerning Mr Don[2].

State Paper Office. Ibid. Original.

1. "I, Gregory Stremer, do testify, that Mr Don said that sir Marshall should make satisfaction for the putting out of this word *papa* in Saint Gregory's works in our library.

2. "I, Edmund Mervyn, testify, that sythe that time, when as sir Martiall laid that same to his charge again, he denied it not, but said these words, 'Mary, and I say yet, that it is not necessary to put out *papa* out of profane books.'

3. "The said Mr Don, when it was his part, in his collation made to the company, to declare the just abrogation of the bishop of Rome's usurped power, went about specially to persuade that the bishop might be called *papa*, and that it was but a foolish phantasy of men to make so much about the name *papa*, because divers bishops, besides the bishop of Rome, were so called.

"Witness of the same { Gregory Stremer,
Hue Goode,
Richard Marshall[3],
Edmund Marvyn,
Richard Wye,
John Wye,
John Bondell.

4. "I, Gregory Stremer, Richard Martiall, and Edmunde Marvyn, were talking with Mr Don in his chamber, and I willed him to teach the youth why the bishop of Rome was expulsed; 'for I think,' said I, 'none of them can tell why it is done.' Then said Mr Don these words: 'No more can I.' 'No?' said I; 'what mean you, Mr Don, by that? Bear record, masters.' Then, after a little deliberation, he said, he could not tell why he was expulsed, by cause he never knew any authority he had here; which interpretation afterwards was allowed of Mr doctor Cotes[4], then being in the commissary's place. In witness whereof we have here subscribed our names.

"Gregory Stremer,
"Edmund Mervyn,
"Richard Marshall.

5. "He affirmed, in a lesson which he read at Wytney, that men make laws now a days for money, not for profit of the commonweal.

"Hue Goode,
"Edmunde Marvyn.

6. "The said Don preached at Wytney in a sermon, that the old time good men were wont to build and maintain churches, and now they be more ready to pluck them down.

"Hue Goode,
"Edmunde Marvyn.

"Mr Slater.

7. "Mr Slater hath accused Hue Goode, Gervase Huche, Richard and John Wye, John Lane, unto their friends wrongfully, and hath continued in troubling of them ever since they began to be conversant with Mr Stremer and Richard Martiall, which hath been abhorred in all the college, syth they began to call upon the officers of the said college for fulfilling of the king's commandments, as touching the abolishing of the pope's name, and preaching against the popish doctrine, and certain other things commanded by the king's commissioners at the last visitation.

"Gregory Stremer,
"Edmunde Marvyn,
"Richard Wye,
"Hue Goode,
"Richard Marshall,
"John Wye.

---

[[1] This paragraph is in Cranmer's own hand.]

[[2] John Dunne was Greek lecturer at C. C. C. about this time. Jenkyns' Remains of Abp. Cranmer, Vol. I. p. 269.]

[[3] He was then dean of Christ Church, "a most furious and zeloticall man, who, to shew his spite against the reformation, had caused Peter Martyr's wife, who deceased while he was the king's professor, to be taken out of her grave, and buried in his dunghill." Strype's Mem. of Abp. Cranmer, Vol. II. p. 535. Ed. Oxon. 1840. Vid. also Wood's Fasti, Vol. II. pp. 136, 8. Ed. (Bliss.) Lond. 1813-20. Dr Marshall was one of the witnesses against Cranmer, Sept. A.D. 1555. Vid. Process. contra Cranmerum, in the Appendix.]

[[4] George Cotes, of Magdalen college, admitted

"SIR TURNBULL.

8. "Sir Turnbull, reader of logic, wresteth good questions, which the scholars put forth in their disputations, to Duns' quiddities.

"Gregory Stremer,
"Hue Goode.

9. "Jo. Edwards, T. Goidge, Jamys Broke[5], William Chedsey[6], masters of arts, keep the youth of this college from the knowledge of God's word, grudging and resisting to their power against such ordinances as make to the spreading of the gospel, and extirping of ungodly and papistical doctrine.

"George Stremer,
"Richard Marshall,
"Hue Goode,
"Richard Wye,
"Edmunde Marvyn,
"John Wye.

"*Papa* was written into a calendar of a book in our college chapel after it had been once put out, by whom we cannot tell.

"John Garrett,
"Richard Marshall,
"George Etherige[7],
"John Morwen[8].

1. "Not fulfilling the king's injunctions, which require preaching. State Paper Office. Ibid.
2. "*Item*, Not singing the collect for the king in the mass, agreeing to the injunctions.
3. "*Item*, Not blotting out *papa*, until it was within this half year, and singing the said *papa* openly in the church.
4. "*Item*, *Papa* written again, after it had been once put out, into a certain church-book, throughout the calendar.
5. "*Item*, A book continual four years suffered in the library, which called them heretics and schismatics that did not set the bishop of Rome above all powers, as kings and emperors, &c.
6. "*Item*, Another book which was named Alexander de Hayles, which proved the bishop of Rome above all powers.
7. "*Item*, They would not suffer the Bible to be read openly in the hall at dinners, as the statute biddeth, till that we ourselves proffered to read it.
8. "*Item*, Mr Chedsay, one of the deans, said, that if he saw any scholar have a New Testament in his hand, he would burn it.
9. "*Item*, Mr Shepreve[9] said, that studying of the scripture was subversion of good order, and that, if he durst, he would bar us from reading of scripture.
10. "*Item*, That Mr Donne would have had satisfaction of sir Marshall for putting out *papa* in Gregory's works in the library.
11. "*Item*, Mr Slater said, that there were some in the house which could prove the bishop of Rome's authority.
12. "*Item*, Mr Goyge reported in Hamsher, that sir Marwin and sir Marshall were heretics, and had heresy books, and were naught.
13. "*Item*, Mr Slater forbade the scholars a company.
14. "*Item*, The divinity lesson, which ought by the statute above all other lessons to be read, is not read.
15. "*Item*, Mr Smythe said, that such as sir Marshall is have done much hurt with preaching.
16. "*Item*, That few or none, except the masters, have any part of scripture in their chamber.
17. "*Item*, Sir Garret for saying that it were better for sir Marshall to let *papa* alone than put it out of the church-books, was punished with losing a fortnight's commons, and had his meat and drink given him.

---

doctor of divinity July 5, A.D. 1536, and elected master of Balliol Nov. 30, A.D. 1539, and bishop of Chester April 1, A.D. 1554. Dr Tresham was commissary of the university of Oxford at this time, having held the office from A.D. 1534 to 1546; Cotes probably acted for him. Wood's Fasti, Vol. II. pp. 98, 104. Le Neve's Fasti, pp. 341, 482. Ed. Lond. 1715.]

[5 Master of Balliol college, A.D. 1547, bishop of Gloucester, April 1, A.D. 1554, and the pope's sub-delegate at the archbishop's trial, A.D. 1555. Wood's Athenæ, Vol. I. pp. 314, 15. Le Neve's Fasti, pp. 101, 482.]

[6 "He was by the protestants accounted a very mutable and unconstant man in his religion, but by the Roman catholics not, but rather a great stickler for their religion, and the chief prop in his time in the university for the cause, as it appeared not only in his opposition of P. Martyr, but of the three bishops that were burnt in Oxon." Wood's Athenæ, Vol. I. p. 323. Vid. Disputations at Oxford, Vol. I. p. 393. et sqq. of this publication.]

[7 George Etheridge, was "the reader of the Greek lecture," (i.e. regius professor) A.D. 1553, and was then a violent persecutor, and proposed at "the communication between Brookes and Ridley," Oct. 15, 1555, that the latter should be gagged. He was also engaged in the proceedings against the archbishop in the same year. Vid. Foxe's Acts and Monuments, p. 1767. Ed. Lond. 1583. Wood's Athen. Oxonien. Vol. I. pp. 546, 7. Process. contra Cranmerum, in Appendix.]

[8 John Morwen, a famous Greek scholar, and private instructor to John Jewel. He was engaged in the disputations at Oxford, A.D. 1555, against Cranmer. Vid. Strype's Mem. of Abp. Cranmer, Vol. II. p. 480. Ed. Oxon. 1840. Wood's Athenæ, Vol. I. pp. 195-7.]

[9 Hebrew professor of the university about A.D. 1538. Vid. Wood's Athen. Oxonien. Vol. I. pp. 134-6.]

18. "*Item*, Sir Turnbull said, when four of Sion, London, and Sheene[1], were put to execution for holding with the bishop of Rome, that he trusted to have a memory of them among other of the saints one day.

19. "*Item*, Sir Bocher said, that all they which be of the new learning, were advoutrers and naughty knaves.

20. "*Item*, Mr Donne called sir Marvin and sir Marshall Neo-Christianos, i. e. a new kind of christian men.

21. "Mr Slater complained of certain to their friends, because he perceived them to favour the truth.

22. "*Item*, Mr Donne forbade reading of the Bible in the hall.

23. "*Item*, The masters and fellows of the house which be counted of the new learning, as they called it, be admitted neither to any office, ne yet to any council of the college business."

---

## CCXLV. TO CRUMWELL.

State Paper Office. Ibid. Original.

My very singular good lord, after my most hearty commendations unto your good lordship; these shall be to yield unto you my most hearty thanks for this bearer Markham, to whom, as I understand, you are so good lord as to prefer him to the farm of the priory of Newsted; beseeching your lordship, as you have herein been his especial good lord, so you will continue; and I doubt not, but that he shall so handle himself, both in the king's service and towards your lordship, that you shall not forthink that you have done for him. Thus, my lord, most heartily fare you well. At Lambeth, the 10th day of October. [1538.]

[2]The two Observants, whom you sent unto me to be examined, have confessed that which I suppose is high treason. I shall send them with their depositions unto your lordship this night or to-morrow.

Your own ever assured,
T. Cantuarien.

*To my very singular good lord,*
*my lord privy seal.*

---

## CCXLVI. TO CRUMWELL.

State Paper Office. Ibid. Original.

My very singular and especial good lord, in my most hearty wise I commend me unto you. And whereas I understand that the town-clerkship of Calais standeth now as void, so that it is in their election there to choose a new officer; forasmuch, my lord, as there is one of Gray's Inn, named Nicolas Bacon[3], whom I know entirely to be both of such towardness in the law, and of so good judgment touching Christ's religion, that in that stead he shall be able to do God and the king right acceptable service: these shall be most heartily to beseech your lordship, by cause I have oftentimes heretofore wished to have that town furnished with some officers of right judgment, that you will direct your favourable letters unto the mayor of Calice and other the king's officers there, moving them to prefer this man in their election to that room; which thing I do more willingly require of your lordship, by cause that I am credibly informed that certain of the head officers there would gladly have him amongst them in this said room; and therefore, not doubting but that your lordship shall think your letters well bestowed hereafter herein, shall now beseech you to be his good lord in this behalf. Thus, my lord, right heartily fare you well. At Lambeth, the xxiii. day of October. [1538.]

Your own ever assured,
T. Cantuarien.

*To my very singular good lord, my lord*
*privy seal.*

---

[[1] Vid. Letter CXLIII. p. 303. *n.* 3.]

[[2] This paragraph is in the archbishop's hand.]

[[3] "Nicholas Bacon, afterwards keeper of the great seal, was now about twenty-eight years of age, and it is not unlikely that this recommendation by Cranmer may have led to his subsequent advancement. His biographers do not mention that he was ever town-clerk of Calais, but he must have been employed early in the king's service; for about 1544 he received a grant of some of the possessions of the dissolved monastery of Bury St Edmund's, as 'a proof of the estimation in which he was held by his majesty.' See Chalmers, Biogr. Dict." Jenkyns' Remains of Abp. Cranmer, Vol. I. p. 273. There is no mention of his name in the Chronicle of Calais, published by the Camden Society.]

## CCXLVII. TO CRUMWELL.

State Paper Office. Ibid. Original.

My very singular good lord, in my right hearty wise I commend me unto your lordship: and whereas I understand, that one Crofts[4], being now in the Tower, and like to be attainted of treason, hath a benefice in Somersetshire, named Shipton Mallet, but of the yearly value of xxvi$^{li.}$; which, being the very parish where doctor Champion[5], my chaplain, was born, and where all his kinsfolk and friends now dwell, is for no man so meet a promotion as for him; and, forasmuch as the said doctor Champion doth trust and hope that your lordship beareth him such favour, that, when occasion should be offered, you would do him a good turn: these shall be heartily to desire you, my lord, to find the means that the said doctor Champion may be preferred unto the said benefice by your favour and aid, or else to shew unto me your good advice how that I may obtain it for him, in case it fall void at this time. The king's majesty and my lord Dalawarre giveth it *alternis vicibus*, and the king's grace gave it last: now whether his grace doth give it again by reason of this attainder, you can best tell: beseeching your lordship so to extend your accustomed benevolence towards the said doctor Champion, that by your procurement he may have the benefice, whosoever giveth it. Wherein I assure your lordship you shall do more for his commodity and preferment, than if you should give him a promotion worth ten of it in value, by cause that thereby he shall not only have occasion to do some good continually in his native country by preaching there the word of God, but also help the judgments of his own kinsmen and friends the sooner by this means. Thus, my lord, most heartily fare you well. At Lambeth, the xiiii. day of November. [1538.]

Your own assured ever,

T. Cantuarien.

*To the right honourable and my singular good lord, my lord privy seal.*

---

## CCXLVIII. TO CRUMWELL.

State Paper Office. Ibid. Original Holograph.

My very singular good lord, after most hearty recommendations; this shall be to signify unto you, that this day the king's highness sent me a commandment to be with him to-morrow at ten of the clock, which I cannot do, if I be with you at Stepney before nine of the clock. But forsomuch as his grace hath appointed me to be at two sundry places about one time, which I cannot accomplish, and I dare disappoint neither of his commandments without his grace countermand the same; therefore I will send unto his grace to know his determinate pleasure herein, and I will not fail to wait upon you at Stepney at your hour assigned, unless the king's pleasure be to the contrary. Thus Almighty God ever preserve your lordship to his pleasure! From Lamehithe, the xix. day of November. [1538.]

Your own ever assured,

T. Cantuarien.

*To my singular good lord, my lord privy seal, be this delivered.*

---

[[4] George Crafte, rector of Shepton Mallet, A.D. 1535. Valor. Eccles. Dr Jenkyns thinks him the same with George Crofts, chancellor of the cathedral of Chichester, who was indicted Dec. 4, A.D. 1538, (Burnet, Hist. of Reformat. Vol. I. p. 719. Ed. Oxon. 1829,) for saying, "the king was not, but the pope was, supreme head of the church;" and was executed with several others.]

[[5] Vid. Letters CXLV. CLXIV. CLXXI. pp. 304, 317, 321.]

## CCXLIX. TO CRUMWELL.

State Paper Office. Ibid. Original.

My singular good lord, after my right hearty recommendations. Whereas I am credibly informed that your servant, doctor Cave[1], (if it may stand with your lordship's pleasure,) is right willing to leave a prebend, which he now hath in the king's majesty's college at Oxforthe, to my chaplain, doctor Barber[2]; albeit I know myself so much bounden unto your lordship, for your ready gentleness towards me in all my suits heretofore, that I would not gladly at this time trouble your lordship with this thing, yet having no other mean to the king's highness, of whose gift the said prebend is, for the obtaining of the same, and considering the qualities and learning of the said doctor Barber, which I think be not to your lordship all unknown, I am compelled in this, as in all other my business, to have recourse to your lordship, heartily desiring your favour towards him herein; whereby your lordship shall not only do for an honest and meet man, but also bind me to do you any pleasure as may lie in my power. From Lambethe, the 21. day of November. [1538.]

Your own ever assured,

T. Cantuarien.

*To the right honourable and my singular good lord, my lord privy seal.*

## CCL. TO CRUMWELL.

State Paper Office. Ibid. Original.

My very singular good lord, in my most hearty wise I commend me unto your lordship. And so herewithal send unto you sir Henry ad Cortbeke, the Dutch priest, to receive the 20li. which on Tuesday last your lordship said you would deliver unto him; and farther, I desire your lordship that he may have the king's letters patents freely to be a denizen, and in that behalf to appoint one to procure it forth for him, to whom he may resort for the same; or else he shall never obtain it himself, by cause he can neither speak English, nor hath no manner of acquaintance to promote his cause in mine absence: beseeching your lordship also to have the said sir Henry in remembrance unto the king's majesty for some honest stipend for the maintenance of his living; wherein your lordship shall do a right good and meritorious deed. Thus, my lord, right heartily fare you well. At Lambeth, the 28th day of November. [1538.]

Your own ever assured,

T. Cantuarien.

*To the right honourable and my singular good lord, my lord privy seal.*

## CCLI. TO CRUMWELL.

State Paper Office. Ibid. Original.

After most hearty commendations unto your good lordship; these shall be to signify unto the same, that I have received your letters dated at Hampton Court, the 12th day of December, by which I perceive that the king's majesty hath nominated and appointed you to the offices of the high stewardship of all my franchises, and master of the game of all my chases and parks, by reason of the attainder of Sir Edward Nevell[3], knight; and thereupon you require for your better assurance my confirmation

[1 Vid. Letter XLIII. p. 256.]

[2 Vid. Letters CCXII. CCXXXVII. pp. 360, 378.]

[3 "On the fourth of December were indicted sir Geofrey Pool, sir Edward Nevill, brother to the lord Abergavenny," with the marquis of Exeter and several others, for saying "the king was a beast, and worse than a beast." Sir Edward was condemned for treason, and was executed with the marquis of Exeter and lord Montacute, on Tower Hill, Jan. 9, 1539. Burnet's Hist. of Reformat. Vol. I. pp. 717, 719. Stow's Annals, p. 575. Ed. Lond. 1615.]

in that behalf. Surely, my lord, I am right glad that you of all other hath the preferment thereof; and if it shall please you to send unto me the tenor of the king's letters patents to you made for the same, I will make unto you such lawful assurance as in me shall be: and to the intent your lordship may be ascertained what grants my predecessor made of the said office, I send unto you herewithal the copies of the said grants. And as touching the said office of the stewardship of the liberties, the same of late hath not been duly exercised as it ought to have been, by reason whereof, as I am informed by the learned counsel, the interest therein by the said grant heretofore made is forfeited; so that, if the law will permit, I will be glad to assure it to you for a term of your life, or else it will appertain unto the lord of Burgayveny[4]. Thus, my lord, right heartily fare you well. At Ford, the 14th day of December. [1538.]

My lord, I pray you accomplish my suit for this bearer, my servant, Francis Basset, concerning the monastery of Croxden[5], and I will not fail to accomplish my promise unto you concerning the same.

Your own assured ever,

T. Cantuarien.

*To the right honourable and my singular good lord, my lord privy seal.*

## CCLII. TO CRUMWELL.

My singular good lord, in my most hearty wise I commend me unto your lordship: signifying to the same, that there is brought before me one Henry Totehill for naughty communication which he should speak concerning the bishop of Rome and Thomas Beckett[6]; which matter I have examined, as your lordship shall farther perceive by a bill of the depositions herein inclosed[7]. And forasmuch as John Alforde, the principal accuser, is one that hath no certain biding-place, I have sent him with the said Totehill unto your lordship, to the intent that he may avouch his words before you in the presence of the said Totehill. State Paper Office. Ibid. Original.

Farther, this shall be to advertise your lordship, that I have taken upon me your office in punishing of such transgressors as break the king's Injunctions[8]: for already I have committed two priests unto the castle of Canterbury, for permitting the bishop of Rome's name in their books; the one of them lay there until it had cost him four or five mark, and yet notwithstanding I commanded him to give 4$^{li.}$ in alms after I had delivered him out of the castle, which he refused to do, and then was again committed unto the castle: at length, considering his expenses and punishment in prison, it is concluded that he shall give 40 shillings unto his poor neighbours, at the distribution of sir Edward Ringeley and other justices. As for the other priest, being but a curate, I have still in the castle until such time as he be condignly punished; for he hath little store of money to bestow in alms: howbeit I have commanded the parson where he was curate, to give 40 shillings in alms unto his poor neighbours. Thus much have I done on your behalf, remitting the rest unto your discretion, if you think it otherwise to be punished, beseeching your lordship to send me word, how I shall behave myself hereafter in punishing of such offences. Thus most heartily fare you well. At Ford, the 11th day of January. [1539.]

Your own ever assured,

T. Cantuarien.

*To the right honourable and my singular good lord, my lord privy seal.*

[4 Vid. Letters XXXI. CCLIII. pp. 253, 389.]
[5 Vid. Letter CCXXXIX. p. 380. This latter paragraph is in the archbishop's handwriting.]
[6 Vid. Letter CCXXXVII. p. 378.]
[7 The depositions follow at the end of this letter.]
[8 Vid. Letter CCXXIX. p. 369.]

[AN INCLOSURE IN ARCHBISHOP CRANMER'S LETTER OF 11 JAN. [1539.]

State Paper Office. Ibid. Original.

WITNES examined the x[th] daye of January, in the xxx yere of the Reign of our Soveraign Lorde King Henry the VIII[th], of certen wourdes whiche one Henry Totehill, of the Parishe of Saincte Kateryns bisides the Tower Hill, shipman, should speke in the house of one Thomas Brown, of Shawlteclyf, within the countie of Kente, concerning the Bisshop of Rome and Thomas Becket some tyme Archebisshop of Canterbury.

John Alforde, of thage of 18 yeres, examined, saith, that by reason that he had ben in Christmas tyme at my Lorde of Canterbury's, and ther had harde an enterlude concernyng King John [1], aboute 8 or 9 of the clocke at night; and Thursdaye, the seconde daye of Januarye last paste, spake theis wourdes folowing in the house of the said Thomas Brown,—That it ys petie that the Bisshop of Rome should reigne any lenger, for if he should, the said Bisshop wold do with our King as he did with King John. Wherunto (this deponent saith) that Henry Totehill answered and said, That it was petie and nawghtely don, to put down the Pope and Saincte Thomas; for the Pope was a good man, and Saincte Thomas savid many suche as this deponent was from hangyng: whiche wourdes were spoken in the presence of Thomas Browne and one William servaunte unto the said Totehill.

Thomas Brown, of the age of 50 yeres, examined, saith, that about 8 of the clocke on Fridaye the 3 daye of Januarye laste paste, as he remembereth, one Henry Totehill beyng in this deponente's house at Shawlteclyf, this deponent tolde that he hadde bene at my Lorde of Canterbury's, and there hadd harde one of the beste matiers that ever he sawe, towching King John; and than sayd that he had harde divers tymes preistes and clerkes say, that King John did loke like one that hadd run frome brynnyng of a house, butt this deponent knewe now that yt was nothing treu; for, as farr as he perceyved, King John was as noble a prince as ever was in England; and therby we myght perceyve that he was the begynner of the puttyng down of the Bisshop of Rome, and therof we myght be all gladd. Then answerd the said Totehill, that the Bisshope of Rome was made Pope by the clergie and by the consent of all the Kinges Christen. Than said this deponent, Holde your peace, for this communication ys nawght. Than said Totehill, I am sorye if I have said amysse, for I thought no harme to no man. This communication was made in the presence of John Alforde and a laborer of the said Totehill, and this deponente saithe that the said Totehill was dronken.

This deponent, examyned wherfore he thought the wourdes of Totehill so nawght, saith, bycause he thought that he spake theym in the mayntenaunce of the Bisshop of Rome.

Also concernyng the wourdes spoken of Thomas Beckette, this deponente aggreeth with the firste witnes.

Antony Marten, examyned what he harde spoken of Henry Totehill syns he was in his custodie, or at any tyme before, saith, that he harde John Halforde reporte that Henry Totehill should saye, that it was petie that Saincte Thomas was put down, and that the olde lawe was as good as the newe. And farther sayth, that the said John Halforde reported that Totehill said, that the Bisshop of Rome was a good man; and this he harde the said Halforde reporte before he toke hym. And farther the forsaid Antony Marten saith, that he demanded one Thomas Brown (in whose house the said Totehill spake theis wourdes above rehersid) what said Totehill; and he saithe, that the said Brown said that the said Totehill hath spoken very evill, and whan he shoulde be examined he would tell the trueth.

## CCLIII. TO CRUMWELL.

State Paper Office. Ibid. Original.

MY singular good lord, after my most hearty commendations unto your lordship; these shall be to signify unto the same, that I have received your letters with two patents, one of them concerning the stewardship of my liberties, the other of the mastership of my game; which patents I have sealed, and sent unto your lordship by Nevell, my steward, whom nevertheless I have commanded not to deliver, until such time as your counsel and mine have concluded that I may justly deliver them: for although, as I am bound, I am very glad and ready to do for your lordship that I may do, yet to do more than I may justly do neither standeth with justice, nor will at length be to your honour and benefit, nor mine neither; for if I should grant your patents, the state of things standing as they do at this present, so far as yet I do know, surely as well the heirs of the lord of Bargaveney [2], as the son of sir Edward Nevell, may hereafter not only recover of me the arrearages, but also bring your patents in question; which I were very loth should chance, for default of an oversight at the beginning. But by cause your counsel have informed your lordship that these patents may justly pass, and I am not instructed as yet how it may be done, nor I have not my counsel here at this time; therefore I beseech your lordship that your counsel learned may commune with Mr James Halis [3] and Mr Boys, my

[[1] The interlude concerning king John, which is here mentioned, is probably bishop Bale's "King Johan," published by the Camden Society in 1838.]

[[2] Vid. Letters XXXI. CCLI. pp. 253, 387.]

[[3] Probably "Sir James Hales, knight, a pious and good man, and a just and able judge under

counsel herein, that by them I may be certified the truth and justice of these things. And surely, whatsoever justice will serve to do for your lordship, that will I do and maintain it unto the uttermost. And yet surely my heart is much moved with pity towards the young lord of Bargavenny[4] and sir Edward Nevell's son[5]; the one, by cause he is within orphany, the other by cause he hath lost all his inheritance. Nevertheless your lordship may do more for them than this matter is worth, if the king's pleasure so be; and they both have justly forfeit their patents, as I am informed by my counsel, for abusing the same; and so I told the lord Bargaveney and Edward Nevell divers times in their lives. Thus, my lord, most heartily fare you well. At Ford, the xxi day of January. [1539.]

Your own ever assured,

T. Cantuarien.

*To my very singular good lord, my lord privy seal.*

---

## CCLIV. TO CRUMWELL.

State Paper Office. Ibid. Original.

My very singular good lord, in my most hearty wise I commend me unto your lordship; signifying to the same, that I have sent unto you another copy of the sermon which doctor Cronkehorne[6] should preach, beseeching you, my lord, to peruse the same, and to add and take away as you shall think convenient; and that you will either enjoin him to do it, or else to signify unto me your mind what I shall do therein. Thus, my lord, most heartily fare you well. At Ford, the last day of January. [1539.]

Your own ever assured,

T. Cantuarien.

*To my very singular good lord, my lord privy seal.*

---

## CCLV. TO CRUMWELL.

State Paper Office. Ibid. Original.

My very singular good lord, after my most hearty commendations unto your lordship; and whereas upon the death of my loving friend, Mr Thomas Wiate, (his son being ward unto the king's majesty,) you obtained the wardship of his said son, and gave the same unto Mr Wrothe, who then likewise gave the said wardship unto mistress Wiate his sister, and mother unto the said ward: and now forasmuch as the said mistress Wyate[7] is not only departed this miserable life, leaving the said ward in the custody of William Morice, Edward Isaac, and Thomas Isaac, her sons and executors, but also hath as yet left unobtained the king's grace's grant under seal, so that without the same the executors are without surety to perform that legacy, which they are bound

---

king Henry and king Edward," who was the only person that refused to sign the letters patent of Edward VI. settling the crown upon lady Jane Grey. In the reign of queen Mary he fell into trouble, and was imprisoned for his religious sentiments. He was prevailed upon to recant by Day, bishop of Chichester, and Portman, a judge;...... but "the trouble that arose in his conscience filled him with great terror, and overwhelmed him with sorrow, so that he attempted to kill himself." Having recanted, and being "dismissed home into his own country and habitation, conquered with grief and despair, he drowned himself in a shallow pond near his own house,...about the beginning of the month of February, or the month of January before, A. D. 1555." Vid. Strype's Eccl. Mem. Vol. III. Part I. pp. 274—276. Ed. Oxon. 1822. Burnet's Hist. of Reformat. Vol. II. p. 456. Ed. Oxon. 1829. Foxe's Acts and Monuments, pp. 1410, 1467, 1532, 3. Ed. Lond. 1583.]

[4 i. e. Henry Nevill, lord Abergavenny, who by the death of his father, A. D. 1535, was left an orphan, and was not of age to be summoned to the house of lords till A. D. 1552. Nicolas' Synopsis of the Peerage, *art.* Abergavenny, Vol. I. p. 13. Ed. Lond. 1825.]

[5 Afterwards baron Abergavenny, succeeding to the barony by the death of Henry Nevill, his cousin, without male issue, A. D. 1586. Id. ibid.]

[6 "This far passeth the calking of Dr Cronkehorne with his secret revelations, and also the pretty practices of Dr Bockynge and the holy maid of Kent." Bale's "Yet a Course at the Romish Fox," fol. 34.]

[7 Vid. Letter CCXV. p. 362.]

to do by her testament; these shall be to desire and pray your lordship to be so good lord unto the said executors, as by your means they may procure the king's grant unto you already made, under the seal, and so your grant over again unto them thereof; and for your lordship's pains to be taken herein, they shall give you a pleasure, howbeit the wardship, as I am informed, is but 10li. yearly, which is little enough to find the child at his learning, and to keep the house in reparations. Wherefore eftsoons I beseech your lordship to shew them herein your lawful favour, and that the rather, because the said mistress Wiate was not only my special friend, but also a very good and perfect woman. Thus, my lord, most heartily fare you well. At Canterbury, the vith day of April. [1539.]

Your own assured ever,

T. Cantuarien.

*To the right honourable and my very singular good lord, my lord privy seal.*

---

## CCLVI. TO LORD LISLE[1].

State Paper Office. Lisle Papers, Vol. II. No. 72. Original.

After most hearty commendations: these shall be to advertise you that whereas certain witnesses were sworn here before us, the king's commissioners under written, to depose against Raaff Hare, as Edward Malpas, Richard Sandes, and Thomas Boys; against the which witness the said Raaff Hare hath objected certain exceptions, which we do send you here inclosed, desiring you most heartily in the king's behalf to take the pains to examine John A. Caleys, John Nycholas, Piers Hedge, and Richarde Swyfte, upon the said exceptions, upon their oaths, and to send hither again unto us the same exceptions, with all such depositions as the said four men shall make thereupon, and that with as much speed as ye can possibly: also we most heartily desire you to call to remembrance whether you can prove any article of heresy against the said Raaff Hare, which he hath spoken or maintained sithens the king's proclamation late made, pardoning all anabaptists and sacramentaries which had offended before the date of the said proclamation; and in case be that you can, we desire you also instantly to send unto us with all speed convenient all the same articles with all such persons as can and will depose thereupon, and prove the same. And that all this may be done with such diligence that we may be certified from you thereupon by the 22nd day of this month or before, not forgetting the other letter which we have written unto you before concerning the commissary of Calais with other, and Thomas Broke, customer of Calais, that such proves as we have written for in that behalf fail not to be here by the day appointed. And thus our Lord Jesus have you to his pleasure! At Lambeth, the 5th day of July. [1539.]

Your loving friends,

(Signed) T. Cantuarien.
Rich. Cicestr.
Richard Gwent.

*To the right honourable my lord viscount Lysle, deputy of the town of Caleys, with other of the king's council there.*

---

## CCLVII. TO LORD LISLE.

State Paper Office. Calais Ecclesiastical Papers. A. D. 1347—1541. No. 1. Original.

My very good lord, after my right hearty commendations; these shall be to signify to you, that I have received your letters dated the 7th day of July, and also your other letters dated the day of , and therewith certain depositions, the contents of the which your said letters I have thoroughly pondered and considered. And first, as touching the said depositions, process shall be made accordingly as justice shall require in that

[1 This letter has not appeared in any previous collection.]

behalf; and as for to get you a discreet priest for your parish, I shall do what I can to provide you one with expedition; and likewise to provide you a learned man to be my commissary[2], I will do the best that lieth in me. Howbeit, I fear me, that I shall with much difficulty obtain such a one, by reason that learned men are not willing to demore continually beyond the sea and out of the realm, without great stipend, which will be to me no small charge over that it was. Nevertheless I do little pass of any charge, so that I may get one that will mind the advancement of God's glory, the king's honour, and the quietness of your town. And as to your request, that none should be suffered to preach nor expound the holy scripture with you, but such as shall be authorised by the king's majesty or by me, I shall not fail to give such a commandment unto him that shall be my commissary, that he shall suffer no person to preach out of his own cure, but such as shall have the said authority, either from the king's grace or from me.

As concerning such persons as in time of divine service do read the bible, they do much abuse the king's grace's intent and meaning in his grace's injunctions[3] and proclamations; which permitteth the bible to be read, not to allure great multitudes of people together, nor thereby to interrupt the time of prayer, meditation, and thanks to be given unto Almighty God, which, specially in divine service, is and of congruence ought to be used; but that the same be done and read in time convenient, privately, for the condition and amendment of the lives both of the readers and of such hearers as cannot themselves read, and not in contempt or hinderance of any divine service or laudable ceremony used in the church; nor that any such reading should be used in the church, as in a common school, expounding and interpreting scriptures, unless it be by such as shall have authority to preach and read; but that all other readers of the bible do no otherwise read thereupon, than the simple and plain text purporteth and lieth printed in the book[4]. And if

---

[[2] "1539. The x. of Awgust, the xxxi. of Henry the Eighth, ser John Butlar, priest, comyssary of Caleis and marches there, and Thomas Broke, chefe clerke of the exchеqwere, and customar of the towne of Calles, were sent to the Flete." "The crime of this person was, it appears, of a religious complexion. At a privy council held at Windsor, 7th Nov. 1540, 'lettres were browght from the depute and counsail of Calais, declaring that Sir [John] Butler, prist, sone and heyre unto the late lady Banestre, decessed, was endited for a sacramentary,'" &c. Chronicle of Calais, pp. 47, 180. Camden Soc. Ed. 1846. "By the archbishop's letters, bearing date May 20, [A. D. 1540] he (i. e. Cranmer) made Robert Harvey, B.LL. his commissary in Calais, and in all the neighbouring places in France, being his diocese: a man surely, wherein the good archbishop was mistaken, or else he would never have ventured to set such a substitute, of such bigoted cruel principles, in that place......He was hanged, drawn and quartered for treason in the said town of Calais." Strype's Mem. of Abp. Cranmer, Vol. I. pp. 124, 5. Ed. Oxon. 1840. Foxe's Acts and Monuments, p. 1229. Ed. Lond. 1583.]

[[3] "It was one of Crumwell's injunctions in the preceding September, that a copy of the bible should be placed in every parish-church." Jenkyns. See Letter CXCVIII. *n.* 3, p. 346.]

[[4] "Now, viz. 1538, the holy bible was divulged and exposed to common sale, and appointed to be had in every parish-church. And then, that the sacred book might be used with the more benefit both of the clergy and lay people, for this reason a declaration was issued out, to be read openly by all curates upon the publishing of this bible, shewing the godly ends of his majesty in permitting it to be in English; and directions how they should read and hear it." Strype's Mem. of Abp. Cranmer, Vol. I. p. 90. Ed. Oxon. 1840. The following is the

"*Declaration, to be read by all Curates upon the publishing of the Bible in English.*" Cleop. E. v. f. 327. British Museum. Original. Strype's Memoirs of Abp. Cranmer, Vol. II. App. No. 23. pp. 735, 6. Ed. Oxon. 1840.

"WHERE it hath pleased the king's majesty, our most dread sovereign lord and supreme head under God of this church of England, for a declaration of the great zeal he beareth to the setting forth of God's word, and to the virtuous maintenance of his commonwealth, to permit and command the bible, being translated into our mother-tongue, to be sincerely taught and declared by us the curates, and to be openly laid forth in every parish-church: to the intent that all his good subjects, as well by reading thereof, as by hearing the true explanation of the same, may first learn their duties to Almighty God and his majesty, and every of us charitably to use other; and then applying themselves to do according to that they shall hear and learn, may both speak and do christianly, and in all things as it beseemeth christian men: because his highness very much desireth that this thing, being by him most godly begun and set forward, may of all you be received as is aforesaid; his majesty hath willed and commanded this to be declared unto you, that his grace's pleasure and high commandment is, that in the reading and hearing thereof, first most humbly and reverently using and addressing yourselves unto it, you shall have always in your remembrance and memories, that all things contained in this book is the undoubted will, law, and commandment of Almighty God, the only and straight mean to know the goodness and benefits of God towards us, and the true duty of every christian man to serve him accordingly: and that therefore reading this book with such mind and firm faith as is aforesaid, you shall first endeavour yourselves to conform your own livings and conversation to the contents of the same; and so by your good and virtuous example to encourage your wives, children, and servants to

it chance that any doubt or question do arise, or seem to the readers and hearers of the said bible by reason of the text, then they always, for the declaration of the said doubts and questions, to resort unto such preachers as shall be lawfully admitted to preach. Which manner of reading and using of the bible I pray you, my lord, that now, in the absence of my commissary, the same may by your authority be published in your church and all other churches within the marches of Calyce, with all convenient expedition. Thus, my lord, right heartily fare you well. At Croydon, the 13th day of July. [1539.]

[1] I pray your lordship to send unto me with expedition other articles which you have against Rauff Hare[2], or Broke, if you have any against them, specially since the king's pardon, other than you have before sent hither; for the mo matters that be against them, the more it is to their condemnation.

Your loving friend,

T. Cantuarien.

*To the right honourable my lord Lyle, the king's deputy at Calyce.*

---

## CCLVIII. TO CRUMWELL.

State Paper Office. Miscellaneous Letters. Temp. Hen. VIII. Third Series. Vol. IX. Original. State Papers, Vol. I. Part. II. Lett. xcii. Todd's Life of Cranmer, Vol. I. p. 129.

My very singular good lord, after my most hearty commendations; these shall be to signify unto your lordship, that I have overseen the Primer[3] which you sent unto me,

---

live well and christianly, according to the rule thereof.

"And if at any time by reading any doubt shall come to any of you, touching the sense and meaning of any part thereof; that then, not giving too much to your own minds, fantasies, and opinions, nor having thereof any open reasoning in your open taverns or alehouses, ye shall have recourse to such learned men as be or shall be authorised to preach and declare the same: so that avoiding all contentions and disputations in such alehouses, and other places unmeet for such conferences, and submitting your opinions to the judgments of such learned men as shall be appointed in this behalf, his grace may well perceive, that you use this most high benefit quietly and charitably every one of you, to the edifying of himself, his wife, and family, in all things answering to his highness' good opinion conceived of you, in the advancement of virtue and suppressing of vice; without failing to use such discreet quietness and sober moderation in the premises, as is aforesaid; as you tender his grace's pleasure, and intend to avoid his high indignation, and the peril and danger that may ensue to you and every of you for the contrary.

"And God save the king."

Also in "a proclamation," (Regist. Bonner, f. 21) "ordained by the king's majesty, with the advice of his honourable council, for the bible of the largest and greatest volume to be had in every church, devised the sixth day of May, the 33rd year [A.D. 1541] of the king's most gracious reign," it is commanded that "by the injunctions,—set forth by the authority of the king's majesty, supreme head of the church of this his realm of England—the king's royal majesty intended that his loving subjects should have and use the commodities of the reading of the said bibles......humbly, meekly, reverently, and obediently; and not that any of them should read the said bibles, with high and loud voices, in time of the celebration of the holy mass, and other divine services used in the church; or that any his lay subjects, reading the same, should presume to take upon them any common disputation, argument, or exposition of the mysteries therein contained, but that every such layman should humbly, meekly, and reverently read the same for his own instruction, edification, and amendment of his life, according to God's holy word therein mentioned." Burnet's Hist. of Reformat. Vol. I. App. Book III. No. 24. pp. 378, 9. Ed. Oxon. 1829. In the "admonition and advertisement given [A.D. 1542] by Bonner, bishop of London," (Regist. Bonner) "to all readers of this bible in the English tongue," it was also advised, "that no number of people be specially congregate therefore to make a multitude; and that no exposition be made thereupon, otherwise than it is declared by the book itself; and that especially regard be had, that no reading thereof be used, allowed, and with noise in the time of any divine service or sermon; or that in the same be used any disputation, contention, or any other misdemeanour." Id. Vol. I. App. Book III. No. 25. p. 380, 1. Vid. Cranmer's Preface to the Bible, pp. 118—125, supra.]

[[1] This paragraph is in the archbishop's hand.]

[[2] Foxe gives a long account of the examinations of Ralph Hare, a private soldier, and of Thomas Brooke, (vid. Letter CCLVI. p. 390.) and others, "before the archbishop of Canterbury, the bishop of Winchester, the bishop of Chichester, and ten others, appointed by the king's majesty's commission for the examination of them," under A. D. 1544. Acts and Monuments, pp. 1224, 5. Ed. Lond. 1583.]

[[3] This letter is placed under A.D. 1537, in the State Papers, (Vol. I. Part II. p. 559) with the following note: "The Primer here alluded to is probably that which was printed in English and Latin, by Robert Redman, in 1537. There was one printed by John Byddell, in 1535; but that could not be the edition here referred to,......Crumwell had not then become keeper of the privy seal." Cranmer, however, writes July 21, 1537, to Crumwell, beseeching him "to be intercessor unto the king's highness for us all, that we may have his grace's licence to depart for this time, until his

and therein I have noted and amended such faults as are most worthy of reformation: divers things there are besides therein, which, if before the printing of the book had been committed unto me to oversee, I would have amended; howbeit they be not of that importance, but that for this time they may be well enough permitted and suffered to be read of the people: and the book of itself, no doubt, is very good and commendable. Thus, my lord, most heartily fare you well. At Croydon, the xxiith day of July. [1539.]

Your own ever assured,

T. CANTUARIEN.

*To the right honourable and my singular good lord, my lord privy seal.*

---

## CCLIX. TO LORD LISLE[4].

State Paper Office. Lisle Papers, Vol. II. No. 73. Original.

MY lord, in my right hearty wise I commend me to you. And whereas Rauf Hare with other are enjoined penance to be done in Calice according to such form and manner as I have prescribed in my late letters to you directed; forsomuch as they do fear to be imprisoned and farther corrected by you and the council; I shall desire you, my lord, although I myself suspect no such thing by you, that they may do their penance quietly without farther let or perturbation, so that they may go and come freely; for else it may be thought that justice is not indifferently ministered. Howbeit, I know your lordship's discretion is such that there need no such monition in this behalf. Thus, my lord, right heartily fare you well. At Lambeth, the 28th day of July. [1539.]

Your loving friend,

T. CANTUARIEN.

*To my very loving lord my lord Lisle, lord deputy of Calice.*

---

## CCLX. TO CRUMWELL.

State Paper Office. Ibid. Original.

MY very singular good lord, after my most hearty commendations; these shall be to signify unto your lordship, that it chanced in time of my being at Lambeth on Sunday at night last past, between ten and eleven of the clock of the same night, a priest and a woman were very suspiciously taken at Croidon by the constable there, and by the said constable kept in ward until my coming home, which was on Monday last past; since which time I have examined both parties, as farther your lordship shall perceive by their examinations, which I send unto you herewithal. And forasmuch as there is no commission out as yet for the due correction and punishment of such offenders according to the act[5] in this behalf, I shall desire your lordship to advertise me with convenient

---

grace's further pleasure be known; for they die [of the plague] almost every where in London, Westminster, and in Lambeth they die at my gate, even in the next house to me." Vid. Letter CXC. p. 338. The probability, therefore, is, that this letter was written two years later than that above referred to, and that the Primer, of which the archbishop writes as having been sent to him for revision, was that printed by John Maylart for John Waylande in 1539, with this title: "The Primer in English, most necessary for the education of children, abstracted out of the Manual of Prayers, or Primer in English and Latin, set forth by John [Hilsey], late bishop of Rochester, at the commandment of the right hon. lord Thomas Crumwell, lord privy seal," &c. Descriptions of the smaller and larger work of the bishop of Rochester may be found in Ames' Typogr. Antiq. Vol. III. p. 518. Ed. Lond. (Dibdin.) 1812—1819.]

[[4] This letter has not appeared in any former collection.]

[[5] Act of the Six Articles. "All the marriages of priests are declared void; and if any priest did still keep any such woman, whom he had so married, and lived familiarly with her, as with his wife, he was to be judged a felon: and if a priest lived carnally with any other woman, he was upon the first conviction to forfeit his benefices, goods, and chattels, and to be imprisoned during the king's pleasure; and upon the second conviction, was to suffer as a felon. The women so offending were also to be punished in the same manner as the priests." Burnet's Hist. of Reformat. Vol. I. p. 519. Ed. Oxon. 1829.]

expedition of the king's grace's pleasure, how and in what manner they shall be ordered. And as concerning the woman, if it be true which she hath confessed, as it seemeth to be, then she hath deserved somewhat the more favour for the plain confession of the truth. Thus, my lord, right heartily fare you well. At Croidon, the xxxti day of July. [1539.]

Your own assured ever,

T. CANTUARIEN.

*To my very singular good lord, my lord privy seal.*

State Paper Office. Ibid. Original.

[EXAMINATIONS OF NICOLAS SOMER AND JULIAN BAYLIE, 28 JULY, 1539. INCLOSED IN CRANMER'S LETTER OF 30 JULY.]

*The Examynation of sir Nicolas Somer, chauntrie priest of saint Nicolas Chauntrie in Croydon, the* 28 *day of July, Anno Reg. R. H. VIII.* 31.

Examyned, saith apon his othe, that he spake not with Julian Baily sith the 12th day of July untill this last nyght paste, and that he never sent unto her sith the said 12th daye untill aboute 10 dayes agoo, at what tyme he sent unto her, by a child callid Anne Bailie, a blew lace with a treu love, whiche she had sent unto hym aboute a twelve moneth and a half past with this message, "I have sente you blewe bycause you should be treu." And moreover syns the 12th day of July she never sent unto hym any thing or message. Nevertheles about 6 daies paste the said Anne seyd that she marvelid whie he should be angrie, seyng she hadd not deservyd his angar. And he gave her no occasion to thinke he was angrie with her, saving that he loked not upon her with so mery a countenaunce as he was wonte to do, bycause he would have had her to have withdrawne her mynde frome hym.

Moreover he saith, he had never . . . . . . with her syns the tyme of my lord of Canterbury's injunctions to him, which were that thei should not company together. Ferthermore he saith, that he never talked with the said Juliane concernyng thacte of Parliament, that preistes should have no wyves nor concubynes. Moreover he saith that yesternyght before 11 of the clocke the said Juliane came unto his chamber wyndow, he being in his bedde, as she said, only to knowe wherfore he was grevid with her. And whan she knocked at the dore, he came to the wyndowe and asked who was there; and she said, "I," and asked him howe he did. He answered, the wurse for her. Than she asked, why soo? to whom he said, bycause she was a nawtie hore: than said she, she was no mannys hore but his. And as she said soo, one knocked at Curties doore nexte house unto her mother's; then said she, "Alas! what shall I do?" and this deponent badd her shifte for her self; and so she wente over the pale and departid, and he neither opened the dore nor came forthe to her[1].

## CCLXI. TO CRUMWELL.

State Paper Office. Ibid. Original.

MY very singular good lord, after my most hearty commendations; these shall be to advertise your lordship, that I have received your letters for the preferment of Mr doctor Peter[2] unto doctor Wotton's[3] room of the faculties, when it shall chance by the promotion of the said doctor Wotton to be void. Surely, my lord, I would be as glad of Mr Peter's preferment as of any man's living to that office, for such good qualities as I know in him of old; but indeed, my lord, I have promised it unto my commissary doctor Nevynson[4], who hath of me twenty marks by year, and can spend no penny, with condition that he should surrender it into my hands when I had given him a benefice: wherefore if your lordship of your goodness will provide some benefice for my commissary, I shall both satisfy your lordship's request, and deliver myself of my promise:

[[1] In the examination of Julian Baylie, which follows the above among the State Papers, the confession is more circumstantial than Sir Nicholas's, and in some important points contradictory to it; but the whole character of it is too gross to be here printed.]

[[2] Vid. Letter CLX. p. 315.]

[[3] [A.D. 1538.] "This year, Oct. 6, I meet with a commission 'ad facultates,' granted by the archbishop to a famous man, Nicholas Wotton, LL.D., a man of great learning......In this office he constituted Wotton his commissary or deputy for the term of his natural life. He succeeded Edmund Boner, master of the archbishop's faculties, now preferred to the bishopric of Hereford." Strype's Mem. of Abp. Cranmer, Vol. I. p. 102 Ed. Oxon. 1840. [A.D. 1539] "he was appointed archdeacon of Gloucester, and refused a bishopric." Chalmers, Biogr. Dict. *art.* Wotton. Le Neve's Fasti, p. 104.]

[[4] Probably Christopher Newinson or Nevison, LL.D. one of the royal visitors "appointed by the king's majesty, to visit the churches of Westminster, London, Norwich, and Ely;" and one of "the honourable umpires" at Oxford, A.D. 1549, in "the disputation concerning transubstantiation ......wherein P. Martyr the respondent did acquit himself very sufficiently." Strype's Eccl. Mem. Vol. II. part I. p. 74. Ed. Oxon. 1822. Mem. of Abp. Cranmer, Vol. I. p. 286.]

and this I write, by cause I have many to provide for, and little to provide them of. As concerning the king's majesty, I will not strive with his highness: howbeit I suppose the gift should appertain unto me, considering Mr Wotton hath it but only at my pleasure. Thus, my lord, most heartily fare you well. At Ford, the xth day of September. [1539.]

Your own assured ever,

T. Cantuarien.

*To my very singular good lord, my lord privy seal.*

---

### CCLXII. TO CRUMWELL.

State Paper Office. Ibid. Original.

My very singular good lord, after my right hearty commendations unto your lordship, these shall be to desire you to have in your remembrance sir Henry Corbett[5], the Dutch priest, for whom I have sued divers times unto your lordship for some honest stipend, beseeching your lordship to move the king's grace in his favour in this behalf. I ensure you he is almost in despair of a living, forsomuch as he supposeth your lordship hath utterly forgotten him; and for so doing your lordship shall not only do a very good deed, and dispatch yourself of an importunate suitor, but also discharge me of such costs as I am at in keeping of him. Thus, my lord, right heartily fare you well. From Croydon, the 7th day of October. [1539.]

Your own ever assured,

T. Cantuarien.

*To my very singular good lord, my lord privy seal.*

---

### CCLXIII. TO CRUMWELL[6].

From a copy of an original letter of Abp. Cranmer, formerly in the possession of Mr Leman of the State Paper Office.

My very singular good lord, after my right hearty commendations unto your lordship, these shall be to signify unto the same, that all such examinations, inquisitions, and other such writings as I have concerning any matters of Calyce, be in the hands and custody of my register, Antony Hussey, unto whom I have direct my letters, that he shall with all expedition repair unto your lordship with all such writings as he hath concerning the said matters. Thus, my lord, right heartily fare you well. At Croydon, this 2nd of November. [1539.]

Your own assured ever,

T. Cantuarien.

*To my very singular good lord, my lord privy seal.*

---

### CCLXIV. TO CRUMWELL[7].

State Paper Office. Ibid. Original. State Papers, Vol. I. part ii. Let. CXVI. pp. 589, 90.

My very singular good lord, after my most hearty commendations; these shall be to signify unto your lordship, that Bartelett and Edward Whitechurche hath been with me,

[[5] See Letter CCL. p. 386.]

[[6] This letter has not been printed in any former collection. The date is probably A.D. 1539, and the letter itself may refer to the examinations of Hare, Brook, and others. Vid. Letters CCLVI. CCLVII. p. 390.]

[[7] The date assigned to this letter in the State Papers is A.D. 1538, which in all probability arose from "the popular mistake of ascribing the bibles issuing from the press in 1539 to Cranmer." The great bible, which appeared April, A.D. 1540, as observed by Dr Jenkyns, is undoubtedly that here referred to by the archbishop; and his allusion in the above letter to the preface, which was first prefixed to that edition, confirms the supposition that it had reference only to this copy. For a full account of this bible and the circumstances connected with its publication, vid. Anderson's Annals of the English Bible, Vol. II. pp. 86, 7, 130, et sqq. Vid. also Todd's Life of Abp. Cranmer, Vol. I. p. 238. Strype's Mem. of Cranmer, Vol. I. p. 120. State Papers, Vol. I. pp. 589, 90. Lewis's Hist. of Eng. Bibles, pp. 121, 136. Ed. Lond. 1818. Cotton's List of Editions, pp. 6, 118. Ed. Oxon. 1821.]

and have by their accounts declared the expenses and charges of the printing of the great bibles; and by the advice of Bartelett I have appointed them to be sold for 13*s*. 4*d*. apiece, and not above. Howbeit Whitechurche informeth me, that your lordship thinketh it a more convenient price to have them sold at 10*s*. apiece, which in respect of the great charges, both of the paper, which in very deed is substantial and good, and other great hinderances, Whitechurche and his fellow[1] thinketh it a small price. Nevertheless they are right well contented to sell them for 10*s*., so that you will be so good lord unto them as to grant henceforth none other licence to any other printer saving to them, for the printing of the said bible; for else they think that they shall be greatly hindered thereby, if any other should print, they sustaining such charges as they already have done. Wherefore I shall beseech your lordship, in consideration of their travail in this behalf, to tender their requests[2]; and they have promised me to print in the end of their bibles the price thereof, to the intent the king's liege people shall not henceforth be deceived of their price.

Farther, if your lordship hath known the king's highness' pleasure concerning the preface[3] of the bible which I sent to you to oversee, so that his grace doth allow the same, I pray you that the same may be delivered unto the said Whitchurche unto printing, trusting that it shall both encourage many slow readers, and also stay the rash judgments of them that read therein. Thus our Lord have your good lordship in his blessed tuition. At Lambeth, the 14th day of November. [1539.]

Your own ever assured,
T. CANTUARIEN.

*To my singular good lord, my lord privy seal.*

---

## CCLXV. TO CRUMWELL.

Cott. MSS. Cleop. E. IV. f. 302. British Museum. Original. Burnet's Hist. of Reformat. Vol. III. part II. Book iii. No. 65. pp. 213—216. Ed. Oxon. 1829.

MY very singular good lord, after my most hearty commendations; these shall be to advertise your lordship, that I have received your letters dated the xxvii. day of November; and therewith a bill concerning the device[4] for the new establishment to be made in the metropolitan church of Canterbury; by which your lordship requireth mine advice thereupon by writing, for our mutual consents.

Surely, my lord, as touching the book drawn and the order of the same, I think that it will be a very substantial and godly foundation: nevertheless in my opinion the prebendaries, which be allowed 40*l*. apiece yearly, might be altered to a more expedient use. And this is my consideration; for having experience both in time past and also in our days, how the said sect of prebendaries have not only spent their time in much idleness, and their substance in superfluous belly cheer, I think it not to be a convenient state or degree to be maintained and established, considering first, that commonly a prebendary is neither a learner, nor teacher, but a good viander. Then by the same name they look to be chief, and to bear all the whole rule and preeminence in the college where they be resident: by means whereof the younger, of their own nature given more to pleasure, good cheer, and pastime, than to abstinence, study, and learning, shall easily be brought

---

[1 i. e. Grafton. Vid. Anderson's Annals of the English Bible, Vol. II. p. 87. Neither of the editions which appeared in A. D. 1539 appear to have been printed by Berthelet and Whitechurch jointly. State Papers, Vol. I. pp. 589, 90.]

[2 "This advice was followed by a proclamation, to which the date of 14 Nov. 31 Hen. VIII, (i. e. 1539) is assigned by Rymer (Vol. XIV. p. 649). The 14th of Nov. is more likely to be the true date of the document; for it would then precede (as it probably did) all the editions of Cranmer's bible, and would be contemporaneous with this volume, which was manifestly written before the first of those editions was published. This proclamation prohibited any bible being printed in English for five years without Crumwell's licence." State Papers, Vol. I. pp. 561, 590. For "the king's letters patents for printing the bible in English," and "the proclamation ordained by the king's majesty, with the advice of his honourable council, for the bible of the largest and greatest volume to be had in every church, devised 6th of May, the 33rd year" of Hen. VIII., vid. Burnet's Hist. of Reformation, Vol. I. part II. Book III. Nos. XV. and XXIV. pp. 291, 2. 376—80. Ed. Oxon. 1829.]

[3 Vid. pp. 118—125 supra.]

[4 The bill concerning the device is printed after this letter.]

from their books to follow the appetite and example of the said prebendaries, being their heads and rulers. And the state of prebendaries hath been so excessively abused, that when learned men hath been admitted unto such room, many times they have desisted from their good and godly studies, and all other christian exercises of preaching and teaching. Wherefore, if it may so stand with the king's gracious pleasure, I would wish that not only the name of a prebendary were exiled his grace's foundations, but also the superfluous conditions of such persons. I cannot deny but that the beginning of prebendaries was no less purposed for the maintenance of good learning and good conversation of living, than religious men were: but forasmuch as both be gone from their first estate and order, and the one is found like offender with the other, it maketh no great matter if they perish both together: for, to say the truth, it is an estate which St Paul, reckoning up the degrees and estates allowed in his time, could not find in the church of Christ. And I assure you, my lord, that I think it will better stand with the maintenance of christian religion, that in the stead of the said prebendaries were twenty divines at £10. apiece, like as it is appointed to be at Oxford and Cambridge; and forty students in the tongues, and sciences, and French, to have 10 marks apiece; for if such a number be not there resident, to what intent should so many readers be there? And surely it were great pity that so many good lectures should be there read in vain: for as for your prebendaries, they cannot attend to apply lectures, for making of good cheer. And as for your sixty children in grammar, their master and their usher be daily otherwise occupied in the rudiments of grammar, than that they may have space and time to hear the lectures: so that to these good lectures is prepared no convenient auditory. And therefore, my lord, I pray you let it be considered, what a great loss it will be to have so many good lectures read without profit to any, saving to the six preachers. Farther, as concerning the reader of divinity and humanity, it will not agree well that one man should be a reader of both lectures. For he that studieth in divinity, must leave the reading of profane authors, and shall have as much to do as he can to prepare his lecture to be substantially read. And in like manner, he that readeth in humanity, had not need to alter his study, if he should make an erudite lecture. And therefore in mine opinion it would be two offices for two sundry learned men.

Now concerning the dean and other to be elected into the college, I shall make a bill of all them that I can hear of in Cambridge, Oxford, or elsewhere, meet to put into the said college, after my judgment; and then of the whole number the king's highness may choose the most excellent: assuring you, my lord, that I know no man more meet for the dean's room in England than doctor Crome[5], who by his sincere learning, godly conversation, and good example of living, with his great soberness, hath done unto the king's majesty as good service, I dare say, as any priest in England. And yet his grace daily remembereth all other that doth him service, this man only except, who never had yet, besides his gracious favour, any promotion at his highness' hands. Wherefore, if it would please his majesty to put him in the dean's room, I do not doubt but that he should shew light to all the deans and masters of colleges in this realm. For I know that when he was but president of a college in Cambridge, his house was better ordered than all the houses in Cambridge besides.

And thus, my lord, you have my final advice concerning the premises, which I refer unto the king's grace's judgment, to be allowed or disallowed at his highness' pleasure; sending unto your lordship herewithal the bill again, according to your request. Thus, my lord, most heartily fare you well. At Croydon, the xxix. day of November. [1539.]

Your own ever assured,

T. CANTUARIEN.

*To my very singular good lord, my lord privy seal.*

---

[[5] Dr Crome was not appointed.—Vid. Examination of Roland Philips, p. 339, supra. *n.* 9. "About the month of December, A.D. 1545, the next Lent following, Dr Crome preaching in the Mercers' Chapel, among other reasons and persuasions to rouse the people from the vain opinions of purgatory, inferred this,.......that if trentals and chauntry masses could avail the souls in purgatory, then did the parliament not well in giving away monasteries, colleges, and chauntries, which served principally to that purpose. But if the parliament did well (as no man could deny) in dissolving

Cott. MSS. Cleop. E. IV. f. 301. British Museum. Original.

"CHRIST'S CHURCH, IN CANTERBURY.

| | £. | s. | d. |
|---|---|---|---|
| "First, A provost | 150 | 0 | 0 |
| "*Item*, Twelve prebendaries, every of them at 40*l*. by the year, sum | 480 | 0 | 0 |
| "*Item*, Six preachers, every of them 20*l*. a year | 120 | 0 | 0 |
| "*Item*, A reader of humanity, in Greek, by year | 30 | 0 | 0 |
| "*Item*, A reader in divinity in Hebrew by year | 30 | 0 | 0 |
| "*Item*, A reader both in divinity and humanity, in Latin, by the year | 40 | 0 | 0 |
| "*Item*, A reader of civil | 20 | 0 | 0 |
| "*Item*, A reader of physic | 20 | 0 | 0 |
| "*Item*, Twenty students in divinity, to be found ten at Oxford, and ten at Cambridge, every of them 10*l*. by the year | 200 | 0 | 0 |
| "*Item*, Sixty scholars to be taught both grammar and logic in Hebrew, Greek, and Latin, every of them five marks by the year | 200 | 0 | 0 |
| "*Item*, A school-master 20*l*. and an usher 10*l*. by the year | 30 | 0 | 0 |
| "*Item*, Eight petty canons to sing in the choir, every of them 10*l*. by the year | 80 | 0 | 0 |
| "*Item*, Twelve laymen to sing also, and serve in the choir, every of them 6*l*. 13*s*. 4*d*. by the year | 80 | 0 | 0 |
| "*Item*, Ten choristers, every of them five marks by the year | 33 | 2 | 4 |
| "*Item*, A master of the children | 10 | 0 | 0 |
| "*Item*, A gospeler | 6 | 13 | 4 |
| "*Item*, An epistler | 5 | 6 | 8 |
| "*Item*, Two sacristans | 6 | 13 | 4 |
| "*Item*, One chief butler, his wages and diets | 4 | 13 | 4 |
| "*Item*, One under butler, his wages and diets | 3 | 6 | 8 |
| "*Item*, A cater to buy their diets, for his wages, diets, and making of his books | 6 | 13 | 4 |
| "*Item*, One chief cook, his wages and diets | 4 | 13 | 4 |
| "*Item*, One under cook, his wages and diets | 3 | 6 | 8 |
| "*Item*, Two porters | 10 | 0 | 0 |
| "*Item*, Twelve poor men, being old and serving men, decayed by the wars or in the king's service, every of them at 6*l*. 13*s*. 4*d*. by the year | 80 | 0 | 0 |
| "*Item*, To be distributed yearly in alms | 100 | 0 | 0 |
| "*Item*, For yearly reparations | 100 | 0 | 0 |
| "*Item*, Six to be employed yearly, for making and emending of highways | 40 | 0 | 0 |
| "*Item*, A steward of the lands | 6 | 13 | 4 |
| "*Item*, An auditor | 10 | 0 | 0 |
| "*Item*, For the provost's expenses in receiving the rents and surveying the lands, by the year | 6 | 13 | 4 |

Harl. MSS. 419. f. 115. British Museum. Original.

"At what time the Cathedral Church of Canterbury [was] newly erected, altered, and changed from monks to secular men of the clergy, in the time of king Henry the VIII., as to prebendaries, canons, petty canons, choristers, and scholars, there were present at that erection Thomas Cranmer, archbishop of Canterbury, the lord Riche, chancellor of the court of the augmentation of the revenues of the crown, sir Christopher Hallis, knight, the king's attorney, sir Antony Senteleger, knight, with divers other commissioners. And taking upon them to nominate and elect such convenient and apt persons, as should serve for the furniture of the said cathedral church, according to the new foundation, it came to pass, that when they should elect the children of the grammar-school, there were of the commissioners mo than one or two, which would have none admitted but younger brethren and gentlemen's sons. As for other husbandmen's children, they were more meet, they said, for the plough and to be artificers, than to occupy the place of the learned sort; so that they wished none else to be put to school but only gentlemen's children.

"Whereunto that most reverend father, Thomas Cranmer, archbishop of Canterbury, being of a contrary mind, said, that he thought it not indifferent so to order the matter. For (said he), poor men's children are many times endued with more singular gifts of nature, which are also the gifts of God, as with eloquence, memory, apt pronunciation, sobriety, with such like, and also commonly more given to apply their study, than is the gentleman's son delicately educated.

"Whereunto it was on the other part replied, that it was meet for the ploughman's son to go to plough, and the artificer's son to apply the trade of his parent's vocation, and the gentlemen's children are meet to have the knowledge of government and rule in the commonwealth: for we have as much need of ploughmen as of any other state, and all sorts of men may not go to school.

"I grant (quoth the archbishop) much of your meaning herein, as needful in a commonwealth; but yet utterly to exclude the ploughman's son and the poor man's son from the benefit of learning, as though they were unworthy to have the gifts of the Holy Ghost bestowed upon them, as well as upon others, is as much to say, as that Almighty God should not be at liberty to bestow his great gifts of grace upon any person, nor no where else but as we and other men shall appoint them to be employed, according to our fancy, and not according to his most godly will and pleasure; who giveth his gifts, both of learning and other perfections in all sciences, unto all kinds and states of people indifferently. Even so doth he many times withdraw from them and their posterity again those beneficial gifts, if they be not thankful. If we should shut up into a strait corner the bountiful grace of the Holy Ghost, and thereupon attempt to build our fancies, we should make as perfect a work thereof, as those that took upon them to build the tower of Babelon. For God would so provide, that the offspring of other best born children should peradventure become most unapt to learn and very dull, as I myself have seen no small number of them very dull and without all manner of

---

them, and bestowing the same upon the king; then is it a plain case, that such chauntries and private masses do nothing confer to relieve them in purgatory. This dilemma of Dr Crome, no doubt, was insoluble. But notwithstanding, the charitable prelates, for all the king's late exhortation unto charity, were so charitable to him, that on Easter next they brought him 'coram nobis,' where they so handled him that they made him to recant. And if he had not, they would have dissolved him and his argument in burning fire." Foxe's Acts and Monuments, p. 1234. Ed. Lond. 1583.]

capacity. And, to say the truth, I take it that none of us all here, being gentlemen born, (as I think), but had our beginning that way from a low and base parentage: and through the benefit of learning and other civil knowledge, for the most part, all gentles ascend to their estate.

"Then it was again answered, that the most part of the nobility came up by feat of arms and martial acts.

"As though (quoth the archbishop) that the noble captain was always unfurnished of good learning and knowledge, to persuade and dissuade his army rhetorically, which rather that way is brought unto authority than else his manly looks. To conclude, the poor man's son by pains-taking will for the most part be learned, when the gentleman's son will not take the pains to get it. And we are taught by the scriptures, that Almighty God raiseth up from the dunghill and setteth him in high authority; and, when so it pleaseth him, of his divine providence, deposeth princes unto a right humble and poor estate. Wherefore if the gentleman's son be apt to learning, let him be admitted: if not apt, let the poor man's child apt enter his room. With such like words in effect."

---

## CCLXVI. TO CRUMWELL[1].

State Paper Office. Miscellaneous Letters. Temp. Hen. VIII. Third series. Vol. IX. Original.

My very singular good lord, after most hearty recommendations; this shall be to signify unto your lordship, that at my first being archbishop of Canterbury, my lord of Wiltshire desired me to grant unto master Heath the deanery of South Mallyng, which I did; and after that time master Heath was much slandered with the name thereof, and called master dean of South Mallyng, until such time as I gave the advowson thereof unto you, by the which Mr Herytage obtained the same, and so master Heath lost it at that time. In consideration whereof, forasmuch as Mr Heath was then disappointed thereof by your lordship's suit, and considering also how small a living he hath, and that he had never but one small benefice of my gift, and also considering how meet a man he is to have some good thing, I trust, knowing my mind that I am purposed to bestow this on him, you will be very glad thereof, and not require it from him. I consider how necessary it were for your lordship to plant your friends about those parties, forasmuch as you have now so much land there; and therefore I would very fain satisfy your request herein: but I trust surely that you can put in that deanery no man that shall be more assured unto you, and do you better service, than Mr Heath shall do. Thus Almighty God preserve your lordship in long health and wealth to his pleasure! From Ford, the 18th day of December. [1539.]

Your own ever assured,

T. Cantuarien.

*To my very singular good lord, my lord privy seal.*

---

## CCLXVII. TO CRUMWELL.

State Paper Office. Ibid. Original.

My singular good lord, in my most hearty wise I commend me to your lordship; and whereas I am informed that this bearer Edward Askew, my servant, son unto Sir William Askewe, knight, is by some nobleman preferred unto the room of one of these new spears[2] in the court, which, because it is done both without my knowledge and his, I shall beseech you, my lord, inasmuch as I have no friend to sue unto for me and mine, but only unto your lordship, that you will, at this my request, bear unto him your lawful favour and furtherance in the same; assuring your lordship that he, the young man, is of a very gentle nature, right forward, and of good activity, so that I think he shall be meet to furnish such a room, and to do unto the king's majesty diligent and faithful service. Thus, my lord, right heartily fare you well. At Ford, the 28th day of December. [1539.]

Your own assured ever,

T. Cantuarien.

*To my very singular good lord, my lord privy seal.*

---

[1 This letter has not been printed in any previous collection.]

[2 "In December [A.D. 1539] were appointed to wait on the king's highness' person, fifty gentlemen called pensioners or spears, like as they were in the first year of the king." Hall's Chronicle, fol. ccxxxvii. 2. Ed. Lond. 1548.]

## CCLXVIII. TO CRUMWELL.

State Paper Office. Ibid. Original. Todd's Life of Abp. Cranmer, Vol. I. p. 206.

My very singular good lord, after my most hearty commendations; these shall be to advertise your lordship, that I have received by my servant Eaton fifty sovereigns from you, which shall be delivered to-morrow, and presented unto my lady Anne's[1] grace, according to your lordship's advertisement in your letters; and if I may compass and bring it to pass, the town of Canterbury shall put thereunto fifty angels, to be all together presented in one cup. And whereas this bearer Mr Pheneux, your servant, by his demore here in giving attendance upon me whiles my said lady Anny's grace was received at Canterbury, hath longer absented himself from you than he thought to have done, I trust your lordship will accept the same in the best part; assuring you, my lord, that in case he and other gentlemen of the country, with mine own retinue, had not the better assisted me, over and besides the number appointed, I should have received her grace but with a slender company. For the whole number appointed to me, besides mine own company, was not six score, and yet some of them failed; so that if, partly by mine own company, and partly by other gentlemen's assistance, it had not been supplied, I should not have received her with a convenient number. Thus, my lord, most heartily fare you well. At Canterbury, the xxixth day of December.

Your own ever assured,

T. Cantuarien.

*To my very singular good lord,*
*my lord privy seal.*

---

## CCLXIX. TO CRUMWELL.

State Paper Office. Ibid. Original.

My very singular good lord, in my most hearty wise I commend me unto your lordship; always thanking you for your benevolence towards me and my poor servant, for which I am not able to recompense as my mind is; signifying to your lordship, that you shall receive of my servant Nevell this bearer £20. for your half year's fee[2] now due. And whereas my said servant Nevell informeth me, that Mr Chancellor of the Augmentation told him, that the king's majesty was content that he should have some recompence for his farm of the parsonage of Bowghton[3]; these shall be to desire you, my lord, to bear him your lawful favour for his furtherance unto such recompence: for the which you shall bind him to be at your lordship's commandment during his life. Thus, my lord, right heartily fare you well. At Ford, the xx. day of January. [1539-40.]

Your own assured ever,

Thomas Cantuarien.

*To my very singular good lord, my*
*lord privy seal.*

---

[1 i. e. Anne of Cleves. For an account of her reception at Calais, A.D. 1539, with "the order taken for the receiving" her "repairing into England," with "the names of them which should receive" her, "and wait on the king Henry VIII." including the archbishop of Canterbury, the bishops of Chichester, Richard Sampson; of Ely, Thomas Goodrich, lord chancellor; of Durham, Cuthbert Tonstall; of Hereford, John Harley; of Lincoln, John Longland; of St Asaph, Robert Warton, or Parfew; vid. Chronicle of Calais, pp. 167, et sqq., Camden Soc. Ed. 1846; in which (p. 169) "it is appointed that beyond Canterbury, in such place as shall be convenient, the archbishop of Canterbury, certain other bishops, and gentlemen assigned to keep her company, shall meet her grace, and so with the rest convey her to her lodging in Canterbury, and in like manner to attend upon her until her meeting with the king's highness." These documents are printed from Harl. MSS. 295. f. 152. b, 296. f. 169, and 171, and Cotton. MSS. Vitellius, c. xi. f. 220. b. 222, preserved in the British Museum. Hall gives a narrative of the progress of the princess from Calais to Greenwich, and says: "On which day (Monday) [Dec. 29, A.D. 1539] for all the storm that then was, she marched toward Canterbury, and on Baram down met her the archbishop of Canterbury, accompanied with the bishop of Ely, St Asse, St Davies, and Dover, and a great company of gentlemen well apparelled, and so brought her to St Austen's without Canterbury, where she lay that night." Hall's Chronicle, fol. ccxxxviii. The above letter was consequently written on the same day of the arrival at Canterbury.]

[2 Besides the other offices which Crumwell held, he was also steward of the liberties of the archbishop, and master of his game. The fee above named may have had reference to one of these appointments. Vid. Letters CCLI. CCLIII. pp. 386, 388.]

[3 Vid. Letter CCXXXIII. p. 374.]

## CCLXX. TO KING HENRY VIII.[4]

Kennet's Hist. of England, Vol. II. Lord Herbert's Life of Henry VIII. p. 223, Ed. Lond. 1706.

. . . . . . . I heard yesterday in your grace's council, that he [Crumwell] is a traitor: yet who cannot be sorrowful and amazed that he should be a traitor against your majesty, he that was so advanced by your majesty; he whose surety was only by your majesty; he who loved your majesty (as I ever thought) no less than God; he who studied always to set forwards whatsoever was your majesty's will and pleasure; he that cared for no man's displeasure to serve your majesty; he that was such a servant, in my judgment, in wisdom, diligence, faithfulness, and experience, as no prince in this realm ever had; he that was so vigilant to preserve your majesty from all treasons, that few could be so secretly conceived, but he detected the same in the beginning? If the noble princes of memory, king John, Henry the Second, and Richard II. had had such a councillor about them, I suppose that they should never have been so traitorously abandoned and overthrown as those good princes were. . . . . . . I loved him as my friend, for so I took him to be; but I chiefly loved him for the love which I thought I saw him bear ever towards your grace, singularly above all other. But now, if he be a traitor, I am sorry that ever I loved him or trusted him, and I am very glad that his treason is discovered in time: but yet again I am very sorrowful; for who shall your grace trust hereafter, if you might not trust him? Alas! I bewail and lament your grace's chance herein, I wot not whom your grace may trust. But I pray God continually night and day, to send such a counsellor in his place whom your grace may trust, and who for all his qualities can and will serve your grace like to him, and that will have so much solicitude and care to preserve your grace from all dangers as I ever thought he had . . . . . . [14 June, 1540.]

---

## CCLXXI. TO WRIOTHESLEY[5].

State Paper Office. Domestic Papers, A. D 1534—1540. Vol. III. Original holograph. Todd's Introduction to Cranmer's Defence, p. 73.

MASTER Wrythiosley, after my right hearty commendations; these be to signify unto you, that I have received out of the realm of Pole letters from Dantiscus, bishop of Vermien., who was many years the king of Pole his ambassador unto the emperor, and was with the emperor the same time that I was the king our master his ambassador[6]: in whom I found at that time great humanity and faithfulness; and, as I could perceive, as ready an heart he had to serve the king's majesty our master, as if he had been his own subject; and as lovingly he entreated me, as if he had been my own brother, notwithstanding that we were of two contrary judgments; for he was a mere papist. Nevertheless he would hear me diligently and patiently to say all my mind concerning the bishop of Rome, and seemed many times to condescend unto my judgment, and to allow the same. Howbeit, after he came home into his own country, and had two bishoprics given unto him, "Jordanus conversus est retrorsum:" for he returned again wholly "ad papismum." And now they say that he is the greatest persecutor of God's word that is in all the land of Pole; and you may perceive by his letter, (which herewith you shall receive,) how much he is offended with me, for that, according to God's word, I wrote myself in the subscription of my letter, *ecclesiæ Cantuarien. ministrum.*

Now since I received this letter, I have been much inquieted therewith, considering

---

[4 Lord Herbert merely quotes this fragment from "Records," so that it is doubtful whence he obtained it. The execution of Crumwell, "brought about by means of the bishop of Winchester (Gardiner) and the popish faction," took place on Tower-hill, the 28th July, A.D. 1540. Vid. Strype's Eccl. Mem. Vol. I. p. 561. Ed. Oxon. 1822. Burnet's Hist. of Reformat. Vol. I. p. 569. Ed. Oxon. 1829.]

[5 Sir Thomas Wriothesley "at first was taken into some office belonging to the treasury. . . . . . And when Gardiner went ambassador, he took him along with him. Afterwards he fell under the observation of Crumwell, who was delighted with his wit and dexterity. Then he went ambassador to Holland and Flanders, to the emperor's sister, the queen of Hungary; and after lord Audley's death was advanced to be lord chancellor, and was the root of the noble family of the earls of Southampton." Strype's Eccl. Mem. Vol. III. pp. 466, 7, A. D. 1544. In this year, during the absence of Henry VIII., he was one of the commissioners appointed to superintend the government of the kingdom. He was created earl of Southampton A.D. 1547. Burnet's Hist. of Reformat. Vol. I. p. 63. Vol. II. p. 30.]

[6 Vid. Letters II, III, pp. 231, 2.]

what heinous rumours by mischievous tongues be spread into so far countries of the king's majesty, which would make any true and loving subject's heart bleed in his body to hear or read of his prince. And by cause you should the better perceive the same, I have sent you Dantiscus' own letter[1], interlined in places most notable concerning that matter; desiring you to declare the same to the king's highness at convenient opportunity, and to know his pleasure, whether I shall make any answer unto the said Dantiscus, and what answer I shall make: for the matter is of such importance, that I dare not presume to make a slender answer upon mine own head. Nevertheless, I think it not good to open this matter unto the king's grace, until he be well recovered of his disease, (which I pray God shortly to put away,) lest peradventure it might trouble and move his grace, and rather be occasion of longer continuance of the said disease. And if that had not been, I would have come to the court this day myself; but I thought it very evil that any person or matter should at this present disquiet his grace. Wherefore I refer unto your wisdom to break this matter unto his grace at such time as you shall think most expedient. From Lambith, this saint Matthies day. [21 Sept. 1540.]

Your assured,

T. CANTUARIEN.

*To my loving friend sir Thomas Wrythisley,*
*secretary unto the king's majesty.*

---

## DANTISCUS TO CRANMER.

State Paper Office. Domestic Papers, A. D. 1534-1540. Vol. III. Original.

Rumorem de morte mea ad te, mi humanissime Cramere, perlatum, eo auctum scribis, quod a me intra triennium nullas acceperis. Hoc quidem non incurantia aut mutuæ nostræ amicitiæ oblivione contigit, verum ob similem de te rumorem, qui apud nos percrebuit, quem certe, amantissimus utpote tui, dolenter accepi, *Te, inquam, jussu Regis tui, cum multis aliis bonis viris, præter omnem æquitatem fuisse e viris sublatum.* Quo intime permotus, non secus atque tu meis, ita et ego tuis manibus æternam non semel beatitudinem sum precatus. Qua de re, quum ejusmodi rumor (Deo gratia!) utrique falsus evanuit, gaudendum nobis, et ad pristinum benevolentiæ officium et animo et scripto redeundum est. *Tu tamen, ne te* [*Salamandræ fatum*[2]] *πυραύστου μόρος occupet, quum ea sint apud vos tempora, quæ in nulla prius orbis Christiani regione fuerunt unquam, caveas:* plura adderem, nisi vererer has fraudi tibi futuras, si in alterius quam in tuas manus inciderent.

Quid apud vos agatur, gratius mihi fuisset scire a te, quam de iis qui multa incerta pro certis nobis denunciant. Tot scilicet bonorum Ecclesiæ di[reptiones] . . . . . . . *quæ modum et numerum non habent, in utrumque promiscue sexum supplicia, quodque magis hic omnes in admirationem ac detestationem inducit, tot conjugia, totque contra omnes tum humanas tum etiam divinas leges repudia, quæ tamen, quamvis passim hic in vulgus sparsa, pro veris habentur, apud me adhuc sunt ambigua.* Nonnihil ad credendum me compellit, quod tu, quum sis et Archiepiscopus et regni vestri Primas, Ministrum ecclesiæ tuæ, longe alio quam prius nomine, te subscribis. Ministri quidem sumus omnes ecclesiarum, qui sumus Episcopi; hoc tamen titulo quo Paulus usus est, abuti non deberemus. Is etenim qui speculatur, non est sine ministerio, sua tamen ob id vocatione non privatur. Nos porro hic sub christianissimo pientissimoque rege[3] degentes, Phavorini apud Gellium præcepto, utimur verbis præsentibus, et moribus vivimus antiquis[4], in quibus et vos olim non infelices inter alios mortales fuistis; adeo etiam quemadmodum *recens nosti, quod de insigni ad te conjugio scripserim, hoc si ad eum modum, ut cum Juliacense successisset, in quas me turbas non conjecissem. Eas a me Deus per suam misericordiam avertit. Quem vero apud vos exitum hoc turbulentissimum cum tot commutatis Helenis malum, et hæc tanta et tam impia diritas aliquando habebit, nemo sanæ mentis non videt, quantumvis lento divina ira gradu procedat.* Quam ut ab hac vestra prædivite insula, quæ mihi ob multam humanitatem in ea perceptam carissima est, et a vobis omnibus mihi carissimis, diutissime Dominus Deus contineat, immo nunquam exerceat, impense oro; tantum abest ut quicquam adversi imprecer. Ceterum quod honorificis illis relictis titulis usu receptis adeo me . . . . . . . . . . Magnas gratias habeo, quod puerum, quem Ratisbonæ ad Danubium in Aula Cæsaris quondam famulatui tuo addixeram, adeo liberaliter educari commiseris: hunc revera, quum tuis me verbis et literis salutaret, a facie non minus quam alium quempiam exoticum a me nunquam prius visum, noveram; fuitque eo mihi gratior, quod tua opera et adminiculo in adolescentem, moribus et literis non incultum, excreverit; qui si institutum quod cœpit,

---

[[1] The letter of Dantiscus is subjoined. It has been much injured by damp. The passages in Italic are underlined in the original, evidently by the archbishop.]

[[2] The Latin of this proverb is inserted in Cranmer's own hand above the Greek words.]

[[3] "Sigismund I. a monarch 'modest, humble humane, enlightened, indefatigable, the father of his people.' A victory gained by him over the Waywode of Moldavia in August 1531, is recorded by Dantiscus in a letter printed in Schardii German. Antiq. p. 1275." Jenkyns' Remains of Abp. Cranmer. Vol. I. p. 301.]

[[4] Gellius' Noctes Atticæ, Lib. I. cap. X. p. 66. Ed. Lugd. Bat. 1706.]

prosequi non intermiserit, quod ad reliquum vitæ tempus pertinebit, facile assequetur. Tibi vero iterum atque iterum gratias ago, quod illum, ad meam commendationem et nostræ inter nos amicitiæ rationem, tam benigne et largiter tuo impendio in literarum studiis exercitum foveris, hucque ad me non sine viatico remiseris. Hinc clare liquet Athenæum non recte sensisse, amicos non esse qui procul degunt[5]; quum tu, ab orbe nostro divisus, in hoc juvene, cujus parentes [non] nisi fama agnovi[sti], mihi fueris officiosissimus: proinde ubi vicissim gratum tibi facere, tibique aut tuis ex usu et re esse possum, propensissimam meam offero operam; qua in eventis periculosi hujus temporis, proque fortunarum et facultatum mearum satis lauta (Deo gratia!) conditione, libere atque tuto utere, tibique persuade, me tui esse assiduissime memorem. Itaque, si me amas, quod certo existimo, copiose de tuo ac rerum vestrarum statu rescribe. Idipsum per mercatores, gentiles meos, qui Londini agunt, commode, quandocunque libuerit, facies, mihique mirum in modum gratificaberis. Dat. ex arce nostra Heilsberg prima Septembris 1540.

. . . . . . . . . . . . . . . . . . . . . . . . . .

. . . . [6]item ad se vitæ meæ cursum (de quo sæpe inter nos, quando una essemus, collocutio incidit) atque institutum, prælis, me invito etiamnum et inscio, excusum mitterem. In eo vivum tibi tui Dantisci simulachrum seu iconisma depinxi; hocque ob id, ut et tu mihi quam ducas vitam, et si comparem, quemadmodum Paulo tribuitur, duxeris, significationem facias. Apud nos cœlibatu et libero lectulo nihil est jucundius ac dulcius. Jocari libuit. Hæc enim scribens, visus sum mihi tecum vel in symposio, ut solebamus, vel in nave Danubiana, ad quam me comiter ex Ratisbona superioribus annis comitasti abeuntem, confabulari. Quod pro jure veteris inter nos comparatæ necessitudinis nedum familiaritatis, boni te puto consulturum. Tuus ille, inquam, totus

Tuus Joannes Dantiscus Episcopus
Vermien: manu mea script.

Rmo. in Christo Patri Domino Thomæ Cranmero Archiepiscopo Cantuarien. et regni Angliæ Primati, fratri carissimo et honorando.

## [TRANSLATION.] DANTISCUS TO CRANMER.

In your letter you say that the report of my death which reached you, was confirmed by the fact that you had not received a letter from me for three years. This has, I assure you, happened neither from carelessness nor forgetfulness of our mutual friendship, but in consequence of a similar report concerning yourself, which was very general among us; and of a truth, as being greatly attached to you, with much sorrow did I hear that by the command of your king you in particular, as well as many other good men, had been removed from the living, in violation of every principle of equity. Being deeply affected by it, I offered up many a prayer for the eternal blessedness of your spirit, as you had done for mine: but as in this matter such a report hath in both cases, by God's grace, turned out false, we must rejoice, and in mind, as well as by letter return to our ancient manifestation of good will. I pray you, however, to take care lest the fate of the moth should overtake you, since the times are such among you, as never before have happened in any country of the christian world. More I would add, did I not fear that this might do you an injury, if it were to fall into any other person's hands than your own.

As to what is being done among you, it would give me greater pleasure to hear it from yourself than from men who announce to us as indisputable many circumstances which are doubtful. So many pillagings of the property of the church, cases which are beyond all bounds and innumerable, promiscuous punishments of both sexes, and, what produces more astonishment and detestation in the minds of all, so many marriages and so many divorces, in violation of every law, as well human as divine; which, although they are every where commonly reported and credited, yet I still regard as doubtful. I am somewhat however constrained to credit them from the circumstance that you, who are both archbishop and primate of your realm, nevertheless subscribe yourself as minister of your church, a title very different from that of former days. No doubt all you who are bishops are ministers of the churches; yet we ought not to abuse this title which Paul used. For he who is an overseer is not without the ministerial office, but still he is not from such a cause deprived of his peculiar calling. Moreover, we who live here under a most christian and pious king, according to Phavorinus his precept in Gellius, make use of common phraseology, and live in accordance with ancient customs, in which even yourselves amongst other men in former days lived not devoid of happiness; so also as you lately heard in what I wrote to you of the extraordinary marriage, if it is in the same manner, I should have thrown myself into extraordinary troubles. God in his mercy averts them from me. But what will be the issue amongst you some time or other of this most turbulent mischief, with his Helens so often changed, and such huge and impious ferocity, every man of sound mind can see, although the divine anger does proceed with a slow step. So far am I from wishing you any ill, that earnestly do I pray the Lord God very long to withhold it, nay more, never to exercise it upon your wealthy island, which is very dear to me from the many acts of kindness which I have received there, or upon you all, to whom I am most attached. But that relinquishing those honourable titles, received by common usage, thus . . . . . . I am much obliged to you for causing to be so well educated the youth whom I formerly assigned to your suite in the imperial court at Ratisbon on the Danube. When he addressed me with your message and letter, I had, I assure you, no more knowledge of his person than your other exotic, which I had never before seen, and he gave me greater pleasure because, by your aid and support, he had grown into a young man of polished manners and education; and if he does not cease to pursue the course which he has begun, as far as concerns the rest of his life, he will succeed without any

[[5] Τηλοῦ φίλοι ναίοντες οὐκ εἰσὶν φίλοι. Athen. v p. 187, init.]

[[6] This paragraph is in Dantiscus' handwriting. The commencement is much injured by damp.]

difficulty. But again and again do I thank you for having, in accordance with my commendation and the nature of the friendship that was between us, supported him so kindly and so liberally at your own expense, while he was employed in the study of literature, and for sending him back hither to me with his travelling expenses paid. From this circumstance it is very clear that Athenæus was wrong when he thought 'that persons who live at a distance cannot be friends:' for you who are separated from our world have been most attentive to me in the case of this youth, whose parents you only know by report; and therefore whenever it is in my power to repay the favour to you, and to be of use or aid to you or yours, I offer you my services most readily. Freely and without any fear make use of them in the events of the most perilous times, so far as the state of my fortune and power will allow, which, thanks be to God! is very comfortable; and be assured that I have a continual regard for you. Therefore if you have any affection for me, on which point I have no doubt, send back by letter a full account of your own position and the state of your affairs. This you will have no difficulty in doing, whenever you please, through the merchants of our country who live at London, and in so doing you will exceedingly oblige me. Given at our castle of Heilsberg, 1 September, 1540.

. . . . . . . . . . . . . . . . . . . . . . .

. . . . . I would also send you an account of the tenour of my life (about which we had many a conversation when we were together) and its employments, which has been printed without my consent or knowledge. I have described in it to the life the image or likeness of your friend Dantiscus, and I have done it for this reason, that you may give me information both what kind of life you are leading, and whether you lead one like that which is allotted to Paul. With us nothing is more pleasant and delightful than celibacy and an unfettered bed. I must have a joke; for while I write this I fancy that I am conversing with you, either at the table, as was our habit, or in the boat on the Danube, to which in former years you have so kindly escorted me when I was leaving Ratisbon. I think you will take in good part all that concerns the claims of that long-standing connexion, not to say friendship, which has obtained between us. Yours, I say, entirely.

Your friend,

JOHN DANTISCUS, bishop of Vermein.
Written with mine own hand.

*To the most reverend father in Christ, master Thomas Cranmer, archbishop of Canterbury, and primate of the realm of England, my most dear and honoured brother.*

---

## CCLXXII. TO OSIANDER[1].

Cott. MSS. Cleop. E. v. fol. 111. British Museum. Original. Strype's Mem. of Abp. Cranmer, Vol. II. App. No. 29. pp. 752-756. Ed. Oxon. 1840.

SALVE plurimum! Vix tribus abhinc diebus elapsis, Osiander dilectissime, literas ad te scriptitabam, quas per subitum et festinatum tabellarii discessum coactus sum abbreviare, imo abrumpere plane, prætermisso eo, quod et tunc quam maxime scriptum volui, et nunc otii plusculum nactus, nescio quam nervose, verbose certe decrevi pertractare. Res est, ut mihi quidem videtur, non parva, neque leniter animadvertenda, ut quæ ad omnium evangelicam veritatem profitentium sugillationem, ne dicam ignominiam et culpam manifeste pertineat. Proinde te rogo, ut et scriptum hoc meum legas attente, et tuum vicissim responsum super eo conficias accurate, matureque remittas, quo habeam tandem quod respondeam iis qui me interrogant. Nosti enim, opinor, ut soleant homines hic omnium quæ istic geruntur a me rationem exigere: alii quidem bono animo, et communis evangelicæ causæ studio soliciti, nequid a vobis fieret secus quam oporteret; aliis autem malus est animus, mala mens. Nihil magis cupiunt, aut captant, quam ut justam aliquam vos et vestra facta dictave reprehendendi ansam undecunque apprehendant; et gaudent si mihi in os subinde talia possint objicere. Quibus duobus inter se diversis hominum generibus respondeo ego persæpe, quæ vel ipse comminisci possum, vel quæ ex scriptis vestris, sive in publicum emissis, sive ad me privatim missis, possim colligere. Incidunt tamen persæpe nonnulla, quæ nec negare possum, nec absque rubore fateri; nequeo denique quo pacto a vobis honeste aut pie fieri doceantur, rationem ullam saltem excogitare sufficientem. Nam ut interim de usuris taceam, a vobis aut vestrum certe nonnullis (ut apparet) approbatis, deque eo, quod magnatum filiis concubinas habendas permittitis, (videlicet ne per nuptias legitimas hæreditates dispergantur,) qui concubinatum in sacerdotibus tantopere aversati estis: quid poterit a vobis in excusationem allegari pro eo, quod permittitis a divortio, utroque conjuge vivo, novas nuptias coire, et, quod adhuc deterius est, etiam absque divortio uni plures permittitis uxores? Id quod et tute, si recte memini, in quibusdam tuis ad me literis apud vos

---

[1 This letter is headed, "Doctissimo Andree Osiandro Concionatori Xtiorenbergensi," in a more modern hand.]

factum diserte expressisti, addens Philippum[2] ipsum sponsalibus posterioribus, ut paranymphum credo atque auspicem, interfuisse.

Quæ ambo tum ipsius conjugii rationi, quæ non duo, sed unam carnem facit, tum etiam scripturis sunt expresse et manifeste contraria: ut patet Matth. xix., Mark x., Luke xvi., Rom vii., 1 Cor. vii. Quibus locis perspicuum fit, ex apostolorum, atque adeo Christi ipsius, institutione, unum uni debere matrimonio conjungi; nec posse sic conjunctos postea, nisi interveniente morte alterutrius, denuo contrahere. Quod si responderitis, hoc intelligi excepta causa fornicationis; an uxoris adulterium fuerit causa cur Philippus marito permiserit aliam superducere, vos melius nostis. Quod si fuerit, tunc objiciemus, ab ineunte hucusque ecclesia (cujus exemplis oportet scripturarum interpretationes conformari confirmarique) nunquam, quod scimus, hoc sic fuisse acceptum. Augustinus, quid ipse de hoc senserit, imo quid ecclesia ante ipsum et usque ad ipsum, clare docet, *Li. De adulterinis conjugiis, Ad Pollentium.* Quid igitur ad hæc dicetis, libenter vellem audire abs te quidem, si et ipse in eadem cum ceteris es sententia: sin minus, per te saltem vellem cognoscere, quid ab illis exploraveris ad talia responsum iri. Nam quum eorum nonnulli, ut audio, statuta nostra parlamentalia censorie nimis ac superciliose condemnent, quorum tamen gravissimas justissimasque causas ac rationes ignorant; mirum est quod interim ipsi non advertant apud ipsos plurima designari, quæ optimis atque gravissimis viris jure optimo displiceant. Scire atque aveo, an ista tanquam honesta, et promiscue quibusvis licita, ac evangelicæ veritati non repugnantia defendant; an secundum indulgentiam (ut dixit Apostolus) ad ea, dum a quibusdam fiunt, connivent, nequid gravius contingat, non idem omnibus itidemque permissuri. Illud prius haud equidem credo illos esse facturos, nisi legis Mahometanæ potius quam Christianæ assertores videri voluerint. Posterius hoc si faciunt, videant quomodo permittant, quæ Christus, Apostoli, Evangelistæ, atque adeo totius ecclesiæ consensus districte ab initio huc usque prohibuit.

Quod si forte dixerint, ea jam quoque tolerari posse, eo quod ante Christum natum fuerunt vel approbata vel tolerata; tunc enimvero causam nobis reddant, cur non et cetera toleremus, quæcunque tunc legimus pari jure usitata; aut definiant quænam hujus generis, ac quatenus erunt admittenda. Nam in veteri Testamento expressum habemus, olim patrem concubuisse cum filiabus, ut Loth; socerum cum nuru, ut Judam; patrem familias, nempe Abraham, cum ancilla pellice, conscia uxore atque etiam id ultro suadente, nempe Sara; eundem ipsum uxorem suam, adhuc juvenculam ac formosam, sororem nominasse, eamque regibus, Pharaoni et Abimelech, ultro in concubinam permisisse; præterea, unum sæpe hominem plures habuisse uxores, ut Jacob et Mosen ipsum, legis latorem a Deo constitutum: postremo, principes multos, eosque nec illaudatos, præter uxorum numerosa contubernia, concubinarum etiam greges aluisse, ut Davidem, Solomonem, etc. Nec Assuero vitio datur, quod singulis pæne noctibus concubinam novam asciverit. Et Hester fœmina laudatissima, utpote quam ad salutem populi sui Deus excitavit, quum esset Judæa et legi Mosaicæ obnoxia, Assueri regis cubiculum ante nuptias intravit. Quid pluribus opus, quum gravissimi auctores Ambrosius et Augustinus disertis verbis affirment, hic polygamiam, ille concubinatum, peccato tum caruisse, quando nec contra morem nec contra præceptum fierent; quæ nunc et legibus et moribus pronuntiant esse contraria? Talia, inquam, constat apud veteres fuisse usitata, nec a bonis quidem viris tunc temporis improbata. Quæ vel omnia probabunt novi isti homines et rerum novarum introductores, vel aliqua, vel nulla. Quod si nulla dicant nobis, cur ista admiserunt? Si aliqua, cur non et reliqua? et præscribant nobis regulam, qua sciamus, quæ sunt admittenda, quæ vero rejicienda. Si omnia, (in qua sententia videtur esse Bucerus,) quæso te, qualem rerum faciem quantumque a priore mutatam in ecclesia videbimus? Quam erunt confusa, inversa, atque

[[2] i. e. Melancthon: he and Bucer were present at the marriage of Philip, landgrave of Hesse, who married (March 3, A.D. 1540) Margaret de Sala, during the lifetime of his first wife. Seckendorf gives an account of the circumstances connected with this marriage, whilst endeavouring to refute "Antonius de Varillas, in Hist. de Hæres. Lib. XII. Ed. Belg. 1687, p. 87," and "Jac. Benignus Bossuetus, de variat. Eccl. Prot. anno. 1688. Ed. Belg. Lib. VI. p. 226," and others. Comment. Hist. Apol. de Lutheran. Lib. III. Sect. 21. § lxxix. Add. 3. pp. 277 et seqq. Vid. also Fuesslin's Epist. Reformat. pp. 198, 9. Ed. Tigur. 1742.]

præpostera omnia? Sed adhuc propius urgebimus eos, interrogabimusque: An non tantum quæ sub lege facta sunt, sed etiam quæ ante legem; et an non tantum quæ a Judæis, sed et quæ a gentibus fuerint usitata, veluti jure postliminii, ad exemplum revocabunt? Et si illa tantum, cur non hæc æque atque illa? præsertim quæ a sanctioribus et sapientioribus viris, ut Socrate, Platone, Cicerone, etc. fuerint vel facta vel approbata. Quod si utraque concedent, concedant et nobis Britannis, more majorum nostrorum, denas duodenasque uxores habere insimul communes, et maxime fratres cum fratribus, parentes cum liberis: quod aliquando in hac insula usitatum fuisse, Cæsar, non ignobilis auctor, testatur in Commentariis. Concedant fœminis Christianis, quod Solon suis Atheniensibus concesserat, ut quæ viros parum ad rem veneream idoneos sortitæ fuissent, aliquem ex mariti propinquis impune admitterent. Concedant quod Lycurgus concessit viris Lacedæmoniis, ut qui minus esset ad procreandam prolem idoneus, alteri cui vellet suam conjugem impregnandam daret, et prolem precario sibi natam, ut propriam, suo nomine nuncuparet. Aut denique quod Romanorum legibus permissum erat, ut qui satis liberorum procreasset, uxorem suam alteri commodaret prolem desideranti: id quod et Cato, vir gravissimus sapientissimusque habitus, Hortensio amico suo legitur fecisse. Talia cum probata fuerint antiquitus viris sapientissimis, ac philosophorum legumque latorum optimis et sanctissimis, ut Platoni, Xenophonti, Catoni, etc.; quum eadem fuerint moribus recepta Hebræorum, Græcorum, Latinorum, (quorum populorum respublicas et politias constat optime fuisse constitutas, et ab omnibus scriptoribus maxime celebratas,) age, faciamus et nos, si Deo placet, similia, et Christianis fratribus permittamus facienda. Imo Christus Opt. Max. tam fœda tamque incestuosa connubiorum portenta a sua sancta ecclesia dignetur avertere, nunc et in diem Domini! Amen.

Hæc ego ad te potissimum, carissime Osiander, in præsentia scribenda duxi, propter eam quæ inter nos est et jam diu fuit summa necessitudo et familiaritas; quamvis putem, atque adeo certo sciam, te ab hujusmodi tam absurdis et moribus et opinionibus quam alienissimum esse. Cum ceteris vestratibus doctoribus levior et minus arcta mihi intercedit amicitia; cujus ipsius quoque (fateor) me multum pœniteret, si scirem hos esse fructus novi evangelii ab ipsis tantopere jactitati, et a nobis quoque hactenus, ut putabamus, non temere aliqua ex parte probati. Bene vale. Dat. Lambeth, xxviimo. Decembr. [1540.]

Tui amantissimus,

T. Cantuarien.

[TRANSLATION.]

To the most learned master Andrew Osiander, preacher of Nuremburg.

My right hearty salutations. Scarcely three days have elapsed, my most beloved Osiander, since I was writing a letter to you, which by the sudden and hurried departure of the letter-carrier I was compelled to shorten, or rather to end very abruptly, without mentioning that which I then most wished to have written, and now, having a little leisure, I have decided to treat it throughout, I know not with what power, but at all events at full length. The subject, as of a truth it seems to me, is neither one of trifling import, nor to be commented on lightly, as it is one which is evidently connected with a lasting stain, not to say disgrace and accusation, of those who profess the truth of the gospel. Wherefore I beg you both attentively to peruse this letter of mine, and to compose carefully your answer with reference to it, and also to send it early, that I may have somewhat at length to answer to those who inquire of me. For you are aware, I suppose, that men here are in the habit of requiring from me an account of all that is doing in those parts; some, no doubt, with the best feelings, and from anxiety in behalf of the cause of our common gospel, that nothing may be done by you which is not becoming; while others have malicious feelings and dispositions. They long for and catch at nothing so much as to discover, no matter from what cause, some suitable handle for blaming you and your doings or sayings; and glad they are if in consequence they can cast such things in my teeth. To these two classes of men, widely differing one from the other, I very frequently reply either from my own imaginings, or from what I can infer from your writings, whether published or sent to me privately. Nevertheless some things are frequently occurring, which I can neither deny, nor can I admit them without shame; nor lastly am I able to imagine any sufficient reason by which they may be shewn to have been done consistently with honour or piety. For, not to say a word at the present time on usury, which it is clear is approved by you, or at all events some of you, or concerning the fact that you allow the sons of your nobles to have concubines (with a view, doubtless, to prevent the breaking up of inheritances through lawful marriages), and yet you are so strongly opposed to priests having concubines; leaving this out of the question, what can possibly be alleged in your excuse when you allow a man after a divorce, while both man and woman are living, to contract a fresh marriage, and, what is still worse, even without a divorce you allow one man to have several wives? And this you yourself, if I remember right, in some of your letters expressly declared to have been done; adding thereto that Philip himself was present at a second marriage, acting as, I believe, a bridesman, and taking it under his countenance.

These two things are expressly and undeniably contrary both to the nature of marriage, which does not make two but one flesh, as well as also to the scriptures, as will be seen from Matthew xix., Mark x., Luke xvi., Romans vii.; 1 Cor. vii.: from which passages it is clear that, according to the institution of the apostles, and therefore of Christ himself, one person ought to be joined in matrimony with one person, and that persons so joined together cannot again contract marriage until the death of one of the parties shall have happened. But if your reply is, that we must understand it in such a sense as to except the case of fornication; I ask, whether adultery on the part of the wife was the reason why Philip allowed the husband to marry a second wife in addition to the first? You know better than I. But even if it were so, we shall then object that from the origin of the church up to this hour, (and according to examples in it interpretations of the scriptures must be conformed and by them confirmed,) at no time, as far as we know, has this been so received. Augustine clearly shews what were his own sentiments on the point; nay, more, what were those of the church before and up to his own days, in his book *De adulterinis Conjugiis*, addressed to Pollentius. I am very desirous of hearing from yourself, if you also are of the same opinion with the rest, what answer you make to this; but if you differ from them, at all events I am anxious to learn from you, what answer you have found to be given by them to similar objections. And since some of them, as I hear, too captiously and superciliously condemn the statutes of our parliament, of which, howbeit, they are ignorant of the most weighty and satisfactory causes and reasons; it is astonishing that at the same time they are not aware that very many things among themselves are pointed out as displeasing, for the very best reasons, to men who are the best and whose judgment is most weighty. I am also anxious to know whether they would defend these things as honourable and allowable for every person without distinction, and as not contrary to the truth of the gospel; or whether according to indulgence (as the apostle saith), without any intention to make the same allowance and in the same way to all, they connive at these things while they are done by certain parties, lest a worse evil should happen. The first I do not verily believe they would do, unless they are anxious to appear as the supporters of the law of Mahomet rather than Christianity. If they do the latter, let them beware how they allow what Christ, the apostles, evangelists, and moreover, the consent of the whole church, from its commencement up to this day, hath straitly forbidden.

But perchance they affirm, that these things may even now be endured, because they were approved or tolerated before the birth of Christ: then truly let them give a reason why they do not allow also the other things which in those times we read were equally allowed and customary; or let them define which are of this class, and how far they are to be admitted. For in the old Testament we find it written that a father formerly lay with his daughters, as Lot; that a father-in-law with his daughter-in-law, as Judah; that the master of a house, namely, Abraham, had his maid as a concubine, his wife knowing it, and even of her own accord advising it, namely, Sarah; and that this same man called his wife, when still young and beautiful, his sister, and allowed her willingly for concubinage to the kings Pharaoh and Abimelech: added to this, that one man often had several wives, as Jacob, and Moses, who was appointed a legislator by God; lastly, that many princes, and these such as were not without commendation, besides numberless societies of wives, supported also companies of concubines, as David, Solomon, &c. Nor is it laid to the charge of Ahasuerus that almost every night he had a fresh concubine; and Esther, a woman most commended, as one whom God raised up for the safety of his people, though she was a Jewess and subject to the Mosaic law, yet before marriage entered the bed of king Ahasuerus. What need is there of more, since those most weighty authorities, Ambrose and Augustine, expressly declare, the one that polygamy, the other that concubinage, was then without sin, because they were done neither contrary to custom nor precept; and yet they proclaim these things now to be contrary both to law and morals? Such things, I say, are well known to have been usual among the ancients, nor were they disapproved even by good men in those days. Which of these, all of them, any, or none, will these novel-men and introducers of novelties approve? If they say to us, none, why then have they allowed these? If they reply, some, why not also the rest? And let them appoint us a rule by which we may know which are to be allowed, or which to be rejected. If all (in which opinion Bucer seems to be), I pray you what a face of things and how changed from the former shall we see in the church! How confused, overturned, and preposterous will all things be! But we will press them still closer, and inquire whether they will recal for example, not merely such things as were done under the law, but even such as before the law; and again, whether not merely such things as were done by Jews, but also such as were common to Gentiles, as it were by the right of restoration. And if they merely allow the one, why not the other, especially such as have either been done or commended by the more holy and wise men, as Socrates, Plato, Cicero, &c.? And if they allow both, let them grant also to us Britons, after the manner of our ancestors, to have ten or twelve wives together in common, and especially brothers with brothers, parents with their children; which Cæsar, no mean authority, testifies in his Commentaries to have been customary at one time in this island. Let them grant to christian women that which Solon granted to his Athenians, that they who had husbands ill suited for family life, should receive without blame some one of their husband's relatives. Let them grant that which Lycurgus granted to the Lacedæmonian men, that any man who was unable to beget children, might deliver his wife for the purpose to any whom he pleased, and call by his own name as his own the children so doubtfully born to him. Or lastly, that which was allowed by the laws of the Romans, that he who had begotten enough children should lend his wife to another that desired offspring; which thing even Cato, a man esteemed most strict and wise, is written to have done to his friend Hortensius. Since such things have received the approbation in ancient times of men the most wise, and the best and most holy of philosophers and legislators, as Plato, Xenophon and Cato, &c.; since they have been the received practices of the Hebrews, Greeks and Latins, (which people we know have had states and governments the best constituted and most admired by all writers,) well, let us, if it please God, both do such things and allow them to be done by the christian brethren! Rather, may Christ the great God deign to avert from his holy church such foul, incestuous and portentous marriages, both now and unto the day of the Lord! Amen.

I have thought it, my dearest Osiander, specially becoming that I should write thus to you at the present time, because of that close connexion and friendship which is between us, and has long subsisted, although I think, nay more, I know for a certainty, that you are most opposed to such absurd morals and opinions. With the rest of your doctors my intimacy is of a lighter character and less close; and even of this I should not a little repent, if I knew that such were the fruits of the new gospel so greatly vaunted by them, and approved by us up to this time, in some measure, as we thought, not without reason. Farewell. Given at Lambeth, xxvii. Dec.

Your most affectionate,

T. CANTUARIEN.

---

## CCLXXIII. TO KING HENRY VIII.

State Paper Office. Domestic Papers. A.D. 1541. Vol. IV. Original holograph. State Papers, Vol. I. pt. ii. Lett. CLXII. pp. 689-91.

It may please your majesty to understand, that at my repair unto the queen's grace[1] I found her in such lamentation and heaviness, as I never saw no creature; so that it would have pitied any man's heart in the world to have looked upon her: and in that vehement rage she continued, as they informed me which be about her, from my departure from her unto my return again; and then I found her, as I do suppose, far entered toward a frenzy, which I feared before my departure from her at my first being with her: and surely, if your grace's comfort had not come in time, she could have continued no long time in that condition without a frenzy, which, nevertheless, I do yet much suspect to follow hereafter.

And as for my message from your majesty unto her, I was purposed to enter communication in this wise; first, to exaggerate the grievousness of her demerits; then to declare unto her the justice of your grace's laws, and what she ought to suffer by the same; and last of all to signify unto her your most gracious mercy: but when I saw in what condition she was, I was fain to turn my purpose, and to begin at the last part first, to comfort her by your grace's benignity and mercy; for else the recital of your grace's laws, with the aggravation of her offences, might peradventure have driven her unto some dangerous ecstasy, and else into a very frenzy; so that the words of comfort coming last might peradventure have come too late. And after I had declared your grace's mercy extended unto her, she held up her hands and gave most humble thanks unto your majesty, who had shewed unto her more grace and mercy than she herself thought meet to sue for or could have hoped of; and then, for a time, she began to be more temperate and quiet, saving that she still sobbed and wept; but after a little pausing she suddenly fell into a new rage, much worse than she was before.

Now I do use her thus: when I do see her in any such extreme braids, I do travail with her to know the cause, and then, as much as I can, I do labour to take away, or at the least to mitigate the cause; and so I did at that time. I told her there was some new fantasy come into her head, which I desired her to open unto me; and after a certain time, when she had recovered herself that she might speak, she cried and said: "Alas, my lord, that I am alive! the fear of death grieved me not so much before, as doth now the remembrance of the king's goodness: for when I remember how gracious and loving a prince I had, I cannot but sorrow; but this sudden mercy, and more than I could have looked for, shewed unto me, so unworthy, at this time, maketh mine offences to appear before mine eyes much more heinous than they did before: and the more I consider the greatness of his mercy, the more I do sorrow in my heart that I should so

---

[[1] i. e. Catharine Howard. Cranmer had been the means of discovering the character of his queen to the king. Vid. Burnet's Hist. of Reformat. Vol. I. pp. 624, 5. Ed. Oxon. 1829. "Upon the subject of her crimes, the queen was spoken withal in it by the archbishop of Canterbury, the lord chancellor, the duke of Norfolk, the lord great chamberlain of England, and the bishop of Winchester; to whom at the first she constantly denied it; but the matter being so declared unto her, that she perceived it to be wholly disclosed, the same night she disclosed the whole to the archbishop of Canterbury, who took the confession of the same in writing, subscribed with her hand." Kennet's Hist. of England, Vol. II.; lord Herbert's Life of Hen. VIII. p. 534. Ed. Lond. 1706. The confession here spoken of is probably that which Catharine Howard signed, and which is printed by Burnet, Hist. of Reformat. Vol. III. Part II. pp. 230—233. The queen, and lady Rochford, who had been the chief cause of Anne Boleyn's and her husband's death, were beheaded on Tower Hill, Feb. 12, A. D. 1542. Dereham and Culpeper suffered for their participation in her crime, Dec. 10, A. D. 1541. Id. Vol. I. pp. 625, 627. Vid. also Letters in State Papers, Part II. pp. 689 et sqq.]

misorder myself against his majesty." And for anything that I could say unto her, she continued in a great pang a long while; but after that she began something to remit her rage and come to herself, she was meetly well until night, and I had very good communication with her, and, as I thought, had brought her unto a great quietness.

Nevertheless, at night, about six of the clock, she fell into another like pang, but not so outrageous as the first was; and that was, as she shewed me, for the remembrance of the time; for about that time, as she said, master Hennage was wont to bring her knowledge of your grace. And because I lack time to write all things unto your majesty, I have referred other things to be opened by the mouth of this bearer, sir John Dudlay; saving that I have sent herewith inclosed all that I can get of her concerning any communication of matrimony with Derame; which, although it be not so much as I thought, yet I suppose, surely, it is sufficient to prove a contract, with carnal copulation following; although she think it be no contract, as indeed the words alone be not, if carnal copulation had not followed thereof.

The cause that master Baynton[2] sent unto your majesty was partly for the declaration of her estate, and partly because, after my departure from her, she began to excuse and to temper those things which she had spoken unto me, and set her hand thereto[3]; as at my coming unto your majesty I shall more fully declare by mouth: for she saith, that all that Derame did unto her was of his importune forcement, and, in a manner, violence, rather than of her free consent and will. Thus Almighty God have your majesty in his preservation and governance! [Nov. 1541.] From

Your grace's most bounden chaplain,

T. CANTUARIEN.

*To the king's majesty.*

---

## CCLXXIV. TO KING HENRY VIII.

IT may please your majesty to be advertised, that yesterday the ambassador of Cleve came unto my house at Lamhith, and delivered me letters from Oslynger, vice-chancellor unto the duke of Cleve, which letters I have sent unto your majesty herewith inclosed: the purport whereof, after he hath set forth my lauds and commendations like an orator, when he cometh to the substance of the matter, is nothing else but to commend unto me the cause of the lady Anne of Cleve. Which although he trusteth that I would do of myself, undesired, yet he saith that the occasion is such, that he will not omit to put spurs to the horse that runneth of his own courage. When I had read the letter, and considered that no cause was expressed specially, but only in general that I should have commended the cause of the lady Anne of Cleve; although I suspected the true cause of his coming, yet I would take upon me no knowledge of any special matter, but said thus unto him: "Master ambassador, I have perused Oslynger's letters, by the which he commendeth unto me the lady Anne of Cleve's cause; but forasmuch as he declareth no certain cause, I trust you have some other instructions to inform me of some particular matter." Whereunto he answered, that the cause was, the reconciliation of your majesty unto the lady Anne of Cleve. Whereunto I answered, that I thought not a little strange, that Oslynger should think it meet for me to move a reconciliation of that matrimony, of the which I, as much as any other person, knew most just causes of divorce. And here I moved him to consider your grace's honour and the tranquillity of this realm, with the

State Paper Office. Domestic Papers. A.D. 1541. Vol. IV. Original holograph. State Papers, Vol. I. pt. ii. Lett. CLXXVII. pp. 716, 17.

---

[2 It was the king's pleasure that Baynton "should attend on the queen, to have the rule and government of the whole house; and with him the almoner [Nicholas Hethe] to be also associate." Letter from the Council to Cranmer in State Papers, Vol. I. p. 692.]

[3 Probably the document printed by Burnet, Hist. of Reformat. Vol. III. App. B. iii. No. 72, Part II. pp. 230—233. (vid. supra), which was signed by the queen, and chiefly refers to her contract of matrimony with Dereham; but also gives positive evidence of her crime. Vid. State Papers, Vol. I. p. 692; Kennet's Hist. of England, Vol. II.; Lord Herbert's Life of Henry VIII. p. 532.]

surety of your grace's succession; and further, how this should agree with Oslynger's opinion of me, as he writeth in his letters, that I should study to the commodity and tranquillity of this realm, if I should move your grace to receive her in matrimony, from whom your majesty was upon most just causes divorced[1]; whereupon might grow most uncertitude of your grace's succession, with such unquietness and trouble to this realm, as heretofore hath not been seen. And when he would have begun something, as appeared unto me, more largely to have reasoned the matter, and to grope my mind, I finished our communication in this sort: "Master ambassador, this is a matter of great importance, wherein you shall pardon me; for I will have no communication with you therein, unless it please the king's majesty to command me. But I shall signify unto his highness your request, and thereupon you shall have an answer." Now what shall be your majesty's pleasure that I shall do, whether that I shall make him any answer or no, and what answer it shall be, and whether I shall make a general answer to Oslynger by writing, because he writeth generally not touching this matter, or that I shall make a certain answer in this point to the ambassador by mouth, I most humbly beseech your majesty that I may be advertised; and according thereto I shall order myself, by the grace of God: whom I beseech daily to have your majesty evermore in his protection and governance. From my manor of Lamhith, this Tuesday the 13 Januarii[2]. [1540-1.]

Your grace's most bounden

chaplain and beadsman,

*To the king's majesty.* THOMAS CANTUARIEN.

[OLYSLEGER'S LETTER TO CRANMER.]

"SALUS et pax a Deo Patre, et Jesu Christo Domino ac Salvatore nostro. Reverendissime Præsul ac Domine, multis modis venerande. Quoniam singularis candor plurimorumque officiorum tuorum præstationes multis bonis viris tam extra quam intra hoc florentissimum regnum Angliæ, cognita atque perspecta, de tua celsitudine eam opinionem statuerunt, eandemque celsitudinem tuam ita suspicentur, ut quod ad Omnipotentis Dei ac Benedicti Filii ejus gloriam illustrandam imprimis, ac deinde ad reipublicæ Christianæ, præsertim Anglicanæ, tranquillitatem ac commoditatem conservandam, augendam, promovendamque quovis modo pertinere videatur, id semper singulari studio, opera, atque industria, celsitudo tua fuerit prosecuta; fieri non potest, quin in eadem spe firmiter consistamus, etiam nunc idipsum celsitudinem tuam pro sua virili curaturam. Itaque, quantum plurimum possumus, celsitudinem tuam flagitamus, uti causam illustrissimæ Dominæ Annæ, sororis Principis nostri, pro rei commoditate sibi quam commendatissimam habere non gravatim velit. Et quamvis existimemus idipsum celsitudinem tuam sine nostra interpellatione æque facturam, nolui tamen committere, quin, pro hujus temporis occasione, hoc calcar equo sponte currenti admoverem. Et oro Dominum nostrum Jesum Christum, ut gratiam suam alioqui plus satis infusam in celsitudinem tuam augere, ac diu incolumem servare dignetur. Datum Duysseldorpii, pridie Calendas Decembris, 1541.

"Ejusdem celsitudinis tuæ addictissimus,

"HENR. OLISL. Doct.

"Vicecancellarius Clevensis.

"*Reverendissimo Præsuli ac Domino, plurimisque dotibus insigni, Domino Thomæ, per Dei gratiam archiepiscopo Cantuariensi, ac per regnum Angliæ primario præsidi, Domino plurimum venerabili.*"

---

[1 Vid. the judgment of the convocation for annulling of the marriage with Anne of Cleves. Burnet's Hist. of Reformat. Vol. I. App. B. iii. No. 19, pp. 308—312, and in State Papers, Vol. I. Part II. No. CXXXVIII. pp. 629—635, where the signatures of the members are added, as well as Hen. VIII.'s declaration of the causes of the separation.]

[2 "This date is manifestly erroneous, for the 13th of January did not fall on a Tuesday between 1540, when the king was recently married to Anne of Cleves, and 1545, when he was the husband of Catharine Parr. There can be little doubt that January is written by mistake instead of December, for the 13th of December, 1541, was Tuesday; and this supposition makes this letter coincide with lord Southampton's of the preceding day, which, from the other circumstances adverted to in it, is fixed beyond dispute to that month and year." Note to State Papers, Vol. I. p. 717. "This morning [12 Dec.] the ambassador of Cleves was here at my house, and advertised me, that he hath letters of credence to your highness from the duke his master, with two other letters; the one addressed to my lord of Canterbury from Olisleger, the other from the said duke to my lord great master; and hath also delivered letters to me from the same Olisleger." Lord Southampton then proceeds to give an account of the ambassador's conversation; which was to the same effect as that which is related by Cranmer. Letter from the earl of Southampton to king Henry VIII. in State Papers, Vol. I. Part II. Letter CLXXVI. p. 714.]

[TRANSLATION.]

Health and peace from God the Father and Jesus Christ our Lord and Saviour! Most reverend prelate and lord, in many ways honourable. Since your special purity and your very many kind attentions shewn to many good men beyond the bounds of, as well as within, the most flourishing realm of England, are known and understood; and have established this opinion of your highness, and they so regard the same your highness, that your highness has followed out with special earnestness, labour and industry, at all times such things above all as appear in any way to concern the setting forth of the glory of Almighty God and his blessed Son, and secondly the preservation, increase and advancement, of the peace and advantage of the christian commonweal, especially that of England; it is therefore impossible but that we should rest strongly on the same hope that even now your highness will attend to the same thing, to the extent of your power. Therefore as earnestly as is in our power we beg of your highness, that it would not be disinclined to regard as most warmly commended according to the soundness of the cause the case of our most illustrious lady Anne, the sister of our prince. And although we feel that your highness would no less do it without our interference, I was however unwilling to omit the application in this suitable time of a spur to the willing horse. And I pray our Lord Jesus Christ to increase his grace in other points more than enough poured into your highness, and long to preserve you. Given at Dusseldorf, 30 Nov. 1541.

The same your highness' most devoted

Henry Olisleger, D.D.

Vice-chancellor of Cleves.

*To the most reverend prelate and lord, and illustrious for many endowments, Lord Thomas, by God's grace archbishop of Canterbury and throughout the realm of England lord primate, and most venerable lord.*

---

## CCLXXV. TO LORD COBHAM[3].

My lord, after my right hearty commendations; these are to advertise you, that I have received your letters dated at Calais the xi[th] of April: and as concerning your request, that I should revoke the inhibition brought unto the arches by John Holland, in the matter between him and William Porter; forasmuch as the said Holland hath appealed to the arches, I cannot with justice interrupt his appellation, so that the same be again remitted unto the commissary of Calais; for then the said Holland should have just occasion to appeal from me: but for the better expedition of the matter, I have sent to the dean of the arches, commanding him to surcease therein, and have wholly resumed the matter into my hands. Wherefore, my lord, I pray you let both the interrogatories and the testament, with all the acts before the judge, be sent unto me, and I shall take such an order therein as shall stand with equity and justice. I will stay the matter for a time, that you may make an end therein, if you can, shortly; and if you cannot, then I shall proceed as to the law appertaineth.

Harl. MSS. No. 283, Plut. lxvii. E. I. 205. British Museum. Original.

Moreover, I most heartily thank your lordship for your wine, which I trust to remember; and if at any time this year there come any to be sold at any reasonable price, I pray you that I may have part thereof. Praying you to have me heartily commended to my lady Cobham, to Mr Treasurer[4], to Mr Marshall, to Mr Wenteworthe, and to my lady. Thus heartily, my lord, fare you well. At Bekisborne, the xviii[th] of April. [1544.]

Your assured,

T. Cantuarien.

And as concerning my lady Baynton's request, you write that you are content that she shall have the college[5], and not to meddle with Cobham hall: I pray, my lord, to send your mind herein to him that hath the ordering of that house and your affairs there; for

---

[[3] George Brook, lord Cobham, lord deputy of Calais. Vid. Letter CLXXXVII. p. 335. Much of his correspondence is preserved in the Harl. MSS. No. 283.]

[[4] "In the month of July, [A.D. 1543], the king sent over 6000 men under the leading of Sir John Wallope, accompanied with Sir T. Seimer, marshal, Sir Robert Bowes, treasurer," &c. Stow's Annals, p. 585. Ed. Lond. 1615. The capture of Boulogne occurred A.D. 1544.]

[[5] Cobham college was sold to lord Cobham, about A.D. 1538, by the master and brethren themselves, from the supposition that it would be dissolved. Vid. Hasted's Hist. of Kent, Vol. I. p. 503.]

my lady is willing to have the same, so that she may have convenient ground thereunto. Wherefore your lordship shall do well to send your determined mind, what commodities she shall have with the college, and the prices thereof, appointing one to whom she may resort, and commune, and conclude withal in that behalf.

*To my very loving lord, my lord Cobham,*
*lord deputy of Calis.*

---

## CCLXXVI. TO KING HENRY VIII[1].

State Paper Office. Domestic Papers. A.D. 1544. Vol. V. Original. State Papers, Vol. I. pt. ii. Lett. CXCVI. pp. 760—1. Collier's Eccles. Hist. Vol. V. pp. 147, 8. Ed. Lond. 1840, 41. Todd's Life of Abp. Cranmer, Vol. I. p. 355.

It may please your majesty to be advertised, that according to your highness' commandment, sent unto me by your grace's secretary, Mr Pagett, I have translated into the English tongue, so well as I could in so short time, certain processions, to be used upon festival days, if after due correction and amendment of the same your highness shall think it so convenient. In which translation, forasmuch as many of the processions, in the Latin, were but barren, as meseemed, and little fruitful, I was constrained to use more than the liberty of a translator: for in some processions I have altered divers words; in some I have added part; in some taken part away; some I have left out whole, either for by cause the matter appeared to me to be little to purpose, or by cause the days be not with us festival-days; and some processions I have added whole, because I thought I had better matter for the purpose, than was the procession in Latin: the judgment whereof I refer wholly unto your majesty; and after your highness hath corrected it, if your grace command some devout and solemn note to be made thereunto, (as is to the procession which your majesty hath already set forth in English,) I trust it will much excitate and stir the hearts of all men unto devotion and godliness: but in mine opinion, the song that shall be made thereunto would not be full of notes, but, as near as may be, for every syllable a note; so that it may be sung distinctly and devoutly, as be in the Matins and Evensong, *Venite*, the Hymns, *Te Deum*, *Benedictus*, *Magnificat*, *Nunc dimittis*, and all the Psalms and Versicles; and in the mass *Gloria in Excelsis*, *Gloria Patri*, the Creed, the Preface, the *Pater noster*, and some of the *Sanctus* and *Agnus*. As concerning the *Salve festa dies*, the Latin note, as I think, is sober and distinct enough; wherefore I have travailed to make the verses in English, and have put the Latin note unto the same. Nevertheless they that be cunning in singing can make a much more solemn note thereto. I made them only for a proof, to see how English would do in song. But by cause mine English verses lack the grace and facility that I would wish they had, your majesty may cause some other to make them again, that can do the same in more pleasant English and phrase. As for the sentence, I suppose will serve well enough. Thus Almighty God preserve your majesty in long and prosperous health and felicity! From Bekisbourne, the 7th of October. [1544.]

Your grace's most bounden
chaplain and beadsman,

*To the king's most excellent majesty.* T. Cantuarien.

### PRINCE EDWARD TO CRANMER.

Foxe's Acts and Monuments, p. 1398. Ed. Lond. 1583.

"Etsi puer sum, colendissime susceptor, non tamen immemor sum vel officii erga te mei, vel humanitatis tuæ, quam indies mihi exhibere studes. Non exciderunt mihi humanissimæ tuæ literæ pridie divi Petri ad me datæ. Quibus antehac respondere nolui, non quod illas neglexerim, aut non meminerim, sed ut illarum diuturna meditatione fruerer, fidelique memoria reponerem, atque demum bene ruminatis pro mea virili

---

[1 In the State Papers this letter is printed under A.D. 1543. By Dr Jenkyns and Mr Todd it is placed under 1544, and by Collier under 1545. It is doubtful to which of the two latter years it may be correctly assigned, but that of A.D. 1544 is here adopted, as being the most probable. The mandate of Henry VIII. June, 1544, authorised the procession which is here spoken of. Dr Jenkyns thinks that as Henry VIII. returned from Boulogne Oct. 1st, he might have been proud of his success, and so probably commanded it to be celebrated by religious processions. Vid. Stow's Annals, p. 587.]

responderem. Proinde affectum erga me tuum vere paternum, quem in illis expressisti, amplector et veneror, optoque ut multos vivas annos, tuoque pio ac salubri consilio pergas esse mihi venerandus pater. Nam pietatem ante omnia mihi amplectendam et exosculandam esse duco, quoniam divus Paulus dicit, 'Pietas ad omnia utilis est.' Optime valeat tua paternitas in plurimos annos. Hartefordiæ, 13. Januarii.

"Tui studiosissimus,

"Edwardus Princeps."

[TRANSLATION.]

Albeit I am a boy, most honourable tutor, yet I am not unmindful either of your attention to me or your kindness which you study every day to shew me. Your very kind letter sent to me on St Peter's eve has not escaped me, but I was unwilling to reply to it heretofore, not because I have neglected or forgotten, but that I might enjoy a daily consideration of it and treasure it up with a tenacious memory, and when at length I should well consider it, might reply to the best of my ability. Accordingly I affectionately receive and honour that truly paternal affection which you have expressed in it, and I hope that you may live many years, and continue to be my honoured father by your godly and wholesome advice. For I think that godliness above all things is to be embraced and loved by me, since St Paul says, "Godliness is profitable for all things." May you, my father, live in much happiness for very many years! Hertford, 13. Jan.

Your most attached,

Edward, Prince.

## CCLXXVII. TO PRINCE EDWARD[2].

Foxe's Acts and Monuments. Ibid.

Non magis poterat ipse me [mea] servare salus, fili in Christo carissime, quam salus tua. Mea vita non dicenda est vita absque tua et salute et valetudine. Quapropter cum te incolumem ac salvum intelligo, vitam etiam mihi integram esse et incolumem sentio. Neque certe absentia mea tam est injucunda tibi, quam sunt literæ tuæ perjucundæ mihi. Quæ arguunt tibi juxta adesse et ingenium dignum tanto principe, et præceptorem dignum tanto ingenio. Ex quibus tuis literis te sic literas video colere, ut interim doctrinæ cœlestis tua nequaquam minima sit cura: quæ cuicunque sit curæ, non potest illum quævis cura frangere. Perge igitur qua via incepisti, princeps illustrissime, et Spartam quam nactus es, hanc orna; ut quam ego per literas video in te virtutis lucem, eadem olim illuminet universam tuam Angliam. Non scribam prolixius, tum quidem ut me intelligas brevitate nonnihil affici, tum etiam quod credam, te ætate quidem adhuc parvulum parvo gaudere, et similem simili; tum etiam præterea, ne impolita mea oratio in causa sit, quo generosa illa tua indoles barbariæ vitium contrahat.

TRANSLATION.

The health of my own self, my dearest son in Christ, could not be more serviceable to me than is your own. My life is not to be called living unless you are in health and strength; and therefore as I hear that you are safe and well, I feel also that my life is complete and uninjured. Nor at all events does my absence deprive you of so much pleasure as your letter adds to mine; for it shews no less that you have ability worthy of so great a prince, than that you have a tutor worthy of such great ability. And from this letter of yours I find that you so study letters that meanwhile you have no small care for heavenly teaching; and whatever person has a care for it, him no care can ever destroy. Proceed then, most illustrious prince, in the same way as you have begun, and adorn this Sparta which you have obtained; so that the same light of excellency which I see from your letter is in you, may hereafter illuminate the whole of your realm of England. I will not write at greater length, both that you may see that I am in a measure pleased with brevity, and also because I believe that as you are still small in age, you delight in that which is small, and like is pleased with like; and furthermore, that my unpolished style may not be the cause of your noble mind contracting the fault of baldness in your own.

[2 This is said by Foxe to be the answer of the archbishop to the above letter of prince Edward, who also gives the following letter, written when the prince "seemed to be very young, not above seven years of age, lying then at Antill."

"An Epistle of young prince Edward to the archbishop of Canterbury, his godfather.

"Impertio te plurima salute, colendissime præsul, et carissime susceptor. Quia abes longe a me, vellem libenter audire te esse incolumem. Precor autem ut vivas diu, et promoveas verbum Dei. Vale. Antilæ decimo octavo Junii. [1544.]

"Tuus in Christo filius,

"Edwardus Princeps."

[Translation:]

"I most heartily commend me to you, most worshipful primate and dearest tutor. As you are at a great distance from me, I am exceedingly anxious to hear that you are well. I pray that you may long live, and promote the word of God. Farewell. From Antill, June xviii.

"Your son in Christ,

"Edward the Prince."]

## CCLXXVIII. TO SIR WILLIAM PAGET[1].

State Paper Office. Domestic Papers. A.D. 1546. Vol. VIII.

AFTER my very hearty commendations. Having sent by this bearer letters to be delivered unto the king's majesty by you, with a minute of another letter in the same inclosed (the copy whereof you shall herewith receive) to be sent unto me from the king's majesty; these shall be to desire you to peruse the said minute; and if it be not formably made, I pray you to reform the same with such correction as shall seem unto you most requisite, and thereupon to deliver it unto the king's majesty, knowing his grace's further pleasure in the same. Thus right heartily fare ye well. From my manor at Bekesbourne, the 20th of January. [1545-6.]

Your assured
T. CANTUARIEN.

*To the right honourable sir William Paget, knight, one of the king's majesty's two principal secretaries.*

---

Domestic Papers, A.D. 1546. Vol. VIII. State Paper Office. Ibid. Burnet's Hist. of Reformat. Vol. II. pt. ii. pp. 334, 5. Ed. Oxon. 1829. Collier's Eccles. Hist. Vol. V. p. 138. Ed. Lond. 1840—41.

The minute of the king's majesty's letters to be addressed to the archbishop of Canterbury.

FORASMUCH as you, as well in your own name as in the name of the bishops of Worcester[2] and Chichester[3], and other our chaplains and learned men, whom we appointed with you to peruse certain books of service which we delivered unto you, moved us, that the vigil and ringing of bells all the night long upon Alhallow-day at night, and the covering of images in the church in time of Lent, with the lifting up of the veil that covereth the cross upon Palm-sunday, with the kneeling to the cross the same time, might be abolished and put away, for the superstition and other enormities and abuses of the same: First, forasmuch as all the vigils of our lady and the apostles, and all other vigils, which in the beginning of the church were godly used, yet for the manifold superstition and abuses which after did grow by means of the same, they be many years passed taken away throughout all Christendom, and there remaineth nothing but the name of the vigil in the calendar, the thing clearly abolished and put away, saving only upon Alhallow-day at night, upon which night is kept vigil, watching, and ringing of bells all the night long; forasmuch as that vigil is abused as other vigils were, our pleasure is, as you require, that the said vigils shall be abolished as the other be, and that there shall be no watching, nor ringing, but as be commonly used upon other holydays at night. We be contented and pleased also, that the images in the churches shall not be covered, as hath been accustomed in times passed; nor no veil upon the cross; nor no kneeling thereto upon Palm-sunday, nor any other time. And forasmuch as you make no mention of creeping to the cross, which is a greater abuse than any of the other; (for there you say, *Crucem tuam adoramus, Domine;* and the ordinal saith, *Procedant clerici ad crucem adorandum nudis pedibus;* and after followeth in the same ordinal, *Ponatur crux ante aliquod altare, ubi a populo adoretur;* which by your own book, called, "A Necessary Doctrine," is against the second commandment:) therefore our pleasure is, that the said creeping to the cross shall likewise cease from henceforth and be abolished, with the other abuses before rehearsed. And this we will, and straitly command you to signify unto all the prelates and bishops of your province of Canterbury, charging them, in our name, to see the same executed, every one in his diocese, accordingly.

---

## CCLXXIX. TO KING HENRY VIII.

*The copy of the letter to the king's majesty.*

State Paper Office. Domestic Papers. A.D. 1546. Vol. VIII. Burnet's Hist. of Ref. Vol. II. pt. ii. fol. 8. B. i. No. 61. pp. 332, 4. Ed. Oxon. 1829.

IT may please your highness to be advertised, that forasmuch as I might not tarry myself at London, because I had appointed the next day after that I departed from your majesty to be at Rochester, to meet the next morning all the commissioners of Kent at Sittingbourn; therefore the same night that I returned from Hampton court to Lambhith,

---

[1 This letter has not appeared in any previous collection.]

[2 Nicholas Hethe. Vid. Letter LXXXVIII. p. 276.]

[3 George Day.]

I sent for the bishop of Worcester incontinently, and declared unto him all this your majesty's pleasure, in such things as your majesty willed me to be done. And first, where your majesty's pleasure was, to have the names of such persons as your highness in times passed appointed to make laws ecclesiastical for your grace's realm[4], the bishop of Worcester promised me with all speed to inquire out their names and the book which they made, and to bring the names and also the book unto your majesty; which I trust he hath done before this time. Todd's Life of Abp. Cranmer, Vol. I. pp. 359—362.

And as concerning the ringing of bells upon Allhallow-day at night, and covering of images in Lent, and creeping to the cross, he thought it necessary that a letter of your majesty's pleasure therein should be sent by your grace unto the two archbishops; and we to send the same to all other prelates within your grace's realm. And if it be your majesty's pleasure so to do, I have, for more speed, herein drawn a minute of a letter, which your majesty may alter at your pleasure. Nevertheless, in my opinion, when such things be altered or taken away, there would be set forth some doctrine therewith, which should declare the cause of the abolishing or alteration, for to satisfy the conscience of the people: for if the honouring of the cross, as creeping and kneeling thereunto, be taken away, it shall seem to many that be ignorant, that the honour of Christ is taken away, unless some good teaching be set forth withal to instruct them sufficiently therein: which if your majesty command the bishops of Worcester and Chichester with other your grace's chaplains to make, the people shall obey your majesty's commandment willingly, giving thanks to your majesty if they know the truth; which else they would obey with murmuration and grutching. And it shall be a satisfaction unto all other nations, when they shall see your majesty do nothing but by the authority of God's word, and to the setting forth of God's honour, and not diminishing thereof. And thus Almighty God keep your majesty in his preservation and governance! And thus, &c. From my manor at Bekisbourne, the 24th of January, 45. [1545-6[5].]

Your grace's most bounden chaplain and beadsman.

---

[[4] Burnet's Hist. of Reformat. Vol. I. p. 661; Vol. III. p. 308. Ed. Oxon. 1829; Strype's Mem. of Abp. Cranmer, Vol. I. p. 190. Ed. Oxon. 1840.]

[[5] The date of the original paper preserved in the State Paper Office, and from which the above documents are printed as they stand, and contrary to the position given to them by Burnet, is 45, i.e. 1545. The date has been enlarged by Burnet to 1545-6. Mr Todd is inclined to reduce it to 1544-5. But it is probable that Burnet is accurate, as Foxe, under A. D. 1546, gives the following narrative of the matter to which the above letters refer: "Whilst the said bishop of Winchester [Gardiner] was now remaining beyond the seas about the affairs aforesaid," [i.e. to conclude a league between Henry VIII., the emperor Charles V., and Francis I. the French king, 'in whose absence the archbishop of Canterbury sought occasion somewhat to further the reformation of the corrupt religion,'] "the king's majesty and the said archbishop, having conference together for reformation of some superstitious enormities in the church, amongst other things, the king determined forthwith to pull down the roods in every church, and to suppress the accustomed ringing on Allhallow night, with a few such like vain ceremonies; and therefore, when the said archbishop, taking his leave of the king, to go into Kent, his diocese, his highness willed him to remember that he should cause two letters to be devised; 'for me,' quoth the king, 'to be signed, the one to be directed unto you, my lord, and the other unto the archbishop of York, wherein I will command you both to send forth your precepts unto all other bishops within your provinces, to see those enormities and ceremonies reformed undelayedly, that we have communed of.'

"So upon this the king's pleasure known, when the archbishop of Canterbury was then come into Kent, he caused his secretary to conceive and write these letters according to the king's mind, and being made in a readiness, sent them to the court to Sir Anthony Denie, for him to get them signed by the king. When master Denie had moved the king thereto, the king made answer: 'I am now otherways resolved; for you shall send my lord of Canterbury word, that since I spake with him about these matters, I have received letters from my lord of Winchester, now being on the other side of the sea, about the conclusion of a league between us, the emperor, and the French king, and he writeth plainly unto us, that the league will not prosper nor go forward, if we make any other innovation, change, or alteration, either in religion or ceremonies, than heretofore have been already commenced and done. Wherefore my lord of Canterbury must take patience herein, and forbear until we may espie a more apt and convenient time for that purpose.' Which matter of reformation began to be revived again at what time the great ambassador from the French king came to the king's majesty at Hampton Court, not long before his death. It is not our purpose here......but only to consider the note of the conference and communication had the first night after the said banquet was finished, between the king's majesty, the said ambassador, and the archbishop of Canterbury, (the king's highness standing openly in the banqueting house, in the open face of all the people, and leaning one arm upon the shoulder of the archbishop of Canterbury, and the other arm upon the shoulder of the ambassador,) touching the establishment of godly religion between those two princes in both their realms; as by the report of the said archbishop unto his secretary

I beseech your majesty, that I may be a suitor unto the same for your cathedral church of Canterbury; who, to their great unquietness and also great charges, do alienate

---

[Morice] upon occasion of his service to be done in king Edward's visitation, then being register in the same visitation, relation was made in that behalf in this sort.

"When the said visitation was put in a readiness, before the commissioners should proceed in their voyage, the said archbishop sent for the said register his man, unto Hampton Court, and willed him in any wise to make notes of certain things in the said visitation, whereof he gave unto him instruction, having then further talk with him touching the good effect and success of the said visitation. Upon which occasion the register said unto his master the archbishop: 'I do remember that you not long ago caused me to conceive and write letters, which king Henry the VIII. should have signed and directed unto your grace and the archbishop of York, for the reformation of certain enormities in the churches, as taking down of the roods, and forbidding of ringing on Allhallow night, and such like vain ceremonies; which letters your grace sent to the court to be signed by the king's majesty, but as yet I think that there was never any thing done therein.'

"'Why,' quoth the archbishop again, 'never heard you how those letters were suppressed and stopped?' Whereunto the archbishop's servant answering again: 'As it was' (said he) 'my duty to write those letters, so was it not my part to be inquisitive what became thereupon.' 'Mary,' quoth the archbishop, 'my lord of Winchester then being beyond the seas about a conclusion of a league between the emperor, the French king, and the king our master, and fearing that some reformation should here pass in the realm touching religion in his absence against his appetite, wrote to the king's majesty, bearing him in hand that the league then towards would not prosper nor go forwards on his majesty's behalf, if he made any other innovation or alteration in religion or ceremonies in the church, than was already done; which his advertisement herein caused the king to stay the signing of those letters, as Sir Antony Denie wrote to me by the king's commandment.'

"Then said his servant again unto him: 'Forasmuch as the king's good intent took no place then, now your grace may go forward in those matters, the opportunity of the time much better serving thereunto than in king Henry's days.'

"'Not so,' quoth the archbishop. 'It was better to attempt such reformation in king Henry the VIII. his days, than at this time, the king being in his infancy. For if the king's father had set forth any thing for the reformation of abuses, who was he that durst gainsay it? Mary, we are now in doubt how men will take the change or alteration of abuses in the church; and therefore the council hath forborne especially to speak thereof, and of other things which gladly they would have reformed in this visitation, referring all those and such like matters to the discretion of the visitors. But if king Henry the VIII. had lived unto this day, with the French king, it had been past my lord of Winchester's power, to have visored the king's highness, as he did when he was about the same league.'

"'I am sure you were at Hampton Court,' quoth the archbishop, 'when the French king's ambassador was entertained there at those solemn banquetting houses, not long before the king's death: namely, when after the banquet was done the first night, the king leaning upon the ambassador and upon me, if I should tell what communication between the king's highness and the said ambassador was had, concerning the establishing of sincere religion then, a man would hardly have believed it. Nor I myself had thought the king's highness had been so forward in those matters as then appeared. I may tell you, it passed the pulling down of roods, and suppressing the ringing of bells. I take it that few in England would have believed, that the king's majesty and the French king had been at this point, not only within half a year after to have changed the mass into a communion, as we now use it, but also utterly to have extirped and banished the bishop of Rome and his usurped power out of both their realms and dominions.

"'Yea, they were so thoroughly and firmly resolved in that behalf, that they meant also to exhort the emperor to do the like in Flanders and other his countries and seignories, or else to break off from him. And herein the king's highness willed me,' quoth the archbishop, 'to pen a form thereof to be sent to the French king to consider of. But the deep and most secret providence of Almighty God, owing to this realm a sharp scourge for our iniquities, prevented (for a time) this their most godly device and intent, by taking to his mercy both these princes.'" Foxe's Acts and Monuments, pp. 1244, 45. Ed. Lond. 1583. Foxe also, in relating the manner of the death of Henry VIII. (p. 1291) says: "And thus much touching the end of king Henry, who if he had continued a few months longer (all those obits and masses, which appear in his will, made before he went to Boulogne notwithstanding,) most certain it is, and to be signified to all posterity, that his full purpose was to have repurged the estate of the church, and to have gone through with the same, so that he would not have left one mass in all England. For the more certain intelligence whereof, two things I have to lead me. The one is the assured report and testimony of Tho. Cranmer, archbishop of Canterbury, hearing the king declare the same out of his own mouth, both to himself and to Mounsieur de Annehault, lord admiral, the French ambassador, in the month of August a little before his death. The other cause, which leadeth me thereunto, is also of equal credit, grounded upon the declaration of the king's own mouth after that time, more near to his death, unto Bruno, ambassador of John Frederick, duke of Saxony. Unto the which ambassador of Saxony the king gave this answer openly, that if the quarrel of the duke of Saxony were nothing else against the emperor but for religion, he should stand to it strongly, and he would take his part, willing him not to doubt nor fear; and so with this answer dismissed the ambassador unto the duke openly, in the hearing of these four sufficient witnesses, the L. Seymer, earl of Harforde, lord Lisley, then admiral, the earl of Bedford, lord privy seal, and lord Paget. But the secret working of God's holy providence, which disposeth all things after his own wisdom and purpose, thought it good rather by taking the king away to reserve the accomplishment of this reformation of his church to the peaceable time of his son Edward, and Elizabeth his daughter, whose hands were yet undefiled with any blood, and life unspotted with any violence or cruelty."]

their lands daily, and, as it is said, by your majesty's commandment. But this I am sure, that other men have gotten their best lands, and not your majesty. Wherefore this is mine only suit, that when your majesty's pleasure shall be to have any of their lands, that they may have some letter from your majesty to declare your majesty's pleasure, without the which they be sworn that they shall make no alienation; and that the same alienation be not made at other men's pleasures, but only to your majesty's use. For now every man that list to have any of their lands, makes suit to get it into your majesty's hands; not that your majesty should keep the same, but, by sale or gift from your majesty, to translate it from your grace's cathedral church unto themselves.

T. CANTUARIEN.

## CCLXXX. TO THE CHAPTER OF CANTERBURY.

Strype's Mem. of Abp. Cranmer, Vol. I. p. 198. Ed. Oxon. 1840. From the Register of Christ Church, Canterbury.

AFTER my hearty commendations: whereas I am informed that you be in doubt, whether any prebendary of that my church may exchange his house or garden with another prebend of the same church living, and that you be moved by this statute so to think, which here followeth; "Statuimus ut canonicus de novo electus et demissus in demortui aut resignantis aut quovis modo cedentis ædes succedat:" these be to signify unto you, that neither this statute, nor any other reason that I know, maketh any thing against the exchange between two prebends living, but that they may change house, orchard, or garden during their life, this statute or any other reason contrary notwithstanding. And whereas you have appointed your preachers at your last chapter their chambers and commodities, I require you that they may be indelayedly admitted thereunto, according to that your order. Thus fare you well. From my manor of Croydon, the 12th of December, 1546.

T. CANTUARIEN.

*To my loving friends, the vice-dean and prebendaries of my church in Canterbury.*

## CCLXXXI. TO BONER.

Wilkins' Concilia, Vol. IV. p. 22. from Boner's Regist. fol. 110.

THIS is to advertise your lordship, that my lord protector's grace, with advice of others the king's majesty's council, for certain considerations them thereunto moving, hath fully resolved, that no candles should be boren upon Candlemas-day, nor also from henceforth ashes or palms used any longer. Wherefore I beseech your lordship to cause admonition thereof to be given in all parish churches throughout your diocese with all celerity; and likewise unto all other bishops that be hereabouts, that they may do the semblable in their dioceses before Candlemas-day. And as for other bishops that cannot have knowledge so soon, you may give them knowledge hereof at more leisure, so that it be done before Ash-Wednesday. Thus fare your lordship well. Lambeth, Jan. 27, 1547. [1548.]

Your loving friend,

T. CANTUAR.

## CCLXXXII. TO THE DEAN AND CHAPTER OF ST PAUL'S.

Cranm. Regist. f. 55. Strype's Mem. of Abp. Cranmer, Vol. I. pp. 219, 20. Ed. Oxon. 1840.

AFTER our right hearty commendations: whereas it hath pleased Almighty God to send the king's majesty such victory against the Scots[1], as was almost above the expectation of man, and such as hath not been heard of in any part of Christendom this many years: in which victory above the number of fifteen thousand Scots be slain, two thousand taken prisoners; and among them many noblemen and others of good reputation; all their ordnance and baggage of their camp also won from them: the king's majesty, with

[[1] Viz. At the battle of Pinkey, in which the Scots were defeated, Sept. 10, A. D. 1547.]

advice of his highness' privy council, presently attending upon his majesty's most royal person, well knowing this, as all other goodness, to be the gifts of God, hath and so doth account it; and therefore rendereth unto him the only glory and praise for the same: and so hath willed me, not only in his majesty's cathedral church, and other churches of my diocese, to give thanks to Almighty God, but also to require in his name all other bishops of the province of Canterbury to do or cause to be done semblably in their cures[1]. Which his majesty's pleasure I have thought good to signify unto you: requiring you, not only to cause a sermon to be made in your cathedral church the next holy-day after receipt thereof, declaring the goodness of God, and exhorting the people to faith and amendment of life; and to give thanks to God for this victory; but also at the same time, immediately after the sermon, and in presence of the mayor, aldermen, and other the citizens of London, to cause the procession in English, and *Te Deum* to be openly and devoutly sung. And that you do also cause the like order to be given in every parish church of your diocese, upon some holy-day, when the parishioners shall be there present, with as much speed as you may; not failing, as you tender his majesty's pleasure. Thus fare you heartily well. From Otelands, the 18th day of December[2], the year of our Lord God 1547.

Your loving friend,

T. CANTUARIEN.

The council's pleasure is, you shall see this executed on Tuesday next.

*To the dean and chapter of St Paul's, in London, this be given in haste*[3].

---

## CCLXXXIII. TO MATTHEW PARKER.

C.C.C.C. MSS. CVIII. p. 3. Original.

I COMMEND me unto you; signifying, that the lord protector, conceiving good opinion of your wisdom, learning, and earnest zeal which you bear to the setting forth of God's word among the people, hath, by the advice of the council, appointed you to preach one sermon at Paul's cross in London on Sunday, being the 22. day of July next; not doubting but that you will purely and sincerely set out the holy scriptures, so as God's glory may be advanced, and the people with wholesome doctrine edified. These therefore shall be to require you to prepare yourself ready in the mean season to supply the day, time, and place to you appointed accordingly; foreseeing that you present yourself unto the dean of Paul's, resiant at his house in Paul's church-yard, or unto his deputy there, the Saturday before noon that you shall preach, or at the least to signify then unto him by your letters, or some sure messenger, that you will not fail to preach the Sunday; because the cross must in no wise be disappointed or destitute of a preacher. Thus heartily fare you well. From my manor at Lambith, the 5. day of May. [1548.]

Your loving friend,

T. CANTUARIEN.

---

## CCLXXXIV. TO KING EDWARD VI.

*To the most excellent prince Edward VI., by the grace of God king of England, France, and Ireland, defender of the faith, and in earth of the church of England and Ireland immediately under God supreme head, your grace's humble subject and chaplain Thomas, archbishop of Canterbury, wisheth abundance of all grace and godliness with a long and prosperous reign.*

Catechism of Justus Jonas, set forth by Abp. Cranmer, Ed. 1548.

IT is not unknown unto the whole world, most excellent prince, that your grace's father, a king of most famous memory, of a fervent and earnest godly disposition and

---

[1 In their course. Strype.]

[2 "It should be September, I suppose." Strype. It is, however, "December" in Cranmer's register, which in all probability is a mistake for "September." Vid. Heylyn's Eccles. Restaur. Edw. VI. p. 47. Ed. Lond. 1670.]

[3 "Expressions in the letter itself prove that it was addressed to the bishop of London." Jenkyns, Remains of Abp. Cranmer, Vol. I. p. 324. *n.* r.]

tender zeal towards the setting forth of God's glory, most diligently travailed for a true and a right reformation and a quiet concord in Christ's religion throughout all his dominions; wherein undoubtedly he brought many things to a godly purpose and effect, and did abolish and take away much blindness and ignorance of God, many great errors, fond and pernicious superstitions and abuses, that had crept into this church of England and Ireland a long time. And I, perceiving that your majesty, by the advice of your most dear uncle my lord protector, and the rest of your grace's most honourable council, is most desirous perfectly to finish and bring to pass that your father did most godly begin, do think that there is nothing more necessary for the furtherance hereof, then that it might be foreseen how the youth and tender age of your loving subjects may be brought up and traded in the truth of God's holy word.

For it is thought, not to me only but to many others, that neither your grace's father should have been inforced in his time to have taken so great pains for the reformation of Christ's religion, neither yet your highness in this your time should need with such great difficulty go about to further God's cause and his true service with so many laws, injunctions, and proclamations, if so great negligence of the education of the youth had not been so much suffered, and the necessary points and articles of our religion and profession omitted, of those whose office and bounden duty was to have most diligently instructed the youth in the same; or if the ancient and laudable ceremony of confirmation had continued in the old state, and been duly used of the ministers in time convenient, where an exact and strait examination was had of all such as were of full age, both of their profession that they made in baptism touching their belief and keeping of God's commandments, with a general solemn rehearsal of the said commandments and of all the articles of their faith.

Surely there can be no greater hope of any kind of persons, either to be brought to all honest conversation of living, or to be more apt to set forth and maintain all godliness and true religion, than of such as have been from childhood nourished and fed with the sweet milk, and as it were the pap, of God's holy word, and bridled and kept in awe with his holy commandments. For commonly as we are in youth brought up, so we continue in age, and savour longest of that thing that we first receive and taste of. And as a fair table finely polished, though it be never so apt to receive either pictures or writings, yet it doth neither delight any men's eyes, neither yet profit any thing, except the painter take his pencil, set to his hand, and with labour and cunning replenish it with scriptures or figures as appertaineth to his science; even so the tender wits of young children, being yet naked and bare of all knowledge, through the grace of God, be apt to receive God's gifts, if they be applied and instructed by such schoolmasters as have knowledge to bring them up and lead them forward therein. And what can be more apt to be grown or painted in the tender hearts of youth, than God's holy word? What can lead them a righter way to God, to the obedience of their prince, and all virtue and honesty of life, than the sincere understanding of God's word, which alone sheweth the way how to know him, to love him, and to serve him? What can better keep and stay them, that they do not suddenly and lightly fall again from their faith? What can cause them more constantly to withstand the assaults of the devil, the world, and the flesh, and manfully to bear the cross of Christ, than to learn in their youth to practise the same? And verily it seemeth no new thing, that the children of them that be godly should be thus instructed in the faith and commandments of God even from their infancy. For doth not God command his people to teach his law unto their children and childer's children? Deut. xi. Hath not this knowledge continued from time to time amongst them, to whom God promised to be their God, and they his people? Doth it not appear by plain expressed words of Paul, that Timothy was brought up even from a child in holy scriptures? 2 Tim. iii. Hath not the commandments of Almighty God, the articles of the christian faith, and the Lord's prayer, been ever necessarily, since Christ's time, required of all, both young and old, that professed Christ's name, yea, though they were not learned to read? For doubtless in these three points is shortly and plainly included the necessary knowledge of the whole sum of Christ's religion, and of all things appertaining unto everlasting life.

In consideration whereof, in this time of your gracious reformation of all ungodliness, and the setting forth of God's true glory, I, knowing myself as a subject greatly bounden, and much the more by reason of my vocation, to set forward the same, am persuaded that this my small travail in this behalf taken shall not a little help the sooner to bring to pass your godly purpose. For by this little treatise[1] not only the youth of your grace's realm may learn to know God, and how they may most purely and sincerely honour, glorify, and serve him, and may also learn their office and duty how they ought to behave themselves, first toward God, secondly towards your majesty, and so towards all ministers under the same, towards their fathers and mothers, and all other persons, of what sort or degree soever they be: but also many of the older sort, such as love God and have a zeal to his honour and glory, and yet in their youth, through negligence, were brought up in ignorance, may, by hearing of their children, learn in their age that which passed them in their youth.

And as mine intent and endeavour is to profit both, and according to mine office to bring both to the right knowledge of God, so my most earnest and humble prayer unto God continually shall be that my good mind and desire may have good success, and take effect according to mine expectation. Which thing I assuredly hope shall come to pass, if it would please your highness to suffer this little book, by me offered unto your majesty, to be read, taught, and learned of the children of your most loving subjects, in whom is great hope of all grace, godliness, and virtue.

Your grace's humble subject and chaplain,

THOMAS, archbishop of Canterbury.

## CCLXXXV. TO JOHN A LASCO[2].

Gabbema, Epist. Claror. Virorum, Epist. LII. pp. 108, 9. Ed. Harlin. Fris. 1669.

ADVENTUM tuum ad nos alterius cujusdam negotii subito interventu impeditum esse doleo: non enim dubito, quin de tua vocatione[3] facile tibi satisfecissem, si coram tecum mihi potestas colloquendi fuisset. Sed quia hoc tempore venire non potuisti, scribis tamen te venturum esse posthac, si prius ex literis nostris intellexeris, qualis vocationis tuæ ratio apud nos futura sit: literis tecum agam, et quod coram copiosius fortassis dicturus eram, id per literas explicabo brevi. [4]Cupimus nostris ecclesiis veram de Deo doctrinam proponere, nec volumus cothurnos facere aut ambiguitatibus ludere; sed semota omni prudentia carnis, veram, perspicuam, sacrarum literarum normæ convenientem doctrinæ formam ad posteros transmittere; ut et apud omnes gentes exstet

[1 Viz. the translation of the Catechism of Justus Jonas.]

[2 For an account of John a Lasco, who was a Polish reformer, vid. Gerde's Hist. Reformat. Vol. III. p. 145; and Gerde's Scrin. Antiq. Tom. II.]

[3 From the following passage in Gerdes' Scrin. Antiq. Tom. II. p. 635, Dr Jenkyns thinks (Remains of Abp. Cranmer, Vol. I. p. 329. *n.* x.) that John a Lasco had been invited to England in the preceding year: "Nuntium mittimus Witebergam ad Philippum [Melancthonem], aut ubi is sit, scribimusque ad illum de vocatione in Angliam, de qua hodie ad te scripsi." Letter from John a Lasco to Albert Hardenberg, Embd. 11 Oct. 1547.]

[4 "In the year 1548 Cranmer propounded a great and weighty business to Melancthon; and a matter that was likely to prove highly useful to all the churches of the evangelic profession. It was this: The archbishop was now driving on a design for the better uniting of all protestant churches; viz. by having one common confession and harmony of faith and doctrine drawn up out of the pure word of God, which they might own and agree in. He had observed what differences there arose among protestants in the doctrine of the sacrament, in the divine decrees, in the government of the church, and some other things. These disagreements had rendered the professors of the gospel contemptible to those of the Roman communion, which caused no small grief to the heart of this good man, nearly touched for the honour of Christ his master, and his true church, which suffered hereby; and, like a person of a truly public and large spirit, as his function was, seriously debated and deliberated with himself for the remedying this evil. This made him judge it very advisable to procure such a confession. And in order to this, he thought it necessary for the chief and most learned divines of the several churches to meet together, and with all freedom and friendliness to debate the points of controversy according to the rule of the scripture; and after mature deliberation, by agreement of all parties, to draw up a book of articles and heads of christian faith and practice, which would serve for the standing doctrine of the protestants, &c. But the troubles at home and abroad frustrated this excellent purpose, which for two years he had been labouring to bring to some good issue." Strype's Mem. of Abp. Cranmer, pp. 584, 588. Ed. Oxon. 1840. Vid. Letters CCLXXXVI. CCLXXXIX. CCXCVI. CCXCVII. CCXCVIII. pp. 422, 425, 430, 431, 433; Strype's Eccl. Mem. Vol. II. p. 87. Ed. Oxon. 1822; and Latimer's 3rd Sermon, preached before Edward VI. Vol. I. p. 141. Park. Soc. Ed.]

illustre testimonium de doctrina nostra, gravi doctorum et piorum auctoritate traditum, et universa posteritas normam habeat quam sequatur. Ad perficiendam rem tantam eruditorum hominum præsentia nobis opus esse judicavimus, qui, collatis nobiscum judiciis, doctrinæ controversias tollant, et integrum corpus veræ doctrinæ extruant. Accersivimus igitur et te et alios quosdam doctos viros[5]; qui cum non gravatim ad nos venerint, ita ut nullum fere ex iis præter te et Melancthonem desideremus, summopere te rogamus, ut et ipse ad nos venias, et Melancthonem, si ullo modo fieri poterit, tecum adducas. [6]Tertiam nunc epistolam ad Melancthonem mitto, qua eum hortor, ut ad nos veniat; quibus meis epistolis si tuæ adhortationes accesserint, non diffido eum persuaderi posse, ut toties iteratam vocationem sequatur[7]. Nullas, ut arbitror, insidias hostium, nulla itinerum pericula pertimescit, quæ, si qua sunt, minora tamen sunt iis, quibus nunc est[8]. Adde, quod exigui temporis molestiis multorum annorum quietem sibi, reipub. vero utilitatem adferet æternam. Quod si ei commigrationem ad nos aut inutilem aut injucundam fore prospicerem, nemo certe me dissuaderet vehementius. Nunc vero, cum videam nihil ab eo aut ipsi aut reipub. posse fieri utilius, quam ut hoc tempore ad nos veniat, insto vehementius, teque hortor, ut omnem curam cogitationemque tuam in hoc unice convertas, ut Philippum nostrum plane nostrum facias. Qualis et tua et ipsius futura sit conditio, paulo ante ostendi. Ita tamen ostendi, ut experientia vestra potius quam prædicatione mea Angliam vobis placere cupiam. Bene et feliciter vale. Londini, die iv. Julii, MDXLVIII.

Tuæ præsentiæ cupidiss.

T. CANTUARIENSIS.

*Illustri Viro D. Joanni a Lasco, amico suo carissimo, S.D.P.*

[TRANSLATION.]

I AM sorry that your coming to us has been prevented by the unlooked-for intervention of some other engagement; for I have no doubt but that I should easily have satisfied you as to your invitation, if I had an opportunity of conversing with you upon the subject. But as you are not able to come at present, but write word that you intend to come at some future time, if you shall have previously been informed by a letter from me as to the nature of your vocation amongst us; I will converse with you by letter, and briefly

---

[[5] July 9, A.D. 1548. John a Lasco wrote as follows to Albert Hardenberg: "Contentio sacramentaria cœpit illic exagitari per quosdam, estque instituta ea de re publica disputatio, ad quam magnis multorum precibus vocor. Bucerus exspectatur. Franciscus noster Dryander jam adest. Et de Calvino mussatur, nisi quod Gallus est." Gerdes' Scrin. Antiq. Tom. II. p. 644. "I find divers outlandish learned and godly men this year [A. D. 1547] at Canterbury: among the rest was John Utenhovius, a person of honourable rank and quality, afterwards elder and assistant to John a Lasco's church in London. Here was also Valerandus Pollanus, and one Franciscus; and the year after Bucer was here. Now, I conjecture, were the beginnings of the foreigners' church planted in Canterbury, by the countenance and influence of archbishop Cranmer. There was a loving correspondence held between the said Utenhovius here, and Peter Martyr now at Lambeth." Strype's Eccl. Mem. Vol. II. p. 123. A further account of the attention of the archbishop to the foreign divines may be seen in Abp. Parker's Antiq. Brit. Eccl. p. 508. Ed. Lond. 1729.]

[[6] "During the short reign of Edward, solicitations of a similar nature appear to have been frequent. Latimer, in a sermon preached before the King, March 22, A. D. 1549, thus alludes to a report of the time: 'I heard say, Master Melancthon, that great clerk, should come hither. I would wish him, and such as he is, to have £200 a year. The king should never want it in his coffers at the year's end.' In the subsequent year his presence here was a second time requested. 'Ego,' he remarks in a letter to J. Camerarius, 'rursus in Angliam vocor.' Epist. Lib. IV. 780. May 17, 1550. And lastly, again before the death of that much-lamented prince: 'Regiis literis vocor in Angliam, quæ scriptæ sunt mense Maio. Postea secuta est mors nobilissimi adolescentis.' Epist. Lib. IV. 813. A.D. 1553. 'Had not the king died so soon, the moderate, learned, and wise Melancthon would have come into England, and been placed in the University of Cambridge.'" Strype's Eccl. Mem. Vol. II. Part II. p. 76. Vid. Laurence's Bampton Lect. pp. 186, 227. Ed. Oxon. 1805. These invitations were sent subsequently to that upon which this and the following letter treat.]

[[7] The archbishop's letter to Melancthon was sent by John a Lasco through the hands of Æpinus, as appears from a letter to Hardenberg, July 28, A. D. 1548. "Te rogo ut ad illum [i. e. Melancthonem] per occasionem scribas, num literas Cantuarienses a me ad se per Æpinum transmissas acceperit, et ut respondeat." Gerdes' Scrin. Antiq. Tom. II. p. 646.]

[[8] The archbishop here evidently refers to the attempts which were made by Charles V. A. D. 1548, to force the Interim upon the German protestants; for an account of which, vid. Sleidan, de Statu Religionis et Reipub. (A. D. 1548.) Lib. XX. XXI. Ed. Francof. 1568. Mosheim's Eccl. Hist. Book IV. §§ 3, 4, Vol. III. pp. 152, 3. Ed. Lond. 1845; Burnet's Hist. of Reformat. Vol. III. p. ii. Book. IV. No. 3, pp. 264, 5. Ed. Oxon. 1829.]

explain in writing, what I should perhaps have stated somewhat more copiously to you in person. We are desirous of setting forth in our churches the true doctrine of God, and have no wish to be shifting and unstable, or to deal in ambiguities; but, laying aside all carnal considerations, to transmit to posterity a true and explicit form of doctrine agreeable to the rule of the sacred writings; so that there may not only be set forth among all nations an illustrious testimony respecting our doctrine, delivered by the grave authority of learned and godly men, but that all posterity may have a pattern to imitate. For the purpose of carrying this important design into execution we have thought it necessary to have the assistance of learned men, who, having compared their opinions together with us, may do away with doctrinal controversies, and build up an entire system of true doctrine. We have therefore invited both yourself and some other learned men; and as they have come over to us without any reluctance, so that we scarcely have to regret the absence of any of them, with the exception of yourself and Melancthon, we earnestly request you, both to come yourself, and, if possible, to bring Melancthon with you. I am now sending a third letter to Melancthon, in which I exhort him to come to us: and if your exhortation be added to my letter, I have no doubt but that he will be persuaded to accept an invitation so often repeated. He need not, I think, be under any fear of the attacks of enemies, or the dangers of the journey, which, if they exist at all, are however far less than where he now is. You may add too, that by undergoing a little inconvenience for a short time he will procure to himself ease for many years, and to the state everlasting benefit. If I anticipated that his visit to us would be either useless or unpleasant, no one would dissuade him from it more earnestly than myself. But now, when I perceive that he can in no wise act more advantageously either for himself or for the state, than by coming over to us at this juncture, I am the more urgent upon the subject, and exhort you to exert all your diligence and consideration to this one end, namely, to make our friend Philip ours in reality. I explained to you, a short time since, what will be the situation of you both; but I so explained it, as desiring that you should learn to be pleased with England from your own experience rather than by my commendation of it. Farewell and happily. London, July 4, 1548.

Exceedingly desirous of your presence.

T. CANTUAR.

---

## CCLXXXVI. TO ALBERT HARDENBERG[1].

Copia manu Huberti in MSS. Vol. IX. p. 36. Scrin. Eccl. Argent.

. . . . Cupimus nostris ecclesiis veram de Deo doctrinam proponere, nec volumus cothurnos facere aut ambiguitatibus ludere: sed semota omni prudentia carnis, veram, perspicuam, ac S. litterarum normæ convenientem doctrinæ formam ad posteros transmittere; ut et apud omnes gentes exstet testimonium doctrinæ nostræ gravi doctorum et piorum auctoritate traditum, et universa posteritas normam habeat quam sequatur. Ad perficiendam rem totam eruditorum hominum præsentia nobis opus esse judicavimus, qui, collatis nobiscum judiciis, doctrinæ controversias tollant, et integrum corpus veræ doctrinæ extruant. Accersivimus igitur plerosque pios et doctos viros, quorum alios habemus jam, alios vero brevi exspectamus. Sed de Philippo Melancthone nihil adhuc certi habemus. Quare te summopere rogamus, ut illum, si id ullo modo facere possis, ad iter ad nos suspiciendum inducas. Tertiam nunc ad ipsum epistolam misi, qua illum hortor ut ad nos veniat; quibus epistolis si tuæ adhortationes accesserint, non diffido illum persuaderi posse, ut toties iteratam vocationem sequatur. Nullas, ut arbitror, insidias hostium, nullaque itinerum pericula pertimescit, quæ si quæ sunt, minora tamen sunt iis, in quibus nunc est. Adde, quod exigui temporis molestiis multorum annorum quietem sibi, reipublicæ vero utilitatem adferet æternam. Quod si ei hoc ad nos iter aut inutile aut injucundum fore prospicerem, nemo me certe hoc illi vehementius dissuaderet: sed cum videam nihil ab eo aut ipsi aut reipublicæ posse fieri utilius, quam ut hoc tempore ad nos veniat, opto vehementius, teque oro, ut omnem curam cogitationemque tuam in hoc convertas, ut Philippum nostrum plane nostrum facias. Qualis ipsius hic futura sit conditio, jam ostendi. Ita tamen ostendi, ut experientia ipsa potius quam mea prædicatione Angliam nostram ei placere cupiam. Quod si noster Philippus videat, ad quid vocetur, a quibus autem hominibus, certe et ipsius et veræ religionis amantissimis, et quanto studio vocetur simul et exspectetur; profecto non video et nescio an vocationem

---

[[1] "Albert Hardenberg, the friend and correspondent of John a Lasco, was educated at the university of Louvain. He commenced his ministerial labours at a monastery in Groningen; from whence he moved to Cologne, on the invitation of archbishop Herman. At the date of this letter he was at the head of the reformed church at Bremen, over which he presided from 1547 to 1561. He then retired, to avoid the troubles of the Ubiquitarian controversy, to Embden; where he died in 1574." His character is thus given by Gerdes, Hist. Evang. Renov. Vol. III. p. 158. "Erat theologus insignis, atque tum doctrina excellebat, tum facundia præstabat, et recte de religione sentiebat; præterea, prudentia, moderatione animi, morum commoditate valebat, et has dotes singulari pietate ornabat." Jenkyns' Remains of Abp. Cranmer, Vol. I. pp. 331, 2, *n. d.*]

hanc negligere possit, præsertim cum nullam pene certam se vocationem illic habere videat, quam huic merito opponere queat. Si in simili vocatione deesse noluit sanctissimo illi seni Electori Coloniensi[2], sane ne nunc quidem illi licebit in causa multo graviore et magis etiam necessaria. Inviti fortasse sui illum dimittent, et ipse quoque invitus suos dimittet, hoc potissimum tempore; sed interim metuo, ne illum omnes istic pro eo ac vellemus audiant, et ut audiant, non scio an tanto cum fructu illic nunc esse possit, quantum ex sua præsentia in Anglia nostra nunc haberi possit; qui tamen negligendus nobis non est, siquidem nobis Christi Domini gloriam vere et ex animo quærendam esse putamus. Utinam semel aliquid statuat, et nos de animo suo certiores faciat, aut ipse mox accurrat, omnesque nuntios prævertat. De sumptu prospiciemus, vel apud te, vel alibi, modo sciamus, quantum et quo loco curari velit. Cantabrigiæ, 28 Julii, 1548.

[TRANSLATION.]

.... We are desirous of setting forth in our churches the true doctrine of God, neither have we any wish to be shifting and unstable, or to deal in ambiguities: but, laying aside all carnal considerations, to transmit to posterity a true and explicit form of doctrine agreeable to the rule of the scriptures; so that there may be set forth among all nations a testimony respecting our doctrine, delivered by the grave authority of learned and pious men; and that all posterity may have a pattern which they may imitate. For the purpose of carrying this important design into effect we have thought it necessary to have the assistance of learned men, who, having compared their opinions together with us, may do away with doctrinal controversies, and establish an entire system of true doctrine. We have therefore sent for many pious and learned men, some of whom we have already with us, and others we are expecting will arrive shortly. But respecting Philip Melancthon we have as yet no certain intelligence. For which cause we most earnestly entreat you, if by any means you can accomplish it, that you will endeavour to induce him to undertake the journey hither. I have already sent a third letter to him, in which I entreat him to come to us; to which letters if you will add your entreaties, I have no doubt but that he may be persuaded to accept an invitation which has so frequently been repeated. I do not think that he need be under any apprehension of the treachery of enemies, nor of the dangers of the journey; which if there were any, are much less than those are where he now is. You may also add, that by his undergoing a little present inconvenience he will secure quiet to himself for many years to come, and unending benefit to the state. If I could foresee that this journey hither would be either useless or disagreeable to himself, truly none would more earnestly dissuade him from undertaking it than I would; but since I perceive that nothing can be more useful both to himself and the state than that he should come over to us at this juncture, I desire it the more earnestly, and beg of you, that you will exert all your diligence and consideration to this end, that you may make our friend Philip ours in reality. I have already explained what his future situation will be here; but I so explained it, as desiring that you should learn to be pleased with our England from your own experience, rather than by my report of it. But if our friend Philip will consider for what purpose he is invited, and also by what persons, those, assuredly, who are most friendly both to himself and to true religion; and also with how great anxiety he is both invited and expected; truly I do not see, and I know not whether he can neglect this summons, especially as he must perceive that he has no certain vocation yonder which he can properly place in opposition to it. If he felt unwilling to refuse the venerable elector of Cologne upon a like invitation, he cannot certainly decline the present one, upon an occasion of much greater importance and necessity. His friends perhaps will be unwilling to let him go, and he too will be unwilling to part with them at this particular juncture: but I fear in the mean time that all parties yonder do not attend to him from such motives as we could wish; and even if they do, I know not whether he can now remain there with as much advantage as can be derived from his presence in our England, and which nevertheless ought not to be disregarded by us, inasmuch as we think it our duty to seek truly and heartily the glory of Christ our Lord. I wish he would at once make up his mind, and acquaint us with his intention, or that he would come over to us immediately, and anticipate every messenger. We will provide for the expense, either through you, or elsewhere, as soon as we know to what extent, and in what place, he wishes provision to be made. Cambridge, July 28, 1548.

## CCLXXXVII. TO MARTIN BUCER[3].

GRATIAM et pacem Dei in Christo. Legi tuas literas ad Johannem Halesium, in quibus tristissimos Germaniæ casus commemorans, te in tua urbe verbi ministerio vix Buceri Scrip. Anglic. pp. 190, 1. Ed. Basil. 1577.

[2 Herman, archbishop of Cologne, whose invitation Melancthon accepted, April, 1543, and remained with him at Bonn till the month of August in the same year. Vid. some account of the "Simple and religious consultation," &c. which he and Bucer then compiled, in Strype, Eccl. Mem. Vol. II. pp. 41, 42, and of the use made of it in drawing up the English Book of Common Prayer, Laurence's Bampton Lectures, p. 439. Herman's attempts at effecting reformation being unsuccessful, he resigned his see, A.D. 1547. He died, August, A.D. 1552. Strype's Mem. of Cranmer, Vol. I. pp. 410, 11; Sleidan, De Statu Religionis et Reipub. (A.D. 1552.) Lib. XXIV. p. 572. Ed. Francof. 1568.]

[3 For an account of "the first occasion of Bucer's call into England," vid. Strype's Mem. of Abp. Cranmer, Vol. I. pp. 280, 81. Ed. Oxon. 1840.]

Strype's Mem. of Abp. Cranmer, Vol. II. App. No. 43, p. 844. Ed. Oxon. 1840.

diutius præesse posse scribis. Gemens igitur prophetæ illud exclamavi, "Mirifica misericordias tuas, qui salvos facis sperantes in te a resistentibus dexteræ tuæ." Nec dubito quin Deus hoc et similes piorum gemitus exauditurus sit; et veram doctrinam, quæ hactenus in vestris ecclesiis sincere propagata est, et conservaturus et defensurus sit adversus omnes diaboli et mundi furores. Interim sævientibus fluctuum procellis, in portus confugiendum est iis, qui vela in altum tendere non possunt. Tibi igitur, mi Bucere, portus longe tutissimus erit nostrum regnum, in quo, Dei beneficio, semina veræ doctrinæ feliciter spargi cœperunt. Veni igitur ad nos; et te nobis operarium præsta in messe Domini. Non minus proderis catholicæ Dei ecclesiæ cum apud nos fueris, quam si pristinas sedes retineres. Adde, quod adflictæ patriæ vulnera absens melius sanare poteris, quam nunc possis præsens. Omni igitur semota cunctatione, quamprimum ad nos venias. Ostendemus nobis præsentia Buceri nihil gratius aut jucundius esse posse. Sed cave ne quid ex itinere incommodi accipias. Nosti quos habeas vitæ insectatores: eorum manibus ne te commiseris. Est istic mercator quidam Anglus Richardus Hils[1], vir pius et summa fidelitate præditus, cum quo de tota itineris ratione te conferre velim. Præterea, Deum æternum Patrem Domini nostri Jesu Christi toto pectore oro, ut in ira misericordiæ recordetur, et afflictæ ecclesiæ calamitates respiciat, et lucem veræ doctrinæ apud nos magis magisque accendat; apud vos vero jam multos annos præclare lucentem non extingui patiatur. Is te quoque, mi Bucere, regat et servet, et incolumem ad nos traducat. Bene et feliciter vale. Londini, 2 Octob. Anno 1548.

Tui ad nos accessus cupientissimus,

THOMAS CRANMERUS, Archie. Cantu.

[TRANSLATION.]

THE grace and peace of God in Christ. I have read your letter to John Hales,[2] in which you relate the miserable condition of Germany,[3] and inform us that you can scarcely preside in the ministry of the word in your city. With groanings therefore I call out with the prophet, "Shew thy marvellous loving-kindness, O thou that savest them which trust in thee from those that rise up against thy right hand." Nor do I doubt but that God will regard both this and the like lamentations of godly men, and that he will preserve and defend the true doctrine, which has hitherto been sincerely set forth in your churches, against all the rage of the devil and of the world. Those, in the mean time, who are unable amidst the raging storm to launch out into the deep, must take refuge in harbour. To you, therefore, my Bucer, our kingdom will be a most safe harbour, in which, by the blessing of God, the seeds of true doctrine have happily begun to be sown. Come over therefore to us, and become a labourer with us in the harvest of the Lord. You will not be of less benefit to the universal church of God while you are with us, than if you retain your former position. In addition to this, you will be better able to heal the wounds of your distressed country in your absence, than you are now able to do in person. Laying aside therefore all delay, come over to us as soon as possible. We will make it manifest that nothing can be more gratifying or agreeable to us than the presence of Bucer. But take care that you suffer no inconvenience from the journey. You are aware of those who pursue your life: do not therefore commit yourself into their hands. There is an English merchant yonder, Richard Hilles, a godly and most trustworthy man, with whom I would have you confer respecting all the arrangements for your journey. Moreover, I pray God, the eternal Father of our Lord Jesus Christ, with my whole heart, that in the midst of wrath he may remember mercy, and look upon the calamities of his afflicted church, and kindle the light of true doctrine increasingly among us, and not suffer it to be extinguished, after having now shone with so much splendour for many years, among yourselves. May he likewise, my Bucer, guide and preserve you, and bring you over to us in safety. Farewell and happily. London, Oct. 2, 1548.

Ps. xvii. 7, marg. ver.

Most anxious for your arrival,

THOMAS CRANMER, archbishop of Canterbury.

---

[1 "Among the papers that were sent me from Zurich, there is a long and particular account of many passages in this matter, (i. e. Henry VIIIth's marriage with Ann of Cleves,) writ by one Richard Hill, who writes very piously and sensibly," &c. Burnet's Hist. of Reformat. Vol. III. pp. 275, 6, 282, 84. See also Original Letters relative to the English Reformation (Parker Society), First Portion, Letter CV.]

[2 "John Hales, a learned and good man, clerk of the hanaper." Strype's Eccl. Mem. Vol. I. Part I. p. 47. Vid. Bp. Keith's Affairs of Church and State in Scotland, Vol. II. pp. 226, 7. Spottiswode Soc. Ed. The names of John and Christopher Hales are inserted amongst the chief of the exiles at Frankfort, A. D. 1555. ib. Vol. III. Part I. pp. 404, 5. Ed. Oxon. 1822.]

[3 Vid. Letter CCLXXXVI. p. 422.]

## CCLXXXVIII. TO MATTHEW PARKER[4].

I COMMEND me heartily unto you; signifying, that my lord protector's grace, having good opinion of your learned knowledge and godly zeal in the advancement of God's word, hath, by the advice of the council, specially appointed you to preach one sermon before the king's majesty's person the third Sunday of Lent, now coming. Wherefore I pray you in the mean season to prepare yourself in a readiness for the purpose, and to repair unto the court against the day appointed, to satisfy the office whereunto you are called accordingly. Thus heartily fare ye well. From my manor at Lambhith, the 17th of Februarii, anno 1548. [1549.]

MSS. C.C.C.C. CXIV. p. 395. Original.

Your loving friend,
T. CANT.

---

## CCLXXXIX. TO MELANCTHON.

Ex copia manu Huberti in MSS. Vol. IX. p. 37. Scrin. Eccl. Argent.

VERISSIMA esse experimur, Melancthon doctissime, quæ Dominus noster Jesus Christus de cruce ecclesiæ suæ prædixit; "sed fidelis est Deus, qui non patietur suos tentari supra id quod possunt, sed faciet una cum tentatione proventum ut possimus sustinere." Etsi enim odio Filii Dei diabolus horribilem tyrannidem exercet in membra Christi, tamen promisit Deus ecclesiam suam non interituram esse. Imo de ultimis temporibus diserte inquit: "Ego senescentem gestabo: ego feram: ego salvabo[5]." Et semper Deus aliquas politias voluit esse hospitia ecclesiarum, et aliquot gubernatores fovere studiosos doctrinæ cœlestis, ut Abdias pavit auditores Heliæ, quos reges Israel undique pellebant. Quamobrem tibi, æterne Pater Domini nostri Jesu Christi, ingentes ago gratias, quod insulam nostram non aliter quam arcam Noæ e fluctibus eripuisti, nobisque tales dederis gubernatores, qui tui gloriam quærunt, et suas ædes ditionesque ecclesiæ et studiis patere cupiunt, ut olim viduæ Sareptanæ casa præbebat hospitium Heliæ. Oroque Deum, ut nos regat, et colligat sibi inter nos perpetuam ecclesiam, non solum ex nostratibus, sed etiam ex peregrinis; id quod facere pro sua immensa misericordia jam incepit.

Multi enim pii doctique viri[6], partim ex Italia, partim ex Germania, ad nos convenerunt, et plures quotidie exspectamus, cujus ecclesiæ chorum si ipse tua præsentia ornare et augere non gravaberis, haud scio qua ratione gloriam Dei magis illustrare poteris. Scio te sæpius optasse[7], ut pii et sapientes viri, communicato consilio et collatis sententiis, gravi auctoritate opus aliquod conderent, quod præcipuas materias ecclesiasticæ doctrinæ complecteretur, et veritatem ad posteros incorruptam transmitteret. Hoc nos sedulo pro virili conamur. Quare te rogamus, ut præsens cum præsentibus sententiam tuam et consilium communices, et ne animum ita obfirmes, ut tuis ipsius votis deesse, aut tam manifeste Dei vocationi repugnare videaris. Plurima hoc loco recensere poteram, quæ te in nostram sententiam flecterent; sed ea omnia non capit epistolæ brevitas. Proinde ex hoc tabellario, D. Joanne a Lasco, viro optimo, ea te cognoscere malim. Is enim mecum hosce aliquot menses conjunctissime et amantissime vixit, cui in his, quæ tibi meo nomine narrabit, fidem adhibeas oro. Dominus noster Jesus Christus, custos ecclesiæ, qui dixit, "Nemo rapiet oves meas de manibus meis," servet et defendat ministerium evangelii sui, et te ad ecclesiæ nostræ hospitium tuto deducat. Vale. Londini, 10. Februarii, 1549.

Tui ad nos accessus avidissimus,
THOMAS CANTUARIENSIS.

*Viro tum eruditione tum pietate clarissimo D. Philippo Melancthoni dentur hæ litteræ.*

Nostri Germani, qui nobiscum sunt, rogant, ut adducas tecum Doctorem Albertum Hardenbergium[8], ut Jonas[9] referet tibi nostro nomine.

---

[4 "In Lent, archbishop Cranmer writ to him (i.e. Parker) to preach before the king; advising him, that it was the lord protector's order for him so to do, on a certain Sunday in the Lent season, by him appointed." Strype's Life of Abp. Parker, Vol. I. pp. 49, 50. Ed. Oxon. 1821.]

[5 Vid. Isaiah xlvi. 4.]

[6 Vid. Letters CCLXXXV., CCLXXXVI., pp. 420, 422.]

[7 "Opto autem, ut antea sæpe scripsi, consensum piæ doctrinæ constitui in iis ecclesiis omnibus, quæ Romani episcopi tyrannidem et impietatem damnant." Letter of Melancthon to Henry VIII., dated March 26, A. D. 1539. (Cott. MSS. Vid. E. v. f. 239. British Museum. Original holograph. Vide also Strype's Eccl. Mem. Vol. I. Part II. App. No. 101, pp. 393, 4.]

[8 Letter CCLXXXVI. p. 422.]

[9 "The son of the great German divine of the same name,"... who "came over with letters com-

[TRANSLATION.]

We are experiencing, most learned Melancthon, the truth of all that our Lord Jesus Christ has foretold respecting the trials of his church. "But God is faithful, who will not suffer his people to be tempted above that they are able, but will also with the temptation make a way to escape, that we may be able to bear it." For though from his hatred to the Son of God the devil exercises a horrible tyranny over the members of Christ, yet God has promised that his church shall never perish; nay, of these last times he expressly declares, "To hoar hairs will I carry her: I will bear, I will deliver her." And God has always willed some civil societies to be the refuge of his churches, and that their rulers should support the friends of heavenly doctrine; just as Obadiah befriended the hearers of Elias, whom the kings of Israel were persecuting on every side. Wherefore, eternal Father of our Lord Jesus Christ, I give thee thanks for having rescued our island from the waves, like the ark of Noah, and for having granted us such rulers as seek thy glory, and who devote their houses and possessions to the church and its service, as in old time the cottage of the widow of Sarepta afforded a home to Elias. And pray God to direct us, and to gather unto himself a perpetual church amongst us, not only out of our own countrymen, but also from among those of foreign nations, as according to his infinite mercy he has already begun to do. For many pious and learned men have come over to us, some from Italy, some from Germany, and we are daily expecting more; which society of the church if you will vouchsafe to increase and adorn with your presence, I know not by what means you will be able more effectually to set forth the glory of God.

I am aware that you have often desired that wise and godly men should take counsel together, and, having compared their opinions, send forth under the sanction of their authority some work, that should embrace the chief subjects of ecclesiastical doctrine, and transmit the truth uncorrupted to posterity. This object we are anxiously endeavouring to accomplish to the utmost of our power. We therefore request you to communicate your counsel and opinions with us in person, and not so to shut up your mind as to seem wanting even to your own wishes, or acting in opposition to so manifest a calling of God. I could relate many things upon this subject, which would bring you over to our opinion; but the brevity of a letter will not contain them all. I would rather, therefore, that you should learn them from the bearer, John a Lasco, a most excellent man. For he has resided with me upon the most intimate and friendly terms for some months past; and I pray you to give credit to whatever he may relate to you in my name. May our Lord Jesus Christ, the guardian of his church, who has said, "None shall pluck my sheep out of my hands," preserve and defend the ministry of his gospel, and bring you in safety to the harbour of our church! Farewell. London, Feb. 10, 1549.

Most anxious for your arrival,

Thomas Cantuar.

Our German friends who are with us, request you to bring with you doctor Albert Hardenberg, as Jonas will tell you in my name.

*To that most illustrious man, as well for his learning as his piety, D. Philip Melancthon, these letters are to be given.*

---

## CCXC. TO MARTIN BUCER.

C.C.C.C. MSS. CXIX. p. 27. Original.

Quanto dolore animum meum vulneravit Fagii nostri mors[1], Bucere doctissime, non est nunc instituti mei narrare, ne vulnus tuum, jam (ut opinor) tum theologiæ tuæ medelis, tum ipso temporis progressu aliquo modo curatum, refricare videar. Quin potius impræsentiarum tecum communicare decrevi, quibus curationibus me ipsum consolatus sum; non quod prudentia tua mea consolatione indigeat, (novi enim animi tui moderationem et æquitatem,) sed ut his sæpius repetendis et mecum revolvendis ægritudinem meam quodammodo discuterem. Primum sic cogitabam, Humanum quidem fuit, cum amicus noster gravi morbo diu multumque cruciaretur, συμπαθεῖν condolere, et collacrymari: nunc vero, postquam omnibus miseriis defunctus, a bello ad pacem, a fluctibus ad portum tranquillissimum, ab ærumnis ad felicitatem perpetuam translatus est, illius statum deplorare invidi esset, non amici. "Sanctorum enim animæ in manu Dei sunt, et non tanget illos tormentum." Et Psalmista ait, "Pretiosa est in conspectu Domini mors sanctorum ejus." Quum enim Deum vera pietate hic noster coluerit, et contulit industriam et operam suam ad studia literarum propaganda, nihil est causæ cur non speremus, eum vitam æternam, quam hic tanta diligentia inchoaverit, jam agonothetæ gratia, nactum esse. Optarem quidem (si sic Deo placuisset) ut diutius in hoc curri-

---

mendatory from Melancthon." ... "This man the archbishop was very kind to, gave him harbour, and admitted him freely into his society and converse: insomuch that Justus Jonas the father entreated Melancthon, that he would take particular notice to the archbishop of his great favour shewed to his son." Strype's Mem. of Cranmer, Vol. II. p. 581.]

[[1] The death of Fagius, who had been professor of Hebrew and rabbinical learning in the university of Cambridge, occurred Nov. 15, A. D. 1549, at that place, where he had arrived on the 5th of the same month. Strype mentions that the archbishop wrote the above letter to Bucer, Nov. 30, A. D. 1549. Mem. of Abp. Cranmer, Vol. I. p. 282.]

culo nobiscum versari potuisset. Sed quum benignissimo Patri nostro visum sit, eum in aliam meliorem et eruditiorem scholam evocare, debemus ei gratulari, quod Paulus Fagius ad Christi et Divi Pauli consuetudinem, et ad sanctissimum collegium angelorum, prophetarum, et apostolorum evocatus sit.

His aliisque rationibus ego animum jacentem excito, inducoque in spem cogitationemque meliorem. Eas autem ad te scribens commemoro, non quod tibi his opus sit, sed potius, ut his similibusque fomentis dolores fœminæ optimæ uxoris Fagii nostri lenias et mitiges. Et ne angoribus se dedat ut horteris, magnopere a te peto quæsoque.

"Ploratur lacrymis amissa pecunia veris,"

dixit poeta quidam. Quare ut hac in parte ego illam aliquo pacto recrearem, mitto ad eam per hunc tabellarium viginti septem libras monetæ nostratis. Quam quidem summam etsi adhuc a quæstore regis pro stipendio Pauli Fagii non acceperim, brevi tamen me accepturum spero. Interim, ut viduæ dolorem aliquo modo levarem, de meo hanc pecuniam numerare visum est. Debebantur quidem illius marito pro stipendio quinquaginta libræ, sed tres decedunt a summa pro impensis in regia diplomata, &c., viginti autem a me numeratæ sunt. Quod tu adhuc literas a regia majestate commendatitias ad academiam Cantabrigiensem, et stipendium tuum in præsentia non acceperis, imputabis non negligentiæ meæ, sed consiliariorum et quæstorum fere omnium occupationibus, quos hoc comitiorum[2] tempore publica negotia sic distrahunt, ut privatas causas tractare non vacet. Interim tamen si quid desideres, significes oro, et ego omni cum diligentia illud ad te mitti curabo. Vale. Lambethi, ultimo Novembris. [1549.]

Tuæ paternitatis amantissimus,

T. CANT.

[TRANSLATION.]

MOST learned Bucer, it is not now my intention to tell you how deep a wound of sorrow has been caused to my feelings by the death of our friend Fagius, lest I should seem to irritate your wound, which, as I suppose, has been healed by the aid of your theology, as well as also in some sense by the lapse of time. But rather for the present I have determined to communicate to you the thoughts by which I myself gained consolation; not that, prudent as you are, you stand in need of consolations which I can give (for I know the moderation and reasonableness of your mind), but that by frequent repetition and consideration in my own mind I might by some means shake off this grief. In the first place, my thoughts took this turn, that it was in accordance with our nature to sympathise, condole, and weep with our friend, while he was for so long a time very grievously suffering from that painful disease: but now after that he has been freed from all sufferings, and has been translated from warfare to peace, from troublous waves to a haven the most still, from toils to endless felicity, it would be the act of an enemy, not of a friend, to bewail his state. "For the souls of the righteous are in the Lord's hand." And the Psalmist saith: "Right dear in the sight of the Lord is the death of his saints." Since therefore our friend worshipped God with true piety, and gave his attention and labour to the extension of the study of learning, there is no reason why we should not hope that, by the mercy of the Judge, he hath obtained that eternal life which he here commenced with such diligence. I could indeed wish, if so it had pleased God, that he might have sojourned with us for a longer period in the course of this life; but since it hath seemed good to our most merciful Father to call him away to a better and more learned school, we ought to congratulate him that Paul Fagius hath been summoned to the company of Christ and St Paul, and to the most holy college of angels, prophets, and apostles.

By these and other means I uplift my prostrate mind, and produce better hopes and thoughts. By my letter I put you in mind of these, not because they are needful for you, but rather that by these and similar consolations you may soften and assuage the grief of that excellent woman, the wife of our friend Fagius. And I earnestly beg and entreat of you to exhort her not to give up herself to sorrow.

A certain poet hath written,

"With sincerity of grief the loss of money is lamented;"

and therefore that in this respect I may in some way recover her, by this messenger I send to her twenty-seven pounds of our money; which sum although as yet I have not received it from the king's treasurer for Fagius' salary, yet I expect soon to receive it. Meanwhile that in some way I might alleviate the widow's grief, I think it better to pay this money from my own resources. There was indeed due to her husband for salary fifty pounds, but three are to be deducted from the total amount, for expenses on royal diploma, &c., and twenty I have paid. That you have not up to this time received letters recommendatory from the king's majesty to the university of Cambridge, and your salary for the present, you must not impute to negligence on my part, but to the occupation of the members of council, and generally all the officers, who are so distracted by public business in the sitting of parliament, that they

[[2] The parliament assembled November 4, A.D. 1549.]

have no leisure to treat of private matters. Meanwhile, if you are in want of anything, I beg you to declare it, and with all diligence I will take care that it be sent to you. Farewell. Lambeth, the last day of November. [1549.]

Your reverence's most affectionate,

T. Cant.

## CCXCI. TO VOYSEY, BISHOP OF EXETER.

Wilkins' Concilia, Vol. IV. p. 62, from Voysey's Regist. f. 117. Todd's Life of Abp. Cranmer, Vol. II. p. 200.

After my hearty commendations; the king's majesty's pleasure and high commandment to me is, that I shall will and charge you to ascertain me the names of all such benefices within your diocese, as at any time have been or yet be impropried, in whose hands and possession the same been, either in his majesty or any his grace's subjects, with your true certificate also of all vicarages endowed within your said diocese, and of all other churches impropried, having no vicarages endowed, being either served by a manual priest, or destitute of a curate, with the several values of such vicarages and benefices, as nigh as you may: fail you not this to do with all celerity, as you tender the accomplishment of his grace's pleasure. Fare you well. From my manor of Lambehith, this xx. of April, anno 1550.

Your loving brother,

T. Cant.

## CCXCII. TO MARTIN BUCER[1].

Todd's Life of Abp. Cranmer, Vol. II. pp. 229, 30, from A brief Examination for the time of a certain declaration lately put in print, in the name and defence of certain ministers of London refusing to wear the apparel prescribed by the laws of the realm.

After my hearty salutations, right well beloved master Bucer; I have read that book which you have sent to doctor Peter Alexander concerning the controversy betwixt master Hooper and the bishop of London[2]; in which book many things are learnedly declared, and largely handled: wherefore now I pray you that you would send unto me your judgment of these questions, expressed with as short brevity of words as you can.

Whether, without the offence of God, it may be lawful to the ministers of the church of England to use those vestures which at these days they wear, and are so prescribed of the magistrate?

Whether he that shall affirm that it is unlawful, or shall refuse to wear this apparel, offendeth against God, for that he sayeth that thing to be unclean that God hath sanctified; and offendeth against the magistrate, for that he disturbeth the politic order?

To these questions, if you will make most brief answer[3], and send unto me your judgment as soon as you may possibly, you shall do me great pleasure. God be with you! From Lambeth, the second of December. [1550.]

[[1] The original Latin copy of this letter, and of which the above is a translation, could not be discovered by Dr Jenkyns, neither has a further search been successful for this edition.]

[[2] For an account of the controversy with bishop Hooper about the ecclesiastical habits, vid. Strype's Eccl. Mem. Vol. II. Part 1. pp. 350 et seq. Mem. of Abp. Cranmer, Vol. I. pp. 302 et seq. Burnet's Hist. of Reformat. Vol. II. pp. 314—318. Todd's Life of Cranmer, Vol. II. pp. 226 et seq.—Bishop Ridley's answer to Hooper's objections to the Romish habits of the prelates, quoted by Archbishop Whitgift in his controversy with Cartwright, was long supposed to be lost: but it has lately been discovered among the large and valuable collection of MSS. belonging to Sir Thomas Phillipps.]

[[3] Bucer, in his reply, says:
1. "Qui jam ecclesiarum Anglicarum ministri hujusmodi sunt, eos sentio posse vestibus illis, quarum hodie usus est, uti cum gratia Dei.—De altera quæstione mea est sententia, hausta, ut credo, ex divinis literis: eos, qui dicunt vestibus de quibus agitur quovis modo uti, etiam eo quem descripsi, nefas esse, ad minimum errare; et hoc eo, quod negant sanctificatis esse sancta omnia. Idem affirmo de iis, qui ex eadem causa vestibus illis nolunt uti."—"Cum constet hodie, vestes has esse occasioni aliis ad superstitionem, aliis ad perniciosam contentionem; præstare eas tollere." Vid. Bucer's Scripta Anglicana, p. 681, and Bucer's Letter to Hooper, ibid. p. 705. Ed. Basil. 1577.]

## CCXCIII. TO MATTHEW PARKER.

C. C. C. C. MSS. CXIV. p. 391. Original. Strype's Life of Abp. Parker, Vol. I. p. 55. Ed. Oxon. 1821.

I COMMEND me heartily unto you; and whereas the king's majesty, by the advice of his most honourable council, hath appointed you to preach one sermon before his highness' person at the court, upon Sunday the 22nd of March next coming, being the sixth Sunday in Lent, and hath commanded me to signify unto you his grace's pleasure in this behalf; these therefore shall be to require you to put yourself in a readiness in the meantime to satisfy the day and place to you appointed, according to the king's majesty's expectation, and not to fail in any wise. Thus heartily fare ye well. From my manor at Lambeth, the xiith of February, 1550. [1551.]

Your loving friend,

T. CANT.

*To my loving friend, Mr. doctor Parker.*

---

## CCXCIV. TO CECIL.

MSS. Strype, preserved in Ball. Coll. Library, Oxford.

AFTER my very hearty commendations. Whereas the bearer hereof, Mr Coverdale, bishop elect of Exeter, is now through in all matters to the consecration, save only in doing his homage and in the dispatch of his first-fruits[4]: these shall be heartily to desire, that, in consideration of his long attendance and of the great lack that the West parts have of him, you will shew him your accustomable favour and help at this present: that by your procurement he may the sooner take his oath, and have your gentle assistance for the obtaining of his suit concerning the first-fruits. For I mind, by God's grace, the 30th day of this month to accomplish the king's majesty's mandate concerning the consecration of him and of the bishop of Rochester[5]. And thus I bid you most heartily well to fare. From my manor at Croydon, the 23rd of August, 1552[6]. [1551.]

Your loving friend,

T. CANT.

*To the right worshipful and my very good friend, Mr William Cecil, one of the king's majesty's two principal secretaries.*

---

## CCXCV. TO CECIL, OR CHEKE.

Strype's Mem. of Abp. Cranmer, Vol. II. App. No. 62, pp. 901, 2. Ed. Oxon. 1840. from Sir W. Hicks's MSS.

AFTER my very hearty commendations; these be to signify unto you, that Rayner Wolf, at my desire, hath fully finished the printing of my book[7], for answer to the late[8] bishop of Winchester's, written against mine of the doctrine of the sacrament. And forasmuch as both printing and selling of any matters in the English tongue is prohibited by

[4 A. D. 1551. Coverdale had previously been coadjutor with Voisey, bishop of Exeter, who greatly spoiled the bishoprick of its revenues: he resigned this year, and Coverdale was appointed to succeed him; but "being a poor man" he was discharged of the payment of this year's tenths, viz. £50, and all arrearages of the old bishop's time. He was discharged from the payments of first-fruits on account of his poverty. Strype's Mem. of Abp. Cranmer, Vol. I. pp. 382, 3; Eccl. Mem. Vol. II. Part II. pp. 265, 6.]

[5 "And also—he (Cranmer) was minded, on the 30th of August, to consecrate him (Coverdale) and the bishop of Rochester (Scory), according to the king's mandate." He was consecrated with Coverdale at Croydon on that day. Strype's Mem. of Abp. Cranmer, Vol. I. pp. 383, 389.]

[6 The date stands thus in Strype's MSS., which is evidently an error, as the events referred to occurred A. D. 1551.]

[7 i. e. "An answer by the Right Rev. Father in God, Thomas, Abp. of Canterbury, unto a crafty and sophistical cavillation, devised by Stephen Gardiner, doctor of law, late bishop of Winchester, against the true and godly doctrine of the most holy sacrament of the body and blood of our Saviour Jesus Christ;" contained in Vol. I. Park. Soc. Ed. 1844.]

[8 The date of Gardiner's deprivation was Feb. 14, A. D. 1551. Vid. Foxe's Acts and Monuments, p. 1539, 40. Ed. 1583.]

a proclamation set forth, unless the same matter be first allowed by the king's majesty, or six of his majesty's privy council, as you shall more plainly perceive by the proclamation, which herewith I send unto you; therefore I heartily pray you to be a suitor to the king's majesty, or to the privy council, that Mr Rayner may have licence for the printing and selling of my said book accordingly; and the same so obtained to send me with convenient speed. For in the beginning of the term I think it were very necessary to be set forth, for the contentation of many which have had long expectation of the same. As soon as I shall receive advertisement, when the king's majesty will be at Hampton Court, I will come thither to see his grace, and do my duty towards the same. Thus fare ye heartily well. From my manor at Croydon, the xxix. of September, 1551.

Your loving friend,

T. CANT.

*To my very loving friends, Mr Cecil, one of the king's majesty's two principal secretaries. Or to Mr Checke.*

---

## CCXCVI. TO BULLINGER.

In Archiv. Eccles. Tig. ex autogr. originali. Epist. Tom. VII. part. prior. p. 2187. Kasten. B. Original.

S. P. QUOD ad litteras tuas Tiguri datas 24 Februarii post annum respondeo, imputabis partim occupationibus meis, partim indiligentiæ cuidam meæ in hoc officii genere, quam in me hærere ingenue confiteor. Sed quia præstat sero quam nunquam officium facere, nunc ad omnia accipies [responsum].

Duas apud me causas agis, publicam et privatam. Quod ad publicam attinet[1], nempe ut consultor esse velim, ne regia majestas legatum ad concilium Tridentinum[2] mitteret, non fuit opus me consultore ad dissuadendum ab eo, quod nunquam illi in mentem venit: sed potius consilium dandum esse duxi, ut quemadmodum adversarii nostri nunc Tridenti habent sua concilia ad errores confirmandos, ita ejus pietas auxilium suum præbere dignaretur, ut in Anglia, aut alibi, doctissimorum et optimorum virorum synodus convocaretur, in qua de puritate ecclesiasticæ doctrinæ et præcipue de consensu controversiæ sacramentariæ tractaretur. Ad quod institutum (quia reipublicæ Christianæ utilissimum esse judicavit) animum majestatis illius admodum propensum esse sensi. Quare non est nobis committendum, ut ecclesiæ Dei in re tam ardua deesse velimus. Scripsi hac de re ad D. Philippum et ad D. Calvinum[3], oroque ut consultetis, qua ratione synodus hæc aut in Anglia aut alibi congregari commodissime possit.

Privata causa, de qua ad me scripsisti, fuit, ut controversiam inter D. Londinensem et D. Hoperum Gloucestrensem componerem, de qua nunc nimis serum est respondere. Nam diu abhinc audisse te sat scio controversiam illam compositam et penitus sublatam fuisse[4]. Et D. Hoperus ea est apud nos æstimatione, ut Wigorniensis episcopus jam sit designatus; et hoc tempore, quo comitia apud nos Londini congregantur, in ædibus

[1 Strype gives the substance of a letter written by Bullinger to Henry Grey, marquis of Dorset, on this subject, March, A.D. 1551. Strype's Eccl. Mem. Vol. II. pp. 397—99. Ed. Oxon. 1822.]

[2 The eleventh session of the council of Trent, and the first under pope Julius III., was held May 1, A.D. 1551. "The protestants were induced to think of attending the council, and to prepare accordingly; but they desired a safe conduct in the name, not of the emperor, but of the council; for they remembered the council of Constance, and the fate of Huss." Mendham's Memoirs of the Council of Trent, p. 141. Ed. London. 1834. Canon. et Decret. Concil. Trident. pp. 56 et seq. Ed. Lips. 1842. An account of the proceedings of this session, which was adjourned to the 1st of the following September, and from that day to Oct. 11th, will be found in Burnet's Hist. of Reformat. Vol. II. pp. 386 et seq. Ed. Oxon. 1829.]

[3 Vid. the next and two following letters.]

[4 Hooper himself informed Bullinger of this settlement of the differences between himself, Cranmer, and others, by a letter dated August 1, A.D. 1551, which is printed in the first Portion of Original Letters relative to the English Reformation, p. 91. Park. Soc. Ed. 1846. Peter Martyr also signified the same news in a letter to Gualter. Hooper was consecrated bishop of Gloucester, March, A.D. 1551, and "the diocese of Worcester becoming void by the deprivation of Heath in October, (A.D.) 1551,......it was given to Hooper to hold *in commendam*." Vid. Strype's Mem. of Abp. Cranmer, Vol. I. pp. 309, 312. Ed. Oxon. 1840.]

meis mecum conjunctissime vivit. Dominus Jesus Spiritu suo sancto te gubernet et tueatur. Vale. Lambethi, 20 Martii, 1552.

Tuæ paternitatis studiosissimus,

THOMAS CANTUARIENSIS.

*Eximio Viro D. Heinricho Bullingero,*
*Tigurinæ ecclesiæ ministro fidelissimo,*
*dentur hæ litteræ.*

[TRANSLATION.]

MUCH health. That I reply, after a year's interval, to your letter dated at Zurich on the 24th of February, you must impute partly to my want of leisure, and partly to a kind of dislike to a duty of this nature, and which I must candidly admit myself to entertain. But as it is better to perform a duty tardily than not at all, you shall now receive a reply to the whole of your letter.

You write to me upon two subjects, one of a public, the other of a private nature. With respect to that which is public, namely, that I would advise the king's majesty not to send any delegate to the council of Trent, there was no need of any advice of mine to dissuade him from a measure which never came into his mind: but I considered it better, forasmuch as our adversaries are now holding their councils at Trent to confirm their errors, to recommend his majesty to grant his assistance, that in England, or elsewhere, there might be convoked a synod of the most learned and excellent persons, in which provision might be made for the purity of ecclesiastical doctrine, and especially for an agreement upon the sacramentarian controversy. To which plan (as considering it most useful to the christian commonwealth) I perceived that the mind of his majesty was very favourably disposed. We must not therefore suffer ourselves to be wanting to the church of God in a matter of such importance. I have written upon the subject to masters Philip [Melancthon] and Calvin; and I pray you to devise the means by which this synod may be assembled with the greatest convenience, either in England or elsewhere.

The private affair upon which you wrote to me, was, that I should put an end to the controversy between the bishop of London and Hooper, bishop of Gloucester, respecting which it is now too late to reply. For I am aware that you have been informed long since that this controversy has been entirely settled. And master Hooper is in such great esteem among us, that he is now appointed bishop of Worcester; and he is at this time living in my house upon the most intimate terms, during the sitting of parliament. May the Lord Jesus guide and defend you by his holy Spirit! Farewell. Lambeth, March 20, 1552.

Your reverence's most attached,

THOMAS CANTUAR.

*To that excellent man, Mr Henry Bullinger, a most faithful minister of the church at Zurich, these letters be given.*

---

## CCXCVII. TO CALVIN.

S. P. Ut nulla res ecclesias magis dissipat, quam hæreses et dissidia circa dogmata religionis, ita nihil efficacius ecclesias Dei congregat et potentius ovile Christi munit, quam incorrupta evangelii doctrina et dogmatum consensus. Quare sæpius optavi atque etiamnum opto, ut docti et pii viri, qui alios antecellunt eruditione et judicio, in tutum aliquem locum convenirent, ubi communicato consilio et collatis sententiis capita omnia ecclesiasticæ doctrinæ tractarent, et non solum de rebus ipsis, sed etiam de formis loquendi, gravi auctoritate opus aliquod posteritati traderent. Adversarii nostri habent nunc Tridenti sua concilia, ut errores stabiliant; et nos piam synodum congregare negligemus, ut errores refutare, dogmata repurgare et propagare possimus? Illi περὶ τῆς ἀρτολατρείας (ut audio) decreta condunt;[5] quare nos omnem lapidem movere debemus, non solum ut alios adversus hanc idololatriam muniamus, sed etiam ut ipsi in doctrina hujus sacramenti consentiamus. Quantum ecclesiam Dei labefactarint circa hoc unitatis sacramentum dissensiones et opinionum varietates, prudentiam tuam latere non potest: quæ etsi nunc alicubi sublatæ sint, tamen in hac doctrina consensionem optarem, non solum de rebus ipsis, sed etiam de verbis et loquendi formulis. Habes meum

Arch. Eccles. Tig. Calvin. Opera. Tom. IX. p. 268. Amst. 1667. Original.

[[5] The thirteenth session of the council of Trent, and the third under pope Julius III. was held, Oct. 11, A. D. 1551, at which the decree concerning the eucharist was determined. Vid. Can. et Decret. Concil. Trident. pp. 58—65. Mendham's Memoirs of the Council of Trent, pp. 145, 6.]

votum, de quo etiam scripsi ad D. Philippum et ad D. Bullingerum, oroque ut vos inter vos deliberetis, qua ratione synodus hæc congregari commodissime possit[1]. Vale. Lambethi, 20 Mart. 1552.

Frater tuus in Christo carissimus,

T. Cantuariensis.

*Th. Cranmerus Calvino.*

[TRANSLATION.]

Much health. As nothing tends more injuriously to the separation of the churches than heresies and disputes respecting the doctrines of religion; so nothing tends more effectually to unite the churches of God, and more powerfully to defend the fold of Christ, than the pure teaching of the gospel, and harmony of doctrine. Wherefore I have often wished, and still continue to do so, that learned and godly men, who are eminent for erudition and judgment, might meet together in some place of safety, where by taking counsel together, and comparing their respective opinions, they might handle all the heads of ecclesiastical doctrine, and hand down to posterity, under the weight of their authority, some work not only upon the subjects themselves, but upon the forms of expressing them. Our adversaries are now holding their councils at Trent for the establishment of their errors; and shall we neglect to call together a godly synod, for the refutation of error, and for restoring and propagating the truth? They are, as I am informed, making decrees respecting the worship of the host: wherefore we ought to leave no stone unturned, not only that we may guard others against this idolatry, but also that we may ourselves come to an agreement upon the

---

[[1] The following from Calvin to Abp. Cranmer is in all probability the answer to the above letter.

*Calvinus Cranmero Archiep. Cantuariensi S. D.*

"Tu quidem, illustrissime Domine, vere et prudenter in hoc tam confuso ecclesiæ statu nullum aptius afferri posse remedium judicas, quam si inter se conveniant pii, cordati, et in Dei schola probe exercitati homines, qui suum in pietatis doctrina consensum profiteantur. Videmus enim quam variis artibus Satan evangelii lucem, quæ mirabili Dei bonitate nobis exorta passim refulget, conetur obruere. Conductitii papæ canes latrare non desinunt, ne purus Christi sermo exaudiatur. Tanta licentia passim ebullit et grassatur impietas, ut parum a manifestis ludibriis absit religio. Qui professi non sunt veritatis hostes, ea tamen protervia lasciviunt, quæ brevi, nisi obviam eatur, fœdam nobis confusionem pariet. Neque solum in hominum vulgo regnat hic tum stultæ curiositatis, tum intemperantis audaciæ morbus: sed, quod magis pudendum est, in ordine quoque pastorum nimis jam grassatur. Quibus deliriis seipsum deludat et quosdam alios fascinet Osiander, plus satis notum est. Et Dominus quidem, ut ab initio usque mundi solitus est, sinceræ fidei veritatem, ne laceretur hominum dissidiis, mirabiliter, et modo nobis incognito, servare poterit. Quos tamen ipse in excubiis locavit, minime torpere vult: quando et eosdem sibi destinavit ministros, quorum opera sanam in ecclesia doctrinam ab omnibus corruptelis purget, ac incolumem ad posteros transmittat. Tibi præsertim, ornatissime Præsul, quo altiore in specula sedes, in hanc curam, ut facis, incumbere necesse est. Quod non ideo dico, quasi tibi addendum esse novum calcar existimem; qui non modo sponte præcurris, sed aliis quoque instas voluntarius hortator; verum ut te in tam fausto præclaroque studio, mea gratulatione confirmem. Lætum quidem esse in Anglia evangelii successum audimus. Sed istic quoque usu venire, quod suo tempore expertus est Paulus, non dubito: ut ostio ad recipiendam puram doctrinam aperto, multi repente adversarii contra insurgant. Etsi vero me non latet, quam multi sint vobis ad manum idonei ad refellenda Satanæ mendacia vindices: facit tamen eorum improbitas, qui ad turbandum satagunt, ut bonorum sedulitas hac in parte nunquam nimia sit aut supervacua. Deinde scio non ita unius Angliæ haberi abs te rationem, quin orbi simul universo consulas. Regis quoque serenissimi non modo generosa indoles, sed rara etiam pietas merito exosculanda, quod sanctum consilium de habendo ejusmodi conventu favore suo prosequitur, et locum in regno suo offert. Atque utinam impetrari posset, ut in locum aliquem docti et graves viri ex præcipuis ecclesiis coirent, ac singulis fidei capitibus diligenter excussis, de communi omnium sententia certam posteris traderent scripturæ doctrinam. Ceterum in maximis seculi nostri malis hoc quoque numerandum est, quod ita aliæ ab aliis distractæ sunt ecclesiæ, ut vix humana jam inter nos vigeat societas, nedum emineat sancta membrorum Christi communicatio, quam ore profitentur omnes, pauci reipsa sincere colunt. Quod si frigidius, quam par esset, se gerunt doctores, gravissima penes ipsos principes est culpa, qui vel, profanis suis negotiis impliciti, ecclesiæ salutem et totam pietatem negligunt; vel singuli privata pace contenti, aliorum cura non tanguntur. Ita fit, ut membris dissipatis lacerum jaceat ecclesiæ corpus. Quantum ad me attinet, si quis mei usus fore videbitur, ne decem quidem maria, si opus sit, ob eam rem trajicere pigeat. Si de juvando tantum Angliæ regno ageretur, jam mihi ea satis legitima ratio foret. Nunc cum quæratur gravis et ad scripturæ normam probe compositus doctorum hominum consensus, qua ecclesiæ procul alioqui dissitæ inter se coalescant; nullis vel laboribus vel molestiis parcere fas mihi esse arbitror. Verum tenuitatem meam facturam spero, ut mihi parcatur. Si votis prosequar quod ab aliis susceptum erit, partibus meis defunctus ero. D. Philippus [i. e. Melancthon] longius abest, quam ut ultro citroque commeare brevi tempore literæ queant. D. Bullingerus tibi forte jam rescripsit. Mihi utinam par studii ardori suppeteret facultas! Porro quod me facturum principio negavi, ipsa rei quam sentis difficultas tentare me cogit: non ut te horter modo, sed etiam obtester ad pergendum, donec aliquid saltem effectum fuerit, si non omnia ex voto succedant. Vale, ornatissime Præsul, et mihi ex animo reverende. Dominus te Spiritu suo regere, sanctosque tuos conatus benedicere pergat. Genevæ." Calvini Op. Epist. col. 134, 5. Ed. Genev. 1617.]

doctrine of this sacrament. It cannot escape your prudence, how exceedingly the church of God has been injured by dissensions and varieties of opinion respecting this sacrament of unity; and though they are now in some measure removed, yet I could wish for an agreement in this doctrine, not only as regards the subject itself, but also with respect to the words and forms of expression. You have now my wish, about which I have also written to masters Philip [Melancthon] and Bullinger; and I pray you to deliberate among yourselves as to the means by which this synod can be assembled with the greatest convenience. Farewell. Lambeth, March 20, 1552.

You very dear brother in Christ,

THOMAS CANTUAR.

---

## CCXCVIII. TO MELANCTHON.

Ex Epist. ad Camer. MSS. in Bibl. Cl. Meisteri Past. in Küssnach prope Tigur. Original.

LEGIMUS in Actis Apostolorum, cum orta esset controversia, an ii qui ex gentibus conversi fuerant ad Deum, adigendi essent ad circumcisionem et observationem legis Mosaicæ, convenisse apostolos ac presbyteros ut dispicerent de hoc negotio, et collatis inter se sententiis, decretum concilii sui epistola scripta edidisse. Hoc exemplum utinam et nos imitaremur, in quorum ecclesiis evangelii doctrina restituta et repurgata est! Etsi autem omnes controversiæ in hoc mundo non possint dirimi, (quia pars inimica veritati non adsentitur judicio ecclesiæ,) tamen optandum est ut veræ ecclesiæ membra de præcipuis ecclesiasticæ doctrinæ capitibus inter se consentirent.

Quantum autem ecclesiam dilacerarint dissensiones religionis, maxime in causa sacramentaria, prudentiam tuam latere non potest, quæ si antea compositæ fuissent, nunquam (opinor) Cæsar bellum vobis intulisset. Et dolendum sane est, sacramentum unitatis invidia diaboli factam esse escam dissidii, et veluti μῆλον ἔριδος. Quare optarem ut ii, qui alios antecellunt eruditione et judicio, exemplo apostolorum congregarentur, et sententiam tum de aliis capitibus controversis, tum de hac controversia, mutuum exponerent, et consensum edito in publicum scripto testarentur. Sed fortasse dices: Idem et ego sæpissime optavi[2]; verum hæc res sine principum ope ad effectum deduci non potest. Ego igitur hac de re cum regia majestate[3]...., quæ Angliam suam vobis apertam esse vult, et ad hos pios conatus non solum locum tutum et quietem, verum etiam operam et auxilium suum, benignissime pollicetur. Scripsi etiam ad D. Calvinum et ad D. Bullingerum, eosque hortatus sum, ne operi tam necessario adeoque utili reipublicæ Christianæ deesse vellent. In proximis ad me literis scripsisti Areopagitas concilii Tridentini περὶ τῆς ἀρτολατρείας decreta condere. Quare cum adversarii evangelii tanto studio conveniunt ad errores stabiliendos, non est nobis committendum, ut illi sint diligentiores ad confirmandam impietatem, quam nos ad piam doctrinam propagandam et illustrandam.

Amori meo erga D. Georgium Majorem[4], quem merita illius apud me pepererunt, magnam accessionem attulit commendatio tua, cui si qua in re gratificari potero, citius facultatem quam voluntatem mihi deesse experietur. Bene et feliciter vale. Lambethi, 27 Martii a. 1552.

Tui aliquando videndi cupidissimus,

T. CANTUARIENS.

*Doctissimo viro et amico suo singulari D. Philippo Melancthoni dentur hæ litteræ.*

[TRANSLATION.]

WE read in the Acts of the Apostles, that when a dispute had arisen, as to whether those, who from among gentiles had been turned to God, should be compelled to be circumcised and keep the law of Moses, the apostles and elders came together to consider of this matter; and having compared their opinions delivered the judgment of their council in a written epistle. This example I wish we ourselves could imitate, in whose churches the doctrine of the gospel has been restored and purified. But although all controversies cannot be removed in this world, (because the party which is hostile to the truth, will not assent to the judgment of the church,) it is nevertheless to be desired that the members of the true church should agree

---

[2 Vid. Letter CCLXXXIX. p. 425, n. 8.]

[3 One or more words are wanting in the original.]

[4 "George Major was a zealous disciple of Luther, and minister at Eisleben. He died A. D. 1574."]

among themselves upon the chief heads of ecclesiastical doctrine. But it cannot escape your notice, how greatly religious dissensions, especially in the matter of the Lord's supper, have rent the churches asunder: had they been settled before, the emperor, I think, would never have made war against you. And it is truly grievous that the sacrament of unity is made by the malice of the devil food for disagreement, and (as it were) the apple of contention. I could wish therefore, that those who excel others in erudition and judgment, should be assembled together, after the example of the apostles, and declare their judgment as well respecting other subjects of dispute, as likewise especially respecting this controversy, and attest their agreement by some published document. But you will perhaps say, "And I also have often expressed the same wish; but this matter cannot be effected without the aid of princes." I have therefore [consulted with] the king's majesty, who places his kingdom of England at your disposal, and most graciously promises not only a place of security and quiet, but also his aid and assistance towards these godly endeavours. I have written likewise to masters Calvin and Bullinger, and exhorted them not to be wanting to a work so necessary, and so useful to the commonwealth of Christendom. You wrote me word in your last letter that the Areopagites of the council of Trent are making decrees respecting the worship of the host. Wherefore, since the adversaries of the gospel meet together with so much zeal for the establishment of error, we must not allow them to be more diligent in confirming ungodliness, than we are in propagating and setting forth the doctrine of godliness. Your commendation of master George Major has greatly increased that regard for him, which his merits have produced in me; and if I can be of service to him in any way, he shall find my ability will fail sooner than my inclination. Farewell and happily. Lambeth, March 27, 1552.

Very desirous of seeing you for some time past,

THOMAS CANTUAR.

*To the very learned man, and his singular friend*
*M. Philip Melancthon, let these letters be given.*

---

## CCXCIX. TO BUCER'S WIDOW[1].

Arch. S. Thom. Strasburg. Copy.

S. P. BENEVOLENTIA singularis qua virum tuum cum adhuc viveret sum prosecutus, post mortem ejus nequaquam est imminuta: siquidem egregia ejus pietas et insignis doctrina non momentaneos, verum æternos, fructus ecclesiæ attulit; quibus non tantum omnes pios, verum et me omnium maxime in perpetuum sibi devinxit. Quare a scribendo ad me ne ulla ratione patiaris te deterreri, si quid erit quod tibi aut rebus tuis adjumento esse possim. Nam literis tuis excitatus, et amici carissimi jucundam memoriam non absque voluptate mecum repetam, et tibi ejus viduæ propenso animo illa caritatis officia præstabo, quæ verbum Dei suadet impendenda, et pietati tuæ pro re nata exhibenda fuerint. Atque de eo quod mihi nuper significasti negotiis tuis expediendis opus esse, ut aliquo scripto certum ac testatum fieret, summam illam centum marcarum quam dono accepisti a majestate regia, cum hinc discederes, ad te ipsam proprie ac singulariter pertinere, literas ad tutores[2] liberorum Buceri dedi; ex quibus apertis cognoscere poterunt, quænam fuerit ea de re serenissimi regis nostri voluntas. Mitto ad te exemplar literarum a dominis consiliariis ad D. Joannem Hales[3] quæstorem regiæ majestatis (qui nunc opinor est Argentorati), aut eo absente ad ejus vicarium, Anglice scriptarum, quæ clare testantur tibi a regia majestate centum marcas dono datas, idque post obitum mariti tui, quod literæ illæ ultimo Martii fuerunt scriptæ, quum maritus tuus præcipitato Februario ex hac vita decesserit. Deus qui fons est et pater universæ consolationis te consolari dignetur, et in utroque nomine cum tota familia servet!

Vale. Lambeti xx$^{mo}$ Aprilis, a$^{o}$ 1552.

Tuus quantum potest,

T. CANTUARIEN.

[TRANSLATION.]

GREETING. The especial favour with which I regarded your husband during his lifetime, is by no means diminished now that he is no more. His remarkable piety indeed, and profound learning, has produced not a transient but an everlasting benefit to the church; whereby he has not only bound all godly persons, but myself more than all of them, under perpetual obligations to him. You must not therefore on any account allow yourself to be deterred from writing to me, should there be any thing in which I can be of use to you or to your affairs. For, stirred up by your letters, I shall not only recal to myself, and not without satisfaction, the agreeable remembrance of a very dear friend; but will also most readily perform to you, his widow, those offices of kindness, which the word of God commands to be paid, and which shall be afforded you as occasion shall offer. With respect to what you have lately informed me, that it is necessary for the ex-

---

[1 This has not appeared in any former collection of the archbishop's letters.]

[2 Viz. Conrad Hubert, Quinter Andernach, and Huldric Chelius, to whom the following letter was addressed.]

[3 Vid. Letter CCLXXXVII. p. 424, *n.* 2.]

pediting of your affairs that it should be certified and attested by some formal document, that the sum of a hundred marks which you received as a present from the king's majesty, when you left this country, belongs especially and exclusively to yourself, I have written a letter to the guardians of Bucer's children, whereby they may clearly ascertain what was the intention of our most serene king upon the matter in question. I send you a copy of the letter of the lords of the council to master John Hales, his majesty's treasurer, (who is now, I think, at Strasburgh,) or to his deputy in his absence, written in English, which clearly testifies that a hundred marks were presented to you by his majesty, and that too, after the death of your husband, inasmuch as that letter was written on the last day of March, and your husband departed this life at the end of February. May God, who is the fountain and father of all comfort, vouchsafe to comfort you, and preserve you with all your family! Farewell. Lambeth, April 20, 1552.

Yours to the utmost of his power,

THOMAS CANTUAR.

## CCC. TO CONRAD HUBERT AND OTHERS[4].

S. P. QUUM nuper intellexerim ex literis quas vidua[5] D. Buceri piæ memoriæ huc scripserat, ad facultates viri ejus jam defuncti partiendas inter liberos[6] opus esse certa notitia seu fide quoad summam pecuniæ centum marcarum quæ donata est a regia majestate, an ad viduam pertineat an ad liberos; ideo ut res liquida fiat, et ambiguitas prorsus tollatur, affirmo ac testor summam illam centum marcarum a serenissimo rege nostro post obitum D. Buceri viduæ peculiariter fuisse donatam, ut ad ipsam proprie pertineret: ut ex literis quas Domini consiliarii ad quæstorem scripserunt manifeste liquet, quarum exemplar ad viduam D. Buceri misi. Deus Spiritu Sancto suo vos gubernet, et successum in laboribus vocationis vestræ vobis donet! Valete. Lambethi, xx$^{mo}$ Aprilis, 1552. Arch. S. Thom. Strasburg.

Vester ex animo,

T. CANTUARIEN.

*Viris eruditione et pietate præstantibus, D. Conrado Huberto, verbi Dei ministro, D. Quintero Andernaco et D. Hulrico Chelio, medicinæ doctoribus, et ceteris tutoribus liberorum D. Buceri, dentur hæ literæ.*

[TRANSLATION.]

GREETING. As I have lately understood, from a letter written to this place by the widow of master Bucer of pious memory, that, for the purpose of dividing the property of her deceased husband amongst his children,[6] a certain declaration or certificate is necessary respecting the sum of a hundred marks, presented by his majesty, as to whether it belongs to the widow or to the children; whereby the fact may be ascertained, and all doubt entirely removed; I affirm and attest that the said sum of a hundred marks was especially bestowed by his most serene majesty upon master Bucer's widow, after his death, and intended for her especial use; as is clearly manifest from the letter which the lords of the council wrote to the treasurer, a copy of which I have sent to master Bucer's widow. May God direct you by his holy Spirit, and grant you success in the labours of your calling! Farewell. Lambeth, April 20, 1552.

Yours heartily,

T. CANT.

*To M. Conrad Hubert, minister of the word of God, M. Quinter Andernach and M. Hulric Chelius, doctors of medicine, men illustrious for their learning and piety, and to the other guardians of M. Bucer's children, let these letters be given.*

## CCCI. TO KING EDWARD VI.

*Thomas Cantuariensis archiepiscopus R. Edwardo VI. Gratia et pax a Deo Patre et Domino nostro Jesu Christo.*

ETSI prudenter moneat Horatius, illustrissime princeps, Bodl. Libr. Oxford. Smith's MSS. LXIX. f. 229. ex autographo.

"Qualem commendes etiam atque etiam adspice, ne mox
Incutiant aliena tibi peccata pudorem:"

[4 This has not appeared in any former collection of the archbishop's letters.]

[5 The name of Bucer's widow was Wibrand Bucerin. "The university gave her an hundred crowns: the king an hundred marks more, besides her husband's half year's pension, though he died before Lady-day, when it came due." Strype's Mem. of Abp. Cranmer, Vol. I. p. 358. Ed. Oxon. 1840.]

[6 For particulars respecting Bucer's property, see the Original Letters relative to the English Reformation, published by the Parker Society, Letters CLXXIX. and two following.]

tamen quum D. Radulphus Chevalærus[1] Gallus me oraverit, ut aditum aliquem ad gratiam tuam commendatione mea illi aperirem, non potui juveni optimo hoc officii denegare, tum quod is olim a piæ memoriæ viro D. Bucero commendatus mihi fuerat, tum quod hoc merentur singularis ejus modestia et eruditio, quæ domestica consuetudine mihi cognita et explorata sunt. Nam annum integrum aut amplius domi meæ vixit, ubi eximiæ pietatis et ingenii excellentis plurima documenta dedit: postea Cantabrigiam profectus, Hebraicas literas, non sine magna auditorum laude et utilitate, gratis professus est. Victum autem non aliunde habet, quum ex me et Domino Eliensi[2] cancellario, qui pro facultatibus nostris annuum quoddam stipendium illi numeramus. Sed quum nunc tanta sit temporum iniquitas, ut omnia fere duplo carius quam antea veneant, necessitas eum cogit ad tuam Majestatem omnium piorum et eruditorum asylum confugere, et a tua benignitate subsidium petere. Nihil attinet me plura scribere, cum norim voluntatem majestatis vestræ erga pios et doctos esse benignissimam: tantum significare volui D. Radulphum in talium catalogo esse numerandum, illud obsecrans ut ad eam voluntatem quam sua sponte M. T. erga Radulphum propter præclaras illius dotes habitura esset, aliquis cumulus accedat, quod peregrinus sit: nam de talibus diserte dicit Moses, "Deus amat peregrinum, et dat ei victum et vestitum, et vos ergo amate peregrinos." Debent vero præ aliis hi qui dii in scripturis dicuntur, Deum in hoc pietatis genere imitari, et ad illius similitudinem quam proxime accedere. Quod si curarit majestas tua, Dominus noster Jesus Christus (qui sibi acceptum fert quod hospitibus datur) non solum in hac vita te gubernabit, et mansionem apud te faciet, sed et hac vita defunctum in æterna sua tabernacula introducet, et pro regno temporario perpetuum daturus est. [1552.]

Serenissima tuæ majestatis famulus,

T. CANT.

[TRANSLATION.]

THOMAS, archbishop of Canterbury, to king Edward VI. Grace and peace from God the Father and our Lord Jesus Christ. Although, most illustrious prince, Horace wisely admonishes, "Look once and again what kind of person you recommend, lest by and bye the faults of others bring shame upon yourself;" yet since Mr Ralph Cavalier, of France, has entreated that I would open for him a means of access to your grace through my recommendation, I could not deny this excellent young man this obligation, both inasmuch as he was formerly recommended to me by master Bucer, a man of pious memory, and that his remarkable modesty and learning, which were known and tried through my private intimacy with him, also deserve it. For he lived in my house a whole year or more, where he exhibited very many proofs of his eminent piety and his surpassing ability: having afterwards proceeded to Cambridge, he gave gratuitous lectures on Hebrew literature, to the great satisfaction and advantage of his hearers. He has no other means of livelihood than from myself, and the bishop of Ely, the lord chancellor, who pay him a certain yearly salary, according to our means. But since from the severity of the times every thing at present is sold for twice as much as formerly, necessity compels him to have recourse to your majesty, the refuge of all pious and learned men, and to beg assistance from your bounty. It is unnecessary that I should write at greater length, since I am well aware that the disposition of your majesty is most gracious towards learned and pious men: I merely wish to intimate that master Ralph is to be accounted amongst such persons; entreating that in addition to that good-will which your majesty spontaneously would feel towards Ralph, because of his excellent endowments, something further may be added on the ground of his being a stranger: for concerning such persons Moses expressly saith, "God

[1 "Rafe Cavelarius, or Cavalier, ... a native of France,......in the year 1552, (if not before) did not so much succeed, as assist Tremellius," (whose wife's sister he had married) "in reading Hebrew in that university [i. e. Cambridge]. For which he was gratified by the state, in a grant to be free denizen, and in the same patent to enjoy the advowson of a prebend in Canterbury, in consideration of reading the Hebrew lecture freely in Cambridge. This was dated in August, 1552." (A.D. 1569) "By means of the learned sir Anthony Cook, and sir William Cecil," he was "appointed to be professor of the Hebrew language and learning in the university of Cambridge," and was sent down with a recommendatory letter, dated May 20, from archbishop Parker and bishop Grindal, in which he is named as "Rodolphus Cavellerius, otherwise called Mr Anthony." In this year he was also appointed to the seventh prebend of the cathedral of Canterbury. Strype supposes that he died at Guernsey, "whither he went A.D. 1569," from his will being dated at that place, Oct. 8, A.D. 1572. Vid. Strype's Eccl. Mem. Vol. II. Part I. pp. 323, 4. Part II. p. 272. Ed. Oxon. 1822. Strype's Annals, Vol. I. Part II. pp. 288, 9. and Appendix, No. 41. p. 552. Strype's Life of Abp. Parker, Vol. II. pp. 146, 7. Le Neve's Fasti, p. 16. Ed. Lond. 1716.]

[2 Thomas Goodrich, bishop of Ely, was sworn lord chancellor, January 22, A.D. 1552. Stow's Annals, p. 607. Ed. Lond. 1615.]

loveth the stranger, giving him food and raiment; love ye therefore the stranger." But those who are called gods in the scriptures, ought above others to imitate God in this kind of piety, and to approach to his likeness as nearly as they possibly can. Which if your majesty should regard, our Lord Jesus Christ (who esteems that which is done to strangers as received by himself) will not only guide you in this life, and take up his dwelling with you; but when you shall depart this life, will bring you into his eternal mansion, and for a temporal will give you an everlasting kingdom.

The servant of your most serene majesty,

T. Cant.

## CCCII. TO CECIL.

Strype's Mem. of Abp. Cranmer, Vol. II. App. No. 67. pp. 908, 9. Ed. Oxon. 1840. from Sir Wm. Hickes' MSS.

After my most hearty commendations and thanks, as well as for your gentle letters, as for the copy of the Pacification[3], and for your good remembrance of the two matters, which I desired you not to forget, the one concerning the bishop of Colen's[4] letters, and the other, Mr Mowse[5]: for whom eftsoons I give you my most hearty thanks.

As for your admonition[6], I take it most thankfully, as I have ever been most glad to be admonished by my friends, accounting no man so foolish as he that will not hear friendly admonishments. But as for the saying of St Paul, "Qui volunt ditescere, incidunt in tentationem," I fear it not half so much as I do stark beggary. For I took not half so much care for my living, when I was a scholar of Cambridge, as I do at this present. For although I have now much more revenue, yet I have much more to do withal; and have more care to live now as an archbishop, than I had at that time to live like a scholar. I have not so much as I had within ten years passed by 150*l.* of certain rent, besides casualties. I pay double for every thing that I buy. If a good auditor have this account, he shall find no great surplusage to wax rich upon.

And if I knew any bishop that were covetous, I would surely admonish him; but I know none, but all beggars, except it be one[7]; and yet I dare well say he is not very rich. If you know any, I beseech you to advertise me; for peradventure I may advertise him better than you. To be short, I am not so doted to set my mind upon things here, which neither I can carry away with me, nor tarry long with them.

If time would have served, I would have written of other things unto you; but your servant making haste compelleth me here to cut off the thread; beseeching Almighty

[3 "A little before this sickness befel him," (i. e. ague, which was prevalent A. D. 1552) "something fell out, which gave him great joy. Cecil knew how welcome good news out of Germany would be to him, and therefore in July sent him a copy of the Pacification," (viz. of Passau) "that is, the emperor's declaration of peace throughout the empire, after long and bloody wars; which consisted of such articles as were favourable unto the protestants, after much persecution of them." Strype's Mem. of Abp. Cranmer, Vol I. p. 409. Ed. Oxon. 1840. The date of the Pacification was July 31, A. D. 1552, upon which a definite arrangement was based for the future peace of Germany in matters of religion, A. D. 1557. Vid. Sleidan, De Statu Religionis et Reipub. Lib. XXIV. pp. 562 et sqq. Ed. Francof. 1568. Vid. also Letter CCCIV. p. 439.]

[4 i. e. Herman, archbishop and elector of Cologne. Vid. Letter CCLXXXVI. p. 423, *n.* 2. "What the contents of these letters of the archbishop of Colen (i. e. Cologne) were, it appeareth not: but I am very apt to think the purport of them was, that Cranmer would solicit some certain business in the English court relating to the affairs of religion in Germany, and for the obtaining some favour from the king in that cause." Strype's Mem. of Abp. Cranmer, Vol. I. pp. 410, 11.]

[5 For an account of Dr William Mowse, vid. Strype's Mem. of Abp. Cranmer, Vol. II. pp. 574—576.]

[6 For an account of the archbishop being charged with covetousness, and the cause of his writing this letter, vid. Strype's Mem. of Abp. Cranmer, Vol. I. pp. 401 et sqq. Vid. also Vol. II. pp. 621 et sqq.]

[7 "In this month of May (A.D. 1552) did Holgate archbishop of York," (to whom Cranmer probably here alludes,) "the only wealthy bishop then in England, bestow some part of his wealth very commendably, for the benefit of his successors in that see. For he made purchase from the king of the site, circuit, and precincts, capital messuage and mansion, lordship and manor of Scroby, in Scroby, with the appurtenances, in the county of Nottingham, lately parcel of the possessions of the archbishop of York," &c. Strype's Eccl. Mem. Vol. II. Part II. p. 77. Ed. Oxon. 1822.]

God to preserve the king's majesty with all his council and family, and send him well to return from his progress[1]. From my manor of Croydon, the xxi. of July.

Your own ever,

T. CANT.

*To my loving friend, sir William Cycil, one of the king's majesty's principal secretaries.*

---

## CCCIII. TO CECIL.

Strype's Mem. of Abp. Cranmer, Vol. II. App. No. 65, pp. 905, 6. Ed. Oxon. 1840. from Sir Wm. Hickes' MSS.

THOUGH in England there be many meet men for the archbishoprics of Ireland, yet I know very few that will gladly be persuaded to go thither. Nevertheless I have sent unto you the names of four[2], viz. Mr Whitehead of Hadley, Mr Tourner of Canterbury, sir Thomas Rosse[3], and sir Robert Wisdome; which, being ordinarily called, I think for conscience sake will not refuse to bestow the talent committed unto them, wheresoever it shall please the king's majesty to appoint them. Among whom I take Mr Whitehead for his good knowledge, special honesty, fervent zeal, and politic wisdom, to be most meet. And next him Mr Tourner, who, besides that he is merry and witty withal, "nihil appetit, nihil ardet, nihil somniat, nisi Jesum Christum;" and in the lively preaching of him and his word declareth such diligence, faithfulness, and wisdom, as for the same deserveth much commendation. There is also one Mr Whitacre[4], a man both wise and well learned, chaplain to the bishop of Winchester, very meet for that office, if he might be persuaded to take it upon him.

I pray you commend me unto Mr Cheke, and declare unto him, that mine ague, whether it were a quotidian or a double tertian (whereof my physicians doubted), hath left me these two days, and so I trust I am quit thereof: notwithstanding my water keepeth still an high colour. Now the most danger is, that if it come again this night, it is like to turn to a quartan. However the matter chance, the most grief to me is, that I cannot proceed in such matters as I have in hand, according to my will and desire. This "terrenum domicilium" is such an obstacle to all good purposes. Forasmuch as I perceive that the king's majesty's progress is altered, I pray you send me the gests of the latter end of his progress, from this time unto the end, that I may from time to time know where his majesty shall be: whom I beseech Almighty God to preserve and prosper in all his affairs, with his most honourable council and all his court. From my manor of Croydon, the xxvth of August, 1552.

Your own assured,

THOMAS CANT.

*To my very loving friend, sir William Cecyl, knight, one of the king's majesty's principal secretaries.*

---

## CCCIV. TO CECIL.

Strype's Mem. of Abp. Cranmer, Vol. II. App. No. 106. pp. 1035, 6. Ed. Oxon. 1840, from Sir Wm. Hickes' MSS.

AFTER my very hearty commendations; I thank you for your news, but specially for that ye advertise me that the king's majesty is in good health: wherein I beseech God long to continue his highness, as he hath twice (as I trust) restored me to the same.

---

[1 "To divert the king after the loss of his uncle, whom he dearly loved, Northumberland took him in progress in the summer of this year," [A.D. 1552.] Strype's Mem. of Abp. Cranmer, Vol. I. p. 401.]

[2 An account of these four divines, whom the archbishop nominated for the archbishoprick of Armagh, is given by Strype, Mem. of Abp. Cranmer, Vol. I. pp. 393—400.]

[3 This was the same Sir Thomas Rose concerning whom the archbishop wrote to the inhabitants of Hadleigh, March 20, 1533. Vid. Letter XCVII. p. 280, n. 3.]

[4 "I suppose this might be a slip of the archbishop's pen or memory, writing Whitacre for Goodacre, who afterwards was placed in that Irish see, [i.e. Armagh,] and had been Poynet's chaplain." Strype's Mem. of Abp. Cranmer, Vol. I. p. 393. See also ibid. p. 400.]

It seemeth by your letters, that a peace should be concluded betwixt the emperor and duke Morrise; which, whether it be according to the articles that afore ye sent unto me[5], or otherwise, I would gladly understand.

The commodity that might arise by printing the Book of Common Prayer and Administration of Sacraments in the French tongue[6], (if any be,) I reckon it were meet that it should come to them which have already taken pains in translating the same: which was first done by sir Hugh Paullet's commandment, and overseen by my lord chancellor, and other at his appointment; and now altered according to that which must be put in execution at the feast of All Saints next, at the appointment of my lord chancellor, by a learned Frenchman, a doctor in divinity: and therefore needless of any other to be travelled in. Aug. 26, 1552.

## CCCV. TO CECIL.

Strype's Mem. of Abp. Cranmer, Vol. II. App. No. 66, p. 907. Ed. Oxon. 1840. from Sir W. Hickes' MSS.

AFTER my very hearty recommendations: now at the last, against his will, Turner is come up unto the court. He preached twice in the camp that was by Canterbury[7]; for the which the rebels would have hanged him; and he seemed then more glad to go to hanging, than he doth now to go to Armachane; he alleged so many excuses, but the chief is this, that he shall preach to the walls and stalls, for the people understand no English. I bear him in hand, Yes; and yet I doubt whether they speak English in the diocese of Armachane. But if they do not, then I say, that if he will take the pain to learn the Irish tongue, which with diligence he may do in a year or two, then both his person and doctrine shall be more acceptable not only unto his diocese, but also throughout all Ireland. I commit him to your cure, praying you to help him to have as ready a dispatch as may be; for he hath but a little money.

I have sent the book of articles for religion[8] unto Mr Cheke, set in a better order than it was, and the titles upon every matter, adding thereto that which lacked. I pray

[5 Vid. Letter CCCII. p. 437; also Strype's Mem. of Abp. Cranmer, Vol. I. pp. 409, 10.]

[6 "Provision also was made for the king's French dominions, that this book (i. e. the second service book of Edward VI. A.D. 1552.) with the amendments should be used there. And the bishop of Ely, lord chancellor, (a great forwarder of good reformation,) procured a learned Frenchman, who was a doctor of divinity, carefully to correct the former French book by this English new one, in all the alterations, additions, and omissions thereof. For the first Common Prayer Book also was in French, for the use of the king's French subjects; being translated by commandment of Sir Hugh Paulet, governor of Calais; and that translation overseen by the lord chancellor and others at his appointment. The benefit of this last book was such, that one of the French congregation in London sought, by the means of A Lasco's interest with secretary Cecil, for a licence under the king's letters patents, to translate this Common Prayer, and the Administration of Sacraments, and to print it, for the use of the French islands of Jersey and Guernsey. But Cecil, after a letter received from A Lasco in August to that effect, not willing to do this of his own head, and reckoning it a proper matter to be considered by the archbishop, who were to be intrusted with the translating of such a book, desired him,....to give him his advice and judgment herein, both as to the work, and as to the benefit. To whom the archbishop gave this answer; 'that the commodity that might arise by printing of the book was meet to come to them who had already taken the pains in translating the same;' informing the secretary who they were; namely, those formerly and now of late employed by Sir Hugh Paulet and the lord chancellor. But I find this book was not presently finished, being not printed till the year 1553, for the use of Jersey and Guernsey." Strype's Mem. of Abp. Cranmer, Vol. I. pp. 416, 17.]

[7 "And this I judge to be that Turner, whom the archbishop nominated for Ireland, having lived long in his diocese, and so well known to him; and whom he had, I suppose, removed to Canterbury, to a prebend, or some other preferment there. Here he did this remarkable and bold piece of service, that when, about three years past, (i.e. A. D. 1549.) the rebels were up in Kent, he then preached twice in the camp near Canterbury; for which the rebels were going to hang him. But God preserved him." &c. Strype's Mem. of Abp. Cranmer, Vol. I. p. 395.]

[8 i. e. The forty-two articles, which were agreed to in the convocation of A.D. 1552, and published by the king's authority both in Latin and English, A.D. 1553. "These articles the archbishop was the penner, or at least the great director of, with the assistance (as is very probable) of bishop Ridley. And so he publicly owned afterwards, in his answer to certain interrogatories put to him by queen Mary's commissioners; viz. that the catechism, the book of articles, and the book against Winchester, were his doings." Strype's Mem. of Abp. Cranmer, Vol. I. p. 390. Vid. Interrogatories objected to the archbishop and his answers, p. 220, supra.]

you, consider well the articles with Mr Cheke; and whether you think best to move the king's majesty therein before my coming, I refer that unto your two wisdoms.

I pray you, let me have your advice unto whom I might best write concerning Rayner Wolfe[1]; for I wot not to whom I might write, but to my lord of Northumberland. The everliving God ever preserve you in this life, and in the life to come! From Croydon, the xixth of September. [1552.]

Your assured friend,

T. CANT.

*To my loving friend, sir William Cecyl, knight, one of the king's majesty's principal secretaries.*

---

## CCCVI. TO CECIL.

Strype's Mem. of Abp. Cranmer, Vol. II. App. No. 107, p. 1036. Ed. Oxon. 1840, from Sir Wm. Hickes' MSS. Todd's Life of Abp. Cranmer, Vol. II. p. 354.

AFTER my very hearty recommendations, and no less thanks for your friendly letters and advertisements; be you assured, that I take the same in such part, and to proceed of such a friendly mind, as I have ever looked for at your hands. Whereof I shall not be unmindful, if occasion hereafter shall serve to requite the same. I have written letters unto my lord of Northumberland, declaring unto him the cause of my stay in the commission[2]; which is, because that all the gentlemen and justices of the peace of Kent, which be in commission with me, be now at London: before whose coming home, if I should proceed without them, I might perchance travail in vain, and take more pain than I should do good. I have written also unto him in the favour of Michael Angelo[3]; whose cause I pray you to help so much as lieth in you.

The Sophy and the Turk, the emperor and the French king[4], (not much better in religion than they,) rolling the stone, or turning the wheel of fortune up and down, I pray God send us peace and quietness with all realms, as well as among ourselves; and to preserve the king's majesty, with all his council. Thus fare you well. From my house of Ford, the xx. day of November, anno 1552.

Your assured,

T. CANT.

*To my loving friend sir William Cecil, knight, and secretary to the king's majesty.*

---

## CCCVII. TO THE LORDS OF THE COUNCIL.

Strype's Mem. of Abp. Cranmer, Vol. II. App. No. 64, p. 905. Ed. Oxon. 1840, from Sir Wm. Hickes' MSS. Todd's Life of Abp. Cranmer, Vol. II. p. 289.

AFTER my very humble recommendations unto your good lordships; I have sent unto the same the book of articles[5] which yesterday I received from your lordships. I have sent also a cedule inclosed, declaring briefly my mind upon the said book: beseeching your lordships to be means unto the king's majesty, that all the bishops may have authority from him to cause all their preachers, archdeacons, deans, prebendaries, parsons,

---

[1 Vid. Letter CCXCV. p. 429; and Strype's Annals, Vol. II. Part I. p. 530. Ed. Oxon. 1824.]

[2 "Another (of the businesses the archbishop was employed in while he was in his retirement at his house in Canterbury) was, the sitting upon a commission to him, and other gentlemen of Kent, for inquiry after such as had embezzled the plate and goods belonging to chauntries, &c. given by the parliament to the king, and converting them to their own uses. But this, being somewhat an odious work, he was not very forward to enter upon, especially because he thought, whatsoever he and the other commissioners should recover, would be but swallowed up by the duke of Northumberland and his friends, and the king be little the better. But, because he did not make haste, he was charged by his enemies at court as a neglecter of the king's business," &c. Strype's Mem. of Abp. Cranmer, Vol. I. p. 419.]

[3 "The minister of the Italian protestant church in London." Todd's Life of Abp. Cranmer, Vol. II. p. 354. *n*. 2.]

[4 "Alluding to the contests then existing between the emperors of Persia and the Turks, and between Charles V. of Germany and Henry II. of France." Id. ibid. *n*. 3.]

[5 Vid. Letter CCCV. p. 439, *n*. 8.]

vicars, curates, with all their clergy, to subscribe to the said articles[6]. And then I trust that such a concord and quietness in religion shall shortly follow thereof, as else is not to be looked for many years. God shall thereby be glorified, his truth shall be advanced, and your lordships shall be rewarded of him, as the setters forward of his true word and gospel. Unto whom is my daily prayer, without ceasing, to preserve the king's majesty, with all your honourable lordships. From my house at Ford, the 24 of this present month of November. [1552.]

Your lordships' ever to command,

T. CANT.

*To my very good lords of the king's majesty his most honourable council.*

## CCCVIII. TO CECIL.

Strype's Mem. of Abp. Cranmer, Vol. II. App. No. 108, p. 1037. Ed. Oxon. 1840. from Sir Wm. Hickes' MSS.

AFTER my hearty commendations and thanks for your letters; there is no man more loth to be in contention with any man, than I am, specially with my lord Warden[7], my near neighbour, dwelling both in one country, and whose familiar and entire friendship I most desire, for the quietness of the whole country. For the example of the rulers and heads will the people and members follow.

And as touching learned men I shall send you my mind with as much expedition as I can, which by this post I cannot do, even in the cold snow, sitting upon coals, until he be gone. But heartily fare you well in the Lord Jesus. From Ford, the last day of November. [1552.]

Your loving friend,

T. CANT.

*To my loving friend sir William Cecill, knight, secretary to the king's majesty, yeve these.*

## CCCIX. TO CECIL.

Strype's Mem. of Abp. Cranmer, Vol. II. App. No. 109, pp. 1037, 8. Ed. Oxon. 1840, from Sir Wm. Hickes' MSS.

AFTER my very hearty recommendations; yesternight I heard reported that Mr Cheke is indicted[8]: I pray you heartily, if you know any thing thereof, to send me

[6 The authority here sought by the archbishop was not granted till June 9, A. D. 1553, when Edward VI. issued a mandate "willing and exhorting" the bishops of the realm, "to subscribe the forty-two articles, and to observe them in their preachings, readings, and teachings, and to cause them to be subscribed and observed of all other, which do or hereafter shall preach or read within their diocese." Another mandate was also issued in king Edward's name, June 19, A. D. 1553, requiring all rectors, vicars, &c., to see that the articles of religion should be signed. Both the letter and the mandate will be found in the Appendix. Vid. Interrogatory 12, objected to the archbishop, and his answer, p. 220, supra.]

[7 "There happened once, in the year 1552, a contest between him and the lord warden of the Cinque-ports, who lived not far from him; and so probably it might be about some worldly matters. It was sir Thomas Cheyny, who, in the year 1549, was one of those that met with Warwick in London, and published a proclamation against the archbishop's friend, the duke of Somerset, as a traitor; which might be an occasion that the archbishop did not much affect Cheyny, nor Cheyny the archbishop." Strype's Mem. of Abp. Cranmer, Vol. II. p. 651.]

[8 "King Edward being dead, and the lady Jane set up and proclaimed queen, letters at this time were sent from the council to the gentry, and other state-letters were written by Cheke as secretary. He checked his brother Cecil, who would not be induced to meddle in this matter, but endeavoured to be absent; and to the very utmost day of queen Jane's reign, viz. to July 19th (A.D. 1553) he acted as secretary to her and her council.——And within eight or nine days after, viz. July the 28th, together with the duke of Suffolk," he was "committed to the Tower as a traitor. And whereas the rest that acted as queen Jane's counsellors, being either papists, or indifferent in religion, were easily pardoned; Cheke and some few others (as the archbishop of Canterbury and the lord Russel) were sent to the Tower, or kept under harder and longer restraint. An indictment was drawn against him the 12th or 13th day of August; and his friends feared it would go hard with him.——The next year, being almost spoiled of all his substance, he

Todd's Life of Abp. Cranmer, Vol. II. pp. 371, 2.

knowledge, and whereupon he is indicted. I had great trust that he should be one of them that should feel the queen's great mercy and pardon, as one who hath been none of the great doers in this matter against her: and my trust is not yet gone, except it be for his earnestness in religion: for the which if he suffer, blessed is he of God, that suffereth for his sake, howsoever the world judge of him. For what ought we to care for the judgment of the world, when God absolveth us? But, alas! if any means could be made for him, or for my lord Russel, it were not to be omitted, nor in any wise neglected. But I am utterly destitute both of counsel in this matter and of power, being in the same condemnation that they be[1]. But that only thing which I can do, I shall not cease to do; and that is only to pray for them and for myself, with all other that be now in adversity. When I saw you at the court, I would fain have talked with you, but I durst not: nevertheless, if you could find a time to come over to me, I would gladly commune with you. Thus fare you heartily well, with my lady your wife. From Lamhith, this 14. day of this month of August. [1553.]

Your own assured,

T. Cant.

*To my very loving friend, sir William Cecil, knight.*

## CCCX. TO QUEEN MARY.

Coverdale's Letters of the Martyrs, pp. 1—3. Ed. Lond. 1564.

Most lamentably mourning and moaning himself unto your highness, Thomas Cranmer[2], although unworthy either to write or speak unto your highness, yet having no

obtained the favour of the queen's pardon." Strype's Life of sir John Cheke, chap. v. sect. 1 and 2. pp. 93—95. Ed. Oxon. 1821.]

[1 "About the beginning of August he was before the council, about the lady Jane's business... and then, with the severe reprimands he received, was charged to keep his house, and be forthcoming. At that time he espied Cecil, who was in the same condemnation; and would fain have spoken with him, but durst not......as it seems, out of his love and care of him, lest his very talking with Cecil might have been prejudicial to that pardon, which he now lay fair for.—September 13, following, the archbishop was again summoned to appear that day before the queen's council. Then he appeared and was dismissed; but commanded to be the next day in the Star-chamber. And so he was. The effect of which appearing was, that he was committed to the Tower, partly for setting his hand to the instrument of the lady Jane's succession, and partly for the public offer he made a little before of justifying openly the religious proceedings of the deceased king. But the chief reason was, the inveterate malice his enemies conceived against him for the divorce of king Henry from the queen's mother; the blame of which they laid wholly upon him, though bishop Gardiner and other bishops were concerned in it as deep as he." Strype's Mem. of Abp. Cranmer, Vol. II. p. 439. "The rest of the nobles paying fines, were forgiven, the archbishop of Canterbury only excepted: who, though he desired pardon by means of friends, could obtain none; insomuch that the queen would not once vouchsafe to see him, for as yet the old grudges against the archbishop for the divorcement of her mother remained hid in the bottom of her heart. Besides this divorce, she remembered the state of religion changed; all which was reputed to the archbishop as the chief cause thereof." Foxe's Acts and Monuments, p. 1871. Ed. Lond. 1583.]

Manet alta mente repostum Judicium Paridis, spretæque injuria *matris*. Virgil. *Æneid.* I.

[2 "On the 13th of November, archbishop Cranmer, the lord Guilford Dudley, and the lady Jane his wife, with two other sons of the duke of Northumberland ...... were brought to their trial. These all confessed their indictments. Only Cranmer appealed to those that judged him, how unwillingly he had consented to the exclusion of the queen; that he had not done it till those whose profession it was to know the law had signed it; upon which he submitted himself to the queen's mercy. But they were all attainted of high treason for levying war against the queen, and conspiring to set up another in her room. So these judgments, with those that had passed before, were now confirmed by act of parliament. And now Cranmer was legally divested of his archbishoprick, which was hereupon void in law, since a man that is attainted can have no right to any church benefice; his life was also at the queen's mercy. But it being now designed to restore the ecclesiastical exemption and dignity to what it had been anciently, it was resolved that he should be still esteemed archbishop, till he were solemnly degraded according to the canon law. The queen was also inclined to give him his life at this time, reckoning, that thereby she was acquitted of all the obligations she had to him; and was resolved to have him proceeded against for heresy, that so it might appear she did not act out of revenge, or on any personal account. So all that followed on this against Cranmer was, a sequestration of all the fruits of his archbishoprick; himself was still kept in prison:—the queen was desirous to seem willing to pardon injuries done against herself, but was so heated in the matters of religion, that she was always inexorable on that head." Burnet's Hist. of Reformat. Vol. II. pp. 515, 16. Ed. Oxon.

person that I know to be mediator for me, and knowing your pitiful ears ready to hear all pitiful complaints, and seeing so many before to have felt your abundant clemency in like case, am now constrained most lamentably, and with most penitent and sorrowful heart, to ask mercy and pardon for my heinous folly and offence, in consenting and following the testament and last will of our late sovereign lord king Edward VI. your grace's brother: which will, God he knoweth, I never liked; nor never anything grieved me so much that your grace's brother did. And if by any means it had been in me to have letted the making of that will, I would have done it. And what I said therein, as well to the council as to himself, divers of your majesty's council can report: but none so well as the marquis of Northampton, and the lord Darcy, then lord chamberlain to the king's majesty; which two were present at the communication between the king's majesty and me. I desired to talk with the king's majesty alone, but I could not be suffered, and so I failed of my purpose. For if I might have communed with the king alone, and at good leisure, my trust was, that I should have altered him from that purpose; but, they being present, my labour was in vain.

Strype's Mem. of Abp. Cranmer, Vol. II. App. No. 74. pp. 919—921. Ed. Oxon. 1840.

He desired to be released of his offence for consenting unto king Edward's will, and so he was; but after was accused of heresy; which he best liked, for then he knew his cause was Christ's. [Coverdale.]

Then when I could not dissuade him from the said will, and both he and his privy council also informed me that the judges and his learned counsel said, that the act of entailing the crown, made by his father, could not be prejudicial to him, but that he, being in possession of the crown, might make his will thereof; this seemed very strange unto me; but being the sentence of the judges, and other his learned counsel in the laws of this realm, (as both he and his council informed me,) methought it became not me, being unlearned in the law, to stand against my prince therein. And so at length I was required by the king's majesty himself to set to my hand to his will; saying, that he trusted that I alone would not be more repugnant to his will than the rest of the council were: (which words surely grieved my heart very sore,) and so I granted him to subscribe his will, and to follow the same. Which when I had set my hand unto, I did it unfeignedly and without dissimulation[3].

For the which I submit myself most humbly unto your majesty, acknowledging mine offence with most grievous and sorrowful heart, and beseeching your mercy and pardon: which my heart giveth me shall not be denied unto me, being granted before to so many, which travailed not so much to dissuade both the king and his council as I did[4].

And whereas it is contained in two acts of parliament[5], (as I understand,) that I,

---

1829. The degradation of the archbishop from his office, in obedience to the sentence definitive from the pope, took place two years afterwards, Dec. A.D. 1555. Vid. p. 224, supra; and Foxe's Acts and Monuments, pp. 2132, 3.]

[3 "Cecil, in a relation which he made one write of this transaction, for clearing himself afterwards, says, that when he had heard Gosnald and Hales declare how much it was against law," (i.e. the alteration of the succession to the throne in favour of the lady Jane Grey by Edward VIth's will,) "he refused to set his hand to it as a counsellor, and that he only signed as a witness to the king's subscription. But Cranmer still refused to do it after they had all signed it, and said, he would never consent to the disinheriting of the daughters of his late master. Many consultations were had to persuade him to it. But he could not be prevailed on, till the king himself set on him; who used many arguments, from the danger religion would otherwise be in, together with other persuasions: so that by his reasons, or rather importunities, at last he brought him to it. But whether he also used that distinction of Cecil's, that he did it as a witness, and not as a counsellor, I do not know: but it seems probable, that if that liberty was allowed the one, it would not be denied the other." Burnet's Hist. of Reformat. Vol. II. p. 458. Vid. Letter CCCXII. p. 445.]

[4 "The said bishop (Heath, abp. of York) declared afterwards to one of Doctor Cranmer's friends, that notwithstanding his attainder of treason, the queen's determination at that time was, that Cranmer should only have been deprived of his archbishoprick, and have had a sufficient living assigned him, upon his exhibiting a true inventory," (i.e. of all his goods, which he had been commanded to give in to the queen's commissioners,) "with commandment to keep his house without meddling in matters of religion. But how that was true, I have not to say. This is certain, that not long after this he was sent unto the Tower, and soon after condemned of treason. Notwithstanding, the queen, when she could not honestly deny him his pardon, seeing all the rest were discharged, and specially seeing he last of all other subscribed to king Edward's request, and that against his own will, released to him his action of treason, and accused him only of heresy: which liked the archbishop right well, and came to pass as he wished, because the cause was not now his own, but Christ's, not the queen's, but the church's." Foxe's Acts and Monuments, p. 1871.]

[5 "One of these acts probably is 1 Mary, St. ii. c. 16, 'for confirming the attainder of the late duke of Northumberland and others,' the preamble to which names Cranmer among those who 'have with the duke of Northumberland, should devise and compass the deprivation of your majesty from your royal crown, surely it is untrue. For the duke never opened his mouth to me, to move me any such matter, nor I him; nor his heart was not such toward me, (seeking long time my destruction,) that he would either trust me[1] in such matter, or think that I would be persuaded by him. It was other of the council that moved me, and the king himself, the duke of Northumberland not being present. Neither before, neither after, had I ever any privy communication with the duke of that matter, saving that openly at the council-table the duke said unto me, that it became not me to say to the king as I did, when I went about to dissuade him from the said will.

Now as concerning the estate of religion, as it is used in this realm of England at this present, if it please your highness to license me, I would gladly write my mind unto your majesty. I will never, God willing, be author of sedition, to move subjects from the obedience of their heads and rulers: which is an offence most detestable. If I have uttered my mind to your majesty, being a christian queen and governor of this realm, (of whom I am most assuredly persuaded, that your gracious intent is, above all other regards, to prefer God's true word, his honour and glory,) if I have uttered, I say, my mind unto your majesty, then I shall think myself discharged. For it lieth not in me, but in your grace only, to see the reformation of things that be amiss. To private subjects it appertaineth not to reform things, but quietly to suffer that they cannot amend. Yet nevertheless to shew your majesty my mind in things pertaining unto God, methink it my duty, knowing that I do, and considering the place which in times past I have occupied. Yet will I not presume thereunto without your grace's pleasure first known, and your licence obtained: whereof I most humbly prostrate to the ground do beseech your majesty; and I shall not cease daily to pray to Almighty God for the good preservation of your majesty from all enemies bodily and ghostly, and for the increase of all goodness heavenly and earthly, during my life, as I do and will do, whatsoever come of me.

## CCCXI. TO MRS WILKINSON[2].

MSS. Emmanuel Coll. Camb. Original. Coverdale's Letters of the Martyrs, p. 23. Ed. Lond. 1564. Strype's Mem. of Abp. Cranmer, Vol. II. App. No. 72, pp. 916, 7. Ed. Oxon. 1840. Foxe's Acts and Monuments, pp. 1892, 3. Ed. Lond. 1583.

THE true comforter in all distress is only God, through his Son Jesus Christ; and whosoever hath him, hath company enough, although he were in a wilderness all alone. And he that hath twenty thousand in his company, if God be absent, he is in[3] a miserable wilderness and desolation. In him is all comfort, and without him is none. Wherefore, I beseech you, seek your dwelling there, where as you[4] may truly and rightly serve God, and dwell in him, and have him ever dwelling in you. What can be so heavy a burden as an unquiet conscience, to be in such a place as a man cannot be suffered to serve God in Christ's true religion?[5] If you be loth to part from your kin and friends, remember, that Christ calleth them his mother, sisters, and brothers, that do his Father's will. Where we find therefore God truly honoured according to his will, there we can lack neither friend nor kin.

Matt. 3. [Coverdale.]

committed many detestable and abominable treasons, to the most fearful peril and danger of the destruction of your most royal person, and to the utter loss, and disherison, and destruction of this your realm of England.' Statutes of the Realm, Vol. IV. p. 217." Jenkyns' Remains of Abp. Cranmer, Vol. I. p. 362.]

[1 Would ever trust me. Strype.]

[2 "The favourers of religion, seeing it was now determined to proceed in all manner of severity against them, began to flee into other countries for their safety as fast as they could. Indeed there were some that made a case of conscience of it: among the rest, one Mrs Wilkinson, a woman of good quality, and a great reliever of good men. Her the archbishop out of prison advised to escape, and avoid a place where she could not truly and rightly serve God." Strype's Mem. of Abp. Cranmer, Vol. II. p. 449. Ed. Oxon. 1840. Vid. "Defensio veræ et Catholicæ doctrinæ de Sacramento." (Emb. ed.). Vol. I. p. 8. Park. Soc. Ed. 1844. "This mistress Wilkinson afterward died in exile at Frankfort." Foxe's Acts and Monuments, &c. p. 1517, Ed. Lond. 1583; who also gives a letter from Bishop Hooper to her. Several other letters to her from Bradford are printed in Coverdale's Letters of the Martyrs, pp. 280, 342, 3.]

[3 Be absent, is in. Coverdale, Strype and Foxe.]

[4 There, as you. Coverdale and Foxe.]

[5 In Christ's religion. Strype and Foxe.]

If you be loth to depart for slandering of God's word[6], remember, that Christ, when his hour was not yet come, departed out of his country into Samaria, to avoid the malice of the scribes and Pharisees; and commanded his apostles, that if they were pursued in one place, they should fly to another. And was not Paul let down by a basket out at a window, to avoid the persecution of Aretas? And what wisdom and policy he used from time to time, to escape the malice of his enemies, the Acts of the Apostles do declare. And after the same sort did the other apostles. Mary, when it came[7] to such a point, that they could no longer escape danger of the persecutors of God's true religion; then they shewed themselves, that their flying before came not of fear, but of godly wisdom to do more good, and that they would not rashly, without urgent necessity, offer themselves to death; which had been but a temptation of God. Yet, when they were[8] apprehended, and could no longer avoid, then they stood boldly to the profession of Christ: then they shewed how little they passed of death; how much they feared God more than men; how much they loved and preferred the eternal life to come above this short and miserable life.

John 4. [Coverdale.] Matt. 5. [Id.] 1 Cor. ii. [Id.]

Wherefore I exhort you, as well by Christ's commandment as by the example of him and his apostles, to withdraw yourself from the malice of your and God's enemies, into some place where God is most truly served[9]: which is no slandering of the truth, but a preserving of yourself to God and the truth, and to the society and comfort of Christ's little flock. And that you will do, do it with speed, lest by your own folly you fall into the persecutors' hands. And the Lord send his Holy Spirit to lead and guide you, wheresoever you go! And all that be godly will say, Amen.

T. Cranmer.

---

## CCCXII. TO THE LORDS OF THE COUNCIL.

In most humble wise sueth[10] unto your right honourable lordships, Thomas Cranmer, late archbishop of Canterbury[11]; beseeching the same to be a means for me unto the queen's highness for her mercy and pardon. Some of you know by what means I was brought and trained unto the will of our late sovereign lord king Edward VI., and what I spake against the same; wherein I refer me to the reports of your honours[12].

Furthermore, this is to signify unto your lordships, that upon Monday, Tuesday, and Wednesday last past were open disputations here in Oxford against me, master Ridley, and master Latimer, in three matters concerning the sacrament: first, of the real presence: secondly, of transubstantiation: and thirdly, of the sacrifice of the mass[13]. How the other two were used[14], I cannot tell[15]; for we were separated: so

MSS. Emmanuel Coll. Camb. Original. Coverdale's Letters of the Martyrs, p. 16. Ed. Lond. 1564. Strype's Mem. of Abp. Cranmer, Vol. II. App. No. 79. pp. 944—6, Ed. Oxon. 1840. Foxe's Acts and Monuments, p. 1464. Ed. Lond. 1583.

---

[6 For slandering God's word. Strype.]

[7 Albeit when it came. Coverdale, Strype and Foxe.]

[8 Yea, when they were. Coverdale, Strype and Foxe.]

[9 Most purely served. Coverdale.]

[10 In right humble wise sheweth unto Strype and Foxe.]

[11 "Thus stood the cause of Cranmer, (Vid. p. 443, supra, n. 4.) till at length it was determined by the queen and the council, that he should be removed from the Tower, where he was prisoner, to Oxford, there to dispute with the doctors and divines.—And although the queen and the bishops had concluded before what should become of him, yet it pleased them that the matter should be debated with arguments, that under some honest shew of disputation the murder of the man might be covered." Foxe's Acts and Monuments, p. 1871. Ed. Lond. 1583. Vid. Disputations at Oxford. Vol. I. pp. 391, et sqq. Park. Soc. Ed. and pp. 212, et sqq. supra. "On Monday next ensuing, after these things done and past, being the 23rd of the said month of April, D. Weston, prolocutor, took his journey up to London, with the letters certificatory from the university unto the queen, by whom the archbishop of Canterbury directed his letters supplicatory unto the council. The which letters after the prolocutor had received, and had carried them well near half way to London, by the way he opened the same, and seeing the contents thereof, sent them back again, refusing to carry them." Foxe's Acts and Monuments, p. 1464, who gives the above as the copy of the archbishop's letter to the council, sent by Dr Weston, who refused to deliver it.]

[12 Your honours and worships. Strype and Foxe. Vid. Letter CCCX. p. 443, n. 3.]

[13 Concerning the sacrifice of the mass, Coverdale, Foxe and Strype, who here add: "Upon Monday against me, upon Tuesday against doctor Ridley, and upon Wednesday against master Latimer."]

[14 Two were ordered I know not. Strype and Foxe.]

[15 But as concerning myself I can report. Doctor Chedsey was appointed to dispute against me; but the disputation was so confused, that I never knew the like, every man bringing forth what he liked without order. Strype and Foxe.]

They put to him three questions, but they suffer him not to answer fully in one. [Coverdale.]

that none of us knew what the other said, nor how they were ordered. But as concerning myself, I can report, that I never knew nor heard of a more confused disputation in all my life. For albeit there was one appointed to dispute against me, yet every man spake his mind, and brought forth what him liked without order. And such haste was made, that no answer could be suffered to be given fully[1] to any argument, before another brought a new argument[2]. And in such weighty and large matters there was no remedy, but the disputations must needs be ended in one day[3], which can scantly well be ended in three months[4]. And when we had answered them, then they would not appoint[5] us one day to bring forth our proofs, that they might answer us again, being required of me thereunto[6]: whereas I myself have more to say, than can be well discussed in twenty days[7]. The means to resolve the truth had been, to have suffered us to answer fully to all that they could say, and then they again to answer to all that we could say[8]. But why they would not answer us, what other cause can there be, but that either they feared the matter[9], that they were[10] not able to answer us; or else (as by their haste might well appear) they came, not to speak the truth, but to condemn us in post haste, before the truth might be thoroughly tried and heard?[11] for in all haste we were all three condemned of heresy upon Friday. Thus much[12] I thought good to signify unto your lordships[13], that you may know the indifferent handling of matters, leaving the judgment thereof unto your wisdoms. And I beseech your lordships to remember me, a poor prisoner, unto the queen's majesty; and I shall pray, as I do daily, unto God for the long preservation of your good lordships in all godliness and felicity. April 23. [1554.]

Behold Satan sleepeth not. Their cruel desire to revenge could abide no delay. [Coverdale.]

---

## CCCXIII. TO MARTYN AND STORY[14].

Certain Letters to the queen, &c. Foxe's Acts and Monuments, p. 1892. Ed. Lond. 1583.

I HAVE me commended unto you; and, as I promised, I have sent my letters unto the queen's majesty unsigned, praying you to sign them, and deliver them with all speed. I might have sent them by the carrier sooner, but not surer: but hearing master Bailiff say, that he would go to the court on Friday, I thought him a meeter messenger to send my letters by; for better is later and surer, than sooner and never to be delivered. Yet one thing I have written to the queen's majesty inclosed and sealed, which I require you may be so delivered without delay, and not to be opened until it be delivered into her grace's own hands. I have written all that I remember I said, except that which I spake against the bishop of Gloucester's own person, which I

---

[1 Suffered to be taken fully. Strype and Foxe.]

[2 The words, "before another brought a new argument," are omitted by Coverdale.]

[3 And in such weighty matters the disputations must needs be ended in one day. Strype and Foxe.]

[4 Which can scantly be ended in three months. Strype.]

[5 Answered them, they would not appoint. Strype and Foxe.]

[6 That they might answer us, being required by me. Strype and Foxe.]

[7 Well discussed, as I suppose, in more than twenty days. Strype and Foxe.]

[8 To answer us fully to all that we can say. Strype and Foxe.]

[9 Feared their matter. Strype and Foxe.]

[10 Or that they were. Strype.]

[11 Or else for some consideration they made such haste, not to seek the truth, but to condemn us, that it must be done in post haste, before the matters could be thoroughly heard. Strype and Foxe.]

[12 Condemned of heresy. Thus much, &c. Strype and Foxe. This much. Coverdale.]

[13 To your lordships. Strype.]

[14 Cranmer, Ridley and Latimer "had been all three condemned and adjudged heretics by Dr Weston, in the university of Oxford, after their disputations. But that sentence was void in law, because the authority of the pope was not yet received. —But there was a new commission sent from Rome for the conviction of Cranmer. Brokes, (bishop) of Glocester, was the pope's sub-delegate under cardinal Puteo, to whom the pope had committed this process; and Martyn and Story, doctors of the civil law, were the queen's commissioners." Strype's Mem. of Abp. Cranmer, Vol. II. pp. 532, 3. Ed. Oxon. 1840. Vid. "Examination at Oxford before Brokes," pp. 212 et sqq. supra. The above Letter was probably written after the termination of the proceedings; and "there is a strong presumption that the letters here described are the two which follow." Vid. Jenkyns' Remains of Abp. Cranmer, Vol. I. p. 367, *nn.* i and k.]

thought not meet to write. And in some places I have written more than I said, which I would have answered to the bishop, if you would have suffered me.

You promised I should see mine answers to the sixteen articles[15], that I might correct, amend, and change them, where I thought good: which your promise you kept not. And mine answer was not made upon my oath, nor repeated; nor made *in judicio*, but *extra judicium*, as I protested; nor to the bishop of Gloucester as judge, but to you the king's and queen's proctors. I trust you deal sincerely with me, without fraud or craft, and use me as you would wish to be used in like case yourselves. Remember, that *Qua mensura mensi fueritis, eadem remetietur vobis;* i. "What measure you mete, the same shall be measured to you again." Thus fare you well, and God send you his Spirit to induce you into all truth! [Sep. 1555.]

## CCCXIV. TO QUEEN MARY[16].

It may please your majesty to pardon my presumption, that I dare be so bold to write to your highness; but very necessity constraineth me, that your majesty may know my mind rather by mine own writing, than by other men's reports. So it is, that upon Saturday[17], being the seventh day of this month, I was cited to appear at Rome the eightieth day after, there to make answer to such matters as should be objected against me upon the behalf of the king and your most excellent majesty: which matters the Thursday following were objected against me by Dr Martin and Dr Storie, your majesty's proctors, before the bishop of Gloucester, sitting in judgment by commission from Rome. But, alas! it cannot but grieve the heart of any natural subject, to be accused of the king and queen of his own realm, and specially before an outward judge, or by authority coming from any person out of this realm: where the king and queen, as if they were subjects[20] within their own realm, shall complain, and require justice at a stranger's hands against their own subject[21], being already condemned to death by their own laws. As though the king and queen could not do or have justice within their own realms against their own subjects, but they must seek it at a stranger's hands in a strange land: the like whereof, I think, was never seen. I would have wished to have had some meaner adversaries: and I think that death shall not grieve me much more, than to have my most dread and most gracious sovereign lord and lady (to whom under God I do owe all obedience) to be mine accusers in judgment within their own realm, before any stranger and outward power. But forasmuch as in the time of the prince of most famous memory, king Henry the Eighth, your grace's father, I was sworn never to consent that the bishop of Rome should have or exercise any authority or jurisdiction in this realm of England; therefore, lest I should allow his authority contrary to mine oath, I refused to make answer to the bishop of Gloucester, sitting here in judgment by the pope's authority, lest I should run into perjury.

Certain Letters to the queen, &c. Coverdale's Letters of the Martyrs, p. 3, Ed. Lond. 1564. Foxe's Acts and Monuments, pp. 1889—1891. Ed. Lond. 1583.

The king and queen make themselves no better than subjects in complaining[18] of their own subject to an outward judge[19], as though they had no power to punish him. [Coverdale.]

The first cause why the archbishop would not make answer to the pope's commissary[22], is to avoid perjury. [Certain Letters to the queen and Coverdale.]

Another cause why I refused the pope's authority is this, that his authority, as he claimeth it, repugneth to the crown imperial of this realm, and to the laws of the same, which every true subject is bounden to defend. First, for that the pope saith[24], that all manner of power, as well temporal as spiritual, is given first to him of God; and that the temporal power he giveth unto emperors and kings, to use it under him, but so as it be always at his commandment and beck. But contrary to this claim,

The second cause is[23], that the pope's laws are contrary to the crown and laws of England. [Id.]

The crown and temporal

[15 Vid. "Interrogatories objected to the archbishop, with his answers to the same," and "his appeal at his degradation," pp. 219—228, supra.]

[16 Where the side notes are found in the Letters, as they stand in Coverdale and Foxe, no reference is made to them in the foot notes, but the omissions and alterations are noticed.]

[17 "Upon Wednesday being the twelfth." Foxe.]

[18 Subjects complaining. Foxe.]

[19 "Subject unto the pope." Foxe, who omits the remainder of the side note.]

[20 As they were subjects. Id.]

[21 Their own subjects. Id.]

[22 The pope's delegate. Id.]

[23 For that the pope's. Coverdale.]

[24 So that the pope saith. Id.]

power is taken immediately from God.
[Certain Letters to the queen.]
The oath of the king and justices, and the duty of subjects.

the imperial crown and jurisdiction temporal of this realm is taken immediately from God, to be used under him only, and is subject unto none but to God alone.

Moreover, the imperial laws[1] and customs of this realm, the king in his coronation, and all justices when they receive their offices, be sworn, and all the whole realm is bounden, to defend and maintain. But contrary hereunto, the pope by his authority maketh void[2], and commandeth to blot out of our books all laws and customs, being repugnant to his laws; and declareth accursed all rulers and governors, all the makers, writers, and executors of such laws or customs: as it appeareth by many of the pope's laws, whereof one or two I shall rehearse. In the Decrees, *Dist.* 10. is written thus, *Constitutiones contra canones et decreta præsulum Romanorum vel bonos mores nullius sunt momenti*[3]. That is, "The constitutions or statutes enacted against the canons and decrees of the bishops of Rome or their good customs are of none effect." Also, *Extra. De Sententia Excommunicationis*, "*Noverit:*" *Excommunicamus omnes hæreticos utriusque sexus, quocunque nomine censeantur, et fautores et receptatores et defensores eorum; nec non et qui de cetero servari fecerint statuta edita et consuetudines introductas contra*[4] *ecclesiæ libertatem, nisi ea de capitularibus suis intra duos menses post hujusmodi publicationem sententiæ fecerint amoveri. Item, excommunicamus statutarios, et scriptores statutorum ipsorum, nec non potestates, consules, rectores, et consiliarios locorum, ubi de cetero hujusmodi statuta et consuetudines editæ fuerint vel servatæ; nec non et illos qui secundum ea præsumpserint judicare, vel in publicam formam scribere judicata*[5]. That is to say, "We excommunicate all heretics of both sexes, what name soever they be called by, and their favourers[6] and receptors and defenders; and also them that shall hereafter cause to be observed the statutes[7] and customs made against the liberty of the church, except they cause the same to be put out of their records and chapters[8] within two months after the publication of this sentence[9]. Also we excommunicate the statute-makers and writers of those statutes, and all the potestates, consuls, governors and counsellors of places where such statutes and customs shall be made or kept; and also those that shall presume to give judgment according to them, or to write into public form the matters so adjudged[10].

Dist. 10. Constitutiones. [Foxe.]
Extrav. De Sententi. et reindic. Noverit. [Id.]

Either the pope's laws be unlawful, or else all England is accursed. [Certain Letters to the queen[11].]

Now by these laws, if the bishop of Rome's authority, which he claimeth by God, be lawful, all your grace's laws and customs of your realm, being contrary to the pope's laws, be naught: and as well your majesty, as your judges, justices, and all other executors of the same, stand accursed among heretics; which God forbid! And yet this curse can never be avoided, if the pope have such power as he claimeth, until such times[12] as the laws and customs of this realm, being contrary to his laws, be taken away and blotted out of the law-books. And although there be many laws of this realm contrary to the laws of Rome, yet I named but a few; as to convict a clerk before any temporal judge of this realm for debt, felony, murder, or for any other crime; which clerks by the pope's laws be so exempt from the king's laws, that they can be no where sued but before their ordinary.

Note wherein the pope's laws and the laws of England do vary[13]. [Id.]

Cases wherein the pope's laws repugn against our laws. [Foxe.]

Also the pope by his laws may give all bishopricks and benefices spiritual, which by the laws of this realm can be given but only by the king and other patrons of the same, except they fall into the lapse.

By the pope's laws, "jus patronatus" shall be sued only before the ecclesiastical judge, but by the laws of this realm it shall be sued before the temporal judges.[14]

Provision against the pope's laws by Præmunire. [Id.]

And to be short, the laws of this realm do agree with the pope's laws like fire

[[1] To the imperial laws. Id.]

[[2] Vid. Collection of Tenets from the Canon Law, pp. 68-75.]

[[3] Corpus Juris Canonici. Decreti I. Pars. Dist. 10. can. iv. Tom. I. p. 8. Ed. Paris. 1687.]

[[4] Consuetudines, contra. Foxe.]

[[5] Corpus Juris Canonici. Decretal. Gregor. IX. Lib. v. Tit. 39. De sentent. excommunicat. cap. xlix. "Noverit." Tom. II. p. 276.]

[[6] And their fautors. Foxe.]

[[7] Observed, statutes. Coverdale.]

[[8] Out of their books or records. Id.]

[[9] The publication hereof. Foxe.]

[[10] Or put into public form of writing the matters so judged. Coverdale. Or shall notify in public form the matters so judged. Foxe.]

[[11] Foxe and Coverdale omit this side note entirely.]

[[12] Such time. Foxe.]

[[13] The pope's law and the laws of England are contrary. Coverdale. The pope's laws and the laws of England do vary, how and wherein. Foxe.]

[[14] Temporal judge. Coverdale and Foxe.]

and water. And yet the kings of this realm have provided for their laws by the "præmunire;" so that if any man have let the execution of the laws of this realm by any authority from the see of Rome, he falleth into the "præmunire."

But to meet with this, the popes have provided for their laws by cursing. For whosoever letteth the pope's laws to have full course within this realm, by the pope's power standeth accursed. So that the pope's power treadeth all the laws and customs of this realm under his feet, cursing all that execute them, until such time as they give place unto his laws.

The proviso of the pope against our præmunire[15]. [Id.]

But it may be said, that notwithstanding all the pope's decrees, yet we do execute still the laws and customs of this realm. Nay, not all quietly without interruption of the pope. And where we do execute them, yet we do it unjustly, if the pope's power be of force, and for the same we stand excommunicate, and shall do, until we leave the execution of our own laws and customs. Thus we be well reconciled to Rome, allowing such authority, whereby the realm standeth accursed before God, if the pope have any such authority.

Mark this well. [Id. and Certain Letters to the queen.]

These things, as I suppose, were not fully opened in the parliament-house, when the pope's authority was received again within this realm; for if they had, I do not believe that either the king or queen's majesty, or the nobles of this realm[16], or the commons of the same, would ever have consented to receive again such a foreign authority, so injurious, hurtful, and prejudicial, as well to the crown as to the laws and customs, and state of this realm, as whereby they must needs acknowledge themselves to be accursed. But none could open this matter well but the clergy, and that such of them as had read the pope's laws, whereby the pope hath made himself[18] as it were a god. These seek to maintain the pope, whom they desired to have their chief head, to the intent they might have as it were a kingdom and laws within themselves, distinct from the laws of the crown, and wherewith the crown may not meddle; and so being exempt[19] from the laws of the realm, might live in this realm like lords and kings, without damage or fear of any man, so that they please their high and supreme head at Rome. For this consideration, I ween, some that knew the truth held their peace in the parliament; whereas if they had done their duties to the crown and whole realm, they should have opened their mouths, declared the truth, and shewed the perils and dangers that might ensue to the crown and realm.

The duty of the clergy neglected in the parliament[17]. [Certain Letters to the queen.] The clergy's duty in the parliament. [Foxe.]

The papists to set up a kingdom of their own, dissemble the known truth, and are false to the crown. [Coverdale.] The clergy of England more addicted to the pope than to their true allegiance to their country[20]. [Foxe.]

And if I should agree to allow such authority within this realm, whereby I must needs confess that your most gracious highness, and also your realm, should ever continue accursed, until you shall cease from the execution of your own laws and customs of your realm; I could not think myself true either to your highness, or to this my natural country, knowing that I do know. Ignorance, I know, may excuse other men; but he that knoweth how prejudicial and injurious the power and authority, which he challengeth every where, is to the crown, laws, and customs of this realm, and yet will allow the same, I cannot see in any wise, how he can keep his due allegiance, fidelity, and truth to the crown and state of this realm.

Another cause I alleged, why I could not allow the authority of the pope, which is this, that by his authority he subverteth not only the laws of this realm, but also the laws of God: so that whosoever be under his authority, he suffereth them not to be under Christ's religion purely, as Christ did command. And, for one example, I brought forth, that whereas by God's laws all christian people be bounden diligently to learn his word, that they may know how to believe and live accordingly, for that purpose he ordained holy days, when they ought, leaving apart all other business, to give themselves wholly to know and serve God. Therefore God's will and commandment is, that when the people be gathered together, ministers should use such language as the people may understand and take profit thereby, or else hold their peace. For as

The third cause why he could not allow the pope. The pope's religion is against Christ's religion[21].

[15 The side-notes from Foxe are not found either in Certain Letters to the queen, or in Coverdale.]

[16 The noblest of this realm. Foxe.]

[17 These notes are omitted altogether by Coverdale.]

[18 The pope had made himself. Foxe.]

[19 Being exempted. Coverdale and Foxe.]

[20 Both of these side-notes are omitted in Certain Letters to the queen.]

[21 Foxe omits this note: it is found in Coverdale and Certain Letters to the queen.]

Why Latin service ought not to be restored in England.

an harp or lute, if it give no certain sound, that men may know what is stricken, who can dance after it? for all the sound is in vain: so is it vain and profiteth nothing, saith Almighty God by the mouth of St Paul, if the priest speak to the people in a language which they know not; "for else he may profit himself, but profiteth not the people," saith St Paul. But herein I was answered thus; that St Paul spake only of preaching, that the preacher should preach in a tongue which the people did know, or else his preaching availeth nothing. [This I would have spoken, and could not be suffered.][1] But if the preaching availeth nothing, being spoken in a language which the people understand not, how should any other service avail them, being spoken in the same language? And yet that St Paul meant not only of preaching, it appeareth plainly by his own words. For he speaketh by name expressly of praying, singing, lauding, and thanking of God[2], and of all other things which the priests say in the churches, whereunto the people say Amen; which they used not[3] in preaching, but in other divine service: that whether the priests rehearse the wonderful works of God, or the great benefits of God unto mankind above all other creatures, or give thanks unto God, or make open profession of their faith, or humble confession of their sins, with earnest request of mercy and forgiveness, or make suit or request unto God for any thing; that then all[4] the people, understanding what the priests say, might give their minds and voices with them, and say Amen, that is to say, allow what the priests say; that the rehearsal of God's universal works and benefits, the giving of thanks, the profession of faith, the confession of sins, and the requests and petitions of the priests and the people[5] might ascend up into the ears of God all together, and be as a sweet savour, odour, and incense in his nose: and thus was it used many hundred years after Christ's ascension. But the aforesaid things cannot be done, when the priests speak to the people in a language not known; and so they (or their clerk in their name) say Amen, but they cannot tell whereunto. Whereas St Paul saith, "How can the people say Amen to thy well saying, when they understand not what thou sayest?" And thus was St Paul understanden of all[6] interpreters, both the Greeks and Latins, old and new, school-authors and others, that I have read, until about thirty years past: at which time one Eckius, with other of his sort, began to devise a new exposition, understanding St Paul of preaching only.

The papists can say Yea and Nay to one thing with one breath. [Certain Letters to the queen.]

The papists and protestants both agreed in Windsor, the service of the church to be in the mother tongue. Anno 1549[9]. [Foxe.]

1 Cor. xiv. [Foxe.]

But when a good number of the best learned men reputed within this realm, some favouring the old, some the new learning, as they term it, (where indeed that which they call the old is the new, and that which they call the new is indeed the old;) but when a great number of such learned men of both sorts were gathered together at Windsor[7], for the reformation of the service of the church; it was agreed by both, without controversy (not one saying contrary[8]), that the service of the church ought to be in the mother-tongue, and that St Paul in the fourteenth chapter to the Corinthians was so to be understanden. And so is St Paul to be understanden in the civil law, more than a thousand years past, where Justinianus, a most godly emperor, in a synod writeth on this manner: "*Jubemus, ut omnes episcopi pariter et presbyteri non tacito modo, sed clara voce, quæ a fideli populo exaudiatur, sacram oblationem et preces in sacro baptismate adhibitas celebrent, quo majori exinde devotione in depromendis Domini Dei laudibus audientium animi efferan-*

---

[1 This sentence is omitted by Coverdale and Foxe.]

[2 Singing and thanking of God. Foxe.]

[3 Which they use not. Id.]

[4 Thing, then all. Coverdale and Foxe.]

[5 And of the people. Foxe.]

[6 Understood of all. Foxe.]

[7 "These were the commissioners who drew up Edward VI.'s first Communion Book, and first Common Prayer Book. King Edward in his Journal mentions them thus: 'A parliament was called, when an uniform order of prayer was institute, before made by a number of bishops and learned men gathered together in Windsor.' Journal, Ann. 2." Jenkyns' Remains of Cranmer, Vol. I. p. 375.—See also Original Letters relative to the English Reformation (Park. Soc.) Letter CLII. and note 3.]

[8 "When I was in office, all that were esteemed learned in God's word agreed this to be a truth in God's word written, that the common prayer of the church should be had in the common tongue. You know I have conferred with many, and I ensure you I never found man, (so far as I do remember,) neither old nor new, gospeller nor papist, of what judgment soever he was, in this thing to be of a contrary opinion." Ridley's letter to West, Coverdale's Letters of the Martyrs, p. 42. Ed. Lond. 1564. Strype's Mem. of Abp. Cranmer, Vol. II. p. 967. Ed. Oxon. 1840.]

[9 Both these side-notes are omitted in Coverdale, and the former of them is not found in Foxe.]

*tur*[10]. *Ita enim et Divus Paulus docet in epistola ad Corinth. Si solummodo benedicat spiritus, quomodo is qui privati locum tenet, dicet ad gratiarum actionem tuam, Amen? quandoquidem quid dicas non videt. Tu quidem pulchre gratias agis, alter autem non ædificatur*[11]. That is to say: "We command that all bishops and priests celebrate the holy oblation and prayers used in holy baptism, not after a still, close manner, but with a clear, loud voice, that they may be plainly heard of the faithful people, so as the hearers' minds may be lifted up thereby with the greater devotion in uttering the praises of the Lord God. For so Paul teacheth also in the epistle to the Corinthians: 'If the spirit do only bless (or say well), how shall he that occupieth the place of a private person, say Amen to thy thanksgiving? for he perceiveth not what thou sayest. Thou dost give thanks well, but the other is not edified.'" And not only the civil law and all other writers a thousand and five hundred years continually together have expounded St Paul not of preaching only, but of other service said in the church; but also reason giveth the same, that if men be commanded to hear any thing, it must be spoken in a language which the hearers understand, or else (as St Paul saith) what availeth it to hear? So that the pope giving a contrary commandment, that the people coming to the church shall hear they wot not what, and shall answer they know not whereto[12], taketh upon him to command, not only against reason, but also directly against God.

**The pope commandeth both against God and natural reason.**

And again I said, whereas our Saviour Christ ordained the sacrament of his most precious body and blood to be received of all christian people under the forms of both bread and wine, and said of the cup, "Drink ye all of this;" the pope giveth a clean contrary commandment, that no lay-man shall drink of the cup of their salvation; as though the cup of salvation by the blood of Christ pertained not to lay-men. And whereas Theophilus Alexandrinus (whose works St Jerome did translate about eleven hundred years past) saith, "That if Christ had been crucified for the devils, his cup should not be denied them[14];" yet the pope denieth the cup of Christ to christian people, for whom Christ was crucified. So that if I should obey the pope in these things, I must needs disobey my Saviour Christ.

**The sacrament ought to be received in both kinds of all Christians.**

**Ex Theophilo Alexandrino[13]. [Foxe.]**

But I was answered hereunto (as commonly the papists do answer), that under the form of bread is whole Christ's flesh and blood: so that whosoever receiveth the form of bread, receiveth as well Christ's blood as his flesh. Let it be so: yet in the form of bread only Christ's blood is not drunken, but eaten; nor is it received in the cup in the form of wine, as Christ commanded, but eaten with the flesh under the form of bread. And, moreover, the bread is not the sacrament of his blood, but of his flesh only; nor the cup is not the sacrament of his flesh, but of his blood only. And so the pope keepeth from all lay-persons the sacrament of their redemption by Christ's blood, which Christ commandeth to be given unto them.

**The excuse of the papists why they take away the cup[13]. [Foxe.]**

And furthermore, Christ ordained the sacrament in two kinds, the one separated from the other, to be a representation of his death, where his blood was separated from his flesh; which is not represented in one kind alone: so that the lay people receive not the whole sacrament, whereby Christ's death is represented, as he commanded.

Moreover, as the pope taketh upon him to give the temporal sword, or royal[15] and imperial power, to kings and princes; so doth he likewise take upon him to depose them from their imperial states, if they be disobedient to him, and commandeth the subjects to disobey their princes, assoiling the subjects as well of their obedience as of their lawful oaths made unto their true kings and princes, directly contrary to God's commandment, who commandeth all subjects to obey their kings, or their rulers under them.

**Misorder in the pope in assoiling the disobedience of subjects towards their princes[13]. [Foxe.]**

One John, patriarch of Constantinople in the time of St Gregory, claimed superiority

[10 Animi afficiantur. Foxe.]

[11 Novell. Constitut. cxxiii. de ecclesiast. divers. capit. p. 215. Ed. Paris. 1562, where, *in sancto baptismo;—et divus apostolus docet, dicens in prima ad Corinthios epistola, Enimvero si solummodo benedicas spiritu private, locum implet; actionem tuam Deo ipsum Amen.*]

[12 They not whereunto. Foxe.]

[13 Omitted in Certain Letters to the queen, and Coverdale.]

[14 Si enim et pro dæmonibus crucifigetur, per hæc impossibile esse demonstrat, dæmones de calice Domini bibere—Ex quibus omnibus approbatur, Christum pro dæmonibus non posse crucifigi, ne dæmones corporis et sanguinis ejus participes fiant. Theoph. Alex. in Mag. Biblioth. Vet. Patr. Epist. Pasch. i. Cap. XI. Tom. VII. p. 619. Ed. Venet. 1765—1781.]

[15 Sword by royal. Foxe.]

above all other bishops. To whom St Gregory writeth, that therein he did injury to his three brethren, which were equal with him, that is to say, the bishop of Rome, the bishop of Alexandria, and of Antiochia: which three were patriarchal sees as well as Constantinople, and were brethren one to another. "But," saith St Gregory, "if any one shall exalt himself above all the rest, to be the universal bishop, the same passeth in pride[2]." But now the bishop of Rome exalteth himself not only above all bishops, but also[3] above all kings and emperors, and above all the whole world, taking upon him to give and take away, to set up and put down, as he shall think good. And as the devil, having no such authority, yet took upon him to give unto Christ all the kingdoms of the world, if he would fall down and worship him: in like manner the pope taketh upon him to give empires and kingdoms, being none of his, to such as will fall down and worship him and kiss his feet.

Note the saying of Gregory[1]. [Foxe.]

The devil and the pope are like[4]. [Certain Letters to the queen, and Foxe.]

And moreover his lawyers and glosers so flatter him, that they feign he may command emperors and kings to hold his stirrup when he lighteth upon his horse, and to be his foot-men; and that, if any emperor and king gave him any thing, they give him nothing but that is his own; and that he may dispense against God's word, against both the old and new Testament, against St Paul's epistles, and against the gospel. And furthermore whatsoever he doth, although he draw innumerable people by heaps with himself into hell, yet may no mortal man reprove him, because he, being judge of all men, may be judged of no man[5]. And thus he sitteth in the temple of God, as if he were a God[6], and nameth himself God's vicar, and yet he dispenseth against God. If this be not to play antichrist's part, I cannot tell what is antichrist, which is no more to say but Christ's enemy and adversary, who shall sit in the temple of God, advancing himself above all other, yet by hypocrisy and feigned religion shall subvert the true religion of Christ, and under pretence and colour of christian religion shall work against Christ, and therefore hath the name of antichrist. Now if any man lift himself higher than the pope hath done, who lifteth himself above all the world; or can be more adversary to Christ, than to dispense against God's laws, and where Christ hath given any commandment, to command directly the contrary, that man must needs be taken for antichrist. But until the time that such a person may be found, men may easily conjecture where to find antichrist.

Emperors and kings made the pope's footmen[1]. [Foxe.]

The pope is antichrist, that is, Christ's enemy. Therefore the pope is antichrist. True marks proving that the pope is antichrist[7].

Wherefore, seeing the pope thus (to overthrow both God's laws and man's laws) taketh upon him to make emperors and kings to be vassals and subjects unto him, and specially the crown of this realm, with the laws and customs of the same; I see no mean how I may consent to admit his usurped power within this realm, contrary to mine oath, mine obedience to God's law, mine allegiance and duty to your majesty, and my love and affection to this realm.

Note this conclusion[8].

This that I have spoken against the power and authority of the pope, I have not spoken (I take God to record and judge) for any malice I owe to the pope's person, whom I know not; but I shall pray to God to give him grace that he may seek above all things to promote God's honour and glory, and not to follow the trade of his predecessors in these latter days.

The cause why the archbishop spake and wrote thus[8].

Nor I have not spoken it for fear of punishment, and to avoid the same, thinking it rather an occasion to aggravate than to diminish my trouble: but I have spoken it for my most bounden duty to the crown, liberties, laws, and customs of this realm of England; but most specially to discharge my conscience in uttering the truth to God's glory, casting away all fear by the comfort which I have in Christ, who saith: "Fear not them that kill the body, and cannot kill the soul; but fear him that can cast both body and

Matt. x. [Foxe.] Luke xii. [Coverdale.]

[1 Omitted in Certain Letters to the queen, and Coverdale.]

[2 Ego autem fidenter dico, quia quisquis se universalem sacerdotem vocat, vel vocari desiderat, in elatione sua antichristum præcurrit, quia superbiendo se ceteris præponit. Greg. Epist. Lib. VI. Epist. XXX. p. 888. Ed. Basil. 1564.]

[3 Foxe omits the words "above all bishops, but also."]

[4 Omitted in Coverdale.]

[5 Vid. Collection of Tenets from the Canon Law, 9. q. 3. p. 70, supra.]

[6 As he were God. Foxe.]

[7 The first part of this note to "Christ's enemy," is found in all the copies; the last clause only in Foxe.]

[8 Omitted by Coverdale.]

soul into hell-fire." He that for fear to lose this life will forsake the truth, shall lose the everlasting life: and he that for the truth's sake will spend his life, shall find everlasting life. And Christ promiseth to stand fast with them before his Father, which will stand fast with him here. Which comfort is so great, that whosoever hath his eyes fixed upon Christ, cannot greatly pass on this life, knowing that he may be sure to have Christ stand by him in the presence of his Father in heaven.

The sacrament. [Foxe.]

The sacraments have the names of those things whereof they are sacraments. [Coverdale.]

A double error of the papists in the words of the sacrament.

Cranmer standeth to be judged by the old church[9]. [Foxe.]

And as touching the sacrament, I said: forasmuch as the whole matter standeth in the understanding of these words of Christ, "This is my body, This is my blood;" I said that Christ in these words made demonstration of the bread and wine, and spake figuratively, calling bread his body and wine his blood, because he ordained them to be sacraments of his body and blood. And where the papists say in these two points contrary unto me, that Christ called not bread his body, but a substance uncertain, nor spake figuratively: herein I said I would be judged by the old church; and which doctrine could be proved the elder, that I would stand unto. And forasmuch as I have alleged in my book[10] many old authors, both Greeks and Latins, which above a thousand years after Christ continually taught as I do; if they could bring forth but one old author, that saith in these two points as they say, I offered six or seven years ago, and do offer yet still, that I will give place unto them.

The papists not able to bring forth one old author above a thousand years to make with the sacrament. [Foxe.]

But when I bring forth any author that saith in most plain terms as I do, yet saith the other party[11], that the authors meant not so: as who should say, that the authors spake one thing, and meant clean contrary. And upon the other part, when they cannot find any one author that saith in words as they say; yet say they, that the authors meant as they say. Now, whether I or they speak more to the purpose herein, I refer me to the judgment of all indifferent hearers: yea, the old church of Rome, above a thousand years together, neither believed nor used the sacrament as the church of Rome hath done of late years.

With the substance the use also changed of the sacrament[12]. [Foxe.]

For in the beginning the church of Rome taught a pure and a sound doctrine of the sacrament. But after that the church of Rome fell into a new doctrine of transubstantiation; with the doctrine they changed the use of the sacrament, contrary to that Christ commanded, and the old church of Rome used above a thousand years. And yet, to deface the old, they say that the new is the old: wherein for my part I am content to stand to the trial. But their doctrine is so fond and uncomfortable, that I marvel that any man would allow it, if he knew what it is. But, howsoever they bear the people in hand, that which they write in their books hath neither truth nor comfort.

The papists make Christ two bodies.

Neither truth nor comfort in the pope's doctrine of the sacrament.

Mark the errors of the papists in their doctrine of the sacrament[14].

For by their doctrine[13], of one body of Christ is made two bodies; one natural, having distance of members, with form and proportion of man's perfect body, and this body is in heaven; but the body of Christ in the sacrament, by their own doctrine, must needs be a monstrous body, having neither distance of members, nor form, fashion, or proportion of a man's natural body. And such a body is in the sacrament, teach they, and goeth into the mouth with the form of bread, and entereth no farther than the form of bread goeth, nor tarrieth no longer than the form of bread is by natural heat in digesting: so that when the form of bread is digested, that body of Christ is gone. And forasmuch as evil men be as long in digesting as good men, the body of Christ, by their doctrine, entereth as far and tarrieth as long in wicked men as in godly men. And what comfort can be herein to any christian man, to receive Christ's unshapen body, and it to enter no farther than the stomach, and to depart by and bye as soon as the bread is consumed?

The sound true doctrine of the sacrament. [Certain Letters to the queen.]

It seemeth to me a more sound and comfortable doctrine, that Christ hath but one body, and that hath form and fashion of a man's true body; which body spiritually entereth into the whole man, body and soul: and though the sacrament be consumed,

---

[9 Omitted in Certain Letters to the queen, and Coverdale.]

[10 Vid. Vol. I. p. 110, et sqq.]

[11 Saith the other part. Coverdale and Foxe.]

[12 Omitted by Coverdale and Foxe.]

[13 Vid. Disputations at Oxford with Harpsfield, Vol. I. p. 423, et sqq.]

[14 The latter clause from "neither truth, &c." is only found in Foxe.]

The protestants' doctrine of the sacrament more comfortable than the doctrine of the papists[1].

yet whole Christ remaineth, and feedeth the receiver unto eternal life, (if he continue in godliness,) and never departeth until the receiver forsake him. And as for the wicked, they have not Christ within them at all, who cannot be where Belial is. And this is my faith, and (as meseemeth) a sound doctrine, according to God's word, and sufficient for a Christian to believe in that matter. And if it can be shewed unto me that the pope's authority is not prejudicial to the things before mentioned, or that my doctrine in the sacrament is erroneous, which I think cannot be shewed; then I never was nor will be so perverse to stand wilfully in mine own opinion, but I shall with all humility submit myself unto the pope, not only to kiss his feet, but another part also.

Another respect why the archbishop refused bishop Brokes to be his judge. [Foxe.]

The bishop of Gloucester twice perjured. [Certain Letters to the queen.]

Another cause why I refused to take the bishop of Gloucester for my judge, was the respect of his own person being more than once perjured. First, for that he being divers times sworn never to consent that the bishop of Rome should have any jurisdiction within this realm, but to take the king and his successors for supreme heads of this realm, as by God's laws they be; contrary to that lawful oath, the said bishop sat then in judgment by authority from Rome: wherein he was perjured and not worthy to sit as a judge.

Double perjury in bishop Brokes[1]. [Foxe.]

The bishop of Gloucester a traitor and an enemy to the realm[2].

The second perjury was, that he took his bishoprick both of the queen's majesty and of the pope, making to each of them a solemn oath: which oaths be so contrary, that the one must needs be perjured. And furthermore in swearing to the pope to maintain his laws, decrees, constitutions, ordinances, reservations, and provisions, he declareth himself an enemy to the imperial crown, and to the laws and state of this realm: whereby he declared himself not worthy to sit as a judge within this realm. And for these considerations I refused to take him for my judge. [Sept. 1555.]

---

## CCCXV. TO QUEEN MARY[3].

Certain Letters to the queen, &c. Coverdale's Letters of the Martyrs, p. 15, Ed. Lond. 1564. Foxe's Acts and Monuments, pp. 1891, 2. Ed. Lond. 1583.

Contradiction in the queen's oaths, sworn both to the realm and to the pope in one day. [Foxe.]

I LEARNED by doctor Martin, that at the day of your majesty's coronation you took an oath of obedience to the pope of Rome, and the same time you took another oath to this realm, to maintain the laws, liberties, and customs of the same. And if your majesty did make an oath to the pope, I think it was according to the other oaths which he useth to minister to princes; which is, to be obedient to him, to defend his person, to maintain his authority, honour, laws, lands, and privileges. And if it be so, (which I know not but by report,) then I beseech your majesty to look upon your oath made to the crown and realm, and to expend and weigh the two oaths together, to see how they do agree, and then to do as your grace's conscience shall give you: for I am surely persuaded that willingly your majesty will not offend, nor do against your conscience for nothing. But I fear me that there be contradictions in your oaths, and that those which should have informed your grace thoroughly, did not their duties therein. And if your majesty ponder the two oaths diligently, I think you shall perceive you were deceived; and then your highness may use the matter as God shall put in your heart. Furthermore, I am kept here from company of learned men, from books, from counsel, from pen and ink, saving at this time to write unto your majesty; which all were necessary for a man being in my case. Wherefore I beseech your majesty, that I may have such of these as may stand with your majesty's pleasure. And as for mine appearance at Rome[4], if your majesty will give me leave, I will appear there: and I trust that God shall put in my mouth to defend his truth there as well as here. But I refer it wholly to your majesty's pleasure[5]. [Sept. 1555.]

Your poor orator,

T. C.

---

[[1] These notes are not found in Coverdale.]

[[2] Omitted in Foxe and Coverdale.]

[[3] Foxe calls this "a piece of another letter to the queen;" and heads it, "This was written in another letter to the queen."]

[[4] Vid. Letter CCCXIV. p. 447.]

[[5] "These and other his smart and learned letters, no question, made impression upon the queen, or at least upon those that read them; for they were delivered by the queen to no less a person than the holy father cardinal Pole himself; who was advised to frame an answer to them."—"By comparing of

## CCCXVI. TO A LAWYER.

NATURÆ lex hoc ab omnibus postulat, ut quatenus citra divini numinis injuriam fieri potest, quisque vitam tueatur suam. Quod cum tribus abhinc diebus mihi in mentem venisset, simulque memoriæ occurrisset appellatio Martini Lutheri a Leone decimo ad concilium generale, constitui et ipse concilium generale legitimum et liberum appellare, ne temere et inconsulto vitam proderem meam. Verum cum appellationis materia ad legisperitos spectet, cujus ego ignarus sum, cumque Lutheri appellatio ad manum mihi non sit; decrevi amico alicui fido et jurisperito consilium meum hac in re pandere, cujus opera in hoc negotio uterer: ac tu quidem unus occurristi, qui mihi in hac academia visus est ad hoc munus idoneus. Sed summam hæc res taciturnitatem postulat, ut antequam res fiat, nemo resciscat. Dies mihi dictus est, ut respondeam Romæ decimo sexto hujus mensis, ante quem mihi provocandum esse puto, ac post sententiam appellandum. Sed an primum mihi provocandum et appellandum sit a judice delegato ad ipsum pontificem, ac deinde ad concilium generale[6], an omisso pontifice ad concilium primum appellandum sit, consilio mihi opus est tuo.

Coverdale's Letters of the Martyrs, p. 19. Ed. Lond. 1564. Foxe's Acts and Monuments, &c. 1st Edit. p. 1492.

Porro appellationis causæ mihi multæ sunt.

Primo quod juramento astrictus sim, nunquam me consensurum in auctoritatem Romani pontificis.

Deinde cum ego respondere omnino renuerem ad articulos mihi objectos ab episcopo Gloucestrensi judice delegato, responderam tamen Doctori Martino et Storeo cum hac protestatione, quod responsio mea non daretur judici, neque in judicio, sed extrajudicialis esset, et post responsum datum petebam responsionis meæ copiam, ut eandem mihi emendare liceret, vel addendo, vel mutando, vel subtrahendo; quanquam hæc mihi promissa sunt, et a Gloucestrensi et a procuratoribus regis et reginæ, omnino tamen fefellerunt fidem, non dantes emendandæ responsionis meæ copiam, et nihilominus (ut audio) inter acta judicialia adscripserunt[7].

Postremo, cum causa defectionis a Romano pontifice et papistica religione in jus vocor, ut jam mihi lis sit adversus pontificem Romanum, et nemo æquus judex sit in causa propria; æquum mihi videtur ut concilium appellem, præsertim cum jus naturæ (ut aiunt) appellationis remedium nemini negandum censeat.

Jam cum ad hanc rem maxima taciturnitate opus sit, si forsan ob rerum imperitiam aliorum consiliis tibi opus sit, obtestor tum te per christianam fidem ac caritatem, ut cujus causa sit, nemini significes. Et cum jam instet tempus, et mature opus sit facto, hoc me sinas a te impetrare, ut sepositis aliis studiis atque negotiis huic uni incumbas quousque perfeceris. Potissima sane appellationis meæ causa est, ut (si ita Deus voluerit) donetur eousque vivendi tempus, quousque cœptum contra Marcum Antonium Constantium responsum absolvero. Quod si veritatis hostes meæ appellationi deferre nolint, (quod existimo,) fiat voluntas Dei, susque deque fero, modo glorificetur Deus, sive per vitam, sive per mortem. Melius est enim multo mori pro Christo et cum illo regnare, quam in hoc carnis ergastulo concludi, nisi in fratrum utilitatem ad majorem Dei gloriam propagandam liceat aliquamdiu militare; cui sit omnis gloria in ævum. Amen.

---

this letter of Pole's with that of Cranmer's, any one may see a mighty difference: strength, evidence, and conviction in the archbishop's, who had truth on his side; but a flashiness and debility in the cardinal's, made up of poor shifts, and weak arguings, and impertinent allegations of scripture, and personal reflections, to help out a weak cause."—"To which I might have added another letter of the said cardinal to the same archbishop, concerning the sacrament, a little after the disputation at Oxford, but that it would be too prolix, being a treatise against Cranmer's book of that argument. This treatise bears this title: Reginaldi Pole, Cardinalis Legati Apostolici, Epistola ad Thomam Cranmerum, qui Archiepiscopalem sedem Cantuariensis Ecclesiæ tenens novam de sacramento eucharistiæ doctrinam contra perpetuam catholicæ ecclesiæ consensum professus est ac tradidit. Qua epistola eum nec magistrum tanti mysterii, neque discipulum idoneum esse posse, simulque unde hic ejus error manarit, ostendit, et ad pœnitentiam hortatur." Strype's Mem. of Abp. Cranmer, Vol. II. pp. 547—549. Ed. Oxon. 1840. The answer of cardinal Pole to the above Letters will be found in the Appendix.]

[6 Cum ergo talibus præjudiciis valde se gravari sentiat (i.e. Luther) eam ob causam, a pontifice Romano minus edocto, quantum quidem ad hoc pertinet, provocare se ad pontificem rectius edocendum, atque hoc ita protestari palam.—He also appealed from the pope to a general council. Sleidan, De Statu Religionis et reipub. Lib. I. pp. 9, 13. Ed. Francof. 1568. Luth. Op. Lat. I. p. 219.]

[7 Vid. Letters CCCXIII. CCCXIV; pp. 446, 7, and Examination before Brokes, pp. 212, et sqq. sup.]

Est et alia appellationis causa, quod cum Romam vocatus sim illic dicturus causam, interim carcere detineor, ut comparere mihi ad dictum diem non liceat. Cum autem de statu et vita mea agitur, et pro defensione mea jurisperitorum consilio mihi opus esset, quum id peterem, negatum est omne advocatorum, procuratorum, et jurisconsultorum consilium et auxilium. Vale. [Nov. 1555.]

[TRANSLATION.]

## A LETTER OF DOCTOR CRANMER, ARCHBISHOP OF CANTERBURY, TO A LAWYER FOR THE DRAWING UP OF HIS APPEAL[1].

Foxe's Acts and Monuments, p. 1892. Ed. Lond. 1583. Coverdale's Letters of the Martyrs, p. 16, Ed. Lond. 1564. Another Letter of the archbishop to a certain learned lawyer, his friend, about his appeal.

THE law of nature requireth of all men, that so far forth as it may be done without offence to God, every one should seek to defend and preserve his own life. Which thing when I about three days ago bethought myself of, and therewithal remembered how that Martin Luther appealed in his time from pope Leo the X. to a general council, (lest I should seem rashly and unadvisedly to cast away myself,) I determined to appeal in like sort to some lawful and free general council. But seeing the order and form of an appeal pertaineth to men learned in the law [2], whereof I myself am ignorant, and seeing that Luther's appeal cometh not to my hand, I proposed to break my mind on this matter to some faithful friend, and skilful in the law, whose help I might use in this behalf; and you only among others came to my remembrance, as a man most meet in this university for my purpose. But this is a matter that requireth great silence, so that no man know of it before it be done. It is so that I am summoned to make mine answer at Rome the xvi. day of this month: before the which day I think it good, [as well as][3] after sentence pronounced, to make mine appeal. But whether I should first appeal from the judge delegate to the pope, and so afterward to the general council, or else, leaving the pope, I should appeal immediately to the council, herein I stand in need of your counsel.

Many causes there be for the which I think good to appeal. First, because I am by an oath bound never to consent to the receiving of the bishop of Rome's authority into this realm. Besides this, whereas I utterly refused to make answer to the articles objected unto me by the bishop of Gloucester, appointed by the pope to be my judge, yet I was content to answer Martyn and Story, with this protestation, that mine answer should not be taken as made before a judge, nor yet in place of judgment, but as pertaining nothing to judgment at all; and moreover, after I had made mine answer, I required to have a copy of the same, that I might, either by adding thereunto, or by altering or taking from it, correct and amend it as I thought good: the which though both the bishop of Gloucester, and also the king and queen's proctors, promised me, yet have they altogether broken promise with me, and have not permitted me to correct my said answers according to my request; and yet, notwithstanding, have (as I understand) registered the same as acts formally done in place of judgment.

Finally, forasmuch as all this my trouble cometh upon my departing from the bishop of Rome, and from the popish religion, so that now the quarrel is betwixt the pope himself and me, and no man can be a lawful and indifferent judge in his own cause; it seemeth (methink) good reason that I should be suffered to appeal to some general council in this matter; specially seeing the law of nature (as they say) denieth no man the remedy of appeal in such cases.

Now, since it is very requisite that this matter should be kept as close as may be, if perhaps for lack of perfect skill herein you shall have need of further advice, then I beseech you, even for the fidelity and love you bear to me in Christ, that you will open to no creature alive whose the case is. And forasmuch as the time is now at hand, and the matter requireth great expedition, let me obtain this much of you, I beseech you, that, laying aside all other your studies and business for the time, you will apply this my matter only, till you have brought it to pass. The chiefest cause in very deed (to tell you the truth) of this mine appeal is, that I might gain time (if it shall so please God) to live until I have finished mine answer against Marcus Antonius Constantius, which I have now in hand. But if the adversaries of the truth will not admit mine appeal, (as I fear they will not,) God's will be done! I pass not upon it, so that God may therein be glorified, be it by my life, or by my death. For it is much better for me to die in Christ's quarrel, and to reign with him, than here to be shut up, and kept in the prison of this body, unless it were to continue yet still awhile in this warfare for the commodity and profit of my brethren, and to the further advancing of God's glory: to whom be all glory for evermore. Amen.

This Constantius was Stephen Gardiner, as constant indeed as a weathercock: who thus named himself, writing against this good archbishop.

There is also yet another cause why I think good to appeal, that whereas I am cited to go to Rome to answer there for myself, I am notwithstanding kept here fast in prison, that I cannot there appear at the time appointed. And moreover, forasmuch as the state I stand in is a matter of life and death, so that I have great need of learned counsel for my defence in this behalf; yet when I made my earnest request for the same, all manner of counsel and help of proctors, advocates, and lawyers, was utterly denied me. Farewell[4].

---

[[1] It is probable that the formal appeal from the pope to a general council, which Cranmer delivered to Thirlby, bishop of Ely, immediately before his degradation, Feb. 14, A. D. 1556, originated from the application contained in this letter to the lawyer to whom it was addressed. Vid. the Appeal at his Degradation, pp. 224, et sqq.]

[[2] Pertaineth to the lawyers. Foxe.]

[[3] Wanting in Foxe.]

[[4] Instead of "Farewell," Foxe concludes, "Your loving friend, Thomas Cranmer."]

## CCCXVII. TO P. MARTYR.

Ex hologr. Simler Coll. Libr. Zurich, 87. 3.

Post plurimam in Christo Servatore nostro salutem. Quando tum demum necessariæ sunt literæ, quum aut non satis prudens est nuncius, aut rerum quas significare volumus ignarus, aut non fidus cui arcana credas; quumque mihi Dei benignitate sese obtulisset hic tabellarius, vir et prudentia (ut nosti) insigni, et qui rebus in credendis fidissimus sit, et nostrum utriusque amantissimus, et rerum nostratium scientissimus, e cujus ore quæ hic acta fuerint intelligas omnia; non necessarium existimavi ut prolixius ad te scriberem, præsertim quum scripturæ tot pericula damnaque afferre soleant. Illud tamen unum prætermittendum non censui, quod expertus didici, nunquam Deum splendidius illucescere, et clementiæ suæ, consolationis, aut roboris ac fortitudinis animi radios suorum mentibus clarius aut pressius infundere, quam in summis animi corporisque angoribus atque pressuris; ut tum vel maxime sese declaret suorum esse Deum, quum illos deseruisse prorsus videtur; tum erigere quum dejicere atque prosternere, tum glorificare quum confundere, tum denique vivificare quum occidere putetur. Ut cum Paulo dicere liceat, 'Quando infirmor tunc fortior sum, et si gloriari oportet, in infirmitatibus meis gloriabor, in carceribus, in contumeliis, in necessitatibus, in persecutionibus, in angustiis pro Christo.' Faxit obsecro Deus, ut in finem perseveremus. Hodie nihil magis animum angit meum, quam quod hactenus M.A. nihil est responsum; ad cujus astutias, præstigias, et insanias jamdudum non defuisset responsum, nisi mihi defuissent et libri et libertas. Præterquam tibi scripsi nemini, nec scire velim quenquam quod ad te scripserim: proinde nomine meo salutabis neminem.

Thomas Crammerus[5].

*Hæc in manu Archiepiscopi Cantuarensis. Scripsit hæc ex carcere ad D. Pet. Martyrem. M.A. significant Marc. Antonium, nimirum Wintoniensem.* 1555.

[TRANSLATION.]

### CRANMER TO PETER MARTYR.

After much health in Christ our Saviour. As letters are then only necessary, when the messenger is either not sufficiently discreet, or is unacquainted with the circumstances we wish to communicate, or not thought worthy to be entrusted with secrets; and since by the goodness of God the bearer of this[6] has fallen in my way, a man, as you know, of signal discretion, most faithful in all matters entrusted to him, exceedingly attached to us both, and possessing an entire acquaintance with the circumstances of our country, from whose mouth you may learn all that has taken place here; I have not thought it needful to write to you more at length, especially as letters are wont to occasion so much danger and mischief. Yet I have not deemed it right to pass over this one thing, which I have learned by experience, namely, that God never shines forth more brightly, and pours out the beams of his mercy and consolation, or of strength and firmness of spirit, more clearly or impressively upon the minds of his people, than when they are under the most extreme pain and distress, both of mind and body, that he may then more especially shew himself to be the God of his people, when he seems to have altogether forsaken them; then raising them up when they think he is bringing them down,

---

[5 "The signature is added by another hand, and the subjoined note is in that of Bullinger. Cranmer was burned at Oxford, March 21, 1556: this letter, which appears undoubtedly to be his autograph, was written only a few months previously." Original Letters relative to the English Reformation (Parker Society), Letter XVIII. note 2, p. 31.—This letter was discovered at Zurich by the Rev. S. A. Pears in 1843, in his examination of the Archives and Library there for the Parker Society. A facsimile of it is given at the commencement of this volume, presenting a specimen of the *latest* handwriting of this venerable prelate. This important and interesting document had escaped all former researches, and supplies a most valuable testimony respecting the principles and views by which he was enabled to endure his cruel imprisonment and death.]

[6 There are some grounds of probability for supposing that the bearer of this letter was Jewel, afterwards bishop of Salisbury.]

and laying them low; then glorifying them, when he is thought to be confounding them; then quickening them, when he is thought to be destroying them. So that we may say with Paul, "When I am weak, then am I strong; and if I must needs glory, I will glory in my infirmities, in prisons, in revilings, in distresses, in persecutions, in sufferings for Christ." I pray God to grant that I may endure to the end! Nothing is at this time more distressing to me, than that no answer has as yet been given to M. A., to whose subtilties, and juggling tricks, and ravings, a reply would not have been wanting long since, had not books and liberty been wanting to myself. I have written to no one but you, nor do I wish any one to know that I have written to you: wherefore salute no one in my name.

THOMAS CRANMER.

*This is in the hand-writing of the archbishop of Canterbury. He wrote it from prison to master Peter Martyr. M. A. signifies Marcus Antonius, meaning the bishop of Winchester.* 1555.

---

## CCCXVIII. (or CCLXXII.*)[1] TO THE KING.

Public Record Office, State Papers of the Treasury of the receipt of the Exchequer, Royal Letters, &c. Vol. I. B. 3. 3.

PLEASETH it your highness to be advertised, that there is a gentleman named Edward Isaac, my servant this bearer, who hath a farm of very good pasture and meadow, worth by the year xx$^{li}$, lying very commodiously for the provision of my household, whether I lie at Canterbury or at Ford, for which he is content to make exchange with me, so that he might have a certain messuage with the appurtenance named Bekisbourne, belonging to Christ's church in Canterbury, worth by the year xx$^{li}$, or thereabout, adjoining to the lands of the said Edward Isaac[2]. Upon which messuage of Bekisbourne there is a house of recreation for the monks, which would be very commodious for the said Edward Isaac, and nothing prejudicial or hurtful unto them: for they have another house for recreation much better than this is at Chartcham, being as nigh unto Canterbury as this is. In consideration hereof, if it would please your highness to be so good and gracious lord unto me as to require the said Bekisbourne, with the appurtenance of the prior and convent of Christ's church aforesaid, to your grace's use, promising them to have as much of my land, value for value, at your grace's appointment, so that I might have the said Bekisbourne at your grace's hands, to accomplish mine exchange with the said Edward Isaac for his said farm; I should not only be greatly bound unto your majesty for the same, but also thereby should have no small commodity for the maintenance of my house during such time as I should lie in Kent. And if it would please your highness at my humble suit to accept my said servant into your grace's service, I doubt not (having such experience of his qualities) but that he shall do unto your majesty right acceptable service within the county of Kent: for besides his good judgment in the truth of God's word, he may spend in Kent six score pounds or better. Beseeching your grace farther to give credence unto my said servant touching this my suit unto your highness. Thus Almighty God have your grace in his most blessed tuition! At Ford, the xviiith day of February. [1541.]

Your grace's most humble chaplain and bedesman,

T. CANTUARIEN.

*To the king's highness.*

---

[[1] This letter has not appeared in any previous collection. It was not discovered in sufficient time to place it in its proper position after the translation of the archbishop's letter to Osiander, p. 408, supra.]

[[2] The exchange was made, A.D. 1541. Vid. Strype's Mem. of Abp. Cranmer, Vol. I. p. 133.]

## THE QUEEN TO MR HERD[3].

As we are greatly bound to the high providence of Almighty God, the fountain only of all good things; so likewise your diligence in the same Lord is not unworthy of due commendation, for that you have so studiously hitherto kept and conserved in your custody the collections or common-places gathered and written by the late archbishop of Canterbury, Thomas Cranmer. And now, forasmuch as such a rare and precious a treasure we think is not to be kept in secret oblivion, as a candle under a bushel, but rather ought to be set abroad, to the public use of the church of Christ; our request therefore to you is, that upon the sight hereof you will commit to the bearer of the same all and singular parts of the said common-places written by the aforesaid archbishop; or if you have any other monument else of the like sort with you remaining: to the intent they may be perused and serve more publicly to the greater fruit and better furtherance of Christ's church. Giving you not only thanks for this your safe custody of such a jewel, but also promising to stand in like case beneficial to you again, so much as this your accomplishing of our request shall require.

State Paper Office. Domestic Papers, A. D. 1563.

(The above is written as a minute, after which, upon the same page, follows the minute of a letter from sir W. Cecil, written all in his own hand.)

After my very hearty commendations. Where I understand that you have very fortunately and studiously preserved certain collections or common-places, gathered and written by the late most reverend and godly father, Thomas, archbishop of Canterbury, the same being monuments of great price and estimation: the queen's majesty hath willed me to write to you, and require you that the same may be sent hither in safety, to the intent only to be copied and returned to you again; wherein you shall well please her majesty, and shall bind me to acquit the same with any pleasure in my power. And hereof I pray you make me answer.

Mr Herd.

Indorsed: "14 *April* 1563. *Copy of my mistress's letter to Mr Herd for the copy of his monument of Mr Cranmer's collections.*"

[[3] It has been conjectured that the first part of the above paper was written by queen Elizabeth, although not in her own hand, but at her dictation, and that secretary Cecil, thinking probably that it would appear of too much importance for the queen to interfere personally, took the same paper and wrote his own minute of a letter under it. It is, perhaps, however, more probable, that the first part was a draft prepared by a secretary, which Cecil did not approve, since the queen's own dictation was not a matter which he would have lightly thrown aside.]

# APPENDIX.

## I. *Cranmer's Oath to the King for his Temporalties.*

Cott. MSS. Cleop. E. vi. f. 246. British Museum. Original. Strype's Mem. of Abp. Cranmer, Vol. II. App. No. 7. p. 685. Ed. Oxon. 1840.

I, Thomas Cranmer, renounce and utterly forsake all such clauses, words, sentences, and grants, which I have of the pope's holiness in his bulls of the archbishoprick of Canterbury, that in any manner was, is, or may be hurtful, or prejudicial to your highness, your heirs, successors, estate, or dignity royal: knowledging myself to take and hold the said archbishoprick immediately, and only, of your highness, and of none other. Most lowly beseeching the same for restitution of the temporalities of the said archbishoprick; promising to be faithful, true, and obedient subject to your said highness, your heirs and successors, during my life. So help me God and the holy evangelists!

## II. *This is an order taken for preaching, and bidding of the beads in all sermons to be made within this realm*[1]. 1534.

Cott. MSS. Cleop. E. v. f. 286. British Museum. Original. Burnet's Hist. Reformat. Vol. III. App. B. ii. No. 29. pp. 79—84. Ed. Oxon. 1829.

First, Whosoever shall preach in the presence of the king's highness and the queen's grace, shall, in the bidding of the beads, pray for the whole catholic church of Christ, as well quick as dead, and specially for the catholic church of this realm: and first, as we be most bounden, for our sovereign lord king Henry the VIIIth, being immediately next unto God the only and supreme head of this catholic church of England, and for the most gracious lady queen Anne his wife; and for the lady Elizabeth, daughter and heir to them both, our princess, and no further.

*Item*, The preacher in all other places of this realm, than in the presence of the king's said highness and the queen's grace, shall, in the bidding of the beads, pray first in manner and form, and word for word, as is above ordained and limited; adding thereunto in the second part, for all archbishops and bishops, and for all the whole clergy of this realm; and specially for such as shall please the preacher to name of his devotion: and thirdly, for all dukes, earls, marquisses, and for all the whole temporalty of this realm; and specially for such as the preacher shall name of devotion: and finally for the souls of all them that be dead, and specially of such as it shall please the preacher to name.

*Item*, It is ordained, that every preacher shall preach once in the presence of his greatest[2] audience against the usurped power of the bishop of Rome, and so after at his liberty: and that no man shall be suffered to defend or maintain the foresaid usurped power.

Furthermore, to keep unity and quietness in this realm, it is ordained, that no preachers shall contend openly in pulpit one against another, nor uncharitably deprave one another in open audience: but if any of them be grieved one with another, let them complain to the king's highness, or to the archbishop or bishop of the diocese where such chance shall happen, and there to be remedied, if there be cause why; and if the complaint be not true, the complainer to be punished.

*Item*, Also to forfend, that no preachers for a year shall preach neither with nor against purgatory, honouring of saints, that priests may have wives, that faith only justifieth, to go on pilgrimages, to forge miracles; considering these things have caused

[1 "About the month of June this year, [A. D. 1534,] was a book drawn up for bishops and priests, wherein was an order for preaching; and in the same were forms devised for the beads, as well for preachers as curates: in which forms the king's title of Supreme head was specified.... This book the archbishop, who, we may well suppose, had a great hand in it, sent by the king's commandment to all the bishops, and to the archbishop of York, though out of his province." Strype's Mem. of Abp. Cranmer, Vol. I. p. 35. Vid. Letters C. CXIX. pp. 283, 292.]

[2 Of the greatest. Burnet.]

dissension amongst the subjects of this realm already, which, thanked be God, is now well pacified.

*Item*, That from henceforth all preachers shall purely, sincerely, and justly preach the scripture and word of Christ, and not mix them with man's institutions, nor make men believe that the force of God's law and man's law is like; nor that any man is able or hath power to dispense with God's law.

*Item*, It is also ordained, that the declaration of the sentence which hath been used in the church four times in the year, shall not from henceforth neither be published[3] nor esteemed in any point contrary to the pre-eminence and jurisdiction royal of our king and his realm, or laws and liberties of the same; and any so doing to be competently punished by the bishop of that diocese where it shall fortune him to be or inhabit: and this throughout the realm and dominions of our sovereign, shortly the bishops to set order in.

*Item*, It is also ordained, that the Collects for the preservation of the king and queen by name be from henceforth commonly and usually used and said in every cathedral church, religious house, and parish-church, in all their high masses, throughout all the realm and dominions of our king and sovereign.

*Item*, It is further ordained, that wheresoever the king's just cause of matrimony hath either been detracted, and the incestuous and unjust set forth, or in places where as it hath not been dilated, that in all those places, till the people be fully satisfied and justly instruct, all manner of preachers, whatsoever they be, happening to come into any such part of the realm, shall from henceforth open and declare the mere verity and justness of this latter matrimony, as nigh as their learning can serve them, and according to the true determinations of a great number of the most famous and esteemed universities of Christendom; according also to the just resolution and definition of both the convocations of this realm, concurring also in the same opinion; by the whole assent of parliament, our prince, the lords spiritual and temporal, and commons of this realm: wherefore now they must declare this matter neither doubtful nor disputable, but to be a thing of mere verity, and so to be allowed in all men's opinions.

*Item*, It is further ordained, that the foresaid preachers shall also declare the false and unjust handling of the bishop of Rome, pretending to have jurisdiction to judge this cause at Rome; which in the first hearing thereof did both declare and confess in word and writing the justness thereof to be upon our sovereign's side, insomuch as by a decretal delivered to the legate, here then sitting for the same cause, he did clearly determine, that if prince Arthur was our prince's brother, and then of competent age allowed in the law, when he married the lady Katharine, she being so likewise, and that, as far as presumptions can prove, carnal copulation ensued between them; that these proved before the said cardinals and legates, (which indeed were according to the laws justly proved,) that then the unjust copulation between our sovereign and the said lady Katharine was neither lawful, nor longer to be[4] suffered; and so, *eo facto*, pronounced in the foresaid decretal the nullity, invalidity, and unlawfulness of their pretensed matrimony, which was by his law sufficient judgment of the cause; which decretal by his commandment, after and because he would not have the effect thereof to ensue, was, after the sight thereof, imbesiled by the foresaid cardinals, and one which then was here his cubicular, contrary to all justness and equity: wherein he hath done our sovereign most extreme wrong.

Secondly, contrary to all equity and determinations[5] of general councils, he hath called the cause (which ought to be determined here) to Rome, where our sovereign is neither bound to appear, nor to send proctor: and yet hath he detained wrongfully the cause there these three or four years at the instance of the other party, which sued to have it there, because they knew he durst not displease the emperor, who maketh himself a party in it, as by the sequel it doth evidently appear; and so could our prince get no justice at his hand, but was wrongfully delayed to no small hinderance, both to his succession, and this his realm, eminent danger.

Thirdly, where it is a natural defence that the subject ought and may defend his

---

[[3] Vid. Letter XCVIII. p. 281. *n.* 5.]

[[4] Nor ought to be. Burnet.]

[[5] And determination. Id.]

natural sovereign or master, both in word and deed, and ought thereto to be admitted; this foresaid bishop of Rome, contrary to this equity in nature, hath rejected our sovereign's excusator, contrary both to his own laws, (which he most setteth by,) and also God's law, which he ought to prefer. Upon which cause, and other great injuries, our sovereign did appeal to the general council; notwithstanding the which, he hath, contrary to all justice, proceeded *ad ulteriora*, wherein by a general council he is damned as an heretic; yet thus injuriously, from the beginning hitherto, he hath handled our prince's cause and matter there.

Fourthly, the said bishop of Rome, since our prince's appeal, hearing of the laws and acts of parliament which we then went about, and that our king having just ground (the premises considered) would provide according to his bounden duty, both for the surety of his succession and realm, gave out a sentence in manner of excommunication and interdiction of him and his realm; in which when he was spoken to for the iniquity and unjustness thereof by our prince's agents, he and his council could nor did otherwise excuse them, (the fact being so contrary to all laws and right,) but that the fault was in a new officer late come to the court, which for his lewd doing should grievously be punished, and the process to cease. This they promised our prince's agents; which notwithstanding was set up in Flanders to the great injury of our prince, and for partiality to the other part, as it may well appear by the foresaid sentence.

Fifthly, the said bishop of Rome sought all the ways possible with fair words and promises both by his ambassadors and our sovereign's own, which by any means could be invented, to have abused our prince and sovereign: which when he saw that by none of his crafts our prince would be no longer abused with them, then sued he to the French king, to be a mediator between our sovereign and him; declaring to him and his council that he would gladly do for our sovereign, allowing the justness of his cause, so that they would find the means that our sovereign would not proceed in his acts and laws till that were proved; and that he would meet with him at Marcelles for the finishing thereof, for at Rome he durst not do it for fear of the emperor. The good French king admonished our prince hereof, offering to him to do all pleasure and kindness that lay in him in this cause, trusting that if the bishop of Rome came once to Marcelles, he should give sentence for our sovereign in his just cause, and therefore prayed our prince to be content with that meeting, in which he would labour for it effectuously; and so he did: to the which our prince answered, that touching the meeting he was content, but touching the forbearing of making laws, he prayed his good brother to hold him excused, for he knew well enough both the craft and delays of the bishop of Rome; by which from thenceforth he would never be abused: and that likewise he feared that he would abuse his good brother, which so indeed after followed; for after he had gotten the marriage of the duke of Orleance, he then promised the French king to give judgment for our master, so he would send a proxy, which the said bishop of Rome knew well before that he neither would, nor was bound to do; yet notwithstanding his subtle imagination, his promise was to the French king, that our prince, sending a proctor, should there before his departure have judgment for him in the principal cause; for he openly confessed further, that our master had the right: but because our prince and master would not prejudicate princes' jurisdiction[1], and uphold his usurped power by sending a proctor, ye may evidently here see that this was only the cause why the judgment of the bishop of Rome was not given in his favour; whereby it may appear that there lacked not any justness in our prince's cause, but that ambition, vain-glory, and too much mundanity, were the letts thereof. Wherefore, good people, I exhort you to stick to the truth and our prince according to our bounden duties, and despise these naughty doings of this bishop of Rome; and charitably pray that he and all others, abusers of Christ's word and works, may have grace to amend.

---

[[1] Would not prejudicate for his jurisdiction. Burnet.]

### III. *Inhibitio pro Visitatione Regia.*

Wilkins' Concilia, Vol. III. p. 797. ex Reg. Voisey. f. 66.

THOMAS, permissione divina Cant' archiepiscopus, &c., venerab' confratri nostro domino Johanni, London' episcopo, salutem et fraternam in Domino caritatem. Cum nuper receperimus serenissimi domini nostri regis Henrici octavi, Dei gratia Angliæ et Franciæ regis, Fidei Defensoris, dominique Hiberniæ, ac in terris supremi ecclesiæ Anglicanæ sub Christo capitis, literas inhibitorias sub verborum tenore sequent': "Henricus octavus Dei gratia Angliæ et Franciæ rex, Fidei Defensor, dominus Hiberniæ, ac in terris supremum ecclesiæ Anglicanæ sub Christo caput, dilecto nobis reverendissimo in Christo patri, Thomæ, miseratione divina Cant. archiepiscopo, ac totius Angliæ primati, salutem. Cum nos auctoritate nostra suprema ecclesiastica omnia ac singula monasteria, domos, prioratus, et loca alia ecclesiastica quæcunque, totumque clerum intra et per totum nostrum Angliæ regnum constituta propediem visitare statuerimus; vobis tenore præsentium stricte inhibemus atque mandamus, et per vos suffraganeis vestris confratribus episcopis, ac per illos suis archidiaconis intra vestram provinciam Cant' ubilibet constitutis, sic inhiberi volumus atque præcipimus, quatenus, pendente visitatione nostra hujusmodi, nullus vestrum monasteria, ecclesias, ac loca alia prædicta, clerumve visitare, aut ea quæ sunt jurisdictionis exercere, seu quicquam aliud in præjudicium dictæ nostræ visitationis generalis quovis modo attemptare præsumat, sub pœna contemptus. In cujus rei testimonium has præsentes literas inde fieri, et sigilli nostri, quo ad causas ecclesiasticas utimur, appensione communiri curavimus. Dat' 18. die mensis Septembris, A.D. MDXXXV."

Quocirca fraternitati vestræ committimus et mandamus, quatenus omnibus et singulis episcopis et suffraganeis nostris, in nostra provincia Cant' constitutis, ac eorum archidiaconis, commissariis, officialibus, et ministris quibuscunque, secundum tenorem et effectum literarum domini nostri regis inhibentis, quibus nos etiam tenore præsentium ex mandato regiæ majestatis prædict' inhibemus, quatenus, pendente visitatione regia hujusmodi, nullus eorum monasteria, ecclesias, ac alia loca ecclesiastica, clerumve visitare, aut ea quæ sunt jurisdictionis exercere, seu quicquam aliud in præjudicium regiæ visitationis quovis modo attemptare præsumat; vobis insuper mandantes, quatenus præfatos coepiscopos et suffraganeos nostros moneatis peremptorie, quos nos etiam tenore præsentium sic monemus, quatenus ipsi modum et formam concionand' ac preces inter prædicand' juxta tenorem articulorum alias ad annum et dimidium ultimo claps' eis transmiss' observent; literas quoque jurisdictionis a Romano pontifice et ejus prædecessoribus usurpatæ expulsionem concernentes, eis etiam jam nuper missas, secundum formam in eis traditam, publice apud populum declarare non omittant. Et quid in præmissis feceritis, nos, cum ad hoc fueritis requisiti, debite certificare curetis per literas vestras patentes, harum seriem in se continentes, auctentice sigillat'. Dat' in manerio nostro de Lamehith, secundo die mensis Octobris, A.D. MDXXXV. et nostræ consecrat' anno tertio.

---

### IV. *The Judgment of the Convocation concerning General Councils.*

Kennet's Hist. of Eng. Vol. II. Lord Herbert's Life of Hen. VIII. pp. 203,4. Ed. Lond. 1706. Burnet's Hist. of Reformat. Vol. III. App. B. 3, No. 5, pp. 244—246. Ed. Oxon. 1829.

As concerning general councils, like as we (taught by long experience) do perfectly know, that there never was, ne is, any thing devised, invented, nor instituted by our forefathers more expedient, or more necessary for the establishment of our faith, for extirpation of heresies, and the abolishing of sects and schisms, and finally, for the reducing of Christ's people unto one perfect unity and concord in his religion, than by the having of general councils, so that the same be lawfully had, and congregated in *Spiritu Sancto*, and be also conform and agreeable, as well concerning the surety and indifferency of the places, as all other points requisite and necessary for the same, unto that wholesome and godly institution and usage, for the which they were at first devised and used in the primitive church: even so on the other side, taught by like experience, we esteem, repute, and judge, that there is, ne can be any thing in the world more pestilent and pernicious to the common-weal of Christendom, or whereby the truth of God's word hath in times past, or hereafter may be sooner defaced and subverted[1], or whereof hath and may ensue more contention, more discord, and other devilish effects, than when such general councils have or shall be assembled, not christianly nor charitably, but for and upon private malice and ambition, or other worldly and carnal respects and considerations, according to the saying of Gregory Nazianzenus, in his epistle to one Procopius, wherein he writeth this sentence following; *Sic sentio, si verum scribendum est, omnes conventus episcoporum fugiendos esse, quia nullius synodi finem vidi bonum, neque habentem magis solutionem malorum, quam incrementum: nam cupiditates contentionum et gloriæ (sed ne putes me odiosum ista scribentem) vincunt rationem*[2]. That is to say: "I think this, if I should write truly, that all general councils be to be eschewed; for I never saw that they produced any good end or effect, nor that any provision or remedy, but rather increase of mischiefs, proceeded of them. For the desire of maintenance of men's opinions, and ambition of glory (but reckon not that I write this of malice) hath always in them overcomed reason." Wherefore we think, that christian princes, especially and above all things, ought and must, with all their wills, power, and diligence, foresee and provide, *Ne sanctissima hac in parte majorum instituta ad improbissimos ambitionis aut malitiæ effectus explendos diversissimo suo fine et sceleratissimo pervertantur; neve ad alium prætextum possint valere, et longe diversum effectum orbi producere, quam sanctissima rei facies præ se ferat.* That is to say: "Lest the most noble wholesome institutions of our elders in this behalf be perverted to a most contrary and most wicked end and effect; that is to say, to fulfil and satisfy the wicked affections of men's ambition and malice; or lest they might prevail for any other colour, or bring forth any other effect, than their most virtuous and laudable countenance doth outwardly to the world shew or pretend." And first of all, we think they ought principally to consider, who hath the authority to call together a general council. Secondly, whether the causes alleged be so weighty and so urgent, that necessarily they require a general council, nor can otherwise be remedied. Thirdly, who ought to be judges in the general council. Fourthly, what order of proceeding is to be observed in the same; and how the opinions or judgments of the fathers are to be consulted or asked. Fifthly, what doctrines are to be allowed or defended:—with divers other things which in general councils ought of reason and equity to be observed. And as unto the first point, we think that neither the bishop of Rome, nor any one prince, of what estate, degree, or pre-eminence soever he be, may, by his own authority, call, indict, or summon any general council, without the express consent, assent, and agreement of the residue of christian princes, and especially such as have within their own realms and seignories *imperium merum*, that is to say, of such as have the whole, entire, and supreme government and authority over all their subjects, without knowledging or recognising of any other supreme power or authority. And this to be true, we be induced to think by many and sundry, as well examples, as great reasons and authority. The which forasmuch as it should be over long and tedious to express here particularly, we have thought good to omit the same for this present. And in witness that this is our plain and determinate sentence, opinion, and judgment, touching the premises, we the prelates and clergy under-written, being congregate together in the convocation of the province of Canterbury, and representing the whole clergy of the same, have to these presents subscribed our names the 20th of July, in the year of our Lord 1536, 28 Hen. VIII.

THOMAS CROMWELL,
THOMAS CANTUARIENSIS,
JOHANNES LONDON.

With 13 bishops; and of abbots, priors, archdeacons, deans, proctors, clerks, and other ministers, 49.

---

[1 Defaced or subverted.]

[2 Ἔχω μὲν οὕτως, εἰ δεῖ τἀληθὲς γράφειν, ὥστε πάντα σύλλογον φεύγειν ἐπισκόπων, ὅτι μηδεμιᾶς συνόδου τέλος εἶδον χρηστὸν, μηδὲ λύσιν κακῶν μᾶλλον ἐσχηκυῖαν ἢ προσθήκην. Ἀεὶ γὰρ φιλονεικίαι καὶ φιλαρχίαι (ἀλλ' ὅπως μή με φορτικὸν ὑπολάβῃς οὕτω γράφοντα,) καὶ λόγου κρείττονες.—Greg. Nazian. Epist. CXXX. Procopio. Tom. II. p. 110. Ed. Paris. 1778—1840.]

V. *Some Queries put by Cranmer in order to the correcting of several abuses*[3].

Cott. MSS. Cleop. E. v. f. 48. British Museum. Original. Burnet's Hist. Reformat. Vol. I. pt. ii. Add. No. 2, pp. 476—479. Ed. Oxon. 1829.

First, What causes, reasons, or considerations, hath or might move any man to desire to have the bishop of Rome restored in any point to his pretended monarchy, or to repugn against the laws and statutes of this realm made for the setting forth of the king's title of supreme head?

2. *Item*, Whether a man offending deadly after he is baptized may obtain remission of his sins by any other way than by contrition, through grace?

3. *Item*, If the clergy know that the common sort of men have them in an higher estimation, because they are persuaded that it lieth in the will and power of priests to remit or not remit sins at their pleasure, whether in such case the said clergy offend, if they wink at this, and voluntarily suffer the people to continue in this opinion?

4. *Item*, Whether a sinner, being sorry and contrite for his sins, and forthwith dying, shall have as high a place in heaven as if he had never offended?

5. *Item*, Whether any, and what difference may be assigned betwixt two men, whereof the one, being very sorry and contrite for his sins, dieth without absolution of the priest, and the other, which being contrite is also absolved by the priest, and so dieth?

6. *Item*, If it may appear that the common people have a greater affiance or trust in outward rites and ceremonies than they ought to have, and that they esteem more virtue in images and adoring of them, kissing their feet, or offering candles unto them, than they should esteem; and that yet the curates knowing the same, and fearing the loss of their offerings, and such other temporal commodities, do rather encourage the people to continue after this sort, than teach them the truth in the premises according to scripture; what the king's highness and his parliament may do, and what they are bound in conscience to do in such case?

7. *Item*, Whether now in time of the new law the tithes or tenth be due to curates by the laws of God, or of man; and if the same be due by the laws of man, what man's laws they be?

8. *Item*, Whether the clergy only, and none but they, ought to have voices in general councils?

9. *Item*, Whether the ninth canon[4] of the council of Chalcedon, wherein is contained that one clerk may not sue another before any secular judge, but only before his bishop, and such other canons of like effect, have been generally received or not? and whether the same be contrary to the king's prerogative and laws of this realm; and whether it be expedient that it were declared by the parliament that the said canons being at no time received, especially within this realm, be void and of none effect?

10. *Item*, Of the 24th canon[5] of the said council, wherein is contained that monasteries once consecrate by the bishop may not after be made dwelling-houses for laymen, whether that canon have been received and observed, and whether the same be against the power of the king and authority of his parliament?

11. *Item*, If it may appear that the bishops have not, ne yet do maturely examine and diligently inquire of the conversation and learning of such as be ordered or admitted to cures by them, but rather without examination or inquisition indistinctly admit persons unable, whereof ensueth great peril of souls, and innumerable inconveniences otherways; what the king's highness or his parliament ought to do, or may do for reformation in the premises?

---

[[3] These questions were probably drawn up by Crumwell. Vid. Cat. of Cotton Library, British Museum. Burnet refers them to Cranmer, as above. In Strype's Observations, &c. of the two Vols. of the Hist. of the Reformation, he says: "Two papers," (i. e. the above and the following) "said to be Cranmer's, but they are not written by him, nor by his secretary; so it does not appear that they are his." Burnet's Hist. of Reformat. (Corrections of Burnet) Vol. III. Part II. Appendix, p. 544.]

[[4] *Eἴ τις κληρικὸς πρὸς κληρικὸν πρᾶγμα ἔχοι, μὴ καταλιμπανέτω τὸν οἰκεῖον ἐκίσκοπον, καὶ ἐπὶ κοσμικὰ δικαστήρια κατατρεχέτω· ἀλλὰ πρότερον τὴν ὑπόθεσιν γυμναζέτω παρὰ τῷ ἰδίῳ ἐπισκόπῳ.* Labb. et Cossart. Concil. Calchedon. Can. ix. Tom. IV. p. 760. Ed. Lutet. Paris. 1671.]

[[5] *Τὰ ἅπαξ καθιερωθέντα μοναστήρια κατὰ γνώμην ἐπισκόπου μένειν εἰς τὸ διηνεκὲς μοναστήρια, καὶ τὰ προσήκοντα αὐτοῖς πράγματα φυλάττεσθαι τῷ μοναστηρίῳ, καὶ μηκέτι δύνασθαι γίνεσθαι ταῦτα κοσμικὰ καταγώγια.*—Id. ibid. Can. XXIV. Tom. IV. p. 768.]

12. *Item*, If such as have deaneries, archdeaconries, chancellorships, and other offices or promotions of the clergy, use not themselves in their own persons after such sort as the primary institution of these offices or promotions require, and according to the wills of them that endowed the same, what the king and his parliament may do, or ought to do in this case?

13. *Item*, For what causes and to what ends and purposes, such offices and promotions of the clergy were first instituted?

14. *Item*, If curates, having benefices with cure, for their more bodily ease refuse to dwell upon any of their said cures, and remain in idleness continually in cathedral or collegial churches upon their prebends, whether it be in this case expedient that the king's highness or his parliament take any order for the redress of the same?

15. *Item*, Of the sacraments of confirmation, order, matrimony, and extreme unction, what the external signs and inward graces be in every of the said sacraments, what promises be made to the receivers of them by God, and of what efficacy they be of, and every of them?

---

## VI. *Some Considerations offered to the King to induce him to proceed to further Reformation*[1].

Cott. MSS. Cleop. E. v. f. 50. British Museum. Original.
Burnet's Hist. Reformat. Vol. I. pt. ii. Add. No. 4, pp. 480—482, Ed. Oxon. 1829.
Collier's Eccles. Hist. Vol. V. pp. 33—35. Ed. Lond. 1840, 41.[2]

Pleaseth it your highness graciously to consider, deeply to ponder and weigh by your high wisdom these considerations following.

1. First, How no great thing is to be determined, principally matters of Christ's religion, without long, great, and mature deliberation.

2. Secondly, How evil it hath succeeded, when in provincial, yea, or yet in general councils, men have gone about to set forth any thing as in the force of God's law, without the manifest word of God, or else without apparent reasons infallibly deduced out of the word of God.

3. Thirdly, How all christian regions[3] are now full of learned men in the scripture, which can well espy out and judge how things that be, or shall be set forth, are agreeable with scripture or not.

4. Fourthly, Of what audacity men be of now-a-days, which will not spare to write against high princes, as well as against private persons, without any respect to their high estates, only weighing the equity or the iniquity of the cause.

5. Fifthly, How not only men of the new learning (as they be called), but also the very papistical authors, do allow, that by the word of God priests be not forbidden to marry, although they were not ignorant that many expounders of scripture were of the contrary judgment.

6. Sixthly, How that it is not possible that all learned men should be of one mind, sentence, and opinion, as long as the cockle is mingled with the wheat, the godly with the ungodly, which certainly shall be, as long as this world endureth.

7. Seventhly, How variety of opinions have been occasion of the opening of many verities heretofore taken for heresy, yea, and yet so esteemed and taken of many in other regions; as namely the usurped authority of the bishop of Rome hath by that occasion come into light, with effusion of the blood not of a few, such as were the first stirrers up thereof.

8. Lastly, There be also other opinions not spoken of, which have made, and yet will make as much variance in your grace's realm, as any of them treated of; namely, whether the holy scripture teacheth any purgatory to be after this life or not? whether the same scripture teacheth the invocation of dead saints? whether there be any unwritten verities necessary to be believed, not written in scripture, nor deducted by

---

[[1] Although Strype has decided that neither this nor the preceding document is Cranmer's, (vid. p. 465. *n*. 3. supra,) yet both Collier (Eccl. Hist. Vol. V. p. 33. Ed. Lond. 1840, 41) and Todd (Life of Abp. Cranmer, Vol. I. p. 189, Vol. II. p. 520,) agree with Burnet in attributing it to him.]

[[2] This document has been much altered by Collier, who has given the substance of it after his own rendering.]

[[3] All christened regions. Burnet.]

infallible arguments out of the open places of scripture? whether there be any satisfaction beside the satisfaction of Christ? whether free-will by his own strength[4] may dispose itself to grace of a conveniency (as it is said), "*de congruo?*" whether it be against scripture to kiss the image of Christ in the honour of him? and generally, whether images may be used any other wise[5] than your grace setteth forth in your Injunctions[6].

Wherefore in consideration of the premises it may please your highness to suspend your judgment for a time, and not to determine the marriage of priests to be against scripture; but rather to put both parts to silence, commanding them neither to preach, dispute, nor openly to talk thereof under pain of —— &c. And in case these premises do not move your highness to stay, that then it may please the same to grant that the article of priests' marriage may be openly disputed in both universities, under indifferent judges, before it be determined: all the arguments of the contrary part first to be delivered in writing to the defenders, twelve days before the disputation; to the intent they may the more maturely and deliberately make answer to the same; and they that shall enter as defenders into this disputation, to do it under this condition, that if their judges discern them to be overcome, they be right well contented to suffer death therefore: and if their adversaries cannot prove their purpose, their desire is no more, but that it may please your highness to leave your most humble subjects to the liberty that God's word permitteth them in that behalf; and your said humble subjects shall pray unto Almighty God for the preservation of your most royal estate long to continue, to God's glory and honour.

---

## VII. *The Opinion of certain of the Bishops and Clergy of this Realm, subscribed with their hands, touching the General Council*[7].

For the General Council.

Though that, in the old time, when the empire of Rome had his ample dominion over the most part of the world, the first four general councils, which at all times have been of most estimation in the Church of Christ, were called and gathered by the emperor's commandment, and for a godly intent, that heresies might be extinct, schisms put away, good order and manners in the ministers of the Church and the people of the same established; like as many councils more were called, till now of late by the negligence, as well of the emperor as other princes, the bishop of Rome hath been suffered to usurp this power: yet now, forsomuch that the empire of Rome and the monarchy of the same hath no such general dominion, but many princes have absolute power in their own realms, and an whole and entire monarchy, no one prince may by his authority call any general council; but if that any one or mo of these princes, for the establishing of the faith, for the extirpation of schisms, &c. lovingly, charitably, with a good sincere intent, to a sure place, require any other prince, or the rest of the great princes, to be content to agree, that for the wealth, quietness, and tranquillity of all christian people, by his or their free consent, a general council might be assembled; that prince, or those princes so required, are bound by order of charity, for the good fruit that may come of it, to condescend and agree thereunto, having no lawful impediment, nor just cause to the contrary. The chief causes of the general councils are before expressed. State Papers, Vol. I. pt. ii. No. 84, pp. 543, 4.

In all the ancient councils of the church, in matters of the faith and interpretation of scripture, no man made definitive subscription, but bishops and priests; forsomuch as the declaration of the word of God pertaineth unto them.

---

[4 By its own strength. Burnet.]

[5 Any other way. Id.]

[6 Vid. Injunctions, A.D. 1536. Burnet's Hist. of Reformat. Vol. I. App. B. iii. No. 7. Part II. pp. 250—256.]

[7 "There is no date to this paper; but as it must have been signed after John Hilsey became bishop of Rochester in Oct. 1535, and before his death in 1538, and as the pope summoned a council to be held at Mantua in May 1537, it must have reference to that council, to which Henry VIII. apprehended that the emperor and the king of France would accede: as appears by a letter from Fitzwilliam to Crumwell, in the Chapter House." State Papers. Vol. I. p. 543. *n.* 1.]

[1] The words of John in his 20th chapter, *Sicut misit me Pater, et ego mitto vos, &c.* hath no respect to a king's or a prince's power, but only to shew, how that the ministers of the word of God, chosen and sent for that intent, are the messengers of Christ, to teach the truth of his gospel, and to loose and bind sin, &c. as Christ was the messenger of his Father. The words also of St Paul, in the 20th chap. of the Acts, *Attendite vobis et universo gregi, in quo vos Spiritus Sanctus posuit episcopos, regere ecclesiam Dei*, were spoken to the bishops and priests, to be diligent pastors of the people, both to teach them diligently, and also to be circumspect that false preachers should not seduce the people, as followeth immediately after in the same place. Other places of scripture declare the highness and excellency of christian princes' authority and power; the which of a truth is most high, for he hath power and charge generally over all, as well bishops and priests, as other. The bishops and priests have charge of souls within their own cures, power to minister sacraments, and to teach the word of God, to the which word of God christian princes knowledge themselves subject; and in case the bishops be negligent, it is the christian princes' office to see them do their duty.

T. CANTUARIEN[2].
JOANNES LONDON[3].
CUTHBERTUS DUNELMS[4].
JO. BAT. WELLES'[5].
THOMAS ELIEN[6].
JOHANNES BANGOR[7].
NICOLAUS SARISBURIEN[8].
HUGO WYGORN'[9]
JOANNES ROFFENS'[10].
WILHELMUS ABBAS MO'-STERII S'CI' B'N'DICTI'[11].
ROBERTUS ALDRYDGE[12].
RICARDUS COREN[13].
EDVARDUS LEYGHTON[14].

---

VIII. *Mandatum Archiepiscopi Cantuar' de Festo D. Marci Evangelistæ celebrando.*

Wilkins' Concilia, Vol. III. p. 826, ex excerpt. actor. convoc. Heylyn.

THOMAS, miseratione divina Cant' Archiepiscopus, totius Angliæ primas et metropolitanus, dilecto nobis in Christo Mag' Roberto Colyns, in legibus baccalaureo, intra civitatem et diœcesin nostras Cant' commissario et officiali, salutem, gratiam, et benedictionem. Licet serenissima regia majestas, tanquam supremum in terris sub Christo ecclesiæ Anglicanæ caput, atque ea auctoritate, de consensu et assensu prælatorum et cleri hujus regni sui Angliæ in convocatione legitime congregatorum, inter cetera decrevit et ordinavit, quod omnes dies festi quorumcunque sanctorum contingentes in tempore messium sive autumni, computando hujusmodi tempus a 1° die Julii usque ad 29m diem Septembris, sive temporibus quibus jura apud Westmon' per suos justitiarios reddi solent, non observabuntur in hoc suo regno tanquam solennes more solito; sed quod liceret unicuique suo subdito in hujusmodi diebus operibus tam mechanicis quam aliis (ut in diebus profestis fieri solet) operam dare (diebus, in quibus præfecti justitiarii ad jura reddenda apud aulam Westmonast' sedere non solent, duntaxat exceptis;) nuperrime tamen eadem sua majestas ex causis justis et rationalibus animum suum in ea parte moventibus voluit et decrevit, quod festum D. Marci evangelistæ (prædicta ordinatione non obstante) solenniter ad instar festorum Apostolorum deinceps annis singulis observabitur more ab antiquo solito; sive intra dies, quibus jus apud Westmonast' reddi solet, sive extra illud tempus contigerit. Tibi igitur committimus, et firmiter injungendo mandamus, quatenus cum omni celeritate qua decet diem D. Marci prædict' solenniter more solito celebrand' clero et populo intra civitat' et dioces' nostras Cant' constituto

---

[[1] This paragraph, signed by the eight bishops named below, omitting Johannes Bangor. and the last four signatures, is printed by Burnet, (Hist. of Reformat. Vol. I. Part II. Appendix, Book iii. No. 10. p. 278. ex MSS. D. Stillingfleet.]
[[2] Cranmer.] [[3] Stokesley.]
[[4] Tonstall.] [[5] Clerk.]
[[6] Goodrich.] [[7] Salcot.]
[[8] Shaxton.] [[9] Latimer.]
[[10] Hilsey.] [[11] Benson.]
[[12] Canon of Windsor and Provost of Eton.]
[[13] Archdeacon of Oxford and Colchester.]
[[14] Archdeacon of Sarum.]

publices, seu publicari facias. Et quid in præmissis feceris, dicto negotio expedito, nobis, quam cito fieri poterit, debite certifices. In cujus rei testimonium sigillum nostrum præsentibus est appensum. Dat' in manerio nostro de Lamehythe, 19° die mensis Aprilis, anno Dom. MDXXXVII. et consecrat' nostræ anno V.

---

IX. [*Minute of an answer of Henry VIII. to a letter from the commissioners prefixed to the Institution of a Christian man*[15].]

Public Record Office. State Papers of the Treasury of the Receipt of the Exchequer. Tractat. Theol. et Polit. Vol. IX. pp. 145—151. A. I. 15.

ALBEIT that hitherto we have had no time convenient to overlook your great pains-taking in the long search and diligent debating of this your book, entitled "The Institution of a Christian Man," much less time to pound and weigh such things as you therein have written: yet, according to your humble suit and petition, we have caused your said book both to be printed, and will the same to be conveyed into all the parties of our realm, nothing doubting but that you, being men of such learning and virtue, as we know you to be, have indeed performed in the whole work that that you do promise in the preface. Our desire was (and ye say you have endeavoured yourselves to accomplish the same) to have a sure and certain kind of doctrine, not as made by men, but by them searched out of the holy scripture. And such things chiefly elected and chosen as were both best to be known, and also meetest to be observed, of men that profess Christ and his religion, you, as you say, thought this thing best contained in such parts of scripture as ye have here handled. We nothing myslyle[16] your judgment, so that ye have in such wise handled those places that every man may know both his whole duty towards God, his Creator and Saviour, and also know how he hath to govern himself in this political life, as a utile member of the same, and also toward God's ministers, the heads and governors of states, and towards his neighbours, much better than they have done heretofore. Notwithstanding that we are otherwise occupied, [we] have taken as it were a taste of this your book, and have found therein nothing but that is both meet to come from you, and also worthy our praise and commendation. Wherefore as you have shewed yourselves very ready to accomplish our desire and request in the gathering of this wholesome doctrine, so we now do require you that ye be as earnest in setting of it forth to the people, as ye have been diligent in searching thereof, that they by your true teaching and virtuous example may learn to know the true service of God, and also their bounden duty to their prince, and diligently to be exercised in the same; expelling from them, and extinguishing for ever, as much as in you shall be, all manner of idolatry, superstition, hypocrisy, with such other errors and abuses as ye have in this book reformed, or be worthy to be reformed, that they may be also amended among our subjects committed by us to your cure and charge. For experience hath taught us that it is much better no laws to be made, than, when many be well made, none to be kept. Even so it is much better nothing to be written concerning religion than, when many things be well written, nothing of them to be taught and observed. Wherefore our pleasure is, that all archbishops and bishops, archdeacons, deans, abbots and priors, doctors, preachers, and, to be short, all that have any jurisdiction or cure in their hands under us, do their uttermost diligence that the people may have the contents of that book so oft declared and instilled into their ears, that all the points of their creed, the effects of the sacraments, the promises made to them that observe the ten commandments, what, of whom, and how they ought to desire, may well be fixed and graven in their hearts; which things, we doubt not, but if ye have gathered them well and godly, they will well agree in the setting of them forth truly. And forasmuch as we trust that the preachers agreeing in the true and sincere word of God, the diligent setting forth and declaring of this book, with other our commandments and injunctions before this, and faithfully following and observing of the same, shall be the occasion that all the rest of our subjects, as well our nobility and clergy, as the commons, shall establish their opinions, and willingly and gladly to hear God's word, and each one according to his vocation to learn and practise it, following the same as the very rule of every christian

---

[15 Vid. Letter CXC. p. 337, *n.* 3. supra.]

[16 Probably for *myslyke.*]

man's life, much to the glory of God and also for our honour, with the maintenance and increase of the commonwealth, both by their virtuous exercise and good example: our commandment therefore is that you agree in your preachings, and that, vain praise of crafty wits and worldly estimation laid aside, and true religion sought for, you serve God in your calling, and not your own glory or vile profit. We will no wrestling of things, no glosses that take away the text: much desirous notwithstanding that if in any place you have not written so plainly or so plenteously as you with more leisure might have done, you in your sermons to the people utter all that is God's word purely and plainly. For we will no more thwarting, no more contentions, whereby the people are much more set one against another than any taketh the profit by such undiscreet doctrine. We had much leaver to pray you than command you. And if the first will serve, we will leave out the second. Howbeit in any case we will that all preachers agree. For if any two shall dissent, let him that will defend the worser part assure himself that he shall run into our displeasure. Wherefore it shall be your parts whom we have chosen our bishops, not only to see this your book, with other our commandments and injunctions before this given, well taught to the people, but also you yourselves to teach them in the most part of your diocese. And also we charge you, that ye suffer no curate within your diocese that either will not or cannot set forth the contents of this book, with other our commandments and injunctions given heretofore unto you for that purpose: but that also ye command the said book, or some convenient part thereof, may every Sunday and every other festival day be at the least read unto our people in every parish-church and other eccle-[si]astical place within this our realm, by the curates of the same, continually by the space of three whole years now next to come; to the intent that the same book and the whole contents thereof may, by the continual reading and preaching thereof in the hearts of our said people, reading and preaching thereof, be ingrave in the hearts of our said people.

---

## X. *Mandatum Archiepiscopi Cantuar' de non celebrandis Festis Diebus jussu Regio in Synodo Provinciali abrogatis.*

Wilkins' Concilia, Vol. III. p. 827, ex excerpt. actor. Convocat. Heylyn.

THOMAS, miseratione divina Cant' archiepiscopus, totius Angliæ primas et metropolitanus, dilecto nobis in Christo decano nostræ peculiaris jurisdictionis ecclesiæ nostræ Christi Cant' immediatæ de Bocking, ejusve in absentia commissario, salutem, gratiam, et benedictionem. Cum serenissimus noster princeps Henricus VIII. Dei gratia, &c. in convocatione præsulum et cleri Cant' provinciæ, anno Dom' MDXXXVI. apud ædes D. Pauli London legitime indicta, cum consensu omnium et singulorum interessentium, inter alia pie sanxierat et ordinaverat quasdam ferias, justissimis causis id exigentibus, abrogari ac penitus tolli; cujus quidem statuti[1] seu ordinationis tenorem clero nostræ peculiaris jurisdictionis ante hæc tempora, literis in illum usum impressis, promulgari fecimus et curavimus; cumque idem serenissimus noster princeps visitatione sua regia eodem anno habita injunctiones[2] quasdam, subditorum salutem et gloriam Dei promoventes, per commissarios suos ad hoc deputatos, clero nostræ peculiaris jurisdictionis de Bocking prædict' observandas exhibuerit; quia tamen accepimus et comperimus quosdam, imo quamplurimos (quod dolemus) nostræ peculiaris jurisdictionis hujusmodi statutis non obtemperare, præmissa observare non curantes; nos, qui potius clementia quam severitate præesse volumus, quique hujusmodi hominum malitiam pietate paterna vincere conamur, ea demum vobis aut uni vestrum per præsentes mandamus, quatenus clericis nostræ peculiaris jurisdictionis prædictæ, ad subsequentia convocatis in capellis vestris, auctoritate nostra (seu potius regia) præcipiatis, quibus et nos sic præcipimus, uti sano consilio obtemperantes, omnia et singula præmissa summo cum studio et maxima cum diligentia, sub pœna privationis beneficiorum, observare curent: intimando iisdem, quod si aliqui in posterum circa

---

[1 i.e. "A copy of the act made for the abrogation of certain holy days, according to the transumpt lately sent by the king's highness to all bishops, with his grace's strict commandment to signify his farther pleasure to all colleges, religious houses, and curates within their diocese, for the publication, and also effectual and universal observation of the same." Wilkins' Concilia. Vol. III. pp. 823, 4.]

[2 Vid. Burnet's Hist. of Reformat. Vol. I. Part II. Append. Book iii. Nos. 7, and 9, pp. 250, 279.]

præmissa se præstiterint culpabiles, nos, si beneficiati fuerint, sine dubio contra eosdem ad beneficiorum privationem, contra alios legitimis juris censuris processuros. Et quoniam nuper in eruditissimo concilio archiepiscoporum, episcoporum, ac aliorum doctorum virorum hujus regni, de rebus religionis consultantium, multa de religione controversa definita sunt, multaque populo ad vitæ institutionem explicata, quæ propediem uno volumine[3] congesta regiæ majestatis auctoritate emittentur; vobis mandamus, uti omnes et singulos clericos, quibus cura animarum committitur, moneatis, ut voluminis prædicti partem, sub pœna prædicta, ordine singulis diebus dominicis clara apertaque voce et suggesto populo legant. Et quid in præmissis feceritis, ille vestrum, qui præmissa executus fuerit, cum ad hoc requisitus fuerit, debite certificet. In cujus rei testimonium sigillum nostrum præsentibus apponi fecimus. Dat' in manerio nostro apud Ford, 10. die mensis Sep' A.D. MDXXXVII. et nostræ consecrat' v.

---

### XI. *Archiepiscopi Cantuar' Epistola ad Regem pro Suffraganeo Dovorensi.*

Strype's Mem. of Abp. Cranmer, Vol. II. Appendix. No. 21, pp. 732, 3. Ed. Oxon. 1840, from Cranmer's Register.

EXCELLENTIS' et potentiss' in Christo principi et D'no' nostro D'n' Henrico Octavo Dei gra' Angliæ et Fr' regi, fidei defensori, et D'no' Hiberniæ, ac in terris supremo ecclesiæ Angl' capiti, vester humilis orator et subditus Thomas, permissione divina Cantuar' archiepiscopus, totius Angliæ primas et metropolit' omnimod' reverentiam et observantiam tanto principi debit' et condignas cum omni subjectionis honore. Ad sedem episcopalem de Doveria intra Cantuar' dioc' existen' dilectos mihi in C'to' Richardum Yngworth priorem domus sive prioratus de Langley regis, et Johannem Codenham, sacræ theolog' professores, juxta et secundum vim, formam, et effectum statuti parlamenti hujus inclyti regni vestri Angliæ in hoc casu editi et provisi, vestræ regiæ majestati per has literas meas nomino et præsento; ac eidem majestati vestræ humiliter supplico, quatenus alteri eorum (cui vestra regia majestas id munus conferend' præoptaverit) titulum, nomen, stylumq; et dignitatem episcopalem ac suffraganeam ad sedem prædictam misericorditer conferre: ipsumque mihi præfato archiepiscopo, intra cujus dioc' et provinciam sedes antedicta consistit, per literas vestras patentes regias intuitu caritatis punctare, mihique mandare dignetur vestra regia majestas, quatenus ipsum sic nominatum et præsentatum in episcopum suffraganeum sedis prædict' juxta formam statuti prædict' effectualiter consecrem et benedicam; ceteraque faciam et exequar in ea parte, quæ ad effectum meum archiepiscopale spectaverint, seu requisita fuerint in præmissis. Vivat denique et valeat in multos annos vestra regia celsitudo prælibata in eo per quem reges regnant et principes dominantur. Dat' apud Lambeth primo die mensis Decembr', anno Domini millesimo quingentesimo tricesimo septimo, et regni vestri florentiss. vicesimo nono.

---

### XII. *Archiepiscopi Cantuar' Litera Commissionalis ad Richardum, suffraganeum Dovorensem.*

Strype's Mem. of Abp. Cranmer, Vol. II. Appendix. No. 22, pp. 733, 4. Ed. Oxon. 1840, from Cranmer's Register.

THOMAS, permissione divina Cant' archiep' tot' Angl' primas et metropolitanus, venerabili confratri nostro Dom' Richardo, Dei gra' sedis Doveriæ nostræ diocesios Cant' suffraganeo, salutem, et fraternam in Domino caritatem. De tuis fidelitate et circumspectionis industria plenam in Domino fiduciam obtinentes, ad confirmandum sacri chrismatis unctione pueros quoscunque intra civitatem et diocesin nostras Cant', et jurisdictiones nostras, et ecclesiæ nostræ Christ' Cant' immediatas, ac jurisdictionem nostram villæ Calisiæ, et marchias ejusdem sub obedientia excellentiss' principis et domini nostri, domini Hen' Oct' Dei gratia Angl' et Fr' regis, fidei defensoris, et domini Hib', ac in terris sub Christo ecclesiæ Anglic' capitis supremi ubilibet constitut': necnon altaria, calices, vestimenta, et alia ecclesiæ ornamenta quæcunque et ea concernen' benedicend', locaque profana si quæ inveneris, de quibus te inquirere volumus, a divinorum celebratione ultime suspendend', ecclesias etiam et cœmiteria sanguinis vel seminis effusione polluta forsan vel polluend' reconciliand', ecclesias et altaria noviter ædificat' consecrand', omnes ordines

---

[[3] i.e. The Institution of a Christian Man. Vid. Letter CXC. p. 337, n. 3, and the preceding document, No. IX. p. 469.]

minores quibuscunque civitatis, diocesios, et jurisdictionum nostrarum prædictarum ipsos ordines a te recipere volentib' et ad hoc habilibus ad jurejurandum de renuntiando Rom' episcopo et ejus auctoritati ac de acceptando regiam majestatem pro supremo capite ecclesiæ Anglic' juxta statuta hujus regni in hac parte edita ab eisdem ordinand' et eorum quolibet per te primitus recepto conferend': ac etiam oleum sanctum chrismatis et sacræ unctionis consecrand': ceteraque omnia et singula, quæ ad officium pontificale in præmissis vel aliquo præmissorum quovis modo pertinent, vel pertinere poterunt, faciend' exercend' et expediend', tibi tenore præsentium committimus vices nostras, et plenam in Domino potestatem: teque quoad præmissa suffraganeum nostrum ordinamus et præficimus per præsentes; donec eas ad nos duxerimus revocand'. Et ut officium tuum hujusmodi possis in præmissis liberius exercere, universis et singulis decanis, rectoribus, vicariis, capellanis, curatis, et non curatis, clericis et apparitoribus quibuscunque in virtute sacræ [suæ] obedientiæ firmiter tenore præsentium injungendo mandamus, quatenus tibi in præmissis et quolibet præmissorum sint obedientes, assistentes, et intendentes in omnibus, prout decet. In cujus rei testimonium sigillum nostrum præsentibus est appensum. Dat' in manerio nostro de Lamehith, decimo die Decembr' anno Domini mill' quin' xxxvii. et nostræ consecrationis anno quinto.

---

## XIII. *A Book containing divers Articles, De Unitate Dei et Trinitate Personarum, de Peccato Originali*[1], *&c.*

TABLE.



### 1. *De Unitate Dei et Trinitate Personarum.*

State Paper Office, Ecclesiastical Papers. Archbishop Cranmer's Papers on the Doctrine and Discipline of the Church, 2. B. No. 19. Original.

De unitate essentiæ divinæ et de tribus personis, censemus decretum Nicenæ synodi verum, et sine ulla dubitatione credendum esse; videlicet, quod sit una essentia divina, quæ et appellatur et est Deus, æternus, incorporeus, impartibilis, immensa potentia, sapientia, bonitate, Creator et Conservator omnium rerum visibilium et invisibilium, et tamen tres sint personæ ejusdem essentiæ et potentiæ, et coæternæ, Pater, Filius, et Spiritus Sanctus; et nomine personæ utimur ea significatione qua usi sunt in hac causa scriptores ecclesiastici, ut significet non partem aut qualitatem in alio, sed quod proprie subsistit. Damnamus omnes hæreses contra hunc articulum exortas, ut Manicheos, qui duo principia ponebant, bonum et malum; item Valentinianos, Arianos, Eunomianos, Mahometistas, et omnes horum similes. Damnamus et Samosatenos, veteres et neotericos, qui cum tantum unam personam esse contendant, de Verbo et Spiritu Sancto astute et impie rhetoricantur, quod non sint personæ distinctæ, sed quod Verbum significet verbum vocale, et Spiritus motum in rebus creatum.

### 2. *De Peccato Originali.*

Omnes homines, secundum naturam propagati, nascuntur cum peccato originali; hoc est, cum carentia originalis justitiæ debitæ inesse, unde sunt filii iræ, et deficiunt cognitione Dei, metu Dei, fiducia erga Deum, etc. Et habent concupiscentiam, repugnantem legi Dei: estque hic morbus seu vitium originis vere peccatum, damnans et afferens nunc quoque æternam mortem his qui non renascuntur per baptismum et Spiritum Sanctum. Damnamus Pelagianos, et alios, qui vitium originis negant esse peccatum, et, ut extenuent gloriam meriti et beneficiorum Christi, disputant hominem viribus naturalibus sine Spiritu

---

[[1] This book was probably drawn up for the agreement of the protestant English and German divines, who held their conferences in London, A.D. 1538. There is much similarity between the clauses of this document and the Augsburg Confession, especially in the first seventeen articles. Vid. Jenkyns' Remains of Abp. Cranmer, Vol. IV. p. 273. et sqq. Portions of this book have been printed by Strype and Burnet, which are noted in the margin.]

Sancto posse legi Dei satisfacere, et propter honesta opera rationis pronunciari justum coram Deo.

### 3. *De Duabus Christi Naturis.*

ITEM docemus, quod Verbum, hoc est Filius Dei, assumpserit humanam naturam in utero beatæ Mariæ Virginis, ut sint duæ naturæ, divina et humana, in unitate personæ inseparabiliter conjunctæ, unus Christus, vere Deus, et vere homo, natus ex Virgine Maria, vere passus, crucifixus, mortuus, et sepultus, ut reconciliaret nobis Patrem, et hostia esset non tantum pro culpa originis, sed etiam pro omnibus actualibus hominum peccatis. Item descendit ad inferos, et vere resurrexit tertia die; deinde ascendit ad cœlos, ut sedeat ad dexteram Patris, et perpetuo regnet et dominetur omnibus creaturis, sanctificet credentes in ipsum, misso in corde eorum Spiritu Sancto, qui regat, consoletur, ac vivificet eos, ac defendat adversus diabolum et vim peccati. Idem Christus palam est rediturus, ut judicet vivos et mortuos, &c. juxta symbolum apostolorum.

### 4. *De Justificatione.*

Cott. MSS. E. v. f. 1, b. British Museum. Original. Strype's Eccl. Mem. Vol. I. pt. ii. App. No. 112. pp. 443, 4. Ed. Oxon. 1822.

ITEM de justificatione docemus, quod ea proprie significat remissionem peccatorum et acceptationem seu reconciliationem nostram in gratiam et favorem Dei; hoc est, veram renovationem in Christo, et quod peccatores, licet non assequantur hanc justificationem absque pœnitentia, et bono ac propenso motu cordis quem Spiritus Sanctus efficit erga Deum et proximum, non tamen propter dignitatem aut meritum pœnitentiæ aut ullorum operum seu meritorum suorum justificantur, sed gratis propter Christum per fidem, cum credunt se in gratiam recipi, et peccata sua propter Christum remitti, qui sua morte pro nostris peccatis satisfecit. Hanc fidem imputat Deus pro justitia coram ipso. Rom. 3°. et 4°. Fidem vero intelligimus non inanem et otiosam, sed eam "quæ per dilectionem operatur." Est enim vera et Christiana fides, de qua hic loquimur, non sola notitia articulorum fidei, aut credulitas doctrinæ Christianæ duntaxat historica; sed una cum illa notitia et credulitate, firma fiducia misericordiæ Dei promissæ propter Christum, qua videlicet certo persuademus ac statuimus eum etiam nobis misericordem et propitium. Et hæc fides vere justificat, vere est salutifera, non ficta, mortua, aut hypocritica, sed necessario habet spem et caritatem sibi individue conjunctas, ac etiam studium bene vivendi, et bene operatur pro loco et occasione. Nam bona opera ad salutem sunt necessaria, non quod de impio justum faciunt, nec quod sunt pretium pro peccatis, aut causa justificationis; sed quia necessum est, ut qui jam fide justificatus est et reconciliatus Deo per Christum, voluntatem Dei facere studeat juxta illud: "Non omnis qui dicit mihi Domine, Domine, intrabit regnum cœlorum, sed qui facit voluntatem Patris mei, qui in cœlis est." Qui vero hæc opera facere non studet, sed secundum carnem vivit, neque veram fidem habet, neque justus est, neque vitam æternam (nisi ex animo resipiscat, et vere pœniteat) assequetur.

Ut hanc fidem consequamur, institutum est ministerium docendi evangelii et porrigendi sacramenta. Nam per verbum et sacramenta tanquam per instrumenta donatur Spiritus Sanctus, qui fidem efficit, ubi et quando visum est Deo, in his qui audiunt evangelium, scilicet quod Deus non propter nostra merita sed propter Christum justificet pœnitentes, qui credunt se propter Christum in gratiam recipi. Damnamus anabaptistas, et alios, qui sentiunt Spiritum Sanctum contingere sine verbo externo hominibus per ipsorum præparationes et opera.

### 5. *De Ecclesia*[2].

Cott. MSS. Cleop. E. v. f. 1. British Museum. Original.

ECCLESIA præter alias acceptiones in scripturis duas habet præcipuas: unam, qua ecclesia accipitur pro congregatione omnium sanctorum et vere fidelium, qui Christo capiti vere credunt et sanctificantur Spiritu ejus. Hæc autem vivum est et vere sanctum Christi corpus mysticum, sed soli Deo cognitum, qui hominum corda solus intuetur.

---

[[2] The above MS. from the Cotton MSS. preserved in the British Museum, is a draft of the article, "de Ecclesia," which was corrected by Henry VIII., in his own hand. As the readings are somewhat different from the copy in the State Paper Office, which the text follows, it has been printed in smaller type at the end of this article. The words inclosed in brackets were erased by Henry VIII.; those which he proposed to substitute are placed in the margin.]

Altera acceptio est, qua ecclesia accipitur pro congregatione omnium hominum qui baptizati sunt in Christo, et non palam abnegarunt Christum, nec juste et per ejus verbum sunt excommunicati. Ista ecclesiæ acceptio congruit ejus statui in hac vita duntaxat, in qua boni malis sunt admixti, et debet esse cognita ut possit audiri, juxta illud: "Qui ecclesiam non audierit," &c. Cognoscitur autem per professionem evangelii et communionem sacramentorum. Hæc est ecclesia catholica et apostolica, quæ non episcopatus Romani aut cujusvis alterius ecclesiæ finibus circumscribitur, sed universas totius Christianismi complectitur ecclesias, quæ simul unam efficiunt catholicam. In hac autem catholica ecclesia nulla particularis ecclesia, sive Romana illa fuerit sive quævis alia, ex institutione Christi supra alias ecclesias eminentiam vel auctoritatem ullam vindicare potest. Est vero hæc ecclesia una, non quod in terris unum aliquod caput seu unum quendam vicarium sub Christo habeat aut habuerit unquam, (quod sibi jam diu pontifex Romanus divini juris prætextu vindicavit, cum tamen revera divino jure nihil amplius illi sit concessum quam alii cuivis episcopo;) sed ideo una dicitur, quia universi Christiani in vinculo pacis colligati unum caput Christum agnoscunt, cujus se profitentur esse corpus, unum agnoscunt Dominum, unam fidem, unum baptisma, unum Deum ac Patrem omnium.

Traditiones vero, et ritus, atque ceremoniæ, quæ vel ad decorem vel ordinem vel disciplinam ecclesiæ ab hominibus sunt institutæ, non omnino necesse est ut eædem sint ubique aut prorsus similes. Hæ enim et variæ fuere, et variari possunt pro regionum et morum diversitate, ubi decus, ordo, et utilitas ecclesiæ videbuntur postulare[1]:

[Hæ enim et variæ fuere, et variari possunt pro regionum et morum diversitate, ubi decus decensque ordo principibus rectoribusque regionum videbuntur postulare; ita tamen ut nihil varietur aut instituatur contra verbum Dei manifestum.]

Et quamvis in ecclesia secundum posteriorem acceptionem mali sint bonis admixti, atque etiam ministeriis verbi et sacramentorum nonnunquam præsint; tamen cum ministrent non suo sed Christi nomine, mandato, et auctoritate, licet eorum ministerio uti, tam in verbo audiendo quam in recipiendis sacramentis, juxta illud: "Qui vos audit, me audit." Nec per eorum malitiam minuitur effectus aut gratia donorum Christi rite accipientibus; sunt enim efficacia propter promissionem et ordinationem Christi, etiamsi per malos exhibeantur.

*De Ecclesia.*

Strype's Eccl. Mem. Vol. I. pt. ii. pp. 442, 3. Ed. Oxon. 1822.

"Ecclesia præter alias acceptiones in scripturis duas habet præcipuas: unam, qua ecclesia accipitur pro congregatione sanctorum et vere fidelium, qui Christo capiti vere credunt, et sanctificantur Spiritu ejus: hæc autem [unum*] est, et vere [†sanctum corpus Christi], sed soli Deo ‡cognitum, qui hominum corda solus [§intuetur.] Altera acceptio est, qua ecclesia accipitur pro congregatione omnium hominum qui baptizati sunt in Christo, et non palam abnegarint Christum, nec sunt ||excommunicati ¶: quæ ecclesiæ acceptio congruit ejus statui in hac vita duntaxat, ubi habet malos bonis simul admixtos**, [et debet esse cognita per verbum et legitimum usum sacramentorum] ut possit audiri; sicut docet Christus, 'Qui ecclesiam non audierit.' Porro ad veram unitatem ecclesiæ requiritur, ut sit consensus in recta doctrina fidei et administratione sacramentorum.

"Traditiones vero et ritus atque ceremoniæ, quæ vel ad decorem, vel ordinem, vel disciplinam ecclesiæ ab hominibus sunt institutæ, non omnino necesse est ut eædem sint ubique aut prorsus similes: hæ enim et variæ fuere et variari possunt†† pro regionum atque morum diversitate et commodo, [sic tamen ut sint consentientes verbo Dei:] et quamvis in ecclesia secundum posteriorem acceptionem mali sint bonis admixti, atque etiam ministeriis verbi et sacramentorum nonnunquam præsint, tamen cum ministrent non suo sed Christi nomine, mandato, et auctoritate, licet eorum ministerio uti, tam in verbo audiendo quam recipiendis sacramentis, juxta illud, 'Qui vos audit, me audit:' nec per eorum malitiam imminuitur effectus aut gratia donorum Christi rite accipientibus; sunt enim efficacia propter promissionem et ordinationem Christi, etiamsi per malos exhibeantur[2]."

* *una.*
† *Sponsa Christi.*
‡ *cognita.*
§ *intuitur.*
|| *Juste.*
¶ *Aut obstinati.*
** *Et cognitio hujus ecclesiæ pervenit per usum verbi et sacramentorum acceptione perfecta unitate ac unanimi consensu acceptata. Ista est ecclesia nostra catholica et apostolica, cum qua nec pontifex Romanus, nec quivis aliquis prælatus aut pontifex, habet quicquid agere præterquam in suas dioceses.*
†† *Modo rectoribus placeant, quibus semper obtemperandum est, sic tamen ut eorum jussio atque lex verbo Dei non adversetur.*

## 6. *De Baptismo.*

Cott. MSS. Cleop. E. v. f. 2. b. British Museum. Original.

De Baptismo dicimus, quod baptismus a Christo sit institutus, et sit necessarius ad salutem, et quod per baptismum offerantur remissio peccatorum et gratia Christi

[[1] In the MS. a space is here left vacant, and the following passage within brackets is written on a loose slip of paper.]

[[2] "Annotationes in margine sunt D. Regis Henrici VIII. manu propria scripta." Strype.]

infantibus et adultis. Et quod non debeat iterari baptismus, et quod infantes debeant baptizari. Et quod infantes per baptismum consequantur remissionem peccatorum et gratiam, et sint filii Dei, quia promissio gratiæ et vitæ æternæ pertinet non solum ad adultos, sed etiam ad infantes. Et hæc promissio per ministerium in ecclesia infantibus et adultis administrari debet. Quia vero infantes nascuntur cum peccato originis, habent opus remissione illius peccati, et illud ita remittitur ut reatus tollatur, licet corruptio naturæ seu concupiscentia manet in hac vita, etsi incipit sanari, quia Spiritus Sanctus in ipsis etiam infantibus est efficax et eos mundat. Probamus igitur sententiam ecclesiæ quæ damnavit Pelagianos, quia negabant infantibus esse peccatum originis. Damnamus et anabaptistas, qui negant infantes baptizandos esse. De adultis vero docemus, quod ita consequuntur per baptismum remissionem peccatorum et gratiam, si baptizandi attulerint pœnitentiam veram, confessionem articulorum fidei, et credant vere ipsis ibi donari remissionem peccatorum et justificationem propter Christum, sicut Petrus ait in Actis: "Pœnitentiam agite, et baptizetur unusquisque vestrum in nomine Jesu Christi in remissionem peccatorum, et accipietis donum Spiritus Sancti."

Strype's Eccl. Mem. Vol. I. pt. ii. App. No. 112 pp. 444, 5. Ed. Oxon. 1822.

## 7. *De Eucharistia.*

De eucharistia constanter credimus et docemus, quod in sacramento corporis et sanguinis Domini vere, substantialiter, et realiter adsunt corpus et sanguis Christi sub speciebus panis et vini; et quod sub eisdem speciebus vere et realiter exhibentur et distribuuntur illis qui sacramentum accipiunt, sive bonis sive malis[3].

Cott. MSS. Cleop. E. v. f. 2. b. British Museum. Original. Strype's Eccl. Mem. Vol. I pt. ii. App. p. 444. Ed. Oxon. 1822.

## 8. *De Pœnitentia*[4].

Summam et ineffabilem suam erga peccatores clementiam et misericordiam Deus Opt. Max. apud prophetam declarans hisce verbis, "Vivo ego, dicit Dominus Deus, nolo mortem impii, sed ut impius convertatur a via sua et vivat," ut hujus tantæ clementiæ ac misericordiæ peccatores participes efficerentur, saluberrime instituit pœnitentiam, quæ sit omnibus resipiscentibus velut antidotum quoddam et efficax remedium adversus desperationem et mortem. Cujus quidem pœnitentiæ tantam necessitatem esse fatemur, ut quotquot a baptismo in mortalia peccata prolapsi sint, nisi in hac vita resipiscentes pœnitentiam egerint, æternæ mortis judicium effugere non poterint. Contra [vero] qui ad misericordiam Dei per pœnitentiam tanquam ad asylum confugerint, quantiscunque peccatis obnoxii sunt, si ab illis serio conversi pœnitentiam egerint, peccatorum omnium veniam ac remissionem indubie consequentur. Porro quoniam peccare a nobis est, resurgere vero a peccatis Dei opus est et donum; valde utile et necessarium esse arbitramur docere, et cujus beneficium sit ut veram salutaremque pœnitentiam agamus, et quænam illa sit ac quibus ex rebus constet, de qua loquimur, pœnitentia.

Cott. MSS. Cleop. E v. ff. 115—121.

Dicimus itaque pœnitentiæ, per quam peccator a morte animæ resurgit, et denuo in gratiam cum Deo redit, Spiritum Sanctum auctorem esse et effectorem, nec quemquam posse sine hujus arcano afflatu peccata sua salutariter vel agnoscere vel odio habere, multo minus remissionem peccatorum a Deo sperare aut assequi. Qui quidem sacer Spiritus pœnitentiæ initium, progressum, et finem, ceteraque omnia quæ veram pœnitentiam perficiunt in anima peccatrice, hoc (quem docebimus) ordine ac modo operatur et efficit.

Principio, facit ut peccator per verbum peccata sua agnoscat, et veros conscientiæ terrores concipiat, dum sentit Deum irasci peccato, utque serio et ex corde doleat ac ingemiscat, quod Deum offenderit: quam peccati agnitionem, dolorem, et animi pavorem ob Deum offensum, sequitur peccati confessio, quæ fit Deo dum rea conscientia peccatum suum Deo confitetur, et sese apud Deum accusat et damnat, et sibi petit ignosci. Psalm 31. [32.] "Delictum meum cognitum tibi feci, et injustitiam meam non abscondi. Dixi, confitebor adversum me injustitiam meam Domino, et tu remisisti

[3 Vid. Seckendorf. Comment. Hist. Apol. de Lutheran. Lib. III. Sect. xiii. § xxxix. Add. (f) pp. 111, 12. Ed. Francof. et Lips. 1792; where the agreement of the English and German divines, A. D. 1535, upon the doctrine of the above article is given almost verbatim as in this article.]

[4 There are four drafts of this article in the Cotton MSS., two in Strype, and one other besides the above in the State Paper Office, which was corrected by Abp. Cranmer himself in his own hand. Those inserted in the copy, from which the above is printed, are marked by brackets. The suggestions which were not adopted are placed in the margin.]

impietatem peccati mei." Atque hæc coram Deo confessio conjunctam habet certam fiduciam misericordiæ divinæ et remissionis peccatorum propter Christum, qua fiducia conscientia jam erigitur et pavore liberatur, ac certo statuit Deum sibi esse propitium, non merito aut dignitate pœnitentiæ, aut suorum operum, sed ex gratuita misericordia propter Christum, qui solus est hostia, satisfactio, ac unica propitiatio pro peccatis nostris. Ad hæc adest et certum animi propositum vitam totam in melius commutandi, ac studium faciendi voluntatem Dei et perpetuo abstinendi a peccatis. Nam vitæ novitatem sive fructus dignos pœnitentiæ ad totius pœnitentiæ perfectionem necessario requirit Deus, juxta illud, Rom. 6º: "Sicut exhibuistis membra vestra servire immunditiæ et iniquitati ad iniquitatem, ita nunc exhibete membra vestra servire justitiæ in sanctificationem."

Atque hæc quidem omnia, agnitionem peccati, odium peccati, dolorem pavoremque pro peccatis, peccati coram Deo confessionem, firmam fiduciam remissionis peccatorum propter Christum, una cum certo animi proposito postea semper a peccatis per Dei gratiam abstinendi et serviendi justitiæ, Spiritus Sanctus in nobis operatur et efficit, modo nos illius afflatui obsequamur, nec gratiæ Dei nos ad pœnitentiam invitanti repugnemus.

Ceterum cum has res, quæ pœnitentiam efficiunt, maxima pars Christiani populi ignoret, nec quomodo agenda sit vera pœnitentia intelligat, nec ubi speranda sit remissio peccatorum norit; ut in his rebus omnibus melius instituatur et doceatur, non solum concionatores et pastores diligenter in publicis concionibus populum de hac re informare, et quid sit vera pœnitentia, ex sacris literis sincere prædicare debent, verum etiam valde utilem ac summe necessariam* esse dicimus peccatorum confessionem, quæ auricularis dicitur, et privatim fit ministris ecclesiæ.

*"Commodissimam" for "summe necessariam." Cranmer.

Quæ sane confessio modis omnibus in ecclesia retinenda est et magni facienda, cum propter hominum imperitorum institutionem in verbo Dei, et alia commoda non pauca, (de quibus mox dicemus,) tum præcipue propter absolutionis beneficium, hoc est, remissionem peccatorum, quæ in hac confessione confitentibus offertur et exhibetur per absolutionem et potestatem clavium, juxta illud Christi, Joan. 20. "Quorum remiseritis peccata," &c. Cui absolutioni certo oportet credere. Est enim vox evangelii, qua minister per verbum, non suo sed Christi nomine et auctoritate, remissionem peccatorum confitenti annuntiat ac offert. Cui voci evangelii per ministrum sonanti dum confitens certa fide credit et assentitur, illico conscientia ejus fit certa de remissione peccatorum, et jam certo secum statuit Deum sibi propitium ac misericordem esse. Quæ una profecto res Christianos omnes magnopere debet permovere, ut confessionem, in qua per absolutionem gratiæ et remissionis peccatorum certitudo concipitur et confirmatur, modis omnibus et ament et amplectantur. Et in hac privata absolutione sacerdos potestatem habet absolvendi confitentem ab omnibus peccatis, etiam illis qui soliti sunt vocari casus reservati, ita tamen ut ille privatim absolutus nihilominus pro manifestis criminibus (si in jus vocetur) publicis judiciis subjaceat.

Accedunt huc et alia confessionis arcanæ commoda, quorum unum est, quod indocti ac imperiti homines nusquam [commodius*] aut melius quam in confessione de doctrina Christiana institui possint, [modo confessorem doctum et pium nacti fuerint.] Nam cum animos attentos ac dociles in confessione afferunt, diligenter ad ea quæ a sacerdote dicuntur animum advertunt. Quocirca et fides eorum explorari potest, et quid peccatum sit, quamque horrenda res sit, et quæ sint peccatorum inter se discrimina, ac quam graviter contra peccata irascitur Deus, a doctis ac piis pastoribus seu confessoribus [ex verbo Dei] doceri possunt ac informari. Multi enim, propterea quod hæc ignorent, in conscientiis sæpe graviter anguntur, illic trepidantes timore, ubi timor non est, qui (ut Servator ait) "culicem excolantes, camelum deglutiunt;" in minimis levissimisque peccatis valde anxii, de maximis et gravissimis non perinde pœnitentes. Sunt porro qui simili laborantes inscitia propter immodicum timorem et animi pusillanimitatem de peccatorum venia fere desperant. Contra sunt, qui per hypocrisim superbientes seipsos adversus Deum erigunt, quasi aut sine peccato sint, aut ipsos pro peccatis Deus nolit punire.

*Substituted for "rectius." Cranmer.

Jam quis nescit quam utilis et necessaria* istiusmodi hominibus confessio sit, in qua hi verbo Dei dure increpandi arguendique sunt, ut peccatores se agnoscant, atque intelligant, quam horribiliter Deus peccata puniat? Contra, illis qui nimio timore desperant, suavissima evangelii consolatio afferenda est. Ad hæc, in confessione [ex verbo Dei] doceri homines possunt, non solum qua ratione Diaboli tentationes vincant, et carnem mortificent, ne ad priores vitæ sordes postea relabantur; verum etiam quibus

*"Commoda" for "necessaria." Cranmer.

remediis peccata omnia fugiant, ut non regnent in ipsis. Præterea illa animi humilitas, qua homo homini propter Deum sese submittit, et pectoris sui arcana aperit, multarum profecto virtutum custos est et conservatrix. Quid quod pudor ille et erubescentia peccati quæ ex confessione oritur, præterquam quod animum a peccato ad Deum vere conversum indicat, etiam multos mortales a turpibus factis retrahit ac cohibet? Postremo, ut ille qui simpliciter et tanquam coram Deo peccata sua ministro ecclesiæ confitetur, declarat se verum Dei timorem habere; ita hac animi humilitate discit Deum magis et timere et revereri, et innatam in corde superbiam reprimere, ut Dei voluntati facilius obsequatur et obtemperet. Jam vero, cum hæc ita se habeant, nihil dubitamus, quin omnes viri boni hanc confessionem tot nominibus utilem ac *necessariam, non solum in ecclesia retinendam esse, sed magno etiam in pretio habendam judicent. Quod si qui sunt qui eam* vel damnant, vel rejiciunt, hi profecto se et in verbo Dei institutionem, et absolutionis beneficium (quod in confessione datur), et alia multa atque ingentia commoda Christianis valde utilia, negligere et contemnere ostendunt; nec animadvertunt se in orbem Christianum maximam peccandi licentiam invehere, et magnam in omne scelus ruendi occasionem præbere.

* "Commodam" for "necessariam;" and adds, "licet non sit præcepta in scripturis, tamen prædictis de causis." Cranmer.

"Eam temere." Cranmer.

Quod vero ad enumerationem peccatorum spectat, quemadmodum non probamus scrupulosam et anxiam, ne laqueum injiciat hominum conscientiis, ita censemus segnem et supinam negligentiam in re tam salutari magnopere periculosam esse et fugiendam.

["Ut cujus conscientia de peccato uno aut pluribus affligitur, is consolationem, consilium, et absolutionem singulatim a sacerdote petere, et rem tam salutarem non negligere debeat." Cranmer.]

### 9. *De Sacramentorum Usu.*

Docemus, quod sacramenta, quæ per verbum Dei instituta sunt, non tantum sint notæ professionis inter Christianos, sed magis certa quædam testimonia et efficacia signa gratiæ, et bonæ voluntatis Dei erga nos, per quæ Deus invisibiliter operatur in nobis, et suam gratiam in nos invisibiliter diffundit, siquidem ea rite susceperimus, quodque per ea excitatur et confirmatur fides in his qui eis utuntur. Porro docemus, quod ita utendum sit sacramentis, ut in adultis, præter veram contritionem, necessario etiam debeat accedere fides, quæ credat præsentibus promissionibus, quæ per sacramenta ostenduntur, exhibentur, et præstantur. Neque enim in illis verum est, quod quidam dicunt, sacramenta conferre gratiam ex opere operato sine bono motu utentis; nam in ratione utentibus necessum est, ut fides etiam utentis accedat, per quam credat illis promissionibus, et accipiat res promissas, quæ per sacramenta conferantur. De infantibus vero, cum temerarium sit eos a misericordia De iexcludere, præsertim cum Christus in evangelio dicat, "Sinite parvulos ad me venire, talium est enim regnum cœlorum;" et alibi, "Nisi quis renatus fuerit ex aqua et Spiritu Sancto, non potest intrare in regnum cœlorum;" cumque perpetua ecclesiæ catholicæ consuetudine, jam inde ab ipsis apostolorum temporibus, receptum sit infantes debere baptizari in remissionem peccatorum et salutem, dicimus quod Spiritus Sanctus efficax sit in illis, et eos in baptismo mundet, quemadmodum supra in articulo de baptismo dictum est.

Cott. MSS. Cleop. E v. f. 122. British Museum. Original. Strype's Eccl. Mem. Vol. I. pt. ii. pp. 449, 50. Ed. Oxon. 1822.

### 10. *De Ministris Ecclesiæ.*

De ministris ecclesiæ docemus, quod nemo debeat publice docere, aut sacramenta ministrare, nisi rite vocatus, et quidem ab his, penes quos in ecclesia, juxta verbum Dei, et leges ac consuetudines uniuscujusque regionis, jus est vocandi et admittendi. Et quod nullus ad ecclesiæ ministerium vocatus, etiamsi episcopus sit sive Romanus sive quicunque alius, hoc sibi jure divino vindicare possit, ut publice docere, sacramenta ministrare, vel ullam aliam ecclesiasticam functionem in aliena diocesi aut parochia exercere valeat; hoc est, nec episcopus in alterius episcopi diocesi, nec parochus in alterius parochia. Et demum quod malitia ministri efficaciæ sacramentorum nihil detrahat, ut jam supra docuimus in articulo de ecclesia.

### 11. *De Ritibus Ecclesiasticis.*

Ritus, ceremoniæ, et ordinationes ecclesiasticæ humanitus institutæ, quæcunque prosunt ad eruditionem, disciplinam, tranquillitatem, bonum ordinem, aut decorem in ecclesia, servandæ sunt et amplectendæ, ut stata festa, jejunia, preces, et his similia.

De quibus admonendi sunt homines quod non sint illi cultus, quos Deus in scriptura præcipit aut requirit, aut ipsa sanctimonia, sed quod ad illos cultus et ipsam sanctimoniam admodum utiles sunt, ac tum placent Deo, cum ex fide, caritate, et obedientia servantur. Sunt autem veri et genuini cultus timor Dei, fides, dilectio, et cetera opera a Deo mandata. Ad quæ consequenda et præstanda quoties ritus et traditiones adjumentum adferunt, diligenter servandæ sunt, non tanquam res in scripturis a Deo exactæ, aut illis veris et genuinis cultibus æquandæ, sed tanquam res ecclesiæ utiles, Deo gratæ, et adminicula veræ pietatis. Et quamvis ritus ac traditiones ejusmodi a Christianis observari debeant, propter causas quas ante diximus; tamen in illarum observatione ea libertatis Christianæ ratio habenda est, ut nemo se illis ita teneri putet, quin eas possit omittere, modo adsit justa violandi ratio et causa, et absit contemptus, nec per ejusmodi violationem proximi conscientia turbetur aut lædatur. Quod si ejusmodi ritus aut ordinationes alio animo ac consilio instituuntur aut observantur, quam ut sint exercitia quædam, admonitiones, et pædagogiæ, quæ excitent et conducant ad eas res in quibus sita est vera pietas et justitia; nos talem institutionem et observationem omnino improbandam et rejiciendam esse dicimus. Non enim remissio peccatorum, justificatio, et vera pietas tribuenda est ejusmodi ritibus et traditionibus, (nam remissionem peccatoris et justificationem propter Christum gratis per fidem consequimur;) sed hoc illis tribuendum est, quod quemadmodum nec sine legibus politicis civitas, ita nec sine ritibus ac traditionibus ecclesiæ ordo servari, confusio vitari, juventus ac vulgus imperitum erudiri potest; quodque ejusmodi ritus et traditiones ad pietatem et spirituales animi motus non parum adminiculantur et prosunt. Quod si ullæ traditiones aliquid præcipiunt contra verbum Dei, vel quod sine peccato præstari non potest, nos ejusmodi traditiones, tanquam noxias et pestiferas, ab ecclesia tollendas esse censemus: impias etiam opiniones et superstitiones, quæ Christi gloriam ac beneficium lædunt atque obscurant, quoties vel populi ignorantia ac simplicitate, vel prava doctrina aut negligentia pastorum, traditionibus ullis annectuntur et hærent, resecandas penitus et abolendas esse judicamus. Præterea etiam hoc docendi sunt homines, quod ejusmodi rituum ac traditionum externa observatio Deo minime grata sit, nisi his, qui illis utuntur, animus adsit qui eas referat ad pietatem, propter quam institutæ sunt: ad hæc, quod inter præcepta Dei, et ritus sive traditiones quæ ab hominibus instituuntur, hoc discrimen habendum sit, nempe quod ritus sive traditiones humanitus institutæ mandatis ac præceptis Dei (quæ in scripturis traduntur) cedere semper et postponi ubique debeant. Et nihilominus, quoniam ordo et tranquillitas ecclesiæ absque ritibus et ceremoniis conservari non potest, docemus adeo utile esse et necessarium, ecclesiam habere ritus et ceremonias, ut si ab ecclesia tollerentur, ipsa illico ecclesia et dissiparetur et labefactaretur.

Postremo ritus, ceremoniæ, sive traditiones, de quibus antea diximus, non solum propter causas prædictas, verum etiam propter præceptum Dei, qui jubet nos potestatibus obedire, servandæ sunt.

### 12. *De Rebus Civilibus*[1].

Misera mortalium conditio, peccato corrupta, præceps ad iniquitatem et ad flagitia ruit, nisi salubri auctoritate retineatur, nec potest publica salus consistere sine justa gubernatione et obedientia: quamobrem benignissimus Deus ordinavit reges, principes, ac gubernatores, quibus dedit auctoritatem non solum curandi ut populus juxta divinæ legis præscripta vivat, sed etiam legibus aliis reipublicæ commodis et justa potestate eundem populum continendi ac regendi; hos autem in publicam salutem deputavit Deus suos in terra ministros, et populi sui duces ac rectores, eisque subjecit universam cujusvis sortis multitudinem reliquam. Atque ob eam causam multa ac diligenter de illis in scripturis tradit. Primum quidem, ut ipsi cœlestibus præceptis erudiantur ad sapientiam et virtutem, quo sciant cujus sint ministri, et concessum a Deo judicium et auctoritatem legitime atque salubriter exerceant; juxta illud, "Erudimini qui judicatis terram, servite Domino in timore." Deinde vero præcipit, atque illis in hoc ipsum auctoritatem dat, ut pro conditione reipublicæ suæ salutares ac justas leges (quoad pro virili

---

[[1] The title is in the archbishop's hand in another copy of this article preserved in the State Paper Office.]

possint) provideant atque legitime condant, per quas non solum æquitas, justitia, et tranquillitas in republica retineri, sed etiam pietas erga Deum promoveri possit; atque insuper ut legis Dei atque Christianæ religionis tuendæ curam habeant, quemadmodum Augustinus diserte fatetur, dicens: "In hoc reges, sicut eis divinitus præcipitur, Deo serviunt, in quantum reges sunt, si in suo regno bona jubeant, mala prohibeant, non solum quæ pertinent ad humanam societatem, verum etiam quæ ad divinam religionem[2]." Proinde principum ac gubernatorum potestas et officium est, non solum pro sua et reipublicæ incolumitate ac salute justa bella suscipere, probos amplecti et fovere, in improbos animadvertere, pauperes tueri, afflictos et vim passos eripere, arcere injurias, et ut ordo et concordia inter subditos conservetur, atque quod suum est cuique tribuatur, curare; verum etiam prospicere, et (si causa ita postulaverit) etiam compellere, ut universi tam sacerdotes quam reliqua multitudo officiis suis rite et diligenter fungantur; omnem denique operam suam adhibere, ut boni ad bene agendum invitentur, et improbi a malefaciendo cohibeantur. Et quamvis illi qui timore legum et pœnarum corporalium cohibentur a peccando, aut in officio continentur, non eo ipso fiunt pii vel accepti Deo; tamen hucusque proficit salubris coercio, ut et illi qui tales sunt, interim vel minus sint mali, vel saltem minus flagitiorum committant, viamque nonnunquam facilius inveniant ad pietatem, et reliquorum quies ac pietas minus turbetur, scandala et perniciosa exempla auferantur a Christianis cœtibus, et apertis vitiis aut blasphemiis nomen Dei et religionis decus quam minimum dehonestetur.

Ad hæc, quia necessum est, ut auctoritatem principum, reipublicæ atque rebus humanis summopere necessariam, populus tanquam Dei ordinationem agnoscat et revereatur; idcirco Deus in scripturis passim præcipit, ut omnes, cujuscunque in republica gradus aut conditionis fuerint, promptam et fidelem obedientiam principibus præstent, idque non solum metu corporalis pœnæ, sed etiam propter Dei voluntatem; quemadmodum Petrus diligenter monet: "Subditi (inquiens) estote omni humanæ creaturæ propter Deum, sive regi quasi præcellenti, sive ducibus, tanquam ab eo missis ad vindictam malefactorum, laudem vero bonorum, quia sic est voluntas Dei." Paulus vero in hunc modum: "Admone illos principibus et potestatibus subditos esse, magistratibus parere, ad omne opus bonum paratos esse, neminem blasphemare." Quod si malus princeps aut gubernator quicquam injuste aut inique imperat subdito, quamvis ille potestate sua contra Dei voluntatem abutatur, ut animam suam lædat, nihilominus subditus debet ejusmodi imperium, quantumvis grave, pati ac sustinere, (nisi certo constet id esse peccatum,) potius quam resistendo publicum ordinem aut quietem perturbare: quod si certo constet peccatum esse quod princeps mandat, tum subditus neque pareat neque reipublicæ pacem quovis modo perturbet, sed pace servata incolumi, et causæ ultione Deo relicta, vel ipsam potius mortem sustineat, quam quicquam contra Dei voluntatem aut præceptum perpetret.

Porro quemadmodum de obedientia principibus exhibenda scriptura diligenter præcipit, ita etiam ut cetera officia alacriter illis præstemus, monet atque jubet; qualia sunt tributa, vectigalia, militiæ labor, et his similia: quæ populus, ex Dei præcepto, principibus pendere et præstare debet, propterea quod respublicæ absque stipendiis, præsidiis, et magnis sumptibus neque defendi possunt neque regi. Est præterea et honos principibus deferendus, juxta Pauli sententiam, qui jubet, ut principibus honorem exhibeamus. Qui sane honos non in externa duntaxat reverentia et observantia positus est, sed multo verius in animi judicio et voluntate; nempe ut agnoscamus principes a Deo ordinatos esse, et Deum per eos hominibus ingentia beneficia largiri: ad hæc, ut principes propter Deum et metuamus et amemus, et ut ad omnem pro viribus gratitudinem illis præstandam parati simus: postremo ut Deum pro principibus precemur, uti servet eos, ac eorum mentes semper inflectat ad Dei gloriam et salutem reipublicæ. Hæc si fecerimus, vere principes honorabimus, juxta Petri præceptum, "Deum timete, regem honorificate."

Quæ cum ita sint, non solum licet Christianis principibus ac gubernatoribus regna et ditiones possidere, atque dignitatibus et muneribus publicis fungi, quæ publicam salutem spectant, et undecunque promovent vel tuentur, uti supra diximus; verum etiam, quando in ejusmodi functionibus respiciunt honorem Dei, et eodem dignitatem suam atque

[[2] August. ad Bonifacium. Epist. i. Tom. II. p. 83. Ed. Paris. 1635. (Epist. clxxxv. 19. Ed. Bened. 1679—1700); where the above passage is found in sense, and partly in the same words.]

potestatem referunt, valde placent Deo, ejusque favorem ac gratiam ampliter demerentur. Sunt enim bona opera quæ Deus præmiis magnificentissimis non in hac duntaxat vita, sed multo magis in æterna, cohonestat atque coronat.

Licet insuper Christianis universis, ut singuli quique pro suo gradu ac conditione, juxta divinas ac principum leges et honestas singularum regionum consuetudines, talia munia atque officia obeant et exerceant, quibus mortalis hæc vita vel indiget, vel ornatur, vel conservatur: nempe ut victum quærant ex honestis artibus, negotientur, faciant contractus, possideant proprium, res suas jure postulent, militent, copulentur legitimo matrimonio, præstent jusjurandum, et hujusmodi. Quæ omnia, quemadmodum universis Christianis, pro sua cujusque conditione ac gradu, divino jure licita sunt, ita cum pii subditi propter timorem Dei principibus ac gubernatoribus suis promptam atque debitam præstent obedientiam, ceteraque student peragere, quæ suum officium et reipublicæ utilitas postulat, placent etiam ipsi magnopere Deo, et bona faciunt opera, quibus Deus ingentia præmia promittit, et fidelissime largitur.

### 13. *De Corporum Resurrectione et Judicio Extremo.*

Credendum firmiter atque docendum censemus, quod in consummatione mundi Christus, sicut ipsemet apud Matthæum affirmat, venturus est in gloria Patris sui cum angelis sanctis, et majestate, ac potentia, sessurusque super sedem majestatis suæ; et quod in eodem adventu, summa celeritate, in momento temporis, ictu oculi, divina potentia sua suscitabit mortuos, sistetque in eisdem in quibus hic vixerunt corporibus ac carne coram tribunali suo cunctos homines, qui unquam ab exordio mundi fuerunt, aut postea unquam usque in illam diem futuri sunt. Et judicabit exactissimo atque justissimo judicio singulos, et reddet unicuique secundum opera sua, quæ in hac vita et corpore gessit: piis quidem ac justis æternam vitam et gloriam cum sanctis angelis; impiis vero et sceleratis æternam mortem atque supplicium, cum diabolo et prævaricatoribus angelis. Præterea quod in illo judicio perfecta et perpetua fiet separatio proborum ab improbis, et quod nullum erit postea terrenum regnum aut terrenarum voluptatum usus, qualia quidam errore decepti somniaverunt. Demum quod nullus post hoc judicium erit finis tormentorum malis, qui tunc condemnabuntur ad supplicia, sicut nec ullus finis beatitudinis bonis, qui in illo die acceptabuntur ad gloriam.

---

## XIV. *Articuli de Missa Privata, De Veneratione Sanctorum, et De Imaginibus*[1].

### 1. *De Missa Privata.*

State Paper Office. Ecclesiastical Papers. Abp. Cranmer's Papers on the Doctrine and Discipline of the Church, 2 B. No. 19. Original.

[Lectiones[2].] [Conciones.]

Lectiones sacras [ac conciones] in missa recitari, et precationis pro rebus vel in singulos vel etiam in universos necessariis fieri, [et eucharistiam in missa populo exhiberi,] non est dubium quin Paulus et reliqui apostoli ecclesiis ordinaverint. Quem morem, a primis Christianitatis incunabulis observatum, nullo nunc pacto abolendum, sed omni reverentia et religione in ecclesiam retinendum atque conservandum judicamus. Nam lectiones illæ permultum habent efficaciæ ad excitandas hominum mentes, vel ad fidem, vel ad [amorem ac] timorem Dei et obedientiam præceptorum ejus, maxime si populo satis intelligantur, vel a concionatore docto et pio explicentur. Siquidem et fides ex auditu est, et quid operis faciendum sit ut Deo placeas, non aliunde melius aut certius quam ex ipsius verbo discas.

[Precationes.]

Precationes autem, quæ in communi cœtu fiunt, promissiones a Christo quam amplissimas adjunctas habent; cum ait, "Si duo ex vobis consenserint super terram de omni re quacunque petierint, fiet illis a Patre meo qui in cœlis est; ubi

---

[1 "These three papers, De Missa Privata, De Veneratione Sanctorum, et De Imaginibus, seem to be drafts for some of the Articles on which the English and German divines, assembled in London in 1538, could not agree." Jenkyns, Remains of Cranmer, Vol. I. p. 293. *n.* e. Letter of German Ambassadors to Hen. VIII. (Cott. MSS. E. v. f. 172, British Museum, Original.) Vid. Burnet's Hist. of Reformat. Vol. I. Add. No. 7. pp. 493—517. Ed. Oxon. 1829; and Seckendorf, Comment. Hist. Apol. de Lutheran. Lib. III. Sect. 21. § lxxviii. Add. 3. pp. 266, 7. Ed. Francof. et Lips. 1692.]

[2 The side-notes are the additions of the archbishop, which are found in the MS. in his own hand.]

enim sunt duo vel tres congregati in nomine meo, ibi sum in medio eorum." Voluit igitur Christus, ut oraturi congregaremur, et nos ecclesiæ aggregaremus. Voluit ecclesiam totam sic inter se devinctam esse, ut haberet cor unum et animam unam, et invicem alii aliorum necessitatibus afficerentur, et pro illis communibus precibus Deum orarent, ratas fore promittens et sibi gratas hujusmodi precationes. Præterea ecclesiam sic convenire et junctim Deum precari, valde etiam prodest ad exemplum. Ibi enim alii aliorum exemplis vel ignari docentur vel segnes excitantur, ut et ipsi credant et Deum invocent. Quam multos necessitatum publicarum vel nulla vel minima cura tangeret, nisi ibi admonerentur singulos debere affici publicis curis, et orare non solum pro ecclesia universa, ut liberetur ab erroribus, scandalis, dissidiis, impiis cultibus, ut vera doctrina propagetur, ut veri cultus (pulsa superstitione) Deo præstentur, ut pax et tranquillitas ecclesiæ conservetur, sed etiam pro principum salute et felici gubernatione, pro proventu frugum, contra pestilentiam, cum similibus! Hujusmodi precationes in missa et ceremoniis publicis censemus pie et necessario institutas esse, vel ob hoc quoque, ut assuescant homines in omnibus periculis Deum invocare, in illum fiduciam collocare, ab illo pendere, et auxilium petere et exspectare. Sed precationes communes communi lingua fieri consentaneum foret; ut omnes astantes communiter atque unanimiter orare Deum possint, tam mente quam spiritu. Ita enim oratio et Deo fieret acceptior, et hominibus haud dubie fructuosior, si populus intellecta sacerdotis verba, non minus animorum interius consensu, quam vocis exterius consono concentu approbaret. Nam, ut inquit Paulus, "Si orem lingua, spiritus meus orat, at mens mea fructu vacat:" et iterum, "Si incertam vocem tuba dederit, quis apparabitur ad bellum? sic et vos per linguam nisi significantem sermonem dederitis, quomodo intelligetur quod dicitur?" et mox ibidem, "Alioqui si benedixeris spiritu, is qui implet locum indocti quomodo dicturus est, Amen, ad tuam gratiarum actionem?" Peractis vero lectionibus, concionibus, et precationibus, populus corpus Christi quod pro nobis traditum est, et sanguinem ejus qui pro nobis effusus est, in eucharistia sumebat, in memoriam videlicet mortis suæ, uti ipse pridie passionis instituerat. Quo factum est, ut illi, veluti Christo incorporati et connati, et cum illo peccatis mortui, denuo in novæ vitæ emendationem sæpissime resurgerent. Hodie vero adeo prævaluit Romani Antichristi tyrannis non solum adversus mundi monarchas, sed etiam contra veterem ecclesiæ morem et sinceram ac puram doctrinæ christianæ religionem, ut quæ sanctissime primitus fuerunt instituta, illa in sui suorumque gloriam ac commodum impurissime profanaverit. Lectiones sacræ et precationes hodie apud sacerdotes manent, sed ea lingua ut a populo non intelligantur, et populus ipse quod precatur (quia peregrino sermone id facit) non intelligit. Conciones sacræ vel nullæ vel rarissimæ sunt; eucharistia a solo sumitur sacerdote, qui illa in turpissimum quæstum pro vivis ac defunctis applicat; populo christiano vix in paschate datur, et ne tunc quidem integrum sacramentum. Ceterum quanto missa res est sacratior, tanto minus decet eam impiis opinionibus profanari, aut ad libidinem quorundam et quæstum in sinistrum usum converti. Damnanda est igitur impia illa opinio sentientium usum sacramenti cultum esse a sacerdotibus applicandum pro aliis, vivis et defunctis, et mereri illis vitam æternam et remissionem culpæ et pœnæ, idque ex opere operato. Talis siquidem doctrina ignota erat veteri ecclesiæ, et aliena est a scripturis sacris, et subvertit rectam de fidei justificatione doctrinam, et parit alieni operis fiduciam. Christus autem, cum institueret hoc sacramentum, dixit, "Hoc facite in meam commemorationem;" volens nimirum, ut ibi fieret in vera fide recordatio mortis ipsius, et beneficiorum quæ nobis sua morte meruit. Quæ beneficia per sacramentum applicantur sumenti, cum fidem tali recordatione exsuscitat. Non possunt autem aliis, quam sacramentum sumentibus, per sumentes applicari. Sed quemadmodum unusquisque pro seipso tantum, et non pro alio baptizatur; ita et eucharistia a Christo est instituta, ut illam nemo pro alio, sed pro sese quisque Christianus sumeret. Talis quippe est sacramentorum ratio et natura, ut signa[3] sint visibilia, certa, et efficacia, per quæ Deus invisibiliter in recte utentibus operatur; verum non nisi in ipsis tantum utentibus per illa operatur, nec aliis per alios, sive sacerdotes seu cujuscunque ordinis aut conditionis fuerint, accommodari possunt. Qua re una animadversa ac perpensa, facile apparebit privatarum missarum applicationes et nundinationes non amplius esse ferendas. Nam cum, teste

[Eucharistia. Cranmer.]

[[3] Vid. De sacramentorum usu, supra. p. 477.]

Augustino, quæcunque sunt in missa præter eucharistiam nihil aliud sint quam laudes, gratiarum actiones, obsecrationes, et fidelium petitiones; eucharistia autem non alii quam ipsi sumenti prosit aut applicari possit; reliqua vero, ut laudes, gratiarum actiones, obsecrationes, &c. tam a laicis quam a sacerdotibus afferri Deo possint et debeant; non erit jam amplius cur missas emere quisquam debebit. Porro, quia sine gratiarum actione recordatio mortis Christi rite non peragitur, ideo veteres hanc sacramenti perceptionem eucharistiam appellarunt, quam et sacrificium nonnulli orthodoxi patres nominaverunt, quod videlicet in memoriam illius unici et semel peracti sacrificii fiat, non quod ipsum opus sit sacrificium applicabile vivis et mortuis in remissionem peccatorum. Id quod papisticum duntaxat est figmentum; et quoniam ab hac tam impia opinione et quæstu inde proveniente missæ privatæ, illæque pro magna parte satisfactoriæ, in tantam multitudinem excreverunt, quarum nec mentionem nec exemplum ullum apud antiquiores invenimus, satisfactorias quidem prorsus abolendas, ceteras vero privatas vel in totum abrogandas, vel certe minuendas et reprimendas judicamus: summam denique curam adhibendam, ut hujus sacramenti verus ac genuinus usus ad gloriam Christi et ecclesiæ salutem restituatur.

### 2. *De Veneratione Sanctorum*[1].

Quamquam credimus et confitemur Deum omnis boni datorem ac largitorem esse, uti Jacobus testatur dicens, "Omne datum optimum et omne donum perfectum desursum est descendens a Patre luminum;" et Christus apud Johannem ait, "Quicquid petieritis Patrem in nomine meo, dabit vobis;" et Psal. "Invoca me in die tribulationis," &c.; quibus scripturæ locis aperte docemur, quicquid ad corporis aut animi salutem pertinet, id a solo Deo petendum esse, et ab eo nobis dari, quoties in Christi nomine petimus: tamen cum jam inde ab exordio ecclesiæ receptum sit, sanctorum memorias et dies festos celebrare, valde utile ac necessarium putamus, eam de his rebus doctrinæ formam tradere, quæ Dei gloriam nulla in parte lædat aut imminuat, et tamen doceat perpetuam ecclesiæ consuetudinem in divorum memoriis ac festis celebrandis laudabilem esse, nec scripturæ sacræ adversari. Et cum non ignoramus in hanc quoque religionis christianæ partem, quæ sanctorum venerationem continet, multos abusus ac superstitiones irrepsisse; curandum censemus, ut eo, quod vanum aut noxium est, improbato et rejecto, illud solum, quod utile ac verum est, retineatur ac probetur. Quod ut rectius et facilius fiat, docendum ducimus, quod sanctorum, qui corporibus exuti cum Christo vivunt, memoria in ecclesiis multis de causis utiliter habeatur.

Primum quod nobis in mentem suggerit illa eximia Dei in sanctis opera, quæ ut olim, dum per sanctos fierent, Dei potentiam et gloriam apud homines illustrabant, ita nunc vel sola recordatione ad Deum in sanctis laudandum nos invitant. Adde huc, quod in his sanctorum memoriis præclarissima fidei, caritatis, patientiæ, et ceterarum virtutum exempla nobis proponuntur, quæ nos exstimulent ad illorum imitationem: ut quemadmodum illi "per fidem vicerunt regna, operati sunt justitiam, adepti promissiones," ita nos, illorum vestigiis insistentes, ad victoriæ coronam, qua illi nunc ornantur, perveniamus. Quam sane sanctorum imitationem summum et maximum honorem esse arbitramur, quem vel nos sanctis impendere possumus, vel illi a nobis flagitant. Quamvis enim solus Christus sit unicum illud et numeris omnibus perfectum vitæ exemplar, quod imitari pro viribus omnes debemus, sunt tamen Christi beneficio et munere etiam in sanctis proposita nobis exempla, quæ utiliter et multo cum fructu sequi possumus. Quos enim non animabit stupenda in tormentis martyrum constantia, ut omnia quantumvis aspera et dura propter Christi gloriam pati velint? Cui non Josiæ, Ezechiæ, et aliorum piorum regum pietas, in vera Dei religione tuenda, et abolendis idololatricis cultibus, exemplo esse potest, ut illorum pietatem imitari pro viribus studeat? Jam vero et lapsus quoque et pœnitentiæ sanctorum, dum ex historiis cognoscuntur, magnam nobis utilitatem adferre poterunt. Nam cum Davidis, Petri, Magdalenæ, et aliorum condonatos fuisse lapsus cognoscimus, quis dubitet quin et nostra peccata, nobis pœnitentiam agentibus, Deus velit similiter

[[1] A copy of this treatise and the following, de Imaginibus, are preserved in Archbishop Cranmer's Collection of Law, Lambeth Library, 1107, fol. 116, 121. The title of this and the following treatise are in the archbishop's own hand in the State Paper Office MS.]

condonare? Porro in sanctorum memoriis gratiæ Deo agendæ sunt, quod sanctis varia dona contulit, quibus illi insigniter ecclesiæ profuerunt, dum vel doctrinæ vel vitæ exemplo quamplurimos Christo lucrati sunt; quæ Dei in sanctis dona non solum magnopere laudare oportet, sed etiam sanctos ipsos, quia his donis bene usi sunt, laudibus attollere, amare, et suspicere, quemadmodum scribit Augustinus *De Civitate*, Lib. VIII. "Honoramus," inquit, "memorias martyrum tanquam sanctorum hominum Dei, qui usque ad mortem suorum corporum pro veritate certarunt,—ut ea celebritate et Deo vero de illorum victoriis gratias agamus, et nos ad imitationem talium coronarum atque palmarum, eodem invocato in auxilium, ex eorum memoriæ renovatione adhortemur[2]." Et alibi, "Colimus... martyres eo cultu dilectionis et societatis, quo et in hac vita coluntur sancti homines Dei, quorum corda ad talem pro evangelica veritate passionem parata esse sentimus; sed illos tanto devotius quanto securius post incerta omnia superata: quanto etiam fidentiore laude prædicamus jam in vita feliciori victores, quam in ista adhuc usque pugnantes![3]" Et Basilius, *Concione de Martyre Gordia:* "Sanctis non est opus additione ad gloriam, sed nobis eorum memoria opus est ad imitationem[4]." Et alibi, "Hoc est martyrum encomium, adhortari ecclesiam ad virtutis imitationem[5]." Atque hactenus quidem de sanctorum veneratione, quæ partim in laudatione Dei in illis, partim in illorum imitatione constitit, diximus. Nunc vero ad alteram venerationis speciem veniamus, quæ de sanctorum interpellatione tractat.

Est sane hæc duplex, et vel sanctorum pro nobis ad Deum precationes, vel nostram ad sanctos interpellationem significat. De priore dicimus, sanctos qui devicto peccato et morte in Christo obdormierunt, cum sunt unius atque ejusdem nobiscum corporis membra, nobis qui adhuc cum carne et mundo conflictamur, bene velle et bene precari. De posteriore vero, qua illorum opem imploramus, docemus, quod cum corporis et animi salus, remissio peccatorum, gratia, vita æterna, et his similia solius Dei munera sint, nec a quoquam alio quam a solo Deo dari possint; quisquis pro his donis sanctos invocat ac solicitat, et hæc petit ab illis, quæ nisi a solo Deo dari nequeunt, quasi ipsimet sancti hæc petentibus largiri possent, is graviter sane errat, et Deum gloria sua spolians, creaturæ eam tribuit.

Ceterum si sanctorum suffragia imploraverimus, et ab illis petierimus, ut nobiscum, et pro nobis, Deum precentur ac orent, ut illas res a Deo citius impetremus, quas nemo nisi Deus largiri potest; hæc sane interpellatio tolerabilis est, et diuturno catholicæ ecclesiæ usu approbata et confirmata.

Neque enim periculum erit, ne Dei gloriam creaturis tribuamus, si modo populus doceatur, istud duntaxat a sanctis petendum esse, ut sua apud Deum intercessione nos adjuvent. Quod caritatis officium cum in hac vita degentes, et cum carne et sanguine decertantes, alacriter præstiterunt, nihil ambigimus, quin nunc, cum Christo suo propius fruuntur, idem officium nobis præstent.

Porro quoniam multi certis divis certorum morborum remedia, et aliarum rerum curam assignaverunt, et unum sanctum pro vitanda peste coluerunt, alium propter pecorum incolumitatem et salutem, alium ut res perditas citius invenirent, atque ita a certis divis res certas petierunt, quasi Deus hunc sanctum huic morbo curando, alium vero alii malo medendo, peculiariter præfecisset, et singulorum morborum curationem in singulos divos distribuisset: ut hic error a simplicioribus omnino tollatur, censemus populum docendum esse, ut in rebus tum prosperis tum adversis Deo, tanquam omnis boni et salutis auctori, suas preces offerat; sanctis vero non aliter utatur, quam ut intercessoribus pro nobis ad Deum, in quo nostra omnis spes ac fiducia ubique et semper collocanda est.

Quamquam non negamus quin, ad fidem et spem in Deum excitandam, possimus Deum velut admonere eorum miraculorum quæ ad sanctorum preces jam olim ostendit, quibus admoniti majori fide Dei beneficia petamus; veluti cum quis febre correptus

---

[2 August. De Civitate Dei. Lib. VIII. cap. xxvii. Tom. V. p. 516. Ed. Paris. 1635.]

[3 Id. Contra Faust. Manich. Lib. xx. cap. xxi. Tom. VI. p. 156, where *cor—paratum esse.*]

[4 ἀλλὰ τὴν μαρτυρίαν τῶν πεπραγμένων ἀντ' ἐγκωμίων λογίζεσθαι, ὡς καὶ τοῖς ἁγίοις ἐξαρκοῦσαν πρὸς ἔπαινον, καὶ τοῖς ὡρμημένοις πρὸς ἀρετὴν αὐτάρκη οὖσαν εἰς ὠφέλειαν. Basil. Hom. xix. In Gord. Martyr. Tom. I. p. 444. Ed. Paris. 1638.]

[5 τοῦτο γάρ ἐστι μαρτύρων ἐγκώμιον, ἡ πρὸς ἀρετὴν παράκλησις τῶν συνειλεγμένων. Id. Hom. xx. In quadraginta Martyr. Tom. I. p. 453.]

Dominum orat, ut quemadmodum ad D. Petri preces ejus socrum febricitantem sanitati restituit, ita velit nunc quoque febris ardores ab ægroto corpore depellere; sive cum oramus, ut Deus, qui Paulum in carcere cum collega Sila vinctum miraculo liberavit, idem nos e morborum aut peccatorum vinculis eripere dignetur.

### 3. *De Imaginibus*[1].

Quoniam imagines Christi et divorum illiteratis esse possunt vice librorum, dum velut scripti libri eos admoneant historiarum et rerum gestarum, censemus eas utiliter in templis Christianorum, aut alibi, statui ac poni posse. Quæ quidem imagines, præterquam quod illiteratis plurimum conducunt ad memoriam et intellectum historiæ, etiam eruditis utilitatem adferunt: nam doctus interdum vehementius afficitur, dum conspicit Christi imaginem in cruce pendentem, quam dum illum legit crucifixum et passum.

Ceterum cum in imaginum usu graviter a populo peccatum sit, cum alii in templis posuerunt illarum rerum imagines, quarum nullum vel in sacris libris vel apud probatos auctores exstet testimonium; alii, neglectis Christi pauperibus, in supervacaneo statuarum ornatu ingentes sumptus fecerint, et hanc esse vel præcipuam pietatis partem falso sunt arbitrati; nonnulli (quod vehementer dolendum est) imagines quasdam collocata in ipsis fiducia coluerunt, eas virtutis ac numinis aliquid præ ceteris habere persuasi; alii imaginibus vota fecerunt, et illarum videndarum causa longas profectiones susceperunt, credentes Deum, in ipsius imaginis gratiam, in uno potius loco quam in alio exauditurum esse: has et alias harum similes opiniones ac judicia præpostera, cum dissimulari non possit, quin plebs indocta de imaginibus habuerit; ut imagines ipsæ in ecclesia retineantur, et abusus omnes ac superstitiones penitus tollantur, pastorum et concionatorum officium esse judicamus, ut populum de his rebus melius instituant ac informent, utque verum imaginum usum esse doceant, intellectum et memoriam illarum rerum quas representant animis hominum suggerere atque subjicere, et intuentis animum nonnunquam exstimulare. In hunc finem imagines in templis positas fuisse nihil dubitamus; nempe ut imaginum aspectus nobis in memoriam revocaret illorum sanctorum virtutes et vitæ exempla, quorum imagines intuemur; ut quoniam oculis subjecta magis movent quam audita, nos sanctorum virtutibus et exemplis, quæ in ipsorum imaginibus repræsentantur, magis inflammaremur ad Deum in sanctis laudandum, ad nostra peccata deflenda, et Deum orandum ut sanctorum virtutes et vitam per illius gratiam imitari possimus.

Quod si quis, conspecto crucifixi signo, caput aperit aut inclinat, lignum illud non honorat, sed ad imaginis occasionem et aspectum veneratur Christum quem ea representat. Is honor, qui non statuis, sed Christo per statuæ aspectum impenditur, et Deo placet, et ab idololatria procul abest.

Ceterum vel imagines adorare, vel divinam aliquam vim aut numen illis tribuere, vel putare, quod Deus aut statuæ alicujus gratia aut loci, quia illic statua collocatur, invocantes citius sit exauditurus, vel ipsas statuas lascive ac juxta seculi vanitates pingere aut formare, vel denique præteritis et neglectis Christi pauperibus, quoties illis ex præcepto Dei subveniendum est, illas ornare, hæc omnia et magnopere improbamus, et Christianis fugienda esse docemus.

---

## XV.

### *De Ordine et Ministerio Sacerdotum et Episcoporum.*

State Paper Office. Ecclesiastical Papers. Abp. Cranmer's Paper on the Doctrine and Discipline of the Church, 2 B. No. 19. Original.

SACERDOTUM et episcoporum ordinem ac ministerium non humana auctoritate sed divinitus institutum, scriptura aperte docet: quippe quæ tradit Dominum ac Servatorem nostrum, Jesum Christum, in ecclesia instituisse certos quosdam verbi sui ministros, tanquam legatos suos et dispensatores mysteriorum Dei, (sic enim eos Paulus vocat,) qui non modo sana doctrina Christi gregem pascant, verum etiam vitæ ac morum sanctitate piisque exhortationibus sedulo incumbant, ut omnes a peccandi consuetudine, tum ad perfectam Dei cognitionem, amorem, ac timorem, tum ad sinceram proximi dilectionem adducant, qui in altaris sacramento Christi corpus et sanguinem consecrent, qui Christi sacramenta

[[1] Vid. p. 482, *n.* 1, supra.]

aliis ministrent, qui ligent et excommunicent, qui solvant ac nexu liberent, ubi et quemadmodum res postulabit; qui cetera munia omnia, quæ ad ejusmodi ministrorum officium pertinent, (quemadmodum in variis hujus articuli locis ostenditur,) exequi debeant. Et horum quidem ministrorum potestas, functio, sive administratio admodum necessaria est ecclesiæ, quamdiu hic in terris contra carnem, mundum, et Satanam militamus, nec ulla unquam occasione aboleri debet; idque propter tres præcipuas (quæ sequuntur) et primarias causas.

Primum, quia Dei præceptum est, ut hæc potestas seu functio in ecclesia perpetuo habeatur et exerceatur, quemadmodum ex variis scripturæ locis apertissime liquet.

Deinde, quia nullam aliam certam et constitutam rationem sive modum Deus instituit, quo nos sibi in Christo reconciliet, et Spiritus sancti dona nobis impertiat, vitæque æternæ hæredes nos faciat, quam verbum duntaxat suum et sacramenta.

Postremo, quia rerum maxime eximiarum certissimas promissiones functio hæc et potestas (de qua agimus) sibi annexas habet. Nam per hanc verbi et sacramentorum administrationem Spiritus sanctus confertur, tot amplissima ejusdem Spiritus dona credentibus impertiuntur, demum et justificatio nostra et vita æterna nobis datur.

Proinde potestatem seu functionem hanc Dei verbum et sacramenta ministrandi, ceterasque res agendi quas ante recensuimus, Christus ipse apostolis suis dedit, et in illis ac per illos eandem tradidit, haud promiscue quidem omnibus, sed quibusdam duntaxat hominibus, nempe episcopis et presbyteris, qui ad istud muneris initiantur et admittuntur.

Qua quidem in re episcoporum valde interest, summa vigilantia et circumspectione curare, ut illos solos, quantum in ipsis erit, ordinent et admittant, quos et ad dictum munus rite exequendum, et ad verbum Dei sinceriter ac pure docendum, admodum aptos et idoneos esse judicabunt, eos vero, quos parum idoneos comperient, a dicto munere arceant atque repellant.

Quod si contingat (ut interdum fit) ad hanc functionem aliquos admitti, qui sese postea indignos reddunt ut eam exerceant, atque id constiterit; ne horum quidem tanta ratio habenda est, præsertim si aliis legitimis rationibus corrigi noluerunt, quin eos propter justas et urgentes causas, justo ordine, a dicta functione et officio (quo indigne abutuntur) amovere penitus et dejicere queant.

Atque hanc sane circumspectionem et vigilantiam episcopi omnes, cum alias semper, tum vero potissimum adhibere debent in illis admittendis, quos vel ipsi suo jure delegerint, vel qui a patronis aut fundatoribus (ut vocant) ecclesiarum, juxta leges et consuetudines singularum regionum, nominantur, et episcopis offeruntur, seu (ut vocant) præsentantur, ut ecclesiæ curam et regimen suscipiant.

Itaque episcopi officium est, juxta nominis sui interpretationem, qua Latine superintendens dicitur, prospicere gregi suo, pro cujus etiam commodo et salute niti semper et curare debet, non modo ut Christi religio et doctrina juxta verum et germanum scripturæ sensum gregi suo sinceriter ac pure prædicetur; verum etiam ut omnia erronea dogmata exterminentur, et talium zizaniorum doctores emendentur vel abjiciantur.

Quæ profecto res ad ecclesiæ pacem et evangelicæ veritatis sinceritatem conservandam usque adeo necessaria est, ut episcopi et presbyteri summo studio, labore, et diligentia niti debeant, ne qua uspiam doctrina erronea, ne superstitio, ne idololatria, ne denique quippiam quod vel Christi gloriam imminuere, vel christianæ pietati incommodare poterit, aut per ipsos aut per alios (quantum in ipsis fuerit) in ecclesiam introducatur.

Porro autem, quamvis ligandi excommunicandique potestas a Christo presbyteris et episcopis (ut supra diximus) data est, nemo tamen putet illis ex evangelio potestatem esse concessam, ut eos quos excommunicent, violentia aliqua corporali, vel ab ecclesia ejiciant, vel a sacramentorum communione arceant et repellant; neque etiam ad hanc excommunicationis pœnam infligendam ullo divino præcepto presbyteros et episcopos ita teneri, quin eandem (ubi ratio aut æquitas postularit) moderari, aut penitus ab eadem supersedere poterint.

Jam vero cum animarum, pro quibus Christus mortuus est, curam ac solicitudinem Omnipotens Deus presbyteris et episcopis, manifestis scripturæ verbis, commisit atque credidit, ut et illi, quibuscunque poterint honestis modis, et plebis animas ad virtutem excitare ac inflammare, et Christi religionem ac Dei gloriam illustrare teneantur; facile liquet ipsorum officium esse, regulas quasdam sive canones, qui ad dictos obtinendos fines necessarii aut utiles esse videantur, quoties opus fuerit, non solum excogitare, et ad earundem observationem populum adhortari, verum etiam benignitate et consensu principis sic ordinare ac statuere, ut vim habeant obligandi: cujusmodi sunt, canones de temporibus conveniendi ad orandum, verbum Dei audiendum, et reliqua sacra facienda; præterea de ritibus ac ceremoniis, quibus sacramenta administrentur, atque orationes publice celebrentur; denique de ceteris ritibus ac ceremoniis, quæ ad Dei gloriam illustrandam, virtutis incrementum, et religionis christianæ propagationem ac decus, utcunque prosint.

Postquam itaque summatim et velut in typo explicuimus, et quæ sit potestas ac functio quam Deus in scriptura episcopis et presbyteris dedit, et quibus in rebus posita sit; ne homines in scripturis et veterum scriptorum monumentis leviter versati potestates illas et jurisdictiones, quas patriarchæ, primates, archiepiscopi, et metropolitani, vel nunc exercent, vel olim super alios unquam episcopos juste et legitime exercuerunt, a Deo in scriptura ipsis datas fuisse falso arbitrentur; nos qui veritatem et studiose sane quærimus, et inventam libenter aliis communicamus, haud alienum ab officio nostro esse ducimus, istiusmodi homines docere et admonere, ut sciant ejusmodi omnes justas potestates, quas unus aliquis episcopus super alium episcopum vel olim exercuit, vel hodie exercet, non divina in scripturis ordinatione, sed hominum consensu, ordinationibus, ac legibus, illis qui ejusmodi potestatibus funguntur collatas fuisse.

Quo utique consequitur, ut quamcunque potestatem ullus episcopus super alium episcopum exercuerit, quam hominum legitimo consensu non acceperit, ea non legitima sane potestas, sed injuria et tyrannis merito nuncupetur.

Quamobrem, cum Romani pontifices sibi ante hæc tempora eam potestatem vindicaverunt, qua seipsos tum omnium episcoporum tum totius catholicæ ecclesiæ capita et rectores constituerunt, manifestum sane est eam potestatem penitus vanam ac fictam esse, quæque ipsis Romanis pontificibus nec a Deo in sacris libris, nec a sanctis patribus in antiquis generalibus conciliis, nec demum ecclesiæ catholicæ consensu, unquam data fuerit. Id quod nos argumentis paucis quidem illis, sed tamen irrefutabilibus, omnino demonstrabimus.

Et primum quidem, constat Christum nec divo Petro, nec apostolorum cuiquam, nec eorum successoribus, ejusmodi universalem potestatem super alios omnes unquam dedisse; quinimo eos omnes ab ipso Christo in pari potestatis, honoris, et auctoritatis consortio constitutos fuisse apertissime declarant, cum loca omnia in novo Testamento quæcumque potestatem ullam a Christo apostolis datam commemorant, tum Paulus ipse ad Galatas scribens, ubi parem sibi cum Jacobo, Petro, et Joanne potestatem vindicat, et sese illis tribus, qui inter alios omnes maxime insignes fuere, æquare haud formidat.

Secundo loco, ut ad concilia generalia veniamus, et ea præsertim, quæ sanctimoniæ et antiquitatis nomine omnium celeberrima semper habita fuere, liquido patet ea talem Romanis pontificibus auctoritatem nunquam dedisse, utpote in quibus nonnulla decreta exstant, quæ diversum plane testantur ac docent.

Atque ut a priore Niceno concilio exordiamur, in hoc utique concilio decretum quoddam vel hodie exstat, quo cautum est, ut Alexandriæ et Antiochiæ patriarchæ talem super regiones illis urbibus adjacentes potestatem haberent, qualem in regionibus quæ circa Romam sunt Romanus episcopus eo tempore obtinebat[1]. Porro in concilio Milevitano, cui ipse divus Augustinus interfuit, et decretis concilii subscripsit, sancitum fuit ut si quis regionis Africanæ clericus ad episcopos transmarinos extra Africam appellasset, is illico in omnibus Africæ regionibus pro excommunicato haberetur[2].

Ad hæc, in primo generali concilio, [quod] in urbe Constantinopolitano habitum est, similiter decretum fuit, tum ut omnes lites et controversiæ inter clericos susceptæ in illis ipsis provinciis, in quibus et exortæ et agi cœptæ sunt, per earundem vel saltem vicinarum regionum episcopos finirentur, tum ne quis episcopus extra propriam diocesim aut provinciam potestatem ullam exerceret[3]. Atque in hac sane sententia sanctissimus præsul

[[1] Labb. et Cossart. Conc. Nicæn. I. A.D. 325. Can. vi. Tom. II. col. 31. Ed. Paris. 1671.]

[[2] Id. Conc. Milevit. II. A.D. 416. Can. xxii. Tom. II. col. 1542, 3.]

[[3] Id. Conc. Constant. I. A.D. 381. Cann. ii. vi. Tom. II. col. 948, et sq.]

ac martyr divus Cyprianus fuit, et ceteri Africanæ regionis sanctissimi patres, idque priusquam ulla generalia adhuc haberentur concilia.

Porro autem, ut omnes qui veritate delectantur satis compertum et exploratum habeant, Romanum episcopum neque divinæ legis auctoritate, neque ulla alicujus antiqui catholici concilii constitutione, ejusmodi universalem potestatem habere, animadvertendum est, Romanum pontificem ad sextum Carthaginense concilium legatos suos misisse, quo et universalem sibi primatum assereret ac vindicaret, et illius titulo defenderet ac comprobaret, se haud injuste fecisse, quod appellationes, quas ad exteros episcopos fieri totum Africanum concilium jam ante decreto suo prohibuisset, ipse Romæ admisisset. In qua re tractanda et discutienda Romanus episcopus, sui tituli asserendi gratia, nihil aliud quam canonem quendam allegavit, in priore (ut ille videri voluit) Niceno concilio institutum ac editum: contra vero Africani episcopi talem in eo concilio canonem esse non agnoscebant[4].

Quibus ita contendentibus, tandem ad patriarchales in oriente sedes missi sunt nuncii, qui integros illius concilii canones magno studio exquirerent: quid multis? post longam et diligentem inquisitionem, cum jam canones integri ab oriente allati essent, nullus profecto canon inter illos inveniri potuit, qualem pro sui primatus titulo Romanus pontifex allegaverat.

Ex cujus disceptationis, quam tituli sui gratia Romanus episcopus cum Carthaginensis concilii patribus habuit, progressu et exitu, duo quædam tanquam compertissima et maxime certa consequuntur:

Alterum, quod Romanus pontifex nullum talem, qualem falso jactitat, divino jure primatum habeat, nec ullis sacræ scripturæ verbis eum sibi poterit vindicare. Quod si posset, haud dubie eo tempore id fecisset, et scripturæ auctoritatem pro se adduxisset, quum legatos suos ad concilium Carthaginense misit. Ad hæc, sanctissimi patres qui illi concilio frequentes et magno numero interfuerunt, inter quos erat etiam doctissimus præsul Augustinus, tantam sacrarum literarum peritiam habebant, ut si quippiam tale pro Romani pontificis primatu in scripturis contineretur, illud profecto eos latere haud potuisset: qui iidem tanta morum sanctitate pollebant, ut si istud in scripturis esse cognovissent, neque diversum et plane huic universali potestati contrarium decretum jam ante statuissent, neque illo tempore (quo tantopere hac de re contendebatur) tam serio eam recusassent.

Alterum, quod ex prædicta pontificis cum concilio contentione æque clarum et manifestum evadit, est, nempe nullum antiquum generale concilium Romanis episcopis ejusmodi potestatem aliquando dedisse. Nam si concilii cujuspiam auctoritate talem sibi datam potestatem Romani pontifices habuissent, non dubium est, quin illius Africani concilii tempore concilium istud pro se adducere et allegare voluissent. Quod illi non fecerunt, nec quicquam a quoquam generali concilio pro primatus sui defensione adduxerunt, præterquam e priore Niceno concilio unum duntaxat fictum canonem, qui (ut paulo ante diximus) diligentissime et summo studio multo tempore quæsitus, numquam inter authenticos canones a quoquam potuit inveniri. Et caput illud authenticum, quod ex omnibus Niceni concilii canonibus ad Romanos episcopos maxime spectat, cum ficto hoc universali primatu directe et a diametro pugnat, dans aliis etiam (ut supra diximus) patriarchis in suis regionibus parem potestatem atque Romanus episcopus in regionibus Romæ vicinis eo tempore usus est.

Tertio in loco probandum suscipimus, Romanos episcopos hunc universalem (quem hodie jactitant) primatum communi totius ecclesiæ catholicæ consensu nunquam fuisse adeptos. Id quod clarum sane et perspicuum vel ex eo evadat, quod ante aliquot secula complures patriarchæ et archiepiscopi, ut patriarcha Constantinopolitanus et alii in oriente, archiepiscopus vero Ravennas et Mediolanus in occidente, obedientiam et subjectionem Romanis episcopis, quam illi universalis primatus prætextu super eos vindicabant, sese debere recusaverint.

Jam Agatho ipse, qui diu post illa quatuor prima generalia concilia Romanæ sedis episcopatum tenuit, cum ad imperatorem, qui concilium generale in urbe Constantinopolitana futurum indixerat, literas daret, in suis illis ad Cæsarem literis aperte docet ac confitetur, primatum suum ad solos occidentalis et septentrionalis ecclesiæ episcopos

[[4] Vid. Labb. et Cossart. Conc. Carthag. VI. A. D. 419. Tom. II. col. 1589, et sqq.]

pertinere. Cujus confessione manifestum est, talem universalem primatum, qualem hodie sibi vindicant, neque ullis sacræ scripturæ verbis, neque generalium conciliorum decretis, neque catholicæ demum ecclesiæ consensu, Romanos episcopos illis temporibus habuisse.

Verum enimvero, si ad posteriora hæc concilia, nempe Constantiense, Basiliense, et Florentinum Romani pontifices confugere velint, ut dejectum jam et tot argumentis explosum hunc universalem primatum per illa saltem concilia rursus erigant, nihil profecto inde lucrifacient: nam cui non est exploratum et cognitum, utrumque tam Constantiense, quam Basiliense concilium, schismatum temporibus habitum fuisse?

Quo tempore principum christianorum quidam uni schismatis parti, quidam alteri favebant. Quo factum est, ut multi mortales, qui illis conciliis interfuerunt, principum suorum votis et studiis obsequentes, etiam ipsi in contrarias factiones dissecti atque divisi fuerint.

Quid quod eorum, qui in illis conciliis pro viris doctis ac eruditis habiti sunt, maxima pars ex monachis et istis nuper institutis (ut vocant) religionibus constaret, eoque esset Romani pontificis voluntati obsequentissima? Qui porro (quod ad doctrinam attinet) in solis quæstionibus et recenti scholasticorum doctrina enutriti et educati, in literis sacris aut veterum scriptorum monumentis minime fuerunt exercitati. Atque horum præterea conciliorum ut exitus intueamur, utrumque diruptum potius quam dimissum fuit. Neutrum certe perfecto fine et consummatione potitum est.

Quo fit, ut ex eo semper tempore istorum conciliorum canones pragmatici, nusquam gentium dictorum conciliorum auctoritate roboris aliquid habentes, afferantur et citentur.

Atque hactenus de Constantiensi et Basiliensi concilio diximus, quæ quantum pro Romani pontificis primatu faciant, nemo non (qui mentem habet) facile videt atque intelligit. Nunc ad Florentinum concilium veniamus. In hoc concilio, præterquam quod ipsum (quemadmodum duo superiora concilia) schismatum tempore celebratum fuit, et plerique omnes docti viri, qui concilio interfuerunt, ejusdem erant farinæ cum iis de quibus ante diximus; etiam ille orientalium et Græcorum qui tunc aderant hac in re consensus regionibus, a quibus missi fuerant, adeo iniquus visus est, ut neque tunc illam partem definitionis concilii de universali pontificis Romani primatu approbare voluerint, neque unquam ex eo tempore, ut ei assentirent, potuerint induci. Probabile autem est, eos legatorum suorum consensum haud aspernaturos fuisse, præsertim cum ipsorum imperator illi concilio interesset, nisi certo credidissent illam concilii definitionem de Romani pontificis primatu et sacris Dei scripturis, et generalibus conciliis, et antiquis ac sanctis ipsorum patribus manifeste repugnare.

Ex his itaque omnibus, quæ hactenus dicta sunt, luce clarius apparet, Romanos episcopos hunc fictum universalem primatum non modo contra omnem scripturæ auctoritatem, et absque ullo catholicæ ecclesiæ consensu, verum etiam contra ejusmodi generalium conciliorum determinationes et decreta, quæ jam seculis bene multis usque in hodiernum diem Romani omnes episcopi in sua (ut vocant) creatione se diligenter ac bona fide observaturos esse verbis solemnibus et expressis profitentur, sibi petere et vindicare. Nam ut ex ipsorum actis legibusque liquet, Romanorum pontificum unusquisque, eo tempore quo ceremoniis pontificalibus initiatur, sese octo primorum generalium conciliorum canones omnes, inter quos sunt illi de quibus antea diximus canones, (huic ficto universali primatui plane repugnantes,) sancte et inviolabiliter observaturum esse, publice et coram omnibus profitetur et promittit.

Postremo, postquam nunc et rationibus solidis ostensum, et argumentis irrefutabilibus comprobatum est, nullam ejusmodi super episcopos et clerum universalem potestatem ad Romanos pontifices juste et legitime pertinere, sapientes sane ac cordati viri omnes facile videant atque perspiciant, multo minus eos posse sibi vindicare christiani orbis monarchiam, et eam in reges ac principes omnes potestatem, qua regnis suis et imperiis ipsos privare, eaque aliis pro suo arbitrio donare poterint; cum scriptura plane diversum docet atque præcipit, nempe ut principibus ac potestatibus mundi Christiani omnes, tam presbyteri et episcopi quam reliqua populi multitudo, subditi sint atque obediant.

Verissimum enim profecto est, Deum ita instituisse et ordinasse, ut regum ac principum christianorum auctoritas in populi gubernatione summa ac suprema esset, aliisque omnibus potestatibus et officiis emineret atque excelleret.

Et regibus quidem, tanquam supremis reipublicæ capitibus, totius sine ulla exceptione populi, qui ipsorum regnis ac dominatu vivit, curam ac gubernationem Deus commisit.

Quocirca christianorum principum interest, non solum illis rebus incumbere, quæ ad civilem reipublicæ gubernationem spectant, verum etiam christianam doctrinam tueri ac defendere, et abusus, hæreses, atque idololatriam abolere; curare præterea et modis omnibus prospicere, ut presbyteri et episcopi officium et functionem sibi commissam pure, sinceriter, et diligenter obeant, nec ea ullo pacto abutantur. Id quod si facere obstinate recusaverint, adeo ut ipsorum culpa et obstinatia Christi gregem illis creditum in exitium ruere, et quotidie perire, manifeste constiterit, tunc principum est, huc curam suam adhibere, ut, ejusmodi nequam et inutilibus servis ab officio justo ordine amotis, alii meliores in illorum loca substituantur.

---

XVI. *Breve Regis et Mandatum Archiepiscopi de Nominibus Beneficiatorum et Beneficiorum.*

THOMAS, &c. dilecto nobis in Christo archidiacono nostro Cantuarien' aut ejus officiali, salutem, gratiam, et benedictionem. Breve supra dicti metuendissimi domini nostri regis, una cum articulis eidem annexis nobis directum, nuper cum ea qua decuit reverentia accepimus, tenorem subsequentem in se continens:

Wilkins' Concilia, Vol. III. p. 857. ex Reg. Cran. f. 53. a.

Henricus Octavus, Dei gratia Angliæ et Franciæ rex, fidei defensor, dominus Hiberniæ, ac in terra supremum caput Anglicanæ ecclesiæ, reverendissimo in Christo patri Thomæ archiepiscopo Cantuarien' salutem. Volentes certis de causis certiorari de et super quibusdam articulis præsentibus annexis, vobis mandamus, quod de veritate eorundem nos in curia nostra primorum fructuum et decimarum in octavis sancti Michaelis proxime futuri, sub sigillo vestro reddatis certiores, remittentes nobis in curiam prædictam articulos prædictos una cum hoc brevi. Teste Johanne Baker, milite, apud Westmonasterium vigesimo quarto die Junii, anno regni nostri trigesimo tertio.

First, to certify how many benefices or other spiritual dignities and promotions have been void within your diocese or jurisdiction, the names of them and every of them, how long they have been void, of whose presentation, nomination, or donation, they and every of them be, and the names of them and every of them that have perceived and taken the mean profits of the said promotions, since the last becoming void of the said dignity or benefice.

*Item*, To certify as well the name and names of all such parson and parsons, as have been collated, institute, or induct in any promotion spiritual within your diocese or jurisdiction, since the feast of the nativity of St John Baptist, which was in the reign of our sovereign lord the king that now is the xxxii. unto the same feast next following, as the name and names of all and every such promotion, whereunto any person hath been collated, institute, or induct from the said feast of St John Baptist, in the xxxii. year aforesaid, unto the same feast next following; as also the name of the county where the same promotion doth lie.

Nos ejusdem domini nostri regis mandatis, pro officii nostri erga suam majestatem debito, parere et omni subjectionis honore obedire, uti par est, volentes, cupientesque de omnibus et singulis articulis supradictis, et in eis contentis et comprehensis quibuscunque, mature fieri certiores, vobis pro parte suæ regiæ majestatis tenore præsentium districte præcipiendo mandamus, quatenus cum ea, qua poteritis, celeritate et diligentia, de et super articulis præmissis, et in eis declaratis quibuscunque, maturam et sedulam faciatis apud singulas ecclesias infra diocesin nostram Cantuarien' utilibet constitutas, modo ac via, quibus melius et efficacius poteritis, inquisitionem pariter et indagationem; reddentes nos de omni eo, quod in hac parte per vos fuerit compertum et inquisitum, certiores per literas vestras patentes, auctentice sigillatas, tenorem præsentium, et totum et integrum processum vestrum, inquisitionem, et indagationem vestram in se continentes; et hoc sub pœna contemptus nostri, et prout eidem domino nostro regi in hac parte sub periculo vestro respondere volueritis, facere et sedulo exequi curetis, et fieri causetis indilate. In cujus rei, &c. Datum in manerio nostro de Lambehith undecimo die Augusti, anno MDXLI. et nostræ consecrationis nono.

XVII. *The King's Letter [and the Mandate of the Archbishop of Canterbury] for taking away Shrines and Images.*

Wilkins' Concilia, Vol. III. p. 857. ex Reg. Cran. f. 18. a.

THOMAS, permissione divina Cantuarien' archiepiscopus, totius Angliæ primas et metropolitanus, per illustrissimum in Christo principem et dominum nostrum, dominum Henricum octavum, Dei gratia Angliæ et Franciæ regem, fidei defensorem, et dominum Hiberniæ, ac in terra supremum ecclesiæ Anglicanæ sub Christo caput, ad infrascripta sufficienter auctorizatus, dilecto nobis in Christo magistro Richardo Liell, legum doctori, decano decanatuum de Shoreham, Croydon, Bocking, Risburghe, Terringe, et Pageham, ecclesiæ Christi Cantuarien' jurisdictionis immediatæ, seu ejus in hac parte deputato, salutem, gratiam, et benedictionem. Literas missivas dicti metuendissimi domini nostri regis signatas, et nominibus dominorum consiliariorum suorum in calce earundem subscriptas, signeto suo obsignatas, nobis inscriptas et datas, nuper debitis cum honore et reverentia accepimus, tenorem sequentem complectentes:

Most reverend father in God, right trusty and right entirely well-beloved, we greet you well. Letting you wit, that whereas heretofore, upon the zeal and remembrance which we had to our bounden duty toward Almighty God, perceiving sundry superstitions and abuses to be used and embraced by our people, whereby they grievously offended him and his word, we did not only cause the images[1] and bones of such as they resorted and offered unto, with the ornaments of the same, and all such writings and monuments of feigned miracles wherewith they were illuded, to be taken away in all places of our realm; but also by our injunctions commanded, that no offering or setting of lights or candles should be suffered in any church, but only to the blessed sacrament of the altar[2]: it is lately come to our knowledge that, this our good intent and purpose notwithstanding, the shrines, covering of shrines, and monuments of those things do yet remain in sundry places of our realm, much to the slander of our doings and to the great displeasure of Almighty God, the same being means to allure our subjects to their former hypocrisy and superstition, and also that our injunctions be not kept as appertaineth: for the due and speedy reformation whereof, we have thought meet by these our letters expressly to will and command you, that incontinently, upon the receipt hereof, you shall not only cause due search to be made in your cathedral churches for those things, and if any shrine, covering of shrine, table, monument of miracles, or other pilgrimage do there continue, to cause it to be taken away, so as there remain no memory of it; but also that you shall take order with all the curates, and other, having charge within your diocese, to do the semblable, and to see that our injunctions be duly kept, as appertaineth, without failing, as we trust, and as you will answer for the contrary. Yeven under our signet at our town of Hull, the 4th day of October, in the thirty-fourth[3] year of our reign.

In capite vero eorundem sic scriptum est: By the king. In calce hæc nomina habentur: Wm. Southamton, Robert Sussex, J. Russell, Cuthbert Dunelmen.[4], Anthony Browne, Anthony Winkfyld, John Gage. Inscriptio hæc est: To the most reverend father in God, our right trusty and right entirely well-beloved counsellor the archbishop of Cantur., and our trusty and well-beloved his vicar-general and the dean of the cathedral church of the same.

Nos vero, affectantes ex animo ejusdem domini nostri regis literis et mandatis obtemperare, volentesque, pro nostro erga suam regiam celsitudinem officio, nobis demandatis negotiis omnem nostram curam et solertem adhibere diligentiam, vobis pro parte suæ regiæ majestatis tenore præsentium mandamus, et præcipiendo injungimus, quatenus, receptis præsentibus, cum omni qua poteritis celeritate et matura diligentia omnes et singulos ecclesiarum collegiatarum magistros, ecclesiarumque parochialium rectores, vicarios, et presbyteros quoscunque infra decanatus prædictos degentes, coram vobis diebus et locis pro vestro sano arbitratu, quam citissime tamen fieri possit, assignandis, convocari possitis,

[1 Vid. "Another letter from Winchester (i. e. Gardiner) to the lord protector" (i. e. Somerset.) Foxe's Acts and Monuments, pp. 1345, 6. Ed. Lond. 1583; in which he relates the subject of a conversation between Henry VIII. and Cranmer respecting images and their use.]

[2 Vid. Injunctions to the Clergy made by Crumwell, A.D. 1538. Burnet's Hist. of Reformat. Vol. I. Part ii. Append. Book III. No. 11, pp. 279—284. Ed. Oxon. 1829.]

[3 Rectius, "third." Wilkins.]

[4 i. e. Tonstall.]

eisque coram vobis constitutis contenta et comprehensa in prædictis literis pro parte suæ regiæ majestatis denuncietis, declaretis, exponatis, et dilucidetis ac demonstretis; eaque et contenta quæcunque in dictis literis, necnon et injunctiones alias, a sua majestate clero et plebi suo editas et promulgatas, ab omnibus et singulis subditis suis infra nostros decanatus prædictos degentibus firmiter et exacte atque ad unguem observari, et debitæ executioni demandari curetis, et efficaciter absque ullo fuco fieri causetis, prout eidem domino nostro regi sub vestro periculo respondere volueritis. Et quid in præmissis feceritis, nos citra ultimum diem mensis Novembris proxime futuri per literas vestras, auctentice sigillatas, reddatis certiores. In cujus rei testimonium sigillum nostrum præsentibus est appensum. Datum in manerio nostro de Lambehith decimo quinto die mensis Octobris, anno Domini MDXLI. et nostræ consecrationis anno nono.

---

## XVIII. *Constitutio Thomæ Cranmeri, Archiepiscopi, et aliorum Fratrum suorum de apparatu escarum moderando.*

Wilkins' Concilia, Vol. III. p. 862. ex MSS. C. C. C. C. Misc. Papers, p. 630. Strype's Life of Abp. Parker, Vol. III. pp. 117, 18. Ed. Oxon. 1821.

IN the year of our Lord MDXLI. it was agreed and condescended upon, as well by the common consent of both the archbishops and most part of the bishops within this realm of England, as also of divers grave men of that time[5], both deans and archdeacons, the fare of their tables[6] to be thus moderated.

First, that th' archbishops should never exceed six divers kinds of flesh, or six of fish on the fish days; the bishop not to exceed five, the dean and archdeacon not above four, and all other under that degree not above three.

Provided also, that the archbishop might have of second dishes four, the bishop three, and all others under the degree of a bishop but two; as custard, tart, fritter, cheese, or apples, pears, or two of other kinds of fruits.

Provided also, that if any of the inferior degree did receive at their table any archbishop, bishop, dean, or archdeacon, or any of the laity of like degree, viz. duke, marquis, earl, viscount, baron, lord, knight, they might have such provision as were meet and requisite for their degrees.

Provided alway, that no rate was limited in the receiving of any ambassador.

It was also provided, that of the greater fishes or fowls there should be but one in a dish, as crane, swan, turkeycock, haddock, pike, tench; and of less sorts but two, viz. capons two, pheasants two, conies two, woodcocks two: of less sorts, as of partridges, the archbishop three, the bishop, and other degrees under him, two; of blackbirds, the archbishop six, the bishop four, the other degrees three; of larks and snytes, and of that sort, but twelve.

It was also provided, that whatsoever is spared by the cutting off the old superfluity, should yet be provided and spent in plain meats for the relieving of the poor.

*Memorandum*, that this order was kept for two or three months, till, by the disusing of certain wilful persons, it came to the old excess.

---

## XIX. *Statutum de Numero Procuratorum Curiæ Cantuar', confirmatum per dominum Thomam Cranmer, Cantuar' Archiepiscopum.*

Wilkins' Concilia, Vol. III. p. 858. ex MSS. Sancroft. Arch. Cant. apud Th. Tanner, episc. Assaph.

THOMAS, permissione Cant' Archiepiscopus, totius Angliæ primas et metropolitanus, illustrissimi et potentissimi in Christo principis et domini nostri Henrici VIII. Dei gratia Angliæ et Franciæ regis, fidei defensoris, et domini Hiberniæ, ac sub Christo in terra supremi capitis ecclesiæ Anglicanæ, ad infrascripta etiam parliamenti auctoritate legitime fulcitus, dilectis nobis in Christo filiis, vicario nostro in spiritualibus generali, officiali curiæ nostræ Cant' de Arcubus nuncupat', decanoque decanatus ecclesiæ beatæ Mariæ de Arcubus prædict', ac prærogativæ nostræ commissario generali; necnon Johanni Hering, Johanni Talcorne, Richardo Watkins, Anthonio Hussaws, Thomæ Stacey, Richardo

[5 At that time. Strype.] [6 At their tables. Id.]

Feyld, Johanni Trevison, Johanni Clerk, Simoni Leston, Henrico Bosfell, Thomæ Dockery, Roberto Johnson, Willielmo Coveyke, et Davidi Clopham, dictæ curiæ procuratoribus generalibus, ac ceteris earundem curiarum nostrarum ministris, tam præsentibus quam futuris, ac aliis quibuscunque, quos infrascripta tangunt, seu tangere poterunt quomodolibet in futurum, salutem, gratiam, et benedictionem, ac fidem indubiam præsentibus adhibere.

Cum non sit minus pium atque laudabile lapsa reficere, quam nova condere; cura et solicitudine pastorali animadvertere et providere tenemur, ne quæ olim a sanctis patribus nostræ metropoliticæ Cant' archiepiscopis prædecessoribus nostris pie et sancte, tam pro honore et celebri fama dictæ curiæ nostræ Cant', quibus antiquitus præ ceteris fulgere dignoscitur, quam pro consideratione ministrorum ejusdem statuta, ordinata, stabilita, et fundata fuerunt, nostris temporibus labantur, deficiant, aut pereant; imo ut consimilibus honore et fama dictæ curiæ nostræ audient' et prærogativæ fulciantur et decorentur: Nos igitur Thomas Cranmer, archiepiscopus, primas, et metropolitanus antedictus, præmissa attente pensantes, et oculate considerantes, ad quem non solum conservatio, continuatio, et confirmatio statutorum prædecessorum nostrorum prædictorum, verum etiam eorundem augmentatio et incrementum notorie dignoscitur pertinere; vestris supplicationibus inclinati, et grato annuentes assensu; ac tam dictæ curiæ nostræ Cant' de Arcubus London', et aliarum curiarum nostrarum hujusmodi honori, quam vestris quieti et commoditati consulere volentes; statutum felic' rec' Roberti de Winchelsey, olim Cant' archiepiscopi, sic incipiens, "Statuimus insuper, ut XVI advocati et X procuratores duntaxat," etc. una cum ordinatione, statuto, stabilitione, et confirmatione bonæ memoriæ Will. Warham Cant' archiepiscopi, prædecessorum nostrorum, desuper fact', edit' et ordinat', auctoritate etiam capitulari dictæ ecclesiæ nostræ metropoliticæ Cant' confirmat', quorum tenores, quatenus expedit, pro his insertis haberi et inscribi volumus, pro nobis et futuris successoribus nostri Cant' archiepiscopis, in quantum eadem statuta, ordinatio, stabilitio, et cetera præmissa dictos procuratores et hujusmodi eorum numerum tangunt et concernunt, etiam ex mero motu et certa scientia nostris præsentium tenore reintegramus, ratificamus, approbamus, confirmamus, corroboramus, et pro perpetuo consolidamus perenniter observand', atque perpetuis futuris temporibus inviolabiliter observari volumus et mandamus. Volumus insuper, ac ex mero motu et certa scientia nostris, ut supra, ordinamus, atque pro nobis et futuris successoribus nostris Cant' archiepiscopis perpetue statuendo, ordinando, et stabiliendo mandamus, quatenus de cetero nullus prorsus in numerum procuratorum præfatarum curiarum nostrarum, aut alicujus earundem admittatur, seu procuratoris officium in eisdem curiis aut earum aliqua exercere quovis modo permittatur, donec et quousque numerus præfat' procuratorum superius nominatorum jam existentium usque ad numerum novem decreverit et pervenerit, nec numerus ipsorum decem procuratorum ullatenus deinceps excedatur, etiamsi in contrarium, a nobis aut dictis successoribus nostris Cant' archiepiscopis, vobis in mandatis haberi, seu alias indulgeri vel dispensari contigerit; quibusvis clausulis dispensationum, commissionum, privileg' seu indult' præsentium derogatoriis, ceterisque in contrarium facientibus, non obstant', nec in futurum valituris quibuscunque, etiamsi de hujusmodi statuto, ordination', stabilition', confirmation,' et corroboration,' ac ceteris præmissis, seu de præsenti ordinatione nostra hujusmodi de verbo ad verbum specialis, specifica, expressa, et individua fiat mentio; decernentes, quod in contrarium fieri contigerit, exnunc prout extunc, et extunc prout exnunc, irritum et inane, viribus quoque et effectu juris et facti omnino carere, prout tenore præsentium sic decernimus. Volentes præterea ac vobis vicario generali, officiali, decano, et prærogativæ commissario hujusmodi præsentibus, et quibuscunque in eisdem officiis futuris firmiter injungendo mandamus, quatenus vos proximis sessionibus in dictis curiis nostris audientiæ, de Arcubus, et Prærogativæ Cant' præsentationem et intimationem præsentium vobis factas immediate sequentibus, has præsentes literas nostras publicari et divulgari, ac inter alia statuta et ordinationes ipsarum curiarum nostrarum registrari et inseri faciatis, necnon pro statutis haberi et reputari, et debite ac inviolabiliter observari, vestris respective decretis judicialibus ibidem publice decernatis, et vestrum quilibet respective decernat. Ut autem præmissa omnia et singula per nos, ut præmittitur, superius facta et gesta, perpetuæ firmitatis robur perenniter obtineant, nec super illis ulla dubietatis seu ambiguitatis valeat quæstio suboriri; nos Thomas archiepiscopus, primas, et metropolitanus antedictus, has nostras præsentes literas sigilli nostri ad facultates, quo utimur in ea parte, fecimus appensione muniri. Dat' in manerio nostro de Lambith 12 die mensis Januarii anno Domini secundum cursum et computationem ecclesiæ Anglicanæ MDXLI. felicissimi regni dicti potentissimi et invictissimi principis et domini nostri regis anno XXXIII. et nostræ consecrationis anno nono.

T. CANT.

---

XX. *Literæ Regis, et Archiepiscopi Cantuar' Mandatum Episcopo London' pro Orationibus pro Cessatione Pluviæ.*

THOMAS, &c. venerabili confratri nostro domino Edmundo[1], eadem permissione Londinensi episcopo, vestrove vicario in spiritualibus generali, et officiali principali, salutem et fraternam in Domino caritatem. Literas supradicti invictissimi domini nostri regis nuper recepimus, tenorem subsequentem continentes: Wilkins' Concilia, Vol. III. p. 868. ex Reg. Cran. f. 22. a.

Most reverend father in God, right trusty and right entirely beloved, we greet you well. And forasmuch as there hath been now a late and still continueth much rain, and other unseasonable weather, whereby is like to ensue great hurt and damage to the corn, and fruits now ripe upon the ground, unless it shall please God of his infinite goodness to stretch forth his holy hand over us; considering by sundry examples heretofore, that God at the contemplation of the earnest and devout prayers ofttimes extended his mercy and grace, and hath also assuredly promised that whensoever we call upon him for things meet for us, he will grant unto us the same; we, having the government and charge of his people committed unto us, have thought good to cause the same to be exhorted by you and other the prelates of this our realm, with an earnest repentant heart for their iniquities, to call unto God for mercy, and with devout and humble prayers and supplications every person, both by himself apart, and also by common prayer, to beseech him to send unto us seasonable and temperate weather, to have in those fruits and corn on the ground, which hitherto he hath caused so plenteously to grow: for the which purpose we require you, and nevertheless command you, to send unto all your brethren the bishops within your province, to cause such general rogations and processions to be made incontinently within their dioceses, as in like case heretofore hath been accustomed in this behalf accordingly. Yeven under our signet at our manor of the Moore, the 20th day of August, the XXXV. year of our reign. In capite vero earundem sic scriptum est: by the king. Inscriptio autem hæc est: to the most reverend father in God, our right trusty, and entirely beloved counsellor, the bishop of Canterbury. Strype's Mem. of Abp. Cranmer, Vol. I. pp. 182, 3. Ed. Oxon. 1840.[2]

Quibus quidem literis pro nostro erga suæ regiæ majestatis excellentiam officio obtemperare, uti par est, summopere cupientes, vestræ fraternitati tenore præsentium committimus, et regiæ majestatis vice et nomine, quibus in hac parte fungimur, mandamus, quatenus attentis præmissis sævientis pestis rigore et bellorum tumultibus, quibus orbis christianus inpræsentiarum, proh dolor! undique æstuat, omnibus et singulis confratribus nostris coepiscopis nostris, et ecclesiæ nostræ Christi Cantuarien' suffraganeis, cum ea qua poteritis celeritate accommoda præcipiatis, ut ipsorum singuli in suis cathedralibus et civitatum et diœcesium suarum parochialibus ecclesiis, exposito publice literarum regiarum hujuscemodi pio et sancto tenore, clericos et laicos infra suas dioceses degentes sedulo et accurate moveant et inducant, aut moveri et induci faciant sanctis monitis et salubribus præceptis, (atque sic a vobis in civitate et diocesi vestra London' fieri volumus,) qualibet quarta et sexta feriis publicis supplicationibus et suffragiis Altissimum devote adorent, eorumque precibus, uti fieri assuevit, suam immensam misericordiam implorent, quatenus in ira sua, quam nostris male meritis juste provocavimus, misericordiæ suæ recordatus, quibus offensus hujuscemodi super nos merito immisit afflictiones, propitiatus misericorditer nobis resipiscentibus submoveat: ab orationibus et suffragiis hujuscemodi non cessantes, donec aliud a nobis in hac parte habueritis in mandatis. Dat' in manerio nostro de Croydon 23 die mensis Augusti, anno Domini MDXLIII. nostræ consecrationis anno undecimo.

---

[[1] i. e. Bonner.] [[2] The English portion of this document only is given in Strype.]

XXI. *Literæ Regiæ Archiepiscopo Cantuar. pro Publicatione Regiarum Injunctionum*[1].

Wilkins'Concilia, Vol. III. pp. 869, 70. ex Reg. Cran. f. 48. b.

THOMAS, permissione divina, &c. illustrissimi in Christo principis et domini nostri Henrici Octavi, Dei gratia Angliæ, Franciæ, et Hiberniæ regis, fidei defensoris, ac in terra ecclesiæ Anglicanæ et Hiberniæ supremi capitis, auctoritate legitime fulcitus, venerabili confratri nostro domino Edmundo, eadem permissione Londinensi episcopo, salutem et fraternam in Domino caritatem. Literas supradicti invictissimi domini nostri regis, manu sua signatas, et signeto suo obsignatas, nobis inscriptas, et ad nos datas, nuper debitis cum honore et reverentia accepimus, tenorem subsequentem complectentes:

Burnet's Hist. of Reformat. Vol. I. Pt. ii. Book III. No. 28, pp. 398, 9. Ed. Oxon. 1829.[3]

[2]Most reverend father in God, right trusty and right well-beloved, we greet you well; and let you wit that, calling to our remembrance the miserable state of all Christendom, being at this present, besides all other troubles, so plagued with most cruel wars, hatreds, and dissensions[4], as no place of the same almost, being the whole reduced to a very narrow corner, remaineth in good peace, agreement, and concord, the help and remedy whereof, far exceeding the power of any man, must be called for of him who only is able to grant our petitions, and never forsaketh nor repelleth any that firmly believe and faithfully call on him; unto whom also the examples of scripture encourageth us in all these and other our troubles and necessities to fly, and to cry for aid and succour: being therefore resolved to have continually from henceforth general processions in all cities, towns, churches, and parishes of this our realm, said and sung with such reverence and devotion, as appertaineth, forasmuch as heretofore the people, partly for lack of good instruction and calling, partly for that they understood no part of such prayers or suffrages, as were used to be sung and said, have used to come very slackly to the procession, when the same have been commanded heretofore: we have set forth certain godly prayers and suffrages[5] in our native English tongue, which we send you herewith, signifying unto you, that for the special trust and confidence we have of your godly mind and earnest desire to the setting forward of the glory of God and the true worshipping of his most holy name within that province committed by us unto you, we have sent unto you these suffrages, not to be for a month or two observed, and after slenderly considered, as other our injunctions have to our no little marvel been used; but to th' intent that as well the same as other our injunctions may earnestly be set forth by preaching, good exhortations, and otherways to the people, in such sort as they, feeling the godly taste thereof, may godly and joyously with thanks receive, embrace, and frequent the same, as appertaineth. Wherefore we will and command you, as you will answer unto us for the contrary, not only to cause these prayers and suffrages aforesaid to be published frequently[6], and openly used in all towns, churches, villages, and parishes of your own diocese; but also to signify this our pleasure unto all other bishops of your province, willing and commanding them in our

---

[[1] "Occasional prayers and suffrages, to be used throughout all churches, began now to be more usual than formerly. For these common devotions were twice this year [A.D. 1544] appointed by authority, as they had been once the last; which I look upon the archbishop to be the great instrument in procuring: that he might by this means, by little and little, bring into use prayer in the English tongue, which he so much desired; and that the people, by understanding part of their prayers, might be the more desirous to have their whole service rendered intelligible; whereby God might be served with the more seriousness and true devotion." Strype's Mem. of Abp. Cranmer, Vol. I. pp. 181, 2. Ed. Oxon. 1840.]

[[2] "It" (i.e. the king's letter) "runs in such pious strain, as though none but the archbishop had been the suggester thereof." Id. p. 183.]

[[3] The English portion of this document only is given in Burnet.]

[[4] "Henry VIII. was now at war with France and Scotland, and was on the point of invading the former country in conjunction with the emperor Charles V." Jenkyns' Remains of Abp. Cranmer, Vol. IV. p. 320, *n.* r.]

[[5] "I have not met with these suffrages; which if I had, I should have been inclined to publish them here, and the rather because I believe they were of Cranmer's own composing." Strype's Mem. of Cranmer, Vol. I. p. 184. Burnet and Todd suppose these prayers and suffrages formed the Litany published June 16, 1544, by Thomas Barthelet, "cum privilegio," of which the following is the title: A Letany with Suffrages to be sayd or sung in Time of Processions. With an Exhortation to Prayer, thought meet by the King and his Clergy to be read to the People in every Church, afore Processions. Vid. Ames' Typogr. Antiq. Vol. III. p. 450. (Dibdin) Ed. Lond. 1810—1819. Burnet's Hist. of the Reformat. Vol. III. p. 315, 16. Todd's Life of Abp. Cranmer, Vol. I. p. 354. "The Litany contained in it was inserted in the Primer of 1545, and differs but little from that still in use." Jenkyns' Remains of Abp. Cranmer, Vol. IV. p. 321, *n.* s.]

[[6] Published, frequented. Burnet.]

name, and by virtue hereof, to do and execute the same accordingly; unto whose proceedings in th' execution of this our commandment we will that you have a special respect, and make report unto us, if any shall not with good dexterity accomplish the same, not failing, as our spiritual trust [7] is in you. Yeven under our signet at our manor of St James, the eleventh of June, the XXXVI. year of our reign. In capite vero eorundem sic scriptum est: By the king. Inscriptio autem hæc est: To the most reverend father in God, our right trusty and right well-beloved counsellor, the archbishop of Canterbury.

Nos vero pro nostra erga suam celsitudinem observantia, toto pectore affectantes literis et mandatis suis regiis, uti decet, obtemperare, volentesque pro debito nostri officii omnem curam et solertem nostram in commissis et demandatis a sua majestate adhibere diligentiam, vobis pro parte regiæ suæ majestatis tenore præsentium mandamus et præcipiendo injungimus, quatenus, receptis præsentibus, non solum injunctiones omnes regias ad sacrosanctam religionem firmandam et stabiliendam antehac per auctoritatem regiam promulgatas cum omni reverentia observandas edicatis et mandetis; verum etiam omni sedulitate et celeritate accommodis sancta hæc suffragia et salubres orationes, quarum unum exemplar præsentibus annexum vobis per latorem præsentium mittimus, tum quidem in omnibus et singulis ecclesiis cathedralibus, collegiatis, et parochialibus per diocesim et jurisdictionem vestras Londonienses ubilibet sitis et existentibus, tum etiam ab omnibus et singulis aliis episcopis, et confratribus nostris, nostræ Cantuarien' provinciæ suffraganeis, ubilibet locorum per dioceses et jurisdictiones suas juxta et secundum literarum regiarum suprascriptarum tenorem et continentiam, in omnibus et per omnia exponi, declarari, denunciari, cantari, dici, publicari, et observari facias et faciant, et fieri sedulo procures et procurent. In cujus rei testimonium sigillum nostrum præsentibus est impensum. Dat' [decimo] octavo die mensis Junii, Anno Domini MDXLIV. et nostræ consecrationis anno XII.

---

## XXII. *Mandate by the Archbishop of Canterbury to the Bishop of London for keeping Processions in English.*

THOMAS, permissione divina, &c. venerabili confratri nostro domino Edmundo permissione eadem London' episcopo, &c. vestrove vicario in spiritualibus generali et officiali principali, salutem, et fraternam in Domino caritatem. Literas missivas clarissimorum et prudentissimorum dominorum de privatis consiliis suæ regiæ majestatis manibus subscriptas, nobis inscriptas et per equos dispositos [advectas,] nuper recepimus, tenorem sequentem complectentes. Cranm. Register, f. 26. b.

[8]After our right hearty commendations to your good lordship, these shall be to signify unto the same, that the king's highness having so provided for the safety of his grace's realm, as the great malice of his enemies shall by the grace of God take small effect[9]; (for the repulsing of the which his highness hath in a readiness to set abroad, at the furthest on Wednesday next[10], such a puissant navy as hath not been seen Strype's Mem. of Abp. Cranmer, Vol. I. p. 185. Ed. Oxon. 1840.

---

[7 Our special trust. Id.]

[8 The date of this letter in Cranmer's Register is A. D. 1545. Strype places it under A. D. 1544, which is evidently an error. Mem. of Abp. Cranmer, Vol. I. p. 185.]

[9 "The 21. July [A.D. 1545.] the French galleys and navy came afore Portsmouth haven, and landed certain of their army in the Isle of Wight, at St Helen's point, and there burned and encamped about 2000 men; but they were soon driven away with loss of their captain and many soldiers. Within few days after, the whole fleet removed from the Wight to a place in Sussex, called Newhaven, four miles from Lewes, and there landed many captains and soldiers, who by the valiantness of the gentlemen and yeomen of Sussex were slain and drowned in the haven a great number of them and the rest hardly recovered their ships and gallies." Stow's Annals, p. 589. Ed. Lond. 1615.]

[10 "I trust in God that we shall depart hence (Portsmouth) upon Tuesday (August 11th), if the wind will serve us." State Papers, Letter CCXXV. John Dudley, Lord Lisle, to Paget, dated August 9, p. 808. "At this present it may like your majesty that the enemies and we have sight one of the other, striving who shall get the advantage of the wind." Id. Letter CCXXVII. Lisle to Henry VIII. dated August 15, p. 815. No "engagement, however, took place; for they say it is not possible for their army to return any more to the sea this year, both for scarcity of victuals and for lack of men. For the most part of these that have been out, had rather be hanged than go forth again. There is no manner of courage, nor gladness, nor appearance of comfort among them. The common people (talking as they dare) grudgeth, saying, their king hath been

assembled in the remembrance of man[1]:) considering nevertheless that all victories and good successes cometh only at the direction and appointment of God, following herein the trade of such a christian prince as he is, hath devised to have processions throughout the realm in such sort as in like cases hath heretofore laudably been accustomed: requiring your lordship therefore to take order incontinently, that from henceforth throughout your province the said processions be kept continually upon the accustomed days and none otherwise, and sung or said, as the number of the quire shall serve for the same, in the English tongue, to the intent that there may be an uniformity in every place; whereby it may please God at all times to prosper his majesty in all his affairs, and the rather to have regard at this time unto the uprightness of his grace's quarrel, and to send his highness victorious success of the same. And thus we bid your good lordship most heartily well to fare. From Petworth, the 10th day of August. Your lordship's assured loving friends, W. Essex, Ste. Wynton., Anthonye Browne, William Paget.

Quibus pro nostro officio obtemperare, uti decet, summopere cupientes, vestræ fraternitati tenore præsentium committimus, et regiæ majestatis vice et nomine, quibus fungimur, mandamus, quatenus attentis diligenter literarum hujuscemodi tenore et bellorum tam terrestrium quam maritimorum tumultubus, quibus hoc inclitum regnum Angliæ undique per mare et terram tum in Gallia et Scotia, tum in partibus Boloniæ assidue infestatur et gravatur, omnibus et singulis confratribus, coepiscopis nostris et ecclesiæ nostræ Christi Cant' suffraganeis, cum ea qua poteritis celeritate accommoda præcipiatis, ut ipsorum singuli in suis cathedralibus et civitatum ac dioc' suarum parochialibus ecclesiis, exposito publice literarum hujuscemodi pio et sancto tenore, clericos et laicos infra suas dioc' degentes sedulo et accurate moveant et inducant, aut moveri et induci sanctis monitionibus et salubribus præceptis faciant, (atque sic a vobis in civitate et dioc' London' fieri volumus) qualibet quarta et sexta feria publicis supplicationibus et suffragiis dudum Angliæ [sermone] conceptis et publicatis, concinna modulatione et una voce, cunctipotentem Deum Sabaoth, omnis victoriæ largitorem unicum, sancte et pie, non labiis sed corde puro adorent, et precibus in perpetuum ipsius auxilium implorent; quatenus eidem domino nostro regi, exercitubus et classi suæ navali, (quam non solum ad propulsandos verum etiam ad opprimendos et profligandos hostium suorum sceleratos cornatus habet instructissimam,) de immensa misericordia et justitia suis, victoriam pariter et triumphum clementer et benigne in tam probato certantibus agone largiri et concedere dignetur, ut devictis hostibus nostris, et rebus ex sententia feliciter gestis, illi concordibus animis assidue hymnos cantemus triumphales. Quibus vos tantisper volumus immorari, quoad aliud a nobis inde habueritis in mandatis: vos etiam harum scire in Domino hortamur. Quod si quid superiori anno in his orationibus decantandis et dicendis a vestris gregibus fuerit oscitanter omissum, id nunc resarcire et in melius reformare, habita hujus turbulentæ tempestatis congrua ratione, summo studio prout fieri confidimus curetis. Bene valeatis, frater carissime. Ex ædibus nostris de Bekysborne nostræ Cant' dioc' 11° Aug. A.D. 1545, et nostræ consecr' an' 13.

---

## XXIII. *A Preface made by the King's most excellent Majesty unto his Primer Book.*

Wilkins' Concilia, Vol. III. p. 873.

HENRY the VIIIth, by the grace of God King of England, France, and Ireland, defender of the faith, and in earth supreme head of the church of England and

---

at great charges, and nothing done." Id. Letter CCXXXII. Lisle to Henry VIII. dated August 21, p. 823. "In September the English fleet in their turn made a descent on the coast of Normandy." "My Lord of Canterbury, having required certain pieces of artillery to be drawn to and from sundry places upon the cliffs, with horses at the charge of the country, for the repelling of the enemies, shall be furnished of the same, if Mr Seymour, upon view of the places, shall think it expedient." Id. Report of the "State of Things," &c. p. 786.]

[[1] "The 'puissant navy' consisted of 104 sail, carrying 12,738 men. The names of the vessels and of their captains, their tonnage, and the number of their crews, with the orders issued on sailing, will be found in the State Papers, Vol. I. p. 810." Jenkyns.]

Ireland, to all and singular our subjects, as well of the clergy as also of the laity, within our dominions, whatsoever they be, greeting. It is the part of kings (whom the Lord hath constituted and set for pastors of his people) not only to procure that a quiet and peaceable life may be led of all his universal subjects, but also that the same life may be passed over godly, devoutly, and virtuously, in the true worshipping and service of God, to the honour of him, and to the sanctifying of his name, and to the everlasting salvation of their own selves. But to godly devotion there belongeth many points, of which that same is not the least, the which doth purely and with perfect understanding make invocation to God the Father, and of the Author and Giver of all goodness earnestly craveth such things as be good, and for the soul health, for that part of the life that is behind to be well ordered; and rendereth thanks for the bounteous giving of good things past, and also for the putting away of evils; and therefore doth sacrifice unto God with the calves and burnt-offering of the lips. But the pureness thereof consisteth in this point, if the heavenly Father of lights be worshipped and served according to the prescription and appointment of the word of God; if we be wary and circumspect in this behalf, that we talk with him in our prayers according to his will: after whose appointing if we direct our prayers, we have assured trust and affiance (as the writing of the apostle teacheth) that we be heard of him. Now prayer is used or made with right and perfect understanding, if we sing with our spirit, and sing with our mind or understanding; so that the deep contemplation or ravishing of the mind follow the pithiness of the words, and the guiding of reason go before: lest when the spirit doth pray, the mind take no fruit at all, and the party that understandeth not the pith or effectualness of the talk, that he frankly maketh with God, may be as an harp or pipe, having a sound, but not understanding the noise that itself hath made. And forasmuch as we have bestowed right great labour and diligence about setting a perfect stay in the other parts of our religion, we have thought good to bestow our earnest labour in this part also, being a thing as fruitful as the best, that men may know both what they pray, and also with what words, lest things special good and principal, being inwrapped in ignorance of the words, should not perfectly come to the mind and to the intelligence of men; or else things being nothing to the purpose, nor very meet to be offered unto God, should have the less effect with God, being the distributor of all gifts.

In consideration whereof we have set out and given to our subjects a determinate form of praying in their own mother tongue, to the intent that such as are ignorant of any strange or foreign speech may have what to pray in their own acquainted and familiar language with fruit and understanding; and to the end that they shall not offer unto God (being the searcher of the reins and hearts) neither things standing against true religion and godliness, nor yet words far out of their intelligence and understanding.

Nevertheless, to the intent that such as have understanding of the Latin tongue, and think that they can with a more fervent spirit make their prayers in that tongue, may have wherein to do their devotion to God, being none acceptor neither of any person ne tongue; we have provided the selfsame form of praying to be set forth in Latin also, which we had afore published in English, to the intent that we should be all things to all persons, and that all parties may at large be satisfied, and as well the wills and desire of them that perceive both tongues, as also the necessity and lack of them that do not understand the Latin.

And we have judged it to be of no small force, for the avoiding of strife and contention, to have one uniform manner or course of praying throughout all our dominions: and a very great efficacy it hath to stir up the ferventness of the mind, if the confuse manner of praying be somewhat holpen with the fellowship or annexion of understanding; if the ferventness of the prayer being well perceived do put away the tediousness or fainting of the mind, being otherwise occupied and turned from prayer; if the plenteousness of understanding do nourish and feed the burning heat of the heart; and finally, if the cheerfulness of earnest minding the matter put clean away all slothfulness of the mind tofore gathered.

Wherefore as great as our will and forwardness hath been to set forth and publish these things, so great ought your diligence and industry to be towards well and fruitfully using the same; that when all things hath been prepared and set forth to the glory of God and for your wealth, yourselves only may not be slack or negligent towards your own behoof, and toward your own benefits.

---

XXIV. *Injunctions given by the most Excellent Prince, Edward the Sixth, by the grace of God, King of England, France, and Ireland, Defender of the Faith, and in earth under Christ of the Church of England and of Ireland the Supreme Head: To all and singular his loving subjects, as well of the Clergy as of the Laity.*

Wilkins' Concilia, Vol. IV. p. 3. Sparrow's Collection of Records, p. 1.

THE king's most royal majesty, by the advice of his most dear uncle the duke of Somerset, lord protector of all his realms, dominions, and subjects, and governor of his most royal person, and residue of his most honourable council, intending the advancement of the true honour of almighty God, the suppression of idolatry and superstition throughout all his realms and dominions, and to plant true religion, to the extirpation of all hypocrisy, enormities, and abuses, as to his duty appertaineth, doth minister unto his loving subjects these godly Injunctions hereafter following; whereof part were given unto them heretofore by the authority of his most dear beloved father, king Henry the Eighth, of most famous memory, and part are now ministered and given by his majesty: all which Injunctions his highness willeth and commandeth his said loving subjects, by his supreme authority, obediently to receive, and truly to observe and keep, every man, in their offices, degrees, and states, as they will avoid his displeasure, and the pains in the same Injunctions hereafter expressed.

The first is, That all deans, archdeacons, parsons, vicars, and other ecclesiastical persons, shall faithfully keep and observe, and, as far as in them may lie, shall cause to be kept and observed of other, all and singular laws and statutes, made as well for the abolishing and extirpation of the bishop of Rome, his pretensed and usurped power and jurisdiction, as for the establishment and confirmation of the king's authority, jurisdiction, and supremacy of the church of England and Ireland. And furthermore, all ecclesiastical persons, having cure of souls, shall, to the uttermost of their wit, knowledge, and learning, purely, sincerely, and without any colour or dissimulation, declare, manifest, and open four times every year at the least, in their sermons and other collations, that the bishop of Rome's usurped power and jurisdiction, having no establishment nor ground by the laws of God, was of most just causes taken away and abolished; and that therefore no manner of obedience or subjection, within his realms and dominions, is due unto him: and that the king's power, within his realms and dominions, is the highest power under God, to whom all men, within the same realms and dominions, by God's laws, owe most loyalty and obedience, afore and above all other powers and potentates in earth.

Besides this, to the intent that all superstition and hypocrisy, crept into divers men's hearts, may vanish away; they shall not set forth or extol any images, relics or miracles, for any superstition or lucre, nor allure the people by any enticements to the pilgrimage of any saint or image: but, reproving the same, they shall teach, that all goodness, health, and grace, ought to be both asked and looked for only of God, as of the very author and giver of the same, and of none other.

*Item*, That they, the persons above rehearsed, shall make or cause to be made in their churches, and every other cure they have, one sermon every quarter of the year at the least, wherein they shall purely and sincerely declare the word of God: and in the same exhort their hearers to the works of faith, mercy, and charity, specially prescribed and commanded in scripture; and that works devised by men's fantasies, besides scripture, as wandering to pilgrimages, offering of money, candles, or tapers, or relics, or images, or kissing and licking of the same, praying upon beads, or such like superstition, have not only no promise of reward in scripture for doing of them, but contrariwise great threats and maledictions of God, for that they be things tending to idolatry and superstition, which of all other offences God Almighty doth most detest and abhor, for that the same diminish most his honour and glory.

*Item*, That such images as they know in any of their cures to be or to have been abused with pilgrimage or offering of any thing made thereunto, or shall be hereafter censed unto, they (and none other private persons) shall, for the avoiding of that most detestable offence of idolatry, forthwith take down, or cause to be taken down, and destroy the same; and shall suffer from henceforth no torches nor candles, tapers, or images of wax, to be set afore any image or picture, but only two lights upon the high altar, before the sacrament, which, for the signification that Christ is the very true light of the world, they shall suffer to remain still: admonishing their parishioners, that images serve for no other purpose but to be a remembrance, whereby men may be admonished of the holy lives and conversations of them that the said images do represent: which images if they do abuse for any other intent, they commit idolatry in the same, to the great danger of their souls.

*Item*, That every holy day throughout the year, when they have no sermon, they shall, immediately after the gospel, openly and plainly recite to their parishioners in the pulpit the Pater Noster, the Credo, and Ten Commandments in English, to the intent the people may learn the same by heart: exhorting all parents and householders to teach their children and servants the same, as they are bound by the law of God and in conscience to do.

*Item*, That they shall charge fathers and mothers, masters and governors, to bestow their children and servants, even from their childhood, either to learning or to some honest exercise, occupation, or husbandry: exhorting and counselling, and by all the ways and means they may, as well in their sermons and collations as otherwise, persuading the said fathers and mothers, masters and other governors, diligently to provide and foresee that the youth be in no manner or wise brought up in idleness, lest at any time afterward, for lack of some craft, occupation, or other honest means to live by, they be driven to fall to begging, stealing, or some other unthriftiness: forasmuch as we may daily see, through sloth and idleness, divers valiant men fall, some to begging, and some to theft and murder; which, after brought to calamity and misery, do blame their parents, friends, and governors, which suffered them to be brought up so idly in their youth, where, if they had been well brought up in learning some good occupation or craft, they would, being rulers of their own household, have profited as well themselves as divers other persons, to the great commodity and ornament of the commonwealth.

*Also*, That the said parsons, vicars, and other curates shall diligently provide that the sacraments and sacramentals be duly and reverently ministered in their parishes. And if at any time it happen them in any of the cases expressed in the statutes of this realm, or of special licence given by the king's majesty, to be absent from their benefices, they shall leave their cure not to a rude and unlearned person, but to an honest, well learned, and expert curate, that can by his ability teach the rude and unlearned of their cure wholesome doctrine, and reduce them to the right way that do err; which will also execute these Injunctions, and do their duty otherwise, as they are bound to do in every behalf, and accordingly may and will profit their cure, no less with good example of living than with the declaration of the word of God; or else their lack and default shall be imputed unto them, who shall straitly answer for the same if they do otherwise. And always let them see, that neither they nor their curates do seek more their own profit, promotion, or advantage, than the profit of the souls they have under their cure, or the glory of God.

*Also*, That they shall provide, within three months next after this visitation, one book of the whole bible, of the largest volume in English; and, within one twelve months next after the said visitation, the Paraphrasis of Erasmus, also in English, upon the gospels, and the same set up in some convenient place within the said church that they have the cure of, where as their parishioners may most commodiously resort unto the same, and read the same. The charges of which books shall be rateably borne between the parson and approprietary, and parishioners aforesaid, that is to say, the one half by the parson or proprietary, and the other half by the parishioners. And they shall discourage no man, authorised and licensed thereto, from the reading any part of the bible, either in Latin or in English; but shall rather comfort and exhort every person to read the same, as the very lively word of God, and the special food of man's soul, that all christian persons are bound to embrace, believe, and follow, if they look to be saved: whereby they may the better know their duties to God, to their sovereign lord the king, and their neighbour; ever gently and charitably exhorting them, and in his majesty's name straitly charging and commanding them, that in the reading thereof no man to reason or contend, but quietly to hear the reader.

*Also*, The said ecclesiastical persons shall in no wise, at any unlawful time, nor for other any cause than for their honest necessity, haunt or resort to any taverns or alehouses. And after their dinner or supper they shall not give themselves to drinking or riot, spending their time idly, by day or by night, at dice, cards, or tables playing, or any other unlawful game; but at all times, as they shall have leisure, they shall hear and read somewhat of holy scripture, or shall occupy themselves with some other honest exercise: and that they always do the things which appertain to honesty, with endeavour to profit the commonweal; having always in mind that they ought to excel all other in purity of life, and should be an example to the people to live well and christianly.

*Item*, That they shall in confessions every Lent examine every person that cometh to confession to them, whether they can recite the Articles of their Faith, the Pater Noster, and the Ten Commandments in English, and hear them say the same particularly: wherein if they be not perfect, they shall declare then, that every christian person ought to know the said things before they should receive the blessed sacrament of the altar, and admonish them to learn the said necessary things more perfectly, or else they ought not to presume to come to God's board, without a perfect knowledge and will to observe the same; and if they do, it is to the great peril of their souls, and also to the worldly rebuke that they might incur hereafter by the same.

*Also*, That they shall admit no man to preach within any their cures, but such as shall appear unto them to be sufficiently licensed thereunto, by the king's majesty, the lord protector's grace, the archbishop of Canterbury, the archbishop of York in his province, or the bishop of the diocese: and such as shall be so licensed, they shall gladly receive to declare the word of God, without any resistance or contradiction.

*Also*, If they have heretofore declared to their parishioners any thing to the extolling or setting forth of pilgrimages, relics, or images, or lighting of candles, kissing, kneeling, decking of the same images, or any such superstition, they shall now openly before the same recant and reprove the same; shewing them, as the truth is, that they did the same upon no ground of scripture, but were led and seduced by a common error and abuse, crept into the church through the sufferance and avarice of such as felt profit by the same.

*Also*, If they do or shall know any man within their parish or elsewhere, that is a letter of the word of God to be read in English, or sincerely preached, or the execution of these the king's majesty's Injunctions, or a fautor of the bishop of Rome's pretensed power, now by the laws of this realm justly rejected, extirpated, and taken away utterly, they shall detect and present the same to the king or his council, or to the justice of peace next adjoining.

*Also*, That the parson, vicar, or curate, and parishioners of every parish within this realm, shall in their churches and chapels keep one book or register, wherein they shall write the day and year of every wedding, christening, and burial, made within their parish for their time, and so every man succeeding them likewise; and therein shall write every person's name that shall be so wedded, christened, or buried. And for the safe keeping of the same book, the parish shall be bound to provide of their common charges one sure coffer, with two locks and keys, whereof the one to remain with the parson, vicar, or curate, and the other with the wardens of every parish church or chapel, wherein the said book shall be laid up: which book they shall every Sunday take forth, and in the presence of the said wardens, or one of them, write and record in the same all the weddings, christenings, and burials made the whole week before; and that done, to lay up the book in the said coffer as afore. And for every time that the same shall be omitted, the party that shall be in the fault thereof shall forfeit to the said church 3*s*. 4*d*., to be employed to the poor men's box of that parish.

Furthermore, Because the goods of the church are called the goods of the poor, and at these days nothing is less seen than the poor to be sustained with the same, all parsons, vicars, pensioners, prebendaries, and other beneficed men within this deanery, not being resident upon their benefices, which may dispend yearly £20. or above, either within this deanery or elsewhere, shall distribute hereafter among their poor parishioners, or other inhabitants there, in the presence of the churchwardens, or some other honest men of the parish, the fortieth part of the fruits and revenues of their said benefices, lest they be worthily noted of ingratitude, which, reserving so many parts to themselves, cannot vouchsafe to impart the fortieth portion thereof among the poor people of that parish, that is so fruitful and profitable unto them.

And to the intent that learned men may hereafter spring the more for the execution of the premises, every parson, vicar, clerk, or beneficed man within this deanery, having yearly to dispend in benefices and other promotions of the church an hundred pounds, shall give competent exhibition to one scholar; and for so many hundred pounds more as he may dispend, to so many scholars more shall he give like exhibition in the university of Oxford or Cambridge, or some grammar school; which, after they have profited in good learning, may be partners of their patron's cure and charge, as well in preaching as otherwise, in the execution of their offices, or may, when need shall be, otherwise profit the commonweal with their counsel and wisdom.

*Also*, That the proprietaries, parsons, vicars and clerks, having churches, chapels, or mansions within this deanery, shall bestow yearly hereafter upon the same mansions or chancels of their churches, being in decay, the fifth part of that their benefices, till they be fully repaired; and the same so repaired shall always keep and maintain in good estate.

*Also*, That the said parsons, vicars, and clerks shall, once every quarter of the year, read these Injunctions given unto them, openly and deliberately before all their parishioners, to the intent that both they may be the better admonished of their duty, and their said parishioners the more moved to follow the same for their part.

*Also*, Forasmuch as by a law established every man is bound to pay his tithes, no man shall, by colour of duty omitted by their curates, detain their tithes, and so redub and requite one wrong with another, or be his own judge; but shall truly pay the same, as he hath been accustomed, to their parsons, vicars, and curates, without any restraint or diminution: and such lack and default as they can justly find in their parsons and curates, to call for reformation thereof at their ordinaries' and other superiors' hands, who upon complaint and due reproof thereof shall reform the same accordingly.

*Also*, that no person shall from henceforth alter or change the order and manner of any fasting day that is commanded, or of common prayer or divine service, otherwise than is specified in these Injunctions, until such time as the same shall be otherwise ordered and transposed by the king's authority.

*Also*, That every parson, vicar, curate, chauntry-priest, and stipendiary, being under the degree of a bachelor of divinity, shall provide and have of his own, within three months after this visitation, the new Testament both in Latin and in English, with the paraphrase upon the same of Erasmus, and diligently study the same, conferring the one with the other. And the bishops and other ordinaries, by themselves or their officers, in their synods and visitations, shall examine the said ecclesiastical persons how they have profited in the study of holy scripture.

*Also*, In the time of high mass, within every church, he that saith or singeth the same shall read or cause to be read the epistle and gospel of that mass in English, and not in Latin, in the pulpit, or in such convenient place as the people may hear the same. And every Sunday and holy day they shall plainly and distinctly read, or cause to be read, one chapter of the new Testament in English in the said place at matins immediately after the lessons; and at evensong, after Magnificat, one chapter of the old Testament. And to the intent the premises may be more conveniently done, the king's majesty's pleasure is, that when nine lessons should be read in the church, three of them shall be omitted and left out with the responds; and at evensong-time the responds, with all the memories, shall be left off for that purpose.

*Also*, Because those persons which be sick and in peril of death, be oftentimes put in despair by the craft and subtlety of the devil, who is then most busy, and especially with them that lack the knowledge, sure persuasion, and stedfast belief that they may be made partakers of the great and infinite mercy which Almighty God of his most bountiful goodness and mere liberality, without our deserving, hath offered freely to all persons that put their full trust and confidence in him: therefore, that this damnable vice of despair may be clearly taken away, and firm belief and stedfast hope surely conceived of all their parishioners, being in any danger, they shall learn and have always in a readiness such comfortable places and sentences of scripture as do set forth the mercy, benefits, and goodness of Almighty God towards all penitent and believing persons, that they may at all times, when necessity shall require, promptly comfort their flock with the lively word of God, which is the only stay of man's conscience.

*Also*, To avoid all contention and strife, which heretofore hath risen among the king's majesty's subjects in sundry places of his realms and dominions, by reason of fond courtesy, and challenging of places in procession, and also that they may the more quietly hear that which is said or sung to their edifying, they shall not from henceforth in any parish church at any time use any procession about the church or churchyard, or other place; but immediately before high mass the priests, with other of the quire, shall kneel in the midst of the church, and sing or say plainly and distinctly the Litany, which is set forth in English, with all the suffrages following; and none other procession or Litany to be had or used but the said Litany in English, adding nothing thereto, but as the king's grace shall hereafter appoint: and in cathedral or collegiate churches, the same shall be done in such places as our commissaries in our visitation shall appoint. And in the time of the Litany, of the mass, of the sermon, and when the priest readeth the scripture to the parishioners, no manner of persons, without a just and urgent cause, shall depart out of the church; and all ringing and knolling of bells, shall be utterly forborne at that time, except one bell in convenient time to be rung or knolled before the sermon.

*Also*, Like as the people be commonly occupied the work-day with bodily labour for their bodily sustenance, so was the holy day at the first beginning godly instituted and ordained, that the people should that day give themselvss wholly to God. And whereas in our time God is more offended than pleased, more dishonoured than honoured upon the holy day, because of idleness, pride, drunkenness, quarrelling, and brawling, which are most used in such days, people nevertheless persuading themselves sufficiently to honour God on that day, if they hear mass and service, though they understand nothing to their edifying: therefore all the king's faithful and loving subjects shall from henceforth celebrate and keep their holy day according to God's holy will and pleasure; that is, in hearing the word of God read and taught, in private and public prayers, in knowledging their offences to God, and amendment of the same, in reconciling their selves charitably to their neighbours where displeasure hath been, in oftentimes receiving the communion of the very body and blood of Christ, in visiting of the poor and sick, in using all soberness and godly conversation. Yet notwithstanding all parsons, vicars, and curates shall teach and declare unto their parishioners, that they may with a safe and quiet conscience, in the time of harvest, labour upon the holy and festival days, and save that thing which God hath sent: and if for any scrupulosity, or grudge of conscience, men should superstitiously abstain from working upon those days, that then they should grievously offend and displease God.

*Also*, Forasmuch as variance and contention is a thing which most displeaseth God, and is most contrary to the blessed communion of the body and blood of our Saviour Christ; curates shall in no wise admit to the receiving thereof any of their cure and flock, who hath maliciously and openly contended with his neighbour, unless the same do first charitably and openly reconcile himself again, remitting all rancour and malice, whatsoever controversy hath been between them: and nevertheless their just titles and rights they may charitably prosecute before such as have authority to hear the same.

*Also*, That every dean, archdeacon, master of collegiate church, master of hospital, and prebendary being priest, shall preach by himself personally twice every year at the least, either in the place where he is intituled, or in some church where he hath jurisdiction, or else which is to the said place appropriate or united.

*Also*, That they shall instruct and teach in their cures, that no man ought obstinately and maliciously to break and violate the laudable ceremonies of the church, by the king commanded to be observed, and as yet not abrogated. And on the other side, that whosoever doth superstitiously abuse them, doth the same to the great peril and danger of his soul's health: as in casting holy water upon his bed, upon images, and other dead things, or bearing about him holy bread or St John's gospel, or making of crosses of wood upon Palm Sunday, in time of reading of the passion, or keeping of private holy days, as bakers, brewers, smiths, shoemakers, and such other do; or ringing of holy bells, or blessing with the holy candle, to the intent thereby to be discharged of the burden of sin, or to drive away devils, or to put away dreams and fantasies; or in putting trust or confidence of health and salvation in the same ceremonies, when they be only ordained, instituted, and made to put us in remembrance of the benefits which we have received by Christ. And if he use them for any other purpose, he grievously offendeth God.

*Also*, That they shall take away, utterly extinct, and destroy all shrines, covering of shrines, all tables, candlesticks, trindles or rolls of wax, pictures, paintings, and all other monuments of feigned miracles, pilgrimages, idolatry, and superstition; so that there remain no memory of the same in walls, glass windows, or elsewhere within their churches or houses. And they shall exhort all their parishioners to do the like within their several houses. And that the churchwardens, at the common charge of the parishioners, in every church, shall provide a comely and honest pulpit, to be set in a convenient place within the same, for the preaching of God's word.

*Also*, They shall provide and have within three months after this visitation a strong chest, with a hole in the upper part thereof, to be provided at the cost and charge of the parish, having three keys; whereof one shall remain in the custody of the parson, vicar, or curate, and the other two in th custody of the churchwardens, or any other two honest men to be appointed by the parish from year to year: which chest you shall set and fasten near unto the high altar, to the intent the parishioners should put into it their oblation and alms for their poor neighbours. And the parson, vicar, or curate, shall diligently from time to time, and specially when men make their testaments, call upon, exhort, and move their neighbours, to confer and give, as they may well spare, to the said chest; declaring unto them, whereas heretofore they have been diligent to bestow much substance otherwise than God commanded, upon pardons,. pilgrimages, trentals, decking of images, offering of candles, giving to friars, and upon other like blind devotions, they ought at this time to be much more ready to help the poor and needy, knowing that to relieve the poor is a true worshipping of God, required earnestly upon pain of everlasting damnation; and that also, whatsoever is given for their comfort, is given to Christ himself, and so is accepted of him, that he will mercifully reward the same with everlasting life: the which alms and devotion of the people the keepers of the keys shall at times convenient take out of the chest, and distribute the same in the presence of their whole parish, or six of them, to be truly and faithfully delivered to their most needy neighbours; and if they be provided for, then to the reparation of highways next adjoining. And also the money which riseth of fraternities, guilds, and other stocks of the church, (except by the king's majesty's authority it be otherwise appointed,) shall be put into the said chest, and converted to the said use; and also the rents and lands, the profit of cattle, and money given or bequeathed to the finding of torches, lights, tapers, and lamps, shall be converted to the said use, saving that it shall be lawful for them to bestow part of the said profits upon the reparation of the church, if great need require, and where as the parish is very poor, and not able otherwise to repair the same.

And forasmuch as priests be public ministers of the church, and upon the holy days ought to apply themselves to the common administration of the whole parish, they shall not be bound to go to women lying in childbed, except in time of dangerous sickness, and not to fetch any corpse before it be brought to the churchyard; and if the woman be sick, or the corpse brought to the church, the priest shall do his duty accordingly, in visiting the woman, and burying the dead person.

*Also*, To avoid the detestable sin of simony, because buying and selling of benefices is execrable before God; therefore all such persons as buy any benefices, or come to them by fraud or deceit, shall be deprived of such benefices, and be made unable at any time after to receive any other spiritual promotion. And such as do sell them, or by any colour do bestow them for their own gain and profit, shall lose the right and title of patronage and presentment for that time, and the gift thereof for that vacation shall appertain to the king's majesty.

*Also*, Because, through lack of preachers in many places of the king's realms and dominions, the people continue in ignorance and blindness, all parsons, vicars, and curates shall read in the churches every Sunday one of the homilies, which are and shall be set forth for the same purpose by the king's authority, in such sort as they shall be appointed to do in the preface of the same.

*Also*, Whereas many indiscreet persons do at this day uncharitably contemn and abuse priests and ministers of the church, because some of them, having small learning, have of long time favoured fancies rather than God's truth; yet, forasmuch as their office and function is appointed of God, the king's majesty willeth and chargeth all his loving subjects, that from henceforth they shall use them charitably and reverently, for their office and administration sake, and especially such as labour in the setting forth of God's holy word.

*Also*, That all manner of persons which understand not the Latin tongue, shall pray upon none other Primer, but upon that which was lately set forth in English by the authority of king Henry the Eighth, of most famous memory; and that no teachers of youth shall teach any other than the said Primer. And all those which have knowledge of the Latin tongue, shall pray upon none other Latin Primer, but upon that which is likewise set forth by the said authority. And that all graces to be said at dinner and supper shall be always said in the English tongue. And that none other grammar shall be taught in any school or other place within the king's realms and dominions, but only that which is set forth by the said authority.

*Item*, That all chauntry-priests shall exercise themselves in teaching youth to read and write, and bring them up in good manners and other virtuous exercises.

*Item*, When any sermon or homily should be had, the prime and hours shall be omitted.

*The Form of bidding the Common Prayers.*

You shall pray for the whole congregation of Christ's church, and especially for this church of England and Ireland: wherein, first, I commend to your devout prayers the king's most excellent majesty, supreme head, immediately under God, of the spirituality and temporality of the same church; and for queen Catharine, dowager; and also for my lady Mary and my lady Elizabeth, the king's sisters.

Secondly, You shall pray for the lord protector's grace, with all the rest of the king's majesty's council; for all the lords of this realm, and for the clergy and commons of the same: beseeching Almighty God to give every of them, in his degree, grace to use themselves in such wise as may be to God's glory, the king's honour, and the weal of this realm.

Thirdly, Ye shall pray for all them that be departed out of this world in the faith of Christ, that they with us, and we with them, at the day of judgment may rest, both body and soul, with Abraham, Isaac, and Jacob in the kingdom of heaven.

All which singular Injunctions the king's majesty ministereth unto his clergy and their successors, and to all his loving subjects; straitly charging and commanding them to observe and keep the same, upon pain of deprivation, sequestration of fruits or benefices, suspension, excommunication, and such other coercion, as to ordinaries, or other having ecclesiastical jurisdiction, whom his majesty hath appointed for the due execution of the same, shall be seen convenient; charging and commanding them to see these Injunctions observed and kept of all persons, being under their jurisdiction, as they will answer to his majesty for the contrary: and his majesty's pleasure is, that every justice of peace, being required, shall assist the ordinaries, and every of them, for the due execution of the said Injunctions.

---

## XXV. *King Edward VI.'s Injunctions particularly delivered to the Bishops.*

Foxe's Acts and Monuments, pp. 1298, 9. Ed. Lond. 1583.

First, that they should, to the uttermost of their wit[1] and understanding, see and cause all and singular the king's Injunctions theretofore given, or after to be given from

[[1] To the utmost of their power, wit. Heylyn and Wilkins.]

time to time, in and through their diocese[2], duly, faithfully, and truly to be kept, observed, and accomplished; and that they should personally preach within their diocese every quarter of a year once at the least, that is to say, once in their cathedral churches, and thrice in other several places of their dioceses, where as they should see it most convenient[3] and necessary, except they had a reasonable excuse to the contrary. Likewise, that they should not retain into their service or household any chaplain, but such as were learned, or able to preach the word of God, and those they should also cause to exercise the same.

Heylyn's Eccles. Restaur. p. 37. Ed. Lond. 1670. Wilkins' Concilia, Vol. IV. p. 9.

Moreover, that they should not[4] give orders to any person, but such as were learned in holy scripture; neither should deny them to such as were learned[5] in the same, being of honest conversation and living. And lastly, that they should not at any time or place preach or set forth unto the people any doctrine contrary or repugnant to the effect and intent contained and set forth in the king's highness's homilies, neither yet should admit or give licence to preach to any within their diocese, but to such as they should know (or at the least assuredly trust) would do the same. And if at any time by hearing, or by report proved, they should perceive the contrary, they should then incontinent not only inhibit that person so offending, but also punish him, and revoke their licence.

---

## XXVI. *Letter from the Privy Council concerning Homilies and Injunctions.*

After our most hearty commendations unto your good lordship. Where the king's majesty, with the advice and consent of my lord protector and the whole council, hath commanded a general visitation to be begun through his majesty's realm, in the which his majesty's commissioners, for the better setting forth of the true honouring of God and extinguishment of all superstition and popery, have in commandment to deliver to men of all sorts several Injunctions meetest for their vocations, and to the priest and curates certain Homilies to be by them read to their parishioners, according to the order of the said Injunctions: forasmuch as we would wish the same to be in like sort set forth with you, whereas yet no commissioners be specially addressed, we have thought good to send you herewith certain of the said Homilies and Injunctions, which your lordship may cause to be delivered to the curates, and others, within the limits of your jurisdiction, by the            of high Bolloigne; after the delivery whereof, we trust that as the same be godly, and set forth by the king's majesty for the good instruction of his majesty's loving subjects, so you will both yourselves in your own families observe the same, and help also to have them well obeyed and kept of others.

State Paper Office. Domestic Papers. Temp. Edw. VI. A.D. 1547—48. No. 1.

T. Cantuarien. Antony Wyngfeld.
W. Seint John. William Paget.
T. Seymour. Edward North.
Richard Ryche. William Petre.
Anthone Browne.

---

## XXVII. *A Proclamation concerning the irreverent Talkers of the Sacrament. Dated the 27th day of December, anno regni reg. Edward. primo.* [1547.]

Whereas the king's highness hath of late, with the assent and consent of the lords spiritual and temporal, and the commons in the parliament held the fourth day of November[7], in the first year of his most gracious reign, made a good and godly act and estatute against those who do contemn, despise, or with unseemly and ungodly words deprave and revile the holy sacrament of the body and blood of our Lord, commonly called the "sacrament of the altar;" and the said estatute hath most prudently declared,

Wilkins' Concilia, Vol. IV. p. 18. Strype's Eccl. Mem. Vol. II. pt. ii. a Repository of Originals, M. pp. 340—343. Ed. Oxon. 1822. Penes Rev. D. Joh. Ep. Elien.[6]

---

[2 Our diocese. Foxe.]
[3 More convenient. Wilkins.]
[4 And secondly, that they should not. Heylyn and Wilkins.]
[5 Them that were learned. Foxe.]
[6 i.e. Bishop Moore.]
[7 A blank space is left in Strype for the words, fourth, and November.]

by all the words and terms which scripture speaketh of it, what is undoubtedly to be accepted, believed, taken and spoken by and of the said sacrament: yet this notwithstanding, his majesty is advertised, that some of his subjects, not contented with such words and terms as scripture doth declare thereof, nor with that doctrine which the Holy Ghost by the evangelists and St Paul hath taught us, do not cease to move contentious and superfluous questions of the said holy sacrament and supper of the Lord, entering rashly into the discussing of the high mystery thereof, and go about in their sermons or talks arrogantly to define the manner, nature, fashion, ways, possibility or impossibility, of those matters; which neither make to edification, nor God hath by his holy word opened:

Which persons,—not contented reverently and with obedient faith to accept that the said sacrament according to the saying of St Paul, "The bread is the communion," or partaking, "of the body of the Lord; the wine," likewise, "the partaking of the blood of Christ," by the words instituted and taught of Christ; and that the body and blood of Jesus Christ is there; which is our comfort, thanksgiving, love-token of Christ's love towards us, and of ours as his members within ourself,—search and strive unreverently, whether the body and blood aforesaid is there really or figuratively, locally or circumscriptly, and having quantity and greatness, or but substantially and by substance only, or else but in a figure and manner of speaking; whether his blessed body be there, head, legs, arms, toes and nails, or any other ways, shape, and manner, naked or clothed; whether he is broken or chewed, or he is always whole; whether the bread there remaineth, as we see, or how it departeth; whether the flesh be there alone, and the blood, or part, or each in other, or in the one both, in the other but only blood; and what blood, that only which did flow out of the side, or that which remained: with other such irreverent, superfluous, and curious questions, which, how and what, and by what means, and in what form may bring into them, which of human and corrupt curiosity hath desire to search out such mysteries as lieth hid in the infinite and bottomless depth of the wisdom and glory of God, and to the which our human imbecility cannot attain; and therefore ofttime turneth the same to their own and others' destruction, by contention and arrogant rashness; which simple and christian affection reverently receiving, and obediently believing, without further search, taketh and useth to most great comfort and profit:

For reformation whereof, and to the intent that further contention, tumult, and question, might not rise amongst the king's subjects, the king's highness, by the advice of the lord protector, and other his majesty's council, straitly willeth and commandeth, that no manner person from henceforth do in any wise contentiously and openly argue, dispute, reason, preach or teach, affirming any more terms of the said blessed sacrament, than be expressly taught in the holy scripture, and mentioned in the foresaid act; nor deny none, which be therein contained and mentioned; until such time as the king's majesty, by the advice of his highness' council and the clergy of this realm, shall define, declare, and set forth an open doctrine thereof; and what terms and words may justly be spoken thereby, other than be expressly in the scripture contained in the act before rehearsed.

In the meanwhile the king's highness' pleasure is, by the advice aforesaid, that every his loving subjects shall devoutly and reverently affirm and take that holy bread to be Christ's body, and that cup to be the cup of his holy blood, according to the purport and effect of the holy scripture, contained in the act before expressed, and accommodate themselves rather to take the same sacrament worthily, than rashly to enter into the discussing of the high mystery thereof.

Yet the king's highness mindeth not hereby to let or stop the ignorant and willing to learn, reverently or privately to demand of those, whom he thinketh knoweth more, the further instruction and teaching in the said blessed sacrament; so that the same be not done with contention, nor in open audience, with a company gathered together about them, nor with tumult: nor doth prohibit any man hereby likewise so quietly, devoutly, and reverently to teach or instruct the weak and unlearned, according to the more talent and learning given to him of God: but only, that all contention, strife and tumult, and irreverentness might be avoided, and in open audience and preaching nothing taught, but which may have the holy scripture for warrant.

Upon pain that whosoever shall openly, with contention or tumult, and in a company gathered together, either in churches, alehouses, markets, or elsewhere, contrary to the form and effect of this proclamation, defend and maintain, or irreverently and contentiously demand of any man, any of the questions before rehearsed, either on the one part or of the other, or any such like, or do otherwise revile, contemn, or despise the said sacrament, by calling it an "idol," or other such vile name, shall incur the king's high indignation, and suffer imprisonment; or to be otherwise grievously punished at his majesty's will and pleasure.

Giving further in authority to all justices of peace within the shires where they dwell, to apprehend and take all such as contentiously and tumultuously, with companies or routs assembled about them, do dispute, argue, or reason, or stiffly maintain, or openly preach and define the questions before rehearsed, or any of them, or such like, either on the one part or the other; and to commit the same to prison, until such time as the king's majesty's pleasure herein be known; and that they immediately do certify the name or names of the party so offending, and of them who were there at the same time present, making the rout or assemble, to the king's highness's council: willing and commanding the said justices, with all diligence, to execute the premises, according to the purport, effect, and true meaning of the same, and their most bound duties, as they tender his highness's will and pleasure, and will answer to the contrary upon their peril.

---

## XXVIII. *A Proclamation for the abstaining from Flesh in Lent time. Dated the 16th day of January, an. reg. prim.* [1548.]

Wilkins' Concilia, Vol. IV. p. 20. Strype's Eccl. Mem. Vol. II. pt. ii. N. a Repository of Originals, pp. 343–346. Ed. Oxon. 1822. E Biblioth. Rev. Joh. Ep. Elien.

The king's highness, by the advice of his most entirely beloved uncle, Edward duke of Somerset, governor of his person, and protector of all his realms, dominions, and subjects, and other of his privy council; considering that his highness hath not only cure and charge of the defence of his realms and dominions, as a king, but also as a christian king, and supreme head of the church of England and Ireland, a desire, will, and charge, to lead and instruct his people, to him committed of God, in such rites, ways, and customs, as might be acceptable to God, and to the further increase of good living and virtue; and that his subjects, now having a more perfect and clear light of the gospel and true word of the Lord, through the infinite clemency and mercy of Almighty God by the hands of his majesty, and his most noble father of famous memory, promulgate, shewed, declared, and opened unto them, should and ought thereby in all good works and virtues increase, be more forward, and diligent, and plentiful; as in fasting, prayer, and alms-deeds, in love, charity, obedience, and other such good works commanded to us of God in his holy scripture:

Yet his highness is advertised and informed, that divers of his subjects be not only to all these more slow and negligent, but rather contemners and despisers of such good and godly acts and deeds; to the which if they were of their own minds bent and inclined, they needed not by outward and princely power be appointed and commanded. But forsomuch as at this time now alate, more than at any other time, a great part of his subjects do break and contemn that abstinence, which of long time hath been used in this his majesty's realm upon the Fridays and Saturdays, and the time commonly called Lent, and other accustomed times; his highness is constrained to see a convenient order herein set and appointed: not minding thereby that his subjects should think any difference to be in the days or meats, or that the one should be to God more holy, more pure, or more clean, than the other; for all days and all meats be of one and equal purity, cleanness, and holiness, that we should in them, and by them, live to the glory of God, and at all times, and for all meats, give thanks unto him, of the which none can defile us at any time, or make us unclean, being christian men, to whom all things be holy and pure, so that they be not used in disobedience and vice: but his majesty hath allowed and approved the days and times before accustomed to be continued and still observed here in this church of England; both that men should on those days abstain and forbear their pleasures, and the meats wherein they have more delight, to the intent to subdue their bodies unto the soul and spirit; unto the which to exhort and move men is the office of a good and godly head and ruler; and also for worldly and civil policy certain days in the year to spare flesh, and use fish, for the benefit of the commonwealth and profit of his majesty's realm; whereof many be fishers, and men using that trade of living unto the which this realm on every part environed with the seas, and so plentiful of fresh waters, doth easily minister occasion; to the great sustenance of this his highness's people: so that hereby both the nourishment of the land might be increased by saving flesh, and specially at the spring time, when Lent doth commonly fall, and when the most common and plenteous breeding of flesh is; and also, divers of his loving subjects have good livings, and get great riches thereby, in uttering and selling such meats as the sea and fresh water doth minister unto us; and this his majesty's realm hath more plenty of ships, boats, crays, and other vessels, by reason of those which by hope of lucre do follow that trade of living.

Wherefore, his majesty, having consideration, that where men of their own minds do not give themselves, so oft as they should do, to fasting, a common abstinence may and should be by the prince enjoined and commanded; and having an eye and mind to the profit and commodity of his realm and subjects, and to a common and civil policy, hath willed and commanded, and by these presents doth will and command, by the advice aforesaid, all manner of person and persons, of what estate, degree, or condition he or they be, (other than such as already be, or hereafter shall be excused by law, or licensed or authorised sufficiently to the contrary,) to observe and keep from henceforth such fasting days, and the time commonly called Lent, in abstaining from all manner of flesh, as heretofore in this realm hath been most commonly used and accustomed: upon pain that whosoever shall, upon any day heretofore wont to be fasted from flesh, and not by the king's highness or his predecessors abrogate and taken away, eat flesh contrary to this proclamation, shall incur the king's high indignation, and shall suffer imprisonment, and be otherwise grievously punished, at his majesty's will and pleasure.

And further the king's highness, by the advice aforesaid, straitly chargeth and commandeth all mayors, bailiffs, and other head-officers and rulers of cities and towns, and all justices of peace in the shires where they be in commission, to be attendant and diligent to the execution of this proclamation; in committing to prison the offenders contrary to this proclamation[1], upon sufficient proof thereof by two sufficient witnesses, before them had and made, there to remain during the king's pleasure, according to the true purport, effect, and meaning of the same; as they tender the king's majesty's will and pleasure, and will answer the contrary at their peril.

And where the late king of most famous memory, father to his highness, hath given divers years licence to his subjects in the time of Lent to eat butter, cheese, and other meats, commonly called white meats; the king's highness, by the advice aforesaid, considering the same to have been done not without great considerations, doth give likewise licence and authority to all his loving subjects from henceforth freely for ever in the time of Lent, or other prohibited times by law or custom, to eat butter, eggs, cheese, and other white meats, any law, statute, act, or custom to the contrary notwithstanding.

---

XXIX. *A Proclamation against those that do innovate, alter, or leave undone any Rite or Ceremony in the Church, of their private authority; and against them which preach without licence. Set forth the 6th day of February, in the second year of the King's Majesty's most gracious reign.* [1548.]

Wilkins' Concilia, Vol. IV. p. 21. Burnet's Hist. of Ref. Vol. II. pt. ii. App. Book I. No. 22. pp. 185—187. Ed. Oxon.

THE King's Majesty, by the advice of his most entirely beloved uncle, the duke of Somerset, governor of his most royal person, and protector of all his realms, dominions, and subjects, and others of his council; considering nothing so much to tend to the disquieting of this realm, as diversity of opinions, and variety of rites and ceremonies concerning religion and worshipping of Almighty God; and therefore studying all the ways and means which can be to direct this church, and the cure committed

[[1] To the proclamation. Strype.]

to his highness, in one and most true doctrine, rite, and usage; yet is advertised, that certain private curates, preachers, and other laymen, contrary to their bounden duty of obedience, do rashly attempt, of their own and singular wit and mind, in some parish churches, and otherwise, not only to persuade the people from the old and accustomed rites and ceremonies, but also themselves bringeth in new orders every one in their church, according to their fantasies; the which, as it is an evident token of pride and arrogance, so it tendeth both to confusion and disorder, and also to the high displeasure of Almighty God, who loveth nothing so much as order and obedience: Wherefore his majesty straitly chargeth and commandeth, that no manner of person, of what estate, order, or degree soever he be, of his private mind, will, or fantasy, do omit, leave undone, change, alter, or innovate any order, rite, or ceremony commonly used and frequented in the church of England, and not commanded to be left undone at any time in the reign of our late sovereign lord, his highness' father, other than such as his highness, by the advice aforesaid, by his majesty's visitors, injunctions, statutes, or proclamations, hath already, or hereafter shall command to be omitted, left, innovated, or changed; but that they be observed after that sort as before they were accustomed, or else now sith prescribed by the authority of his majesty, or by the means aforesaid, upon pain, that whosoever shall offend contrary to this proclamation, shall incur his highness's indignation, and suffer imprisonment and other grievous punishment, at his majesty's will and pleasure. Provided always, that for not bearing a candle upon Candlemass-day; not taking ashes upon Ash-Wednesday; not bearing palm upon Palm-Sunday; not creeping to the cross; not taking holy bread or holy water; or for omitting other such rites and ceremonies concerning religion and the use of the church, which the most reverend father in God, the archbishop of Canterbury, by his majesty's will and commandment, with the advice aforesaid, hath declared, or hereafter shall declare, to the other bishops[2], by his writing under seal, as heretofore hath been accustomed, to be omitted or changed, no man hereafter be imprisoned, nor otherwise punished; but all such things to be reputed for the observation and following of the same, as though they were commanded by his majesty's injunctions. And to the intent that rash and seditious preachers should not abuse his highness's people, it is his majesty's pleasure, that whosoever shall take upon him to preach openly in any parish church, chapel, or any other open place, other than those which be licensed by the king's majesty, or his highness' visitors, the archbishop of Canterbury, or the bishop of the diocese where he doth preach, except it be bishop, parson, vicar, dean, warden, or provost, in his or their own cure, shall be forthwith, upon such attempt and preaching, contrary to this proclamation, be committed to prison, and there remain until such time as his majesty, by the advice aforesaid, hath taken order for the further punishment of the same. And that the premises should be more speedily and diligently done and performed, his highness giveth straitly in commandment to all justices of peace, mayors, sheriffs, constables, headboroughs, churchwardens, and all other his majesty's officers and ministers, and rulers of towns, parishes, and hamlets, that they be diligent and attendant to the true and faithful execution of this proclamation, and every part thereof, according to the intent, purport, and effect of the same. And that they of their proceedings herein, or, if any offender be, after they have committed the same to prison, do certify his highness the lord protector, or his majesty's council, with all speed thereof accordingly, as they tender his majesty's pleasure, the wealth of the realm, and will answer to the contrary at their uttermost perils.

1829. Ex reg. Cran. f. 111. Strype's Eccl Mem. Vol. II. pt. ii. a Repository of Originals, pp. 346—348. Ed. Oxon. 1822. Ubi supra.

God save the King.

---

## XXX. *Mandatum ad amovendas et delendas Imagines.*

THOMAS, permissione divina Cantuariensis archiepiscopus, totius Angliæ primas et metropolitanus, per illustrissimum in Christo principem et dominum nostrum dominum Edvardum Sextum Dei gratia Angliæ, Franciæ, et Hiberniæ Regem, Fidei Defensorem, et in terra Ecclesiæ Anglicanæ et Hiberniæ supremum caput, sufficienter et legitime

Wilkins' Concilia, Vol. IV. p. 22. Ex reg. Cran. f. 32 a.

---

[[2] Vid. Letter CCLXXXI. p. 417.]

auctorizatus; venerabili confratri nostro domino Edmundo eadem permissione Londoniensi episcopo, vestrove vicario in spiritualibus generali et officiali principali, salutem et fraternam in Domino caritatem. Literas missivas clarissimorum et prudentissimorum dominorum de privato consilio suæ regiæ majestatis manibus subscriptas, nobis inscriptas et directas, nuper recepimus, tenorem subsequentem complectentes.

Foxe's Acts and Monuments, p. 1300. Ed. Lond. 1583. Burnet's Hist. of Ref. Vol. II. pt. ii. App. Book I. No. 23. pp. 187—189. Ed. Oxon. 1829. Heylyn's Eccles. Restaur. Edw. VI. p. 55. Ed. Lond. 1670.

After our right hearty recommendations[1] to your good lordship, where now of late, in the king's majesty's visitation, among other godly injunctions commanded to be generally observed through all parts of this his highness' realm, one was set forth for the taking down of all such images as had at any time been abused with pilgrimages, offerings, or censings[2]: albeit that this said injunction hath in many parts of the realm been well and quietly obeyed[3] and executed, yet in many other places much strife and contention hath risen, and daily riseth, and more and more increaseth about the execution of the same; some men being so superstitious, or rather wilful, as they would by their good wills retain all such images still, although they have been most manifestly abused; and in some places also the images, which by the said injunctions were taken down, be now restored and set up again; and almost in every place is contention for images, whether they have been abused or not; and whiles these men go about on both sides[4] contentiously to obtain their minds, contending whether this[5] or that image hath been offered unto, kissed, censed, or otherwise abused, parties have in some places been taken, in such sort as further inconvenience is very like to ensue, if remedy be not provided in time[6]: considering therefore that almost in no places of this realm[7] is any sure quietness, but where all images be wholly taken away[8] and pulled down already; to the intent that all contention in every part of this realm for this matter may be clearly taken away, and that the lively images of Christ should not contend for the dead images, which be things not necessary, and without which the churches of Christ continued most godly for many years; we have thought good to signify unto you, that his highness's pleasure, with the advice[9] and consent of us the lord protector and the rest of the council, is, that immediately upon the sight hereof, with as convenient diligence as you may, you shall not only give order that all the images remaining in any church or chapel within your diocese be removed and taken away, but also by your letters signify unto the rest of the bishops within your province his highness' pleasure[10] for the like order to be given by them and every of them within their several dioceses: and in the execution thereof we require both you and the rest of the bishops foresaid[11], to use such foresight as the same may be quietly done with as good satisfaction of the people as may be. Thus fare your good lordship well[12]. From Somerset Place, the twenty-first of February, 1547. [1548.] Your lordship's assured friends[13], E. Somerset, Jo. Russell, Henricus Arundell, T. Seymour, Anthony Wyngefelde, William Pagett.

Quibus quidem literis pro nostro erga suam regiam majestatem officio, uti decet, obtemperare summopere cupientes, vestræ fraternitati tenore præsentium committimus, et regiæ majestatis vice et nomine, quibus in hac parte fungimur, mandamus, quatenus attento diligenter literarum hujuscemodi tenore, omnibus et singulis confratribus coepiscopis nostris, et ecclesiæ nostræ Christi Cantuariensis suffraganeis, cum ea qua poteritis celeritate accommoda præcipiatis, ut ipsorum singuli in suis cathedralibus, necnon civitatum et diocesium suarum parochialibus ecclesiis, exposito publice literarum hujuscemodi tenore, omnia et singula in literis præinsertis comprehensa, deducta et descripta, quatenus eos concernunt, in omnibus et per omnia exequi et perimpleri sedulo et accurate curent, et fieri non postponant; sicque a vobis, frater carissime, in civitate et diocesi vestris London' per omnia fieri et perimpleri volumus et mandamus. Dat'

[1 Hearty commendations. Foxe and Burnet.]
[2 Vid. supra, p. 499.]
[3 Been quietly obeyed. Foxe.]
[4 Go on both sides. Id.]
[5 Whether this image. Id.]
[6 Further inconveniences be like to ensue, if remedy be not found in time. Id.]
[7 No places of the realm. Burnet. No place of this realm. Foxe.]
[8 Be clean taken away. Foxe.]
[9 With advice. Burnet.]
[10 This his highness' pleasure. Burnet and Foxe.]
[11 Rest of the said bishops. Burnet and Foxe.]
[12 Lordship heartily well. Foxe.]
[13 Assured loving friends. Id.]

in manerio nostro de Lambehithe vigesimo quarto die mensis Februarii, anno Domini, juxta computationem ecclesiæ Anglicanæ, 1547, 8, et nostræ consecrationis anno decimo quinto.

---

## XXXI. *Letter Missive from the Council to the Bishops of the Realm concerning the Communion to be ministered in both Kinds.*

AFTER our most hearty commendations unto your lordship. Where in the parliament lately holden[14] at Westminster it was, amongst other things, most godly established, that, according to the first institution and use of the primitive church, the most holy sacrament of the body and blood of our Saviour Jesus Christ should be distributed to the people under the kinds of bread and wine: according to the effect whereof, the king's majesty, minding, with the advice and consent of the lord protector's grace, and the rest of the council, to have the said statute well executed in such sort, or like as is agreeable[15] with the word of God, (so the same may be also faithfully and reverently received of his most loving subjects, to their comforts and wealth,) hath caused sundry of his majesty's most grave and well learned prelates, and other learned men in the scripture[16], to assemble themselves for this matter; who, after long conference together, have with deliberate advice finally agreed upon such an order to be used in all places of the king's majesty's dominions, in the distribution of the said most holy sacrament, as may appear to you by the book thereof, which we send herewith unto you: albeit, knowing your lordship's knowledge in the scriptures, and earnest good-will and zeal to the setting forth of all things according to the truth thereof, we be well assured you will of your own good-will, and upon respect to your duty, diligently set forth this most godly order here agreed upon, and commanded to be used by the authority of the king's majesty; yet, remembering the crafty practice of the devil, who ceaseth not, by his members, to work by all ways and means the hinderance of all godliness; and considering furthermore that a great number of the curates of the realm, either for lack of knowledge cannot, or for want of good mind will not, be so ready to set forth the same as we would wish, and as the importance of the matter and their own bounden duty requireth[17]; we have thought good to pray and require your lordship, and nevertheless in the king's majesty our most dread lord's name to command you, to have an earnest diligence and careful respect both in your own person and by all your officers and ministers; also to cause these books to be delivered to every parson, vicar, and curate, within your diocese, with such diligence as they may have sufficient time well to instruct and advise themselves for the distribution of the most holy communion according to the order of this book before this Easter time; and that they may by your good means be well directed to use such good, gentle, and charitable instruction of their simple and unlearned parishioners, as may be to all their good satisfactions as much as may be: praying you to consider, that this order is set forth to the intent there should be in all parts of the realm, and among all men, one uniform manner quietly used; the execution whereof, like as it shall stand very much in the diligence of you and others of your vocation, so do we eftsoons require you to have a diligent respect thereunto, as ye tender the king's majesty's pleasure, and will answer for the contrary. And thus we bid your lordship right heartily farewell. From Westm', the thirteenth of March, 1548.

[Wilkins' Concilia, Vol. IV. p. 31. Foxe's Acts and Monuments, pp. 1300, 1. Ed. Lond. 1583.]

Your lordship's loving friends,

THO. CANTERBURY,
R. RICH,
[JOHN RUSSELL,[18]]
EDWARD NORTH,
EDWARD WOOTON,
ANTHONY WINGFIELD,
WILLIAM PETRE,
WIL. SAINT JOHN,
HENRY ARUNDELL.

---

[[14] Late holden. Foxe.]
[[15] As it is agreeable. Id.]
[[16] In the Scriptures. Id.]
[[17] Duties requireth. Id.]
[[18] This name is omitted in Wilkins' Concilia.]

XXXII. *A Letter sent to all those Preachers which the King's Majesty hath licensed to preach, from the Lord Protector's Grace and other of the King's Majesty's most honourable Council, the 13th day of May, in the second year of the reign of our Sovereign Lord, King Edward the VIth.* [1548.]

Wilkins' Concilia, Vol. IV. p. 27. Burnet's Hist. of Ref. Vol. II. pt. ii. App. Book I. No. 24. pp. 189—192. Ed. Oxon. 1829.

AFTER our right hearty commendations: as well for the conservation of the quietness and good order of the king's majesty's subjects, as that they should not by evil and unlearned preachers be brought unto superstition, error, or evil doctrine, or otherwise be made stubborn and disobedient to the king's majesty's godly proceedings, his highness, by our advice, hath thought good to inhibit all manner of preachers, who have not such licence as in the same proclamation is allowed, to preach, or stir the people in open and common preaching of sermons, by any means; that the devout and godly homilies might the better in the mean while sink into his subjects' hearts, and be learned the sooner, the people not being tossed to and fro with seditious and contentious preaching, while every man, according to his zeal, some better some worse, goeth about to set out his own fantasy, and to draw the people to his opinion. Nevertheless it is not his majesty's mind hereby clearly to extinct the lively teaching of the word of God by sermons made after such sort, as for the time the Holy Ghost shall put into the preacher's mind, but that rash, contentious, hot, and undiscreet preachers should be stopped; and that they only which be chosen and elect, be discreet and sober men, should occupy that place, which was made for edification, and not for destruction; for the honour of God, and peace and quietness of conscience to be set forward, not for private glory to be advanced; to appease, to teach, to instruct the people with humility and patience, not to make them contentious and proud; to instil into them their duty to their heads and rulers, obedience to laws and orders, appointed by the superiors who have rule of God, not that every man should run before their heads have appointed them what to do, and that every man should choose his own way in religion: the which thing yet being done of some men, and they being rather provoked thereto by certain preachers, than dehorted from it, it was necessary to set a stay therein. And yet, forasmuch as we have a great confidence and trust in you, that you will not only preach truly and sincerely the word of God, but also will use circumspection and moderation in your preaching, and such godly wisdom as shall be necessary and most convenient for the time and place, we have sent unto you the king's majesty's licence to preach; but yet with this exhortation and admonishment, that in no wise you do stir and provoke the people to any alteration or innovation, other than is already set forth by the king's majesty's injunctions, homilies, and proclamations; but contrarywise, that you do in all your sermons exhort men to that which is at this time more necessary; that is, to the emendation of their own lives, to the observance of the commandments of God, to humility, patience, and obedience to their heads and rulers: comforting the weak, and teaching them the right way, and to flee all erroneous superstitions, as the confidence in pardons, pilgrimages, beads, religious images, and other such of the bishop of Rome's traditions and superstitions, with his usurped power; the which things be here in this realm most justly abolished: and straitly rebuking those, who of an arrogancy and proud hastiness will take upon them to run before they be sent, to go before the rulers, to alter and change things in religion without authority; teaching them to expect and tarry the time which God hath ordained to the revealing of all truth, and not to seek so long blindly and hidlings after it, till they bring all orders into contempt. It is not a private man's duty to alter ceremonies, to innovate orders in the church; nor yet it is not a preacher's part to bring that into contempt and hatred, which the prince doth either allow, or is content to suffer. The king's highness, by our advice, as a prince most earnestly given to the true knowledge of God, and to bring up his people therein, doth not cease to labour and travail by all godly means that his realm might be brought and kept in a most godly and christian order, who only may and ought to do it. Why should a private man, or a preacher, take this royal and kingly office upon him; and not rather, as his duty is, obediently follow himself, and teach likewise others to follow and observe, that which is commanded? What is abolished, taken away, reformed, and commanded, it is easy to see by the acts of parliament, the Injunctions, Proclamations, and Homilies; the which things most earnestly it behoveth all preachers in their sermons to confirm and approve accordingly: in other things which be not yet touched, it behoveth him to think, that either the prince doth allow them, or else suffer them; and in those it is the part of a godly man, not to think himself wiser than the king's majesty and his council, but patiently to expect and to conform himself thereto, and not to intermeddle further to the disturbance of a realm, the disquieting of the king's people, the troubling of men's consciences, and disorder of the king's subjects.

These things we have thought good to admonish you of at this time, because we think you will set the same so forward in your preaching, and so instruct the king's majesty's people accordingly, to the most advancement of the glory of God, and the king's majesty's most godly proceedings, that we do not doubt but much profit shall ensue thereby, and great conformity in the people, the which you do instruct: and so we pray you not to fail to do; and having a special regard to the weakness of the people what they may bear, and what is most convenient for the time, in no case to intermeddle in your sermons, or otherwise, with matters in contention or controversion, except it be to reduce the people in them also to obedience, and following of such orders as the king's majesty hath already set forth, and no others; as the king's majesty's and our trust is in you, and as you tender his highness' will and pleasure, and will answer to the contrary at your peril.

Fare you well.

*Printed at London, June* 1, 1548.

---

XXXIII. *A Proclamation for the Inhibition of all Preachers; the second of Edward the VIth, September* 23.

Fuller's Church Hist. of Britain, Vol. IV. Book vii. Cent. xvi. pp. 32—34. Ed. Oxon. 1845. Wilkins' Concilia, Vol. IV. p. 30.

Whereas of late, by reason of certain controversious and seditious preachers, the king's majesty, moved of tender zeal and love which he hath to the quiet of his subjects, by the advice of the lord protector, and other his highness' council, hath by proclamation inhibited and commanded, that no manner of person, except such as was licensed by his highness, the lord protector, or by the archbishop of Canterbury, should take upon him to preach in any open audience, upon pain in the said proclamation contained, and that upon hope and esperance[1] that those being chosen and elect men should preach and set forth only to the people such things, as should be to God's honour and the benefit of the king's majesty's subjects; yet nevertheless his highness is advertised, that certain of the said preachers so licensed, not regarding such good admonitions as hath been by the lord protector and the rest of the council on his majesty's behalf by letters or otherwise given unto them, have abused the said authority of preaching, and behaved themselves irreverently and without good order in the said preachings, contrary to such good instructions and advertisements as were given unto them; whereby much contention and disorder might rise and ensue in this his majesty's realm: wherefore his highness, minding to see very shortly one uniform order throughout this his realm, and to put an end of all controversies[2] in religion, so far as God shall give[3] grace, (for which cause at this time certain bishops, and notable learned men, by his highness' commandment are congregate,) hath by the advice aforesaid thought good, although certain and many of the said preachers so before licensed have behaved themselves very discreetly and wisely, and to the honour of God and to his highness' contentation; yet at this present, and until such time as the said order shall be set forth generally throughout his majesty's realm, to inhibit, and by these presents doth inhibit[4] generally, as well the said preachers so before licensed, as all manner of persons whosoever they be, to preach in open audience in the pulpit or otherwise, by any sought colour or fraud, to the disobeying of this commandment; to the intent that the whole clergy in this mean space might apply

---

[[1] Assurance. Wilkins.]
[[2] To all controversies. Id.]
[[3] God should give. Id.]
[[4] Do inhibit. Id.]

themselves to prayer to Almighty God for the better achieving of the same most godly intent and purpose; not doubting but that also his loving subjects in the mean time will occupy themselves to God's honour, with due prayer in the church and patient hearing of the godly Homilies heretofore set forth by his highness' Injunctions unto them; and so endeavour themselves that they may be the more ready, with thankful obedience, to receive a most quiet, godly, and uniform order to be had throughout all his said realms and dominions: and therefore hath willed all his loving officers and ministers, as well justices of peace as mayors, sheriffs, bailiffs, constables, or any other his officers, of what estate, degree, or condition soever they be, to be attendant upon this proclamation and commandment, and to see the infringers or breakers thereof to be imprisoned, and his highness or the lord protector's grace, or his majesty's council, to be certified thereof immediately, as they tender his majesty's pleasure, and will answer to the contrary at their peril.

## XXXIV. *Of Unwritten Verities*[1].

Strype's Eccl. Mem. Vol. II. pt. ii. A Repository of Originals, AA. pp. 410—415. Ed. Oxon. 1822. Ex MSS. D. Joh. D. Episc. Elien.

In the day of Pentecost, when the Holy Ghost descended upon the apostles and disciples of Christ, they received such grace and ghostly knowledge, that they had forthwith the gift of the understanding of scripture, to speak in the tongues of all men; and also that, upon whomsoever they laid their hands, the Holy Ghost should descend upon them. And thereupon they by their preaching and good doctrine converted in short time great multitudes of people unto the faith of Christ. And after that, divers blessed men, in strength of the faith, wrote the life, miracles, doctrine, passion, death, and resurrection of our master Christ: but four of those writings were only received by all the whole church of Christ, that is to say, of Matthew, Mark, Luke, and John. And they received them to be of such authority, that it should not be lawful to any man, that would confess Christ, to deny them. And they were called "The four gospels of Christ." And the Epistles of Paul, the Acts of the Apostles, the Epistles that be called canonic, and the Apocalypse, were received to be of like authority as the gospels were. And thus by assent as well of the people as of the clergy, was the new Testament affirmed to be of such authority as it is now taken to be of, and as it is of indeed. So that it is not lawful to deny any thing that it affirmeth, ne to affirm any thing that it denieth. And it is no marvel though it be taken to be of such strength. For it was authorised, when the people that were newly converted to the faith were full of grace and of devotion, replenished with virtues, desiring alway the life to come, and the health of their own souls and of their neighbours.

Then also were blessed bishops, blessed priests, and other blessed persons of the clergy. And what could such men ask of God right wisely, that should be denied them? And who may think but that they and all the people, at the said authorising of the scripture, prayed devoutly for the assistance of the Holy Ghost, that they might have grace to authorise such as should be to his honour, to the increase of his faith, and to the health of the souls of all his people?

The time also that this authorising of the new Testament, and the gathering it together was made, was, as I suppose, the time of the most high and gracious shedding out of the mercy of God into the world, that ever was from the beginning of the world unto this day: and I mean the time that was from the incarnation of Christ unto the said authorising of the new Testament was accomplished. For in part of that time our Lord was here himself in bodily presence, preaching and teaching his laws, gathering and choosing his apostles and disciples, that should teach and preach his laws, when he was gone: which they did not only by word, but also by good examples, that yet remain unto this day. So that all that time may in manner be called "the golden time." And not only the new Testament was then received, but also the old Testament. And by preaching and teaching of these Testaments was the faith of Christ marvellously increased in many countries.

After all this, by a common speaking among the people, the bishops, priests, and

[[1] Vid. supra, p. 5.]

other of the clergy, which were as lanterns unto the people, and the special maintainers of the christian faith, were called "The church," or men of the church: and under the colour of that name "church," many of the clergy in process of time pretended that they might make expositions of scripture, as the universal church of Christ, that is to say, as the whole congregation of christian people might. And thereupon, when covetyse and pride somewhat increased in many of the clergy, they expounded very favourably divers texts of scripture, that sounded to the maintenance of their honour, power, jurisdiction, and riches; and over that take upon them to affirm that they were the "church" that might not err; and that Christ and his apostles had spoken and taught many things that were not expressly in scripture, and that the people were as well bound to love them, and that under like pain, as if they had been expressed in scripture, and called them "Unwritten Verities." Whereof I shall, as for an example, recite part.

First, That Christ after his Maundy, and after he had washen the feet of his apostles, taught them to make holy cream, for ministration of the sacraments; and that they have as full authority to do the same, as if it had been contained in scripture, that Christ had given them power to do it.

That it is a tradition of the apostles, that *images* ought to be set up.

That the apostles ordained that all faithful people should resort to the church of Rome, as to the most high and principal church of all other: and yet it cannot be proved by scripture, ne by anẏ other sufficient authority, that they made any such ordinance.

Also, that the *Creed*, which is commonly and universally used to be said by the common people, was made by the twelve apostles: and though the articles thereof are firmly and stedfastly to be believed of every christian man, as articles sufficiently proved by scripture; yet that they were gathered together by the twelve apostles, and specially that every one of the apostles made one article, as painters shew that they did, cannot be proved by scripture, ne is it not necessary to be believed for our salvation. And though it were but a small offence in the people to believe that it were an article necessary to be believed for our salvation, because the clergy, which be the lanterns and leaders unto the people, do instruct them that it is so; and it is neither against the law of God nor the law of reason but that it may be so; yet it is a great offence to the clergy to affirm for certain the thing that is to themselves uncertain; and therefore it would be reformed for eschewing of offences unto the clergy.

Also, that the people shall pray into the east is not proved by scripture. And yet they say, that by the tradition of the apostles it is to be believed.

Also, that our lady was not born in original sin.

That she was assumpt into heaven, body and soul.

All these, and many others, divers of the clergy call "Unwritten Verities," left in the world by the tradition and relation of the apostles, which (as they say) the people are bound to believe as well as scripture: for they say, that sith no man were bound to believe scripture, but because the church saith, This is scripture; so they say, that in the things before rehearsed, the church witnesseth them to be true; and that the people have assented to them many years; wherefore it is not lawful to doubt at them, ne to deny them. To this reason it may be answered, that if it can be proved by as good and as high authority, that these things were left in the world by the tradition and relation of the apostles, as the authorising of scripture was, that then they are to be believed as verily as scripture: but if they be witnessed to be so by some bishops and priests, and some other of the clergy only, or that they be witnessed to be so by decrees and laws made by bishops of Rome, and by the clergy of Rome, or by opinion of doctors only; then no man is bound to accept them, ne believe them, as they are bound to believe scripture. For scripture, as it is said before, was authorised by the whole church of God, and in the most elect and most gracious time that of likelihood hath been sith the beginning of Christ's church. And if it be said that many of the said opinions have been affirmed and approved by general councils, in whom no error may be presumed; it may be answered, that though the church gathered together in the Holy Ghost may not err in things pertaining to the faith, that yet, forasmuch as some general councils have been gathered, and not by the power of kings and princes that be heads of the church, and that laws have been also made at such general councils, of divers things which have not pertained to the faith, but to the maintenance of the authority or profit of the clergy, or of such articles as are before rehearsed, that they call "Unwritten Verities," which undoubtedly pertain not merely to the faith; that it may therefore be lawfully doubted whether such councils were gathered in the Holy Ghost or not; and whether they erred in their judgments or not. And it is no doubt but that in some general councils they have done so indeed.

And I suppose that there be but few matters more necessary ne more expedient for kings and princes to look upon, than upon these unwritten verities, and of making of laws by the clergy. For if they be suffered to maintain that there be any verities which the people are bound to believe, upon pain of damnation, beside scripture, it will persuade partly an insufficiency in scripture; and thereupon might follow great dangers many ways. And if it were admitted that the clergy might be received to affirm that there be such verities beside scripture, yet they could not prove them. For if they would in proof thereof say, that the apostles first taught those verities, and that they have so continued from one to another unto this day, and shew none other authority thereof but that; then all the saying may as lightly be denied as it was affirmed, and with as high authority. And if they will further attempt to approve it by laws made by the bishops of Rome, and by the clergy at Rome, yea, or by laws and decrees made at general councils; yet these laws and decrees may be lawfully doubted at, as before appeareth. So that they cannot by reason thereof drive any necessity of belief into any person.

Wherefore kings and princes, that have received of God the high power and charge over the people, are bound to prohibit such sayings upon great pains; and not to suffer a belief to be grounded upon things uncertain.

But yet if some of the said articles, that be called "Unwritten Verities," were suffered to continue as things that be more like to be true than otherwise, and no necessity of belief to be derived thereupon; I suppose verily it might well be suffered that they should stand still, not prohibit: as it is of that article, that the twelve apostles made the creed; that it is good to pray into the east; that our lady was not born in original sin; that she was assumpted body and soul. And therefore if it were ordained by kings and princes that no man, upon pain to be taken as a breaker of the quietness of the people, should deny any of the said articles, it were well done to keep unity among the people. But divers realms may order such things diversely, as they shall seem convenient, after the disposition of the people there. For they be but things indifferent to be believed, or not believed, and are nothing like to scripture, to the Articles of the Faith, the Ten Commandments, ne to such other moral learnings, as are merely derived out of scripture: for they must of necessity be believed and obeyed of every christian man. For, after St Paul, ad Ephes. iv., there must be "one God, one faith, and one baptism." But to suffer them to stand as "Unwritten Verities" that may not be denied, and to have their authority only by laws made by the clergy, it seemeth dangerous. For it might cause many of the clergy to esteem more power in the clergy than there is indeed. And that might lift many of them into a higher estimation of themselves than they ought to have: whereby might follow great danger unto the people. For as long as there be disorders in the clergy, it will be hard to bring the people to good order.

And all this that I have touched before may be reformed, without any rebuke to the clergy that now is. For the pretence of such "Unwritten Verities," ne yet of making of laws, to bind kings and princes and their people, ne yet that both powers, that is to say, spiritual and temporal, were in the clergy, began not in the clergy that now is, but in their predecessors.

And as to the said other pretensed Unwritten Verities; that is to say, that all men should resort to Rome, as to the most high and principal church; and that it is a tradition and unwritten verity that images ought to be set up; it were well done that they and such other opinions, whereby pride, covetyse, or vain glory might spring hereafter, were prohibit by authority of the parliament upon great pains. And as to the said Unwritten Verity, that holy cream should be made after the Maundy; it pertaineth only to them that have authority to judge whether it be an Unwritten Verity or not, and to judge also, what is the very authority for making that cream. And therefore I will no further speak of that matter at this time.

## XXXV. 1. *Preface to the Book of Common Prayer*, 1549. 2. *Of Ceremonies.* 3. *Preface to the Ordination Services*, 1550.

### 1. Preface to the Book of Common Prayer[1].

Liturgies of Edw. VI. A.D. 1549. pp. 17—19. Park. Soc. Ed. 1844.

There was never any thing by the wit of man so well devised, or so surely established, which (in continuance of time) hath not been corrupted; as (among other things) it may plainly appear by the common prayers in the church, commonly called Divine Service; the first original and ground whereof if a man would search out by the ancient fathers, he shall find that the same was not ordained, but of a good purpose, and for a great advancement of godliness. For they so ordered the matter, that all the whole bible (or the greatest part thereof) should be read over once in the year; intending thereby, that the clergy, and specially such as were ministers of the congregation, should (by often reading and meditation of God's word) be stirred up to godliness themselves, and be more able also to exhort other by wholesome doctrine, and to confute them that were adversaries to the truth: and further, that the people, by daily hearing of holy scripture read in the church, should continually profit more and more in the knowledge of God, and be the more inflamed with the love of his true religion. But these many years passed, this godly and decent order of the ancient fathers hath been so altered, broken, and neglected, by planting in uncertain stories, legends, responds, verses, vain repetitions, commemorations, and synodals, that commonly, when any book of the bible was begun, before three or four chapters were read out, all the rest were unread. And in this sort, the book of Esaie was begun in Advent, and the book of Genesis in Septuagesima; but they were only begun, and never read through. After a like sort were other books of holy scripture used. And moreover, whereas St Paul would have such language spoken to the people in the church, as they might understand and have profit by hearing the same; the service in this church of England (these many years) hath been read in Latin to the people, which they understood not; so that they have heard with their ears only, and their hearts, spirit, and mind, have not been edified thereby. And furthermore, notwithstanding that the ancient fathers had divided the psalms into seven portions, whereof every one was called a nocturn; now of late time a few of them have been daily said (and oft repeated) and the rest utterly omitted. Moreover, the number and hardness of the rules called the pie, and the manifold changings of the service, was the cause, that to turn the book only was so hard and intricate a matter, that many times there was more business to find out what should be read, than to read it when it was found out.

These inconveniences therefore considered, here is set forth such an order, whereby the same shall be redressed. And for a readiness in this matter, here is drawn out a calendar for that purpose, which is plain and easy to be understanded; wherein (so much as may be) the reading of holy scripture is so set forth, that all things shall be done in order, without breaking one piece thereof from another. For this cause be cut off anthems, responds, invitatories, and such like things as did break the continual course of the reading of the scripture. Yet because there is no remedy, but that of necessity there must be some rules, therefore certain rules are here set forth; which, as they be few in number, so they be plain and easy to be understanded. So that here you have an order for prayer (as touching the reading of holy scripture) much agreeable to the mind and purpose of the old fathers, and a great deal more profitable and commodious than that which of late was used. It is more profitable, because here are left out many things, whereof some be untrue, some uncertain, some vain and superstitious; and is ordained nothing to be read but the very pure word of God, the holy scriptures, or that which is evidently grounded upon the same; and that in such a language and order as is most easy and plain for the understanding both of the readers and hearers. It is also more commodious, both for the shortness thereof and for the plainness of the order, and for that the rules be few and easy. Furthermore, by this order the curates shall need none other books for their public

---

[[1] This Preface, as well as that to the form and manner of making and consecrating archbishops, &c. (vid. p. 519, infra) are attributed to Cranmer by Bale. It is doubtful, however, whether he wrote them, though they had his approbation and sanction.]

service, but this book and the bible: by the means whereof the people shall not be at so great charge for books as in time past they have been.

And where heretofore there hath been great diversity in saying and singing in churches within this realm; some following Salisbury use, some Hereford use, some the use of Bangor, some of York, and some of Lincoln; now from henceforth all the whole realm shall have but one use. And if any would judge this way more painful, because that all things must be read upon the book, whereas before, by the reason of so often repetition, they could say many things by heart; if those men will weigh their labour with the profit in knowledge which daily they shall obtain by reading upon the book, they will not refuse the pain in consideration of the great profit that shall ensue thereof.

And forsomuch as nothing can, almost, be so plainly set forth, but doubts may rise in the use and practising of the same: to appease all such diversity, (if any arise,) and for the resolution of all doubts concerning the manner how to understand, do, and execute the things contained in this book, the parties that so doubt, or diversely take anything, shall alway resort to the bishop of the diocese, who by his discretion shall take order for the quieting and appeasing of the same; so that the same order be not contrary to anything contained in this book.

¶ Though it be appointed in the afore written Preface, that all things shall be read and sung in the church in the English tongue, to the end that the congregation may be thereby edified: yet it is not meant but when men say matins and evensong privately, they may say the same in any language that they themselves do understand: neither that any man shall be bound to the saying of them, but such as from time to time, in cathedral and collegiate churches, parish churches, and chapels to the same annexed, shall serve the congregation.

## 2. Of Ceremonies.

### Why some be abolished and some retained.

Liturgies of Edw. VI. A.D. 1549. pp. 155—157. Park. Soc. Ed. 1844.

Of such ceremonies as be used in the church, and have had their beginning by the institution of man, some at the first were of godly intent and purpose devised, and yet at length turned to vanity and superstition: some entered into the church by undiscreet devotion, and such a zeal as was without knowledge; and for because they were winked at in the beginning, they grew daily to more and more abuses, which not only for their unprofitableness, but also because they have much blinded the people and obscured the glory of God, are worthy to be cut away and clean rejected. Other there be, which although they have been devised by man, yet it is thought good to reserve them still, as well for a decent order in the church, (for the which they were first devised,) as because they pertain to edification, whereunto all things done in the church (as the apostle teacheth) ought to be referred. And although the keeping or omitting of a ceremony (in itself considered) is but a small thing; yet the wilful and contemptuous transgression and breaking of a common order and discipline is no small offence before God. "Let all things be done among you" (saith St Paul) "in a seemly and due order." The appointment of the which order pertaineth not to private men: therefore no man ought to take in hand nor presume to appoint or alter any public or common order in Christ's church, except he be lawfully called and authorised thereunto. And whereas in this our time the minds of men be so diverse, that some think it a great matter of conscience to depart from a piece of the least of their ceremonies (they be so addicted to their old customs), and again on the other side, some be so new fangle that they would innovate all thing, and so do despise the old, that nothing can like them but that is new: it was thought expedient not so much to have respect how to please and satisfy either of these parties, as how to please God, and profit them both. And yet, lest any man should be offended (whom good reason might satisfy), here be certain causes rendered why some of the accustomed ceremonies be put away, and some be retained and kept still.

Some are put away, because the great excess and multitude of them hath so increased in these latter days, that the burden of them was intolerable: whereof Saint Augustine in his time complained, that they were grown to such a number, that the state of christian people was in worse case (concerning that matter) than were the Jews. And he counselled that such yoke and burden should be taken away, as time would serve quietly to do it. But what would St Augustine have said, if he had seen the ceremonies of late days used among us, whereunto the multitude used in his time was not to be compared? This our excessive multitude of ceremonies was so great, and many of them so dark, that they did more confound and darken, than declare and set forth Christ's benefits unto us. And besides this, Christ's gospel is not a ceremonial law (as much of Moses' law was); but it is a religion to serve God, not in bondage of the figure or shadow, but in the freedom of spirit, being content only with those ceremonies which do serve to a decent order and godly discipline, and such as be apt to stir up the dull mind of man to the remembrance of his duty to God by some notable and special signification, whereby he might be edified.

¶ Furthermore, the most weighty cause of the abolishment of certain ceremonies was, that they were so far abused, partly by the superstitious blindness of the rude and unlearned, and partly by the insatiable avarice of such as sought more their own lucre than the glory of God; that the abuses could not well be taken away, the thing remaining still. But now as concerning those persons, which peradventure will be offended for that some of the old ceremonies are retained still: if they consider, that without some ceremonies it is not possible to keep any order or quiet discipline in the church, they shall easily perceive just cause to reform their judgments. And if they think much that any of the old do remain, and would rather have all devised anew: then such men (granting some ceremonies convenient to be had,) surely where the old may be well used, there they cannot reasonably reprove the old (only for their age) without bewraying of their own folly. For in such a case they ought rather to have reverence unto them for their antiquity, if they will declare themselves to be more studious of unity and concord, than of innovations and new fangleness; which (as much as may be with the true setting forth of Christ's religion) is always to be eschewed. Furthermore, such shall have no just cause with the ceremonies reserved to be offended: for as those be taken away which were most abused, and did burden men's consciences without any cause; so the other that remain are retained for a discipline and order, which (upon just causes) may be altered and changed, and therefore are not to be esteemed equal with God's law. And moreover they be neither dark nor dumb ceremonies, but are so set forth that every man may understand what they do mean, and to what use they do serve. So that it is not like that they, in time to come, should be abused as the other have been. And in these all our doings we condemn no other nations, nor prescribe any thing but to our own people only. For we think it convenient that every country should use such ceremonies as they shall think best to the setting forth of God's honour and glory, and to the reducing of the people to a most perfect and godly living, without error or superstition; and that they should put away other things, which from time to time they perceive to be most abused, as in men's ordinances it often chanceth diversely in diverse countries.

3. Preface [to "The Form and Manner of making and consecrating of Archbishops, Bishops, Priests, and Deacons." Printed by Grafton, March 1549-50.]

Liturgy of Edw. VI. A.D. 1549. p. 161. Park. Soc. Ed. 1844.

It is evident unto all men diligently reading holy scripture and ancient authors, that from the apostles' time there hath been these orders of ministers in Christ's church; bishops, priests, and deacons: which offices were evermore had in such reverent estimation, that no man, by his own private authority, might presume to execute any of them, except he were first called, tried, examined, and known to have such qualities as were requisite for the same; and also by public prayer, with imposition of hands, approved and admitted thereunto. And therefore, to the intent these orders should be continued, and reverently used and esteemed, in this church of England, it is requisite that no man (not being at this present bishop, priest, nor deacon) shall execute any of them, except he be called, tried, examined, and admitted, according to the form hereafter following. And none shall be admitted a deacon, except he be twenty-one years of age at the least. And every man which is to be admitted a priest, shall be full twenty-four years old. And every man which is to be consecrated a bishop, shall be fully thirty years of age.

And the bishop knowing, either by himself or by sufficient testimony, any person to be a man of virtuous conversation, and without crime, and after examination and trial, finding him learned in the Latin tongue, and sufficiently instructed in holy scripture, may upon a Sunday or holy day, in the face of the church, admit him a deacon, in such manner and form as hereafter followeth.

---

## XXXVI. *Three Letters from the Lords of the Council at Windsor to the Lords of the Council in London*[1].

### 1.

Stow's Annals, pp. 597, 8. Ed. Lond. 1516.

My lords, we commend us most heartily unto you: and where the king's majesty was informed that you were assembled in such sort as ye do now remain there, was advised by us, and such other of his council as were here about his person, to send master secretary Peter unto you with such a message, as whereby might have ensued the surety of his majesty's person, with preservation of his realm and subjects, and the quiet both of us and yourselves, as master secretary can declare unto you: his majesty and we of his council here do not a little marvel that you stay still with you the said master secretary; and have not (as it were) vouchsafed to send an answer to his majesty, neither by him, nor yet by any other. And for ourselves we do much more marvel, and are right sorry, as we and you have good cause to be, to see the manner of your doings, bent with force and violence to bring the king's majesty and us to those extremities, which as we do intend, if you will take none other way but violence, to defend us, as nature and our allegiance doth bind us, to extremity of death, and put it unto God's hands, who giveth victory as pleaseth him; so if our reasonable conditions and offers will take no place, as hitherto none hath been signified unto us from you, nor we do not understand what ye do require or seek, nor what ye do mean; and that ye speak no hurt of the king's majesty's person: as touching all other private matters, to avoid the effusion of christian blood, and to preserve the king's majesty's person, his realm, and subjects, ye shall find us agreeable to any reasonable conditions that you will require; for we do esteem the king's wealth and tranquillity of the realm more than all other worldly things, yea, more than our own lives. Thus praying you to send us determinate answer herein by master secretary Peter, or, if ye will not let him go, by this bearer, we beseech God to give both you and us grace to determine this matter as may be to God's honour, the preservation of the king, and the quiet of us all; which may be, if the fault be not in you. And so we bid you heartily farewell. From the king's majesty's castle of Windsor, the 7th day of October, 1549.

### 2.

Stow's Annals, pp. 598, 9. Ed. Lond. 1516. Todd's Life of Abp. Cranmer, Vol. II. p. 157.

After our hearty commendations unto your good lordships: we have received from the same a letter by master Hunnings, dated at London yesterday; whereby you do us to understand the causes of your assembly there; and, charging the lord protector with the manner of government, require that he withdraw himself from the king's majesty, disperse the force which he hath levied, and be contented to be ordered according to justice and reason; and so you will gladly commune with us, as touching the surety of the king's majesty's person, and the order of all other things, with such conformity on that behalf as appertaineth; and otherwise you must (as you write) make other account of us than you trust to have cause, and burden (of) us, if things come to extremities.

---

[1 Vid. Burnet's Hist. of the Reformation, Vol. II. Part II. App. Book i. No. 41, p. 261. &c. Ed. Oxon. 1829. Stow's Annals, pp. 597, 8. Ed. Lond. 1516. Ellis' Original Letters, 1st ser. Letter CLXXI. Vol. II. p. 171, &c. "The second of them has been attributed wholly to the pen of Cranmer by Mr Turner (Hist. Edw. VI. p. 176) and Mr Todd, who affirm that 'it breathes all his spirit in its genuine nature.' Strype also seems to have been of the same opinion." Jenkyns, Remains of Abp. Cranmer, Vol. IV. p. 369, *n.* d.]

To the first point, we verily believe, that as bruits, rumours, and reports that your lordships intended the destruction of the lord protector, induced his grace to fly to the defence which he hath assembled, excuse your lordships, [who,] hearing that his grace intended the like destruction towards you, have been moved to do as you have done; so as for lack of understanding one of another's right meaning things be grown to such extremities, as if the saving of the king's majesty's person and the common weal take not more place in his grace and your lordships than private respect or affairs, you see, we doubt not, as we do, that both our king, our country, and also ourselves shall, as verily as God is God, be utterly destroyed and cast away. Wherefore might it please you, for the tender passion of Jesus Christ, use your wisdom, and temper your determination in such sort, as no blood be shed, nor cruelty used, neither of his grace's part nor of your lordships': for, if it come to the point, both you and we are like to see presently with our eyes that which every vein of all our hearts will bleed to behold.

Wherefore, as true subjects to the king's majesty, as faithful counsellors, though unworthy counsellors, to his majesty and his realm, and as lamentable petitioners, we beseech your lordships most humbly, and from the bottom of our hearts, to take pity of the king and the realm, whereof you be principal members, and to set apart *summum jus*, and to use at this time *tum bonum et æquum:* and think not that this is written for any private fear or other respect of ourselves, but for that undoubtedly we hear and know more of this point, with your favours, than you there do know: yea, and howsoever it shall please you to account of us, we are true men to God, to the king, to the realm, and so will we live and die wheresoever we be; and in respect of them three esteem little any other person or thing, no, not our own lives: and having clear consciences, as to whatsoever ill may follow upon the use of extremity there, that neither now is nor shall be found fault in us; and so quieting ourselves we rest.

Now to that you would have the lord protector to do for his part, his grace and we have communed herein; and much to our comforts, and yours also, if it shall like you to weigh the case: who is contented, if you will again for your parts use equity, to put that now in execution which many times he hath declared by his words; that is to say, so as the king and the realm may be otherwise well served, he passeth little for the place he now hath. Mary, he doth consider, that by the king's majesty, with all your advices and the consents of the nobles of the realm, he was called to the place, (as appeareth in writing under his majesty's great seal and sign; whereunto your own hands also, and ours, with all others the lords of the upper house in the parliament are subscribed;) and therefore in violent sort to be thus thrust out against his will, he thinketh it no treasonable. He is here with the king's person, where his place is to be; and we be here with him, we trust in God, for the good service of the king, the weal of the realm, and the good acquitting both of his grace and of your lordships; which we most heartily desire, and see such hope here thereof, as, if you be not too sore bent upon the extremities, as is reported, and as equity can take no place, my lord's grace may live in quiet, and the king's majesty's affairs maintained in such order as by his majesty's counsellors shall be thought convenient.

Mary, to put himself simply into your hands, having heard as both we and he have, without first knowledge upon what conditions, it is not reasonable. Life is sweet, my lords, and they say you seek his blood and his death: which if you do, and may have him otherwise conformable to reason, and by extremity drive him to seek extremity again, the blood of him and others that shall die on both sides innocently, shall be by God justly required at your hands. And when peradventure you would have him again, upon occasion of service, you shall forthink to have lost him. Wherefore, good my lords, we beseech you again and again, if you have conceived any such determination, to put it out of your heads, and incline your hearts to kindness and humanity; remembering that he hath never been cruel to any of you, and why should you be cruel to him? as we trust you be not, whatsoever hath been said, but will shew yourselves as conformable for your parts, as his grace is contented, for the zeal he beareth to the king and the realm, to be for his part, as this bearer, sir Phillip Hobie, will declare unto you; to whom we pray you to give credit, and to return him hither again with answer hereof. And thus, beseeching the living God to direct your hearts to the making of a quiet end of these terrible tumults, we bid your lordships most heartily well to fare. From the king's majesty's castle of Windsor, the eight of October, 1549.

3.

Cott. MSS. Calig. B. vii. f. 412. British Museum. Original. Ellis' Original Letters, 1st series, Let. clxxiv. Vol. II. pp. 171—3. Burnet's Hist. of Reformat. Vol. II. pt. ii. App. Book I. No. 45. pp. 267, 8. Ed. Oxon. 1829.

It may like your good lordships, with our most hearty commendations, to understand, that this morning sir Phillip Hobbey hath, according to the charge given to him by your lordships, presented your letters to the king's majesty, in the presence of us and all the rest of his majesty's good servants here; which was there read openly, and also the others to them of the chamber and of the household, much to their comforts, and ours also; and according to the tenours of the same, we will not fail to endeavour ourselves accordingly.

Now touching the marvel of your lordships, both of that we would suffer the duke of Somerset's men to guard the king's majesty's person, and also of our often repeating the word cruel... although we doubt not but that your lordships hath been thoroughly informed of our estates here, and upon what occasion the one hath been suffered, and the other proceeded; yet at our convening together (which may be when and where please you) we will, and are able to make your lordships such an account, as wherewith we doubt not you will be satisfied, if you think good to require it of us. And for because this bearer, Mr Hobbey, can particularly inform your lordships of the whole discourse of all things here, we remit the report of all other things to him; saving that we desire to be advertised, with as much speed as you shall think good, whether the king's majesty shall come forthwith thither, or remain still here, and that some of your lordships would take pain to come hither forthwith. For the which purpose, I the comptroller will cause three of the best chambers in the great court to be hanged and made ready. Thus, thanking God that all things be so well acquieted, we commit your lordships to his tuition. From Windsor, the xth of October, 1549.

Your lordship's assured loving friends,

T. CANT. WILLIAM PAGET.

T. SMITH.

*To our very good lords and others of the king's majesty's privy council at London.*

---

## XXXVII. *The king's Order, and the Mandate of the Archbishop of Canterbury, for bringing in Popish Rituals.*

Wilkins' Concilia, Vol. IV. p. 37. Ex Reg. Cran. f. 25. b.

THOMAS, permissione divina Cantuariensis archiepiscopus, totius Angliæ primas et metropolitanus, per illustrissimum et invictissimum in Christo principem et dominum nostrum, dominum Edvardum Sextum, Dei gratia Angliæ, Franciæ, Hiberniæ regem, &c. ad infrascripta sufficienter et legitime fulcitus, dilecto filio archidiacono nostro Cantuariensi, seu ejus officiali, salutem, gratiam, et benedictionem. Literas missivas dicti metuendissimi domini nostri regis signatas, et nominibus honorabilium virorum dominorum consiliariorum suorum in calce earundem subscriptas, signeto suo obsignatas, nobis inscriptas et datas, nuper cum honore et reverentia debitis accepimus, tenorem subsequentem complectentes[1]:

Burnet's Hist. of Ref. Vol. II. pt. ii. App. Book I. No. 47. pp. 272, 3. Ed. Oxon. 1829.

By the king. Right reverend father in God, right trusty and well-beloved, we greet you well. And whereas the book entitled, "The Book of Common Prayers and administration of the Sacraments and other Rites and Ceremonies of the Church, after the use of the Church of England," was agreed upon and set forth by act of parliament, and by the same act commanded to be used of all persons within this our realm; yet nevertheless we are informed, that divers unquiet and evil-disposed persons, sithence the apprehension of the duke of Somerset, have noised and bruited abroad that they should have again their old Latin service, their conjured bread and water, with such like vain and superstitious ceremonies[2], as though the setting forth of the said book had been the

---

[[1] Vid. Strype's Eccl. Mem. Vol. II. pp. 329—334. Ed. Oxon. 1822.]
[[2] Superfluous ceremonies. Burnet.]

only act of the said duke: we therefore, by the advice of the body and state of our privy council, not only considering the said book to be our own act, and the act of the whole state of our realm assembled together in parliament, but also the same to be grounded upon holy scripture, agreeable to the order of the primitive church and much to the re-edifying of our subjects, to put away all such vain expectation of having the public service, the administration of the sacraments, and other rites and ceremonies again in the Latin tongue; which were but a preferment of ignorance to knowledge, and darkness to light, and a preparation to bring in papistry and superstition again; have thought good, by the advice of the aforesaid, to require and nevertheless straitly to charge and command you, that, immediately upon the sight hereof[3], you do command the dean and prebendaries of the cathedral church, the parson, vicar, or curate, and church-wardens of every parish within your diocese, to bring and deliver unto you or your deputy, any of them for their church and parish, at such convenient place as you shall appoint, all antiphoners, missals, grayles, processionals, manuals, legends, pies, portases, journals, and ordinals, after the use of Sarum, Lincoln, York, or any other private use; and all other books of service, the keeping whereof should be a let to the usage of the said book of Common Prayers: and that you take the same books into your hands, or into the hands of your deputy, and them so deface and abolish, that they never after may serve either to any such use as they were provided for, or be at any time a let to that godly and uniform order which by a common consent is now set forth: and if you shall find any persons stubborn or disobedient, in not bringing in the said books, according to the tenour of these our letters, that then ye commit the said person to ward, unto such time as you have certified us of his misbehaviour. And we will and command you, that you also search, or cause search to be made, from time to time, whether any book be withdrawn or hid, contrary to the tenour of these our letters; and the same book to receive into your hands, and to use as[4] in these our letters we have appointed.

And furthermore, whereas it is come to our knowledge, that divers froward and obstinate persons do refuse to pay towards the finding of bread and wine for the holy communion, according to the order prescribed by the said book, by reason whereof the holy communion is many times omitted upon the Sunday; these are to will and command you to convent such obstinate persons before you, and them to admonish and command to keep the order prescribed in the said book; and if any shall refuse so to do, to punish them by suspension, excommunication, or other censures of the church. Fail you not thus to do, as you will avoid our displeasure. Given under our signet, at our palace of Westminster, the 25th of December, the third year of our reign. By the king. Inscriptio hæc est: To the most reverend father in God, our right trusty and well-beloved counsellor, the archbishop of Canterbury. In calce hæc nomina habentur, Thomas Cantuarien', R. Ryche, Canc', Wm. Seint John, J. Russell, H. Dorsett, W. Northampton.

Nos vero affectantes ex animo domini nostri regis literis et mandatis obtemperare, volentesque pro nostro erga regiam celsitudinem officio in demandatis negotiis omnem nostram curam et solertem adhibere diligentiam, vobis pro parte suæ majestatis districte præcipiendo mandamus harum serie, quatenus receptis præsentibus, cum omni qua poteritis celeritate et diligentia maturis, dilectos filios nostros decanum, canonicos, et præbendarios ecclesiæ Christi Cantuarien', necnon rectores, vicarios, curatos, plebanos, ac syndicos et iconicos[5] quarumcunque ecclesiarum parochialium nostræ diœcescos Canturien' moneatis, hortemini, et præcipiendo mandetis, quatenus ipsi et eorum quilibet vel singuli omnes et singulos libros in eisdem literis regiis specifice nominatos nobis, aut nostro in hac parte commissario vel deputato infra palatium nostrum Cantuarien', infra novem dies monitionem et intimationem vestras eis fiendas proxime sequentes, realiter afferant, adducant, et penes nos vel nostrum deputatum hujuscemodi relinquant et deponant; ceteraque omnia et singula in dictis literis descripta perimpleant, exequantur, et sedulo fieri curent, quatenus eos et eorum quemlibet contingunt vel concernunt; sicque vos et vestrum alter sedulo exequatur, sincere perimpleat, et diligenter obediat, quæ ad vestram in hac parte functionem pro congrua executione literarum prædictarum dignos-

[[3] The receipt hereof. Burnet.] [[4] To use all in. Id.] [[5] "Forte, œconomos." Wilkins.]

cuntur pertinere, omnibus mora, dilatione, conniventia, et fuco penitus remotis, prout eidem domino nostro regi sub tui et deputati tui periculo incumbente obtemperare et respondere velitis, et vult vestrum alter. Et quid in hac parte feceritis, et exequi curaveritis, id totum et omne nobis quam citissime significatum iri non postponatis. Dat' in manerio nostro de Lambithe, decimo quarto die mensis Februarii, anno Domini 1549. [1550.] et regni dicti invictissimi in Christo principis et domini nostri Edwardi Sexti quarto, et nostræ consecrationis decimo septimo.

---

## XXXVIII. *The Council's Letter to Bp. Ridley to take down Altars, and place Communion Tables in their stead.*

Foxe's Acts and Monuments, p. 727. Ed. 1563. Wilkins' Concilia, Vol. IV. p. 65. Heylyn's Eccles. Restaur. p. 96. Ed. Lond. 1670.

RIGHT reverend father in God, right trusty and well-beloved, we greet you well. And where it is come[1] to our knowledge that, being the altars within the more part of the churches of this realm[2] already upon good[3] and godly considerations taken down, there doth yet remain altars standing in divers others churches, by occasion whereof much variance and contention ariseth among sundry of our subjects, which, if good foresight were not had, might perchance engender great hurt and inconvenience; we let you wit, that minding to have all occasion[4] of contention taken away, which many times groweth by those and such like diversities, and considering that, amongst other things belonging to our royal office and cure[5], we do account the greatest to be, to maintain the common quiet of our realm; we have thought good by the advice of our council to require you, and nevertheless specially to charge and command you, for the avoiding of all matters of further contention and strife about the standing or taking away of the said altars, to give substantial order throughout all your diocese, that with all diligence all the altars in every church or chapel, as well in places exempted, as not exempted, within your said diocese, be taken down, and in the stead of them a table to be set up in some convenient part of the chancel, within every such church or chapel, to serve for the ministration of the blessed communion. And to the intent the same may be done without the offence of such our loving subjects as be not yet so well persuaded in that behalf as we would[6] wish, we send unto you herewith certain considerations[7] gathered and collected, that make for the purpose; the which, and such other as you shall think meet to be set forth to persuade the weak to embrace our proceedings in this part, we pray you cause to be declared to the people by some discreet preachers, in such places as you shall think meet, before the taking down of the said altars; so as both the weak consciences of others may be instructed and satisfied as much as may be, and this our pleasure the more quietly executed. For the better doing whereof, we require you to open the foresaid considerations in that our cathedral church in your own person, if you conveniently may, or otherwise by your chancellor, or some other grave[8] preacher, both there and in such other market towns and most notable places of your diocese, as you may think most requisite.

*Given under our signet, at our place of Westminster, the 24th day of November, the fourth year of our reign.*

E. Somerset, Thomas Cant., W. Wiltsher, Jhon Warwike, J. Bedford, W. Northe, E. Clinton, H. Wentworth, T. Ely.

---

## XXXIX. *Reasons why the Lord's Board should rather be after the form of a Table than of an Altar.*

### *The first reason.*

Foxe's Acts and Monuments, p. 1331. Ed. Lond. 1583.

FIRST, the form of a table shall more move the simple from the superstitious opinions of the Popish mass unto the right use of the Lord's Supper. For the use of an altar is to

[1 Whereas it is come. Heylyn and Wilkins.]
[2 Of the realm. Wilkins.]
[3 Realm, upon good. Heylyn and Wilkins.]
[4 All occasions. Heylyn.]
[5 Care. Heylyn and Wilkins.]
[6 Could. Id.]
[7 Vid. No. XXXIX. infra.]
[8 Or other grave. Heylyn and Wilkins.]

make sacrifice upon it: the use of a table is to serve for men to eat upon. Now when we come unto the Lord's board, what do we come for? To sacrifice Christ again, and to crucify him again; or to feed upon him that was once only crucified and offered up for us? If we come to feed upon him, spiritually to eat his body, and spiritually to drink his blood, which is the true use of the Lord's Supper; then no man can deny but the form of a table is more meet for the Lord's board than the form of an altar.

Considerations and reasons why the table were more convenient in the church than the altar.

*The second reason.*

*Item,* whereas it is said the Book of Common Prayer maketh mention of an altar; wherefore it is not lawful to abolish that which that book alloweth; to this it is thus answered: The Book of Common Prayer calleth the thing whereupon the Lord's Supper is ministered indifferently a table, an altar, or the Lord's board, without prescription of any form thereof, either of a table or of an altar: so that whether the Lord's board have the form of an altar, or of a table, the book of Common Prayer calleth it both an altar and a table. For, as it calleth it an altar, whereupon the Lord's Supper is ministered, a table, and the Lord's board; so it calleth the table where the holy Communion is distributed, with lauds and thanksgiving unto the Lord, an altar; for that there is offered the same sacrifice of praise and thanksgiving. And thus it appeareth that here is nothing either said or meant contrary to the book of Common Prayer.

The second reason. Answer to certain cavillers which take hold of the term of the altar in the king's book.

The table how it may be called an altar, and in what respect.

*The third reason.*

*Thirdly,* the Popish opinion of mass was, that it might not be celebrated but upon an altar, or at the least upon a super-altar, to supply the fault of the altar, which must have had his prints and characters; or else it was thought that the thing was not lawfully done. But this superstitious opinion is more holden in the minds of the simple and ignorant by the form of an altar than of a table: wherefore it is more meet, for the abolishment of this superstitious opinion, to have the Lord's board after the form of a table than of an altar.

The third reason. This reason, for taking away the superstitious opinion, serveth also as well for the abolishing of other things more besides altars, &c.

*The fourth reason.*

*Fourthly,* the form of an altar was ordained for the sacrifices of the law, and therefore the altar in Greek is called *θυσιαστήριον*, *quasi sacrificii locus.* But now both the law and the sacrifices thereof do cease: wherefore the form of the altar used in the law ought to cease withal.

The fourth reason. The name of an altar, how it is derived, and what it signifieth.

*The fifth reason.*

*Fifthly,* Christ did institute the sacrament of his body and blood at his last supper at a table, and not at an altar, as it appeareth manifestly by the three Evangelists. And Saint Paul calleth the coming to the holy Communion the coming unto the Lord's Supper. And also it is not read, that any of the Apostles or the primitive Church did ever use any altar in ministration of the holy Communion.

The fifth reason. Christ used a table, and not an altar. The altar never used among the apostles.

Wherefore, seeing the form of a table is more agreeable with Christ's institution, and with the usage of the Apostles and of the primitive Church, than the form of an altar, therefore the form of a table is rather to be used than the form of an altar in the administration of the holy Communion.

*The sixth reason.*

*Finally,* it is said in the preface of the Book of Common Prayer, that if any doubt do arise in the use and practising of the same book; to appease all such diversity, the matter shall be referred unto the Bishop of the diocese, who by his discretion shall take order for the quieting and appeasing of the same, so that the same order be not contrary unto anything contained in that book.

The sixth reason.

### XL. *Letter from the Council to the Princess Mary*[1].

Foxe's Acts and Monuments, &c. p. 1335. Ed. 1583.

AFTER our due commendations to your grace. By your letters to us, as an answer to ours, touching certain process against two of your chaplains, for saying mass against the law and statute of the realm, we perceive both the offence of your chaplains is otherwise excused than the matter may bear, and also our good wills otherwise misconstrued than we looked for. And for the first part, where your greatest reason for to excuse the offence of a law is a promise made to the emperor's majesty; whereof you write, that first some of us be witnesses, next that the ambassador for the emperor declared the same unto you, and lastly, that the same promise was affirmed to you before the king's majesty at your last being with him: we have thought convenient to repeat the matter from the beginning, as it hath hitherto proceeded; whereupon it shall appear how evidently your chaplains hath offended the law, and you also mistaken the promise. The promise is but one in itself, but by times thrice (as you say) repeated. Of which times, the first is chiefly to be considered; for upon that do the other two depend. It is very true the emperor made request to the king's majesty, that you might have liberty to use the mass in your house, and to be as it were exempted from the danger of the statute. To which request divers good reasons were made, containing the discommodities that should follow the grant thereof, and means devised, rather to persuade you to obey and receive the general and godly reformation of the whole realm, than by a private fancy to prejudice a common order. But yet, upon earnest desire and entreaty made in the emperor's name, thus much was granted, that for his sake and your own also it should be suffered and winked at, if you had the private mass used in your own closet for a season, until you might be better informed, (whereof was some hope,) having only with you a few of your own chamber, so that for all the rest of your household the service of the realm should be used, and none other; further than this the promise exceeded not. And truly such a matter it then seemed to some of us, as indeed it was, that well might the emperor have required of the king's majesty a matter of more profit, but of more weight or difficulty to be granted his majesty could not. After this grant in words, there was by the ambassador now dead oftentimes desired some writing, as a testimony of the same. But that was ever denied, not because we meant to break the promise, as it was made, but because there was a daily hope of your reformation.

Now to the second time, you say the emperor's ambassador's declaration made mention of a promise to you. It might well so be, but we think no otherwise than as it appeareth before written. If it were, his fault it was to declare more than he heard; ours it may not be, that deny not what we have said. As for the last time, when you were with the king's majesty, the same some of us (whom by these words your letter noteth) do well remember, that no other thing was granted to you in this matter, but as the first promise was made to the emperor: at which time you had too many arguments made to approve the proceedings of the king's majesty, and to condemn the abuse of the mass, to think that where the private mass was judged ungodly, there you should have authority and ground to use it. About the same time the ambassador made means to have some testimony of the promise under the great seal; and, that not heard, to have it but by a letter; and that also was not only denied, but divers good reasons [alleged,] that he should think it denied with reason, and so to be contented with an answer. It was told him, in reducing that which was commonly called the mass to the order of the primitive church and the institution of Christ, the king's majesty and his whole realm had their consciences well quieted; against the which if any thing should be willingly committed, the same should be taken as an offence to God, and a very sin against a truth known. Wherefore to license by open act such a deed, in the conscience of the king's majesty and his realm were even a sin against God. The most that might herein be borne was, that the king's majesty might, upon hope of your grace's reconciliation, suspend the execution of his law, so that you would use the licence as it was first granted.

[[1] "This excellent letter, which I suppose was drawn by the pen of Abp. Cranmer, is extant in Foxe." Strype's Eccl. Mem. Vol. II. p. 450. Ed. Oxon. 1822. "The council writ a long letter, which, being in the style of a churchman, seems to have been penned either by Cranmer or Ridley." Burnet's Hist. of Reformat. Vol. II. p. 357. Vid. Foxe's Acts and Monuments, ubi supra.]

Whatsoever the ambassador hath said to others, he had no other manner grant from us; nor, having it thus granted, could allege any reason against it. And where in your letter your grace noteth us as breakers of the promise made to the emperor, it shall appear who hath broken the promise; whether we that have suffered more than we licensed, or you that have transgressed that was granted. Now therefore we pray your grace confer the doing of your chaplains with every point of the premises; and if the same cannot be excused, then think also how long the law hath been spared. If it prick our consciences somewhat, that so much should be used as by the promise you may claim, how much more should it grieve us to license more than you can claim? And yet could we be content to bear great burden to satisfy your grace, if the burden pressed not our consciences: whereof we must say as the apostle said, *Gloriatio nostra est hæc, testimonium conscientiæ nostræ.*

For the other part of your grace's letter, by the which we see you misconstrue our good wills in writing to you; howsoever the law had proceeded against your chaplains, our order in sending to you was to be liked, and therein truly had we special regard of your grace's degree and estate. And because the law of itself respecteth not persons, we thought to give respect to you, first signifying to you what the law required, before it should be executed; that, being warned, your grace might either think no strangeness in the execution, or for an example of obedience cause it to be executed yourself. Others we see perplexed with suddenness of matters; your grace we would not have unwarned, to think any thing done on a sudden. Truly we thought it more commendable for your grace to help the execution of a law, than to help the offence of one condemned by law. And in giving you knowledge what the king's laws required, we looked for help in the execution by you, the king's majesty's sister. The greater personage your grace is, the nigher to the king, so much more ought your example to further the laws. For which cause it hath been called a good commonwealth, where the people obeyed the higher estates, and they obeyed the laws. As nature hath joined your grace to the king's majesty to love him most entirely, so hath reason and law subdued you to obey him willingly. The one and the other we doubt not but your grace remembereth: and as they both be joined together in you, his majesty's sister, so we trust you will not sever them; for indeed your grace cannot love him as your brother, but you must obey his majesty as his subject. Example of your obedience and reverence of his majesty's laws is instead of a good preacher to a great number of his majesty's subjects; who, if they may see in you negligence of his majesty or his laws, will not fail but follow on hardly, and then their fault is not their own but yours, by example; and so may the king's majesty, when he shall come to further judgment, impute the fault of divers evil people (which thing God forbid!) to the sufferance of your grace's doings. And therefore we most earnestly from the depth of our hearts desire it, that as nature hath set your grace nigh his majesty by blood, so your love and zeal to his majesty will further his estate by obedience.

In the end of your letter two things be touched which we cannot pretermit: the one is, you seem to charge us with permission of men to break laws and statutes. We think indeed it is too true, that laws and proclamations be broken daily, (the more pity it is;) but that we permit them, we would be sorry to have it so proved. The other is, that we have suffered bruits to be spoken of you; and that also must be answered as the other. It is pity to see men so evil, as whom they may touch with tales and infamies they care not, so they miss not the best. Such is the boldness of people, that neither we can fully bridle them to raise tales of you, nor of ourselves. And yet whensoever any certain person may be gotten, to be charged with any such, we never leave them unpunished. Indeed the best way is, both for your grace, and also us, that when we cannot find and punish the offender, let us say as he said that was evil spoken of: "Yet will I so live, as no credit shall be given to my back-biters." Certainly, if we had credited any evil tale of your grace, we would friendly have admonished you thereof, and so also proceeded, as either the tale-tellers should have been punished, or else to have proved their tales. And therefore we pray your grace to think no unkindness in us, that any evil bruits have been spread by evil men; but think rather well of us, that howsoever they were spread, we believed them not.

Hitherto your grace seeth we have written somewhat at length of the promise made to you, and our meanings in our former writings. And now for the latter part of our letter, we will, as briefly as we can, remember to you two special matters; whereof the one might suffice to reform your proceedings, and both together, well considered, we trust shall do your grace much good. The one is, the truth of that you be desired to follow; the other is, the commodity that thereby shall ensue. They both make a just commandment; and because of the first the latter followeth, that shall be first entreated. We hear say, your grace refuseth to hear any thing reasoned contrary to your old determination; wherein you make your opinion suspicious, as that you are afraid to be dissuaded. If your faith in things be of God, it may abide any storm or weather; if it be but of sand, you do best to eschew the weather. That which we profess hath the foundation in scriptures, upon plain texts and no glosses, the confirmation thereof by the use in the primitive church, not in this latter corrupted. And indeed our greatest change is not in the substance of our faith, no, not in any one article of our creed. Only the difference is, that we use the ceremonies, observations, and sacraments of our religion, as the apostles and first fathers in the primitive church did: you use the same that corruption of time brought in, and very barbary and ignorance nourished, and seem to be bold for custom against truth, and we for truth against custom. Your grace in one or two places of your letter seemeth to speak earnestly in the maintenance of your faith; and therein, so that your faith be according to the scriptures, we must have the like opinion. The saying is very good, if the faith be sound. But if every opinion your grace hath (we cannot tell how) conceived, shall be your faith, you may be much better instructed. St Paul teacheth you, that faith is by the word of God. And it was a true saying of him that said, *Non qui cuivis credit, fidelis est, sed qui Deo.* For where hath your grace ground for such a faith, to think common prayer in the English church should not be in English; that images of God should be set up in the church; or that the sacrament of Christ's body and blood should be offered by the priests for the dead; yea, or that it should be otherwise used than by the scripture it was instituted? Though you have no scripture to maintain them, we have evident scriptures to forbid them. And although fault may be found, that of late baptism hath been used in your grace's house, contrary to law, and utterly without licence; yet is it the worse, that, contrary to the primitive church, it hath been in a tongue unknown, by the which the best part of the sacrament is unused, and as it were a blind bargain made by the godfathers in a matter of illumination: and thus in the rest of the things in which your grace differeth from the common order of the realm, where have you ground or reason, but some custom, which oftentimes is mother of many errors? And although in civil things she may be followed, where she causeth quiet, yet not in religious, where she excuseth no error; as in Leviticus it is said, "Ye shall not do after the custom of Egypt, wherein ye dwelled, nor after the custom of Canaan; no, you shall not walk in their laws, for I am your Lord God; keep you my laws and commandments." The points wherein your grace differeth in your faith, as you call it, may be shewed where, when, how, and by whom they began since the gospel was preached, the church was planted, and the apostles martyred: at which time your faith depended upon the scripture, and otherwise there was no necessity to believe. For, as Hierome saith: *Quod de scripturis non habet auctoritatem, eadem facilitate contemnitur qua probatur*[1]. And because your grace, as we hear say, readeth sometimes the doctors, we may allege unto you two or three places of other principal doctors. Augustine saith: *Cum Dominus tacuerit, quis nostrum dicat, Illa vel illa sunt; aut si dicere audeat, unde probat?* And Chrysostom's saying is not unlike: *Multi, inquit, jactant Spiritum Sanctum; sed qui propria loquuntur, falso illum prætendunt*[2]. And if you will have their meaning plain, read the fifth chapter of the first book of Ecclesiastica Historia; and where Constantine had these words in the council: *In disputationibus, inquit, rerum divinarum habetur præscripta Spiritus Sancti doctrina; evangelici et apostolici libri cum prophetarum oraculis plene nobis ostendunt sensum numinis: proinde, discordia posita, sumamus ex verbis Spiritus quæstionum explicationes.* What plainer sayings may be than these to answer

---

[[1] Vid. p. 28, *n.* 3.] [[2] Vid. p. 26, *n.* 1.]

your fault? Again, too infinite it were to remember your grace of the great number of particular errors crept into the church, whereupon you make your foundation. The fables of false miracles and lewd pilgrimages may somewhat teach you. Only this we pray your grace to remember with yourself, the two words that the Father said of his Son Jesus Christ, *Ipsum audite.*

To the second point, of the commodity that may follow your obedience, we, having by the king's authority in this behalf the governance of this realm, must herein be plain with your grace. And if our speech offend the same, then must your grace think it is our charge and office to find fault where it is, and our duty to amend it as we may. Most sorry truly we be, that your grace, whom we should otherwise honour for the king's majesty's sake, by your own deeds should provoke us to offend you: we do perceive great discommodity to the realm by your grace's singularity (if it may be so named) in opinion; and in one respect, as you are sister to our sovereign lord and master, we most humbly beseech your grace to shew your affection continually towards him, as becometh a sister. And as your grace is a subject, and we counsellors to his majesty's estate, we let you know, the example of your grace's opinion hindereth the good weal of this realm: which thing we think is not unknown unto you; and if it be, we let your grace know it is too true. For God's sake, we beseech your grace, let nature set before your eyes the young age of the king your brother. Let reason tell you the looseness of the people: how then can you without a wailing heart think that you should be the cause of disturbance? If your grace see the king, being the ordinary ruler under God, not only of all others in the realm, but of you also, call his people by ordinary laws one way, with what heart can your grace stay yourself without following; much worse, to stay other that would follow their sovereign lord? Can it be a love in you to forsake him, his rule, and law, and take a private way by yourself? If it be not love, it is much less obedience. If your grace think the king's majesty to be over his people, as the head in a man's body is over the rest, not only in place but in dignity and science; how can you, being a principal member in the same body, keep the nourishment from the head? We pray your grace most earnestly, think this thing so much grieveth us, as for our private affection and good wills to you though we should dissemble, yet for our public office we cannot but plainly inform your grace, not doubting but that your wisdom can judge what your office is; and if it were not your own cause, we know your grace by wisdom could charge us, if we suffered the like in any other. Truly every one of us apart honoureth your grace for our master's sake; but when we join together in public service, as in this writing we do, we judge it not tolerable, to know disorder, to see the cause, and leave it unamended. For though we would be negligent, the world would judge us. And therefore we do altogether eftsoons require your grace, in the king's majesty's name, that if any of your two chaplains, Mallet or Barkley, be returned, or as soon as any of them shall return to your grace's house, the same may be, by your grace's commandment or order, sent or delivered to the sheriff of Essex, who hath commandment from the king's majesty, by order of the law and of his crown, to attach them; or if that condition shall not like your grace, yet that then he may be warned from your grace's house, and not kept there, to be as it were defended from the power of the law. Which thing we think surely neither your grace will mean, nor any of your counsel assent thereto.

And so to make an end of our letter, being long for the matter, and hitherto deferred for our great business, we trust your grace first seeth how the usage of your chaplains differeth from the manner of our licence, and what good intent moved us to write unto you in our former letters; lastly, that the things whereunto the king and the whole realm hath consented, be not only lawful and just by the policy of the realm, but also just and godly by the laws of God: so that if we, which have charge under the king, should willingly consent to the open breach of them, we could neither discharge ourselves to the king for our duties, neither to God for our conscience. The consideration of which things we pray Almighty God by his holy Spirit to lay in the bottom of your heart, and thereupon to build such a profession in you, as both God may have his true honour, the king his due obedience, the realm concord, and we most comfort. For all the which we do heartily pray, and therewith, for the continuance of your grace's health to your heart's desire. From Westminster, the xxv. of December. [1550.]

---

### XLI. *Mandatum pro publicatione Actus Parliamenti contra Rebelles.*

Wilkins' Concilia, Vol. IV. p. 68. Ex Reg. Cran. f. 61. a.

THOMAS, &c. per illustrissimum et invictissimum in Christo principem et dominum nostrum, dominum Edwardum sextum, &c. ad infra scripta rite suffultus, dilecto in Christo filio archidiacono nostro Cantuarien', seu ejus officiali, salutem, gratiam, et benedictionem. Literas missivas dicti metuendissimi domini nostri regis, manu sua regia signatas, ejusque signeto obsignatas, nominibus illustrissimorum virorum dominorum a secretis consiliis suis regiis in calce earundem subscriptas, nobis inscriptas et directas, nuper cum debito officii nostri obsequio accepimus, tenorem subsequentem complectentes:

Most reverend father in God, right trusty and right well-beloved counsellor, we greet you well. And whereas it is come to our knowledge that there be divers lewd and seditious persons in certain parts of our realm, that practise and devise the means to stir up unlawful assemblies and commotions, to the trouble and unquiet of us and our loving subjcts; forasmuch as we intend to meet with the said practisers in time, we have thought good, among other things that we have set forth for the purpose, to address unto you, as we have done the like to all other prelates of our realm, the books of an act of parliament made and established in the third year of our reign, for the containing of our subjects in quiet and good order, and the suppression of the rebellion, if at any time any should happen to be practised or begun within our realm. Wherefore we require, and straitly charge and command you, to give substantial order throughout all your diocese, that within every parish church within the same the said act may be openly and distinctly read by the parson or curate to the parochians every Sunday, or second Sunday at the least, at such time in the morning as the assembly of the said parochians is most frequent; to the end they may be from time to time admonished of their duties, and of the peril that shall ensue to them that shall devise or attempt any thing contrary to the said act. And like as we in this perilous time have thought it necessary, for the preservation of the common quiet of our realm, to address to you and the rest of our prelates these our letters with our said act; so our special trust is, that you for your part will see the same effectually done and executed throughout your diocese, so duly and with such regard and care as the importance of the case requireth: whereof fail you not, as you tender our pleasure, and will avoid our indignation. Yeven under our signet at our manor of Grenewhyche, the sixth of May, in the fifth year of our reign.

In calce hæc nomina habentur: E. Somersett, R. Ryche, Canc', W. Wilteshire, J. Warwick, J. Bedford, E. Clinton. Inscriptio talis est: To the most reverend father in God, our right trusty and right well-beloved counsellor, the archbishop of Canterbury.

Nos vero affectantes ex animo ejusdem domini nostri regis literis et mandatis obtemperare, volentesque pro nostro erga suam regiam celsitudinem officio in demandatis nobis negotiis omnem nostram curam et solertem adhibere diligentiam, vobis pro parte suæ regiæ majestatis districte præcipiendo mandamus harum serie, quatenus receptis præsentibus, cum omni qua poteritis celeritate et diligentia maturis, dilectos filios nostros rectores, vicarios, et curatos quarumcunque ecclesiarum parochialium nostræ diœceseos Cantuariensis moneatis, et præcipiendo mandetis, quatenus ipsi et eorum quilibet vel singuli actum sive statutum parliamenti in eisdem literis regiis specificatum, cujus unum exemplar typis excusum vobis una cum præsentibus per latorem præsentis nostri mandati transmittimus, singulis diebus dominicis, vel saltem qualibet secunda die dominica, in ecclesia sua parochiali coram parochianis ejusdem, mane quum et quando parochiani cujuslibet parochiæ ad divina audienda in ecclesia sua frequentes adfuerint, publice, distincta, aperta, ac alta et intelligibili voce perlegant, ac cetera omnia et singula in dictis literis regiis descripta perimpleant, exequantur, et sedulo fieri curent, omnibus mora, dilatione, et fuco penitus remotis, prout eidem domino nostro regi sub vestro incumbente periculo obtemperare et respondere velitis, et vult vestrum alter. Et quid in præmissis feceritis, et exequi curaveritis, id totum et omne nobis quam citissime significatum iri non postponatis. Dat' in manerio nostro de Lambehith, nono die mensis Maii, anno Domini 1551, regnique ejusdem felicissimi domini nostri regis anno quinto, et nostræ consecrationis decimo nono.

---

XLII. *Letter from Edward VI. to the Bishops, on occasion of the Sweating Sickness*[1].

EDWARD[2].

By the King.

Right reverend father in God, right trusty and well-beloved, we greet you well. And being not a little disquieted to see the subjects of our realm vexed with this extreme and sudden plague, that daily increaseth over all, we cannot but lament the people's wickedness, through the which the wrath of God hath been thus marvellously provoked. For the more we study how to instruct them in the knowledge of God and of his most holy word, that consequently they might follow and observe his laws and precepts, so much the more busy is the wicked spirit to alienate their hearts from all godliness; and his malice hath so much prevailed, that because the people are become as it were open rebels against the divine majesty, God after one plague hath sent another and another, increasing it so from one to one, till at length, seeing none other remedy, he hath thrown forth this extreme plague of sudden death. And because there is no other way to pacify his fury, and to recover his grace and mercy, but by prayer and amendment of life; considering the cure and charge committed unto you, we have thought good to call upon you to use all diligence possible throughout your whole diocese, as well by yourself as by good ministers, to persuade the people to resort more diligently to common prayer than they have done, and there not only to pray with all their hearts, in the fear of God, as good and faithful men should do, but also to have a better regard unto their livings, and specially to refrain their greedy appetites from that insatiable serpent of covetousness, wherewith most men are so infected, that it seemeth each one would devour another without charity or any godly respect to the poor, to their neighbours, or to their commonwealth: for the which God hath not only now poured out this plague upon them, but also prepared another plague, that after this life shall plague them everlastingly. Wherein you must use those persuasions that may engender a terror, to reduce them from their corrupt, naughty, and detestable vices. But as the body and members of a dull or sick head cannot be lusty, or apt to do well; so in many cures of this our realm, as well the chief as the particular ministers of the church have been both so dull and so feeble in discharging of their duties, that it is no marvel, though their flocks wander, not knowing the voice of their shepherd, and much less the voice of their principal and sovereign Master. We trust ye are none of those: but if there have been such negligence within your jurisdiction, we exhort and pray you, and nevertheless charge and command you, by the authority given us of God, to see it reformed; increasing also amendment in that that already is well begun, in such sort as your diligence may declare you worthy of your vocation, and the effects thereof yield unto God an obedient, faithful, and fearful flock: which we wish to God we may shortly see. Yeven under our signet, at our honour of Hampton Court, the 18th of July, the fifth year of our reign.

State Paper Office. Domestic Papers. Temp. Edw. VI. A.D. 1551, 2. No. 6. Original.

E. Somerset, W. Wiltesh^r. J. Bedford,
F. Huntyngdon,
T. Darcy, G. Cobham, T. Cheyne,
John Gage.

---

[1 "The sweating sickness breaking out this year in great violence, (whereby the two sons of the Duke of Suffolk were taken off,) letters from the Council, dated July 18, were sent to all the bishops, to persuade the people to prayer, and to see God better served." Strype's Mem. of Abp. Cranmer, Vol. I. p. 388. Ed. Oxon. 1840. Strype's Eccl. Mem. Vol. II. pp. 494, 5. Ed. Oxon. 1822. Burnet's Hist. of Reformat. Vol. II. p. 363. Edward VI's Journal, ibid. Vol. II. Part II. App. 44. Ed. Oxon. 1829.]

[2 The signature "Edward," is not written, but stamped at the head of this document.]

## XLIII. *Mandates by Edward VI. for Subscription to the Articles of* 1552[1].

### 1. The King's Mandate to the Bishop of Norwich, sent with the Articles to be subscribed by the Clergy.

Burnet's Hist. of Reformat. Vol. III. pt. ii. Book IV. No. 8, pp. 275–277. Ed. Oxon. 1829. From Thirlby's Regist. Strype's Eccl. Mem. Vol. II. pt. ii. App. pp. 105—107. Ed. Oxon. 1822. From Ridley's Regist.

By the King.

RIGHT reverend father in God, right trusty and well-beloved, we greet you well. And because it hath pleased Almighty God in this latter time of the world, after long darkness of knowledge, to reveal to this his church of England, whereof we have under Christ the chief charge in earth, a sincere knowledge of the gospel, to the inestimable benefit of us and our people, redeemed by our Saviour Christ: we have thought it meet and our duty, for the pure conservation of the same gospel in our church, with one uniform profession, doctrine, and preaching, and for the avoiding of many perilous and vain opinions and errors, to send unto you certain Articles, devised and gathered with great study, and by counsel and good advice of the greatest learned part of our bishops of this realm, and sundry others of our clergy; which Articles we will and exhort yourself to subscribe, and in your preachings, readings, and teachings to observe, and cause to be subscribed and observed of all other, which do, or hereafter shall preach, or read, within your diocese. And if any person or persons, having benefice within your diocese, shall from henceforth not only refuse wilfully to set their hands to these Articles, but also obstinately exhort their parochians to withstand the same, and teach the people in a contrary way; our pleasure is, that, being duly proved, ye shall advertise us, or our council, of the whole matter fully, to the intent such further order may by direction from us, or our said council, be taken, as the case shall require, and shall stand with justice and the order of our laws. And further, that when and as often as ye shall have any manner of person presented unto you to be admitted by you as the ordinary to any ecclesiastical order, ministry, office, or cure within your diocese, that ye shall, before you admit him, confer with him in every these Articles; and finding him thereto consenting, to cause him to subscribe the same in one ledger book to be formed for that purpose, which may remain as a register for a concord, and to let him have a copy of the same Articles. And if any men in that case shall refuse to consent to any of the said Articles, and to subscribe the same, then we will and command you, that neither ye, nor any for you, or by your procurement in any wise shall admit him, or allow him as sufficient and meet to take any order, ministry, or ecclesiastical cure. For which your so doing we shall discharge you from all manner of penalties, or dangers of actions, suits, or pleas of præmunires, *quare impedit*, or such like. And yet our meaning is, that if any party refuse to subscribe any of these Articles for lack of learning and knowledge of the truth, ye shall in that case by teaching, conference, and proof of the same by the scriptures, reasonably and discreetly move and persuade him thereto, before you shall peremptorily judge him as unable and a recusant. And for the trial of his conformity, ye shall, according to your discretion, prefix a time and space convenient to deliberate and give his consent, so that be betwixt three weeks and six weeks from the time of the first access unto you. And if after six weeks he will not consent and agree willingly to subscribe, then ye may lawfully, and shall in any wise, refuse to admit or enable him. And where there is of late set forth by our authority a catechism for the instruction of young scholars in the fear of God, and the true knowledge of his holy religion, with express commandment from us to all schoolmasters to teach and instruct their scholars the said catechism, making it the beginning and first foundation of their teaching in their schools; our pleasure is, that for the better execution of our said commandment, ye shall yearly at the least once visit, or cause to be visited, every school within your said diocese; in which visitation it shall be inquired both how the schoolmaster of every such school hath used himself in the teaching of the said catechism, and also how the scholars do receive and follow

[[1] Vid. Letter CCCVII. p. 440. The above mandate is printed from Burnet; whose copy in some respects differs verbally from that in Strype.]

the same; making plain and full certificate of the offenders contrary to this our order, and of their several offences, to the archbishop of that province, within the months from time to time after every such offence. Yeoven under our signet, at the manor of Grenewich, the IXth day of June, the VIIth year of our reign.

## 2. A Mandate in King Edward's name to the officers of the Archbishop of Canterbury; requiring them to see that the Articles of Religion should be subscribed.

*Mandatum pro publicatione nonnullorum Articulorum, veram Christi fidem concernentium.*

Wilkins' Concilia, Vol. IV. p. 79. Burnet's Hist. of Reformat. Vol. III. pt. ii. Book IV. No. 7, pp. 273, 4. Ed. Oxon. 1829. Ex Reg. Cran. f. 65.

EDWARDUS Sextus, Dei gratia, Angliæ, et Franciæ, et Hiberniæ Rex, Fidei Defensor, et in terra ecclesiæ Anglicanæ et Hiberniæ supremum caput, dilectis sibi officiali curiæ Cantuar' et decano decanatus de arcubus Londin' ac eorum surrogatis, deputatis aut locum tenentibus, uni vel pluribus, salutem. Quoniam nuper, per literas nostras regias, signeto nostro obsignatas, reverendissimo in Christo patri, consiliario nostro fidelissimo, Thomæ Cantuariensi archiepiscopo, totius Angliæ primati et metropolitano, dederimus in mandatis, quatenus ipse, ad Dei optimi maximi gloriam illustrandam, nostrumque et ecclesiæ nostræ Anglicanæ (cujus caput supremum post Christum esse dignoscimur) honorem, et ad tollendam opinionis dissensionem, et consensum veræ religionis firmandum, nonnullos articulos, et alia rectam Christi fidem spirantia, clero et populo nostris ubilibet infra suam jurisdictionem degentibus, pro parte nostra exponeret, publicaret, denunciaret, et significaret; prout in literis nostris (quarum tenores pro hic insertis habere volumus) latius continetur et describitur: vobis igitur, et eorum cuilibet, tenore præsentium, districte præcipiendo nostra sublimi regia auctoritate mandamus, quatenus moneatis, monerive faciatis peremptorie, omnes et singulos rectores, vicarios, presbyteros, stipendiarios, curatos, plebanos, ministros, ludimagistros cujuslibet scholæ grammatices, aut aliter vel alias grammaticam aperte vel privatim profitentes, aut pubem instituentes, verbi Dei prædicatores vel prælectores, necnon quoscunque alios quamcunque aliam functionem ecclesiasticam (quocunque nomine aut appellatione censetur, habetur, aut nuncupatur) obtinentes et habentes, œconomos quoque cujuslibet parochiæ infra decanatum de arcubus prædictum existentes aut degentes; quod ipsi omnes, et eorum quilibet, per se compareant vel compareat personaliter, coram dicto reverendissimo patre Cantuar' archiepiscopo, in aula ædium suarum apud Lambehithe, die Veneris vicesimo tertio die præsentis mensis Junii, inter horas septimam et nonam, ante meridiem ejusdem diei, his quæ tunc iis ex parte nostra fuerint significanda humiliter obtemperaturi, facturique ulterius et recepturi, quod consonans fuerit rationi, ac suo convenerit erga nostram regiam dignitatem officio; mandantes, quatenus dictis die, loco, et horis, eundem reverendissimum, de executione hujus regii nostri mandati, una cum nominibus et cognominibus omnium et singulorum per vos monitorum, rite, recte, et auctentice reddatis certiorem, una cum præsentibus uti decet. Teste Thoma Cant' archiepiscopo prædicto, decimo nono die Junii, anno regni nostri septimo.

### Certificatorium factum super Executione Mandati prædicti.

REVERENDISSIMO in Christo patri et domino, domino Thomæ, permissione divina, Cantuariensi archiepiscopo, totius Angliæ primati et metropolitano; auctoritate illustrissimi in Christo principis, et domini nostri domini Edwardi Sexti, Dei gratia, Angliæ, Franciæ, et Hiberniæ regis, fidei defensoris, ac in terra ecclesiæ Anglicanæ et Hibernicæ supremi capitis, sufficienti auctoritate fulcito, Johannes Gibbon civilium legum professor, vestræ celsitudinis observantissimus, pariter eidem addictissimus, decanatus vestr' beatæ Mariæ virginis de arcubus London' commissarius, omnem quæ decet reverentiam et obedientiam tanto reverendissimo patri debitam cum honore. Mandatum illustrissimi et potentissimi domini nostri regis, præsentibus annexum, nuper accepimus, cujus vigore pariter et auctoritate omnes et singulos rectores, presbyteros, &c. Dat' vicesimo secundo die mensis Junii, anno Domini millesimo quingentesimo quinquagesimo tertio.

XLIV. *Pole, Cardinal Legate, to Archbishop Cranmer, in answer to the letter he had sent to the Queen*[1].

Strype's Mem. of Abp. Cranmer, Vol. II. pp. 972—988. Ed. Oxon. 1840. Ex Foxii MSS.

ALMIGHTY God the Father, by the grace of his only Son, God and man, that died for our sins, may give you true and perfect repentance. This I daily pray for myself, being a sinner; but, I thank God, never obstinate sinner. And the same grace the more earnestly I do pray for to be given to them that be obstinate, the more need they have thereof, being otherwise past all man's cure and admonition to save them: as your open sayings, in open audience, doth shew of you. Which hath caused, that those judges, that hath sit upon the examination of your grievous faults, seeing no likelihood of any repentance in you, hath utterly cast away all hope of your recovery: whereof doth follow the most horrible sentence of condemnation, both of your body and soul, both your temporal death and eternal. Which is to me so great an horror to hear, that if there were any way, or mean, or fashion, that I might find to remove you from error, bringing you to the knowledge of the truth, for your salvation; this I testify to you afore God, upon the salvation of mine own soul, that I would rather choose to be that mean, that you might receive this benefit by me, than to receive the greatest benefit for myself, that can be given under heaven in this world: I esteem so much the salvation of one soul.

And because it happened to me to see your private letters directed to the queen's highness, sent by the same unto me, wherein you utter and express such apparent reasons, that cause you to swerve from the rest of the church in these articles of the authority of the pope, and of the sacrament of the altar, concluding with these words: "That if any man can shew you by reason, that the authority of the pope be not prejudicial to the wealth of the realm, or that your doctrine in the sacrament be erroneous, then you would never be so perverse to stand wilfully in your own opinion; but shall with all humility submit yourself to the truth in all things, and gladly embrace the same:" these your words, written in that letter, giveth me some occasion, desiring your wealth, not utterly to despair thereof; but to attempt to recover you by the same way that you open unto me: which is, by reason to shew you the error of your opinion, and withal the light of the truth in both causes. But whether this may help you indeed, or bring you to revoke the same with true repentance, this I know not; and I fear much the contrary; for that I see the ground and beginning, how you fell into error in both these articles, not to be of that sort that maketh men commonly to fall into errors and heresies. Which sort and way is, by meddling with your wit and discourse natural, to examine the articles of the faith; making your reason judge thereof, which ought to be judged and ruled by the tradition of the faith: which abuse causeth men daily to fall into errors and heresies. And the same also is in you, and is joined with that you have done. But here standeth not the ground of your error; nor yet in this other common manner of falling from the truth, which St Paul noteth in the Gentiles, and is in all men commonly that followeth their sensual appetites, *qui veritatem Dei in injustitia detinent:* which thing also hath been occasion of your error. But yet not this is the very ground thereof, but a further fault: that you giving your oath to the truth, you mocked with the same, as the Jews mocked with Christ, when they saluted him saying, *Ave Rex Judæorum*, and afterwards did crucify him. For so did you to the vicar of Christ, knowledging the pope of Rome by the words of your oath to be so, and in mind intending to crucify the same authority; whereof came the plague of deep ignorance and blindness unto you: which is now that bringeth you to this grievous peril, to perish both body and soul. From which peril no reason can deliver you.

But you discovering yourself, touching the entry, when you should make the customable oath of all legitimate bishops in Christendom, which is the door for you to enter to the service of God, in the highest spiritual office within this realm, and seeing you made the same but for a countenance, nothing meaning to observe that you promised by the oath; this is a door that every thief may enter by. This is not the door that they enter by, that mean earnestly the service of God. Wherein the prophet's sentence is

[[1] Vid. p. 454, *n.* 5.]

plain, asking this question, *Quis ascendet in montem Domini? aut quis stabit in loco sancto ejus?* And then answering to the same saying, *innocens manibus, et mundo corde, qui non accepit in vano animam suam, nec juravit in dolo proximo suo. Hæc est generatio quærentium Dominum, quærentium faciem Dei Jacob.* So that you now entering to the mountain of God, which was to that high archbishoprick, and to the primacy in the realm, by a clean contrary way, which is, as you confess yourself, by a feigned oath, by fraud, and dissimulation; what more plain sentence can be against you, if you have a thousand reformations in your mind, than that all this doth not make that this should be the way to the true service of God, nor that you, using a false oath, should be of that generation, which with their heart sought God, but utterly concludeth against you, that if those that abstain from all deceit with their neighbour, specially in oath, be blessed of God, he that confesseth to have used such dissimulation in his oath, not with one neighbour or twain, but with the whole realm, with the whole church, what can he receive, but the malediction of God? What can more evidently shew that man to be none of that generation that seeketh God? As, if there were none other proof, that followed in your acts, such a deceitful and shameful entry doth manifestly declare: and most of all, one of the first acts you did after this; which was to pluck the rest of the realm (of whom you had chief cure) out of the house of God, bringing them forthwith into the schism.

And that we see now, that the whole realm by the high mercy of God being brought into the house of God again, there to receive his grace and benediction; and this to be done by those princes, and those ministers, *qui non acceperunt in vano animam suam, nec juraverunt in dolo proximo suo;* your person yet remaining without, deprived of the grace granted to them; what doth this shew, but that it is the just sentence of God against you, for your deceitful entry into his service; and the mercy of God toward them, that not willingly went forth, but by your traiterous means were thrust out?

So that here now I have told you, whether you hear me, or no, the very cause of your blindness and ignorance: which is the vengeance of God against you for your dissimulation and perjury to him and to the whole church, at your entering to the high service thereof. Whereby you have deserved to be cast out of the house of God, which is the church, *in tenebras exteriores, ubi est fletus et stridor dentium.* Which is the place and state wherein I see you now lie; and the same I saw so evidently in your letters, from the beginning to the end, as nothing can be more plain: you shewing yourself in the same to be so ignorant, that you know not those things which be evident to every man; which every man, that hath any exterior light, by experience and knowledge of things past, doth know....

*Here much is wanting.*

that be once of the church as dead bodies, when the spirit is out. But to all that be within the body of the church, this giveth comfort and life, as the spirit doth to the body. And this shall be sufficient to say for every man's information of the truth in this matter, that will believe, either that old or late experience, or the continual doctrine of the whole church, hath taught in every christian realm: whereof none ever found this fault, that the pope's laws spiritual were not to be exercised, because the same could not agree with their politic laws; but rather found fault, when the pope himself, or his ministers, did let the course of those laws, which agreed with every politic body, as the soul of man with all complexions and form of body. And when they were stopped, then seemed to be stopped the breath and life of justice, as no realm can give (as I said before) greater or surer testimony than ours. For when the authority and laws of the pope did flourish in the realm, all justice flourished withal; and, that stopped and cast out, as it was these latter years, all good justice and civil manner of living was stopped and cast forth withal.

So that, when you came first to marvel of a thing never seen nor heard of afore in this realm, that a bishop, made by the pope's authority, should not be deposed without his authority; what doth this shew, but a deep blindness and ignorance of the use of the law in this realm, ever continual, and never broken of any just prince, until you yourself were made bishop; which helped them to break all good laws and customs of the realm; and then afterward to make this for a great reason, that the pope's laws should not be now again admitted? for then, you say, all the whole realm that cast out his authority, must needs acknowledge themselves accursed: which God, you say, forfend. And this you shew you cannot abide for nothing by any manner, that the realm should knowledge themself accursed: which they cannot, you say, avoid, if they admit the pope's law as good. This word you should have said afore the realm had cast forth the pope's authority, for to have letted them from their fall into the curse; and this had been the very part of a good bishop. But after that they were fallen from the laws, which they had admitted afore, and thereby run into the curse, (which you say cannot be avoided of them that hath once admitted them,) then I with all good and catholic men do say, God forfend they after this should not knowledge their state to be accursed. Which if they did not, they could never be absolved from the curse. And he that forbiddeth now the knowledge of the same, doth in effect procure that, being accursed indeed, they remain ever accursed. This is your monstrous and blind love you pretend to bear to the realm, being accursed yourself, and blinded in the knowledge of your state, to have the whole realm remain still accursed. But the true affection these two catholic princes bear to the realm, with the blood of those that resisted the swerving from the pope's authority, hath obtained of the high mercy of God, that the whole realm hath with repentance knowledged their evil state they stood in since the leaving of the authority of the pope in the realm, and with repealing of those laws, made contrary, have asked absolution, and received it, and be delivered of all curse, received into the grace of God, and brought into the church's lap again; they only left out, that doth refuse this grace, and hath not so much grace to accept it. Whereof if any should be deprived, none hath deserved it more by the just wrath of God to be deprived, than he that was chief doer to make the realm leave it, as you; by shewing yourself in this to be the very member of Satan, both then, but most of all now: which, deprived of grace of repentance himself, would draw all other to his damnation, and dissuadeth all return to grace.

This your charity you now shew to your country, which, as I said hitherto, is very vengeance of God toward you. Of the which this great blindness giveth a great testimony, that you shew in your letter, writing of these things, as though you had never knowledge what had been done in the realm afore your time, nor what was the state of your time, nor yet what is the state of the realm at this present; bringing for a great inconvenient, that if the parliament should accept the laws of the pope, they should be constrained to repeal those that were done against his laws and authority: as though this were not so done already. And shewing so great ignorance, both touching the doctrine of the church, and in this point touching the pope's authority, and the experience of the custom of the realm, yet you conclude, that ignorance might excuse other men, how prejudicial the canon laws be to the wealth of the realm, if they would accept the same. But you cannot be excused by ignorance. And seeing in this the very truth, that ignorance cannot excuse you, as in truth it cannot, being of that kind it is. But if that do not excuse you, then malice doth condemn you: which is the very cause to bring you to ignorance inexcusable, both in this point of the authority of the pope, as in the doctrine of the sacrament; wherein it is no less monstrous. And this you shew most, where you think to speak with less obstinacy; as where you say, that "if they that follow the pope's doctrine herein could bring in but one old ancient doctor of the church of their opinion, you have offered afore, as you offer yet, to give place unto them, and to consent to the same." What a proof is this to shew your profound blindness! If there be no let but this, because you see not of the old doctors at the least one, that were against your opinion, in the defence of the pope's doctrine, other men seeing so many, and not one ancient approved doctor that ever dissented; what a wonderful blindness is this, not to see one against you! For this is plain, when the pope sheweth his sense and doctrine in this article, he doth not speak thereof, as of an article that he himself hath newly found, nor yet any of his predecessors, but that all hath uniformly received one of another of their fathers, unto the apostles' time, and they of Christ. Which argument is so strong, so evident to the condemnation of your opinion and confirmation of the pope's, that many sage and learned men, writing against the opinion you follow, being divers sorts of arguments to confound the same, set apart all form of reasoning, and only stick upon the testimony and uniform consent of all the old doctors of the church to this day. Which testimonies be so many, that they fill up great books; as, amongst other, my lord of Durham at this present, in his book written of this matter, taketh this way, to ground himself most upon, the perpetual consent of the old doctors, continuing unto this age: and all against your opinion. Which book is abroad, and hath been seen of you.

Then if ye will think him of so small judgment or knowledge, that in such a number as he bringeth there is not one that maketh to his purpose, but all for your purpose, whom he intendeth to oppugn, either this must prove a wonderful blindness in him, and not in him alone, but in so many learned men, that taketh the same way; or else in you, that amongst so many testimonies, some more clearer than some, not to see so much as one alone: this is an evident proof that ye be stark blind. For if ye were not, if it were but one brought forth unto you, as is mentioned in that book, the condemnation of Berengarius, that was of your opinion; and that done by a general council of all the nations in Christendom; grounding itself upon the uniform doctrine of their forefathers; were not this enough, if you had eyes to see, to shew that more than one old doctor were of the pope's doctrine? And if this be not sufficient proof unto you, the same being enough to Berengarius himself, which was converted thereby, and persuaded to recant his opinion; what doth this shew, but that he was not utterly blinded, but that he saw some testimony against him, you utterly to have lost all sight, that see not so much as one?

But of this your monstrous blindness I marvel the less, the more I see the same to proceed of the very justice and wrath of God against you; with whom you mocking on that manner as you shewed in coming in such a high place, in service of the church, as was to be archbishop and primate of the realm, as to swear *in dolo*, not only *proximo*, but *universæ ecclesiæ;* willing afterward to pervert the old order of the church, which you called a reformation, meseemeth to hear the very words and curse of St Paul, that lighted upon the false prophet Barjesu, letting the course of the doctrine evangelical preached by him, when he then cursing him said: *O plene omni malo, et omni fallacia, fili diaboli, inimice omnis justitiæ, non desinis pervertere vias Domini rectas? Et ecce nunc manus Domini super te, et eris cæcus, non videns solem, usque ad tempus.* The effect of this I do see hath lighted upon you, for entering by deceit to be a chief doctor in the church, perverting *vias Domini rectas*, to be blinded, I pray God it be but *ad tempus*. But hitherto I have not known a more deeper blindness. And if that was punishment of that false prophet, to lose his corporal sight for a time, that, being an infidel, for very ignorance did put obstacle to the very true doctrine of the faith never heard of afore, to be blinded corporally for a time; you that first knew the doctrine, and preached the same, which afterward you do pervert, if you were stricken with a greater and more notable blindness, the which you shew now, this is evident to come of the very hand of God, which man's hand cannot heal, but only the hand of God, that justly punished you therewithal. And the sorer and more desperate cure is of this your blindness, the more you acquit yourself therein: as though you had a great gift of light above all other. For so you shew in your letters, persuading yourself to have found a way in teaching the doctrine of the sacrament of the altar, that other hath not seen: which is to take away the absurdity both to the sense and reason of man, that is in the catholic doctrine, touching the sacrament of the altar, as you say, in that form of bread and wine to be the very true real presence of the body of Christ, and that it is his body and blood that is shewed in the form of bread and wine, what reason will admit this? What sense? And how much probable were this, if this doctrine were taught as you teach it, to say, that you see in the form of bread and wine, is a figure only of the body of Christ that is in heaven; whom in spirit in that figure you do honour. This manner no doubt were more probable saying to the ears of men that judge things either by reason or by sense. But the more probable it is, the more false it is; the great sophister and father of all lies ever deceiving us by probability of reason, proponing ever that which is more agreeable to the sense, but the true doctrine of Christ is taught by another way.

*Here is another deficiency.*

being fallen therein not so much for fault or abuse of reason, as by malice against reason. And such, I say, no hand can cure, no reason, no discourse; but only that it please the high mercy of God, that doth chastise your malicious handling of the truth with such ignorance and darkness, to withdraw his hand of vengeance upon you: for otherwise you hearing reason, and seeing some light thereof, yet you have not so much grace as to receive it nor follow it.

This is the thing I greatly fear in you, having knowledge of your proceeding since your first notable error in rejecting the doctrine of the pope's supremacy, and afterward of the sacrament; which, as I said afore, was not after the common manner of falling, as other did, by curiosity, or by frailty, but by deliberate malice, to forsake the truth in both points, to satisfy your carnal appetites, to the which your dissembling first, and mocking with the truth, and afterward openly forsaking the same, did serve you. Which as yet you do not knowledge: and this must be the first thing that you should knowledge, making open confession with repentance thereof, if you shall ever come to receive any fruit of the mercy of God.

So that if I now, that desire your recover, should go about by way of discourse or argument to bring you from your error to the truth, this must be the first point, to shew how you fell into the same darkness, to the intent that God so much remitting his hand of justice, that you may see your abomination in abusing the truth, you might knowledge by fear the justice of God in letting you fall into so great darkness; and by the hope of his infinite mercy call to him for grace to be restored to some light of his infallible verity. And this I with all my heart praying for you, in the mean season, until God give you the grace to do the same for yourself, shall withal open unto you the manner of your fall.

Touching your first article of the pope's authority, which I need not open any further than you have opened yourself, nor cannot better express it, than you have set it forth, I having no knowledge thereof, but by your own saying and writing, for defence of perjury objected to you. And now mark you well, if you have any sense of knowledge left unto you to see yourself and your own deeds, if ever there were heard such kind of a defence, in any perjury of any man, that had left him any light of reason or knowledge of justice. Which for to know, first you must be put in remembrance of the kind of your oath, and the manner of making thereof. The kind was such, that it was no new oath, but the very same that all archbishops of Canterbury, which be primates of this realm, all archbishops and bishops in every christian realm, doth accustomable make to the pope's holiness, as to the vicar of Christ in earth, swearing to him obedience: such was your oath. And as touching the manner of making of it, none could be more solemn; being made in the hand of a bishop, with the testimony and assistance of other bishops, openly in the church, in the presence of as much people as the church could hold; at such time as you, arrayed with the sacred vesture of a bishop, came afore the altar to be consecrated archbishop. All this you cannot, nor do not deny; nor yet that, after all this solemn and open oath, you did directly and openly against the same. Which must necessarily condemn you of perjury.

But this necessary consequence you deny; granting notwithstanding, to have done contrary to the oath. But you say for your defence, that "where you went to make the oath, even then you never thought to observe it." And lest this should be an inconvenient, and a thing much damageous unto your fame and estimation, if it were not well known, that you swore one thing in the most solemn fashion you could, and meant another; here you bring such a testimony by writing: you bring forth a privy protestation, made with privy witnesses, having the hand and sign of the notary, to prove that when you went to make that solemn oath, you were nothing minded to observe it. Which former protestation, whereto doth it serve, but to testify a double perjury, which is to be forsworn afore you did swear? Other perjurers be wont to break their oath after they have sworn, you break it afore. *Quis sapiens et intelliget hæc, et intelliget malitiam Satanæ?* And a wonderful aggravation of the wrath of God towards you.

But let the malice of Satan be first considered, in deluding you, when you thought to delude other. This delusion was this: that because it had been heard some protestations to be made, also of some good men, in a case when they not being at their own choice and liberty, when *per vim et metum, qui aliquando cadit in constantem virum*, they be made to swear to that which afterward they have done contrary to their former oath; in which case a protestation, excusing the will, and alleging the fear, hath some colour of defence: this, I say, you hearing, and Satan putting you in remembrance hereof, with the similitude of this deluded you; making you believe, that such a kind of protestation might serve for a premeditate perjury. Whereunto you were not driven, neither *vi*, nor *metu*, as you were not in this your case: except you call that a just fear, that you did see, if you did not swear, you could not satisfy your ambition and covetousness in having the bishoprick. For so it was, leave you these two affections, care ye not for to be made bishop; and who did constrain you to swear? Were ye not by that refuse quite delivered of all necessity to swear? This also ye cannot deny. Whereunto therefore serveth your protestation made by the hand of a notary, but to make your privy perjury more notoriously known, but to make it known to the world, that you entering to the rule of a part of the flock of Christ, you entered not in by the door; and not entering by the door, but *aliunde*, what comfort could your flock look for to have by you, but that which Christ saith to follow of those, *qui non intrant per ostium, sed aliunde*, to be stealers and thieves, *qui non intrant nisi ut mactent et perdant;* as the effect hath shewed by you?

But here you deceive yourself again, and would deceive other, making your defence of your simulate oath, that "you did the same so, for the more service of God, having in your mind then to reform the church:" to the which being no way but to make that oath for a countenance, this you thought for such a purpose might be acceptable afore God: and also entering by the authority of the pope, called by him, that had authority to name you, then you think it cannot be justly of any man objected unto you, that you did not enter by the door. And this truly, if you could have kept your own counsel touching me, I durst not object the same unto you, seeing nothing outwardly but as that you were lawfully called and institute bishop; and of your inward I would not make myself judge.

*More wanting here.*

and see, as is the first point in your letters; where you make a great marvel, saying "it to be a thing that was never seen in the realm, that, to condemn any subject thereof, justice should be sought of a foreign power, as is the pope's." How this is to be called a foreign power, I will declare afterward. For this I do not marvel, if you do not well know, not being so open to them that lacketh spiritual doctrine, nor of that ignorance I do not speak now, but of that outward light and knowledge, which is open to every man by experience. The which you not knowing, it may be well said, you be cast *in tenebras exteriores*, and that you have lost both interior and exterior knowledge of things. For so you shew in this case, where you say, "it was never seen in the realm, that to condemn any subject thereof to death, should be required any other sentence than that cometh from the imperial crown of the realm and their temporal laws." Wherein that which I note first is this, that in that place you seem to lament, that being condemned already, as you say, by the laws of the realm, of high treason, this dilation is given to your death, not to suffer, afore all such things as be laid to your charge were first known at Rome, this being natural unto all that be in jeopardy of life, if they cannot hope by any just defence to extue the same, at the least to have time all desire, following that proverb, "in space cometh grace." The which natural effect being extinct in you, this followeth withal, natural knowledge to be extinct, as in the proeme of your letter is more declared.

And now to come nearer to that you say was never seen, that "any subject to be condemned, had need of any outward justice," calling outward justice the canon laws, that come from the pope. To this I say, the experience and use of the laws, and justice in this realm, doth shew clean contrary to your marvel, that it was never seen in the realm, afore the time of your malicious oath, that there was ever any man condemned for the crime of heresies, by the mere justice that cometh from the temporal laws, but all were first declared to be such by the spiritual laws of the canons, which you call "foreign laws." And this beside I say, afore that same time, of all other crimes, as treason and other, there was never spiritual man put to execution, according to the order of the laws of the realm, but he were first by the canon laws condemned, dis-graded, and then given to the temporal hands. Whereof there be as many examples, afore the time of breaking the old order of the realm these last years, as hath been delinquents. Let all the records be seen; and specially this is notable of the bishop of ———, which being imprisoned here for high treason, the king would not proceed to his condemnation and punishment, afore he had the pope's bull given him.

And this is the trade of justice, which the king and queen use with you at this time, being condemned of treason, being consecrate bishop, to have the pope's sentence from Rome afore you suffer: which manner of proceeding, you say, was never afore in the realm; and the practice and experience in like cases doth shew never to have been otherwise, afore the time of your notable perjury. And so catholic kings, as it pertaineth to the privilege of the see of Rome, when they be crowned, doth swear.

And now look what ignorance is this, to think that the like was never seen in the realm, when it was never seen otherwise amongst those princes, that were counted to be in the obedience of the laws of Christ, and of the church!

But now to come to that you speak of, the pope's law and power, which after a seditious manner of speaking you call "a foreign power:" this standeth under such a fashion, if God leave you so much sense to understand what I say, that the pope's power can no more be called foreign power, coming not of man alone, but of him that is God and man, that was *secundus homo de cœlo cœlestis*, than may be called a foreign power, that the soul of man, coming from heaven, hath in the body generate in earth. And so it is in the politic body of this realm, ruled with politic laws, founded by man's reason, that be called temporal laws: to them coming the pope's laws spiritual doth no other, but that the soul in the body, to give life to the same, to confirm and strengthen the same. And this is it the angel, speaking in Christ's conception, and declaring what his authority should be, signified, saying, he should sit *super domum David*, which was a temporal reign, *ut confirmet illud et corroboret*. And so doth the spiritual laws, proceeding of his Spirit: as be the laws of the church, and canon laws. Which wheresoever they be well observed, doth this effect, ever to confirm and stablish the temporal laws of the realm: as no realm hath had more experience than this, ever since the time they received the faith and obedience of the pope; from whom came their doctrine of the faith. There was never notable trouble in the realm of any kind, if it dured any space, but it was ever lightly eased, and the realm established by some legate sent from the pope and the see of Rome, following the prescript of the canons and the spiritual law: without the which no realm can well be governed, but all be like to the thorn-bush; whereof it is written *in libro judicum*, when the Sichimites had chosen a tyranny over them, against the law of God, then it was prophesied unto them, what should come thereof, which was that fire should come forth of that thorn, which was their king, that should devour the people, and from the people, to burn him, as it was, and ever shall be, where mere temporal laws without spiritual doth rule. Which state may be compared to be like such a thorn, whereof fire doth come forth, to the destruction both of the governor and the people. And how the laws of the realm might be well likened to such a thorn, after that the spiritual authority was cast forth, the destruction of such a sort of men, of all degrees, both great and small, the great spoils that were taken, may give sufficient proof to all them that hath any sense or remembrance of things so lately done.

And now coming again to the spiritual authority and law, to join itself with the temporal, this is like to the fire that Moses saw *in rubo;* which gave light, and did not burn, nor never doth, when it is well used. And if it be not well used, the fault is in the persons, and not in the thing; as the fault is not in the temporal laws, when the prince doth abuse them; howbeit of their nature they be *tanquam spinæ*, as was also Moses' law, sharp to which was mitigate; and so shall be in every when they be joined with the spiritual ought not to be called "foreign laws"

*More here wanting.*

*Non in probabilibus humanæ sapientiæ verbis, ne evacuetur Christi:* as it should be in this case. For if this probability were followed, the slander of the cross should be void. For this were no slander to the Jews, to hear Christ honoured in a figure, they being ever used to the same: nor it would seem so much foolish to the gentiles and infidels, after we had accepted Christ for God, to honour him in a figurative manner. But this being the counsel of Christ, to utter his great mystery in form that he should have it slander to both the Jews, that seek signs, and were used to be taught by figures; and also the gentiles, that stick upon the judgment of reason; the more probable you make it, the further you swerve from the true doctrine of Christ, and very true manner to teach it. And here may no new manner be taught. What a heinous pride is this, this doctrine passing a thousand year, and as many hundred beside as hath been since this sacrament was instituted, by the midst of the Jews and gentiles, with this slander and appearance of foolishness, never being found faulty in any one of the bishops and preachers of the word of God, that they confessed the real presence of the body of Christ in the sacrament of the altar; but all found faulty and condemned of heresy, which denied the same! And ever the doctrine of the presence, prevailing and triumphing above man's reason or sense, may be capace of the same: which both God will have mortified and die utterly, when this mystery and meat of life is spoken and taken. For as that was the beginning of the destruction of man, when following the probability of reason, he would feed himself with meat prohibit unto him; so the counsel of God hath ordained this to be the beginning of the life of man, to take a sensible meat, wherein neither reason nor sense can find any probability, or make any judgment thereof.

But because I have entreated this part more largely in another epistle that I send unto you, wherein I shew that standing, as you do, without repentance of the manner of your entry to the service of the church, you could never be neither good scholar of this doctrine, and much less a master; I will now proceed no further to reason with you herein, knowing all to be in vain, and no help nor mean to recover you, but only prayer. Which with all my heart, as I would for mine own soul, I will not fail to use for you to him whom you have so greatly offended, as I never read of any bishop that ever was in the church. But the fountain of his mercy is never closed to them that will call for it: as mine own entire prayer is to the infinite mercy of God, that you may have the grace so to do; sending you for obtaining of that, his holy Spirit, *qui condemnat mundum de peccato, de judicio, et de justitia:* that, seeing first your sore condemnation, you may therewith be stirred with all humility and contrite heart to demand some comfort; which cannot be hoped of without your former condemnation of yourself. Whereunto to bring you, it hath caused me by writing to set forth so earnestly some part of your grievous offences afore you: willing you no less comfort, than I would to mine own soul.

And the same I say, concluding and ending, as I began: it may please the paternal love, that God beareth unto all sinners, for his sake, that being his only Son, God and man, died to pay their ransom, for to forgive you, and to deliver you *ex ore leonis*, which hath so devoured you, that if you be not plucked out as the prophet Amos saith of Israel, *quomodo si eruat pastor duo crura aut extremum auriculæ;* I say, if you be not plucked out by the ear, you be utterly undone both body and soul. Which yet again, and ever, the infinite mercy of God may defend you from! Written in the court at St James', the vi. of November, 1555.

Your very true comforter in God, you not refusing his grace,

R. Pole. Car. Leg.

---

## XLV. *Processus contra Thomam Cranmer.*

Reverendissimo in Christo patri et domino, domino Jacobo miseracione divina tituli sancte Marie in via sacrosancte Romane ecclesie presbitero cardinali de Puteo nuncupato, causeque et causis ac partibus infrascriptis judice ac commissario a sanctissimo domino nostro papa specialiter deputato, seu alii vestro in hac parte surrogato sive surrogando cuicunque, vester humilis Jacobus, permissione divina Glocestrensis episcopus ac vestre reverendissime paternitatis, immo verius sanctissimi domini nostri pape vigore literarum

MSS. Lambeth Library, No. 1136. Original. Strype's Mem. of Abp. Cranmer, Vol. II. pp. 1069—1113. Ed. Oxon. 1840.

commissionalium presentibus annex' commissarius sive subdelegatus sufficienter et legitime deputatus, omnimodas obediencias et reverencias tanto reverendissimo patri ac sedi apostolice debitas cum omni subjectionis honore. Ad noticiam vestram deducimus et deduci volumus, vestreque reverendissime paternitati significamus et certificamus per presentes, quod die lune, nono viz. die mensis Septembris, anno Domini millesimo quingentesimo quinquagesimo quinto, indictione decima tercia pontificatus sanctissimi in Christo patris et domini nostri, domini Pauli divina providentia pape quarti anno primo, in ecclesia parochiali dive virginis Marie in Oxonia, in providi et circumspecti viri magistri Johannis Clerk, sedis apostolice auctoritate notarii publici, et testium in actis hujus diei (ut inferius statim apparebit) presenciis coram nobis ad effectum infrascriptum judicialiter et pro tribunali sedentibus, comparens et personaliter constitutus preclarus et venerabilis vir magister Johannes Story legum doctor quasdam literas vestras commissionales vestre paternitatis reverendissime, immo verius apostolicas presentibus annex' sigillo vestro cera rubea impressa in quadam alba lignea capsula inclusa cum filis sive cordulis rubei coloris pendentibus sigillatas, ac signo, nomine, et subscripcione providi viri Claudii Badii clerici Bismitine diocesis publici auctoritate apostolica et imperiali notarii et scribe vestri (ut apparuit) in hac parte specialiter assumpti munitas et subscriptas, non viciatas, non rasas, non abolitas, non cancellatas, nec in aliqua sui parte suspectas, sed sanas et integras ac omni vicio et sinistra suspicione carentes, nobis directas et per partem illustrissimorum serenissimorumque Philippi et Marie Anglie regis et regine in ipsis literis commissionalibus nominat' ex parte dicti sanctissimi domini nostri pape et vestra realiter presentavit. Post quarum literarum commissionalium presentacionem nobis et recepcionem per nos humiliter factas, ipsisque per dominum Christoferum Smythe apostolice sedis auctoritate notarium publicum usque ad subscripcionem notarii in eisdem exclusive tunc ibidem publice perlectis, per prefatum venerabilem virum magistrum Johannem Story fuimus debite requisiti, quatenus onus execucionis earundem in nos assumere et acceptare ipsasque exequi dignaremur. Post cujus requisicionem sic ut premittitur nobis factam, ob honorem et reverenciam sacrosancte sedis apostolice et paternitatis vestre reverendissime onus execucionis earundem in nos assumpsimus, atque juxta vim, formam, tenorem et effectum earundem procedendum fore decrevimus; prenominatumque magistrum Johannem Clerk notarium publicum in nostrum et actorum nostrorum agendorumque et expediendorum per nos et coram nobis in causa et causis inferius descriptis ac inter partes infra nominatas scribam assumpsimus, deputavimus, et constituimus. Quo facto, egregius vir magister Thomas Martyn legum doctor exhibuit procuratorium suum a serenissimis Philippo et Maria Anglie rege et regina sibi et dicto venerabili viro magistro Johanni Story ac Davido Lewis conjunctim et divisim in hac parte concessis ac sigillo magno eorundem serenissimorum et illustrissimorum regis et regine in cera crocei coloris sigillatis; lectoque procuratorio hujusmodi de mandato nostro, prenominatus venerabilis vir magister Thomas Martin exhibens ut prefertur procuratorium suum pro dictis illustrissimis rege et regina fecit se partem pro eisdem et dedit articulos ex parte ipsorum serenissimorum dominorum regis et regine contra prefatum dominum Thomam Cranmerum propositos et conceptos una cum scedula eisdem articulis annexa: etiam libros dedit in ipsis articulis mencionatos et in margine eorundem specificatos; petiitque procurator hujusmodi quatenus dignaremur decernere dictum dominum Thomam Cranmerum, se archiepiscopum Cantuarie pretendentem, citandum fore ad comparendum coram nobis die Jovis prox' tunc sequente, duodecimo viz. die dicti mensis Septembris in ecclesia predicta hora octava ante meridiem ad respondendum, et procedi videndum contra eum juxta tenorem dicte commissionis sive subdelegacionis, et ad objiciendum contra articulos et cetera predicta contra eum in hac parte modo premisso exhibita si voluerit. Ad cujus quidem procuratoris peticionem, quia justa nobis videbatur ac juri et racione consona, decrevimus ipsum Thomam Cranmerum citandum juxta peticionem procuratoris predicti. Quo facto, prefatum Christoferum Smythe publicum apostolica auctoritate notarium in nostrum mandatarium in hac parte cum potestate citandi, certificandi, et exequendi dictam cicationem et quemcunque alium processum et ad alia facienda ad mandatarii officium spectantia deputavimus et admisimus; ipsumque Christoferum notarium publicum et mandatarium nostrum hujusmodi de fideliter exequendo, referendo, et certificando, et de ejus officio in ea parte juste exercendo juramento ad sancta Dei evangelia oneravimus et juravimus. Deinde vero articulos predictos et contenta in eisdem per dictum Christoferum Smythe notarium publicum publice in judicio perlegi fecimus, necnon prenominatum dominum Johannem Clerk notarium publicum ac scribam nostrum predictum ad conficiendum instrumentum seu instrumenta publica unum vel plura de et super premissis omnibus et singulis per nos et coram nobis istis die et loco qualitercumque habitis et factis mandavimus, et eundem ad sic conficiendum ac testes infra nominatos inde testimonium perhibere prefatus magister Thomas Martyn instanter requisivit; presentibus tunc ibidem venerabilibus viris Richardo Marshall, Commissario Universitatis predicte, Waltero Wright legum doctore, Archidiacono Oxon', Arthuro Cole sacre theologie baccalario, preside Collegii dive Magdalene in eadem Universitate, Richardo Cawdewell in medicinis doctore, Henrico Joilyff sacre theologie baccalario, Thoma Pygott et Edmundo Powell armigeris, cum multis aliis ad numerum ducentarum personarum et ultra. Tenor vero procuratorii illustrissimorum Philippi et Marie Regis et Regine predictorum, de quo superius fit mencio, per prefatum venerabilem virum magistrum Thomam Martyn procuratorem in eodem nominatum ut prefertur productum et exhibitum sequitur, et est talis: "Universis pateat per presentes, quod nos Philippus et Maria Dei gracia Anglie Francie Neapolis Jerusalem et Hibernie Rex et Regina, fidei defensores, Principes Hispaniarum et Cicilie, Archiduces Austrie, Duces Mediolani Burgundie et Brabancie, Comites Haspurgi Flandrie et Tirolis, dilectos nobis in Christo Thomam Martyn, Johannem Story et Davidum Lewis legum doctores absentes tanquam presentes omnibus melioribus et efficacioribus modo via et forma conjunctim, et eorum quemlibet per se divisim et in solidum, ita quod non sit melior conditio occupantis nec deterior subsequentis, sed quod unus eorum inceperit id ipsorum quilibet per se libere prosequi valeat, mediare pariter et finire, nostros veros legitimos et indubitatos procuratores, actores, factores, negociorumque nostrorum gestores et nuncios speciales nominamus, ordinamus, facimus, et constituimus per presentes, damusque et concedimus eisdem procuratoribus nostris conjunctim ut prefertur et eorum cuilibet per se divisim et in solido potestatem generalem et mandatum speciale, ita quod specialitas generalitati non derogat nec e contra, pro et nominibus nostris coram reverendis in Christo patribus Wigornien' et Glocestren' Episcopis ac Decano Londonien' et Archidiacono Cantuar', seu coram eorum tribus, duobus, sive uno, reverendissimi in Christo patris et domini, domini Jacobi, miseratione divina tituli sancte Marie in via sacrosancte Romane ecclesie presbyteri Cardinalis de Puteo nuncupat' sanctissimi in Christo patris et domini nostri domini Pauli divina providentia illius nominis Pape quarti, in causa et causis heresim aliaque enormia crimina, in quibus Thomas Cranmerus nuper metropolitane ecclesie Cant' Archiepiscopus assertus sit prolapsus, sapientibus, per nos nostrisque vice et nominibus contra ipsum Thomam Archiepiscopum pretensum mota et motis indecisis adhuc penden', Commissarii sive Judicis delegati, Subdelegatis sive Commissariis sufficienter et legitime deputatis, comparendi absenciamque nostram quoad personalem comparacionem in omnibus excusandi ac causam et causas absentie nostre (si opus fuerit) allegandi, proponendi, et probandi, ac fidem faciendi super eisdem, literasque commissionales remissorial' sive subdelegatorum prefati reverendissimi Jacobi Cardinalis ac Judicis delegat' sive Commissarii antedicti realiter producend' ostendendi et exhibendi. Necnon articulos, capitula, positiones sive interrogatoria, ac alias materias, objectiones, allegaciones seu peticiones quascunque verbo vel in scriptis dandi, faciendi, ministrandi, proponendi et exhibendi, posicionibus et articulis excepcionibusque ex adversis fiendis respondendi et suis responderi petendi, videndique juramentum quodcunque licitum et honestum ac de jure in hac parte requisitum in animas nostras prestand' subeund' et jurand'. Testes, literas et instrumenta, ac alia quecunque probacionum genera producend' ostendend' et exhibend', productaque et exhibita ex adverso reproband' et impugnandi, crimina et defectus objiciendi et objectis respondendi, decreta quecunque fieri decernique petendi et obtinendi, alium insuper procuratorem sive procuratores loco eorum seu eorum alicujus substituendi, ac substitutum sive substitutos hujusmodi revocandi, procuratorisque officium in se reassumendi, quotiens et quando id eis seu eorum alicui melius videbitur expedire. Ceteraque omnia et singula faciendi, exercendi et expediendi, que in premissis aut circa ea necessaria fuerint seu quomodolibet opportuna, etiam si mandatum de se magis exigant speciale quam superius est expressum. Et promittimus nos ratos, gratos, et firmos perpetuo habituros totum et quicquid dicti procuratores nostri seu eorum aliquis fecerit in premissis aut aliquo premissorum sub ypotheca et obligatione omnium bonorum nostrorum, et in ea parte caucionem exponimus per presentes. Dat' sub magno sigillo nostro apud honorium nostrum de Hamtoncorte Londonien' dioces' xxiiii$^{to}$ die mensis Augusti anno Domini millesimo quingentesimo quinquagesimo quinto ac annis regnorum nostrorum secundo et tercio." Adveniente vero dicto die Jovis, xii$^{o}$. viz. die predicti mensis Septembris, annoque Domini indictione et pontificatu predictis, coram nobis prefato Jacobo Glocestren' Episcopo ac Judice subdelegato sive Commissario supra nominato in ecclesia parochiali dive Virginis Marie superius specificat' loco in hac parte assignat' et deputat' judicialiter et pro tribunali seden' in prenominati magistri Johannis Clerk Notarii publici et scribe nostri predicti presentia, prefatus venerabilis vir magister Thomas Martyn ex superabundanti exhibuit procuratorium suum predictum pro illustrissimis rege et regina predictis, et se partem fecit pro eisdem ac eorum nomine procuratorio mandatum nostrum citatorium contra dictum dominum Thomam Cranmerum modo superius specificat' per nos decretum et sub sigillo nostro emanatum una cum certificatorio in dorso ejusdem sub instrumento publico de et super execucione ejusdem per prenominatum Christoferum Smythe Notarium publicum et Mandatarium nostrum predictum die et loco ac sub modo et forma in eodem certificatorio specificatis et contentis concepto, ac signis et subscripcionibus tam prefati domini Johannis Clerk auctoritate apostolica notarii publici et scribe nostri predicti, quam etiam dicti Christoferi Smythe eadem etiam auctoritate apostolica notarii publici nostrique in hac parte Mandatarii specialiter ut prefertur deputati, admissi et jurati, consignat' et subscript' ac nostro sigillo etiam sigillat' realiter exhibuit, et contra prefatum dominum Thomam Cranmerum tunc in judicio personaliter presentem ex parte dictorum serenissimorum dominorum Philippi et Marie, Regis et Regine predict', ac procuratorio nomine pro eisdem denuo dedit articulos prius ut prefertur per eum coram nobis datos et porrectos, atque in partem et subsidium probacionis articulorum hujusmodi et contentorum in eisdem exhibuit libros mencionatos in dictis articulis vestre reverendissime paternitati originaliter una cum presentibus transmissos. Qui quidem libri atque articuli ac subdelegatio et mandatum nostrum citatorium predict' in eorum formis originalibus tempore execucionis nostri hujusmodi mandati citatorii eidem Thome publice ostensi, ac ipsi seu saltem vere copie collacionate eorundem ac signo et nomine prefati domini Johannis Clerk, notarii publici nostrique actorum scribe antedicti, signat' eidem domino Thome Cranmero de facto realiter tradite fuerunt et penes eum dimisse, prout ex tenore certificatorii dicti nostri mandati citatorii plenius ac manifeste liquet et apparet, in presentia ejusdem domini Thome Cranmer personaliter ut prefertur presentis et comparentis, ac primo et ante omnia protestantis quod per suam comparicionem aut per aliqua per eum dicta seu dicenda, gesta vel gerenda, seu aliquo modo per eum facta seu fienda, non intendit consentire in nos subdelegatum sive commissarium antedictum aut in aliquem alium auctoritate domini pape seu Romani pontificis fulgentem, tanquam in judicem sibi in hac parte (ut asseruit) competentem, seu aliquo pacto admittere aliquam auctoritatem dicti Romani pontificis, asserendo et constanter affirmando eundem Romanum pontificem nullum in hoc regno habere seu habere debuisse aut debere auctoritatem seu potestatem, quodque ex eo etiam ipsius Romani pontificis auctoritatem ut prefertur admittere non intendit pro eo quod alias prestitit juramentum contrarium (ut asseruit) Henrico tunc Anglie illius nominis regi octavo, viz. de renunciando Romano pontifici et de admittendo et acceptando eundem regem Henricum octavum pro supremo capite ecclesiæ Anglicane, et protestabatur ulterius se paratum esse ad respondendum coram quocumque judice potestatem, auctoritatem, seu commissionem dictorum illustrissimorum regis et regine habente. Idem dominus Thomas Cranmerus tunc incontinenti ibidem multis variisque modis ac verbis suis nephariis, famosis et protervis publice in judicio dixit, opposuit, et objecit contra auctoritatem potestatemque dicti domini nostri Pape et Romani pontificis, et inter cetera audacter et sine pudore aut verecundia asserendo ipsum Romanum pontificem per leges et canones suos non solum pervertisse et pervertere leges hujus regni Anglie, sed etiam sacras scripturas et leges divinas, etiam asserendo et constanter affirmando inter cetera Christum in eucharistia spiritualiter tantum et non corporaliter esse, sed in corpore in celo tantum esse et non alibi. Asseruitque quod casu quo papam sive Romanum pontificem modernum imitari contigerit vestigia predecessorum suorum

Romanorum pontificum, aut si ejus auctoritate potestate et legibus in regnis et dominiis aliorum principum uti contigerit, quod per hoc perverteret et destrueret tam leges divinas quam etiam leges regum, et in hoc utitur (ut asseruit) vice antechristi et pro antechristo et Christi adversario censeri deberet. Ac etiam addendo asseruit et publice affirmavit, quod quisquis receperit seu admiserit auctoritatem domini Pape seu Romani pontificis in hoc Anglie regno, adversaretur et Deo et corone Anglie, atque eo facto excommunicatus est. Ulteriusque asseruit et publice dixit prefatus Thomas Cranmerus nos Subdelegatum ac Commissarium predictum nullo modo fuisse aut esse judicem sibi in hac parte competentem, sed incompetentem et perjurum eo quod admisimus auctoritatem Romani pontificis et eo quod juramentum alias prestitimus contrarium viz. de renunciando auctoritati ejusdem Romani pontificis ac de acceptando et admittendo prenominatum Regem Henricum octavum pro supremo capite ecclesie Anglicane. Et quia dictus dominus Cranmerus negavit Romanum pontificem esse supremum caput ecclesie Christi, ideo interrogatus per prefatum procuratorem dominorum Regis et Regine "quisnam tunc" (ejus judicio et opinione) "caput esset ecclesie," hujusmodi respondebat, "Regem quemcumque in regno suo." Et cum dictus Procurator replicavit dicens, "Ergo Nero qui interfecit Petrum caput fuit ecclesie Christi," ipse dominus Cranmerus affirmavit eundem Neronem sic fuisse caput ecclesie Christi, et etiam Turcam sue ecclesie caput esse. Deinde prenominatus venerabilis vir magister Thomas Martyn procurator antedictus in subsidium probationis contentorum in dictis articulis exhibuit quoddam instrumentum publicum manu propria magistri Richardi Watkyns notarii publici (ut apparuit) subscriptum, et ejus signo (ut apparuit) signatum, continens in se inter cetera tenorem juramenti fidelitatis obediencie per ipsum Thomam Cranmerum tempore ejus prefectionis sive consecracionis in Archiepiscopum Cantuar' beato Petro et sedi apostolice ac domino nostro Pape Clementi ejusque successoribus Romanis pontificibus prestiti, petiitque procurator predictus memoratum dominum Thomam Cranmerum per nos juramento onerari de fideliter respondendo tam dictis articulis et scedule annex' quam etiam ceteris per eum superius respective exhibitis in presencia ejusdem domini Thome Cranmeri recusantis subire juramentum hujusmodi pro eo (ut asseruit) quod nos procedimus in hac parte auctoritate Romani pontificis. Ceterum salvis protestacionibus suis previis et etiam sub protestacione quod non intendebat respondere nobis subdelegato predicto, sed prefato magistro Thome Martyn procuratori antedicto, tunc incontinenti idem Thomas Cranmerus dictis articulis omnibus et singulis superius ut prefertur contra eum datis et objectis ad peticionem prefati magistri Thome Martyn procuratoris predicti et de mandato nostro tam Latine quam Anglice plene et articulatim ac publice perlectis et declaratis sceduleque dictis articulis annexe et ceteris exhibitis antedictis, absque tamen aliquo juramento, deliberate et constanter coram nobis in publico judicio pro tribunali seden' respondebat ut sequitur. Ad primum articulum respondet se recepisse bullas a curia Romana et a Romano pontifice pro recepcione Archiepiscopatus Cantuar', quas bullas (ut asseruit) obtulit dicto tunc Regi Henrico octavo et ab eodem Rege et ejus auctoritate (ut etiam asseruit) eundem Archiepiscopatum recepit: et aliter negat hunc articulum esse verum. Ad secundum fatetur contenta in eodem esse vera. Ad tercium fatetur se acceptasse et duxisse mulierem in uxorem, postquam recepit sacrum ordinem sacerdotalem et circa viginti annos post mortem prime uxoris sue: et aliter hunc articulum negat esse verum. Ad quartum fatetur contenta in eodem esse vera. Ad quintum fatetur se secrete tenuisse dictam mulierem secundo per eum acceptam, quousque per statuta et leges hujus regni Anglie (ut asseruit) ei licitum fuit habere uxorem, et quod tunc eam publice tenuit et ab eadem plures proles habuit: et aliter negat articulum hujusmodi. Ad vj fatetur eundem esse verum, tamen sine pudore aut verecundia ut dicit. Ad septimum fatetur se edidisse librum in hac parte exhibitum et in articulo mencionatum vocat' "A defense of the true and catholicke feithe" etc. et negat se edidisse librum in eodem articulo etiam mencionatum vocat' "A discourse of Peter Martir" etc.; et quoad tercium librum vocat' "A discourse of the Lord's supper" etc. negat se illum edidisse, tamen credit quod hujusmodi liber est bonus et catholicus, et quoad cathechismum et articulos in eodem fatetur se adhibuisse ejus consilium circa edicionem ejusdem: et quoad librum vocat' "An aunswer of the moste reuerende father in God" etc. fatetur se edidisse illam partem ejusdem libri que continet ejus responsa ad librum editum per reverendum patrem Winton' Episcopum.

Ad octavum respondet se nunquam coegisse aliquos hujusmodi articulis subscribere, tamen dicit quod plures clericorum provincie Cant' eisdem articulis voluntarie subscripserunt, quorum subscripciones recepit ut dicit: et aliter negat articulum hujusmodi. Ad nonum fatetur quod a turri London' ad academiam Oxon' ductus fuit: et aliter negat contenta in eodem. Ad decimum fatetur se pro viribus defendisse libros et articulos mencionatos in hoc articulo (et in loco articulato) et contenta in eisdem: et aliter negat. Ad undecimum fatetur sententiam de facto fuisse contra eum latam eo quod defendebat libros et articulos predictos, et tamen dicit quod in illis libris et articulis non sunt hereses alique contente: et aliter respondet negative. Ad duodecimum respondet quod recessit ab auctoritate Romani pontificis, et aliis (quantum potuit) persuasit ut sic recederent, propter enormitates illic (ut dixit) regnantes; tamen per hoc dicit eum non esse schismaticum nec per hoc recessisse ab ecclesia catholica: et aliter credit hunc articulum non esse verum in aliquo. Ad decimum tercium et scedulam fatetur se prestitisse juramentum obediencie prout continetur in scedula huic articulo annexa; tamen hoc fecit (ut asseruit) sub protestacione in instrumento publico (ut prefertur) in hac parte exhibito contenta; et non aliter. Ad xiiij respondet et fatetur se recessisse (ut prefertur) ab auctoritate Romani pontificis et aliis sic recedere persuasit; hoc tamen (ut dicit) non fecit ante legem inde factam auctoritate parliamenti Anglie: et etiam dicit quod post leges hujusmodi et earum auctoritate consecravit episcopos et cetera fecit que ante legem hujusmodi factam ad Romanum pontificem pertinebant et que per ipsum Romanum pontificem antea fieri solebant: et aliter negat. Ad xv respondet quod ante recepcionem Romani pontificis auctoritatem et ante reconciliacionem nuperrime in hoc Anglie regno factam hoc regnum in bono statu remansit, atque maxime optat quod modo in eodem statu remaneret; et fatebatur (ut prius) se recessisse ab auctoritate Romani Pontificis, et quod non intendit ad illam auctoritatem redire vel eandem aliquo modo admittere, ut dicit. Ad ultimum negat contenta in eodem aliter esse vera quam superius respondebat, ut dicit. Ac incontinenti (responsionibus predicti domini Thome Cranmeri modo premisso publice et judicialiter factis, receptis, et conscriptis) dictus venerabilis vir magister Thomas Martyn procurator predictus ac nomine procuratorio quo supra acceptavit responsa superius facta et contenta in eisdem, quatenus faciunt pro parte et intencione dictorum illustrissimorum dominorum suorum, atque super articulis et exhibitis predictis produxit venerabiles viros magistros Will'm Tresham, Richardum Marshall, Richardum Smythe, et Richardum Croke, sacre theologie doctores, Jacobum Curtopp, Robertum Warde, Georgium London, et Robertum Serles, in testes, quos nos ad peticionem procuratoris hujusmodi in testes admisimus, et in forma jurandorum testium tactis per eos sacrosanctis scripturis de fideliter deponendo et de dicendo omnem et meram veritatem, cum fuerint examinati in hac parte de et super premissis super quibus modo premisso producti fuerunt, omni amicicia, favore, affectione, odio, timore et displicentia postpositis et semotis, juxta formam, modum et morem in simili testium admissione et juramenti prestacione solit' et consuet' et in hac parte de jure requisit', jurari fecimus in presentia dicti domini Thome Cranmeri sub ejus protestacionibus previis allegantis quod dicti testes nullo modo in hac parte sunt testes idonei, nec eisdem fides aliqua in hac parte fuit aut est (ut asseruit) adhibenda pre eo (ut etiam asseruit) sunt perjuri in eo quod subierunt juramentum domino Regi Anglie tanquam supremo capiti, ac modo contra hujusmodi juramentum (ut prefertur) per eos prestitum admiserunt auctoritatem Romani pontificis. Et tunc idem dominus Thomas interrogatus, an velit aliquibus aliis excepcionibus uti contra testes predictos seu aliqua interrogatoria contra eos ministrare, respondebat quod noluit nec ulterius aliquid in hac parte dicere, proponere, vel objicere. Super quibus omnibus et singulis modo premisso dicto duodecimo die Septembris ac anno Domini indictione pontificatuque et loco antedictis habitis factisque et expeditis, prefatum dominum Johannem Clerk Notarium publicum ac nostrum in hac parte auctorum Scribam predictum mandavimus, eundemque dictus magister Thomas Martyn procurator antedictus et procuratorio nomine predicto ad conficiend' instrumentum sive instrumenta publicum seu publica ac testes infra nominatos tunc presentes inde testimonium perhibitur' instanter rogavit et requisivit, presentibus tunc ibidem venerabilibus viris Waltero Wright legum doctore Archidiacono Oxon', Will'mo Tresham, Richardo Marshall, Richardo Smythe publico prelectore sacre theologie in eadem academia, et Richardo Croke sacre theologie professoribus, Arthuro Cole sacre theologie baccalario ac preside Collegii dive Magdalene in Oxonia, Richardo Cawdewell in medicinis doctore, Roberto Morwent sacre theologie baccalario, preside Collegii vulgo Anglice dict' "Oriell Colledge," Mauricio Bullock artium magistro, vicegardiano Novi Collegii Winton' in Oxon', Richardo Busshop artium magistro, Griffino Willyams in legibus baccalario, Philippo Randall principali Aule Cervine Oxon,' Will'mo Hawarden sacre theologie baccalario, principali Collegii Enei Nasi vocat' "brase nose," et Georgio Edrigio artium magistro ac publico Grecarum literarum prelectore, ac Johanne Pollard, Thoma Pygott, et Edmundo Powell armigeris, cum multitudine copiosa tam clericorum et scholarium dicte Universitatis quam etiam laicorum ad numerum quadringentarum personarum et ultra existen'. Postremo vero decimo tercio die mensis Septembris anno Domini indictioneque ac anno pontificatus supradictis, in quadam superiori camera sive pergula gardiani Collegii Novi dicte Universitatis, in presentia prefati domini Johannis Clerk Notarii publici ac Scribe nostri predicti, etiam presentibus Thoma Owen in legibus baccalario et Christofero Smythe Notariis publicis London' commoran', testes infra nominatos (ut prefertur) productos et juratos examinavimus, eorumque testium dicta et depositiones seriatim sequuntur et sunt tales.

Richardus Croke sacre theologie doctor in Universitate Cantabrigie, sexaginta sex vel quinque annorum, libere (ut dicit) condicionis, de noticia partium examinatus dicit, quod novit prefatum Thomam Cranmerum circiter triginta sex annos, Reginam Mariam a bimatu, Regem Philippum ex quo venit in Angliam, viz. circiter annum. Ad primum secundum tercium quartum quintum sextum septimum octavum et nonum respondet, quod credit articulos veros esse et omnia in eis contenta, quodque de eisdem fama laborat per universum regnum Anglie et in multis etiam partibus transmarinis; et aliter nescit deponere. Ad decimum dicit articulum esse verum, quia ipse personaliter disputacioni predicte in publica scola theologica Oxon' facte interfuit. Ad undecimum dicit articulum esse verum, ipse enim presens erat in ecclesia parochiali dive Virginis Marie Oxon' quando decretum in articulo specificatum adversus eundem Thomam pronunciatum fuit. Ad duodecimum respondet articulum esse verum, excepto eo quod iste deponens certo affirmare non potest quod prefatus Thomas Cranmer aliquos per vim coegerit et compulerit ad renunciandum auctoritati sedis apostolice, quanquam et illud publice a fide dignis audivit. Dicit insuper quod prefatus Cranmer multos seduxerit non tantum ab auctoritate ecclesie Romane, sed etiam a veritate in multis aliis fidei catholice articulis: et aliter nescit deponere ad articulum predictum. Ad decimumtercium dicit quod audivit ipsum Cranmerum publice confitentem se in consecracione sua prestitisse sacrum obediencie summo pontifici: et aliter nescit deponere in articulo predicto. Ad decimumquartum dicit et deponit ut supra: dicit insuper quod prefatus Cranmer pro Archiepiscopo Cant' se gerens consecravit et transtulit complures in Anglie episcopos, viz. consecravit quendam doctorem Poynett in Winton' Ep'm et quendam Coverdale in Ep'm Exon' et quendam Johannem Hoper in Ep'm Glocestr' et quod transtulit quendam doctorem Rydley a Roffen' in Londonien' episcopatum. Ad xv dicit articulum esse verum, quia heri audivit eum publice detestantem auctoritatem Pape et apostolice sedis: et aliter nescit deponere. Ad xvi dicit famam de premissis divulgatam esse per universum regnum Anglie.

Robertus Warde artium magister et publicus philosophie in Academia Oxon' prelector, quadraginta vel circiter annorum, testis (ut prefertur) productus et juratus, libere condicionis, interrogatus de noticia personarum dicit, quod novit Regem Philippum ab eo tempore quo primum appulit in Anglia, hoc est per integrum annum et ultra, Mariam Reginam ab inicio regni Edwardi sexti, viz. circiter novem annos, Thomam Cranmerum per duodecim annos vel circiter novit. Ad primum secundum tercium quartum quintum et sextum dicit, quod credit articulos veros esse et omnia in eis contenta, quia sepius publice audivit contenta in eisdem vera esse tam Oxonie quam alibi in multis Anglie partibus. Ad septimum dicit, quod credit prefatum Thomam vix adeo eruditum ut possit ipse ejus proprio ingenio hujusmodi libros componere, certo tamen scit ejus nomine et auctoritate eos circumferri, ipsumque Thomam dixisse libros predictos seu saltem plurimos ex illis fuisse proprio ingenio confectos, et ut suos agnovisse, et quod novit ipsum Thomam sepius defendisse plurimas hereses in libris predictis contentas in publicis disputacionibus Oxonie habitis, in quibus iste deponens publico certamine contra dictum Thomam congressus est: et aliter nescit deponere. Ad octavum credit esse verum, quia publice a fide dignis audivit: et aliter nescit. Ad nonum dicit esse verum, quia vidit quum prefatus Thomas Oxoniam primum a Londino ductus est, et in aliis rebus credit articulum esse verum. Ad decimum dicit articulum esse verum, quia interfuit disputacionibus predict', et in eisdem disputacionibus eidem Thome publice respondebat dum predict', hereses pro viribus confirmare satageret. Ad undecimum dicit articulum verum esse; ipse enim interfuit in ede dive Marie Oxon' quum decretum in articulo specificatum contra prefatum Thomam Cranmerum et duos alios publice legeretur per Doctorem Weston. Ad xij dicit quod credit esse verum, quia publice et sepius a fide dignis audivit. Ad xiij dicit verum esse, quia vidit publicum instrumentum super juramento predicto confectum publice contra eundem Thomam exhibitum: et aliter nescit. Ad xiiij dicit quod prefatus Thomas Cranmerus consecravit in episcopos Johannem Hooper in Gloucestren' Milonem Couerdale in Exonien' Hugonem Holbache et postea quendam doctorem Taylor in episcopos Lincoln', et insuper quod consecravit doctorem Rydley in Roffen' episcopum, quem postea transtulit ad episcopatum Londoniensem; et in aliis credit articulum esse verum. Ad xv dicit verum esse, quia heri xij° Septembris audivit eum animo obstinato contempnentem primatum Romane ecclesie, et insuper protestantem se nolle aliquo pacto in eundem consentire. Ad xvj dicit famam de premissis publice divulgatam esse tam Oxonie quam alibi in Anglia.

Robertus Serles sacre theologie baccalaurius in Universitate Oxon' commorans lx^ta. annorum vel circiter, libere (ut dicit) condicionis, testis (ut prefertur) productus et juratus de noticia partium examinatus dicit, quod novit Regem Philippum a tempore adventus sui in Angliam, viz. per annum aut circiter, ac Reginam Mariam per triginta annos vel circiter, Thomam Cranmerum circiter viginti annos. Ad primum secundum tercium quartum quintum sextum septimum octavum et nonum dicit, quod credit articulos veros esse et omnia contenta in eisdem, quia eadem publice audivit tam Oxonie quam in aliis hujus regni Anglie partibus: et aliter nescit deponere. Ad decimum dicit quod ipse presens personaliter non interfuit publice disputacioni habite Oxon' cum prefato Thoma Cranmer; credit tamen articulum per omnia verum esse, quia publica (ut asserit) per universum Anglie regnum fama erat et est, ipseque a nonnullis fide dignis qui disputacioni predicte intererant personaliter audivit prefatum Cranmerum in Academia predicta publica disputacione libros et articulos suos predictos pro viribus defendisse, tandemque convictum et exsibilitatum a multis fuisse: et aliter nescit deponere. Ad undecimum dicit similiter, quod credit et ex frequenti fide dignorum relacione audivit, omnia et singula in articulo contenta vera esse: et aliter nescit deponere. Ad xij dicit quod credit dictum Thomam fuisse et esse notorium scismaticum et hereticum, quia sepius audivit eundem tam privatim quam publice multas impias et execrandas hereses docentem, efferentem et pertinaciter defendentem, et quod idem deponens circa id temporis, quo ecclesia Anglicana primum cepit desistere ab auctoritate Pape et sedis apostolice, fuit vicarius de Lenham dioces' et provinc' Cantuar', et ideo tum subjectus (seu saltem publice habitus pro subjecto) jurisdictioni prefati Thome Cranmeri, qui tum publice pro episcopo Cant' se gessit, et quod ab ipso Thoma Cranmero seu saltem ab ejus Cancellario (mandatum et auctoritatem regiam in ea parte habere pretendente) idem deponens inductus et compulsus sit ad renunciandum auctoritati domini Pape et ad prestandum juramentum contra eundem et contra sedem apostolicam. Dicit insuper quod ipse circiter xv hinc annos unus erat ex publicis concionatoribus domini Regis in dioces' Cant', quodque ex predicto officio ignominiose expulsus fuit per prefatum Thomam Cranmerum Archiepiscopum Cant' pretens' pro eo viz. quod idem Robertus Serles publice in concionibus affirmavit realem presenciam corporis et sanguinis Christi in eucharistia, et quod recusavit subscribere certis articulis per prefatum Thomam Cranmerum editis et divulgatis qui sibi a fide Christiana in multis dissentire et penitus heretice videbantur, quodque eo nomine per prefatum Thomam (seu saltem ejus jussu et mandato) idem deponens bis in carceres conjectus fuit et ibidem diu detentus, hocque fuit et est notorium per universam Cant' dioc': et aliter nescit deponere de articulo predicto. Ad xiij dicit quod credit et quod publice audivit esse verum; et aliter nescit deponere. Ad xiiij dicit quod postquam in Anglia publice renunciatum est auctoritati sedis apostolice, maxime queque negocia ad jurisdictionem spiritualem pertinencia, ut consecraciones episcoporum et similia, sub umbra et auctoritate regii nominis per ipsum Thomam Cranmerum se (ut prefertur) tum pro Archiepiscopo Cant' gerentem agebantur et fiebant: et aliter nescit deponere. Ad xv dicit articulum esse verum, quia nuperrime viz. hesterna die audivit ipsum impia et execranda contra sedem apostolicam predict' publice in judicio dicentem, et protestantem quod nullo modo intendit in eandem consentire neque se eidem reconciliare: et aliter nescit deponere. Ad xvj dicit famam de premissis laborare.

Willielmus Tresham sacre theologie professor et ecclesie Christi Oxon' canonicus, sexaginta annorum etatis aut circiter, libere (ut dicit) condicionis, testis productus juratus et examinatus super articulis et exhibitis ex parte illustrissimorum principum Philippi et Marie Regis et Regine Anglie contra dominum Thomam Cranmerum pretensum Archiepiscopum Cant' propositis dicit et deponit in vim juramenti sui prestiti ut sequitur. Primo quoad noticiam partium dicit, quod dictum Regium Philippum per annum integrum ac dominam Mariam Reginam per viginti annos jam ult' ac dictum Thomam Cranmerum per idem tempus bene novit, ut dicit. Ad primum secundum tercium quartum quintum et sextum articulos dicit et deponit contenta in eisdem fuisse et esse vera ac tanquam vera publica, notoria, manifesta pariter et famosa in hoc Anglie regno habita de auditu istius deponentis, et quod sic sepius audivit dici, ut dicit: et aliter nescit deponere. Ad septimum dicit et deponit, quod prenominatus dominus Cranmerus libros sequentes edidit et orbi publicavit, viz. "A defense of the true and catholique feithe" etc. Item librum vocat' "An aunswer of the most reuerende father in God" etc. atque etiam quod idem Thomas Cranmerus ejus consilium adhibuit circa edicionem libri vocat' "Catachismum," in hoc articulo respective mencionat', quos quidem respective libros iste deponens dicit se audivisse prenominatum dominum Thomam Cranmerum in publico judicio fateri et confiteri se modo et forma quibus supra edidisse, et ejus consilium adhibuisse: et aliter nescit deponere. Ad octavum nescit deponere. Ad nonum dicit et deponit contenta in hoc articulo esse vera de certa sciencia et noticia hujus deponentis, ut dicit. Ad x et xj dicit et deponit, quod quia dictus dominus Thomas Cranmerus in Academia Oxon' publica disputacione secum ex more scolarum habita contenta in dictis libris et articulis publice pro viribus defendebat, et sic quatenus potuit defendens convictus fuit, et circiter duos aut tres dies prox' sequen' intra ecclesiam parochialem dive Marie Virginis Oxon', ex eo quod ab eisdem recedere pertinaciter recusavit, scolastico et academico Oxon' decreto pro heretico et impio pronunciatus fuit et declaratus, librique et articuli predicti pro hereticis et impiis pronunciati et declarati, de certa sciencia visu et auditu istius jurati, ut dicit; addendo ac causam sciencie sue in hac parte reddendo dicit se fuisse presentem tempore defensionis et convictionis predict', et dicit se contra eundem Thomam et ejus libros predictos in publica scola disputasse, et quod audivit ipsum Thomam ejus libros et hereses predict' modo et forma quibus supra defendentem, et in ea parte (ut prefertur) convictum, ut dicit: Presentibus tunc ibidem Richardo Smythe, Richardo Marshall, et Richardo Crook, sacre theologie professoribus, contestibus suis cum multis aliis, ut dicit, premissa videntibus et audientibus. Ad duodecimum dicit et deponit contenta hujusmodi articulo fuisse et esse vera, ac in Anglie regno publica, notoria, manifesta pariter et famosa de auditu, scientia, et noticia istius jurati, except' tantum quod ignorat de aliqua compulsione per eundem Thomam Cranmerum cuiquam facta, ut dicit. Ad xiij dicit contenta in hujusmodi articulo fuisse et esse vera ut credit, eo quod tunc Romanus pontifex suam auctoritatem exercebat in hoc regno Anglie de certa sciencia et noticia istius deponentis, ut dicit. Et ulterius dicit et deponit se audivisse dictum Thomam Cranmerum in publico judicio coram reverendo domino Subdelegato pro tribunali in hac parte seden' fateri se tale prestitisse juramentum obediencie, prout continetur in scedula huic articulo annexa; hoc tamen fecit sub protestacione in instrumento publico in hac parte contra eum exhibito contenta, ut idem Thomas asseruit: et aliter nescit. Ad xiiij et xv dicit et deponit contenta in eisdem articulis (except' hoc tantum quod aliquem coegit ad consenciendum contentis in eisdem articulis) fuisse et esse vera, publica, et notoria de certa sciencia et noticia hujus deponentis, ut dicit. Ad ultimum dicit et deponit predeposita per eum fuisse et esse vera, publica, et notoria, ac juxta eadem famam presertim in hoc Anglie regno laborasse et laborare juxta depositionem suam predictam.

Jacobus Curtopp artium magister decanusque Ecclesie Cath' Petriburgen', triginta octo annorum etatis aut circiter, libere (ut dicit) condicionis, testis productus juratus et examinatus super articulis et exhibitis in hac parte contra Thomam Cranmerum pretensum Archiepiscopum Cant' ex parte illustrissimorum dominorum nostrorum Regis et Regine propositis et datis. Primo quoad noticiam partium litigantium dicit, quod dictum dominum nostrum Regem per tres quarterios anni ult' ac dominam Reginam per xxv annos jam ult' elapsos respective bene novit, ut dicit. Ad primum et secundum dicit et deponit, quod sic dici audivit prout continetur in istis articulis: et aliter nescit deponere. Ad tercium dicit et deponit, quod audivit dici quod idem Thomas Cranmerus quandam mulierem secundo in uxorem duxit, sed an eidem mulieri fuit nuptus necne, nescit (ut dicit) nisi per auditum aliorum, sed pro certo dicit et deponit se vidisse eandem mulierem quam idem Thomas Cranmerus tanquam uxorem suam (ut asseruit) tenuit cum ipso Thoma in ejus mensa sedentem, comedentem et bibentem: et aliter nescit deponere. Ad iiij et quintum dicit et deponit, quod dici audivit quod dictus Thomas Cranmerus ejus secundam uxorem predictam tempore regis Henrici octavi clanculum et secrete tenuit, atque tempore Edwardi sexti etiam hujus regni nuper Regis idem Thomas eandem suam uxorem aperte et publice tenuit de visu et noticia istius deponentis: et aliter nescit deponere. Ad sextum dicit et deponit, quod dici audivit quod idem Thomas dictam uxorem suam secundo (ut prefertur) per eum acceptam, antequam prefectus fuit Cant' Archiep', duxit et tenuit Osiandro benedicente nupciis: et aliter nescit deponere. Ad septimum dicit et deponit, quod ex certa sua sciencia dictus Thomas Cranmerus sequentes libros suo nomine edidit et orbi publicavit, viz. "A defense of the true and Catholique doctrine," etc. item "Cathachismum brevem Christiane discipline" etc. atque "articulos" in eodem Cathachismo mencionat'; necnon, "An aunswer of the most reuerende father" etc. Et aliter nescit deponere. Ad octavum nescit deponere. Ad ix x et xj dicit et deponit, quod sic dici audivit quod idem Thomas Cranmerus dictos suos libros et articulos ac contenta in eisdem publice et in publica scola pro viribus defendebat, atque ab heresibus in hujusmodi libris et articulis contentis recedere pertinaciter recusavit, et propterea publico Oxon' decreto tam ipse quam ejus libri et articuli predicti pro hereticis et impiis pronunciati et declarati: et aliter nescit deponere. Ad xij (hoc excepto, quod non novit eundem Thomam aliquem coegisse ad contenta in hoc articulo facienda) dicit et deponit eundem articulum et contenta in eodem fuisse et esse vera, publica, notoria et manifesta in hoc Anglie regno: et aliter nescit. Ad xiij dicit et deponit contenta in eodem fuisse et esse vera, et etiam dicit quod audivit eundem Thomam coram reverendo domino Subdelegato in hac parte procedente in publico judicio pro tribunali seden' confiteri se tale prestitisse juramentum obediencie prout continetur in scedula huic articulo annexa: et aliter nescit deponere. Ad xiiij et xv dicit et deponit contenta in eisdem articulis fuisse et esse vera, except' quod non novit de aliqua coactione per eundem Thomam Cranmerum facta. Ad ultimum dicit predeposita per eum fuisse et esse vera, ac juxta eadem famam laborasse et laborare.

Georgius London sacre theologie baccalarius, Collegii Glocestren' in Academia Oxon', quinquaginta duorum annorum etatis aut circiter, libere (ut dicit) condicionis, testis in hac parte productus et juratus, quoad partes dicit quod dominum Regem modernum non novit, ac dictam dominam Reginam circiter xxviij annos jam ult' elapsos ac Thomam Cranmerum per quindecim annos bene novit, ut dicit. Ad primum secundum tercium quartum quintum et sextum dicit et deponit, contenta in eisdem articulis fuisse et esse vera et in hoc Anglie regno publica, notoria et manifesta, etiam per dictum Thomam Cranmerum coram domino Subdelegato in hac parte procedente publice in judicio saltem in effectu confessa, ut dicit: et aliter nescit deponere. Ad septimum dicit et deponit dictum Thomam Cranmerum libros sequentes edidisse saltem suo nomine, viz. "A defense of the true and Catholique doctrine" etc. "An aunswer of the moste reuerende father in God" etc. necnon ejus consilium adhibuisse circa edicionem Cathachismi brevis Christiane discipline etc. in hoc articulo mencionat', prout dictus Thomas Cranmerus publice fatebatur coram domino Subdelegato in hac parte pro tribunali seden': et aliter nescit deponere. Ad octavum nescit deponere. Ad ix x et xj dicit et deponit, quod dictus Thomas Cranmerus in publica scola theologica Academie Oxon' dictos libros et articulos ac contenta in eisdem aliasque nonnullas hereses publice defendebat, et inter cetera negavit presenciam corporis Christi in sacrocancta, eucharistia ut dicit; et sic defendendo et negando scholastico et academico Oxon' decreto pro heretico et impio in ecclesia parochiali dive Marie Virginis civitatis Oxon' pronunciatus et declaratus, ut iste deponens dici audivit, tamen eidem decreto non interfuit, ut dicit: et aliter nescit deponere. Ad duodecimum dicit et deponit eundem Thomam Cranmerum fuisse et esse (premissorum obtentu) Schismaticum, et quod idem Thomas Cranmerus publice fatebatur se adhibuisse ejus consilium Regi Henrico et quamplurimis aliis personis hujus regni ut recederent ab auctoritate Romani pontificis: et aliter dicit quod nescit deponere. Ad xiij dicit se audivisse dictum Thomam Cranmerum coram prefato domino Subdelegato publice in judicio fassum esse et confiteri se tale prestitisse juramentum, prout continetur in scedula huic articulo annexa; tamen hoc fecit (ut asseruit) sub protestacione in instrumento publico in hac parte exhibito contenta: et aliter nescit deponere. Ad xiiij et xv dicit et deponit contenta in eisdem articulis fuisse et esse vera, publica, et notoria etiam de certa sciencia auditu et noticia istius deponentis, ut dicit. Ad ultimum dicit predeposita per eum esse vera, atque juxta eadem famam laborasse et laborare.

MAGISTER RICHARDUS SMYTHE sacre theologie professor, ecclesie Christi in Academia Oxon' prebendarius ac publicus prelector sacre theologie in eadem Academia, quinquaginta trium aut circiter annorum etatis, libere (ut dicit) condicionis, testis super articulis capitulis sive interrogatoriis ex parte illustrissimorum dominorum Regis et Regine contra Thomam Cranmerum pro Archiepiscopo Cantuar' se gerentem datis et propositis productus, juratus et examinatus dicit, quod citra adventum ejusdem Regis ad hoc Anglie regnum eum tam tempore nuptiarum inter eum et serenissimam dominam Mariam Anglie Reginam Winton' celebrat' quam etiam pluries citra illud tempus vidit, quodque serenissimam dominam Mariam Reginam per xiiij aut xv annos, necnon prefatum dominum Thomam Cranmerum per xviij annos, aut circiter novit. Ad primum secundum tercium quartum quintum et sextum articulos predictos dicit et deponit iste deponens, quod a pluribus sepius audivit dici prout in eisdem articulis continetur quodque sic in quamplurimis hujus regni civitatibus et oppidis ac in utraque Universitate sive Academia Oxon' viz. et Cantabrigien' et in nonnullis aliis locis publicis hujus regni contenta in eisdem articulis fuerunt et sunt communiter dicta, et publica, notoria, et famosa etiam de auditu et sciencia hujus deponentis. Dicitque iste deponens quod firmiter credit contenta in articulis hujusmodi fuisse et esse vera; et aliter dicit quod nescit deponere. Ad septimum dicit et deponit iste juratus, quod liber vulgo nominatus "The defence of the true and Catholicke doctrine of the sacrament of the bodie and blodd of ower Lord" etc. editus fuit ac publicatus et orbi traditus per dictum Thomam Cranmerum ac ejus nomine, auctoritate et mandanto, non solum prout iste juratus sepius hoc verum esse audivit a pluribus aliis, verum etiam ex eo quod sub nomine ipsius Thome editus et impressus fuit. Cui quidem libro et contentis in eisdem iste juratus respondens confutacioni ejusdem alium librum edidit et scripsit nominatum vulgariter et Anglice "A confutacion of the true and Catholique doctrine" etc. Et quod attinet ad catachismum et articulos annexos et ad librum continentem responsa ejusdem Thome Cranmeri contra librum reverendi patris domini Stephani Winton' episcopi vulgariter dictum "An aunswer of the moste reuerende father in God Thomas Archebushop of Canterbury" etc. dicit quod tam per titulum et inscripcionem eorundem et per publicam famam, quam per confessionem dicti Thome, apparet eosdem libros per eundem Thomam editos fuisse et publicatos: et aliter dicit quod super contentis in hoc articulo nescit deponere. Ad octavum et nonum dicit quod nescit deponere. Ad decimum et undecimum dicit iste deponens, quod intra festa Pasche et Pentecostes ad annum elapsum, viz. anno Domini millesimo quingentesimo quinquagesimo quarto, presens fuit in scola theologica Oxonien' quando dictus Thomas Cranmerus publice et pertinaciter pro viribus defenderat hereses contentas in libris et articulis predictis, viz. non esse corpus Christi realiter in eucharistia, et non esse transubstanciationem panis et vini, tercio missam non esse sacrificium propiciatorium pro vivis et defunctis: quodque propterea post disputacionem aliquot dierum in ea parte publice et solemniter factam tandem sentencia duodecim doctorum virorum, viz. sex de Universitate Oxon' et sex de Universitate Cantabrigien', et aliorum multorum virorum doctorum specialiter in ea parte a Convocatione Cleri tunc Londini celebrat' missorum, convictus fuit, et postea in Ecclesia parochiali dive Marie Oxon' pro heretico judicatus, ejusque opiniones predicte tanquam heretice dampnate fuerunt: Presentibus etiam tunc ibidem ac premissa audientibus venerabilibus viris Richardo Marshall sacre theologie professore ac dicte Universitatis Oxonien' tunc et in presenti vicecancellario, Will'mo Tresham et Richardo Croke theologie doctoribus, ac Georgio London theologie baccalario, Roberto Warde artium magistro, Johanne Smythe artium magistro, Richardo Bruern sacre theologie baccalario et prelectore Hebraice lingue in dicta Universate, una cum aliis pluribus ad numerum millenarium et ultra, ut credit et ut modo recolit: et aliter dicit quod super contentis in istis articulis nescit deponere. Ad xij xiij xiiij xv et xvj dicit aliter super contentis in eisdem articulis deponere nescit quam ex auditu famaque publica et ex propria confessione predicti Thome Cranmeri hesterna luce, viz. duodecimo die instantis mensis Septembris, coram domino Subdelegato pro tribunali sedente publice facta, dicitque iste juratus in vim juramenti sui quod non est doctus neque instructus preceve aut precio aliquo in hac parte corruptus.

Magister Richardus Marshall sacre theologie professor ac decanus Ecclesie Cathedralis Collegii Christi in Alma Academia Oxon' et ejusdem Academie commissarius, xxxvij annorum etatis aut circiter, libere (ut dicit) condicionis, testis super articulis ex parte serenissimorum dominorum Philippi et Marie Anglie Regis et Regine contra dominum Thomam Cranmerum assertum Episcopum Cantuar' datis et propositis productus, juratus et examinatus, primo de partium noticia dicit, quod illustrissimum dominum Philippum Anglie Regem primo Winton' tempore nuptiarum inter eum et serenissimam dominam Mariam Anglie Reginam celebrat' vidit, quodque citra pluries eum vidit; et dicit quod prefatam serenissimam dominam Mariam Anglie Reginam per octo aut novem annos aut circiter ac Thomam Cranmerum per xvi annos aut circiter novit. Ad primum secundum tercium quartum quintum et sextum articulos predictos dicit, quod super contentis in eisdem aliter deponere nescit quam ex ipsius Thome confessione tam hesterna luce, viz. xij° die hujus mensis Septembris, coram reverendo patre domino Jacobo Glocestren' episcopo Subdelegato in hac causa judicialiter et publice facta, quam etiam antea isti jurato per eundem dominum Thomam Cranmerum declarata, atque ex publica et communi voce et fama super contentis in eisdem tam in utraque Universitate viz. Oxonien' et Cantabrigien' ac in pluribus aliis locis publicis hujus regni Anglie laborante; tamen dicit quod firmiter credit contenta in eisdem fuisse et esse vera: et aliter dicit quod super contentis in hujusmodi articulis nescit deponere. Ad septimum articulum dicit et deponit iste juratus, quod tam liber vocatus "A discourse of the true and catholike faithe" etc. "Cathachismus brevis" etc. cum articulis annexis, quam etiam liber vocatus "An aunswer of the most reuerende father in God Thomas Archebushop of Canterbury" etc. editi, publicati, et in publico producti et destinati fuerunt sub nomine dicti domini Thome Cranmeri, atque pro editis per eum publice et communiter dicti, nominati et reputati tam per ipsum Thomam quam per alios quamplurimos, et etiam judicialiter coram domino Judice Subdelegato predicto xij° die hujus mensis Septembris superius mencionat' sic recognit' et confessat.' Et ideo iste juratus etiam firmiter credit libros et articulos hujusmodi per ipsum Thomam Cranmerum saltem ejus nomine sic editos publicatosque et omnibus destinatos fuisse: et aliter nescit deponere. Ad octavum et nonum dicit iste juratus, quod firmiter credit contenta in eisdem vera esse ex eo quod sic communiter dicitur etiam ab aliquibus eorum qui articulis hic mencionatis subscripserunt, et quod sic communis fama laboravit de hujus deponentis auditu proprio: et aliter dicit quod nescit deponere. Ad decimum et undecimum dicit iste juratus, quod intra festa Pasche et Pentecostes ad annum elapsum, viz. in anno Domini millesimo quingentesimo quinquagesimo quarto jam ult' preterit', presens fuit iste juratus in scola theologica dicte Universitatis Oxonien', ubi dictus Thomas Cranmerus publice pro viribus defendebat hereses in libris et articulis predictis contentas, viz. denegando presenciam corporis et sanguinis Christi in eucharistia ac transubstancionem panis et vini in corpus et sanguinem Christi, etiam misse sacrificium denegando, propter quod post longam et prolixam disputacionem per quinque aut sex dies idem Thomas in ea parte convictus fuit: atque sentencia sex virorum doctorum Universitatis Oxon' et sex virorum doctorum Universitatis Cantabrigien', necnon sex etiam doctorum virorum ex

Convocacione sive Sinodo Cleri tunc Londini celebrat' et Oxonie pro dicta disputacione specialiter transmissorum, in choro Ecclesie beate Marie Virginis Oxon' predict' condempnatus fuit pro heretico, et similiter ejus opiniones predicte pro hereticis dampnate ac condempnate et pronunciate fuerunt: Presentibus tunc ibidem et premissa etiam audientibus venerabilibus viris Will'mo Tresham, Richardo Smythe, et Richardo Croke sacre theologie professoribus, Roberto Warde artium magistro, Georgio London sacre theologie baccalario, necnon Hugone Weston sacre theologie professore ac Convocacionis predicte proloquutore, Will'mo Chedsey sacre theologie professore, ac Will'mo Cole legum doctore, et Morgano Philipps sacre theologie baccalario, cum aliis quamplurimis ad numerum (ut credit) quadringentorum: et aliter dicit quod de contentis in istis articulis deponere nescit. Ad reliquos articulos viz. ad xij xiij xiiij xv et xvj articulos dicit et deponit, quod tam racione confessionis prefati Thome Cranmeri hesterna die coram reverendo patre domino Jacobo Brokes Judice in hac parte Subdelegato judicialiter et publice facte, quam etiam racione fame publice et communiter in ea parte tam in hac Academia Oxonien' quam etiam in aliis plurimis hujus regni oppidis et locis publicis laborantis, etiam de istius deponentis certo auditu credit contenta in articulis predictis fuisse et esse vera. Et aliter dicit quod de et super contentis in articulis predictis nescit deponere, dicitque iste juratus quod non est doctus neque instructus preceve aut precio in hac parte corruptus.

Tenores autem mandati nostri citatorii predicti una cum certificatorio in dorso ejusdem, necnon articulorum et scedule annexe, ac instrumenti publici de quibus superius fit mencio, seriatim sequuntur et sunt tales. Jacobus Brokes permissione divina Glocestren' Episcopus reverendissimi in Christo patris et domini domini Jacobi miseracione divina tituli sancte Marie in via sacrosancte Romane ecclesie presbyteri Cardinalis de Puteo nuncupati, cause et causis ac partibus infra nominatis Judicis et Commissarii a sanctissimo domino nostro Papa specialiter deputati, una cum reverendo in Christo patre Wigorn' Episcopo ac venerabilibus viris Decano Londonien' et Archidiacono Cantuarien' cum illa clausula et vestrum cuilibet insolid' etc. sub modo et forma infrascript'. Judex Subdelegatus sive Commissarius sufficienter et legitime deputatus universis et singulis prepositis decanis archidiaconis prebendariis rectoribusque vicariis capellanis curatis et non curatis scolaribus ac notariis publicis et tabellionibus clericisque et literatis quibuscumque per provinciam Cantuar' ac alias ubilibet constitutis, Salutem in Domino, ac nostris hujusmodi et dicti reverendissimi domini Cardinalis Judicis delegati antedicti, immo verius apostolicis, volentibus firmiter obedire mandatis literas commissionales sive subdelegatorias prefati reverendissimi patris et domini domini Jacobi Cardinalis et Judicis delegati predicti ipsius sigillo cera rubea impressa in quadam alba lignea capsula inclusa cum cordulis rubei coloris oblongo dependentibus sigillat' ac signo, nomine et subscripcione providi viri Claudii Badii clerici Bismitin' dioces' publici auctoritate apostolica et imperiali ut apparuit Notarii munitas et subscriptas, non viciatas, non rasas, non obolitas, non cancellatas, nec in aliqua sui parte suspectas, sed sanas et integras ac omni vicio et sinistra suspicione carentes, Nobis directas et per partem illustrissimorum serenissimorumque Philippi et Marie Dei gratia Anglie Regis et Regine in ipsis literis commissionalibus nominat' anno Domini millesimo quingentesimo quinquagesimo quinto inditione decima tercia pontificatus dicti sanctissimi domini nostri Pauli Pape eo nomine quarti anno primo, mensis vero Septembris die nono, in Ecclesia parochiali dive Virginis Marie in Alma Academia Oxoniensi scituat' realiter presentatas: Noveritis nos cum ea qua decuit reverencia recepisse tenorem infra scriptum in se continentem, Jacobus miseracione divina tituli sancte Marie in via sacrosancte Romane ecclesie presbiter Cardinalis de Puteo nuncupatus, causeque et causis ac partibus infra scriptis Judex ac Commissarius a sanctissimo domino nostro Papa specialiter deputatus, Reverendis in Christo patribus et dominis dominis Dei et apostolice sedis gracia Wigorn' et Glocestren' Episcopis ac Decano Londonien' et Archidiacono Cantuar' et vestrum cuilibet insolido, Salutem in Domino et presentibus fidem indubiam adhibere ac hujusmodi in commissis diligenciam facere nostrisque hujusmodi, immo verius apostolicis, firmiter obedire mandatis. Noveritis quod nuper sanctissimus in Christo pater et dominus noster dominus Paulus divina providencia Papa quartus quandam commissionis sive supplicacionis papiri scedulam nobis per certos cursores suos presentari fecit, quam nos cum ea qua decuit reverencia recepimus hujusmodi sub tenore motu proprio etc. Quoniam, sicut nuper nobis significatum fuit per literas dilectorum in Christo filiorum nostrorum Philippi Regis et Marie Regine Anglie, Thomas Cranmerus, qui olim sedis apostolice auctoritate metropolitane ecclesie Cantuarien' prefectus fuerat, in heresis aliaque tam grandia tamque enormia crimina sit prolapsus, ut non solum dicte metropolitane ecclesie regimine indignum se reddiderit, sed cum omnem fere divini et humani juris racionem abjecisse videatur, majori pena meritum se fecerit, prout etiam ex complurimis dicti regni Anglie prelatorum attestacionibus dicitur apparere, asseriturque etiam omnia esse notoria: Nos de premissis certam aliter quam ut prefertur noticiam non habentes, et tanta crimina (si vera sint) impunita dictamque metropolitanam ecclesiam sine pastore idoneo derelinquere, ad aliquam tamen execucionem aliter quam rei veritate per legitime receptas probaciones habita procedere nolentes, dilecto filio nostro Jacobo tituli sancti Simeonis sancte Romane Cardinali, ut de premissis etiam summarie simpliciter et de plano, sine strepitu et figura judicii ac sine ulla terminorum substancialium vel tele judiciarie observacione, citato dicto Thoma se informet, et quicquid inveniet nobis referat, committimus et mandamus cum potestate in Curia et extra citandi et inhibendi literas compulsoriales generales ac remissorias in forma consueta ad partes decernendi personasque quascumque (si opus esse arbitrabitur) sive ad exhibenda jura sive ad perhibendum testimonium, etiam per censuras ecclesiasticas cogendi et compellendi, seu si pro celeriori expedicione sibi videbitur ad recipiend' informacionem hujusmodi aliquem probum virum in dignitate ecclesiastica constitutum in partibus illis commorantem cum simili citandi, inhibendi, cogendi, facultatem deputandi ac compellendi et subdelegandi, cumque aliis facultatibus necessariis consuetis et opportunis, presentium tenore committimus et mandamus, non obstan' constitucione et ordinacione apostolicis dicti regni legibus statutis et consuetudinibus etiam juramento roboratis ceterisque contrariis quibuscunque, statum merita et tenores predictorumque aliorumque forsan latius exprimendorum pro sufficienter expressis habentes. Que quidem commissio binas in ejus fine habebat signaturas, quarum prior talis erat viz. de mandato domini nostri Pape, Audiam, idem reverendissimus dominus Cardinalis citet, decernat, deputet, subdeleget et referat ut petitur. Secunda vero sic subsequebatur viz. placet. J. Cujus quidem commissionis pretextu per nos citacione legitime extra Romanam Curiam et ad partes contra et adversus reverendum patrem dominum Thomam Cranmerum prefect' metropolitane ecclesie Cantuar' in forma solita et consueta decreta et concessa. Subsequenter vero constitutus legitime coram nobis providus vir, magister Petrus Renilius, in Romana Curia causarum et serenissimorum Philippi Regis et Marie Regine Anglie procurator assertus, prout de sue procuracionis mandato nobis legitimam promisit facere fidem et eo nomine procuratorio et ad recipiend' informacionem contentorum in preinserta commissione aliquem probum virum in dignitate ecclesiastica constitutum in partibus illis commorantem juxta et secundum predicte commissionis vim, formam, continenciam, et tenorem subdelegari, vicesque nostras committi per nos debita cum instancia postulavit. Nos tunc Jacobus Puteus Cardinalis et Judex prefatus, attendentes postulacionem hujusmodi fore justam et racioni consonam, vos reverendos dominos Wigornien' et Glocestren' Episcopos ac Decanum Londonien' et Archidiaconum Cantuarien' et vestrum quemlibet insolid' ad recipiend' informacionem premissorum narratorum et contentorum in preinserta commissione juxta dicte commissionis vim, formam, continenciam, et tenorem subdelegand' ac vices nostras committend' duximus, et per presentes subdelegamus et committimus has nostras literas nostro sigillo munitas decernentes. Que omnia et singula premissa vobis omnibus et singulis predictis intimamus, insinuamus, et notificamus, ac ad vestram et cujuslibet vestrum noticiam deducimus et deduci volumus per presentes. In quorum omnium et singulorum fidem et testimonium premissorum presentes literas sive presens publicum instrumentum, hujusmodi subdelegacionem in se continentes sive continens, exinde fieri et per notarium publicum nostrumque et hujusmodi cause coram nobis scribam infra scriptum subscribi et publicari mandavimus, sigillique nostri jussimus et fecimus appensione communiri. Dat' et actum Rome in domo habitacionis nostre solite residen' sub anno a Nativitate Domini millesimo quingentesimo quinquagesimo quinto, indictione decima tercia, die vero Mercurii decima nona mensis Junii, pontificatus sanctissimi in Christo patris et domini nostri domini Pauli divina providencia Pape quarti anno ejus primo: Presentibus ibidem venerabilibus viris dominis Menelao de Bazzanis et Augustino Ferragutt clericis, Parmen' et Majoricen' respective civitatum testibus ad premissa vocatis specialiter et rogatis et speciales, et ego Claudius Badius clericus Bismitin' diocesis, publicus apostolica et imperiali auctoritatibus notarius reverendissimique domini Cardinalis prefati et hujus cause coram eo in locum venerabilis viri domini Parii de Fabianis clerici Arben' notarii scriba deputatus: Quia dict' subdelegacioni, peticioni, et decreto, omnibusque aliis et singulis premissis, dum sic ut premittitur fierent et agerentur, una cum prenominatis testibus presens interfui, eaque omnia et singula sic fieri vidi et audivi ac in notam sumpsi, ex qua presens publicum instrumentum manu alterius scriptum exinde confeci et subscripsi, signoque et nomine meis solitis et consuetis una cum ipsius reverendissimi Cardinalis sigilli appensione signavi in fidem premissorum rogatus et requisitus: Post quarum quidem literarum commissionalium predict' presentacionem et earum recepcionem nobis et per nos sic ut premittitur fact' fuimus per partem prefatorum illustrissimorum Regis et Regine debita cum instancia requisiti, quatenus onus execucionis earundem literarum et contentorum in eisdem in nos assumere, et eas juxta formam in eis annotatam et secundum juris exigentiam debite exequi et citacionem legitimam contra et adversus prenominatum Thomam Cranmerum pro Cantuar' Archiepiscopo se gerentem in predictis literis ex adverso principaliter nominatum, sub modo et forma inferius descript' decernere et concedere dignaremur. Unde nos Jacobus Episcopus et Subdelegatus sive Commissarius antedictus, attendentes requisicionem hujusmodi nobis ut premittitur factam justam fore et racioni consonam, ob reverenciam dicti reverendissimi domini Cardinalis Judicis delegati committentis onus commissionis hujusmodi in nos assumentes, necnon juxta ipsius commissionis vim, formam, et effectum procedere volentes in hac parte, citacionem hujusmodi etiam ad diem et locum inferius descript' fieri decernimus, justicia id poscente. Vobis igitur conjunctim et divisim auctoritate apostolica (qua fungimur in hac parte) committimus et firmiter injungendo mandamus, quatenus citetis seu citari faciatis peremptorie prefatum Thomam Cranmerum Archiepiscopum assertum antedictum, quod compareat coram nobis in Ecclesia parochiali dive Virginis Marie in Alma Academia Oxon' situat' duodecimo viz. die instantis mensis Septembris hora octava ante meridiem ejusdem diei cum continuacione et prorogacione dierum, horarum, et locorum tunc sequend' et limitand', si oporteat in hac parte fiend' causam racionabilem et legitimam, si qua pro se habeat aut dicere sciat, objectionemve sive excepcionem si quam proponere, facere, aut objicere velit aut possit contra literas sive instrumentum subdelegacionis predict' aut contra articulos in hac parte datos seu contra instrumenta processum sive jura aliqua in hac parte producta in debita juris forma dictur' ostensur' et allegatur'; necnon testes aliasque probaciones super articulis ceterisque juribus et instrumentis hujusmodi produci, jurari, et fieri visur' et auditur', interrogatoriaque si quedare voluerit datur' et ministratur', necnon ad omnia et singula acta in hac parte necessaria atque juxta premissa et juxta vim, formam, et tenorem literarum commissionalium sive subdelegatoriarum predictarum successive expediend' processur' et procedi visur' ulteriusque factur' et receptur' quod tenor et effectus dictarum literarum commissionalium sive subdelegatoriarum et contenta in eisdem de se exigunt et requirunt, et quod justicia in hac parte suadebit, intimantes nihilominus eidem Thome Cranmero Archiepiscopo asserto sic citato, quod sive ipse in dicto citacionis et decreti nostri hujusmodi termino comparuerit sive non, Nos juxta juris exigentiam ac juxta vim, formam, tenorem et effectum dictarum literarum commissionalium sive subdelegatoriarum tam ad testium productionem, juramenti prestacionem, et eorum examinacionem, ceterorumque probacionem recepcionem et admissionem, quam etiam ad omnia et singula acta necessaria in hac parte successive expediend', prout justum fuerit, procedemus ipsius Thome citati absencia sive contumacia in aliquo non obstante. Et quid in premissis feceritis, nos Subdelegatum antedictum dictis die et loco debite certificet ille vestrum qui presens nostrum mandatum fuerit executus personaliter vel per suas literas patentes harum seriem in se continentes una cum presentibus auctentice sigillat'. In cujus rei testimonium sigillum nostrum presentibus apposuimus. Dat' nono die mensis Septembris anno Domini millesimo quingentesimo quinquagesimo quinto. IN DEI NOMINE AMEN. Universis et singulis presens publicum instrumentum inspecturis pateat evidenter et sit notum, quod anno a Nativitate Domini millesimo quingentesimo quinquagesimo quinto, indictione decima tercia pontificatusque sanctissimi in Christo patris et domini nostri domini Pauli divina providencia hujus nominis Pape quarti anno ejus primo, mensis vero Septembris die nono, in domo Rogeri Taylor alias Cooke infra parochiam beate Marie Magdalene in suburbiis civitatis Oxon' diocesisque Oxon' notorie situat', in providi et circumspecti viri domini Johannis Clerk notarii publici subscripti testiumque infra nominatorum ad hæc specialiter vocatorum et rogatorum presencia, Ego Christoferus Smythe notarius publicus ac mandatarius in hac parte specialiter deputatus juratusque et admissus ex parte illustrissimorum serenissimorumque Philippi et Marie Anglie Regis et Regine in retroscriptis literis citatoriis principaliter nominatorum, ad assumend' in me execucionem retroscriptarum literarum citatoriarum et ad illas exequend' instanter requisitus, tanquam obediencie filius, literas hujusmodi humiliter et reverenter recepi, ac ipsarum execucionem juxta officii mei debitum suscepi, et eidem Thome Cranmero ex adverso principali in retroscriptis literis ex adverso principaliter nominato presenti easdem literis et contenta in eisdem insinuavi, publicavi, notificavi et ad ejus noticiam, quantum melius potui et debui, deduxi, ac earundem vigore eundem Thomam citavi, quatenus post hujus citacionis execucionem infra terminum in ea prefixum in judicio coram reverendo in Christo patre et domino domino Jacobo permissione divina Glocestren' Episcopo, reverendissimi in Christo patris et domini domini Jacobi miseracione divina tituli sancte Marie in via sacrosancte Romane ecclesie presbyteri Cardinalis de Puteo nuncupati cause et causis ac partibus infra nominatis Judicis et Commissarii a dicto sanctissimo domino nostro Papa specialiter deputati sub modo et forma infrascript' Judice Subdelegato sive Commissario, sufficienter et legitime deputato, in retroscriptis literis nominato modo et forma in eisdem literis expressis, compareat, et alias dictas citatorias literas juxta vim, formam, tenorem et effectum earundem executus fui, nihil de contentis in eisdem omittendo, et in signum vere et realis execucionis hujusmodi ipsi Thome veram earundem literarum copiam, necnon copiam veram articulorum, capitulorum, sive interrogatoriorum ex parte dictorum serenissimorum dominorum nostrorum Regis et Regine in hac parte contra eum proposit' dat' et exhibit' collacionatas, ac manu et signo dicti domini Johannis Clerk notarii publici predicti, ac hujus cause in actorum scribam specialiter assumpti, subscriptas et firmatas, una cum libris, munimentis, et documentis in ipsis articulis sive capitulis specificatis, et in hac parte coram retro nominato domino Subdelegato etiam exhibitis, tradidi et dimisi. Super quibus omnibus et singulis tam Ego notarius et mandatarius antedictus, quam etiam prefatus dominus Johannes Clerk notarius publicus predictus, tunc etiam personaliter presens ex parte dictorum serenissimorum dominorum nostrorum Regis et Regine, et eorum nomine ad conficiend' instrumentum sive instrumenta publicum seu publica unum vel plura, ac testes infra nominatos inde testimonium perhibere specialiter fuimus respective requisiti. Acta fuerunt hec omnia et singula prout suprascribuntur et recitantur sub anno Domini indictione pontificatusque ac mense die et loco supradictis: Presentibus tunc ibidem Griffino Willyams Oxon' commorante, et Thoma Owen London' commorante, notariis publicis, ac Rogero Taylor alias Cooke Oxon' dioc' et Rolando Grene literato London' etiam commorante, Testibus ad premissa vocatis specialiter et rogatis. Et ego Christoferus Smythe Lincoln' diocesis publicus (apostolica auctoritate) notarius, quia dictam citacionem contra memoratum dominum Thomam Cranmerum modo et forma quibus supra debite executus fui, omnibusque aliis et singulis premissis, dum sic ut premittitur sub anno Domini indictione pontificatusque ac mense die et loco supradictis fierent et agerentur (una cum prenominato domino Johanne Clerk notario publico et actorum scriba predicto hic inferius se subscribente) prenominatisque testibus presens personaliter interfui, eaque omnia et singula sic feci, executus fui, et expedivi ac in notam sumpsi. Ideo hoc presens publicum instrumentum manu mea propria exinde confeci, scripsi et subscripsi, signoque[a] et nomine meis solitis et consuetis una cum signo et nomine prefati Johannis Clerk notarii predicti atque dicti reverendi patris domini Jacobi Glocestren' Episcopi subdelegati supradicti sigilli appensione signavi in fidem premissorum rogatus specialiter et requisitus. Et ego Johannes Clerk, Bathon' et Wellen' diocesis publicus sacra auctoritate apostolica notarius, et alme Curie Cantuarien' procuratorum generalium unus, in causaque et causis retroscriptis actorum scriba specialiter assumptus, admissus, et assignatus, Quia dictarum literarum citatoriarum recepcioni et execucioni ac vere copie earum

[a] The device is in the margin of the MS.

etiam manu nomineque et signo meis propriis et solitis signate et firmate tradicioni ceterisque premissis omnibus et singulis, dum sic ut premittitur sub anno Domini indictione pontificat' menseque ac die et loco superius specificatis agerentur et fierent, una cum memorato domino Christofero Symthe notario publico et mandatario predicto (ut prefertur) se superius subscribente testibusque prenominatis presens personaliter interfui, eaque omnia et singula sic fieri vidi, scivi, et audivi, Ideo hoc presens publicum instrumentum, manu propria supra nominati domini Christoferi Smythe notarii publici predicti scriptum et exinde confectum, etiam subscripsi, signoque[a] et nomine meis solitis et consuetis signavi una cum appensione sigilli supradicti reverendi domini Subdelegati in fidem et testimonium premissorum rogatus (ut prefertur) et requisitus. In dei nomine amen coram vobis reverendo in Christo patre et domino domino Jacobo permissione divina Glocestren' Episcopo, reverendissimi in Christo patris et domini domini Jacobi miseracione divina tituli sancte Marie in via sacrosancte Romane ecclesie presbiteri Cardinalis de Puteo nuncupati, a sanctissimo domino nostro domino Paulo divina providencia illius nominis Papa quarto Judicis delegati, Commissario sive Subdelegato in hac parte sufficienter auctorisato, Articulos, capitula, posiciones sive interrogatoria infra scripta, ac omnia et singula in eisdem contenta, omnibus melioribus validioribusque et efficatioribus via modo et juris forma, quibus melius validius et efficatius de jure potuit aut debeat atque ad omnem juris effectum exinde sequi valen' Procurator, et eo nomine illustrissimorum serenissimorumque principum Philippi et Marie Anglie Regis et Regine contra et adversus Thomam Cranmerum pro Archiepiscopo metropolitane ecclesie Cantuar' se gerentem dat, proponit, et exhibet conjunctim et divisim ac articulatim prout sequitur. In primis procurator dictorum illustrissimorum Regis et Regine ac procuratorio nomine pro eisdem ponit et articulatur, et si negatum fuerit probare intendit, Quod idem Thomas Craumerus ad viginti seu circiter annos elapsos in Archiepiscopum Cantuarien' (tunc ipsa sede Archiepiscopali et ecclesia metropolitana Cantuar' per mortem recolende memorie Will'mi Warrham ultimi Archiepiscopi ibidem et illius Thome immediati predecessoris vacante) auctoritate sedis apostolice utcumque prefectus fuit, atque per nonnullos citra annos pro Archiepiscopo metropolitanoque ejusdem ecclesie metropolitice se gessit, et aliquo modo se gerit pretenditque in presenti, hocque fuit et est verum, publicum, notorium, manifestum pariter et famosum: ponit et articulatur conjunctim, divisim, et de quolibet. Item ponit et articulatur, et si negatum fuerit probare intendit, procurator prefatus et procuratorio nomine quo supra, Quod olim antequam dictus Thomas Cranmerus dicte Cantuar' ecclesie (ut prefertur) prefectus fuit, et ante ullos sacros ordines ab eo susceptos, ad xxx[ta] et ultra annos elapsos quandam mulierem communiter et vulgo nominatam Johannam alias "black Johanne of the dolphin" in Cantabrigia Elien' diocesis (seu alio forsan nomine sive cognomine vocatam) in uxorem duxit: ponit et articulatur ut supra. Item ponit et articulatur, et si negatum fuerit probare intendit, procurator antedictus, Quod dictus Thomas Cranmerus post mortem dicte uxoris sue, presbiter effectus ac in sacro ordine sacerdotali constitutus, quandam aliam mulierem Annam nominatam, seu forsan aliter vocatam de facto quum de jure non deberet, in suam conjugem accepit, et in Archiepiscopum Cantuar' auctoritate predicta utcumque prefectus fuit: ponit et articulatur ut supra. Item ponit et articulatur, et si negatum fuerit probare intendit, idem procurator, Quod ipse Thomas Cranmerus mulierem hujusmodi sic per eum secundo tanquam uxorem acceptam pro uxore usque ad mortem Henrici octavi nuper Anglie Regis, clanculum tamen et (ut fieri potuit) secrete tenuit, habuit, et custodivit. Item procurator predictus ponit et articulatur, et si negatum fuerit probare intendit, Quod memoratus Thomas Cranmerus a morte dicti Regis Henrici et tempore Edwardi sexti tunc immediate Anglie Regis eandem mulierem sic secundo acceptam non secrete, ut prius, sed palam, publice, notorieque et manifeste citra ullum pudorem et verecundiam tanquam suam uxorem et pro sua uxore tam in mensa quam alibi de facto tenuit, acceptavit, et tractavit, et cum ea tanquam cum sua uxore cohabitavit, prolesque et liberos multos ex eadem suscitavit et habuit: ponit et articulatur ut supra. Item ponit et articulatur antedictus procurator, et si negatum fuerit probare intendit, Quod dictus Thomas Cranmerus, adeo impudens existens ut turpitudinem suam in hac parte manifeste jactando detegeret, et in publicum totius hujus regni Anglie conspectum notorie deduceret, tempore dicti Regis Edwardi (et ipso regnante) publice asseruit et

[a] The device is in the margin of the MS.

affirmavit, inter cetera, se dictam mulierem secundam ex multis antea annis in uxorem suscepisse et cum ea cohabitasse, necnon proles et liberos (ut prefertur) ab eadem suscitasse: ponit et articulatur ut supra. Item ponit et articulatur procurator antedictus, et si negatum fuerit probare intendit, Quod prelibatus Thomas Cranmerus ad profundum malorum veniens (Christiana fide et religione penitus contemptis) in hereses suas, quas longe antea imbiberat, et maxime contra venerabile eucharistie sacramentum, libros una cum copia istorum articulorum sibi ostensos, propositos et traditos, ac in margine hujus articuli expressos sive designatos, eorumque vim, formam, tenorem et effectum edidit lingua partim Latina partim Anglicana saltem sic edi imprimique et orbi publicari fecit etiam suo nomine, ipsasque hereses publice asseruit et docuit: ponit ut supra. Item ponit et articulatur procurator supra nominatus, et si negatum fuerit probare intendit, Quod prefatus Thomas Cranmerus articulis quibusdam hereticis, maxime inter cetera contra veritatem veramque presentiam corporis et sanguinis Christi in eucharistia editis et conceptis, verumque et reale ac perfectum Christi corpus in ipso sacramento sub specie sive forma panis et vini notorie denegantibus, sub nomine Cleri Cantuarien' falso editis et publicatis, pastores, rectores et ecclesiarum curatos non paucos subscribere coegit, fecit et compulit: ponit et articulatur ut supra. Item procurator antedictus ponit et articulatur, et si negatum fuerit probare intendit, Quod dictus Thomas, quia libros et articulos antedictos modis quibus potuit non cessabat defendere, tum ut factionis et heresis sue participes in impietate retineret, tum ut alios ad eandem nequiciam pertraheret, auctoritate serenissime domine Marie Regine predicte (et ejus consiliariis suadentibus) e turri et carcere London', ubi ob sua enormia nephandaque scelera, delicta, et crimina detentus fuit, ad Academiam Oxonien', ubi tunc parliamentum futur' sperabatur, mittebatur: Hocque fuit et est verum, publicum, notorium, manifestum pariter et famosum: ponit et articulatur ut supra. Item ponit et articulatur, et si negatum fuerit probare intendit, procurator antedictus, Quod idem Thomas Cranmerus in dicta Academia Oxonien' (publica disputacione secum ex more scolarum habita) libros et articulos predictos publice pro viribus defendebat, et sic quatenus potuit defendens exsibilatus et convictus fuit: ponit et articulatur ut supra. Item ponit et articulatur procurator sepe dictus, et si negatum fuerit probare intendit, Quod memoratus Thomas Cranmerus, quia sic libros, articulos, et hereses predict' pro viribus defendebat, et quia modo premisso convictus cedere et ab eisdem recedere pertinaciter recusavit, scolastico et academico Oxonien' decreto pro heretico et impio execratoque pronunciatus fuit et declaratus, librique et articuli predicti pro hereticis impiis et execratis pronunciati similiter et declarati fuerunt: ponit et articulatur ut supra. Item ponit et articulatur procurator predictus, et si negatum fuerit probare intendit, Quod prefatus Thomas Cranmerus fuit et est merus et notorius schismaticus, ex eo presertim quod non solum ab unitate catholice et universalis ecclesie ipsiusque ecclesie constitucionibus, ordinacionibus, ritibus, decretis, sanisque doctrinis et determinacionibus variis et innumeris modis, atque a sede apostolica ecclesiaque Romana totius ecclesie catholice sola matrice summoque et Romano pontifice et domino nostro Papa ejusdem ecclesie catholice et universalis solo sub Christo capite, recessit, verum etiam ex eo quod tum hujus regni Anglie Regem Henricum octavum, tum etiam plures alios hujus regni Anglie episcopos, prelatos, et proceres et magnates, atque utriusque sexus personas quamplurimas, sic recedere summoque pontifici et ejus ac sedis apostolice auctoritati renunciare procuravit et fecit, et in ea parte ejus consilium et auxilium adhibuit, etiam pluribus et variis modis quosdam eorum ad sic recedendum et renunciandum compulit et coegit, necnon in ea parte specialis precipuusque et principalis seu quasi instigator et fautor fuit, pro talique et ut talis fuit et est communiter dictus, tentus, habitus, nominatus et reputatus palam, publice et notorie: ponit et articulatur ut supra. Item ponit et articulatur, et si negatum fuerit probare intendit, sepe dictus procurator, Quod prefatus Thomas Cranmerus auctoritate sedis apostolice et domini nostri Pape Cantuarien' Archiepiscopus (ut prefertur) consecratus et prefectus (inter cetera tempore consecrationis sue hujusmodi paulove antea aut citra) fidelitatem et obedienciam beato Petro sancteque et apostolice Romane ecclesie et sanctissimo domino nostro Pape tunc existenti ejusque successoribus juxta tenorem scedule presentibus annexe saltem in effectu

*A defence of the true and catho' doctrine of the sacrament of the bodie and bloode of our saivo*r*. Christe* etc. *A discourse vpon the sacrament of the Lords supper solemplie handled at the vniuersitie of Oxforde by doctor*r*. Petir Martir* etc. *Catachismus brevis Christiane discipline* etc. *Articuli de quibus in Sinodo Londonien'* a°. dn$^{i}$. 1552. etc. *An Aunswer of the most reuerende father in God Thomas Archebushop of Cant' vnto a craftie and sophisticall cavillacion deuised by Steven Gardiner* etc.

prestitit, et in ea parte juramentum ad sancta Dei evangelia subivit: ponit et articulatur ut supra. Item ponit et articulatur procurator predictus, Quod dictus Thomas Cranmerus ejus fidelitatis obedienciequ e et juramenti prestacione predictis et ceteris premissis non obstantibus (sed penitus spretis et postpositis) spiritu perversi consilii ductos, immo verius seductos, non solum modo premisso ab ecclesie unitate sedeque apostolica et domino nostro domino Papa ejusque auctoritate recessit, et alios supra nominatos recedere et (ut prefertur) renunciare fecit, procuravit, et coegit, in plurimasque et varias hereses lapsus sit; verum etiam ipsius summi pontificis et sedis apostolice auctoritatem in se assumere et usurpare presumendo, saltem prophana et illicita auctoritate utendo (et omnino absque hujusmodi summi pontificis et sedis apostolice auctoritate) tam episcopos consecrare ceteraque ad solam sedem apostolicam et dominum nostrum Papam et ad nullum alium spectantia attemptare et peragere presumpsit: Quorum premissorum pretextu idem Thomas Cranmerus tum reatum crimenque heresis et schismatis, tum etiam reatum perjurii etiam voluntarii, notorie et manifeste incurrebat et incurrit: Hocque fuit et est verum, publicum, notorium, manifestum pariter et famosum: ponit et articulatur ut supra. Item ponit et articulatur procurator predictus, et si negatum fuerit probare intendit, Quod licet hujus regni Anglie subditi et utriusque sexus persone nuper ad octo seu novem menses aut circiter elapsos a schismate pernicioso, quo hoc regnum antea pestifere infectum fuit, recesserunt, atque ad ecclesie unitatem redierunt, sedisque apostolice et sacrosancte Romane ecclesie ac domini nostri domini Pape auctoritatem receperunt, acceptarunt et admiserunt, et in ea parte a schismate et ab heresibus quibus infecti et involuti fuerunt reconciliacionem auctoritate dicte sedis apostolice et domini nostri Pape obtinuerunt, Prefatus tamen Thomas Cranmerus animo perverso, indurato corde, in heresibus suis et in schismatis reatu (quibus antea infectus fuit) adhuc involutus remanet et jacet infectus, atque se in ea parte debite reconciliare ejusque heresi errori et schismati renunciare ad unitatemque ecclesie catholice et dominum nostrum Papam summumque pontificem caput ejusdem ecclesie redire contempsit et neglexit, ac sic pertinaciter contempnuit et negligit in presenti: Hocque fuit et est verum, publicum, notorium, manifestum pariter et famosum: ponit et articulatur ut supra. Item ponit et articulatur procurator predictus, ac si negatum fuerit probare intendit, Quod premissa omnia et singula presertim in hoc regno Anglie fuerunt et sunt vera, publica, notoria, manifesta pariter et famosa apud omnis ordinis homines, etiam tam publica, vera, notoria, manifesta et famosa, quod ulla tergiversacione celari non possunt, atque pro talibus et ut talia taliterque facta et perpetrata communiter dicta, tenta, habita, nominata et reputata palam, publice et notorie. UNDE petit procurator illustrissimorum et serenissimorum dominorum Regis et Regine predict' ac procuratorio nomine pro eisdem jus et justiciam de et super premissis et ea continentibus quibuscunque conjunctim et divisim fieri et ministrari: Non arctans se ad omnia et singula premissa probanda, nec ad onus superflue probacionis eorundem de quo protestatur specialiter in hac parte, Juris beneficio in omnibus semper salvo ac vestrum officium, domine Judex, antedict' in hac parte humiliter implorando. IN DEI NOMINE AMEN. Ego Thomas electus Cantuarien' ab hac hora inantea fidelis et obediens ero beato Petro sancteque apostolice Romane ecclesie ac domino nostro domino Clementi Pape septimo suisque successoribus canonici intrantibus. Non ero in consilio aut consensu vel facto ut vitam perdant aut membrum, seu capiantur aut in eos manus violenter quomodolibet ingerantur, vel injurie alique inferantur quovisquesito colore. Consilium vero quod mihi credituri sunt per se aut nuncios seu literas, ad eorum dampnum (me sciente) nemini pandam. Papatum Romanum et regalia sancti Petri adjutor eis ero ad retinendum et defendendum contra omnem hominem. Legatum apostolice sedis in eundo et redeundo honorifice tractabo et in suis necessitatibus adjuvabo. Jura, honores, privilegia, et auctoritatem Romane ecclesie et domini nostri Pape et successorum predictorum conservare et defendere, augere et promovere curabo, nec ero in consilio vel tractatu in quibus contra ipsum dominum nostrum vel eandem Romanam ecclesiam aliqua sinistra vel prejudicialia personarum, juris, honoris, status, et potestatis eorum machinentur; et si talia a quibuscumque procurari novero (vel tractari), impediam hoc pro posse, et quantocius potero commode significabo eidem domino nostro vel alteri per quem ad ipsius noticiam pervenire possit. Regulas sanctorum patrum, decreta, ordinaciones, sentencias, disposiciones, reservaciones, provisiones, et mandata apostolica totis viribus observabo et faciam ab aliis observari. Hereticos, schismaticos, et rebelles domino nostro et successoribus predictis pro posse persequar et impugnabo. Vocatus ad sinodum veniam, nisi prepeditus fuero canonica prepedicione. Apostolorum limina Romana Curia existentia citra singulis annis, ultra vero montes singulis bienniis visitabo aut per me aut per meum nuncium, nisi apostolica absolvar licencia. Possessiones vero ad mensam meam pertinentes non vendam neque donabo nec impignorabo, neque de novo infeudabo vel aliquo modo alienabo etiam cum consensu capituli ecclesie mee, inconsulto Romano pontifice. Sic me Deus adjuvet et hec sancta Dei Evangelia.—In dei nomine amen. Per presentis publici Instrumenti seriem cunctis appareat evidenter et sit notum, quod anno Domini millesimo quingentesimo tricesimo tercio, indictione sexta, regni illustrissimi metuendissimi ac invictissimi principis et domini nostri supremi Henrici octavi, Dei gracia Anglie et Francie Regis, fidei defensoris, et domini Hibernie excellentissimi, anno vicesimo quarto, mensis vero Marcii die tricesimo, in domo capitulari Collegii Regii sancti Stephani prothomartyris prope palacium Regium Westm' London' diocesis notorie situat', constitutus personaliter reverendissimus in Christo pater dominus Thomas in Cant' Archiepiscopum (ut dicebat) electus, in mea prothonotarii Regii ac notarii subscripti ac venerabilium virorum magistri Johannis Tregonwell legum doctoris, et Thome Bedyll clerici a consiliis dicti domini nostri Regis, Richardi Gwent decretorum doctoris Curie Cantuar' Officialis principalis, et Johannis Cocks legum doctoris, dicti reverendissimi patris audiencie causarum et negociorum Auditoris ac Vicarii in spiritualibus generalis, testium in hac parte specialiter adhibitorum presentia, protestaciones quasdam fecit, legit, et interposuit, ac cetera fecit prout in quadam papiri scedula quam tunc ibidem in manibus suis tenuit et perlegit plenius continebatur. Cujus quidem scedule verus tenor (nil addito vel dempto) de verbo ad verbum sequitur et est talis: In dei nomine amen. Coram vobis auctentica persona et testibus fide dignis hic presentibus, Ego Thomas in Cant' Archiepiscopum electus dico, allego, et in hiis scriptis palam publice et expresse protestor, quod cum juramentum sive juramenta ab electis in Cant' Archiepiscopos summo pontifici prestari solita me ante meam consecracionem aut tempore ejusdem pro forma potius quam pro esse aut re obligatoria ad illam obtinend' oporteat, non est nec erit mee voluntatis aut intencionis per hujusmodi juramentum vel juramenta, qualitercunque verba in ipsis posita sonare videbuntur, me obligare ad aliquod racione eorundem posthac dicendum, faciendum, aut attemptandum, quod erit aut esse videbitur contra legem Dei vel contra illustrissimum Regem nostrum Anglie aut rempublicam hujus sui regni Anglie, legesve aut prerogativas ejusdem: Et quod non intendo per hujusmodi juramentum aut juramenta quovismodo me obligare, quo minus libere loqui, consulere et consentire valeam in omnibus et singulis reformacionem religionis Christiane, gubernacionem ecclesie Anglicane, aut prerogativam corone ejusdem reipubliceve commoditatem quoquomodo concernen', et ea ubique exequi et reformare que michi in Ecclesia Anglicana reformanda videbuntur. Et secundum hanc interpretacionem et intellectum hunc, et non aliter neque alio modo, dicta juramenta me prestaturum protestor et profiteor: protestorque insuper, quodcunque juramentum sit quod meus procurator summo pontifici meo nomine antehac prestitit, quod non erat intencionis aut voluntatis mee sibi aliquam dare potestatem, cujus vigore aliquod juramentum meo nomine prestare potuerit contrarium aut repugnans juramento per me prestito aut imposterum prestando prefato illustrissimo Anglie Regi. Et casu quo aliquod tale contrarium aut repugnans juramentum meo nomine prestitit, protestor quod illud me inscio et absque mea auctoritate prestitum pro nullo et invalido esse volo. Quas protestaciones in omnibus clausulis et sentenciis dictorum juramentorum repetitas et reiteratas volo, a quibus per aliquod meum factum vel dictum quovismodo recedere non intendo nec recedam, sed eas mihi semper salvas esse volo. Super quibus omnibus et singulis premissis dictus reverendissimus pater me prothonotarium et notarium predictum unum vel plura publicum seu publica instrumentum sive instrumenta exinde conficere, ac testes superius nominatos testimonium perhibere rogavit et requisivit. Et deinde die, mense, et anno predictis dictus reverendissimus dominus Thomas electus in me[a] et prelibatorum venerabilium virorum presentia testium ad hoc etiam adhibitorum dict' domum capitularem exivit, et ad gradus summi altaris dicti Collegii vestibus sacerdotalibus amictus ad recipiendum munus consecracionis perrexit, ac ibidem coram reverendo in

Christo patre domino Johanne permissione divina Lincoln' Episcopo pontificalibus induto super cathedram honorifice ornatam sedente, reverendis patribus Johanne Exon' et Henrico Assaven' Episcopis eidem Lincoln' Episcopo in actu consecracionis dicti reverendissimi electi assistentibus, genibus innixus quandam pergameni scedulam tenoris sequentis, viz. IN DEI NOMINE AMEN. Ego Thomas electus Cantuarien' ab hac hora inantea fidelis et obediens ero beato Petro sancteque apostolice Romane ecclesie ac domino nostro domino Clementi Pape septimo suisque successoribus canonice intrantibus. Non ero in consilio aut consensu vel facto ut vitam perdant aut membrum, seu capiantur, aut in eos manus violenter quomodolibet ingerantur, vel injurie alique inferantur quovisquesito colore. Consilium vero, quod mihi credituri sunt per se aut nuncios seu literas, ad eorum dampnum (me sciente) nemini pandam. Papatum Romanum et regalia sancti Petri adjutor eis ero ad retinendum et defendendum contra omnem hominem. Legatum apostolice sedis in eundo et redeundo honorifice tractabo, et in suis necessitatibus adjuvabo. Jura, honores, privilegia, et auctoritatem Romane ecclesie, domini nostri Pape et successorum suorum predictorum, conservare et defendere, augere et promovere curabo. Nec ero in consilio vel tractatu quibus contra ipsum dominum nostrum vel eandem Romanam ecclesiam aliqua sinistra vel prejudicialia personarum, juris, honoris, status et potestatis eorum machinentur; et si talia a quibuscunque procurari novero vel tractari, impediam hoc pro posse, et quantocius potero commode significabo eidem domino nostro vel alteri per quem ad ipsius noticiam pervenire possit. Regulas sanctorum patrum, decreta, ordinaciones, sentencias, disposiciones, reservaciones, provisiones et mandata apostolica totis viribus observabo et faciam ab aliis observari. Hereticos, scismaticos, et rebelles domino nostro et successoribus predictis pro posse persequar et impugnabo. Vocatus ad sinodum veniam nisi prepeditus fuero canonica prepedicione. Apostolorum limina Romana Curia existentia citra singulis annis, ultra vero montes singulis bienniis, visitabo aut per me aut per meum nuncium, nisi apostolica absolvar licencia. Possessiones vero ad mensam meam pertinentes non vendam neque donabo nec impignorabo neque de novo infeudabo vel aliquo modo alienabo etiam cum consensu capitali ecclesie mee, inconsulto Romano pontifice. Sic me Deus adjuvet et hec sancta Dei Evangelia: manibus suis tenens ante lecturam ejusdem scedule et juramenti in eadem contenti prestacionem in mea et eorundem testium presentia, asseruit et potestatus est se dictam scedulam lecturum ac juramentum inibi insertum prestiturum sub premissis protestacionibus alias per eundem eodem die in dicto domo Capitulari in mea et eorundem testium presentia habitis et factis, et non aliter neque alio modo. Et incontinenter post premissa eandem scedulam perlegit, et ut in eadem continetur juravit. Super quibus assercione et protestacione per eundem modo premisso tunc ibidem factis unum vel plura publicum seu publica exinde conficere instrumentum sive instrumenta ac testes prescriptos testimonium perhibere etiam tunc ibidem rogavit et requisivit. Quibus sic peractis die, mense, et anno predictis, ac solenni consecracione ejusdem reverendissimi patris finita et expedita, idem reverendissimus pater dominus Thomas Cantuar' Archiepiscopus ante dictum summum altare pallium recepturus in mea et dictorum mag' Johannis Tregunwell, Thome Bedill, et Richardi Gwent testium predictorum ad hoc specialiter adhibitorum presentia, ante prestacionem juramenti infra scripti iterum protestatus est se hujusmodi sequens juramentum sub eisdem protestacionibus ut premittitur in dicto domo Capitulari habitis et factis ac superius descriptis, et non aliter neque alio modo prestiturum et juraturum, ac ibidem immediate post premissa juramentum sub forma que sequitur—IN DEI NOMINE AMEN. Ego Thomas Archiepiscopus Cant' ab hac hora inantea fidelis et obediens ero beato Petro sancteque apostolice Romane ecclesie et domino nostro domino Clementi Pape septimo suisque successoribus canonice intrantibus. Non ero in consilio aut consensu vel facto ut vitam perdant aut membrum, seu capiantur mala capcione. Consilium vero quod mihi credituri sunt per se aut nuncium seu literas, ad eorum dampnum me sciente nemini pandam. Papatum Romanum et regalia sancti Petri adjutor eis ero ad retinendum et defendendum salvo meo ordine contra omnem hominem. Legatum apostolice sedis in eundo et redeundo honorifice tractabo, et in suis necessitatibus adjuvabo. Vocatus ad sinodum veniam nisi prepeditus fuero canonica prepedicione. Apostolorum limina Roman' Cur' existentia citra singulis annis, ultra vero montes singulis bienniis, visitabo aut per me aut meum nuncium, nisi apostolica absolvar licencia. Possessiones vero ad mensam mei archiepiscopatus pertinentes non vendam neque donabo nec impignorabo neque de novo infeudabo vel aliquo modo alienabo, inconsulto Romano Pontifice. Sic me Deus adjuvet et hec sancta Dei evangelia—prestitit et juravit.—Super qua protestacione sic ut premittitur per eundem reverendissimum tercio facta et habita, idem reverendissimus pater me prothonotarium et notarium publicum subscriptum unum vel plura publicum seu publica instrumentum sive instrumenta exinde conficere, ac testes predictos testimonium perhibere de et super eisdem etiam tercio rogavit et requisivit. Acta fuerunt hec omnia et singula prout supra scribuntur et recitantur respective sub anno Domini, indictione, anno regni Regis predicti mense, die, et locis predictis, presentibus tunc ibidem venerabilibus viris prenominatis testibus ad premissa respective ut premittitur adhibitis et requisitis. Et ego Richardus Watkyns in legibus baccalaurius, dicti domini nostri Regis prothonotarius, quia premissis omnibus et singulis, dum sic ut premittitur sub anno Domini et regni dicti domini nostri Regis mense, die, et loco predictis agebantur et fiebant, una cum prenominatis testibus presens personaliter interfui, eaque omnia et singula sic fieri vidi et audivi ac in notam sumpsi, Ideo hoc presens publicum instrumentum manu alterius (me interim aliter occupato) fideliter scriptum exinde confeci, publicavi, atque in hanc publicam formam redegi, [a] signavi et nomine meis solitis signavi, rogatus et requisitus in fidem et testimonium omnium et singulorum premissorum. Quibus quidem processis et actis nostris antedictis plenariam et indubitatam fidem tam in judicio quam extra ac alias ubilibet in agendis adhibend' fore volumus, et per presentes decernimus, Vobisque reverendissimo patri domino Jacobo Cardinali et Delegato antedicto de premissis omnibus et singulis per presentes presentiumque vigore cum omni debita reverencia et honore certificamus, informacionem damus et referimus. In quorum omnium et singulorum fidem et testimonium premissorum presentes literas sive hoc presens publicum instrumentum processum nostrum hujusmodi in se continen' exinde fieri, et per prefatum providum virum magistrum Johannem Clerk notarium publicum scribam nostrum predict' subscribi et publicari mandavimus, nostroque sigillo jussimus et fecimus appensione communiri. Data et acta fuerunt hec omnia et singula prout supra scribuntur et recitantur, sub anno Domini, indictione, pontificatuque ac mense, diebus, et locis superius respective specificatis, presentibus venerabilibus et circumspectis viris et personis superius respective etiam nominatis cum multis et quasi innumeris aliis testibus ad perhibendum exinde testimonium specialiter rogatis et requisitis.

[a] It is *signavi* in the MS. but *signoque* was probably intended.

Et Ego Johannes Clerk, Bathon' et Wellen' diocesis publicus sacra auctoritate apostolica notarius ac alme Curie Cantuar' procuratorum generalium unus, necnon actorum ceterorumque per supra nominatum reverendum dominum Subdelegatum et coram eo habitorum factorum et gestorum scriba in hac parte specialiter assumptus, Quia literarum commissionalium sive subdelegatoriarum predict' presentacioni onerisque suscepcioni earundem ac procuratorii exhibitioni et articulorum dationi prefatique domini Thome Cranmeri partis ex adverso principalis responsioni testiumque productioni et examinacioni predictis modo premisso respective factis, atque ceteris premissis omnibus et singulis, dum sic ut premittitur sub anno Domini, indictione, pontificatu menseque ac diebus et locis superius respective specificatis coram prenominato reverendo domino Subdelegato et per eum agerentur et fierent, una cum testibus prenominatis presens personaliter interfui, eaque omnia et singula sic fieri vidi et audivi, Ideo exinde notam sumpsi et hoc presens publicum instrumentum manu aliena (me interim aliis impedito negociis) fideliter scriptum exinde confeci, subscripsi et publicavi, atque in hanc publicam et auctenticam formam redegi. Signoque et nomine meis solitis et consuetis signavi et [in] fidem et testimonium premissorum rogatus specialiter et requisitus.

Jo. Clerk.

XLIII. [1]*All the Submissions and Recantations of Thomas Cranmer, late Archbishop of Canterbury, truly set forth both in Latin and English, agreeable to the Originals, written and subscribed with his own hand.* Todd's Life of Abp. Cranmer, Vol. II. pp. 472, et sqq. from an original copy published by Cawood, A.D. 1556.

VISUM ET EXAMINATUM PER REVERENDUM PATREM ET DOMINUM, DOMINUM EDMUNDUM EPISCOPUM LONDON. ANNO MDLVI.

1. The true copy of the first submission of Thomas Cranmer, late archbishop of Canterbury, which afterward by inconstancy and unstableness he the said Thomas Cranmer did cancel, the original whereof was sent to the queen's majesty and her privy council, as followeth:

Forasmuch as the king and queen's majesties, by consent of their parliament, have received the pope's authority within this realm, I am content to submit myself to their laws herein, and to take the pope for chief head of this church of England, so far as God's laws and the laws and customs of this realm will permit.

THOMAS CRANMER.

2. The true copy of the second submission of the said Thomas Cranmer, which he the said Thomas did advisedly subscribe with his own hand, and did not afterward revoke it, the original whereof was also sent up to the queen's majesty and her said council, as before.

I, Thomas Cranmer, doctor in divinity, do submit myself to the catholic church of Christ, and to the pope, supreme head of the same church, and unto the king and the queen's majesties, and unto all their laws and ordinances.

THOMAS CRANMER.

3. Tertium scriptum Cranmeri sua ipsius manu exaratum, et per eum in Buccardo exhibitum London' episcopo.

I am content to submit myself to the king and queen's majesties, and to all their laws and ordinances, as well concerning the pope's supremacy as others. And I shall from time to time move and stir all other to do the like, to the uttermost of my power, and to live in quietness and obedience unto their majesties, most humbly, without murmur or grudging against any of their godly proceedings. And for my book which I have written, I am contented to submit me to the judgment of the catholic church, and of the next general council.

THOMAS CRANMER.

4. Quartum scriptum Cranmeri sua ipsius manu exaratum, et per eum in Buccardo exhibitum London' episcopo.

Be it known by these presents, that I, Thomas Cranmer, doctor of divinity, and late archbishop of Canterbury, do firmly, stedfastly, and assuredly believe in all articles and points of the christian religion and catholic faith, as the catholic church doth believe, and hath ever believed from the beginning. Moreover, as concerning the sacraments of the church, I believe unfeignedly in all points as the said catholic church doth and hath believed from the beginning of christian religion. In witness whereof I have humbly subscribed my hand unto these presents, the xvi. day of February, MDLV. [$155\frac{5}{6}$.]

THOMAS CRANMER.

5. The true copy of a fifth submission of the said Thomas Cranmer, written and subscribed with his own hand in the presence of master Henry Syddall, and of one called Frater Johannes de Villa Garcina, a notable learned man, as followeth.

EGO, Thomas Cranmer, anathematizo omnem Lutheri et Zuinglii hæresim et quodcunque dogma sanæ doctrinæ contrarium: confiteor vero et credo firmissime unam sanctam

[1 Vid. Strype's Eccl. Mem. Vol. III. pt. i. pp. 390, et sqq. Ed. Oxon. 1822.—Also, Sampson's letter to Bullinger, dated April 6, 1566, in the *Original Letters relative to the English Reformation*, (Park. Soc.) p. 173, with the note there; and the quotation from Todd, infra pp. 567—9.]

et catholicam ecclesiam visibilem, extra quam salus non est; atque ejusdem in terris supremum agnosco caput episcopum Romanum, quem fateor summum esse pontificem et papam ac Christi vicarium, cui omnes tenentur subesse fideles. Jam quod ad sacramenta attinet, credo et colo in sacramento eucharistiæ verum Christi corpus et sanguinem sub speciebus panis et vini verissime citra ullum tropum et figuram contenta, conversis et transubstantiatis pane in corpus et vino in sanguinem Redemptoris divina potentia. Atque in sex aliis sacramentis (sicut in hoc) id credo et teneo quod universa tenet ecclesia ac sentit Romana. Credo insuper purgatorium locum, ubi ad tempus cruciantur defunctorum animæ, pro quibus sancte et salubriter orat ecclesia, sicut et sanctos colit, ad illosque preces effundit. Demum in omnibus me profiteor non aliud sentire quam ecclesia catholica et Romana tenet; ac per me pœnitet quod aliud unquam tenuerim ac senserim. Deum autem supplex oro, ut pietate sua mihi condonare dignetur, quæ in illum et ejus ecclesiam commisi: fideles simul rogo et obsecro, ut pro me preces effundant; eos autem qui meo aut exemplo aut doctrina seducti sunt, per sanguinem Jesu Christi obtestor, ut ad ecclesiæ redeant unitatem, idemque dicamus omnes, ut non sint in nobis schismata. Postremo sicut me subjicio catholicæ Christi ecclesiæ ejusdemque supremo capiti, ita me submitto Philippo et Mariæ Angliæ Regibus, atque eorum legibus et decretis, et testor Deum optimum maximumque, hæc in nullius gratiam, nullius metu a me confessa, sed ex animo et libentissime, ut meæ et aliorum simul conscientiis consulam et prospiciam.

Per me, THOMAM CRANMER.

Testes hujus subscriptionis, Frater Joannes de Villa Garcina.
Henricus Sidallus.

6. The true Copy of a Sixth Submission of the said Thomas Cranmer, written and subscribed with his own hand, as followeth.

EGO, Thomas Cranmer, pridem archiepiscopus Cantuarien', confiteor, et doleo ex animo, quod gravissime deliquerim in cœlum et adversus Anglicanum regnum, immo in universam Christi ecclesiam, quam longe sævius persecutus sum quam olim Paulus, qui fui blasphemus, persecutor, et contumeliosus. Atque utinam qui Saulum malitia et scelere superavi, possem cum Paulo quem detraxi honorem Christo et ecclesiæ utilitatem recompensare! Verum meum utcunque animum latro ille evangelicus solatur. Ille namque tunc tandem ex animo resipuit, tunc illum furti pertæsum est, quum furari amplius non liceret: et ego (qui, meo officio et auctoritate abusus, et Christo honorem et huic regno fidem et religionem abstuli) jam tandem Dei maximi beneficio ad me reversus, agnosco me omnium maximum peccatorem, et cupio (si qua possem) Deo primum, deinde ecclesiæ, et ejus capiti supremo, atque regibus, toti demum Anglicano regno condignam reddere satisfactionem. Verum sicut latro ille felix, quum non esset solvendo quas pecunias et opes abstulit (quum nec pes nec manus affixæ cruci suum officium facerent) corde et lingua duntaxat (quæ non erat ligata) testatus est quod reliqua membra essent factura, si eadem qua lingua libertate gauderent; illa confessus est Christum innocentem, ea objurgabat impudentiam socii, eadem anteactam vitam detestatus et peccatorum veniam impetravit, et veluti clavi quadam paradisi fores aperuit: hujus exemplo non mediocrem concipio de Christi misericordia spem, fore ut mihi peccata condonet. Manibus et pedibus careo, quibus quod destruxi iterum reædificare valeam, (relicta enim sunt tantummodo labia circa dentes meos;) sed vitulos labiorum nostrorum recipiet, qui est supra quam credi possit misericors. Hac igitur concepta spe libet hunc offerre vitulum, hanc minimam et corporis et vitæ partem litare. Confiteor in primis meam erga Deum opt. max. ingratitudinem, agnosco me omni indignissimum beneficio et pietate, dignissimum vero omni non tantum humano ac temporali, sed divino et æterno supplicio, quod in Henricum VIII. et maxime in ejus uxorem reginam Catherinam vehementissime deliqui, quum divortii causa et auctor extiti: quæ sane culpa omnium hujus regni malorum et calamitatum seminarium fuit. Hinc tot proborum neces, hinc totius regni schisma, hinc hæreses, hinc tot animorum et corporum strages obortæ sunt, ut vix possim vel ratione complecti. Sed quum adeo sint hæc gravia initiaque dolorum, aperui fateor ingentem fenestram hæresibus cunctis, quarum ego præcipuum egi doctorem et ducem. In primis vero illud vehementer meum excruciat animum, quod sacrosanctum eucharistiæ sacramentum tot blasphemiis et contumeliis affecerim, negans Christi corpus et sanguinem vere et realiter sub speciebus panis et vini contineri; editis etiam libellis, quibus veritatem pro viribus impugnabam: in hac sane parte non solum Saulo et latrone deterior, verum omnium quos terra unquam sustinuit sceleratissimus. Domine, peccavi in cœlum et coram te: in cœlum, quod mea causa tot caret cœlicolis, quod cœleste hoc beneficium nobis exhibitum negavi impudentissime: peccavi et in terram, quæ tamdiu hoc sacramento misere caruit, in homines quos ab hac supersubstantiali esca revocavi, tot occisor hominum, quot inedia perierunt. Defraudavi defunctorum animas hoc jugi et celeberrimo sacrificio. Atque ex his omnibus manifestum est, quantopere etiam post Christum in ejus vicarium injurius extiti, quem libris etiam editis potestate privavi. Propterea magnopere et impensissime oro summum pontificem, ut mihi ob Christi clementiam condonet, quæ adversus illum ejusque apostolicam sedem commisi. Ac serenissimos reges Angliæ, Hispaniæ, &c. Philippum et Mariam supplex oro, ut regia qua pollent clementia mihi velint ignoscere: totum etiam regnum, immo universam ecclesiam rogo et obsecro, misereantur hujus miseræ animæ, cui jam præter linguam nihil est reliquum, quo possim illatas injurias et damna resarcire. Præcipue vero, quia tibi soli peccavi, oro, clementissime Pater, (qui omnes ad te venire, quamlibet facinorosos, et cupis et præcipis,) me propius et cominus digneris intueri, sicut Magdalenam et Petrum respexisti; vel certe sicut latronem ex cruce aspiciens, tuæ gratiæ et gloriæ promissione dignatus es pavidum et trementem animum consolari, ita etiam solita et nativa tua pietate oculos misericordiæ ad me convertas, necnon tuo me digneris alloquio, dicens, Salus tua ego sum, et in die mortis, Hodie mecum eris in Paradiso. Scriptum est hoc anno Domini 1555. [155$\frac{5}{6}$.] mensis Martii 18.

Per me, THOMAM CRANMER.

---

*The Prayer and Saying of Thomas Cranmer, a little before his death, all written with his own hand, as followeth*[1].

GOOD christian people, my dear beloved brethren, and my sisters in Christ, I beseech you most heartily to pray for me to Almighty God, that he will forgive me all my sins and offences, which be many without number, and great above measure: but yet one thing grieveth my conscience more than all the rest, whereof, God willing, I intend to speak more hereafter. But how many and how great soever they be, I beseech you to pray God of his mercy to pardon and forgive me all.

O Father of heaven, O Son of God, Redeemer of the world, O Holy Ghost, proceeding from them both, three Persons and one God, have mercy upon me, a most wretched caitiff and miserable sinner. I have offended both heaven and earth, more than my tongue can express. Whither then may I go, or whither shall I flee for succour? To heaven I may be ashamed to lift up mine eyes, and in earth I find no refuge or succour. What shall I then do? Shall I despair? God forbid. O God, thou art merciful, and refusest none that cometh unto thee for succour. To thee, therefore, do I run; to thee do I humble myself, saying, O Lord God, my sins be great, but have mercy upon me for thy great mercy. God was not made man for our small offences. Thou didst not give thy Son unto death for small sins only, but for all and the greatest sins of the world, so that the sinner return to thee in his heart, as I do here at this present. Wherefore have mercy on me, O Lord; for although my sins be great, yet thy mercy is greater. I crave nothing, O Lord, for mine own merits, but for thy name's sake, that it may be hallowed thereby, and for thy dear Son, Jesus Christ's sake. And now therefore, O Father, that art in heaven, hallowed be thy name. Thy kingdom come, &c.

Every man desireth, good people, at the time of their death to give some exhortation, that good folks may remember after their death, and be the better for the same:

---

[[1] This prayer, &c. will also be found in Vol. I. pp. xxvi. et sqq., but it is again inserted here in order to give Cawood's book entire. It will be seen that the report here printed, as published by Boner, agrees with Foxe's account, *except in the last paragraph* and the line immediately preceding it.]

so I beseech God grant unto me that I may speak something, whereby he may be glorified, and you edified.

First, it is an heavy case to see how many folks be so much doted of this present world, and be so careful of it, that for the world to come they seem to care very little or nothing. Therefore this shall be my first exhortation, that you set not over much by this present world, but upon the world to come and upon God; and to learn to know what this lesson meaneth of St John. "The love of this world," saith he, "is hatred unto God."

The second exhortation is, that, next unto God, you obey your king and queen, willingly and gladly, without murmuring or grudging, not for fear of them, but much more for fear of God, knowing that they be God's ministers, appointed by God for to govern and rule you; and therefore they that resist them, resist God's ordinance.

The third exhortation is, that you love together like brethren and sistern. But, alas! pity it is to see how faint this love is, many taking other not as brother and sisters, but rather as strangers or mortal enemies. And yet, I pray you, learn this one lesson, to do good unto all men, as much as in you lieth, and to hurt no man, no more than you would do to your natural loving brother and sister. For whosoever hateth any person, and goeth about maliciously to hurt him, surely, without doubt, God is not with that man, although he think himself never so much in God's favour.

The fourth exhortation shall be to them that have substance and riches of the world, that they well consider and remember three sayings of the scripture. One is of our Saviour Christ himself, who saith, that "rich men hardly come into heaven:" a sore saying, and yet spoken of him that knew the truth. The second is of St John, who saith thus: "He that hath the substance of this world, and seeth his brother in necessity, and shutteth up his mercy from him, how can he say that he loveth God?" The third is of St James, who saith to covetous rich men after this manner: "Weep and howl, you rich men, for the misery that shall come upon you: your riches do rot, your clothes be moth-eaten, your gold and silver wax cankery and rusty, and their rust shall bear witness against you, and consume you like fire: you make a hoard and treasure of God's indignation against the last day." Let them that be rich ponder well these three sentences; for if ever they had occasion to shew their charity, they have it now, the poor people being so many, and victuals so dear.

Here to declare the queen's just title to the crown.

And now, forasmuch as I am come to the last end of my life, whereupon hangeth all my life past, and all my life to come, either to live with my Saviour Christ for ever in joy, or else to be in pains ever with the wicked devils in hell; and I see before mine eyes presently either heaven ready to receive me, or else hell ready to swallow me up; I shall therefore declare unto you my very faith, without colour or dissimulation; for now is no time to dissemble, whatsoever I have said, preached, or written in time past.

First, I believe in God the Father Almighty, maker of heaven and earth, &c. And I believe every article of the catholic faith, every clause, word, and sentence taught by our Saviour Jesus Christ, his apostles, and prophets, in the new and old Testament, and all articles explicate and set forth in the general councils.

And now I come to the great thing that so much troubleth my conscience, more than any other thing that ever I did; and that is, setting abroad untrue books and writings, contrary to the truth of God's word; which now I renounce and condemn, and refuse them utterly as erroneous, and for none of mine. But you must know also what books they were, that you may beware of them, or else my conscience is not discharged; for they be the books which I wrote against the sacrament of the altar sith the death of king Henry VIII. But, whatsoever I wrote then, now is time and place to say truth: wherefore, renouncing all those books, and whatsoever in them is contained, I say and believe that our Saviour Christ Jesu is really and substantially contained in the blessed sacrament of the altar, under the forms of bread and wine.

*Excusum Londini in ædibus Johannis Cawodi*
*Typographi Regiæ Majestatis.*

*Anno* MD.LVI. *Cum privilegio.*

[With regard to these recantations of Cranmer, the following extract from Boner's own Register, fol. 423, utterly overthrows the falsehood set forth in the concluding paragraph:

"Notandum est quod dictus Thomas Cranmerus fuit potestea [postea], viz. die Sabbati, xxi° die mensis Marcii, anno Domini secundum cursum et computationem ecclesiæ Anglicanæ millesimo quingentesimo quinquagesimo sexto, in quodam loco extra muros borealis partis civitatis Oxoniensis, combustus et in cineres concrematus, &c. et quod idem Cranmer tempore ejusdem concremationis, et immediate ante illam suam concremationem, publice revocavit recantationes suas antea per eum factas, persistendo in erroribus et hæresibus suis, &c."

The extract from Sampson's letter referred to, p. 563, note, is as follows:

"Recantatio quædam absurda et a papistis conficta cœpit eo vivente spargi, quasi ille eam palinodiam cecinisset: sed auctores ipsi eam eo vivo revocarunt, et ille fortiter reclamabat vivens pernegabatque." *Original Letters relating to the English Reformation*, (Park. Soc.) Lett. XC. p. 173.

On the whole question Archdeacon Todd writes as follows:

"The sentence of the Ecclesiastical Court now remained to be executed by the secular power. But ere the order was issued to this purpose (and a few days only passed before it was issued), another trial of his constancy was made, and he sunk under it. With expressions of pity for his situation, but with a design of leading him to recant, some of the principal academics seem to have immediately visited him in prison. He whose deposition is the last of those who were witnesses against him[1], is now said to have invited the archbishop to his deanery at Christ Church; but the invitation could not have been accepted till after the 16th of February, as on that day one of his recantations is signed, which appears to have been delivered, as a preceding recantation was, to Boner personally, in the Bocardo prison. These, in Boner's narrative of 'All the Submissions that Cranmer made,' are the third and fourth. The first and second will shew how the archbishop hesitated ere he fell. Perhaps they were proposed by Thirlby. Before the proceedings on the 14th had ended, they could not have been made. The language of Cranmer was then undauntedly opposed to them. He probably listened at the close of that day to the persuasions of his friend, and signed what by him was hoped might propitiate the queen; of which the copy being seen by others, after it had been dispatched, it was considered not sufficiently explicit, and therefore was followed by the second, without delay we may suppose, retracting what is said in the first. It is remarkable, however, that neither of them is dated."—Todd's Life of Archbishop Cranmer, Vol. II. pp. 470-472.

"These papers," (*i. e.* the first four recantations attributed to the archbishop,) "as might be expected, were not sufficient to satisfy the Romish party. Other concessions must be obtained from their great opponent, they said, by intimidation as well as by artful proposals, and by insidious suggestions. It was immediately after the fourth recantation, I have no doubt, that to the deanery of Christ Church he was conducted for the visit of a few days, to partake of a treacherous hospitality; that there the Spanish friar, John de Villa Garcina, then the Regius Professor of Divinity at Oxford, and Henry Sydall, a canon in the dean's cathedral, were the principal managers of the allurements and the threats, by which themselves and other Romanists at length subdued him to their purpose. To the king and queen his absolute recantation, these egregious tempters urged, would be highly acceptable. Nor to the lords of the council and other noblemen, they added, who much respected him, could it be less so. They put him in hope that not only his life might be spared, but that his former dignity might be restored; saying that for such boons it was but a small and easy matter they required of him, his sub-

[1] i. e. Dr Marshall. Vid. p. 382, *n.* 3.

scription only to a few words in 'a little leaf of paper,' with his own hand; and that then, whether he would have rank or wealth, or would prefer the quietness of private life, his choice might be secured by the regal power; but that if he refused, of pardon there was no hope; for the queen was so purposed that she would have Cranmer a Roman Catholic, or else no Cranmer at all.

"To these artifices he yielded; and to the words on the little leaf of paper which they brought, subscribed, as it should seem, in their presence. 'This recantation,' says Foxe[1], 'was not so soon conceived, but the doctors and prelates, without delay, caused the same to be imprinted and set abroad in all men's hands. Whereunto, for better credit, first was added the name of Thomas Cranmer, with a solemn subscription; then followed the witnesses, Henry Sydall, and John de Villa Garcina.' The privy council were displeased at the hasty publication of this paper, and the two printers of it were commanded to deliver all the copies to be burned. It was reserved to be the fifth recantation in Boner's account, where it appears in Latin, bearing, however, an English title, and has been translated by Foxe[2]."—Id. Vol. II. pp. 474-476.

"To this recantation" (*i. e.* the fifth, witnessed by J. de Villa Garcina, and H. Sydall) "there is no date. But it was probably made immediately after the writ for burning him had been sent to Oxford, as Noailles, the French ambassador to Mary (whose character for veracity, however, is not spotless), mentions to his court, that with this fifth paper Cranmer sent a letter to Pole, begging the respite of a few days, that he might yet give to the world a more convincing proof of his repentance. Mary is said to have 'cheerfully' granted what Cranmer asked; but, determined not to spare him, she only ordered the day of his approaching fate to be concealed from him. Meantime the sixth recantation was prepared. To a more laboured disavowal (more complete it could not be than what the fifth recites) of tenets he had maintained, to louder cries for mercy, to deeper expressions of self-abasement, he was now to be earnestly pressed under the fallacious persuasion that from the terror of the stake he might be wholly freed. That this outrageous composition was drawn up by Pole, Strype long since assumed, by comparing it with the tedious prolixity and style of the recantation, which the cardinal prepared for the friend of Cranmer, Sir John Cheke[3]."—Id. Vol. II. pp. 479, 80.

"For what purpose, it may be asked, were this and the preceding instrument formed in a language known only to the learned? Were they to be detailed only so far, in our own, to the common people, as not to lead them to a belief that other words than Cranmer's were recited? But whatever was the intention, and admitting the contents of both the instruments, though paltering in a double tongue, to be universally known, numbers still disbelieved that Cranmer was entirely lost, that yet he would not redeem himself. When he ascended the platform at St Mary's on the morning of his martyrdom, numbers wept, says the Roman Catholic who witnessed the scene, having indeed 'conceived an assured hope of his conversion and repentance[4],' which, ere a few minutes had elapsed, was disappointed. But again, when the fallen prelate began to pray, this honest spectator divides the listening audience into 'those that hated him before, [the Romanists] who now loved him for his [fancied] conversion and hope of continuance,' and 'those that loved him before, [the protestants] who could not suddenly hate him, having hope of his confession again of his fall[5].' Why also was the fifth recantation, published by prelates and divines, immediately after it was made, suppressed by an order of the privy council? Was it because a suspicion was believed to exist, that Cranmer's assent to it was incapable of proof? No, says the apologist for this questionable proceeding: 'Perhaps it was incorrectly printed; perhaps they waited for that which he said God would inspire him to make[6].' What the privy council are thus conjectured as expecting from the archbishop, is nothing more than what

[1] Vid. Foxe's Acts and Monuments, p. 1884. Ed. Lond. 1583.

[2] Id. ibid.

[3] Vid. Strype's Eccl. Mem. Vol. III. part I. p. 395. Ed. Oxon. 1822.

[4] Vid. Strype's Mem. of Abp. Cranmer, Vol. II. p. 552. Ed. Oxon. 1840.

[5] Id. p. 554.

[6] Lingard, Hist. Eng. 8vo. VII. 276, *n.*

is flippantly pretended as his expression by the French ambassador; not a shadow of authority for which is any where to be found. That it was *incorrectly* printed is probable enough. But Pole and Boner intended not merely to correct it, but to reprint it with the four preceding papers, and with the production of a sixth. Indeed this is the only recantation, to which historians formerly drew the attention of their readers. Hence Collier, after Foxe[7], relates, that on the day of Cranmer's execution the Spanish friar, (J. de Villa Garcina,) 'who was a witness to his recantation, proposed the reading his recantation to a public audience, and to this purpose desired him to subscribe the instrument with his own hand and sign it[8].' Of any new submission on the fatal morning, this historian seems to have entertained no belief. Burnet is alike silent. Thus too the Romish biographer of Pole, with the printed submissions of the archbishop at his service, speaks apparently of none but that which is numbered the fifth by Boner; and after noticing the writ for burning him, says, 'Cranmer had again renewed his subscription, and transcribed a fair copy of the whole; but, having some misgivings of his approaching punishment, he secretly wrote another declaration, which contradicted, in every point, the doctrine he had before signed.' What here is called a renewed subscription, is affirmed, however, in the recent history of our country, to be nothing less than the copy of a 'seventh instrument of abjuration.' Is it improbable, however, that what the friar proposed was merely the fifth recantation more correctly written than the hastily printed copy had given it? To this the signature of Cranmer was requisite, and it was made together with that of the friar; but, it is especially to be observed, is undated. It would now be ready for Boner's publication, as the fifth instrument; while a written abbreviation of the material parts of it would be sufficient for Cranmer 'openly to profess before the people;' and accordingly Boner, without the statement of its being a new subscription, without the pretence of its being a seventh recantation, prints only what the martyr was to have spoken, but basely conceals the fact that he did not speak it. The faith that he was to assert was thus worded for him: 'First, I believe in God, the Father Almighty, Maker of heaven and earth, &c., &c. I believe every article of the catholic faith, every clause, word, and sentence taught by our Saviour Christ, and his apostles and prophets, in the new and old Testament, and all articles explicate and set forth in general councils. And now I come to the great thing that so much troubleth my conscience, more than any other thing that ever I did; that is, setting abroad untrue books and writings, contrary to the truth of God's word, which now I renounce and condemn, and refuse them utterly as erroneous and for none of mine. But you must know also what books they were, that you may beware of them; or else my conscience is not discharged. For they be the books which I wrote against the sacrament of the altar since the death of king Henry the Eighth. But whatsoever I wrote then, now is time and place to say truth. Wherefore, renouncing all those books, and whatsoever is in them contained, I say and believe, that our Saviour Christ Jesus is really and substantially contained in the blessed sacrament of the altar under the forms of bread and wine.'

"So ends the tract, affirmed in the title page 'to have been seen and examined by Boner.' Upon him, therefore, rests the responsibility of the compilation, even if by any other hand than his own it had been compiled; upon him the shame also,

---

[7] Foxe calls it "a paper with articles, which Cranmer should openly profess in his recantation before the people, earnestly desiring him that he would write the said instrument (with the articles) with his own hand, and sign it with his name: which when he had done, the said friar desired that he would write another copy thereof, which should remain with him, and that he did also." (Vid. Foxe's Acts and Monuments, p. 1885. Ed. Lond. 1583.) Hence the interpretation of Burnet: "he was (now) dealt with to renew his subscription and to write the whole over again." (Burnet's Hist. of Reformat. Vol. II. p. 670. Ed. Oxon. 1829.) But the most curious, and I believe hitherto unnoticed, mention in regard to this fifth recantation, and what was selected from it for Cranmer to avow before the people at his execution, occurs in the continuation of "the Chronicles of Fabian," Lond. 1559. Vol. II. p. 564. "In this year (1556) in Lent, Thomas Cranmer, Archbishoppe of Canterbury, after that he had recanted his *supposed* recantation, was brent at Oxford." Note, Todd's Life of Abp. Cranmer, Vol. II. p. 486.

[8] Collier's Eccl. Hist. Vol. VI. p. 139. Ed. Lond. 1840, 1.

which, if not to other parts of it, at least to the conclusion, belongs, where what the sufferer really spoke is concealed, but what was prepared for him to have spoken is related, and by many of the compiler's party was afterwards reported, as if indeed he did speak it."—Id. Vol. II. pp. 484—489. Vide also Todd's Vindication of Archbishop Cranmer, pp. 116 et sqq. 2nd Ed. Lond. 1826. Soames' Hist. of Reformat. Vol. IV. pp. 515, et sqq., who enters largely into an examination of this portion of the archbishop's history. Wordsworth's Eccl. Biog. Vol. IV. pp. 258—260. Ed. Lond. 1839. Original Letters relative to the English Reformation, Letter XC. p. 173, n. 1, Park. Soc. Ed. 1846.]

# INDEX.

Printed in the United States
48629LVS00006B/2